CCH
a Wolters Kluwer business

2011 GAAP Guide, Volume II

By Judith Weiss

Highlights

CCH's *GAAP Guide, Volume II,* provides an analysis of the following authoritative pronouncements that have been incorporated in the FASB Accounting Standards Codification™ (ASC):

- FASB Technical Bulletins, FASB Staff Positions, and FASB Implementation Guides;
- EITF Consensus positions and FASB and SEC staff announcements (Topic Ds);
- AICPA Accounting Interpretations of APB Opinions, AICPA Statements of Position, and AICPA AcSEC Practice Bulletins.

> The *GAAP Guide, Volume II,* is organized into chapters that are listed in the Table of Contents alphabetically by topic. To aid users of the Guide in doing their research, each chapter includes pronouncements on the same topic.

2011 Edition

In June 2009, the FASB issued Statement No. 168, *The FASB Accounting Standards Codification™ and the Hierarchy of Generally Accepted Accounting Principles,* under which all of the existing accounting and reporting standards in the hierarchy of generally accepted accounting principles (GAAP), issued by standard-setting bodies other than the SEC (i.e., FASB, AICPA, EITF), have been superseded by the FASB Acccounting Standards Codification™ (ASC) as of July 1, 2009. The ASC, which is effective for financial statements issued for interim and annual reporting periods ending after September 15, 2009, is now the sole source of *authoritative* U.S. GAAP for nongovernmental entities.

The ASC includes only pre-codification pronouncements that are deemed to be authoritative. Pronouncements that are no longer relevant or those that amend other pronouncements have been eliminated from the FASB's cross-reference to the ASC. Certain pre-codification pronouncements are not included in the ASC, but have been grandfathered because they continue to apply to limited transactions, such as guidance for employee stock ownership plans that had been established before the issuance of SOP 93-6, *Employers' Accounting for Stock Ownership Plans*. Pronouncements that amend other pronouncements are included in the *GAAP Guide, Volume II* in a separate section of the applicable chapters under the heading, "Authoritative Guidance Not Included Separately in the Codification, but Incorporated in Other Pronouncements in the Codification," and pronouncements that have been grandfathered also are presented in separate sections of the applicable chapters, because of their potential usefulness to the Guide's users.

The ASC is organized into 90 topics that are further subdivided into subtopics, sections, and paragraphs. As a result, pre-codification pronouncements that frequently provide guidance on more than one subject, for example, accounting for convertible debt and earnings per share treatment, are discussed in the ASC under separate topics. To help you in your research, each pre-codification pronouncement discussed in the *GAAP Guide, Volume II*, includes all of the ASC references for that pronouncement. In addition, all paragraph references to pre-codification pronouncements also include the ASC references by topic, subtopic, section, and paragraph number. In the future, the FASB will issue new guidance as Accounting Standards Updates (ASUs) rather than in the form of Statements, FASB Staff Positions, and EITF Issues to which we have become accustomed. That guidance will be discussed in the applicable chapters in the *GAAP Guide, Volume II*.

This edition of *GAAP Guide, Volume II*, includes discussions of the following new pronouncements:

- Chapter 9, "Computer Software"—Analysis of the EITF's consensus positions in EITF Issue 09-3, *Applicability of SOP 97-2 to Certain Arrangements That Include Software Elements*, which was codified in the ASC as the result of the FASB's issuance of ASU 2009-14, *Certain Revenue Arrangements That Include Software Elements*.

- Chapter 10, "Consolidated Financial Statements"—Analysis of the EITF's consensus positions in EITF Issue No. 09-B, *Consideration of an Insurer's Accounting for Majority-Owned Investments When the Ownership Is through a Separate Account*, which was codified in the ASC as the result of the FASB's issuance of ASU 2010-15, *How Investments Held through Separate Accounts Affect an Insurer's Consolidation Analysis of Those Investments*.

- Chapter 35, "Results of Operations"—Analysis of the EITF's consensus positions in EITF Issue 09-K, *Health Care Entities: Presentation of Insurance Claims and Related Insurance Recoveries*, which was codified in the ASC as the result of the FASB's issuance of ASU 2010-24, *Presentation of Insurance Claims and Related Insurance Recoveries*.

- Chapter 36, "Revenue Recognition"—Analysis of the EITF's revised consensus positions in EITF Issue 08-1, *Revenue Arrangements with Multiple Deliverables*, which was codified in the ASC as the result of the FASB's issuance of ASU 2009-13, *Multiple-Deliverable Revenue Arrangements*; the consensus positions in EITF Issue 08-9, *Milestone Method of Revenue Recognition,* which was codified in the ASC as the result of the FASB's issuance of ASU 2010-17, *Milestone Method of Revenue Recognition*; EITF Issue 09-F, *Casino Base Jackpot Liabilities,* which was codified in the ASC as the result of the FASB's issuance of ASU 2010-16, *Accruals for Casino Jackpot Liabilities*; and EITF Issue 09-L, *Health Care Entities: Measuring Charity Care For Disclosure,* which was codified in the ASC as the result of the FASB's issuance of ASU 2010-23, *Measuring Charity Care For Disclosure*.
- Chapter 38, "Share-Based Payments"—Analysis of the EITF's consensus positions in EITF Issue 09-J, *Effect of Denominating the Exercise Price of a Share-Based Payment Award in the Currency of The Market in Which the Underlying Equity Security Trades*, which was codified in the ASC as the result of the FASB's issuance of ASU 2010-13, *Effect of Denominating the Exercise Price of a Share-Based Payment Award in the Currency of The Market in Which the Underlying Equity Security Trades*.
- Chapter 39, "Stockholders' Equity"—Analysis of the EITF's consensus positions in Issue 09-E, *Accounting for Distributions to Shareholders With Components of Stock and Cash*, which was codified in the ASC as the result of the FASB's issuance of ASU 2010-1, *Accounting for Distributions to Shareholders With Components of Stock and Cash*.
- Chapter 41, "Troubled Debt Restructuring"—Analysis of the EITF's consensus positions in Issue 09-I, *Effect of a Loan Modification When the Loan Is Part of a Pool That is Accounted for as a Single Asset*, which was codified in the ASC as the result of the FASB's issuance of ASU 2010-18, *Effect of a Loan Modification When the Loan Is Part of a Pool That is Accounted for as a Single Asset*.

CCH Learning Center

CCH's goal is to provide you with the clearest, most concise, and up-to-date accounting and auditing information to help further your professional development, as well as a convenient method to help you satisfy your continuing professional education requirements. The CCH Learning Center* offers a complete line of self-study courses covering complex and constantly evolving accounting and auditing issues. We are continually adding new courses to the library to help you stay current on all the latest developments. The CCH Learning Center courses are available 24 hours a day, seven days a week. You'll get immediate exam results and certification. To view our complete accounting and auditing course catalog, go to: **http://cch.learningcenter.com**.

Accounting Research Manager™

Accounting Research Manager is the most comprehensive, up-to-date, and objective online database of financial reporting literature. It includes all authoritative and proposed accounting, auditing and SEC literature, plus independent, expert-written interpretive guidance.

Our Weekly Summary e-mail newsletter highlights the key developments of the week, giving you the assurance that you have the most current information. It provides links to new FASB, AICPA, SEC, PCAOB, EITF, and IASB authoritative and proposal-stage literature, plus insightful guidance from financial reporting experts.

Our outstanding team of content experts takes pride in updating the system on a daily basis, so you stay as current as possible. You'll learn of newly released literature and deliberations of current financial reporting projects as soon they occur! Plus, you benefit from their easy-to-understand technical translations.

With **Accounting Research Manager**, you maximize the efficiency of your research time, while enhancing your results. Learn more about our content, our experts and how you can request a FREE trial by visiting us at **http://www.accountingresearchmananager.com**.

12/10

© 2010 CCH. All Rights Reserved.

---

[*] CCH is registered with the National Association of State Boards of Accountancy (NASBA) as a sponsor of continuing professional education on the National Registry of CPE Sponsors. State boards of accountancy have final authority on the acceptance of individual courses for CPE credit. Complaints regarding registered sponsors may be addressed to the National Registry of CPE Sponsors, 150 Fourth Avenue North, Nashville, TN 37219-2417. Telephone: 615-880-4200.

[*] CCH is registered with the National Association of State Boards of Accountancy as a Quality Assurance Service (QAS) sponsor of continuing professional education. Participating state boards of accountancy have final authority on the acceptance of individual courses for CPE credit. Complaints regarding QAS program sponsors may be addressed to NASBA, 150 Fourth Avenue North, Suite 700, Nashville, TN 37219-2417. Telephone: 615-880-4200.

2011

GAAP

GUIDE, VOLUME II

Restatement and Analysis of
Other Current FASB, EITF,
and AICPA Pronouncements

JUDITH WEISS, CPA

CCH
a Wolters Kluwer business

This publication is designed to provide accurate and authoritative information in regard to the subject matter covered. It is sold with the understanding that the publisher is not engaged in rendering legal, accounting, or other professional services. If legal advice or other professional assistance is required, the services of a competent professional person should be sought.

—From a *Declaration of Principles* jointly adopted by a Committee of the American Bar Association and a Committee of Publishers and Associations

ISBN: 978-0-8080-2402-6

© 2010 CCH. All Rights Reserved.
4025 W. Peterson Avenue
Chicago, IL 60646-6085
1 800 248 3248
http://CCHGroup.com

No claim is made to original government works; however, within this Product or Publication, the following are subject to CCH's copyright: (1) the gathering, compilation, and arrangement of such government materials; (2) the magnetic translation and digital conversion of data, if applicable; (3) the historical, statutory and other notes and references; and (4) the commentary and other materials.

Portions of this work were published in a previous edition.

Printed in the United States of America

SUSTAINABLE FORESTRY INITIATIVE Certified Fiber Sourcing
www.sfiprogram.org

Contents

Our Peer Review Policy   v
Peer Review Statement   vi
Preface   vii
About the Author   xiii

Generally Accepted Accounting Principles

Accounting Changes	1.01
Accounting Policies and Standards	2.01
Advertising	3.01
Balance Sheet Classification and Related Display Issues	4.01
Bankruptcy and Reorganization	5.01
Business Combinations	6.01
Capitalization and Expense Recognition Concepts	7.01
Cash Flow Statement	8.01
Computer Software	9.01
Consolidated Financial Statements	10.01
Contingencies, Risks, and Uncertainties	11.01
Convertible Debt and Debt with Warrants	12.01
Earnings per Share	13.01
Equity Method	14.01
Extinguishment of Debt	15.01
Fair Value	16.01
Financial Instruments	17.01
Foreign Operations and Exchange	18.01
Impairment of Long-Lived Assets	19.01
Income Taxes	20.01
Intangible Assets	21.01
Interest on Receivables and Payables	22.01
Interim Financial Reporting	23.01
Inventory	24.01

Investments in Debt and Equity Securities	25.01
Leases	26.01
Long-Term Construction Contracts	27.01
Nonmonetary Transactions	28.01
Pension Plans—Employers	29.01
Pension Plans—Settlements and Curtailments	30.01
Personal Financial Statements	31.01
Postemployment and Postretirement Benefits Other Than Pensions	32.01
Real Estate Transactions	33.01
Research and Development	34.01
Results of Operations	35.01
Revenue Recognition	36.01
Segment Reporting	37.01
Stock-Based Payments	38.01
Stockholders' Equity	39.01
Transfer of Financial Assets	40.01
Troubled Debt Restructuring	41.01
Appendix: Listing of Specialized Industry Guidance	APP.01
Accounting Resources on the Web	WEB.01
Cross-Reference—Original Pronouncements to **GAAP Guide**, *Volumes* **I** *and* **II**	CR.01
Index	IND.01

> For the most recent activities of the FASB, the EITF, and the AICPA, refer to the *GAAP Update Service* and the **GAAP** *Library* (http://www.accountingresearchmanager.com).

Our Peer Review Policy

Thank you for ordering the 2011 *GAAP Guide, Volume II*. Each year we bring you the best accounting and auditing reference guides available. To confirm the technical accuracy and quality control of our materials, CCH voluntarily submitted to a peer review of our publishing system and our publications (see the Peer Review Letter on the following page).

In addition to peer review, our publications undergo strict technical and content reviews by qualified practitioners. This ensures that our books and practice aids meet "real world" standards and applicability.

Our publications are reviewed every step of the way—from conception to production—to ensure that we bring you the finest guides on the market.

Updated annually, peer-reviewed, technically accurate, convenient, and practical—the 2011 *GAAP Guide, Volume II* shows our commitment to creating books and practice aids and workpapers you can trust.

Peer Review Statement

Caldwell, Becker, Dervin, Petrick & Co., L.L.P.
CERTIFIED PUBLIC ACCOUNTANTS

Quality Control Materials Review Report

November 12, 2009

Executive Board
CCH, a Wolters Kluwer business
and the National Peer Review Committee

We have reviewed the system of quality control for the development and maintenance of GAAP Guide (2010 Edition) (hereafter referred to as *materials*) of CCH, a Wolters Kluwer business (the organization) and the resultant materials in effect at October 31, 2009. Our quality control materials peer review was conducted in accordance with the Standards for Performing and Reporting on Peer Reviews established by the Peer Review Board of the American Institute of Certified Public Accountants. The organization is responsible for designing a system of quality control and complying with it to provide users of the materials with reasonable assurance that the materials are reliable aids to assist them in conforming with those professional standards that the materials purport to encompass. Our responsibility is to express an opinion on the design of the system and the organization's compliance with that system based on our review. The nature, objectives, scope, limitations of, and the procedures performed in a Quality Control Materials Review are described in the standards at www.aicpa.org/prsummary.

In our opinion, the system of quality control for the development and maintenance of the quality control materials of CCH, a Wolters Kluwer business was suitably designed and was being complied with during the year ended October 31, 2009, to provide users of the materials with reasonable assurance that the materials are reliable aids to assist them in conforming with those professional standards the materials purport to encompass. Also, in our opinion, the quality control materials referred to above are reliable aids at October 31, 2009. Organizations can receive a rating of *pass, pass with deficiency(ies)*, or *fail*. CCH, a Wolters Kluwer business has received a peer review rating of *pass*.

Caldwell, Becker, Dervin, Petrick & Co., LLP
CALDWELL, BECKER, DERVIN, PETRICK & CO., L.L.P.

20750 Ventura Boulevard, Suite 140 • Woodland Hills, CA 91364
(818) 704-1040 • FAX (818) 704-5536

Preface

The 2011 *GAAP Guide, Volume II,* shows you how FASB and AICPA accounting pronouncements and EITF consensus positions apply to specific business transactions. It is designed with one goal in mind: To give you what you need to find answers quickly. We have taken the complex and often lengthy technical implementation guidance contained in the original text of those pronouncements and restated and analyzed it in clear, understandable terms.

The 2011 *GAAP Guide, Volume I,* which is the companion volume to this Guide, provides an incisive analysis of FASB Standards and Interpretations, APB Opinions, and Accounting Research Bulletins. As part of CCH's **Complete GAAP Library for Business,** the following types of authoritative pronouncements, which have been incorporated in the FASB Accounting Standards Codification™ (ASC), are discussed in this innovative Guide:

- Statements of Position of the AICPA's Accounting Standards Executive Committee
- Technical Bulletins issued by the FASB
- FASB Staff Positions
- Consensus positions of the Emerging Issues Task Force (EITF)
- Practice Bulletins of the AICPA's Accounting Standards Executive Committee
- FASB and SEC staff announcements
- Accounting Interpretations of the AICPA associated with Accounting Principles Board Opinions that remain in effect
- Implementation Guides (Q&A) issued by the FASB

Statements of Position (SOPs) of the AICPA Accounting Standards Executive Committee are the primary source of generally accepted accounting principles for the following significant business events for which there is no other accounting guidance:

- Accounting for start-up costs (SOP 98-5)
- Software revenue recognition (SOPs 97-2)
- Environmental remediation liabilities (SOP 96-1)
- Disclosure of certain risks and uncertainties (SOP 94-6)
- Reporting on advertising costs (SOP 93-7)
- Employers' accounting for employee stock option plans (SOP 93-6)

- Financial reporting by entities in reorganization under the Bankruptcy Code (SOP 90-7)
- Accounting and financial reporting for personal financial statements (SOP 82-1)
- Accounting for performance of construction-type and certain production-type contracts (SOP 81-1)

The following types of pronouncements in the *GAAP Guide, Volume II*, answer specific questions that have been asked as a result of the application of GAAP in practice:

1. FASB Technical Bulletins (FTBs) address a limited number of narrow financial accounting and reporting issues in a question and answer format. For example, FTB 85-6 provides accounting guidance to an entity that repurchases its own stock at a price significantly in excess of the prevailing market price prior to the purchase.
2. Consensus positions of the Emerging Issues Task Force mostly address issues related to the implementation of authoritative pronouncements issued by the FASB and the AICPA or previously issued EITF consensus positions.
3. FASB Staff Positions (FSPs) provide application guidance related to authoritative pronouncements issued by the FASB, the EITF, and the AICPA. They are written by the FASB Staff, deliberated by the FASB, exposed to the public for comments, and approved for final issuance by the FASB.
4. Practice Bulletins, which were issued by the Accounting Standards Executive Committee, address a limited number of narrow accounting issues.
5. Accounting Interpretations, which were issued by the Accounting Principles Board are similar to FASB Technical Bulletins because they address a limited number of narrow accounting issues in a question and answer format.
6. The inclusion of FASB Implementation Guides, which provide additional guidance for some of the FASB's more complex accounting standards, is a significant feature of this Guide. Implementation Guides, which tend to be lengthy, provide detailed financial accounting and reporting guidance in a question and answer format, as well as additional examples for the following FASB Statements:

    (a) FAS-109 (Accounting for Income Taxes)

    (b) FAS-115 (Accounting for Certain Investments in Debt and Equity Securities)

    (c) FAS-140 (Accounting for Transfers and Servicing of Financial Assets and Extinguishments of Liabilities)

EITF consensus positions are a particularly important part of this Guide. They interpret or provide implementation guidance on existing authoritative pronouncements. They also represent the best thinking on some issues for which there is no specific guidance elsewhere in GAAP, such as for environmental liabilities. The following is the EITF's procedure for the issuance of final consensus positions:

- Before reaching a consensus on an Issue, the EITF first agrees on a consensus-for-exposure that has to be ratified by the FASB and approved for exposure before issuance for a minimum 15-day public comment period.

- EITF Issues are exposed for comment in the form of proposed Updates, which are posted on the FASB's web site.

- The EITF reviews comments on the exposure draft, if any, at a future meeting and decides whether to affirm a consensus-for-exposure as a consensus on the Issue. At the Chairman's discretion, an EITF meeting may be held in the form of a web cast or a public conference call for the purpose of approving a consensus-for-exposure as a consensus after exposure for comment. Notice of such a web cast or public conference call will be given on the FASB's web site at least one week before a scheduled meeting. The EITF's approval of a consensus-for-exposure as a consensus during a web cast or public conference call will be conducted by a voice vote following the same procedure as at a regular EITF meeting.

- After the EITF has reached a consensus on an Issue, a majority of the FASB must ratify the consensus position, as written, at a public meeting before it is issued as an accounting pronouncement.

- After the FASB has ratified the EITF's consensus positions on an Issue, an Accounting Standards Update (ASU) is issued by the FASB and posted on the FASB's web site. The guidance in ASUs, which are numbered consecutively each year beginning with the number 1, e.g., 2010-1, is then incorporated in the applicable sections of the FASB Accounting Standards Codification™ (ASC).

Also discussed in this Guide are announcements of authoritative guidance made at EITF meetings by the FASB staff, the SEC Observer, and others, such as the AICPA Observer, on technical matters that usually are related to FASB pronouncements. Those announcements are reviewed and discussed by the EITF. They may be subsequently issued as ASUs and incorporated in the ASC.

Format and Practical Features

The *GAAP Guide, Volume II,* is organized in chapters that are listed in the Table of Contents alphabetically by topic. To aid users of the Guide, each chapter includes pronouncements on the same topic.

The *GAAP Guide, Volume II,* is written in clear, understandable language. Each pronouncement is presented in a format that makes it easy to understand and apply the guidance discussed. Each pronouncement discussed in the Guide includes detailed cross-references to the ASC. Abundant illustrations demonstrate and clarify specific accounting principles. The Cross-Reference in the back of the Guide and the Index provide quick, accurate references to needed information.

Additional tools provided in the 2011 *GAAP Guide, Volume II,* enable users to locate correct and complete information quickly. First, the Cross-Reference to the **Complete GAAP Library for Business** is included at the end of this volume to help you locate specific pronouncements easily. The pronouncements are listed in the Cross-Reference section in chronological order by type of pronouncement. The listing of each pronouncement includes its chapter location and status, as well as the ASC section in which it is discussed. Second, to facilitate your research, pronouncements related to specialized industries are listed in the Appendix to this volume.

The 2011 *GAAP Guide, Volume II,* meets accounting industry standards overseen by the peer review system. A document related to the peer review of this book is reprinted for your reference.

Abbreviations

The following abbreviations are used throughout the text to represent the various sources of authoritative literature covered in this book:

AcSEC	AICPA Accounting Standards Executive Committee
AIN-APB	AICPA Accounting Interpretation
APB	Accounting Principles Board Opinion
ARB	Accounting Research Bulletin
ASC	FASB Accounting Standards Codification™
ASR	Accounting Series Release
CON	FASB Concepts Statement
EITF	Emerging Issues Task Force
FAS	FASB Statement
FASB	Financial Accounting Standards Board
FSP	FASB Staff Position
FIG-FAS	FASB Implementation Guide
FIN	FASB Interpretation
FRR	Financial Reporting Release
FTB	FASB Technical Bulletin
PB	AICPA AcSEC Practice Bulletin
SAB	SEC Staff Accounting Bulletin
SAS	Statement on Auditing Standards
SOP	AICPA Statements of Position

Acknowledgments

The author gives thanks to the late Thomas W. McRae and to Paul Rosenfield, formerly of the AICPA, who taught her about writing and the accounting standards-setting process; former colleagues and friends who helped to make the Guide a reality; and four very important CPAs: her husband, Carl, sons, Daniel and Jonathan, and daughter-in-law, Robyn, for their interest and tireless encouragement in this project.

About the Author

Judith Weiss, CPA, has an M.S. in Accounting from Long Island University, Greenvale, New York, and an M.S. in Education from Queens College, Flushing, New York. After several years in public accounting and private industry, she worked as a technical manager in the AICPA's Accounting Standards Division, where she helped industry committees to develop Audit and Accounting Guides and Statements of Position. As a senior manager in the national offices of Deloitte & Touche LLP and Grant Thornton LLP, she was involved in projects related to standard-setting by the FASB and the AICPA. Ms. Weiss has followed the work of the EITF since its inception and has attended its meetings regularly since 1991.

Since 1993, Ms. Weiss has combined her extensive experience in the development and implementation of accounting and auditing standards with her technical writing background in writing projects related to accounting standards. She has contributed to several books in the area of accounting and auditing. She also has coauthored articles on accounting standards for several publications, including the *Journal of Accountancy, The CPA Journal, The Journal of Real Estate Accounting and Taxation,* and the *Journal of Corporate Accounting and Finance.* Ms. Weiss is also one of the authors of the *GAAP Update Service.*

**Generally Accepted
Accounting Principles**

CHAPTER 1
ACCOUNTING CHANGES

CONTENTS

Overview	1.01
Authoritative Guidance	
ASC 810 Consolidation	1.03
EITF Issue 06-9 Reporting a Change in (or the Elimination of) a Previously Existing Difference between the Fiscal Year-End of a Parent Company and That of a Consolidated Entity or between the Reporting Period of an Investor and That of an Equity Method Investee	1.03
Nonauthoritative Guidance	
EITF/FASB/SEC Staff Announcements	1.04
Topic D-1 Implications and Implementation of an EITF Consensus	1.04
Related Chapter in 2011 GAAP Guide, Volume II	1.05
Related Chapters in 2011 GAAP Guide, Volume I	1.05
Related Chapters in 2011 International Accounting/Financial Reporting Standards Guide	1.06

OVERVIEW

Accounting changes are broadly classified as (*a*) changes in an accounting principle, (*b*) changes in an accounting estimate, and (*c*) changes in the reporting entity. *Corrections of errors in previously issued financial statements are not accounting changes but are covered in the same pronouncement because of their similarity.*

Three different accounting methods are used to account for accounting changes and corrections of errors: (1) current and prospective, (2) retrospective application, and (3) restatement. These methods are not alternatives—the authoritative literature is specific concerning which method should be used for each type of accounting change or correction of error.

1.02 *Accounting Changes*

Guidance on the treatment of accounting changes in the following pronouncements is discussed in the *GAAP Guide, Volume I*, Chapter 1, "Accounting Changes":

ASC 250	Accounting Changes and Error Corrections ((FAS-154, (Accounting Changes and Error Corrections)
ASC 250-10 and 330-10	Accounting Changes and Error Corrections—Overall (FIN-1, (Accounting Changes Related to the Cost of Inventory)

AUTHORITATIVE GUIDANCE

ASC 810 Consolidation

EITF Issue 06-9 (Reporting a Change in (or the Elimination of) a Previously Existing Difference between the Fiscal Year-End of a Parent Company and That of a Consolidated Entity or between the Reporting Period of an Investor and That of an Equity Method Investee) (ASC 810-10-45-13; 50-2)

OVERVIEW

Under the guidance in the FASB Accounting Standards Codification™ (ASC) 810, *Consolidation* (ARB-51, *Consolidated Financial Statements*) and ASC 323 (APB-18, *The Equity Method of Accounting for Investments in Common Stock*), a parent company's reporting year-end is permitted to be different from that of a consolidated entity's year-end for the purpose of consolidating the entity's operations; and an investor's reporting year-end is permitted to be different from its equity-method investee's year-end for the purpose of recognizing a change in an equity investment's net assets. Parent companies and investors who want to obtain financial results that are more consistent with, or the same as, their respective entity's results have asked for guidance on how to account for a change in or an elimination of a previously existing difference (lag period) in a consolidated entity's or equity method investee's reporting year-end.

SCOPE

ASC 810-10-45-13; 50-2 (Issue 06-9) applies to all entities that change or eliminate an existing difference between a parent company's reporting year-end and that of a consolidated entity or that of an investor and its equity method investee. The guidance in Issue 06-9 does *not* apply if a parent company changes its fiscal year-end.

ACCOUNTING ISSUE

How should a parent company recognize the effect of a change to or the elimination of an existing difference between a parent company's reporting period and a consolidated entity's reporting period or between an investor's reporting period and an equity-method investee's reporting period?

1.04 Accounting Changes

EITF CONSENSUS

The EITF reached a consensus that a change or elimination of an existing difference between a parent company's reporting period and that of an entity consolidated in its financial statements or between an investor's reporting period and the reporting period of an equity method investee should be accounted for in a parent company's or an investor's financial statements as a change in accounting principle in accordance with the guidance in ASC 250-10-05, 10-15, 10-45, 10-50, 10-55, 10-60 (FAS-154, *Accounting Changes and Error Corrections*). The EITF reached that consensus based on the view that a change to or elimination of a lag period is a change in accounting principle. The EITF also noted that, although voluntary changes under the guidance in ASC 250 (FAS-154) are required to be reported retrospectively, according to the guidance in ASC 250-10-45-9, 45-10 (paragraph 11 of FAS-154), retrospective application is *not* required if applying the effects of a change would be impracticable.

DISCLOSURE

The EITF reached a consensus that information required under the guidance in ASC 250-10-50 (FAS-154) should be disclosed.

TRANSITION

The EITF reached a consensus that ASC 810-10-45-13; 50-2 (Issue 06-9) should be effective for changes that occur in interim or annual reporting periods that begin *after* the FASB's ratification of the consensus. Earlier application of the guidance is permitted in periods for which financial statements have *not* yet been issued.

FASB RATIFICATION

The FASB ratified the EITF's consensus position on Issue 06-9 at its November 29, 2006, meeting.

NONAUTHORITATIVE GUIDANCE

EITF/FASB/SEC Staff Announcements

Topic D-1 (Implications and Implementation of an EITF Consensus)

> **OBSERVATION:** The guidance in ASC 250-10-05, 10-15, 10-45, 10-50, 10-55, 10-60 (FAS-154, *Accounting for Changes*

and Error Corrections) superseded the guidance in APB-20 (Accounting Changes), FAS-3 (Reporting Accounting Changes in Interim Financial Statements), and FIN-20 (not in ASC). The EITF continues to establish transition provisions for EITF consensus positions based on the transition that is most appropriate for an Issue's specific circumstances. In choosing retrospective application as the default method for new accounting principles and the required transition for voluntary changes in accounting principles, the EITF should consider the FASB's concerns about financial statement comparability between periods. If the EITF decides that a consensus should be accounted for as a cumulative-effect adjustment, the EITF should consider including guidance on the transition date and a requirement that any adjustment be made to retained earnings or other appropriate components of equity or net assets. For accounting changes made in fiscal years that begin after December 15, 2005, the transition guidance and disclosures in ASC 250-10-45-5 through 45-10 (paragraphs 7–11 of FAS-154), and ASC 250-10-45-15 and 45-16 and ASC 250-10-50-1 through 50-3 (paragraphs 15 through 18 of FAS-154) should be applied to all prior periods and should be followed if an EITF Issue does not include specific transition guidance, unless doing so would be impractical.

Shortly after the EITF was established, the SEC's Chief Accountant, who is an observer at EITF meetings with the privilege of the floor, indicated that he believes EITF consensus positions will set the tone for future accounting and that the SEC would question accounting practices used by SEC registrants that differ from EITF consensus positions. He noted, however, that accounting followed in good faith in financial statements filed with the SEC would not be challenged as the result of a subsequent EITF consensus.

RELATED CHAPTERS IN 2011
GAAP GUIDE, VOLUME II

Chapter 6, "Business Combinations"
Chapter 10, "Consolidated Financial Statements"

RELATED CHAPTERS IN 2011
GAAP GUIDE, VOLUME I

Chapter 1, "Accounting Changes"
Chapter 4, "Business Combinations"
Chapter 7, "Consolidated Financial Statements"

**RELATED CHAPTERS IN 2011
*INTERNATIONAL ACCOUNTING/FINANCIAL
REPORTING STANDARDS GUIDE***

Chapter 5, "Accounting Policies, Changes in Accounting Estimates, and Errors"
Chapter 12, "Earnings per Share"
Chapter 22, "Interim Financial Reporting"

CHAPTER 2
ACCOUNTING POLICIES AND STANDARDS

CONTENTS

Overview		2.01
Authoritative Guidance		
FASB Staff Positions		2.03
ASC 255	Changing Prices	2.03
SOP 93-3	Rescission of Accounting Principles Board Statements	2.03
ASC 310	Receivables	2.05
PB-1	Purpose and Scope of AcSEC Practice Bulletins and Procedures for Their Issuance	2.05
Nonauthoritative Guidance		
FASB Technical Bulletins		2.10
FTB 79-1(R)	Purpose and Scope of FASB Technical Bulletins and Procedures for Issuance	2.10
Related Chapter in 2011 GAAP Guide, Volume II		2.11
Related Chapters in 2011 GAAP Guide, Volume I		2.11
Related Chapter in 2011 International Accounting/Financial Reporting Standards Guide		2.12

OVERVIEW

Information about an entity's accounting policies is an important aid in helping users to understand the content of financial statements. FASB (Financial Accounting Standards Board) and APB (Accounting Principles Board) standards provide guidance related to the presentation of required disclosures about an entity's accounting policies as an integral part of financial statements that are intended to present an entity's financial position, cash flows,

2.02 *Accounting Policies and Standards*

and results of operations in conformity with generally accepted accounting principles (GAAP).

The guidance in the following pronouncement, which is the primary source that addresses the disclosure of accounting policies, is discussed in the 2010 *GAAP Guide, Volume I,* Chapter 2, "Accounting Policies and Standards":

ASC-235 Notes to Financial Statements (APB-22, Disclosure of Accounting Policies)

AUTHORITATIVE GUIDANCE

FASB Staff Positions

The FASB staff frequently receives questions on the application of various pronouncements. In the past, when the FASB's staff viewed the question as having broad applicability, and when the staff viewed only one answer as acceptable, guidance on that inquiry was issued in the form of Staff Implementation Guide or, from time to time, in the form of a FASB staff announcement at EITF meetings . Staff Implementation Guides (FASB staff announcements) were considered "Level D" pronouncements in the generally accepted accounting principles (GAAP) hierarchy in accordance with the provisions of AICPA Statement on Auditing Standards No. SAS-69 (The Meaning of Present Fairly in Conformity with Generally Accepted Accounting Principles), which had to be followed in determining whether a set of financial statements were prepared in accordance with GAAP. When the FASB staff began issuing FASB Staff Positions (FSPs), the FASB discontinued the issuance of Staff Implementation Guides.

The guidance in SAS-69 was removed from the auditing literature issued by the AICPA's Auditing Standards Board and transferred to the FASB's authoritative accounting literature by the FASB's issuance of FAS-162, The Hierarchy of Generally Accepted Accounting Principles. Since the establishment of the FASB Accounting Standards Codification™ (ASC) on July 1, 2009, drafts of pronouncements formerly known as FASB Statements of Financial Accounting Standards, FASB Interpretations, EITF Consensus positions, and FASB Staff Positions will be exposed for public comment and issued as final pronouncements in the form of Accounting Standards Updates (ASUs), which will be used to amend the related Topics in the Codification. ASUs will not be considered to be authoritative until they have actually been incorporated in the Codification.

ASC 255 Changing Prices

SOP 93-3 (Rescission of Accounting Principles Board Statements) (ASC 255-10-15-2; 15-45-2 through 4)

BACKGROUND

Statements of Position presented the conclusions of at least two-thirds of the Accounting Standards Executive Committee (AcSEC). AcSEC was a senior technical body of the AICPA authorized to represent the AICPA on matters involving industry specific accounting and financial reporting guidance.

2.04 *Accounting Policies and Standards*

The FASB's predecessor, the APB, issued both Opinions and Statements. The APB issued 31 Opinions between 1959 and 1973. Any of those Opinions that had not been superseded by an FASB Statement have been part of the literature encompassed by Rule 203 of the AICPA's Code of Professional Conduct.

The APB also issued four Statements. Those Statements never were considered rules or standards that AICPA members had to follow (i.e., they were not encompassed by the Code of Professional Conduct). In addition, SAS-69 (The Meaning of "Present Fairly in Conformity with Generally Accepted Accounting Principles" in the Independent Auditor's Report) listed APB Statements as a source of "other accounting literature. " Before the FASB's issuance of the Accounting Standards Codification on July 1, 2009, which considers that guidance to be nonauthoritative, practitioners were permitted to choose to follow items included in that category; but they were not required to do so. However, even though APB Statements never represented a source of authoritative literature, some practitioners erroneously viewed APB Statements as authoritative. SOP 93-3 was issued to rectify this situation.

STANDARDS

As the result of the provisions of SOP 93-3, the four Statements issued by the APB were rescinded. The ACIPA's Accounting Standards Executive Committee (AcSEC) took that action to eliminate any confusion as to whether APB Statements represented a source of authoritative literature. Also, FASB pronouncements had effectively superseded each of those four APB Statements. The following APB Statements were rescinded:

- APB Statement No. 1 (Statement by the Accounting Principles Board)
- APB Statement No. 2 (Disclosure of Supplemental Financial Information by Diversified Companies)—effectively superseded by FAS-14 and FAS-14 has been superseded by FAS-131
- APB Statement No. 3 (Financial Statements Restated for General Price-Level Changes)—partially superseded by FAS-89
- APB Statement No. 4 (Basic Concepts and Accounting Principles Underlying Financial Statements of Business Enterprises)— effectively superseded by the various FASB Statements of Financial Accounting Concepts

APB-3 (Financial Statements Restated for General Price-Level Changes) provided guidance for a comprehensive application of price-level adjusted financial statements. ASC 255 (FAS-89, Financial Reporting and Changing Prices) effectively superseded a portion of APB-3. However, ASC 255-10-50-1, 50-3, 50-5, 50-7 through 50-55, 55-1 through 55-89 continues to provide guidance for the presentation of partial price-level data only. Although APB Statement 3 has been rescinded by this SOP, entities are not precluded from following the guidance presented in APB-3 for preparing a comprehensive set of price-level adjusted financial statements (assuming those statements are not inconsistent with the guidance in ASC 255 regarding historical cost/constant purchasing power accounting, such as the classification of assets and liabilities as monetary or nonmonetary).

ASC 310 Receivables

PB-1 (Purpose and Scope of AcSEC Practice Bulletins and Procedures for Their Issuance) (ASC 310-10-05-9; 10-15-5; 10-25-15 through 25-30; 10-35-55 through 35-61; 10-40-3 through 40-5; 10-45-15; ASC 360-10-35-3, 35-9)

BACKGROUND

The AICPA issued Practice Bulletins to disseminate the views of the AICPA Accounting Standards Executive Committee (AcSEC) (now known as the Financial Reporting Executive Committee) on narrow financial accounting and reporting issues. AcSEC was a senior technical body of the AICPA authorized to represent the AICPA on matters that addressed accounting and financial reporting unique to specific industries.. Practice Bulletins addressed issues that were not addressed and are not expected to be addressed by either the FASB or the Governmental Accounting Standards Board (GASB).

STANDARDS

Before 1987, when AcSEC began to issue Practice Bulletins, similar guidance was provided in "Notices to Practitioners," which were published in either *The CPA Letter* or the *Journal of Accountancy*. Unlike Notices to Practitioners, which are not numbered for retrievability, Practice Bulletins are numbered and designed to convey information that will enhance the quality and comparability of financial statements.

Drafts of proposed Practice Bulletins, which have been discussed at AcSEC open meetings, are available to the public as part of the meeting's agenda. However, Practice Bulletins have not been exposed for public comment, and their issuance is not subject to public hearings.

A Practice Bulletin is issued if both of the following conditions are met: (a) two-thirds or more of AcSEC's members vote to issue the proposed Bulletin, and (b) after reviewing the proposed Bulletin, the FASB and GASB indicate that neither plans to address the particular issue.

Most of the Notices to Practitioners that preceded the issuance of Practice Bulletins have been superseded. Three Notices to Practitioners continue to be in effect, however, and are discussed in the appendix to PB-1, "Purpose and Scope of AcSEC Practice Bulletins and Procedures for Their Issuance." The following is a brief discussion of the three Notices to Practitioners that were not superseded.

ACRS Lives and GAAP

In most cases, the number of years specified by the ACRS for recovery deductions will not bear any reasonable resemblance to the asset's useful life. In these cases, ACRS recovery deductions cannot be used as the depreciation expense amount for financial reporting purposes. Rather, depreciation for financial reporting purposes should be based on the asset's useful life.

Accounting by Colleges and Universities for Compensated Absences

Note: The following discussion pertains solely to private (nonpublic) colleges and universities.

When FASB Accounting Standards Codification™, ASC 710, *Compensation—General*, (FAS-43, Accounting for Compensated Absences) and ASC 420, *Exit or Disposal Cost Obligations* (FAS-146, Accounting for Costs Associated with Exit or Disposal Activities) were issued, there was some discussion as to whether the guidance in ASC 710 (FAS-43) would apply to colleges and universities. The FASB decided *not* to exempt colleges and universities from the provisions of that standard. A Notice to Practitioners was issued to assist colleges and universities in applying that guidance. The essential conclusions of the Notice were as follows:

- In recognizing the liability, and the associated charge, for compensated absences in the current and prior years, the unrestricted current fund is to be used (use of the plant fund is specifically prohibited).
- In some cases, the liability for compensated absences might be recoverable from future state and federal grants and contracts for funded research. A receivable, and the associated revenue, can be recognized to offset a portion of the liability only in limited situations. More specifically, a receivable can be recognized only if it meets the definition of an *asset* in Statement of Financial Accounting Concepts No. 6 (Elements of Financial Statements of Business Enterprises). In evaluating the receivable, the college or university should consider the measurability and collectibility of the receivable and the institution's legal right to it.

- The reduction in the unrestricted current fund balance caused by recognizing the liability for compensated absences may be reduced by interfund transfers. These interfund transfers may be recognized only if (*a*) unrestricted assets are available for permanent transfer and (*b*) payment (or other settlement) to the unrestricted current fund is expected within a reasonable period.

ADC Arrangements

This Notice to Practitioners addresses the funding provided by financial institutions for real estate acquisition, development, and construction (ADC). In some cases, financial institutions enter into ADC agreements where the institution has essentially the same risks and rewards as an investor or a joint venture participant. In these cases, treating the ADC funding as a loan would not be appropriate.

The notice applies only to ADC arrangements in which a financial institution is expected to receive some or all of the residual profit. Expected residual profit is the amount of funds the lender is expected to receive—whether these funds are referred to as interest, as fees, or as an equity kicker—above a customary amount of interest and fees normally received for providing comparable financing.

The profit participation between the lender and the developer is not always part of the mortgage loan agreement. Therefore, the auditor should be cognizant that such side agreements may exist and should design the audit to detect such profit participation agreements between the lender and the developer.

> ☞ **PRACTICE POINTER:** A side agreement may exist to provide the lender with a profit participation in ADC loans. This side agreement may not be referred to in the mortgage agreement between the lender and the developer. The auditor should specifically ask the lender to confirm whether it is party to a profit participation agreement on a particular loan.

A number of characteristics, in addition to the sharing of the expected residual profit, indicate that the ADC arrangement is more akin to an investment or a joint venture than to a loan. These characteristics are as follows:

- The financial institution provides all, or substantially all, of the funds necessary to acquire, develop, and construct the project. The developer has title but little or no equity investment in the project.
- The financial institution rolls into the loan any commitment and/or origination fees.

- The financial institution adds to the loan balance all, or substantially all, interest and fees during the term of the loan.
- The financial institution's only security for the loan is the ADC project. There is no recourse to other assets of the borrower. Also, the borrower does not guarantee the debt.
- The financial institution recovers its investment in one of three ways: (a) the project is completed and sold to an independent third party, (b) the borrower obtains refinancing from another source, or (c) the project is completed and placed in service, and cash flows are sufficient to fund the repayment of principal and interest.
- Foreclosure during the development period due to delinquency is unlikely, because the borrower is not required to make any payments during this period.

In some cases, even though a lender is expected to participate in the residual profit from the project, the facts and circumstances of the borrowing arrangement are consistent with a loan. The following characteristics of an ADC arrangement are consistent with a loan:

- The lender's participation in the expected residual profit is less than 50%.
- The borrower has a substantial equity investment in the project, not funded by the lender. This equity investment can be either in the form of cash or in the form of the contribution of land to the project.
- Either (a) the lender has recourse to other substantial, tangible assets of the borrower, which have not already been pledged under other loans, or (b) the borrower has secured an irrevocable letter of credit from a creditworthy, independent third party for substantially all of the loan balance and for the entire term of the loan.
- A take-out commitment for the entire amount of the loan has been secured from a creditworthy, independent third party. If the take-out commitment is conditional, the conditions should be reasonable and their attainment should be probable.

Some ADC loans contain personal guarantees from the borrower or from a third party. AcSEC believes that such guarantees are rarely sufficient to support classifying the ADC arrangement as a loan.

In evaluating the substance of a personal guarantee, the following factors should be considered: (1) the ability of the guarantor to perform under the guarantee, (2) the practicality of enforcing the guarantee in the applicable jurisdiction, and (3) a demonstrated intent on the part of the lender to enforce the guarantee. Factors that might indicate the ability to perform under the guarantee include placing liquid assets in escrow, pledging marketable securities, and obtaining irrevocable letters of credit from a creditworthy, independent third party.

In the absence of the support discussed above for a guarantee, financial statements of the guarantor need to be evaluated. In evaluating the financial statements of the guarantor, the auditor should consider both the guarantor's liquidity and net worth. A guarantee has little substance if its only support is assets already pledged as security for other debt. Also, guarantees made by the guarantor on other projects should be considered.

If the lender expects to receive more than 50% of the residual profit from the project, the lender should account for the income or loss from the arrangement as a real estate investment. The guidance in ASC 970, Real Estate-General (FAS-67, Accounting for Costs and Initial Rental Operations of Real Estate Projects) and in ASC 360, Property Plant and Equipment and ASC 976, Real Estate-Retail Land (FAS-66, Accounting for Sales of Real Estate) should be followed.

If a lender expects to receive less than 50% of the residual profit from the project, the ADC arrangement should be accounted for as a loan or as a joint venture, depending on the applicable circumstances. If an ADC arrangement is classified as a loan, interest and fees may be recognized as income if they are recoverable. In assessing the recoverability of loan amounts and accrued interest, the guidance in both ASC 974, Real Estate-Real Estate Investment Trusts (SOP 75-2, Accounting Practices of Real Estate Investment Trusts) and the guidance in ASC 942 (Audit and Accounting Guide, *Banks and Savings Institutions*) might be useful. If an ADC arrangement is classified as a joint venture, the primary accounting guidance may be found in ASC 970 (SOP 78-9, Accounting for Investments in Real Estate Ventures) and in ASC 835-20, Interest-Capitalization (FAS-34, Capitalization of Interest Cost).

ADC arrangements classified as investments in real estate or as joint ventures should be combined and reported separately from those ADC arrangements treated as loans for balance sheet reporting purposes.

In some cases, the lender's share of the expected residual profit is sold before the project is completed. The applicable accounting in these cases hinges on whether the ADC arrangement was treated as a loan, as an investment in real estate, or as a joint venture. If the ADC arrangement was treated as a loan, proceeds received from the sale of the expected residual profit should be recognized as additional interest income over the remaining term of the loan. If the ADC arrangement was treated as a real estate investment or a joint venture, any gain to be recognized upon sale of the expected residual profit is determined by reference to ASC 976 (FAS-66).

The accounting treatment of an ADC project should be periodically reassessed. For example, an ADC arrangement originally classified as an investment or a joint venture might subsequently be classified as a loan if the lender is not expected to receive more than 50% of the residual profit and if the risk to the lender has decreased significantly. It is important to note that a change in the accounting for an ADC arrangement depends on a change in the facts that were relied upon when the ADC arrangement was initially classified. The absence of, or a reduced participation in, a residual profit is not sufficient to change the categorization of the ADC arrangement. In addition, it is possible for an ADC arrangement initially classified as a loan to be reclassified as a real estate investment or a joint venture. The lender may take on additional risks and rewards of ownership by releasing collateral to support a guarantee and by increasing its percentage of profit participation. An improvement in the economic prospects for the project does not justify a change in how the ADC arrangement is categorized. A change in classification is expected to be rare and needs to be supported by adequate documentation.

Finally, regardless of the accounting treatment for an ADC arrangement, it is necessary to continually assess the collectibility of principal, accrued interest, and fees. Also, ADC financing often entails a heightened risk of related-party transactions. The auditor needs to design the audit accordingly.

NONAUTHORITATIVE GUIDANCE

FASB Technical Bulletin

FTB 79-1 (R) (Purpose and Scope of FASB Technical Bulletins and Procedures for Issuance)

BACKGROUND

Between 1979 and 2001, the FASB staff was authorized to prepare Technical Bulletins to provide timely guidance on certain financial accounting and reporting issues. FTB 79-1 (R) (Purpose and Scope of FASB Technical Bulletins and Procedures for Issuance) describes the purpose and scope of Technical Bulletins and the procedures for their issuance.

STANDARDS

FASB Technical Bulletins provide guidance in applying Accounting Research Bulletins, APB Opinions, and FASB Statements and Interpretations and guidance for resolving issues that are not directly addressed in those pronouncements. The following kinds of guidance are provided in Technical Bulletins:

- To clarify, explain, or elaborate on an underlying standard
- To provide guidance for a particular situation (e.g., a specific industry) in which application of a standard may differ from its general application
- To address areas not directly covered by existing standards

Problems and issues that are brought to the FASB's attention are the basis for issuing a Technical Bulletin if the financial reporting problem or issue can be resolved within all of the following guidelines:

- The guidance is not expected to cause a major change in accounting practice for a large number of entities.
- The administrative cost that may be involved in implementing the guidance is not expected to be significant for most affected entities.
- The guidance does not conflict with a broad fundamental principle or create a new accounting practice.

Proposed Technical Bulletins are available to the public, and interested individuals may comment in writing to the FASB. Issues proposed for Technical Bulletins are discussed by the FASB at a public meeting, and FASB members are provided copies of all proposed Bulletins before their issuance. FASB members are also provided copies of a summary of the comments that are received before a Technical Bulletin is issued. Technical Bulletins are generally in a question and answer format.

> **OBSERVATION:** The FASB's issuance of Technical Bulletins has decreased markedly since the creation of the FASB's Emerging Issues Task Force. For example, only three Technical Bulletins were issued during the 1990s. The FASB appears to have largely delegated the responsibility for providing guidance on FASB Statements and Interpretations to the EITF.

RELATED CHAPTER IN 2011
GAAP GUIDE, VOLUME II

Chapter 26, "Leases"

RELATED CHAPTERS IN 2011
GAAP GUIDE, VOLUME I

Chapter 2, "Accounting Policies and Standards"
Chapter 29, "Leases"

RELATED CHAPTER IN 2011 INTERNATIONAL ACCOUNTING/FINANCIAL REPORTING STANDARDS GUIDE

Chapter 5, "Accounting Policies, Changes in Accounting Estimates, and Errors"

CHAPTER 3
ADVERTISING

CONTENTS

Overview		3.01
Authoritative Guidance		
ASC 340 and 720	Other Assets and Deferred Costs; Other Expenses	3.02
SOP 93-7	Reporting on Advertising Costs	3.02
PB-13	Direct-Response Advertising and Probable Future Benefits	3.08

OVERVIEW

Although advertising is a common business expenditure, before 1993 there were no stand-alone authoritative accounting pronouncements on the treatment of advertising costs. Given this lack of authoritative guidance, a wide diversity in practice developed as to how these costs were treated. Some entities expensed advertising costs as incurred; other entities deferred these costs, with subsequent amortization, in an attempt to match revenues with expenses. The AICPA Accounting Standards Executive Committee (AcSEC) (now known as the Financial Reporting Executive Committee) issued ASC 340 and 720 (SOP 93-7, Reporting on Advertising Costs) to narrow the range of acceptable practices in reporting advertising costs.

The guidance in that pronouncement and in ASC 340 (PB-13, Direct-Response Advertising and Probable Future Benefits) established accounting and reporting standards for advertising costs.

In general, advertising expenditures should be expensed either as incurred or the first time the advertisement appears. There are two exceptions to this general rule. First, direct-response advertising, which meets certain conditions, should be capitalized and amortized against revenues in future periods. Second, expenditures for advertising costs that are made after the recognition of revenues related to those costs should be capitalized and charged to expense when the related revenues are recognized.

AUTHORITATIVE GUIDANCE

ASC 340 and ASC 720
Other Assets and Deferred Costs; Other Expenses

SOP 93-7 (Reporting on Advertising Costs) (ASC 340-20-05-2; 15-3, 15-4; 25-1 through 25-4, 25-6, 25-8 through 25-16; 30-2; 35-1 through 35-6; 45-1; 50-1; 55-1; ASC 720-35-05-1 through 05-5; 15 through 14-4; 25-1 through 25-6; 35-1; 50-1; 55-1; ASC 958-720-25-5)

BACKGROUND

Before ASC 340 (SOP 93-7) was issued, there was a lack of broad authoritative guidance on the treatment of advertising costs. Entities accounted for these costs in diverse ways. Some entities charged advertising expenditures to expense as incurred. Other entities, believing that advertising created a probable future economic benefit that was sufficiently measurable, capitalized these costs and amortized them against future revenues.

Advertising is defined as the promotion of an industry, company, brand, product name, or specific product or service for the purpose of improving an entity's image and/or increasing future revenues. Advertising is typically distributed via one or more media outlets (e.g., television, radio, magazines, direct mail).

STANDARDS

In most cases, the costs of advertising should be expensed as incurred or the first time the advertisement appears. There are two exceptions to this general rule. First, entities are to capitalize certain direct-response advertising. Second, expenditures for advertising costs that are made subsequent to the recognition of revenues related to those costs are to be capitalized and charged to expense when the related revenues are recognized. For example, some entities enter into an arrangement whereby they are responsible for reimbursing some or all of their customers' advertising costs. In most cases, revenues related to the transactions creating these obligations are earned before the reimbursements are made. The entity responsible for reimbursing advertising expenditures would recognize a liability and the related advertising expense concurrently with the recognition of revenue.

There are two general types of advertising costs: the costs of producing advertisements and the costs of communicating them. Costs of communicating advertisements should not be expensed until the dissemination service has been received. For example, the costs of purchasing television or radio airtime should not be expensed until the advertisement is aired (the costs of communicating certain direct-response advertisements will be charged to expense as the advertising benefit is received).

Illustration of Expensing Advertising Costs

Ace Motor Company plans to introduce a series of new cars (the A series). Ace Motor agrees to reimburse dealerships for advertising costs they incur during January of 20X5 to promote this new series of cars. The reimbursement rate is set at 20% of the value of orders placed by the dealership for cars in the A series (up to 50% of the advertising costs incurred by the dealership). Russell Ace, a dealership in Waterbury, Connecticut, incurs $100,000 of advertising costs during January 20X5 and places $300,000 of orders for cars from the A series during that month. When the automobiles are shipped, Ace Motor will record $300,000 of revenue. Concurrently with recognizing the revenue, Ace Motor is to record a liability and a charge to advertising expense for $50,000 (Ace's reimbursement obligation to the Russell Ace dealership).

Direct-Response Advertising

Direct-response advertising must meet two conditions in order to be capitalized. First, the primary purpose of the advertising must be to generate sales, and these sales must be capable of being traced specifically to the advertising. Second, the direct-response advertising must result in probable future economic benefits.

Generation of Sales and Traceability to Direct-Response Advertising

In order for the costs of direct-response advertising to be capitalized, sales derived therefrom must be traceable directly to the advertising. The entity must maintain records that identify customers making purchases and the advertisement that customers responded to. Acceptable documentation includes the following examples:

- Files indicating customer names and the applicable direct-response advertisement
- A coded order form, coupon, or response card, included with an advertisement that includes the customer name
- A log of customers placing phone orders in response to a number appearing in an advertisement, linking those calls to the advertisement

Illustration of Direct-Response Advertising

Fantastic Systems, Inc., has developed a new product—an aerobic exercise machine called the Air Flyer. In order to elicit sales of this product, Fantastic Systems produces a 30-minute infomercial. Fantastic Systems has obtained a unique toll-free telephone number to facilitate sales that result from the airing of this infomercial. This toll-free number is displayed frequently throughout the infomercial. Assuming this infomercial results in probable future economic benefits to Fantastic Systems (discussed below in the section titled "Probable Future Economic Benefits of Direct-Response Advertising"), the cost of producing and airing this infomercial would be capitalizable as direct-response advertising. Given the targeted toll-free number used, the resultant sales and the customer names can be traced to a specific advertisement (i.e., the infomercial).

Certain advertising costs may be related to a direct-response advertising campaign and yet still not be capitalizable. If the subsequent sale cannot be traced to the direct-response advertising, the related advertising costs cannot be capitalized.

Illustration of Advertising Costs Not Capitalized

Fleet Foot, Inc., a large athletic-shoe manufacturer, incurs costs to produce and air a television advertisement for a new running shoe. The commercial states that order forms, with discount coupons, will soon be distributed to certain consumers (this is the direct-response advertisement). The costs of producing and airing the television commercial are not capitalizable, since there is no link between subsequent sales and the television commercial. However, the cost of producing and distributing the order forms would be capitalizable (assuming this direct-response advertisement provided Fleet Foot with future economic benefits).

Probable Future Economic Benefits of Direct-Response Advertising

Probable future economic benefits are expected future revenues from direct-response advertising minus the costs to be incurred in generating those revenues. In order for the costs of direct-response advertising to be capitalized, there must be *persuasive evidence* that the effect of the current advertising campaign will be similar to that of previous advertising campaigns that generated future economic benefits. In terms of probable future benefits, attributes to consider in evaluating the similarity between the current direct-response advertising campaign and prior campaigns include audience demographics, the advertising method, the product, and economic conditions.

A specific entity needs to base its decision about whether to capitalize direct-response advertising costs on its past results with other direct-response advertising campaigns. In the absence of prior experience with direct-response advertising, an entity cannot rely on industry statistics as support for capitalizing advertising costs. The most persuasive type of evidence in support of the capitalization of direct-response advertising costs is a prior history of similar advertising for similar products that resulted in future economic benefits. Although an entity may not have a prior history of advertising a similar product, it may have used direct-response advertising to promote a related product or service. An entity may be able to support the capitalization of direct-response advertising for the new product or service if it can document that the results from a prior advertising campaign for a related product or service are likely to be highly correlated with the current advertising campaign. Test market results may suggest that the reaction of prospective consumers to the advertising campaign for a new product or service is likely to be similar to consumer reaction to a similar campaign for a different product or service.

> **PRACTICE POINTER:** In the absence of a high degree of correlation between the current campaign and advertising campaigns for other products in the past, a success rate based on the historical ratio of successful products or services to total products or services introduced to the marketplace would not be sufficient to support capitalization.

Illustration of Capitalizing Costs of Subsequent Products

As discussed in a previous illustration, Fantastic Systems, Inc., marketed a new fitness product, the Air Flyer, via a direct-response television campaign. This product was introduced in 20X4, and the costs of the campaign were capitalized as direct-response advertising. Fantastic Systems plans to introduce a new product, the Magic Club, in 20X5. The Magic Club, which is a new type of golf club, clearly represents a different product than the Air Flyer. On the basis of test market results, however, Fantastic Systems believes that there will be a high degree of correlation between the response of consumers to the ads for the Air Flyer and the response to the ads for the Magic Club. Therefore, Fantastic Systems can capitalize the costs of producing and distributing an infomercial for the Magic Club.

Direct-response advertising that is not capitalized, because future economic benefits are uncertain, should not be retroactively capitalized if future results indicate that the advertisement did produce economic benefits.

Measurement of the Costs of Direct-Response Advertising

Each separate direct-response advertising campaign that meets the capitalization criteria represents a *separate stand-alone cost pool*.

The costs of direct-response advertising that should be capitalized include both of the following:

- Incremental direct costs of direct-response advertising incurred in transactions with independent third parties (e.g., idea development, writing advertising copy, artwork, printing, magazine space, and mailing).

- Payroll and payroll-related costs for the direct-response advertising activities of employees who are directly associated with and devote time to the advertising reported as assets (e.g., idea development, writing advertising copy, artwork, printing, and mailing). The costs of payroll and fringe benefits for these employees should be capitalized only to the extent of the time spent working on the particular advertising project (i.e., if 10% of an employee's time is spent working on a direct-response advertising campaign that is subject to capitalization, 10% of that employee's compensation and fringe benefit costs would be included among the costs to be capitalized).

If the criteria for capitalization are met, the entire cost of the direct-response campaign, not just a pro rata share of the cost based on the expected response rate of consumers to the campaign, is capitalizable. For example, an entity distributes one million order forms and coupons to target customers and expects to receive 10,000 orders as a result of this mailing. In this case, orders can be directly traced to the advertisement. If this advertising campaign is likely to generate future economic benefits, the cost of the entire mailing campaign should be capitalized (not just the cost of mailing to the 10,000 individuals who are likely to place an order).

Amortization of Capitalized Advertising Costs

Amortization of direct-response advertising costs for a particular cost pool is as follows: Current Period Revenues Attributable to the Direct-Response Advertising Cost Pool/(Current Period Revenues Attributable to the Direct-Response Advertising Cost Pool + Estimated Future Revenues Attributable to the Direct-Response Advertising Cost Pool). Estimated future revenues may change over time, and the amortization ratio is to be recalculated each period.

Direct-response advertising costs are typically amortized over a period of not more than one year or one operating cycle. This suggests that future revenues attributable to the advertisement are limited to those likely to result within the next year (or within the next operating cycle). AcSEC bases this recommendation on the belief that the reliability of future revenue estimates decreases as the length of time for which such estimates are made increases. However, a possible exception to this general recommendation is illustrated below.

Illustration of Amortizing Advertising Costs

An entity undertakes a direct-response advertising campaign, via a series of television commercials and a dedicated toll-free number, to sell classic works of literature (e.g., *Moby Dick* and *A Tale of Two Cities*). Because sales can be tied directly to the advertisement, the costs of this campaign will be capitalized if the campaign is likely to generate probable future economic benefits. For this entity such benefits exist. Customers who buy the first book are sent a response card on a monthly basis thereafter, asking them if they would like to order another book in the set (there are 24 books in the collection). These future advertising efforts (mailing the response card on a monthly basis) are viewed as minimal. The entity also knows that a certain percentage of the customers who buy the first book will buy a quantifiable percentage of the remaining books. In this case, the amortization ratio used will include total revenues expected from all sales, including an estimate of future book sales. If a significant advertising effort was necessary for each book sold, however, each of these advertising efforts would be treated separately—in terms of both initial capitalization and subsequent amortization.

Assessment of Realizability of Capitalized Advertising Costs

The realizability of capitalized direct-response advertising costs should be evaluated at each reporting date on a cost-pool-by-cost-pool basis. The unamortized direct-response advertising costs are to be compared to probable future *net* revenues that are expected to be generated directly from such advertising. *Net revenues* are gross revenues less costs to be incurred in generating those revenues, excluding the amortization of advertising costs. Examples of costs to be included in making this evaluation are cost of goods sold, sales commissions, and payroll and payroll-related costs.

If the carrying amount of unamortized direct-response advertising exceeds probable future net revenues, the difference should be charged to advertising expense in the current period.

Illustration of Write-Off of Unamortized Advertising Costs

MMX Enterprises has $400,000 of unamortized direct-response advertising costs at December 31, 20X5; probable future net revenues are $300,000. This difference—$100,000—would be reported as advertising expense in 20X5.

Any later-period increase in probable future net revenue cannot be used to increase the carrying amount of the unamortized advertising costs (i.e., the write-down cannot be reversed on the basis of a subsequent increase in probable net revenues).

Miscellaneous Issues

Certain tangible assets (e.g., blimps and billboards) may be used in a number of different advertising campaigns. These tangible assets are to be capitalized and depreciated over their estimated useful lives. The related depreciation charge is a cost of advertising to the extent that the tangible asset was used for an advertising-related purpose.

Costs to produce film or audio, and video tape used to communicate advertising, do not constitute tangible assets under the provisions of this SOP. Sales materials, such as brochures and catalogs, should be classified as prepaid supplies until they are no longer owned or expected to be used. At that point, the related cost would be considered a cost of advertising.

Disclosures

The notes to the financial statements should contain the following disclosures:

- The accounting policy selected for non-direct-response advertising costs. The two choices are to (a) expense these costs as incurred or (b) expense them the first time the advertising takes place.
- A description of the direct-response advertising reported as assets (if any), the related accounting policy, and the amortization period.
- The total amount charged to advertising expense for each income statement presented, with a separate disclosure (if any) of amounts representing a write-down to net realizable value.
- The total amount of advertising expenditures reported as an asset for each balance sheet presented.

PB-13 (Direct-Response Advertising and Probable Future Benefits) (ASC 340-20-25-17, 25-18; 35-7)

BACKGROUND

Under the provisions of ASC 340 and ASC 720 (SOP 93-7, Reporting on Advertising Costs), a direct-response advertisement must provide an entity with probable future economic benefits in order for the related advertising costs to be capitalized. In determining whether an advertisement provides an entity with probable future economic benefits, an entity estimates future revenues (derived from the advertisement) less costs incurred in generating those revenues. There has been diversity in practice as to which revenues are considered in making this determination.

Some entities have limited their consideration of future revenues to primary revenues, that is, revenues derived from sales to customers receiving and responding to the direct-response advertisement. Other entities have taken a more expansive view of the appropriate revenues to consider. These entities consider both primary and secondary revenues in evaluating whether the advertisement provides probable future economic benefits. Secondary revenues are revenues other than those derived from sales to customers receiving and responding to the direct-response advertisement. For example, revenues that publishers receive from subscriptions are considered primary revenues. Revenues resulting from advertisements placed in the magazine are secondary revenues.

STANDARDS

In determining probable future revenues, an entity should consider only primary revenues—revenues expected from customers receiving and responding to the direct-response advertisement. In addition, only primary revenues should be considered for purposes of amortizing direct-response advertising costs and for assessing realizability of these same costs.

CHAPTER 4
BALANCE SHEET CLASSIFICATION AND RELATED DISPLAY ISSUES

CONTENTS

Overview		4.02
Authoritative Guidance		
ASC 325 Investments—Other		4.04
FTB 85-4	Accounting for Purchases of Life Insurance	4.04
EITF Issue 06-5	Accounting for Purchases of Life Insurance—Determining the Amount That Could Be Realized in Accordance with FASB Technical Bulletin No. 85-4	4.05
ASC 470 Debt		4.08
FTB 79-3	Subjective Acceleration Clauses in Long-Term Debt Agreements	4.08
EITF Issue 86-5	Classifying Demand Notes with Repayment Terms	4.08
EITF Issue 86-15	Increasing-Rate Debt	4.09
EITF Issue 86-30	Classification of Obligations When a Violation Is Waived by the Creditor	4.11
EITF Issue 88-15	Classification of a Subsidiary's Loan Payable in Consolidated Balance Sheet When Subsidiary's and Parent's Fiscal Years Differ	4.13
EITF Issue 88-18	Sales of Future Revenues	4.14
EITF Issue 95-22	Balance Sheet Classification of Borrowings Outstanding under Revolving Credit Agreements That Include both a Subjective Acceleration Clause and a Lock-Box Arrangement	4.16
Topic D-23	Subjective Acceleration Clauses and Debt Classification	4.18

4.02 *Balance Sheet Classification and Related Display Issues*

Topic D-61	Classification by the Issuer of Redeemable Instruments That Are Subject to Remarketing Agreements	4.19
ASC 480	Distinguishing Liabilities from Equity	4.20
EITF Issue 89-11	Sponsor's Balance Sheet Classification of Capital Stock with a Put Option Held by an Employee Stock Ownership Plan	4.20
ASC 505	Equity	4.23
EITF Issue 85-1	Classifying Notes Received for Capital Stock	4.23
ASC 958	Not-for-Profit Entities	4.25
FSP FAS-117-1	Endowments of Not-for-Profit Organizations: Net Asset Classification of Funds Subject to an Enacted Version of the Uniform Prudent Management of Institutional Funds Act, and Enhanced Disclosures	4.25
Related Chapters in 2011 GAAP Guide, Volume II		4.29
Related Chapters in 2011 GAAP Guide, Volume I		4.29
Related Chapters in 2011 International Accounting/Financial Reporting Standards Guide		4.29

OVERVIEW

The balance sheet (i.e., statement of financial position) is presented in three major categories: assets, liabilities, and equity (stockholders' equity for the equity form of ownership). In a classified balance sheet, the distinction between current and noncurrent assets and liabilities is particularly important. There is considerable interest in the liquidity of the reporting enterprise, and the separate classification of current assets and liabilities is an important part of liquidity analysis.

Guidance on balance sheet classification is provided in the following pronouncements, which are discussed in the 2011 *GAAP Guide, Volume I,* Chapter 3, "Balance Sheet Classification and Related Display Issues."

ASC 605; 505	Chapter 1A, Receivables from Officers, Employees, or Affiliated Companies (ARB-43)
ASC 210; 310	Chapter 3A, Current Assets and Current Liabilities (ARB-43)

ASC 210; 605	Omnibus Opinion—1966 (APB-10)
ASC 470	Classification of Short-Term Obligations Expected to Be Refinanced (FAS-6)
ASC 710	Accounting for Compensated Absences (FAS-43)
ASC 470	Classification of Obligations That Are Callable by the Creditor (FAS-78)
ASC 480	Accounting for Certain Financial Instruments with Characteristics of both Liability and Equity (FAS-150)
ASC 470	Classification of a Short-Term Obligation Repaid Prior to Being Replaced by a Long-Term Security (FIN-8)
ASC 210; 815	Offsetting of Amounts Related to Certain Contracts (FIN-39)

AUTHORITATIVE GUIDANCE

ASC 325 Investments—Other

FTB 85-4 (Accounting for Purchases of Life Insurance) (ASC 325-30-05-3 through 05-5; 15-2 through 15-3; 25-1; 35-1 through 35-2)

BACKGROUND

The premium paid by a purchaser of life insurance serves several purposes. Part of it pays the insurer for assumption of mortality risk and provides for recovery of the insurer's contract acquisition, initiation, and maintenance costs. Part of the premium contributes to the accumulated contract value. The relative amounts of premium payment credited to various contract attributes change over time as the age of the insured person increases and as earnings are credited to previous contract values. An insurance contract is significantly different from other investment agreements. The various attributes of the policy could be obtained separately through term insurance and the purchase of separate investments, but the combination of benefits and contract values typically could not be acquired without the insurance contract.

STANDARDS

Question: How should an entity account for an investment in life insurance?

Answer: The amount that could be realized under the contract at the date of the financial statements (i.e., the contract's cash surrender value) should be reported as an asset. The change in that value during the period is an adjustment to the amount of premium paid in recognizing expense or income for that period.

Illustration of the Accounting for a Life Insurance Contract

Roth Enterprises carries a "key-person" life insurance policy on its CEO, Susan Ray. The face value of the policy is $1 million. The cash surrender value of the policy was $50,000 at 1/1/20X4. During 20X4 Roth Enterprises paid premiums of $10,000, and the cash surrender value of the policy was $55,000 at 12/31/20X4. The cash surrender value at 12/31/20X4, $55,000, would be included as an asset on the balance sheet of Roth Enterprises. The insurance premium expense recognized on the income statement, $5,000, is the net of premiums paid, $10,000, and the increase in the policy's cash surrender value, $5,000 [$55,000−$50,000].

EITF Issue 06-5 (Accounting for Purchases of Life Insurance—Determining the Amount That Could Be Realized in Accordance with FASB Technical Bulletin No. 85-4) (ASC 325-30-05-2, 05-6 through 05-9; 15-4; 30-1; 35-3 through 35-7; 50-1; 55-2 through 4)

OVERVIEW

Some entities purchase insurance policies—corporate-owned life insurance (COLI) or bank-owned life insurance (BOLI)—to fund the cost of providing employee benefits; others do so to protect the entity against the loss of "key" employees. COLI and BOLI may be structured as:

- *Individual-life policies*, which have a contract value component and may include a surrender charge and a cash surrender value that represents the amount that could be realized if the policy is surrendered.
- *Multiple individual-life policies*, which are individual-life policies on which an employer has taken a rider at an additional cost so that the surrender charges on individual policies would be waived if all of the individual policies are surrendered at once.
- *Group life policies*, which are legal contracts with an insurance company that enables an employer to cover multiple employees with individual-life insurance. Although separate certificates are issued to the covered individuals, the group policy contract is the controlling document. Under a group life policy, a policyholder receives the full cash surrender value if an individual policy is surrendered separately.

Many policies include provisions to make them more attractive to a policyholder, such as a provision that allows the policyholder to recover certain costs. However, the policies may also include provisions, such as a prohibition against a change of control or a restructuring that occurs within the last 24 months, a prohibition against a planned restructuring within the prior 12 months, or a limit on a policyholder operating a loss carryforward position, that would limit the amount that an entity may be able to recover in cash. Additionally, a policy may require that a policyholder meet certain criteria to recover any amount. Further, the amount due to the policyholder may be received over an extended period after the insurance policy or certificate has been surrendered.

There has been diversity in practice in the calculation of the amount that would be realized on multiple individual policies with a separate group-level rider agreement, multiple individual policies with a contractual requirement in each individual policy referring to the other policies as a group, or a group life policy with multiple certificates in the form of individual life insurance for multiple

4.06 *Balance Sheet Classification and Related Display Issues*

employees. The issues addressed in this Issue are related to an interpretation of the phrase "the amount that could be realized under an insurance contract" in ASC 325-30 (FTB 85-4, Accounting for Purchases of Life Insurance), which requires that this amount be reported in the balance sheet as an asset. To calculate that amount, it is necessary to assume how the contracts are settled and whether they are surrendered individually or as a group.

ACCOUNTING ISSUES

1. Should a policyholder consider any additional amounts included in an insurance policy's contractual terms, other than its cash surrender value, when calculating the amount of cash into which an insurance policy could be converted under the guidance in ASC 325-30 (FTB 85-4)?
2. Should a policyholder consider its contractual ability to surrender all of the individual life insurance policies or certificates in a group policy at once when calculating the amount of cash into which the insurance policy could be converted under the guidance ASC 325-30 (FTB 85-4)?

EITF CONSENSUS

The EITF reached the following consensus positions:

- In determining the "amount that could be realized under the life insurance contract," policy holders should to take into account any contractual amounts that are included in addition to the policy's cash surrender value. Contractual limitations also should be considered when realizable amounts are determined if it is probable that those terms would limit the amounts that could be realized under an insurance contract. Amounts recoverable at an insurance company's discretion should be *excluded* from the computation of the amount that could be realized under an insurance contract. Amounts that policyholders can recover more than one year after a policy has been surrendered should be discounted based on the guidance in ASC 835-30-15 (APB-21, Interest on Receivables and Payables).
- Policyholders should determine the "amount that could be realized under the life insurance contract" by assuming that individual life insurance contracts and individual certificates in group policies will be surrendered individually. In addition, the amount that a policyholder would ultimately realize, if any, on an assumed surrender of a final policy or a final certificate in a group policy should be included in the computation.
- If a policyholder who has made a request to surrender a policy with contractual limitations on the holder's ability to surrender

the policy continues to participate in changes in the policy's cash surrender value in the same manner as before making the request, the policyholder should *not* discount the cash surrender value component of the amount that could be realized under the insurance contract. However, a future amount that could be realized under an insurance contract should be discounted under the guidance in ASC 835-30-15 (APB-21) if the policyholder is not permitted to participate in changes to the policy's cash surrender value because of the policy's contractual restrictions. It was noted that Internal Revenue Code Section 1035 exchanges (Sec. 1035 exchanges) do *not* represent a cash surrender as intended in ASC 325-30 (Technical Bulletin 85-4). A policyholder should determine the amount that could be realized under an insurance contract on a group basis if a group of individual life policies or a group policy only permit that all individual-life policies or certificates be surrendered as a group.

DISCLOSURE

The EITF reached a consensus that policyholders should disclose the existence of contractual restrictions on the ability to surrender a policy.

EFFECTIVE DATE AND TRANSITION

The guidance in this Issue is effective for fiscal years that begin after December 15, 2006, but may be adopted earlier as of the beginning of a fiscal year in which interim or annual financial statements have *not* yet been issued.

The consensus positions in this Issue should be adopted either as:

- A change in accounting principle by making a cumulative-effect adjustment to retained earnings or to other components of equity or net assets in the balance sheet as of the beginning of the year in which a consensus was adopted; or
- A change in accounting principle by *retrospectively* applying the guidance to all prior periods.

A policyholder that applies the guidance in this Issue as a change in accounting principle by making a *cumulative-effect adjustment* to retained earnings should disclose the cumulative effect of the change on retained earnings or other components of equity or net assets in the balance sheet.

A policyholder that applies the guidance in this Issue as a change in accounting principle by *retrospectively* applying the guidance to all prior periods should recognize:

- The cumulative effect of a change in accounting principle on periods *before* those presented in the financial statements by showing the effect of a change in the carrying amounts of assets and liabilities as of the beginning of the first period presented.

FASB RATIFICATION

The FASB ratified the EITF's consensus positions on this Issue at its September 20, 2006, meeting.

ASC 470 Debt

FTB 79-3 (Subjective Acceleration Clauses in Long-Term Debt Agreements) (ASC 470-10-45-2; 50-3)

BACKGROUND

The guidance in ASC 470, Debt (FAS-6, Classification of Short-Term Obligations Expected to Be Refinanced) indicates that a subjective acceleration clause in a financing arrangement that would otherwise permit a short-term obligation to be refinanced on a long-term basis precludes that obligation from being classified as noncurrent. The guidance in ASC 470 (FAS-6) does not, however, address agreements other than those related to short-term obligations.

STANDARDS

Question: Should long-term debt be classified as a current liability if the long-term debt agreement includes a subjective acceleration clause?

Answer: The circumstances dictate the answer to this question. In some circumstances, such as recurring losses or liquidity problems, the long-term debt should be classified as current. Other situations, however, would require disclosure of only the acceleration clause. If the likelihood of the due date being accelerated is remote, neither reclassification nor disclosure would be required.

EITF Issue 86-5 (Classifying Demand Notes with Repayment Terms) (ASC 470-10-45-9, 45-10)

OVERVIEW

In addition to specifying repayment terms, some loan agreements also might include language that enables the creditor to call the loan on demand. For example, the agreement may state that "the term note shall mature in monthly installments as set forth therein *or on demand, whichever is earlier,"* or "principal and interest shall be due *on demand, or if no demand is made,* in quarterly installments beginning on...."

ACCOUNTING ISSUES

- How should a loan agreement that allows the creditor to demand payment at the creditor's discretion be classified in a classified balance sheet?
- What disclosures should be made about maturities of a long-term obligation that includes such a clause?

EITF CONSENSUS

The EITF reached a consensus that in such situations, the debt should be classified as a current liability, in accordance with the guidance in ASC 470-10-45-12 (FAS-78), Classification of Obligations That Are Callable by the Creditor). The Task Force also noted that a demand provision is not the same as a subjective acceleration clause, which is discussed in ASC 470-10-45-2; ASC 470-10-50-3 (FTB 79-3).

DISCUSSION

The guidance in ASC 470-10-45-12 (FAS-78) deals specifically with the classification of an obligation that by its terms can be called by the lender on demand within one year from the balance sheet date (or operating cycle, if longer). It provides that such an obligation should be classified as a current liability, even if the obligation is not expected to be liquidated during that period unless (*a*) the creditor has waived or lost the right to call the debt or (*b*) it is probable that the debtor will cure the violation during the grace period. Some had been treating the "due on demand clause" as a subjective acceleration clause under ASC 470-10-45-2; ASC 470-10-50-3 (FTB 79-3).

ETIF Issue 86-15   (Increasing-Rate Debt) (ASC 470-10-35-1, 35-2; 45-7, 45-8; 835-10-60-9)

OVERVIEW

Whether to classify increasing-rate debt as a current or long-term liability is secondary in ASC 470-10-45-2; 470-10-50-3 (Issue 86-15), which addresses primarily how to determine interest expense on such debt. (See Chapter 22, "Interest on Receivables and Payables," for a detailed discussion of this issue.) Increasing-rate debt that is discussed in this Issue consists of notes that mature three months from the original issue date and that can be extended at the issuer's option for another three months at each maturity date, but not for longer than five years from original issuance. The interest rate on the notes increases each time their maturity is extended.

ACCOUNTING ISSUE

How should the note be classified in the balance sheet?

EITF CONSENSUS

The Task Force reached a consensus that the debt should be classified as current or noncurrent based on whether the borrower anticipates repaying the notes with current assets or noncurrent assets. For example, the debt would be classified as current if repayment were from current assets or from a new short-term borrowing. It would be classified as long-term if repayment were financed by a long-term financing arrangement or from the issuance of equity securities.

DISCUSSION

This consensus is consistent with the guidance in (ARB-43, Chapter 1A, Receivables from Officers, Employers, or Affiliated Companies) and ASC 470 (FAS-6). That is, the guidance in ASC 310-45-13; 505-10-25-1; 605-10-25-1, 25-3, 25-5; 850-10-50-2 (ARB-43) states that liabilities that are expected to be satisfied with current assets should be classified as current liabilities. Based on the provisions of ASC 470 (FAS-6), however, if an entity intends to repay a short-term obligation scheduled to mature within one year of the balance sheet date with (1) proceeds from a long-term obligation, (2) the issuance of equity securities, or (3) by renewing, extending, or replacing it with short-term obligations for an uninterrupted period extending beyond one year (or the operating cycle) from the balance sheet date, the obligation should be classified as a long-term liability, subject to certain criteria.

SUBSEQUENT DEVELOPMENTS

- The SEC staff's discussion in ASC 340-10-S99-2 (Staff Accounting Bulletin (SAB) Topic 2.A.6, Question 2 (Debt Issue Costs in a Business Combination Accounted for as a Purchase) of "bridge financing" that consists of increasing-rate debt refers to Issue 86-15 and requires registrants to follow the consensus.
- The guidance in ASC 815, Derivatives and Hedging (FAS-133, Accounting for Derivative Instruments and Hedging Activities) partially nullifies the EITF's consensus. It requires analysis of provisions that would extend the term of a debt instrument to determine whether those provisions represent an embedded derivative that should be accounted for separately. Under the guidance in ASC 815-15-05-1 (paragraph 12c of FAS-133), as amended by ASC 815-15-25-14 (paragraph C(2)(b) of FAS-150, Accounting for Certain Financial Instruments with Characteristics of Both Liabilities and Equity) of ASC 815 (FAS-133) provides guidance

for that determination. However, the guidance in ASC 480-10-25 (paragraphs 9 through 12 of FAS-150) should be disregarded when the guidance in ASC 480-10-25-8 (paragraph 11(a) of FAS-150) is applied to an embedded derivative instrument as though it were a separate instrument. The guidance in ASC 958-205-45-17, 45-22 (Issue No. A13, Whether Settlement of Provisions That Require a Structured Payout Constitute Net Settlement under Paragraph 9(a) of the Implementation Guide for FAS-133) also may be relevant. ASC 815 (FAS-133) also has been amended by the guidance in ASC 815-15-25-4, 25-5 (FAS-155, Accounting for Certain Hybrid Financial Instruments), which provides that certain hybrid financial instruments with embedded derivatives may be measured at fair value instead of bifurcating the financial instrument. However, a hybrid instrument measured at fair value should not be used as a hedging instrument under the guidance in ASC 815 (FAS-133).

EITF Issue 86-30 (Classification of Obligations When a Violation Is Waived by the Creditor) (ASC 470-10-45-1; 55-3 through 55-6)

OVERVIEW

Under Company F's loan agreement with a financial institution, the company must to comply with certain covenants that, for example, require maintaining a minimum current ratio or debt-to-equity ratio on a quarterly basis. If Company F violates a covenant at specified dates, quarterly or semiannually, the lender may call the loan. However, the lender may waive the right to call the loan for longer than one year while retaining the right to require the company to comply with the covenant requirement during that period.

ACCOUNTING ISSUE

Under such circumstances, can Company F continue to classify the debt as a noncurrent liability or should it reclassify it as a current liability?

EITF CONSENSUS

The Task Force reached a consensus that, unless the facts and circumstances indicate otherwise (e.g., the borrower violates a covenant after the balance sheet date but before the financial statements are issued), noncurrent classification is appropriate unless:

- A covenant was violated at the balance sheet date or would have been violated without a loan modification, and

- It is probable that the borrower will not be able to comply with a loan covenant on measurement dates within the next 12 months.

Furthermore, the EITF noted that borrowers that classify the debt as noncurrent should disclose the negative effects of probable future noncompliance with debt covenants.

DISCUSSION

Resolving how to classify debt when a lender has waived the right to call the debt, but has retained the right to require compliance with debt covenants at interim dates, involves a determination of whether the lender's waiver of the right to call the debt can be considered a grace period as contemplated in FAS-78. Under the guidance in ASC 470-10-45-12 (FAS-78), a grace period is a specified period of time during which the lender has waived the right to call the debt, giving the borrower time to cure the violation. For example, if an agreement provides that a borrower who has violated a covenant at the balance sheet date has a three-month grace period to cure a violation, the lender does not have the right to call the debt at the balance sheet date. The guidance in ASC 470-10-45-12 (FAS-78) provides that the debt can continue to be classified as noncurrent if it is probable (as defined in ASC 450 (FAS-5)) at the balance sheet date that the borrower can comply with the covenant within the grace period, thus preventing the lender from calling the debt. If the concept of a grace period in ASC 470-10-45-12 (FAS-78) is extended to this issue, it would be necessary to assess the probability that the borrower can comply with the covenant by the next measurement date.

The EITF discussed the following five scenarios:

1. The debt covenants apply only after the balance sheet date, and it is probable that the borrower will not be able to comply with the covenants as required three months after the balance sheet date.

2. The borrower complies with the debt covenants at the balance sheet date, but it is probable that the borrower will fail the requirements three months after the balance sheet date.

3. The borrower complies with the debt covenants at the balance sheet date, but it is probable that the borrower will not meet a more restrictive covenant three months later at the next compliance date.

4. On the compliance date, which occurred three months before the balance sheet date, the borrower had complied with the loan covenants. Before the balance sheet date, the borrower negotiates with the lender to modify the loan agreement by eliminating a compliance requirement at the balance sheet date or by modifying a requirement that the borrower would otherwise fail. The borrower must, however, meet the same requirement or a more restrictive requirement three months

later at the next compliance date, and it is probable that the borrower will fail the requirement at that time.

5. The borrower has violated the covenant at the balance sheet date, but obtained a waiver from the lender before issuing the financial statements. The borrower must, however, meet the same or a more restrictive covenant three months later. It is probable that the borrower will not meet the requirement at that date.

Applying the consensus to those five scenarios, it appears that the EITF decided to classify the debt based on existing circumstances at the balance sheet date rather than based on expectations. Thus, the debt in scenarios 1, 2, and 3 can continue to be classified as noncurrent, because in each case the borrower complied with the loan covenants at the balance sheet date. In scenarios 4 and 5, however, in which the borrower failed to comply at the balance sheet date, current classification would be required even though the borrower negotiated a waiver in both cases. Noncurrent classification would, nevertheless, be permitted if the borrower expects to repay the debt with noncurrent assets and meets the conditions in FAS-6 (ASC 470, Debt).

> **OBSERVATION:** Although the consensus does not say so specifically, the presumption is that the waiver of the lender's right to call the debt while retaining the right to require compliance with the debt covenants is, in substance, a grace period, because the EITF has applied the probability test in FAS-78.

EITF Issue 88-15 (Classification of a Subsidiary's Loan Payable in Consolidated Balance Sheet When Subsidiary's and Parent's Fiscal Years Differ) (ASC 470-10-S45-1; S99-4; 810-10-S45-1)

OVERVIEW

Company A, which has a February 28, 20X5, year-end, issues consolidated financial statements that include its subsidiary, Company B, which has a December 31, 20X0, year-end. Company B has a material loan payable with a January 31, 20X6, maturity.

Paragraph 4 of ARB-51 (Consolidated Financial Statements) (ASC 810-10-45-12) permits a parent company to consolidate financial statements of a subsidiary if the difference between their year-ends is no more than three months.

ACCOUNTING ISSUE

How should Company A classify Company B's loan payable in its February 28, 20X5, consolidated financial statements?

4.14 *Balance Sheet Classification and Related Display Issues*

EITF CONSENSUS

The EITF did not reach a consensus on this issue.

> **OBSERVATION:** The FASB may address this issue in its project on the reporting entity, including consolidations and the equity method.

SEC STAFF COMMENT

The SEC Observer stated that the SEC staff would expect registrants to classify the loan as current under those circumstances.

EITF Issue 88-18 (Sales of Future Revenues) (ASC 470-10-25-1, 25-2; 35-3)

OVERVIEW

Company G enters into an agreement with Company H (an investor) to receive a sum of cash in exchange for a specified percentage or amount of Company G's future revenues or another measure of income, such as gross margin or operating income, for a particular product line, business segment, trademark, patent, or contractual right, for a specified period. The future revenue or income may be from a foreign contract, transaction, or operation denominated in a foreign currency.

ACCOUNTING ISSUES

- Assuming the proceeds received from the sale of future revenues are appropriately accounted for as a liability, should the liability be characterized as debt or deferred income?
- How should debt or deferred income be amortized? (Discussed in Chapter 36, "Revenue Recognition.")
- How should foreign currency effects, if any, be recognized? (Discussed in Chapter 18, "Foreign Operations and Exchange.")

> **OBSERVATION:** The distinction between recognizing a liability as debt or as deferred income is significant, because (1) liabilities characterized as deferred income are generally ignored in the calculation of the debt-to-equity ratio and (2) under the provisions of FAS-52 (Foreign Currency Translation) (ASC 830, Foreign Currency Matters) the effects on debt of changes in foreign currency exchange rates are accounted for differently from the effects of such changes on deferred income. (See Chapter 18, "Foreign Operations and Exchange," for a discussion related to recognition of the effects on the liability of changes in foreign currency exchange rates if future revenue is recognized as debt or as deferred revenue.)

EITF CONSENSUS

The EITF reached the following consensus positions on the first issue:
- The liability's characterization depends on the specific facts and circumstances of the underlying transaction.
- The existence of any one of the following factors would result in a rebuttable presumption that the liability should be characterized as debt:
  —The transaction is intended as a borrowing, not a sale.
  —The company has a significant, continuing involvement in generating cash flows that will be paid to the investor.
  —The company or the investor may cancel the transaction, with the company paying a lump sum of cash or transferring other assets to the investor.
  —The terms of the transaction implicitly or explicitly limit the investor's return. (The limitation may be stated explicitly; for example, a rate of return not to exceed 10%. Or the limitation may be implicit in the agreement; for example, if revenues for a particular period do not meet certain expectations, the payment to the investor is calculated in an alternate manner that limits the investor's return.)
  —The investor's rate of return is not significantly affected by variations in the company's measure of performance on which the transaction is based.
  —The investor has recourse to the company for payments due.

DISCUSSION

Some proponents of debt classification analogized the transaction to a lessor's stream of future cash flows from rentals, which is not recorded by the lessor. Paragraph 22 of FAS-13 (Accounting for Leases) (ASC 840-20-40-3) provides that a lessor that sells or assigns such an income stream should account for it as debt if the lessor retains substantial risks and rewards of ownership.

Others analogized the transaction to those discussed in FAS-19 (Financial Accounting and Reporting by Oil and Gas Producing Companies) (ASC 932-10-15), which supports the view that cash advances from customers that will be repaid with goods and services should be accounted for as deferred revenue, while cash received from investors or financial institutions that will be repaid with cash should be accounted for as debt. It was noted that the similarity to transactions reported as debt in accordance with the provisions of FAS-19 is even greater if the company guarantees that it will make minimum payments to the investor, there is a cap on the amount the investor would receive, or both.

A further argument made for debt classification was that future revenue or income is generally sold by companies with predictable cash flows, which help to assure investors that they will collect their investment plus a return. Consequently, such transactions are viewed as similar to a nonrecourse borrowing with an equity kicker, with cash as the collateral rather than a tangible asset.

Some argued that by selling future revenues the company had, in fact, accelerated collection of cash for goods or services that would be delivered in the future and should, therefore, classify those revenues as deferred revenue. Furthermore, they compared the transaction to a sale of a share of the future risks and rewards of a business.

Those Task Force members who supported classifying the transaction as debt or deferred-income based on the specific facts and circumstances believed that FAS-19 provides the best analogy, but also thought that the important factor in determining whether to classify such a transaction as debt or deferred income is the amount of operating risk transferred to those who advanced the funds, not whether the transaction was settled with cash instead of with goods or services.

EITF Issue 95-22 (Balance Sheet Classification of Borrowings Outstanding under Revolving Credit Agreements That Include both a Subjective Acceleration Clause and a Lock-Box Arrangement) (ASC 470-10-45-3 through 45-6)

OVERVIEW

An entity has a revolving credit agreement with a note due in three years. The borrowing, which is collateralized, includes a subjective acceleration clause and is evidenced by a note signed on entering into the agreement. Under the agreement, the borrower is *required* to maintain a lock-box with the lender, to which the borrower's customers must remit their payments. The lender applies the outstanding payments to reduce the debt.

FTB 79-3 (Subjective Acceleration Clauses in Long-Term Debt Agreements) determines the effect of an acceleration clause on balance sheet classification for long-term obligations. However, if a borrowing considered to be a short-term obligation has a subjective acceleration clause, it is classified in the balance sheet as a current liability, under the provisions of FAS-6 (Classification of Short-Term Obligations Expected to Be Refinanced). This Issue does not apply if maintaining a lock-box is at the borrower's discretion.

The Task Force also discussed a related Issue that addresses the balance sheet classification of a borrowing with a subjective acceleration clause and a "springing" lock-box arrangement under which amounts paid by a borrower's customers are deposited in the borrower's general bank account and are not used by the bank to reduce the debt without the lender's activation of the subjective acceleration clause. However, if the lender exercises the subjective acceleration clause, the lender has the right to redirect all of the lockbox's receipts to the lender's loan account and to apply them against the outstanding debt.

ACCOUNTING ISSUE

1. Should a borrowing under a revolving credit agreement be considered a short-term borrowing if it includes a subjective acceleration clause and requires the borrower to maintain a lock-box with the lender so that customers' payments are remitted directly to the lender and applied to reduce the outstanding debt?
2. Does the consensus in (1) apply to a revolving credit arrangement with a springing lock and a subjective acceleration clause?

EITF CONSENSUS

1. A revolving credit agreement should be classified as a short-term borrowing if it includes *both* a subjective acceleration clause and a requirement for the borrower to maintain a lock-box with the lender to which customers remit their payments, which are used to reduce the debt.

    The Task Force observed that the balance sheet classification of debt that includes a subjective acceleration clause should be based on the guidance in FAS-6, which requires short-term debt with an acceleration clause to be classified as a current liability. An obligation may be classified as a long-term obligation, however, if it is refinanced after the balance sheet date on a long-term basis, thus meeting the conditions in paragraphs 10 and 11 of FAS-6 (ASC 470-10-45-14), based on an agreement other than a revolving credit agreement.

    The Task Force also noted that the term *lock-box arrangement* as it is used in this consensus applies to situations in which a debt agreement requires the borrower's cash receipts to be used in the ordinary course of business to repay the debt without the occurrence of another event. Therefore, if the borrower has no alternative but to use working capital to repay the obligation, a revolving credit agreement should be classified as a *short-term* obligation.

2. Debt in an arrangement with a springing lock box should be classified as a *long-term* obligation, because the customers' payments are not used automatically to reduce the debt unless another event has occurred. The guidance in FTB 79-3 (ASC 470-10-45-2) should be used to determine the effect of a subjective acceleration clause on the arrangement discussed in this consensus, because the debt is classified as a long-term obligation.

DISCUSSION

The deciding factor in the EITF's consensus—the borrowing is a short-term obligation—was the fact that the agreement requires the borrower to maintain a lock-box, enabling the lender to use the proceeds to repay the borrowing and then lend the money back to the borrower under the revolving credit agreement, which results in a new borrowing. Those who supported this view argued that because of the lock-box requirement, the borrowing is repaid with current assets.

Because the EITF determined that the borrowing is a short-term obligation, the balance sheet classification falls under the guidance of FAS-6, which applies to the classification of short-term obligations with a subjective acceleration clause.

The Task Force argued that FAS-6 does not apply in the case of a springing lock-box, because under the terms of the arrangement, the debt is not due within the entity's normal operating cycle. The borrower should use the guidance in FTB 79-3 to determine the balance sheet classification of the debt based on the likelihood that the lender will exercise the subjective acceleration clause.

Topic D-23 (Subjective Acceleration Clauses and Debt Classification) (ASC 470-10-55-1)

The FASB staff discussed its response to an inquiry as to whether the treatment of subjective acceleration clauses in FTB 79-3 and FAS-6 is inconsistent. Under FAS-6, short-term obligations can be classified as noncurrent if the entity has the ability and intent to refinance the obligation on a long-term basis. That ability can be demonstrated by an existing financial agreement. FAS-6 states that such an agreement, however, would only qualify if it has no subjective acceleration clauses that enable the lender to accelerate the debt. Conversely, FTB 79-3 states that as long as acceleration of the due date is remote, there is no need to reclassify a noncurrent liability and disclose the existence of a subjective acceleration clause.

The FASB staff explained that the circumstances discussed in the two pronouncements differ. FTB 79-3 deals with loans made initially on a long-term basis; thus, continuing that classification requires a judgment about the likelihood that the loan's due date will be accelerated. Conversely, FAS-6 deals with circumstances under which a short-term obligation may be excluded from classification as a current liability by getting a new loan or refinancing the debt with long-term debt based on conditions at that date. The FASB staff justified the higher standard required in FAS-6 because it deals with a refinancing of a short-term obligation as long-term rather than with the likelihood that existing long-term debt will be accelerated.

Topic D-61 (Classification by the Issuer of Redeemable Instruments That Are Subject to Remarketing Agreements) (ASC 470-10-55-7 through 9)

The FASB staff reported that it received inquiries about the balance sheet classification of debt instruments with the following characteristics:

- The debt has a long maturity (e.g., 30 to 40 years).
- The debt can be put to the issuer for redemption on short notice (within 7 to 30 days).
- The issuer has a remarketing agreement with an agent who agrees to resell redeemed bonds on a best efforts basis under which the agent is required to buy only securities that the agent can sell to the public. The issuer must pay off any debt the agent is unable to resell.
- A short-term letter of credit is used to secure the debt to protect the holder if the redeemed debt cannot be remarketed. The issuer of the redeemable debt must repay the issuer of the letter of credit for amounts drawn down on the same day.

According to ASC 470-10-45-10, obligations that are due on demand within one year of the balance sheet should be classified as current liabilities, even if they will not be repaid during that period. Paragraph 11 of FAS-6 (ASC 470-10-45-14) specifies the following two conditions for a short-term liability to be classified as noncurrent if the debtor intends to refinance the liability:

1. The liability will be refinanced on a long-term basis.
2. Either of the following two events occurs before the issuance of the balance sheet to confirm the debtor's ability to refinance short-debt debt on a long-term basis:
   a. A long-term obligation or equity securities have been issued.
   b. The debtor entered into a *financing agreement* based on readily determinable terms meeting all of the following conditions:
      (1) The agreement does not expire within one year (or the entity's operating cycle) from the balance sheet date and cannot be canceled by the lender or investor (obligations incurred cannot be called) during the period except if the debtor violates a provision with which compliance can be determined or measured objectively.
      (2) The debtor had not violated any of the provisions at the balance sheet date and there is no indication that any occurred after that date but before the balance sheet was issued. Alternatively, the lender has waived any

violation that had occurred at the balance sheet date or before the balance sheet was issued.

(3) The lender or investor is expected to be financially viable to honor the agreement.

The FASB Staff believes that, in accordance with the guidance in ASC 470-1-45-12 (FAS-78), issuers should classify as current liabilities debt instruments that can be redeemed by the holder on demand or within one year, even if a best efforts remarketing agreement exists. In this situation, classification as a long-term liability would be acceptable only if the letter-of-credit arrangement meets the requirements in ASC 470-10-45-14 (paragraph 11 of FAS-6) for a financing agreement, as discussed above.

ASC 480 Distinguishing Liabilities from Equity

EITF Issue 89-11 (Sponsor's Balance Sheet Classification of Capital Stock with a Put Option Held by an Employee Stock Ownership Plan) (ASC 480-10-S45-5; S99-4)

OVERVIEW

(See Chapter 38, "Stock Compensation," for a general discussion of employee stock ownership plans (ESOPs) and the accounting for such plans.)

Federal income tax regulations require employer securities held by an ESOP to have a put option, referred to as a liquidity put, allowing the employee to demand redemption if the securities are not readily marketable. The employer may have the option to satisfy the demand for redemption with cash, marketable securities, or both. Under the provisions of some ESOPs, the ESOP may substitute for the employer in redeeming the employees' shares.

Companies may also issue to their ESOPs convertible preferred stock, which is convertible into the company's common stock. Such stock is not publicly traded and therefore has a put option. The holder generally has the option of when to convert the stock, but under the terms of some convertible stock the issuer/employer is permitted to convert the shares. In some cases, the stock is converted or put to the employer when there is a takeover attempt or a merger. The convertible stock may have the following features:

- It has a "floor put" feature that guarantees the participant a minimum value, and is exercised if the convertible is "out of the money." The employer may have the option of redeeming the stock for cash, giving the participant common stock that would be issuable on conversion plus additional shares, or giving the participant common stock that would be issuable on conversion plus cash. The participant may have the option of receiving cash, common shares, or a combination of both.

- After a certain period of time, the employer may have the option to call the stock at a stipulated price. The ESOP can hold callable stock if it provides for a reasonable period of time after calling for the stock to be converted to common shares instead of cash, if participants so desire.
- The convertible stock can be held only by the ESOP and is automatically converted to common stock when distributed to participants leaving the plan. However, a floor put feature enables participants to require the trustee to put the convertible stock even before it has been distributed to participants if the convertible stock is "out of the money."

SEC Staff Accounting Series Release (ASR) 268 (Presentation in Financial Statements of "Redeemable Preferred Stocks") requires public companies to classify mandatorily redeemable preferred stock or stock whose redemption is outside the issuer's control outside of stockholders' equity.

In a leveraged ESOP, the employer records the ESOP debt as a liability. The liability is offset by a contra-equity account referred to as "unearned ESOP shares," which is recorded as a debit in equity. (Before the issuance of SOP 93-6 (Employers' Accounting for Employee Stock Ownership Plans) (ASC 718-40), such an account was referred to as *loan to ESOP or deferred* compensation.) When the employer issues stock to the ESOP, this contra-equity account is credited and there is no effect on equity.

ACCOUNTING ISSUES

- Under what circumstances should all or a portion of convertible preferred stock with put options held by an ESOP be classified outside of equity?
- If convertible preferred stock with put options issued to a leveraged ESOP is classified outside of stockholders' equity, should the contra-equity account, unearned ESOP shares, be classified in the same manner?

EITF CONSENSUS

- Publicly held companies should classify convertible preferred stock issued to ESOPs in accordance with the provisions of ASR-268, which requires that mandatorily redeemable preferred stock be classified as a separate item between liabilities and equity, commonly referred to as the "mezzanine."
- A proportional amount of the contra-equity account in the employer's balance sheet should be similarly classified.

For example, if $7,500,000 of $10,000,000 of preferred stock issued to an ESOP is convertible and therefore is classified outside of stockholders' equity, 75% of the balance of the contra-equity account would be classified in the same manner. Thus, if the remaining ESOP debt is $8,000,000, 75% (or $6,000,000) of the contra-equity account, unearned ESOP shares, would be classified outside of stockholders' equity.

OBSERVATION: Under paragraph 3 of FIN-45 (Guarantor's Accounting and Disclosure Requirements for Guarantees, Including Indirect Guarantees of Indebtedness of Others) (ASC 460-10-55-5), a put option issued by an ESOP may be a guarantee. If a put is a guarantee that is *not* accounted for under the provisions of FAS-133 (ASC 815-10-15) and the ESOP sponsor's obligations under that guarantee would be reported as a liability under GAAP, the sponsor would be required to recognize a liability for the fair value of the put at its inception and provide the disclosures specified in the Interpretation. The requirement in FIN-45 that the put be recognized as a liability at its inception and the requirement to disclose additional information change the sponsor's reporting and, therefore, partially nullify the consensus.

FAS-150 (Accounting for Certain Financial Instruments with Characteristics of both Liabilities and Equity) (ASC 480-10) provides guidance to issuers on the classification and measurement of financial instruments with characteristics of both liabilities and equity, except for mandatorily redeemable financial instruments of nonpublic entities. Financial instruments under the Interpretation's scope should be classified as liabilities or, in some cases, as assets. Because ESOP shares with embedded repurchase features or freestanding instruments to repurchase ESOP shares are covered under the guidance in SOP 93-6 (Employers' Accounting for Employee Stock Ownership Plans) (ASC 718-40) and related guidance, FAS-150 does *not* apply to those shares. However, the requirement in the SEC's ASR-268 that ESOP shares be reported in temporary equity continues to apply.

EFFECT OF FAS-133

Put options discussed in this Issue should be analyzed to determine whether they meet the definition of a derivative in FAS-133. Contracts classified in temporary equity may qualify for the exception in paragraph 11(a) of the Statement (ASC 815-10-15-74), because temporary equity is considered to be stockholders' equity.

SEC STAFF COMMENT

The SEC Observer stated that under ASR-268, the maximum possible cash obligation related to equity securities that give the holder the option to demand redemption in cash, regardless of the probability of occurrence, should be reported outside of equity. Consequently, employers should report outside of equity all allocated and unallocated convertible preferred securities held by an ESOP that are redeemable in cash. However, if the cash obligation is related only to the market-value guarantee feature of some convertible securities, the SEC staff would not object if registrants report outside of equity only amounts representing the maximum cash obligation based on the market price of the underlying securities at the reporting date. The entire guaranteed amount of such securities may, nevertheless, be reported outside of equity at the registrant's option to recognize the uncertainty of the ultimate cash obligation resulting from possible declines in the market value of the underlying security.

DISCUSSION

- In this Issue, arguments for classification outside stockholders' equity focused on the fact that redemption may be outside the control of the employer as a result of the put and the employer's potential cash obligation.
- Some Task Force members supported classifying all or a portion of the contra-equity account outside of equity because that account, unearned ESOP shares, resulted from a transaction in which the employer issued the securities and incurred the liability. They argued that the purpose of the contra-equity account is to offset shares that have not been paid for, as in a stock subscription. Thus, if shares not paid for are reclassified, the contra-equity account should be treated in the same manner.

ASC 505 Equity

EITF Issue 85-1 (Classifying Notes Received for Capital Stock) (ASC 310-10-45-14; ASC 505-10-45-1, 45-2; ASC850-10-60-4)

OVERVIEW

A contribution to an entity's equity is made by a minority shareholder(s), majority shareholder(s), or an entity's majority or sole owner in the form of a note, rather than in cash. The transaction may occur because a new company is being formed, a company needs additional capital for credit or other purposes, or a parent company wants to make its wholly owned subsidiary more self-sufficient by increasing its equity. Such transactions may be in the form of a sale of stock or a contribution to paid-in capital.

ACCOUNTING ISSUE

Should the note always be classified as a reduction of equity, or are there any circumstances under which it can be classified as an asset?

EITF CONSENSUS

The EITF reached a consensus that recognizing such a note receivable as an asset, even though generally inappropriate, would be permitted only in the following very limited circumstances:

- There is substantial evidence of intent and ability to pay.
- The note will be repaid within a reasonably short period of time.
- Some Task Force members stated that they would also require the note to be collateralized or paid before the financial statements are issued to qualify for asset recognition.

SEC STAFF COMMENT

The SEC Observer reiterated that exceptions from the SEC's rule would be very rare for registrants.

DISCUSSION

Issue 85-1 is one of the rare instances when the EITF has discussed an issue that would apply only to privately held companies. Although there is no guidance on this matter in GAAP, the SEC has developed guidance for its registrants. Rule 5-02.30 of SEC Regulation S-X requires registrants to deduct from equity notes receivable when common stock transactions involve the company's common stock. This rule is restated in SEC Staff Accounting Bulletins, Topics 4E and 4G (ASC 310-10-S99-2, S99-3). In all cases, the presumption is that such notes are seldom paid.

- Proponents of asset recognition suggested that a note should meet the following criteria to qualify as an asset:
- A scheduled repayment date
- Collection within a short period of time (five years suggested as the maximum)
- A market interest rate
- Collateralization by tangible assets with an adequate margin or a letter of credit
- The debtor's representation of intent to pay

ASC 958 Not-for-Profit Entities

FSP FAS-117-1 (Endowments of Not-for-Profit Organizations: Net Asset Classification of Funds Subject to an Enacted Version of the Uniform Prudent Management of Institutional Funds Act, and Enhanced Disclosures) (ASC 958-205-05-10; 45-21A, 45-28 through 45-32; 50-1A, 50-1B; 55-1, 55-31 through 55-53, 65-1)

OVERVIEW

The Uniform Prudent Management Institutional Funds Act of 2006 (UPMIFA) is a model act that was adopted by the National Conference of Commissioners on Uniform State Laws (NCCUSL) to be used as a guideline by states enacting related legislation. It is a modernized version of the Uniform Management of Institutional Funds Act of 1972 (UMIFA) on which 46 states and the District of Columbia have based their primary laws that legislate the manner in which not-for-profit organizations (NFPOs) are required to invest and manage donor-restricted endowment funds.

UPMIFA provides new guidance for the designation of expenditures of a donor-restricted endowment fund, unless it is superseded by explicit donor conditions. While UMIFA dealt with the prudent spending of a fund's net appreciation, UPMIFA addresses the treatment of both the *original* gift and the *net appreciation* of a donor-restricted endowment fund. UPMIFA also replaces UMIFA's historic-dollar-threshold, which was defined in that act as the total fair value in dollars of: (1) the amount of the original endowment gift; (2) subsequent donations to the fund; and (3) "each accumulation made pursuant to a direction in the applicable gift instrument at the time the accumulation is added to the fund," below which an organization could not spend from a fund. Instead, UPMIFA provides guidance on what represents prudent spending while considering a fund's duration and preservation.

Under subsection 4(a) of UPMIFA, an endowment fund's assets are considered to be donor-restricted assets until the NFPO has designated them for disbursement, unless the gift instrument states otherwise. Some have raised questions about how that requirement in subsection 4(a) and the UPMIFA's changed focus from UMFIA's requirement of prudent spending (i.e., historical-dollar-threshold) to the detailed guidelines on what represents prudent spending, which requires consideration of an endowment fund's duration and preservation, would affect (a) the net asset classification of a donor-restricted endowment fund and (b) whether a *temporary* (i.e., time) restriction is imposed on the portion of a donor-restricted endowment fund that normally would be classified as "unrestricted net assets."

4.26 *Balance Sheet Classification and Related Display Issues*

FASB STAFF POSITION

FSP FAS-117-1(FASB Accounting Standards Codification (ASC) 958-205) provides the following guidance to NFPOs in states that have enacted a law based on UPMIFA:

- A portion of a donor-restricted endowment fund that has a *perpetual* duration should be classified as *permanently* restricted net assets. Based on the guidance in paragraph 14 of FAS-116 (Accounting for Contributions Received and Contributions Made) (ASC 948-605-45-4), and paragraph 22 of FASB-117 (Financial Statements of Not-for-Profit Organizations) (ASC 958-205-45-21), the amount of an endowment fund that must be classified as permanently restricted is: (1) the amount that must be retained permanently in accordance with a donor's specific conditions; or (2) if there are *no* specified donor conditions, the portion of an endowment fund that must be permanently retained based on the NFPO's governing board's interpretation of the applicable law that should be applied on a consistent basis from year to year.

  Because legislation based on UPMIFA has only recently been enacted by many states and no case law currently exists for the interpretation of such legislation, it is not yet clear how a particular state will interpret and enforce that legislation. To help NFPOs understand the requirements of the applicable law in their particular states, the following sources of information may be consulted: (1) discussions of a state's legislative committee that have resulted in the law's adoption; (2) announcements from a state's Attorney General; (3) a consensus of scholarly lawyers in that state; or (4) similar information. The governing board of an NFPO in a state that has *not* enacted new legislation based on UPMIFA should interpret the requirements of UPMIFA consistently from year to year based on clarifying court decisions, additional guidance issued by their state's Attorney General, or similar developments.

  In accordance with the guidance in paragraphs 11 and 12 of FAS-124 (Accounting for Certain Investments Held by Not-for-Profit Organizations) (ASC 958-205-45-17, 45-22), *permanently* restricted net assets should *not* be reduced by: (1) losses on a fund's investments, except as required by the donor, including losses related to specific investments required by the donor to be held in perpetuity; and (2) an NFPO's expenditures from the fund.

If the restriction discussed in subsection 4(a) of UPMIFA applies, classify as *temporarily* restricted net assets (i.e., time restricted) the portion of each donor-restricted endowment fund that is *not* classified as permanently restricted net assets until the NFPO has designated that amount for disbursement. Unless court decisions or interpretations of a state's Attorney General exist on when an amount is considered as designated for disbursement, for the purposes of this FSP, an amount is designated for disbursement when an expenditure has been approved. However, an expenditure that has been approved for disbursement in a *future* period is considered to occur in that period. An amount that has been designated for expenditure should be reclassified in *unrestricted net assets* because the time restriction for that amount has expired, unless that amount is also restricted for a specified purpose. If so, in accordance with the guidance in paragraph 17 of FAS-116 (ASC 958-205-45-9), that amount would *not* be reclassified to unrestricted net assets until the purpose restriction also has been met. The guidance related to net asset classification in *EITF Abstracts*, Topic D-49 (Classifying Net Appreciation on Investments of a Donor-Restricted Endowment Fund) (ASC 958-205-45-35), continues to apply to donor-restricted endowment funds under the guidance in UMIFA.

- Regardless of whether it is subject to an enacted version of UPMIFA, a NFPO is required to disclose information about the organization's *donor-restricted* and *board-designated* endowment funds to help users of its financial statements understand: (1) the classification and composition of net assets; (2) changes in the composition of net assets; (3) the organization's spending policies; and (4) related investment policies. At a minimum, the following information should be disclosed for each period for which a NFPO presents financial statements:

  —The governing board's interpretation of the law used to classify net assets of donor-restricted endowment funds.

  —The NFPO's spending policies (i.e., its policies for the designation of funds from endowment assets for disbursement).

  —The NFPO's investment policies for its endowments, including: (1) the organization's goals for returns and risk limits; (2) the relationship of those goals to its spending policies; and (3) the strategies used to achieve those goals.

  —The composition of the NFPO's endowment by net asset class at the end of the period, in total and by type of endowment fund, with donor-restricted endowment funds presented *separately* from board-designated endowment funds.

  —A reconciliation of the beginning and ending balance of the NFPO's endowment, in total and by net asset class, including, at a minimum, the following line items, if applicable: (1) investment return, separated into investment income (e.g., interest, dividends, or rents) and net appreciation or depreciation of investments; (2) contributions; (3) amounts designated for disbursement; (4) reclassifications; and (5) other changes.

  —If it has been determined, the planned amount to be designated for expenditure in the year *after* the most recent period for which the NFPO presents financial statements.

4.28 *Balance Sheet Classification and Related Display Issues*

An NFPO also should provide the following information about the net assets of its endowment funds in accordance with the guidance in ASC 958-205 (FAS-117) and FAS-124:

The nature and types of permanent restrictions or temporary restrictions, as required in paragraphs 14 and 15 of FAS-117 (ASC 958-210-45-9, 45-10).

- The total amount of deficiencies for all donor-restricted endowment funds with assets having a fair value at the reporting date that is *less* than the level required by donor stipulations or law, as required in paragraph 15d of FAS-124 (ASC 958-205-50-2).

Footnote 4 to paragraph 13 of FAS-124 (ASC 958-205-45-33) is amended as follows [added text is underlined and deleted text is struck out]:

> Donors that create endowment funds can require that their gifts be invested in perpetuity or for a specified term. Some donors may require that a portion of income, gains, or both be added to the gift and invested subject to similar restrictions. In states that have enacted a version of the Uniform Management of Institutional Funds Act (UMFIA) or states whose relevant law is based on trust law, it ~~it~~ is generally understood that at least the amount of the original gift(s) and any required accumulations is not expendable, although the value of the investments purchased may occasionally fall below that amount. Future appreciation of the investments generally restores the value to the required level. In states that have enacted its provisions, ~~the Uniform Management of Institutional Funds Act~~ UMIFA describes "historic dollar value" as the amount that is not expendable. In states that have enacted the Uniform Prudent Uniform Management of Institutional Funds Act of 2006 (UPMIFA), the level required by law is the amount that must be retained permanently under the version of UPMIFA enacted in that jurisdiction, as determined by the organization's governing board. This is explained further in FASB Staff Position FAS 117-1, *Endowments of Not-for-Profit Organizations: Net Asset Classification of Funds Subject to an Enacted Version of the Uniform Management of Institutional Funds Act, and Enhanced Disclosures.*

EFFECTIVE DATE AND TRANSITION

The FSP's provisions are effective for fiscal years ending after December 15, 2008. Earlier application is permitted if annual financial statements for that fiscal year have *not* yet been issued.

An NFPO subject to the provisions of UPMIFA that initially applies the guidance in this FSP to donor-restricted endowment funds that existed *before* UPMIFA is first effective should report net asset reclassifications, if any, as the result of the application of the guidance in this FSP in a separate line item in the organization's statement of activities for that period, outside a performance indicator or other intermediate measure of operations, if one is presented. However, an entity applying the guidance in this FSP in a period *after* UPMIFA is first effective should report reclassifications, if any, in the financial statements in the *earliest* comparative period presented for which UPMIFA was effective. The effects of a reclassification, if any, should be reported *retrospectively* in the *earliest* period presented if the period in which UPMIFA first became effective is *not* presented.

When the guidance in this FSP regarding the accounting for donor-restricted endowment funds discussed in subsection 4(a) of UPMIFA is first applied, the portion of a donor-restricted endowment fund that had been considered available to meet a purpose restriction under the guidance in paragraph 17 of FAS-116 (ASC 958-205-45-11), but that had *not* been designated for disbursement, should be considered *unavailable* until it is designated for disbursement, similar to other amounts in that fund that have yet to be designated for disbursement. Consequently, a purpose restriction that was considered to have been met should be considered reinstated.

RELATED CHAPTERS IN 2010
GAAP GUIDE, VOLUME II

Chapter 10, "Consolidated Financial Statements"
Chapter 11, "Contingencies, Risks, and Uncertainties"
Chapter 12, "Convertible Debt and Debt with Warrants"
Chapter 17, "Financial Instruments"
Chapter 25, "Investments in Debt and Equity Securities"
Chapter 39, "Stockholders' Equity"

RELATED CHAPTERS IN 2010
GAAP GUIDE, VOLUME I

Chapter 3, "Balance Sheet Classification and Related Display Issues"
Chapter 7, "Consolidated Financial Statements"
Chapter 8, "Contingencies, Risks, and Uncertainties"
Chapter 9, "Convertible Debt and Debt with Warrants"
Chapter 17, "Financial Instruments"
Chapter 28, "Investments in Debt and Equity Securities"
Chapter 44, "Stockholders' Equity"

RELATED CHAPTERS IN 2010
INTERNATIONAL ACCOUNTING/FINANCIAL REPORTING STANDARDS GUIDE

Chapter 3, "Presentation of Financial Instruments"
Chapter 16, "Financial Instruments"

4.30 *Balance Sheet Classification and Related Display Issues*

Chapter 20, "Income Taxes"
Chapter 23, "Inventories"
Chapter 24, "Investment Property"
Chapter 28, "Provisions, Contingent Liabilities, and Contingent Assets"

CHAPTER 5
BANKRUPTCY AND REORGANIZATION

CONTENTS

Overview		5.01
Authoritative Guidance		
ASC 852	Reorganizations	5.03
SOP 90-7	Financial Reporting by Entities in Reorganization under the Bankruptcy Code	5.03
Authoritative Guidance Incorporated in Other Pronouncements in the Codification		
FSP SOP 90-7-1	An Amendment of AICPA Statement of Position 90-7	5.20
Related Chapters in 2011 GAAP Guide, Volume II		5.21
Related Chapters in 2011 GAAP Guide, Volume I		5.21

OVERVIEW

Before 1990, there was little authoritative accounting and reporting guidance for entities that were operating under Chapter 11 protection or that had recently reorganized under the provisions of the Federal Bankruptcy Code. As a result, great diversity in practice developed. The Statement of Position and the Practice Bulletin discussed in this chapter were issued to provide guidance to entities in bankruptcy that are attempting to reorganize under Chapter 11 of the Federal Bankruptcy Code and to provide guidance to those entities that have emerged from Chapter 11 protection with a confirmed reorganization plan.

The following pronouncements establish accounting and reporting standards for entities in bankruptcy or reorganization: FASB Accounting Standards Codification™ (ASC) 852 (SOP 90-7, Financial Reporting by Entities in Reorganization under the Bankruptcy Code) and ASC 852-10-45-22 to 45-25 (PB-11, Accounting for Preconfirmation Contingencies in Fresh-Start Reporting).

Those pronouncements provide guidance for the presentation of information about an entity operating in reorganization in the balance sheet, income statement, and the statement of cash flows.

Under that guidance, information about the liabilities of an entity operating in reorganization must be segregated on the balance sheet into the following categories: prepetition liabilities subject to compromise, prepetition liabilities *not* subject to compromise (e.g., fully secured liabilities), and postpetition claims. However, that guidance does not affect the manner in which such an entity's assets are reported. Items of revenue, expense, gain, or loss that occur because an entity is operating in reorganization proceedings should be reported separately. In a similar fashion, cash flows from operating, investing, and financing activities related to an entity's reorganization proceedings should be presented separately. The statement of cash flows is viewed as providing the most useful information about an entity operating under bankruptcy-law protection.

In many cases, entities emerging from Chapter 11 protection will implement fresh-start reporting. The adoption of fresh-start reporting gives rise to a new reporting entity, which has no retained earnings or deficit when it begins its operations. Any deficit of the predecessor entity would have been eliminated before the new entity begins its operations. The detailed requirements for implementing fresh-start reporting are discussed in this chapter.

AUTHORITATIVE GUIDANCE

ASC 852 Reorganizations

SOP 90-7 (Financial Reporting by Entities in Reorganization under the Bankruptcy Code) (ASC 210-10-60-3; 852-10-05-3 through 05-16; 10-1; 15-1 through 15-3; 25-1; 30-1; 45-1 through 45-2, 45-4 through 45-21, 45-26 through 45-27, 45-29; 50-2 through 50-4, 50-7; 55-3, 55-5 through 55-11; 852-20-15-3; 740-45-1)

BACKGROUND

Entities experiencing severe financial distress may file for protection from creditors under Chapter 11 of the Bankruptcy Code. An entity filing for protection under Chapter 11 seeks to reorganize and to emerge from bankruptcy as a viable business. The primary objective of the reorganization is to maximize the recovery of creditors and shareholders by preserving the going concern value of the entity.

STANDARDS

Legal Summary of the Reorganization Process

To begin the process of bankruptcy reorganization, an entity would file a petition with the Bankruptcy Court, an adjunct of the United States District Courts. The entity filing the bankruptcy petition typically prepares a reorganization plan, which it submits to the Court for confirmation. This plan specifies the treatment of the entity's assets and liabilities, and it may result in debt being forgiven. For the reorganization plan to be confirmed, the consideration to be received by parties in interest under the plan must exceed what would be received if the entity liquidated under Chapter 7 of the Bankruptcy Code. In most cases, the debtor has the exclusive right to file a reorganization plan during the first 120 days after the bankruptcy filing (this right is lost if the Court appoints a trustee).

In general, the provisions of a confirmed reorganization plan bind all parties connected with the entity. This includes (1) the entity itself (i.e., the debtor); (2) any entity issuing securities under the plan; (3) any entity acquiring assets under the plan; and (4) any creditor, stockholder, or general partner of the debtor. This is the case regardless of whether the claim of any of these parties is impaired by the reorganization plan and irrespective of whether the party accepted the plan.

The requirements that must be met for the Bankruptcy Court to approve a reorganization plan include the following:

- The technical requirements of the Bankruptcy Code have been met.

- In soliciting acceptance of the plan, the entity has provided adequate disclosures.
- A class of individuals whose claims are impaired might consent to the plan and yet have some individual members who dissent from this action. These dissenting members must receive at least as much under the plan as they would receive in a Chapter 7 liquidation.
- Priority claims under the terms of the Bankruptcy Code will be paid in cash.
- If the plan is confirmed, it is not likely to be followed by liquidation or further reorganization.
- At least one class of impaired claims, not including insiders, has accepted the plan.
- The plan proponent, typically the debtor, has obtained the consent of all parties with impaired claims or equity securities, or the plan proponent can comply with the "cram-down" provisions of the Bankruptcy Code. (This means that the plan can be forced on nonassenting creditors by the Bankruptcy Court.) The court can confirm a plan even if one or more parties with impaired claims or equity securities do not accept it. In order for the court to confirm a plan under these circumstances, the plan cannot unfairly discriminate against a nonconsenting class impaired by the plan, and it must treat nonconsenting classes in a fair and equitable manner.
  - —A secured claim is treated in a fair and equitable manner if it remains adequately collateralized and if the present value of the payments it is to receive equals the amount of the secured claim when the plan becomes effective.
  - —An unsecured claim is treated in a fair and equitable manner if the discounted assets it is to receive equal the allowed amount of the claim or if any claim junior to it will not receive or retain any assets.
  - —An equity interest is treated in a fair and equitable manner if the discounted assets it is to receive equal the greatest of (1) any fixed liquidation preference, (2) any fixed redemption price, or (3) the value of such interest. Alternatively, the equity interest is treated fairly and equitably if no junior equity security interest will receive or retain any assets under the plan.

Accounting and Financial Aspects of the Reorganization Process

A central feature of the reorganization plan is to determine the reorganization value of the entity that seeks to emerge from Bankruptcy Court protection. The reorganization value is designed to approximate the fair value of the entity's assets, and it should conform with the amount that a willing buyer would pay for these assets.

The reorganization value is generally determined through the following steps:

Step 1: Consideration of the amount to be received for assets that will not be needed by the reconstituted business

Step 2: Computation of the present value of cash flows that the reconstituted business is expected to generate for some period into the future

Step 3: Computation of the terminal value of the reconstituted business at the end of the period for which future cash flows are estimated

---

Illustration of Estimating Reorganization Value

ERT, Inc., is a debtor-in-possession operating under the protection of Chapter 11 of the Bankruptcy Code. In order to prepare a reorganization plan, ERT needs to estimate its reorganization value. ERT has $150,000 of cash above its likely needs as an ongoing business. (It is not unusual for entities operating under Chapter 11 protection to accumulate excess cash; these entities do not pay most claims during the period of time they are operating under Chapter 11 protection.) Also, ERT is expected to generate $40,000 of net cash flows per month, each year, during the first five years after it emerges from Chapter 11. ERT's terminal value is estimated to be $1,091,456. ERT's reorganization value of approximately $2,816,667 represents the $150,000 of excess cash on hand, the present value of receiving $40,000 per month for the next five years ($1,575,211 discounted at 18%), and the terminal value of the enterprise.

After the entity's reorganization value is determined, it is allocated in interest to parties in accordance with their respective legal priorities. Secured claims have first priority, to the extent of the value of their collateral. Following secured claims are those claims specifically granted priority under the provisions of the Bankruptcy Code. Finally, distributions are made to various classes of unsecured debt and equity interests in accordance with their respective legal priorities, or otherwise as the parties may agree.

Before the reorganization plan is submitted to creditors, equity holders, etc., these groups are provided with a disclosure statement. The disclosure statement must be approved by the Court, and it should contain adequate information for interested parties to make an informed decision as to the appropriateness of the reorganization plan.

The disclosure statement typically contains (1) a description of the reorganization plan, (2) historical and prospective financial information, and (3) a pro forma balance sheet that presents the reorganization value and the capital structure of the new entity. A valuation of the emerging entity is not required for the disclosure statement to be approved by the Bankruptcy Court.

Normally, however, such a valuation would be performed unless (1) the reorganization value of the emerging entity exceeds its liabilities or (2) holders of existing voting shares will own a majority of the emerging entity.

Need for and Scope of SOP 90-7

Before the issuance of the guidance in ASC 210-10-60-3; 852-10-05-3 through 05-16; 10-1; 15-1 through 15- 3; 25-1; 30-1; 45-1 through 45-2, 45-4 through 45-21, 45-26 through 45-27, 45-29; 50-2 through 50-4, 50-7; 55-3, 55-5 through 55-11; 852-20-15-3; 740-45-1 (SOP 90-7), there was no specific guidance for entities operating in reorganization proceedings. This led to wide diversity in practice.

That guidance applies to both (1) entities that are operating under Chapter 11 protection and that expect ultimately to emerge from such protection as a going concern and (2) entities that have emerged from Chapter 11 protection under a confirmed reorganization plan. It does not apply to (1) entities that restructure their debt outside of the Chapter 11 process, (2) entities that liquidate or that plan to do so, and (3) governmental entities.

Financial Reporting—Entity Operating under Chapter 11 Protection

For the most part, filing for Chapter 11 protection does not change the application of generally accepted accounting principles. One difference is that transactions or events that are directly associated with the reorganization proceedings should be kept separate from ongoing operations.

Balance Sheet Reporting

Prepetition liabilities (i.e., liabilities incurred by the enterprise before the Chapter 11 filing) may be subject to compromise. A liability is compromised when it ultimately is settled for less than its allowed amount. The *allowed* amount is that which is permitted by the Bankruptcy Court, even though such liabilities may not be paid in full. Prepetition liabilities subject to compromise should be separated from prepetition liabilities not subject to compromise (e.g., fully secured liabilities) and from postpetition claims. These two latter amounts are combined and reported as one amount. All liabilities should be reported at the amount allowed by the Bankruptcy Court, even though they ultimately may be settled for less than the allowed amount.

Some secured liabilities may be undersecured. An undersecured liability exists when the fair value of the collateral may be less than the allowed liability. In this case, the entire liability should initially be classified as a prepetition claim subject to compromise. The liability would not be reclassified unless it became clear that the secured claim in question would not be compromised. Certain prepetition liabilities may not become known until after the bankruptcy petition is filed. Those liabilities should be reported at the expected amount of the allowed claims (based on the framework of ASC 450-20 (FAS-5, Accounting for Contingencies). If the existence of the liability is at least reasonably possible, this information should be disclosed in the notes to the financial statements even if the amount of the prepetition liability cannot be estimated.

In certain cases, the allowed amount of a prepetition liability may differ from its recorded amount. When this circumstance occurs, the carrying amount of the liability should be adjusted to the allowed amount. If unamortized debt discounts, premiums, or debt issue costs exist, these accounts are used in making the adjustment to record the liability at its allowed amount. Any resulting gain or loss is classified as a reorganization item and, as such, will be reported separately in the income statement.

Details of claims subject to compromise are to be reported in the financial statement notes. Finally, if a classified balance sheet is presented, claims not subject to compromise are to be categorized as current or noncurrent.

Illustration of Balance Sheet Presentation

Hale & Carter filed for protection from creditors under Chapter 11 of the Bankruptcy Code on February 15, 20X4. Its first set of annual financial statements prepared after this date is prepared on December 31, 20X4. The details of Hale & Carter's liabilities and stockholders' equity are as follows:

Prepetition liabilities subject to compromise

Secured debt, 12%, secured by a first mortgage on equipment (the fair value of the collateral is less than the claim)	$200,000
Senior subordinated secured notes, 16%	300,000
Subordinated debentures, 19%	200,000
Trade and other miscellaneous claims	100,000
Priority tax claims	50,000

Prepetition liabilities not subject to compromise

Secured debt, 11%, secured by a first mortgage on a building ($50,000 of principal due on 6/30/X5)	$700,000

Postpetition claims

Accounts payable—trade	$120,000
Short-term borrowings	180,000

Stockholders' equity

Preferred stock	$150,000
Common stock	100,000
Retained earnings (deficit)	(500,000)

5.08 *Bankruptcy and Reorganization*

In its December 31, 20X4, balance sheet, Hale & Carter reports total assets of $1,600,000. (The presentation of the asset side of the balance sheet for an entity operating under Chapter 11 does not present any unique issues.) The right-hand side of Hale & Carter's balance sheet would look as follows:

Liabilities and Shareholders' Deficit	
Liabilities Not Subject to Compromise	
Current liabilities:	
Short-term borrowings	$ 180,000
Accounts payable	120,000
Total current liabilities	$ 300,000
Noncurrent liabilities:	
11%, Long-term note (see Note xx)	$ 700,000
Liabilities Subject to Compromise	$ 850,000(a)
Total liabilities	$1,850,000
Shareholders' (deficit):	
Preferred stock	$ 150,000
Common stock	100,000
Retained earnings (deficit)	(500,000)
Total liabilities & shareholders' deficit	$ 1,600,000

(a) Liabilities subject to compromise consist of the following:

Secured debt, 12%, secured by a first mortgage on equipment (the fair value of the collateral is less than the claim)	$200,000
Senior subordinated secured notes, 16%	300,000
Subordinated debentures, 19%	200,000
Trade and other miscellaneous claims	100,000
Priority tax claims	50,000
	$850,000

Income Statement

Items of revenue, expense, gain, or loss that occur because the entity is operating in reorganization proceedings are to be reported separately. However, under the provisions in ASC 225-20-45 (APB-30, Reporting the Results of Operations) as amended by ASC 360-10 (FAS-144, Accounting for the Impairment or Disposal of Long-Lived Assets) and ASC 470-50-45-1 (FAS- 145, Rescission of FAS-4, 44, and 64, Amendment of FAS-13, and Technical Corrections), this requirement does not apply to an item required to be reported separately as a discontinued operation or as an extraordinary item.

The guidance in ASC 210-10-60-3; 852-10-05-3 through 05-16; 10-1; 15-1 through 15- 3; 25-1; 30-1; 45-1 through 45-2, 45-4 through 45-21, 45-26 through 45-27, 45-29; 50-2 through 50-4, 50-7; 55-3, 55-5 through 55-11; 852-20-15-3; 740-45-1 (SOP 90-7) specifically addresses the treatment of three items on the income statement. First, professional fees related to the reorganization are to be recognized as incurred and categorized as a reorganization expense. Before this guidance was issued, some entities established a liability for professional fees upon filing for bankruptcy; other entities capitalized these fees when incurred and ultimately offset them against debt discharge when the reorganization plan was confirmed. Neither of those treatments is now acceptable. Second, interest expense is *not* a reorganization item. It should be reported only to the extent that interest is paid during the reporting period or to the extent that it will be an allowed claim. In many cases, the interest expense reported will be significantly less than contractual interest. Any difference between reported interest expense and contractual interest is to be disclosed. SEC registrants must disclose this difference on the face of the income statement. Third, any interest income above that which would normally be earned on invested working capital is to be reported as a reorganization item. Entities operating under Chapter 11 protection often generate large amounts of interest income. The entity continues to generate cash flows from operations, and payments under many liabilities are stayed by the bankruptcy proceedings.

Statement of Cash Flows

The guidance in (ASC 210-10-60-3; 852-10-05-3 through 05-16; 10-1; 15-1 through 15- 3; 25-1; 30-1; 45-1 through 45-2, 45-4 through 45-21, 45-26 through 45-27, 45-29; 50-2 through 50-4, 50-7; 55-3, 55-5 through 55-11; 852-20-15-3; 740-45-1 (SOP 90-7) provides that the most beneficial information that can be provided about an entity operating under Chapter 11 protection is the information presented in the statement of cash flows. Cash flows from operating, investing, and financing activities that relate to the reorganization should be shown separately. That treatment is more useful if an entity uses the direct method of preparing the statement. If the indirect method is used, a supplementary schedule (or a note) containing information on operating cash flows due to the reorganization proceedings must be provided.

Other Issues

A company presenting consolidated results may have one or more entities in reorganization proceedings. Assuming that this hypothetical company also has other entities that are not operating under Chapter 11 protection, condensed combined financial statements for the units operating under Chapter 11 must accompany the consolidated financial statements. Those units operating under Chapter 11 must present intercompany receivables and payables in the condensed combined financial statements. In addition, those entities that are not in reorganization proceedings must evaluate the propriety of reporting an intercompany receivable from a unit that is operating in Chapter 11.

In general, earnings per share for entities in reorganization are calculated in a manner similar to the calculation for any other entity.

However, if it is probable that additional shares of stock or common stock equivalents will be issued under the reorganization plan, that fact should be disclosed.

Fresh-Start Reporting—Emergence from Chapter 11

For an entity emerging from Chapter 11 protection to employ fresh-start reporting, two conditions must exist. First, the value of the emerging entity's assets immediately before the reorganization plan is confirmed must be less than the amount of postpetition liabilities and prepetition allowed claims. Second, persons holding existing voting shares immediately before the reorganization plan is confirmed must receive less than 50% of the voting shares of the new entity. Note that the loss of control experienced by the former shareholders must be substantive and not temporary. Fresh-start reporting is to be applied as of the confirmation date, or at a later date when all material conditions precedent to the reorganization plan becoming binding have been resolved.

If an entity emerging from reorganization proceedings does not meet *both* of the criteria outlined in the previous paragraph, the entity is precluded from adopting fresh-start reporting. However, even in this case, the entity needs to ensure that (1) liabilities adjusted as a result of a confirmed reorganization plan are stated at present value and (2) any debt forgiveness received is reported as an extraordinary item.

Implementing Fresh-Start Reporting

In implementing fresh-start reporting, the reorganization value of the emerging entity should be assigned among the tangible and specifically identifiable intangible assets and liabilities of the entity in conformity with ASC 805 (FAS-141(revised 2007), Business Combinations Any excess of reorganization value over that which can be assigned to tangible and specifically identifiable intangible assets is reported as, if any, goodwill in accordance with ASC 350-20-25-2 (paragraph 6 of FAS-142, Goodwill and Other Intangible Assets). Goodwill as a result of the implementation of fresh-start reporting is not amortized, but is periodically evaluated for impairment in accordance with the guidance in ASC 350 (FAS-142).

Deferred income taxes should be reported in conformity with GAAP. If deferred taxes cannot be recognized at the date of a plan's confirmation by eliminating the valuation allowance, tax benefits from preconfirmation net operating loss carryforwards and deductible temporary differences should be reported as a reduction of income tax expense.

An entity emerging from bankruptcy that applies fresh start reporting should follow the guidance in accounting standards that are *effective* when fresh-start reporting is adopted. (See ASC 852-10-45-20 (paragraph 38 of FSP SOP 90-7-1 (not in codification (see below))

Transitioning to Fresh-Start Reporting

Before the confirmation date of the reorganization plan, the accounting should follow that which is required when an entity is operating under Chapter 11 protection. Any adjustments to the recorded asset and liability amounts that result from the adoption of fresh-start reporting would be reported in the predecessor entity's final statement of operations. Also, the effects of debt forgiveness are to be reported in the predecessor entity's final statement of operations. The adoption of fresh-start reporting gives rise to a new reporting entity, which has no retained earnings nor deficit when it begins operations. Any deficit of the predecessor entity would be eliminated before the new entity begins operations.

Disclosures Required by Fresh-Start Reporting

A number of disclosures are required for entities that are exiting Chapter 11 proceedings and are adopting fresh-start reporting. These disclosures are as follows:

- Adjustments to the historical amounts of assets and liabilities.
- The amount of debt that has been forgiven.
- The amount of prior retained earnings or deficit that is eliminated.
- Significant matters in determining reorganization value. These include the following:
    - *The method or methods used to determine reorganization value* This includes disclosing information such as discount rates, tax rates, the number of years for which cash flows are projected, and the method of determining terminal value.
    - *Sensitive assumptions* These are assumptions made where there is a reasonable possibility of divergence from the assumption that could materially affect the estimate of reorganization value.
    - *Assumptions about anticipated conditions that are expected to be different from current conditions (unless these differences are already apparent)*

Other Issues

If, for example, a calendar-year-end entity has its reorganization plan confirmed on June 30, 20X5, and adopts fresh-start reporting on July 1, 20X5, at December 31, 20X5, this new entity should not prepare comparative financial statements. The financial statements presented would be limited to capturing the activity of the new entity for the latter half of 20X5. AcSEC believed that presenting comparative financial statements that straddle a confirmation date would be misleading; therefore, such statements should not be presented.

Illustration of Fresh-Start Reporting

Background

Edison, Inc., filed for protection from creditors under Chapter 11 of the Bankruptcy Code on March 1, 20X5. Edison's reorganization plan was confirmed by the applicable Bankruptcy Court on May 1, 20X5.

Reorganization Value

Edison's reorganization value immediately before the confirmation of the reorganization plan was as follows:

Cash in excess of normal operating requirements generated by operations	$ 85,000
Net realizable value expected from asset dispositions	130,000
Present value of discounted cash flows of the emerging entity	525,000[1]
Terminal value	1,250,000[2]
Reorganization value	$1,990,000

[1] The present value of discounting estimated yearly cash flows, $250,000, over the forecast period, 3 years, by the appropriate interest rate, 20%.

[2] Terminal value is determined via an independent business valuation.

Applicability of Fresh-Start Reporting

Holders of Edison's existing voting shares before the confirmation of the reorganization plan will receive less than 50% of the voting shares in the emerging entity (in fact, these former shareholders will have no interest in the new entity). This meets the first requirement for use of fresh-start reporting. The second requirement, that reorganization value must be less than total postpetition liabilities and allowed claims, is also met, as illustrated below:

Postpetition current liabilities	$ 400,000
Liabilities deferred pursuant to Chapter 11 proceeding	1,700,000
Total postpetition liabilities and allowed claims	$ 2,100,000
Reorganization value	(1,990,000)
Excess of liabilities over reorganization value	$ 110,000

Computing the Total Assets of the Emerging Entity

Total assets of the emerging entity are computed by subtracting assets that will be distributed before or simultaneously with the confirmation of the reorganization plan—in this case, the $85,000 of excess cash—from the new entity's reorganization value. Therefore, the total assets of Edison–New Entity at May 1, 20X6, are $1,905,000 ($1,990,000–$85,000).

Beginning Capital Structure—Emerging Entity

After consideration of the emerging entity's debt capacity, projected earnings to fixed charges, earnings before interest and taxes to interest, free cash flow to interest, etc., the following capital structure for the new entity has been agreed upon:

Capital Structure for the Emerging Entity

Postpetition current liabilities	$ 400,000
IRS note	75,000
Senior debt	610,000(1)
Subordinated debt	420,000
Common stock	400,000

(1) $100,000 due each year for the next five years, at 14% interest; $110,000 due in the sixth year.

Distributions to Be Received by Parties in Interest

Secured Debt—The company's $600,000 of secured debt was exchanged for $85,000 in cash, $400,000 of new senior debt, and $115,000 of subordinated debt. The senior debt carries an interest rate of 14%, and principal payments of $65,574 are due during each of the next five years (the first payment is due on June 30, 20X6). The final payment of $72,130 is due in the sixth year.

Priority Tax Claims—Payroll and withholding taxes of $75,000 are payable in five equal annual installments, with the first payment due on May 31, 20X7. The annual interest rate is 11%.

Senior Debt—The company's $400,000 of senior debt was exchanged for $150,000 of new senior debt, $175,000 of subordinated debt, and 15% of the new issue of voting common stock. The senior debt carries an interest rate of 14%, and principal payments of $24,590 are due during each of the next five years (the first payment is due on June 30, 20X6). The final payment of $27,050 is due in the sixth year. Payments under the subordinated debentures are due in equal annual installments over seven years. The first payment is due September 30, 20X7, and the interest rate is 17%.

Trade and Other Claims—The holders of $200,000 of trade and other claims received the following for their stake: (a) $60,000 of senior debt, (b) $70,000 of subordinated debentures, and (c) 10% of the new issue of voting common stock. The senior debt carries an interest rate of 14%, and principal payments of $9,836 are due during each of the next five years (the first payment is due on June 30, 20X6). The final payment of $10,820 is due in the sixth year. Payments under the subordinated debentures are due in equal annual installments over seven years. The first payment is due September 30, 20X7, and the interest rate is 17%.

Subordinated Debentures—The company's $425,000 of subordinated debt was exchanged for $60,000 of new subordinated debentures and 75% of the new issue of voting common stock. Payments under the subordinated debentures are due in equal annual installments over seven years. The first payment is due September 30, 20X7, and the interest rate is 17%.

5.14 *Bankruptcy and Reorganization*

Common Stock—Edison had 200,000 shares of $1 par value common stock outstanding immediately before the confirmation of its reorganization plan. None of these stockholders will have any interest in the emerging entity. Four hundred thousand shares of new voting common stock, $1 par value, will be issued. These shares will be issued as follows: (*a*) 60,000 shares to holders of the former entity's senior debt, (*b*) 40,000 shares to holders of trade and other claims from the former entity, and (*c*) 300,000 shares to holders of the former entity's subordinated debentures.

Plan of Reorganization—Recovery Analysis

It is necessary to prepare a schedule detailing what the claims of the parties in interest are, and how and to what extent these claims are being satisfied. This schedule facilitates the preparation of the journal entries necessary to implement fresh-start reporting. This type of schedule is included either as a note to the financial statements or as supplementary information to the financial statements.

The following points should be noted about this schedule:

1. All of Edison's liabilities, both prepetition and postpetition, and shareholders' equity accounts are listed in column (a) of the table.

2. Column (b), elimination of debt and equity, represents the difference between the claim held (column (a) amount) and the consideration received for the claim (total recovery listed in column (j)).

3. Columns (c)-(g) represent the book value, which at the date of fresh-start reporting would also equal fair value, of the various items of consideration issued to settle the Chapter 11 claims (e.g., surviving debt, cash, new secured debt).

4. Column (h), common stock percentage, represents the percentage of the voting shares of the emerging entity issued to various parties.

5. Column (i), the value of the common stock issued, is computed by multiplying the net assets of the emerging entity by the percentage of voting shares of common stock received. For instance, the emerging capital structure for Edison will have only $400,000 of common stock (a deficit or retained earnings is always eliminated as part of the fresh-start process). Multiplying this amount by the percentage of common stock received produces the common stock value. Also, although this is not the case for Edison, some entities will have a beginning balance in additional paid-in capital as a result of the fresh-start process.

6. Column (j), total recovery, represents the total of the various types of consideration received.

7. Column (k), total recovery percentage, is computed by dividing the total recovery amount (column (j)) by the amount of the claim.

Journal Entries—Needed to Implement Fresh-Start Reporting

Entry to record debt discharge:

Liabilities subject to compromise	$1,700,000	
Cash		$ 85,000
IRS note		75,000
Senior debt—current		100,000
Senior debt—long-term		510,000
Subordinated debt		420,000
Common stock—new		400,000
Gain on debt discharge		110,000[1]

[1] The gain on debt discharge can be calculated as follows:

Using the recovery analysis schedule, column (b)—elimination of debt and equity, add the amounts in this column for liabilities that have been compromised. In the case of Edison, the $400,000 of senior debt was settled for $385,000, a $15,000 gain. In a similar fashion, there were $30,000 and $65,000 gains on the settlement of trade claims and subordinated debentures, respectively. The sum of these three amounts is $110,000.

5.16 *Bankruptcy and Reorganization*

EDISON, INC.
PLAN OF REORGANIZATION
RECOVERY ANALYSIS

	(a)	(b) Elimination of Debt and Equity	(c) Surviving Debt	(d) Cash	(e) IRS Note	(f) Senior Debt	(g) Subordinated Debt	(h) Common Stock Percentage	(i) Common Stock Value	(j) Total Recovery	(k) Total Recovery Percentage
Postpetition liabilities	$ 400,000		$400,000							$ 400,000	100
Claim/Interest											
Secured debt	600,000			$85,000		$400,000	$115,000			600,000	100
Priority tax claim	75,000				$75,000					75,000	100
Senior debt	400,000	$ (15,000)				150,000	175,000	15%	$ 60,000	385,000	96
Trade and other claims	200,000	(30,000)				60,000	70,000	10%	40,000	170,000	85
Subordinated debentures	425,000	(65,000)					60,000	75%	300,000	360,000	85
	1,700,000	(110,000)									
Common shareholders	200,000	(200,000)						100%	0	0	0
Deficit	(535,000)	535,000									
	$1,765,000	$225,000	$400,000	$85,000	$75,000	$610,000	$420,000		$400,000	$1,990,000	

Entry to retire Edison's (old) common stock:

Common stock—old	200,000	
Additional paid-in capital		200,000

Entry to record the adoption of fresh-start reporting and to eliminate the deficit in retained earnings:

Inventory	50,000[1]	
Property, plant, and equipment	200,000[1]	
Reorganization value in excess of amounts allocable to identifiable assets	375,000[2]	
Gain on debt discharge	110,000[3]	
Additional paid-in capital	200,000[4]	
Goodwill		400,000[2]
Deficit		535,000[2]

---

[1] The fair values of inventory and property, plant, and equipment immediately before the confirmation of Edison's reorganization plan have increased by $50,000 and $200,000, respectively. To implement fresh-start reporting, the recorded values of these assets are written up to their fair values. Note that the staff of the SEC, in their interpretation of *Financial Reporting Release* Section 210 (ASR-25), believes that the recognition of reorganization value in the balance sheet of an emerging entity that meets the criteria for fresh-start reporting should be limited to no net write-up of assets.

[2] To eliminate goodwill and the deficit of the predecessor entity and to record the excess of the emerging entity's reorganization value over amounts allocated to tangible and identifiable intangible assets. These amounts are obtained from the Balance Sheet Worksheet (see next page).

[3] This amount represents the difference between Edison's allowed liabilities of $2,100,000 (see column (a) of Edison's plan of reorganization—recovery analysis) and the amount paid to settle these same liabilities, $1,990,000 (see column (j) of Edison's plan of reorganization—recovery analysis).

[4] The entry to additional paid-in capital is used to balance the entry. In this case, it represents the book value of Edison's former stockholders that is being forfeited as part of the reorganization plan.

Balance Sheet Analysis—Needed to Implement Fresh-Start Reporting

The table that follows illustrates the implementation of Edison's reorganization plan and the preparation of Edison's initial balance sheet as a reorganized entity.

5.18 Bankruptcy and Reorganization

Balance Sheet Worksheet

	Precon-firmation	Adjustments to Record Confirmation of Plan Debt Exchange Discharge of Stock	Fresh Start	Edison, Inc.'s Reorganized Balance Sheet
ASSETS				
Current Assets				
Cash	$ 120,000	$ (85,000)		$ 35,000
Receivables	250,000			250,000
Inventory	350,000		$ 50,000	400,000
Assets to be disposed of valued at market, which is lower than cost	30,000			30,000
Other current assets	15,000			15,000
Total current assets	$ 765,000	$ (85,000)	$ 50,000	$ 730,000
Property, plant, and equipment	500,000		200,000	700,000
Assets to be disposed of valued at market, which is lower than cost	100,000			100,000
Goodwill	400,000		(400,000)	0
Reorganization value in excess of amounts allocable to identifiable assets			375,000	375,000
Total assets	$1,765,000	$ (85,000)	$ 225,000	$1,905,000

LIABILITIES AND SHAREHOLDERS' DEFICIT

Current Liabilities Not Subject to Compromise

Short-term borrowings	$ 250,000		$ 250,000
Current maturities of senior debt		$ 100,000	100,000
Accounts payable–trade	150,000		150,000
Total current liabilities	$ 400,000	$ 100,000	$ 500,000

Liabilities Subject to Compromise

Prepetition liabilities	1,700,000	(1,700,000)	0
IRS note		75,000	75,000
Senior debt, less current maturities		510,000	510,000
Subordinated debt		420,000	420,000
Total Liabilities	$2,100,000	$ (595,000)	$1,505,000

Shareholders' Deficit

Common stock–old	200,000	(200,000)	-0-
Common stock–new		400,000	400,000
Additional paid-in capital		200,000	
		(200,000)	-0-
Retained earnings (deficit)	(535,000)	110,000	
		425,000[(1)]	-0-
Total liabilities in shareholders' deficit	$ (335,000)	$ 510,000	$ 225,000
Total liabilities and shareholders' deficit	$1,765,000	$ (85,000)	$1,905,000

[(1)] Represents the net effect of the elimination of the deficit in retained earnings, via a $535,000 credit to this account, and the debt to retained earnings to eliminate the $110,000 gain on debt discharge.

AUTHORITATIVE GUIDANCE INCORPORATED IN OTHER PRONOUNCEMENTS IN THE CODIFICATION

FSP SOP 90-7-1 (An Amendment of AICPA Statement of Position 90-7)

OVERVIEW

SOP 90-7 (Financial Reporting by Entities in Reorganization under the Bankruptcy Code) provides the primary guidance on financial reporting for entities that file for bankruptcy and expect to reorganize as a going concern under Chapter 11 of Title 11 of the United States Code. Under the guidance in ASC 210-10-60-3; 852-10-05-3 through 05-16; 10-1; 15-1 through 15- 3; 25-1; 30-1; 45-1 through 45-2, 45-4 through 45-21, 45-26 through 45-27, 45-29; 50-2 through 50-4, 50-7; 55-3, 55-5 through 55-11; 852-20-15-3; 740-45-1 (SOP 90-7) entities in Chapter 11 that meet certain criteria are required to adopt fresh-start reporting. In addition, when such an entity first adopts fresh-start reporting, it is required under the guidance in ASC 852-10-45-20 (paragraph 38 of SOP 90-7) to early adopt at that time changes in accounting principles, if any, that the emerging entity will be required to apply in its financial statements within the 12 months after having adopted fresh-start reporting.

Although new pronouncements issued in 1990 encouraged early adoption of those standards, the FASB has prohibited the early adoption of several recently issued standards. As a result, some have noted that the guidance in ASC 852-10-45-20 (paragraph 38 of SOP 90-7) related to the early adoption of changes in accounting principles conflicts with the FASB's guidance regarding the adoption date of some recent pronouncements. The issue is, therefore, whether entities emerging from bankruptcy that apply fresh-start reporting should be permitted to continue following the guidance in the SOP related to the early adoption of changes in accounting standards or whether such entities should be required to adopt new pronouncements based on their stated effective dates.

FASB STAFF POSITION

This FSP's guidance applies to entities that are required to apply fresh-start reporting under the guidance in SOP 90-7.

Recognition and Measurement

This FSP amends the guidance in ASC 852-10-45-20 (paragraph 38 of SOP 90-7), which addresses the early adoption of changes in accounting principles. Consequently, entities emerging from bankruptcy that use fresh-start reporting should follow only accounting standards that are effective at the date the entity adopts fresh-start reporting, including standards eligible for early adoption if an entity elects to adopt early.

Effective Date and Transition

The guidance in this FSP is effective for financial statements issued after the April 24, 2008 date on which the final FSP was issued.

Amendment to SOP 90-7

SOP 90-7 is amended as follows: [Deleted text is ~~struck out~~.]

- Paragraph 38 (ASC 852-10-45-20)—fourth bullet *before* the effective date of FASB Statement No. 141 (revised 2007) (FAS-141R) (Business Combinations) and as amended by FAS-141(R).

  ~~Changes in accounting principles that will be required in the financial statements of the emerging entity within the twelve months following the adoption of fresh start reporting should be adopted at the time fresh start reporting is adopted.~~

RELATED CHAPTERS IN 2011 GAAP GUIDE, VOLUME II

Chapter 4, "Balance Sheet Classification and Related Display Issues"
Chapter 8, "Cash Flow Statement"
Chapter 25, "Investments in Debt and Equity Securities"
Chapter 35, "Results of Operations"
Chapter 39, "Stockholders' Equity"

RELATED CHAPTERS IN 2011 GAAP GUIDE, VOLUME I

Chapter 3, "Balance Sheet Classification and Related Display Issues"
Chapter 5, "Cash Flow Statement"
Chapter 28, "Investments in Debt and Equity Securities"
Chapter 40, "Results of Operations"
Chapter 44, "Stockholders' Equity"

CHAPTER 6
BUSINESS COMBINATIONS

CONTENTS

Overview		6.02
Authoritative Guidance		
ASC 325 Investments—Other		6.03
EITF Issue 91-5	Nonmonetary Exchange of Cost-Method Investments	6.03
ASC 805 Business Combinations		6.05
FSP FAS 141(R)-1	Accounting for Assets Acquired and Liabilities Assumed in a Business Combination That Arise from Contingencies	6.05
EITF Issue 85-21	Changes of Ownership Resulting in a New Basis of Accounting	6.08
EITF Issue 87-21	Change of Accounting Basis in Master Limited Partnership Transactions	6.09
EITF Issue 96-5	Recognition of Liabilities for Contractual Termination Benefits or Changing Benefit Plan Assumptions in Anticipation of a Business Combination	6.12
Topic D-97	(Push Down Accounting) (ASC 805-50-S55-1; S99-2)	6.14
Topic D-108	Use of the Residual Method to Value Acquired Assets Other Than Goodwill	6.17
ASC 930 Extractive Activities		6.18
EITF Issue 04-3	Mining Assets: Impairment and Business Combinations	6.18
Related Chapters in 2011 GAAP Guide, Volume II		6.20

Related Chapters in 2011 GAAP Guide, Volume I   6.20

Related Chapter in 2011 International Accounting/Financial Reporting Standards Guide   6.21

OVERVIEW

A business combination occurs when two or more entities combine to form a single entity. An *asset combination* results when one company acquires the assets of one or more other companies, or when a new company is formed to acquire the assets of two or more existing companies. In an asset combination, the target companies cease to exist as operating entities and may be liquidated or become investment companies. An *acquisition or stock combination* occurs when one company acquires more than 50% of the outstanding voting common stock of one or more target companies, or when a new company is formed to acquire controlling interest in the outstanding voting common stock of two or more target companies.

Until the issuance of FAS-141 (Business Combinations), two basic methods of accounting existed for business combinations: (1) the purchase method (now known as the acquisition method) and (2) the pooling-of-interests method. FAS-141, which has been superseded by FASB Accounting Standards Codification™ (ASC) 805 (FAS-141(R), Business Combinations), eliminated the pooling-of-interests method.

After a business combination has occurred, the combined entity should report the assets and liabilities of the target company at fair value on the date of the acquisition. Any excess of the fair value of consideration given that exceeds the fair value of the net assets acquired is reported as goodwill. If the fair value of the net assets acquired exceeds the fair value of the consideration given, the transaction is considered to be a bargain purchase. In accordance with the guidance in ASC 805-30-25-2 (paragraph 36 of FAS-141(R)), the acquirer should recognize a gain on a bargain purchase in earnings on the acquisition date.

The following pronouncement is discussed in the 2011 *GAAP Guide, Volume I*, Chapter 4, "Business Combinations."

ASC 805   Business Combinations (FAS-141(R), Business Combinations)

AUTHORITATIVE GUIDANCE

ASC 325 Investments—Other

EITF Issue 91-5 (Nonmonetary Exchange of Cost-Method Investments) (ASC 325-20-30-2 through 30-6)

OVERVIEW

A cost-method investor has an investment in the common stock of a company, which is involved in a business combination. The investor will receive either new stock that represents an ownership interest in the combined entity, or the shares currently held by the investor will represent an ownership interest in the combined entity. According to the provisions of ASC 805-10-25-5 (paragraph 8 of FAS 141(R)) the company that will hold a majority interest in the combined entity is considered to be the acquirer. The combined company will continue to be publicly traded.

ACCOUNTING ISSUES

1. Should an investor that uses the cost method to account for an investment in shares of Company B (the *acquiree*) account for an exchange of those shares in a business combination at fair value, thus recognizing a new accounting basis in the investment and a *realized* gain or loss to the extent fair value differs from the investor's cost basis?
2. Should an investor in Company A, which is considered the *acquirer* in a business combination, account for a cost-method investment in the same manner as the investor in Issue 1?
3. Would the consensus on Issues 1 and 2 change if before the business combination, an investor in either company also held an investment in the other company that is a party to the transaction?

EITF CONSENSUS

1. A cost-method investor in a company considered to be the acquiree should recognize the investment at fair value.

    OBSERVATION: Under the guidance in ASC 320-10 (FAS-115) entities report investments in marketable equity securities at fair value. *Realized* gains on securities available for sale (not trading securities) are reported in the financial statements in income. *Unrealized* holding gains and losses are reported in the financial statements in other comprehensive income in accordance with the guidance in ASC 220-10 (FAS-130), which amends ASC 320 (FAS-115), but the total amount of accumulated unrealized gains and losses should continue to be reported in a separate component of shareholders' equity until those amounts are realized. Accordingly, under the consensus in Issue 1, an investor would recognize a new cost basis in the securities of Company B exchanged for securities in the combined entity and report a realized gain or loss in income.

2. A cost-method investor in a company considered to be the acquirer should continue to carry the investment at historical cost.

> **OBSERVATION:** Although an investor would continue carrying the investment at its historical cost, under the provisions of ASC 320 (FAS- 115), as amended (see Observation above), an investor is required to report the fair value of the investment in its financial statements and to report *unrealized* holding gains or losses in comprehensive income.
>
> **OBSERVATION:** FAS-141 has been replaced by ASC 805 (FAS-141(R)), which was issued in December 2007. The guidance in ASC 805-10-25-5 (paragraph 8 of FAS-141(R)) provides guidance for identifying the acquirer in a business combination, but has no effect on the guidance provided in this issue.

3. The conclusion in Issues 1 and 2 would not change if an investor in either company also held an investment in the other company before the merger.

Illustration Using EITF Issue 91-5 Consensus

Company Z has an investment in 1,000 shares of Company T, which it carries at cost ($35,000), and an investment in 1,000 shares of Company A, which it also carries at cost ($50,000). Company T enters into a business combination with Company A. Shareholders of Company T receive 0.5 shares of stock in Company A for each share of Company T. Company A accounts for the transaction as a pooling of interests. After the combination, 1,000,000 shares of the combined entity are outstanding, of which 550,000 (or 55%) are owned by former shareholders in Company A and 450,000 shares are owned by former shareholders in Company T. The fair value of a share in the combined entity is $80.

As a result of the transaction, Company Z would own 1,500 shares of the combined entity (1,000 × .5 shares of Company T plus 1,000 shares of Company A). Based on the consensus in Issue 1, Company Z would change its basis in the 500 shares of Company A received for its stake in Company T to $40,000 (500 × $80) and would realize a gain of $5,000. Under the consensus in Issue 2, Company Z would continue carrying its investment in the combined entity at $50,000, which is the cost basis of its investment in Company A.

DISCUSSION

The underlying question in this Issue is whether the investor's exchange of shares of one entity for shares in the combined entity is an event that culminates the earnings process. That depends on whether the original investment is in the company whose shareholders receive the greater interest in the shares of the combined entity (the acquirer) or in the company whose shareholders receive the lesser interest (the acquiree). The EITF's consensus positions reflect the view that the exchange of shares by the acquiree's shareholders results in the culmination of the earnings process. Those shareholders actually disposed of their investment in Company T (see Illustration) in exchange for shares in the combined entity in which they will not have a controlling interest.

ASC 805 Business Combinations

FASB Staff Position (FSP) FAS 141(R)-1 (Accounting for Assets Acquired and Liabilities Assumed in a Business Combination That Arise from Contingencies) (ASC 805-10-35-1; 20-25-15A, 25-18A, 25-19 through 20B; 30-9, 30-9A, 30-23; 35-3 through 35-4A; 50-1; 30-35-1A)

OVERVIEW

Under the guidance in ASC 805 (FAS-141(R), Business Combinations), which was issued in December 2007 and is effective for business combinations acquired on or after December 15, 2008, the acquirer must recognize at their fair value on the acquisition date all *contractual* contingencies and all *noncontractual* contingencies that more likely than not will result in an asset or liability, as defined in CON-6 (Elements of Financial Statements) (not in ASC). However, *noncontractual* contingencies that are *not* more than likely to result in an asset or a liability as of the acquisition date, would be accounted for in accordance with other U.S. generally accepted accounting principles (GAAP), including ASC 450 (FAS-5, Accounting for Contingencies).

In accordance with the guidance in ASC 805 (FAS-141(R)), such assets and liabilities would continue to be reported at their fair values as of the acquisition date until there is new information about the related contingency's possible outcome. At that time, the resulting liability would be measured at its fair value at acquisition or an amount based on the guidance in ASC 450 (FAS-5), whichever is *lower*. An asset would be measured at its fair value at acquisition or at the best estimate of the amount at which it would be settled in the future. An acquirer would continue to report assets

6.06 *Business Combinations*

and liabilities that resulted from preacquisition contingencies until the related contingencies have been resolved.

Since the issuance of FAS-141(R), constituents have raised issues related to the application of its guidance, which includes guidance to:

- Determine the fair value at acquisition of a contingency related to litigation;
- Support the measurement and recognition of liabilities related to legal contingencies if supporting information is unavailable due to attorney-client privilege;
- Distinguish between contractual and noncontractual contingencies;
- Address a situation in which an acquiree that intends to settle a contingent liability out of court wants to recognize a loss contingency based on the guidance in ASC 450 (FAS-5), but cannot do so because the liability does *not* meet the more-likely-than-not threshold for a noncontractual contingency, as required in ASC 805 (FAS-141(R));
- Derecognize a liability that results from a contingency recognized as of the acquisition date;
- Disclose information in financial statements that is potentially prejudicial;
- Determine whether an acquiree's arrangements for contingent consideration assumed in a business combination should be accounted for in accordance with the guidance for contingent consideration or in accordance with guidance for the accounting of other assets and liabilities resulting from contingencies.

The guidance in ASC 805-10-35-1; 20-25-15A, 25-18A, 25-19 through 20B; 30-9, 30-9A, 30-23; 35-3 through 35-4A; 50-1; 30-35-1A (FSP FAS-141(R)) amends ASC 805 (FAS-141(R)) and clarifies its guidance on initial recognition and measurement, subsequent measurement and accounting, and disclosure of assets and liabilities that result from contingencies in business combinations.

FASB STAFF POSITION

Scope

ASC 805-10-35-1; 20-25-15A, 25-18A, 25-19 through 20B; 30-9, 30-9A, 30-23; 35-3 through 35-4A; 50-1; 30-35-1A (FSP FAS-141(R)) applies to all of a business combination's acquired assets and assumed liabilities that have resulted from contingencies that would be accounted for under the guidance in ASC 450 (FAS-5). That is, in the same manner as contingencies that were *not* acquired or assumed in a business combination. The guidance in this pronouncement does *not* apply to assets or liabilities that result from contingencies for which there is specific accounting guidance in ASC 805 (FAS-141(R)).

Initial measurement and recognition

An asset acquired or a liability assumed in a business combination that has resulted from a contingency should be recognized at the acquisition date at its fair value if that amount can be determined during the measurement period, such as the fair value of an obligation under a warranty. If that fair value cannot be determined during the measurement period, the following two criteria must be met for such assets and liabilities to be recognized at the acquisition date based on the guidance in ASC 450 (FAS-5) and in ASC 450 (FIN-14, Reasonable Estimation of a Loss), for the application of similar criteria in ASC 450-20-25-2 (paragraph 8 of FAS-5):

- Based on information available *before* the end of the measurement period, it is probable that an asset existed and that a liability had been incurred at the acquisition date. This condition intended to imply that it is probable at the acquisition date that one or more future events will occur to confirm the existence of the recognized asset or liability.
- It is possible to reasonably estimate the amount of the asset or liability.

An asset or a liability resulting from a contingency should *not* be recognized as of the acquisition date if the criteria for measurement and recognition discussed above are *not* met at that date based on information available during the measurement period. After the acquisition date, assets and liabilities that result from contingencies that did *not* meet the criteria for recognition at the acquisition date should be accounted for *after* the acquisition date based on other applicable GAAP, including ASC 450 (FAS-5), whichever is appropriate.

An acquirer should initially recognize at fair value an acquiree's arrangements for contingent consideration assumed in a business combination by applying the guidance in ASC 805 (FAS-141(R)) for such arrangements.

Subsequent measurement and accounting

Subsequent to an acquisition, an acquirer should:

- Measure and account for assets and liabilities that result from a contingency using a systematic and rational approach based on the nature of the contingency,
- Measure contingent consideration arrangements assumed from an acquiree in a business combination based on the guidance in ASC 805-30-35-1 (paragraph 65 of FAS-141(R)).

6.08 Business Combinations

Disclosures

Information disclosed by an acquirer in a business combination should enable financial statement users to evaluate the nature of the business combination and how it affects the entity financially during the reporting period in which it occurs or after the reporting period but before financial statements are issued. An acquirer should disclose the following information in the notes to the financial statements about each business combination that occurs during a reporting period:

  a. For assets and liabilities as a result of contingencies recognized at the acquisition date:
    (1) Amounts recognized at the acquisition date and the basis used for recognition, that is, fair value or an amount based on the guidance in ASC 450 (FAS-5) or ASC 450 (FIN-14).
    (2) The nature of the contingencies.
  b. For contingencies not recognized at the acquisition date, disclose information required in ASC 450 (FAS-5) if the criteria for making those disclosures are met.

Effective date and transition

The guidance in ASC 805-10-35-1; 20-25-15A; 25-18A, 25-19 through 20B; 30-9, 30-9A, 30-23; 35-3 through 35-4A; 50-1; 30-35-1A (FSP FAS-141(R)) is effective for assets and liabilities that result from contingencies in business combinations with an acquisition date on or *after* the beginning of the first annual reporting period that begins on or *after* December 15, 2008.

EITF Issue 85-21   (Changes of Ownership Resulting in a New Basis of Accounting) (ASC 805-50-S30-3; S99-4)

OVERVIEW

Company A has acquired the voting common stock of Company B in a business combination accounted for as a purchase transaction. ASC 805 (FAS-141(R)) requires Company A to account for the assets and liabilities acquired in the transactions at their fair values. However, the accounting literature provides no guidance as to whether Company B should report its assets and liabilities on the same basis as Company A, thus adopting a "new basis of accounting."

ACCOUNTING ISSUES

  1. At what level of change in ownership should a company adopt a new basis of accounting to report its assets and liabilities?

2. How should the new basis of accounting be computed?
3. At what amount should minority interests be reported?

EITF CONSENSUS

The EITF did not reach a consensus on this Issue.

SEC OBSERVER COMMENT

The SEC Observer stated that SEC registrants are required to adopt new-basis accounting only if virtually 100% of the stock has been acquired and there is no outstanding publicly held debt or preferred stock. The SEC Observer stated further that net assets (in a business combination) or long-lived assets transferred between companies under common control or between a parent and subsidiary should be reported at their historical cost in the subsidiary's separate financial statements.

DISCUSSION

Although the authoritative accounting literature does not provide guidance on this Issue, SEC SAB-54 (Application of Push-Down Basis of Accounting in Financial Statements of Subsidiaries Acquired by Purchase) provides guidance to SEC registrants. It requires the parent company's cost of acquiring a subsidiary to be "pushed down" to the subsidiary's separate financial statements if "substantially all" of the subsidiary's voting common stock has been acquired and the parent can control the form of ownership. SAB-54 encourages but does not require new-basis accounting if less than "substantially all" of a company's stock has been acquired or there is outstanding publicly held debt or preferred stock.

EITF members noted that the application of SAB-54 is inconsistent when less than 100% of a company is acquired or when there is a step acquisition. The Task Force's views also differed as to whether private companies should apply new-basis accounting.

> **OBSERVATION:** New-basis accounting is a component of the FASB's project on the reporting entity and consolidation. The FASB issued a Discussion Memorandum (New Basis Accounting) in December 1991.

EITF Issue 87-21 Change of Accounting Basis in Master Limited Partnership Transactions (ASC 805-50-05-7; 15-8; S30-2; 30-7, 8, 9; S99-3)

OVERVIEW

The enactment of the Tax Reform Act of 1986 resulted in the formation of an increasing number of Master Limited Partnerships

(MLPs), which are partnerships whose interests are traded publicly. MLPs may be formed to realize the value of undervalued assets; to pass income and deductible losses through to its shareholders; to raise capital; to enable companies to sell, spin off, or liquidate operations; or to combine partnerships. They are generally formed from assets in existing businesses operated in the form of limited partnerships and in connection with a business in which the general partner is also involved.

The following are different methods of creating an MLP:

- In a *roll-up*, two or more legally separate limited partnerships are combined into one MLP.
- In a *drop-down*, units of a limited partnership that was formed with a sponsor's assets (usually a corporate entity) are sold to the public.
- In a *roll-out*, a sponsor places certain assets into a limited partnership and distributes its units to shareholders.
- In a *reorganization*, an entity is liquidated by transferring all of its assets to an MLP.

EFFECTS OF FAS-141 AND ASC 805 (FAS-141(R)/

FAS-141, which superseded APB-16, applies to transactions in which all entities transfer net assets, or the owners of those entities transfer their equity interests to a newly formed entity in a transaction that is referred to as "roll-up." Its scope excludes, however, transfers of net assets or exchanges of equity interests between entities under common control. All the facts and circumstances should be analyzed to determine the nature of the transaction and the appropriate method of accounting for it.

FAS-141 has been replaced by ASC 805 (FAS-141(R)), which was issued in December 2007. Although, its scope continues the exclusion of transfers of net assets or exchanges of equity interests between entities under common control, guidance on the accounting for those transactions is included in Appendix D, "Continuing Authoritative Guidance," of the Statement.

ACCOUNTING ISSUES

1. Can new-basis accounting ever be used for the assets and liabilities of an MLP?
2. How should an MLP account for transaction costs in a roll-up?

EITF CONSENSUS

1. A new basis is not appropriate in the following circumstances:

a. The MLP's general partner in a roll-up was also the general partner of the predecessor limited partnerships, and no cash has been exchanged in the transaction.
   b. A sponsor in a drop-down receives 1% of the units of the MLP as its general partner and 24% of the units as a limited partner, with the remaining 75% of the units sold to the public. The general partner can be replaced by a two-thirds vote of the limited partners.
   c. An MLP is created as a roll-out.
   d. An MLP is created as a reorganization.

   In addition, the conclusion on a roll-up would not change even if the general partner was the general partner of only some of the predecessor limited partnerships. Task Force members noted that if a general partner of predecessor limited partnerships who will not be a general partner of the MLP receives MLP units in settlement of management contracts or for other services that will not carry over to the MLP, those units have the characteristics of compensation rather than equity, and should be accounted for as such by the MLP. The Task Force did not reach a consensus on situations in which new-basis accounting would be appropriate, but did not preclude the possibility.
2. A roll-up's transaction costs should be charged to expense.

SEC OBSERVER COMMENT

The SEC Observer announced that the SEC would not object to new-basis accounting in an MLP created as a drop-down to the extent of the percentage of change in ownership if (1) 80% or more of the MLP is sold to the public and (2) the limited partners can replace the general partner by a "reasonable" vote.

DISCUSSION

Issue 1 The issues of change of control and voting interest would normally be the primary concerns in determining whether there should be new-basis accounting. However, the EITF found it difficult to resolve the issue of control in an MLP. Some argued that there is no change in control in a roll-up of existing limited partnerships because the general partner of the MLP was also the general partner of the limited partnerships that have been combined. Under those circumstances, the transaction would not qualify for accounting as a business combination because APB-16 does not apply to transactions in which there were no outsiders. Others argued that accounting for business combinations may apply if one party's voting control is close to a majority. However, a majority of a working group formed to discuss the issues recommended combining the limited partnerships at carryover basis.

Determining who has control in an MLP is also difficult because control may not be based on a majority ownership of the voting shares. For example, although a general partner may own less than a majority of the voting interest, the limited partners may be able to exercise control only in limited situations, such as the removal of the general partner. ARB-51 discusses situations in which majority ownership may not be indicative of control, but it does not discuss situations in which there may be control without a majority ownership.

Some analogized an MLP created as a drop-down to push-down accounting. However, here again the primary issue was whether there is a new control group. An AICPA Issues Paper on push-down accounting had recommended that a change in basis be "pushed down" to the subsidiary's financial statements in a business combination accounted for as a purchase if there was at least a 90% change in ownership.

A roll-out was considered to be a spin-off, which was being accounted for in practice at carryover basis. A reorganization did not involve a change of owners because it was merely a change in legal entity. In practice, reorganizations were also being accounted for at carryover basis.

Issue 2 The issue was whether transaction costs, such as professional fees, in a roll-up should be accounted for as an expense, as part of the purchase price, or as a reduction of the partners' equity accounts. Treating those costs as part of the purchase would be appropriate under purchase accounting, while reducing the proceeds would be consistent with offerings that are not business combinations. Expense recognition would be most appropriate for a transaction treated like a pooling. (The issue of new basis vs. old basis is analogous to purchase vs. pooling-of-interests accounting.)

EITF Issue 96-5 (Recognition of Liabilities for Contractual Termination Benefits or Changing Benefit Plan Assumptions in Anticipation of a Business Combination) (ASC 420-10-60-3; 450-10-60-7; 710-10-60-4; 712-10-60-1; 715-60-60-2; 805-20-55-50, 51)

OVERVIEW

This Issue addresses the timing of liability recognition for termination benefits paid to involuntarily terminated employees for a plan that is governed by an *existing contractual agreement* that will be implemented only if a business combination occurs.

The Issue applies, but is not limited to, the following types of agreements, which are referred to here as *contractual termination benefits:*

- Golden parachute employment agreements that require payment if control changes in a business combination
- Union agreements requiring payment of termination benefits for involuntary terminations when a plant closes as a result of a business combination
- Postemployment plans requiring payments for involuntary terminations due to a business combination

Curtailment losses also may be incurred as a result of the writeoff of unrecognized prior service costs and a change in the projected benefit obligation from a significant reduction in the expected years of future service of current employees. This Issue refers to payments under the above-mentioned agreements.

Guidance on loss recognition for curtailments and liabilities is found in ASC 450-20-25-1 to 25-7 (FAS-5, Accounting for Contingencies), ASC 715-30 (FAS-88, Employers' Accounting for Settlements and Curtailments of Defined Benefit Pension Plans and for Termination Benefits), ASC 715-20; 715-60: 715-70 (FAS-106, Employers' Accounting for Postretirement Benefits Other Than Pensions), and ASC 712-10 (FAS-112, Employers' Accounting for Postemployment Benefits). To recognize a loss under ASC 450 (FAS-5), which is the primary source of guidance on loss accruals, it must be probable before the financial statements are issued that an asset has been impaired or a liability has been incurred at the date of the financial statements and the amount of the loss is reasonably estimable. ASC 715-30 (FAS-88) states that a loss and a liability should be recognized for a pension plan curtailment and for contractual termination benefits when it is probable that the curtailment will occur or that employees will be entitled to the contractual benefits and the amount can be reasonably estimated. ASC 715-60 (FAS-106) provides comparable guidance for other postretirement curtailment losses. Under the guidance in ASC 712-10 (FAS-112), costs related to the termination of employees under a postemployment benefit plan may result in curtailment losses or accruals for contractual termination benefits.

This Issue addresses a transaction in which a company has agreed to a business combination. The company believes the combination is probable and has developed a plan under which certain employees will be terminated if the combination is consummated. Termination benefits will be paid under a preexisting plan or contractual relationship.

ACCOUNTING ISSUE

Should a liability for contractual termination benefits and curtailment losses under employee benefit plans that will be triggered when a business combination is consummated be recognized when it is probable that the business combination will occur or when the business combination is consummated?

EITF CONSENSUS

The EITF reached a consensus that an entity should recognize a liability for contractual termination benefits and curtailment losses under employee benefit plans triggered by a business combination only when the business combination is consummated.

> **OBSERVATION:** FAS-141 has been replaced by ASC 805 (FAS-141(R)), which was issued in December 2007. The Statement does not affect the EITF's consensus in this Issue.

DISCUSSION

The EITF's consensus is based on the view that a business combination is not merely a confirming event—it is the event necessary to trigger a contractual obligation to pay termination benefits when an entity undergoes a business combination. Proponents argued that the company can avoid the liability until the business combination has been consummated. In addition, the FASB staff believes that if a business combination is considered a discrete event, a liability for contractual termination benefits should be recognized only when the business combination has been consummated, because the effects of a business combination should not be recognized until it has occurred. Because the effects of a business combination cannot be recognized until it has been consummated, and because all those effects should be recognized in the same accounting period, the treatment of the liability for contractual termination benefits should be consistent with that for restructuring costs under the consensus in Issue 95-14 (not in ASC), which prohibits recognition of such costs before the business combination has been consummated. In effect, a business combination is an example of the second type of *subsequent event* discussed in AU Section 560 of the codification of Statements on Auditing Standards—an event that occurs after the year-end but before the issuance of financial statements that should be disclosed but for which a liability need not be accrued.

FASB/SEC Staff Announcements

Topic D-97 (Push Down Accounting) (ASC 805-50-S55-1; S99-2)

This SEC staff announcement discusses the staff's views regarding the facts and circumstances under which push down accounting should be applied. The staff's views on this matter can be found in SAB-54 (Application of "Push Down" Basis of Accounting in Financial Statements of Subsidiaries Acquired by Purchase), which states that push down accounting should be used in a purchase transaction in which an entity becomes substantially wholly owned. Application of that view is *required* if a company becomes substantially wholly owned, that is, 95% or more of the company has been acquired, due to a series of related and anticipated transactions, unless the acquirer's ability to control the company's form of ownership is affected by the existence of outstanding public debt or preferred stock. Push down accounting is permitted if *80 to 95%* of the company has been acquired.

The staff believes that push down accounting should be applied in a subsidiary's financial statements, regardless of a minority interest sold to new investors, if a parent company has purchased all the minority interest of a majority-owned subsidiary in a single transaction or a series of related and anticipated transactions, and subsequently issues shares in the subsidiary to new investors. Further, push down accounting is required even if a subsidiary became wholly owned for a short time and there was a plan for the subsidiary to issue shares after it became wholly owned. Registrants should distinguish between transactions in which only a significant change in ownership occurs, such as in a recapitalization, which would not warrant the use of push down accounting, and those in which a company becomes substantially wholly owned.

The SEC staff believes that a company becomes substantially wholly owned in a single transaction or a series of transactions if a group of investors act together to acquire a company as if they are one investor and can control the company's form of ownership. That is, it is appropriate to combine the holdings of investors that both "mutually promote" the acquisition and "collaborate" on the investee's subsequent control (the collaborative group). Push down accounting applies in those circumstances. To determine whether an investor is part of that group, the SEC staff believes that a rebuttable presumption exists that investors who invest in a company at the same time or within a reasonably close time frame are part of the collaborative group. To rebut that presumption, the following are indicators that an investor is *not* part of a collaborative group:

1. Independence
    a. The investor is an entity with substantial capital and other operations of its own.
    b. The investor is independent of and unaffiliated with the other investors.
    c. The investor's investment in the investee does not depend on investments made by any other investor in the investee.
    d. The investor has no relationships with the other investors that are material to either party.

2. Risk of Ownership
    a. The investor invests at fair value.
    b. The investor uses its own resources to invest.
    c. The investor shares in the risks and rewards of ownership in the investee with the other owners in proportion to its class and amount of investment. Its upside rewards or downside risk are unlimited and the investor receives no other direct or indirect benefits from any other investor for making the investment.
    d. No other investor directly or indirectly provides or guarantees the investor's investment.
    e. The investor does not provide or guarantee any other investor's investment.
3. Promotion
    a. The investor did not ask others to invest in the investee.
4. Subsequent Collaboration
    a. The investor can exercise its voting rights in all shareholder votes.
    b. The investor has no special rights not given to the other investors, such as a guaranteed board seat.
    c. The investor's right to sell its shares is unrestricted, except as required by securities laws or by what is reasonable or customary in individually negotiated investment transactions for closely held companies, such as the investee's right of first refusal on the investor's shares if a third party offers to purchase the shares.

The SEC staff believes that push down accounting also applies when several financial investors act together to acquire ownership interests in a company but no single investor obtains substantially all of the ownership interests even though there is a significant ownership change. In that type of scenario, the presumption that the investors acted as a collaborative group would not be overcome if:

- The investors negotiated their investments in the company at the same time, based on the same contract.
- The investors made their investments to achieve a broad strategic objective that they were pursuing together.
- The investors had several prior business relationships that were material to each of the investors.
- One of the investors does not share fully in the risks and rewards of ownership because of limited first-loss guarantees made by the other investors.

- The board of directors is not controlled by a single investor but as a result of bylaw amendments regarding board representation and voting, one of the investors can block board action. Therefore, the investors must collaborate on controlling the board.
- Each investor's ability to transfer its shares is restricted.

EFFECTIVE DATE

The guidance in this announcement applies prospectively to transactions initiated after April 19, 2001.

Topic D-108 (Use of the Residual Method to Value Acquired Assets Other Than Goodwill) (ASC 805-20-S30-1; S35-1; S99-3)

Under current guidance on accounting for business combinations in ASC 805-20-55-2 (paragraph A19 of FAS-141(R), Business Combinations), intangible assets that result from contractual or legal rights must be recognized separately from goodwill. The SEC Observer reported at the EITF's September 2004 meeting that, in some circumstances, SEC registrants have claimed that they are unable to value a legal or contractual right directly or separately from goodwill in a business combination because the asset's characteristics make it indistinguishable from goodwill. Examples are cellular/spectrum licenses and cable franchise agreements. Some of those entities have assigned a purchase price to all other identifiable assets and liabilities and have assigned the remaining residual amount to the "indistinguishable" intangible asset without recognizing goodwill or recognizing goodwill based on a technique other than that specified in ASC 805-30-30-1, 25-1 (paragraph 34 of FAS-141(R)).

Entities in the telecommunications, broadcasting, and cable industries have been using the residual method to value intangible assets. That method is similar to the allocation methods used to account for business combinations accounted for under the purchase method in APB-16 (Business Combinations), before that Opinion was superseded by FAS-141 and later ASC 805 (FAS-141(R)). He stated that proponents of that approach claim that the residual method results in a value that approximates the value that would be arrived at under a direct value method or that, under the circumstances, it would be impracticable to use other methods. Some believe that the value obtained under the residual method for indistinguishable intangible assets is an acceptable surrogate for fair value because it is very difficult to determine fair value by using a direct value method. Entities that use the residual method to assign the purchase price to indistinguishable intangible assets often also use it to test for impairment.

SEC OBSERVER COMMENT

The SEC Observer stated that registrants must follow the guidance in paragraph 37(e) of FAS-141, which is now ASC 805-30-30-1 (paragraph 34 of FAS-141(R)) under which intangible assets meeting the criteria for recognition should be recognized at fair value. Goodwill differs from other recognized assets because it is specifically stated in ASC 805-30-30-1 (paragraph 34 of FAS-141(R)) that goodwill is the residual of the cost of an acquisition "over the net amounts assigned to assets acquired and liabilities assumed" and is, therefore, defined and measured as an excess. Other recognized intangible assets must be measured at fair value.

The SEC staff does not believe that it can be assumed that using the residual method to value intangible assets will result in amounts that represent the fair value of those assets. In addition, the fact that it is difficult to value certain intangible assets is not an excuse for not following the guidance in paragraphs ASC 805-20-55-2 through 45 (paragraphs A19 through A22 of FAS-141(R)), under which the fair value of intangible assets must be determined separately from goodwill. In addition, the SEC Observer noted that some entities are valuing the same intangible assets by the direct value method. Consequently, entities should use a direct value method rather than the residual value method to determine the fair value of intangible assets other than goodwill. Further, impairment should be tested in accordance with the guidance in ASC 350 (FAS-142, Goodwill and Other Intangible Assets).

The direct value method should be applied to the valuation of assets for acquisitions that are completed after September 29, 2004.

ASC 930 Extractive Activities

EITF Issue 04-3 (Mining Assets: Impairment and Business Combinations) (ASC 930-360-35-1, 2; 930-805-30-1, 2)

OVERVIEW

Some mining entities have been excluding estimated cash flows associated with a mining asset's economic value beyond its proven probable (VBPP) reserves and the effects of anticipated fluctuations in the minerals' future market prices over the period of cash flows when testing such assets for impairment in accordance with the guidance in ASC 360-10 (FAS-144, Accounting for the Impairment or Disposal of Long-Lived Assets) and in making the purchase price allocation of business combinations. Both VBPP and an estimate of the future market price of the minerals are generally included in a mining asset's fair value.

VBPP is defined in the SEC's Industry Guide 7 (Using Cash Flow Information and Present Value in Accounting Measurements) as (1) *proven reserves,* for which quantity is computed from certain dimensions, such as workings or drill holes; for which quality is determined from detailed samplings; and the geologic character of which is well defined because of the close proximity of the sites for inspection, sampling, and measurement and (2) *probable reserves,* the quantity, grade, and quality of which is computed based on information similar to that used for proven reserves, but the sites for inspection, sampling, and measurement are farther apart. The degree of assurance is lower than that of proven reserves, but is high enough that continuity can be assumed between the points observed. Proven and probable reserves are distinguished based on the level of geological evidence and the subsequent confidence in the estimated reserves. In addition to information about VBPP, the SEC also requires registrants to complete a feasibility study before accepting a registrant's statement that mining assets are proven and probable reserves.

The scope of this Issue applies to mining entities—which include entities that find and remove wasting natural resources—other than oil- and gas-producing entities under the scope of ASC 932-10 (FAS-19, Financial Accounting and Reporting by Oil and Gas Producing Companies).

ACCOUNTING ISSUES

1a. Should VBPP be considered when an entity allocates the purchase price of a business combination to mining assets?

1b. Should the effects of anticipated fluctuation in the future market price of minerals be considered when an entity allocates the purchase price of a business combination to mining assets?

EITF CONSENSUS

The EITF reached the following consensus positions:

1a. VBPP should be included in the value allocated to mining assets in the purchase price allocation of a business combination in the same manner that a market participant would include VBPP in determining the asset's fair value.

1b. The effects of anticipated fluctuations in the future market price of minerals should be included when the fair value of the mining assets is determined in a purchase price allocation. Estimates of those effects should be consistent with the expectations of marketplace participants—that is, available information, such as current prices, historical averages, and forward pricing curves should be considered. The assumptions should be consistent with the acquirer's operating plans for developing and producing minerals and should be based on more than one factor.

The cash flows associated with VBPP estimates of future discounted and undiscounted cash flows should be included in the evaluation of mining assets for impairment under ASC 360-10 (FAS-144). In addition, estimated cash flows used to determine impairment should include estimated cash outflows necessary to develop and extract the VBPP.

The effects of anticipated fluctuations in the future market price of minerals should be included when estimating discounted and undiscounted cash flows used to determine impairment under ASC 360-10 (FAS-144). Estimates of those effects should be consistent with the expectations of marketplace participants—that is, available information, such as current prices, historical averages, and forward pricing curves should be considered. The assumptions should be consistent with the acquirer's operating plans for developing and producing minerals and should be based on more than one factor.

TRANSITION

The first and second consensus positions should be applied *prospectively* to business combinations completed and goodwill impairment tests performed in reporting periods that begin after the consensus positions have been ratified by the FASB. The consensus positions may be applied early if financial statements have not been issued. On initial application, an impairment charge, if any, should be reported in income from continuing operations. The third and fourth consensus positions should be applied *prospectively* to asset impairment tests performed in reporting periods that begin after the FASB has ratified the consensuses. They may be applied early if financial statements have not been issued.

The FASB ratified the consensus positions at its March 31, 2004 meeting.

RELATED CHAPTERS IN 2011 GAAP GUIDE, VOLUME II

Chapter 12, "Contingencies, Risks, and Uncertainties"
Chapter 21, "Intangible Assets"
Chapter 28, "Nonmonetary Transactions"
Chapter 29, "Pension Plans—Employers"
Chapter 34, "Research and Development"

RELATED CHAPTERS IN 2011 GAAP GUIDE, VOLUME I

Chapter 4, "Business Combinations"
Chapter 8, "Contingencies, Risks, and Uncertainties"

Chapter 23, "Intangible Assets"
Chapter 32, "Nonmonetary Transactions"
Chapter 33, "Pension Plans"
Chapter 39, "Research and Development"
Chapter 47, "Banking and Thrift Institutions"

RELATED CHAPTER IN 2011
INTERNATIONAL ACCOUNTING/FINANCIAL
REPORTING STANDARDS GUIDE

Chapter 7, "Business Combinations"

CHAPTER 7
CAPITALIZATION AND EXPENSE RECOGNITION CONCEPTS

CONTENTS

Overview		7.02
Authoritative Guidance		
ASC 340 Other Assets and Deferred Costs		7.03
EITF Issue 99-5	Accounting for Pre-Production Costs Related to Long-Term Supply Arrangements	7.03
ASC 350 Intangibles—Goodwill and Other		7.05
EITF Issue 00-2	Accounting for Web Site Development Costs	7.05
ASC 360 Property, Plant, and Equipment		7.07
AUG AIR-1	Accounting for Planned Major Maintenance Activities	7.07
ASC 410 Asset Retirement and Environmental Obligations		7.10
FSP FAS-143-1	Accounting for Electronic Equipment Waste Obligations	7.10
EITF Issue 89-13	Accounting for the Cost of Asbestos Removal	7.13
EITF Issue 90-8	Capitalization of Costs to Treat Environmental Contamination	7.16
ASC 450 Contingencies		7.18
Topic D-77	Accounting for Legal Costs Expected to Be Incurred in Connection with a Loss Contingency	7.18
ASC 710 Compensation—General		7.19
EITF Issue 88-23	Lump-Sum Payments under Union Contracts	7.19
ASC 720 Other Expenses		7.20

EITF Issue 97-13	Accounting for Costs Incurred in Connection with a Consulting Contract or an Internal Project That Combines Business Process Reengineering and Information Technology Transformation	7.20
ASC 740	Income Taxes	7.23
EITF Issue 88-4	Classification of Payment Made to IRS to Retain Fiscal Year	7.23
ASC 932	Extractive Activities—Oil and Gas	7.24
FSP FAS-19-1	Accounting for Suspended Well Costs	7.24
ASC 954	Health Care Entities	7.28
Topic D-89	Accounting for Costs of Future Medicare Compliance Audits	7.28
Related Chapters in 2011 GAAP Guide, Volume II		7.29
Related Chapters in 2011 GAAP Guide, Volume I		7.29

OVERVIEW

The conceptual basis for capitalizing an expenditure is the resulting asset, which is expected to benefit future periods. Expenditures whose benefit is expected to be limited to the current accounting period should be expensed immediately.

This relatively simple concept is difficult to apply in practice, and it has led to a number of accounting complexities, such as accounting for research and development costs, start-up costs, and intangible assets.

AUTHORITATIVE GUIDANCE

ASC 340
Other Assets and Deferred Costs

EITF Issue 99-5 (Accounting for Pre-Production Costs Related to Long-Term Supply Arrangements)
(ASC 340-10-05-6; 25-1, 2, 3; S50-1; 55-2 through 55-5; S99-3; 460-10-60-2; 730-10-60-1)

OVERVIEW

Manufacturers that supply parts to original equipment manufacturers (OEMs), such as manufacturers of automobiles, often incur pre-production costs associated with the design and development of products they will manufacture for their customers. They incur pre-production engineering costs—for example, in designing, developing, and building molds, dies, and other tools—which will be used in manufacturing parts such as seats and instrument panels for automobiles. Those costs are referred to in the Issue as *tooling costs*.

Eligibility to be awarded a contract to supply *production parts* to the automotive industry includes the capability to produce the tooling used to manufacture the parts. Although suppliers begin pre-production activities and incur tooling costs several years before actual production begins, they do so only after they have been awarded a contract to produce specific parts for a specific car or model, approximately two to five years before production begins.

Suppliers recover tooling costs in several ways. An OEM may be contractually obligated to pay the supplier a guaranteed amount for tooling costs, which is included in the price of each part purchased; the OEM may agree to pay the supplier a lump sum for those costs; or if there is no specific agreement for reimbursement, the supplier may include those costs in the price of each part. Even if there is no contractual reimbursement arrangement, OEMs have historically compensated their suppliers for tooling costs if a program terminates early or the number of units purchased is less than expected.

Although this Issue is discussed in terms of the automotive industry, a consensus would also apply to other industries with similar production arrangements.

ACCOUNTING ISSUES

1. How should an entity account for costs incurred to design and develop products sold under long-term supply arrangements?

7.04 *Capitalization and Expense Recognition Concepts*

2. How should an entity account for costs incurred to design and develop molds, dies, and other tools used in producing products sold under long-term supply arrangements?
3. Should customer reimbursement for design and development costs affect the supplier's accounting for such costs?

EITF CONSENSUS

1. Suppliers should expense design and development costs for products sold under long-term supply contracts as they are incurred.
2. Design and development costs for molds, dies, and other tools used in producing products under long-term supply contracts should be accounted for as follows:
   a. Capitalize as part of the cost of molds, dies, and other tools (subject to the impairment test in ASC 360-10 (FAS-144), which superseded FAS-121) that are *owned* by the supplier and will be used to produce products under long-term supply arrangements.
   b. Capitalize as part of the cost of molds, dies, and other tools (subject to impairment test in ASC 360-10) (FAS-144)) that are *not owned* by the supplier and will be used to produce products under long-term supply arrangements if the supplier has a *noncancelable* right under the arrangement (as long as the supplier is performing under the terms of the arrangement) to use the molds, dies, and other tools during the supply arrangement.
   c. Expense design and development costs of *nonowned* molds, dies, and other tools as incurred if the supplier does *not* have a noncancelable right to use the molds, dies, and other tools during the supply arrangement.
   d. Expense as incurred in accordance with the guidance in ASC 730-10-05; 05-1; 05-25; 05-50; 05-55 (FAS-2, Accounting for Research and Development Costs) if design and development costs are for owned or not owned molds, dies, and other tools that involve new technology.
3. Recognize design and development costs as assets as incurred if the supplier has a *contractual guarantee* for reimbursement of those costs. That is, the guarantee is included in a legally enforceable supply arrangement that provides criteria (e.g., a maximum total amount or a specific amount per part) for the objective measurement and verification of the reimbursement.

EFFECTIVE DATE

The guidance in this Issue applies to design and development costs incurred after December 31, 1999, with earlier application encouraged. Entities may choose to adopt the consensus positions as a cumulative effect of a change in accounting principle.

ASC 350 Intangibles—Goodwill and Other

EITF Issue 00-2 (Accounting for Web Site Development Costs) (ASC 350-10-05-7; 350-50-15-2, 3; 25-2 through 25-17; 55-2 through 55-9)

OVERVIEW

Web sites are developed by different kinds of companies. Many are "brick and mortar" companies; others are start-up companies that will be conducting their business operations only on the Internet. There are three broad categories of Internet web sites: (1) sites that provide information only, (2) sites that provide information and a service, and (3) sites that provide information and enter into transactions with customers over the Internet. In addition, Internet web sites can be accessed by the general public, extranet sites can be accessed only by subscribers, and intranet sites can be accessed only by individuals within a specific company.

The stages of web site development include (*a*) planning, (*b*) web application and infrastructure development, (*c*) graphics and content, and (*d*) production. Because there is no specific guidance on the accounting for web site development costs, the accounting for those costs has been diverse.

This Issue does not apply to costs of hardware, such as servers, necessary to support a web site. It also does not apply to costs incurred under web site development contracts for others. Such costs are accounted for under contract accounting.

ACCOUNTING ISSUE

How should an entity account for costs incurred to develop a web site?

EITF CONSENSUS

Planning stage activities *Expense* all costs of web site planning activities, regardless of whether they are related to software. Those costs include, but are not limited to, a business plan, a project plan, or both; identification of specific goals; determining the web site's functions (e.g., order placement, shipment tracking); identifying necessary hardware and web applications; determining whether the technology necessary to achieve the site's intended functions exists; alternative means of achieving the site's functions; identifying software tools; and legal costs to address copyright issues.

Web site application and infrastructure development stage During this stage, the necessary hardware is acquired and software is developed. This Issue does *not* apply to costs of hardware acquired. It is assumed that all costs related to software development are incurred for the purpose of operating the web site (internal-use software). Those costs should be accounted for according to the guidance in ASC 350-10-05-6; 350-40-05-2 through 05-6, 05-8, 05-9; 15-2 through 15-7; 25-1 through 25-16; 30-1 through 30-4; 35-1 through 35-10; 50-1; 55-1 through 55-4; 730-10-60-2; 985-20-60-1 (SOP 98-1). That is, the costs generally should be *capitalized* under the guidance in ASC 350-40-25-2 through 25-15, 05-8 through 5-9, 15-2, 30-1 (paragraphs 21 through 31 of SOP 98-1). An entity that has a plan or is developing a plan to market the software to others should account for those costs under the guidance in ASC 985-20-05-1 through 05-2; 15-2 through 15-4; 25-1 through 25-4, 25-6 through 25-11; 35-1 through 35-4; 50-1 through 50-2; 985-330-40-1; 730-10-60-4; 55-1 (FAS-86, Accounting for the Costs of Computer Software to be Sold, Leased or Otherwise Marketed). Costs of obtaining or registering an Internet name would be capitalized in accordance with the guidance in ASC 350 (FAS-142, Goodwill and Other Intangible Assets). In addition, fees paid periodically to an Internet service provider for hosting a web site on its servers, generally, should be *expensed* over the benefit period.

Graphics development costs Graphics involve the design of a web page and do not change with content. Because they are part of the software, they should be *capitalized* according to the guidance in ASC 350-40-25-2 through 25-4 (paragraph 21 of SOP 98-1) for internal-use software. If those costs are related to software to be sold to others, they should be accounted for based on the provisions of ASC 985-20-05-1 through 05-2; 15-2 through 15-4; 25-1 through 25-4, 25-6 through 25-11; 35-1 through 35-4; 50-1 through 50-2; 985-330-40-1; 730-10-60-4;. 55-1 (FAS-86). Changes to a web site's graphics after the site has been launched may be related to web site maintenance or enhancements. The accounting for such changes is discussed in 5(b) below.

Content development costs A web site's content may consist of articles, pictures, maps, and so forth and may be presented as text or in graphical form. (The graphics discussed above are not included here.) Because the accounting guidance for costs of web site content, which may be acquired from others or developed internally, may not be limited to forms of content found only on web sites, the Task Force decided to address those costs in a separate Issue.

Costs incurred in operating a web site Costs incurred in operating a web site should be accounted for as follows:

- *Costs having no future benefit* Expense operating costs with no future benefit as incurred (e.g., training, administration, maintenance, and other web site operating costs) because the costs of operating a web site should be accounted for in the same way as the costs of operating other kinds of entities.

- *Costs with a future benefit* Costs incurred to develop upgrades and enhancements that increase the functions of web site software should be accounted for in the same way as the costs of developing new software according to the guidance in ASC 350-10-05-6; 350-40-05-2 through 05-6, 05-8, 05-9; 15-2 through 15-7; 25-1 through 25-16; 30-1 through 30-4; 35-1 through 35-10; 50-1; 55-1 through 55-4; 730-10-60-2; 985-20-60-1 (SOP 98-1). Similar costs incurred for upgrades or enhancements to software to be sold to others should be accounted for based on the guidance for product enhancements in ASC 985-20-05-1 through 05-2; 15-2 through 15-4; 25-1 through 25-4, 25-6 through 25-11; 35-1 through 35-4; 50-1 through 50-2; 985-330-40-1; 730-10-60-4; 55-1 (FAS-86). Determining whether a change to web site software is an upgrade or enhancement (product enhancement) or maintenance requires judgment based on the specific facts and circumstances. In addition, the Task Force noted that ASC 350-10-05-6; 350-40-05-2 through 05-6, 05-8, 05-9; 15-2 through 15-7; 25-1 through 25-16; 30-1 through 30-4; 35-1 through 35-10; 50-1; 55-1 through 55-4; 730-10-60-2; 985-20-60-1 (SOP 98-1) provides that if it is not cost-effective to separate internal costs incurred for maintenance from those incurred for minor upgrades and enhancements, the total amount should be expensed as incurred.

Transition The consensus positions are effective for web site development costs incurred for fiscal quarters beginning after June 30, 2000, including costs incurred for projects as of the beginning of the quarter in which the consensus positions are adopted. Alternatively, entities can elect to adopt the consensus positions as a cumulative effect of a change in accounting principle in accordance with ASC 250-10 (FAS-154, Accounting Changes and Error Corrections). Early adoption is encouraged.

ASC 360 Property, Plant, and Equipment

AUG AIR-1 Accounting for Planned Major Maintenance Activities (ASC 340-10-25-5; 360-10-25-5; 45-1; 908-360-45-2)

OVERVIEW

ASC 908 (AICPA Industry Audit Guide, *Audits of Airlines* (Airline Guide)), provides guidance regarding the accounting for planned major maintenance activities, which is also followed by entities in other industries. Under the guidance in ASC 908 (Airline Guide), the following four alternative methods of accounting for planned major maintenance activities are permitted: (1) direct expense; (2) built-in overhaul; (3) deferral; and (4) accrual in advance. The FASB believes that liabilities for planned major maintenance activities recognized under the accrual-in-advance method do *not* meet the definition of a liability in FASB Concepts Statement No. 6 (Elements of Financial Statements (not in ASC), because an expense is recognized in a period before a transaction or event obligating the entity has occurred. Future costs to be incurred for maintenance to improve an asset's operating efficiency, comply with regulatory operating guidelines, or extend an asset's useful life do *not* represent an entity's current duty or responsibility before an obligating transaction or event has occurred. Therefore, the guidance in ASC 908 (Airline Guide) regarding the accounting for planned major maintenance activities is being amended by the guidance in this FSP, which applies to *all* industries.

FASB STAFF POSITION

Under the guidance in this FSP, application of the accrual-in-advance method to account for planned major maintenance activities is prohibited in annual and interim financial reporting periods. Major maintenance activities should be accounted for in the same manner in annual and interim financial reporting periods.

ASC 908 (Airline Guide) is amended as follows:

- ASC 908-360-25-2 (paragraph 3.69)—Modify the last sentence of the paragraph as follows: "The following accounting methods are [most often employed] *permitted*:" Delete the bullet "Accrual method."
- Not in ASC (paragraph 3.73)—Delete the paragraph discussing the accrual method.
- Not in ASC (paragraph 3.74—Delete "and accrual" from the first sentence.)
- Not in ASC (paragraph 4.11.2)—In the first sentence change the number of alternative methods of accounting for scheduled maintenance to three from four and delete all references to the accrual method in the paragraph.

ASC 270-10-45-9 (Paragraph 16(a) of APB-28, Interim Financial Reporting) is amended as follows:

- Delete the parenthetical (e.g., annual major repairs).

EFFECTIVE DATE AND TRANSITION

Entities should apply the guidance in this FSP in the first fiscal year that begins after December 15, 2006, but may apply the guidance earlier as of the beginning of an entity's fiscal year. The guidance in

ASC 340-10-25-5; 360-10-25-5, 45-1; 908-360-45-2 (FSP AUG AIR-1) should be applied *retrospectively* for all financial statements presented unless doing so would be impractical. Retrospective recognition should include the recognition of:

- The cumulative effect of changing to the new accounting principle on periods before those presented in the carrying amounts of assets and liabilities as of the beginning of the first period presented;
- An offsetting adjustment, if any, to the opening balance of retained earnings or other suitable components of equity or net assets in the balance sheet for that period; and
- Adjustments to financial statements for each individual prior period presented to show the effects of the change to a new principle on the specific period in which it was applied.

If it is impractical to apply the guidance in ASC 340-10-25-5; 360-10-25-5, 45-1; 908-360-45-2 (FSP AUG AIR-1) retrospectively to all years presented, the financial statements should be *retrospectively* adjusted for as many consecutive years as practicable and the cumulative effect of applying that guidance should be used to adjust the carrying amounts of assets and liabilities as of the beginning of the earliest period to which that guidance can be *retrospectively* applied. The opening balance of retained earnings or other suitable components of equity or net assets in the balance sheet for that period should be adjusted by an offsetting amount, if any. If *retrospective* application of that guidance to any prior year is impracticable, the cumulative effect should be included in beginning retained earnings in the year in which the guidance in ASC 340-10-25-5; 360-10-25-5; 45-1; 908-360-45-2 (FSP AUG AIR-1) is applied for the first time.

DISCLOSURE

The following disclosures should be made as of the date on which the guidance in ASC 340-10-25-5; 360-10-25-5; 45-1; 908-360-45-2 (FSP AUG AIR-1) is adopted:

- The method used to account for planned major maintenance activities;
- A description of retrospectively adjusted prior-period information, if any;
- How the change in accounting principle affects income from continuing operations, net income, or other suitable captions of changes in the applicable net assets or performance indicator, other affected financial statement line items, if any, and affected per-share amounts, if any, for retrospectively adjusted periods, if any;
- The cumulative effect of a change in accounting principle on retained earnings or other components of equity or net assets

in the balance sheet as of the beginning of the earliest period presented; and

- If it is impractical to apply the provisions in ASC 340-10-25-5; 360-10-25-5; 45-1; 908-360-45-2 (FSP AUG AIR-1) retrospectively to all prior periods, the reasons why doing so would be impracticable and a description of the alternative method used to report the change in accounting principle.

ASC 410 Asset Retirement and Environmental Obligations

FSP FAS-143-1 Accounting for Electronic Equipment Waste Obligations (ASC 410-20-15-2, 15-3; 55-23 through 55-30, 55-64 through 55-67; 720-40-05-1 through 05-4; 15-1; 25-1 through 25-3; 35-1; 55-2, 55-3)

INTRODUCTION

The guidance in ASC 410-20-15-2, 15-3; 55-23 through 55-30, 55-64 through 55-67; 720-40-05-1 through 05-4; 15-1; 25-1 through 25-3; 35-1; 55-2, 55-3 (FSP FAS-143-1)addresses the accounting for obligations related to the European Union's Directive 2002/96/EC on Waste Electrical and Electronic Equipment (the Directive). The Directive refers to two types of waste: (1) "new waste," the term used for products put on the market *after* August 13, 2005, and (2) "historical waste" equipment, the term used for all products that have been on the market on or *before* August 13, 2005. For the purpose of financing the cost of historical waste, the Directive differentiates between such waste from households and from commercial users.

The guidance in ASC 410-20-15-2, 15-3; 55-23 through 55-30, 55-64 through 55-67; 720-40-05-1 through 05-4; 15-1; 25-1 through 25-3; 35-1; 55-2, 55-3 (FSP FAS-143-1)applies only to *historical* waste. The FASB does not expect that there will be diversity in practice in the accounting for new waste because under the Directive the costs related to new waste will be assumed by the producers of such equipment. The following two questions are addressed under the guidance in ASC 410-20-15-2, 15-3; 55-23 through 55-30, 55-64 through 55-67; 720-40-05-1 through 05-4; 15-1; 25-1 through 25-3; 35-1; 55-2, 55-3 (FSP FAS-143-1): (1) should commercial users of electronic equipment or producers of such equipment that sell to private households and to commercial users recognize the Directive's effects on historical waste management under U.S. GAAP and (2) if so, when and how should those effects be accounted for?

FASB STAFF POSITION

Historical waste equipment held by commercial users The Directive provides that a commercial user retains the waste management obligation for historical waste until it replaces the equipment. At the time of replacement, that obligation may be transferred to the entity that has produced the newly acquired equipment, subject to the laws adopted by applicable EU-member countries. A commercial user that does not replace the equipment retains the obligation until the equipment's disposition. Under the Directive, however, EU-member countries have the option of requiring commercial users to retain an obligation for a portion of or all costs associated with historical waste even if the equipment is replaced. In that case, a commercial user may retain a portion or all of the obligation until disposing of the equipment. Therefore, for all intents and purposes, commercial users may be obligated to incur the costs of retiring assets that meet the definition of historical waste equipment.

Commercial users should apply the provisions ASC 410-20 (FAS-143, Accounting for Asset Retirement Obligations) and the related guidance in ASC 410-20-25, 20-55 (FIN-47, Accounting for Conditional Asset Retirement Obligations) to obligations related to historical waste because they are, in effect, asset retirement obligations. The guidance in ASC 410-20-25-1-5; 30-1; 35-1, 2; 360-10-35-18, 35-19 (paragraphs 3 through 12 of FAS-143) applies to the initial recognition and measurement of a liability and the cost of asset retirement. Recognition of that obligation is required regardless of a commercial user's intent and ability to replace the equipment and transfer the obligation. The obligation may be transferred to the producer of replacement equipment, depending on the laws of the applicable EU-member country, and if so, would be reflected in the purchase price of the asset purchased.

The cost related to an asset's retirement should be capitalized when a liability related to historical waste is initially recognized by increasing the related asset's carrying amount by the same amount as the liability. The guidance in ASC 410-20-35-3 through 35-8 (paragraphs 13 through 15 of FAS-143), which requires recognition of changes in the amount of an obligation as a result of the passage of time and changes in the timing or amount of the original estimate of undiscounted cash flows, should be applied in periods following the initial accounting for the liability.

A commercial user that subsequently replaces equipment and transfers its obligation for historical waste to the producer of the newly acquired equipment should determine, based on the fair value of the asset retirement obligation, how much of the purchase price is related to the newly acquired equipment and how much is related to the transferred asset retirement obligation. The cost basis of the newly acquired equipment should equal the difference between the amount paid and the fair value of the obligation transferred. The transferred liability should be removed from the commercial user's balance sheet and a gain or loss should be recognized for the difference between the carrying amount of the liability at the date that replacement equipment was purchased and the portion of the purchase price related to the transferred obligation. Producers of replacement equipment that accept the transfer of and obligation related to historical waste and for whom recycling of electronic waste equipment is *not* a revenue-producing activity should recognize revenue on a net basis based on the amount received less the fair value of the transferred liability for historical waste. The producer should derecognize the transferred obligation when it is settled. Producers that do conduct such recycling as a revenue-producing activity should measure revenue earned on the sale of replacement equipment and the assumption of the obligation based on the guidance in ASC 605-25-05; 05-15, 05-25, 05-30, 05-50, 05-55 (EITF Issue 00-21,Revenue Arrangements with Multiple Deliverables) . In EU countries where commercial users retain their historical waste obligations when purchasing replacement equipment, *no* portion of the purchase price of newly acquired equipment should be allocated to the liability, which remains on the commercial user's balance sheet until it is settled.

Historical waste held by private households   The guidance in this section is not related to the guidance for asset retirement in ASC 410-20 (FAS-143). Under the Directive, historical waste held by private households should be financed collectively by producers that are sellers in the market during each measurement period, which should be defined by each EU member. The amount to be financed is not affected by the volume of equipment qualifying as historical waste sold by electronic equipment producers in the market before the measuring period. Producers will be required to contribute proportionate amounts based on their shares of the market by type of equipment. Each EU-member country will determine the exact method of computation. For example, if the amount of the liability of each producer in the market is computed based on its respective share of the market by type of equipment sold during a measurement period, a producer would recognize a liability for its obligation and an offsetting amount as an expense over the measurement period based on its portion of the estimated total costs of the waste management program to be allocated and its estimated market share. Each producer is required to adjust its liability as information about the actual cost of the program and the producer's actual respective market share becomes available. Because an obligation is triggered by participation in the market during the measurement period, a producer should *not* recognize an obligation *before* that period begins.

EFFECTIVE DATE AND TRANSITION

The guidance in ASC 410-20-15-2, 15-3; 55-23 through 55-30, 55-64 through 55-67; 720-40-05-1 through 05-4; 15-1; 25-1 through 25-3; 35-1; 55-2, 55-3 (FSP FAS-143-1) should be applied on the first reporting period that ends after June 8, 2005, or the date the law is adopted by the applicable EU-member country, whichever is later. Entities are encouraged to apply the guidance earlier for periods for which financial statements had not been issued when this guidance was finalized if the applicable EU-country had adopted the law in those periods.

Commercial users Commercial users should recognize the following items in their balance sheets for amounts related to historical waste equipment recognized on initial application of this guidance:

- A liability for existing asset retirement obligations, if any, adjusted for cumulative accretion to the date of the adoption of the guidance in ASC 410-20-15-2, 15-3; 55-23 through 55-30, 55-64 through 55-67; 720-40-05-1 through 05-4; 15-1; 25-1 through 25-3; 35-1; 55-2, 55-3 (FSP FAS-143-1);
- An asset retirement cost capitalized as an increase to the carrying amount of associated long-lived asset; and
- Accumulated depreciation on the capitalized cost.

Amounts recognized as a result of the initial application of the guidance in ASC 410-20-15-2, 15-3; 55-23 through 55-30, 55-64 through 55-67; 720-40-05-1 through 05-4; 15-1; 25-1 through 25-3; 35-1; 55-2, 55-3 (FSP FAS-143-1) should be measured based on information, assumptions, and interest rates as of the date of adoption. The amount recognized as an asset retirement cost should be measured as of the date on which the asset retirement obligation was incurred. Cumulative accretion and accumulated depreciation should be recognized for the period beginning with the date on which the liability would have been recognized had this guidance been in effect on the date the liability was incurred to the date on which this guidance was actually adopted.

EITF Issue 89-13 (Accounting for the Cost of Asbestos Removal) (ASC 410-20-15-3; 410-30-45-6)

OVERVIEW

Many jurisdictions require that "dangerous asbestos" found in buildings be treated by removal or containment. In addition, many companies have voluntarily treated asbestos in buildings they own.

ACCOUNTING ISSUES

1. Should costs incurred to treat an asbestos problem that was known when a property was acquired be capitalized or recognized as an expense?
2. Should costs incurred to treat an asbestos problem in an existing property that was identified after acquiring the property be capitalized or recognized as an expense?

3. Should these costs be charged to expense, and if so, should they be reported as an extraordinary item? (Discussed in Chapter 35, "Results of Operations.")

EITF CONSENSUS

1. Costs incurred to treat asbestos should be capitalized as part of the cost of the property if they were incurred reasonably soon after the acquisition of a property with a known asbestos problem; the carrying amount of the property should be subject to an impairment test, however.

   > **OBSERVATION:** ASC 360-10 (FAS-144, Accounting for the Impairment or Disposal of Long-Lived Assets), which superseded FAS-121(Accounting for the Impairment of Long-Lived Assets and for Long-Lived Assets to Be Disposed Of), provides guidance on accounting and reporting of impairment or disposal of long-lived assets. Although ASC 360-10 (FAS-144) does not affect the EITF's consensus discussed in this Issue, impairment should be tested based on its provisions.

2. Costs incurred to treat asbestos problems in an existing property may be capitalized as an improvement, subject to an impairment test on the property's carrying amount. Costs incurred while expecting to sell the property should be deferred and recognized in the period a sale is consummated to the extent those costs can be recovered from the estimated selling price.

SEC OBSERVER COMMENT

The SEC Observer noted that registrants should discuss significant exposure to asbestos treatment costs in "Management's Discussion and Analysis" regardless of the treatment of such costs in the financial statements.

DISCUSSION

Issue 1 The question in Issue 1 is whether it is appropriate to capitalize the cost of asbestos treatment as part of the asset if a problem is known at the time the property was purchased. Proponents of capitalization referred to the definition and characteristics of an asset as discussed in paragraphs 25 and 26a of CON-6 (not in ASC). They believed that costs incurred to treat asbestos have a "future economic benefit" that will "contribute directly or indirectly to future net cash inflows." Treatment will improve the property directly by making it more valuable in a future sale. An improvement in employees' safety and morale might be an indirect benefit of treatment.

Proponents also noted that it is accepted practice to capitalize as part of an acquired property costs of preparing it for its intended use. Therefore, costs incurred to treat an asbestos problem known at the time of acquisition should be accounted for in the same manner, based on the presumption that the sales price already considered the cost of asbestos treatment.

Issue 2 The threshold question in Issue 2 is whether costs of treating asbestos that are incurred while owning a building improve the property and extend its useful life, or whether they are incurred to repair the property. Those who supported capitalization argued that the nature and extent of the costs influence the decision whether to capitalize or expense the costs of asbestos treatment. They contended that treatment extends the building's useful life because it cannot continue to be occupied unless the hazardous condition was remedied.

Others noted that if the fair value of the building after asbestos treatment would exceed its book value by more than the cost of treatment, the owner has an economic incentive to incur the cost. They supported capitalizing such costs if they could be recovered from a future sale. Expense recognition would be appropriate, however, if treatment would result in a loss. Still others would have permitted capitalization only if the property is held for sale and the selling price is sufficient to recover the costs. They believed that a gain from the sales transaction and asbestos treatment costs should be recognized in the same operating statement, the same as the deferral of near-term losses after the measurement date of a discontinued operation if an overall gain is expected.

SUBSEQUENT DISCUSSION

The EITF affirmed its consensus on this Issue while discussing related issues in ASC 410-20-15-2, 3; 410-30-15-3; 25-16, 25-18, 25-19; 35-14; 55-19 through 55-26 (Issue 90-8), and noted that capitalization of asbestos treatment costs could be justified based on the criteria in the first consensus in that pronouncement.

ASC 410-20 (FAS-143, Accounting for Asset Retirement Obligations), which is effective for financial statements issued for fiscal years beginning after June 15, 2002, applies to *legal* obligations related to the retirement of tangible long-lived assets that result from the acquisition, construction, or development and the normal operation of those assets. Because the guidance in ASC 410-20 (FAS-143) does *not* apply to an obligation to remove asbestos from other than the normal operation of an asset; this consensus or the guidance in ASC 410-30-05, 05-15, 05-25, 05-30, 05-35, 05-55 (SOP 96-1, Environmental Remediation Liabilities) may apply in those circumstances. Asset retirement obligations under the scope of ASC 410-20 (FAS-143) must be recognized at the fair value of the liability in the period incurred; the associated costs should be capitalized as part of the long-lived asset's carrying amount and amortized to expense using a systematic and rational method over the asset's useful life. A liability should be recognized on the acquisition date for an existing retirement obligation related to acquired tangible long-lived assets as if the obligation had been incurred on that date. The consensus positions in this Issue do *not* apply to asbestos removal obligations under the scope of ASC 410-20 (FAS-143) that occur after the Statement's provisions have been adopted.

EITF Issue 90-8 (Capitalization of Costs to Treat Environmental Contamination) (ASC 410-20-15-2, 3; 410-30-15-3; 25-16, 25-18, 25-19; 35-14; 55-19 through 55-26)

> **OBSERVATION:** The consensus positions in this Issue do not apply to obligations for the treatment of environmental contamination under the scope of ASC 410-20 (FAS-143) that occur after the Statement's provisions have been adopted.

OVERVIEW

Companies may incur environmental contamination treatment costs such as removal costs, containment costs, neutralization costs, and costs to prevent current or future contamination. Examples of these include: costs to remove contamination (e.g., cleaning up a disposal site); costs to acquire tangible property (e.g., air pollution control equipment); costs of environmental studies; and costs of fines.

Such costs may be incurred voluntarily or be required by law. The guidance in ASC 410-20-15-3; 410-30-45-6 (EITF Issue 89-13) specifies that the cost of asbestos removal may be capitalized subject to an impairment test as to recoverability of the recorded cost of the property. As a result, some companies have questioned whether the same reasoning could be applied to costs related to other types of environmental contamination.

This issue does not address the following:

- When to recognize liabilities resulting from environmental contamination
- How to measure such liabilities
- Whether to report costs of treating environmental contamination as an unusual or extraordinary item

ACCOUNTING ISSUE

Should costs of treating environmental contamination be capitalized or expensed?

EITF CONSENSUS

The EITF reached a consensus that environmental cleanup costs should generally be expensed as incurred. Some costs may be capitalized if they are recoverable and meet *one* of the following criteria:

- The cost extends the life, increases the capacity, or improves the safety or efficiency of existing owned property. To determine whether this criterion has been met, the condition of the property after making the expenditure must be compared to its condition when first constructed or acquired. Its condition must be improved to qualify for capitalization.
  For example, reinforcement of an oil tanker's hull would be a qualifying expenditure. Reinforcing the hull makes the tanker safer than it was when originally acquired. Removing toxic waste from a site would not qualify under this criterion, because the expenditure only restores the property to its original condition. (See the third criterion for an exception.)
- The cost prevents or reduces future environmental contamination that may result from an entity's operations or activities (e.g., installing air scrubbers in a factory's smokestack).
- The cost is incurred to treat property currently held for sale (e.g., removing toxic waste from a site would qualify under this criterion, if the property is held for sale).

The Task Force affirmed its consensus in ASC 410-20-15-3; 410-30-45-6 (Issue 89-13) and stated that capitalization of asbestos removal costs would be justified under the first criterion.

DISCUSSION

Proponents of using specific criteria to distinguish between environmental cleanup costs that should be capitalized and those that should be expensed believed that such costs generally should be expensed, but realized that under certain circumstances, it may be appropriate to capitalize those costs. They noted that by establishing specific criteria for capitalization, the predominant practice of expensing environmental cleanup costs would be retained. For example, cleaning up a gasoline station's contaminated soil does not create an asset because it does not increase the station's capacity or improve its safety or efficiency over its condition when it was first constructed. Rather, the soil is restored to its original condition.

If the criterion of improvement rather than repair is applied, some believed it would be appropriate to capitalize asbestos cleanup costs based on the premise that a building containing asbestos was unsafe even when it was built and that removal made it safer. However, others argued that the building was safe when it was built, but the asbestos became unsafe over time because of remodeling and aging that could release asbestos fibers into the air. Thus, treatment would only restore the building to its original safe state.

SUBSEQUENT DEVELOPMENTS

ASC 410-20 (FAS-143, Accounting for Asset Retirement Obligations) , which is effective for financial statements issued for fiscal years beginning after June 15, 2002, applies to *legal* obligations related to the retirement of tangible long-lived assets that result from the acquisition, construction, or development and the normal operation of those assets. Because the guidance in ASC 410-20 (FAS-143) does *not* apply to an obligation to treat environmental contamination from other than the normal operation of an asset; the consensus in this Issue or the guidance in ASC 410-30-05, 05-15, 05-25, 05-30, 05-35, 05-55 (SOP 96-1, Environmental Remediation Liabilities) may apply in those circumstances. Asset retirement obligations under the scope of ASC 410-20 (FAS-143) must be recognized at the fair value of the liability in the period incurred; the associated costs should be capitalized as part of the long-lived asset's carrying amount and amortized to expense using a systematic and rational method over the asset's useful life. A liability should be recognized on the acquisition date for an existing retirement obligation related to acquired tangible long-lived assets as if the obligation had been incurred on that date.

ASC 450 Contingencies

Topic D-77 (Accounting for Legal Costs Expected to Be Incurred in Connection with a Loss Contingency) (ASC 450-20-S25-1; S50-2; S99-2)

At its January 23, 1997, meeting, the EITF discussed a potential new Issue that addressed the accounting for legal costs expected to be incurred in connection with a loss contingency under the guidance in ASC 450 (FAS-5, Accounting for Contingencies). Although Task Force members generally believe that practice is to expense such costs, some members suggested that accounting practice for such costs is mixed. Nevertheless, the Task Force decided not to add the Issue to its agenda.

The SEC Observer stated that the SEC staff expects registrants to apply their accounting policies consistently and to disclose material accounting policies and the methods of applying those policies in accordance with the requirements in ASC 235-10-05, 10-50 (APB-22).

ASC 710 Compensation—General

EITF Issue 88-23 (Lump-Sum Payments under Union Contracts) (ASC 710-10-S15-1; 15-3; S25-1; 25-12, 25-13, 25-14; S99-1)

OVERVIEW

In connection with the signing of a new union contract, a company might give employees one or more lump-sum payments instead of, or in addition to, a base wage rate increase. Typically, employees are not required to refund any portion of such lump-sum payments if they leave the company before the contract period ends. In addition, employees who leave the company generally are replaced by other union members at the same base wage rate but replacements receive no lump-sum payments.

ACCOUNTING ISSUE

Should lump-sum payments made to employees in connection with the signing of a new union contract be (1) charged to expense immediately or (2) deferred and amortized over the contract period or some portion of the contract period?

EITF CONSENSUS

A consensus was reached that lump-sum payments made to employees in connection with the signing of a new union contract may be deferred provided that the payments clearly will benefit future periods in the form of lower base wage rates. The deferred charge should be amortized over periods clearly benefited, but not longer than the contract period.

Task Force members noted that the terms and conditions of those types of arrangements vary and must be reviewed to determine how to account for the lump-sum payments.

DISCUSSION

Those who supported deferral argued that lump-sum payments that result in lower wage costs over the contract period provide a future economic benefit to the entity. They believed that such payments represent a cost of the contract, which will benefit the entity over the entire contract period and consequently should be deferred and recognized in the periods in which services are performed.

Proponents also referred to certain pronouncements that recommend recognition of compensation costs over the periods during which an employee performs services. For example, the goal of recognizing pension costs over the periods in which employees provide services are discussed in ASC 715 (FAS-87, Employers' Accounting for Pensions). Under the guidance in ASC 310-10-45-4; 50-14; 360-10-50-1; 710-10-15-4 through 15-5; 25-9 through 25-11; 30-1 through 30-2; 715-20-60-1; 505-10-50-2; 835-30-35-3 (APB Opinion No. 12 (Omnibus Opinion—1967) employers are required to accrue and amortize amounts to be paid to employees under deferred compensation contracts for current services in a systematic and rational manner over the period of active employment beginning when the employer enters into the contract.

To refute the argument of those who compare lump-sum payments to bonuses for past services, proponents of deferral also argued that such payments had not been promised to the employees before the union contract negotiation; all contractually required payments have already been made to the employees; and the only reason for making these payments is to obtain a lower base wage rate over the contract period.

ASC 720 Other Expenses

EITF Issue 97-13 (Accounting for Costs Incurred in Connection with a Consulting Contract or an Internal Project That Combines Business Process Reengineering and Information Technology Transformation) (ASC 720-45-05-2, 05-3; 15-2; 25-1 through 25-4; 30-1; 55-1)

OVERVIEW

Many companies are installing advanced software packages that will improve their ability to participate in electronic commerce and take advantage of new computer technology. Because the software is often not compatible with the company's existing business processes, the project also involves reengineering the company's business processes to work with the software. Such projects may be carried out through a contract with an outside consulting firm or performed by the company's own personnel. As part of the total project, the company may install new computer hardware, reconfigure work areas, and purchase new furniture, office equipment, and workstations.

A *business process reengineering project* consists of the following activities:

- Documenting the current business processes (not the current software structure), which may be referred to as mapping, developing an "as-is" baseline, flow charting, or determining the current business structure.

- Reengineering business processes for greater efficiency and effectiveness, which may be referred to as analysis, developing "should-be" processes, or improving profit/performance.
- Determining the composition of the workforce required to operate reengineered business processes.

The issue whether to capitalize or expense business process reengineering was excluded from the scope of ASC 350-10-05-6; 350-40-05-2 through 05-6, 05-8, 05-9; 15-2 through 15-7; 25-1 through 25-16; 30-1 through 30-4; 35-1 through 35-10; 50-1; 55-1 through 55-4; 730-10-60-2; 985-20-60-1 (SOP 98-1, Accounting for Computer Software Developed or Obtained for Internal Use), and it is not addressed in ASC 720-15-15-1 through 15-5; 25-1; 55-1, 55-3 through 55-54, 55-6 through 55-7, 55-9 through 55-10 (SOP 98-5, Reporting on the Costs of Start-Up Activities) (see Chapter 35, "Results of Operations"). However guidance is provided in ASC 350-20-25-3 (paragraph 10 of FAS-142, Goodwill and Other Intangible Assets) which states that "costs of internally developing, maintaining, or restoring intangible assets (including goodwill) that are not specifically identifiable, that have indeterminate lives, or that are inherent in a continuing business and related to an enterprise as a whole shall be recognized as an expense when incurred."

ACCOUNTING ISSUES

1. How should the costs of a project to transform a company's information technology and to reengineer its business processes be accounted for if the project is carried out by internal personnel or through a consulting contract with a third party?
2. How should a company allocate the total costs of a business reengineering consulting contract to the project's various activities?

EITF CONSENSUS

1. Costs of business process reengineering activities (such as those described in the Overview) should be *expensed as incurred*, regardless of whether they are performed by internal personnel or through a consulting contract with a third party. This guidance also applies if such activities are included in a project to acquire, develop, or implement internal-use software. However, this consensus does not affect the accounting for internal-use software development costs or for the acquisition of property and equipment.

The Task Force noted that although personnel involved in a business process reengineering project also may have expertise in information technology and software application, the

project's effort is focused on the reengineering process, not on software systems.
2. The total price of a business process reengineering project performed under a consulting contract with a third party should be allocated to each activity based on the relative fair value of the separate activities. Objective evidence of the fair value of the different elements of the contract should be used to make the allocation, rather than basing the allocation solely on the separate prices stated for the various elements of the contract.

APPLICATION GUIDANCE

The staff provided the following application guidance for the recognition of internal costs or costs of work performed by third parties:

- Business process reengineering and information technology transformation costs that should be expensed as incurred in accordance with the consensus:
  — Preparation of request for proposal
  — Current state assessment
  — Process reengineering
  — Workforce restructuring
- Costs of preliminary software project stage activities that should be expensed as incurred in accordance with ASC 350-10-05-6; 350-40-05-2 through 05-6, 05-8, 05-9; 15-2 through 15-7; 25-1 through 25-16; 30-1 through 30-4; 35-1 through 35-10; 50-1; 55-1 through 55-4; 730-10-60-2; 985-20-60-1 (SOP 98-1, discussed in Chapter 9, "Computer Software") on internal-use software:
  — Conceptual formulation of alternatives
  — Evaluation of alternatives
  — Determination of existence of needed technology
  — Final selection of alternatives
- Costs of software application development stage activities that should be capitalized in accordance with the guidance in ASC 350-10-05-6; 350-40-05-2 through 05-6, 05-8, 05-9; 15-2 through 15-7; 25-1 through 25-16; 30-1 through 30-4; 35-1 through 35-10; 50-1; 55-1 through 55-4; 730-10-60-2; 985-20-60-1 (SOP 98-1):
  — Design of chosen path, including software configuration and software interface
  — Coding
  — Installation to hardware
  — Testing, including parallel processing phase

- Data conversion costs to develop or obtain software allowing the new system to access old data
- Costs of software application development stage activities that should be expensed as incurred in accordance with the guidance in ASC 350-10-05-6; 350-40-05-2 through 05-6, 05-8, 05-9; 15-2 through 15-7; 25-1 through 25-16; 30-1 through 30-4; 35-1 through 35-10; 50-1; 55-1 through 55-4; 730-10-60-2; 985-20-60-1 (SOP 98-1):
  - All data conversion processes not included above
  - Training
- Costs of post-implementation/operation stage activities that should be expensed as incurred in accordance with the guidance in ASC 350-10-05-6; 350-40-05-2 through 05-6, 05-8, 05-9; 15-2 through 15-7; 25-1 through 25-16; 30-1 through 30-4; 35-1 through 35-10; 50-1; 55-1 through 55-4; 730-10-60-2; 985-20-60-1 (SOP 98-1):
  - Training
  - Application maintenance
  - Ongoing support
- Costs of acquiring fixed assets accounted for in accordance with a company's existing policy:
  - New computer equipment, office furniture, and workstation purchases
  - Reconfiguration of work area, including architect fees and hard construction costs

(The FASB staff included the information related to the application of the guidance in ASC 350-10-05-6; 350-40-05-2 through 05-6, 05-8, 05-9; 15-2 through 15-7; 25-1 through 25-16; 30-1 through 30-4; 35-1 through 35-10; 50-1; 55-1 through 55-4; 730-10-60-2; 985-20-60-1 (SOP 98-1) for illustrative purposes only. In addition, capitalization of costs under that guidance requires that other criteria be met.)

ASC 740 Income Taxes

EITF Issue 88-4 (Classification of Payment Made to IRS to Retain Fiscal Year) (ASC 740-10-55-69, 55-70, 55-71)

OVERVIEW

The Revenue Act of 1987 changed the requirements of the Tax Reform Act of 1986 by permitting partnerships and S corporations to elect to either retain their fiscal year or adopt a calendar year for tax purposes. If an entity elects to retain its fiscal year, it is required to make one annual deposit that approximates the income tax the partners would have paid on the short-period income tax return had the entity adopted a calendar year.

The election and the deposit are made by the partnership or S Corporation rather than by the partners. The deposit is adjusted annually based on the entity's income in the previous year so the entity either makes a payment to the IRS or receives a refund.

ACCOUNTING ISSUE

Should an entity report the annual payment in the financial statements as a period expense, an asset in the form of a deposit, or as a debit to partners' equity?

EITF CONSENSUS

The EITF reached a consensus that the payment should be reported as an asset.

DISCUSSION

The authoritative literature provides no specific guidance for the resolution of this issue, except for the definition and discussion of the characteristics of assets and expenses in CON-5 (Recognition and Measurement in Financial Statements of Business Enterprises) (not in ASC) and CON-6 (Elements of Financial Statements—A Replacement of FASB Concepts Statement No. 3) (not in ASC).

To support their view that the payment should not be reported as a debit to the partners' equity accounts, proponents argued that the payment was made on behalf of the entity so it could retain the fiscal year for tax purposes. In addition, the IRS does not associate the individual partners with the payment, which is not offset against their actual individual tax liabilities. The argument for recognizing the payment as an asset rather than as a current expense was based on the view that it will not be realized by the entity currently but only if the entity is liquidated, its income declines to zero, or it converts to a calendar year-end.

ASC 932 Extractive Activities—Oil and Gas

FSP FAS-19-1 Accounting for Suspended Well Costs (ASC 932-360-25-18; 932-235-50-16)

OVERVIEW

The guidance in ASC 932-360-25-18; 932-235-50-16 (FSP FAS-19-1) addresses the accounting for costs of exploratory wells by entities that use the successful efforts method of accounting discussed in the FASB Accounting Standards Codification ™ ASC 932 (FAS-19, Financial Accounting and Reporting by Oil and Gas Producing Companies) and amends that guidance.

The guidance in ASC 932-360-25-18; 932-235-50-16 (FSP FAS-19-1) addresses the question of whether there are circumstances in which an entity can continue to capitalize costs related to exploratory wells beyond one year, even if *no* additional exploratory wells are necessary to justify major capital expenditures and the wells are under way or firmly planned for the near future. The guidance in ASC 932-360-35-17 (paragraph 19 of FAS-19) states that the costs of drilling exploratory wells can be capitalized while determining whether proved reserves have been found. If such reserves are found, costs that have been capitalized are recognized as part of the entity's wells, equipment, and facilities. Otherwise, those costs should be expensed, net of salvage value.

Sometimes reserves are found but cannot be classified as proved reserves when drilling is completed, because additional geologic and engineering information is required. In addition, other matters, such as government approvals, sales contracts, and financing must be resolved to verify with "reasonable certainty" that the reserves can be recovered under "existing economic and operating conditions"—that is, based on prices and costs at the date of the estimate. Before ASC 932-360 (FAS-19) was amended by the guidance in ASC 932-360-25-18; 932-235-50-16 (FSP FAS-19-1), the accounting guidance in ASC 932-360-35-6, 35-13, and 35-16 through 35-20 (paragraphs 31 through 34 of FAS-19) was followed under such circumstances. Under that guidance, at least one of the following conditions had to be met in order to capitalize costs of major capital expenditures in an area in which reserves could not be classified as proved reserves:

- A discovery that a well has sufficient reserves to justify making additional capital expenditures towards its completion as a producing well
- Drilling of additional exploratory wells is in process or firmly planned for the near future

Otherwise, exploratory well costs had to be expensed. Capitalized costs related to exploratory wells *not* under the scope of ASC 932-360-35-13 and 35-20 (paragraphs 31(a) and 34 of FAS-19) had to be expensed if reserves could not be classified as proved reserves within one year from the date drilling was completed.

The issue of accounting for the costs of exploratory wells was raised because the manner in which oil and gas companies are performing their exploration activities has changed from that originally contemplated in the guidance in ASC 932-360-35-13 and 35-20 (paragraphs 31(a) and 34 of FAS-19). Exploration activities now frequently occur in more remote areas, go to greater depths, and are undertaken in more complex geological formations than previously.

As a result, some believe that there is a need to extend the one-year capitalization period in which an entity can determine whether found reserves qualify for classification as proved reserves.

FASB STAFF POSITION

An entity should continue capitalizing exploratory well costs if (1) a well has sufficient reserves to justify its completion as a producing well and (2) the entity is making satisfactory progress in evaluating the reserves and the project's economic and operating viability.

Amendment of ASC 932 (FAS-19) The guidance in ASC 932-360-35-16 through 35-18 (paragraph 31 of FAS-19)is amended based on the guidance in ASC 932-360-25-18; 932-235-50-16 (FSP FAS-19-1) for reserves that cannot be classified as proved reserves when drilling is completed. The guidance in paragraphs 31 through 34 (ASC 932-360-35-13, 35-16 through 35-20) also applies to exploratory-type stratigraphic wells.

Paragraphs 31(a) and 31(b) of FAS-19 are replaced by ASC 932-360-35-13 (new paragraph 31(a) of FAS-19), which provides that the value of wells should be assumed to be impaired if the criteria in ASC 932-360-25-18; 932-235-50-16, (FSP FAS-19-1) that have been incorporated in ASC 932-360-35-16 through 20 (new paragraph 31 of FAS-19), are *not* met or an entity has information that raises doubts about a project's economic or operational viability. In that case, capitalized exploration costs incurred, less salvage value, should be expensed. Further, it is required that exploratory well costs *not* continue to be capitalized based on an expectation that economic conditions will change or that technology will be developed to make a project economically or operationally viable.

The following guidance in ASC 932-360-35-19 (new paragraph 32 of FAS-19) provides indicators that should be considered along with other relevant facts and circumstances in determining whether an entity is making enough progress in its evaluation of reserves and a project's economic and operational viability:

- Commitment of appropriate personnel with appropriate skills is being made
- Costs are incurred to assess the reserves and their potential development
- The economic, legal, political, and environmental features of a potential development are being assessed
- Sales contracts (or active negotiations) with customers for oil and gas exist
- Agreements (or active negotiations) with governments, lenders and venture partners exist
- Outstanding requests for proposals for the development of the required facilities exist

- Firm plans, established timetables, or contractual commitments exist
- There is progress on contractual arrangements to permit future development
- Existing transportation and other infrastructure that is or will be available for the project has been identified.

The guidance in ASC 932-360-35-19 (paragraph 33 of FAS-19), as amended, provides that long delays in assessing progress or in a development plan may raise questions about whether an entity should continue to capitalize exploratory well costs after the completion of drilling. Justification for the deferral of well exploration costs becomes more difficult the longer that process continues.

Under the guidance in ASC 932-360-35-20 (new paragraph 34 of FAS-19), capitalized exploratory costs associated with a well, net of salvage value, if any, should be expensed if activities have been suspended or the entity has *not* participated in substantial activities to assess the reserves or a project's development within a "reasonable" time period after drilling has been completed. Planning to undertake activities in the near future is *not* sufficient to continue capitalization. Brief interruptions of activities, however, should *not* affect continued capitalization.

Disclosures Under the amendment of ASC 932 (FAS-19) in ASC 932-360-25-18; 932-235-50-16 (FSP FAS-19-1), management is required to apply more judgment than previously was required in evaluating whether capitalized costs of exploratory wells meet the criteria for continued capitalization. Consequently, the following required disclosures in the notes to the financial statements are intended to provide financial statement users with information about how management is applying that judgment. The disclosures are not required in interim financial statements unless previous information has changed significantly, for example, if exploratory well costs capitalized for more than one year after the completion of drilling are found to be impaired at the most recent balance sheet date. These disclosures are:

- The amount of capitalized exploratory well costs awaiting the determination of proved reserves
- For each annual period that an income statement is presented, changes in capitalized exploratory well costs as a result of
  — Additions to wells awaiting determination of proved reserves
  — Transfer of costs to wells, equipment, and facilities because proved reserves were determined
  — Expensing of capitalized costs

- For exploratory well costs capitalized for a period longer than one year after the completion of drilling at the most recent balance sheet date
  - The amount of such costs and the number of projects to which they are related
  - An aging of the amount by year or by a range of years and the number of projects to which they are related
- For exploratory well costs that continue to be capitalized for a period longer than one year after the completion of drilling at the most recent balance sheet date
  — A description of the projects and activities *undertaken* to date to evaluate the reserves and the projects
  — Remaining activities required to classify the related reserves as proved reserves

EFFECTIVE DATE AND TRANSITION

The guidance in ASC 932-360-25-18; 932-235-50-16 (FSP FAS-19-1) should be applied in the first reporting period beginning after April 4, 2005, the date this guidance was posted on the FASB's web site. The guidance should be applied *prospectively* to existing and newly capitalized exploratory well costs. Exploratory well costs expensed as a result of applying the guidance in this FSP should be recognized in income from continuing operations and should be presented separately as a component of operations or should be disclosed in the notes to the financial statements. Projects to which the costs relate should be quantified and described. Previously expensed exploratory well costs should *not* be capitalized. Early application of the FSP is permitted for periods in which financial statements have not yet been issued.

All of the disclosures required under the guidance in ASC 932-360-25-18; 932-235-50-16 (FSP FAS-19-1) should be made in the period in which that guidance is first adopted, including an interim period. For annual periods *preceding* the adoption of that guidance, the disclosures required in the first three bullets above should be presented. They should be presented based on the accounting method previously used for each prior period for which an income statement is presented.

ASC 954 Health Care Entities

Topic D-89 (Accounting for Costs of Future Medicare Compliance Audits) (ASC 954-405-25-4, 25-5; 958-405-60-1)

Health care providers that have settled allegations of Medicare fraud with the U.S. government must commit under their settlement agreements to engage an independent organization annually for the following five years to test and report on their compliance with Medicare requirements. The FASB staff has received inquiries as to whether those entities may accrue a liability on settlement for costs related to that commitment.

The FASB staff believes that the promise made in the settlement agreement to have future compliance audits creates a current duty and responsibility only if an obligating event has occurred, in accordance with the definition of a *liability* in paragraph 36 of CON-6 (not in ASC), which would allow the provider little or no discretion to avoid incurring that cost. The FASB staff believes further that entering into the agreement is not the obligating event for costs of a future compliance audit and that therefore providers should not recognize a liability on the date of settlement.

RELATED CHAPTERS IN 2011 *GAAP GUIDE, VOLUME II*

Chapter 10, "Computer Software"
Chapter 12, "Contingencies, Risks, and Uncertainties"

RELATED CHAPTERS IN 2011 *GAAP GUIDE, VOLUME I*

Chapter 6, "Computer Software"
Chapter 8, "Contingencies, Risks, and Uncertainties"

CHAPTER 8
CASH FLOW STATEMENT

CONTENTS

Overview		8.01
Authoritative Guidance		
ASC 230 Statement of Cash Flows		8.02
EITF Issue 95-13	Classification of Debt Issue Costs in the Statement of Cash Flows	8.02
EITF Issue 02-6	Classification in the Statement of Cash Flows of Payments Made to Settle an Asset Retirement Obligation within the Scope of FASB Statement No. 143, *Accounting for Asset Retirement Obligations*	8.03
Related Chapter in 2011 GAAP Guide, Volume I		8.04
Related Chapters in 2011 International Accounting/Financial Reporting Standards Guide		8.04

OVERVIEW

A statement of cash flows is required as part of a complete set of financial statements prepared in conformity with GAAP for all business enterprises. Within that statement, cash receipts and payments are classified as operating, investing, and financing activities, which are presented in a manner to reconcile the change in cash from the beginning to the end of the period.

The following pronouncements are discussed in the *GAAP Guide, Volume 1*, Chapter 5, "Cash Flow Statement":

ASC 230; ASC 830; ASC 942	Statement of Cash Flows; Foreign Currency Matters; Financial Services—Depository and Lending (FAS-95, Statement of Cash Flows)
ASC 230-10-15, ASC 230-10-45	Statement of Cash Flows (FAS-102, Statement of Cash Flows—Exemption of Certain Enterprises and Classification of Cash Flows from Certain Securities Acquired for Resale)

ASC 942-230-45-1, 45-2, 45-27   Financial Services—Depository and Lending (FAS-104, Statement of Cash Flows—Net Reporting of Certain Cash Receipts and Cash Payments and Classification of Cash Flows from Hedging Transactions)

AUTHORITATIVE GUIDANCE

ASC 230 Statement of Cash Flows

EITF Issue 95-13 (Classification of Debt Issue Costs in the Statement of Cash Flows) (ASC 230-10-45-15)

OVERVIEW

Entities incur certain costs in connection with issuing debt securities or other short-term or long-term borrowings. Such costs, which include underwriting, accounting, legal fees, and printing, generally are subtracted by the underwriter or lender from the proceeds of the debt or are paid by the borrower directly to the service providers.

Debt issue costs, which are required to be reported in the balance sheet as deferred charges, in accordance with ASC 835-30-45-3 (paragraph 16 of APB-21, Interest on Receivables and Payables) (FASB Accounting Standards Codification™), generally are reported as assets and amortized over the term of the debt.

There has been diversity in practice in the cash flow statement classification of debt issue costs paid directly by a borrower—some have associated such costs with an entity's financing activities while others have associated them with an entity's operating activities. In an informal survey conducted by the FASB staff, debt issue costs were most often classified as a financing activity.

ACCOUNTING ISSUE

How should a borrower's cash payments for debt issue costs be classified in the statement of cash flows?

EITF CONSENSUS

The EITF reached a consensus that a borrower's cash payments for debt issue costs should be classified as a financing activity in the statement of cash flows.

The Task Force agreed that the consensus applies to annual financial statements issued after September 21, 1995.

DISCUSSION

The following arguments support classification of debt issue costs as a financing activity:

- There is a direct relationship between the debt issue and the debt issue costs.
- It is inconsistent to classify such costs as an operating activity, because according to ASC 230-10-45-17 (paragraph 23e of FAS-95, Statement of Cash Flows), cash from operations includes activities that are *other* than financing or investing activities. Also, according to ASC 230-10-45-22 (paragraph 24 of FAS-95), classification depends on the "predominant source of cash flows for the item."
- Additions to property, plant, and equipment, which are subsequently depreciated, are not included in operating cash flows. Likewise, even though the asset is subsequently amortized, it is not meaningful to include payments for debt issue costs in the operating activity classification.

EITF Issue 02-6 (Classification in the Statement of Cash Flows of Payments Made to Settle an Asset Retirement Obligation within the Scope of FASB Statement No. 143, Accounting for Asset Retirement Obligations) (ASC 230-10-45-17; 410-20-45-3)

OVERVIEW

ASC 410-20 (FAS-143, Accounting for Asset Retirement Obligations), which is effective for financial statements issued for fiscal years beginning after June 15, 2002, applies to *legal* obligations related to the retirement of tangible long-lived assets that result from the acquisition, construction, or development and the normal operation of those assets. Asset retirement obligations under the scope of ASC 410-20 (FAS-143) must be recognized at the fair value of the liability in the period incurred; the associated costs should be capitalized as part of the long-lived asset's carrying amount and amortized to expense using a systematic and rational method over the asset's useful life. A liability must be recognized on the acquisition date for an existing retirement obligation related to acquired tangible long-lived assets as if the obligation had been incurred on that date. The consensus positions in this Issue do *not* apply to obligations under the scope of ASC 410-20 (FAS-143) related to the treatment of environmental contamination that occur after the Statement has been adopted.

Although under the guidance in ASC 230 (FAS-95) cash receipts and payments should be classified as operating, investing, or financing activities, the provisions of neither ASC 230 (FAS-95) nor those in ASC 410-20 (FAS-143) provide guidance as to the classification of cash paid for obligations associated with the retirement of tangible long-lived assets and associated retirement costs.

ACCOUNTING ISSUE

How should an entity classify in its cash flow statement cash paid to settle an asset retirement obligation?

EITF CONSENSUS

The EITF reached a consensus that a cash payment made to settle an asset retirement obligation should be classified in the statement of cash flows as an *operating* activity.

RELATED CHAPTER IN 2011 *GAAP GUIDE, VOLUME I*

Chapter 5, "Cash Flow Statement"

RELATED CHAPTERS IN 2011 *INTERNATIONAL ACCOUNTING/FINANCIAL REPORTING STANDARDS GUIDE*

Chapter 3, "Presentation of Financial Statements"
Chapter 8, "Cash Flow Statements"

CHAPTER 9
COMPUTER SOFTWARE

CONTENTS

Overview		9.02
Authoritative Guidance		
ASC 350 Intangibles—Goodwill and Other		9.04
SOP 98-1	Accounting for Costs of Computer Software Developed or Obtained for Internal Use	9.04
ASC 985 Software		9.08
SOP 97-2	Software Revenue Recognition	9.08
EITF Issue 96-6	Accounting for the Film and Software Costs Associated with Developing Entertainment and Educational Software Products	9.15
EITF Issue 00-3	Application of AICPA Statement of Position 97-2 to Arrangements That Include the Right to Use Software Stored on Another Entity's Hardware	9.17
EITF Issue 03-5	Applicability of AICPA Statement of Position 97-2, *Software Revenue Recognition*, to Non-Software Deliverables in an Arrangement Containing More-Than-Incidental Software	9.19
EITF Issue 09-3	Applicability of AICPA Statement of Position 97-2 to Certain Arrangements That Include Software Elements	9.20
Nonauthoritative Guidance		
AICPA Staff Guidance on Implementing SOP 97-2 (Software Revenue Recognition)		9.24
Related Chapters in 2011 GAAP Guide, Volume II		9.44

Related Chapters in 2011 GAAP Guide, Volume I	9.44
Related Chapter in 2011 International Accounting/Financial Reporting Standards Guide	9.44

OVERVIEW

The role of computer software in our economy has increased rapidly over the past 20 years, and its role is likely to continue to grow in the future. Some entities develop computer software for sale to other parties. These entities need guidance on recognizing revenue from the sale of computer software. Entities that sell computer software also need guidance on accounting for the costs of such software development.

Many other entities do not sell computer software, but they do use software internally in running their own businesses. Software used internally may be developed in-house or may be purchased from an outside party. These entities need guidance on accounting for the costs of computer software developed or purchased for internal use.

FASB Accounting Standards Codification™ (ASC) 985-605 (SOP 97-2, Software Revenue Recognition) provides guidance to entities that sell computer software to other parties. In general, revenue should be recognized from the sale of computer software when (1) persuasive evidence of a sale arrangement exists, (2) delivery of the software has occurred, (3) the software's price is fixed or determinable, and (4) collectibility of the selling price is probable. Computer software is frequently sold with other features attached (e.g., post-contract support). If a sale of computer software includes multiple elements, revenue should be allocated to each element based on the vendor-specific objective evidence of the fair value of each element.

ASC 985-20 (FAS-86, Accounting for the Costs of Computer Software to be Sold, Leased, or Otherwise Marketed) provides guidance on accounting for the costs of developing computer software to those entities planning to sell such software. Before technological feasibility is established, costs of developing computer software are expensed as incurred. Technological feasibility is that point where it is evident that the particular software project in development can be produced in accordance with its design specifications, including functions, features, and technical performance requirements. After technological feasibility is established, all costs incurred in developing the computer software product are to be capitalized. The 2011 *GAAP Guide, Volume 1* provides additional details on the requirements of ASC 986-20 (FAS-86).

ASC 350-10-05-6; ASC 350-40-05-2 through 05-6, 05-8, 05-9; 15-2 through 15-7; 25-1 through 25-16; 30-1 through 30-4; 35-1 through 35-10; 50-1; 55-1 through 55-4; 730-10-60-2; 985-20-60-1 (SOP 98-1,

Accounting for Costs of Computer Software Developed or Obtained for Internal Use), which is discussed in this Chapter, provides guidance on accounting for the costs of computer software purchased or developed for internal use. The three stages of software development discussed are (1) preliminary project stage, (2) application development stage, and (3) post-implementation/operation stage. The accounting for software costs, whether incurred internally or externally, depends on the stage in the software development process where those costs are incurred.

The following pronouncements, which are discussed in the *GAAP Guide, Volume I*, Chapter 6, "Computer Software," address the accounting for computer software:

> ASC-985 Software (Accounting for the Costs of Computer Software to be Sold, Leased, or Otherwise Marketed (FAS-86))
>
> ASC 730 Research and Development (Applicability of FASB Statement No. 2 to Computer Software (FIN-6))

AUTHORITATIVE GUIDANCE

ASC 350 Intangibles—Goodwill and Other

SOP 98-1 (Accounting for Costs of Computer Software Developed or Obtained for Internal Use) (ASC 350-10-05-6; 40-05-2 through 05-6, 05-8, 05-9; 15-2 through 15-7; 25-1 through 25-16; 30-1 through 30-4; 35-1 through 35-10; 50-1; 55-1 through 55-4; 730-10-60-2; 985-20-60-1)

BACKGROUND

Diversity in practice has arisen in accounting for costs associated with software purchased for internal use. Some entities capitalize costs of software purchased for internal use, while other entities expense costs of software intended for internal use if the software was developed internally. SOP 98-1 was issued to reduce this diversity in practice.

STANDARDS

Internal-use software is software having the following characteristics: (1) the software is acquired, internally developed, or modified solely to meet the entity's internal needs; or (2) during the software's development or modification, no substantive plan exists or is being developed to market the software externally. If, in the past, the entity has tended to use software internally and to market it externally, a rebuttable presumption is that any software developed by that entity is intended for sale, lease, or other marketing. ASC 986-20 (FAS-86, Accounting for the Costs of Computer Software to Be Sold, Leased, or Otherwise Marketed) provides the applicable authoritative guidance.

Software that becomes part of a product or a process that is sold (e.g., software designed for and embedded in a semiconductor chip) should be accounted for under the provisions of ASC 986-20 (FAS-86), not under the guidance in this pronouncement. However, software used in the production of a product or the provision of a service but not acquired by the customer (e.g., software embedded in a switch used by a telecommunications company to provide telephone service) should be accounted for under the guidance in this pronouncement.

Stages of Computer Software Development

The three stages of computer software development are (1) preliminary project stage, (2) application development stage, and (3) post-implementation/operation stage. The preliminary project stage includes the conceptual formulation of alternatives, evaluation of alternatives, determination of the existence of needed technology, and the final selection of alternatives. The application development stage includes the design of chosen paths, including software configuration and software interfaces, coding, installation of hardware, and testing (including the parallel processing phase). The post-implementation/operation stage includes training and application maintenance.

Internal Computer Software Costs as R&D

Internal-use computer software costs may be incurred for research and development purposes. Such costs are accounted for in accordance with the guidance in ASC 730-20 (FAS-2 Accounting for Research and Development Costs). Those types of costs include:

- Purchased or leased computer software used in R&D activities where the software does not have alternative future uses.
- All internally developed internal-use computer software if (*a*) the software developed represents a pilot project or (*b*) the software is used in a particular R&D project, regardless of whether the software has alternative future uses.

Capitalizing or Expensing Internal Computer Software Costs

The treatment of internal-use computer software costs (i.e., capitalize or expense) largely depends on the nature of the cost incurred. Internal and external costs incurred during the preliminary project stage should be expensed as incurred. Internal and external costs incurred during the application development stage should be capitalized. Software costs that allow for access or conversion of old data by new systems also should be capitalized. Internal and external training costs and maintenance costs should be expensed as incurred.

Upgrades and Enhancements

Upgrades and enhancements are defined as modifications to existing internal-use software that result in additional functionality (e.g., modifications to enable software to perform tasks that it was previously incapable of performing). In order for the costs of upgrades or enhancements to be capitalized, it must be probable that these expenditures will result in additional software functionality. Internal costs of upgrades or enhancements should be expensed if the activity relates to the preliminary project stage or the post-implementation/operation stage; costs incurred during the application development stage are to be capitalized. External costs of upgrades or enhancements should be expensed if the activity relates to the preliminary project stage or the post-implementation/operation stage; costs incurred during the application development stage are to be capitalized.

Applying the Capitalization Criteria

Capitalization of costs should begin when both of the following occur:

- The preliminary project stage is complete.
- Management with applicable authority authorizes, implicitly or explicitly, funding of the project, and it is probable that the project will be completed and the software will be used to perform the function intended.

Capitalization should cease no later than when the software project is substantially complete and ready for its intended use. The software is ready for its intended use after all substantial testing is completed.

The development of new software that is intended to replace existing internal-use software has implications for any unamortized costs. First, the remaining useful lives of software that is to be replaced should be reconsidered. Second, when new software that is to replace existing software is ready for its intended use, the unamortized cost of the old software is to be charged to expense.

The following types of costs, incurred during the application development stage, are eligible for capitalization:

- External direct costs of materials and services consumed in developing or obtaining the software (e.g., fees paid to third-party developers, costs incurred to obtain software from third parties, and travel expenses incurred by employees in their duties directly associated with developing software)
- Payroll and payroll-related costs (e.g., employee benefits) for employees who are directly associated with and who devote time to the internal-use computer software project, to the extent of time spent directly on the project
- Interest costs incurred while developing internal-use computer software (see ASC 835-20 (FAS-34 (Capitalization of Interest Cost)))

General and administrative costs and overhead costs should *not* be capitalized.

Software Purchased for Internal Use with Multiple Elements

In some cases, the purchase price of a software package includes multiple elements. For example, a software product may be purchased from an external vendor for a lump sum that includes the software itself, training, a maintenance agreement, data conversion services, reengineering, and rights to future upgrades and enhancements. The total purchase price should be allocated among all individual elements based on objective evidence of the fair values of the contract components. Such fair values may differ from prices stated within the contract for each element.

Impairment

Impairment of internal-use computer software costs should be recognized and measured in accordance with the provisions of ASC 360 (FAS-144, Accounting for the Impairment or Disposal of Long-Lived Assets). If it is no longer probable that the software being developed will be completed and placed in service, the asset should be reported at the lower of its carrying amount or its fair value less costs to sell. The rebuttable presumption is that such uncompleted software has a fair value of zero. Indications that the software may not be completed and placed in service include the following:

- A lack of expenditures budgeted or incurred for the project
- Programming difficulties that cannot be resolved on a timely basis
- Significant cost overruns
- Management plans to purchase third-party software rather than completing the internally developed software; costs of internally developed software will significantly exceed the cost of comparable software from a third-party vendor
- Management plans to purchase third-party software rather than completing the internally developed software; third-party software has more advanced features
- The business segment or unit to which the software relates is unprofitable or has been or will be discontinued

Amortization

The costs of software developed for internal use are to be amortized. Amortization is on a straight-line basis unless another systematic and rational basis is more representative of the software's use. The amortization period should be relatively short.

External Marketing of Internal-Use Computer Software

In some cases, the entity decides to market software developed for internal use to external parties. Proceeds received from the sale of such software, net of direct incremental costs of marketing, should be applied against the carrying amount of the internal use software.

9.08 *Computer Software*

Direct incremental costs of marketing include commissions, software reproduction costs, warranty and service obligations, and installation costs. No profit should be recognized until the proceeds received from the sale of the internal use software and amortization charges reduce the carrying amount of the software to zero. Subsequent proceeds should be recognized in revenue as earned.

ASC 985 Software

SOP 97-2 (Software Revenue Recognition) (ASC 450-10-60-12; 605-35-15-3; 730-10-60-5; 985-20-60-3; 985-605-05-1, 05-3; 15- 2 through 15-4; 25-1 through 25-19, 25-21 through 25-31, 25-33 through 25-41, 25-44 through 63 through 25-64 through 25-89, 25-91 through 25-107; 55-2, 55-28, 55-127 through 55-129, 55-131 through 55-133, 55-136 through 55-144; 55-146 through 55-148, 55-150, 55-151, 55-154 through 55-160, 55-162 through 55-168, 55-170 through 55-179, 55-181 through 55-184, 55-205 through 55-210)

BACKGROUND

The guidance in this pronouncement supersedes the guidance in SOP 91-1 (Software Revenue Recognition). The AICPA's Accounting Standards Executive Committee (AcSEC) issued this pronouncement for two reasons. First, the AcSEC believed there were practice issues that were not being adequately addressed by SOP 91-1. Second, AcSEC wanted to reconsider some of the provisions of SOP 91-1.

This pronouncement provides guidance on when and how to recognize revenue from the sale, lease, or licensing of computer software. Its guidance does *not* apply to the sale of products containing software that is incidental to the product being sold.

SCOPE

The scope of the guidance in ASC 985-605-15-3 (paragraphs 2 through 4 of SOP 97-2) has been amended by the guidance in Issue 09-3, which is discussed below, by deleting the existing subparagraph 3b and amending ASC 985-605-15-3c to include a service that cannot function without the software element of an arrangement. The guidance in Issue 09-3, which is discussed below, amends the guidance in ASC-985-605-15-4 (paragraphs 2 through 4 of SOP 97-2) to *exclude* application of the guidance in ASC 985-605 to the following transactions and activities:

1. Leases of software that include property, plant, or equipment (tangible products) if the software is incidental to the tangible product as a whole, or if the tangible product's software and nonsoftware components work together to enable the tangible product to perform its essential function (ASC 985-605-15-4b.)
2. Nonsoftware components of tangible products (ASC 985-605-15-4d.)
3. Software components of tangible products that are sold, licensed, or leased with tangible products whose software and nonsoftware components work together to enable the tangible product to perform its essential function (ASC 985-605-15-4e.)
4. Undelivered elements related to software essential to the ability of the tangible product discussed in (3) (above) to function (ASC 985-605-15-4f.)

STANDARDS

If the sale of computer software involves significant customization, modification, or production, the transaction should be accounted for as a long-term contract. In all other cases, revenue should be recognized when the following four conditions are met:

1. Persuasive evidence of an arrangement exists.
2. Delivery has occurred.
3. The vendor's price is fixed or determinable.
4. Collectibility of the selling price is probable.

Evidence an Arrangement Exists

Some entities require a written contract to support the sale of computer software. If the entity customarily uses written contracts to support the sale of software, such a written contract—signed by both parties to the contract—must exist to confirm that a sale arrangement exists. If written contracts are not typically used to support the sale of computer software, other evidence that a sale arrangement exists must be present. This other evidence might include a purchase order from the customer or an electronic order. Even if all the other criteria for software revenue recognition specified in this pronouncement are met, a sale is not to be recorded unless there is persuasive evidence that a sales arrangement exists.

Delivery Has Occurred

In most cases, delivery is deemed to have occurred at the transfer of the product master or, in cases where the product master is not transferred, at the transfer of the first copy. The one exception to this general rule is when the amount of revenue is a function of the number of copies shipped. In this case, revenue is recognized as copies are delivered to the user or reseller. Sometimes the delivery mode for software is electronic dissemination. In these cases, delivery is deemed to have occurred when the buyer: (1) takes possession of the software by downloading it, or (2) has been provided with the access codes necessary to download the software. In addition, if there is uncertainty as to whether the customer has accepted the software, license revenue is to be deferred until such acceptance occurs.

Delivery has not occurred until the software is delivered to the customer's place of business or to an intermediate site designated by the customer. In some cases in which the customer specifies an intermediate site as the delivery point, a substantial portion of the revenue is not due until the vendor moves the software from the intermediate site to another location designated by the customer. In these cases, revenue is not recognized until the software is delivered to that other site.

A delivery agent, acting for the vendor, may distribute software to customers. Revenue is not recognized when the vendor delivers the software to the delivery agent. Rather, revenue is recognized when the delivery agent delivers the software to the customer.

Software may contain authorization keys, which prohibit unauthorized access to the software. The possession of these keys is what allows the customer to access the software. Typically, delivery of the software key is not a prerequisite to the vendor's recognition of revenue.

Price Is Fixed or Determinable and Collectibility Is Probable

A number of situations indicate that the selling price is not fixed or determinable. In these cases, revenue is recognized as payments from customers become due. Situations where the selling price is not fixed or determinable are as follows:

- The selling price is a function of the number of copies distributed or the number of users of the product.
- In general, the presence of extended payment terms exists.
- A significant portion of the license fee is not due until after the expiration of the license period or not due until more than 12 months from the sale date. However, these payments terms are not a problem if the vendor has a history of successfully collecting the sales price using such payment terms, without making concessions.
- The sale includes a cancellation period. The selling price is not fixed or determinable until the cancellation period lapses.

Before revenue can be recognized, collectibility also must be reasonably assured. If a right of return exists, the requirements for revenue recognition in ASC 605-15 (FAS-48, Revenue Recognition When Right of Return Exists) must be met.

Additional criteria must be met when the sale is to a reseller. For example, the following four situations suggest that the sale price may not be fixed or determinable, or that collectibility is not reasonably assured:

1. The vendor's payment is substantially contingent on the reseller's success in distributing the software to end users.
2. The reseller's financial situation may be such that it is unable to make fixed or determinable payments to the vendor until it collects cash from its customers.
3. Uncertainties about the number of copies to be sold by the reseller may preclude reasonable estimates of future returns.
4. The vendor provides the reseller protection against future price changes, and there are significant uncertainties about the vendor's ability to maintain its selling price.

Computer Software—Multiple Elements

Note: See Issue 08-1 in Chapter 36, "Revenue Recognition," for updated guidance on (1) how a vendor should determine whether an arrangement that involves multiple deliverable should be accounted for as more than one unit of accounting, (2) how to measure consideration on such an arrangement and (3) how to allocate that consideration the arrangement's separate units of accounting.

The sale of computer software often includes other elements in addition to the software itself. These other elements might include a service that cannot function without the software element of an arrangement, the delivery of enhancements/upgrades, services of various types, and post-contract support (PCS). If the sales contract includes multiple elements, revenue should be allocated to the multiple elements based on vendor-specific objective evidence (VSOE) of the relative fair values of each element. Separate prices stated within the contract that apply to each element are often not indicative of relative fair values.

> **OBSERVATION:** This pronouncement originally limited VSOE to two criteria:
>
> 1. The price charged when the same element was sold separately
> 2. For an element not yet being sold separately, the price set for the separate element by an appropriate level of management and where it is probable that the price would not change before the separate element is introduced into the marketplace.
>
> Those two criteria were viewed by many as too restrictive as to what constitutes VSOE. The effective date of this provision was deferred by SOP 98-4 (not in ASC) and it was subsequently

permanently eliminated Although the two original limitations on what constitutes VSOE have been eliminated from this pronouncement, entities must still allocate fees received in a multiple element arrangement based on the relative fair values of each element. Those fair values must be supported by VSOE. If VSOE is insufficient to support unbundling of the total fee, the entire fee must be deferred.

In general, if VSOE of relative fair values does not exist, revenue recognition should be deferred until the earlier of (1) the date on which VSOE of relative fair values exists, or (2) the date when all elements under the contract have been delivered. There are four exceptions to this general guidance:

1. If the only undelivered element is PCS, the entire fee is to be recognized ratably.
2. If the only undelivered element are services that do not involve significant production, modification, or customization, the entire fee is to be recognized over the period that the service is performed.
3. If the software sale is essentially a subscription, the entire fee is to be recognized over the subscription period.
4. If the fee is based on the number of copies sold of more than one product, it is often not clear how many of each product will be sold. In most cases, revenue cannot be recognized because total revenue allocable to each software product is not known.

Collectibility may be a problem when software is delivered in installments. The collectibility criterion is not met if the portion of the fee allocated to units already delivered is subject to forfeiture if other elements of the software package are not delivered. In evaluating whether revenue allocated to units already delivered is subject to forfeiture, the focus is on management's intent and not just on the terms of the legal contract. That is, if management typically refunds fees already paid if other elements of the software sale are not delivered, the collectibility criterion is not met even if management is not legally required to provide such refunds.

Multiple Software Elements—Rights to Upgrades and Enhancements

A vendor may deliver a software package and promise to provide upgrades or enhancements to that software as those upgrades/enhancements subsequently become available. The purchase price is allocated between the current software product and the right to future upgrades/enhancements based on VSOE. Some customers may choose not to exercise their right to the upgrade/enhancement. If sufficient evidence exists to estimate the number of customers who will not exercise the upgrade/enhancement right, revenue allocated to this right should be reduced.

Vendors may deliver software and a promise to provide additional software in the future. Again, the fee should be allocated between the current software product and the right to additional software based on VSOE. Unlike the situation of upgrades/enhancements, the fee allocated to the additional software is not reduced for any customers not expected to take delivery of the additional software.

Often the promise to provide customers with future versions of software is, in essence, a subscription agreement. For example, the vendor may promise to deliver all new products that comprise a certain "family" of software that are developed over some number of future years. In the case of subscription agreements, no revenue is allocated to individual software products. Rather, all of the revenue is recognized over the life of the subscription agreement, beginning on the date of delivery of the first product.

Multiple Software Elements—Postcontract Customer Support

Software is often sold with a promise, either contractual or implied by the vendor's normal business practices, to provide postcontract customer support (PCS). An example of postcontract customer support is telephone support (e.g., a help desk maintained by the vendor). Revenue is to be allocated between the software product and the PCS based on the fee to be received if the PCS was sold separately. This fee is best estimated by referring to the rate charged for such service at renewal (i.e., the renewal rate). Revenue allocated to PCS is to be recognized ratably over the PCS period.

In cases where the sale of software includes multiple elements (including PCS), there may not be the VSOE needed to allocate the fee across the multiple elements. In these cases, if the PCS represents the only undelivered element, the entire software fee should be recognized ratably over:

- The PCS contract period if the vendor is contractually obligated to provide these services.
- The estimated period over which the vendor will provide PCS if the vendor's obligation to provide these services is implied based on its past actions.

In some cases, PCS revenue can be recognized along with the initial licensing fee at delivery of the software product if all of the following conditions are met:

- The PCS fee is included with the initial licensing fee.
- The term of the PCS included with the initial license is for one year or less. This criterion is not violated if the vendor provides telephone support for more than one year, if the vendor's past history indicates that the majority of the telephone support will be provided in the first year after the sale.

- The estimated cost of providing the PCS during this period is insignificant.

- Unspecified upgrades/enhancements offered during the PCS period have historically been, and are expected to continue to be, minimal and infrequent.

If PCS revenue is recognized on delivery of the software product, the estimated costs of providing PCS are to be accrued on this date. The estimated costs of providing PCS include the costs of providing software upgrades/enhancements.

Multiple Software Elements—Services

The sale of software may include the provision of future services (non-PCS related) in addition to the software product itself. These services might include installation, consulting, and training. The vendor must determine whether the service elements qualify for separate accounting treatment as the services are performed. If not, the entire purchase price (for both the software and services) is to be accounted for using contract accounting. To conclude that the service element of the contract can be accounted for separately, the following criteria must be met:

- The fair value of the service element of the contract must be supported by sufficient VSOE.

- The ability to use the software (i.e., functionality) must not depend on the service.

- The price of the contract would be expected to vary based on the inclusion or exclusion of the service.

If the service qualifies for separate accounting, revenue allocated should be recognized as the service is performed. If no pattern of performance is obvious, revenue is recognized over the period during which the service is to be performed.

There may be instances in which there is not sufficient VSOE to allocate the sale price between the software product and the services included. If the only undelivered element of the sale is the service and if the service does not involve significant production, modification, or customization, the entire purchase price is recognized as services are performed.

Software is more likely to be functional without any additional services being rendered if the software is viewed as off-the-shelf software. If the software is not off-the-shelf, or if significant modifications to off-the-shelf software are necessary to meet the customer's functionality, no element of the arrangement would qualify as accounting for a service. Rather the entire purchase price, both for the software and for any services, would be accounted for using contract accounting.

Factors that indicate that the service element of the arrangement is essential to the functionality of the software are as follows:

- The software is not off-the-shelf.
- The services to be rendered include significant modifications to off-the-shelf software.
- It is necessary to build complex interfaces for the customer to use the vendor's software in its own environment.
- The customer's obligation to pay for the software is tied to the completion of the services.
- Customer acceptance criteria (i.e., milestones) affect the realizability of the software-license fee.

Multiple Software Elements—Contract Accounting

Software or software systems that require significant production, modification, or customization do not meet the criteria for separate accounting for the service element. In these cases, contract accounting must be applied. Contract accounting is implemented using either the percentage-of-completion method or the completed-contract method. Guidance on applying those methods is provided in Chapter 30, "Long-Term Construction Contracts," of the 2011 *GAAP Guide, Volume I,* and Chapter 27, "Long-Term Construction Contracts," of this *Guide.*

In applying the percentage-of-completion method, both input and output measures of the degree to which the software project is complete can be used. A typical input measure is labor hours incurred. Labor hours incurred provides a good measure of progress toward completion for software projects that are labor intensive (e.g., customization of core software). Milestones toward completion of the software project are examples of output measures. A good example of useful output measures of progress to date is the completion of tasks that trigger independent review.

EITF Issue 96-6 (Accounting for the Film and Software Costs Associated with Developing Entertainment and Educational Software Products) (ASC 985-705-S25-1; S99-1)

OVERVIEW

Games incorporating audio, film, graphics, and interactive software technology on CD-ROM are entertainment and educational software (EE) products, which may include film content taken from an existing film or film developed specifically for the software product. The development of such products by both motion picture companies and software companies differs from the development of software for business applications or operating systems; production costs are a significant component of multimedia entertainment product costs.

Motion picture companies have been capitalizing costs related to EE products as inventory and amortizing them over the product's expected revenue stream under the provisions of FAS-53 (Financial Reporting by Producers and Distributors of Motion Picture Films). In addition, motion picture companies do not apply the provisions of SOP 91-1 or the provisions of SOP 93-7. They believe that accounting treatment under FAS-53 is appropriate, because motion picture companies consider EE products to be entertainment products similar to films for the following reasons: (*a*) the products usually use previously developed or simple software, so technological feasibility is reached at the beginning of the project, and (*b*) the software content often is minimal. In contrast, software companies have been expensing film production and software costs under the provisions of FAS-86. Some software companies have been accounting separately for costs related to the film content under the provisions of FAS-53 and costs related to the software content under the provisions of FAS-86.

ACCOUNTING ISSUE

How should companies developing EE products account for related film and software costs?

SEC OBSERVER COMMENT

At the May 1996 meeting, the SEC Observer announced that based on the educational session presented by a working group from the motion picture and software industries at the EITF's March 1996 meeting, the SEC staff believes that EE products that are sold, licensed, or otherwise marketed should be accounted for based on the requirements of FAS-86. Therefore, subsequent to May 23, 1996, SEC registrants should account for film costs related to those products under the provisions of FAS-86, not the provisions of FAS-53. In addition, registrants should expense exploitation costs incurred subsequent to May 23, 1996, unless they qualify for capitalization under the provisions of SOP 93-7. Registrants that previously capitalized all costs incurred in the development of EE products should restate prior-period financial statements to account for software development costs, in accordance with the provisions of FAS-86, if the related amounts are material. The SEC staff's views are not intended to apply to costs incurred to produce computer generated special effects and images used in products exhibited in theaters or licensed to television stations, which are under the scope of FAS-53.

EITF CONSENSUS

Because of the SEC staff's position, the EITF was not asked to reach a consensus.

EITF Issue 00-3 (Application of AICPA Statement of Position 97-2 to Arrangements That Include the Right to Use Software Stored on Another Entity's Hardware) (ASC 985-605-05-4; 55-121 through 55-125)

OVERVIEW

Instead of licensing software that is installed on a customer's hardware, some software companies and entities referred to as application software providers (ASPs) are offering customers access to software applications without taking possession of the software. Under such arrangements, the customer can access software—which is installed on the vendor's or a third party's hardware—over the Internet or over a dedicated line. This type of storage or access service is known as hosting.

The form of such arrangements consists of a right to (1) use software and (2) store software on hardware owned by a vendor or a third party. Customers in those arrangements may not have a license to the software and may not be able to access the software through a different host. ASPs consider themselves to be service providers that deploy, host, and manage application solutions for rent.

Although the terms of hosting arrangements may differ significantly, the discussion in this Issue applies to arrangements in which a customer purchases a software license as well as a right to store and access the software. It is assumed that payment occurs at the inception of the arrangement.

ACCOUNTING ISSUES

1. Should SOP 97-2 apply to arrangements that require a vendor to host the software?
2. Does SOP 97-2 apply to arrangements in which a customer can choose to take delivery of the software?
3. If the answer to Issue 2 is affirmative, when does delivery occur and how does the vendor's obligation to host the software affect revenue recognition?

EITF CONSENSUS

1. SOP 97-2 applies to the software element of a hosting arrangement if

   a. The customer has a contractual right to take physical possession of the software at any time during the hosting period without significant penalty, and

   b. It is feasible for the customer to run the software on its own hardware or to contract for a hosting arrangement with a third party that is unrelated to the vendor or the host.

   Arrangements that do not give those options to a customer are accounted for as *service arrangements,* which are not covered by SOP 97-2.

2. If a customer in a hosting arrangement can choose whether to take physical possession of the software as discussed above, delivery occurs when the customer is able to takes possession of the software. The Task Force noted that service arrangements could include multiple elements that would affect the allocation of revenue.

3. The Task Force noted that if SOP 97-2 applies to software in a hosting arrangement, revenue for the portion of the fee allocated to the software portion of the arrangement should be recognized on delivery only if *all* of the SOP's revenue recognition requirements are met. This would include the requirement for vendor-specific objective evidence of fair value and that the portion of the fee allocated to the software cannot be forfeited, refunded, or be subject to any other concession. The portion of the fee allocated to the hosting arrangement would be recognized as the service is provided. In addition to the software and the hosting service, arrangements under this Issue that are accounted for under the SOP also may include other elements, such as specified or unspecified upgrade rights.

   The Task Force stated the following regarding the accounting for costs of developing software for hosting arrangements:

   a. The provisions of FAS-86 apply to software development costs incurred by vendors that sell, lease, license, or market to others software that is accounted for under SOP 97-2.

   b. The provisions of SOP 98-1 apply to the development costs of software accounted for under the scope of SOP 97-2 if it is used only to provide services and is not sold, leased, licensed, or marketed to others.

   c. The provisions of FAS-86 also apply to software development costs if in the process of developing or modifying the software, the vendor develops a substantive plan to sell, lease, license, or market the software to others.

EITF Issue 03-5 (Applicability of AICPA Statement of Position 97-2, Software Revenue Recognition, to Non-Software Deliverables in an Arrangement Containing More-Than-Incidental Software) (ASC 985-605-15-3)

OVERVIEW

This Issue has been raised because there is diversity in practice in the application of the provisions of SOP 97-2 (Software Revenue Recognition), in arrangements that include non-software deliverables, such as hardware, in addition to software that is more than incidental to the products or services as a whole. Footnote 2 to paragraph 2 of the SOP (ASC 985-605-15-3) includes the following indicators that software is more than incidental: (*a*) the company's marketing focuses on the software and or it is sold separately, (*b*) the vendor provides postcontract customer support, and (*c*) the vendor incurs significant costs that are accounted for under the scope of FAS-86 (Accounting for the Costs of Computer Software to Be Sold, Leased, or Otherwise Marketed). There has been some confusion, because paragraph 4 of SOP 97-2 (ASC 985-605-15-3, 4) states that revenue related to property, plant, or equipment included in a lease of software should be accounted for under the guidance in FAS-13 (Accounting for Leases) (ASC 840-10), but paragraph 9 of the SOP (ASC 985-605-25-5) discusses accounting for revenue from software arrangements with *multiple elements* and states that "all additional products and services specified in the arrangements" should be accounted for under the SOP.

ACCOUNTING ISSUE

Should non-software deliverables included in an arrangement that contains software that is more than incidental to the products or services as a whole be included under the scope of SOP 97-2?

EITF CONSENSUS

The EITF reached a consensus that software and software-related elements are included under the scope of SOP 97-2 in arrangements that include software that is *more than incidental* to the products or services as a whole. Software-related elements include software products and services, such as upgrades and enhancements and postcontract customer support, as well as non-software deliverables that require a software deliverable for their functionality. Unrelated equipment that does not require a software deliverable for its functionality is not considered to be software-related and should be *excluded* from the scope of SOP 97-2.

TRANSITION

The consensus is effective prospectively based on the guidance in Topic D-1 (Implications and Implementation of an EITF Consensus). The FASB ratified the consensus at its August 13, 2003, meeting.

EITF Issue No. 09-3 Applicability of SOP 97-2 to Certain Revenue Arrangements That Include Software (ASC 985-605-15-3 through 15-4A; 25-10; 50-1; 55-211 through 55-236; 65-1)

OVERVIEW

The guidance in ASC 450-10-60-12; 605-35-15-3; 730-10-60-5; 985-20-60-3; 985-605-05-1, 05-3; 15-2 through 15-4; 25-1 through 25-19, 25-21 through 25-31, 25-33 through 25-41, 25-44 through 25-89, 25-91 through 25-107,;55-2, 55-28, 55-127 through 55-129, 55-131 through 55-133, 55-136 through 55-144; 55-146 through 55-148, 55-150 through 55-151, 55-154 through 55-160, 55-162 through 55-168, 55-170 through 55-179, 55-181 through 55-184, 55-205 through 55-210 (SOP 97-2, Software Revenue Recogniion) applies to products or services that contain software that is "more than incidental" to the products or services as a whole and requires that the selling price of separate deliverables in an arrangement that includes multiple elements be based on vendor-specific objective evidence (VSOE). Certain transactions under the scope of SOP 97-2 (see ASC references above) include software-enabled devices, which are sold only with other deliverables and result in a revenue pattern that is *not* based on the economics of the transaction because VSOE cannot be determined for those devices.

As a result of the EITF's discussion in EITF Issue No. 08-1, "Revenue Arrangements with Multiple Deliverables," (ASC 605, *Revenue Recognition*), which is discussed in Chapter 36, "Revenue Recognition," of this *Guide*, supersedes the guidance in EITF Issue No. 00-21, "Revenue Arrangements with Multiple Deliverables," (see references in Issue 08-1, Chapter 36) some constituents have suggested that the model in SOP 97-2 (see ASC references above) should be amended to exclude some transactions that include software-enabled devices that may *not* have been considered when SOP 97-2 (see ASC references above) was written. During its discussion of Issue 08-1 (ASC 605) at the November 13, 2008 meeting, the EITF recommended that a separate Issue be added to consider changes to the accounting guidance in SOP 97-2. The FASB Chairman and other FASB members present at that meeting agreed with the EITF's recommendation. It was also recommended that the effective date of that Issue be consistent with that of Issue 08-1.

ACCOUNTING ISSUES

1. Whether the measurement criteria or the scope of SOP 97-2 (see ASC references above) should be modified?
2. If so, how should the scope of SOP 97-2 be modified?

SCOPE

The guidance in this Issue applies to arrangements with multiple elements that include both hardware and software elements. However, hardware elements of a tangible product are never accounted for under the scope of software revenue recognition guidance

EITF CONSENSUS

The EITF reached the following consensus positions:

1. The scope of the guidance in ASC 985-605-15-3 (paragraphs 2 through 4 of SOP 97-2) should be amended by deleting the existing subparagraph 3b and amending ASC 985-605-15-3c to include a service that cannot function without the software element of an arrangement.
2. The guidance in this Issue amends the guidance in ASC-985-605-15-4 (paragraphs 2 through 4 of SOP 97-2) to *exclude* application of the guidance in ASC 985-605 to the following transactions and activities in addition to those already listed:
   a. Leases of software that include property, plant, or equipment (tangible products) if the software is incidental to the tangible product as a whole, or if the tangible product's software and nonsoftware components work together to enable the tangible product to perform its essential function (ASC 985-605-15-4b)
   b. Nonsoftware components of tangible products (ASC 985-605-15-4d)
   c. Software components of tangible products that are sold, licensed, or leased with tangible products whose software and nonsoftware components work together to enable the tangible product to perform its essential function (ASC 985-605-15-4e)
   d. Undelivered elements related to software essential to the ability of the tangible product discussed in the previous bullet to function (ASC 985-605-15-4f.)
3. A vendor should consider all of the following factors to determine whether software components that function together and

are delivered with a tangible product are necessary for the tangible product to perform its basic function:

a. There is a rebuttable presumption that a software product is essential to a tangible product's ability to perform its function if the tangible product is rarely sold without the software element.

b. If a vendor sells products that perform similar functions, such as different models of similar products, the products should be considered to be the same products for the evaluation of factor (a) if the only difference between similar products is that one includes software that the other does not.

c. If a vendor sells software separately as well as tangible products containing the same software, it should not be presumed that the software is not essential to the tangible product's functionality because the vendor also sells the software separately.

d. The fact that a software element may not be embedded in a tangible product does not mean that it is not considered to be essential to that product's functionality.

e. Nonsoftware elements of a tangible asset must contribute significantly to a product's essential function. That is, a tangible product should not only be a means of delivering software to a customer. (ASC 985-605-15-4A)

A vendor that has entered into an arrangement that includes software deliverables, which are under the scope of ASC 605-25, Software Deliverables, and nonsoftware deliverables, which are not under the scope ASC 605-25, should allocate consideration under that arrangement to the nonsoftware and software deliverables as a group based on the guidance in ASC 605-25-15-3A. If a nonsoftware deliverable includes software deliverables that are considered to be essential to the tangible product's ability to perform its function and the arrangement includes more than one software deliverable, a portion of the consideration on the arrangement should be allocated to the software deliverables as a group based on the guidance in ASC 605-25-15-3A and should be separated and allocated further based on the guidance in this Subtopic. In addition, software contained in a tangible product that is *not* essential to that product's ability to perform its function as well as nonessential software and other deliverables under an arrangement (other than the nonsoftware components of the tangible product) related to the nonessential software also are included in the scope of this Subtopic. An undelivered element related to a deliverable under the scope of this Subtopic and to a deliverable excluded from this Subtopic's scope should be separated into (a) a software deliverable, which is under the scope of this Subtopic, and (b) a nonsoftware deliverable, which is not under the scope of this Subtopic. (ASC 985-605-25-10(f))

DISCLOSURE

A vendor should disclose the information required under the guidance in Issue 08-1 (see Chapter 36, "Revenue Recognition," of this *Guide*) for arrangements that apply to multiple elements that may or many not be under the scope of ASC 985-605.

EFFECTIVE DATE AND TRANSITION

The EITF reached the following consensus positions regarding the effective date and transition provisions of Issue 09-3:

1. The guidance in Issue 09-3 should be applied *prospectively* for revenue arrangements entered into or materially modified in fiscal years that begin on or after June 15, 2010. However, a vendor may elect to adopt the guidance *retrospectively* in accordance with the guidance in ASC 985-605-25-65-1(d).
2. Early application is permitted as follows:
    a. A vendor that elects to early adopt the guidance in a reporting period other than the first period of the entity's fiscal year should apply the guidance in Issue 09-3 *retrospectively* from the beginning of the entity's fiscal year; and
    b. A vendor that elects to early adopt the guidance in a reporting period other than the first period of the entity's fiscal year should disclose the following information at a minimum for all interim periods previously reported in the fiscal year in which the guidance in Issue 09-3 is adopted:
        i. Revenue
        ii. Net income
        iii. Earnings per share
        iv. The effect of the change for the relevant captions presented
3. A vendor that elects to apply the guidance in Issue 09-3 prospectively should provide the disclosures in ASC 605-25-65-1(c) through 65-1(d).
4. A vendor that elects, but is not required to apply the guidance in Issue 09-3 retrospectively by applying the guidance in ASC 250-10-45-5 through 45-10 should disclose the information required in ASC 250-10-50-1 through 50-3.
5. The guidance in Issue 09-3 should be adopted in the same period as the guidance in Issue 08-1 by applying the same transition method to the adoption of the guidance in both Issues. (ASC 985-605-65-1(a) through (e))

NONAUTHORITATIVE GUIDANCE

AICPA Staff Guidance on Implementing SOP 97-2 (Software Revenue Recognition)

BACKGROUND

The AICPA's staff has received questions on how to implement SOP 97-2 (Software Revenue Recognition). The questions and answers included in this section contain the questions relating to the application of SOP 97-2 that the AICPA's staff has addressed.

STANDARDS

Question 1: The sale of computer software often includes elements other than the software itself. If the sales contract includes multiple elements, revenue should be allocated to the multiple elements based on vendor-specific objective evidence (VSOE) of the relative fair values of each element. If management establishes VSOE of a software element after the balance sheet date but before the issuance of the financial statements, may such evidence be used to support revenue recognition at the balance sheet date?

Answer: No. The establishment of VSOE after the balance sheet date is a Type II subsequent event (i.e., the evidence did not exist at the balance sheet date). As such, any resulting revenue from the sales transaction should be deferred at the balance sheet date. If, however, the VSOE that is compiled existed at the balance sheet date, the VSOE should be examined to determine if it is sufficient to support revenue recognition.

Question 2: A particular customer may enter into more than one contract with a single software vendor. In such cases, should these separate contracts be combined and viewed as a multiple-element arrangement for purposes of applying SOP 97-2's revenue recognition guidance?

Answer: The group of contracts may be so closely related that they constitute, in essence, a single, multiple-element sales arrangement. The following factors, when present, may indicate that a group of separate contracts should be accounted for as a single arrangement for revenue recognition purposes:

- Only a short time elapses between the negotiation of the separate contracts.
- The elements contained in the separate contracts are closely interrelated or interdependent (e.g., design, technology, function).

- The fee for one or more contracts is subject to refund or forfeiture if other elements under different contracts are not performed satisfactorily.
- One or more elements in one contract is dependent on one or more elements in another contract.
- Payment terms under one contract coincide with performance criteria of another contract.
- The negotiations are conducted jointly with two or more parties to do what is in essence a single project.

Question 3: A vendor may commit to provide a Year 2000 compliant version of a software product to an existing customer or to a customer who is purchasing a version of the same software product that is not Year 2000 compliant. Is a vendor's commitment to provide a software upgrade to ensure Year 2000 compliance considered an "upgrade right"?

Answer: Yes. The SOP 97-2 criteria related to upgrades apply regardless of whether or not the vendor's commitment to provide a software upgrade is contained within a warranty provision. If a vendor sells a version of a software product that is not Year 2000 compliant and promises to provide a Year 2000 compliant version at a later date, revenue must be allocated between the software and the upgrade.

Question 4: SOP 97-2 states that if a fee for a software arrangement with extended payment terms is not fixed or determinable at the inception of the arrangement, revenue should be recognized as payments become due. If a vendor receives payments directly from customers in advance of their due dates, should the vendor recognize revenue?

Answer: Yes, provided all the other revenue recognition criteria of SOP 97-2 are met.

Question 5: SOP 97-2 states that the selling price is not fixed or determinable if a significant portion of the fee is due more than one year after the delivery of the software product. Assume that a vendor enters into an arrangement on March 30, 2004, to sell a software product for $250,000. Of this amount, $150,000 is due on April 30, and the remaining $100,000 is due 13 months from March 30 (i.e., April 30, 2005). The vendor's fiscal year-end is March 31. How much revenue should the vendor recognize from this transaction in the fiscal year ended March 31, 2004?

Answer: None. Because the selling price in the above situation is not fixed or determinable, SOP 97-2 specifies that revenue is to be recognized as payments become due. Therefore, $150,000 of revenue would be recognized on April 30, 2004, and the remaining $100,000 would be recognized on April 30, 2005.

Question 6: A software vendor may license a product to customers, and customers may elect whether or not to purchase postcontract support (PCS) services as part of the software arrangement. In order to satisfy warranty obligations, the vendor may provide complimentary "bug fixes"—necessary to maintain the software's compliance with published specifications—to those customers who choose not to purchase PCS. If a vendor provides complimentary bug fixes under a warranty provision, should the vendor account for the estimated costs to correct bugs in accordance with FAS-5 (Accounting for Contingencies), or should the vendor view the complimentary bug fixes as part of PCS? If these complimentary bug fixes are viewed as PCS activity, software revenue may need to be deferred.

Answer: Given the above facts, the software vendor should account for the estimated costs of bug fixes under the provisions of FAS-5.

Question 7: A software vendor enters into an arrangement to deliver software and provide PCS. The software product will be deployed in stages, and the PCS begins some period of time (e.g., three months) after delivery of the product. However, the vendor has a history of providing PCS services and product upgrades/enhancements as soon as the product is delivered. After a certain period of time has elapsed (e.g., two years), the customer has the option of renewing the PCS arrangement. The PCS renewal rate is set at a stipulated rate times the software's aggregate (reflecting all pieces of the software that was deployed in stages) list price. Given the above fact pattern, VSOE of the fair value of the PCS arrangement does not exist when the product is less than fully deployed. VSOE does not exist when the product is less than fully deployed because PCS services are only sold separately (at the predetermined renewal rate) when these services are renewed. Are the PCS services considered to commence at the date of product delivery or at the later date when the PCS services officially begin (three months after delivery in this example)? Does the predetermined renewal rate provide VSOE of the fair value of the PCS services?

Answer: The PCS services are considered to commence at the date of product delivery. The vendor's past practice suggests that these services are provided beginning with product delivery. The predetermined renewal rate provides VSOE of the fair value of the PCS services, since the predetermined renewal rate provides the only indication of the fair value of the PCS services. The vendor should initially defer revenue recognition related to the two years of PCS services provided under the arrangement, and the value of the two years of these PCS services is determined by referring to the predetermined renewal rate.

Question 8: A software vendor may license multiple products to a customer under a single arrangement. The customer may have the right to use at least one copy of each of these multiple products, and the customer has the option of altering the mix of products used. The number of these multiple products that the customer can use at any one time is limited such that the total value of products in use at any one time does not exceed the total license fee. Alternatively, under these types of arrangements, the total number of users that can simultaneously use the products may be limited. When should the vendor recognize revenue for these types of arrangements?

Answer: Revenue should be recognized upon delivery of the first copy (or the product master) for all of the products within the license mix (assuming the other revenue recognition criteria in SOP 97-2 are met).

Question 9: The AICPA has received a number of questions involving nonmonetary exchanges of software products. A software vendor may license a product to another company in exchange for either (1) the right to include the other company's technology/products in the vendor's software product or (2) the right to separately market the other company's technology/products as a stand-alone product. Do these transactions represent the culmination of the earnings process? That is, are these transactions to be accounted for at fair value or at the carryover basis of the vendor's software product?

Answer: It depends on whether the technology/products received are going to be used (sold, licensed, or leased) in the same line of business as the vendor's software product. If so, the earnings process is not complete and the exchange should be recorded at the basis of the vendor's software product (i.e., carryover basis).

If, however, the technology/products received are going to be used in a different line of business from the vendor's software product, the earnings process is complete and the transaction should normally be recorded at fair value. The transaction should be recorded at fair value if both of the following conditions are met:

- VSOE of the fair value of the software given up or of the technology/products received exists.
- The technology/products received are expected to be used by the software vendor and the value assigned to the transaction is consistent with the extent of such expected use.

If the fair value of the software given up or of the technology/products received is not reasonably determinable, the transaction is to be recorded using the software product's basis (i.e., carryover basis).

Question 10: A software vendor may license a product to another company in exchange for the right to use the other company's technology or products for internal purposes. Does this transaction represent the culmination of the earnings process? That is, is this transaction to be accounted for at fair value or at the carryover basis of the vendor's software product?

Answer: This transaction represents the culmination of the earnings process and should generally be recorded at fair value. In order to record the transaction at fair value, both of the following conditions must be met:

- VSOE of the fair value of the software given up or of the technology/products received exists.
- The technology/products received are expected to be used by the software vendor and the value assigned to the transaction is consistent with the extent of such expected use.

If the fair value of the software given up or of the technology/products received is not reasonably determinable, the transaction is to be recorded using the software product's basis (i.e., carryover basis).

Question 11: In certain situations, SOP 97-2 requires vendors to use contract accounting to recognize revenue. There has been some confusion as to the meaning of the phrase "using the relevant guidance herein" in paragraph 7 of SOP 97-2 (ASC 985-605-05-3; 25-1, 2; 15-3). To what does this phrase refer?

Answer: This phrase refers to paragraphs 74-91 of SOP 97-2 (ASC 985-605-25-88 through 107). Those paragraphs discuss how to apply contract accounting to certain software arrangements.

Question 12: Certain software arrangements that are subject to contract accounting also contain PCS services. How should the vendor account for such PCS services?

Answer: If the vendor has VSOE of the value of the PCS services, these services should be separated from the rest of the contract and accounted for separately. The balance of the software arrangement should be accounted for using contract accounting principles.

Question 13: In connection with the licensing of an existing product, a vendor might offer a small or insignificant discount on additional licenses of the licensed product or other products that exist at the time of the offer but are not part of the arrangement. Paragraph 3 of SOP 97-2 (ASC 985-605-15-4) indicates that these discounts are not within the scope of the Statement. However, footnote 3 to paragraph 3 (ASC 985-605-15-3) states that "[i]f the discount or other concessions in an arrangement are more than insignificant, a presumption is created that an additional element(s) is being offered in the arrangement." What is a "more-than-insignificant" discount, as discussed in footnote 3 to paragraph 3 of SOP 97-2 (ASC 985-605-15-3)?

Answer: A more-than-insignificant discount on future purchases exists when the discount is (1) significant, (2) incremental to the discount amount typically given in similar transactions, and (3) incremental to the discount amount given on other elements of the arrangement in question.

Readers should note that footnote 3 to paragraph 3 (ASC 985-605-15-3) does not apply to an arrangement that gives the customer an option to purchase additional copies of a software product that has already been licensed by, or delivered to, the customer. In such instances, revenue is recognized as rights to additional copies are purchased, based on the arrangement's price per copy. Providing additional copies of software that has already been delivered is not considered an undelivered element. The delivery criterion is met when the first software copy or product master is delivered; duplication of additional copies is incidental to the arrangement.

Question 14: How should a software vendor account for significant incremental discounts that are within the scope of SOP 97-2?

Answer: If the software arrangement provides the customer with the right to a significant incremental discount on future purchases of products or services, apply a proportionate amount of the discount to each element in the arrangement using VSOE of each element's fair value before consideration of the incremental discount.

Illustration of Accounting for a Software Arrangement Offering Customers Significant Incremental Discounts on Future Purchases

Xunil Inc., a software vendor, sells Product A for $80 along with a $60 coupon good toward the purchase of Product B. VSOE is $80 for Product A and $120 for Product B. The $60 discount offered on Product B is a significant incremental discount that would not normally be offered in comparable transactions.

The $60 discount is allocated between Products A and B based on the relative fair values of each product. Therefore, $24 or 40% [$80 / ($80 + $120)] of the $60 discount is allocated to Product A. Upon the sale of Product A, $56 of revenue would be recognized ($80 - $24), and $24 would be credited to deferred revenue. Assuming Product B is purchased for $60 ($120 selling price less the $60 coupon), revenue of $84 would be recognized (the $60 of cash received plus the $24 of deferred revenue).

In other cases, the products or services on which a customer can take a significant incremental discount may not be specified in the arrangement (e.g., the customer can take the discount on any future purchases) or the fair value of the future purchases to be made is not known. However, there may be a limit on the maximum amount of incremental discounts on future purchases. The maximum amount of incremental discounts should be allocated between the current purchase and future purchases assuming that sufficient future purchases will exist to absorb the full maximum amount of incremental discounts.

Illustration of Accounting for Significant Future Discounts Where the Product to Which the Future Discount Is to Be Applied Is Not Known Yet

Obacke Inc., a software vendor, sells Product A for $50 along with a $30 coupon good toward the purchase of any other product in Obacke's product line. VSOE is $50 for Product A and ranges from $30 to $100 for the other products in Obacke's product line. The $30 discount offered on future purchases is a significant incremental discount that would not normally be offered in comparable transactions.

The $30 discount is allocated between Product A and whichever of Obacke's other products has the lowest fair value. Assume that Product B has the lowest fair value, $40. Therefore, $16.67 or 55.5% [$50 / ($50 + $40)] of the $30 discount is allocated to Product A. Upon the sale of Product A, $33.33 of revenue would be recognized ($50 - $16.67), and $16.67 would be credited to deferred revenue. Assuming Product B is purchased for $10 ($40 selling price less the $30 coupon), revenue of $26.67 would be recognized (the $10 of cash received plus the $16.67 of deferred revenue).

Illustration of Accounting for Significant Future Discounts Where the Product to Which the Future Discount Is to Be Applied Is Not Known Yet and the Maximum Amount of the Discount Is Limited

Ocsic Inc., a software vendor, sells Product A for $40 along with the right to purchase any of its other products at a 50% discount. The maximum amount of discounts that can be taken is $100. VSOE is $40 for Product A and ranges from $40 to $200 for the other products in Ocsic's product line. The 50% discount offered on future purchases is a significant incremental discount that would not normally be offered in comparable transactions.

In accounting for this transaction, assume a sufficient amount of future purchases to fully utilize the discount. In order to fully utilize the $100 of discounts, $200 of future purchases is necessary given the 50% discount rate. The discount amount allocated to Product A is $16.67 [($40 / $240) × $100], and $23.33 of revenue will be recognized upon the sale of Product A. Assuming that $200 of future purchases are made, revenue of $116.67 will be recognized ($100 of cash received plus the $16.67 of deferred revenue).

Finally, a vendor may offer a significant incremental discount on future sales without any maximum limit on the cumulative discount amount. Revenue recognized at the time of the original sale should be reduced by the discount percentage that will apply to additional purchases. The amount of revenue deferred is to be recognized on a pro rata basis over the discount period or, if no discount period is specified, over the length of time that future purchases are expected to be made. Future purchases are recognized as revenue to the extent of cash received (because the cash received will reflect the discount allowed on future purchases).

Illustration of Accounting for Significant Future Discounts Where the Product to Which the Future Discount Is to Be Applied Is Not Known Yet and the Maximum Amount of the Discount Is Unlimited

Nus Inc., a software vendor, sells Product A for $40 along with the right to purchase any of its other products at a 50% discount. The maximum amount of future discounts that can be taken is unlimited and applies to all future purchases made during the next four years. VSOE is $40 for Product A and ranges from $40 to $200 for the other products in Nus's product line. The 50% discount offered on future purchases is a significant incremental discount that would not normally be offered in comparable transactions.

Revenue of $20 would be recognized upon the sale of Product A ($40 × .50). The $20 of deferred revenue would be recognized ratably over the next four years ($5 per year). All sales over the next four years would be recorded based on their cash selling prices (since cash selling prices would be net of the available discount).

Question 15: The fee for a perpetual software license includes postcontract support PCS services for a term of two years. However, only one-year PCS renewal rates are offered to those holding the perpetual license rights. Do rates for the PCS renewal terms provide VSOE of the fair value of the PCS element included (bundled) in the software arrangement?

Answer: Yes, assuming that the renewal rate and term are substantive. Multiply the one-year renewal rate by two to determine the VSOE of the fair value of the PCS services.

Question 16: A multiple-element software arrangement subject to the accounting requirements of SOP 97-2 provides a 12-month time-based software license that includes (bundles) six months of PCS services for a total fee of $100,000 and specifies a six-month renewal fee for PCS services of $5,000. Are there arrangements that include time-based software licenses and PCS services wherein the duration of the time-based software license is so short that a renewal rate or fee for the PCS services does not represent VSOE of the fair value of the bundled PCS?

Answer: Yes, and the above specifics illustrate such a situation. If a time-based software license has a duration of less than one year, a PCS renewal rate does not provide evidence of the fair value of the bundled PCS services. The short time frame applicable to the PCS renewal precludes an objective determination of the fair value (no VSOE) of the licensee's right to PCS.

Because, in this case, no VSOE of the fair value of the bundled PCS services exists, the total arrangement fee would be deferred.

Revenue would be deferred until all elements under the contract have been delivered.

Question 17: Arrangements for multiyear time-based software licenses may include (1) initial (bundled) PCS services for only a portion of the software license's term (e.g., a five-year time-based software license that includes initial PCS services for one year) and (2) a renewal rate for PCS for an additional year(s) within the time-based license period. Does that renewal rate constitute VSOE of the fair value of the PCS?

Answer: Yes, assuming the renewal rate and term are substantive. The following are among the situations that indicate that the renewal rate and/or term are not substantive:

- The period of the initial (bundled) PCS services is relatively long compared with the period of the software license (e.g., the initial (bundled) PCS services lasts for four of the five years of the software license and a PCS renewal rate is provided for year five).
- The aggregate renewal period is less than the initial (bundled) PCS period (e.g., the initial (bundled) PCS period lasts for three years and there are two separate renewal periods of one year each).
- A time-based software license for a relatively short period is accompanied by a PCS renewal rate that is significantly below the vendor's normal pricing policy (e.g., a two-year time-based software license with one year of initial (bundled) PCS service, with a PCS renewal rate for year two of $10,000 when the vendor's normal pricing policy for PCS services is substantially higher).

Question 18: Does the existence of varying amounts of PCS renewal fees for the same software product (resulting from using a renewal rate that is a consistent percentage of the stipulated software license fee for the same software product) indicate an absence of VSOE of the fair value of PCS?

Answer: No. As long as the PCS renewal rate that is expressed as a consistent percentage of the software license fee is substantive, the renewal rate so determined provides VSOE of the fair value of the PCS.

Question 19: A software product's value may be reduced due to the subsequent introduction of enhanced products by the vendor or its competitors. The possibility that the vendor will provide a refund or concession to a creditworthy customer to liquidate outstanding amounts due under the original terms of the arrangement increases as payment terms become longer. What kinds of changes to an arrangement would be considered concessions?

Answer: A software vendor may provide many different types of concessions. A noninclusive list of such concessions includes, but is not necessarily limited to, the following types of changes to the arrangement: (1) a change that would have affected the original amount of revenue recognized, (2) a reduction in the arrangement fee or an extension of payment terms, and (3) an increase in deliverables or an increase in customer's rights beyond those in the original transaction.

Examples of a reduction in the arrangement fee or an extension of payment terms include the following:

- Extending payment due dates for noncredit-related reasons
- Decreasing total payments due for noncredit-related reasons
- Paying the customer's financing fees when the original arrangement did not call for such payments
- Accepting returns beyond those required under the terms of the original arrangement

Examples of concessions that increase the vendor's deliverables include the following:

- Providing discounted or free post-contract support when not so required
- Providing other types of discounted or free services, upgrades, or products when not so required
- Giving customers access to other products not contemplated by the original arrangement without an appropriate increase in fees
- For term licenses, increasing the amount of time a reseller has to sell the product or increasing the amount of time a purchaser can use the product
- For limited licenses, increasing the geographic area in which a reseller can sell the product or the number of the purchaser's employees who can use the product

Question 20: Per SOP 97-2, if a significant portion of a software licensing fee is not due until after expiration of the license or more than 12 months after delivery, the licensing fee should be presumed not to be fixed or determinable. That presumption may be overcome by evidence that the vendor has a standard business practice of using long-term or installment contracts and a history of successfully collecting under the original payment terms without making concessions. What types of evidence are useful in determining whether the vendor has a history of successfully collecting under the original payment terms without making concessions?

Answer: The vendor would have to have a history of collecting all payments when due under comparable contracts without making concessions. A partial payment history—for example, the receipt of three years of payments on a five-year contract—is not sufficient because all payments due under the contract have yet to be made. In addition to a history of collecting all payments when due, the software vendor must not intend to provide any refunds or concessions beyond those established in the contract.

In evaluating the vendor's payment history, the prior software contracts (arrangements) must be comparable to the current contract in order to conclude that prior contracts are relevant. Examples of factors to consider are the following:

- Similarity of customers (e.g., type or class of customer)
- Similarity of products
  - Types of products (e.g., financial systems, production planning, human resources)
  - Stage of product life cycle (e.g., product maturity and overall stage within product life cycle)
  - Elements included in the arrangement (e.g., rights to services or discounts)
- Similarity of license economics
  - Length of payment terms
  - Economics of license arrangement

Question 21: Extended payment terms may indicate that the software fee is not fixed or determinable. Moreover, the licensing fee is presumed not to be fixed or determinable if a significant portion of a software licensing fee is not due until after expiration of the license or more than 12 months after delivery. Is the presumption overcome if the software vendor transfers the rights to receive amounts due on an extended payment term arrangement to an independent third party without recourse to the vendor?

Answer: No. The transfer of the rights to future payments does not change the nature of the transaction between the vendor and the customer.

Question 22: The presumption that an extended payment term license fee due more than 12 months after delivery of the software is not fixed or determinable *may* be overcome by evidence that the software vendor has a standard business practice of using long-term or installment contracts and has a history of successfully collecting under the original payment terms without making concessions. Assume that an entity does not have a history of using long-term or installment contracts. If a software vendor receives payment in full on a multiyear licensing arrangement after the financial statement date but before the issuance of its financial statements, does the subsequent cash receipt provide sufficient evidence to render the licensing fee fixed or determinable?

Answer: No. The software vendor must determine whether the fee is fixed or determinable at the inception of the software arrangement.

Question 23: How should a software vendor recognize revenue if it enters into an arrangement with an end-user customer that contains customary (that is, non-extended) payment terms and the end-user customer obtains, without the software vendor's participation, financing from a party unrelated to the software vendor?

Answer: The software vendor should recognize revenue upon delivery of the software product, assuming the other requirements of SOP 97-2 are met.

Question 24: How should a software vendor recognize revenue if it enters into an arrangement with an end-user customer that contains extended payment terms and the software vendor receives payments in advance of the scheduled due dates after the software vendor participated in the customer's financing with a party unrelated to the software vendor?

Answer: The fee is not fixed or determinable if the software vendor faces additional risk of being required to provide a refund or concession either to the customer or financing party as a result of its involvement in securing the financing. As such, defer recognizing the advance payments as revenue and recognize these amounts consistent with the customer's payment obligation to make payments under the financing arrangement.

Question 25: A software vendor enters into an arrangement with an end-user customer that contains customary (that is, non-extended) payment terms for which the arrangement fee ordinarily would be considered fixed or determinable. Simultaneously with entering into a software arrangement, or prior to the scheduled payment due date(s), the software vendor participates in the end-user customer's financing with a party unrelated to the software vendor. In what circumstances would the software vendor's participation in the end-user customer's financing (a) preclude a determination by the software vendor that the software arrangement fee is fixed or determinable pursuant to paragraph 28 of SOP 97-2 (ASC 985-605-25-34) or (b) lead to a presumption (that can be overcome) that the fee is not fixed or determinable in accordance with paragraph 28 (ASC 985-605-25-34)?

Answer: The purchase price is not fixed or determinable if the vendor does not have the intent or ability to enforce originally agreed upon terms if the financing is not successful. Also, the purchase price is not fixed or determinable if the vendor has altered past payment terms to provide for an extended payment period consistent with the terms of the financing. Finally, the fee is not fixed or determinable if the software vendor faces additional risk of being required to provide a refund or concession either to the customer or financing party as a result of its involvement in securing the financing.

The following conditions and vendor actions result in a presumption that the fee is not fixed or determinable due to the incremental risk faced by the vendor:

- Contract indemnification provisions that are more generous to the financing party than standard contractual terms, which were included in the contract between the vendor and end user customer
- A requirement that the vendor provide additional representations to the financing party regarding customer acceptance, incremental to any written acceptance documentation already received by the vendor from the end-user customer
- A requirement that the vendor take action (e.g., terminate the licensing agreement) if the end-user customer defaults on payments to the financing party unless:
  — These actions only involve insignificant direct incremental costs *or*
  — The customer explicitly authorizes the vendor to take these actions and no vendor concessions result from this customer authorization
- A provision that limits the vendor's ability to enter into a similar software arrangement with the customer if the customer defaults on payments to the financing party unless the customer explicitly authorizes the vendor to take this action
- A requirement that the vendor guarantee, certify, or attest that the customer meets the financing party's standards
- The software vendor has previously provided concessions to financing parties or customers to facilitate or induce payments to financing parties
- The software vendor guarantees the customer's indebtedness to the financing party
- If the presumption that the fee is not fixed or determinable is not overcome, the vendor will recognize revenue as the customer's payments to the financing party become due and payable (assuming that the other revenue recognition criteria in SOP 97-2 are met).

Question 26: Question 25 lists factors that suggest that the vendor faces increased risk as a result of participating in securing a customer's financing. What evidence should the software vendor consider to overcome the presumption that the fee is not fixed or determinable?

Answer: The vendor should have a history of entering into similar arrangements with financing parties, and the terms of the arrangements should be substantially identical. In addition, the vendor should have a history of not providing refunds or concessions to either the customer or financing party in arrangements similar to the one being analyzed.

In those cases where the vendor is able to overcome the presumption that the fee is not fixed and determinable, the vendor still must evaluate the arrangement for other possible accounting implications presented by the arrangement. For example, any vendor guarantee of the customer's indebtedness would require disclosure under the provisions of FAS-5 (Accounting for Contingencies).

Question 27: Are there examples of software vendor actions that generally do not cause the software vendor to assume incremental risk that the software vendor will provide a refund or concession to either the end-user customer or the financing party related to the software vendor's participation in an end-user customer's financing of a software arrangement?

Answer: Yes. The following are examples of vendor actions that generally do not result in increased risk to the vendor:

- Serving as an intermediary (facilitator) between the customer and financing party
- Assisting the customer in pre-qualifying for financing, as long as the vendor does not guarantee, certify, or otherwise attest to the financing party that the customer meets the financing party's qualification criteria
- Assuming that the same representations are made to the customer, stating to the financing party that the vendor has free and clear title to the software or that the vendor is free to sublicense the software
- Assuming that the same representations are made to the customer, stating to the financing party that the software functions according to the vendor's specifications
- Assuming that the customer has provided the necessary authorization, the vendor acts to terminate the license agreement (including services) or to not enter into a similar arrangement with the customer
- The vendor provides customary warranty provisions to the customer with respect to defective software

Question 28: A customer may desire, and a software vendor may be willing to help the customer, to obtain financing with a party unrelated to the software vendor that has a more attractive interest rate than typically offered by the financing party. For example, a software vendor arranges to "buy down" the interest rate a financing party would otherwise charge to the software vendor's customer. That interest rate "buy down" may occur simultaneously with the original arrangement between the software vendor and customer, or it may occur at a later point in time. Further, that interest rate "buy down" may occur with or without the customer's awareness. Does either the point in time of the interest rate "buy down," or the awareness by the customer of it, affect revenue recognition under SOP 97-2?

Answer: The time when the "buy down" occurs affects revenue recognition, but whether the customer is aware of the buy down is irrelevant. An interest rate buy down that occurs simultaneously with the original arrangement (sale) represents a reduction in the arrangement fee—such buy downs are not to be treated as an interest or financing expense. A buy down that occurs after the original sale is treated as a concession because there is a reduction in the original arrangement fee that was not contemplated at the time of the sale.

Question 29: The preceding six questions all pertained to financing arrangements with end-user customers. Are the replies different if the customer is a reseller?

Answer: The preceding guidance also pertains to a reseller, but the additional revenue recognition criteria applicable to resellers (paragraph 30 of SOP 97-2 (ASC 985-605-25-36)) should be considered. In particular, the following additional risks exist if financing is provided to a reseller:

- Payment of the arrangement fee may hinge on the reseller's success in selling the software
- The reseller may lack the ability (economic substance) to pay the arrangement fee
- Due to increased concession risk, the vendor may be unable to estimate likely returns or price protection payments

Question 30: Paragraph 20 of SOP 97-2 (ASC 985-605-25-21) says, "After delivery, if uncertainty exists about customer acceptance of the software, license revenue should not be recognized until acceptance occurs." In a software arrangement that contains a customer acceptance provision, can a software vendor ever recognize revenue (provided all of the other revenue recognition criteria of SOP 97-2 have been met) before formal customer acceptance occurs?

Answer: Yes. Just because a software arrangement contains a customer acceptance provision does not necessarily indicate that uncertainty exists regarding customer acceptance of the software. The factors to consider in evaluating whether revenue recognition should be deferred until customer acceptance occurs include the following:

- The vendor's previous history with the customer
- Whether the customer acceptance provision is a standard contract term or whether it is unique to the present customer
- The length of the acceptance period

- The vendor's past experience with similar types of products and arrangements

For public entities, additional guidance on the effect of customer acceptance provisions on revenue recognition is contained in SAB-101 (Revenue Recognition in Financial Statements) (ASC 605-10-S99-1) and the questions and answers issued by the SEC's staff applicable to SAB-No. 101.

Question 31: Software licenses for the same product currently are offered by a software vendor as (1) a perpetual license and (2) a multi-year time-based license (for example, two or more years). The pricing of the license reflects the duration of the license rights. Vendor-specific objective evidence (VSOE) of fair value exists for post-contract customer support (PCS) services in the perpetual licenses. For the multi-year time-based licenses, PCS services for the entire license term are included (bundled) in the license fee and there is no renewal rate inasmuch as the time-based license rights are co-terminus with the PCS service period. Do the PCS renewal terms in the perpetual license provide VSOE of the fair value of the PCS services element included (bundled) in the multi-year time-based software arrangement pursuant to the provisions of SOP 97-2?

Answer: No. PCS services under a perpetual license are different from PCS services under a multi-year time-based license. Although product upgrades and enhancements are provided under both types of licenses, the duration of time in which the PCS services are provided is different.

There can be exceptions to this general guidance. Renewal terms for PCS services under a perpetual license can provide VSOE of the fair value of PCS services under a multi-year time-based license if both of the following conditions are met:

- The term of the multi-year time-based software arrangement is substantially the same as the useful life of the software product (and related enhancements)
- The fees from both arrangements—the perpetual license, including renewals during the estimated useful life of the product and the multi-year time—based arrangement—are substantially the same

Another exception occurs if the vendor sells software under a multi-year time-based arrangement and provides PCS services either for the full term of the arrangement or for a partial period. The PCS renewal rate when such services are only provided for a partial period can provide VSOE of the fair value of those PCS services provided for the full term of the multi-year time-based arrangement.

Question 32: Delivery is one of the basic criteria for revenue recognition in SOP 97-2. In an arrangement that requires physical delivery of software, are delivery terms that indicate when the customer assumes the risks and rewards of its licensing rights (e.g., FOB destination and FOB shipping point terms) relevant in the assessment of whether software has been delivered?

Answer: Yes. Delivery has not occurred until the customer receives the software for those products shipped FOB destination. In addition, public entities should consult the guidance in SAB-101 (Revenue Recognition in Financial Statements) for further guidance on determining when delivery has occurred.

Question 33: SOP 97-2 identifies four basic revenue recognition criteria: (1) pervasive evidence of an arrangement; (2) delivery; (3) fixed or determinable fee; and (4) probable collectibility. None of these criteria specifically address whether the license term also must commence. Assuming all other criteria for revenue recognition are met, should the software vendor recognize any of the arrangement fees before the license term begins?

Answer: No. Revenue should not be recognized prior to the commencement of the initial license term.

Question 34: AICPA Technical Practice Aid (TPA) 5100.70 indicates that revenue should not be recognized before the license term commences even if all other criteria for revenue recognition are met. If the license is an extension/renewal of a pre-existing, currently active license for the same product(s), is commencement of the extension/renewal term a prerequisite for revenue recognition?

Answer: The software vendor should recognize the portion of the extension/renewal arrangement fee allocated to the license of the product as revenue if all other revenue recognition criteria are met. In the case of an extension/renewal of a pre-existing, currently active license for the same product(s), the customer already has possession of and the right to use the software to which the extension/renewal applies.

Question 35: TPA5100.71 addresses the effect of commencement of an extension/renewal license term when the extension/renewal arrangement includes only a product(s) already included in the existing, currently active arrangement. If the extension/renewal arrangement includes additional product(s), how should the extension/renewal arrangement fee be allocated to the different products?

Answer: The software vendor should allocate the extension/renewal arrangement fee using vender-specific objective evidence (VSOE) of fair value consistent with SOP 97-2. The software vendor should recognize the portion of the extension/renewal arrangement fee allocated to the original product if all other revenue recognition criteria are met because the customer already has possession of and the right to use the software to which the extension/renewal applies. The portion of the extension/renewal allocated to additional product(s) should be recognized when the criteria of SOP 97-2 are met and the license period for the additional product(s) has commenced.

Question 36: A software vendor sells Product A with post-contract customer support (PCS) under a three-year term license with PCS renewable after the first year. VSOE of fair value exists for PCS. The arrangement specifies that any time during the term, the customer can extend the license for Product A indefinitely for an additional fee. In effect, the arrangement contains an option to convert the three-year terms license into a perpetual license for Product A. Does the option to convert represent an element as that term is used in SOP 97-2? Would the answer differ if the perpetual license for Product A necessitated another delivery of software media because the term license software media contained a self-destruct or similar mechanism to allow the vendor to control the usage of its intellectual property?

Answer: The option itself is not an element as intended in SOP 97-2 because there is no new deliverable. The exercise of the option merely affords the customer a longer period over which to use the same product that it already has as part of the original arrangement. The additional fee to exercise the option is essentially the same as the fee for an extension/renewal of a license. In addition, the need for another delivery of software media as a result of a self-destruct or similar mechanism would not create an element or deliverable to be accounted for in the original arrangement. Such media would need to be delivered before the option exercise price could be recognized as revenue.

Question 37: The term "discount," as used in SOP 97-2 and related TPAs, is the difference between the arrangement fee and VSOE of fair value when VSOE of fair value exists for all elements in the arrangement. A question arises as to how to compute the amount of a discount when the software vendor is applying the residual method because VSOE of fair value does not exist for all of the elements in the arrangement, but does exists for all of the undelivered elements. How should the software vendor determine if the discount on future purchases of future products is significant and incremental since it does not have VSOE of fair value of its software products?

Answer: In this situation, the software vendor should compute the discount provided in the initial arrangement by comparing the published list price of the delivered elements to the residual value attributable to the delivered elements. If the discount on future purchases of products is significant and incremental to the discount provided on the delivered elements, the software vendor should apply the significant and incremental discount on future purchases to the initial arrangement using the guidance in TPA 5100.51.

Question 38: A software vendor offers a perpetual license to an end-user customer for a software product with PCS bundled for the initial year. The end-user is entitled to deploy an unlimited number of copies of the licensed software product for a three-year period. During that three-year period, the end-user customer has an option to renew PCS annually for the second and third years at a stipulated percentage of the stated license fee. After the expiration of the three-year unlimited deployment period, the end-user is required to pay additional license and PCS fees if it deploys additional copies of the software product. The optional PCS fee for subsequent years is based on the ultimate number of copies of the software product deployed by the end-user customer at the end of the three-year unlimited period. Do the annual PCS renewal rates stipulated for the second and third years constitute VSOE of fair value for the first year PCS in accordance with SOP 97-2?

Answer: No. In this arrangement, there are two different pricing methodologies for PCS and no basis for determining which pricing methodology produces the appropriate VSOE of fair value of the PCS bundled in the first year and offered in the second and third years. The vendor should recognize the entire arrangement fee ratably over the three-year deployment period. This presumes that the customer will renew the PCS in the second and third years. If the customer does not renew the PCS, the vendor should recognize the remaining deferred revenue at the time PCS is no longer being provided.

Question 39: Software vendors may enter into various multiple-element arrangements that provide for both licensing rights and PCS and that include contingent usage-based fees. Usage-based fees are determined based on applying a constant multiplier to the frequency that the licensee uses the software. That fee structure is different from fees that are determined based on the number of individuals or workstations that use or employ the software. If usage-based fees are not paid timely, the licensee's perpetual license to use the software is vacated and there is no continuing obligation to provide PCS. The following three scenarios illustrate circumstances in which software functionality is used by the software licensee only in processing the activity that underlies the measurement of the usage-based fee. How should a software vendor recognize revenue for the perpetual license, PCS, and contingent-usage based fee elements in each scenario?

Scenario A: An arrangement provides for a nonrefundable initial fee for the perpetual license and contingent usage-based fees determined monthly or quarterly and due shortly thereafter. PCS is provided at no additional charge for the first year, and the licensee may purchase renewal PCS annually thereafter for a fixed amount that is deemed substantive.

Scenario B: An arrangement provides for a nonrefundable initial fee for the perpetual license and contingent usage-based fees determined monthly or quarterly and due shortly thereafter. PCS is provided at no additional stated charge.

Scenario C: An arrangement provides for a perpetual license solely in exchange for contingent usage-based fees determined monthly or quarterly and due shortly thereafter. PCS is provided at no additional stated charge.

Answer: Usage-based fees are not specifically addressed in SOP 97-2. In describing VSOE, however, SOP 97-2 indicates that when a vendor's pricing is based on factors such as the number of products and the number of users, the amount allocated to the same element when sold separately must consider all of the factors of the vendor's pricing structure. Accordingly, usage-based fees should be considered in determining whether there is sufficient VSOE of fair value of all the elements of an arrangement.

Scenario A: The existence of a substantive renewal rate for PCS allows the determination of the portion of the initial fee that should be allocated to the perpetual license by applying the residual method. That amount should be recognized as revenue when the SOP 97-2 (par. 8) criteria are met, and the amount allocated to PCS should be recognized when the SOP 97-2 criteria (par. 57) are met. The usage-based fee should be recognized when a reliable estimate can be made of the actual usage that has occurred and collectibility is probable.

Scenario B: Because there is no substantive renewal rate for PCS, there is no VSOE of fair value of the PCS that precludes application of the residual method to determine the portion of the initial fee allocable to the perpetual license. Also, there is not subjective evidence that some portion of the initial fee does not represent payment for future PCS. Accordingly, the initial fee should be recognized ratably over the period that the vendor expects to provide PCS. The usage-based fee should be recognized at the time a reliable estimate can be made of the actual usage that has occurred and collectibility is probable.

Scenario C: The usage-based fee represents payment for both the perpetual license right and PCS. That fee becomes fixed or determinable only at the time actual usage occurs, so revenue should be recognized at the time a reliable estimate can be made of the actual usage, assuming collectibility is probable.

RELATED CHAPTERS IN 2011 GAAP GUIDE, VOLUME II

Chapter 7, "Capitalization and Expense Recognition Concepts"
Chapter 36, "Revenue Recognition"

RELATED CHAPTERS IN 2011 GAAP GUIDE, VOLUME I

Chapter 6, "Computer Software"
Chapter 41, "Revenue Recognition"

RELATED CHAPTER IN 2011 INTERNATIONAL ACCOUNTING/FINANCIAL REPORTING STANDARDS GUIDE

Chapter 21, "Intangible Assets"

CHAPTER 10
CONSOLIDATED FINANCIAL STATEMENTS

CONTENTS

Overview		10.03
Authoritative Guidance		
ASC 810 Consolidation		10.04
FSP FIN-46 (R)-1	Reporting Variable Interests in Specified Assets of Variable Interest Entities as Separate Variable Interest Entities under Paragraph 13 of FASB Interpretation No. 46 (Revised December 2003), *Consolidation of Variable Interest Entities*	10.04
FSP FIN-46 (R)-2	Calculation of Expected Losses under FASB Interpretation No. 46 (Revised December 2003), *Consolidation of Variable Interest Entities*	10.05
FSP FIN-46 (R)-5	Implicit Variable Interests under FASB Interpretation No. 46 (Revised December 2003), *Consolidation of Variable Interest Entities*	10.07
FSP FIN-46 (R)-6	Determining the Variability to Be Considered in Applying FASB Interpretation No. 46(R)	10.10
EITF Issue 85-12	Retention of Specialized Accounting for Investments in Consolidation	10.13
EITF Issue 96-16	Investor's Accounting for an Investee When the Investor Has a Majority of the Voting Interest but the Noncontrolling Shareholder or Shareholders Have Certain Approval or Veto Rights	10.16
EITF Issue 97-2	Application of FASB Statement No. 94 and APB Opinion No. 16 to Physician Practice Management Entities and Certain Other Entities with Contractual Management Arrangements	10.22

EITF Issue 97-14	Accounting for Deferred Compensation Arrangements Where Amounts Earned Are Held in a Rabbi Trust and Invested	**10.34**
EITF Issue 04-5	Determining Whether a General Partner, or the General Partners as a Group, Controls a Limited Partnership or Similar Entity When the Limited Partners Have Certain Rights	**10.40**
EITF Issue 08-8	Accounting for an Instrument (or an Embedded Feature) with a Settlement Amount That Is Based on the Stock of an Entity's Consolidated Subsidiary	**10.49**
ASC 944-80 Accounts	Financial Services—Insurance—Separate	**10.54**
Issue 09-8	How Investments Held through Separate Accounts Affect an Insurer's Consolidation Analysis of Those Investments	**10.54**
ASC 946	Financial Services—Investment Companies	**10.56**
FSP SOP 07-1	Clarification of the Scope of the Audit and Accounting Guide *Investment Companies* and Accounting by Parent Companies and Equity Method Investors for Investments in Investment Companies	**10.56**
ASC 970-810 Real Estate—General—Consolidation		**10.71**
FSP SOP 78-9-1	Interaction of AICPA Statement of Position 78-9 and EITF Issue No. 04-5	**10.71**

Authoritative Guidance Not Included Separately in the Codification But Incorporated with Another Pronouncement in the Codification

FSP SOP 07-1-1	Effective Date of AICPA Statement of Position 07-1	**10.74**

Related Chapters in 2011 GAAP Guide, Volume II **10.75**

Related Chapters in 2011 GAAP Guide, Volume I **10.75**

Related Chapter in 2011 International Accounting/Financial Reporting Standards Guide **10.75**

OVERVIEW

Consolidated financial statements represent the results of operations, statement of cash flows, and financial position of a single entity, even though multiple, separate legal entities are involved. Consolidated financial statements are presumed to present more meaningful information than separate financial statements and must be used in substantially all cases in which a parent directly or indirectly controls the majority voting interest (over 50%) of a subsidiary. Consolidated financial statements should not be used in those circumstances in which (*a*) the parent's control of the subsidiary is temporary or (*b*) there is significant doubt concerning the parent's ability to control the subsidiary.

The following pronouncements, which provide authoritative guidance on reporting principles for consolidated financial statements, combined financial statements, and comparative financial statements, are discussed in the *GAAP Guide, Volume I*:

ASC 605   Revenue Recognition (ARB-43)

ASC 205   Presentation of Financial Statements (ARB 43)

ASC 810   Consolidation (ARB-51)

ASC 810 840   Consolidation of All Majority-Owned Subsidiaries (FAS-94)

ASC 810   Consolidation of Variable Interest Entities (revised December 2003) (FIN-46(R))

AUTHORITATIVE GUIDANCE

ASC 810 Consolidation

> **OBSERVATION:** The guidance in ASC 810-10-30-7 through 30-9; 65-2 (FAS-167, Amendments to FASB Interpretation No. 46(R)), which addresses the consolidation of variable interest entities, is effective as of the beginning of an entity's first annual reporting period that begins after November 15, 2009, and for interim periods after that.

FSP FIN-46(R)-1 (Reporting Variable Interests in Specified Assets of Variable Interest Entities as Separate Variable Interest Entities under Paragraph 13 of FASB Interpretation No. 46 (revised December 2003), *Consolidation of Variable Interest Entities*) (ASC 810-10-25-58)

Question: Should a specified asset (or a group of assets) of a variable interest entity (Entity A) and a related liability that is secured only by the specified asset or group of assets be treated as a separate variable interest entity (Entity B), as discussed in the FASB Accounting Standards Codification™ (ASC) 810-10-25-57 (paragraph 13 of FIN-46(R)), if other parties have rights or obligations related to the specified asset or to residual cash flows from the specified asset?

Answer: The FASB staff believes that a separate variable interest entity does not exist under the circumstances in question. Treatment as a separate variable interest entity for accounting purposes is appropriate only if all of Entity B's assets, liabilities, and equity are separate from those of Entity A and can be identified separately. Under those circumstances, Entity A would not be able to use returns on Entity B's assets and Entity B would not be able to use Entity A's assets to settle its liabilities.

EFFECTIVE DATE AND TRANSITION

This FSP supersedes the guidance in FSP FIN-46-2 for all entities to which the guidance in ASC 810-10-05-8 through 05-8A; 15-12 through 15-17; 25-37 through 25-44; 30-1 through 30-4, 30-7 through 30-9; 35-3 through 35-5; 45-25; 50-2AA through 50-7, 50-9 through 50-10; 55-16 through 55-49, 55-93 through 55-181, 55-183 through 55-205; 60-13; 323-10-45-4; 712-10-60-2; 715-10-60-3, 60-7; 860-10-60-2; 954-810-15-3; 45-2; 958-810-15-4 (FIN-46(R)) is applied. The effective date and transition provisions in FIN-46(R) apply to the application of the guidance in this FSP.

FSP FIN-46(R)-2 (Calculation of Expected Losses under FASB Interpretation No. 46 (revised December 2003), *Consolidation of Variable Interest Entities*) (ASC 810-10-55-50 through 55-54)

Question: Is it appropriate to account for an entity as a variable interest entity if it has no history of net losses and expects to continue to be profitable in the foreseeable future?

Answer: Treatment as a variable interest entity is appropriate because even entities that expect to be profitable will have expected losses. The term "expected losses" is used in FIN-46(R) to refer to the negative variability in the fair value of a variable interest entity's net assets, excluding variable interests, and does *not* apply to the expected amount of variability of net income or loss. Appendix A of FIN-46(R) illustrates the calculation of expected losses. A variable interest entity's expected losses are defined in paragraph 8 (ASC, *Glossary*) of the Interpretation as the expected negative variability in the fair value of the entity's net assets without the variable interests.

Example: Company A is formed on January 1, 2004, to purchase a building that is financed with 95% debt and 5% equity. If Company A does not make the required debt payments, the lenders have recourse only to the building. On the same day, Company A leases the building to Company B under a five-year market-rate lease that includes a guarantee of a portion of the building's residual value. The present value of the minimum lease payments, including the residual value guarantee, is less than 90% of the building's fair value. No other entities have interests in Company A. The appropriate discount rate is assumed to be 5%.

In accordance with the definitions of expected losses and expected residual returns in ASC, *Glossary* (paragraph 8 of FIN-46(R)), the entity's estimated annual results in the above example include estimated cash flows and the estimated fair value of Company A's assets that will be distributed to variable interest holders instead of cash, regardless of cash flows or flows of other assets to and from variable interests. The guarantee constitutes a variable interest in the entity because it is an interest in assets with a fair value that is more than half of the total fair value of Company A's assets. Consequently, losses absorbed by the residual value guarantee are Company A's losses and are included in the results used to calculate expected losses. To simplify the calculation, it is assumed that (*a*) the estimated results, which include both cash flows and changes in the fair value of Company A's net assets, and related probabilities are the same each year of the five-year lease and (*b*) the carrying value of the building is its fair value.

The illustration below from this demonstrates the calculation at January 1, 2004, of the expected results at the inception of the guarantee identified as a variable interest. It is assumed that the fair value of the expected result will be equal to the sum of the present values of probability-weighted estimated annual results for the five-year lease term, excluding the effects of the residual value guarantee. A variation in estimated results, if any, as compared to the expected result, constitutes a change in the value of the entity's net assets, excluding variable interests, from the value of those net assets on the calculation date.

Illustration of Expected Results at Inception of Guarantee Identified as Variable Interest
(amounts in thousands)

Estimated Annual Results	Probability	Expected Annual Results	Fair Value of Expected Five-Year Results
$(10,000)	5.0%	$(500)	$(2,165)
(5,000)	10.0	(500)	(2,165)
0	20.0	0	0
10,000	50.0	5,000	21,648
50,000	15.0	7,500	32,471
	100.0	$11,500	$49,789

Estimated annual results include estimated cash flow, excluding cash flow or flows of other assets to and from variable interests, and the estimated fair value of Company A's assets to be distributed to holders of variable interests instead of cash. It is assumed that the fair value of expected five-year results is the sum of the present values of the expected results for each year in the five-year period. In the present value calculations to determine the fair value of the five-year expected results, the expected annual results are treated as level annuities because to simplify the calculation it is assumed that the annual estimated results and probabilities are the same for each year of the five-year period.

The illustration below demonstrates the calculation of expected losses as the negative variability from the fair value of the expected results. It shows that an estimated annual result of $0 and one of $10,000 can contribute to expected losses even though neither is a negative amount, because a company's value will be less relative to its value based on the expected results if a positive estimated result is less than the expected results. The calculation of an expected loss shows that the expected loss is the fair value of the probability-weighted negative variation from the expected results. Expected losses include all negative variations.

**Illustration of Calculation of Expected Losses as Negative Variability from Fair Value of Expected Results
(amounts in thousands)**

Estimated Annual Result	Present Value of Estimated Five-Year Result	Positive Fair Value of Expected Five-Year Results (from above)	(Negative) Variation Expected from Value	Probability	Expected Losses	Residual Returns
$(10,000)	$(43,294)	$49,789	$(93,083)	5.0%	$(4,654)	
(5,000)	(21,648)	49,789	(71,437)	10.0	(7,144)	
0	0	49,789	(49,789)	20.0	(9,958)	
10,000	43,294	49,789	(6,495)	50.0	(3,247)	
50,000	216,473	49,789	166,684	15.0		25,003
				100.0%	$(25,003)	$25,003

The estimated annual results are treated as level annuities in calculating the present value of the estimated five-year results because, in order to simplify the calculation, it is assumed that the annual estimated results are the same for each year of the five-year periods.

EFFECTIVE DATE AND TRANSITION

This FSP replaces FSP FIN-46-5 for all entities to which FIN-46(R) applies. The effective date and transition provisions in FIN-46(R) apply to the application of the guidance in this FSP.

FSP FIN-46(R)-5 (Implicit Variable Interests under FASB Interpretation No. 46 (Revised December 2003), Consolidation of Variable Interest Entities) (ASC 810-10-25-48 through 25-54; 55-89)

> **OBSERVATION:** This FSP applies to public and nonpublic reporting entities. The circumstances discussed in this FSP are common in leasing arrangements among related parties and in other types of arrangements that involve related and unrelated parties.

OVERVIEW

There has been diversity in practice in accounting for situations in which a reporting entity, Entity A, has an interest in or other involvement that is *not* a variable interest with Entity B, which is a variable interest entity (VIE) or a potential VIE. In addition, Entity C, which is *not* a VIE, is a related party to Entity A that also has a variable interest in Entity B. Questions have been raised as to whether the reporting entity (Entity A) should consider whether an *implicit* variable interest has been created between it and the VIE (Entity B). A reporting entity's interest in or other financial involvement with a VIE may be in the form of a lessee under a leasing arrangement, as a party to a supply contract, service contract, derivative contract, or in other forms of involvement.

An *implicit* variable interest is an indirect financial interest in an entity that changes as a result of changes in the fair value of the entity's net assets, not including variable interests. Such variable interests may result from transactions with related parties and other parties. An example is provided in ASC 810-10-55-25 through 55-26 (paragraph B10 of FIN-46(R), Consolidation of Variable Interest Entities, as amended by FAS-167, Amendments to FASB Interpretation 46(R)), which refers to an unspoken agreement to replace impaired assets of a VIE that protects holders of other interests in the VIE from incurring losses.

Explicit variable interests in an entity *directly* absorb or receive the entity's variability, while *implicit* variable interests act the same as explicit variable interests but they absorb or receive variability *indirectly* from the entity.

The FASB directed the FASB staff to issue this FSP to provide guidance as to whether a reporting entity should consider if it has an *implicit* variable interest in a VIE or a potential VIE under specific conditions. Information about implicit and explicit variable interests is necessary in the application of the provisions of ASC 810-10-05-8 through 05-8; 15-12 through 15-17; 25-37 through 25-44; 30-1 through 30-4, 30-7 through 30-9; 35-3 through 35-5; 45-25; 50-2AA through 50-7, 50-9 through 50-10; 55-16 through 55-49, 55-93 through 55-181, 55-183 through 55-205; 60-13; 323-10-45-4; 712-10-60-2; 715-10-60-3, 60-7; 860-10-60-2; 954-810-15-3; 45-2; 958-810-15-4 (FIN-46(R)) because it may affect (*a*) whether a potential VIE should be considered a VIE, (*b*) the calculation of expected losses and residual returns, and (*c*) which party, if any, is a VIE's primary beneficiary.

FASB STAFF POSITION

The guidance in ASC 810-10-25-42 through 25-43 (paragraph 16 of FIN-46(R)) states that an entity with a variable interest in another entity should treat variable interests held by a related party in the same entity as its own interests for the purpose of determining whether it is the VIE's *primary* beneficiary. In addition, under the guidance in ASC 810-10-25-44 (paragraph 17 of FIN-46(R)) a party within a related party group that is the most closely associated with a VIE is considered to be its primary beneficiary if (1) two or more related parties hold variable interests in the same VIE and (2) the total variable interest held by those related parties would cause a single holder to be considered the VIE's primary beneficiary.

Question: Should a reporting entity consider whether it has an *implicit* variable interest in a VIE or potential VIE under the following conditions:

- A reporting entity has an interest in, or other involvement with, a VIE or potential VIE that is *not* considered a variable interest in the VIE under the *explicit* terms of the reporting entity's interest in or involvement with the VIE. Therefore, the entity has *no* explicit variable interest in the VIE. Further, without considering related party relationships, the reporting entity would have *no* implicit variable interest in the entity.
- The reporting entity's related party has a variable interest in the same entity.

Answer: The FASB staff believes that a reporting entity should consider whether it has an *implicit* variable interest in a VIE or potential VIE based on all the facts and circumstances when the reporting entity determines whether it may absorb the VIE's or a potential VIE's variability. If a reporting entity determines that it holds an implicit variable interest in a VIE and it is a related party, as defined in ASC 810-10-25-43 (paragraph 16 of FIN-46(R) as amended by FAS-167), to other holders of the variable interests, it should determine whether it is the VIE's primary beneficiary based on the guidance in ASC 810-10-25-44 (paragraph 17 of FIN-46(R) as amended by FAS-167). That is, a party within a related party group that is most closely associated with a VIE is deemed to be the *primary* beneficiary, if a single party holding the total implicit and explicit variable interests that are held by the reporting entity and its related parties would be identified as the primary beneficiary under those circumstances. Judgment based on all the facts and circumstances is required to determine which party in a related party group is most closely associated with a VIE. Factors stated in ASC 810-10-25-44 (paragraph 17 of FIN 46(R), as amended by FAS-167) that should be considered include (*a*) whether a reporting entity and a VIE are under common control; (*b*) whether a reporting entity has an interest in or other involvement with a VIE and an officer of the reporting entity has an interest in the VIE; or (*c*) whether a reporting entity has a contractual arrangement with an unrelated third party that has a variable interest in the VIE resulting in a related party relationship.

If a reporting entity that holds an implicit variable interest in a VIE is not the primary beneficiary, the entity should disclose the information required in ASC 810-10-50-4 (paragraph 24 of FIN 46(R), as amended by FAS-167).

EFFECTIVE DATE AND TRANSITION

Entities that have applied the guidance in FIN-46(R) should adopt the FSP's guidance in the first reporting period beginning after

March 3, 2005, the date the FSP was posted on the FASB's web site, in accordance with the transition provisions of FIN-46(R). Entities are permitted but are *not* required to restate their financial statements to the date of the initial application of FIN-46(R). Early application is permitted for periods for which financial statements have *not* been issued. Entities that have *not* applied the guidance in FIN-46(R) should apply the guidance in this FSP in accordance with the effective date and transition of FIN-46(R).

FSP FIN-46(R)-6 (Determining the Variability to Be Considered in Applying FASB Interpretation No. 46(R)) (ASC 810-10-15-15, 14; 25-21 through 25-28; 55-56 through 55-85)

OVERVIEW

To apply the guidance in ASC 810-10-05-8 through 05-8A; 15-12 through 15-17; 25-37 through 25-44; 30-1 through 30-4, 30-7 through 30-9; 35-3 through 35-5; 45-25; 50-2AA through 50-7, 50-9 through 50-10; 55-16 through 55-49, 55-93 through 55-181, 55-183 through 55-205; 60-13; 323-10-45-4; 712-10-60-2; 715-10-60-3, 60-7; 860-10-60-2; 954-810-15-3; 45-2; 958-810-15-4 (FIN-46(R), Consolidation of Variable Interest Entities, as amended by FAS-167), it is necessary to determine the variability that should be considered in order to determine (a) whether an entity is a variable entity (VIE), (b) the interests in the entity that are variable interests, and (c) which party, if any, is a VIE's primary beneficiary. Calculations of expected losses, if any, and expected returns are affected by that variability.

Reporting entities are determining the variability to be considered in a variety of ways. Some reporting entities have been considering only variability caused by changes in cash flows under the *cash flow method*; others have been considering only variability caused by changes in fair value under the *fair value method*. Regardless of the method used, entities applying the guidance in FIN-46(R) should reach the same conclusion as to whether the entity is a VIE and which interests should be considered variable interests. However, this is not always the case.

To protect certain equity and liability holders from exposure to (a) variability caused by certain assets and operations held by an entity or (b) divergence in the overall profile of an entity's assets and liabilities, reporting entities may enter into arrangements, such as derivative contracts, which reduce or eliminate those types of variability. During the life of any entity, it may treat those arrangements as recorded or unrecorded assets or liabilities. Application of the cash flow method or the fair value method does not resolve the variety of opinions as to whether such arrangements should be treated as variable interests or should be considered *creators* of variability.

FASB STAFF POSITION

The design of an entity should be analyzed based on the following steps to determine the variability that should be considered when FIN-46(R) is applied:

Step 1. Analyze the *nature* of an entity's risks.

Step 2. Determine (a) the *purpose* for which an entity was established and (b) the variability created by the risks identified in Step 1 that the entity has been designed to create and pass on to its interest holders, including all of an entity's potential variable interest holders (contractual, ownership, or other financial interests).

Assets are *not* variable interests. Rather, an entity's assets and operations *cause* variability, which is absorbed by the entity's liabilities and equity interests. Some contracts or arrangements appear to have the attributes of creating *and* absorbing variability because, at different times in an entity's life, they may be represented as assets or as liabilities that may or may not be recorded. As stated in ASC 810-10-55-19 (paragraph B4 of FIN-46(R), as amended by FAS-167), it was the FASB's intent that a conclusion about whether a contract or arrangement *creates* or *absorbs* variability should be based on the contract's *role* in the entity's design, regardless of the arrangement's legal form or classification.

Once the variability to consider has been determined, the interests designed to absorb that variability may be identified. Although the cash flow and fair value methods are examples of methods that may be used to measure the amount of an entity's variability in the form of expected losses and expected residual returns, the FASB staff believes that such methods do *not* provide an appropriate means for determining which variability should be considered when applying the guidance in FIN-46(R), as amended by FAS-167.

In Step 1, risks that *cause* variability are considered. They include, but are not limited to, credit risk; interest rate risk, including prepayment risk, foreign currency exchange risk; commodity price risk; equity price risk; and operations risk.

In Step 2, which is intended to determine the *purpose* for which an entity was created and the variability it was designed to create and pass on to its interest holders, the relevant facts and circumstances that should be considered include, but are not limited to, the activities of the entity; the terms of contracts into which the entity has entered; the nature of interests the entity has issued; the manner in which the interests were negotiated and marketed to potential investors; and the parties that participated in the design and redesign of an entity.

How to determine variability A review of contracts into which an entity has entered should include an analysis of other documents, such as the original documents prepared to establish the entity, governing documents, marketing materials, and other contractual arrangements into which the entity has entered and has provided to potential investors or other parties with which it is associated. When determining variability, the following should be considered:

- Whether the terms of interests issued, regardless of their legal form or accounting designation, transfer to the interest holders all or a portion of the risk or return, or both, certain assets or operations of the entity. Transfer of variability to interest holders strongly indicates that the entity has been designed to create that variability and to pass it on to its interest holders.

- Whether subordination (i.e., the priority on claims to an entity's cash flows) is *substantive* if an entity issues both senior interests and subordinated interests, which often affect the determination of which variability should be considered. Because expected losses generally are first absorbed by subordinated interests and then by senior interests, the latter have a higher credit rating and a lower interest rate than subordinated interests. The primary factor in determining whether a subordinated interest is substantive is the relationship of its amount to the entity's overall *expected* losses and residual returns. Absorption of variability by a substantively subordinated interest strongly indicates that the entity was designed to create such variability and pass it on to its interest holders. A subordinated interest that is considered equity-at-risk, as the term is used in ASC 810-10-15-14 (paragraph 5 of FIN-46(R), as amended by FAS-167), may be considered substantive for the purpose of determining the variability that should be considered, even if it is not regarded to be sufficient under ASC 810-10-15-14, 25-45 (paragraphs 5(a) and 9 of FIN-46(R) as amended by FAS-167).

- Whether an entity was *designed* to pass interest rate risk to its interest holders. If an entity was *not* designed to create and pass on interest rate risk associated with interest receipts and payments to its interest holders, such periodic interest receipts or payments should be *excluded* from the variability being considered. However, cash proceeds received from anticipated sales of fixed-rate investments in an actively managed portfolio or those held in a static pool that, by design, will be required to be sold before maturity to satisfy the entity's obligations also may vary as a result of interest rate fluctuations. That kind of variability strongly indicates that the entity was designed to create that variability and to pass it on to its interest holders.

The existence of the following two characteristics strongly indicates that a derivative instrument *creates* variability:

1. The underlying is an observable market rate, price, index of prices or rates, or other market observable, which includes the occurrence or nonoccurrence of a specified market observable event.
2. The derivative counterparty is *senior* in priority in relation to the entity's other interest holders.

An entity's design should be analyzed further to determine whether a derivative instrument having the two characteristics discussed above creates variability or is a variable interest if changes in the derivative instrument's fair value or cash flows are expected to offset all, or nearly all, of the risk or return, or both, related to a majority of an entity's assets, excluding the derivative instrument, or the entity's operations.

A qualitative analysis of an entity's design performed in accordance with the guidance is this FSP and that discussed in FIN-46(R), as amended by FAS-167 often will result in a conclusive determination of the variability that should be considered when FIN-46(R), as amended by FAS-167 is applied—that is, the determination as to which interests are variable interests and the ultimate determination of which variable interest holder, if any, is the primary beneficiary.

EFFECTIVE DATE AND TRANSITION

The guidance in this FSP should be applied prospectively to all entities with which the entity first becomes involved and to all entities previously required to be analyzed, including those that are newly created, under the guidance in FIN-46(R) beginning on the first day of the first reporting period that begins after June 15, 2006. The FSP may be applied early for periods for which no financial statements have yet been issued. The FSP may be applied retrospectively to the date on which FIN-46(R) was first applied, but such application is not required. If elected, retrospective application must be completed no later than the end of the first annual reporting period ending after July 15, 2006.

EITF Issue 85-12 (Retention of Specialized Accounting for Investments in Consolidation) (ASC 810-10-25-15; 946-10-65-1)

> **OBSERVATION:** In June 2007, the AICPA issued SOP 07-1 (Clarification of the Scope of the Audit and Accounting Guide Investment Companies and Accounting by Parent Companies and Equity Method Investors for Investments in Investment Companies), which provides guidance on the conditions that

should be met by a parent of an investment company or an equity method investor in an investment company to retain investment company accounting in its financial statements. Accordingly, SOP 07-1 effectively nullified the guidance in Issue 85-12 for equity method investments in or accounting by an investment company's parent. However, subsequent to the issuance of the SOP, the FASB issued FSP SOP 07-1-1 (Effective Date of AICPA Statement of Position 07-1), which delays the SOP's effective date indefinitely, but provides guidance to entities that had early adopted the FSP's provisions and those had not yet adopted the SOP's provisions. Both pronouncements are discussed in this chapter.

OVERVIEW

Some operating companies have subsidiaries that are venture capital investment companies, which provide financing to companies in various stages of development by investing in their securities. Venture capital investment companies generally follow the specialized accounting principles for investment companies and carry their investments at market value.

ACCOUNTING ISSUE

> **OBSERVATION:** FIN-46(R) (Consolidation of Variable Interest Entities) does not affect the consensus positions reached on this Issue, because the entity is not a variable interest entity if (a) its shareholders have the power to control the entity as a group, as discussed in this Issue, because the majority interest holder does not control the entity as a result of a noncontrolling interest's veto rights, and (b) the equity investment meets the Interpretation's other requirements.

Should an operating company report the investments of its venture capital subsidiary in consolidated financial statements at market value based on the subsidiary's specialized accounting principles, or should the investments be reported in the same manner as the parent's investments?

> **OBSERVATION:** When this issue was discussed, companies reported their investments at cost less impairment, lower of cost or market, or by the equity method in accordance with the provisions of FAS-12 (Accounting for Certain Marketable Securities). ASC 320 (FAS-115, Accounting by Debtors and Creditors for Troubled Debt Restructurings), which superseded the guidance in FAS-12, eliminates the lower-of-cost-or-market method for marketable equity securities, which should be reported at fair value.

EITF CONSENSUS

The EITF reached a consensus that a subsidiary's specialized industry accounting principles should be retained in consolidation if they are appropriate at the subsidiary's level.

DISCUSSION

During the discussion of this Issue, the FASB staff voiced their concerns about the use of market-value accounting by venture capital investment companies for their investments in restricted securities or securities without a ready market. In those situations, cost is frequently used as a surrogate for market value. The FASB staff noted that venture capital companies usually do not report the impairment of the cost of such investments in the early years of an investment while increases in value are often reflected in later years.

Another concern was that it may be more appropriate for venture capital companies to account for such investments on the equity method, or that they should be consolidated in the venture capital company's financial statements. Further, there was a concern that operating companies may designate their research and development subsidiaries as investments of venture capital subsidiaries to avoid reporting certain costs in their financial statements.

The SEC Observer was concerned that not all venture capital companies report their investments at market value.

SUBSEQUENT DEVELOPMENT

Subsequent to the EITF's discussion, the AICPA Investment Companies Committee wrote an Issues paper, *Accounting for Venture Capital Investment Companies.* This paper addressed issues related to the use of market value by all venture capital companies to value their investments and the retention of market value for the investments of venture capital company subsidiaries in consolidation. At a meeting with committee representatives, the FASB objected to the paper's conclusions that (1) all venture capital companies should carry their investments at market value and (2) investments of venture capital subsidiaries should be reported at market value in consolidation regardless of the parent company's method of reporting its investments.

The FASB had difficulty with the paper's definition of a venture capital investment company and raised the same objections and concerns about abuses as the staff did at the EITF's discussion. After discussing the results of the meeting with the FASB, the Investment Companies Committee decided to terminate the project.

EITF Issue 96-16 (Investor's Accounting for an Investee When the Investor Has a Majority of the Voting Interest but the Noncontrolling Shareholder or Shareholders Have Certain Approval or Veto Rights) (ASC 810-10-15-10; 25-1 through 25-8, 25-10 through 25-14; 55-1)

OVERVIEW

Under the guidance in ASC 810 (ARB-51, Consolidated Financial Statements) and 810-10-60-4; 840-10-45-4 (FAS-94, Consolidation of All Majority-Owned Subsidiaries), entities holding a controlling financial interest in an investee, which is evidenced by ownership of a majority voting interest, are required to consolidate such investees in their financial statements. There are circumstances, however, under which noncontrolling shareholders are granted certain approval or veto rights that restrict the majority shareholders' powers to control the entity's operations or its assets. The authoritative accounting literature provides no guidance as to whether such restrictions affect the ability of a shareholder with a majority voting interest to control the entity and whether the majority shareholder may be precluded from consolidating such an investee because of a lack of control.

This Issue does not apply to the accounting by entities, such as investment companies, which are required under GAAP to present substantially all of their assets at fair value, including investments in controlled entities, and that report changes in value in a statement of net income or financial performance. Investments in noncorporate entities and special-purpose entities also are outside the scope of this Issue.

ACCOUNTING ISSUES

- Which rights held by noncontrolling shareholders overcome the presumption in 840-10-45-4 (FAS-94) that all majority-owned investments should be consolidated?
- Does the extent of a majority shareholder's financial interest—50.1% versus 99.9%—affect the conclusion to Issue 1?
- Would the conclusions in the above Issues apply in other circumstances under which a corporate investee would otherwise have been consolidated under FAS-94?

EITF CONSENSUS

> **OBSERVATION:** The guidance in ASC 810-10-05-8 through 05; 15-12 through 15-17; 25-37 through 25-44; 30-1 through 30-4, 30-7 through 30-9; 35-3 through 35-5; 45-25; 50-2AA

through 50-7, 50-9 through 50-10; 55-16 through 55-49, 55-93 through 55-181, 55-183 through 55-205; 60-13; 323-10-45-4; 712-10-60-2; 715-10-60-3, 60-7; 860-10-60-2; 954-810-15-3; 45-2; 958-810-15-4 (FIN-46(R) Consolidation of Various Interest Entities) does *not* affect the consensus positions reached on this Issue because the entity is *not* a variable interest entity if (*a*) its shareholders have the power to control the entity as a group, as discussed in this issue, because the majority interest holder does *not* control the entity as a result of a noncontrolling interest's veto rights, and (*b*) the entity's investment meets the Interpretation's other requirements.

Scope The consensus positions apply only to investments with majority voting interests in corporations or similar entities, such as limited liability companies that are equivalent to regular corporations as a result of their governing provisions. The guidance in this Issue also should be used to evaluate the effect of noncontrolling shareholder approval or veto rights in other situations in which consolidation of an investee would normally be required under GAAP (for example, a 49% ownership with 100% control of the board of directors).

> **OBSERVATION:** The EITF reached a consensus in ASC 272-10-053, 4; 323-30-15-4; 35-3 (Issue 03-16, Accounting for Investments in Limited Liability Companies) that when determining whether a noncontrolling investment in an LLC should be accounted for by the cost or the equity method, an investment in an LLC in which each investor has a *specific ownership* account should be considered to be similar to an investment in a limited partnership. That consensus does not affect the guidance in this Issue.

Framework for evaluating the rights of noncontrolling shareholders. Noncontrolling shareholders' rights should be evaluated based on the following framework when the noncontrolling interest is obtained and whenever it is reassessed because the terms of those rights or their exercisability has been changed significantly:

- Judgment, which depends on the facts and circumstances, should be used to determine whether a noncontrolling investor's rights overcome the presumption that an investor with a majority voting interest should consolidate the investee.
- The facts and circumstances should be evaluated based on whether noncontrolling shareholders' rights, individually or in combination, provide the noncontrolling investors with effective participation in significant decisions made in the "ordinary course of business."
- A noncontrolling investor that has *effective participation* can block significant decisions proposed by a majority investor. A noncontrolling investor's ability to block a majority investor from making the investee take a significant action in the

ordinary course of business deprives the majority investor of the ability to control the investee.

The Task Force noted that all noncontrolling shareholders' rights are intended to protect the noncontrolling interests in the investee (protective rights). Such noncontrolling shareholders' rights do not overcome the presumption in ASC 840-10-45-4 (FAS-94) that the majority shareholder should consolidate the investee. However, noncontrolling shareholders may have substantive rights (participating rights) that permit the noncontrolling shareholders to block certain actions proposed by the majority investor concerning the investee's financial and operating decisions made in the ordinary course of business. For the purpose of applying the consensus, decisions made *in the ordinary course of business* are defined as those normally made to deal with matters that are encountered in the current operations of a business. Although it may not necessarily be expected that the events or transactions requiring such decisions to be made will occur in the near term, it must be at least reasonably possible that events or transactions that require making such decisions will occur. This ordinary course of business definition *does not* apply to self-dealing transactions with controlling shareholders. Participating rights enable noncontrolling shareholders to participate in significant decisions, because those holding a majority interest are prevented from making certain decisions in the ordinary course of business without the noncontrolling shareholders's agreement. The Task Force believes that the existence of noncontrolling shareholders' participating rights overcomes the presumption that a majority-owned investee should be consolidated by the majority owner.

Protective rights Contractual or legal rights that enable noncontrolling shareholders to block the following corporate actions are considered to be protective rights that would not overcome the presumption that a shareholder with a majority voting interest should consolidate the investee:

- Amendments to the investee's articles of incorporation
- Pricing of the majority owner's transactions with the investee and related self-dealing transactions
- An investee's liquidation or bankruptcy filing
- Acquisitions and dispositions of assets equal to more than 20% of the fair value of the investee's total assets. (See discussion below in "Factors affecting the determination based on facts and circumstances" and "Additional guidance" for an evaluation of transactions of 20% or less.)

> **OBSERVATION:** As a result of the EITF's consensus reached at its June 15 through 16, 2005, meeting to amend the guidance in this Issue so it will conform with the guidance in ASC 810-20 (Issue 04-5, Determining Whether a General Partner, or the General Partners as a Group, Controls a Limited Partnership or Similar Entity When the Limited Partners Have Certain

Rights), the phrase "equal to more than 20% of the investee's total assets" and the reference in the parentheses are being replaced by the following language: "*not* expected to be undertaken in the ordinary course of business. Noncontrolling shareholders' rights related to acquisitions and dispositions made in the ordinary course of business are considered to be *participating* rights. Therefore, judgment based on the specific facts and circumstances should be used to determine whether such rights are substantive." The EITF also reached a consensus that this amendment should be applied *prospectively* to new investments and to investment agreements that have been modified after June 29, 2005—the date the FASB ratified the consensus to amend this Issue.

- Issuance or repurchase of equity interests

This list illustrates some, but not all, corporate actions that may be blocked as a result of a noncontrolling shareholder's protective rights.

Substantive participating rights Contractual or legal rights that enable noncontrolling shareholders to effectively participate in the following corporate decisions are considered to be substantive participating rights that would overcome the presumption that a shareholder with a majority voting interest should consolidate an investee:

- Hiring, firing, *and* decisions related to the compensation of management implementing the investee's policies and procedures
- Operating *and* capital decisions, including operating and capital budgets that affect management's actions in the ordinary course of business

These items illustrate some, but not all, substantive participating rights that may be granted to noncontrolling shareholders. They are considered to be participating rights, because in their entirety they permit the noncontrolling shareholders to effectively participate in significant decisions required to conduct the investee's business activities in the ordinary course of business. It is necessary to consider the facts and circumstances in determining whether a noncontrolling investor's single right, such as the ability to prevent a majority investor from firing management responsible for implementing an investee's policies and procedures, should be considered in and of itself a substantive participating right. Nevertheless, the presumption that a majority investor should consolidate its investee would not be overcome by noncontrolling shareholders' rights that appear to be participating rights but that are not substantive individually. A determination whether a noncontrolling shareholder's right is a substantive participating right should *not* be based on the likelihood of whether a noncontrolling investor would exercise that right.

Factors affecting the determination based on facts and circumstances Not all noncontrolling shareholders' rights that appear to be participating rights are substantive. The following factors should be considered in determining whether certain rights enable noncontrolling shareholders to effectively participate in significant decisions made in an investee's ordinary course of business:

- *The significance of the majority owner's interest in the investee* The greater the difference between the noncontrolling Interest' and majority's ownership interest in the investee, the more likely that noncontrolling shareholders' rights are protective rights. The greater the noncontrolling shareholders' interest in the investee, the greater the skepticism about the majority owner's ability to control the investee.

- *Whether corporate decisions are made by the shareholders or the board of directors, and the rights of each level* For matters decided by a shareholders' vote, it is necessary to determine whether the ability to vote gives a shareholder participating rights.

- *Related-party relationships, as defined in ASC 850-10 (FAS-57, Related Party Disclosures), between the majority and noncontrolling shareholders* For example, if noncontrolling shareholders are members of the majority shareholder's immediate family, it is likely that noncontrolling shareholders' rights would *not* overcome the presumption that a majority investor should consolidate an investee.

- *The significance of operating or capital decisions affected by noncontrolling shareholders' rights* The presumption that a majority investor should consolidate an investee would not be overcome by noncontrolling shareholders' rights related to operating or capital decisions that are not significant in the investee's ordinary course of business because they are not considered to be substantive participating rights.

- *The chance that significant decisions covered by noncontrolling shareholders' participating rights will occur* If there is only a remote possibility that the noncontrolling shareholders' approval will be required in making certain decisions in the ordinary course of business, the presumption that the majority owner should consolidate the investee is not overcome.

- *The feasibility that the majority owner will exercise a contractual right to acquire the noncontrolling shareholders' interest in the investee at fair value or less* If the majority investor's acquisition of the noncontrolling shareholders' interest in the investee is prudent, feasible, and within the majority owner's control, it demonstrates that the 's participating right is not substantive. However, that would not be true if the noncontrolling shareholders' control critical technology or is the entity's principal source of funding. The Task Force believes that a majority owners' call option on the noncontrolling shareholders' interest overrides the noncontrolling shareholders' rights to veto the majority shareholders' actions, but does not result in an additional ownership interest for the majority shareholders.

Additional guidance The Task Force has provided the following guidance in addition to the factors previously stated to assist in evaluating whether noncontrolling shareholders' rights, individually or in combination, should be considered protective rights or substantive participating rights, which enable noncontrolling shareholders to be involved in significant decisions expected to be made in the ordinary course of business.

- A noncontrolling investor's right to approve acquisitions or dispositions of assets that are (1) 20% or less of the fair value of the investee's total assets and (2) in the same line of business as the investee's existing business may be a substantive participating right. The presumption that a majority investor should consolidate an investee would not be overcome by rights that affect acquisitions that are unrelated to an investee's existing business, which usually are protective rights. A right requiring the noncontrolling interest's approval to incur additional indebtedness to finance an acquisition not in the ordinary course of business (that is, an acquisition of more than 20% of the fair value of the investee's total assets or one that is not in the same line as the investee's existing business) would be considered a protective right.
- The right to approve the incurrence of additional debt should be evaluated based on existing facts and circumstances. If it is reasonably possible or probable that the noncontrolling interest's approval will be required to incur debt in the ordinary course of business, the right would be considered a substantive participating right.
- Rights to dividends or other distributions may be protective or participating and should be evaluated based on the facts and circumstances. Rights to block normal or expected dividend distributions may be substantive participating rights, whereas rights to block extraordinary dividends or distributions would be protective.
- Rights related to a specific action, such as leasing property, may be participating or protective and should be evaluated based on the specific facts and circumstances. If the investee could purchase instead of lease property without the noncontrolling interest's approval, the right to block a lease is not substantive.
- Rights related to negotiations of collective-bargaining agreements with unions may be participating or protective and should be evaluated based on the specific facts and circumstances. The right to approve or veto a new or broader collective bargaining agreement is not substantive if the investee has no collective-bargaining agreement or the union does not represent a substantial number of the investee's employees.
- Determining whether a noncontrolling interest right to block an action is substantive requires consideration of provisions in the shareholder agreement that state what should be done if a

noncontrolling investor has exercised its right. For example, a noncontrolling investor's right to block approval of an operating budget is not substantive and does not permit a noncontrolling investor to effectively participate if the agreement provides that the budget defaults to the previous year's budget adjusted by inflation and the investee is a mature company whose operating budgets do not vary significantly from one year to the next.

- Noncontrolling shareholders' rights related to the initiation or resolution of a lawsuit may be participating or protective and should be evaluated based on the specific facts and circumstances. Such rights would be substantive participating rights if participating in law-suits is commonly a part of the entity's ordinary course of business, as it is for some insurance companies.

- If a noncontrolling investor has the right to block an investee's operating budget for a specified number of years, that right may be a substantive participating right during that specified time period, based on the facts and circumstances. However, if the noncontrolling investor's ability to exercise its right changes after that time period, for example, the right terminates, that right is no longer a substantive participating right from that date forward and the presumption that the majority investor should consolidate the investee can no longer be overcome.

DISCUSSION

The Task Force's consensus is based on the view that only noncontrolling investors' rights that affect the majority owner's ability to control the investee's ongoing operations and assets "in the ordinary course of business" can overcome the presumption that an investee should be consolidated in accordance with ASC 840-10-45-4 (FAS-94). The Task Force agreed on specific guidelines to determine whether those so-called participating rights are substantive, that is, the noncontrolling investors' rights are effective in making important management decisions that affect the operations of the business. The cut made is between the noncontrolling investors' ability to participate in managing the entity by blocking an important transaction instead of merely protecting its investment in the entity.

EITF Issue 97-2 (Application of FASB Statement No. 94 and APB Opinion No. 16 to Physician Practice Management Entities and Certain Other Entities with Contractual Management Arrangements) (810-10-05-15 through 05-16, 15-19 through 15-22; 25-61 through 25-64, 25-66 through 25-72, 25-74 through 25-79, 25-81; 55-90 through 55-92; ASC 718-10-55-85A)

> **OBSERVATION:** As a result of the FASB's issuance of the guidance in ASC 810-10-05-8 through 05, 15-12 through 15-17, 25-37 through 25-44, 30-1 through 30-4, 30-7 through 30-9, 35-3

through 35-5, 45-25, 50-2AA through 50-7, 50-9 through 50-10, 55-16 through 55-49, 55-93 through 55-181, 55-183 through 55-205, 60-13; ASC 323-10-45-4; ASC 712-10-60-2; ASC 715-10-60-3, 60-7; ASC 860-10-60-2; ASC 954-810-15-3, 45-2; ASC 958-810-15-4 (FIN-46(R), Consolidation of Variable Interest Entities), the consensus positions in this Issue apply only to physician practices that are *not* variable interest entities.

OVERVIEW

Current changes in the delivery of medical services, such as the proliferation of health management organizations (HMOs) and preferred provider organizations (PPOs), have caused an increasing number of physician practices to enter into contractual arrangements, under which a physician practice management entity (PPM) acquires and manages the physician practice (medical entity) and may enter into employment and noncompete agreements with the physicians who become its employees. Because a PPM may be precluded from acquiring the physician practice's equity instruments for legal or business reasons (some states restrict ownership of medical practices to physicians), the PPM may acquire some or all of the physician practice's net assets, assume all of its contractual rights and responsibilities, and enter into a long-term management agreement with the physician owners to operate the physician practice in exchange for consideration. To reduce its exposure to malpractice suits, the PPM may acquire the physician practice's shares and transfer them to a physician shareholder of the PPM who has incorporated a nominally capitalized new medical practice and acts as a nominee shareholder of the PPM. The PPM can change the nominee at any time. The following are examples of such arrangements:

    Company A—Existing physician practice

    Company B—New physician practice
    Company C—PPM

    Company D—The PPM's subsidiary

    Dr. Friendly—A physician who acts as nominee shareholder of Company C

- Physicians who are the shareholders of Company A exchange their shares in Company A for shares of Company C and also enter into a long-term management agreement with Company C. Because state law does not permit a non-physician-owned practice to enter into contractual arrangements between physicians and hospitals and between physicians and HMOs, the physicians form Company B concurrently with the merger and transfer their patient contracts to it. The physicians thus become the owners and employees of Company B under an employment contract with Company B.

- Company C creates a wholly owned subsidiary, Company D, which acquires all of Company A's net assets in exchange for some of its shares of voting common stock. At the same time, Company A enters into a long-term management agreement with Company D. The physicians who continue as the owners of Company A enter into new employment agreements with Company D.

- Company C issues shares to the shareholders of Company A, which simultaneously delivers the shares in Company A to Dr. Friendly and enters into a management agreement with Company C. The management agreement gives the rights to the residual interest in Company A to Company C, although the shares held by Dr. Friendly have only a nominal value. The physicians enter into employment agreements with the existing physician practice, which is now owned by Dr. Friendly.

This issue was raised for the following reasons:

1. Although APB-16 (Business Combinations) provides guidance on the accounting for combinations of business entities or their net assets, it does not address whether an ownership interest in an entity can be acquired by acquiring the target's tangible assets and entering into a long-term service agreement with the target, rather than by ownership of its outstanding equity instruments.

2. Under the guidance in ASC 840-10-45-4 and ASC 810-10-60-4 (FAS-94), entities are required to consolidate in their financial statements the financial statements of other entities in which they have a controlling financial interest as evidenced by a majority voting interest. That guidance states, however, that the majority owner may not always control the entity. In addition, the phrase *controlling financial interest* is not defined under that guidance, which also does not address the question of when a contract provides an entity with a controlling financial interest.

ACCOUNTING ISSUES

1. Can a PPM obtain a controlling financial interest (as discussed in ASC 840-10-45-4 and ASC 810-10-60-4 (FAS-94)) in a physician practice through a contractual management agreement without owning a majority of the physician practice's outstanding voting equity instruments?

2. Under what circumstances, if any, would a transaction in which a physician practice enters into a management agreement with a PPM be considered a business combination accounted for under the guidance in ASC 805 (FAS 141(R))?

3. Would the pooling-of-interests method be precluded, if the conclusion in Issue 2 above is that such transactions may qualify as business combinations, under some circumstances?

4. What common types of intangibles should be considered in a purchase price allocation under the purchase method of accounting, if the conclusion in Issue 2 above is that such transactions may qualify as business combinations, under some circumstances?
5. Should employees of a physician practice that is consolidated with a PPM be considered the PPM's employees when determining the method of accounting for the employees' stock-based compensation?

SCOPE

The EITF's consensus positions apply to contractual management relationships with the following types of entities:

- Entities in the health care industry, such as practices of medicine, dentistry, veterinary science, and chiropractic medicine, which are referred to in the Issue as physician practices.
- Entities in which the PPM does not own a majority of the outstanding equity instruments of the physician practice, because the PPM is not permitted to own the equity instruments under the law or the PPM has chosen not to own them.

The Task Force noted that if the circumstances in industries other than the health care industry are similar to those discussed in this Issue, the guidance established in this Issue applies.

SEC OBSERVER COMMENT

The SEC Observer stated that because the Task Force did not identify unique industry characteristics in connection with the guidance in this Issue, the guidance is not unique to PPMs. Therefore, the Task Force's conclusions in this Issue may apply to arrangements in other industries in which one entity has a controlling financial interest in another entity through a contractual arrangement or a nominee structure. The SEC staff will consider the guidance in this Issue when evaluating the accounting for such arrangements.

EITF CONSENSUS

Issue 1

Accounting for the Transactions

1. A controlling financial interest in a physician practice can be achieved by a PPM through a contractual management agreement, if the PPM's control over the physician practice and its financial interest in it meet the following requirements:

a. The term of the contractual arrangement between the PPM and the physician practice is as follows:
   (1) The term of the arrangement spans over the physician practice's remaining legal life or over a period of ten years or longer.
   (2) The physician practice cannot terminate the agreement, except if the PPM commits gross negligence, fraud, other illegal acts, or declares bankruptcy.
b. The PPM's control is evidenced by its exclusive authority over the following:
   (1) The physician practice's ongoing, major, or central operations, including the scope of services, patient acceptance policies and procedures, pricing, negotiation and execution of contracts, approval of operating and capital budgets, and issuance of debt in cases in which the physician practice uses debt financing as an ongoing, major, or primary source of financing. Control over dispensing medical services is excluded.
   (2) Decisions related to total compensation of the practice's licensed medical professionals and to establishing and implementing guidelines for selecting, hiring, and firing those employees.
c. The PPM's financial interest in the physician practice must be significant and must meet the following requirements:
   (1) The PPM has the unilateral ability to sell or transfer its financial interest.
   (2) The PPM has the right to receive income from ongoing fees and the sale of its interest in the physician practice, based on the practice's operating performance and the change in its fair value.

Effective date The guidance in this Issue applies as of November 20, 1997, to all *new* transactions and to *modifications* of existing arrangements that occur after that date.

Transition

A. Change in Consolidation Status

PPMs that change the consolidation status of a physician practice as a result of adoption of the consensus in this Issue should calculate the effect of initial adoption using the terms of the agreement that were effective in periods before the consensus was adopted. Although either of the following two transition methods may be used to report the effect of a change, the method selected should be applied to *all* arrangements:

1. *The cumulative effect method* A change is reported as the effect of a change in accounting principle in accordance with ASC 250-10-45-5 through 10 (paragraphs 7-10 of FAS-154 ,Accounting Changes and Error Corrections)

    The consensus is applied retroactively resulting in the restatement of prior periods' financial statements. Items in prior financial statements that would have been accounted for differently had the consensus on consolidation in this Issue been applied when the transaction was consummated should be *adjusted*.

2. When a PPM applies the transition method discussed above:

    a. The PPM should change the accounting for the transaction that consummated the arrangement between the PPM and the physician practice.

    b. The PPM is *not* required to change the accounting for existing stock-based compensation transactions with the physician practice's employees if the designation of employee or nonemployee would differ under the consensus.

B. No Change in Consolidation Status

1. *Transactions that include a nominee shareholder* PPMs should apply the following guidance to transactions that were consummated before November 21, 1997, using the pooling-of-interests method:

    a. The *consummation* transaction need *not* be adjusted if after November 20, 1997, but before adoption of the guidance in this Issue (*a*) the PPM's existing arrangement with the physician practice was *not modified* or (*b*) the arrangement was modified for *no consideration* or for a nominal amount.

    b. The *consummation* transaction should be *restated* as a purchase business combination if after November 20, 1997, but before adopting the guidance in this Issue, the PPM modified its existing arrangement with a physician practice for *more than a nominal* amount of consideration.

2. *Transactions without a nominee shareholder* Transactions that were consummated before November 21, 1997, using the pooling-of-interests method should be restated as purchase business combinations.

C. Modifications with Consideration

If a PPM gives the physician practice consideration to modify their arrangement, the PPM should account for that transaction in the financial period in which the modification occurs, not in an earlier period, based on the appropriate GAAP accounting for the consideration given. That treatment is required regardless of whether the physician practice's consolidation status has changed as a result of adopting the consensus in this Issue.

Issue 2

> **OBSERVATION:** The EITF's consensus in this Issue has been nullified by the guidance in ASC 805 (FAS-141(R)) under which a business combination is defined as "a transaction or other event in which an acquirer obtains control of one or more businesses." The Statement clarifies that an acquirer might obtain control of an acquiree solely as a result of a contract.

Issue 3

The consensus reached on this Issue was nullified by FAS-141 (Business Combinations). That Statement has been replaced by FAS-141(R), under which the pooling-of-interests method continues to be prohibited.

Issue 4

The EITF did not discuss this Issue. However, FAS-141(R) provides guidance regarding the application of the acquisition method to business combinations accomplished solely by contract.

Issue 5

The EITF noted that regardless of whether or not a physician practice's consolidation status changes, the PPM is *not* required to change the accounting for existing stock-based compensation arrangements with the physician practice's employees and modifications of such arrangements that occurred before November 21, 1997, even if the designation as employee or nonemployee would differ under the consensus. The effective date is discussed in Issue 2.

> **OBSERVATION:** FIN-44 (Accounting for Certain Transactions Involving Stock Compensation) (not in ASC) affirmed the EITF's view on this Issue and clarifies the application of APB-25 (Accounting for Stock Issued to Employees).

APPLICATION GUIDANCE

The application guidance that follows applies to Issue 1.

General The management agreement between the PPM and the physician practice should be reviewed to determine whether it documents the existence of a controlling financial interest. If such documentation is available, it also should be reviewed to determine whether the requirements in the consensus are met, regardless of whether the parties are acting in accordance with the document's provisions. If the existence of a controlling interest is not documented in the agreement, the relevant facts and circumstances (such as the legal rights and obligations of each party and the reasons for undocumented arrangements) should be evaluated to determine whether the requirements of the consensus are met. For example, a controlling financial interest may be undocumented, because the shareholders of the physician practice have not transferred ownership of their outstanding equity interests to the PPM or its nominee. Documentation also may be unavailable in cases in which the PPM and the nominee own the shares collectively, because documentation may not seem necessary when there are no third-party physician practice owners.

Term of the arrangement The term of the management agreement should be evaluated based on its substance, rather than on its form, by considering the original stated contract term and renewal or cancellation provisions. For example, the term of an arrangement that specifies an initial five-year term and that provides for a renewal option that can be exercised unilaterally by the PPM meets the requirements of the consensus, because the initial term and renewal span over a total of ten years.

The adequacy of the term generally should be based on the facts and circumstances of the specific arrangement. The requirement that the term of an arrangement be for at least ten years is intended to imply that the arrangement has an unlimited life. However, the Task Force did not intend for this requirement to apply to all consolidations. Specifically, in other situations involving consolidation, a ten-year term is not necessarily required for a relationship to be considered "other than temporary."

Control

1. *Nominee shareholder situations*
    a. *More than 50% ownership.* There is a rebuttable presumption that the physician practice is under the PPM's control, if the PPM's nominee shareholder or the PPM and the nominee shareholder *together* own a *majority* of the physician practice's outstanding voting equity instruments. That presumption may be rebutted, however, if the PPM does *not* have *exclusive authority* over the decisions discussed in the consensus under Issue 1(*b*) above, because others, such as other physician practice shareholders and physicians employed by the physician

practice, were granted decision-making rights by either (*a*) the PPM under the management agreement or through the nominee, or (*b*) by the physician practice under its corporate governance provisions. The presumption cannot be rebutted if the PPM's exclusive decision-making authority is pursuant to the management agreement, the corporate governance provisions, or obtained through its nominee.

    b. *Less than 50% ownership.* There is no presumption of control if the PPM's nominee shareholder or the PPM and the nominee together own less than a majority of the physician practice's outstanding voting equity instruments. The PPM must demonstrate that it meets the criteria of the consensus in Issue 1(b) above as a result of the combination of its rights under the management agreement, the power of its nominee shareholder, and the physician practice's provisions for corporate governance.

2. *Provisions for binding arbitration* The existence of a provision requiring binding arbitration to settle disagreements between the PPM and the physician practice without overriding the PPM's exclusive decision-making authority, such as disputes about the meaning of contract terms, does not necessarily indicate that the arrangement does not meet the criteria of the consensus in Issue 1(b) above. In contrast, those criteria are not met if binding arbitration can affect the PPM's exclusive decision-making authority.

3. *Powers limited by law* The PPM's exclusive decision-making authority over a matter is not precluded under the consensus, if federal, state, or corresponding non-U.S. laws limit the powers or discretion of any party over a particular decision. For example, a PPM's ability to control patient acceptance policies and procedures within the law is unaffected by "antidumping" statutes that prohibit physicians from refusing to treat certain types of patients.

4. *Scope of service decisions* The PPM is considered to have exclusive decision-making authority over the scope of the physician practice's services, if the PPM and the physician practice agree on the practice's range of medical disciplines, such as cardiology, neurology, or obstetrics, in the initial negotiations of the management agreement. If the PPM does not have exclusive decision-making authority over the initial and ongoing decisions about the practice's scope of services, the PPM does not control the physician practice. Scope-of-service decisions include those about the range of services to be provided within the selected disciplines.

5. *Physician cosigning provisions*

    a. *Perfunctory provisions.* A perfunctory provision requiring the physicians to sign contracts with the practice's customers, in

addition to the PPM's execution of the contracts, does not affect the PPM's exclusive decision-making authority over the execution of customer contracts. The physician's signature is considered to be perfunctory, if the obligations under the contract are no greater than if only the PPM had signed the contract and if either of the following conditions is met:
   (1) The physician is required to sign the contract under state law, or the payor on the contract requested the physician's signature.
   (2) The management agreement or the physician's employment contract provides that the physician's approval is not needed to execute contracts negotiated by the PPM.
  b. *Nonperfunctory provisions.* The physician's signature is not considered to be perfunctory and the control criteria in Issue 1(b) are not met if any one of the following exists:
   (1) The PPM gave signatory authority to the physicians (other than the PPM's nominee).
   (2) The physicians' signature results in obligations in addition to those that would be incurred if only the PPM had signed the contract.
   (3) The physicians can decide which customer contracts the PPM will execute (e.g., whether the physicians alone or together with the PPM decide the terms of an acceptable contract).

Financial interest Although the consensus deliberately does not define a *significant financial interest*, which must be determined based on the facts and circumstances of the particular situation, the Task Force provides the following guidance:

1. *Nominee shareholder situations*
   a. *Presumption of financial interest.* Without citing its current compliance with the consensus in Issue 1(c) above, there is a presumption that the PPM has a significant financial interest in the physician practice, if
   (1) The PPM's nominee shareholder or the PPM together with its nominee own a majority of the outstanding equity instruments of the physician practice, and
   (2) Based on the PPM's and the nominee's rights and their obligations to others, such as other shareholders of the physician practice and the practice's employees, the PPM or its nominee can change the terms of the PPM's financial interest in the physician practice at its own discretion with or without consideration.
      The presumption is rebutted only if the PPM is not permitted to change the terms of its financial interest in

the physician practice so the criteria of the consensus in Issue 1(c) above are met, which would be very unlikely.

b. *No presumption of financial interest.* There is no presumption that the PPM has a significant financial interest in the physician practice, if the nominee shareholder holds less than a majority of the physician practice's outstanding voting equity instruments. If so, the PPM would have to demonstrate that it has a significant financial interest, in accordance with the criteria of the consensus in Issue 1(c) above as a result of its rights under the management agreement and the powers of its nominee shareholder.

2. *Type and level of the PPM's participation in the practice's fair value*

The PPM's financial interest in the physician practice gives it a right to share in the change in the practice's fair value that must be economically similar to a shareholder's normal right. The change in the practice's fair value is composed of a change in its current operating results and the amount available only if the practice were to be sold or liquidated. Under the consensus in Issue 1(c)(2) above, the PPM must be able to share in both amounts, which must represent a significant portion of the change in the practice's total fair value. If the PPM's relationship with the physician practice ends before a sale or liquidation, the PPM should receive an amount equivalent to the change in fair value during the period it was associated with the physician practice. To comply with the consensus, the calculation of ongoing fees and sales proceeds should be evaluated based on their substance rather than their form. Judgment is required in determining whether the requirements of the consensus are met for specific management fee structures.

DISCUSSION

Issue 1

The consensus on Issue 1 addresses when a PPM is required to consolidate a physician practice in its financial statements as a result of a contractual management agreement between the parties, even if the PPM does not own a majority of the physician practice's equity instruments. The working group that developed the guidance cited discussions in the following authoritative pronouncements, which imply that control may be possible through a contractual arrangement without a controlling financial interest: SEC Regulation S-X, Rule No. 1-02(g); SEC Reporting Release No. 25 of SEC Regulation S-X, Rule No. 3A-02(a); APB-18, paragraph 3c; FAS-94, paragraph 10; EITF Issue 90-15; and Topic D-14.

The requirements to demonstrate that the PPM has a controlling financial interest in the physician practice were established based on the premise that the PPM must have the same type of control and financial interest under a contractual management agreement as it would if it owned the physician practice's equity instruments. That is, the PPM should be able to control all of the physician practice's operations and should be required to make major decisions, such as hiring and firing employees. However, the working group did not believe that the PPM's financial interest in the physician practice must be greater than what would be acceptable in other situations, such as partnerships, in which one party may have control without a majority ownership.

The working group believed that the requirement for consolidation under FAS-94 should also apply in this Issue when a nominee shareholder is the sole owner of the physician practice's equity interests, because the nominee shareholder is, in fact, controlled by the PPM. The working group also recommended that to avoid manipulation of the extent of the PPM's financial interest in the physician practice, there should be a presumption that the PPM has a financial interest when a nominee shareholder is involved. To avoid different requirements for the various methods of equity ownership in this Issue, the rights discussed in the application guidance section are those that would lead to a conclusion that the PPM has control regardless of whether a nominee shareholder is the sole shareholder.

The requirement for transferability of a significant financial interest in the physician practice (regardless of whether it is held by the PPM alone, by a nominee shareholder alone, or jointly with a nominee shareholder) and for the right to receive income based on the practice's operating performance and the change in its fair value was intended to address the Task Force's concerns about the PPM's ability to realize the residual value of the physician practice even if it does not own the equity interests.

The Task Force decided that to avoid further diversity in practice, the consensus on Issue 1 should apply immediately to all new transactions and to modifications of existing transactions. As in Issue 96-16, application of the consensus to existing transactions that have not been modified was delayed for one year to give entities with such arrangements additional time to implement the consensus.

Similar to the transition in Issue 96-16, this Issue permits using a cumulative effect method *or* restatement.

Issue 2

The consensus on business combinations is based on the view stated in paragraph 1 of APB-16 that a business combination has occurred when the results of the acquired entity's operations are incorporated with those of the acquiring entity and the two become one accounting entity. This would occur if a PPM has a controlling financial interest in a physician practice that is consolidated in its financial statements.

10.34 Consolidated Financial Statements

EITF Issue 97-14 (Accounting for Deferred Compensation Arrangements Where Amounts Earned Are Held in a Rabbi Trust and Invested) (ASC 810-10-15-10; ASC 260-10-60-1; ASC 710-10-05-8 through 05-9, 15-8 through 15-10, 25-15 through 25-18; 35-2 through 35-4, 45-2 through 45-4; 810-10-15-10)

> **OBSERVATION:** Under the guidance in ASC 810-10-05-8 through 05-8A, 15-12 through 15-17, 25-37 through 25-44, 30-1 through 30-4, 30-7 through 30-9, 35-3 through 35-5, 45-25, 50-2AA through 50-7, 50-9 through 50-10, 55-16 through 55-49, 55-93 through 55-181, 55-183 through 55-205, 60-13; ASC 323-10-45-4; ASC 712-10-60-2; ASC 715-10-60-3, 60-7; ASC 860-10-60-2; ASC 954-810-15-3, 45-2; ASC 958-810-15-4 (FIN-46(R)) as amended by ASC 810-30-7 through 30-9, 65-2 (FAS-167, Amendment of Interpretation 46(R)), an entity is required to consolidate a variable interest entity if the entity has a controlling interest in the variable entity. ASC 810-10-25-38 through 25-38G provides guidance for determining whether an entity has a controlling financial interest in a variable interest entity.

OVERVIEW

Some employers have set up deferred compensation arrangements under which amounts—such as bonuses earned by a select group of management or highly compensated employees—are placed in a grantor trust, which is commonly referred to as a "rabbi trust." Amounts placed in a rabbi trust are *not* tax deductible to the employer, and the employee is *not* taxed on deferred amounts until that compensation is paid. A rabbi trust qualifies for income tax purposes only if its terms state explicitly that the employer can use assets held by the trust to satisfy the claims of its creditors in bankruptcy.

Plans generally invest amounts held by a rabbi trust in the employer's securities, but some plans permit diversification into the securities of other entities either immediately or after a certain time period, such as six months. However, some plans do not permit diversification. Employers may settle their deferred compensation obligation by (*a*) selling the employer's stock or diversified assets and settling the obligation in cash, (*b*) transferring employer stock to the employee, or (*c*) transferring diversified assets to the employee.

This Issue was raised because of diversity in practice. Some companies offset the value of the shares held by the rabbi trust against the liability and do not report the liability in their financial statements, because they believe that the liability is fully funded by the shares.

This Issue does not apply to the accounting for stock appreciation rights (SARs), even if they are funded through a rabbi trust.

ACCOUNTING ISSUES

- Should an employer be required to consolidate the accounts of a rabbi trust in its financial statements?
- How should an employer report investments in a rabbi trust?
- How does an employee's election to diversify the assets held by a rabbi trust into nonemployer securities affect the accounting for the trust's assets and for the deferred compensation obligation?

EITF CONSENSUS

> **OBSERVATION:** An enterprise that has an interest in a variable interest entity and is required to absorb the majority of that entity's expected losses, or is entitled to receive most of the entity's expected residual returns, or both, is required to consolidate that entity in accordance with the guidance in FIN-46(R) (Consolidation of Variable Interest Entities), as amended by the guidance in ASC 810-10-30-7 through 30-9, 65-2 (FAS-167). The Interpretation also provides guidance on the consolidation of many types of trusts. Public entities that are not small business issuers, and that have interests in variable interest entities subject to this Interpretation should apply this Interpretation no later than the end of the first reporting period that ends after March 15, 2004 (or as of March 31, 2004, for calendar-year enterprises).

Deferred compensation invested in an employer's stock and held in a rabbi trust should be accounted for as follows:

1. The employer should consolidate the accounts of a rabbi trust in its financial statements.
2. Assets held by the trust should be accounted for as follows:
    a. Employer stock should be classified in equity and reported in the employer's consolidated financial statements at acquisition cost, without recognizing changes in fair value, similar to treasury stock. This accounting method applies whether the deferred compensation obligation is settled in cash, employer's stock, or diversified assets.
    b. Diversified assets should be accounted for in accordance with generally accepted accounting principles appropriate for the specific asset; for example, marketable equity securities should be accounted for based on the guidance in ASC 320 (FAS-115, Accounting for Certain Investments in Debt and Equity Securities).

c. If diversification is permitted and the obligation is not required to be settled in a fixed number of the employer's shares (see (d) below), the deferred compensation obligation should be recognized as a liability, which should be adjusted for changes in its fair value. Compensation cost should be adjusted by a corresponding charge or credit. Changes in the fair value of the deferred compensation obligation should *not* be recognized in comprehensive income even if changes in the fair value of the assets held by the rabbi trust and classified as available-for-sale are recognized in comprehensive income in accordance with ASC 320 (FAS-115). The Task Force noted that diversified assets held by a rabbi trust may be classified in the trading category at acquisition.

d. If diversification is prohibited and the obligation must be settled in a fixed number of the employer's shares, the deferred compensation obligation should be classified in equity and changes in the fair value of the obligation to the employee should not be recognized.

The Task Force provided the following guidance for *earnings per share* (EPS) calculations:

1. Treat employer shares held by the rabbi trust the same as treasury stock in EPS calculations and exclude the amount from the denominator in the calculation of basic and diluted EPS.
2. Include the deferred compensation obligation in the denominator of the EPS calculation in accordance with FAS-128 (Earnings per Share).
3. Include employer shares in Plan A in the basic and diluted EPS calculations, because ASC 260-10-45-13 (paragraph 10 of FAS-128) requires that treatment if an obligation must be settled by delivering the employer's shares.
4. Include employer shares only in Plans B, C, or D in the diluted EPS calculation, because paragraphs 22 and 29 of FAS-128 (ASC 260-10-45-30, 45-45 through 45-46) require that treatment if an obligation can be settled by delivery of cash, shares of employer stock, or diversified assets.

This consensus applies to all new awards after March 19, 1998, even those made in accordance with existing arrangements.

TRANSITION

1. The Task Force discussed the transition guidance as it applies to each of the following four types of deferred compensation arrangements:

a. Plan A—Diversification is *not* permitted. The employer must settle the obligation by delivering a fixed number of the employer's shares of stock.
b. Plan B—Diversification is *not* permitted. The employer must settle the obligation by delivering cash or the employer's shares of stock.
c. Plan C—Diversification is permitted, but the employee has *not* diversified. The obligation may be settled in cash, employer's shares of stock, or diversified assets.
d. Plan D—Diversification is permitted, and the employee has diversified. The obligation may be settled in cash, employer's shares of stock, or diversified assets.

2. The transition guidance described below should be applied as of September 30, 1998, to awards granted before March 19, 1998, regardless of the prior accounting for those arrangements. It is assumed that the rabbi trust purchased the shares for the exact amount of compensation deferred by the employee and the award has not been settled by September 30, 1998.

3. The Task Force noted that entities may amend the terms of existing type B or type C plans to convert them to type A plans before September 30, 1998, so that the obligation could be settled only by delivering a fixed number of the employer's shares of stock.

4. The following is the transition method for each type of plan:
   a. Plan A—Recognize the employer's stock held by the rabbi trust and the related deferred compensation obligation in equity at the original amount of the deferred compensation.
   b. Plans B or C should be reported as follows:
      (1) Recognize the employer's stock held by the rabbi trust in equity, similar to treasury stock, at its original acquisition cost.
      (2) Recognize the difference between the original cost of the shares acquired by the rabbi trust and their fair value (the transition differential) at September 30, 1998, in a contra-equity account.
      (3) Report the deferred compensation obligation as a liability at the fair value of the shares held by the rabbi trust on September 30, 1998.
      (4) During the period between the transition date and the final settlement, increases or decreases in the deferred compensation liability should be reported in income as an increase or decrease in compensation cost for the amount by which the per share price of the employer's stock exceeds its fair

value on September 30, 1998, or is less than the trust's original acquisition cost of the shares. The portion of the increase or decrease equal to the transition differential, which is the difference between the original cost of the shares acquired by the rabbi trust and their fair value at September 30, 1998, is charged or credited to the contraequity account.

   c. Plan D—Report the diversified assets held by the rabbi trust at fair value at September 30, 1998, and report a corresponding amount as the deferred compensation liability.

5. Entities can elect to adopt the consensus in this Issue as a cumulative effect of a change in accounting principle for awards granted under all the plans discussed above before March 19, 1998, and not settled as of that date. If this approach is adopted for awards under Plans B and C, it would be unnecessary to calculate amounts not previously recognized in income.

DISCUSSION

- The Task Force reached a consensus to consolidate the rabbi trust, because it is not bankruptcy proof so the company can use the trust's assets to settle the claims of general creditors in bankruptcy. It was also noted that consolidation of rabbi trusts is common practice and that consolidation is consistent with the treatment implied in the discussion in ASC 715-60-55-26; ASC 710-10-60-2 (Issue 93-3,Plan Assets under FASB Statement 106).
- Task Force members who supported the consensus argued that a consolidated entity holding the parent's stock must treat it as treasury stock in consolidation and subtract it from equity.
- The Task Force decided to classify the deferred compensation obligation for awards that do not permit diversification and must be settled in the employer's shares as equity instruments, because that treatment conforms to the framework established in Issue 96-13. Subsequent changes in the fair value of the employer's stock are not recognized for the same reason.
- The Task Force's decision to recognize changes in the fair value of the deferred compensation obligation in income by adjusting compensation expense even if the diversified assets are recognized as available-for-sale securities is based on the view of the FASB staff that the award is a stock-based compensation award and that authoritative literature, such as ASC 840-40-25-4 through 25-5, 35-4, 55-79 through 55-80, 55-82 through 55-84, 55-86 through 55-88, 55-90 through 55-92, and 55-94 (FIN-28), requires that changes in the value of such awards subsequent to the employee's service period be recognized in income as an adjustment of compensation expense.

- In its discussion of the transition, the SEC Observer stated that a cumulative catch-up would be the appropriate method for Plans B and C. However, the Task Force argued that because this consensus establishes a new accounting method to correct diversity in practice and is not a correction of an error, it should be applied prospectively by giving companies an opportunity to change their plans to Plan A type of arrangements or to apply the consensus prospectively by a specific date (September 30, 1998) at the fair value of the obligation on that date. Under the method adopted for such plans, if the fair value of the obligation (based on the fair value of the assets in the trust) after initial application of the consensus changes up to the difference between the value of the obligation at the inception of the plan and its fair value at the transition date (the transition differential), there is no effect on income. However, income is affected if the amount of a change exceeds the transition differential, because any excess is charged or credited to compensation expense.

Illustration of the Consensus on the Accounting for Deferred Compensation Held in a Rabbi Trust

CIG Corp. has a plan under which cash bonuses paid to highly compensated employees are deferred to a future date. The company uses the cash bonus to acquire shares of the employer's stock for an equivalent amount. The shares are held in a rabbi trust, which in accordance with IRS rules is not bankruptcy proof. Consequently, the bonus is not taxable to the employee until it has been received, but it is included in the employer's tax return.

The plan permits the employee to diversify into other securities, but the employee has *not* diversified. At the end of the deferral period, the employee will receive an amount equivalent to the fair value of the deferred compensation liability either in cash or in the employer's shares. This Illustration applies to a type C plan:

12/31/X4   CIG's CEO is due a bonus of $6 million. The company accrues a liability and recognizes compensation expense for that amount.

1/6/X5   The company purchases 50,000 shares of CIG stock at a market price of $120 per share and holds them in a rabbi trust. CIG does not recognize the liability or the shares in its financial statements believing that the amounts can be offset because the liability is fully funded by the shares.

9/30/X5   The market price of CIG's shares is $100 per share so the fair value of the total obligation is $5 million. CIG makes the following journal entry to apply the consensus on that date:

Contraequity (shares held by rabbi trust)	6,000,000	
Deferred compensation liability		5,000,000
Contraequity (depreciation of shares held by rabbi trust at transition—transition differential)		1,000,000

(To record the deferred compensation liability and the employer's shares held in a rabbi trust at their fair value at the transition date)

10/31/X5   The market price of the company's stock decreases to $90 per share (total fair value is $4.5 million).

Deferred compensation liability	500,000	
Compensation expense		500,000

(To record a change in the deferred compensation liability)

12/31/X5   The market price of the company's stock increases to $125 per share (total fair value of $6.25 million).

Contraequity	1,000,000	
Compensation expense	750,000	
Deferred compensation liability		1,750,000

(To record a change in the deferred compensation liability)

EITF Issue 04-5 (Determining Whether a General Partner, or the General Partners as a Group, Controls a Limited Partnership or Similar Entity When the Limited Partners Have Certain Rights) (ASC 810-20-15-1 through 15- 3, 25-1 through 25-20; 45-1; 55-1 through 55-16)

OVERVIEW

The EITF agreed to discuss this Issue, because preparers of financial statements and auditors have been asking for guidance on how to determine whether a partnership should be consolidated in the financial statements of the partners. Practice has been to analogize to the guidance in ASC 970-323 (the AICPA's SOP 78-9, Accounting for Investments in Real Estate Ventures), which provides specific guidance on investments in real estate ventures that may include investments in corporate joint ventures, general partnerships, limited partnerships, and undivided interests. The guidance in ASC 970-323-25-8 (paragraph 7 of the SOP 78-9) provides that "a controlling investor should account for its investment under the principles of accounting applicable to investments in subsidiaries" (i.e., by consolidating the limited partnership). The guidance in ASC 970-810-25-1 through 25-2 (paragraph 9 of SOP 78-9), however, provides that the guidance in ASC 970-323-25-8 (paragraph 7 of SOP 78-9) applies only "if the substance of the partnership or other agreements provides for control by the general partners.", The presumption of the general partner's control in ASC 970-323 (SOP 78-9) may be affected by *important* rights held by the *limited* partners, such as the right to replace the general partner(s) and approve the sale, refinancing, or acquisition of the partnership's major assets.

Although there is little authoritative guidance for determining whether rights held by limited partners are important rights, the issuance of certain pronouncements has affected the consolidation of partnerships. In ASC 810-10-15-10; 25-1 through 25-8, 25-10 through 25-14; 55-1 (Issue 96-16, Investor's Accounting for an Investee When the Investor Has a Majority of the Voting Interest but the Noncontrolling Shareholder or Shareholders Have Certain Approval or Veto Rights), which specifically excluded noncorporate entities, the EITF introduced the concept of *participating rights* in its consensus requiring that the rights of *noncontrolling* shareholders be analyzed based on whether those rights enable the noncontrolling shareholders, individually or in total, to participate in significant decisions made in an entity's ordinary course of business. That is, if the noncontrolling shareholders can veto significant decisions made by an investor holding a majority voting interest, the majority investor does *not* have control.

In December 2003, the FASB issued ASC 810-10-05-8 through 05-8A, 15-12 through 15-17, 25-37 through 25-44, 30-1 through 30-4, 30-7 through 30-9, 35-3 through 35-5, 45-25, 50-2AA through 50-7, 50-9 through 50-10, 55-16 through 55-49, 55-93 through 55-181, 55-183 through 55-205, 60-13; ASC 323-10-45-4; ASC 712-10-60-2; ASC 715-10-60-3, 60-7; ASC 860-10-60-2; ASC 954-810-15-3, 45-2; ASC 958-810-15-4 (FIN-46(R), Consolidation of Variable Interest Entities), which is a revision of FIN-46, and has been amended by ASC 810-10-30-7 through 30-9, 65-2 (FAS-167). FIN 46(R), as amended by FAS-167, which applies to entities that are *not* controlled through voting interests or those in which equity investors do *not* have residual economic risks, provides guidance for a consolidation model that is based on the concept of economic risks and rewards. It does *not*, however, provide guidance for partnerships, which are considered voting interest entities, regarding what *important rights* held by the limited partners would preclude a general partner from consolidating a partnership.

ACCOUNTING ISSUE

When does a general partner, or when do the general partners as a group, control a limited partnership or a similar entity if the limited partners have certain rights?

SCOPE

The EITF agreed to limit the scope of this Issue to limited partnerships or similar entities, such as limited liability companies that function like limited partnerships as a result of their governing provisions but which are *not* variable interest entities accounted for under the guidance in ASC 810-10-05-8 through 05-8A, 15-12 through 15-17, 25-37 through 25-44, 30-1 through 30-4, 30-7 through 30-9, 35-3 through 35-5, 45-25, 50-2AA through 50-7, 50-9 through 50-10, 55-16 through 55-49, 55-93 through 55-181, 55-183 through 55-205, 60-13; ASC 323-10-45-4; ASC 712-10-60-2; ASC 715-10-60-3, 60-7; ASC 860-10-60-2; ASC 954-810-15-3, 45-2; ASC 958-810-15-4 (FIN-46(R)). The guidance in this Issue applies to general partners that are required to account for their investments in a limited partnership in accordance with the guidance in ASC 810 (ARB-51, Consolidated Financial Statements) and ASC 840-10-45-4; ASC 810-10-60-4 (FAS-94 (Consolidation of All Majority-Owned Subsidiaries)). Limited partnerships with multiple general partners should determine, based on an analysis of the relevant facts and circumstance, which general partner, if any, controls the partnership and, therefore, should consolidate the limited partnership in its financial statements.

The guidance in this Issue *does not*:

- Apply to entities required under generally accepted accounting principles (GAAP) to carry their investments in limited partnerships at fair value and to report changes in the investments' fair value in their statements of operations or financial performance.
- Affect the guidance in ASC 323-30-25-1; ASC 910-810-45-1; ASC 930-810-45-1; ASC 932-810-45-1; ASC 810-10-45-14 (Issue 00-1, Investor Balance Sheet and Income Statement Display under the Equity Method for Investments in Certain Partnerships and Other Ventures), regarding when general partners should consolidate their investments in limited partnership by the pro rata consolidation method.
- Apply if *no* individual general partner in a group of general partners controls a limited partnership.

Although this Issue does not provide guidance on which general partner in a group of general partners should consolidate an investment in a limited partnership, the EITF agreed that the concepts in this Issue may help in determining which general partner controls the partnership—for example, whether the other general partners' combined rights and those of the limited partners prevail over the conclusion that a single partner controls the limited partnership.

EITF CONSENSUS

The EITF reached a consensus that the following framework should be used by a limited partnership's general partners to determine whether they control the limited partnership.

Presumption of Control

The presumption is that a limited partnership's general partners control a limited partnership regardless of their ownership interests in the partnership. To address comments regarding the relevance of a financial statement presentation in which a general partner consolidates a limited partnership in its financial statements even though its interest in that partnership is insignificant, the EITF referred to the existence of alternative financial statement presentations and disclosures, such as consolidating financial statements or separating classification of the limited partnership's assets and liabilities on the face of the balance sheet.

A decision whether the limited partners' rights should prevail over the presumption of the general partners' control should be based on the facts and circumstances of the particular situation.

- However, the general partners do *not* control a limited partnership if the limited partners have *either* of the following rights, which are referred to as kick-out rights:
- A substantive right to liquidate the limited partnership or to remove the general partners without cause, referred to as *kick-out rights*, or
- Substantive participating rights.

Substantive kick-out rights The relevant facts and circumstances must be considered to determine whether kick-out rights are substantive. Kick-out rights with *both* of the following characteristics are considered to be substantive:

- A single partner, a simple majority, or a lower percentage, of the *limited partner* voting interests held by parties *other than* the general partners, entities under common control with the general partners, and other parties acting on behalf of the general partners can exercise those rights. The following are examples of a simple majority that would qualify for a substantive kick-out right:
  — Two out of three limited partners with equal voting interests and no relationship to the general partners vote for the removal of a general partner under a limited partnership agreement that requires a vote of any individual limited partner or a vote of two of the limited partners for the removal of a general partner.
  — Two limited partners who hold equal voting interests in a limited partnership vote to remove a general partner under a limited partnership agreement that requires a vote of both limited partners or the vote of an individual limited partner.
  — A vote of 101 out of 200 limited partners with equal voting interests and no relationship to the general partners vote for the removal of a general partner under a limited partnership agreement that requires a vote of less than 102 of the limited partners for the removal of a general partner.
  The EITF noted that a kick-out right could be considered to be substantive even if a limited partnership agreement requires *more* than a simple majority (supermajority) of the voting interests of the limited partners' to exercise its

kick-out right. That would be the case if a simple majority of the limited partners' voting interests would result in a vote for the removal of the general partner(s) under every combination of those voting interests. For example, a vote for the removal of a general partner by any two out of three limited partners with *equal* voting interests under an agreement that requires a vote of 66.6% of the voting interests to exercise the limited partners' kick-out rights would represent a simple majority that meets the requirements for a substantive kick-out right. In the following example there are three limited partners with the following voting interests: Limited Partner A has a 30% voting interest and Limited Partners B and C each have a 35% voting interest. A vote of at least 66.6% of the voting interests of the limited partners is required to overcome the presumption that the general partners control the limited partnership. A combination of the votes of limited partners B and C would be a simple majority of 70% of the voting interests that would meet the 66.6% threshold. Although, a combination of the votes of limited partner A and limited partner B *or* limited partner C also would be a simple majority of the partners' voting interests, their total voting interests of 65% would *not* meet the agreement's required 66.6% threshold to remove a general partner. Therefore, the limited partners' kick-out rights in this example would *not* be considered to be substantive, because the votes of the limited partners in *all* combinations did *not* meet the required percentage to remove a general partner.

— All of the facts and circumstances should be considered in determining whether other parties, including but not limited to parties defined as related parties in ASC 850-10-05-2 through 05-5, 10-1, 15- 3 through 15-4, 50-1, 50-3 through 50-6; ASC 958-810-60-2, 60-8; ASC 958-20-50-1 (FAS-57, Related Party Disclosures) may be acting on behalf of the general partners when exercising their voting rights as limited partners. Those considerations also apply in determining whether a single limited partner has the ability to remove a general partner.

- There are no significant barriers to prevent limited partners with kick-out rights to exercise those rights if they choose to do so. The following are examples of such barriers:

  — Conditions making it unlikely that kick-out rights will be exercised, such as a limit on the time during which they can be exercised.

  — Disincentives to dissolution of the partnership or removal of the general partner in the form of financial penalties or operational barriers.

— Inability to replace general partners because of a lack of qualified candidates or inadequate compensation to attract candidates.

— No provision in the limited partnership agreement or the applicable laws or regulations for an explicit and reasonable means by which the limited partners can call for and conduct a vote to exercise their kick-out rights.

— Inability of the limited partners holding kick-out rights to obtain the necessary information to exercise those rights.

A limited partner's right to withdraw from a limited partnership is *not* a kick-out right. Therefore, the presumption that the general partners control a limited partnership would prevail if the limited partners have a unilateral right to withdraw from a partnership *without* dissolving or liquidating the entire limited partnership. To be considered a potential kick-out right, however, the requirement to dissolve or liquidate a limited partnership if a limited partner(s) withdraws need not be contractual.

Each general partner should account for its investment in a limited partnership by the equity method if the presumption that the general partners' control of the limited partnership has been overcome, because the limited partners' kick out rights are substantive based on the previous discussion.

Substantive participating rights Limited partners that have substantive participating rights can participate in significant decisions made in the ordinary course of conducting a limited partnership's business operations. That is, the limited partners participate in making certain of the limited partnership's financial and operating decisions. Participating rights providing the limited partners with the right to block or approve decisions made by the general partners are considered to be substantive. Although the general partners are unable to act without the limited partners' agreement, the lim-ited partners' participation does *not* require the ability to initiate an action.

Participating rights granted to limited partners by contract or by law which enable limited partners to participate in the following activities—which are illustrative and not all-inclusive—should be considered to be substantive and would overcome the presumption that the general partners control the limited partnership:

- Selecting, terminating, and setting the compensation of management responsible for implementing the limited partnership's policies and procedures.
- Establishing the limited partnership's operating and capital decisions, including budgets, in the ordinary course of business.

The EITF believes that those are substantive participating rights, because they allow the limited partners to actively participate in decisions made in a limited partnership's ordinary course of business and are significant in directing and carrying out a limited partnership's activities. Individual rights should be evaluated based on the facts and circumstances to determine whether they are substantive participating rights independent of other rights. Rights that appear to be participating rights but are *not* deemed to be substantive by themselves *do not* overcome the presumption that the general partners control a limited partnership. The probability that a limited partner will use the power to veto the general partners' decisions should *not* be considered in evaluating whether the limited partner's participation right is substantive.

The following factors should be considered to determine whether participating rights are substantive rights providing limited partners with the ability to participate in significant decisions in a limited partnership's ordinary course of business:

- The level at which decisions affecting the limited partnership are made under the agreement, i.e., whether decisions are made by the general partners or the limited partnership as a whole and whether the limited partners have substantive participation rights individually or as a whole as a result of their ability to vote on matters presented for a vote of the limited partnership. Whether matters that can be voted on by the limited partners or the partnership as a whole are substantive should be based on the relevant facts and circumstances.
- Consideration of relationships between the general partners and limited partners that have the characteristics of related party transactions under the guidance in ASC 850-10-05-2 through 05-5, 10-1, 15- 3 through 15-4, 50-1, 50-3 through 50-6; ASC 958-810-60-2, 60-8; ASC 958-20-50-1 (FAS-57). In determining whether the limited partners' participating rights are substantive, for example, if a limited partner is a member of a general partner's family, the presumption of the general partner's control probably would *not* be overcome.
- Whether rights to vote on operating or capital decisions *not* significant to the ordinary course of a limited partnership's business are substantive participating rights. The EITF agreed that such rights are *not* substantive participating rights and would *not* overcome the presumption of the general partners' control. Examples include the ability to vote on the location of a limited partnership's headquarters or the selection of its auditors.
- The likelihood that the limited partners will ever exercise their right to participate in certain significant decisions expected to be made in certain business activities in the ordinary course of business. The presumption that the general partners control a limited partnership would *not* be overcome if that likelihood is remote.
- The feasibility of the general partners' contractual right to buy out the limited partners in the limited partnership for fair value or less. If the general partners' buyout would be prudent, feasible, and substantially within the general partners' control, that

buyout right indicates that the limited partners' participating right is *not* substantive. For the purpose of this Issue, the existence of such call options cancels the limited partners' participating rights required to approve or veto the general partners' actions to create an additional ownership interest for the general partners. It would *not* be prudent, feasible, and substantially within the general partners' control to buy out the limited partners, however, if the limited partners control important technology needed by the limited partnership or if the limited partnership depends on the limited partners for funding.

Each general partner should account for its investment in a limited partnership by the equity method if the presumption that the general partners' control of the limited partnership has been overcome, because the limited partners' participation rights are substantive based on the previous discussion.

Protective rights The EITF believes that the limited partners' ability to block the following actions, among others, would be considered protective rights often provided to limited partners that would *not* overcome the presumption that the general partners control a limited partnership:

- Amendments to the limited partnership agreement.
- Pricing on transactions between the general partners and the limited partnership and related self-dealing transactions.
- The limited partnership's liquidation initiated by the general partners or a decision to put the limited partnership into bankruptcy or receivership.
- Acquisitions and dispositions of assets not in the ordinary course of business.
- Issuance or repurchase of limited partnership interests.

Initial and Continuing Assessment of Limited Partners' Rights

Limited partners' rights and their effect on the presumption that the general partners control a limited partnership should be evaluated when an investor first becomes a general partner and reassessed at each following reporting period for which a general partner prepares financial statements.

TRANSITION

The guidance in this Issue is effective:

- After June 29, 2005, for
  — General partners of all *new* limited partnerships formed, and
  — Limited partnerships that have *modified* their existing partnership agreements.

- No later than the beginning of the first reporting period in fiscal years beginning after December 15, 2005, for all other limited partnership by applying either Transition Method A or Transition Method B.

Transition Method A

Existing limited partnerships that have *not* modified their existing partnership agreements should apply the guidance in this Issue in financial statements issued for the first reporting period in fiscal years that begin after December 15, 2005, but earlier application is encouraged. Therefore, public companies with December 31 fiscal year ends should apply the guidance in this Issue no later than the beginning of the first quarter of 2006, based agreements in effect at adoption. Companies with December 31 year ends that do *not* issue interim financial statement should apply the guidance in the annual financial statements as of the beginning of the year ended December 31, 2006.

The effect of initial application of this guidance for existing limited partnership agreements should be presented as a cumulative-effect-type adjustment. Prior years' financial statements should be presented as previously reported. The cumulative-effect-type adjustment, if any, of adopting the guidance in this Issue on retained earnings (or other appropriate components of equity or net assets) at the beginning of the period in which the guidance is first applied should be included in the opening balance of retained earnings (or other appropriate components of equity or net assets) in the period of change. Entities deciding on early adoption of the consensus in an interim period should recognize a cumulative-effect-type adjustment, if any, in retained earnings (or other appropriate components of equity or net assets) as of the beginning of the year of adoption. Therefore, the provisions of FAS-3 (Reporting Accounting Changes in Interim Financial Statements) should continue to be applied, but the cumulative-effect-type adjustment should be recognized in beginning retained earnings (or other appropriate components of equity or net assets) for that fiscal year. The effect of adopting the new accounting principle should be disclosed in the year in which it is adopted. Pro forma effects of applying the new accounting principle on net income need *not* be disclosed.

Previously reported equity or net income generally would *not* be adjusted as a result of a change in accounting for a general partner's interest in a limited partnership from the equity method to consolidation and vice versa. However, a cumulative-effect-type adjustment might be required if as a result of a change from the equity method to consolidation losses that would *not* have been recognized under the equity method must be recognized in consolidation or vice versa in accordance with ASC 810-10-45-7 (paragraph 15 of ARB-51, Consolidated Financial Statements) and ASC 323-10-35-19 through 35-22 (paragraph 19(i) of APB-18, The Equity Method of Accounting for Investments in Common Stock). Other items that would have been accounted for differently in prior financial statements if this guidance had been applied should *not* be adjusted.

Transition Method B

The guidance in this Issue may be applied retrospectively to existing limited partnership agreements that have *not* been modified. An entity that adopts this transition method should apply the guidance in ASC 250-10-45-5 through 45-6, 45-8 (paragraphs 7, 8, and 10 of FAS-154, Accounting Changes and Error Corrections) and provide the required disclosures in ASC 250-10-50-1 (paragraph 17 of FAS-154). Entities that apply the guidance in this Issue retrospectively should apply it to all existing partnership agreements based on the facts and circumstances when each investment was made and should consider making changes in later periods. Other items that would have been accounted for differently in prior periods had the guidance in this Issue existed at that time should be adjusted in the financial statements under this transition method. Retrospective application is *not* required, however, for investments in limited partnerships if the entity is no longer a general partner of that entity at the date the guidance in this Issue is adopted.

FASB RATIFICATION

The FASB ratified the EITF's consensus positions in this Issue at its June 29, 2005, meeting.

SUBSEQUENT DEVELOPMENT

The FASB issued ASC 970-810-25-1 through 25-3 (FSP SOP 78-9-1, Interaction of AICPA Statement of Position 78-9 and EITF Issue 04-5), which amends the guidance in SOP 78-9 (Accounting for Investments in Real Estate Ventures) to make the SOP's guidance consistent with that in Issue 04-5. (See FSP SOP 78-9-1 elsewhere in this Chapter for detailed information.)

EITF Issue No. 08-8   (Accounting for an Instrument (or an Embedded Feature) with a Settlement Amount That Is Based on the Stock of an Entity's Consolidated Subsidiary) (ASC 810-10-45-17A; 815-10-65-4, 40-15-5C)

OVERVIEW

Under the guidance in ASC 815-10-15-74 (paragraph 11(a) of FAS-133, Accounting for Derivative Instruments and Hedging Activities), a contract issued or held by a reporting entity should not be considered to be a derivative financial instrument when applying the guidance in ASC 815 (FAS-133) if the contract is: (1) indexed to a reporting entity's own stock; *and* (2) classified in stockholders' equity in the entity's balance sheet. A freestanding financial instrument, such as a stock purchase warrant, should be classified as an equity instrument and *not* accounted for as a derivative if it qualifies for the scope exception in ASC 815-10-15-74 (paragraph 11(a) of FAS-133).

Currently, if a counterparty will be paid in whole or in part based on the stock of a reporting entity's consolidated subsidiary, the scope exception in ASC 815-10-15-74 (paragraph 11(a) of FAS-133) is being applied differently under GAAP to a financial instrument than to an embedded feature. The EITF provides conflicting guidance in the following issues:

- The EITF's consensus in ASC 815-10-S99-4, S30-2, S35-1 (Issue 00-6, Accounting for Freestanding Derivative Financial Instruments Indexed to, and Potentially Settled in, the Stock of a Consolidated Subsidiary) provides guidance that applies to *freestanding* financial instruments entered into by a reporting entity, provides that a subsidiary's stock is not considered to be the reporting entity's equity. As a result, derivatives indexed to, and potentially settled in, a consolidated subsidiary's stock do *not* meet the scope exception in ASC 815-10-15-74 (paragraph 11(a) of FAS-133) and must be accounted for as derivatives under that Statement.

- The EITF's consensus in Issue 99-1 (Accounting for Debt Convertible into the Stock of a Consolidated Subsidiary) (not in ASC), provides that debt convertible into a consolidated subsidiary's stock meets the scope exception in ASC 815-10-15-74 (paragraph 11(a) of FAS-133 if) an embedded conversion option is not required to be classified as a liability under other accounting literature, such as Issue 00-19 (Accounting for Derivative Financial Instruments Indexed to, and Potentially Settled in, a Company's Own Stock) (not in ASC), and, therefore, should be accounted for based on the guidance in ASC 470-20-25-2 through 25-3, 25-10 through 25-13, 05-2 through 05-6; ASC 505-10-60-3 (APB-14, Accounting for Convertible Debt and Debt Issued with Stock Purchase Warrants).

Since ASC 810-10-65-1 (FAS-160) has been finalized, questions have been raised about the accounting for financial instruments and embedded features for which a counterparty will be paid totally or partly based on a consolidated subsidiary's stock. The question is whether they should be considered to be indexed to an entity's own stock in the reporting entity's consolidated financial statements. In addition, although ASC 810-10-65-1 (FAS-160) provides that a reporting entity should present a noncontrolling interest in a subsidiary separately from the reporting entity's equity in the subsidiary in the equity section of its consolidated balance sheet, the Statement does *not* amend the accounting guidance for financial instruments that are linked to a consolidated subsidiary's stock, such as warrants to purchase a consolidated subsidiary's shares.

SCOPE

Issue 08-8 applies to freestanding financial instruments and embedded features for which a counterparty will be paid totally or partially based on a consolidated subsidiary's stock. The guidance in Issue 08-8 does *not* affect the accounting for instruments or embedded features that would not otherwise qualify for the scope exception in ASC 815-10-15-74 (paragraph 11(a) of FAS-133), such as freestanding instruments classified as liabilities or assets under the guidance in ASC 480-10-05-1 through 05-6, 10-10-1, 15-3 through 15-5, 15-7 through 15-10, 25-1 through 25-2, 25-4, through 25-15, 30-1 through 30-7, 35-3 thrugh 35-5, 45-1 through 45-4 50-1 through 50-4, 55-1 through 55-12, 55-14 through 55-28, 55-34 through 55-41, 55-64; ASC 835-10-60-13; ASC 260-10-45-70A (FAS-150, Accounting for Certain Financial Instruments with Characteristics of both Liabilities and Equity), and put and call options embedded in a noncontrolling interest that is accounted for as a financing arrangement under the guidance in ASC 810-55-53 through 55-62; ASC 460-10-60-6 (Issue 00-4, Majority Owner's Accounting for a Transaction in the Shares of a Consolidated Subsidiary and a Derivative Indexed to the Noncontrolling Interest in That Subsidiary).

EITF CONSENSUS

The EITF reached the following consensus positions:

Recognition

If a subsidiary is a *substantive* entity, a freestanding financial instrument or an embedded feature under the scope of Issue 08-8 may be considered to be indexed to an entity's own stock in the reporting entity's consolidated financial statements. An instrument or an embedded feature would *not* be considered to be indexed to an entity's own stock if the subsidiary is *not* a substantive entity.

If a subsidiary is considered to be a substantive entity, the consensus in ASC 815-40 (Issue 07-5, Determining Whether an Instrument (or an Embedded Feature) Is Indexed to an Entity's Own Stock) should be applied in determining whether a financial instrument or an embedded feature is indexed to an entity's own stock and should be considered together with other GAAP, such as the guidance in ASC 815-40 (Issue 00-19), in determining how to classify a freestanding financial instrument or an embedded feature in an entity's financial statements.

Measurement

The SEC Observer restated the existing position of the SEC staff that written options that do *not* qualify to be recognized as equity should be reported at fair value and thereafter marked to fair value through earnings.

Other presentation matters

An instrument classified as equity under the scope of Issue 08-8, including an embedded feature that is recognized separately in equity under applicable GAAP, should be presented as a component of noncontrolling interest in the consolidated financial statements, regardless of whether the instrument was entered into by a parent or a subsidiary. However, the carrying amount of an instrument classified in equity and accounted for under the scope of Issue 08-8 that was entered into by a parent and expires unexercised should be reclassified from a noncontrolling interest to a controlling interest in equity.

EFFECTIVE DATE AND TRANSITION

The guidance in Issue 08-8 should be effective for fiscal years beginning on or after December 15, 2008, and interim periods in those fiscal years, but earlier application is prohibited. The consensus positions in Issue 08-8 should be applied to instruments that are outstanding as of the fiscal year in which the guidance in Issue 08-8 is first applied. The fair value of an outstanding instrument that was previously classified as an asset or a liability should become its net carrying amount (i.e., its current fair value) at that date. The net carrying amount should be reclassified as a noncontrolling interest. However, gains or losses recognized during the period in which a financial instrument was classified as an asset or a liability should *not* be reversed. The transition disclosures in ASC 250-10-50-1 through 50-3 (paragraphs 17 and 18 of FAS-154, Accounting Changes and Error Corrections) should be presented.

FASB RATIFICATION

The FASB ratified the EITF's consensus positions at its November 24, 2008, meeting.

AMENDMENTS TO OTHER LITERATURE

Other literature is amended as follows by the guidance in Issue 08-8:

ARB 51

ASC 810-10-45-16A through 45-17 (paragraph 27 of ARB-51, Consolidated Financial Statements) is amended as follows [added text is underlined and deleted text is struck-out]:

> Only the following a financial instrument issued by a subsidiary that is classified as equity in the subsidiary's financial statements can be a noncontrolling interest in the consolidated financial statements:

a. A financial instrument (or an embedded feature) issued by a subsidiary that is classified as equity in the subsidiary's financial statements
b. A financial instrument (or an embedded feature) issued by a parent or a subsidiary for which the payoff to the counterparty is based, in whole or in part, on a stock of a consolidated subsidiary, that is considered indexed to the entity's own stock in the consolidated financial statements of the parent and that is classified as equity

Issues 99-1 and 00-6

Both issues are superseded.

Issue 00-4

The 3rd sentence in the discussion on Derivative 2 in ASC 480-10-55-55 (paragraph 15) is amended as follows (Only the affected portion of the paragraph is shown.) [Added text is underlined and deleted text is ~~struck out~~]:

> If the written put option and the purchased call option in Derivative 2 were issued as freestanding instruments, the written put option is accounted for under Statement 150 as a liability measured at fair value, and the purchased call option would be accounted for under Issue 00-19, Issue 07-5, and Issue 08-8<u>00</u> ~~6~~.

Issue 00-19

Delete the word "purchase" in the second sentence of paragraph 3. The sixth sentence in paragraph 3 is amended as follows [added text is underlined and deleted text is ~~struck out~~]:

This Issue does not address the accounting for <u>a written put option and a purchased call option embedded in the shares of a noncontrolling interest of a consolidated subsidiary</u> if the arrangement is accounted for as a financing under ~~contracts that are indexed to, and potentially settled in, the stock of a consolidated subsidiary (see discussion of Issue No. 00-6, "Accounting for Freestanding Derivative Financial instruments Indexed to, and Potentially Settled in, the Stock of a Consolidated Subsidiary,"~~ Issue No. 00-4, "Majority Owner's Accounting for a Transaction in the Shares of a consolidated Subsidiary and a Derivative Indexed to the ~~Minority~~ <u>Noncontrolling</u> Interest in that Subsidary" (See further discussion paragraph<u>s</u> 62 ~~and 63~~ of the STATUS section).

Paragraph 63 of Issue 00-19 is deleted.

ASC 944-80 Financial Services—Insurance—Separate Accounts

EITF Issue 09-8 How Investments Held through Separate Accounts Affect an Insurer's Consolidation Analysis of Those Investments (ASC 944-80-25-2 through 25-3, 25-12, ASC 944-80-65-1)

OVERVIEW

Some life insurance products (e.g., variable annuity contracts) provide an investment return and sometimes also insure mortality risk. Separate accounts, which are not separate legal entities and are similar to mutual funds, are established by insurance companies to: (1) help pass through investment return risk; and (2) protect the assets that back the separate account component of a variable interest annuity contract from the insurance company's general creditors if the insurance company were to become insolvent. Separate accounts are accounting entities controlled by an insurance company that holds 100 percent of the separate account's assets. The insurance company cannot make investment allocation decisions for contract holders, but it has certain rights (e.g., voting on behalf of the contract holders).

Some separate accounts are required to file standalone financial statements and are considered to be investment companies. Although separate accounts that hold a majority interest in a mutual fund generally do not consolidate the mutual fund in their standalone financial statements, it is unclear whether that treatment is appropriate. In addition, in view of the issuance of FASB Accounting Standards Codification™ (ASC) 810, *Consolidation* (FAS-160, *Noncontrolling Interests in Consolidated Financial Statements*,, questions have been raised about the presentation of a noncontrolling interest if an investment was consolidated. Further, there are questions as to whether an insurer should combine its general account interest with its separate account interest in an investment in determining whether it has a controlling interest in the investment.

ACCOUNTING ISSUES

1. How should an insurer account for a majority owned investment in a mutual fund if the insurer's separate account holds a majority ownership interest?

2. If the EITF concludes that an insurer should consolidate the mutual fund in issue 1, how should the consolidated mutual fund be presented in the insurer's financial statements?

3. How should an insurer account for a majority-owned investment in a mutual fund if its majority ownership is a result of a

combination of interests held by its separate and general accounts, neither of which has a majority interest in the separate account on an individual basis?

SCOPE

The guidance in this Issue applies to an insurance company that holds a majority-owned investment in a voting-interest mutual fund through a separate account that meets all of the conditions in ASC 944-80-25-2 or through the combined interests of a separate account and a general account. However, the guidance in Issue does *not* apply to an insurance company that has a majority interest in a mutual fund held through its general account.

EITF CONSENSUS

At its March 18, 2010 meeting, the EITF made the following decisions:

- Reaffirmed as a consensus its consensus-for-exposure reached at the September 2010 meeting that an insurer that holds a majority interest in a mutual fund through its separate account or through a combination of its general and separate accounts is not required to consolidate the mutual fund if the general account does *not* hold a controlling interest in the fund on its own;
- Reached a consensus to expand the scope of the consensus to apply to investment funds that are considered to be variable interest entities (VIEs) under the guidance in Accounting Standards Update (ASU) 2009-17, *Consolidation (Topic 810): Improvements to Financial Reporting by Enterprises Involved with Variable Interest Entities*, which was issued in December 2009;
- Reached a consensus that an insurance entity that holds investments for the benefit of policyholders through its separate accounts should *not* be required to consider those investments as its own when applying the guidance in ASC 810-10, except if the holder of the separate account is a related party. In that case, the insurance entity should consolidate the separate account; (ASC 944-80-25-3)
- Reached a consensus that if consolidation is required, an insurance entity should include: (1) the portion of a fund's assets that represent the contract holder's interests as separate account assets and liabilities in accordance with the guidance in ASC 944-80-25-3; and (2) the remaining fund assets, including those owned by other investors, in the entity's general account on a line-by-line basis; (ASC 944-80-25-12)
- Determined that noncontrolling assets should be classified as a liability or equity based on other guidance; (ASC 944-80-25-12) and

- Prohibited entities with arrangements that are not separate accounts from applying the guidance in Issue 09-B to other investments by analogy.

EFFECTIVE DATE AND TRANSITION METHOD

The guidance in Issue 09-B is effective for fiscal years and interim periods that begin after December 15, 2010. *Retrospective* application is required to all prior periods on adoption. Early adoption is permitted. (ASC 944-80-65-1)

FASB RATIFICATION

The FASB ratified the EITF's consensus positions at it March 31, 2010 meeting.

ASC 946 Financial Services—Investment Companies

SOP 07-1 (Clarification of the Scope of the Audit and Accounting Guide Investment Companies and Accounting by Parent Companies and Equity Method Investors for Investments in Investment Companies) (ASC 946-10-05-3;15-4 through 15-5; 55-22 through 55-23, 55-25 through 55-71, 65-1; ASC 323-55-2 through 55-5, 55-7 through 55-9; ASC 810-15-2; 55-6, 55-8 through 55-12)

DEFINITION OF AN INVESTMENT COMPANY

An investment company is defined in SOP 07-1 as follows:

- An entity whose business purpose and activity is to invest in various investments, such as the securities of other entities, commodities, securities based on indices, derivatives, real estate, and other forms of investments, for current income, capital appreciation, or both, and has exit strategies for its investments. An investment company does *not* acquire or hold investments for strategic operating purposes and does *not* get benefits from its investees that are *not* available to noninvestors that are *not* related parties to the investees. An investment company: (1) sells its capital shares to investors; (2) invests the proceeds to achieve its investment objectives; and (3) makes distributions to its investors in the form of cash or ownership interests in its investees, income earned on investments, and proceeds realized on investments that have been disposed off, less expenses incurred by the investment company; or
- An entity, including one in a foreign jurisdiction, that is registered or regulated so that it is subject to the requirements

of the 1940 Act, the Small Business Investment Company Act of 1958, or similar requirements, and is required to report its investments at fair value for regulatory or similar reporting purposes. Such entities include: (1) management investment companies; (2) unit investment trusts (UITs); (3) small business investment companies (SBICs); (4) business development companies (BDCs); (5) certain offshore funds; (6) separate accounts of insurance companies; and (7) common (collective) trust funds. To determine whether an entity is subject to reporting requirements sufficiently similar to those of the 1940 Act or the Small Business Investment Company Act of 1958, regulations related to the following should be considered: (1) registration requirements; (2) reporting and disclosure to investors; (3) the investment manager's and related entities' fiduciary duties; (4) investment diversification; (5) recordkeeping and internal controls; and (6) purchases and redemptions of shares at fair value.

The determination of whether an entity meets the definition of an investment company in SOP 07-1 should be made when the entity is formed and should be reconsidered in each reporting period.

Activities Inconsistent with the Definition of an Investment Company

The following factors should be considered in determining whether an entity meets the definition of an investment company in SOP 07-1:

Business purpose. Under the definition in SOP 07-1, an investment company's business purpose is to invest for current income, capital appreciation, or both. How an entity presents itself to other parties may provide evidence about its business purpose. The business purpose of an entity that presents itself as a private equity investor whose objective is to invest for capital appreciation is consistent with SOP 07-1's definition of an investment company. However, the business objective of an entity presenting itself as an investor for strategic operating purposes is *not* consistent with the definition. An entity's prior history of purchasing and selling investments, its offering memorandum, and other corporate partnership documents may provide information about an entity's business purpose.

An entity's activities, assets, and liabilities. To meet the definition of an investment company's business purpose, it should have *no* substantive activities other than its investment activities and *no* significant assets or liabilities other than those related to its investment activities.

Multiple substantive investments. An investment company should invest in and hold multiple substantive investments directly or through another investment company. An entity that has equity investments in other entities should organize those investees as separate legal entities, except for temporary investments as a result of foreclosure or liquidation of the original investment. However, an investment company is *not* required to hold multiple substantive investments at all times (e.g., while completing the entity's initial offering period, while identifying suitable investments, or during an entity's liquidation stage) as long as the entity plans to hold various substantive investments simultaneously.

Exit strategies. The following should exist for each investment:

- A potential exit strategy has been identified, even though a specific method has not yet been identified, such as whether an exit will occur through: (1) a sale of securities in a public market; (2) an initial public offering of equity securities; (3) a private placement of equity securities; (4) distributions to investors of ownership interests in investees; (5) sales of assets; or (6) holding a debt security to maturity.

- The expected time for exiting an investment has been determined in terms of an expected date or a range of dates. It is based on a milestone, the entity's limited life, or an entity's investment objective.

Not for strategic operating purposes. Since investment companies are prohibited from holding investments for strategic purposes, the following relationships and activities are *not* permitted:

- Acquiring, using, exchanging, or exploiting an investee's or its affiliate's technology, intangible assets, or processes;

- Significant sales or purchases of assets between the entity or its affiliates and an investee or its affiliates;

- Joint ventures between the entity or its affiliates and an investee or its affiliates;

- Other arrangements between the entity or its affiliates and an investee or its affiliates for joint development, production, marketing, or provision of products or services;

- Other transactions between the entity or its affiliates and an investee or its affiliates: (1) on terms unavailable to parties unrelated to the investee; (2) at a price not available to other market participants at that date; or (3) that correspond to a significant portion of an investee's or the entity's business activity or that of their affiliates; and

- The entity or its affiliates have disproportionate rights, exclusive rights, or rights of first refusal to purchase or acquire in other ways an investee's or its affiliate's assets, technology, products, or services, held temporarily as a result of a default related to an investment in a collateralized security. However, a right of first refusal to purchase or acquire a direct ownership interest in collateral as a result of a default related to an investment in a collateralized security is *not* inconsistent with the definition of an investment company.

Factors to Consider

When considering whether an entity meets the definition of an investment company in SOP 07-1, all of the following relevant facts and circumstances should be considered.

Number of substantive investors in an entity (pooling of funds). The fact that an entity has many investors who pool their funds in order to benefit from the entity's professional investment management provides significant evidence that the entity's business purpose is to invest for current income, capital appreciation, or both.

Level of ownership interests in investees. The entity's level of ownership interests in its investees and the significance of the investees to the total investment portfolio should be considered. It is more likely that an entity with minor levels of ownership in its investees is investing for current income, capital appreciation, or both, rather than for strategic operating purposes.

Substantial ownership by passive investors. If a substantial amount of an entity whose purpose is to invest for current income and capital appreciation is owned by passive investors rather than by principal investors who determine the entity's strategic direction or run its day-to-day operations, it is a significant indicator that the entity is investing for current income, capital appreciation, or both, rather than for strategic operating purposes.

Substantial ownership by employee benefit plans. Ownership of a substantial amount of an entity by employee benefit plans is a significant indicator that the entity is investing for current income, capital appreciation, or both, rather than for strategic operating purposes.

Involvement in the day-to-day management of investees, their affiliates, or other investment assets. An entity's involvement in investees' day-to-day management activities is an indicator that the entity is investing for strategic operating purposes and consequently would *not* meet the definition of an investment company in SOP 07-1. However, an investment company may occasionally become involved temporarily in an investee's day-to-day operations if the investee is having difficulties and the investment company steps in to maximize the value of its investment. If that involvement continues over an extended period of time, it may be an indicator that the entity made the investment for strategic operating purposes.

Provision of loans by noninvestment company affiliates of the entity to investees or their affiliates. If an affiliate of an investment company that is *not* an investment company provides a loan to an investee or its affiliate, depending on the arrangement's terms and conditions, it may be an indicator that the investment was made for strategic operating purposes. However, if *all* of the following conditions exist, such a loan may *not* be inconsistent with SOP 07-1's definition of an investment company:

- The loan's terms are at fair value.
- The loan is not required as a condition of the investment.

- The loans are not made to most of the entity's investees or their affiliates.
- Making loans is part of the usual business activity of an affiliate that is *not* an investment company.

Compensation of investee's or its affiliate's management or employees depends on the entity's or its affiliate's financial results. If the compensation of an investee's or its affiliate's management or employees depends on the entity's or its affiliate's financial results, it is an indicator that the entity has made the investment for a strategic operating purpose. Options granted to acquire stock are an example of such compensation.

Directing the integration of operations of investees or their affiliates or the establishment of business relationships between investees or their affiliates. An entity's involvement with an investee's or its affiliate's integration of operations or the establishment of business relationships between investees or their affiliates, such as the creation of joint ventures or significant purchases or sales of assets or other transactions between an investee and its affiliate, is an indicator that the investment was made for strategic operating purposes.

Although none of the factors discussed are individually determinative as to whether an entity meets SOP 07-1's definition of an investment company, some should be given more weight than others when the definition of an investment company is applied. Specifically, the indicators related to the number of an entity's investees and an entity's level of ownership interest in its investees provide more significant evidence about an entity's business purpose than the other factors discussed.

ACCOUNTING BY PARENT COMPANIES AND EQUITY METHOD INVESTORS FOR INVESTMENTS IN INVESTMENT COMPANIES.

An investment company under the scope of SOP 07-1 may be: (1) a subsidiary of another entity; or (2) an investor in an investment company that has the ability to exercise significant influence over it and accounts for its investment under the equity method of accounting.

Overview. A parent company or an equity method investor that chooses to retain investment company accounting in its financial statements may do so only if *all* of the following conditions exist:

- A subsidiary or equity method investee under the scope of the Guide meets the definition of an investment company in SOP 07-1.
- The established policies of a consolidated group of a parent company that chooses to retain investment company accounting in consolidation follows established policies that distinguish the nature and type of the investment company's investments from the nature and type of the investments made by other entities in

the consolidated group that are *not* investment companies. At a minimum, those policies should address the following:
— The degree of the investment company's and its related entities' influence over the investment company's investees.
— The extent to which the investment company's investees or their affiliates are in the same line of business as the parent company or its related parties.
— The consolidated group's level of ownership interest in the investment company. The intent of this requirement is to prevent the consolidated group from selectively making investments in the investment company subsidiary that are similar to investments held by members of the consolidated group that are *not* investment companies and that would account for those investments by the equity method, consolidation, or the cost method.
- The purpose of the parent company's or equity method investor's investments are to earn current income, capital appreciation, or both rather than for strategic operating purposes.

The parent company or equity method investor (through the investment company) is investing for current income, capital appreciation, or both, rather than for strategic operating purposes. One of the requirements to retain investment company accounting in the financial statements of a parent company or an equity investor is that a parent company or an equity method investor should hold its investments for current income, capital appreciation, or both, rather than for strategic operating purposes. That requirement is *not* met if a parent company, an equity method investor, or their related parties have benefited or intend to benefit from relationships with their investees or the investees' affiliates that are not available to entities that are *not* investors and are *not* related parties to an investee. The following relationships or conditions violate that requirement:

- Acquiring, using, exchanging, or exploiting an investee's or its affiliate's technology, intangible assets, or processes;
- Significant sales or purchases of assets between the entity or its related parties and an investee or its affiliates;
- Joint ventures between the entity or its related parties and an investee or its affiliates;
- Other arrangements between the entity or its related parties and an investee or its affiliates for joint development, production, marketing, or provision of products or services;
- Other transactions between the entity or its related parties and an investee or its affiliates: (1) on terms unavailable to parties unrelated to the investee; (2) at a price not available to other market participants at that date; or (3) that correspond to a significant portion of the business activities of an investee or its

affiliates, the parent company or equity method investor, or that of their related parties.

- An equity method investor or its related parties (not including insurance companies' separate accounts, trust funds, and other investments held by trust departments of financial institutions, and pension and profit-sharing trusts) have a *direct* investment in an investee or its affiliate enabling the investor to exercise significant influence over the investee or its affiliate.

- The parent company, equity method investor, or their related parties have disproportionate rights, exclusive rights, or rights of first refusal to purchase or acquire an investee's or its affiliate's assets, technology, products, or services in other ways.

- The parent company, equity method investor, or their related parties obtain tax benefits due to their ownership interest in the investment company and obtaining those benefits was a significant reason for making the investment.

Except for certain exceptions to be discussed below, a parent company or equity investor is considered to be holding an interest in an investee for strategic operating purposes, which results in a change in accounting, if transfers of investments, including, but not limited to, transfers made in exchange for cash or other consideration are made:

- From an investment company to its parent company, equity method investor, or to their related parties that are *not* investment companies; or

- From the parent company, equity investor, or their related parties that are *not* investment companies to the investment company.

The following transfers are the exceptions that would *not* lead to a conclusion that a parent company or equity method investor is investing for strategic operating purposes:

- Transfers in circumstances in which the investments and the effects of holding them would be reported in the same manner in the financial statements regardless of which party holds them.

- A transfer that is a pro-rata distribution of an investee's shares to an equity method investor in the investment company if: (1) the equity method investor is not able to initiate the distribution; and (2) the distribution of shares is a final liquidation of the investment company or the shares are publicly traded securities.

- Transfers that occur in rare situations between an investment company and its parent company, equity method investor, or their related parties if there have been: (1) significant changes in the facts and circumstances of the nature of the parent company's, equity method investor's, or their related parties' business activities that are unrelated to the investee or its affiliates; or (2) significant changes in the business activities of an investee or its affiliates that were *not* initiated or directed by the parent company, equity method investor, or their related parties so that retaining the investment in the investment company, parent company, equity method investor, or their related parties would lead to a conclusion that the investment company should *no* longer be accounted for under the Guide's scope.

- Immaterial and insignificant transfers in all respects, for example, in relation to: (1) a parent company's or equity investor's financial statements; (2) a parent company's or equity investor's interest in the investment company; and (3) the total investment portfolio of investment company subsidiaries and investees reported on the equity method.

Factors to Consider

The following factors should be considered in determining whether a parent company or equity method investor is investing in an investment company for strategic operating purposes:

- Involvement in the day-to-day management of investees, their affiliates, or other investment assets;
- Significant administrative or support services provided by the parent company, equity method investor, or their related parties;
- Financial guarantees or assets to serve as collateral provided by investees or their affiliates for borrowing arrangements entered into by the parent company, equity method investor, or their related parties;
- Compensation of an investee's or affiliate's management or employees depends on the parent company's, equity method investor's, or their related parties' financial results;
- Directing the integration of investees' or their affiliates' operations or the establishment of business relationships between investees or their affiliates;
- Active participation in an investee's or its affiliate's organization and formation; and
- Acquiring equity interests in an investment company in exchange for interests in investees.

GUIDANCE FOR EQUITY METHOD INVESTORS (THROUGH THE INVESTMENT COMPANY) THAT INVEST FOR CURRENT INCOME, CAPITAL APPRECIATION, OR BOTH, RATHER THAN FOR STRATEGIC OPERATING PURPOSES

Because an investment company may have a number of equity method investors, those investors should apply the guidance regarding the retention of investment company accounting in a parent company's or equity method investor's financial statements (as discussed in the September 15, 2007, *GAAP Update Service*), based on their *own* facts and circumstances without regard to the relationships and activities of other investors in the investment company that are *not* related to the equity method investor. That is, some equity method investors in an investment may apply investment company accounting when applying the equity method in their financial statements while others may not. The guidance in SOP 07-1 does *not* apply to investors that do not exercise significant influence over an investee, even though the guidance in SOP 78-9 (Accounting for Investments in Real Estate Ventures), EITF Abstracts, ASC 323-30-S55-1; S99-1 (Topic D-46, Accounting for Limited Partnership Investments), andASC 272-10-05-3 through 05-4; 323-30-15-4; 35-3) (EITF Issue 03-16 (Accounting for Investments in Limited Liability Companies) provides that the equity method may be applied in certain situations in which an investor does not exercise significant control. Those investors should retain the specialized accounting for investment companies when applying the equity method to their investment in an investment company.

Changes in Status

An investment company's status as an entity that accounts for its transactions under the guidance in the Guide should be determined when the entity is formed. That determination should be reconsidered at each reporting period based on the guidance regarding the scope of the Guide in SOP 07-1. If an entity's status changes (i.e., an entity previously not under the Guide's scope meets the requirements for investment company accounting or an entity that was under the Guide's scope no longer meets those requirements), the entity should adopt the appropriate accounting as of the date on which its status changed, rather than as of the reporting date. A change in status should be accounted for as follows:

- *Change from investment company accounting.* An entity that no longer meets the scope requirements under the guidance in SOP 07-1 should stop accounting for its transactions in accordance with investment company accounting under the Guide and report its changed status *prospectively* by accounting for its investments in accordance with other generally accepted accounting principles (GAAP) as of the date of the change in status using *fair value* as the carrying amount of the investments in conformity with investment company accounting *at the date of the change.*
- *Change to investment company accounting.* If there is a change in the status of an entity that previously had not met the scope requirements in SOP 07-1 to be accounted for in accordance with the Guide, the effect of the change in status, which is the difference between the carrying amounts of the investments in

conformity with the Guide's provisions and their carrying amounts in accordance with other GAAP should be reported as of the date of the change as an adjustment to retained earnings in the period in which the change occurred.

- *Disclosure of change in status.* All entities that experience a change in status should disclose that fact in their financial statements. However, entities that change to investment company accounting from other GAAP should disclose the effect of the change in status on the financial statements in the period in which it occurred, including the effect of the change on the reported amounts of investments as of the date of the change in status and how that change has affected net income, change in net assets from operations (for investment companies) or change in net assets (for not-for-profit organizations), and related per share amounts. When making their initial investment in an investment company, a parent company or an equity method investor should make their initial determination whether to retain investment company accounting for that investment in their financial statements. The provisions in SOP 07-1 regarding the retention of investment company accounting in a parent company's or an equity method investor's financial statements should be reconsidered at each reporting period and may result in a change in status. A change in status should be accounted for as follows:

- *Parent company no longer meets the requirements for retention of investment company accounting.* If after the initial determination that a parent company should retain investment company accounting for a subsidiary in its financial statements, the parent company no longer meets the requirements in SOP 07-1 for retention of investment company accounting for *any* investment company subsidiary (or if an investment company subsidiary that previously had met the scope requirements under SOP 07-1 and had been consolidated in the parent company's financial statements no longer meets SOP 07-1's scope requirements for investment company accounting), the parent company should discontinue its retention of investment company accounting in its financial statements for *all* of its subsidiaries.

- *Equity method investor no longer meets the requirements for retention of investment company accounting.* If an equity method investor discontinues retention of investment company accounting in its financial statements for its investment in an investment company in accordance with the guidance in SOP 07-1 after it had been determined that investment company accounting should be retained for that investee in the equity method investor's financial statements (or if an equity method investee that previously had met the scope requirements under this SOP and investment company accounting had been retained in the investor's financial statements for that investee no longer meets SOP 07-1's scope requirements for investment company accounting), the equity method investor should stop using investment company accounting to report its investment in *that* investment company and its equity method investments in *other* investment companies that meet both of the following conditions: (1) the equity method investor has the ability to exercise significant influence over the entity; and (2) the entity is managed by the same general partner, investment advisor, a party with an equivalent role, or a related party of that general partner, investment adviser, or party with an equivalent role for which investment company accounting is *not* permitted.

REPORTING A DISCONTINUANCE OF RETENTION OF INVESTMENT COMPANY ACCOUNTING

A parent company or an equity method investor that no longer retains investment company accounting for a subsidiary or investee in its financial statements in accordance with the guidance in SOP 07-1 should report a change in status *prospectively* by accounting for its investment in accordance with *other* GAAP as of the date of the change in status, rather than as of the reporting date, and should report the carrying amount of the investment at *fair value* in accordance with investment company accounting at the date of the change.

- *Adopting retention of investment company accounting.* If after an initial determination that a parent company does *not* meet the conditions in SOP 07-1 for retention of investment company accounting in its financial statements for a subsidiary or an equity method investor for its investee, a change in a parent company's or equity method investor's circumstances may result in the conclusion that investment company accounting should be retained in a parent company's or equity method investor's financial statements in accordance with the guidance in SOP 07-1. In that case, a parent company or equity method investor should change to the appropriate accounting as of the date of the change in status and should report the effect of that change as an adjustment to retained earnings in the period in which it occurred. The effect of that change equals the difference between the carrying amounts of the investments in accordance with the provisions of the Guide and the carrying amounts of the investments (or assets minus liabilities or consolidated investments) in accordance with GAAP other than that in the Guide.

- *Disclosure of a change in status.* All entities that have a change in status should report that fact in their financial statements. Parent companies or equity method investors that had initially determined not to retain investment company accounting for their subsidiary or investee in their financial statements and that due to a change in circumstances have started to retain investment company accounting in their financial statements should disclose: (1) the effect of the change in status on the financial statements in the period in which the change occurred; (2) the effect of the change on the reported amounts of investments as of the date of the change in status; and (3) the related effects on net income, change in net assets from operations (for investment companies) or change in net assets (for not-for-profit organizations), and related share amounts.

DISCLOSURE REQUIREMENT

Disclosures About a Parent Company's Retention of Investment Company Accounting

Parent companies should disclose the following information if investment company accounting is retained for investment company subsidiaries in the parent company's consolidated financial statements:

- Retention of investment company accounting in the consolidated financial statements.
- As of each balance sheet date, the carrying amount (fair value) and cost of the portfolio of investment company subsidiaries for which investment company accounting has been retained.
- Disclosures about significant transactions between the parent company or its related parties and investees of the investment company or their affiliates, including:
  — The nature of the relationships.
  — A description of transactions for each of the periods for which income statements are presented and other information considered necessary to understand the effects of the transactions on the financial statements, such as the amount of gross profit (or similar measure) from the transactions.
  — The dollar amounts of transactions, such as sales and similar revenues, for each of the periods for which income statements are presented and the effects of a change, if any, in the method of establishing the terms of the transactions from that used in the preceding period.
  — Amounts due from or to investees or their affiliates as of the date of each balance sheet presented and, if not otherwise clear, the terms and manner of settlement.
- Gross unrealized total appreciation and total depreciation of investments in the investment company's investment portfolio for each balance sheet date.

- Net realized gains and losses from investments in the investment portfolio of investment company subsidiaries for which investment company accounting has been retained for each year an income statement is presented.
- Net increase (decrease) in unrealized appreciation (or depreciation) of the investment portfolio (change in unrealized amounts during the year) for each year an income statement is presented.
- The policy for distinguishing the nature and type of investments made by the investment company from the nature and type of investments made by other entities within the consolidated group that are *not* investment companies.

Disclosures about an Equity Method Investor's Retention of Investment Company Accounting

Equity method investors should disclose the following information if investment company accounting is retained in the financial statements:

- Retention of investment company accounting for an investment company in the equity method investor's financial statements.
- As of each balance sheet date, the carrying amount (fair value) and cost of the portfolio of equity method investees for which investment company accounting has been retained. Amounts disclosed should correspond to the equity method investor's proportionate interests in the portfolios of its equity method investees.
- Disclosures about significant transactions between the equity method investor or its related parties and investees of the investment company or their affiliates, including:
  — The nature of the relationships.
  — A description of transactions for each of the periods for which income statements are presented and other information considered necessary to understand the effects of the transactions on the financial statements, such as the amount of gross profit (or similar measure) from the transactions.
  — The dollar amounts of transactions, such as sales and similar revenues, for each of the periods for which income statements are presented and the effects of any change in the method of establishing the terms from that used in the preceding period.
  — Amounts due from or to investees or their affiliates as of the date of each balance sheet presented and, if not otherwise clear, the terms and manner of settlement.

Disclosures Related to Changes in Status Related to the Scope of the Guide

The following information should be disclosed if in accordance with the guidance in SOP 07-1 there is a change in the status of an investment company's qualification to be accounted for under the scope of the Guide:

- The nature of and justification for the change in status.
- The disclosures required under the guidance in SOP 07-1 related to the scope of the Guide.

Disclosures Related to Changes in Status Regarding the Retention of Investment Company Accounting in the Financial Statements of a Parent Company and of an Equity Method Investor

The following information should be disclosed in accordance with the guidance in SOP 07-1:

- The nature of and justification for the change in status.
- The disclosures required under the guidance in SOP 07-1 related to the retention of investment company accounting in the financial statements of a parent company and of an equity method investor.

EFFECTIVE DATE AND TRANSITION

SOP 07-1's provisions are effective for fiscal years that begin on or after December 15, 2007, but earlier application is encouraged.

The guidance in SOP 07 1 regarding the scope of the Guide and the guidance regarding the retention of investment company accounting in the financial statements of a parent company for its subsidiary and an equity method investor for its investee should be considered initially as of the beginning of the fiscal year for which SOP 07-1 is first applied. An entity that decides to first apply that guidance in a period other than the first interim period of the year of change should report the change by applying the change *retrospectively* to previous interim periods of that year. If the accounting of an entity that has previously applied the Guide's provisions conforms to SOP 07-1's provisions as of the initial application of this SOP, the entity should continue to apply the Guide's provisions when initially applying SOP 07-1's guidance, even if the entity did not meet all of this SOP's provisions in all periods before the initial application of SOP 07-1.

Entities That Do Not Meet the SOP's Provisions

Entities that had been applying the Guide's provisions, but that do not meet SOP 07-1's provisions regarding the scope of the Guide or regarding the retention of investment company accounting in the financial statements of a parent company and those of an equity method investor should report the effects of adopting this SOP *prospectively* by accounting for their investments in accordance with other applicable GAAP as of the date of adoption of SOP 07-1. The investment's carrying amount should be at *fair value* in accordance with investment company accounting at the date SOP 07-1 is adopted.

Entities That Meet the SOP's Provisions

The cumulative effect of adopting the guidance in SOP 07-1 should be reported by entities that had not been applying the Guide's provisions related to the scope or the retention of investment company accounting in their financial statements, but that (a) meet the provisions of SOP 07-1 regarding the scope of the Guide, or (b) SOP 07-1's provisions regarding the retention of investment company accounting in the financial statements of a parent company or those of an equity method investor should report the *cumulative effect* of adopting the guidance in SOP 07-1, which equals the difference between the investments' carrying amounts in accordance with the Guide's provisions and their carrying amounts (or assets less liabilities for consolidated investments) in conformity with GAAP other than the Guide's provisions. It should be recognized as an adjustment to opening retained earnings as of the beginning of the year in which the guidance in SOP 07-1 is adopted.

Entities with Changes in Accounting

All entities that have changes in accounting as a result of adopting the guidance in SOP 07-1 should disclose the effect of adopting this SOP on: (1) the financial statements of the period of the change, including changes in accounting for investments; (2) changes, if any, on the reported amounts of investments as of the date of adoption; and related effects, if any, on (3) net income, change in net assets from operations (for investment companies) or change in net assets (for not-for-profit organizations), and related share amounts.

The Accounting Standards Executive Committee (AcSEC) notes that only entities that are *separate legal entities*, except for separate accounts of insurance companies, would retain the Guide's specialized accounting practices when the guidance in SOP 07-1 is adopted.

ASC 970-810 Real Estate—General—Consolidation

FSP SOP 78-9-1 (Interaction of AICPA Statement of Position 78-9 and EITF Issue No. 04-5) (ASC 970-810-25-1 through 25-3)

OVERVIEW

For many years, preparers of financial statements and auditors have been asking for guidance on how to determine whether a limited partnership should be consolidated in a general partner's financial statements. Until recently, the practice has been to analogize to the guidance in the ASC 970-323 (AICPA's SOP 78-9, Accounting for Investments in Real Estate Ventures), which provides specific guidance on investments in real estate ventures, which may include investments in corporate joint ventures, general partnerships, limited partnerships, and undivided interests.

In ASC 810-20-15-1 through 15- 3, 25-1 through 25-20; 45-1; 55-1 through 55-16 (Issue 04-5, Determining Whether a General Partner, or the General Partners as a Group, Controls a Limited Partnership or Similar Entity When the Limited Partners Have Certain Rights), the EITF provides guidance for determining whether a limited partnership's general partner, or the general partners as a group, control a limited partnership. Because the EITF believes that such guidance should be consistent for limited partnerships in all industries, the EITF asked the FASB to amend SOP 78-9 so that its guidance would conform to the consensus in Issue 04-5. The FASB, therefore, directed the staff to issue FSP SOP 78-9-1, which amends the guidance in SOP 78-9.

AMENDMENT OF SOP 78-9

The guidance in SOP 78-9 is amended as follows:

- In ASC 970-810-25-2 (paragraph 7 of SOP 78-9), the fourth sentence, which addresses the concept that the majority owners may not control a partnership if *major* decisions must be approved by one or more of the partners, is deleted. It is replaced with the concept that a majority interest holder may *not* control an entity if one or more of the other partners have *substantive participating* rights allowing them to participate in *significant* decisions made in the ordinary course of an entity's business. Whether those rights are substantive and whether the presumption that a majority owner has control has been overcome should be evaluated based on the guidance in ASC 810-20-15-1 through 15- 3, 25-1 through 25-20; 45-1; 55-1 through 55-16 (Issue 04-5).
- Paragraph 9 of the SOP is deleted and replaced with ASC 970-810-25-3, which states that although it is presumed that a limited

partnership's general partners—whose rights and obligations differ from those of the limited partners—control a limited partnership, that presumption of control may be overcome. Readers are referred to the guidance in Issue 04-5 above to make that determination. General partners should account for their interests in a limited partnership by the equity method if (a) the presumption of control is overcome by the limited partners' rights and (b) the presumption of control is *not* overcome by the limited partners' rights, but no single general partner controls the limited partnership. A single general partner that controls a limited partnership should consolidate an interest in a limited partnership in its financial statements and account for that interest in accordance with authoritative guidance for investments in subsidiaries.

TRANSITION

The guidance in this Issue is effective:

- After June 29, 2005, for general partners of:
  - *New* limited partnership formed, and
  - Existing limited partnerships that have *modified* their existing partnership agreements.
- For all *other* limited partnerships, no later than the beginning of the first reporting period in fiscal years beginning after December 15, 2005, by applying either Transition Method A or Transition Method B.

Transition Method A

Existing limited partnerships that have *not* modified their partnership agreements should apply the guidance in this FSP in financial statements issued for the first reporting period of fiscal years that begin after December 15, 2005, but earlier application is encouraged. Public companies with December 31 fiscal year ends therefore should apply the guidance no later than the beginning of the first quarter of 2006, based on agreements in effect at adoption. Companies with a December 31 year end that do *not* issue interim financial statements should apply the guidance in their annual statements as of the beginning of the year ended December 31, 2006.

The effect of initial application of this guidance for existing limited partnership agreements should presented as a cumulative-effect-type adjustment. Prior years' financial statements should be presented as previously reported. A cumulative-effect-type adjustment, if any, of adopting the guidance in this FSP on retained earnings (or other appropriate components of equity or net assets) at the beginning of the period in which the guidance is first applied should be included in the opening balance of retained earnings (or other appropriate components of equity or net assets) in the period of change. Entities that decide on early adoption of the guidance in this FSP in an interim period should recognize a cumulative-effect-type adjustment, if any, in retained earnings (or other appropriate components of equity or net assets) as of the beginning of the year of adoption. Therefore, the provisions of FAS-3 (Reporting Accounting Changes in Interim Financial Statements)) (not in ASC) should continue to be applied, but the cumulative-effect-type adjustment should be recognized in beginning retained earnings (or other appropriate components of equity or net assets) for that fiscal year. The effect of adopting a new accounting principle should be disclosed in the year in which it is adopted. The pro forma effects of applying the new accounting principle on net income need *not* be disclosed.

Previously reported equity or net income generally would not be adjusted if a general partner changes its accounting for an interest in a limited partnership from the equity method to consolidation or vice versa. A cumulative-effect-type adjustment might be required, however, if as a result of a change from the equity method to consolidation, losses that would *not* have been recognized under the equity method must be recognized in consolidation or vice versa, in accordance with ASC 810-10-45-7 (paragraph 15 of ARB-51, Consolidated Financial Statements) and paragraph ASC 323-10-35-19 through 35-22 (19(i) of APB-18, The Equity Method of Accounting for Investments in Common Stock) . Other items that would have been accounted for differently if this guidance had been applied in prior period financial statements should *not* be adjusted.

Transition Method B

The guidance in this FSP may be applied retrospectively to existing limited partnership agreements that have *not* been modified. An entity that adopts this transition method should apply the guidance in ASC 250-10-45-5, 6, 8 (paragraphs 7, 8, and 10 of FAS-154, Accounting Changes and Error Corrections) () and should provide the required disclosures in ASC 250-10-50-1 (paragraph 17 of FAS-154). Entities that apply the guidance in this Issue *retrospectively* should apply it to all existing partnership agreements based on the facts and circumstances when each investment was made and should consider making changes in later periods. Other items that would have been accounted for differently in prior periods had the guidance in this FSP existed at that time should be adjusted in the financial statements under this transition method. Retrospective application is *not* required for investments in limited partnerships if an entity is no longer a general partner in a limited partnership at the date the guidance in this Issue is adopted.

AUTHORITATIVE GUIDANCE NOT INCLUDED SEPARATELY IN THE CODIFICATION BUT INCORPORATED IN ANOTHER PRONOUNCEMENT IN THE CODIFICATION

FSP SOP 07-1-1 (Effective Date of AICPA Statement of Position 07-1)

OVERVIEW

The AICPA issued ASC 946-323-55-2 through 55-5, 55-7 through 55-9; ASC 946-810-15-2; 55-6, 55-8 through 55-12, ASC 946-10-05-3; 15 through 15-5, 55-22 through 55-23, 55-25 through 55-71, 65-1 (SOP 07-1, Clarification of the Scope of the Audit and Accounting Guide *Investment Companies* and Accounting by Parent Companies and Equity Method Investors for Investments in Investment Companies) to provide guidance for determining whether: (1) an entity is required to apply the guidance in ASC 946, (Audit and Accounting Guide, *Investment Companies*); and (2) investment company accounting should be retained by a parent company in consolidation or by an equity method investor. Since the SOP's issuance on June 11, 2007, financial statement preparers have identified significant issues that they believe should be considered and resolved by the FASB before the SOP's provisions can be implemented. Consequently, they have asked the FASB to delay the required application of the provisions in the SOP, which would otherwise be effective for fiscal years beginning on or after December 15, 2007, or earlier.

FASB STAFF POSITION

This FSP, which applies to entities that are required to apply the guidance in SOP 07-1, requires that the SOP's effective date be delayed for an indefinite period of time. Entities that opted to adopt the SOP's provisions before the issuance of this FSP are permitted, but not required, to continue applying the SOP's provisions. However, entities that have *not* yet adopted the SOP's provisions are prohibited from adopting it, except that a consolidated entity must apply the guidance in the SOP in its standalone financial statements if that entity was formed or acquired after its parent company had early adopted the SOP's provisions and it has decided to continue following its guidance.

ASC 946-10-65-1 (paragraph 56 of SOP 07-1) is amended as follows by the guidance in this FSP: (Added text is underlined and deleted text is struck out.)

> The effective date of this SOP is delayed indefinitely. An entity that early adopted the SOP before December 15, 2007, is permitted but not

required to continue to apply the provisions of the SOP. No other entity may adopt the provisions of this SOP, with the following exception. If a parent entity that early adopted the SOP chooses not to rescind its early adoption, an entity consolidated by that parent entity that is formed or acquired after that parent entity's adoption of the SOP must apply the provisions of the SOP in its standalone financial statements. ~~The provisions of this SOP are effective for fiscal years beginning on or after December 15, 2007. Earlier application is encouraged.~~

Because the provisions of FSP FIN-46(R)-7 (Application of FASB Interpretation No. 46(R) to Investment Companies) are *not* amended by the guidance in this FSP, the guidance in FSP FIN-46(R)-7 will be effective only when the guidance in SOP 07-1 is initially adopted.

The guidance in ASC 810-10-25-15 (EITF Issue 85-12, Retention of Specialized Accounting for Investments in Consolidation) and EITF Topic D-74 (Issues Concerning the Scope of the AICPA Guide on Investment Companies) (not in ASC) continue to be effective for entities that did *not* adopt the guidance in SOP 07-1.

EFFECTIVE DATE AND TRANSITION

The provisions of this FSP are effective as of December 15, 2007. An entity that chose early adoption of the guidance in SOP 07-1 and has decided to voluntarily rescind that early adoption should account for that change based on the guidance in ASC 250 (FAS-154, Accounting Changes and Error Corrections).

RELATED CHAPTERS IN 2011
GAAP GUIDE, VOLUME II

Chapter 25, "Investments in Debt and Equity Securities"
Chapter 39, "Stockholders' Equity"

RELATED CHAPTERS IN 2011
GAAP GUIDE, VOLUME I

Chapter 7, "Consolidated Financial Statements"
Chapter 28, "Investments in Debt and Equity Securities"
Chapter 44, "Stockholders' Equity"

RELATED CHAPTER IN 2011
INTERNATIONAL ACCOUNTING/FINANCIAL REPORTING STANDARDS GUIDE

Chapter 10, "Consolidated Financial Statements"

CHAPTER 11
CONTINGENCIES, RISKS, AND UNCERTAINTIES

CONTENTS

Overview		11.02
Authoritative Guidance		
ASC 275 Risks and Uncertainties		11.03
SOP 94-6	Disclosure of Certain Significant Risks and Uncertainties	11.03
ASC 310 Receivables		11.06
SOP 01-6	Accounting by Certain Entities (Including Entities with Trade Receivables) That Lend to or Finance the Activities of Others	11.06
ASC 410 Asset Retirement and Environmental Obligations		11.06
SOP 96-1	Environmental Remediation Liabilities	11.10
ASC 450 Contingencies		11.10
EITF Issue 03-8	Accounting for Claims-Made Insurance and Retroactive Insurance Contracts by the Insured Entity	11.23
ASC 460 Guarantees		11.23
FSP FIN-45-1	Accounting for Intellectual Property Infringement Indemnification under FIN-45	11.32
FSP FIN-45-2	Whether FASB Interpretation No. 45, *Guarantor's Accounting and Disclosure Requirements for Guarantees, Including Indirect Guarantees of Indebtedness of Others*, Provides Support for Subsequently Accounting for a Guarantor's Liability at Fair Value	11.32
FSP FIN-45-3	Application of FASB Interpretation No. 45 in Minimum Revenue Guarantees Granted to a Business or Its Owners	11.33
EITF Issue 85-20	Recognition of Fees for Guaranteeing a Loan	11.35

11.02 *Contingencies, Risks, and Uncertainties*

ASC 715	Compensation—Retirement Benefits	11.38
EITF Issue 92-13	Accounting for Estimated Payments in Connection with the Coal Industry Retiree Health Benefit Act of 1992	11.38
ASC 825	Financial Instruments	11.40
FSP SOP 94-6-1	Terms of Loan Products That May Give Rise to a Concentration of Credit Risk	11.40
ASC 970	Real Estate	11.43
EITF Issue 91-10	Accounting for Special Assessments and Tax Increment Financing Entities	11.43
Related Chapters in 2011 GAAP Guide, Volume II		11.46
Related Chapters in 2011 GAAP Guide, Volume I		11.47
Related Chapters in 2011 International Accounting/Financial Reporting Standards Guide		11.47

OVERVIEW

Accounting for contingencies is an important feature of the preparation of financial statements in accordance with GAAP, because of the many uncertainties that may exist at the end of each accounting period. Standards governing accounting for loss contingencies require accrual and/or note disclosure when specified recognition and disclosure criteria are met. Gain contingencies generally are not recognized in financial statements but may be disclosed.

Guidance on accounting for contingencies in the following pronouncements is discussed in the 2011 *GAAP Guide, Volume I*, Chapter 8, "Contingencies, Risks, and Uncertainties":

ASC 450	Accounting for Contingencies (FAS-5)
ASC 450	Reasonable Estimation of the Amount of a Loss (FIN-14)
ASC 460	Guarantor's Accounting and Disclosure Requirements for Guarantees, Including Indirect Guarantees of Indebtedness of Others (FIN-45)

AUTHORITATIVE GUIDANCE

ASC 275 Risks and Uncertainties

SOP 94-6 (Disclosure of Certain Significant Risks and Uncertainties) (ASC 275-10-05-2 through 05-8; 10-1; 15-3 through 15-6; 50-1 through 50-2, 50-4, 50-6 through 50-21, 50-23; 55-1 through 55-19; 60-3; 205-20-55-80; 330-10-55-8 through 55-13; 814-10-30-55-8 through 55-13; 450-20-50-2; 55-36 through 55-37; 460-10-55-27; 605-35-55-3 through 55-10; ASC 740-10-55-219 through 5-22; 932-360-55-15 through 15-19; 958-205-60-1; 605-55-70; 985-20-55-24 through 5-29)

BACKGROUND

Volatility and uncertainty in the business and economic environment result in the need for disclosure of information about the risks and uncertainties confronted by reporting entities. Under the guidance in this SOP, disclosure is required about significant risks and uncertainties that confront entities in the following areas: nature of operations, use of estimates in the preparation of financial statements, certain significant estimates, and current vulnerability due to certain concentrations.

STANDARDS

Nature of Operations

Financial statements should include a description of the major products or services an entity sells or provides and its principal markets and locations of those markets. Entities that operate in more than one market must indicate the relative importance of their operations in each market. Disclosures concerning the nature of operations are not required to be quantified, and relative importance may be described by terms such as *predominantly, about equally, major,* and *other*.

Illustration of a Nature of Operations Note for a Pharmaceutical Company

Geneca Inc. is a research-driven pharmaceutical company that discovers, develops, manufactures, and markets a broad range of human, animal, and agricultural health products. Human health products include therapeutic and preventive agents, generally sold by prescription, for the treatment of human disorders.

☛ **PRACTICE POINTER:** Entities that operate in more than one market are required to indicate the relative importance of their operations in each market. Similar to the previous illustration, most companies do not include this disclosure in the "nature of operations" note. Rather, information on the relative importance of operations in different markets is typically found in the business segments note.

Use of Estimates

Financial statements should include an explanation that their preparation in conformity with GAAP requires the application of management's estimates.

Illustration of a Use of Estimates Note—Basic

We prepare our financial statements under generally accepted accounting principles, which require management to make estimates and assumptions that affect the reported amounts or certain disclosures. Actual results could differ from those estimates.

Illustration of a Use of Estimates Note—Detailed

We prepare our financial statements under generally accepted accounting principles, which require management to make estimates and assumptions that affect the reported amounts or certain disclosures. Actual results could differ from those estimates. Estimates are used when accounting for certain items such as long-term contracts, allowance for doubtful accounts, depreciation and amortization, employee benefit plans, taxes, restructuring reserves, and contingencies.

Significant Estimates

Disclosure regarding an estimate is required when *both* of the following conditions are met:

- It is at least reasonably possible that the estimate of the effect on the financial statements of a condition, situation, or set of circumstances that existed at the date of the financial statements will change in the near term due to one or more future confirming events.
- The effect of the change would have a material effect on the financial statements.

The disclosure requirements of ASC 450 (FAS-5, Accounting for Contingencies) for contingencies are supplemented by the guidance in this SOP as follows:

- If an estimate requires disclosure under the guidance in ASC 450 (FAS-5) or another pronouncement, there should be an indication that it is at least reasonably possible that a change in the estimate will occur in the near term.

- An estimate that does not require disclosure under ASC 450 (FAS-5) (such as estimates associated with long-term operating assets and amounts reported under profitable long-term contracts) may meet the standards described above and, if so, requires the following:

    —Disclosure of its nature

    —An indication that it is reasonably possible that a change in the estimate will occur in the near term

The following are examples of the types of situations that may require disclosure in accordance with the guidance in this SOP, assuming the conditions stated above are met:

- Inventory subject to rapid technological obsolescence
- Specialized equipment subject to technological obsolescence
- Valuation allowances for deferred tax assets based on future taxable income
- Capitalized motion picture film production costs
- Capitalized computer software costs
- Deferred policy acquisition costs of insurance enterprises
- Valuation allowances for commercial and real estate loans
- Environmental remediation-related obligations
- Litigation-related obligations
- Contingent liabilities for obligations of other entities
- Amounts reported for long-term obligations (e.g., pensions and other post-retirement benefits)
- Estimated net proceeds recoverable, the provisions for expected loss to be incurred, etc., on disposition of a business or assets
- Amounts reported for long-term contracts

Vulnerability from Concentrations

Vulnerability from concentrations exists because of an enterprise's greater exposure to risk than would be the case if the enterprise had mitigated its risk through diversification. Financial statements should disclose concentrations if *all* of the following conditions are met:

- The concentration existed at the date of the financial statements.
- The concentration makes the enterprise vulnerable to the risk of a near-term severe impact.
- It is reasonably possible that the events that could cause the severe impact will occur in the near term.

Information sufficient to inform financial statement users of the general nature of the risk associated with the concentration is required for the following specific concentrations:

- Concentrations in the volume of business transacted with a particular customer, supplier, lender, grantor, or contributor
- Concentrations in revenue from particular products, services, or fundraising events
- Concentrations in the available sources of supply of materials, labor, or services, or of licenses or other rights used in the entity's operations
- Concentrations in the market or geographic area in which an entity conducts its operations

In addition, for concentrations of labor subject to collective bargaining agreements, disclosure shall include both the percentage of the labor force covered by a collective bargaining agreement and the percentage of the labor force covered by a collective bargaining agreement that will expire within one year. For concentrations of operations located outside the entity's home country, disclosure shall include the carrying amounts of net assets and the geographic areas in which they are located.

Illustration of a Note on Concentrations—No Exposure

As of December 31, 20X4, we do not have any significant concentration of business transacted with a particular customer, supplier, or lender that could, if suddenly eliminated, severely impact our operations. We also do not have a concentration of available sources of labor or services that could, if suddenly eliminated, severely impact our operations. We invest our cash with high-quality credit institutions.

Illustration of a Note on Concentrations—Customer Concentration Exposure

The company's five largest customers accounted for approximately 48% of net revenues for 20X4. At December 31, 20X4, these customers accounted for approximately 38% of net accounts receivable.

ASC 310 Receivables

SOP 01-6 (Accounting by Certain Entities (Including Entities with Trade Receivables) That Lend to or Finance the Activities of Others) (ASC 310-10-05-5, 05-7;25-3, 25-6, 25-8; 11-25-13;30-7;35-41 through 35-43, 35-46 through 35-49; 45-2, through 45-3; 50-2 through 50-11; 310-20-15-3;50-1; 460-10-35-3; 45-1; 460-605-25-7; 825-10-35-1 through 35-3; 835-30-15-1; 860-20-50-5; 860-50-15-3; 860-50-40-2, 40-6; 860-942-15-2 through 15-3; 942-210-45-1 through 45-2;

942-305-05-2; 45-1; 50-1; 942-310-15-2; 942-320-50-4;
942-325-25-1 through 25-3; 35-1 through 35-4; 942-360-45-2;
942-405-25-1 through 25-4; 35-1; 45-1 through 45-4; 50-1;
942-470-45-1 through 45-2; 50-2 through 50-3; 942-505-50-1H
through 50-7; 942-825-50-1 through 50-2; 944-320-50-1;
948-10-15-3; 50-2 through 50-5)

BACKGROUND

This SOP was issued to reduce the variability among financial institutions (including entities with trade receivables) in accounting for similar transactions. It provides accounting guidance for entities that lend to or finance the activities of other parties, including entities that simply extend normal trade credit to customers (i.e., accounts receivable).The SOP does *not* apply to entities that carry loans and trade receivables at fair value, with changes in fair value flowing through the current period's income statement. Examples of these entities include: investment companies, broker-dealers in securities, and employee benefit plans.

The discussion of the SOP consists of the portions of the SOP that have broad applicability across different types of business entities. Much of the SOP provides specific guidance for financial institutions (e.g., banks, savings institutions, credit unions, and finance companies). For a discussion of the SOP's provisions that apply to those kinds of entities, refer to the *GAAP Update Service* (Volume 02, Issue 06; March 30, 2002).

> **OBSERVATION:** This SOP applies to all entities that lend to or finance the activities of their customers or other parties, even if an entity is not considered to be a finance company. Therefore, the SOP provides guidance on the recognition, measurement, and disclosure of loans and trade receivables, credit losses, and other items, for manufacturers, retailers, and other non-financial entities. The SOP also provides more specific guidance for finance companies.

STANDARDS

Recognition and Measurement

The SOP provides recognition and measurement guidance for a number of items, including loans and trade receivables not held for sale, nonmortgage loans held for sale, sales of loans not held for sale, credit losses—including losses on off-balance-sheet instruments, standby commitments to purchase loans, delinquency fees, prepayment fees, and rebates.

An entity has a loan or trade receivable not held for sale when management has the intent and ability to hold the loan or receivable for the foreseeable future or until maturity. Such loans and receivables are to be carried at outstanding principal adjusted for charge-offs, the allowance for loan losses (allowance for doubtful accounts), deferred fees or costs on originated loans, and unamortized premiums or discounts for purchased loans. A nonmortgage loan held for sale should be carried at the lower of cost or fair value.

An entity may decide to sell a loan not previously categorized as held for sale. Once a decision is made to sell such a loan, the loan is to be transferred into the held for sale category and carried at the lower of cost or fair value.

Credit losses—whether for loans or trade receivables—are to be subtracted from the related allowance account. The loan or trade receivable itself should be written off in the period in which the particular loan or receivable is deemed uncollectible.

> ☛ **PRACTICE POINTER:** The recognition and measurement of trade receivables should not be changed as a result of the guidance in this SOP. However, it is likely that presentation and disclosure of trade receivables will change as a result of the guidance in the SOP.

An entity may have credit losses arising from off-balance-sheet exposures of the entity. If an entity has such a loss, the loss and a related liability are to be recognized. The loss accrual should be recorded separately from any valuation account related to a recognized financial instrument that may exist.

Entities may enter into standby commitments to purchase loans. In return for a fee, the entity stands ready to purchase loans at a stated price. The applicable accounting treatment depends on whether (1) the settlement date is reasonable and (2) the entity has the intent and ability to accept the loans without selling assets. An example of a reasonable settlement date is one within a normal loan commitment period. If both of the previous criteria are met, the loan is recorded at cost, less any standby commitment fee received, at the settlement date. If either one of the previous criteria are not met, the standby commitment is recorded as a written put option.

Delinquency fees are to be recognized in income when the entity is allowed to charge the fee (i.e., the conditions necessary for charging delinquency fees have been met). This treatment assumes that collection of the delinquency fees is reasonably assured. Prepayment penalties should not be recognized in income until the loans are prepaid.

Borrowers are sometimes entitled to rebates of previous finance charges paid. The calculation of rebate amounts is typically governed by state law, often using the Rule of 78s, rather than reflecting the entity's internal accounting procedures, which typically follow the interest method. Any differences between rebate calculations and interest income previously recognized are treated as adjustments of previously recognized interest income. The difference would be recognized in income when loans (or receivables) are prepaid or renewed.

Presentation and Disclosure

This SOP provides presentation and disclosure guidelines related to (1) accounting policies for loans and trade receivables, (2) accounting policies for credit losses and doubtful accounts, (3) accounting policies for nonaccrual and past due loans and trade receivables, (4) sales of loans and trade receivables, (5) loans or trade receivables, (6) foreclosed or repossessed assets, (7) nonaccrual and past due loans and trade receivables, and (8) assets serving as collateral.

First, the entity must provide a summary of its significant accounting policies for loans and trade receivables. The entity's basis of accounting for loans, trade receivables, and lease financings must be disclosed. In addition, the entity must disclose whether it uses the aggregate or individual asset basis to determine the lower of cost or fair value of nonmortgage loans held for sale. The entity must disclose the classification and method of accounting for interest-only strips, loans, other receivables, and certain retained interests in securitizations. Finally, disclosure of the entity's method of recognizing interest income on loan and trade receivables is required.

Second, an entity must describe its policies and methodology for determining the allowance for loan losses, allowance for doubtful accounts, and any liability for off-balance-sheet credit losses. Moreover, the entity must disclose its policy and methodology for the recognition and measurement of losses related to loans, trade receivables, and other credit exposures.

Third, an entity must provide a number of disclosures related to its policies for nonaccrual and past due loans and trade receivables. The entity must describe its policy for placing loans (or trade receivables) on nonaccrual status, and how payments received on nonaccrual loans (or trade receivables) are treated. The entity's policy for restoring loans (or receivables) to accrual status must be disclosed. The entity must disclose its policy for writing off as uncollectible loans and trade receivables. Finally, the entity must describe whether it evaluates past due (or delinquency) status based on when the most recent payment was received or based on contractual terms.

Fourth, an entity must separately disclose its aggregate gains or losses from its sale of loans or trade receivables.

Fifth, major categories of loans and trade receivables are to be presented separately, either in the financial statements or notes. Moreover, on the balance sheet itself, receivables held for sale should be shown as a separate category.

Sixth, foreclosed or repossessed assets are to be shown as a separate balance sheet amount, or as part of other assets with details representing amounts foreclosed or repossessed appearing in the notes.

Seventh, there are two specific requirements related to nonaccrual and past due loans and receivables. The recorded investment in nonaccrual loans and trade receivables as of each balance sheet date is to be disclosed in the notes. And, the recorded investment in loans (or receivables) that are still accruing interest even though they are past due 90 days or more is to be disclosed in the notes.

Finally, an entity must disclose the carrying amount of loans, receivables, securities, and financial instruments that are serving as collateral for borrowings.

ASC 410 Asset Retirement and Environmental Obligations

SOP 96-1 (Environmental Remediation Liabilities) (ASC 410-30-05-1 through 3, 05-5 through 05-25; 10-1; 15-1 through 15-3; 25-1 through 25-15, 25-17, 25-20 through 25-23; 30-1 through 30-19; 35-1 through 35-5, 35-7 through 35-12, 35-12A; 45-1 through 45-5; 50-1 through 50-17; 55-1 through 55-6, 55-14 through 55-17, 55-27 through 55-51; 60-3, 60-8)

BACKGROUND

This SOP provides accounting guidance for environmental remediation liabilities that relate to pollution resulting from some past act. Generally, these liabilities result from one of the following:

- Superfund provisions
- The corrective-action provisions of the Resource Conservation and Recovery Act (RCRA)
- State and non-U.S. laws and regulations that are analogous to the RCRA

The SOP applies to all entities that prepare financial statements in conformity with generally accepted accounting principles applicable to nongovernmental entities. The provisions of SOP 96-1 are intended to be applied on a site-by-site basis.

The SOP is written in the context of operations taking place in the United States, although the guidance provided is applicable to all of a reporting entity's operations. It is *not* intended to provide guidance for the following:

- Accounting for pollution control costs with respect to current operations
- Accounting for costs of future site restoration or closure that are required upon the cessation of operations or sale of facilities
- Accounting for environmental remediation actions that are undertaken at the sole discretion of management and that are not induced by the threat of litigation or of assertion or by a claim of assessment by governments or other parties

- Recognizing liabilities of insurance companies for unpaid claims
- Asset impairment issues

☞ **PRACTICE POINTER:** Guidance on the accounting for costs of future site restoration or closure that are required upon the cessation of operations or sale of facilities is provided in ASC 410-20; 450-20; 835-20; 360-10-35; 840-40 and 840-10; 980-410 (FAS-143, Accounting for Asset Retirement Obligations). Chapter 11, "Depreciable Assets and Depreciation," of the 2011 GAAP Guide Volume I, for additional details on this pronouncement. In addition, guidance on asset impairment issues is provided in ASC 360-10; ASC 840-30; ASC 840-20; ASC 205-10, ASC 205-20; ASC 958-225-45; ASC 958-360; ASC 855-10; ASC 225-20 (FAS-144, Accounting for the Impairment or Disposal of Long-Lived Assets). See Chapter 20, "Impairment of Long-Lived Assets," of the 2011 GAAP Guide, Volume I, for additional details on this pronouncement.

The SOP is intended to provide guidance for "cleanup" activities rather than preventative or other activities. For example, it does not cover situations in which remediation is required only at the time of sale of a property.

The following discussion is drawn primarily from Part II of the SOP, which provides detailed accounting guidance on accounting and disclosure for environmental remediation liabilities. Three other sections of the SOP that are not discussed here are particularly important for entities applying this standard or auditing entities that are applying this standard. The first is Part I, which presents an overview of environmental laws and regulations that relate to environmental liabilities. The second is Appendix B, which includes an environmental remediation case study that works through a six-year period to illustrate the application of the recognition and measurement guidance provided in the SOP. The third is Appendix C, which provides auditing guidance related to the SOP. Familiarity with those sections of the standard is highly recommended before implementation of the accounting guidance summarized here.

STANDARDS

OBSERVATION: The Governmental Accounting Standards Board has issued an exposure draft (ED) of a proposed standard, *Accounting and Reporting for Pollution Remediation Obligations,* under which an entity would determine whether to accrue a loss based on a probability standard. For example, if there is a 5% probability that a governmental entity will be found liable in a remediation case with a potential total liability of $100 million, the entity would have to accrue a $5 million loss in its statement of net assets. This approach is also discussed in the FASB's Invitation to Comment, *Selected Issues Relating to Assets and Liabilities with Uncertainties,* which also discusses guidance in IAS-37 (Provisions, Contingent Liabilities, and Contingent Assets).

Recognition of Environmental Remediation Liabilities

The SOP builds on the recognition criteria in ASC 450 (FAS-5) by requiring accrual of a liability when *both* of the following conditions are met:

- Information available before issuance of the financial statements indicates that it is probable that an asset has been impaired or a liability has been incurred at the date of the financial statements.
- The amount of the loss can be reasonably estimated.

A liability related to environmental remediation often results over a period of time rather than as a distinct event. The underlying cause of such a liability is the past or present ownership or operation of a site, or the contribution or transportation of waste to a site, at which remedial actions must take place. For the criteria for recognizing a liability to be met, this underlying cause must have occurred on or before the date of the financial statements.

Probability That a Liability Has Been Incurred

Applying the criteria in ASC 450 (FAS-5) to environmental remediation liabilities requires the following:

- It has been asserted (or it is probable that it will be asserted) that the entity is responsible for participating in a remediation process because of a past event. This usually means that litigation has begun, a claim or an assessment has been asserted, or commencement of litigation or assertion of a claim or assessment is considered probable.
- Available evidence indicates that the outcome of such litigation, claim, or assessment will be unfavorable (i.e., the entity will be held responsible for participating in a remediation process because of the past event).

In light of the legal framework in which most environmental remediation liabilities occur, the SOP is based on a presumption that if litigation has commenced (or a claim or an assessment has been asserted or is considered probable), and the reporting entity is associated with the site, the outcome will be unfavorable for the entity.

Ability to Make a Reasonable Estimate

Developing an estimate of environmental remediation liabilities involves a consideration of many factors, such as the following:

- The extent and types of hazardous substances at the site
- The range of technologies that can be used for remediation
- Evolving standards of what constitutes acceptable remediation

- The number and financial condition of other potentially responsible parties and the extent of their responsibility for the remediation

Illustration of Estimating an Environmental Remediation Liability

Foster, Inc., has determined that its environmental remediation obligation meets the recognition criteria in the SOP The company is in the process of estimating the amount of the obligation that will be recognized. The company has further determined that the liability consists of four components, described as follows:

Component	Description
A	Estimated at $750,000
B	Estimated to be within a range of $500,000 to $900,000, with the most likely amount at $625,000
C	Estimated to be within a range of $275,000 to $400,000, with no amount within that range more likely than any other amount
D	Unable to estimate

The environmental remediation liability that should be recognized at this time, subject to adjustment in the future as additional information becomes available, is determined as follows:

Component A	$ 750,000
Component B	625,000
Component C	275,000
Component D	None
	$1,650,000

ASC 450-20-25-5; 30-1; 05-5; 55-23 through 55-34 (FIN-14, Reasonable Estimation of the Amount of a Loss) is particularly important in estimating the amount of an environmental remediation liability. In the early stages of the remediation process, liabilities are not easily quantified. The range and ultimate amount of the liability will be determined as events occur over time. The range of an environmental remediation liability typically is estimated by first estimating the various components of the liability—which may themselves be ranges. As suggested in ASC 450-20-25-5; 30-1; 05-5; 55-23 through 55-34 (FIN-14), if an amount within a range is a better estimate than any other amount within the range, that figure should be used. If no amount within the range is a more reliable estimate than any other, the minimum amount in the range should be used. Thus, the amount of the environmental remediation liability will be a combination of most likely amounts and minimum amounts of the components of the liability. Even if a range for certain components of the liability cannot be estimated, a liability still should be recognized and recorded at the appropriate amount for those components that can be estimated. the various stages (benchmarks) involved in the remediation process and when costs generally should be accrued are discussed in the SOP.

A complexity that arises in estimating environmental remediation liabilities is the assignment and allocation among the various potentially responsible parties (PRPs). The final allocation may not be known until the remediation effort is substantially complete and may depend on factors such as the PRPs' willingness to negotiate a cost allocation. This should not preclude an entity from recognizing its best estimate of its share of the liability if the probability criterion is met. Any change in the estimate of the environmental remediation liability, including those due to negotiations with other PRPs, is accounted for as a change in accounting estimate in accordance with ASC 250 (FAS-154).

Measurement of Environmental Remediation Liabilities

Once an entity determines that it is probable that an environmental remediation liability has been incurred, it must estimate the amount of that liability based on available evidence. The estimate of the liability includes the allocable share of the liability for a specific site, and the share of amounts related to the site that will not be paid by other PRPs or the government.

The following four issues that must be addressed in the measurement of an entity's environmental remediation liability are identified in the SOP:

1. Costs that should be included in the measurement
2. Whether the measurement should consider the effects of expected future events or developments
3. How the measurement should be affected by the existence of other PRPs
4. How the measurement should be affected by potential recoveries

Costs to Be Included

Costs to be included in the measurement of the environmental remediation liability include (*a*) incremental direct costs of the remediation effort and (*b*) costs of compensation and benefits for those employees who are expected to devote a significant amount of time on the remediation effort (e.g., in-house lawyers and engineers).

The remediation effort is considered on a site-by-site basis and includes the following:

- Precleanup activities (e.g., the performance of a remedial investigation, risk assessment, or feasibility study and the preparation of remedial action plan)
- Performance of remedial actions under Superfund, corrective actions under RCRA, and analogous actions under state and non-U.S. laws
- Government oversight and enforcement activities
- Operation and maintenance of the remedy

The following are examples of incremental direct costs of a remediation effort:

- Fees paid to outside law firms for work related to remedial actions
- Costs related to completing the remedial investigation/feasibility study
- Fees to outside engineering and consulting firms for site investigations and the development of remedial action plans and designs
- Costs of contractors performing remedial actions
- Government oversight costs
- Costs of machinery and equipment related to the remedial effort that do not have alternative uses
- The PRP's assessments of the costs it incurred in dealing with a site
- Operating costs and remedial action maintenance

The costs of the following are included in the measurement of the remediation liability:

- Determining the extent of the remedial actions that are required
- Determining the types of remedial actions to be used
- Allocating the costs among PRPs

The costs of routine environmental compliance matters and litigation costs involved with potential recoveries are *not* part of the remediation effort. Further, the SOP does not require that the cost of defense against assertions of liability be included in the measurement of the environmental remediation liability. It notes that the current practice in this regard is diverse: some include legal defense costs in the measurement of liability under the guidance in ASC 450, (FAS-5), while most companies treat litigation costs as period costs.

Effects of Expected Future Events or Developments

Remediation of a site may extend over several years. As a result, the laws that govern the remediation process and the technology available may change during the remediation process. Other factors that may affect estimates of costs to be incurred are the impact of inflation and productivity improvements.

Enacted laws and adopted regulations and policies should provide the basis for measuring a remediation liability. Changes in these factors should not be anticipated, and the impact of changes that are enacted or adopted should be recognized only when they occur. Concerning remediation technology, the remediation plan should be based on the methodology that is expected to be approved, and the liability should be based on that methodology and technology, which should continue to be the basis for the liability until it is probable that a revised methodology will be accepted.

The measurement of environmental remediation liabilities should be based on the reporting entity's estimate of what it will cost to perform each of the elements of the remediation effort (identified earlier) when those elements are expected to be performed. As such, the entity should take into account productivity improvements due to experience, as well as inflation. When it is not practicable to estimate inflation, the cost estimate should include the minimum in the range of the liability until these costs can be more reasonably estimated.

If the amount and timing of cash payments is (reasonably) fixed or reliably determinable, the measurement of the liability, or a component of the liability, may be discounted to reflect the time value of money. The discount rate that should be used is that rate (*a*) that will produce an amount at which the environmental liability theoretically could be settled in an arm's-length transaction with a third party and (*b*) that does not exceed the interest rate on monetary assets that are essentially risk-free and have maturities comparable to that of the environmental liability.

Allocation of the Liability Among PRPs
The environmental remediation liability recorded by an entity should be based on the entity's estimate of its allocable share of the joint and several remediation liability. This requires an identification of the PRPs for the site, an assessment of the likelihood that other PRPs will pay their share of the liability, and a determination of the portion of the liability that will be allocated to the entity.

Identification of PRPs The SOP identifies five categories of PRPs:

1. *Participating PRPs* PRPs that acknowledge their potential involvement with the site. These PRPs also are referred to as "players."
2. *Recalcitrant PRPs* PRPs that adopt an attitude of nonresponsibility, even though evidence suggests their involvement in the site. Typically, parties in this category must be sued in order for their allocable share of the remediation liability to be collected.
3. *Unproven PRPs* Parties that have been identified as PRPs by the Environmental Protection Agency (EPA) but that do not

acknowledge their potential involvement because no substantive evidence currently links them to the site. These PRPs eventually will be reclassified based on evidence that is later discovered.

4. *Parties that have not been identified as PRPs* As the investigation progresses, additional PRPs may be identified. These PRPs will later be reclassified to the participating category or the recalcitrant category.

5. *PRPs that cannot be identified or have no assets* PRPs from which no contributions will be received because they are not found or have no assets. These PRPs are sometimes referred to as "orphan PRPs."

Allocation process The environmental remediation liability is allocated only among participating PRPs. There are several ways to allocate the liability among PRPs. The following are the four principal factors that are considered in a typical allocation process:

1. *Elements of fair share* Examples are the amount of waste based on volume, mass, type, and toxicity and the length of time the site was used.

2. *Classification of PRP* Examples are site operator, transporter of waste, and generator of waste.

3. *Limitations on payments* Any statutory or regulatory limitations on contributions.

4. *Degree of care* Refers to the degree of care exercised in selecting the site or in selecting a transporter.

The environmental remediation liability may be allocated according to any of the following methods: (1) PRPs may agree among themselves as to the allocation, (2) PRPs may hire an allocation consultant whose conclusions may or may not be binding, or (3) PRPs may request a nonbinding allocation of responsibility from the EPA. The allocation method or percentages may change as the project moves forward.

An entity should determine its allocable share of the remediation liability based on its estimate of the allocation method and its percentage of the amount that will ultimately be used for the entire remediation effort. Sources for this estimate should be the allocation method and the percentages that the PRPs have agreed to, the method and percentages that have been assigned by a consultant, or the method and percentages determined by the EPA, depending on the method that is chosen (as described in the preceding paragraph). If the entity's estimate of the ultimate liability differs significantly from the method or percentage from these primary sources, the entity's estimate should be based on objective, verifiable evidence, such as the following:

- Existing data about the kinds and quantities of waste at the site
- Experience with allocation approaches in comparable situations

- Reports of environmental specialists
- Internal data refuting EPA allegations about the entity's contribution of waste to the site

A consideration in estimating an entity's allocable share of the liability is the financial condition of the participating PRPs, including their ability to pay. The entity should include in its liability its share of amounts that are not expected to be paid by other PRPs or by the government.

Impact of potential recoveries Potential recoveries may come from a number of sources, such as insurers, PRPs other than participating PRPs, and government or third-party funds. The environmental remediation liability should be determined without regard to potential recoveries. An asset related to recoveries should be separately recognized only when realization is considered probable. If the claim is subject to litigation, the realization of the recovery claim is not considered probable.

Fair value should be the basis for measuring the potential recovery. This requires consideration of both the transaction costs related to the recovery and the time value of money. The time value of money should not be considered, however, if the liability is not discounted and if the timing of the recovery depends on the timing of the payment of the liability. Usually the point in time when the liability is both probable and reasonably estimable precedes the point in time when any related recovery is probable of realization.

Financial Statement Presentation and Disclosure

The guidelines for financial statement presentation and disclosure are discussed in this section of the SOP. Entities that are subject to the rules and regulations of the Securities and Exchange Commission (SEC) also are required to adhere to various SEC rules that apply to environmental matters.

Financial Statement Presentation

Several assets may result from an environmental remediation obligation, including the following:

- Receivables from other PRPs that are not providing initial funding
- Anticipated recoveries from insurers
- Anticipated recoveries from prior owners as a result of indemnification agreements

ASC 210-20, 815-10 (FIN-39, Offsetting of Amounts Related to Certain Contracts) specifies that offsetting assets and liabilities is appropriate only when a right of setoff exists, which requires *all* of the following:

- Each of the two parties owes the other party a determinable amount.
- The reporting entity has the right to set off the amounts owed with the amount owed by the other party.
- The reporting entity intends to set off.
- The right of setoff is enforceable at law.

For environmental remediation assets and liabilities these rules apply, although SOP 96-1 indicates that it would be rare for the facts and circumstances surrounding environmental remediation liabilities and related assets to -meet these conditions.

Recording an environmental remediation liability usually results in a charge to income. Such a charge does not meet the criteria of ASC 225-20-45-1 through 45-6, 45-8, 45-10 through 45-14, 45-16; 15-2; 50-2 through 50-3; 55-1 through 55-2; 830-10-45-19 (APB-30, Reporting the Results of Operations) for classification as an extraordinary item, because it does not result from an event that is unusual in nature and infrequent in occurrence. Furthermore, it is difficult to substantiate the classification of environmental remediation costs as a component of nonoperating expenses, because the events underlying the obligation are part of the entity's operations. Thus, environmental remediation-related expenses should be reported as a component of operating income in an income statement that separates operating and nonoperating items. Credits (i.e., gains or loss recoveries) that are recognized in the entity's financial statements should be presented in the income statement in the same manner. Any earnings on assets that are reflected in the entity's balance sheet and are reserved for its environmental liabilities should be reported as investment income. Environmental remediation-related expenses and recoveries that are associated with disposals of a segment of a business that are accounted for in accordance with the guidance in ASC 225-20-45-1 through 45-6, 45-8, 45-10 through 45-14, 45-16; 15-2; 50-2 through 50-3; 55-1 through 55-2; 830-10-45-19 (APB-30) should be classified as discontinued operations.

DISCLOSURE

Accounting policies ASC 235-10-05-3 through 05-4; 50-1 through 50-6 (APB-22, Disclosure of Accounting Policies) provides guidance concerning information that must be disclosed about the accounting policies employed by an entity in the preparation of its financial statements. With regard to environmental remediation liabilities, that disclosure should include an indication of whether the accrual is measured on a discounted basis.

Environmental remediation liabilities are increasingly significant and involve subjective judgment. As a result, entities are encouraged, but not required, to disclose the event, situation, or set of circumstances that generally triggers recognition of loss contingencies that arise out of the entity's environmental remediation-related obligations. Entities also are encouraged to disclose their policy with regard to the timing of recognition of recoveries. An example of an accounting policy note is presented in the following Illustration.

Illustration of Accounting Policy Note

Environmental remediation costs—Company X accrues losses associated with environmental remediation obligations when they are probable and reasonably estimable, which usually is no later than the time of completion of the remedial feasibility study. These accruals are adjusted as additional information is available or if circumstances change. Costs of future expenditures for environmental remediation obligations are [not] discounted to their present value. Expected recoveries of environmental remediation costs from other parties are recognized as assets when their receipt is judged to be probable.

Loss contingencies The disclosure requirements in ASC 450 (FAS-5) and SOP 94-6 (see ASC references above) are particularly important for environmental remediation liabilities. FAS-5 requires disclosure of loss contingencies as follows:

- If accrual is possible, the nature of an accrual for a loss contingency and, in some circumstances, the amount accrued to keep financial statements from being misleading
- If no accrual is possible because the loss is either not probable or estimable, or if an exposure to loss exists in excess of the accrued amount, the reasonable possibility of loss, the nature of the loss, and an estimate of the possible range of loss, or a statement that such an estimate cannot be made

The disclosure requirements of SOP 94-6 (see ASC references above) that are particularly important for an environmental remediation liability are the following:

- Estimates used in determining the carrying amount of assets or liabilities or gain or loss contingencies
- Information regarding an estimate when information known before issuance of the financial statements indicates that both of the following are met:
    - It is at least reasonably possible that the estimate of the effect on the financial statements of a condition, situation, or set of circumstances that existed at the date of the financial statements will change in the near term due to one or more future confirming events.

— The effect of the change would be material to the financial statements.
- Information regarding the nature of the uncertainty and an indication that it is at least reasonably possible that a change in the estimate will occur in the near term. (If the estimate involves a loss contingency covered by ASC 450 (FAS-5), the disclosure also should include an estimate of the possible loss or range of loss or state that such an estimate cannot be made.)

Uncertainties associated with environmental remediation loss contingencies are pervasive and may result in wide ranges of reasonably possible loss contingencies. These contingencies may occur over many years. As a result, SOP 96-1 encourages but does not require additional specific disclosures with respect to environmental remediation loss contingencies that would be useful in better understanding the entity's financial statements.

The following Illustration summarizes the disclosure requirements of ASC 450 (FAS-5), SOP 94-6 (see ASC references above), and this SOP for loss contingencies related to environmental remediation liabilities.

Illustration of Disclosures for Loss Contingencies

Related to Recorded Accruals

1. The nature of the accrual (if required to keep financial statements from being misleading), including the total amount accrued
2. If any portion of the accrued obligation is discounted, the undiscounted amount of the obligation and the discount rate used in the present value calculation
3. If the criteria of SOP 94-6 (see ASC references above) are met with respect to the accrued obligation or to any recognized asset for third-party recoveries, an indication that it is at least reasonably possible that a change in the estimate, obligation, or asset will occur in the near term

Related to Reasonably Possible Loss Contingencies

1. The nature of the reasonably possible loss contingency; also, an estimate of the possible loss exposure, or the fact that such an estimate cannot be made
2. If the criteria of SOP 94-6 (see ASC references above) are met with respect to estimated gain or loss contingencies, it is an indication that it is at least reasonably possible that a change in the estimate will occur in the near term

Disclosures Encouraged But Not Required

1. The estimated time frame of disbursements for recorded amounts if expenditures are expected to continue over a long period of time
2. The estimated time frame for realization of recognized probable recoveries if those recoveries are not expected in the near term
3. If the criteria of SOP 94-6 (see ASC references above) are met with respect to the accrued obligation, to any recognized asset for third-party recoveries, or to reasonably possible loss exposures or disclosed gain contingencies, the factors that cause the estimate to be sensitive to change
4. If an estimate of the probable or reasonably possible loss or range of loss cannot be made, the reasons why
5. If information about the reasonably possible loss or the recognized and additional reasonably possible loss for an environmental remediation obligation related to an individual site is relevant to an understanding of the financial statements, the following with respect to that site:
    a. The total amount accrued for the site
    b. The nature of any reasonably possible loss contingency or additional loss, and an estimate of the possible loss or the fact that such an estimate cannot be made and why
    c. Whether other PRPs are involved, and the entity's estimated share of the obligation
    d. The status of regulatory proceedings
    e. The estimated time frame for resolution of the contingency

Probable But Not Reasonably Estimable Losses

1. If the environmental remediation liability may be material, a description of the remediation obligation and the fact that a reasonable estimate cannot be made
2. Disclosure of the estimated time frame for resolution of the uncertainty about the amount of the loss (encouraged, but not required)

Unasserted Claims

1. If an entity is required by existing laws and regulations to report the release of hazardous substances and to begin a remediation study, or if assertion of a claim is considered probable, the matter represents a loss contingency subject to the disclosure requirements for unasserted claims of ASC 450 (FAS-5).

Environmental Remediation Costs Currently Recognized

Entities are encouraged, but not required, to disclose the following details concerning environmental remediation costs:

1. The amount recognized for environmental remediation loss contingencies for each period

2. The amount of any recovery from third parties that is credited to environmental remediation costs in each period
3. The income statement caption in which environmental remediation costs and credits are included

ASC 450 Contingencies

EITF Issue 03-8 (Accounting for Claims-Made Insurance and Retroactive Insurance Contracts by the Insured Entity) (ASC 450-30-60-4; 720-20-05-2 through 05-8; 15-4 through 15-6, 15-8; 25-2 through 25-12, 25-14; 30-2; 35-2 through 35-5, 35-8 through 35-10; 45-1; 50-1; 55-3 through 55-12, 55-14 through 55-20; 954-720-25-4A)

OVERVIEW

This Issue codifies the guidance in the following Issues and FASB staff announcement, which address the accounting for retroactive insurance contracts and claims-made insurance policies by insured entities, including those that purchase insurance unrelated to an entity's core insurance operations:

- EITF Issue 86-12, "Accounting by Insureds for Claims-Made Insurance Policies" (Codified in Issue 03-8)
- EITF Issue 03-3, "Applicability of *EITF Abstracts,* Topic D-79, 'Accounting for Retroactive Insurance Contracts Purchased by Entities Other Than Insurance Enterprises' to Claims-Made Insurance Policies" (Codified in Issue 03-8)
- Topic D-79, "Accounting for Retroactive Insurance Contracts Purchased by Entities Other Than Insurance Enterprises" (Codified in Issue 03-8)

This Issue does *not* apply to reinsurance transactions.

Companies generally purchase claims-made policies to cover product, directors and officers (D&O), and malpractice liabilities. Such coverage insures an entity for claims reported during the policy's term, depending on the policy's retroactive date. Two categories of claims are covered: (*a*) retroactive claims for incidents that occurred *before* the policy's term and reported during its term or (*b*) *prospective* claims for incidents that occur and are reported during the policy's term.

Claims-made policies are generally renewed annually. If a company ceases its operations, it can purchase tail insurance, which insures the entity against claims made *after* the policy has terminated. By renewing its policy annually and purchasing tail insurance, if needed, a company can convert a claims-made policy to one based on occurrence so that the company is covered for any claims made against it. Because the date of occurrence is usually irrelevant in determining whether a claim is covered, a claims-made policy is usually the only form of insurance that covers exposures for which it is difficult to determine the date of occurrence and occurrences that may extend over long periods of time. Some companies that purchase such insurance are frequently unaware of outstanding unasserted claims of liabilities that do not meet the recognition criteria in ASC 450 (FAS-5) or other generally accepted accounting principles (GAAP). Consequently, no liability has been recognized for such claims, including incurred but not reported (IBNR) claims. Other companies that purchase such claims-made coverage may know about potential claims related to specific incidents, and may choose to specifically include those unasserted claims under the coverage or to exclude them.

ACCOUNTING ISSUES

1. How should an insured entity, such as a manufacturer, retailer, service company, or financial institution, including an insurance company that purchases insurance *not* related to its core insurance operations, account for a purchased retroactive insurance policy to cover a liability for a *past* event recognized in accordance with ASC 450 (FAS-5), and does that transaction result in a gain being recognized? (Topic D-79)

2. Does a claims-made insurance policy correspond to a purchased retroactive insurance policy covered by the consensus in Issue 1? (Issue 03-3)

3a. Should an insured entity recognize a liability at the balance sheet date for IBNR claims? (Issue 1 of Issue 86-12)

3b. If it is impossible to reasonably estimate the probable losses from IBNR claims and the number of incidents cannot be reasonably estimated, may a liability be accrued based on the estimated cost of purchasing tail coverage to insure the entity for events that occur during the period of the claims-made policy but that are *not* reported to the insurance carrier in that period? (Issue 2 of Issue 86-12)

4a. If an entity's fiscal year and the term of a prospective policy are the same, how should both of the following be accounted for: (*a*) the IBNR liability in subsequent periods in which the entity purchases another claims-made insurance policy that covers a portion of losses included in the IBNR liability, and (*b*) the premiums for the subsequent claims-made insurance policy? (Issues 4 and 5 of Issue 86-12)

4b. What is the accounting effect on the consensus reached on Issue 4(a) if a prospective claims-made policy's term is *not* the same as the entity's fiscal year? (Issue 6 of Issue 86-12)

5. What disclosures should be made by companies insured under claims-made policies? (Issue 3 of Issue 86-12 and discussion at the July 2003 EITF meeting)

EITF CONSENSUS

1. The consensus on Issue 1 applies only to retroactive insurance contracts that (*a*) do not legally extinguish an entity's liability, (*b*) meet the conditions in ASC 450 (FAS-5) for indemnification against loss or liability, (*c*) indemnify the insured against loss or liability for liabilities that were incurred as a result of a past event, for example, environmental remediation liabilities, and (*d*) are not reinsurance transactions.

    The EITF noted that under the guidance in ASC 450-20-05-3 (paragraph 44 of FAS- 5), entities are required to determine whether an insurance contract results in a transfer of insurance risk. The guidance for insurance enterprises in ASC 944-20 (FAS-113, Accounting and Reporting for Reinsurance of Short-Duration and Long-Duration Contracts) may be useful in making that determination. FAS-113 provides that reinsurance contracts that do *not* transfer insurance risk should be accounted for as deposits.

    Although ASC 944-20 (FAS-113) applies only to insurance companies, the EITF reached a consensus that purchased retroactive insurance contracts that indemnify an insured should be accounted for in a manner similar to that provided in ASC 944-20 (FAS-113) for retroactive reinsurance contracts. The guidance in ASC 944-605-25-35 (paragraphs 22 through 25 of FAS-113) should be applied, if appropriate, based on the facts and circumstances of the specific transaction.

    Amounts paid for retroactive insurance should be expensed immediately, and a receivable should be recognized at the same time for expected recoveries related to the underlying event. If a receivable exceeds the amount paid for the insurance, there is a deferred gain, which should be amortized using the interest method over the estimated period that the entity expects to recover substantially all amounts due under the terms of the insurance contract, provided the amount and timing of the insurance recoveries can be reasonably estimated. Otherwise, amortization should be based on the proportion of actual recoveries to total estimated recoveries.

    A gain should *not* be recognized and a related liability should *not* be derecognized immediately, because the liability has not been completely extinguished. The EITF also noted that amounts receivable on an insurance policy should *not* be offset against a liability for a past insurable event, because those amounts do *not* meet the criteria in ASC 210-20; 815-10 (FIN-39, Offsetting of Amounts Related to Certain Contracts) for offsetting. Legal and other costs covered under purchased insurance contracts should be accounted for in a consistent manner in the related asset and liability accounts. For example, if the costs are covered under the term of the insurance contracts and the entity's policy is to accrue such costs, they should also be included in the insurance receivable.

2. The EITF reached a consensus that a claims-made insurance policy contains a retroactive provision if it provides coverage for specific, known claims that were reportable by the insured entity to the insurance carrier before the period of the policy. Retroactive and prospective provisions of such policies should be accounted for separately, if practicable. Otherwise, the entire policy should be accounted for as a retroactive contract in accordance with ASC 944-605-25-35 (paragraphs 22 through 25 of FAS-113). Claims-made insurance policies that do *not* include retroactive provisions should be accounted for on a *prospective* basis based on the consensus position in Issues 4(a) and Issue 4(b).

The Task Force noted that because ASC 944-20-15-34B (paragraph 95 of FAS-113, Accounting and Reporting for Reinsurance of Short-Duration and Long-Duration Contracts) states that under a claims-made policy, an insured event is the act of *reporting* to an insurer a loss covered by a policy during the period stated in the policy, *prospective* claims-made insurance policies cover only losses reported to an insurer during the term of a policy, regardless of the date on which the incident resulting in the claim occurred. A policy with a retroactive provision covers insured events that occurred or were reportable *before* the term of the policy and, therefore, covers claims for specific, known claims that were reportable before the policy's effective date. The EITF also noted that the fact that a liability for IBNR claims has been recognized is *not* a conclusive factor in determining whether a claims-made insurance policy contains a retroactive provision.

The EITF also noted that all facts and circumstances that are relevant should be considered in determining whether a claims-made policy includes a retroactive provision. The following are indicators that a policy does *not* contain a retroactive provision (i.e., it does not cover previously reportable claims) and should be accounted for on a prospective basis, but no one indicator is determinative:

a. The insured always purchases claims-made insurance policies for the type of risk that is insured, and tail coverage for prior periods and policies can be easily obtained at a reasonable cost compared to tail coverage that does not contain retroactive provisions offered to similar companies.

b. The claims-made policy covers unknown risks for a finite or limited time period, because (*a*) the claims are incurred during the policy's period and paid shortly after the end of the policy's period, (*b*) the policy covers a limited time period, (c) claims-made insurance is the most easily available coverage for this type of insurance risk, and (d) it is difficult to determine the date on which the type of risk covered under the policy will occur.

c. The claims-made insurance policy has clear indicators *not* subject to interpretation, negotiation, or manipulation, that a claim is covered under the policy, such as, a provision requiring (a) notification by an insured of an asserted claim or that an incident occurred during the policy term, or (b) a representation that the insured was not aware of such an incident when the claims-made policy was purchased.

d. The claims-made policy's premium is *not* significantly higher than that for a policy that could be purchased by a similar entity with similar insurance risks that does not know of any circumstances or events that would result in claims, except for a typical number of claims incurred but not reported (IBNR).

e. The policy's premium may be based on estimates and predictions based on the insured's past experience, but not on estimates of settlements of specific, known events expected to be recovered under the policy.

f. The current year's premium does *not* significantly exceed that charged in previous years, except for increases in the amount or type of coverage.

g. The policy is purchased primarily to cover insurance risk, *not* as a financing arrangement. Such claims-made policies usually include (a) no adjustments based on experience, and (b) coverage of the final loss from a claim once it has been made, regardless of when the claim is settled.

h. If a claims-made insurance policy has a specified retroactive date before the relationship with the insurer begins, the period from the specified retroactive date to the date the claims-made relationship with the insurer begins is short or is covered by other insurance.

The EITF noted that the guidance in Issue 1 is *not* intended to preclude prospective accounting for claims-made policies or portions of those policies that contain only prospective provisions even though the guidance applies in situations in which an insured entity uses the policy to finance known losses that occurred or were reportable *before* entering into the insurance contract. In addition, an insured entity that enters into multiple claims-made insurance contracts at the same time should consider whether to combine the insurance contracts so it can determine how to account for them. ASC 944-20-15-40 (paragraph 8 of FAS-113) provides guidance on those matters.

3a. Under the guidance in ASC 450 (FAS-5), insured entities that insure certain risks using a claims-made approach are required to recognize a liability for probable losses from IBNR claims and incidents if the loss is *probable* and *estimable*. The EITF noted that recognition of a liability for an IBNR claim would generally *not* be a determinative indicator that a claims-made insurance policy does *not* contain a retroactive provision. In addition, prepaid insurance or insurance to be recovered should *not* be offset against a recognized IBNR liability or a liability incurred as a result of a past insurable event, unless the conditions in ASC 210-20, 815-10 (FIN-39) are met.

3b. If an entity has not purchased tail insurance coverage, the estimated cost of such coverage is irrelevant in determining a loss accrual. However, the EITF agreed that if an entity has the option to purchase such coverage at a premium that does not exceed a specified fixed maximum and the entity intends to do so, the maximum premium could be used as a ceiling in determining an estimated IBNR liability. Nevertheless, the need to determine whether an additional liability should be accrued as a result of policy limits and other factors is *not* eliminated by purchasing tail coverage.

4a. If an entity's fiscal year and the policy's year are the same, the entity should accrue the total expense of the annual premium and anticipated adjustments of the IBNR liability at year-end on a pro rata basis over the year. Unusual claims or incidents *not* insured under the current claims-made policy should be recognized in the interim period in which they become known. Under this approach, usual recurring losses are accounted for in the interim period as part of annual reporting, but unusual material losses are accounted for as separate items and recognized as they occur. It is assumed under this approach that the purchase of a one-year term claims-made insurance policy is a recurring event and that the premium will be paid on the first day of each policy year.

Task force members noted that when an entity's fiscal year and the policy's term are the same, the entity's liability at year-end for IBNR is for claims and incidents that were incurred *before* the year-end but that will be reportable after year-end. Policyholders that purchase claims-made policies consisting of *prospective* provisions should account for those policies as follows:

a. At the *beginning* of the fiscal year, a prepaid expense should be recognized for the total premium paid for the new policy.

b. At the *beginning* of the fiscal year, the IBNR liability as of the end of the fiscal year should be estimated by considering claims and incidents that occurred before the year-end but that will *not* be reportable until after the year-end. That amount should be roughly the IBNR liability at the beginning of the year plus adjustments for relevant historical patterns and possible adjustments due to new factors that have been identified, such as major changes in products, manufacturing processes, or risk management systems.

c. The estimated annual expense should be computed as the sum of (*a*) the premium paid for the claims-made policy, and (*b*) the difference between the IBNR at the beginning of the year and at the end of the year. That amount should be recognized ratably in interim periods using a method that best represents the manner in which the benefits of the insurance coverage are used up and the IBNR liability is incurred.

d. The estimated IBNR liability should be reviewed at interim reporting dates. Routine adjustments of the estimated liability should be recognized ratably in interim periods, but significant adjustments of the year-end IBNR liability should be recognized in an interim period in which events and circumstances indicate that unusual claims and incidents occurred *before* the end of the interim period but that will probably not be reported until after year-end and, therefore, will *not* be covered under the existing claims-made policy.

e. Unusual claims and incidents that have occurred *before* the end of an interim period but that will probably be reported *before* the year-end do *not* affect net income if they are covered under an existing policy.

The EITF noted that prepaid insurance should *not* be offset against a recognized IBNR liability or a liability incurred as a result of a past insurable event unless the conditions in ASC 210-20; 815-10 (FAS-39) are met.

4b. If an entity's fiscal year and policy year are *not* the same, the accrual in interim periods should be based on the entity's estimated premium for the claims-made policy expected to be purchased later in that fiscal year. At year-end, the entity should recognize the following: (*a*) an IBNR *liability* for the obligation for claims and incidents that occurred *before* year-end but that will be reported *after* year-end and (*b*) an *asset* for prepaid insurance premiums for coverage of claims and incidents that will occur *after* year-end, but will be reported *before* the current policy expires. Policyholders that purchase claims-made policies with terms that are *not* the same as the entity's fiscal year should account for those policies as follows:

a. The estimated premium for a new claims-made policy expected to be purchased during the fiscal year should be estimated at the *beginning* of the fiscal year. The portion of the future premium relating to coverage for claims or incidents that will occur *after* the end of the fiscal year but that will be reported *before* the new claims-made policy expires should also be estimated. That amount is the estimated prepaid asset at end of the fiscal year. An estimate of the future premium considers the effect of past claims and incidents that are expected to affect the premium and the effect of historical patterns and relevant new factors, such as a major change in products, manufacturing processes, or risk management systems.

b. At the *beginning* of the fiscal year, the IBNR liability as of the end of the fiscal year should be estimated by considering claims and incidents that occurred before the year-end but that will not be reportable until after the year-end. That amount should be roughly the IBNR liability at the beginning of the year plus adjustments for relevant historical patterns and possible adjustments due to new factors that have been identified, such as major changes in products, manufacturing processes, or risk management systems.

c. The estimated annual expense should be computed as the sum of (*a*) the estimated premium paid for a new claims-made policy, (*b*) the difference between the beginning prepaid insurance and the estimated year-end prepaid insurance, and (*c*) the difference between the IBNR liability at the beginning of the fiscal year and the estimated IBNR liability at year-end. That amount should be recognized ratably in interim periods using a method that best represents the manner in which the benefits of the insurance coverage are used up and the IBNR liability is incurred.

d. The estimated IBNR liability should be reviewed at interim reporting dates. Routine adjustments of the estimated liability, such as adjustments of the estimated future premium to reflect the actual cost should be recognized ratably in the remaining interim periods, but significant adjustments of the year-end IBNR liability should be recognized in an interim period in which events and circumstances indicate that unusual claims and incidents occurred before the end of the interim period but that will probably not be reportable until after the subsequent interim period.

e. Unusual claims and incidents that occurred before the end of an interim period but that will probably be reported before the new claims-made policy expires do *not* affect net income if they will be covered by insurance.

5. During a discussion of the disclosures that should be made if an entity changes from occurrence-based insurance to claims-made insurance or elects to significantly reduce or eliminate its insurance coverage, members noted that under ASC 450-20-25-2 (paragraph 10 of FAS-5), disclosure is required if it is at least reasonably possible that a loss has been incurred. That paragraph also includes a discussion of disclosures for unasserted claims.

In July 1987, the AICPA's Accounting Standards Executive Committee (AcSEC) issued the Report of the Task Force of Insurance, Disclosure Concerning Insurance Coverage, which encouraged publicly held entities and entities with public accountability, such as governments, to disclose circumstances in which they are exposed to certain uninsured risks of future material loss. Reporting entities can decide on the matters to be disclosed and no specific disclosures are recommended if an entity changes from occurrence-based insurance to claims-made insurance or elects to significantly reduce or eliminate its insurance coverage. The following are the conclusions of the stated in the Report:

1. Publicly held entities and entities with public accountability, such as governments are encouraged, but not required, to disclose the following:
    a. Circumstances in which they are exposed to risks of future material loss related to:
        (1) Torts
        (2) Theft of, damage to, expropriation of, or destruction of assets
        (3) Business interruption
        (4) Errors or omissions
        (5) Injuries to employees, or
        (6) Acts of God, and
    b. Those risks have *not* been transferred to unrelated third parties through insurance.
2. A reporting entity should decide what matters should be disclosed, based on the circumstances. Entities might consider disclosing the following matters:
    a. The actual and potential effects of losses from such risks on the entity's historical or planned operations, including exposure to losses from claims, curtailment of research and development or manufacturing, or contraction or cessation of other activities, such as a discontinued product line
    b. A comparison of current insurance coverage by major categories of risk to coverage in prior periods, without disclosing the amount or changes, if any, of coverage
    c. Recent claims experience
    d. A description of the entity's risk management programs
3. The location of the disclosures in the financial statements depends on the preparer's judgment.

TRANSITION

The transition guidance in the original individual pronouncements applies to the issues discussed in this Issue.

ASC 460 Guarantees

FSP FIN-45-1 (Accounting for Intellectual Property Infringement Indemnification under FIN-45) (ASC 460-10-55-31 through 55-34)

Question: A software vendor-licensor may include an indemnification clause in a software licensing agreement that indemnifies the licensee against liability and damages arising from any claims of patent, copyright, trademark, or trade secret infringement by the software vendor's software. Does an indemnification of that type constitute a guarantee subject to the scope of FASB Accounting Standards Codification™ (ASC) 460 (FIN-45, Guarantor's Accounting and Disclosure Requirements for Guarantees, Including Indirect Guarantees of Indebtedness to Others)?

Answer: Yes. The infringement indemnification arrangement requires the guarantor to make a payment to the guaranteed party if the occurrence of an infringement claim against the licensee results in any liability or damage related to the licensed software. However, because an infringement claim can impair the licensee's ability to use the software, the occurrence of an infringement claim is related to the performance of the licensed software. Therefore, an infringement indemnification arrangement falls under the scope of ASC 460 (FIN-45) and a liability need not be recognized at the inception of the guarantee (i.e., the product scope exception applies). The disclosure requirements of ASC 460 (FIN-45) that relate to guarantees under product warranties would apply to guarantees from infringement indemnification arrangements.

FSP FIN-45-2 (Whether FASB Interpretation No. 45, Guarantor's Accounting and Disclosure Requirements for Guarantees, Including Indirect Guarantees of Indebtedness of Others, Provides Support for Subsequently Accounting for a Guarantor's Liability at Fair Value) (ASC 460-10-35-2)

Question: May a guarantor that wishes to report its liability for obligations under a guarantee (including a seller's recourse obligations, if any, included in ASC 460-10-15-4; 25-34; 55-2, 55-5, 55-12 through 55-13 (paragraph 3 of FIN-45) at fair value after initial recognition cite FIN-45 to justify using that accounting method for subsequent measurement of the liability?

Answer: No. A guarantor may *not* cite ASC 460 (FIN-45) to justify measuring the guarantor's liability for its obligations at fair value after the guarantee has been issued. The guidance in FIN-45 applies only to the measurement of a guarantor's liability for the guarantee when it is initially recognized. In addition, paragraph A49 (not in ASC) states specifically that providing guidance on subsequent accounting is beyond the Interpretation's scope.

The FASB staff notes that although ASC 460-10-35-1 through 35-2, 35-4 (paragraph 12 of FIN-45) discusses three methods that are used in practice to measure the liability *after* initial recognition, the discussion is *not* intended to imply that a guarantor can choose any of those methods to subsequently account for the liability. A guarantor should *not* account for a liability for its obligation under a previously issued guarantee at fair value in subsequent periods unless doing so can be justified under generally accepted accounting principles, for example, accounting for a guarantee as a derivative under ASC 815 (FAS-133, Accounting for Derivative Instruments and Hedging Activities).

Subsequent to initial recognition, a guarantor that is using fair value to measure its obligations under a guarantee, other than one under the scope of ASC 815 (FAS-133), and relying on ASC 460 (FIN-45) to justify that treatment should reconsider the appropriateness of that treatment at the end of the fiscal quarter that includes December 10, 2003, the date on which this FSP was posted on the FASB's web site. If the guarantor cannot justify the use of fair value based on GAAP, the fair value of the liability at the end of that fiscal quarter should be the liability's carrying amount for the future application of the guarantor's new method of measuring the liability in subsequent accounting.

FSP FIN-45-3 (Application of FASB Interpretation No. 45 in Minimum Revenue Guarantees Granted to a Business or Its Owners) (ASC 460-10-55-1, 55-10 through 55-11; 954-460-55-1)

OVERVIEW

This FASB Staff Position (FSP), which amends the guidance in ASC 460 (FIN-45, Guarantor's Accounting and Disclosure Requirements for Guarantees, Including Indirect Guarantees of Indebtedness of Others), is being issued in response to questions raised by constituents regarding its applicability to a guarantee granted to a business or its owner under which the business or the owner is guaranteed a specified minimum amount of revenue for a specified period of time. For example, a not-for-profit health care facility that recruits a nonemployee physician to establish a practice in a certain area guarantees to make a payment to the physician if the physician's gross revenues do not equal or exceed a specified dollar amount during a specified period of time. In another example, a corporation that wants a daycare center to open a facility next to its plant guarantees to the daycare center that it will earn a minimum amount of revenue per month over a specified period of time (e.g., during the first 12 months). If the daycare center does not earn the guaranteed minimum amount during any month in the first 12 months, the corporation guarantees to make up the shortfall.

AMENDMENT TO FIN-45

ASC 460-10-15-4; 25-34; 50-2, 50-5, 50-12 through 50-13 (paragraph 3 of FIN-45) states:

> 3. Except as provided in ASC 460-10-15-7 (paragraphs 6 and 7 of FIN-45), the provisions of this Interpretation apply to guarantee contracts that have any of the following characteristics:
>
> a. Contracts that contingently require the guarantor to make payments (either in cash, financial instruments, other assets, shares of its stock, or provision of services) to the guaranteed party based on changes in an underlying (as defined in ASC, *Glossary*, (paragraph 540 of FAS-133) that is related to an asset, a liability, or an equity security of the guaranteed party. Thus, for example, the provisions apply to the following:

(5) A guarantee granted to a business or its owner(s) that the revenue of the business (or a specific portion of the business) for a specified period of time will be at least a specified amount.

Note: Four examples are listed in ASC 460-10-55-2 (paragraph 3(a) of FIN-45). The amendment adds the above fifth example.

EFFECTIVE DATE AND TRANSITION

The FSP applies to *new* guarantees of minimum revenue. It is effective for such guarantees that have been issued or modified on or *after* the beginning of the first fiscal quarter after November 10, 2005, the date the FSP was posted on the FASB's web site. Although early application is permitted for *new* transactions, guarantors should *not* revise or restate their previous accounting based on the recognition and measurement provisions of ASC 460 (FIN-45) for minimum revenue guarantees that were issued *before* this FSP's effective date.

Guarantors should disclose the information required in ASC 460-10-50-4; 55-8, 55-5, 55-6; 850-10-60-2 (paragraphs 13 through 16 of FIN-45) for all minimum revenue guarantees in interim or annual financial periods ending after the beginning of the first fiscal quarter after November 10, 2005. Those disclosure requirements should be presented for any minimum revenue guarantees issued *before* this

FSP is initially applied, even if those guarantees were *not* recognized and measured under the provisions of ASC 460 (FIN-45).

BASIS FOR CONCLUSION

The FASB reached a conclusion that the guarantee discussed in this FSP meets the characteristics in ASC 460-10-55-2 (paragraph 3(a) of FIN-45), because the guarantee's *underlying*, which, in this case, is the gross revenues of a business or of a business owner, is related to an asset or equity security belonging to the party receiving the guarantee. A business' revenues change as result of transactions with customers. Therefore, a guarantee made to a business meets the characteristics in ASC 460-10-55-2 (paragraph 3(a) of FIN-45), because gross revenues of a business are related to changes in its assets or liabilities. In addition, a guarantee made to an owner of a business meets the characteristics in ASC 460-10-55-2 (paragraph 3(a) of FIN-45), because the gross revenues of the business are related to changes in the owner's investment in the business. The FASB further believes that guarantors should account for minimum revenue guarantees under the provisions in ASC 460 (FIN-45), because a minimum revenue guarantee granted to a business or its owners does *not* meet any of the scope exceptions in ASC 460-10-15-7, 15-9, 15-10; 25-1; 30-1 (paragraphs 6 and 7 of FIN-45).

The FASB noted that the list of examples under ASC 460-10-55-23 (FIN-45, paragraph 11) is not a comprehensive all-inclusive list of contracts that would meet the provisions of that paragraph. In addition, minimum revenue guarantees granted to physicians should be accounted for under the provisions of this FSP regardless of whether the physician's practice is considered a business under the guidance in ASC 718-10-55-85A; 810-10-05-15, 05-16; 15-19 through 15-22; 25-61 through 25-64, 25-66 through 25-72, 25-74 through 25-79, 25-81; 55-90, 55-91, 55-92 (EITF Issue 97-2, Application of FASB Statement No. 94 and APB Opinion No. 16 to Physician Practice Management Entities and Certain Other Entities with Contractual Management Arrangements).

EITF Issue 85-20 (Recognition of Fees for Guaranteeing a Loan) (ASC 460-10-60-8; 605-20-25-8 through 25-12; 15-3; 310-10-60-4)

OVERVIEW

An entity, usually a financial institution or insurance company, guarantees the debt of another entity and is paid a fee for doing so. The guarantee may be in the form of a general guarantee to ensure that the funds will be repaid or in the form of a pledge of assets that could be claimed by the lender if the borrower defaults.

11.36 *Contingencies, Risks, and Uncertainties*

Such guarantees are usually used by entities that would otherwise be unable to borrow or would have to pay a very high interest rate. The following are examples of such transactions:

- A company issues three-to-six-year notes, which are guaranteed with a surety bond issued by an insurance company. The company pays an annual premium to the insurance company based on the company's annual debt service and pledges as collateral to the insurance company assets valued at 110% of the debt.
- A developer issues tax-exempt industrial bonds to finance a project. A financial institution guarantees the debt by pledging specific assets.
- A guarantor and an investment banker establish a special-purpose entity that issues commercial paper for borrowers who would be unable to do so themselves. The guarantor provides a surety bond for each borrower to guarantee repayment of the funds. The investment banker sells the commercial paper and lends the funds to the borrower at a spread above the commercial paper interest rate. The loan and the commercial paper have the same maturity dates.

ACCOUNTING ISSUES

1. Should a guarantor recognize a liability on its balance sheet for guaranteeing the debt?
2. How should the guarantor account for initial and continuing fees received?

EITF CONSENSUS

1. The EITF reached a consensus that the guarantor should determine whether a liability (and a loss) should be recognized in accordance with the guidance in ASC 450 (FAS-5) by evaluating the probability of a loss on an ongoing basis. The guarantee should be disclosed if it is material.

    OBSERVATION: In December 1985, the SEC staff issued Staff Accounting Bulletin (SAB) No. 60, which reaffirms the EITF's consensus and provides guidance on appropriate disclosures.

    The consensus in this Issue is partially nullified by ASC 815 (FAS-133, Accounting for Derivative Instruments and Hedging Activities), which states that a guarantee would meet the definition of a derivative and should be accounted for in accordance with ASC 815 (FAS-133) if a payment on a guarantee depends on changes in an underlying, such as a change in a borrower's creditworthiness. Unless a guarantee is exempt under the scope exception in ASC 815-10-15-13 (paragraph 10(d) of FAS-133), a guarantee contract would be recognized under the Statement as an asset or liability and measured at fair value. The consensus in this Issue applies only to guarantee contracts not covered under the scope of ASC 815 (FAS-133) but are subject to the requirements of this Issue. Although ASC 815 (FAS-133) superseded the disclosure requirements of FAS-105 (not in ASC), some of the disclosures related to concentrations of credit risk have been modified and added to the requirements in ASC 825-10-50-2A through 50-3, 50-8 through 50-23; 55-3 through 55-5; 60-1; 942-470-50-1; 310-10-50-26; 958-320-50-4 (FAS-107, Disclosures about Fair Value Instruments).

2. When the Issue was first discussed in June 1985, the EITF reached a consensus that a guarantor should recognize fee income over the period of the guarantee. One member believed that because the guarantor is paid to assume risk, such fees should be recognized as the risk is reduced (and, presumably, as the principal balance of the loan is reduced). Other members likened the guarantor's risk to that of a primary lender, thus suggesting that fees be recognized over the term of the loan. The Task Force also agreed that direct costs related to the guarantee should be recognized in a comparable manner to the recognition of fee income.

After the issuance of ASC 310 (FAS-91) in December 1985, the Task Force discussed at its December 1987 and January 1988 meetings whether the previous consensus should be amended to state that the guarantor should recognize fee income in accordance with the guidance on the recognition of commitment fees in ASC 310-20-35-3 (paragraph 8 of FAS-91). Such fees are defined in ASC, *Glossary* (paragraph 80 of FAS-91) as "fees charged for entering into an agreement that obligates the enterprise to make or acquire a loan *or to satisfy an obligation* of the other party under a *specified condition.*" [Emphasis added.]

The EITF did not reach a consensus on whether the guidance in ASC 310 (FAS-91) applies to all loan guarantees, but it did agree that the character of each loan guarantee should be considered to determine whether it is more like a lending commitment or insurance. The guidance in ASC 310 (FAS-91) applies to fees for guarantees that are in essence lending commitments. Fees for guarantees that are similar to insurance should be accounted for as insurance premiums.

DISCUSSION

1. The transactions discussed in this Issue differ from usual guarantees, because the guarantor's risk related to this obligation is

almost as great as if the guarantor had borrowed the funds and lent them to the borrower. The EITF's consensus indicates its view that a guarantee is a contingency, not an outright liability, which must be evaluated based on the specific facts and circumstances.

2. A guarantor of a loan usually receives two fees: (*a*) an initial fee, which is paid when the transaction is closed, and (*b*) an annual fee, which is paid over the term of the loan. This Issue addresses the accounting for the initial fee. The Task Force's consensus is based on the notion that the initial fee cannot be separated from annual fees and should thus be recognized over the term of the loan. The guarantor does not earn the total initial fee when the transaction is closed, but rather over the period during which the guarantor will be at risk.

Although the EITF's consensus specified the period over which to recognize the fee, the Task Force did not provide guidance on the method of recognition. The Issue was reconsidered after ASC 310 (FAS-91) was issued, because that Statement provides guidance on the method of recognition. Loan guarantees contemplated in this Issue meet the definition of a commitment fee, as defined in ASC, *Glossary* (paragraph 80 of FAS-91), and should be accounted for in accordance with the guidance in ASC 310-20-35-3 (paragraph 8 of FAS-91) regardless of whether a guarantor is required to satisfy the obligation under the guarantee or the guarantor is ready to perform under the terms of the guarantee.

ASC 715 Compensation—Retirement Benefits

EITF Issue 92-13 Accounting for Estimated Payments in Connection with the Coal Industry Retiree Health Benefit Act of 1992 (ASC 715-60-60-4; ASC930-715-05-2; 25-1; 45-1; 50-1;ASC 450-20-60-18)

OVERVIEW

The United Mine Workers of America (UMWA) and the Bituminous Coal Operators' Association, Inc. (BCOA) established four trusts (1950 and 1974 Pension and Benefit Trusts) to provide pension and health benefits for coal industry retirees and their eligible dependents.

In response to the financial crisis confronting the 1950 and 1974 Benefit Trusts, a commission was appointed to study the funding problem. Based on the results of that study, Congress approved the Coal Industry Retiree Health and Benefit Act of 1992 (the Act).

The Act created a new private plan called the United Mine Workers of America Combined Benefit Fund (Combined Fund), which would provide medical benefits beginning in 1993 to all beneficiaries in the 1950 and 1974 benefit plans who were receiving benefits as of July 20, 1992. The Combined Fund is described by the Act as a multiemployer fund under the Employee Retirement Income Security Act of 1974 (ERISA).

All companies that were party to a coal wage agreement will be responsible for payments to the Combined Fund. Those payments will be based on a formula determined by the Act, which will include assignment of beneficiaries, a per-beneficiary premium, and a percentage of the cost of unassigned beneficiaries (who are referred to as orphans). The premium to be charged will be determined by using the July 1, 1991, cost per individual based on payments required by the 1950 and 1974 Benefits Trusts.

ACCOUNTING ISSUE

How should an entity account for payments required by the Act?

EITF CONSENSUS

- Entities currently involved in operations in the coal industry should account for their obligation under the Act as (1) a participation in a multiemployer plan (on a pay-as-you-go basis) or (2) a liability. Entities that choose to account for the obligation as a liability should recognize the entire obligation as a loss under the provisions of ASC 450 (FAS-5).
- Entities *not* currently involved in operations in the coal industry should account for the obligation as a liability and recognize the entire obligation as a loss under the provisions of SC 450 (FAS-5).
- Entities accounting for the obligation as a loss under the provisions of ASC 450 (FAS-5) should report the estimated loss as an extraordinary item.
- Disclosure about the effect of the Act should include information about the estimated amount of the total obligation and the entity's method of accounting for it.

FASB STAFF COMMENT

A member of the FASB staff stated that companies should not include the obligation imposed by the Act in the cumulative effect of a change in accounting principle when adopting the guidance in ASC 715 (FAS-106), because this obligation is the result of legislation rather than the result of changing to an accrual method to account for the costs of postretirement benefits.

ASC 825 Financial Instruments

FSP SOP 94-6-1 (Terms of Loan Products That May Give Rise to a Concentration of Credit Risk) (ASC 825-10-55-1, 55-2; 310-10-50-25)

OVERVIEW

The FASB staff issued this FSP in response to questions from constituents and as a result of discussions with the staff of the SEC and with regulators of financial institutions. Those questions are related to loan products that have contractual terms and features that may cause the originator, holder, investor, guarantor, or servicer of the loan to experience a greater exposure to nonpayment or realization. The following terms or loan features may increase credit risk:

- The ability to defer principal repayment or to make payments that are smaller than interest accrual and result in negative amortization
- High loan-to-value ratio
- Using the same collateral for multiple loans that result in a high loan-to-value ratio when combined
- Adjustable-rate mortgages (option ARMs) under which a borrower may choose to pay a different amount each month for a specified period of the loan term but eventually may be subject to future increases in repayments that exceed increases solely from increased market interest rates—for example, if a loan to reach a maximum limit for accrual of principal because of negative amortization
- A below market interest rate during the initial period of a loan term that may increase significantly thereafter
- Interest-only loans

Information about credit losses on loans that have reduced payment requirements in the early part of the loans' terms may not be known to creditors until a loan's payment terms change. This delays a creditor's ability to determine that a loss accrual should be recognized and a loan loss allowance should be established under the guidance in ASC 450 (FAS-5, Accounting for Contingencies) and ASC 310-10-30-2, 35-13 through 35-14, 35-16 through 35-22, 35-24 through 35-29, 35-32, 35-34, 35-37, 35-39; 45-5 through 45-6; 50-12 through 50-13, 50-15, 50-19 310-40-35-8 through 35-9, 35-12; 50-2 through 50-3 (FAS-114,Accounting by Creditors for Impairment of a Loan).

Loan products with initial payment requirements for amounts less than or equal to the contractual interest, such as option ARMs, negative amortizing, deferred interest, or interest-only loans, can increase the loan-to-value ratio and reduce a borrower's equity. A borrower's contractually required repayments on such loans may increase in the future as a result of increases in interest rates, a step-up from the initial interest rate, or required amortization of the principal amount. The borrower's ability to repay a loan may be affected by those payment increases and may lead to default and losses. The risk of loss on loans with high loan-to-value ratios that are based on appreciation of the collateral may increase if the expected appreciation does not occur.

The purpose of this FSP is to emphasize the requirement to assess the adequacy of disclosures for secured and unsecured loans and how changes in market and economic conditions affect the adequacy of those disclosures.

FASB STAFF POSITION

Question 1: Under what circumstances, if any, do the terms of loan products cause a *concentration of credit risk* as the term is used in ASC 825-10-50-2A through 50-3, 50-8 through 50-23; 55-3 through 55-5; 60-1; 942-470-50-1; 310-10-50-26; 958-320-50-4, (FAS-107, Disclosures about Fair Value of Financial Instruments)?

Answer: A reporting entity's *concentration of credit risk* may be caused by the terms of certain loan products, either as individual products or as a group of products with similar features. Under the guidance in ASC 958-320-50-4; 825-10-50-20 through 50-21 (paragraph 15A of FAS-107), disclosures are required about each significant concentration, including "information about the (shared) activity, region, or economic characteristic that identifies the concentration." Shared characteristics that may be used to determine significant concentrations may include, but are not limited to:

- Borrowers subject to significant increases in payments
- Loan terms permitting negative amortization
- Loans with high loan-to-value ratios

Judgment should be used in determining whether a loan's terms cause a concentration of credit risk.

Under the guidance in ASC 825-10-50-23 (paragraph 15C of FAS-107), entities are encouraged to disclose "quantitative information about the market risks of financial instruments that is consistent with the way it manages or adjusts those risks." In addition, entities may disclose information about how their underwriting procedures deal with controlling credit risk that may occur as a result of future payment increases on loans.

Question 2: What disclosures or other accounting considerations apply for entities that originate, hold, guarantee, service, or invest in loan products whose terms may give rise to a concentration of credit risk?

Answer: Disclosures in addition to those required in Question 1 should be considered. The type of disclosures and their extent should be influenced by the type of entity making the disclosures and how significant the loan products are to the reporting entity. Under the guidance in ASC 275-10-50-1 (Paragraph 8 of SOP 94-6, Disclosure of Certain Significant Risks and Uncertainties), disclosure is required about the existence of risks and uncertainties as of the date of the financial statements in the following areas:

- Nature of operations
- Estimates used in preparing the financial statements
- Certain significant estimates
- Current exposure as a result of certain concentrations

The contractual terms of certain loan products cause entities to be vulnerable to risks and uncertainties in one or more of those areas. Under the guidance in ASC 275-10-50-18 (paragraph 22 of SOP 94-6), revenue concentrations from particular products should be disclosed. Disclosure of other concentrations is required if they meet the following requirements in ASC 275-20-50-16 (paragraph 21 of the SOP 94-6)):

- A concentration that exists at the date of the financial statements
- The entity is exposed to the risk of a near-term severe impact as a result of that concentration
- There is at least a reasonable possibility that the events that could cause the severe impact will occur in the near term

Disclosure about a possible change in estimate is required under ASC 275-10-50-8 (paragraph 13 of the SOP 94-6) if information available before the issuance of financial statements suggests both that "it is at least reasonably possible that the estimate of the effect on the financial statements of a condition, situation, or set of circumstances that existed at the date of the financial statements will change in the near term because of one or more future confirming events" and "the effect of the change would be material to the financial statements."

If significant, noncash interest income recognized as a result of negative amortization that is added to the principal balance of an outstanding loan before it is received in cash should be included in the reconciliation of an entity's net income to net cash flows from operating activities under the provisions of ASC FAS-95 (Statement of Cash Flows).

An entity should consider whether the principal risk characteristics of a recognized servicing asset related to loan products with terms that may cause a concentration of credit risk would result in a separate stratum when impairment is determined. Disclosure of the risk characteristics used to stratify recognized servicing assets for the measurement of impairment is required under the provisions of ASC 860 (FAS-140, Accounting for Transfers and Servicing of

Financial Assets and Extinguishments of Liabilities) as amended by ASC 860-10-65-3 and ASC 860-10-40-5 through 40-6A (FAS-166). Originators and servicers that have provided guarantees on those loan products also should consider the specific risk characteristics when they estimate the guarantees' fair value. Each product's characteristics should be considered when estimating the fair value of loan products than an entity classifies a held for sale and when fair value is determined for the disclosures required under ASC 825-10-50-2A through 50-3, 50-8 through 50-23; 55-3 through 55-5; 60-1; 942-470-50-1; 310-10-50-26; 958-320-50-4 (FAS-107).

Entities are reminded that interest income must be recognized by the interest method as discussed in ASC 310 (FAS-91, Accounting for Nonrefundable Fees and Costs Associated with Originating or Acquiring Loans and Initial Direct Costs of Leases). If, during the term of a loan, the loan's stated interest rate increases so that interest accrued under the interest method in early periods would exceed interest at the stated rate, interest income should *not* be recognized if the net investment in the loan would increase to such an extent that it would exceed the amount at which the borrower could settle the obligation. The guidance in ASC 310-20-35-18 (paragraph 18a of FAS-91) and the related implementation guidance should be applied if interest income is recognized on loans with interest rates that increase during the term of the loan, such as loans with a reduced initial interest rate.

SEC Rules and Regulations, such as Item 303 of Regulation S-K (Management's Discussion and Analysis of Financial Conditions and Results of Operations), may require public entities to make additional disclosures. Additional disclosures also may be required of banks and bank holding companies that are subject to the requirements of SEC Regulation S-X, rule 9-03, and SEC Industry Guide 3.

EFFECTIVE DATE AND TRANSITION

The guidance in Question 1 is effective for interim and annual periods that end *after* December 19, 2005, the date this FSP was posted on the FASB's web site. The disclosures required in FAS-107 should be made for products determined to represent a concentration of credit risk in accordance with Question 1 for all periods presented.

No effective date or transition guidance is required for Question 2, because it refers to existing literature that is already in effect.

ASC 970 Real Estate

EITF Issue 91-10 (Accounting for Special Assessments and Tax Increment Financing Entities) (ASC 970-470-05-2, 05-3; 25-1, 25-3; 55-2 through 55-14; 460-10-60-40)

OVERVIEW

The construction of infrastructure or improvements may be financed by a municipality through special assessments or by a Tax Increment Financing Entity (TIFE), which is an independent taxing jurisdiction organized under various state statutes to issue bonds used to finance the construction, operation, and maintenance of roads and other capital infrastructure related to a specific project. For example, Company A owns land it wants to develop into an industrial park that requires roads, water, power, and all other infrastructure associated with such a development. Because the only entity receiving direct benefits is Company A, it might be considered unfair to levy an assessment payable by all members of the community. Instead, a TIFE is created to issue bonds to finance the construction and to levy assessments on users (in this case, Company A) to repay the debt and operate and maintain the infrastructure.

A TIFE established for a real estate development may repay a pro rata portion of the bonds as portions of the project are sold or if assessments surpass current tax rates. The company (developer) provides the funds to repay the bonds or reduce future assessments. The bonds are generally nonrecourse to the sponsoring company. If there is a default on a TIFE's bonds, however, the company may be affected because the property would be subject to liens. In some states, such as California, the obligation for repayment of the debt remains with the property as it is sold to new owners. Some states set a minimum amount that must be repaid by the developer.

ACCOUNTING ISSUE

Should a company that uses a TIFE to finance infrastructure construction recognize an obligation for special assessments or the TIFE's debt?

EITF CONSENSUS

- There is a presumption that a company (the property owner) should recognize an obligation if a special assessment or an assessment to be levied by a TIFE on each individual property owner is a fixed or determinable amount for a fixed or determinable period.
- The following factors indicate that the company may be contingently liable for a TIFE's debt; recognition of a liability should therefore be evaluated under the provisions of ASC 450 (FAS-5):
    —A shortfall, if any, in annual debt service obligations must be made up by the company.
    —The company has pledged assets.
    —A letter of credit or other means of supporting the TIFE's debt has been provided by the company.

- There is a presumption that the TIFE's debt should be recognized as the company's obligation if the company is constructing facilities for its own use or operation and any of the criteria stated above is met.

    OBSERVATION: An enterprise entity that has an interest in a variable interest entity and is required to absorb the majority of that entity's expected losses, or is entitled to receive most of the entity's expected residual returns, or both, is required to consolidate that entity in accordance with the guidance in ASC 810 (FIN-46(R), Consolidation of Variable Interest Entities) as amended by ASC 810-10-30-7 through 30-9, 65-2) (FAS-167). ASC 810-10-05-10; 25-38 through 38G (paragraphs 14 through 14G of FIN 46(R)), as amended by FAS-167) provide guidance for determining whether an entity has a controlling interest in a variable interest entity. The Interpretation also provides guidance on the consolidation of many special-purpose entities of the type used as TIFEs.

Illustration Using EITF Issue 91-10 Consensus

A real estate developer organizes a TIFE to issue bonds for the construction of the infrastructure for a subdivision of homes. The infrastructure's assets become the property of the municipality when construction is completed. The company does not guarantee the TIFE's debt.

Case 1

Annual assessments are based on anticipated debt service requirements. Properties are taxed based on their stage of development. (That is, developed property is taxed at the maximum rate, undeveloped property is not taxed or taxed only to supplement shortfalls in the annual debt service requirement. If taxes collected on developed and undeveloped property are not sufficient to meet the obligation, an additional tax may be levied.)

Accounting Because individual properties are assessed based on their rate of development, assessments are not fixed or determinable and no obligation need be recognized. The company should, however, evaluate the recognition of an obligation under ASC 450 (FAS-5) if it is obligated to make up any shortfall in debt service requirements.

Case 2

The total assessment, which is based on the TIFE's annual debt service, is allocated equally to all lots in the development. In addition to their regular property taxes, property owners are assessed over the period that the debt is outstanding. When a portion of the property is sold, the developer must repay a pro rata portion of the TIFE debt or the purchaser must assume the obligation.

Accounting The developer should recognize a liability because the amount of the assessment is fixed and determinable for a fixed or determinable period of time.

DISCUSSION

In the EITF's discussion of the treatment of TIFE debt by entities sponsoring infrastructure construction, it determined that practice among such companies included recognition of the TIFE's debt and assets and treatment of the TIFE as a tax assessor (i.e., recording the annual tax assessments, user fees, or both as incurred in the assessment period).

The EITF's consensus on this Issue applies the guidance in ASC 450-20-25-2 (paragraph 8 of FAS-5, Accounting for Contingencies), which requires recognition of a liability if it is probable that a loss will be confirmed by one or more events that will occur in the future and the amount is estimable. Applying the guidance in ASC 450 (FAS-5), a property owner sponsoring an infrastructure project should account for a TIFE's debt as follows:

- *Debt recognized as a liability* If assessments are fixed or determinable amounts for a fixed or determinable period, required payments can be estimated. In addition, payments are probable because the company is the primary obligor; the only way the company can avoid payment of the obligation is by selling the property. However, even when the property is sold, the company has to satisfy the debt or reduce the selling price by the amount of debt assumed by the buyer.

- *Debt not recognized as a liability* A TIFE's debt need not be recognized as an obligation if debt service requirements are met by other than fixed or determinable assessments, because the amount cannot be estimated. The following are examples:

  —Annual assessments whose rates depend on the land use category (developed or undeveloped)

  —Assessments computed based on the assessed value of the property

  —Normal property tax assessments

- *Debt may be a contingent liability* A developer may remain contingently liable on the TIFE's debt. For example, in certain states, such as California, where the obligation remains with the property, the company has to make up shortfalls in the annual debt service obligation. In other states, such as Colorado, a company is required to guarantee the TIFE's debt. In those cases or if a company guarantees the TIFE's debt by pledging assets, the company has a contingent liability on the debt and therefore must continue to evaluate its obligation to report the debt based on the guidance in ASC 450 (FAS-5).

RELATED CHAPTERS IN 2011 GAAP GUIDE, VOLUME II

Chapter 2, "Accounting Policies and Standards"
Chapter 23, "Interim Financial Reporting"

RELATED CHAPTERS IN 2011
GAAP GUIDE, VOLUME I

Chapter 2, "Accounting Policies and Standards"
Chapter 8, "Contingencies, Risks, and Uncertainties"
Chapter 26, "Interim Financial Reporting"

RELATED CHAPTERS IN 2011
INTERNATIONAL ACCOUNTING/FINANCIAL REPORTING STANDARDS GUIDE

Chapter 3, "Presentation of Financial Instruments"
Chapter 7, "Business Combinations"
Chapter 20, "Income Taxes"
Chapter 28, "Provisions, Contingent Liabilities, Contingent Assets"
Chapter 30, "Revenue"

CHAPTER 12
CONVERTIBLE DEBT AND DEBT WITH WARRANTS

CONTENTS

Overview		12.02
Authoritative Guidance		
ASC 470	Debt	12.03
FSP APB 14-1	Accounting for Convertible Debt Instruments That May Be Settled in Cash upon Conversion (Including Partial Cash Settlement)	12.03
EITF Issue FSP 85-9	Revenue Recognition on Options to Purchase Stock of Another Entity	12.12
EITF Issue 85-17	Accrued Interest upon Conversion of Convertible Debt	12.14
EITF Issue 98-5	Accounting for Convertible Securities with Beneficial Conversion Features or Contingently Adjustable Conversion Ratios	12.15
EITF Issue 00-27	Application of Issue No. 98-5 to Certain Convertible Instruments	12.24
EITF Issue 02-15	Determining Whether Certain Conversions of Convertible Debt to Equity Securities Are within the Scope of FASB Statement No. 84, *Induced Conversions of Convertible Debt*	12.36
EITF Issue 05-1	Accounting for the Conversion of an Instrument That Becomes Convertible upon the Issuer's Exercise of a Call Option	12.37
EITF Issue 08-4	Transition Guidance for Conforming Changes to Issue No. 98-5	12.41

12.02 *Convertible Debt and Debt with Warrants*

EITF Issue 09-1	Accounting for Own-Share Lending Arrangements in Contemplation of Convertible Debt Issuance	12.42
ASC 815	Derivatives and Hedging	12.46
EITF Issue 05-2	The Meaning of "Conventional Convertible Instrument" in EITF Issue No. 00-19, "Accounting for Derivative Financial Instruments Indexed to, and Potentially Settled in, a Company's Own Stock"	12.46
EITF Issue 06-7	Issuer's Accounting for a Previously Bifurcated Conversion Option in a Convertible Debt Instrument When the Conversion Option No Longer Meets the Bifurcation Criteria in FASB Statement No. 133, *Accounting for Derivative Instruments and Hedging Activities*	12.47

Nonauthoritative Guidance

85-29	Convertible Bonds with a "Premium Put"	12.49

Related Chapters in 2011 GAAP Guide, Volume II	12.51
Related Chapters in 2011 GAAP Guide, Volume I	12.51
Related Chapters in 2011 International Accounting/Financial Reporting Standards Guide	12.52

OVERVIEW

Debt may be issued with a conversion feature or a feature that permits the separate purchase of other securities, usually common stock of the issuing company. These "hybrid" debt/equity securities generally derive some portion of their value from the equity component (i.e., the conversion feature or the separate purchase option) that is included in the issue price. The significant accounting question that arises is the recognition, if any, of the equity feature when a hybrid security is issued. That treatment, in turn, affects the subsequent accounting when the conversion feature or separate purchase option is exercised.

- ASC 470 Debt (APB-14, Accounting for Convertible Debt and Debt Issued with Stock Purchase Warrants)
- ASC 470 Debt (FAS-84, Induced Conversions of Convertible Debt)
- ASC 480 Distinguishing Liabilities from Equity (FAS-150, Accounting for Certain Financial Instruments with Characteristics of both Liabilities and Equity)

AUTHORITATIVE GUIDANCE

ASC 470 Debt

FSP APB 14-1 (Accounting for Convertible Debt Instruments That May Be Settled in Cash upon Conversion (Including Partial Cash Settlement)) (ASC 470-20-10-1, 10-2; 15-2, 15-4 through 15-6; 25-21 through 25-27; 30-27 through 30-31; 35-12 through 30-20; 40-19 through 40-26; 45-3; 50-3 through 50-6; 55-70 through 55-82; 65-1; 815-15-55-76A; 825-10-15-5)

OVERVIEW

When EITF Issue 90-19 (Convertible Bonds with Issuer Option to Settle for Cash upon Conversion) was issued, it applied to three types of convertible debt instruments: (1) Type A instruments, which would be settled on conversion in cash based on a fixed number of shares multiplied by the stock price on the conversion date; (2) Type B instruments, which would be settled on conversion in either stock or cash equal to the conversion value; and (3) Type C instruments, which would be settled on conversion in cash for the accreted value of the obligation, separately from the excess conversion value over the accreted value (conversion spread), and in cash or stock for the conversion spread. The guidance for Type A instruments was subsequently nullified by the guidance in ASC 815 (FAS-133, Accounting for Derivative Instruments and Hedging Activities), but Type B and Type C instruments continued to be accounted for under Issue 90-19's original consensus. However, the EITF revised Issue 90-19 in January 2002 by requiring that a Type C instrument be accounted for as a convertible debt instrument in accordance with the guidance in ASC 470-20-05-2 through 05-6; 25-2 through 24-3; 25-11 through 25-13; 30-1 through 30-2. ASC 505-10-60-3 (APB-14, Accounting for Convertible Debt and Debt Issued with Stock Purchase Warrants) with diluted earnings per share on such instruments calculated in the same manner as debt issued with detachable warrants. As a result of that change, Type C instruments had a less dilutive effect on the calculation of diluted earning per share than convertible debt instruments whose earnings per share must be calculated using the if-converted method. Consequently, the issuance of Type C instruments became very popular and caused some practitioners to question whether the accounting for Type C instruments properly represents their economic effects. In addition, the FASB believed that the EITF's revision of its consensus on the accounting for Type C instruments resulted in an inappropriate expansion of the guidance in FASB Accounting Standards Codification™ (ASC) 470-

20-25-12 (paragraph 12 of APB-14), which previously did not apply to convertible debt instruments settled in cash or partial cash, and that the manner in which Type C instruments are accounted for misleads investors.

This FSP nullifies the EITF's guidance in Issue 90-19 (Convertible Bonds with Issuer Option to Settle for Cash upon Conversion) and Issue 03-7 (Accounting for the Settlement of the Equity-Settled Portion of a Convertible Debt Instrument That Permits or Requires the Conversion to Be Settled in Stock (Instrument C of Issue 90-19)). This FSP also amends the guidance in ASC 470-20-05-7, 05-8; 25-4 through 25-6; 30-3, 30-6, 30-8, 30-10, 30-11, 30-15; 35-2, 35-7; 40-2, 40-3; 55-30 through 55-33, 55-35 through 55-38, 55-40 through 55-43, 55-45 through 40-48, 55-50 through 55-54, 55-54A, 55-56 through 55-60, 55-60A, 55-62 through 55-66, 55-69; 505-10-50-8 (Issue 98-5, Accounting for Convertible Securities with Beneficial Conversion Features or Contingently Adjustable Conversion Ratios), ASC 470-20-05-7, 05-8; 25-4 through 25-6; 30-3, 30-6, 30-8, 30-10, 30-11, 30-15; 35-2, 35-7; 40-2, 40-3; 55-30 through 55-33, 55-35 through 55-38, 55-40 through 55-43, 55-45 through 40-48, 55-50 through 55-54, 55-54A, 55-56 through 55-60, 55-60A, 55-62 through 55-66, 55-69; 505-10-50-8 (Issue 99-1, Accounting for Debt Convertible into the Stock of a Consolidated Subsidiary), 470-20-25-8 through 25-9, 25-20; 30-1, 30-5, 30-7, 30-9 through 30-10, 30-12 through 30-13, 30-16 through 30-21; 35-1, 35-4, 35-7 through 35-10; 40-1, 40-4; 45-1; 55-11 through 55-12, 55-14 through 55-17, 55-19 through 55-21, 55-23 through 55-24, 55-26 through 55- 27; 505-10-50-7; 260-10-50-1 (Issue 00-27, Application of Issue No. 98-5 to Certain Convertible Instruments); 260-10-45-43 through 45-44; 55-78 through 55-79, 55-81 through 55-82, 55-84 through 55-84B, (Issue 04-8, The Effect of Contingently Convertible Instruments on Diluted Earnings per Share); 470-20-05-11; 40-4A through 40-10; 55-68 (Issue 05-1, Accounting for the Conversion of an Instrument That Becomes Convertible upon the Issuer's Exercise of a Call Option); and 815-15-35-4; 40-1, 40-2, 40-4; 50-3; 470-20-25-16 (Issue 06-7, Issuer's Accounting for a Previously Bifurcated Conversion Option in a Convertible Debt Instrument When the Conversion Option No Longer Meets the Bifurcation Criteria in FASB Statement No. 133).

FASB STAFF POSITION

Scope

The convertible debt instruments under the scope of this FSP are *not* discussed in ASC 470-20-25-12 paragraph 12 of APB-14). This FSP applies only to convertible debt instruments that, in accordance with their terms, must be settled at conversion in cash or partially in cash, unless an instrument includes an embedded conversion option that must be accounted for separately as a derivative under the provisions of ASC 815 (FAS-133). In addition, mandatorily convertible preferred shares classified as liabilities under the provisions of ASC 480-10-05-1 through 05-6; 10-10-1; 15-3 through 15-5, 15-7 through 15-10; 25-1 through 25-2, 25-4 through 25-15; 30-1 through 30-7; 35-3 through 35-5; 45-1 through 45-4; 50-1 through 50-4; 55-1 through 55-12, 55-14 through 55-28, 55-34 through 55-41, 55-64; 835-10-60-13; 260-10-45-70A (FAS-150, Accounting for Certain Financial Instruments with Characteristics of both Liabilities and Equity) that include an unconditional obligation for an issuer to settle the face amount of the instruments in cash at a specified date are considered to be convertible debt instruments for the purpose of determining whether the instruments should be accounted for under the scope of this FSP. However, convertible preferred shares accounted for as equity or as temporary equity are *not* included under this FSP's scope.

The guidance in this FSP also does *not* apply to convertible debt instruments that:

- Require or permit settlement in cash or other assts on conversion only if the holders of the underlying shares receive the same form of consideration in exchange for their shares.
- Require issuers to settle their obligations for fractional shares on conversion in cash, but otherwise do *not* require or permit settlement on conversion in cash or other assets.

Recognition

The underlying principle of the approach used in this FSP is that interest costs related to convertible debt instruments recognized in periods *after* their initial recognition should represent the borrowing rate an entity would have incurred had it issued a comparable debt instrument *without* the embedded conversion option. That goal is accomplished by requiring issuers to separately account for the liability and equity components of convertible debt instruments.

Initial Measurement

Issuers should apply the following guidance for the *initial* measurement of convertible debt:

- First, determine the carrying amount of an instrument's liability component based on a fair value measurement of a similar liability (including embedded features, if any, other than the conversion option) that has *no* related equity component.
- Next, determine the carrying amount of the instrument's equity component corresponding to the embedded conversion option by deducting the liability component's fair value from the initial proceeds attributed to the total convertible debt instrument.

- For the purpose of the determinations made in the two bullets above and for the purpose of subsequent measurement, evaluate in the context of a total convertible debt instrument whether its embedded features, other than the conversion option (including an embedded prepayment feature) are *substantive* at the issuance date. If, at issuance, an entity has concluded that it is *probable* that a convertible instrument's embedded feature will *not* be exercised, that embedded feature is deemed to be *nonsubstantive* and would *not* affect the initial measurement of an instrument's liability component.
- Attribute a portion of the initial proceeds of a convertible debt instrument to additional unstated (or stated) rights or privileges, if any, included in the transaction based on guidance in other applicable U.S. generally accepted accounting principles (GAAP).
- Apply the guidance in ASC 815 (FAS-133) first if embedded features *other* than the conversion option (e.g., prepayment options) are embedded in a convertible debt instrument accounted for under the guidance in this FSP to determine whether any of those features should be accounted for separately from the liability component as derivative instruments under the guidance in ASC 815 (FAS-133) and its related interpretations. As stated above, the guidance in this FSP does *not* apply if *no* equity component exists because the conversion option is accounted for separately as a derivative under the guidance in ASC 815 (FAS-133). The following steps provide guidance to issuers of convertible debt instruments on how to apply the guidance in ASC 815 (FAS-133) and its related interpretations to the accounting for embedded derivatives:

   Step 1: Identify the embedded features, other than the embedded conversion option, that should be evaluated under the guidance in ASC 815 (FAS-133) and its related interpretations.

   Step 2: Apply the guidance in ASC 815 (FAS-133) and its related interpretations to determine whether any of the embedded features identified in Step 1 should be accounted for separately as derivative instruments. This FSP's guidance does *not* affect the determination of whether an embedded feature needs to be accounted for separately as a derivative.

   Step 3: Apply the guidance in the first two bullets above to separate the liability component, including embedded features, if any, other than the conversion option, from the equity component.

   Step 4: If applicable, separate from the convertible debt instrument's liability component in accordance with the guidance in ASC 815 (FAS-133) and its related interpretations embedded features, if any, that must be accounted for separately as derivates based on the evaluation in Step 2. An embedded derivative's separation from the liability component would *not* affect the accounting for the equity component.

Transaction costs incurred with third parties other than the investors that are directly related to the issuance of convertible debt instruments accounted for under the guidance in this FSP should be allocated to the liability and equity components in the same proportion as the allocation of proceeds and accounted for as costs of issuing debt and equity, respectively.

Because of the separate recognition of a liability component and an equity component for convertible debt instruments accounted for under the guidance in this FSP, a temporary basis difference related to the liability component may occur when the provisions of ASC 740 (FAS-109, Accounting for Income Taxes) are applied. Additional paid-in capital should be adjusted when deferred taxes are initially recognized for the tax effect of that temporary difference.

The fair value option under the scope exception in ASC 825-10-15-5 (paragraph 8(f) of FAS-159, The Fair Value Option for Financial Assets and Financial Liabilities) does *not* apply to convertible debt instruments under this FSP's scope.

Subsequent Measurement

Under the guidance in this FSP, the excess of the principal amount of the liability component *over* its initial fair value must be amortized to interest cost based on the interest method discussed in ASC 835-30-35-2 (paragraph 15 of APB-21, Interest on Receivables and Payables). In accordance with the interest method, debt discounts must be amortized over the expected life of a similar liability that does *not* have a related equity component (considering the effects of embedded features other than the conversion option). An issuer that initially measured the fair value of the liability component based on a valuation technique consistent with an income approach is required to consider the periods of cash flows used initially to determine the appropriate period over which to amortize the debt discount.

A liability component's expected life is *not* affected by embedded features that were determined to be *nonsubstantive* at the time the convertible debt instrument is issued. The third bullet under the discussion related to initial measurement above provides guidance for determining whether or not an embedded feature, other than the conversion option, is substantive.

An equity component that continues to meet the conditions for equity classification in ASC 460-10-60-14; 480-10-55-63; 505-10-60-5; 815-10-15-78, 55-52; 815-15-25-15; 815-40-05-1 through 50-4, 05-10 through 05-12;. 25-1 through 25-5, 25-7 through 25-20, 25-22 through 25-24, 25-26 through 25-35. 25-37 through 25-40; 30-1; 35-1, 35-2, 35-4 through 35-6, 35-8 through 35-13; 40-1, 40-2; 50-1 through 50-5; 55-1 through 55-18 (Issue 00-19, Accounting for Derivative Financial Instruments Indexed to, and Potentially Settled in, a Company's Own Stock) need *not* be remeasured in subsequent periods. If in accordance with the provisions of Issue 00-19 (see ASC reference above), a conversion option must be reclassified from stockholders' equity to a liability measured at fair value, the difference between the amount that had been recognized in equity and the fair value of the conversion option at the reclassification date should be accounted for as an adjustment to stockholders' equity. However, if a conversion option that had been accounted for in stockholders' equity is reclassified as a liability, gains or losses recognized to account for that conversion option at fair value while classified as a liability should *not* be reversed if subsequently the conversion option is reclassified back to stockholders' equity. Reclassifications of a conversion option do *not* affect the accounting for the liability component.

Derecognition

An issuer that derecognizes an instrument under the guidance in this FSP should allocate the consideration transferred and the related transaction costs incurred to the extinguishment of the liability component and the reacquisition of the equity component.

Instruments accounted for under the guidance in this FSP should be derecognized as follows, regardless of the form of consideration transferred at settlement, which may include cash or other assets, stock, or any combination of the two:

- Measure the fair value of the consideration transferred to the holder. In the case of a modification or exchange that results in the original instrument's derecognition, measure the new instrument at fair value (including both the liability and equity components if the new instrument also is accounted for under the provisions of this FSP).
- Allocate the fair value of the consideration transferred to the holder between the liability and equity components of the original debt instrument as follows:
    1. Allocate a portion of the settlement consideration to the liability component's extinguishment at its fair value immediately *before* the extinguishment. Recognize a gain or loss on debt extinguishment in the income statement for a difference, if any, between consideration allocated to the liability component and the sum of (a) the net carrying amount of the liability component, and (b) unamortized debt issuance costs, if any.

2. Allocate the remaining settlement consideration to the equity component's reacquisition and recognize that amount as a reduction of stockholders' equity.

Allocate a portion of the settlement consideration to other unstated(or stated) rights or privileges, if any, included in the derecognition transaction in addition to the settlement of the convertible debt instrument based on guidance in other applicable U.S. GAAP.

Allocate to the liability and equity components transaction costs incurred with third parties other than the investor(s) that are directly related to the settlement of a convertible debt instrument accounted for under the guidance in this FSP in proportion to the allocation of consideration transferred at settlement and accounted for as debt extinguishment costs and equity reacquisition costs, respectively.

Modifications and Exchanges

To determine whether a modification or an exchange of an original instrument accounted for under the scope of this FSP should be accounted for as an extinguishment of that instrument or as a modification to the original instrument's terms, an issuer should apply the guidance in ASC 470-50-40-12, 40-15, 40-16 (Issue 06-6 (Debtor's Accounting for a Modification (or Exchange) of Convertible Debt Instruments) and ASC 470-50-05-4; 15-3; 40-6 through 40-14, 40-17 through 40-20; 55-1 through 55-9 (Issue 96-19, Debtor's Accounting for a Modification or Exchange of Debt Instruments). An issuer of an original instrument that is a modified or exchanged instrument, but *not* derecognized, should reevaluate the liability component's expected life under the guidance in the section for subsequent measurement in this FSP, and determine a new effective interest rate for the liability component in accordance with the guidance in Issues 06-6 and 96-19 (see ASC references above).

The components of an instrument under the scope of this FSP that has been modified to no longer require or permit cash settlement on conversion should continue to be accounted for separately, unless the original instrument must be derecognized under the guidance in Issues 06-6 and 96-19 (see ASC references above). Accounting in accordance with *other* GAAP (e.g., ASC 470-20-25-12 (paragraph 12 of APB-14)), not the guidance in this FSP, is required for a new convertible debt instrument that was issued after the original convertible debt instrument was derecognized under the guidance in Issues 06-6 and 96-19 (see ASC references above) and that may *not* be settled in cash on conversion.

An issuer should apply the guidance in Issues 06-6 and 96-19 (see ASC references above). to determine whether extinguishment accounting is required if a convertible debt instrument *not* originally under the scope of this FSP is modified so that it qualifies to be accounted for under this FSP's scope. If the modification is *not* accounted for as an extinguishment, the guidance in this FSP should be applied *prospectively* from the date of the modification and the liability component should be measured at its fair value as of the date of the modification. The fair value of the liability component should be deducted from the total carrying amount of the convertible debt instrument to determine the carrying amount of the equity component represented by the embedded conversion option. A portion of the unamortized debt issuance costs, if any, should be reclassified at the modification date and accounted for as equity issuance costs based on the proportion of the overall carrying amount of the convertible debt instrument allocated to the equity component.

Induced Conversions

The terms of an instrument under this FSP's scope may be amended to bring about early conversion (e.g., by offering a more favorable conversion ratio or paying an additional amount for conversions that occur *before* a specific date). In that case, an issuer should recognize a loss equal to the fair value of all securities and other amounts transferred in the transaction that exceed the fair value of the consideration that would have been issued under the instrument's original conversion terms. The instruments would be derecognized based on the guidance for derecognition in this FSP using the fair value of the consideration that would have been issued in accordance with the instrument's original conversion terms. This guidance does *not* apply if the holder does not exercise the embedded conversion option.

Balance Sheet Classification of the Liability Component

An issuer's determination whether to classify the liability component as a current or a long-term liability is *not* affected by the guidance in this FSP. All of a convertible debt instrument's terms (including the equity component) should be considered in making that determination by applying other applicable U.S. GAAP. The liability component's balance sheet classification also has *no* effect on that component's measurement in accordance with this FSP's measurement guidance.

Disclosure

The objective of this FSP's disclosure requirements is to provide information to financial statement users about the terms of convertible debt instruments within the scope of those financial statements and how information about those instruments is presented in an issuer's balance sheet and income statement. In addition to the disclosures required in other applicable GAAP, entities should provide the following information in their annual financial statements about convertible debt instruments under the scope of this FSP that were outstanding during any of the periods presented.

An entity should disclose the following information as of each date for which a balance sheet is presented:

a. The carrying amount of the equity component
b. The principal amount of the liability component, its amortized discount, and its net carrying amount.

The following information should be disclosed as of the most recent balance sheet presented:

a. The remaining period over which a discount on the liability component, if any, will be amortized
b. The conversion price and the number of shares used to determine the total consideration to be delivered on conversion
c. The amount by which the instrument's if-converted value exceeds its principal amount, regardless of whether the instrument is currently convertible. This disclosure is required only for public entities, as defined in ASC, *Glossary* (paragraph E1 of FAS-123(R), Share-Based Payment)
d. Information about derivative transactions entered into in connection with the issuance of instruments within the scope of this FSP, including the terms of those derivative transactions, how they relate to the instruments under the scope of this FSP, the number of shares underlying the derivative transactions, and the reasons for entering into those derivative transactions. The purchase of call options that are expected to substantially offset changes in the conversion option's fair value is an example of a derivative transaction entered into in connection with the issuance of an instrument under the scope of this FSP. That disclosure is required regardless of whether the related derivative transactions are accounted for as assets, liabilities, or equity instruments.

An entity should disclose the following information for each period for which an income statement is presented:

a. The effective interest rate on the liability component for the period
b. The amount of interest cost related to both the contractual interest coupon and amortization of the discount on the liability component recognized for the period.

Effective Date and Transition

The guidance in this FSP is effective for financial statements issued for fiscal years that begin after December 15, 2008, and interim periods within those fiscal years. Early adoption is prohibited.

This FSP's requirements should be applied *retrospectively* to all periods presented as follows:

- Recognize the cumulative effect of a change in accounting principles on periods *before* those presented as of the beginning of the first period presented.
- Make an offsetting adjustment to the opening balance of retained earnings or other appropriate components of equity or net assets for that period, presented separately.
- To apply the guidance in this FSP retrospectively, the guidance in ASC 360-10-30-1; 835-15-2, 15-5 through 15-6, 15-8; 30-2 through 30-6, 30-8; 25-2 through 25-8, 50-1; 10-2; 35-3 (FAS-34, Capitalization of Interest Cost) should be applied in all periods in which an instrument under the scope of this FSP was outstanding. However, asset impairment tests should *not* be reperformed nor should additional asset tests be performed in prior periods when the guidance in this FSP is applied restrospectively. Further, a transitional impairment test should *not* be performed when this FSP is adopted.
- Apply the guidance in this FSP *retrospectively* to the modification date of convertible debt instruments modified *after* their original issuance date to provide for cash settlement, including partial cash settlement, on conversion, if a modification transaction is *not* accounted for as an extinguishment. The guidance in this FSP on the accounting for a convertible debt instrument that was *not* under the scope of this FSP but becomes subject to the FSP's guidance after it has been modified should be applied.
- Provide the required transition disclosures in ASC 250-10-50-1 through 50-3 (paragraphs 17 and 18 of FAS-154, Accounting Changes and Error Corrections).

This FSP's guidance should *not* be applied retrospectively to instruments under this FSP's scope that were *not* outstanding for any periods presented in the annual financial statements for the period in which this FSP's guidance is adopted but that were outstanding during an earlier period. Consequently, amounts between an entity's opening equity accounts should *not* be reclassified.

EITF Issue 85-9 (Revenue Recognition on Options to Purchase Stock of Another Entity) (ASC 470-20-S99-1, S25-1)

OVERVIEW

Normally, convertible debt or detachable warrants issued with a company's debt obligations are convertible into the issuer's own equity securities. This Issue discusses a situation in which Company

A issues debt instruments that can be converted by the holder into the securities of Company B, which Company A holds as an investment. Company A may issue such debt in the form of convertible debt instruments that must be tendered by the holder in exchange for a certain number of Company B's equity securities, or in the form of debt instruments with warrants that can be detached from the debt and converted into Company B's securities at a specific price.

ACCOUNTING ISSUES

1. Should the amount of a warrant issued with debt be amortized over its term or should it be credited to income only when it is exercised or has expired?
2. Should debt instruments that must be tendered for conversion into securities other than those of the issuer be accounted for the same as convertible debt, based on the provisions in ASC 470-20-05-2 through 05-6; 25-2 through 24-3; 25-11 through 25-13; 30-1 through 30-2. ASC 505-10-60-3 (APB-14, Accounting for Convertible Debt and Debt Issued with Stock Purchase Warrants), or should the conversion feature be accounted for separately, as in the case of a detachable warrant?

EITF CONSENSUS

1. An issuer of debt with detachable warrants should recognize a liability for the value of a warrant that can be converted into the common stock of an entity in which the issuer has an investment, but should not amortize that amount into income until the warrant has been exercised or has expired.

    OBSERVATION: This consensus is partially nullified by the guidance in ASC 815 (FAS-133, Accounting for Derivative Instruments and Hedging Activities). It applies only to detachable warrants that do *not* meet the definition of a derivative in ASC 815 (FAS-133).

2. The EITF did not reach a consensus on the accounting for debt instruments that must be extinguished on conversion. Task Force members could not agree on whether the provisions for convertible debt in APB-14 (see ASC references above) should apply.

    OBSERVATION: This Issue has been resolved by the guidance in ASC 815-15-05-1; 35-1 through 35-2A; 25-1, 25-4 through 25-6, 25-11 through 25-14, 25-26 through 25-29, 25-54; 30-1; 15-5 through 15-6, 15-8 through 15-10, 15-14; 815-10-15-72 through 15-73, 15-11, 15-84; 815-20-25-71 (paragraphs 12 through 16 of FAS-133).

EITF Issue 85-17 (Accrued Interest upon Conversion of Convertible Debt) (ASC 470-20-05-9; 35-11; 40-11; 835-10-60-10)

OVERVIEW

The conversion terms of some convertible debt instruments provide that former debt holders will forfeit interest accrued but unpaid at the conversion date if they convert zero coupon bonds, which do not pay interest, or other convertible debt securities into the issuer's equity securities between interest payment dates.

ACCOUNTING ISSUES

1. Should interest expense be accrued or imputed on such debt instruments to the date of conversion when it is forfeited?
2. If interest should be accrued to the date of conversion, how should it be recognized when the debt is converted into common stock?

EITF CONSENSUS

1. Accrue or impute interest to the date the debt instrument is converted to equity securities.
2. Interest accrued from the last payment date, if applicable, to the date of conversion should be charged to interest expense and credited to capital as part of the cost of securities issued, net of related income tax effects, the same as the converted debt principal and unamortized issue discount or premium on the debt, if any.

DISCUSSION

This Issue was raised as a result of a comment letter on the guidance in ASC 470-20-05-10; 40-13 through 40-17; 45-2; 55-2 through 55-9 (FAS-84, Induced Conversions of Convertible Debt) exposure draft, which requested clarification of the accounting for accrued interest when debt is converted to equity securities. Some entities, believing that the obligation to pay interest had been forgiven, were reversing accrued interest to income on conversion. The FASB decided that the question was not related to the issue considered in FAS-84 (see ASC reference above) and asked the staff to discuss with the EITF whether the Task Force was aware of such diversity in practice. The EITF's consensus is consistent with the views of the FASB staff on this issue.

EITF Issue 98-5 (Accounting for Convertible Securities with Beneficial Conversion Features or Contingently Adjustable Conversion Ratios)(ASC 470-20-05-7, 05-8, 25-4 through 6, 30-3, 30-6, 30-8, 30-10, 30-11, 30-15, 35-2, 35-7, 40-2, 40-3, 55-30 through 55-33, 55-35 through 55-38, 55-40 through 55-43, 55-45 through 40-48, 55-50 through 55-54, 55-54A, 55-56 through 55-60, 55-60A, 55-62 through 55-66, 55-69. 505-10-50-8)

OVERVIEW

The EITF was asked to address this Issue because some entities have been issuing convertible debt securities and convertible preferred stock with a nondetachable conversion feature that are in-the-money at the commitment date (the beneficial conversion feature), which is the date on which there is an agreement on the terms of the transaction and an investor has committed to purchase the convertible securities based on those terms. The securities may be converted into common stock at a conversion rate that is fixed on the commitment date or at a fixed discount from the common stock's market price at the conversion date, whichever is lower. The conversion price of some convertible securities may vary based on future events—for example, subsequent financing at a lower price than the original conversion price, the company's liquidation or a change of control, or an initial public offering that has a lower price per share than the agreed upon amount.

The scope of the Issue covers convertible debt securities with beneficial conversion features that must be settled in stock and convertible shares with beneficial conversion features that allow an issuer to choose whether to satisfy the obligation in stock or in cash. The scope also covers instruments in which the beneficial conversion features are convertible into more than one instrument, such as convertible preferred stock that can be converted into common stock and detachable warrants. This Issue does *not* apply to instruments under the scope of FSP APB 14-1 (see references above).

ACCOUNTING ISSUES

1. Should a beneficial conversion feature embedded in a convertible security be valued separately at the commitment date?
2. If an embedded beneficial conversion feature should be valued separately, how should it be recognized and measured?

12.16 *Convertible Debt and Debt with Warrants*

3. How should convertible securities issued with conversion ratios that are adjusted as a result of the occurrence of future events be accounted for?

EITF CONSENSUS

1. Beneficial conversion features embedded in convertible securities should be valued *separately* at the commitment date. (See "Effect of FAS-133," below.)

   OBSERVATION: See the consensus on Issue 5 in Issue 00-27 below for a revised definition of *a commitment date*.

   1. The *commitment* date is defined in this Issue as the date on which an entity has reached an agreement with an unrelated party that is binding on both parties and is usually legally enforceable. The agreement has the following two features:
      - It includes specific information about all significant terms, including the quantity to be exchanged, a fixed price, and the timing of the transaction. The price may be stated as a specific amount of an entity's functional currency or of a foreign currency. In addition, a specified interest rate or specified effective yield may be stated.
      - It includes a disincentive for nonperformance that is large enough to make performance probable. For the purpose of applying the definition of a firm commitment, the existence of statutory rights in the legal jurisdiction governing the agreement, such as remedies for default that equal the damages suffered by the counterparty to the agreement, would be a sufficiently large disincentive for nonperformance that makes performance probable.

      EITF members noted that the commitment date of an agreement that includes subjective provisions permitting either party to rescind its commitment to consummate the transaction should *not* occur until the provisions expire or the convertible instrument is issued, whichever occurs first. For example, an investor may be allowed to rescind its commitment to purchase a convertible instrument if a material adverse change occurs in the issuer's operations or financial condition, or the commitment is conditional on customary due diligence or shareholder approval.

      If the securities are purchased by several investors, such as a group of lenders that participate in a syndicate, the commitment date is the latest commitment date for the group or the issuance date for each individual security, whichever comes first.

2. Embedded beneficial conversion features should be *recognized* and *measured* as follows:

b. Allocate a portion of the proceeds equal to the intrinsic value of the embedded beneficial conversion feature to additional paid-in capital at the commitment date. The intrinsic value is calculated as the difference between the *conversion price* and the *fair value* of the common stock or other securities into which the security can be converted multiplied by the *number* of shares into which the security can be converted. Fair value is determined at the market price, if available, or at the best estimate of fair value, without adjustments for transferability restrictions, large block factors, avoided underwriter's fees, or time value discounts. To allocate an amount to the beneficial conversion feature of convertible securities issued with detachable warrants or with another security, such as common stock, the proceeds are first allocated between the convertible instruments and the detachable warrants based on the relative fair value method in ASC 470-20-05-2 through 05-6; 25-2 through 25-3, 25-10 through 25-13; 30-1 through 30-2; 505-10-60-3 (APB-14).

c. If the *intrinsic value* of the beneficial conversion feature is *greater* than the proceeds from the sale of the convertible instrument, the discount assigned to the beneficial conversion feature should *not* exceed the amount of the proceeds allocated to the convertible instrument. *(This consensus has been partially nullified by FAS-133.)*

A discount as a result of the recognition of a beneficial conversion option of a convertible instrument that has a stated redemption date should be amortized from the issuance date to the convertible instrument's stated redemption date regardless of when the instrument's earliest conversion date occurs. However, a discount as a result of the recognition of a beneficial conversion option of a convertible instrument with *no* stated redemption date, such as perpetual preferred stock, should be amortized from the issuance date to the earliest conversion date. (Updated based on the EITF's consensus on issue 6 of Issue 00-27. Also see the Subsequent Development section.)

The issuer should disclose the terms of the transaction in the notes to the financial statements in accordance with FAS-129. That disclosure should also include information about the amount in excess of the instruments' total fair value to be received by the holder at conversion over the proceeds received by the issuer and the amortization period of the discount.

A discount on convertible *preferred* securities resulting from the allocation of proceeds to a beneficial conversion feature is analogous to a *dividend*, which should be recognized as a return to the preferred shareholders by the effective yield method. (Updated based on the EITF's consensus on issue 6 of Issue 00-27. Also see the Subsequent Development section.) A discount on convertible *debt* securities as a result of the allocation of proceeds to the beneficial conversion feature should be recognized as *interest expense* using the effective yield method. (Updated based on the EITF's consensus on issue 6 of Issue 00-27. See discussion of the effect of Issue 00-27.)

d. This Issue's basic accounting model is modified if an instrument has a multiple-step discount to the market price that increases over time (e.g., 10% at three months, 15% at six months, 20% at nine months, and 25% at one year). The EITF reached a consensus that the beneficial conversion feature's intrinsic value should be calculated based on the conversion terms that are most beneficial to the *investor*. The resulting discount is amortized over the shortest period during which the investor can recognize that return (e.g., in the above example, 25% over one year).

A discount on a convertible instrument with a stated redemption date should be amortized from the instrument's issuance date to its stated redemption date, regardless of when the earliest conversion date occurs. In the example above, the discount would be 25% and the amortization period would be from the issuance date to the redemption date. (Updated based on Issue 6 of Issue 00-27. Also see the Subsequent Development section.)

A discount on a convertible instrument that has *no* stated redemption date should be amortized over the minimum period in which the investor can recognize that return. In the example above, the discount would be 25% and the amortization period would be one year. (Updated based on issue 6 of Issue 00-27. Also see the Subsequent Development section.) However, the amortized portion of the discount may have to be adjusted so that, at any point in time, the discount at least equals the amount the investor could obtain if the security were converted at that date. In the example above, a discount of at least 10% should have been recognized at the end of three months. Under this method, the cumulative amortization should equal the *greater of* (a) the amount obtained by using the effective yield method based on the conversion terms most beneficial to an investor or (b) the amount of discount that an investor can realize at that interim date.

If the instrument is converted *before* the discount has been fully amortized, the unamortized portion of the discount at the conversion date should be recognized immediately as interest expense or as a dividend, whichever is appropriate. If the remaining amount of the unamortized discount is recognize as an expense because the convertible instrument was in the form of debt, that expense should *not* be classified as extraordinary. (Updated based on issue 6 of Issue 00-27. Also see the Subsequent Development section.) However, the EITF agreed that no adjustment should be made to amounts previously amortized if the amortized discount is greater than the amount realized by the holder because the instrument was converted at an earlier date. The portion of the discount already amortized need not be adjusted, however, if that amount exceeds the amount the holder realized on an early conversion.

e. If an instrument with an embedded beneficial conversion feature is extinguished before its conversion, a portion of the price to reacquire the security includes a repurchase of the beneficial conversion feature. The amount of the price that is allocated to the beneficial conversion feature should be measured based on the intrinsic value of the beneficial conversion feature at the date of extinguishment. An excess, if any, is allocated to the convertible security. A gain or loss on the extinguishment of *debt* is classified in accordance with FAS-4. A gain or loss on a *preferred security* is accounted for based on the guidance in ASC 260-10-S99-2 (Topic D-42) and ASC 260-10-S99-3 (Topic D-53).

The guidance in ASC 470-50 (Interpretation 1 of APB-26) and in ASC 470-20-05-9; 35-11; 40-11; 835-10-60-10 (Issue 85-17), which provide that a convertible debt's carrying amount, including an unamortized premium or discount, if any, should be credited to equity on conversion, continues to apply to convertible debt that does not include a beneficial conversion option.

> **OBSERVATION:** Although ASC 470-5-45-1 (FAS-145, Rescission of FASB Statements No. 4, 44, and 64, Amendment of FASB Statement No. 13, and Technical Corrections) supersedes FAS-4, which requires that gains and losses on the extinguishments of debt be classified as extraordinary items, the Statement does *not* prohibit using that classification for extinguished debt that meets the criteria in ASC 225-20-45-10 through 45-16; 45-1 through 45-2, 45-8; 15-2; 55-1 through 55-2; 45-3 through 45-6; 50-2 through 50-3; 830-10-45-19 (APB-30).

3. A *contingent* beneficial conversion feature of a security that (*a*) becomes convertible only if a future event not under the holder's control occurs and (*b*) is convertible from inception with conversion terms that change if a future event occurs is *measured* at the stock price on the commitment date, but *recognized* in earnings only when the contingency is *resolved*.

12.20 *Convertible Debt and Debt with Warrants*

EFFECTIVE DATE

The EITF's original consensus positions reached in this Issue applied to convertible instruments issued after May 20, 1999. The changes made to the Issue to conform its guidance to that in ASC 470-20-25-8 through 25-9, 25-20; 30-1, 30-5, 30-7, 30-9 through 30-10, 30-12 through 30-13, 30-16 through 30-21; 35-1, 35-4, 35-7 through 35-10; 40-1, 40-4; 45-1; 55-11 through 55-12, 55-14 through 55-17, 55-19 through 55-21, 55-23 through 55-24, 55-26 through 55- 27; 505-10-50-7; 260-10-50-1 (Issue 00-27) and ASC 480-10-05-1 through 05-6; 10-10-1; 15-3 through 15-5, 15-7 through 15-10; 25-1 through 25-2, 25-4 through 25-15; 30-1 through 30-7; 35-3 through 35-5; 45-1 through 45-4; 50-1 through 50-4; 55-1 through 55-12, 55-14 through 55-28, 55-34 through 55-41, 55-64. ASC 835-10-60-13; 260-10-45-70A (FAS-150) are effective for financial statements issued for fiscal years *after* December 15, 2008. Earlier application is permitted. The effect, if any, of applying those conforming changes should be presented *retrospectively* and the cumulative effect of the change should be reported in retained earnings in the balance sheet as of the beginning of the first period presented.

EFFECT OF ASC 815 (FAS-133)

The guidance in ASC 815 (FAS-133) partially nullifies the consensus Issue 1. An issuer and a holder of a security with an embedded conversion feature should analyze the terms of the entire embedded conversion feature to determine whether the guidance in ASC 815-15-25-1 (paragraph 12 of FAS-133) from the host contract for separation and accounting of embedded derivatives applies. Although instruments that meet the criteria under ASC 815-10-15-74 (paragraph 11(a) of FAS-133) may not be considered derivatives for the purpose of the issuer's accounting and, therefore, would be exempted from the requirements in ASC 815 (FAS-133), this exemption does not apply to a holder's accounting for a security that is convertible into an issuer's stock. In addition, a holder will generally find that the conversion feature can be separated from the instrument if it meets the requirement for separation in ASC 815-15-25-1 (paragraph 12(a))—that is, its economic characteristics and risks are not clearly and closely related to those of the host contract.

Under the guidance in ASC 815-15-25-4 through 25-5 (FAS-155, Accounting for Certain Hybrid Financial Instruments), which amends the guidance in ASC 815 (FAS-133), entities are permitted to measure at fair value certain hybrid financial instruments with embedded derivatives that otherwise would have to be separated. A hybrid financial instrument that is accounted for entirely at fair value cannot be used as a hedging instrument in a hedging relationship under FAS-133. During the discussion of this Issue, some stated that an issuer of such securities would usually be unable to make a reliable measurement of the fair value of an embedded conversion feature. Similarly, that also would apply to the holder of such securities. Under the guidance in ASC 815-15-25-52 (paragraph 301 of FAS-133) however, it would be unusual for an entity to conclude that it cannot reliably separate an embedded derivative from its host contract.

EFFECT OF ASC 480 (FAS-150)

ASC 480-10-05-1 through 05-6; 10-1; 15-3 through 15-5, 15-7 through 15-10; 25-1 through 25-2, 25-4 through 25-15; 30-1 through 30-7; 35-3 through 35-5; 45-1 through 45-4; 50-1 through 50-4; 55-1 through 55-12, 55-14 through 55-28, 55-34 through 55-41, 55-64; 835-10-60-13;. 260-10-45-70A (FAS-150, Accounting for Certain Financial Instruments with Characteristics of Both Liabilities and Equity) establishes classification and measurement guidance for certain financial instruments that have the characteristics of both liabilities and equity. An issuer is required to classify a financial instrument under the scope of the Statement as a liability or as an asset in some circumstances.

SUBSEQUENT DEVELOPMENT

If the commitment date defined in this Issue did not occur before November 16, 2000, the EITF's consensus in Issue 00-27 (Application of Issue 98-5 to Certain Convertible Instruments) (discussed below) should be applied to all instruments issued after that date. See Issue 00-27 below for the SEC Observer's comments, which provide specific guidance for SEC registrants.

Illustrations of the Accounting for a Beneficial Conversion Feature of a Convertible Security

Example 1—Instruments that are convertible at issuance

(Example A has been modified for the guidance in Issue 00-27.)

A. *Fixed dollar conversion terms*—Convertible debt issued at a $600,000 face value is convertible at issuance into the issuer's common stock at $20 a share. The redemption date is on the fifth anniversary of issuance. The fair value of each share is $25 on the commitment date. The accounting for such instruments is as follows:

1. Calculate the number of shares into which the debt will be converted at the conversion price: $600,000/$20 = 30,000 shares.

2. Calculate the intrinsic value of the beneficial conversion feature at the commitment date: fair value of $25 − $20 conversion price at the commitment date = $5 × 30,000 shares = $150,000.

3. The debt is recognized at $600,000, with the $150,000 intrinsic value of the debt credited to additional paid-in capital.

12.22 Convertible Debt and Debt with Warrants

4. The debt discount should be amortized over a period of five years from the issuance date to the redemption date, because the debt has a stated redemption on the fifth anniversary of the issuance date.

5. Entry at issuance date:

Cash	$600,000	
Debt discount	150,000	
Debt		$600,000
Additional paid-in capital		150,000

(Examples B and C were deleted as a result of the guidance in Issue 00-27.)

D. *Instrument with fixed terms that change when a future event occurs*—Convertible debt issued at a $600,000 face value is convertible at issuance and redeemable on the fifth anniversary of issuance. The instrument is convertible into the issuer's common stock at $24, 80% of the stock's $30 fair value at the commitment date. However, if the company has an IPO, the convertible debt can be converted at 80% of the fair value of the IPO price or the fair value on the commitment date, whichever is less. Such debt instruments should be accounted for as follows:

1. The instrument includes a "basic" beneficial conversion feature that does not depend at issuance on the occurrence of a future event. its intrinsic value is calculated as follows: (600,000/24) = 25,000 × (30−24) = $150,000, which is calculated at the commitment date and recognized at the issuance date. The debt discount (equal to the intrinsic value of the beneficial conversion feature) should be amortized over a five year period from the issuance date to the stated redemption date. (For guidance on recognition and measurement of the contingent beneficial conversion feature, see the EITF's consensus on issues 3 and 7 of Issue 00-27.)

2. The accounting entry at issuance date:

Cash	$600,000	
Debt discount	150,000	
Debt		$600,000
Additional Paid-in Capital		150,000

Under the terms of the convertible debt instrument, a calculation of the number of shares that would be received on conversion if an IPO occurs is not permitted at the commitment date.

E. *Instrument with variable terms that depend on the occurrence of a future event*—Convertible debt issued at $600,000 face value is redeemable on the fifth anniversary of the issuance date. The instrument is convertible at issuance into the issuer's common stock at 80% of the $30 stock price at the commitment date. However, if the price of each common share has increased by at least 20% one year after an IPO, the debt can be converted at 60% of the stock price. Such instruments should be accounted for as follows:

1. The intrinsic value of the beneficial conversion feature is measured based on the terms at issuance. Calculated at the commitment date, it equals $150,000 (calculated in the same manner as in example D above) and is recognized at issuance. The debt discount is amortized over the five-year redemption period.
2. The accounting entry is the same as the one in example D above.
3. Under the terms of the convertible debt instrument, a calculation of the number of shares that would be received on conversion if an IPO occurs is not permitted at the commitment date. (For guidance on recognition and measurement of the contingent beneficial conversion feature, see the EITF's consensus on issues 3 and 7 of Issue 00-27.)

(Example F has been deleted as a result of the guidance in Issue 00-27.)

Example 2—Instruments that are *not* convertible at issuance

A. *Fixed dollar conversion terms*—(This Example, formerly Example A, has been modified as a result of the guidance in Issue 00-27.)

Convertible debt with a $600,000 face value redeemable on the fifth anniversary of issuance is convertible any time after one year into the issuer's common stock at $24 per share. The fair value of each share is $30 at the commitment date. The accounting for such instruments is as follows:

1. Calculate the intrinsic value of the beneficial conversion feature as in the previous examples.
2. A portion of the proceeds from the issuance of the convertible debt, equal to the intrinsic value is allocated to additional paid-in capital.
3. The debt discount should be amortized over the five-year redemption period.
4. The accounting entry is the same as above.

(Example B has been deleted as a result of the guidance in Issue 00-27.)

Example 3—Extinguishment of convertible debt with a beneficial conversion feature before conversion

(This example has been modified as a result of the guidance in Issue 00-27.)

Proceeds from the issuance of zero coupon debt	$600,000
The intrinsic value of the beneficial conversion feature	$540,000

The issuer recognizes $540,000 at the commitment date as a discount on the debt. The offsetting entry is a credit to additional paid-in capital. The remaining $60,000 is recognized as debt and is accreted to its full face value of $600,000 over the five-year redemption period of the debt. The debt is extinguished one year after the issuance date.

Facts at the extinguishment date:

Reacquisition price	$700,000
Intrinsic value of beneficial conversion feature	432,000

12.24 *Convertible Debt and Debt with Warrants*

Carrying value of debt   140,000

At the extinguishment date, the proceeds from the extinguishment first should be allocated to the beneficial conversion feature ($432,000) with the remainder allocated to the extinguishment of the convertible debt security.

The accounting entry to record the extinguishment is as follows:

*Debt	$140,000	
Additional paid-in capital	432,000	
Loss on extinguishment	128,000	
Cash		$700,000

---

*The net carrying amount of the debt one year after issuance is calculated using the effective interest method to amortize the debt discount over the five-year redemption period.

> **OBSERVATION:** See Chapter 39, "Stockholders' Equity," for a discussion of FSP FAS 129-1 (Disclosure Requirements under FASB Statement No. 129, "Disclosure of Information about Capital Structure Relating to Contingently Convertible Securities").

EITF Issue 00-27 (Application of Issue No. 98-5 to Certain Convertible Instruments) (ASC 470-20-25-8 through 25-9, 25-20, 30-1, 30-5, 30-7, 30-9 through 30-10, 30-12 through 13, 30-16 through 30-21, 35-1, 35-4, 35-7 through 35-10, 40-1, 40-4, 45-1, 55-11 through 12, 55-14 through 55-17, 55-19 through 55-21, 55-23 through 55-24, 55-26 through 55- 27. ASC 505-10-50-7. ASC 260-10-50-1)

OVERVIEW

In ASC 470-20-05-7, 05-8, 25-4 through 6, 30-3, 30-6, 30-8, 30-10, 30-11, 30-15, 35-2, 35-7, 40-2, 40-3, 55-30 through 55-33, 55-35 through 55-38, 55-40 through 55-43, 55-45 through 40-48, 55-50 through 55-54, 55-54A, 55-56 through 55-60, 55-60A, 55-62 through 55-66, 55-69. 505-10-50-8 (Issue 98-5, Accounting for Convertible Securities with Beneficial Conversion Features or Contingently Adjustable Conversion Ratios), the EITF reached a consensus that in-the-money nondetachable beneficial conversion features embedded in convertible securities should be valued separately at the issue date. Under that consensus, embedded beneficial conversion features are recognized and measured based on their intrinsic value at the commitment date. Issue 98-5 also provides guidance on the measurement and recognition of beneficial conversion features *contingent* on future events. The EITF decided to readdress the Issue because certain practice questions have been raised about the application of the guidance in Issue 98-5.

> **OBSERVATION:** Paragraph 1 of this Issue has been amended by the guidance in FSP APB 14-1 (Accounting for Convertible Debt Instruments That May Be Settled in Cash upon Conversion (Including Partial Cash Settlement)). which was issued in May 2008. Consequently, financial instruments accounted for under the scope of that FSP are exempted from following the guidance in Issue 98-5 and this Issue.

> **OBSERVATION:** See Chapter 20, "Income Taxes," for a discussion of EITF Issue 05-8 (Income Tax Consequences of Issuing Convertible Debt with a Beneficial Conversion Feature).

ACCOUNTING ISSUES

1. Is the intrinsic value model discussed in ASC 470-20-05-7, 05-8, 25-4 through 6, 30-3, 30-6, 30-8, 30-10, 30-11, 30-15, 35-2, 35-7, 40-2, 40-3, 55-30 through 55-33, 55-35 through 55-38, 55-40 through 55-43, 55-45 through 40-48, 55-50 through 55-54, 55-54A, 55-56 through 55-60, 55-60A, 55-62 through 55-66, 55-69. 505-10-50-8 (Issue 98-5) sufficiently operational to address practice Issues or should embedded beneficial conversion options be measured based on a fair value method?

2. If the intrinsic value model is retained, in determining whether an instrument includes a beneficial conversion feature, should an issuer calculate the intrinsic value of a conversion option based on (*a*) a conversion price specified in the instrument or (*b*) an effective conversion price based on the proceeds received for or allocated to the convertible instrument?

3. Under the guidance in Issue 98-5 (see ASC references above), if a convertible instrument includes an embedded *contingent* conversion option, the intrinsic value of the contingent conversion option is measured based on the fair value of the underlying stock at the commitment date, but that amount is not recognized unless an event occurs that causes the contingency to be resolved. In applying the model in Issue 98-5, which conversion option should be considered an "initial" conversion option and which should be considered a "contingent" conversion option?

4. Is a contingent conversion feature that will reduce the conversion price if the value of the underlying stock declines after the commitment date to or below a specified price a beneficial conversion option if (*a*) the initial active conversion price equals or exceeds the price of the underlying stock at the commitment date and (*b*) at the future date on which the conversion price is adjusted, the *contingent* conversion price exceeds the fair value of the underlying stock at the commitment date?

5. When does a commitment date occur for the purpose of determining the fair value of an issuer's common stock used to measure an embedded conversion option's fair value?
6. Should the commitment date, as defined in Issue 5 above, also be the date on which the assumptions, including the fair value of an issuer's stock, are determined for the purpose of allocating the proceeds, in accordance with the guidance in ASC 470-20-05-2 through 05-6;. 25-2 through 25-3, 25-10 through 25-13, 30-1 through 30-2;. 505-10-60-3 (APB-14), on a relative fair value basis to separate instruments in a financing transaction that includes a convertible instrument with an embedded conversion feature?
7. Is it appropriate to accrete (a) a discount that results from an allocation of proceeds on a relative fair value basis to a transaction's separate instruments over the convertible instrument's life and (b) a discount from recording a beneficial conversion option under Issue 98-5 over the period to the first date the convertible instrument may be converted?
8. How should an issuer apply Issue 98-5 if a contingent conversion option's terms do not permit calculation at the commitment date of the number of shares a holder would receive when the price is adjusted on the occurrence of a contingent event until the contingent event actually occurs?
9. How should Issue 98-5 be applied if a beneficial conversion option terminates after a specified period of time and the instrument is mandatorily redeemable at a premium at that date?
10. How should a convertible instrument issued to a provider of goods or services be accounted for?
11. Is a commitment date for convertible instruments issued as paid-in-kind (PIK) interest or dividends (a) the commitment date of the original convertible instrument to which the PIK issuance relates or (b) the date on which interest is recognized as a liability or a dividend is declared?
12. How should an issuer account for the issuance of a convertible instrument to repay its debt on a nonconvertible instrument when the nonconvertible instrument's matures, including whether the Issue 98-5 model applies to the embedded conversion option in the instrument issued as payment of the matured debt?
13. The following Issues are related to the application of Issue 98-5 to a reacquisition of an embedded conversion option if a convertible instrument that included a beneficial conversion option under Issue 98-5 is extinguished before its stated maturity date:
    a. Is it appropriate to allocate a portion of the reacquisition price to the conversion option based on that option's intrinsic value

at the extinguishment date if the conversion option has not been accounted for separately under Issue 98-5?
b. How should the requirement to allocate a portion of the reacquisition price to the beneficial conversion option for convertible debt be applied if the option's intrinsic value at the extinguishment date exceeds the originally measured intrinsic value?
c. Is it ever appropriate to allocate a portion of a reacquisition price to an embedded beneficial conversion option on an issuer's common stock on an early redemption of convertible preferred stock?

14. This Issue addresses how to measure and when to recognize a beneficial conversion option in an underlying warrant, which is classified as an *equity* instrument, that allows a holder to acquire a convertible instrument for a stated exercise price and requires physical delivery of the convertible instrument for the stated exercise price.

   a. Should the commitment date used to measure the intrinsic value of the conversion option in the convertible instrument that is the underlying for the warrant be (a) the commitment date for the warrant or (b) the warrant's exercise date?
   b. How should the deemed proceeds for the convertible instrument be calculated when measuring the intrinsic value of a conversion option embedded in a convertible instrument?
   c. Should the measured intrinsic value of a beneficial conversion option in a convertible instrument that is the underlying for a warrant be recognized at (*a*) the date the warrant is issued or (*b*) the date the warrant is exercised and the convertible instrument is issued?

15. This Issue addresses how to measure and when to recognize a beneficial conversion option in an underlying warrant, which is classified as a *liability* instrument, that allows a holder to acquire a convertible instrument for a stated exercise price and requires physical delivery of the convertible instrument for the stated exercise price.

   a. Should the commitment date used to measure the intrinsic value of the conversion option in the convertible instrument that is the underlying for the warrant be (*a*) the commitment date for the warrant or (*b*) the warrant's exercise date?
   b. How should the deemed proceeds for the convertible instrument be calculated when measuring the intrinsic value of a conversion option embedded in a convertible instrument?

12.28 *Convertible Debt and Debt with Warrants*

    c. Should the measured intrinsic value of a beneficial conversion option in a convertible instrument that is the underlying for a warrant be recognized at (*a*) the date the warrant is issued or (*b*) the date the warrant is exercised and the convertible instrument is issued?

16. How should a beneficial conversion feature be measured when a convertible instrument is issued, if the holder will receive the issuer's common stock and other equity instruments of the issuer, such as warrants to acquire the issuer's common stock on conversion?

17. This Issue addresses questions related to presentation, disclosure, and classification of convertible equity instruments subject to the requirements of Issue 98-5.

    a. Should there be specific presentation or disclosure requirements for those instruments?

    b. Should convertible *preferred* stock with a conversion option under the scope of Issue 98-5 be classified as permanent or temporary equity in accordance with the guidance in ASC 460-10-60-14; 480-10-55-63; 505-10-60-5; 815-10-15-78; 55-52; 815-15-25-15; 815-40-05-1 through 05-4, 05-10 through 05-12; 25-1 through 25-5, 25-7 through 25-20, 25-22 through 25-24, 25-26 through 25-35. 25-37 through 25-40; 30-1; 35-1, 35-2, 35-4 through 35-6, 35-8 through 35-13; 40-1, 40-2; 50-1 through 50-5; 55-1 through 55-18 (Issue 00-19)?

EITF CONSENSUS

1. The intrinsic value model in ASC 470-20-05-7, 05-8; 25-4 through 25-6; 30-3, 30-6, 30-8, 30-10, 30-11, 30-15; 35-2, 35-7; 40-2, 40-3; 55-30 through 55-33, 55-35 through 55-38, 55-40 through 55-43, 55-45 through 55-48, 55-50 through 55-54, 55-54A, 55-56 through 55-60, 55-60A, 55-62 through 55-66, 55-69; 505-10-50-8 (Issue 98-5) should be retained.

2. The intrinsic value, if any, of an embedded conversion option should be computed using the effective conversion price based on the proceeds received for, or allocated to, the convertible instruments. Consequently, an issuer would account for a financing transaction that includes a convertible instrument as follows: (*a*) allocate the proceeds received on a fair value basis to the convertible instrument and other detachable instruments, such as detachable warrants, if any, included in the exchange, and (*b*) apply the Issue 98-5 model to the amount allocated to the convertible instrument and calculate an effective conversion price, which will be used to measure an embedded conversion option's intrinsic value, if any.

3. The intrinsic value of an embedded conversion option should be measured using the most favorable conversion price that would be in effect at the conversion date assuming that the current circumstances will not change, except for the passage of time. An issuer should account for changes to conversion terms that would be triggered by future events not under the Issuer's control as contingent conversion options of which the intrinsic value is not recognized until the triggering event occurs.

Excess amortization should not be reversed if the amortized amount of a discount on a convertible instrument as a result of an initial measurement of a conversion option's intrinsic value (before the conversion option is adjusted due to the occurrence of a future event) is greater than the remeasured amount of the conversion option's intrinsic value after the conversion option has been adjusted. In contrast, a debit should be recognized in paid-in-capital to adjust an amount initially recognized inequity for the conversion option's intrinsic value if the unamortized portion of an original discount is greater than the amount required for the total discount (amortized and unamortized) to equal the adjusted conversion option's intrinsic value if the unamortized portion of an original discount is greater than the amount required for the total discount (amortized and unamortized) to equal the adjusted conversion option's intrinsic value. An adjusted unamortized discount, if any, should be amortized based on the interest method and the guidance in Issue 8 below.

4. A beneficial conversion amount must be recognized when a conversion price is reduced (reset) under the circumstances discussed in this Issue as a result of a contingent conversion feature, because the holder realizes the instrument's enhanced economic value when the price is reset. A convertible instrument should be considered to be debt settled in stock if the price of the instrument's conversion option is continuously reset based on price increases or decreases of the underlying stock so that the value of the common stock to the holder is fixed at any conversion date. In that case, the guidance in Issue 98-5 would apply only to the initial accounting for the convertible instrument, including an initial active beneficial conversion feature, if any, but the provisions related to the contingent beneficial conversion option apply only the first time the option price is reset.

5. For consistency with the definition of a firm commitment in FAS-133 and in Implementation ASC 815-25-55-84 (Issue F3 of FAS-133), the definition of a commitment date in Issue 98-5 is replaced by the following definition:

> The date on which a legally enforceable agreement having the following characteristics that is binding on both parties is reached with an unrelated party:

a. All significant terms are specified, including the quantity to be exchanged in the transaction, a fixed price in the entity's functional currency or a foreign currency or as a specified interest or specified effective yield, and its timing.
b. Performance is probable because there is a sufficiently large disincentive for nonperformance. The existence of statutory rights in the legal jurisdiction governing the agreement under which the nondefaulting party can pursue remedies equivalent to the damages suffered provides, in and of itself, a sufficiently large disincentive for nonperformance to apply the definition of a firm commitment.

The Task Force noted that a commitment date would *not* occur until an agreement's subjective provisions that would permit either party to rescind its commitment to consummate a transaction have expired or the convertible instrument has been issued, whichever occurs earlier.

6. The same measurement date should be used in applying the guidance in ASC 470-20-05-2 through 05-6; 25-2 through 25-3, 25-10 through 25-13; 30-1 through 30-2; 505-10-60-3 (APB-14) and in ASC 470-20-05-7, 05-8; 25-4 through 25-6; 30-3, 30-6, 30-8, 30-10, 30-11, 30-15; 35-2, 35-7; 40-2, 40-3; 55-30 through 55-33, 55-35 through 55-38, 55-40 through 55-43, 55-45 through 55-48; 55-50 through 55-54, 55-54A, 55-56 through 55-60, 55-60A, 55-62 through 55-66, 55-69; 505-10-50-8 (Issue 98-5) so that (*a*) the proceeds from a transaction are allocated to the separable components and (*b*) the intrinsic value of a conversion option is measured based on measurement attributes as of the same point in time. Therefore, when the proceeds of a convertible instrument are allocated under the guidance in APB-14 to the separate instruments issued together with it, the allocation should be determined based on the relative fair values of the of all the instruments at the commitment date defined in Issue 5 above.

7. The Task Force provided the following guidance on the accretion of discounts:

    a. The Issue 98-5 model should be modified to require that issuers of convertible instruments that have a *stated* redemption date be required to recognize a discount when they recognize a beneficial conversion option that will be accreted from the date of issuance to the stated convertible instrument's redemption date, regardless of the earliest conversion date.
    b. The guidance in Issue 98-5 should continue to apply to convertible instruments without a stated redemption date.
    c. At the date of conversion, interest expense or a dividend, as appropriate, should be immediately recognized for the remaining unamortized discount due to (*a*) an allocation of

proceeds under the guidance in ASC 470-20-05-2 through 6; 25-2, 3, 10 through 13;. 30-1, 2;. 505-10-60-3 (APB-14) to other separable instruments included in instruments with beneficial conversion features and (*b*) the discount that results from the accounting for the beneficial conversion. If an expense is recognized, it should not be classified as extraordinary.

d. The calculation of an embedded conversion option's intrinsic value is not affected by costs of issuing convertible instruments. Such costs should also not be offset in the calculation of the conversion option's intrinsic value against proceeds received from the issuance. The Task Force noted that issuance costs in this consensus are limited to incremental and direct costs incurred with parties other than the investor in the convertible instrument. Amounts paid to an investor when the transaction is consummated should be accounted for as a reduction in the issuer's proceeds, not as issuance costs, they do affect the calculation of an embedded option's intrinsic value.

8. If under the terms of a contingent conversion option, an issuer is not permitted to calculate the number of shares the holder would receive when the price is adjusted on the occurrence of a contingent event, the issuer should calculate the number of shares that the holder would receive based on the new conversion price. That number of shares should be compared to the number that would have been received before the contingent event occurred. The incremental intrinsic value from the resolution of the contingency and the adjustment to the conversion price, which is recognized when the contingent event occurs, equals the difference between the number of shares in the two calculations multiplied by the stock price at the commitment date. The discount would be accreted in accordance with the guidance in Issue 5 above.

> **OBSERVATION:** This Issue applies to convertible instruments with a beneficial conversion feature that ends after a specified period of time. A convertible financial instrument under the scope of this Issue that was issued in the form of equity shares and whose terms require the holder to redeem the shares if the conversion feature expires becomes a liability under the guidance in ASC 480-10-05-1 through 05-6; 10-10-1; 15-3 through 15-5, 15-7 through 15-10; 25-1 through 25-2, 25-4 through 25-15; 30-1 through 30-7; 35-3 through 35-5; 45-1 through 45-4; 50-1 through 50-4; 55-1 through 55-12, 55-14 through 55-28, 55-34 through 55-41, 55-64; 835-10-60-13; 260-10-45-70A (FAS-150, Accounting for Certain Financial Instruments with Characteristics of both Liabilities and Equity) when the conversion feature expires. Under the guidance in ASC 480-10-30-2 (paragraph 23 of FAS-150), an instrument that becomes redeemable and is reclassified as a liability should be measured at its fair value. A corresponding reduction should be made to equity by adjusting paid-in capital if the fair value of the liability

is different from the amount at which the convertible debt was reported. No gain or loss should be recognized. If a convertible instrument in the form of shares is convertible into a variable number of shares based mainly or exclusively on one of the conditions stated in ASC 480-10-25-14 (paragraph 12 of FAS-150), but must be redeemed by transferring assets if the instrument is *not* converted, the convertible instrument becomes a liability under the guidance in ASC 480-10-25-14 (paragraph 12 of FAS-150) because the outstanding shares represent an unconditional obligation to be redeemed. That instrument is no longer accounted for under the scope of Issue 00-27.

9. If a beneficial conversion option terminates after a specified time period and the instrument becomes mandatorily redeemable at a premium, the guidance in ASC 470-20-05-7, 05-8; 25-4 through 25-6, 30-3, 30-6, 30-8, 30-10, 30-11, 30-15; 35-2, 35-7; 40-2, 40-3; 55-30 through 55-33, 55-35 through 55-38, 55-40 through 55-43, 55-45 through 55-48, 55-50 through 55-54, 55-54A, 55-56 through 55-60, 55-60A, 55-62 through 55-66, 55-69; 505-10-50-8 (Issue 98-5) should be applied with the discount accreted to the mandatory redemption amount, because a holder who received an in-the-money embedded conversion option is entitled to receive a premium when the instrument is redeemed.

10. See Issue 01-1 in Chapter 38. ASC 480-10-05-1 through 05-6; 10-10-1; 15-3 through 15-5, 15-7 through 15-10; 25-1 through 25-2, 25-4 through 25-15; 30-1 through 30-7, 35-3 through 35-5; 45-1 through 45-4; 50-1 through 50-4; 55-1 through 55-12, 55-14 through 55-28, 55-34 through 55-41, 55-64; 835-10-60-13; 260-10-45-70A (FAS-150) provides guidance to issuers on the classification and measurement of certain financial instruments with the characteristics of both liabilities and equity and requires issuers to classify financial instruments under the Statement's scope as liabilities or as assets, under certain circumstances.

11. The original commitment date for convertible instruments on which interest or dividends must be paid-in-kind (PIK) with the same convertible instruments as those originally issued is the commitment date for the convertible instruments issued to satisfy the agreement if the issuer or holder cannot choose another form of payment, and the holder will always receive the number of shares on conversion as if all accumulated dividends or interest have been PIK, even if the original instrument or a portion of it has been converted before accumulated dividends or interest were declared or accrued. If so, the fair value of the issuer's underlying stock at the commitment date for the original issuance is used to measure the intrinsic value of the embedded conversion option in the PIK instruments. In other situations, the date that interest is recognized as a liability or a dividend is declared is the commitment date for convertible instruments issued as PIK interest or dividends with the intrinsic value of the conversion option embedded in such

PIK instruments being measured based on the fair value of the issuer's underlying stock at that date.

12. The fair value of a convertible instrument issued to repay a nonconvertible instrument at maturity should be equal to the redemption amount owed on the nonconvertible debt if the old debt has matured and the Issuer's exchange of debt instruments is *not* a troubled debt restructuring under the guidance in ASC 310; ASC 470 (FAS-15). The fair value of the convertible debt should not exceed the amount at which the nonconvertible debt must be redeemed, because the issuer could have paid that amount in cash. The intrinsic value, if any, of the new debt's embedded conversion option should be measured and accounted for after the exchange under the Issue 98-5 model based on the fair value of the proceeds received. The Task Force noted that the guidance in ASC 470-50-05-4; 15-3; 40-6 through 40-14, 40-17 through 40-20; 55-1 through 55-9 (Issue 96-19, Debtor's Accounting for a Modification or Exchange of Debt Instruments) should be applied first if the original instrument is extinguished before its maturity.

TENTATIVE CONCLUSIONS

> **OBSERVATION:** At its March 12, 2008, meeting, the EITF agreed not to finalize the following tentative conclusions.

13. The following tentative conclusions apply to the accounting for a reacquisition of a beneficial conversion option if the convertible debt in which it is embedded is reacquired before maturity:

    a. If a conversion option embedded in a convertible security had no intrinsic value required to be accounted for under Issue 98-5, no portion of the price paid to reacquire the convertible instrument should be allocated to the conversion option.

    b. At the extinguishments date of convertible debt, if the intrinsic value of a conversion option embedded in a convertible security *exceeds* the amount measured at the commitment date, the amount of the reacquisition price allocated to the conversion option should be calculated based on the option's intrinsic value at the date of reacquisition. Consequently, paid-in capital might be reduced by an amount that exceeds the amount at which the conversion option was recognized in additional paid-in capital when the debt was issued.

    c. At the January 2001 meeting, the Task Force reconsidered its tentative conclusion reached at the November 2000 meeting because the SEC staff decided not to modify its announcement in ASC 260-10-S99-2 (Topic D-42, The Effect on the Calculation of Earnings per Share for the

12.34 *Convertible Debt and Debt with Warrants*

Redemption or Induced Conversion of Preferred Stock)). Although it conflicts with the tentative conclusion in Issue 13b, the Task Force reached a tentative conclusion that an issuer that redeems a convertible preferred security with a beneficial conversion option should calculate the effect of that transaction on net earnings available to common shareholders for the purpose of computing earnings per share as follows: Subtract the total of (*a*) the carrying amount of the convertible preferred security in the issuer's balance sheet plus (*b*) the intrinsic value originally recognized for the beneficial conversion option from (*c*) the fair value of consideration transferred to holders of the preferred security. Subtract from net earnings an excess, if any, over the total of (*a*) and (*b*). If the reacquisition price of the convertible preferred security is less than its carrying amount, the shortfall would increase the amount of net earnings available to common shareholders in the computation of earnings per share.

14a. Under the circumstances discussed in Issue 13 above, the intrinsic value of the conversion option should be measured on the *commitment date* for the warrant, if the issuer receives the fair value of the warrant (or the fair value of the warrant and other instruments issued at the same time) on issuance. However, the intrinsic value of the conversion option should be measured on the *warrant's exercise date* if the consideration transferred by the holder on the warrant's issuance date is less than the warrant's fair value (or the fair value of the warrant and other instruments issued at the same time).

14b. The deemed proceeds for the convertible instrument under the circumstances discussed in this Issue should equal the total proceeds received for the warrant and its exercise price.

14c. If the fair value of common stock that a holder would receive when exercising the conversion option of the convertible stock underlying the warrant exceeds the sum of (1) the proceeds received for or allocated to the warrant and (2) the warrant's exercise price, the excess, which is limited to the original proceeds received or allocated to the warrant, is considered to be a deemed distribution to the holder of the warrant for the convertible instrument. That excess amount should be recognized over the life of the warrant. If the intrinsic value of the warrant exceeds the proceeds received for or allocated to the warrant at issuance, it should be recognized when the warrant is exercised. That excess intrinsic value should be combined on the warrant's exercise date with the remainder, if any, of the unamortized intrinsic value measured at the warrant's issuance date. That amount should be amortized over the period specified in ASC 470-20-05-7, 05-8; 25-4 through 25-6; 30-3, 30-6, 30-8, 30-10, 30-11, 30-15; 35-2, 35-7; 40-2, 40-3; 55-30 through 55-33,

55-35 through 55-38, 55-40 through 55-43, 55-45 through 55-48, 55-50 through 55-54, 55-54A, 55-56 through 55-60, 55-60A, 55-62 through 55-66, 55-69; 505-10-50-8 (Issue 98-5) (as interpreted by Issue 7) based on the convertible instrument's characteristics.

15. A *warrant's exercise date* should be the *measurement date* for the intrinsic value of a conversion option in a convertible instrument as described in Issue 14 above. Because the warrant is classified as a liability, it is marked to fair value through earnings while it is outstanding and depends partly on the fair value of the conversion option in the underlying convertible instrument.

16. A conversion option's intrinsic value should be calculated by comparing (*a*) the proceeds of the convertible instrument that are allocated to the common stock portion of the conversion option and (*b*) the fair value at the commitment date of the common stock that the holder will receive on conversion. At the convertible instrument's issuance date, the issuer should recognize the amount by which (*b*) exceeds (*a*) as the intrinsic value of the embedded conversion option.

17a. The Task Force discussed the Issue and noted that ASC 505-10-50-3 (paragraph 4 of FAS-129) provides relevant disclosure guidance and that ASC 260-10-50-1 (paragraph 40c of FAS-128) requires disclosure of the terms and conditions of such securities, even if they were not included in the current period's diluted earnings per share. The Task Force was *not* asked to reach a consensus on this Issue and asked the Working Group to continue its consideration of disclosure and presentation guidance of the instruments discussed in this Issue.

17b. An issuer's ability to control the necessary actions or events to issue the number of required shares under a conversion option if the holder exercises the option should be evaluated based on the guidance in ASC 460-10-60-14; 480-10-55-63; 505-10-60-5; 815-10-15-78; 55-52; 815-15-25-15; 815-40-05-1 through 05-4, 05-10 through 05-12; 25-1 through 25-5, 25-7 through 25-20, 25-22 through 25-24, 25-26 through 25-35. 25-37 through 25-40; 30-1; 35-1, 35-2, 35-4 through 35-6, 35-8 through 35-13; 40-1, 40-2; 50-1 through 50-5; 55-1 through 55-18 (Issue 00-19). There is a presumption that the option will be settled in *cash* if the issuer cannot control the conversion option's exercise by delivering shares. Under those circumstances, SEC registrants should classify convertible preferred stock as temporary equity.

TRANSITION

All the consensus positions reached on this Issue should be applied *prospectively* for instruments issued after November 16, 2000, if a

12.36 *Convertible Debt and Debt with Warrants*

commitment date, as *previously* defined in Issue 98-5, had not occurred before that date.

SEC OBSERVER COMMENT

The SEC Observer stated that registrants are expected to apply the consensus in Issue 2 to all transactions accounted for under the guidance in ASC 470-20-05-7, 05-8; 25-4 through 25-6, 30-3, 30-6, 30-8, 30-10, 30-11, 30-15; 35-2, 35-7; 40-2, 40-3; 55-30 through 55-33, 55-35 through 55-38, 55-40 through 55-43, 55-45 through 55-48, 55-50 through 55-54, 55-54A, 55-56 through 55-60, 55-60A, 55-62 through 55-66, 55-69; 505-10-50-8 (Issue 98-5), including those for which a commitment date occurred before November 16, 2000. Registrants should report the initial application of that consensus to all existing, terminated, and converted transactions subject to the guidance in ASC 470-20-05-7, 05-8; 25-4 through 25-6; 30-3, 30-6, 30-8, 30-10, 30-11, 30-15; 35-2, 35-7; 40-2, 40-3; 55-30 through 55-33, 55-35 through 55-38, 55-40 through 55-43, 55-45 through 55-48, 55-50 through 55-54, 55-54A, 55-56 through 55-60, 55-60A, 55-62 through 55-66, 55-69; 505-10-50-8 (Issue 98-5), as of the beginning of the registrant's quarter that includes November 16, 2000, in a manner similar to a cumulative effect of a change in accounting principle in accordance with the guidance in ASC 250 (FAS-154). A cumulative effect, if any, should be recognized and accounted for in accordance with the guidance in Issue 98-5 before recognizing the effect of other consensus positions in this Issue.

STATUS

The EITF will discuss this Issue again after the FASB has made further progress on Phase II of its liabilities and equity project.

EITF Issue 02-15 (Determining Whether Certain Conversions of Convertible Debt to Equity Securities Are within the Scope of FASB Statement No. 84, Induced Conversions of Convertible Debt) (ASC 470-20-40-13)

OVERVIEW

Under the guidance in ASC 470-50 (APB-26, Early Extinguishment of Debt), all extinguishments of debt were accounted for the same, regardless of how the extinguishment was accomplished. FAS-84 (Induced Conversions of Convertible Debt), which amends the guidance in APB-26, excludes from the scope of APB-26 convertible debt that is converted to a debtor's equity securities based on conversion privileges that (*a*) differ from those stated in the original terms of the debt when it was originally issued, (*b*) are effective for a limited period of time, (*c*) include additional consideration, and (*d*) are intended to induce conversion. Convertible debt having those characteristics is covered under the scope of ASC 470-20-05-10; 40-13 through 40-17; 45-2; 55-2 through 55-9 (FAS-84).

The EITF was asked to address this Issue, because some have asked whether the guidance in FAS-84 would apply to offers to induce conversion made by a debt *holder* to a debtor in which the conversion terms of the convertible debt are increased from the original terms, for example, to include cash or an additional number of shares. In addition, such offers to induce conversion may not be extended to all debt holders, but may apply only to the debt holders making the offer to the debtor.

ACCOUNTING ISSUE

Does the guidance in ASC 470-20-05-10; 40-13 through 40-17; 45-2; 55-2 through 55-9 (FAS-84) apply if an offer for consideration that exceeds a debt instrument's original terms is made by a debt *holder*, including if (a) a third party that purchases the debt in the open market at a significant discount from face value asks the debtor to increase the instrument's conversion terms, and (b) the offer is not made to all debt holders?

EITF CONSENSUS

The EITF reached a consensus that the guidance in ASC 470-20-05-10; 40-13 through 40-17; 45-2; 55-2 through 55-9 (FAS-84) applies to *all* conversions of convertible debt if (a) the conversion is a result of changes in conversion privileges that can be exercised only for a limited time period, and (b) include the issuance of all of the equity securities that can be issued for each converted debt instrument under the conversion privileges stated in the terms of the debt at issuance, regardless of whether the offer has been made by the issuer or the holder of the debt or whether the offer applies to all debt holders.

EFFECTIVE DATE

This consensus applies to conversion transactions completed after September 12, 2002.

EITF Issue 05-1 (Accounting for the Conversion of an Instrument That Becomes Convertible upon the Issuer's Exercise of a Call Option) (ASC 470-20-05-11. 40-4A through 40-10. 55-68)

OVERVIEW

Contingently convertible debt instruments (CoCos), which were discussed in ASC 260-10-45-43 through 45-44; 55-78 through

55-79, 55-81 through 55-82, 55-84 through 55-84B (Issue 04-8, The Effect of Contingently Convertible Instruments on Diluted Earnings per Share), are convertible debt instruments that include a contingent feature and are generally convertible into an issuer's common shares after the stock price of the issuer's common stock exceeds a predetermined amount, known as a market price trigger, for a specified period of time. A CoCo's conversion price usually is higher than the underlying stock's market price when the CoCo is issued and its market price trigger usually is higher than the conversion price.

Since the EITF reached its consensus on Issue 04-8, some have asked whether CoCos also may include embedded call options under which issuers can call such debt instruments when they would not be otherwise convertible. Holders would have the option to receive cash for the call price or a specified number of shares of the issuer's stock. For example, a CoCo with a $1,000 par amount matures on September 30, 2012. The holder can convert the debt to the issuer's securities if the price of the debt security exceeds $1,500. The issuer has the option to call the debt between 2008 and the debt's maturity date. The holder may choose to receive cash for the call amount or a fixed number of shares, regardless of whether the price trigger of $1,500 has been met.

SCOPE

This Issue applies only to accounting for the issuance of equity securities to settle a debt instrument that has become convertible because the issuer has exercised a call option included in the original terms of the debt instrument and that otherwise would *not* have been convertible at the conversion date. Conversions based on terms that include changes made by a debtor to conversion privileges under the terms of the debt at issuance in order to encourage conversion are accounted for according to the guidance in ASC 470-20-05-10; 40-13 through 40-17; 45-2; 55-2 through 55-9 (FAS-84, Induced Conversions of Convertible Debt), and guidance for modifications to embedded conversion options is discussed in ASC 470-50-40-12; 40-15 through 40-16 (Issue 06-6, Debtor's Accounting for a Modification (or exchange) of Convertible Debt). The consensus in this Issue does *not* apply to convertible debt instruments accounted for under the scope of FSP APB 14-1 (Accounting for Convertible Debt Instruments That May Be Settled in Cash upon Conversion (Including Partial Cash Settlement)) (see ASC references above).

ACCOUNTING ISSUE

How should an issuer account for the conversion of a debt instrument that becomes convertible when the issuer exercises its call option under the original terms of the debt instrument?

EITF CONSENSUS

The EITF reached the following consensus positions:

- Equity securities issued on the conversion of a debt instrument that include a *substantive* conversion feature at the issuance date should be accounted for as a *conversion* if the debt instrument becomes convertible because the issuer has exercised a call option based on the debt instrument's original conversion terms. *No* gain or loss should be recognized on the issuance of equity securities to settle the debt instrument.

- Equity securities issued on the conversion of a debt instrument that does *not* include a *substantive* conversion feature at the issuance date should be accounted for as a *debt extinguishment* if the debt instrument becomes convertible because the issuer has exercised a call option based on the debt instrument's original conversion terms. In that case, the equity securities' fair value should be considered a part of the price of reacquiring the debt.

- A convertible debt instrument's issuance date is its *commitment* date, as defined in Issue 4 of EITF Issue 00-27 (Application of EITF Issue 98-5, "Accounting for Convertible Securities with Beneficial Conversion Features or Contingently Adjustable Conversion Ratios," to Certain Convertible Instruments). The determination as to whether a conversion feature is substantive should be based on the assumptions, considerations, and information about the marketplace available as of the issuance date, although that determination may be made *after* the issuance date.

The EITF's consensus positions should be applied in accordance with the following guidance:

- A conversion feature is considered to be *substantive* if it is at least *reasonably possible*, as defined in ASC 450 (FAS-5, Accounting for Contingencies), that the conversion feature will be exercisable in the future without the issuer's exercise of its call option. The holder's intent need not be evaluated to make such a determination.

- The EITF noted that for the purpose of this Issue, a conversion feature would *not* be considered to be substantive if the debt instrument's conversion price at issuance is so high that it would *not* be regarded at least *reasonably possible* at the date of issuance that a conversion would occur—even if the instrument includes a feature that would permit conversion *before* the maturity date. Further, a debt instrument does *not* include a substantive conversion feature if a conversion can only occur if the issuer exercises its call option.

- The determination as to whether a debt instrument's conversion feature is *substantive* should be based solely on assumptions, considerations, and marketplace information that were available as of the instrument's *issuance* date, even though that determination may be made *after* the debt instrument has been issued.

The following guidance, which is *not* all inclusive, may be useful in determining whether a conversion feature is substantive—that is, that it is at least reasonably possible that the conversion feature will exercised in the future:

- Compare the fair value of the conversion feature to the fair value of the debt instrument.

- Compare the effective annual interest rate based on the terms of the debt instrument to the estimated effective annual rate that an issuer estimates it could get on a similar nonconvertible debt instrument with an equivalent expected term and credit risk.

- Compare the fair value of the debt instrument to the fair value of an identical convertible instrument that has a *noncontingent* conversion option to determine the effect of a contingency. Similarity in the fair value of the two instruments may indicate that the conversion feature is substantive. To use this approach, it must be clear that the conversion feature, without considering the contingencies, is substantive.

- Consider the nature of the conditions required for the instrument to become convertible by a qualitative evaluation of the conversion provisions. For example, if it is likely that a contingent event will occur *before* an instrument's maturity date, it may indicate that a conversion feature is substantive. To use this approach, it must be clear that the conversion feature, without considering the contingencies, is substantive.

The EITF noted that a consensus on this Issue does *not* deal with the accounting for a contingently convertible debt instrument when the guidance in FAS-128 (Earnings per Share) and related interpretive guidance, including the guidance in ASC 260-10-45-43 through 45-44; 55-78 through 55-79, 55-81 through 55-82, 55-84 through 55-84B (Issue 04-8,The Effect of Contingently Convertible Instruments on Diluted Earnings per Share), is applied.

TRANSITION

The EITF reached a consensus that this Issue should apply to all conversions under its scope that occur when a call option is exercised and is effective for annual or interim reporting periods that begin after June 28, 2006, the date the FASB ratified this consensus, regardless of whether the instruments were entered into *before* or *after* that date. Only assumptions, considerations, and information available in the marketplace as of the instrument's *issuance* date should be used to determine whether the conversion feature of a debt instrument issued *before* the effective date of the consensus is *substantive*.

The FASB ratified the EITF's consensus positions at its June 28, 2006, meeting.

EITF Issue 08-4 (Transition Guidance for Conforming Changes to Issue No. 98-5) (ASC 470-20-65-2)

OVERVIEW

The guidance in EITF Issue ASC 470-20-25-8 through 25-9, 25-20; 30-1, 30-5, 30-7, 30-9 through 30-10, 30-12 through 30-13, 30-16 through 30-21; 35-1, 35-4, 35-7 through 35-10; 40-1, 40-4; 45-1; 55-11 through 55-12, 55-14 through 55-17, 55-19 through 55-21, 55-23 through 55-24, 55-26 through 55- 27; 505-10-50-7; 260-10-50-1 (00-27, Application of Issue No. 98-5 to Certain Convertible Instruments) nullified portions of the guidance in EITF Issue 98-5 (Accounting for Convertible Securities with Beneficial Conversion Features or Contingently Adjustable Conversion Ratios). However, Issue 98-5 has not been updated to identify the specific paragraphs that were affected nor were the illustrations in Issue 98-5 updated for the change.

Further, as a result of the issuance of ASC 480-10-05-1 through 05-6; 10-10-1; 15-3 through 15-5, 15-7 through 15-10; 25-1 through 25-2, 25-4 through 25-15; 30-1 through 30-7; 35-3 thrugh 35-5; 45-1 through 45-4; 50-1 through 50-4; 55-1 through 55-12, 55-14 through 55-28, 55-34 through 55-41, 55-64; 835-10-60-13; 260-10-45-70A (FAS-150, Accounting for Certain Financial Instruments with Characteristics of both Liabilities and Equity), in May 2003, certain guidance in Issues 98-5 and 00-27 no longer applies to financial instruments accounted for under the scope of FAS-150 (see ASC reference above).. Although Issue 00-27 has been updated to note that fact, Issue 98-5 has not.

ACCOUNTING ISSUE

What is the effective date and transition for entities that adopt the conforming changes to Issue 98-5 as a result of the issuance of Issue 00-27 and ASC 480-10-05-1 through 05-6; 10-10-1; 15-3 through 15-5, 15-7 through 15-10; 25-1 through 25-2, 25-4 through 25-15; 30-1 through 30-7; 35-3 thrugh 35-5; 45-1 through 45-4; 50-1 through 50-4; 55-1 through 55-12, 55-14 through 55-28, 55-34 through 55-41, 55-64; 835-10-60-13; 260-10-45-70A (FAS-150)?

SCOPE

The guidance in Issue 08-4 applies to changes made to ASC 470-20-05-7, 05-8; 25-4 through 25-6; 30-3, 30-6, 30-8, 30-10, 30-11, 30-15; 35-2, 35-7; 40-2, 40-3; 55-30 through 55-33, 55-35 through 55-38, 55-40 through 55-43, 55-45 through 55-48, 55-50 through 55-54, 55-54A, 55-56 through 55-60, 55-60A, 55-62 through 55-66, 55-69; 505-10-50-8 (Issue 98-5) as a result of the issuance of Issue 00-27 and FAS-150 (see ASC reference above).

TRANSITION

The EITF reached a consensus that conforming changes made to Issue 98-5 as a result of the issuance of Issue 00-27 and ASC 480-10-05-1 through 05-6; 10-10-1; 15-3 through 15-5, 15-7 through 15-10; 25-1 through 25-2, 25-4 through 25-15; 30-1 through 30-7; 35-3 through 35-5; 45-1 through 45-4; 50-1 through 50-4; 55-1 through 55-12, 55-14 through 55-28, 55-34 through 55-41, 55-64; 835-10-60-13; 260-10-45-70A (FAS-150) should be effective for financial statements issued for fiscal years that end *after* December 15, 2008, but early application is *permitted*. The effect of applying the conforming changes, if any, should be presented *retrospectively* and the cumulative effect of the change should be reported in retained earnings in the balance sheet as of the beginning of the first period presented.

If an entity changes its accounting as a result of applying the conforming changes in Issue 08-4, the disclosure requirements in ASC 250 (FAS-154) should be followed.

FASB RATIFICATION

At its meeting on June 25, 2008, the FASB ratified the EITF's amendments to Issue 98-5 and the consensus in Issue 08-4.

EITF Issue No. 09-1: Accounting for Own-Share Lending Arrangements in Contemplation of Convertible Debt Issuance (ASC 470-20-05-1, 05-12A through 12C; 15-2; 25-1, 20A; 30-26A; 35-11A; 45-2A; 50-2A through 2C; 65-3; ASC 260-10-45-70B)

OVERVIEW

Under the current market conditions, entities that need financing find it easier to place convertible debt rather than straight debt and issuing such debt may also be more attractive to the issuer because such debt has a lower interest rate. Investors that purchase convertible debt frequently use a hedging technique called "delta neutral" hedging to hedge changes in the value of an option to buy shares, such as the one embedded in convertible debt, with a "short" position on the shares. By using a hedge, an investor offsets gains on the conversion option if the price of the stock increases and offsets losses on the conversion option if the stock's price decreases.

Many issuers of convertible debt have also been entering into separate arrangements with the investment bank that underwrites their offering under which the entity issues legally outstanding shares of its own common stock and lends those shares to the investment bank in exchange for a loan processing fee that usually equals the par value of the common stock. Even though the holders of the shares are legally entitled to receive dividends and to vote, such arrangements require that during the period that the shares are loaned to the investment bank, it must reimburse the issuer for dividends paid on the shares even if those shares have been sold in the market. In addition, as long as the investment bank is the owner of record, it is precluded from voting on matters submitted to the issuer's shareholders for a vote. Some agreements include a provision requiring the investment bank to post collateral during the loan term. However, issuers usually do not enforce that requirement.

Investment banks use those shares to enter into equity derivative contracts, such as options, forwards, and total return swaps, on their own behalf with investors in the issuers' convertible debt instruments. Those equity derivative contracts enable the investors to hedge the long position in the issuer's stock that they hold through the convertible debt's embedded conversion option. The investment bank may also sell the loaned shares in equity markets.

Investment banks enter into share loan arrangements, which create a short position, to hedge their own market risk related to their long position as a result of the equity derivative contracts entered into with the investors. By borrowing issuers' shares and the sale of derivatives to investors, investment banks eliminate their own exposure to changes in the issuers' stock prices and create a short position that hedges the investors' conversion option in the convertible debt instruments.

When the convertible debt matures, the investment bank generally must return the loaned shares to the issuer without additional consideration. An issuer may be entitled to a cash payment for the fair value of its common stock if an investment bank does not return the loaned shares.

SCOPE

Issue 09-1 applies to an equity-classified share-lending arrangement on an entity's own shares that is executed in contemplation of a convertible debt offering or other financing.

EITF CONSENSUS

At its June 18, 2009 meeting, the EITF reached the following consensus positions:

- *Measurement.* An entity that plans to issue convertible debt instruments or other financing should: (1) measure a share-lending arrangement of its own shares at the fair value of the shares at the date of issuance; and (2) recognize the arrangement

in its financial statements as an issuance cost with an offset to additional paid-in capital.
- *Subsequent measurement.* If the default of a counterparty to a share-lending arrangement becomes probable, the issuer of the share-lending arrangement should recognize an expense that equals the then fair value of the unreturned shares, net of the fair value of probable recoveries, with an offset to additional paid-in capital. An issuer of a share-lending arrangement should remeasure the fair value of unreturned shares each reporting period through earnings until consideration on the arrangement payable by the counterparty becomes fixed. Subsequent changes in the amount of probable recoveries also should be recognized in earnings.
- *Earnings per share presentation.* Loaned shares should be excluded from the basic and diluted earnings-per-share calculations unless there is a default of the share-lending arrangement. In that case, the loaned shares would be included in the calculation of basic and diluted earnings per share. If dividends on the loaned shares are not reimbursed to the entity, amounts, if any, including contractual (accumulated) dividends and participation rights in undistributed earnings that may be attributed to the loaned shares should be deducted in the computation of income available to common shareholders, as required in the "two-class" method discussed in ASC 260-10-45-60B (paragraph 61 of FAS-128)

DISCLOSURE

The following disclosures should be made by entities that enter into a share-lending arrangement on their own shares in contemplation of a convertible debt offering or other financing arrangement. The information should be disclosed in the interim and annual financial statements, in any period in which a share-lending arrangement is outstanding:

- A description of outstanding share-lending arrangements, if any, on an entity's own stock and all significant terms of such arrangements, including the number of shares, the term, the circumstances under which cash settlement would be required, and requirements, if any, for the counterparty to provide collateral.
- The entity's reason for entering into a share-lending arrangement.
- The fair value of outstanding loaned shares as of the balance sheet date.
- How the share-lending arrangement is treated in the earnings per share calculation.
- The unamortized amount and classification of issuance costs related to the share-lending arrangement at the balance sheet date.

- The amount of interest cost recognized in conjunction with the amortization of the issuance costs related to the share-lending arrangement for the reporting period.
- The amounts of dividends, if any, paid for loaned shares that will not be reimbursed.

The disclosures required in FASB Statement No. 129, *Disclosure of Information about Capital Structures* (FAS-129) (ASC 505, *Equity*) (ASC 505-10-50) apply to entities that enter into share lending arrangements on their own shares in contemplation of a convertible debt offering or other financing and should disclose:

- The amount of expense reported in the income statement that is related to a default in the period the entity concludes that it is probable that a counterparty to its share-lending arrangement will default.
- In any subsequent period, material changes, if any, in the amount of expense as a result of changes in the fair value of the entity's shares or the probable recoveries.
- If a default is probable but has not yet occurred, the number of shares related to a share-lending arrangement that will be shown in basic and diluted earnings per share when the counterparty's default occurs.

EFFECTIVE DATE AND TRANSITION

The guidance in this Issue is effective for fiscal years that begin on or after December 15, 2009, and interim periods within those fiscal years for arrangements outstanding as of the beginning of those fiscal years. *Retrospective* application is required for all arrangements that are outstanding as of the beginning of those fiscal years. The guidance in this Issue is effective for interim and annual periods beginning on or after June 15, 2009 for share-lending arrangements entered into in those periods. Early application of Issue 09-1 is *not* permitted.
Share lending arrangements that have been terminated because a counterparty has defaulted before Issue 09-1's effective date but for which the entity has *not* reached a final settlement as of the effective date should be accounted for under the guidance in Issue 09-1. The transition disclosures in ASC 250-10-50-1 through 50-3 (paragraphs 17 and 18 of FAS-154, Accounting Changes and Error Corrections) should be provided.

FASB RATIFICATION

The FASB ratified the EITF's consensus positions in this Issue at its July 1, 2009 meeting. The EITF will discuss Issue 09-1 again at a future meeting.

ASC 815 DERIVATIVES AND HEDGING

EITF Issue 05-2 (The Meaning of "Conventional Convertible Instrument" in EITF Issue No. 00-19, "Accounting for Derivative Financial Instruments Indexed to, and Potentially Settled in, a Company's Own Stock") (ASC 815-40-25-41 through 42)

OVERVIEW

ASC 815-10-15-74 (paragraph11 (a) of FAS-133, Accounting for Derivative Instruments and Hedging Activities) provides that contracts issued or held by a reporting entity should *not* be considered to be derivative instruments if they are (*a*) indexed to that entity's *own* stock and (*b*) reported in the entity's balance sheet in stockholders' equity. In ASC 460-10-60-14; 480-10-55-63; 505-10-60-5; 815-10-15-78, 55-52; 815-15-25-15; 815-40-05-1 through 50-4; 05-10 through 05-12; 25-1 through 25-5, 25-7 through 25-20, 25-22 through 25-24, 25-26 through 25-35, 25-37 through 25-40, 30-1; 35-1, 35-2, 35-4 through 35-6, 35-8 through 35-13; 40-1, 40-2; 50-1 through 50-5; 55-1 through 55-18 (Issue 00-19, Accounting for Derivative Financial Instruments Indexed to, and Potentially Settled in, a Company's Own Stock), which applies only to *freestanding* derivatives such as forward contracts, options, and warrants, the EITF provides guidance for determining whether an embedded derivative would be classified in stockholders' equity in accordance with ASC 815-10-15-74 (paragraph 11(a) of FAS-133) (if it were freestanding. However, in Issue 00-19, the EITF provided that a *conventional convertible debt instrument* should be exempted from the evaluation of whether it contains an embedded derivative indexed to the company's own stock that would require bifurcation if the holder of that debt instrument can realize the value of the conversion option only by exercising the option and receiving the proceeds, at the issuer's discretion, in a fixed number of shares or an equivalent amount of cash.

Because the guidance in ASC 460-10-60-14; 480-10-55-63; 505-10-60-5; 815-10-15-78, 55-52; 815-15-25-15; 815-40-05-1 through 50-4; 05-10 through 05-12; 25-1 through 25-5, 25-7 through 25-20, 25-22 through 25-24, 25-26 through 25-35. 25-37 through 25-40; 30-1; 35-1, 35-2, 35-4 through 35-6, 35-8 through 35-13; 40-1, 40-2; 50-1 through 50-5; 55-1 through 55-18 (Issue 00-19) does not specifically define the term *conventional convertible debt*, there has been diversity in practice in determining which convertible debt instruments qualify for the exemption.

ACCOUNTING ISSUE

Should the exemption for applying the Accounting Model discussed in paragraphs 12 to 32 of Issue 00-19 for "conventional convertible debt instruments" be deleted from the Issue or clarified?

EITF CONSENSUS

The EITF reached the following consensus positions:

- The exemption under Issue 00-19 for conventional convertible debt instruments should be *retained*.
- A convertible debt instrument should be considered to be *conventional* for the purpose of applying the guidance in ASC 460-10-60-14; 480-10-55-63; 505-10-60-5; 815-10-15-78; 55-52; 815-15-25-15; 815-40-05-1 through 05-4, 05-10 through 05-12; 25-1 through 25-5, 25-7 through 25-20, 25-22 through 25-24, 25-26 through 25-35, 25-37 through 25-40; 30-1; 35-1, 35-2, 35-4 through 35-6, 35-8 through 35-13; 40-1, 40-2; 50-1 through 50-5; 55-1 through 55-18 (Issue 00-19) if the holder has an option under the debt instrument's provisions to convert it into a fixed number of shares or an equivalent amount of cash at the issuer's discretion based on the passage of time or the occurrence of a contingent event. The existence of a standard antidilution provision does *not* prohibit the conversion of an instrument into a fixed number of shares.
- Convertible preferred stock having a mandatory redemption date may qualify for the exemption provided in Issue 00-19 (see ASC references above) for conventional convertible debt if the instrument's economic characteristics are more similar to debt than equity.

The applicable information required in ASC 505-10-15-1; 50-3 to 50-5, 50-11 (FAS-129, Disclosure of Information about Capital) should be disclosed for instruments under the scope of this Issue.

TRANSITION

Entities should apply the guidance in this Issue to new instruments entered into and instruments modified in periods beginning after June 29, 2005—the date on which the FASB ratified the EITF's consensus positions in this Issue.

EITF Issue 06-7 (Issuer's Accounting for a Previously Bifurcated Conversion Option in a Convertible Debt Instrument When the Conversion Option No Longer Meets the Bifurcation Criteria in FASB Statement No. 133, *Accounting for Derivative Instruments and Hedging Activities*) (ASC 815-15-35-4; 40-1, 40-2, 40-4; 50-3; 470-20-25-16)

OVERVIEW

Under the guidance in ASC 815 (FAS-133, Accounting for Derivative Instruments and Hedging Activities) convertible debt with an embedded conversion option must be bifurcated to separate the conversion option from its host contract and accounted for separately as a derivative if the three conditions discussed in ASC 815-15-25-1 (paragraph 12 of FAS-133) are met. Because under the guidance in ASC 815 (FAS-133) an entity must reassess in each reporting period whether an embedded conversion option meets the conditions for bifurcation, sometimes an embedded conversion option that has been separated from its host contract no longer meets the conditions for separate accounting as a derivative. This Issue was undertaken by the EITF because opinions vary as to how to account for the change. Some believe that the change should be recognized by combining the liability related to the derivative with the liability on the debt instrument. Proponents of this view believe that a premium resulting from the change should be amortized over the remaining term of the debt. Others reclassify the carrying value of the liability on the derivative and combine it with the liability on the debt instrument only as long as the future amortization of a premium that results from the transaction does *not* result in a negative effective yield.

ACCOUNTING ISSUE

How should an issuer account for a previously bifurcated conversion option in a convertible debt instrument if that conversion option no longer meets the criteria for bifurcation in ASC 815 (FAS-133)?

EITF CONSENSUS

The EITF reached the following consensus positions:

- An issuer should reclassify the carrying amount of a liability related to an embedded conversion option in a convertible debt instrument that had been bifurcated but that no longer meets the criteria for bifurcation in FAS-133 to shareholders' equity at its fair value on the date the liability is reclassified. Amortization of a debt discount, if any, recognized when a conversion option was originally bifurcated from a convertible debt instrument should continue.

- An issuer should immediately recognize as interest expense the unamortized amount of a discount, if any, which remains at the conversion date, if a holder exercises a conversion option whose carrying amount had been reclassified to shareholders' equity under the guidance in this Issue.

- If a convertible debt instrument with a conversion option whose carrying amount had been reclassified to shareholders' equity according to the guidance in this Issue is extinguished for cash or other assets before its stated maturity date, the issuer should allocate the reacquisition price as follows: (a) allocate to equity the portion that equals the fair value of the conversion option at the extinguishment date, and (b) allocate the remaining amount to the debt extinguishment to determine the amount of a gain or loss.

The EITF believes that this consensus is *not* inconsistent with the guidance in ASC 470-20-05-2 through 05-6; 25-2, 25-3, 25-10 through 25-13; 30-1, 30-2; 505-10-60-3 (APB-14, Accounting for Convertible Debt and Debt Issued with Stock Purchase Warrants), because *(a)* the instrument was bifurcated initially in accordance with the guidance in FAS-133, and *(b)* APB-14's guidance applies to convertible debt instruments only at issuance, not to subsequent changes.

DISCLOSURE

The EITF reached a consensus that issuers should disclose the following information for the period in which an embedded conversion option that was previously accounted for as a derivative under the guidance in ASC 815 (FAS-133) no longer meets the criteria for bifurcation:

- A description of the principal changes as a result of which an embedded conversion option is no longer required to be bifurcated under the guidance in FAS-133.
- The amount of a liability that is reclassified to stockholders' equity.

FASB RATIFICATION

The FASB ratified the consensus positions in this Issue at its November 29, 2006, meeting.

NONAUTHORITATIVE GUIDANCE

EITF Issue 85-29 (Convertible Bonds with a "Premium Put)"

OVERVIEW

Some convertible bonds are issued at par with a "premium put," which allows the holder to redeem the bond for cash at a multiple of its par value (e.g., 110%) on a specific date or dates before the bond matures. The put expires if not exercised. On issuance of such bonds, their carrying amount exceeds the market value of the common stock into which the bonds could be converted.

ACCOUNTING ISSUES

1. Should the issuer accrue a liability over the period that the premium put is outstanding, so that the total liability would equal the redemption price when the put is exercisable?

12.50 *Convertible Debt and Debt with Warrants*

2. Should the issuer continue accruing a liability if it is unlikely that the put will be exercised because the value of the debt or the common stock has subsequently changed?
3. If the put is not exercised, should the accrued liability be recognized as income, credited to capital, included in the carrying amount of the debt, or amortized as a yield adjustment over the remaining term of the debt?

EITF CONSENSUS

1. The issuer should accrue a liability for the put premium from the date the debt was issued to the date the put can first be exercised.
2. The issuer should continue accruing a liability regardless of changes in the market value of the debt or the underlying stock.
3. If the holder of the bond does not exercise the put, the issuer should account for the liability for the put premium based on the relationship between the put price and the market value of the underlying common stock into which the bond would be converted at the put's expiration date, as follows:
   a. Credit the liability to additional paid-in capital if the market value of the common stock exceeds the price of the put.
   b. Amortize the liability as a yield adjustment over the remaining term of the debt if the price of the put exceeds the market value of the common stock.

> **OBSERVATION:** Under the provisions of ASC 460 (FIN-45, Guarantor's Accounting and Disclosure Requirements for Guarantees, Including Indirect Guarantees of Indebtedness of Others), guarantors are required to recognize a liability at the inception of a guarantee for the obligation assumed. The put option discussed in this Issue is considered to be a guarantee under the provisions of ASC 460-10-55-2 (paragraph 3(a)(2)) of FIN-45 that should be accounted for according to the Interpretation's initial recognition and initial measurement requirements with disclosure of the required information. However, in accordance with ASC 460-10-25-1 (paragraph 7(a) of FIN-45), only the Interpretation's disclosure requirements apply to written options accounted for under the provisions of ASC 815 (FAS-133, Accounting for Derivative Instruments and Hedging Activities)

EFFECT OF FAS-133

FAS-133 applies if an embedded feature qualifies as a derivative under the guidance in ASC 815-15-25-1 (paragraphs 12 and 13 of FAS-133). The EITF's consensus positions continue to apply, however, to derivatives embedded in hybrid instruments issued before 1998 or 1999, if the issuer decides not to account for that feature separately, as permitted under the guidance in paragraph 50 of FAS-133.

> **OBSERVATION:** The guidance in FAS-133 has been amended by FAS-155 (Accounting for Certain Hybrid Financial Instruments), which permits an entity to elect to measure at their fair value certain hybrid financial instruments with embedded derivatives that otherwise would have to be bifurcated. If an entity elects to measure an entire hybrid instrument at its fair value, that financial instrument *cannot* be used as a hedging instrument in a FAS-133 hedging relationship.

DISCUSSION

The EITF's conclusions on Issues 1 and 2 indicate that the Task Force rejected the notion suggested by some that accrual of a liability should be influenced by the probability that the put would be exercised, based on the movement of interest rates and the market value of the stock into which the bonds could be converted.

The EITF's conclusion on Issue 3 indicates the Task Force's view that the amount accrued for a put premium should be considered on expiration as (1) an equity transaction if the market value of the stock exceeds the put price or (2) a transaction affecting periodic income if the put price exceeds the market value of the common stock.

RELATED CHAPTERS IN 2011 GAAP GUIDE, VOLUME II

Chapter 4, "Balance Sheet Classification and Related Display Issues"
Chapter 15, "Extinguishment of Debt"
Chapter 17, "Financial Instruments"
Chapter 39, "Stockholders' Equity"

RELATED CHAPTERS IN 2011 GAAP GUIDE, VOLUME I

Chapter 3, "Balance Sheet Classification and Related Display Issues"
Chapter 9, "Convertible Debt and Debt with Warrants"
Chapter 15, "Extinguishment of Debt"
Chapter 17, "Financial Instruments"
Chapter 44, "Stockholders' Equity"

RELATED CHAPTERS IN 2011 INTERNATIONAL ACCOUNTING/FINANCIAL REPORTING STANDARDS GUIDE

Chapter 3, "Presentation of Financial Statements"
Chapter 12, "Earnings per Share"
Chapter 16, "Financial Instruments"

CHAPTER 13
EARNINGS PER SHARE

CONTENTS

Overview		13.02
Authoritative Guidance		
ASC 260 Earnings Per Share		13.03
FSP EITF 03-6-1	Determining Whether Instruments Granted in Share-Based Transactions Are Participating Securities	13.03
EITF Issue 03-6	Participating Securities and the Two-Class Method under FASB Statement No. 128, *Earnings per Share*	13.05
EITF Issue 04-8	The Effect of Contingently Convertible Instruments on Diluted Earnings per Share	13.08
EITF Issue 07-4	Application of the Two-Class Method under FASB Statement No. 128, *Earnings per Share*, to Master Limited Partnerships	13.09
Topic D-42	The Effect on the Calculation of Earnings per Share for a Period that Includes for the Redemption or Induced Conversion of Preferred Stock	13.13
Topic D-53	Computation of Earnings per Share for a Period That Includes a Redemption or an Induced Conversion of a Portion of a Class of Preferred Stock	13.14
Topic D-62	Computing Year-to-Date Diluted Earnings per Share under FASB Statement No. 128	13.15
Topic D-72	Effect of Contracts That May Be Settled in Stock or Cash on the Computation of Diluted Earnings per Share	13.17
Topic D-82	Effect of Preferred Stock Dividends Payable in Common Shares on Computation of Income Available to Common Stockholders	13.19
ASC 815	Derivatives and Hedging	13.20

13.02 *Earnings per Share*

EITF Issue 00-19	Accounting for Derivative Financial Instruments Indexed to, and Potentially Settled in, a Company's Own Stock	13.20
Related Chapters in 2011 GAAP Guide, Volume II		13.22
Related Chapters in 2011 GAAP Guide, GAAP Guide, Volume I		13.22
Related Chapters in 2011 International Accounting/Financial Reporting Standards Guide		13.22

OVERVIEW

Earnings per share (EPS) is an important measure of corporate performance for investors and other users of financial statements. Publicly held companies are required to present EPS amounts in the income statement in a manner consistent with the statement's captions. Holders of certain securities, such as convertible bonds, preferred stock, and stock options, may become common stockholders or may add to the number of shares of common stock already held. When potential reduction, called *dilution*, of EPS amounts is inherent in a company's capital structure, a dual presentation of EPS is required—primary and fully diluted EPS.

The following pronouncements, which address the calculation and presentation of EPS information in financial statements, are discussed in the *GAAP Guide, Volume I*, Chapter 13, "Earnings per Share."

ASC 260	Earnings per Share (FAS-128)
ASC 480	Accounting for Certain Financial Instruments with Characteristics of both Liabilities and Equity (FAS-150)

AUTHORITATIVE GUIDANCE

ASC 260 Earnings Per Share

FSP EITF 03-6-1 Determining Whether Instruments Granted in Share-Based Transactions Are Participating Securities (ASC 260-10-45-61A, 45-68B, 65-2, 55-76A through 55-D)

OVERVIEW

Participating securities are defined in FASB Accounting Standards Codification™ ASC 260-10-45-59A (paragraph 60(a) of FAS-128, Earnings per Share) as:

> Securities that may participate in dividends with common stocks according to a predetermined formula (for example, two for one) with, at times, an upper limit on participation (for example, up to, but not beyond a specified amount per share).

Further, under the guidance in ASC 260 (FAS-128), entities that have participating securities or multiple classes of securities with a different dividend rate for each class of security are required to compute their earnings per share by the two-class method.

The EITF's consensus on issue 2 of Issue 03-6 (Participating Securities and the Two-Class Method under FASB Statement No. 128) states that a participating security is one that may participate in undistributed earnings with common stock in its current form, regardless of whether or not participation depends on the occurrence of a specific event. Because the guidance in issue 2 applies *only* to share-based payment awards that are *fully* vested and ASC 260-10-45-60, 45-60A through 45-68; 55-24 through 55-30, 55-71 through 55-75 (Issue 03-6) does *not* address whether unvested share-based payment awards are participating securities, the EITF discussed that question in Issue 04-12 (Determining Whether Equity-Based Compensation Awards Are Participating Securities) (not in ASC). However, the EITF was unable to reach a consensus on that Issue and consequently removed it from its agenda.

ACCOUNTING ISSUE

Can instruments granted in share-based payment transactions be participating securities before the required service has been rendered?

FASB STAFF POSITON

The computation of basic earnings per share under the two-class method should include *unvested* share-based payment awards, which include *nonforfeitable* rights to paid or unpaid dividends or dividend equivalents, because securities that include such rights are considered to be participating securities. A share-based payment award that includes a right to receive a dividend that is *not* forfeited regardless of whether the award becomes vested or remains unvested is a participating right, because it is *not* contingent on the performance of additional services after the dividend has been declared. However, an award under which the right to dividends would be forfeited if the award does *not* vest would *not* be treated as a participating right, because it does not meet the definition of a participating security. In addition, an award whose exercise price would be reduced by amounts equivalent to distributions to common shareholders would *not* be treated as a participating right; the transfer of value to the holder of the award is not a nonforfeitable right, because it would occur only if the award is exercised. That conclusion is consistent with the consensus in Issue 2(b)(i) of Issue 03-6.

Under the guidance in ASC 718-10-55-45 (paragraph A37 of FAS-123(R) (Revised 2004), Share-Based Payment), nonrefundable dividends or dividend equivalents paid on awards for which the required service has *not* been or is *not* expected to be rendered and therefore do *not* vest must be recognized as additional compensation cost and dividends or dividend equivalents paid on awards for which the required service has been or is expected to be performed must be recognized in retained earnings. Consequently, dividends or dividend equivalents recognized as compensation cost on unvested share-based payment awards that are *not* expected to or do *not* vest should *not* be included in the earnings allocation for the computation of earnings per share because doing so would result in a double reduction of earnings available to common shareholders—as compensation cost and as a distribution of earnings. However, *undistributed* earnings should be allocated to all outstanding share-based payment awards, including those for which the required service is *not* expected to be performed. For the purpose of calculating EPS under the guidance in this FSP, the estimated number of awards for which it is expected that the required service will *not* be performed should be consistent with an entity's estimate used to recognize compensation cost under the guidance in ASC 718 (FAS-123(R)). A change in estimate of the number of awards for which the required service is *not* expected to be performed should be applied in the period in which the change in estimate occurs. Although that change in estimate will affect an entity's current period income, an entity's change in the current period of its expected forfeiture rate would *not* affect its EPS calculations in prior periods.

EFFECTIVE DATE AND TRANSITION

This FSP is effective for financial statements issued for fiscal years that begin after December 15, 2008, and interim periods in those years. Entities would be required to retrospectively adjust all earnings per share information presented in prior periods to conform with the guidance in this FSP. That requirement also applies to interim financial statements, summaries of earnings, and selected financial data. Early application is prohibited.

EITF Issue 03-6 (Participating Securities and the Two-Class Method under FASB Statement No. 128, *Earnings per Share*) (ASC 260-10-45-60, 45-60A through 45-68; 55-24 through 55-30, 55-71 through 55-75)

OVERVIEW

Under the guidance in ASC 260 (FAS-128, Earnings per Share), entities that have issued participating securities, which are defined in ASC 260-10-45-59A (paragraph 60(a) of FAS-128) as securities that may participate in dividends with common stock according to a prescribed formula, are required to compute earnings per share (EPS) by the two-class method. ASC 260-10-45-60B (paragraph 61 of FAS-128) states further that the two-class method should be used for securities that are *not* convertible into a class of common stock.

In Topic D-95 (Effect of Participating Convertible Securities on the Computation of Basic Earnings per Share) (nullified by this Issue), the FASB staff clarified that participating securities convertible into common stock should be included in the computation of basic EPS if the effect of doing so is dilutive. In addition, the FASB staff stated that the decision whether basic EPS should be computed by the if-converted or the two-class method is an accounting policy. The if-converted method should *not* be used to compute basic EPS, however, if the result would be *less* dilutive than if the security were not convertible to common stock and basic EPS were computed by the two-class method. This Issue addresses questions about the application of the two-class method and its interaction with the guidance in Topic D-95.

ACCOUNTING ISSUES

1. Does the two-class method require the presentation of basic and diluted EPS for all participating securities?

1a. When should basic and diluted EPS be presented if the two-class method does not require the presentation of basic and diluted EPS for all participating securities?

2. How should a participating security requiring the application of ASC 260-10-45-60B (paragraph 61 of FAS-128 be defined?

2a. Should all potential common shares, that is, securities or other contracts that may entitle their holders to obtain common stock (such as options, warrants, forwards, convertible debt, and convertible preferred stock), be participating securities?

2b. Do dividends or dividend equivalents paid to the holder of a convertible participating security that are applied to either reduce the conversion price or increase the conversion ratio of the security represent participation rights?
3. How should undistributed earnings be allocated to a participating security?
4. Would an entity that allocated undistributed earnings to a nonconvertible participating security continue to do so in a period of net loss if the effect is anti-dilutive?
5. Would a convertible participating security be excluded from the computation of basic EPS if an entity has a net loss from continuing operations?
6. How should a convertible participating security be included in the computation of diluted EPS?

EITF CONSENSUS

The EITF reached the following consensus positions:

1. Under the two-class method, presentation of basic and diluted earnings per share is *not* required for all participating securities.
2. For the purpose of applying the requirements in ASC 260-10-45-59A, 45-60B (paragraphs 60 and 61 of FAS-128), a participating security is defined as one that may participate with common stocks in undistributed earnings without considering (*a*) the form of participation and (*b*) whether participation depends on the occurrence of a specific event.
3. Dividends or dividend equivalents transferred to a holder of a convertible security in the form of a reduction of the conversion price or an increase in the security's conversion ratio are not participation rights. This consensus would also apply to other contracts or securities to issue an entity's common stock if the exercise price would be adjusted as a result of an issuer's declaration of dividends. However, the EITF noted that this consensus does *not* apply to forward contracts to issue an entity's own equity shares because forward contracts are participating securities.
4. An issuer should consider whether a dividend or dividend equivalent applied to reduce the conversion price or increase the conversion ratio of a convertible security in its financial statements is a contingent beneficial conversion feature. That decision should be made in accordance with the guidance in ASC 470-20-05-7, 05-8; 25-4 through 6; 30-3, 30-6, 30-8, 30-10, 30-11, 30-15; 35-2, 35-7; 40-2, 40-3; 55-30 through 55-33, 55-35 through 55-38, 55-40 through 55-43, 55-45 through 55-48, 55-50 through 55-54, 55-54A, 55-56 through 55-60, 55-60A, 55-62 through 55-66, 55-69; 505-10-50-8 (EITF Issue 98-5, Accounting for Convertible Securities with Beneficial Conversion Features

or Contingently Adjustable Conversion Ratios) and EITF Issue 00-27 (Application of Issue No. 98-5 to Certain Convertible Instruments).

5. Undistributed earnings for a period should be allocated based on a security's contractual participation rights to share in current earnings as if all of the earnings for the period had been distributed. Undistributed earnings should *not* be allocated based on arbitrary assumptions if the participating security's terms do *not* state objectively determinable, nondiscretionary participation rights. The EITF noted that this consensus is based on the guidance in ASC 260-10-45-60B (paragraph 61(b) of FAS-128), which states that under the two-class method, "the remaining earnings shall be allocated to common stock and participating securities to the extent that each security may share in earnings as if all the earnings for the period had been distributed," even though this is a pro forma allocation and may not represent the economic probabilities of actual distributions to the holders of the participating securities.

6. An entity should allocate losses to a nonconvertible participating security in a period in which the entity has a net loss if the security's contractual terms provide that, in addition to the right to participate in the issuer's earnings, the security also has an obligation to share in the issuer's losses on an objectively determinable basis. A holder of a nonconvertible participating security has an obligation to share in the issuer's losses if either of the following conditions exists:

   a. The holder has an obligation to commit assets in addition to the initial investment to fund the issuing entity's losses without increasing the holder's investment interest in the entity.

   b. The participating security's contractual principal or mandatory redemption amount is reduced by the issuing entity's incurred losses.

7. The basis for the consensus in item 6 (above) also applies to the inclusion of convertible securities in basic EPS when an issuer has a net loss and the security's contractual terms provide that the participating security has an obligation to share in the issuer's losses on an objectively determinable basis. The existence of an obligation to share in an issuer's losses should be determined in the applicable reporting period based on the security's contractual rights and obligations.

8. The computation of basic EPS using the two-class method should include participating securities. This consensus *nullifies* the guidance in EITF Abstracts, Topic D-95, "Effect of Participating Convertible Securities on the Computation of Basic Earnings per Share" (Topic D-95).

9. All securities that meet the definition of a participating security in item 2 (above) should be included in the computation of basic

EPS under the two-class method, regardless of whether they are convertible, nonconvertible, or potential common stock securities.

10. Until options or shares are fully vested, the guidance in this Issue does not apply to stock-based compensation, accounted for under the provisions of ASC 718 (FAS-123(R), Share-Based Payments), such as options and nonvested stock that include a right to receive dividends declared on an issuer's common stock.

EITF Issue 04-8 (The Effect of Contingently Convertible Instruments on Diluted Earnings per Share) (ASC 260-10-45-43 through 45-44; 55-78 through 55-79, 55-81 through 55-82, 55-84 through 55-84B)

OVERVIEW

This issue addresses the question of when to include the dilutive effect of contingently convertible debt instruments (Co-Cos) in diluted earnings per share (EPS). Co-Cos are convertible debt instruments that include a contingent feature and are generally convertible into an issuer's common shares after the stock price of the issuer's common stock exceeds a predetermined amount for a specified period of time, known as the market price trigger. A Co-Co's conversion price usually is higher than the underlying stock's market price when the Co-Co is issued and its market price trigger usually is higher than the conversion price. Because the market price trigger is higher than the conversion price, a Co-Co is less likely to be converted than is a convertible debt instrument without a market price trigger.

The Issue was brought to the EITF's attention because some issuers are accounting for Co-Cos differently than for convertible debt without a market price trigger. That is, most issuers of Co-Cos are not including the instrument's dilutive effect in diluted EPS until the market price trigger has been reached. Some issuers, however, are including the dilutive effect of convertible debt without a market price trigger in diluted EPS as of the instrument's issue date.

ACCOUNTING ISSUE

When should the dilutive effect of a contingently convertible instrument be included in diluted earnings per share calculations?

EITF CONSENSUS

The EITF reached a consensus to include all instruments with embedded contingent conversion features, such as contingently convertible debt, contingently preferred stock, and instruments such as Instrument C discussed in Issue 90-19 (Convertible Bonds with

Issuer Option to Settle for Cash upon Conversion) (nullified by FSP APB 14-1) in the calculation of diluted earnings per share, if dilutive, without considering whether the market conditions for conversion have been met. The EITF believes that the economics of such instruments do not differ from conventional convertible debt with a market price conversion premium. Also included under the consensus are instruments with more than one contingency if at least one of the instrument's contingencies requires the occurrence of a market condition that would trigger conversion, regardless of whether a non-market condition, such as a change in control, has been met. Instruments requiring that both a market trigger *and* a substantive non-market-based contingency be met for conversion to occur, however, are *not* included under the scope of this Issue until the non-market-based contingency has occurred.

FASB RATIFICATION

The FASB ratified the consensus positions in this Issue at its October 13, 2004, and November 30, 2004, meetings.

EITF Issue 07-4 (Application of the Two-Class Method under FASB Statement No. 128, *Earnings per Share*, to Master Limited Partnerships) (ASC 260-10-05-3 through 05-5; 15-5; 45-72 through 45-73; 55-103 through 55-110; 65-1)

OVERVIEW

Master limited partnerships (MLPs) that are publicly traded may issue several classes of securities with the right to participate in a partnership's distributions based on a formula that is specified in the partnership agreement. Generally, an MLP's capital structure is composed of publicly traded "common units" that are held by its limited partners (LPs), a general partner (GP) interest, and holders of incentive distribution rights (IDRs), which may be a separate class of non-voting LP interests depending on the MLP's capital structure. In some cases, IDRs may initially be held by a GP that may transfer or sell them separately from its general interest, but sometimes IDRs are embedded in a GP's interest so that they cannot be detached and sold separately from the GP's interest in the MLP.

In accordance with the provisions of a partnership agreement, a GP usually is required to distribute 100% of an MLP's "available cash" (as defined in the partnership agreement) to the GP and the LPs at the end of each reporting period. That distribution is based on a schedule referred to as a "waterfall," which stipulates the distributions at each threshold. As certain thresholds are met, available cash is distributed further to holders of IDRs or to a GP whose IDRs are embedded in the GP's interest in the MLP. The timing of a distribution after the end of a reporting period is stipulated in an MLP's contract. "Available cash" is defined as all cash on hand at the end of each reporting period *less* cash retained by the partnership as capital to: (1) operate the business; (2) meet debt obligations and other legal obligations; and (3) provide funds for distribution to the holders of common units, the GP, and the IDR holders for one or more of the following reporting periods. After considering priority income allocations as a result of incentive distributions, a partnership's net income or loss is distributed to its GP's and LPs' capital accounts based on their respective sharing of income and losses stated in the partnership agreement.

Because of their capital structure, MLPs must compute earnings per unit (EPU) under the provisions for the two-class method discussed in ASC 260 (FAS-128, Earnings per Share), which requires that undistributed earnings be allocated to common units and participating securities as if all of the period's earnings had been distributed. However, under the guidance in Issue 3 of EITF Issue 03-6, (Participating Securities and the Two-Class Method under FASB Statement No. 128), a reporting period's undistributed earning are allocated to a participating security based on its contractual participation rights to share in the current period's earnings as if *all* of that period's earnings had been distributed. Consequently, the FASB has received requests for guidance on the effect of IDRs on the computation of EPU when the two-class method is applied to the interests of an MLP's LPs and its GP.

EITF CONSENSUS

The EITF reached the following consensus positions:

- *Scope*. Issue 07-4 applies to MLPs making incentive distributions that are treated as equity distributions when certain thresholds are met. This Issue does *not* provide guidance for determining whether an incentive distribution should be accounted for as an equity distribution or as compensation cost.
- *IDRs that are a separate class of LP interest*. IDRs that are held separately are participating securities because they are entitled to participate in earnings with common equity holders. Consequently, an MLP's earnings for a reporting period should be allocated to the GP, LPs, and IDR holders using the two-class method discussed in FAS-128 to calculate EPU as follows:
  — When the two-class method is used to calculate an MLP's EPU, the current period's net income (or loss) should be reduced (or increased) by the amount of available cash that has been or will be distributed for that period to the GP, LPs, and IDR holders. For example, under the XYZ MLP's partnership agreement, its GP is required to distribute available cash within 60 days after the end of each fiscal quarter. Because XYZ must file its financial statements with a regulatory agency within 45 days after the end of each fiscal quarter, the amount of available cash that will be distributed to the GP, LPs, and IDR holders must be determined in order to

calculate the MLP's EPU for the first quarter. Further, XYZ's income or loss must be reduced (or increased) by the amount of available cash to be distributed in order to compute the *undistributed* earnings that must be allocated to the GP, LPs, and IDR holders in the computation of the first quarter's EPU.

— *Undistributed earnings*, if any, should be distributed to the GP, LPs, and IDR holders based on the terms of the partnership agreement. Although available cash must be distributed for the period presented based on the distribution waterfall specified in the partnership agreement, undistributed earning must be distributed to IDR holders based on an IDR's *contractual participation rights* to share in the current period's earnings. However, if a partnership agreement includes a "specified threshold" for the distribution of undistributed earnings (e.g., 5% of earnings), as discussed in ASC 260-10-55-24 (Example F of paragraph 16 of Issue 03-6) in the FASB's *EITF Abstracts*, undistributed earnings should *not* be distributed to an IDR holder beyond that specified threshold.

— To determine whether there is a specified threshold for distributions to IDR holders, it is necessary to evaluate whether such distributions are contractually limited to available cash, as defined in the partnership agreement, if all of a period's earnings have been distributed. In that case, an IDR holder that has received a distribution of available cash up to its specific threshold would *not* be eligible to share *in undistributed* earnings. However, if a partnership agreement's provisions do *not* specifically limit distributions to IDR holders to available cash, undistributed earnings should be distributed to IDR holders based on the partnership agreement's distribution waterfall for available cash.

— If cash distributions *exceed* current-period earnings, such excess distributions over earnings should be allocated to the GP and LPs based on the partnership agreement's provisions for the allocation of losses to the respective partners' capital accounts. If IDR holders do *not* have a contractual obligation to share in an MLP's losses, *no* portion of an excess distribution over earnings would be allocated to them. However, if IDR holders have a contractual obligation to share in an MLP's losses on an objectively determined basis, excess distributions, if any, would be allocated to the GP, LPs, and IDR holders based on the partnership agreement's provisions for their respective sharing of losses.

- *IDRs embedded in a GP's interest.* Although IDRs embedded in a GP's interest are not separate participating securities, the two-class method should be used to calculate EPU for the GP's and LPs' interests because those interests are separate classes of equity:

- When an MLP's EPU is calculated under the two-class method, the current period's net income (or loss) should be reduced (or increased) by the amount of available cash that has been or will be distributed for that period to the GP (including the embedded IDR's distribution rights) and LPs. For example, under the XYZ MLP's partnership agreement, its GP is required to distribute available cash within 60 days after the end of each fiscal quarter. Because XYZ must file financial statements with a regulatory agency within 45 days after the end of each fiscal quarter, the amount of available cash that will be distributed to the GP and LPs must be determined in order to calculate the MLP's EPU for the first quarter. Furthermore, XYZ's income or loss should be reduced (or increased) by the amount of available cash to be distributed in order to compute the *undistributed* earnings that must be allocated to the GP and LPs in the computation of the first quarter's EPU.

- *Undistributed earnings.* Undistributed earnings, if any, should be distributed to the GP (including the embedded IDR's distribution rights) and LPs based on the terms of the partnership agreement. Although *available cash* must be distributed for the period presented based on the distribution waterfall specified in the partnership agreement, undistributed earning should be distributed to the GP based on an embedded IDR's *contractual participation rights* to share in the current period's earnings. However, if a partnership agreement includes a specified threshold for the distribution of undistributed earnings (e.g., 5% of earnings), as discussed in ASC 260-10-55-24 (Example F of paragraph 16 of Issue 03-6) in the FASB's *EITF Abstracts*, undistributed earnings should *not* be distributed to the GP for the embedded IDR's distribution rights beyond that specified threshold:

  - To determine whether there is a specified threshold for distributions to a GP for the embedded IDR's distribution rights, it is necessary to evaluate whether such distributions are contractually limited to available cash, as defined in the partnership agreement, if all of a period's earnings have been distributed. In that case, a GP that has received a distribution of available cash up to its specific threshold for the embedded IDR's distribution rights would *not* be eligible to share in undistributed earnings. However, if a partnership agreement's provisions do *not* specifically limit distributions to a GP for the distribution rights of embedded IDRs to available cash, undistributed earnings should be distributed to the GP for the distribution rights of embedded IDRs based on the partnership agreement's distribution waterfall for available cash.

  - If cash distributions *exceed* current-period earnings, such excess distributions over earnings would be allocated to the GP and LPs based on the partnership agreement's provisions for their respective sharing of losses for the period.

TRANSITION

The EITF reached a consensus that the guidance in this Issue should be effective for financial statements in fiscal years that begin after December 15, 2008, and interim periods in those years. Earlier application is prohibited. The guidance in this Issue should be applied *retrospectively* for all financial statements presented.

FASB RATIFICATION

The FASB ratified the EITF's consensus reached in this Issue at its March 26, 2008 meeting.

Topic D-42 The Effect on the Calculation of Earnings per Share for a Period that Includes the Redemption or Induced Conversion of Preferred Stock (ASC 260-10-99S-2)

The guidance in this SEC staff announcement has been amended by ASU 2009-8.

The SEC staff's guidance applies to redemptions and induced conversions of preferred stock instruments that are classified in equity. Such transactions should be accounted for as follows:

- An exchange or modification of preferred stock instruments is considered a redemption if the transaction is accounted for as an extinguishment and results in a new basis of accounting for the modified or exchanged preferred stock.
- The guidance in this pronouncement applies to redemptions and induced conversions of preferred stock classified in temporary equity under the guidance in ASR 268 and ASC 480-10-S99-3A (Topic D-98), which are considered to be classified in equity.
- A subsequent reclassification of an equity security to a liability based on guidance in other GAAP (e.g., if a preferred share becomes mandatorily redeemable under the guidance in ASC 480-10) is considered to be a redemption of equity by means of issuing a debt instrument.

This announcement does not affect the accounting for conversions of preferred stock into other securities classified as equity as a result of conversion privileges included under the terms of instruments at issuance.

The SEC staff believes that on such redemptions or conversions, the difference between the fair value of the consideration transferred to the preferred stockholders and the carrying amount of the preferred stock in the registrant's balance sheet (net of issuance costs) should be subtracted from or added to net income for the calculation of income available to common stockholders used in computing earnings per share. The SEC staff believes that the difference between the fair value of the consideration transferred to the preferred stockholders and the carrying amount of the preferred stock in the registrant's balance sheet represents a return to the preferred shareholder that should be treated similarly to dividends paid on preferred stock whether or not the embedded conversion feature is "in the money" or "out of the money" at redemption. If a redemption includes the reacquisition of a beneficial conversion feature in a convertible preferred stock that had previously been recognized, the fair value of the consideration transferred should be reduced by the intrinsic value of the conversion option at the commitment date.

The SEC Staff believes that if the fair value of securities and other consideration transferred by a registrant to the holders of convertible preferred stock as a result of an offer inducing conversion exceeds the fair value of the securities that would have been issued based on the original conversion terms, the difference should be subtracted from net earnings used to calculate net earnings available to common shareholders in the earnings per share calculation. Registrants should follow the guidance in ASC 470-20-05-10; 40-13 through 40-17; 45-2; 55-2 through 55-9 (FAS-84) to determine whether conversion occurred as a result of an inducement offer.

SEC OBSERVER COMMENT

At a subsequent EITF meeting, the SEC Observer responded to a question about the accounting for redemption of convertible preferred stock that has appreciated since issuance. He reiterated that the guidance stated above applies to all classes of preferred stock and that the entire redemption amount that exceeds the *carrying amount* of the preferred stock should be deducted from earnings available to common shareholders. (See Topic D-53 and the discussion in ASC 470-20-40-13 (Issue 02-15).)

Topic D-53 (Computation of Earnings per Share for a Period That Includes a Redemption or an Induced Conversion of a Portion of a Class of Preferred Stock) (ASC 260-10-S99-3)

If only a portion of the outstanding securities of a class of preferred stock is redeemed or converted as a result of an induced conversion, the SEC staff believes that to determine whether the "if converted" method is dilutive for the period, those shares should be considered separately from other shares of the same class that have not been redeemed or converted. The staff also believes that preferred securities with different effective dividend yields should not be combined in testing whether the "if converted" method is dilutive.

To illustrate, a registrant has 100 shares of convertible preferred stock outstanding at the beginning of the period and redeems 20 convertible preferred shares during the period.

FACTS:

Fair value at issuance: $10 per share
Par value: $10 per share
Stated dividend: 5 percent
Dividend for the period: $0.125
Conversion ratio: 1 share of convertible preferred into 1 share of common stock
Redemption premium: $2

The SEC staff believes that the registrant should determine whether the conversion is dilutive:

1. For the 80 preferred shares not redeemed—Apply the "if converted" method from the beginning of the period to the end of the period using the stated 5 percent dividend
2. For the 20 preferred shares redeemed—Apply the "if converted" method from the beginning of the period to the date of redemption using the stated 5 percent dividend and the $2 redemption premium per share.

CALCULATION:

1. To determine whether the 20 redeemed shares are dilutive, compare the effect of $2 plus $0.125 = $2.125 per share if the shares were converted into 20 shares of common stock to the effect if they had not been converted, weighted for the period for which were outstanding.
2. The "if converted" effect of the 80 shares should be determined separately from the redeemed shares by comparing the EPS effect of the $0.125 dividend per share to the effect of those 80 shares if they had been converted into 80 shares of common stock.

Topic D-62 (Computing Year-to-Date Diluted Earnings per Share under FASB Statement No. 128) (ASC 260-10-55-3A, 55-3B, 55-85 through 55-87)

BACKGROUND

A member of the FASB staff discussed their view on the computation of a company's year-to-date diluted EPS if it has a year-to-date loss from continuing operations but has had income from continuing operations in one or more quarters. The question was raised because the guidance in ASC 260-10-45-17; 260-10-55-3 (paragraphs 13 and 46 of FAS-128) seems to conflict when a company has a year-to-date loss for a period of more than three months but has had income in some quarters during the year. ASC 260-10-55-3 (Paragraph 46 of FAS-128) provides the following computational guidance for applying the treasury stock method; the number of incremental shares that will be included in the denominator is determined by computing the year-to-date weighted average of incremental shares included in each quarterly computation of diluted EPS, however, the antidilution rule in ASC 260-10-45-19 (paragraph 16 of FAS 128) states that the conversion, exercise, or contingent issuance of securities should not be assumed if the effect on EPS is antidilutive.

FASB STAFF VIEW

The FASB staff believes that the guidance in ASC 260-10-45-17 (paragraph 13 of FAS-128) should be followed; therefore, no potential common shares (incremental shares) should be included in the computation of diluted EPS if the result is antidilutive.

Illustration of Quarterly and Year-to-Date Calculation

ABC Company has:
- 20,000 common shares outstanding
- 2,000 shares of preferred stock convertible into 4,000 common shares
- Quarterly income (loss) (same as income from continuing operations) as follows:

Q1: $20,000 Q2: ($30,000) Q3: ($8,000) Q4: $10,000

Quarterly EPS

	Q1	Q2	Q3	Q4
Income	$20,000	$(30,000)	($8,000)	$10,000
Common shares	20,000	20,000	20,000	20,000
Incremental shares	4,000	0*	0*	4,000
Basic EPS	$1.00	($1.50)	($.40)	$.50
Diluted EPS	$.83	($1.50)	($.40)	$.42

Year-to-date EPS

	Q1	Q2	Q3	Q4
Income	$20,000	($10,000)	($18,000)	$(8,000)
Common shares	20,000	20,000	20,000	20,000
Incremental shares	4,000	0*	0*	0*
Basic EPS	$1.00	($.50)	($.90)	($.40)
Diluted EPS	$.83	($.50)	($.90)	($.40)

*Incremental shares are not included because they are antidilutive.

Topic D-72 Effect of Contracts That May Be Settled in Stock or Cash on the Computation of Diluted Earnings per Share (ASC 260-10-55-32, 55-34, 55-36, 55-36A; 45-22)

> **OBSERVATION:** The requirements for calculating earnings per share (EPS) in this announcement and for mandatorily redeemable financial instruments and forward contracts requiring physical settlement by repurchasing a fixed number of shares in exchange for cash are partially nullified by the guidance in ASC 480-10-05-1 through 05-6; 10-1; 15-3 through 15-5, 15-7 through 15-10; 25-1 through 25-2, 25-4 through 25-15; 30-1 through 30-7; 35-3 through 35-5; 45-1 through 45-4; 50-1 through 50-4; 55-1 through 55-12, 55-14 through 55-28, 55-34 through 55-41, 55-64; 835-10-60-13. ASC 260-10-45-70A (FAS-150), which requires that such instruments be classified as liabilities. Consequently, ASC 480-10-45-4 (paragraph 25 of FAS-150) requires that common shares redeemed or repurchased be excluded from the calculation of basic and diluted earnings per share. Amounts, if any, related to such shares that have not been recognized as interest cost, such as participation rights, should be deducted from the numerator in the calculation, which is income available to common shareholders. This treatment is consistent with the "two-class" method discussed in ASC 260-10-45-60B (paragraph 61 of FAS-128). The guidance in this announcement continues to apply to other financial instruments, including those that are recognized as liabilities under the provisions of FAS-150.

A FASB staff representative announced the staff's view on the effect on a company's computation of diluted EPS for contracts indexed to and potentially settled in the company's own stock.

The consensus in EITF Issue 96-13 (codified in Issue 00-19) states that freestanding contracts that must be settled in net cash generally should be recognized as assets or liabilities and contracts that must be settled in shares should be recognized as equity instruments. It is assumed that contracts that permit the *company* to choose whether to settle in net cash or in net shares are settled in net shares. Similarly, it is assumed that contracts that permit the *counterparty* to choose whether to settle in net cash or in net shares are settled in net cash.

ASC 260-10-45-45 through 45-46 (paragraph 29 of FAS-128) provides guidance on the effect of such contracts on the issuer's calculation of EPS. It provides that if the issuer or the counterparty can choose the method of settling a contract, it is presumed that the contract will be settled in shares and the potential common shares should be included in diluted EPS, if the effect is dilutive. That presumption may be overcome, however, if it is reasonable to believe that the contract will be settled in cash based on the company's stated policy on the settlement method or past practice.

That guidance is inconsistent with the guidance in Issue 00-19, because under the consensus, initial balance sheet recognition of such contracts does not consider a company's stated policy on the settlement method or past experience. Nevertheless, ASC 260-10-45-45 through 45-46) (paragraph 29 of FAS-128) addresses the effect of that inconsistency on the computation of diluted earnings per share for contracts classified as assets or liabilities according to the guidance in Issue 00-19. It states that the numerator of contracts reported as assets or liabilities for accounting purposes may need to be adjusted for the difference between the reported income or loss, if any, and the amount that would have been reported had the contracts been accounted for as equity instruments during the reporting period.

Likewise, the FASB staff believes that the numerator should be adjusted for contracts accounted for as equity instruments under the guidance ASC 460-10-60-14; 480-10-55-63; 505-10-60-5; 815-10-15-78; 55-52; 815-15-25-15; 815-40-05-1 through 05-4, 05-10 through 05-12; 25-1 through 25-5, 25-7 through 25-20, 25-22 through 25-24, 25-26 through 25-35; 25-37 through 25-40; 30-1; 35-1, 35-2, 35-4 through 35-6, 35-8 through 35-13; 40-1, 40-2; 50-1 through 50-5; 55-1 through 55-18 in (Issue 00-19), if it is reasonable to believe that those contracts will be settled partially or wholly in cash based on the company's stated policy or past practice. The numerator for such contracts may need to be adjusted for the difference between the reported income or loss, if any, and the amount that would have been reported had the contracts been accounted for as assets or liabilities during the reporting period. In addition, the denominator would not include potential dilutive shares. The FASB staff noted that such adjustments to the numerator for the purpose of computing diluted earnings per share should be made only for contracts that qualify to be accounted for based on the guidance in Issue 00-19, because net income would be affected differently by the classification of the contract as an asset or liability or as an equity instrument. The guidance in ASC 260-10-45-45 through 45-46 (paragraph 29 of FAS-128) should be used to determine whether shares issued for stock-based compensation arrangements that are payable in common stock or in cash at the election of the entity or the employee should be included in the denominator in computing diluted EPS. In those situations, the numerator is not adjusted.

The FASB staff clarified that under the guidance in ASC 260-10-45-45 through 45-46 (paragraph 29 of FAS-128), it is assumed that the company will settle the contract in shares if the company can choose the settlement method under the contract. This presumption can be overcome based on the company's past practice or policy. However, if the counterparty chooses the settlement method, the company's past practice or policy would not affect the accounting. In that case, the company should use the more dilutive settlement method in its EPS calculation.

Under certain circumstances, it may be necessary to adjust the numerator in year-to-date diluted EPS calculations. If, for example, the counterparty can choose the settlement method and a settlement in shares would have a more dilutive effect, the numerator would be adjusted for the effect on earnings of the asset or liability's change in fair value recognized during the year-to-date period in accordance with Issue 00-19. The number of additional shares included in the denominator in that example is calculated by determining the number of shares necessary to settle the contract at the average price per share during the year-to-date period.

The staff noted that the calculation of diluted earnings per share should exclude antidilutive contracts such as purchased put options and purchased call options.

The FASB staff summarized the interaction between the requirements in FAS-128 and Issue 00-19 as follows:

Settlement method assumed*	Accounting method (per 96-13)	Should recorded earnings (numerator) be adjusted to compute diluted earnings per share?	Should number of shares included in denominator be adjusted?
Shares	Asset/liability	Yes (according to ASC 260-10-45-45 through 45-46 (paragraph 29 of FAS-128)	Yes
Shares	Equity	No	Yes
Cash	Asset/liability	No	No
Cash	Equity	Yes (according to this staff announcement)	No

*For the purpose of computing EPS, it is assumed that an exchange of the full amount of cash for the full stated number of shares (physical settlement) is considered a share settlement.

Topic D-82 (Effect of Preferred Stock Dividends Payable in Common Shares on Computation of Income Available to Common Stockholders) (ASC 260-10-45-11, 45-12)

This announcement clarifies the accounting for preferred stock dividends that an issuer has paid or intends to pay in its own common shares when the issuer computes income available to common stockholders. The FASB staff announced that in accordance with the definition of income available to common stockholders in ASC, *Glossary* (paragraph 171 of FAS-128) and the guidance in ASC 260-10-45-11 (paragraph 9 of FAS-128), issuers should adjust the amount of net income or loss for dividends on preferred stock, regardless of the method of payment. The staff noted that this approach is consistent with the accounting for common stock issued for goods and services. To apply the guidance in this announcement, issuers should restate earnings per share reported in prior periods.

13.20 *Earnings per Share*

ASC 815 Derivatives and Hedging

EITF Issue 00-19 (Accounting for Derivative Financial Instruments Indexed to, and Potentially Settled in, a Company's Own Stock) (ASC 460-10-60-14; 480-10-55-63; 505-10-60-5; 815-10-15-78; 55-52; 815-15-25-15; 815-40-05-1 through 50-4, 05-10 through 05-12; 25-1 through 25-5, 25-7 through 25-20, 25-22 through 25-24, 25-26 through 25-35, 25-37 through 25-40; 30-1; 35-1 through 35-2, 35-4 through 35-6, 35-8 through 35-13; 40-1 through 40-2; 50-1 through 50-5; 55-1 through 55-18)

[*Note:* The EITF incorporated all the consensus positions in Issue 87-31 into Issue 96-13 (Accounting for Sales of Options or Warrants on Issuer's Stock with Various Forms of Settlement), which has been codified in Issue 00-19. Although the remaining consensus positions in Issue 00-19 are discussed in Chapter 17, "Financial Instruments," this Issue—which was affirmed by the guidance in FAS-128 (Earnings per Share)—is discussed here separately.]

The guidance in ASC 480-10-05-1 through 05-6; 10-10-1; 15-3 through 15-5, 15-7 through 15-10; 25-1 through 25-2, 25-4 through 25-15; 30-1 through 30-7; 35-3 through 35-5; 45-1 through 45-4; 50-1 through 50-4; 55-1 through 55-12, 55-14 through 55-28, 55-34 through 55-41, 55-64; 835-10-60-13. ASC 260-10-45-70A (FAS-150, Accounting for Certain Financial Instruments with Characteristics of both Liabilities and Equity) amends ASC 260 (FAS-128, Earnings per Share) for forward-purchase contracts that must be physically settled by repurchasing a fixed number of the issuer's equity shares of common stock for cash. Diluted earnings per share can no longer be computed by the reverse treasury stock method for those contracts. Therefore, common shares subject to the forward-purchase contracts should be excluded from the calculation of basic and diluted earnings per share (EPS). (See Topic D-72 above for additional guidance.)

OVERVIEW

A company sells put options that are publicly traded and expire two years from the date of issuance. The puts obligate the company to purchase from the holder one share of the company's stock at a fixed price, which is lower than the market price of the company's stock at the date of issuance. The company may repurchase the puts in the open market at any time during the redemption period.

ACCOUNTING ISSUE

Although none of the issues specifically addresses the calculation of EPS, one of the Task Force's consensus positions provides related guidance.

EITF CONSENSUS

The EITF stated in its consensus that an issuer should use the reverse treasury stock method to calculate the potential dilutive effect of put options having a higher exercise price than the market price of the stock ("in the money") during the reporting period. Under the reverse treasury stock method, the number of additional shares to be included in the calculation of EPS is equal to the number of shares the company must issue for cash at the current market price to satisfy the put obligation minus the number of shares repurchased from the holder of the puts.

The EITF reached a consensus that to calculate the *dilutive* effect of written put options and similar contracts when the contract's exercise price *exceeds* its market price during the reporting period (the contract is in the money), the *average* market price of the contract *during the period* should be used (instead of the then current market price required under Issue 96-13) in calculating the incremental number of shares that would have to be issued to obtain the cash to satisfy a *put* obligation under the reverse treasury method.

> **OBSERVATION:** It is assumed that company shares will be issued if the company can choose the settlement method. However, that presumption may be overcome if the company has a stated policy that requires contracts to be settled in cash or has historically settled contracts wholly or partially in cash. If the counterparty can choose the settlement method, the more dilutive method should be used in computing EPS. (See Topic D-72.)

DISCUSSION

The treasury stock method discussed in ASC 260-10-45-23 (paragraph 17 of FAS-128) is used to calculate the incremental number of shares to be issued for options under which the holder can purchase a company's stock at less than its market price. This calculation assumes that the company receives cash, satisfies a portion of its obligation by repurchasing an equivalent number of shares in the open market, and satisfies the remainder of the obligation by issuing stock. The EITF's consensus in this Issue requires using the *reverse treasury stock method* ASC 260-10-45-35 (paragraph 24 of FAS-128) ,under which it is assumed that the company (1) finances the cash payment to the holder of the put option by issuing new shares at the market price (in this case, a lower price than the amount at which the put will be exercised), and (2) sells the shares obtained by redeeming the put options at the market price for cash. The difference between (1) and (2) is the *incremental number of shares,* for example:

Number of puts outstanding	$1000
Exercise price	$50
Market price at 12/31/X4	$40
Shares to be sold to satisfy puts ($50,000/$40)	1,250
Less: Treasury shares obtained from satisfaction of put options	1,000
Incremental shares	250

RELATED CHAPTERS IN 2011
GAAP GUIDE, VOLUME II

Chapter 17, "Financial Instruments"
Chapter 39, "Stockholders' Equity"

RELATED CHAPTERS IN 2011
GAAP GUIDE, VOLUME I

Chapter 13, "Earnings per Share"
Chapter 17, "Financial Instruments"
Chapter 44, "Stockholders' Equity"

RELATED CHAPTERS IN 2011
INTERNATIONAL ACCOUNTING/FINANCIAL
REPORTING STANDARDS GUIDE

Chapter 3, "Presentation of Financial Statements"
Chapter 5, "Accounting Policies, Changes in Accounting Estimates, and Errors"
Chapter 12, "Earnings per Share"
Chapter 16, "Financial Instruments"

CHAPTER 14
EQUITY METHOD

CONTENTS

Overview		14.02
Authoritative Guidance		
ASC 272	Limited Liability Entities	
EITF Issue 03-16	Accounting for Investments in Limited Liability Companies	14.04
ASC 323	Investments—Equity Method and Joint Ventures	14.06
EITF Issue 98-13	Accounting by an Equity Method Investor for Investee Losses When the Investor Has Loans to and Investments in Other Securities of the Investee	14.06
EITF Issue 99-10	Percentage Used to Determine the Amount of Equity Method Losses	14.13
EITF Issue 00-1	Investor Balance Sheet and Income Statement Display under the Equity Method for Investments in Certain Partnerships and Other Ventures	14.14
EITF Issue 00-12	Accounting by an Investor for Stock-Based Compensation Granted to Employees of an Equity Method Investee	14.16
EITF Issue 02-14	Whether an Investor Should Apply the Equity Method of Accounting to Investments Other than Common Stock	14.17
EITF Issue 02-18	Accounting for Subsequent Investments in an Investee after Suspension of Equity Method Loss Recognition	14.20
EITF Issue 08-6	Equity Method Investment Accounting Considerations	14.23

14.02 *Equity Method*

FSP APB 18-1	Accounting by an Investor for Its Proportionate Share of Accumulated Other Comprehensive Income of an Investee Accounted for under the Equity Method in Accordance with APB Opinion No. 18 upon a Loss of Significant Influence	**14.25**
Topic D-46	Accounting for Limited Partnership Investments	**14.26**
Topic D-68	Accounting by an Equity Method Investor for Investee Losses When the Investor Has Loans to and Investments in Other Securities of an Investee	**14.26**
FSP APB 18-1	The Equity Method of Accounting for Investments in Common Stock: Accounting Interpretations of APB Opinion No. 18	**14.28**

Nonauthoritative Guidance

FASB Technical Bulletins		**14.30**
FTB 79-19	Investor's Accounting for Unrealized Losses on Marketable Securities Owned by an Equity Method Investee	**14.30**
Related Chapters in 2011 GAAP Guide, Volume II		**14.31**
Related Chapters in 2011 GAAP Guide, Volume I		**14.31**
Related Chapters in 2011 International Accounting/Financial Reporting Standards Guide		**14.31**

OVERVIEW

The equity method of accounting for investments in common stock should be used to account for an investment if the investor has significant influence over the investee's operating or financial decisions. In those circumstances, the investor has a degree of responsibility for the investee's return on investment, and therefore, the investor's results of operations should include its share of the investee's earnings or losses. The equity method is not intended as a substitute for consolidated financial statements when the conditions for consolidation exist.

The guidance in the following pronouncements, which address the equity method, are discussed in the 2011 *GAAP Guide, Volume 1*, Chapter 14, "Equity Method."

ASC 323	The Equity Method of Accounting for Investments in Common Stock (APB-18)
ASC 810 and 840	Consolidation of All Majority-Owned Subsidiaries (FAS-94)
ASC 323	Criteria for Applying the Equity Method of Accounting for Investments in Common Stock (FIN-35)

AUTHORITATIVE GUIDANCE

ASC 272 Limited Liability Entities

EITF Issue 03-16 (Accounting for Investments in Limited Liability Companies) (ASC 272-10-05-3, 4; ASC 323-30-35-3, 15-4)

OVERVIEW

Although limited liability companies (LLCs) are similar both to corporations and to partnerships, LLCs also differ in many ways from those types of entities. LLCs are similar to corporations because their members generally are *not* personally liable for the LLC's liabilities. They differ from corporations in that owners of LLCs control the operations of those entities, whereas the operations of corporations are controlled by their Boards of Directors and their committees rather than by their common shareholders.

LLCs are *similar* to partnerships in the following ways: (*a*) the members of LLCs are taxed on their shares of the LLCs' earnings; (*b*) LLC members generally cannot assign their financial interests without the consent of *all* members; and (*c*) most LLCs are dissolved as a result of a member's death, bankruptcy, or withdrawal.

LLCs *differ* from partnerships in that (*a*) it is *not* necessary for *one* owner to be liable for the LLC's liabilities, such as the general partner in a limited partnership; (*b*) the owners of LLCs control the operations of those entities, unlike limited partnerships, whose operations are managed by the general partner; and (*c*) all partners in a general partnership have *unlimited* liability.

Although the authoritative accounting literature provides no specific guidance regarding the accounting for noncontrolling LLCs, the guidance in ASC 323 (APB-18,The Equity Method of Accounting for Investments in Common Stock) currently is being applied in accounting for those entities. Under the provisions of APB-18, the equity method should be used to account for investments in which an investor can exercise *significant influence* over an investee's operating and financial policies. It is presumed that investments of at least 20% meet that requirement. Even though the Opinion does *not* specifically apply to partnerships, ASC 323-30-15-3; 25-2; 30-1 through 30-2; 35-1 through 35-2; 810-10-45-14 (AICPA Accounting Interpretation 2 of APB-18, Investments in Partnerships and Ventures) states that many of APB-18's provisions would be "appropriate in accounting" for partnerships.

ASC 970-323 (SOP 78-9, Accounting for Investments in Real Estate Ventures) states that noncontrolling interests in limited partnerships should be accounted for under the equity method, unless a limited partner's interest is "so minor that the limited partner may have virtually no influence over partnership operating and financial policies." The SOP requires that the cost method should be used under those circumstances. Another source of guidance is EITF Topic D-46 (Accounting for Limited Partnership Investments) (discussed in this chapter), in which the SEC staff clarifies what percentage is considered minor. It states that investments in limited partnerships of *more* than 3%–5% should be accounted for by the equity method, because they are more than minor investments.

The EITF was asked to consider this Issue because diverse guidance has resulted in diversity in practice—for example, a 10% investment in a corporation's common stock may be accounted for under the cost method, whereas a 10% investment in a limited partnership may be accounted for under the equity method. Guidance is required on how to account for noncontrolling interests in LLCs because practice would differ significantly if such entities were accounted for based on the guidance for corporations in APB-18 rather than on the guidance for limited partnerships in SOP 78-9 and Topic D-46, or vice versa.

ACCOUNTING ISSUE

To determine whether *noncontrolling* investments in an LLC should be accounted for by the cost method or by the equity method, should an LLC be considered to be similar to a corporation or to a partnership?

EITF CONSENSUS

The EITF reached a consensus position regarding whether a limited liability company should be considered to be similar to a corporation or to a partnership when determining how to account for a noncontrolling investment in an LLC.

- The EITF agreed that the guidance in this Issue does *not* apply to:
- Investments in LLCs that must be accounted for as debt securities under ASC 860-20-35-2 (paragraph 14 of FAS-140, Accounting for Transfers and Servicing of Financial Assets and Extinguishments of Liabilities) ;
- Equity interests in LLCs that must be accounted for under the consensus positions in Issue 99-20 (Recognition of Interest Income and Impairment on Purchased and Retained Beneficial Interests in Securitized Financial Assets) (see chapter 40); and
- LLCs that must be accounted for under the guidance in EITF Issue 96-16 (Investor's Accounting for an Investee When the Investor Has a Majority of the Voting Interest but the Noncontrolling Shareholder or Shareholders Have Certain Approval or Veto Rights) (see chapter 10).

An LLC that maintains a "specific ownership account" for each investor in the LLC is treating its investors in a manner similar to the way partnership capital accounts are structured. Consequently, investments treated in that manner should be considered to be similar to limited partnerships (LPs) when determining the appropriate accounting. Such LLCs should be accounted for under the guidance in ASC 970-323 (SOP 78-9) and the guidance in the SEC's announcement in Topic D-46, which is discussed below. It was noted that specific ownership accounts may exist in entities using other forms of organization. The EITF did *not* consider the characteristics of those organizations, but some members suggested that it may be appropriate for such entities to analogize to the guidance in this Issue.

ASC 323 Investments—Equity Method and Joint Ventures

EITF Issue 98-13 Accounting by an Equity Method Investor for Investee Losses When the Investor Has Loans to and Investments in Other Securities of the Investee (ASC 323-10-35-23 through 35-26, 55-30 through 55-32, 55-34 through 55-47; ASC 320-10-35-3)

OVERVIEW

In ASC 323-10-35-19 (Topic D-68),, which is discussed below, the FASB staff clarified the guidance in ASC 323-10-35-23 through 35-28 (paragraph 19 of APB-18) regarding how an equity method investor in an investee's common or other voting stock should account for the investee's operating losses when the investment has been reduced to zero *and* the investor also has one or more of the following: (*a*) the investee's debt securities, which include mandatory redeemable preferred stock; (*b*) the investee's preferred stock; or (*c*) loans to the investee.

The FASB staff believes that the guidance in ASC 323-10-35-19 (paragraph 19i of APB-18) indicates that an equity method investor's *total* investment in an investee includes, in addition to its investment in the investee's common stock or other voting stock, the investor's additional support committed to or made to the investee in the form of capital contributions, investments in additional common or preferred stock, loans, debt securities, or advances. The investor should, therefore, report an investee's losses up to the amount of the *total* investment.

This Issue is a follow-up to the FASB staff's guidance in Topic D-68 It is intended to clarify the relationship among the guidance in ASC 323 (APB-18), the guidance on impaired loans in ASC 310-10-30-2; 35-13 through 35-14, 35-16 through 35-22, 35-24 through 35-29, 35-32, 35-34, 35-37, 35-39; 45-5 through 45-6; 50-12 through 50-13, 50-15, 50-19; 310-40-35-8 through 35-9, 35-12; 50-2 through 50-3 (FAS-114 (Accounting by Creditors for Impairment of a Loan—An Amendment of FASB Statements No. 5 and 15) as amended by FAS-118 (Accounting by Creditors for

Impairment of a Loan—Income Recognition and Disclosures), and that in ASC 320-10 (FAS-115, Accounting for Certain Investments in Debt and Equity Securities) in accounting for an equity method investor's *total* investment in an investee.

ACCOUNTING ISSUE

If the carrying value of an equity method investee's common stock has been reduced to zero, how does the investor's accounting under the guidance in ASC 323 (APB-18) interact with the investor's accounting for its investments in the investee's other securities in accordance with FAS-114 or FAS-115?

EITF CONSENSUS

1. An investor should continue to report its share of equity method losses in an investee in the income statement up to the balance of and as an adjustment of the adjusted basis of the investor's other investments in the investee—such as preferred stock, debt securities, and loans—if (*a*) the investor is not required to advance additional funds to the investee and (*b*) the investment in the investee's common stock has been reduced to zero.

    OBSERVATION: See the guidance in Issue 99-10 and Topic D-84 in this chapter.

    The equity method losses should be distributed to the other investments according to the order of seniority (that is, priority in liquidation) of the other investments. In each period, the investor should first charge the adjusted basis of the other investments with equity method losses incurred during the period, and then should apply the provisions of FAS-114 and FAS-115 to those other investments, as appropriate.

    The *cost basis* of the other investments as defined under the consensus is their original cost, which has been adjusted for other-than-temporary write-downs and amortization of a discount or premium, if any, on debt securities and loans. The *adjusted basis* of the other investments is the cost basis adjusted for a valuation allowance under FAS-114 for loans to the investee and the cumulative amount of losses under the equity method that have been charged to those other investments. Subsequent income earned on the equity method investment should be attributed to the adjusted basis of the other investments in reverse of the order in which losses were attributed to those other investments.

2. To determine the amount of a loss on the equity method that should be reported at the end of the period, an investor that holds an investee's securities and debt under the scope of FAS-114 and FAS-115 should perform the following tasks:

   a. Determine the maximum amount of equity method losses under the provisions of APB-18.

   b. Account for equity method losses as follows:

      (1) If the adjusted basis of the other investments in the investee is positive, adjust the balance of the other investment for the amount of the loss on the equity method based on that investment's seniority. The adjusted basis of an investment accounted for in accordance with FAS-115 becomes the security's basis used to measure subsequent fair value changes.

      (2) If the adjusted basis of the other investment is zero, further losses on the equity method investment should *not* be reported. The investor, however, should continue to keep track of unrecorded equity method losses in order to apply ASC 323-10-35-19 (paragraph 19i of APB-18). If one of the other investments is sold when its carrying amount is greater than its adjusted basis, the difference between the investment's cost basis and its adjusted basis on sale equals the equity method losses that were attributed to that other investment and that difference should be reversed when the asset is sold. Such amounts are considered unreported equity losses that should be tracked before the investor can report future income on the equity method investment.

   c. The provisions in FAS-114 and FAS-115 should be applied to the adjusted basis of the other investments in the investee, if appropriate, after the provisions of APB-18 have been applied. Other generally accepted accounting principles not within the scopes of FAS-114 and FAS-115 should also be applied to the other investments, if appropriate.

The provisions of the consensus should be applied prospectively in interim or annual periods beginning after December 31, 1998.

OBSERVATION: An enterprise that has an interest in a variable interest entity and is required to absorb the majority of that entity's expected losses or is entitled to receive most of the entity's expected residual returns, or both, must consolidate that entity in accordance with the guidance in ASC 323-10-45-4; 810-10-05-8 through 05-13; 15-12, 15-13B, 15-14, 15-15 through 15-17; 25-37 through 25-47, 25-55 through 25-57; 30-1 through 30-4, 30-7 through 30-9; 35-3 through 35-5; 45-25; 50-2 through 50-4 through 50-7, 50-9 through 50-10;

55-16 through 55-49, 55-93 through 55-181, 55-183 through 55-205; 860-10-60-2; 954-810-15-3; 45-2; 958-810-15-4; 715-60-60-3; 715-30-60-7; 712-10-60-2; 460-10-60-13 (FIN-46(R), (Consolidation of Variable Interest Entities).as amended by ASC 810-10-65-2; 30-7 through 30-9 (FAS-167, Amendments to FASB Interpretation No. 46(R)), That Interpretation also provides guidance on the consolidation of some corporations that investors previously may have accounted for under the equity method. Public entities that have interests in variable interest entities or potential variable interest entities commonly referred to as special-purpose entities (SPEs) should apply this Interpretation in financial statements for periods ending after December 15, 2003. Public entities (other than small business issuers) should apply the Interpretation for all other types of entities in financial statements for periods ending after March 15, 2004 (or as of March 31, 2004, for calendar-year enterprises). Small business issuers that are public entities should apply the Interpretation to entities considered to be special-purpose entities no later than the end of the first reporting period ending after December 15, 2003 (or as of December 31, 2003, for a calendar-year enterprise). Nonpublic enterprises should apply this Interpretation by the beginning of the first annual period beginning after December 15, 2004, to all entities that are subject to this Interpretation. Nonpublic enterprises should apply this Interpretation immediately to interests in entities subject to this Interpretation that were created after December 31, 2003.

SUBSEQUENT DEVELOPMENT

In Issue 02-14 (Whether an Investor Should Apply the Equity Method of Accounting to Investments Other Than Common Stock) (discussed below), the EITF reached a consensus that when applying the guidance in ASC 323 (APB-18,The Equity Method of Accounting for Investments in Common Stock), the term "common stock" also applies to "in-substance common stock," as defined in Issue 02-14. Consequently, investors who have significant influence over their investees' operating and financial policies should apply the guidance in Issue 98-13 only to investments in common stock or in-substance common stock.

Illustration of the Application of the Consensus to Equity Method Investments and Other Investments in an Investee

At the beginning of 20X9, Company A has a 45% equity method investment in Company B's common stock, which has been reduced to zero as a result of losses in previous years. On that date, the carrying amounts of Company A's other investments in Company B are as follows:

- Preferred stock at $35,000, which constitutes 45% of Company B's outstanding preferred stock.
- A $60,000 loan, which constitutes 45% of Company B's loan indebtedness.

Company A has no obligation to fund Company B's additional losses.

This illustration assumes that all of Company B's operating income and losses discussed below have been adjusted for intercompany interest on the loan and dividends received on the preferred stock in accordance with ASC 323-10-35-19 (paragraphs 19a and 19k of APB-18).

The table on the following pages summarizes the following information about Company A's accounting for income or loss on its equity method investment in Company B and for changes in the value of its other investments in Company B after its common stock investment in Company B has been reduced to zero:

- *12/31/X9*—Company B has a loss of $50,000. The fair value of the preferred stock is $30,000 and the carrying value of the loan is $54,000.
- *12/31/X0*—Company B has a loss of $150,000. The fair value of the preferred stock is $15,000 and the carrying value of the loan is $45,000.
- *12/31/X1*—Company B has no income. The fair value of the preferred stock is $29,000 and the carrying value of the loan is $40,000.
- *12/31/X2*—Company B has $200,000 income. The fair value of the preferred stock is $30,000 and carrying value of the loan is $55,000.
- *12/31/X3*—Company B has no income. The fair value of the preferred stock is $32,000 and the carrying value of the loan is $58,000.
- *12/31/X4*—Company B has income of $100,000. Company A sells the preferred stock for $33,000. The carrying value of the loan is $60,000.

Summary of Transactions
(Amounts are in thousands)

Year	Inc/Loss (Equity Loss)	Preferred Stock Fair Value	Preferred Stock Adjusted Basis	Loan	Common Stock	Investment in Company B Carrying Amount	Investment in Company B Adjusted Basis	OCI	P&L	Cash	Unrecognized Loss
1/1/X9		35.0	35.0	60.0	0.00	95.0	95.0				
20×9	(22.5)	(22.5)	(22.5)			(22.5)	(22.5)		(22.5)		
		17.5(a)		(6.0)		17.5		17.5			
						(6.0)	(6.0)		(6.0)		
		30.0	12.5	54.0		84.0	66.5	17.5	28.5		
20×0	(67.5)	(12.5)	(12.5)	(54.0)		(66.5)	(66.5)(b)		(66.5)		(1.0)(b)
		(2.5)				(2.5)		(2.5)			
		15.0	0.0	0.0		15.0	0.0	15.0	(66.5)		(1.0)
									0.0		
20×1	0.0	14.0		(c)		14.0		14.0			
		29.0				29.0		29.0	0.0		
20×2	72.0	17.0	17.0	54.0		71.0	71.0		71.0(d)		1.0
		(16.0)		1.0		(16.0)	1.0	(16.0)			
		30.0	17.0	55.0		85.0	72.0	13.0	71.0		
20×3	0.0	2.0				2.0		2.0	0.0		
				3.0		3.0	3.0		3.0		
		32.0	17.0	58.0		90.0	75.0	15.0	3.0		

14.12 Equity Method

Summary of Transactions
(Amounts are in thousands)

	Preferred Stock				Investment in Company B					
Year	Inc/Loss (Equity Loss)	Fair Value	Adjusted Basis	Loan	Common Stock	Carrying Amount	Adjusted Basis	OCI	P&L	Cash	Unrecognized Loss
20×4	45.0	(32.0)	(17.0)		27.0	27.0	27.0		27.0(e)		
				2.0		(32.0)	(17.0)	(15.0)	15.0	32.0	
		___	___	___	___	___	___	___	2.0	___	___
		0.0	0.0	60.0	27.0	87.0	87.0	0.0	44.0	32.0	0.0

(a) Because the carrying amount of the preferred stock was reduced to $12,500 when Company B's $22,500 equity method loss was applied against the balance of the preferred stock investment in Company B, an unrealized gain of $17,500 is recognized to adjust the preferred stock to its fair value of $30,000.

(b) A portion of the $67,500 loss is recognized by reducing the $12,500 adjusted cost basis of the preferred stock investment to zero. The $54,000 adjusted basis of the loan is then reduced to zero. Because the equity method loss is limited to Company A's total adjusted basis of its total investments in Company B, the remaining $1,000 of equity method loss is unrecognized but should be tracked.

(c) Because the loan has been reduced to zero, no additional reduction in the value of the loan would be recognized.

(d) In accordance with APB-18, the equity method income of $72,000 must be reduced by the unrecognized $1,000 loss in 20×0 when the preferred stock investment and the loan were reduced to zero. The adjusted cost bases of the other investments are reinstated in reverse of the order in which the equity method loss was applied. That is, the loan is reinstated first to its adjusted amount of $54,000 and the remaining $17,000 is allocated to the preferred stock.

(e) During the previous years, Company A recognized $18,000 in losses related to its investment in Company B's preferred stock ($35,000 cost less $17,000 adjusted basis). Although the $15,000 gain recognized on the sale of the investment ($35,000 cost basis less $32,000 proceeds). Therefore, only $27,000 of the equity method income should incurred a $3,000 loss on the sale of the investment ($35,000 cost basis less $32,000 proceeds). Therefore, only $27,000 of the equity method income should be recognized ($45,000 less $18,000 losses on the preferred stock). That amount is used to reinstate a portion of the common stock investment in Company B.

EITF Issue 99-10 (Percentage Used to Determine the Amount of Equity Method Losses) (ASC 323-10-35-27 and 28; 55-49 through 57)

OVERVIEW

In Topic D-68, the FASB staff stated that APB-18 provides that an investor that is not obligated to provide additional financing after its common stock investment in an equity method investee has been reduced to zero must apply subsequent equity method losses—such as debt securities, preferred stock, and loans—to its other investments in the investee. In EITF Issue 98-13 (discussed above), the Task Force reached a consensus on the interaction of APB-18, FAS-114, and FAS-115 in equity method losses under those circumstances.

ACCOUNTING ISSUE

How should an investor who is *not* obligated to provide additional financing after its common stock investment in an equity method investee has been reduced to zero measure and recognize subsequent equity method losses applied to its other investments in the investee?

EITF CONSENSUS

The Task Force discussed the Issue based on the following example:

> An investor owns 40% of an investee's outstanding common stock, 50% of the investee's outstanding preferred stock, and has extended loans that represent 60% of the investee's outstanding loans. The common stock investment has been reduced to zero and the investor is not obligated to provide additional funds.

The Task Force reached a consensus that an investor should *not* recognize equity method losses based exclusively on the investor's percentage ownership of the investee's common stock.

The Task Force discussed whether equity method losses should be recognized based on (a) the specific ownership percentage of the investment to which the equity method losses are applied or (b) the change in the investor's claim on the investee's book value. Although the results were the same under both approaches for the example discussed at the meeting, it was not clear whether the results might differ in other situations. The Task Force was not asked to reach a consensus on the merits of one approach over the other and noted that both approaches would be acceptable and that other approaches not discussed may also be acceptable. However, once the authoritative literature has been applied to the other investments, as discussed in Issue 98-13, no additional adjustments would be necessary.

Task Force members believe that entities should choose one approach that should be applied entitywide to distribute equity method losses to the other investments after the common stock investment has been reduced to zero as a result of previous losses. The policy should be disclosed in the notes to the financial statements.

SEC OBSERVER COMMENT

The SEC Observer stated that the transition guidance in this Issue does not apply to Topic D-68 or Issue 98-13, which should have been followed to date. Registrants that have not been following that guidance will be required to restate their financial statements.

SUBSEQUENT DEVELOPMENT

In Issue 02-14 (Whether an Investor Should Apply the Equity Method of Accounting to Investments Other Than Common Stock), the EITF reached a consensus that when applying the guidance in APB-18 (The Equity Method of Accounting for Investments in Common Stock), the term "common stock" also applies to "in-substance common stock," as defined in Issue 02-14. Consequently, investors that have significant influence over their investees' operating and financial policies should apply the guidance in Issue 98-13 only to investments in common stock or in-substance common stock.

EITF Issue 00-1 (Investor Balance Sheet and Income Statement Display under the Equity Method for Investments in Certain Partnerships and Other Ventures) (ASC 323-30-25-1; 910-810-45-1; 810-1-45-14; 930-810-45-1; 932-810-45-1)

OVERVIEW

Although APB-18 applies only to corporate entities, partnerships and other unincorporated entities have analogized to that Opinion and applied the equity method when accounting for investments in investees over which they can exercise significant influence. Generally, such investments are reported as a single amount in the balance sheet with the investor's share of the investee's earnings or losses displayed as a single amount in the income statement. Although the guidance in ASC 323 (APB-18) does not apply to situations in which an investor has an undivided interest in each asset and a proportionate obligation for each liability of a partnership or other venture, which is not a separate legal entity, it has been the practice of companies in some industries (e.g., oil and gas, mining, and construction) to report their investments in other entities by the equity method on a proportionate gross basis. Those companies present a proportionate share of the investee's revenues and expenses under each major revenue and expense caption of their income statement and may present their proportionate share of the investee's assets and liabilities separately under each related major caption in the balance sheet.

The pro rata consolidation method is discussed in several pronouncements of the authoritative accounting literature. Interpretation 2 of APB-18 states that in industries in which it is established industry practice, an investor-venturer in an unincorporated joint venture who owns an undivided interest in each asset and is proportionately liable for its share of each liability may account in its financial statements for a pro rata share of the venture's assets, liabilities, revenues, and expenses.

The guidance in ASC 970-323 (AICPA SOP 78-9), which is sometimes applied by analogy to nonreal estate ventures, also provides guidance on pro rata consolidation. It is stated in ASC 970-810-45-1 (paragraph 11 of SOP 78-9) that an investor-venturer may present its undivided interest in a venture's assets, liabilities, revenues, and expenses if (*a*) decisions related to the venture's financing, development, sale, or operations can be made without the approval of two or more of the owners, (*b*) each investor venturer is only entitled to its share of the income, (*c*) each is responsible only for its pro rata share of the venturer's expenses, and (*d*) each is liable only for liabilities incurred for its proportionate interest in the entity.

Real estate entities under the scope of SOP 78-9 should apply the guidance in ASC 970-810-45-1 (paragraph 11 of SOP 78-9). That is, real property owned by undivided interests that is under joint control should be presented under the equity method, like investments in noncontrolled partnerships.

ACCOUNTING ISSUE

Are there circumstances under the equity method in which it is appropriate to use a proportionate gross presentation in the financial statements of a legal entity?

EITF CONSENSUS

- A proportionate gross financial statement presentation may *not* be used to report on investments in unincorporated *legal* entities, which are normally accounted for on the equity method, except by entities in the construction industry or the extractive industries, because that type of reporting has been a longstanding practice in those industries. Under this consensus, entities are considered to be in the extractive industries only if their activities are limited to the extraction of mineral resources, such as those involved in oil and gas exploration and production. The consensus does *not* apply to companies involved in refining, marketing, or transporting extracted mineral resources.

- APB-18 applies to common stock investments of *all* corporate entities in which an investor has significant influence over the investee. Consequently, the guidance in ASC 323-10-35-19 (paragraph 19c of APB-18), which requires the display of a single amount for such investments, should be applied. This consensus does not affect the accounting for undivided interests under the circumstances discussed in the Overview.

SEC OBSERVER COMMENT

The SEC Observer indicated that the SEC staff expects corporate entities to follow the provisions of APB-18 if an investor has significant influence over the investee. Further, the use of pro rata consolidation by such entities is not acceptable in SEC filings even if under an agreement, the benefits and risks are attributed to the owners as if they held undivided interests in the entity.

EITF Issue 00-12 (Accounting by an Investor for Stock-Based Compensation Granted to Employees of an Equity Method Investee) (ASC 323-10-25-25-3 through 25-5; 30-3; S45-1; S99-4; 55-19 through 55-20; 718-10-S60-1)

OVERVIEW

ASC 323 (APB-18) provides guidance to investors on the accounting for gains or losses on investments accounted for under the equity method. It does not, however, provide guidance to investors on how they should account for unreimbursed costs incurred on behalf of an investee, such as the cost of stock-based compensation granted to an investee's employees. Under the circumstances considered in this Issue, the entity's other investors do not contribute a proportionate amount and the investor's relative ownership percentage of the investee does not increase. It is assumed in this Issue that the grant of stock-based compensation to the investee's employees did not occur as a result of the investor's agreement to acquire an interest in the investee.

ACCOUNTING ISSUES

1. Should a contributing investor and an equity method investee capitalize or expense stock-based compensation costs incurred

by the investor on behalf of the investee and when should the investee and the contributing investor account for those costs?
2. How should noncontributing equity method investors in an investee account for stock-based compensation costs incurred by a contributing equity method investor on behalf of the investee if they do not fund a proportionate amount of those costs?

EITF CONSENSUS

1. A contributing investor that incurs stock-based compensation cost on behalf of an equity method investee should expense those costs as incurred (i.e., in the same period in which the investee recognizes those costs) in so far as the investor's claim on the investee's book value does not increase.

    An investee should recognize an expense and a corresponding cost incurred on its behalf by a contributing investor as the investor incurs those costs, as if the investor had paid cash to the investee's employees according to the guidance in Issue 2 of Issue 96-18, which is discussed in Chapter 38.

2. Noncontributing investors should recognize income for an amount that corresponds to their increased interest in the investee's net book value (i.e., their proportionate share of the increase in the investee's contributed capital) because of the contributing investor's funding of stock-based compensation for the investee's employees. They also should recognize their percentage share of the investee's gains or losses, which would include the expense recognized for the cost of stockbased compensation incurred by the contributing investor on the investee's behalf.

SEC OBSERVER COMMENT

The SEC Observer stated that registrants should classify income or expense, if any, as a result of the consensus in this Issue under the same income statement caption that includes the registrant's equity in the investee's earnings.

Issue 02-14 Whether an Investor Should Apply the Equity Method of Accounting to Investments Other than Common Stock (ASC 323-10-15-3 through 15-5, 15-13 through 15-18, 55-1 through 55-18)

OVERVIEW

According to ASC 323-10-15-3, 15-4, 15-6 through 15-8 (paragraphs 2 and 17 of APB-18, The Equity Method of Accounting in Common Stock, and Interpretation 2 of APB-18, Investments in Partnerships and Ventures), the guidance in ASC 323 (APB-18) applies only to an interest in an entity's voting *common stock*. However, in recent years investments in such vehicles as convertible debt, preferred equity securities, options, warrants, interests in unincorporated entities, complex licensing and management arrangements, and other types of financial instruments have been giving investors rights, privileges, or preferences that in the past were limited to investors in common stock. Rights, privileges, or preferences—such as (*a*) the right to vote with common stockholders, (*b*) the right to appoint directors to the company's board, (*c*) important participating and protective rights as discussed in Issue 96-16 (Investors Accounting for an Investee When the Investor Has a Majority of the Voting Interest but the Minority of Shareholder or Shareholders Have Certain Approval or Veto Rights), (*d*) the right to cumulative and participating dividends, and (*e*) liquidation preferences—may enable investors in such financial instruments to exercise significant influence over an investee's operating and financial policies even though they do not own the company's voting common stock.

ACCOUNTING ISSUE

Should an investor who exercises significant influence over an investee by means other than an ownership of the investee's voting common stock account for the investee by the equity method of accounting?

EITF CONSENSUS

The EITF reached the following consensus positions:

- Investors that have significant influence over their investees' operating and financial policies should apply the equity method of accounting as discussed in ASC 323 (APB-18) only if those investments are in common stock or in-substance common stock.
- The risk and reward characteristics of an entity's in-substance common stock must be substantially the same as those of the entity's common stock. An investment in an entity is *not* in-substance common stock if one of the following characteristics indicates it is *not* substantially similar to an investment in that entity's common stock:
    - *Subordination* An investment's subordination characteristics must be substantially similar to those of the entity's common stock. If an investment has a substantive liquidation preference over common stock, it is not substantially similar to the common stock.
    - *Risks and rewards of ownership* An investment's risk and reward of ownership characteristics must be substantially similar to those of the entity's common stock. For example, an investment that is not expected to participate in an

entity's earnings and losses and capital appreciation and depreciation in substantially the same manner as common stock is not substantially similar to common stock. In contrast, if an investment participates in an investee's dividend payments in a manner that is substantially similar to the participation of common stock in such dividend payments, the investment is substantially the same as common stock. It was noted that the right to convert certain investments to common stock would indicate that those investments can participate in the investee's earnings and losses and in capital appreciation and depreciation in a substantially similar manner as common stock.

—*Obligation to transfer value* Obligation to transfer value If an investee is obligated to transfer substantive value to an investor, but the entity's common stockholders do not participate in the same manner, the investment is not substantially similar to common stock. An example is an investment's substantive redemption provision, such as a mandatory redemption provision or a put option at other than fair value, which is not offered to common shareholders.

An investment is in-substance common stock if its subordination and risk and reward characteristics are substantially similar to an investee's common stock and the investee is *not* required to transfer value to the investor in a manner that differs from the participation of common shareholders. If, based on the characteristics discussed previously, an investor is unable to determine whether an investment in an entity is substantially similar to the entity's common stock, the investor should determine whether it is expected that there will be a high correlation between future changes in the investment's fair value and changes in the fair value of the common stock. The investment is not in-substance common stock if that high correlation is not expected to exist.

An investor that has significant influence over an investee's operating and financial policies should determine whether an investment is substantially similar to common stock on the date on which the investor makes the investment. That determination should be reconsidered if one or more of the following circumstances occur:

- An investment's contractual terms change so that there is a change in any of the characteristics previously discussed.
- The investee's capital structure changes significantly, including the receipt of additional subordinated financing.
- The amount of an existing interest has increased. Consequently, the investor's method of accounting for its cumulative interest should be based on the characteristics of the investment on which the additional investment was made so that one method will be used by the investor to account for the cumulative interest in an investment of the same issuance.

An investee's losses, however, should not cause an investor to reconsider the determination of whether an investment is substantially similar to common stock.

An investor that gains the ability to exercise significant influence over an investee's operating and financial policies after the date on which the investment in the entity was made should determine whether the investment is substantially similar to common stock by considering the characteristics previously discussed and the relevant information existing on the date the investor obtained significant influence.

The EITF was not asked to reach a consensus on how to apply the equity method to investments other than common stock. Although the EITF also was not asked to reach a consensus on whether investments other than common stock that have a "readily determinable fair value" under the guidance in ASC 470-60-15-7 (paragraph 3 of FAS-115) should be accounted for in accordance with FAS-115 rather than based on this Issue, the EITF noted that the equity method of accounting should be applied in all cases under the scope of this Issue in which an investor has significant influence over an investee's operating and financial policies and owns the investee's common stock or in-substance common stock.

FASB RATIFICATION

At its July 16, 2004, meeting, the FASB ratified the EITF's consensus positions reached on this Issue.

SEC OBSERVER COMMENT

The SEC Observer advised that the Securities and Exchange Commission (SEC) staff has required registrants with significant influence over their investees to apply the equity method to interests in other than common stock if it was obvious that those investments did *not* differ substantively from the investee's common stock. In those circumstances, the SEC staff has required registrants to restate their financial statements for the correction of an error and will continue requiring such restatement, if appropriate.

EITF Issue 02-18 (Accounting for Subsequent Investments in an Investee after Suspension of Equity Method Loss Recognition) (ASC 323-10-35-29, 35-30)

OVERVIEW

According to the guidance in ASC 323-10-35-20 (paragraph 19(i) of APB-18, The Equity Method of Accounting for Investments in

Common Stock) an investor should discontinue applying the equity method of accounting when the investment (and net advances) equal zero. Further, an investor should recognize losses only if the investor has guaranteed an investee's obligations or is committed to provide financial support to an investee. Even after an investee has resumed recognition of net income, an investor should *not* resume applying the equity method until the investor's share of net income equals the amount of net losses not recognized after application of the equity method was suspended.

Although the following pronouncements provide guidance on related matters, none addresses the question addressed in this Issue:

- In Topic D-68 (Accounting by an Equity Method Investor for Investee Losses When the Investor Has Loans to and Investments in Other Securities of an Investee) (see below), which was issued in March 1998, the FASB staff stated that an equity method investor should report its losses in an investee up to its *total* investment in the investee, which in the staff's view includes additional support to an investee in the form of capital contributions, investments in additional common or preferred stock, loans, debt securities, or advances.

- Issue 98-13 (Accounting by an Equity Method Investor for Investee Losses When the Investor Has Loans to and Investments in Other Securities of the Investee), which was issued in January 1999, addresses the interaction of an investor's accounting for an investee under APB-18 with the investor's accounting for its investments in the investee's other securities in accordance with FAS-114 (Accounting by Creditors for Impairment of a Loan—An Amendment of FASB Statements Nos. 5 and 15) and FAS-115. The EITF reached a consensus that an investor should continue reporting its share of equity method losses in an investee up to the balance of and as an adjustment of the adjusted basis of an investor's other investments in an investee, such as preferred stock, debt securities, and loans, if *(a)* the investor is *not* required to advance additional funds to the investee and *(b)* the investment in the investee's common stock has been reduced to zero.

- Issue 99-10 (Percentage Used to Determine the Amount of Equity Method Losses), which was issued in September 1999, addresses how an investor who is *not* obligated to provide additional support to an equity method investee after its common stock investment has been reduced to zero should measure and recognize subsequent equity method losses applied to its other investments in an investee. The EITF reached a consensus that an investor should *not* recognize equity method losses based exclusively on its percentage ownership of the investee's common stock. Two methods of recognizing equity method losses were discussed: (1) based

14.22 *Equity Method*

on an investor's specific ownership percentage of an investment to which the equity method losses are applied or (2) based on a change in an investor's claim on an investee's book value.

- In Topic D-84 (Accounting for Subsequent Investments in an Investee after Suspension of Equity Method Loss Recognition When an Investor Increases Its Ownership Interest from Significant Influence to Control through a Market Purchase of Voting Securities), which was issued in January 2000, the SEC Observer stated the view of the SEC staff that if an investor who is *not* committed or obligated to provide additional support to an equity method investee purchases additional shares of an investee's securities in the market to increase its ownership interest from significant influence to control, the investor should account for the transaction as a step acquisition; the investor should *not* recognize a loss on the purchase or restate prior period financial statements.

ACCOUNTING ISSUE

If an investor that has suspended equity method loss recognition in an investee in accordance with ASC 323-10-35-19 (paragraph 19(i) of APB-18) and Issue 98-13 (see above) subsequently makes an additional investment in an investee but *does not* increase its ownership from significant influence to one of control, should that investor (*a*) account for the transaction as a step acquisition, or (*b*) recognize a loss in the amount of previously suspended losses?

EITF CONSENSUS

The EITF reached the following consensus positions on the issues:

- If all or part of an additional investment made by an investor who has appropriately suspended recognition of equity method losses in accordance with the guidance in ASC 323-10-35-19 (paragraph 19(i) of APB-18) and Issue 98-13 is in substance used to fund earlier losses, the investor should recognize previously suspended losses only up to the amount that the additional investment is considered to be a funding of earlier losses discussed in (b) below.
- The facts and circumstances of the investment should be considered.

The EITF believes that determining whether an additional investment is, in substance, the funding of prior losses requires judgment. The following factors should be considered in making that determination, but no one factor alone should be considered presumptive or determinative:

— *The source of the investment, a third party or the investee* If an investor purchases an additional investment in an investee from a third party and neither the investor nor the third party provide additional funds to the investee, it is unlikely that prior losses are being funded.

— *Whether the amount paid to acquire an additional investment in an investee represents the fair value of the additional ownership interest received* A payment that exceeds the fair value of an additional investment in an investee would indicate that the excess paid over fair value is intended to fund prior losses.

— *Whether an additional investment in an investee increases the investor's ownership percentage of the investee* If an investment is made directly with an investee, the form of the investment should be considered and whether other investors are also making investments proportionate to their interests in the investee. It may be an indication that prior losses are being funded if (*a*) an additional investment in an investee does not increase the investor's ownership or other interests in the investee, or (*b*) if all other existing investors are also making additional pro rata equity investments in the investee.

— *Seniority of an additional investment* If an investor's additional investment in an investee has a *lower* seniority than the investor's existing investment in the investee, it may be an indication that an additional investment is funding previous losses.

It was noted that an investor making an additional investment in an investee should also consider whether as a result of the additional investment the investor becomes "otherwise committed" to provide financial support to the investee. The EITF will provide guidance in a separate Issue on how to make that determination.

FASB RATIFICATION

At its meeting on February 5, 2003, the FASB ratified the EITF's consensus positions reached on this Issue.

EITF Issue 08-6 (Equity Method Investment Accounting Considerations) ASC 323-10-25-2A; 30-2A through 30-2B; 35-14A, 35-32A; 40-1; 65-1

OVERVIEW

The FASB and the International Accounting Standards Board (IASB) recently collaborated on a project to converge the guidance on accounting for business combinations and that on accounting and reporting for noncontrolling interests. That project resulted in the issuance of ASC 805 (FASB Statement No. 141 (Revised 2007),

Business Combinations (FAS-141R)), and ASC 810-10-65-1 (FASB Statement No. 160, *Noncontrolling Interests in Consolidated Financial Statements* (FAS-160)), whose principles are based on the premise that a reporting entity has gained or lost control of a business or a subsidiary. Although it was not the objective of that project to reconsider the accounting for equity method investments, the issuance of FAS-141R and FAS-160 has affected the application of the equity method. Consequently, some constituents have asked whether all of the provisions of those Statements must be applied when accounting for an equity method investment because an entity's ability to control differs substantially from its ability to exert significant influence.

SCOPE

The guidance in Issue 08-6 applies to all investments accounted for under the equity method.

EITF CONSENSUS

The EITF reached the following consensus positions:

Initial measurement. An equity-method investment's initial carrying value should be measured based on the cost accumulation model discussed in ASC 805-50-25-1; 30-1 through 30-3; 35-1 (paragraphs D3 through D7 of FAS-141R) for asset acquisitions. The initial measurement of an equity method investment should include contingent consideration only if doing so is required in specific authoritative guidance other than FAS-141R. Nevertheless, if there is an arrangement for contingent consideration in an agreement in which the fair value of the investor's share of an investee's net assets exceeds the investor's initial cost, the entity should recognize a liability for one of the following amounts, whichever is less:

- The maximum amount of consideration not otherwise recognized; or
- The amount by which the investor's share of an investee's net assets exceeds the initial cost measurement that includes contingent consideration otherwise recognized.

If a contingency related to a liability recognized based on the guidance above is resolved and the consideration is issued or becomes issuable, the amount by which the fair value of the contingent consideration exceeds the amount of the recognized liability should be added to the cost of the investment. However, the cost of the investment should be reduced if the recognized liability exceeds the fair value of the consideration.

Decrease in the value of an investment. In accordance with the guidance in ASC 323-10-35-32 (paragraph 19(h) of Accounting Principles Board (APB) Opinion No. 18, *The Equity Method of Accounting for Investments in Common Stock* (APB-18)), an equity method investor should recognize other-than-temporary impairments related to an equity method investment. Although that investor should not perform a separate impairment test of an investee's asset, the investor should recognized its share of an impairment, if any, recognized by an investee in accordance with the guidance in ASC 323-10-35-7, 35-13 (paragraphs 19(b) and 19(c) of APB-18) and should consider how the impairment, if any, affects the investor's basis difference in the assets that caused the investee to recognize an impairment.

Change in level of ownership or degree of influence. An equity method investor should account for an investee's issuance of shares as if the investor had sold a proportionate share of its investment with a gain or loss recognized in earnings.

TRANSITION

This guidance in this Issue should be effective in fiscal years that begin on or after December 15, 2008, and the interim periods within those fiscal years and should be applied *prospectively*. An entity that had previously adopted an alternative accounting policy is *not* permitted to apply the guidance earlier. The transition disclosures in ASC 250-10-50-1 through 50-3 (paragraphs 17 and 18 of FASB Statement No. 154, *Accounting Changes and Error Corrections* (FAS-154)), should be made, if applicable.

FASB RATIFICATION

The FASB ratified the EITF's consensus positions in this Issue at its November 24, 2008 meeting.

FSP APB 18-1 (Accounting by an Investor for Its Proportionate Share of Accumulated Other Comprehensive Income of an Investee Accounted for under the Equity Method in Accordance with APB Opinion No. 18 upon a Loss of Significant Influence) (ASC 323-10-35-37 through 35-39; 323-30-35-4)

OVERVIEW

The FASB staff issued this FSP at the direction of the FASB and posted the final FSP on the FASB's web site on July 12, 2005. This FSP provides guidance regarding an investor's accounting for its proportionate share of an investee's equity adjustments for other comprehensive income (OCI) if the investor loses significant influence.

Under the guidance in ASC 323-10-35-18 (paragraph 121 of FAS-130 (Reporting Comprehensive Income), an investor is required to recognize its proportionate share of an investee's equity adjustments in other comprehensive income, such as unrealized gains and losses on available-for-sale securities, minimum pension liability adjustments, and foreign currency items, as increases or decreases in the investment account with corresponding adjustments to equity in accordance with the guidance in ASC 323-10-35-15 (paragraph 19(e) of APB-18 (The Equity Method of Accounting for Investments in Common Stock), as amended by paragraph C3(b) of FAS-160. Constituents have asked the question below.

Question: How should an investor account for its proportionate share of an investee's adjustments of other comprehensive income (OCI) if the investor has lost significant influence in the investee?

FASB STAFF POSITION

The FASB believes that when an investor loses significant influence, the investor should offset its proportionate share of the investee's equity adjustments of OCI against the investment's carrying value. If the offset would reduce the carrying value of the investment to *less than* zero, however, the investor should (*a*) reduce the carrying amount to zero, and (*b*) recognize the remaining amount as income.

Topic D-46 (Accounting for Limited Partnership Investments) (ASC 323-30-S99-1; S55-1)

The Acting Chief Accountant of the SEC announced at the May 1995 EITF meeting that the SEC staff will no longer accept cost method accounting for an investment in a limited partnership, even though the partner has an interest of 20% or less and has no significant influence over an investee. The staff now believes that investors in limited partnerships should follow the guidance in ASC 970-323-25-6 through 25-7 (paragraph 8 of SOP 78-9), which requires limited partners to use the equity method to account for such investments, unless their interest is so minor that they have virtually no influence over the partnership's operating and financial policies. According to the SEC staff, investments of more than 3%–5% generally have been considered to be more than minor in practice. The announcement applies to all investments in limited partnerships made after May 18, 1995, not just to those holding real estate.

Topic D-68 (Accounting by an Equity Method Investor for Investee Losses When the Investor Has Loans to and Investments in Other Securities of an Investee) (ASC 323-10-35-19)

The FASB staff's announcement is intended to clarify the guidance in ASC 323-10-35-3 through 35-4, 35-6 through 35-7, 35-13, 35-15 through 35-16, 35-19 through 35-22, 35-20, 35-32 through 35-33 through 35-36; 45-1 through 45-2; 15-12; 225-20-60-1; 250-10-60-2; 460-10-60-1 (paragraph 19 of APB-18) regarding whether an investor in an investee's common or other voting stock should provide for the investee's operating losses if the common stock investment has been reduced to zero, but in addition, the investor: (*a*) owns the investee's debt securities, which may include mandatorily redeemable preferred stock, (*b*) owns the investee's preferred stock, or (*c*) has made loans to the investee.

The FASB staff believes that the carrying amount of an equity method investor's *total* investment includes additional support committed to or made by the investor in the form of capital contributions, investments in additional common or preferred stock, loans, debt securities, or advances. The investee's losses, therefore, should be reported up to the *total* investment.

The staff believes that this position is consistent with the provisions of ASC 970-323-35-34, 35-5, 35-12 (paragraphs 15 and 20 of SOP 78-9). It provides the following examples of circumstances in which an investor would reduce its equity in a real estate venture for losses that exceed the investment:

- The investor is legally obligated because of its position as guarantor or general partner.
- The investor's commitment to provide additional support is implied based on considerations such as the investor's business reputation, intercompany relationships, or the investor's credit standing. A commitment may also be implied by an investor's previous support to the investee or the investor's statements to other investors or third parties about its intentions.

OBSERVATION: See Issue 98-13 and Issue 02-14.

FSP APB 18-1 (The Equity Method of Accounting for Investments in Common Stock: Accounting Interpretations of APB Opinion No. 18) (ASC 323-10-35-7 through 11; 55-through 55-29; 15-5; 323-30-15-3; 25-2; 35-1 through 35-2; 810-10-45-14)

BACKGROUND

FSP APB 18-1 provides guidance on two implementation issues associated with APB-18: (1) elimination of intercompany profit or loss and (2) its applicability to partnerships and joint ventures.

STANDARDS

Question 1: ASC 323 (APB-18) and ASC 810 (ARB-51, Consolidated Financial Statements) require that intercompany profits or losses on assets still remaining with an investor or an investee at a reporting date are to be eliminated. Should all of the intercompany profit or loss be eliminated, or should only that portion related to the investor's common stock interest in the investee be eliminated?

Answer: The extent of the intercompany profit or loss to be eliminated depends on the relationship between the investor and the investee. Given certain relationships between the investor and the investee, none of the intercompany profit or loss should be recognized by the investor until it has been realized through transactions with third parties. The following are examples of situations where this accounting treatment would be appropriate:

- The investor owns a majority of the voting shares of the investee and enters into a transaction with the investee that is not on an arm's-length basis.

- An investee is established with the cooperation of the investor, and the investor controls the investee through guarantees of indebtedness, through extension of credit by the investor for the benefit of the investee, or through warrants or convertible securities of the investee owned by the investor. An example of this type of arrangement is where the investee is established for the financing and operation of property that the lessor sells to the lessee.

In other cases, it is acceptable for the investor to eliminate intercompany profit based on its percentage ownership of the investee; the elimination of intercompany profit would be the same regardless of whether the transaction is "downstream" (a sale by the investor to the investee) or "upstream" (a sale by the investee to the investor). The elimination of intercompany profit is to be performed on a net-of-tax basis.

Illustration of Intercompany Profit Elimination

On December 31, 20X5, an investor holds $800,000 worth of inventory items that were sold to it during the year by the investee. The investee's gross profit rate on sales of inventory is 25%. Both the investor and the investee face a 36% tax rate. The investor owns 40% of the outstanding voting stock of the investee. At year-end, the investor holds inventory items for which the investee recognized $200,000 of gross profit ($800,000 × 25%). In computing the investor's equity "pickup," $128,000 would be deducted from the investee's net income [$200,000 × (1 − 36%)]. The investor's share of the intercompany gross profit after tax, $51,200, would be eliminated from the investor's equity income ($128,000 × 40%). The offsetting credit recorded by the investor would be either to the investor's investment account (the most common method) or to the inventory account.

Question 2: Do the provisions of APB-18 apply to investments in partnerships and joint ventures?

Answer: Not directly. APB-18 applies only to investments in common stocks of corporations. It does not pertain to partnerships or unincorporated joint ventures. However, many of the provisions of APB-18 would be applicable in accounting for these unincorporated ventures. For example, partnership profits and losses accrued by investor-partners are generally reflected in their financial statements at a single amount. In addition, and consistent with APB-18, the following additional provisions would apply to a partnership: (1) the elimination of intercompany profits and losses and (2) the accrual of income taxes on the profits accrued by investor-partners regardless of the tax basis employed in the partnership return.

For the most part, the preceding discussion as to the applicability of APB-18 to partnerships would also apply to unincorporated joint ventures. However, in one divergence from APB-18, where it is established industry practice, the investor-venturer may account in its financial statements for its pro rata share of the assets, liabilities, revenues, and expenses of the venture.

> **PRACTICE POINTER:** The G4+1 (standard setters representing Australia, Canada, New Zealand, the United Kingdom, the United States, and the International Accounting Standards Committee (IASC)) released a Special Report titled *Reporting Interests in Joint Ventures and Similar Arrangements*. The Special Report recommends the use of the equity method in accounting for joint ventures. In addition, the Special Report rejects the notion that joint venture participants should depart from the equity method by recognizing their pro rata share of the assets, liabilities, revenues, and expenses of the venture. Although G4+1 Special Reports do not represent the promulgation of binding accounting standards, they do represent the best thinking of standard-setters from both the IASC and every major English-speaking country in the world. More importantly, future accounting standards on this topic in the United States are likely to borrow heavily from this Special Report.

NONAUTHORITATIVE GUIDANCE

FASB Technical Bulletins

FTB 79-19 (Investor's Accounting for Unrealized Losses on Marketable Securities Owned by an Equity Method Investee)

BACKGROUND

A subsidiary or investee may be required to account for investments at market value with an associated adjustment made directly to stockholders' equity.

STANDARDS

Question: How should a parent or investor account for its share of unrealized holding gains or losses on investments in debt and equity securities included in stockholders' equity of an investee accounted for by the equity method?

Answer: If a subsidiary or other investee that is accounted for by the equity method is required to include unrealized holding gains or losses on investments in debt and equity securities in other comprehensive income, the parent or investor should adjust its investment by its proportionate share of the unrealized gains or losses and the same amount should be included in other comprehensive income of the parent or investor.

Illustration of Equity Method Application—Recognition of Shareholders' Equity Valuation Allowance Account in the Investor's Financial Statements

Roth Corp. owns 40% of the outstanding voting common stock of Rose & Rose Inc. and is able to exercise significant influence over the affairs of Rose & Rose. Rose & Rose holds "available-for-sale" investment securities. At December 31, 20X4, the cost of Rose & Rose's available-for-sale investment portfolio is $1 million, and the portfolio's fair market value is $1.5 million. Consistent with the provisions of FAS-115, Rose & Rose carries this investment portfolio at its fair value, $1.5 million, and recognizes the $500,000 increase in fair value above cost in other comprehensive income. Roth Corp., which accounts for its investment in Rose & Rose using the equity method, would increase its investment account by $200,000 (40% of the $500,000 increase in the investment portfolio), and $200,000 would be included in other comprehensive income.

RELATED CHAPTERS IN 2011
GAAP GUIDE, VOLUME II

Chapter 20, "Income Taxes"
Chapter 25, "Investments in Debt and Equity Securities"

RELATED CHAPTERS IN 2011
GAAP GUIDE, VOLUME I

Chapter 14, "Equity Method"
Chapter 21, "Income Taxes"
Chapter 28, "Investments in Debt and Equity Securities"

RELATED CHAPTERS IN 2011
INTERNATIONAL ACCOUNTING/FINANCIAL REPORTING STANDARDS GUIDE

Chapter 7, "Business Combinations"
Chapter 10, "Consolidated Financial Statements"
Chapter 14, "Equity Method"
Chapter 16, "Financial Instruments"
Chapter 20, "Income Taxes"
Chapter 24, "Investment Property"

CHAPTER 15
EXTINGUISHMENT OF DEBT

CONTENTS

Overview		**15.02**
Authoritative Guidance		
ASC 310 Receivables		**15.03**
EITF Issue 01-7	Creditor's Accounting for a Modification or an Exchange of Debt Instruments	**15.03**
ASC 470 Debt		**15.04**
FTB 80-1	Early Extinguishment of Debt through Exchange for Common or Preferred Stock	**15.04**
EITF Issue 96-19	Debtor's Accounting for a Substantive Modification and Exchange of Debt Instruments	**15.05**
EITF Issue 98-14	Debtor's Accounting for Changes in Line-of-Credit or Revolving-Debt Arrangements	**15.14**
EITF Issue 02-4	Debtor's Accounting for a Modification or an Exchange of Debt Instruments in Accordance with FASB Statement No. 15, *Accounting by Debtors and Creditors for Troubled Debt Restructurings*	**15.16**
EITF Issue 06-6	Debtor's Accounting for a Modification (or Exchange) of Convertible Debt Instruments	**15.19**
AIN-APB 26	Early Extinguishment of Debt: Accounting Interpretations of APB Opinion No. 26	**15.22**
Related Chapter in 2011 GAAP Guide, Volume I		**15.23**
Related Chapters in 2011 International Accounting/Financial Reporting Standards Guide		**15.23**

15.02 *Extinguishment of Debt*

OVERVIEW

An *extinguishment of debt* is the reacquisition of debt, or removal of debt from the balance sheet, prior to or at the maturity date of that debt. Gain or loss on the extinguishment is the difference between the total reacquisition cost of the debt to the debtor and the net carrying amount of the debt on the debtor's books at the date of extinguishment.

The following pronouncements, which provide guidance on accounting for the extinguishment of debt, are discussed in the 2011 *GAAP Guide, Volume 1*, Chapter 15, "Extinguishment of Debt."

ASC 470	Debt (APB-26, Early Extinguishment of Debt)
ASC 840	Leases (FAS- 22, Changes in the Provisions of Lease Agreements Resulting from Refundings of Tax-Exempt Debt)
ASC 860	Transfers and Servicing (FAS-140, Accounting for Transfers and Servicing of Financial Assets and Extinguishments of Liabilities)
ASC 470	Debt (FAS-145, Rescission of FASB Statements No. 4, 44, and 64, Amendment of FASB Statement No. 13, and Technical Corrections)

> **OBSERVATION:** The FASB issued ASC 470 (FAS-145, Rescission of FASB Statements 4, 44, and 64, Amendment to FASB Statement No. 13, and Technical Corrections) in April 2002. The primary effect of this standard on the material in this chapter is that gains and losses on extinguishments of debt no longer are required to be classified as extraordinary items in an entity's income statement unless an extinguishment of debt meets the criteria in ASC 225-20-45 (APB-30) for such classification.

AUTHORITATIVE GUIDANCE

ASC 310 Receivables

EITF Issue 01-7 (Creditor's Accounting for a Modification or an Exchange of Debt Instruments) (ASC 310-20-35-11)

OVERVIEW

The authoritative accounting literature provides different guidance to creditors and debtors as to how to determine whether a modification or exchange of a debt instrument should be accounted for as an extinguishment of a debt instrument and its replacement with a new debt instrument or as a continuation of a debt instrument that has been modified. ASC 310 (FAS-91, Accounting for Nonrefundable Fees and Costs Associated with Originating or Acquiring Loans and Initial Direct Costs of Leases) provides such guidance for creditors and ASC 470-50-05-4. 15-3; 40-6 through 40-14, 40-17 through 40-20; 55-1 through 55-9 (Issue 96-19, Debtor's Accounting for a Modification or Exchange of Debt Instruments) provides such guidance for debtors. Under the guidance in that Issue, which is discussed below, a debtor is required to account for a modification or exchange of debt as new debt if it is *substantially different* from the original debt. Whereas, under the guidance in ASC 310 (FAS-91), a creditor is not permitted to account for an original debt instrument that has been modified as a new instrument unless the modification is *more than minor*. However, ASC 310 (FAS-91) provides no guidance on how to evaluate what is more than a minor modification.

ACCOUNTING ISSUE

How should a creditor evaluate whether a modification of a debt instrument's terms as a result of a refinancing or restructuring (other than in a troubled debt restructuring) should be considered to be more than *minor* in applying the guidance in ASC 310-20-35-10 (paragraph 13 of FAS-91)?

EITF CONSENSUS

The Task Force reached the following consensus positions:

- In applying the guidance in ASC 310-20-35-10 (paragraph 13 of FAS-91), a modification or an exchange of debt instruments should be considered *more than minor* if the present value of the cash flows under the new debt instrument differs by at least 10% from the present value of the remaining cash flows under the terms of the original debt instrument.

15.04 *Extinguishment of Debt*

- If the difference between the present value of the cash flows of a new and an existing debt instrument differs by *less than* 10%, the creditor should evaluate whether a modification or exchange of debt instruments is *more* than minor based on the facts and circumstances and other relevant information related to the modification.

- Creditors should apply the guidance in ASC 470-50-05-4; 15-3; 40-6 through 40-14, 40-17 through 40-20; 55-1 through 55-9 (Issue 96-19, Debtor's Accounting for a Modification or Exchange of Debt Instruments) to calculate a debt instrument's present value of cash flows when applying the 10% test.

ASC 470 Debt

FTB 80-1 (Early Extinguishment of Debt through Exchange for Common or Preferred) (ASC 470-50-05-1; 15-2, 3; 40-3)

BACKGROUND

Under the guidance in ASC 470-50-05-1; 15-3 through 15-4; 40-2, 40-4; ASC 850-10-60-3 (APB-26, Early Extinguishment of Debt), conversion of debt to common or preferred stock is not an extinguishment if the conversion represents the exercise of a conversion right contained in the terms of the debt issue. Other exchanges of common or preferred stock for debt would constitute extinguishment.

STANDARDS

Question: Does the guidance in (APB-26) apply to extinguishments of debt effected by issuance of common or preferred stock, including redeemable and fixed-maturity preferred stock?

Answer: All extinguishments of debt must be accounted for in accordance with the guidance in ASC 310-40-15-3 through 15-12; 10-1 through 10-2; 25-1 through 25-2; 35-2, 35-5, 35-7; 40-2 through 40-6, 40-8; 50-1 through 50-2; 55-2; ASC 470-60-15-3 through 15-12; 35-1 through 35-12; 45-1 through 45-2; 55-3; 10-1 through 10-2; ASC 450-20-60-12 (FAS-15, Accounting by Debtors and Creditors for Troubled Debt Restructurings) as amended by FAS-145 (Rescission of FASB Statements No. 4, 44, and 64, Amendment of FASB Statement No. 13, and Technical Corrections). The guidance in ASC 470-50-05-1; 15-3 through 15-4; 40-2, 40-4; ASC 850-10-60-3 (APB-26) applies to all extinguishments except those subject to the requirements of ASC 310-40-15-3 through 15-12; 10-1 through 10-2; 25-1 through 25-2; 35-2, 35-5, 35-7; 40-2 through 40-6, 40-8; 50-1 through 50-2; 55-2; ASC 470-60-15-3 through 15-12; 35-1 through 35-12; 45-1 through 45-2; 55-3;

10-1 through 10-2; ASC 450-20-60-12 (FAS-15), which applies to extinguishments in troubled debt restructurings. In accordance with the guidance in guidance in ASC 470-50-05-1; 15-3 through 15-4; 40-2, 40-4; ASC 850-10-60-3 (APB-26), the difference between the net carrying amount of the extinguished debt and the reacquisition price is recognized currently in income of the period of extinguishment. In this situation, the reacquisition price of the extinguished debt is the value of the common or preferred stock issued or the value of the debt, whichever is more clearly evident.

EITF Issue 96-19 (Debtor's Accounting for a Substantive Modification and Exchange of Debt Instruments) (ASC 470-50-05-4; 15-3; 40-6 through 40-14, 40-17 through 40-20; 55-1 through 55-9)

> **OBSERVATION:** FAS-140 (Accounting for Transfers and Servicing of Financial Assets and Extinguishments of Liabilities) superseded FAS-125 but did not change that guidance on the extinguishment of liabilities. The guidance in this Issue was not reconsidered in ASC 860-10-35-4, 35-6; 05-8; 860-20–25-5, 55-46 through 55-48; 860-50-05-2 through 05-4; 30-1 through 30-2; 35-1A, 35-3, 35-9 through 35-11; 25-2, 25-3, 25-6; 50-5; 460-10-60-35 (FAS-166), which amended the guidance in ASC 860 (FAS-140).
>
> **NOTE:** The guidance in this Issue has been amended by the guidance in Issue 06-6, which is discussed below.

OVERVIEW

The EITF reached a consensus in Issue 86-18 (not in ASC) that an exchange of callable debt for noncallable debt constitutes an extinguishment that should be accounted for as an extraordinary gain or loss. Although the Task Force's discussion of the accounting for substantive modifications of existing debt terms, such as changes in principal, interest rate, maturity, or call provisions, did not result in a consensus, many Task Force members believed that such transactions should be accounted for as the extinguishment of old debt and the issuance of new debt. Other members believed that unless the conditions in FAS-76 (not in ASC) have been met, extinguishment accounting is inappropriate. The Task Force also provided guidance on determining what is a substantial modification, although it did not reach a consensus on that matter.

Under the provisions of ASC 405-20-40-1 (paragraph 16 of FAS-140 as amended by FAS-166), which nullified the first two consensus positions in Issue 86-18 and superseded existing guidance on extinguishment of debt, a liability is extinguished and derecognized only if one of the following two conditions exists:

15.06 Extinguishment of Debt

1. The debtor is relieved of the obligation by paying the creditor in cash, other financial assets, goods, or services, or the debtor has reacquired the outstanding debt securities, which are either canceled or held as treasury bonds, *or*
2. The debtor obtains a legal release from being primarily liable on the obligation.

Exchanges of debt or modifications of debt that have a substantive effect on the amount and timing of the future cash flows of the debt instruments are not treated as extinguishments under the guidance in ASC 860 (FAS-140, as amended by FAS-166). Because that guidance does not address the accounting for such transactions, the FASB asked the EITF to resolve that matter.

ACCOUNTING ISSUES

- How should a debtor account for an exchange of debt instruments with substantially different terms?
- How should a debtor account for a substantial modification of terms of an existing debt agreement that is not a troubled debt restructuring?
- Should a gain or loss recognized on an exchange or modification of debt be reported as extraordinary?

EITF CONSENSUS

- An *exchange* of debt instruments with substantially different terms is accounted for as a debt extinguishment, with the liability for the existing debt derecognized in accordance with the guidance in ASC 405-20-40-1 (paragraph 16 of FAS-140 as amended by FAS-166).
- A substantial modification of the terms of existing debt is accounted for and reported as an extinguishment the same as an exchange of debt with substantially different terms, because the debtor can achieve the same economic result in the two transactions.
- From the debtor's perspective, if the present value of the cash flows under the terms of a new debt instrument differ by at least 10% from the present value of the cash flows remaining under the original debt instrument, the exchange of debt instruments with the creditor or the modification of debt in a nontroubled debt restructuring is achieved with substantially different debt instruments. Present value is calculated based on the following guidance:
  —The new debt instrument's cash flows include all cash flows stated in the terms of the new debt instrument as well as amounts paid by the debtor to the creditor less amounts

received by the debtor from the creditor in the exchange or modification.
- —For debt instruments (original or new) that have a floating interest rate, the variable rate effective on the date of the exchange or modification is used to calculate the instrument's cash flows.
- —For debt instruments (original or new) that are callable or puttable, cash flows are analyzed separately assuming exercise and nonexercise of the put option. Cash flow assumptions that result in a smaller change are used to determine whether the 10% difference for substantially different instruments is met.
- —Judgment should be used to determine the appropriate cash flows of debt instruments with contingent payment terms or unusual interest rate terms.
- —For accounting purposes, the effective interest rate of the original debt instrument is used as the discount rate to calculate the present value of cash flows.
- —If debt exchanged or modified within one year before the current transaction was determined not to be substantially different, the debt terms existing before that exchange are used to determine whether the current exchange or modification is substantially different.
- Changes in the amount of principal, interest rates, or maturity of the debt can affect cash flow. Fees exchanged between a debtor and a creditor for the purpose of changing any of the following features or provisions of the debt also can affect cash flows:
  - —Recourse or nonrecourse features
  - —Priority of the obligation
  - —Collateralization (including changes in collateral) or noncollateralization features
  - —A guarantor or elimination thereof
  - —Option features

  Debt instruments are *not* substantially different if a debt instrument is changed or modified as discussed above, but the effect on the present value of cash flow is less than 10%.
- New debt instruments as a result of exchanges or modifications of old debt that are considered to be substantially different (the old debt is extinguished) are recognized initially at fair value. That amount is used to determine the gain or loss on extinguishment and the effective interest rate of the new debt instrument.

15.08 *Extinguishment of Debt*

- New debt instruments as a result of exchanges or modifications of old debt that are *not* considered to be substantially different are *not* accounted for as extinguishments of the old debt. A new effective interest rate is calculated on the date of the exchange or modification based on the carrying amount of the original debt instrument and the revised cash flows.
- For exchanges or modifications that result in an extinguishment of the old debt and the new debt is initially recognized at fair value:
  —Fees paid by the debtor to the creditor or received by the debtor from the creditor (for example, to cancel the debtor's call option or to extend a no-call period) in the exchange or modification are associated with the extinguishment transaction and included in determining the gain loss on the extinguishment.
  —Amounts paid to third parties as a result of the exchange or modification (such as legal fees) are associated with the new or modified debt instruments and amortized over the term of the new or modified debt based on the interest method similar to debt issue costs.
- For exchanges or modifications that do *not* result in an extinguishment of the old debt:
  —Fees paid by the debtor to the creditor or received by the debtor from the creditor (for example, to cancel the debtor's call option or to extend a no-call period) in the exchange or modification are associated with the new or modified debt instruments and amortized with existing unamortized discount or premium to adjust interest expense over the remaining term of the new or modified debt based on the interest method.
  —Amounts paid to third parties as a result of the exchange or modification, such as legal fees, are expensed as incurred.
- The consensus positions in this Issue supersede the consensus positions in Issue 95-15. The transactions discussed in that Issue are accounted for according to the consensus positions in this Issue.
- The guidance in the third consensus of EITF Issue 86-18 (not in ASC) is retained. That consensus addresses the accounting for a transaction in which a borrower, who instead of acquiring debt securities directly, loans money to a third party to acquire the borrower's debt securities. The borrower and third party agree to offset the payments of their payables and receivables as they become due as long as the third party retains the borrower's debt. The EITF's consensus on that Issue was that the original debt securities are not extinguished and that the securities should not be offset in the borrower's financial statements against the receivable from the third party.

- The guidance in Issue 87-20 was superseded by Issue 96-19.

Because the above consensus positions contemplate only single debtors and creditors and do not consider the effect on the debtor's accounting of actions taken by third-party intermediaries acting as agent or principal, the Task Force reached a consensus on the following implementation guidance at its July 1998 meeting:

- A transaction in which a debtor pays cash to a creditor to extinguish its current debt and the creditor issues new debt in exchange should be accounted for as an extinguishment of the current debt only if the new debt instrument has substantially different terms, as defined in the Issue. The consensus in this Issue does *not* apply to exchanges of cash between debtors and creditors, because such transactions already meet the requirement for extinguishment of debt in ASC 405-20-40-1 (paragraph 16 of FAS-140 as amended by the guidance in FAS-166).
- In determining whether there has been an exchange of debt instruments or a modification of the terms of an existing debt instrument between a debtor and a creditor, the actions of a third-party intermediary acting as an *agent* for the debtor should be considered in the same manner as if they had been taken by the debtor.
- In determining whether there has been an exchange of debt instruments or a modification of the terms of an existing debt instrument between a debtor and a creditor, the actions of a third-party intermediary acting as a *principal* should be considered to be those of a third-party creditor in the same manner as the actions of any other creditor.
- The debtor's accounting for a debt is not affected by transactions among debt holders, because such actions do not cause a modification of the terms of the original debt or an exchange of debt instruments between the debtor and the debt holders.
- To determine whether a gain or loss should be recognized on transactions between a debtor and a third-party creditor, the guidance in ASC 405-20-40-1 (paragraph 16 of FAS-140) and the EITF's consensus positions in the Issue should apply.

When applying the above consensus, it may be necessary to determine whether a third-party intermediary is acting as an agent or as a principal. Legal definitions of those terms and an evaluation of the facts and circumstances related to a third-party intermediary's involvement may be useful. The Task Force discussed the following indicators that should be considered:

- If an intermediary is only required to place or reacquire debt for a debtor but does not risk its own funds, it is an indicator that the third-party intermediary is acting as an *agent* for the debtor. For example, an intermediary that uses its own funds is acting as an agent if the debtor will compensate the intermediary for any incurred losses. However, an intermediary is acting as a *principal* if the intermediary risks losing its own funds.

- If an intermediary places notes issued by a debtor in accordance with a best-efforts agreement under which the intermediary agrees to buy only securities that can be sold to others and otherwise the debtor must repay the debt, it is an indicator that the intermediary is acting as an *agent* for the debtor. An intermediary can be deemed to be acting as a *principal* if the intermediary acts on a firmly committed basis and must hold debt that is not sold.
- An indicator that an intermediary is acting as an *agent* is an arrangement in which the intermediary can act only on an exchange of debt or a modification of debt terms based on the debtor's instructions. However, an intermediary that acquires debt from or exchanges debt with another debt holder in the market and the transaction exposes the intermediary to the risk of loss may be deemed to be acting as a *principal*.
- If an intermediary is paid only a specified fee to act for the debtor, it is an indicator that the intermediary is acting as an *agent*. An intermediary's ability to realize a gain on the transaction based on the value of the security issued by the debtor is an indicator that the intermediary is acting as a *principal*.

The EITF reached a consensus that debtors can recognize gains or losses on transactions related to a modification or exchange of debt instruments only for transactions meeting the conditions in ASC 405-20-40-1 (paragraph 16 of FAS-140 as amended by FAS-166) or the requirements for extinguishment under the consensus in this Issue. Consequently, the guidance in this Issue supersedes the guidance in Issue 87-20 on loss recognition. The principles discussed in this Issue would apply to the transaction discussed in Issue 87-20.

Illustrations of Debtor's Accounting for a Substantive Modification and Exchange of Debt Instruments

Identification of Debtor and Creditor

1. XYZ Bank (lead bank/creditor) makes a $10 million loan to ABC Construction Co. (debtor). The debt instrument is a contract between the bank and the debtor. Subsequently, the bank transfers a $1 million undivided interest in the debt to each of nine banks that have a participating interest in the loan, as evidenced by a certificate of participation, but that are not direct creditors in accordance with the guidance in paragraph 74 of FAS-125. The debtor would apply the provisions of this Issue only if the debtor and the lead bank agree to exchange the debt or to modify its terms.

2. A syndicate of ten banks (creditors) jointly funds a $10 million loan to ABC Construction Co. (debtor). In this transaction, each member of the syndicate individually loans $1 million to the debtor and issues a sepa-

rate debt instrument. After one year, the debtor asks the creditors to modify the terms of the debt instruments. Six creditors agree to the modification, but four do not. Because each of the creditors has a separate right to repayment under the provisions of ASC 860-10-55-4 and ASC 310-10-25-4 (paragraphs 102 through 103 of FAS-140. as amended by FAS-166), the debtor accounts for the modified loans in accordance with the guidance in this Issue. The loans from creditors who would not modify the terms of the debt instruments are unaffected.

3. IHT Manufacturing Corp. issues identical debt instruments to an underwriter who sells them in the form of securities to the public. Each investor (creditor) holding a security (debt instrument) is considered to be a separate creditor for the purpose of applying the consensus in this Issue. If IHT asks the holders of the securities for a modification in the terms of the debt instruments (or an exchange of debt instruments), the debtor applies the consensus only to debt instruments held by creditors that agree to an exchange or modification. Debt instruments held by the other security holders are unaffected.

Exchanges or Modifications of Debt Involving a Third-Party Intermediary

1. In the following three scenarios, the actions of an investment banker acting in the capacity of a third-party intermediary for a debtor (*agent*) are viewed as the actions of the debtor:

   a. The investment banker acquires debt instruments from holders for cash and later transfers debt instruments with the same or different terms to the same or different investors. The debtor accounts for the cash transaction as an extinguishment of the debt, because it meets the criterion in ASC 405-20-40-1 (paragraph 16a of FAS-140, as amended by FAS-166)).

   b. The investment banker redeems the debtor's outstanding debt instruments in exchange for new debt instruments. The debtor must account for that transaction under the provisions of this Issue. The transaction would be accounted for as an extinguishment only if the terms of the new debt are substantially different from those of the debt exchanged.

   c. The investment banker acquires debt instruments from holders for cash and at the same time issues new debt instruments for cash. This transaction is also accounted for under the consensus in this Issue; the original debt is extinguished only if the terms of the new debt are substantially different from those of the original debt.

2. In this transaction, a third-party investment banker acts as a *principal* and is treated the same as other debt holders. If the investment banker acquires debt instruments from other debt holders, the transaction does not affect the debtor's accounting. Exchanges and modifications between the investment banker and the debtor are accounted for under the consensus in this Issue based on whether the terms of the new or modified debt instrument differ substantially from those of the original debt instrument.

Transactions among Debt Holders

An investment banker intermediary acting as a *principal* for a debt holder exchanges a debt instrument for cash with another party in the marketplace.

15.12 *Extinguishment of Debt*

Because the funds do not pass through the debtor or its agent, the debtor's accounting is not affected by that transaction. However, if the cash exchanged by the debt holders passes through the debtor, the debtor would account for the transaction as an extinguishment.

Gain or Loss Recognition

A debtor cannot recognize a gain or loss in the following situations until the debt has been extinguished under the provisions of ASC 405-20-40-1 (paragraph 16 of FAS-140) and the consensus in this Issue:

1. A debtor announces it intends to call a debt instrument at the first call date. (The SEC Staff Accounting Bulletin No. 94 (Recognition of a Gain or Loss on Early Extinguishment of Debt) states that the staff would object to gain or loss recognition in a period other than the period in which the debt is extinguished.)

2. A debtor places amounts equal to the principal, interest, and prepayment penalties of the debt instrument in an irrevocable trust established for the benefit of the creditor. (Under FAS-140, debt is not extinguished in an in-substance defeasance.)

3. The debtor and a creditor agree that the debtor will redeem a debt instrument issued by the debtor from a third party.

SUBSEQUENT DEVELOPMENT

At its November 29, 2006 meeting, the FASB ratified the EITF's consensus positions in Issue 06-6 (Debtor's Accounting for a Modification (or Exchange) of Convertible Debt Instruments), which supersedes the guidance in Issue 05-7 (Accounting for Modifications to Conversion Options Embedded in Debt Instruments and Related Issues) and amends the guidance in Issue 96-19. Issue 06-6, which is discussed in this Chapter, provides the following guidance:

- If a debt instrument is exchanged or its terms are modified, the resulting change in the embedded conversion option's fair value should *not* be included in the cash flow test used to determine under the guidance in Issue 96-19 whether a new debt instrument's terms are *substantially* different from those in the original debt instrument. If the results of the cash flow test under the guidance in Issue 96-19 are inconclusive as to whether a *substantial* modification or an exchange has occurred, a separate analysis should be performed. Debt extinguishment accounting is required if:

    —A *substantial* modification or an exchange is deemed to have occurred based on the results of a separate analysis, because the change in the embedded conversion option's fair value that is calculated as the difference between the fair value of the embedded conversion option immediately *before* and *after* a modification or exchange has occurred equals at least 10% of the carrying amount of the *original* debt instrument immediately *before* the modification or exchange occurred.

— A modification or exchange is considered to be substantial if a *substantive* conversion option is *added* or a conversion option that was substantive at the date of a modification or exchange of a convertible debt instrument is *eliminated*. To determine whether an embedded conversion option is substantive on the date it is added to or eliminated from a debt instrument, the guidance in EITF Issue No. 05-1 (Accounting for Conversion of an Instrument That Became Convertible upon the Issuer's Exercise of a Call Option), which is discussed in Chapter 12, "Convertible Debt and Debt with Warrants," should be considered.

- If a modification or exchange of a convertible debt instrument is *not* accounted for as a debt extinguishment, the debt instrument's carrying amount should be reduced by an *increase* in the embedded conversion option's fair value, which is calculated as the difference between the fair value immediately *before* and *after* the modification or exchange, by increasing a debt discount or reducing a debt premium. A corresponding increase should be made to additional paid-in capital. However, a decrease in an embedded conversion option's fair value should *not* be recognized. Further, if a modification or exchange of a convertible debt instrument is *not* accounted for as a debt extinguishment, the issuer should *not* recognize a beneficial conversion feature or reevaluate an existing one as a result of that transaction.

DISCUSSION

The Task Force based its consensus in this Issue on a determination of whether the economics of the exchanged or modified debt instrument differ substantially from the original debt instrument. Members argued that the guidance in ASC 860 (FAS-140) permitting extinguishment accounting only for transactions with a different lender is counterintuitive when the same economic result might be achieved in a transaction with the same lender. Consequently, the Task Force decided that the decision whether to account for an exchange or modification of debt instruments as an extinguishment should be based on whether the instruments exchanged or modified are substantially different and the debtor is in a different *economic* position after the exchange or modification than before the transaction. It was noted that a lender would recognize an extinguishment under the same circumstances.

The Task Force used the criteria suggested by the EITF in Issue 86-18 (not in ASC) as a starting point in developing criteria for substantially different terms of debt instruments in this Issue. A cutoff of 10% rather than 5% was used to determine whether debt instruments are substantially different to compensate for using the

15.14 *Extinguishment of Debt*

historical effective interest rate instead of a market rate in computing the present value of cash flows. The difference in the present value of cash flows is used as the primary test. A working group suggested that negotiated fees exchanged between the debtor and the creditor to change debt terms other than the principal amount, interest rate, or maturity of the debt should be used as a surrogate for measuring the significance of the other changes.

Issue 98-14 (Debtor's Accounting for Changes in Line-of-Credit or Revolving-Debt Arrangements) (ASC 470-50-40-21 through 40-22; 45-2; 55-11 through 55-13)

OVERVIEW

A line-of-credit or a revolving-debt arrangement enables a debtor to borrow up to an agreed amount, to repay some of the indebtedness, and to borrow additional amounts. Such arrangements may include amounts borrowed by the debtor and a lender's commitment to make additional funds available under specified terms. Usually, a debtor incurs a cost to establish a line-of-credit or a revolving-credit arrangement. Such costs are usually deferred and amortized over the term of the arrangement. The EITF's consensus in Issue 96-19 (see ASC references above) did not specifically address modifications or exchanges of revolving debt arrangements or lines of credit on which amounts have been drawn. It specifically excluded those on which no funds had been drawn because of their unique characteristics.

Application of the consensus in Issue 96-19 to *revolving-debt* arrangements and to *lines of credit* is unclear, because of the difficulty of determining whether a change is substantial when there is an outstanding balance and a lender has committed to lend additional amounts. Issue 98-14 applies to modifications and exchanges of lines-of-credit and revolving-debt arrangements.

ACCOUNTING ISSUE

How should a debtor account for modifications to or exchanges of line-of-credit or revolving-debt arrangements, including the accounting for unamortized costs at the time of the change, fees paid to or received from the creditor, and third-party costs incurred?

EITF CONSENSUS

- A modification to or exchange of a line-of-credit or a revolving debt arrangement that results in a new line-of-credit or revolving-debt arrangement or in a traditional term debt arrangement should be evaluated as follows:

The debtor should compare the product of the remaining term and the maximum available credit of the *old* arrangement (referred to as the borrowing capacity) with the borrowing capacity under the *new* arrangement and should account for related costs in the following manner:

—*Fees paid to the creditor, and third-party costs incurred, if any* Associate those costs with the *new* arrangement, regardless whether the borrowing capacity of the new arrangement is *greater* than, *equal* to, or *less* than under the old arrangement, by deferring and amortizing those costs over the term of the new arrangement.

—*Unamortized deferred costs of the old arrangement* Account for the unamortized, deferred costs of the *old* arrangement as follows:

(1) *Borrowing capacity of the new arrangement is greater than or equal to the new arrangement* Amortize over the term of the *new* arrangement.

(2) *Borrowing capacity of the new arrangement is less than that under the old arrangement* Write off the unamortized deferred costs of the *old* arrangement at the time of the change in proportion to the decrease in borrowing capacity. Defer and amortize the remaining amount related to the *old* arrangement over the term of the *new* arrangement.

- Charges to earnings, if any, as a result of the write-off of unamortized costs of the old arrangement under b(ii) above should *not* be classified as an extraordinary expense.

The Task Force also clarified that the scope of the Issue is limited to modifications of or exchanges of line-of-credit or revolving-debt arrangements in *nontroubled* situations involving a debtor and creditor who were involved in the original arrangement.

Illustration of a Debtor's Accounting for Changes in a Line of Credit or Revolving Credit Arrangement

On 1/1/X9 Company M has a revolving credit arrangement with Bank X that has a 6-year term with 4 years remaining and a $12 million commitment. The company's borrowing capacity under this arrangement is $48 million (4 years × $12 million commitment).

On 4/1/X9, the company renegotiates its credit arrangement with Bank X. At that time, $250,000 in unamortized costs relating to the company's current credit arrangement remain on its balance sheet. To change the credit arrangement, the company will have pay a $150,000 fee to the bank and will also incur $250,000 in third-party costs. The company can choose among the following changes to its current arrangement:

- **Terms** (1) Increase the amount of the bank's commitment to $18 million with the term remaining at 4 years, or (2) replace the original revolving agreement with a 4-year, $12 million term loan on which the principal is due at the end of 4 years. Thus, the loan has a $48 million borrowing capacity.

Accounting Result (1) The company's borrowing capacity increases from $48 million to $72 million. The $250,000 of unamortized costs of the original arrangement is amortized over the 4-year term of the new arrangement. The $400,000 in fees to the bank and third parties is deferred and amortized over 4 years. (2) The company's borrowing capacity is unchanged. The accounting for unamortized deferred costs of the old arrangement and costs of the new arrangement is the same as in (1).

- **Terms** Decrease the amount of the bank's commitment to $6 million and increase the term to 5 years.

   Accounting Result The company's borrowing capacity decreases from $48 million to $30 million, a reduction of 37.5%. Therefore, $93,750 ($250,000 × .375) of the unamortized costs of the original arrangement is written off. The remaining $156,250 is amortized over the 5-year term of the new arrangement. The $400,000 in fees to the bank and third parties is deferred and amortized over 5 years.

- **Terms** Replace the bank's revolving credit arrangement with a $6 million term loan on which the principal is due at the end of 3 years.

   Accounting Result The company's borrowing capacity decreases from $48 million to $18 million, a reduction of 62.5%. Therefore, $156,250 ($250,000 × .625) of the unamortized costs of the original arrangement is written off. The remaining $93,750 is amortized over the 3-year term of the new arrangement. The $400,000 in fees to the bank and third parties is deferred and amortized over 3 years.

EITF Issue 02-4 (Debtor's Accounting for a Modification or an Exchange of Debt Instruments in accordance with FASB Statement No. 15, *Accounting by Debtors and Creditors for Troubled Debt Restructurings*) **(ASC 470-60-55-4 through 55-14; 15-13)**

OVERVIEW

FAS-15 provides some guidance on determining whether a modification or exchange of debt constitutes a troubled debt restructuring. The guidance in ASC 470-60-15-9 (paragraph 5 of FAS-15) includes a list of factors that may exist in a troubled debt restructuring and ASC 470-60-15-12 (paragraph 7 of FAS-15) lists factors that *may* indicate that a modification or exchange of debt does *not* "necessarily" constitute a troubled debt restructuring. However, it appears that further clarification is required. For example, there is some question whether a reduction in the face amount of a debt instrument should always be accounted for as a troubled debt restructuring based on the guidance in ASC 470-60-15-9 (paragraph 5(c)(3) of FAS-15), and whether FAS-15 applies to a transaction in which a debtor exchanges its existing debt by issuing new marketable debt that meets the criterion in ASC 470-60-15-12 (paragraph 7(d) of FAS-15) for a nontroubled debt restructuring. In the latter situation, the new debt's effective interest rate is based on a market price that approximates the price of debt with similar maturity dates and stated interest rates that has been issued by a nontroubled borrower.

ACCOUNTING ISSUE

Does any single characteristic or factor, taken alone, determine whether a debtor should account for a modification or exchange as a troubled debt restructuring under FAS-15?

EITF CONSENSUS

The EITF reached a consensus that in determining whether a modification or an exchange of debt instruments is within the scope of the guidance in ASC 310-40-15-3 through 15-12; 10-1 through 10-2; 25-1 through 25-2; 35-2, 35-5, 35-7; 40-2 through 40-6, 40-8; 50-1 through 50-2; 55-2; ASC 470-60-15-3 through 15-12; 35-1 through 35-12; 45-1 through 45-2; 55-3; 10-1 through 10-2; ASC 450-20-60-12 (FAS-15), a debtor should consider (*a*) whether the entity is experiencing financial difficulty and (*b*) whether the creditor has granted a concession to the debtor. A debtor would follow FAS-15) (see ASC reference above) if both questions are answered affirmatively. If the answer to either question is negative, a debt modification or exchange should *not* be accounted for under the provisions of FAS-15 (see ASC reference above).

The EITF also reached a consensus that the following factors are irrelevant in determining whether FAS-15 (see ASC reference above) applies to a debt modification or exchange:

- The amount that current creditors had invested in the old debt.
- A comparison of the fair value of new debt at issuance to the fair value of the old debt immediately before a modification or exchange.
- Transactions among debt holders.

In addition, the Task Force observed that the length of time that current creditors have held an investment in the old debt is also irrelevant in determining whether a modification or exchange is under the scope of FAS-15 (see ASC reference above) *unless* all the current creditors recently acquired the debt from the previous debt holders in what is effectively a planned refinancing.

Determining Whether a Debtor Is Experiencing Financial Difficulties

A debtor should evaluate whether it is experiencing financial difficulties if its creditworthiness has deteriorated since the debt was first issued. A debtor is experiencing financial difficulties if the following indicators exist:

- The debtor is currently in default on any of its debt.
- The debtor has declared or is declaring bankruptcy.
- Significant doubt exists whether the debtor will continue as a going concern.
- The debtor's securities have been delisted, are in the process of being delisted, or are under the threat of being delisted from an exchange.
- The debtor forecasts that based on estimates covering only its current business capabilities, the debtor's entity-specific cash flows will be insufficient to service interest and principal on the debt through maturity in accordance with the contractual terms of the existing agreement.
- The debtor cannot obtain funds from other sources at an effective interest rate that equals the current market interest rate for similar debt for a nontroubled debtor.

Despite the above criteria, if *both* of the following factors exist, there is determinative evidence that a debtor is *not* experiencing financial difficulties and a modification or exchange is *not* under the scope of FAS-15 (see ASC reference above):

- The debtor is servicing the old debt on a current basis and can obtain funds to repay the old debt from sources other than the current creditors at an effective interest rate that equals the current market interest rate for a nontroubled debtor *and*
- The creditors agree to restructure the old debt only to show a decrease in current interest rates for the debtor or positive changes in the debtor's creditworthiness since the original issuance of the debt.

Determining Whether a Creditor Granted a Concession

- A creditor has granted a concession if the debtor's effective borrowing rate on restructured debt is less than the effective borrowing rate of the old debt immediately before it was restructured. To calculate the effective borrowing rate of restructured debt, after considering all the terms including new or revised options or warrants, if any, and new or revised guarantees or letters of credit, if any, all cash flows under the new terms should be projected and the discount rate that equates the present value of the cash flows under the *new* terms to the debtor's current carrying amount of the *old* debt should be computed.
- Although this is rare, if persuasive evidence exists that the decrease in the borrowing rate is attributed exclusively to a factor that is not depicted in the computation, such as additional col-

lateral, the creditor may not have granted a concession and the modification or exchange should be evaluated based on the substance of the modification.

Despite the consensus reached above, an entity that is currently restructuring its debt after having done so recently should calculate the effective borrowing rate of the restructured debt, after considering all the terms including new or revised options or warrants, if any, and new or revised guarantees or letters of credit, if any, by projecting all cash flows under the new terms and determining the debtor's previous carrying amount of the debt immediately before the previous restructuring. To determine whether the effective borrowing rate has decreased and therefore the creditor has granted a concession, the debtor should compare the effective borrowing rate of the debt immediately before the previous restructuring.

EITF Issue No. 06-6 (Debtor's Accounting for a Modification (or Exchange) of Convertible Debt Instruments) (ASC 470-50-40-12, 40-15 through 40-16)

OVERVIEW

The EITF reached the following consensus positions in EITF Issue No. 05-7 (Accounting for Modifications to Conversion Options Embedded in Debt Instruments and Related Issues) (not in ASC):

- The consensus in Issue 1 provides that an issuer that modifies a convertible debt instrument should include a change in the fair value of the related embedded conversion option as cash flow in the current period when determining whether the debt instrument has been extinguished under the guidance in ASC 470-50-05-4; 15-3; 40-6 through 40-14, 40-17 through 40-20; 55-1 through 55-9 (EITF Issue No. 96-19 (Debtor's Accounting for a Modification or Exchange of Debt Instruments), which is discussed above;

- The consensus in Issue 2 provides that fair value changes in an embedded conversion option as a result of a modification of the associated convertible debt instrument would affect subsequent recognition of interest expense on that debt instrument; and

- The consensus in Issue 3 provides that if a convertible debt instrument is modified, the issuer should not recognize a beneficial conversion feature or reassess it, if one exists.

After the Financial Accounting Standards Board ratified the consensus in Issue 05-7 at its September 28, 2005, meeting, the FASB staff was informed that some constituents question whether its guidance applies to debt instruments that are modified to either add or eliminate an embedded conversion option, including one in an original or a modified instrument that the issuer has been required to bifurcate from its host in accordance with the guidance in ASC 815 (FAS-133, Accounting for Derivative Instruments and Hedging Activities).

At the EITF's March 16, 2006, meeting, the FASB staff stated the view that modifications to debt instruments that add or eliminate an embedded conversion option are included under the scope of Issue 05-7, but that its guidance should not apply to modifications of debt instruments that an issuer must bifurcate from their hosts under the guidance in ASC 815 (FAS-133) because the EITF did not discuss those types of instruments in its deliberations of Issue 05-7. The EITF, therefore, agreed to add a paragraph to Issue 05-7 and to Issue 96-19 (see ASC references above) to clarify that the scope of Issue 05-7 is based on the FASB staff's view discussed above. However, because of concerns about the accounting for modifications that *decrease* the value of or *eliminate* an embedded conversion option, the EITF agreed to reconsider the issues in Issue 05-7.

ACCOUNTING ISSUES

1. How should an issuer consider a modification of a debt instrument (or an exchange of debt instruments) that affects an embedded conversion option's terms in analysis to determine whether debt extinguishment accounting applies?

2. How should an issuer account for a debt instrument's modification or an exchange of debt instruments that affects an embedded conversion option's terms if extinguishment accounting does *not* apply?

SCOPE

The guidance in this Issue applies to modifications and exchanges of debt instruments that (*a*) add or eliminate an embedded conversion option or (*b*) affect an existing embedded conversion option's fair value. This Issue does *not* provide accounting guidance for a modification or exchange of a debt instrument if its embedded conversion option is separately accounted for as a derivative under the guidance in ASC 815 (FAS-133, Accounting for Derivative Instruments and Hedging Activities) before a modification occurs, after the modification or in both instances.

EITF CONSENSUS

At its November 16, 2006, meeting, the EITF reached the following consensus positions on Issues 1 and 2 of this Issue based on further discussion:

1. If a debt instrument is exchanged or its terms are modified, the resulting change in the embedded conversion option's fair value should *not* be included in the cash flow test used to

determine under the guidance in Issue 96-19 (see ASC references above) whether the new debt instrument's terms are substantially different from those in the original debt instrument. If the results of the cash flow test under the guidance in Issue 96-19 (see ASC references above) are inconclusive as to whether a *substantial* modification or an exchange has occurred, a separate analysis should be performed. Debt extinguishment accounting is required if:

   a. A *substantial* modification or an exchange is deemed to have occurred based on the results of a separate analysis, because the change in the embedded conversion option's fair value that is calculated as the difference between the fair value of the embedded conversion option immediately *before* and *after* a modification or exchange has occurred equals at least 10% of the carrying amount of the *original* debt instrument immediately *before* the modification or exchange occurred.
   b. A modification or exchange is considered to be substantial if a *substantive* conversion option is *added* or a conversion option that was substantive at the date of a modification or exchange of a convertible debt instrument is *eliminated*. To determine whether an embedded conversion option is substantive on the date it is added to or eliminated from a debt instrument, the guidance in ASC 470-20-05-11; 40-4A through 40-10; 55-68 (EITF Issue 05-1, Accounting for the Conversion of an Instrument That Became Convertible upon the Issuer's Exercise of a Call Option) should be considered.

2. If a modification or exchange of a convertible debt instrument is *not* accounted for as a debt extinguishment, the debt instrument's carrying amount should be reduced by an *increase* in the embedded conversion option's fair value, which is calculated as the difference between the fair value immediately *before* and *after* the modification or exchange, by increasing a debt discount or reducing a debt premium. A corresponding increase should be made to additional paid-in capital. However, a decrease in an embedded conversion option's fair value should *not* be recognized. Further, if a modification or exchange of a convertible debt instrument is not accounted for as a debt extinguishment, the issuer should *not* recognize a beneficial conversion feature or reevaluate an existing one as a result of that transaction.

This Issue supersedes the guidance in Issue 05-7. Issue 96-19 should be amended by replacing the guidance from Issue 05-7 with the guidance in this Issue.

FASB RATIFICATION

The FASB ratified the EITF's consensus positions at its November 29, 2006.

AIN-APB 26 (Early Extinguishment of Debt: Accounting Interpretations of APB Opinion No. 26) (ASC 470-50-40-5; 15-3; ASC 470-20-40-4)

BACKGROUND

The guidance in ASC 470-50-40-5; 15-3; ASC 470-20-40-4 (AIN-APB 26) clarifies the applicability of ASC 470-50-05-1; 15-3 through 15-4; 40-2, 40-4; ASC 850-10-60-3 (APB-26, Early Extinguishment of Debt) to debt tendered to exercise warrants).

STANDARDS

Question: The guidance in ASC 470-50-05-1; 15-3 through 15-4; 40-2, 40-4; ASC 850-10-60-3 (APB-26) indicates that a gain or loss should be recognized currently in income when a debt security is reacquired by the issuer except through conversion by the holder. Does that guidance apply to debt tendered to exercise warrants that were originally issued with that debt, but which were detachable?

Answer: The guidance in ASC 470-50-05-1; 15-3 through 15-4; 40-2, 40-4; ASC 850-10-60-3 (APB-26) does not apply to debt tendered to exercise detachable warrants that were originally issued with that debt if the debt is permitted to be tendered toward the exercise price of the warrants under the terms of the securities at issuance. In this circumstance, the debt is considered a conversion. (APB-26 does not apply to conversion of debt. In practice, however, the carrying amount of the debt, including any unamortized premium or discount, is transferred to capital accounts when the debt is converted. No gain or loss is recognized.)

Illustration of Debt Tendered to Exercise Detachable Warrants

DeVries Chemical originally issued a $100 million bond issue at par. In addition, each bond contained two detachable warrants, enabling the holder to purchase DeVries? stock at $50 per warrant. DeVries allocated $3 million of the purchase price to the detachable stock warrants. Therefore, the net carrying amount of the bonds at issuance was $97 million.

The terms of the indenture permitted holders to tender their bonds toward the exercise price of the warrants. The carrying value of the $100 million bond issue on 7/15/20X4 was $98.5 million. Given a decline in interest rates since the bonds were issued, the market price of DeVries? bonds on 7/15/20X4 had risen to $100 million.

Institutional Equities International holds 20% of the DeVries bond issue. On 7/15/20X4 Institutional Equities exercises all of its warrants, 40,000 [($20,000,000 / $1,000) × 2], by tendering bonds with a market value of $2 million (40,000 × $50). The par value of DeVries? common stock is $1 per share.

DeVries Chemical would prepare the following journal entry to record the issuance of its stock as the result of Institutional Equities exercising its warrants and tendering bonds with a market value of $2 million.

Bonds payable		2,000,000
Discount on bonds payable	30,000	
Common stock	40,000	
Additional paid-in capital	1,930,000	

RELATED CHAPTER IN 2011 *GAAP GUIDE, VOLUME I*

Chapter 15, "Extinguishment of Debt"

RELATED CHAPTERS IN 2011 *INTERNATIONAL ACCOUNTING/FINANCIAL REPORTING STANDARDS GUIDE*

Chapter 3, "Presentation of Financial Statements"
Chapter 16, "Financial Instruments"
Chapter 25, "Leases"

CHAPTER 16
FAIR VALUE

CONTENTS

Overview		**16.02**
Authoritative Guidance		
ASC 820 Fair Value Measurements and Disclosures		**16.04**
EITF Issue 08-5	Issuer's Accounting for Liabilities Measured at Fair Value with a Third-Party Credit Enhancement	**16.04**
FSP FAS 157-4	Determining Fair Value When the Volume and Level of Activity for the Asset or Liability Have Significantly Decreased and Identifying Transactions That Are Not Orderly	**16.05**
ASC 825 Financial Instruments		**16.10**
FSP FAS 107-1 and APB 28-1	Interim Disclosures about Fair Value of Financial Instruments	**16.10**
ASC 840 Leases		**16.12**
FTB 79-13	Applicability of FASB Statement No. 13 to Current Value Financial Statements	**16.12**
Authoritative Guidance Not Included Separately in the Codification But Incorporated in Another Pronouncement		**16.13**
FSP FAS 157-1	Application of FASB Statement No. 157 to FASB Statement No. 13 and Other Accounting Pronouncements That Address Fair Value Measurements for Purposes of Lease Classification or Measurement under Statement 13	**16.13**
Related Chapter in 2011 GAAP Guide, Volume II		**16.15**
Related Chapters in 2011 GAAP Guide, Volume I		**16.15**
Related Chapter in 2011 International Accounting/Financial Reporting Standards Guide		**16.15**

OVERVIEW

The early years of the 21st century have introduced a new era in which fair value measurement is gradually replacing historical cost as the primary measurement approach for certain assets and liabilities. Evidence suggests that fair value measurement and reporting will be extended to a wide range of balance sheet items as experience with developing and auditing fair value information becomes more widespread.

To date, the FASB has issued two primary standards on fair value: ASC 820 (FAS-157, Fair Value Measurements) and ASC 825 (FAS-159, The Fair Value Option for Financial Assets and Financial Liabilities). In addition, fair value measurement is currently required in accounting for a wide range of financial instruments discussed in other FASB pronouncements. A broad overview of fair value, focusing primarily on the following standards, is presented in this chapter:

ASC 255	Financial Reporting and Changing Prices (FAS-89)
ASC 820	Fair Value Measurement (FAS-157)
ASC 825	The Fair Value Option for Financial Assets and Financial Liabilities (FAS-159)

FAS-33 (Financial Reporting and Changing Prices) was issued in 1979 during a period of the highest inflation in the United States in recent history. Under that standard, which was subsequently superseded by the guidance in ASC 255 (FAS-89 Financial Reporting and Changing Prices), entities that met a specified size criterion were required to report supplemental information on a current value basis. That requirement was later eliminated because of a reduction in inflation and the belief that the information was of limited value to financial statement users.

Financial statements prepared in conformity with GAAP are based on the assumption there is a stable monetary unit. That is, it is assumed that the monetary unit used to convert all financial statement items into a common denominator (i.e., dollars) does not vary sufficiently over time that it would result in material distortions in the financial statements. Also, financial statements prepared in conformity with GAAP are primarily historical-cost based (i.e., most items reported in financial statements are measured and presented at their historical cost.

Over the years, two approaches, current value accounting and general price-level accounting, have been proposed and procedures have been developed to compensate for changes in the monetary unit and changes in the value of assets and liabilities after their acquisition. Under *Current value accounting* a measure of the current value of the components of financial statements is substituted for their historical cost as the primary valuation method. Under *general price-level accounting* historical cost is used as the primary valuation basis but the current value of a dollar is substituted for its historical value by using price indexes. Currently, neither current value accounting nor general price-level accounting is required. Procedures have been established in the accounting literature for use by entities that choose to develop either general price-level or current value financial statements. In ASC 255 (FAS-89, Financial Reporting and Changing Prices), the FASB has developed disclosure standards that are optional to address the effect of changing prices on financial statements.

Guidance on accounting for changing prices in the following pronouncements is discussed in the 2011 *GAAP Guide, Volume I*, Chapter 16, "Fair Value":

- ASC 255 Financial Reporting and Changing Prices (FAS-89)
- ASC 820 Fair Value Measurement (FAS-157)
- ASC 825 The Fair Value Option for Financial Assets and Financial Liabilities (FAS-159)

AUTHORITATIVE GUIDANCE

ASC 820 Fair Value Measurements and Disclosures

EITF Issue 08-5 (Issuer's Accounting for Liabilities Measured at Fair Value with a Third-Party Credit Enhancement) (ASC 820-10-05-3, 55-23C through 55-23D, 25-1 through 25-2, 55-8 through 55-9, 50-4A)

OVERVIEW

Issuers of debt securities sometimes issue their securities combined with a financial guarantee made by an unrelated third party (i.e., a credit enhancement), which the issuer purchases to guarantee its credit obligations. The guarantee gives investors additional assurance that the debt will be paid by the issuer or the guarantor and usually enables the issuer to: (1) pay a lower interest rate on the debt securities; (2) receive higher proceeds; or (3) both.

Generally, if an issuer that has issued debt securities with a credit enhancement defaults on its debt, the issuer is *not* released from its obligation, because the issuer is required to reimburse the guarantor for payments made to investors. Consequently, if an issuer of debt securities defaults on its obligation, that obligation still exists but the investor has been paid by a different creditor.

Under the guidance in ASC 825 (FAS-159, The Fair Value Option for Financial Assets and Financial Liabilities), which was effective for fiscal years that began after November 15, 2007, an entity is permitted to measure its financial assets and liabilities at fair value depending on certain requirements. Therefore, an entity is permitted to measure the liability discussed in this Issue at fair value. In addition, under the guidance in ASC 825 (FAS-107, Disclosures about Fair Value of Financial Instruments) requires entities to disclose the fair value of all financial instruments (with some exceptions). Because under the guidance in ASC 820 (FAS-157, Fair Value Measurements), the fair value of a liability must include the risk that an obligation will *not* be satisfied, some have questioned whether a debt instrument that includes an *inseparable* credit enhancement should be accounted for as one unit of accounting or as two if the debt instrument is measured at fair value.

ACCOUNTING ISSUE

Should a debt instrument that includes an *inseparable* credit enhancement be accounted for as one unit of accounting or as two if the debt instrument is measured at fair value?

SCOPE

The guidance in this Issue applies to the accounting for a debt instrument measured at fair value that is issued with a contractual guarantee from a third party (i.e., credit enhancement) that cannot be separated from the debt instrument. It does *not* apply to the accounting for guarantees, such as deposit insurance, provided by a government or a government agency.

MEASUREMENT

The EITF reached a consensus that an issuer's fair value measurement of its liability for a debt instrument issued with a credit enhancement purchased from an unrelated third party should *not* include the effect of the credit enhancement in the liability's fair value measurement, which is not the issuer's asset but was purchased by the issuer for the investor's benefit. By purchasing a credit enhancement, an issuer transfers its debt obligation from the investor to the guarantor. Proceeds received by the issuer from an investor who has purchased the liability with the credit enhancement should be allocated to the premium paid for the credit enhancement and to the issued liability.

DISCLOSURE

The EITF reached a consensus that an issuer should disclose the existence of a credit enhancement on its issued debt that the issuer purchased from an unrelated third party.

TRANSITION

The EITF reached a consensus that the guidance in this Issue should be effective *prospectively* in the first reporting period that begins on or after December 15, 2008. The effect of initial application of the guidance in this Issue should be included in the change in fair value in the year in which the guidance is adopted, but earlier application is prohibited.

In addition, the EITF reached a consensus that in the period in which an entity adopts the guidance in this Issue, it should disclose its valuation techniques used to measure the fair value of liabilities accounted for under the scope of this Issue and should provide information about changes, if any, in the valuation techniques used to measure those liabilities in prior periods.

FSP FAS 157-4 (Determining Fair Value When the Volume and Level of Activity for the Asset or Liability Have Significantly Decreased and Identifying Transactions That Are Not Orderly) (ASC 820-10-35-51A through 35-51H)

OVERVIEW

With the issuance of the guidance in ASC 820 (FAS-157 (Fair Value Measurements) in September 2006, the FASB has established

16.06 *Fair Value*

a single definition of fair value and a framework for measuring fair value under U.S. generally accepted accounting principles (GAAP) for the purpose of increased consistency and comparability of fair value measurements. Although constituents believe that ASC 820 (FAS-157) and FSP FAS 157-3 (superseded by the guidance in this FSP) have helped to improve the presentation and disclosure of fair value information, they have asked for additional guidance on determining when a market for a financial asset is no longer active and whether a transaction is not orderly.

As a result of a mandate in the October 3, 2008, Emergency Economic Stabilization Act of 2008 (EESA), the Securities Exchange Commission (SEC) conducted a study on mark-to-market accounting standards, which recommended that to improve the existing fair value requirements, application and best practice guidance for determining fair value in illiquid or inactive markets should be developed. The SEC suggested providing additional guidance for determining (1) when markets become inactive and significant adjustment of transactions or quoted prices might be required; and (2) whether a transaction or group of transactions is not orderly. The FASB believes that a decrease in the number of transactions involving an asset or liability indicates that quoted market prices may not represent fair value because under those market conditions the transactions may not be orderly. Therefore, to estimate fair value in accordance with the guidance in ASC 820 (FAS-157), the transactions or quoted prices may need to be adjusted after additional analysis.

The guidance in FSP FAS 157-4 supersedes the guidance in ASC 820-10-35-15A; 820-10-35-55A; 820-10-65-2 (FSP FAS 157-3).

Scope

All assets and liabilities under the scope of accounting pronouncements that permit or require fair value measurements, except as discussed in ASC 820-10-15-1 through 15-3 (paragraphs 2 and 3 of FAS-157), are covered under the guidance in FSP FAS 157-4. However, FSP FAS 157-4 does *not* apply to quoted prices for an identical asset or liability in an active market (i.e., a Level 1 input), which continue to be accounted for under the guidance in ASC 820-10-35-41 through 35-44 (paragraphs 24 through 27 of FAS-157).

Determining the fair value of assets and liabilities if volume and level of activity decrease significantly and identifying transactions that are not orderly

To determine whether there has been a significant decrease in the volume and level of activity for an asset or liability, a reporting entity should evaluate, based on the weight of the evidence, the significance and relevance of the following factors, among others:

- Few recent transactions;
- Price quotations based on outdated information;
- Substantial variance in price quotations either over time or among market makers;
- Lack of correlation between indexes and recent indications of the fair value of assets and liabilities that previously were highly correlated;
- Based on all available market data about credit and other non-performance risk for an asset or liability, a significant increase in indirect liquidity risk premiums, yields, or performance indicators (e.g., delinquency rates or loss severities) for observed transactions or quoted prices as compared to a reporting entity's estimate of expected cash flows;
- Wide bid-ask spread or significant increase in bid-ask spread;
- Significant decline or lack of a market for new issuances (i.e., a primary market) for an asset or liability or similar assets or liabilities; and
- Not much public information (e.g., a principal-to-principal market).

A reporting entity that concludes that the volume and level of activity for an asset or liability has significantly decreased in comparison to normal market activity for that asset or liability should perform further analysis of the transactions or quoted prices to determine whether an adjustment is necessary in order to estimate fair value in accordance with the guidance in ASC 820 (FAS-157). Significant adjustments to fair value estimates also may be necessary if the price of a similar asset requires significant adjustment for comparability to the asset being measured or if a price is out-of-date.

Although the use of valuation techniques to estimate fair value is discussed in ASC 820-10-35-24 through 35-26, 35-28, 35-30, 35-31, 35-33, 35-35, 50-5, 50-7 (paragraphs 18 through 20 of FAS-157), no guidance is provided on how to make significant adjustments to transactions or quoted prices in the process of estimating fair value. It is suggested in this FSP that a different valuation technique or multiple valuation techniques should be used if the volume and level of activity for an asset or liability has decreased significantly. A range of fair value estimates may result when multiple valuation techniques are used to estimate fair value. The reasonableness of the range of fair values should be considered with the objective of determining the amount in the range that best represents the fair value of an asset or liability under the existing conditions. Further analysis may be required if a wide range of fair value estimates results from the use of multiple valuation techniques.

The objective of a fair value measurement does *not* change, regardless of the circumstances or the valuation techniques used. Paragraph 15 of this FSP states:

16.08 Fair Value

Fair value is the price that would be received to sell an asset or paid to transfer a liability in an orderly transaction (that is, not a forced liquidation or distressed sale) between market participants at the measurement date under current market conditions.

The price at which willing market participants would enter into a transaction considering the conditions that exist at the measurement date if there has been a significant decrease in the volume and level of activity for an asset or liability depends on the facts and circumstances and requires using significant judgment. Paragraph 15 also notes that "[f]air value is a market-based measurement, not an entity-specific measurement." Therefore, it is irrelevant in estimating fair value whether a reporting entity intends to hold an asset or liability.

The fact that there has been a significant decrease in the volume and level of activity for an asset or liability should not lead to a presumption that all transactions are distressed or forced (i.e., not orderly). The following circumstances, among others, may indicate that a transaction is *not* orderly:

- The lack of an adequate period of market exposure before the measurement date to carry out the usual and customary marketing activities for transactions related to such assets or liabilities under current market conditions.
- The asset or liability was marketed only to one market participant during the usual and customary marketing period.
- The seller is in or close to bankruptcy or receivership, or the sale was forced to meet regulatory or legal requirements.
- The transaction price is outside the range of fair value estimates in comparison to other recent transactions for the same or similar asset or liability.

To determine whether a transaction is orderly, an entity should evaluate the circumstances based on the weight of the evidence.

If there has been a significant decrease in the volume or level of activity for an asset or liability, an entity should consider the following guidance in its determination of whether a transaction is or is not orderly:

- Little, if any, significance, as compared to other indicators of fair value, should be placed on a transaction price in an entity's estimate of fair value or market risk premiums if the weight of the evidence indicates that the transaction is *not* orderly.
- A transaction price should be considered in an entity's estimate of fair value or market risk premiums if there is significant evidence to indicate that a transaction is orderly. The importance of a transaction price as compared to other indicators of fair value depends on the facts and circumstance, such as the volume of the transaction, comparability of the transaction to the asset or

liability being measured at fair value, and the period of time between the transaction and the measurement date.
- An entity should consider a transaction price in estimating fair value or market risk premiums even if the information is insufficient to indicate whether the transaction was orderly. However, that transaction price should *not* be used as the only or primary basis for making that estimate. Less significance should be placed on transactions for which the reporting entity has insufficient information to reach a conclusion about whether the transaction is orderly in comparison to other known orderly transactions.

Although a reporting entity should *not* ignore information that is easily accessible at a reasonable cost, it need not make all possible efforts to determine whether a transaction is orderly. If a reporting entity is a party to a transaction, it is expected to have sufficient evidence as to whether a transaction is orderly.

Regardless of the technique that an entity uses to estimate fair value, it should adjust the fair value of an asset or liability to consider the risk related to cash flows. The inclusion of a risk premium suggests that an orderly transaction has occurred between market participants under current market conditions at the measurement date.

Under the guidance in ASC 820 (FAS-157, fair value may be estimated by using quoted prices from third parties, such as pricing services or brokers, if a reporting entity finds that those amounts were determined in accordance with ASC 820 (FAS-157). However, if there is a significant decrease in the volume or level of activity for an asset or liability, the reporting entity needs to evaluate whether the information is based on current orderly transactions or a valuation technique that represents the assumptions of market participants, including assumptions about risk. Less significance should be placed on quoted prices that are not related to transactions. In addition, the nature of a quote (i.e., whether it is an indicative price or a binding offer) should be considered in determining the significance of available evidence. Binding offers should be considered to be more significant.

Disclosures

The guidance in ASC 820 (FAS-157) is amended to require disclosure of the following information:

- In interim and annual financial statements, the inputs and valuation techniques used to measure fair value and a discussion of changes in valuation techniques and related inputs, if any, during the period.
- Definition of "major category," as discussed in ASC 820-10-50-1 through 50-3, 50-5 (paragraphs 32 and 33 of FAS-157) and ASC 270-10-60-1 for equity and debt securities to be major security types as discussed in ASC 320-10-50-2, 50-5 (paragraph 19

of FAS-115, Accounting for Certain Investments in Debt and Equity Securities), as amended by ASC 320-10-65-1 (FSP FAS 115-2 and FAS 124-2) for all equity and debt securities measured at fair value, including equity or debt securities *not* under the scope of ASC 320 (FAS-115), such as securities measured at fair value in accordance with the guidance in the AICPA Audit and Accounting Guide (Investment Companies) (AAG-INV) (ASC 946, Financial Services—Investment Companies).

ASC 825 Financial Instruments

FSP FAS 107-1/APB 28-1 (Interim Disclosures about Fair Value of Financial Instruments) (ASC 825-10-50-2A through 50-3, 50-8, 50-10 through 50-12; ASC 320-10-35-26; ASC 270-10-50-1(m))

OVERVIEW

The FASB has issued FSP FAS 107-1/APB 28 (Interim Disclosures about Fair Value of Financial Instruments) to address the concerns of constituents regarding a lack of comparability between the financial statements of entities that report the values of their financial instruments based on different measurement attributes, for example, at fair value or at amortized cost. Although the FASB and the International Accounting Standards Board (IASB) have undertaken a joint project to address the recognition and measurement of financial instruments, the FASB decided that the clarity and quality of financial information in financial statements would be improved if reporting entities disclose the information about fair value more frequently. In addition, the FASB believes that such disclosures about fair value would stimulate the discussion between financial statement users and preparers regarding the current valuations of financial instruments.

This FSP amends the guidance in ASC 825 (FAS-107, Disclosures about Fair Value of Financial Instruments) by requiring that publicly traded companies disclose information about the fair value of financial instruments for interim periods in addition to those in their annual financial statements. The guidance in ASC 270 (APB-28, Interim Financial Reporting) is also amended to require that the disclosures be made in summarized financial information at interim reporting periods.

FASB STAFF POSITION

Scope

The guidance in FSP FAS 107-1/APB-28 applies to all financial instruments under the scope of FAS-107 that are held by publicly traded companies, as defined in ASC 270 (APB-28).

Amendment to Disclosure Requirements of FAS-107/APB-28

Disclosures about the fair value of a publicly traded company's financial instruments, if it is practicable to estimate that value, should be included in the body and the accompanying notes of an entity's summarized financial information issued for interim periods and its financial statements issued for annual periods.

As required in ASC 825 (FAS-107), the disclosures should be made, regardless of whether the financial instruments are recognized in the entity's balance sheet. The manner in which information about the fair value and carrying amount of financial instruments is disclosed in the notes to the financial statements should be unambiguous as to whether the instruments are assets or liabilities and should clarify how the carrying amounts are related to the information reported on the balance sheet.

The methods and significant assumptions used to estimate the fair value of financial instruments should be disclosed and should describe changes in methods and significant assumptions, if any, made during the period.

EFFECTIVE DATE AND TRANSITION

The guidance in FSP FAS 107/APB-28 is effective for interim periods ending after June 15, 2009, but early adoption is permitted for periods ending after March 15, 2009. Early adoption of this FSP is permitted only if an entity also chooses early adoption of FSP FAS 157-4 (Determining Fair Value When the Volume and Level of Activity for the Asset or Liability Have Significantly Decreased and Identifying Transactions That Are Not Orderly), and FSP FAS 115-2 and FAS 124-2 (Recognition and Presentation of Other-Than-Temporary Impairments). Disclosures are *not* required for earlier periods presented for comparative purposes when the guidance in this FSP is initially adopted. After initial adoption, comparative disclosures are required only for periods ending after the initial adoption of the guidance in this FSP.

AMENDMENTS TO EXISTING PRONOUNCEMENTS

[Added text is underlined, deleted text is struck out:]
The guidance in ASC 825 (FAS-107) is amended as follows:
- ASC 825-10-50-8, ASC 50-2A through 50-3 (Paragraph 7)—
Second sentence: For annual reporting periods, it It ...
Add as a third sentence: For interim reporting periods, it applies to all entities but is optional for those entities that do not meet the definition of a publicly traded company, as defined by APB Opinion No. 28, *Interim Financial Reporting*.

16.12 *Fair Value*

- ASC 825-10-50-10 through 50-12 (Paragraph 10)—First sentence: An entity shall disclose in annual reporting periods and, for publicly traded companies, in interim reporting periods . . . Add at the end of the paragraph's last sentence: and shall describe changes in the method(s) and significant assumptions used to estimate the fair value of financial instruments, if any, during the period.

The guidance in APB-28 is amended as follows:

- Footnote 1 to paragraph 6 (not in ASC)—Last sentence: Additionally, when a company is required to file or furnish financial statements with the SEC or . . .
- ASC 270-10-50-1(m) Add as (paragraph 30(n)): The information about fair value of financial instruments as required by FASB Statement No. 107, *Disclosures about Fair Value of Financial Instruments*.

The guidance in FSP FAS 115-1 and FAS 124-1 is amended as follows:

- ASC 320-10-35-26 (Paragraph 10, footnote 3, , first sentence): For example, an investor may not estimate the fair value of a cost-method investment during a reporting period for Statement 107 disclosure because (a) Statement 107 requires disclosure only for annual reporting periods; (b) the investor determined that, in accordance with paragraphs 14 and 15 of Statement 107, it is not practicable to estimate the fair value of the investment; or (c)(b) the investor is exempt from providing the disclosure for annual reporting periods under FASB Statement No. 126, *Exemption from Certain Required Disclosures about Financial Instruments for Certain Nonpublic Entities*; or (c) the investor is exempt from providing the disclosure for interim reporting periods because the investor does not meet the definition of a publicly traded company, as defined by APB Opinion No. 28 , *Interim Financial Reporting*.

ASC 840 Leases

FTB 79-13 (Applicability of FASB Statement No. 13 to Current Value Financial Statements) (ASC 840-10-45-2 through 45-3)

BACKGROUND

Uncertainty has existed concerning the applicability of FAS-13 (Accounting for Leases) in current value financial statements.

STANDARDS

Question: Are financial statements prepared on a current value basis subject to the provisions of FAS-13?

Answer: FAS-13 is not inapplicable merely because financial statements are prepared on a current value basis. Under FAS-13, the carrying amount of a capitalized lease would be adjusted in accordance with the valuation techniques employed in the preparation of the financial statements on a current value basis.

AUTHORITATIVE GUIDANCE NOT INCLUDED SEPARATELY IN THE CODIFICATION BUT INCORPORATED IN ANOTHER PRONOUNCEMENT

FSP FAS 157-1 Application of FASB Statement No. 157 to FASB Statement No. 13 and Other Accounting Pronouncements That Address Fair Value Measurements for Purposes of Lease Classification or Measurement under Statement 13

OVERVIEW

The FASB's goal in drafting ASC 820 (FAS-157, Fair Value Measurements) was to create one definition of fair value and a framework under which fair value would be measured under generally accepted accounting principles (GAAP) so that fair value measurements would be applied consistently and result in better comparability of financial statements.

In its first exposure draft (ED) of FAS-157 (Fair Value Measurements), the FASB proposed that the Statement's guidance should *not* apply to the guidance in ASC 840 (FAS-13, Accounting for Leases) and other pronouncements that require fair value measurements for leasing transactions. The FASB was concerned that applying the fair value measurement proposed in the ED to leasing transactions may result in unintended consequences that could not be considered in the ED. However, commentators on the ED indicated that the fair value guidance for leasing transactions in ASC 840 (FAS-13) generally was not inconsistent with the guidance in the proposed Statement. As a result, the FASB did not exempt lease accounting pronouncements from the guidance in ASC 820 (FAS-157).

Nevertheless, since the issuance of FAS-157, constituents have noted situations in which the interaction between the objective of the fair value measurement guidance in FAS-13 and that in FAS-157 could cause a change in lease classifications and measurements in leasing transactions accounted for under the guidance in FAS-13, such as a change in the classification of a lease that otherwise would be accounted for as a direct financing lease.

16.14 *Fair Value*

In developing this FSP, the FASB had considered expanding the scope exception of this FSP to the required fair value measurements in FAS-144 (Accounting for Impairment or Disposal of Long-Lived Assets), FAS-146 (Accounting for Costs Associated with Exit or Disposal Activities), and fair value measurements for leases under the guidance in FIN 21 (Accounting for Leases in a Business Combination). In the final analysis, the FASB decided to limit the scope exception to FAS-13, because the issuance of this FSP was primarily motivated by the conflict between the objectives of the fair value measurements in FAS-13 and FAS-157.

The FASB decided to partially defer the effective date of FAS-157, as discussed in FSP FAS-157-2 elsewhere in this chapter, to give constituents time to resolve implementation issues for the required measurements in FAS-144, FAS-146, and for the initial fair value measurement of nonfinancial assets in a business combination. Although the definition of fair value in FAS-13 differs from that in FAS-157, the FASB believes that the accounting for leases under FAS-13 should only change as a result of a comprehensive reconsideration of the guidance in FAS-13, its amendments, and its interpretations. The FASB has such a project on its agenda, which also will address the Statement's definition of fair value.

FASB STAFF POSITION

The guidance in ASC 820 (FAS-157) does *not* apply to the application of the guidance in FAS-13 and other pronouncements that provide fair value measurement guidance for the classification or measurement of leases under FAS-13. However, this scope exception does *not* apply to assets acquired and liabilities assumed in a business combination that should be measured at fair value using the guidance in FAS-141 (Business Combinations) or FAS-141(R) (Business Combinations), regardless of whether those assets and liabilities are related to leases.

Amendments to FAS-157

FAS-157 is amended as follows: [Added text is underlined and deleted text is struck out.]

- ASC 820-10-15-1 (paragraph 2(c)) is added as follows:

    This Statement does not apply under FASB Statement No. 13, *Accounting for Leases*, and other accounting pronouncements that address fair value measurements for purposes of lease classification or measurement under Statement 13. This scope exception does not apply to assets acquired and liabilities assumed in a business combination that are required to be measured at fair value under Statement 142 or Statement 141(R), regardless of whether those assets and liabilities are related to leases.

- Appendix D-The following pronouncements have been deleted from the list of pronouncements that refer to fair value:

FAS-13 (Accounting for Leases), FAS-23 (Inception of the Lease), FAS-28 (Accounting for Sales with Leasebacks), FAS-98 (Accounting for Leases), FIN-23 (Leases of Certain Property Owned by a Governmental Unit or Authority), FIN-24 (Leases Involving Only Part of a Building), FTB 86-2 (Accounting for an Interest in the Residual Value of a Leased Asset), FTB 88-1 (Issues Relating to Accounting for Leases).

Amendments to FAS-13

ASC *Glossary* (paragraph 5(c) of FAS-13) is amended as follows:

Fair Value of the leased property. ~~The price that would be received to sell the property in an orderly transaction between market participants at the measurement date. Market participants are buyers and sellers that are independent of the reporting entity, that is, they are not related parties at the measurement date.~~ The price for which the property could be sold in an arm's length transaction between unrelated parties.

EFFECTIVE DATE AND TRANSITION

This FSP is effective when the guidance in FAS-157 is initially adopted. An entity that has applied the guidance in FAS-157 in a manner that is consistent with this FSP's provisions should continue to apply the provisions of FSP FAS-157 from the date that the guidance in FAS-157 is adopted. Entities that have not done so should retrospectively apply the provisions in this FSP to the date on which the guidance in FAS-157 was initially adopted.

RELATED CHAPTER IN 2011
GAAP GUIDE, VOLUME II

Chapter 26, "Leases"

RELATED CHAPTERS IN 2011
GAAP GUIDE, VOLUME I

Chapter 16, "Fair Value"
Chapter 29, "Leases"

RELATED CHAPTER IN 2011
INTERNATIONAL ACCOUNTING/FINANCIAL
REPORTING STANDARDS GUIDE

Chapter 9, "Changing Prices and Hyperinflationary Economies"

CHAPTER 17
FINANCIAL INSTRUMENTS

CONTENTS

Overview		**17-03**
Authoritative Guidance		
ASC 310 Receivables		**17-05**
EITF Issue 84-19	Mortgage Loan Payment Modifications	**17-05**
EITF Issue 92-5	Amortization Period for Net Deferred Credit Card Origination Costs	**17-06**
EITF Issue 93-1	Accounting for Individual Credit Card Acquisitions	**17-08**
ASC 320 Investments—Debt and Equity Securities		**17-10**
EITF Issue 96-12	Recognition of Interest Income and Balance Sheet Classification of Structured Notes	**17-10**
EITF Issue 98-15	Structured Notes Acquired for a Specified Investment Strategy	**17-15**
ASC 480 Distinguishing Liabilities from Equity		**17-17**
FSP FAS-150-1	Issuer's Accounting for Freestanding Financial Instruments Composed of More Than One Option or Forward Contract Embodying Obligations under FASB Statement No. 150, *Accounting for Certain Financial Instruments with Characteristics of both Liabilities and Equity*	**17-17**
FSP FAS-150-2	Accounting for Mandatorily Redeemable Shares Requiring Redemption by Payment of an Amount That Differs from the Book Value of Those Shares, under FASB Statement No. 150, *Accounting for Certain Financial Instruments with Characteristics of both Liabilities and Equity*	**17-19**
FSP FAS-150-3	Effective Date and Transition for Mandatorily Redeemable Financial Instruments of Certain Nonpublic Entities of FASB Statement No. 150, *Accounting for Certain Financial Instruments with Characteristics of both Liabilities and Equity*	**17-20**

FSP FAS-150-5	Issuer's Accounting under FASB Statement No. 150 for Freestanding Warrants and Other Similar Instruments on Shares That Are Redeemable	17-23
EITF Issue 00-4	Majority Owner's Accounting for a Transaction in the Shares of a Consolidated Subsidiary and a Derivative Indexed to the Noncontrolling Interest in That Subsidiary	17-24
Topic D-98	Classification and Measurement of Redeemable Securities	17-27
ASC 815	Derivatives and Hedging	17-36
FSP FAS-133-1/ FIN-45-4	Disclosures about Credit Derivatives and Certain Guarantees: An Amendment of FASB Statement No. 133 and FASB Interpretation No. 45; and Clarification of the Effective Date of FASB Statement No. 161	17-36
EITF Issue 99-2	Accounting for Weather Derivatives	17-39
EITF Issue 99-9	Effect of Derivative Gains and Losses on the Capitalization of Interest	17-42
EITF Issue 00-19	Accounting for Derivative Financial Instruments Indexed to, and Potentially Settled in, a Company's Own Stock	17-43
EITF Issue 02-3	Issues Involved in Accounting for Derivative Contracts Held for Trading Purposes and Contracts Involved in Energy Trading and Risk Management Activities	17-65
EITF Issue 03-11	Reporting Realized Gains and Losses on Derivative Instruments That Are Subject to FASB Statement No. 133, *Accounting for Derivative Instruments and Hedging Activities*, and Not "Held for Trading Purposes" as Defined in EITF Issue No. 02-3, "Issues Involved in Accounting for Derivative Contracts Held for Trading Purposes and Contracts Involved in Energy Trading and Risk Management Activities"	17-68
EITF Issue 07-5	Determining Whether an Instrument (or Embedded Features) Is Indexed to an Entity's Own Stock	17-69

Topic D-102	Documentation of Methods Used to Measure Hedge Ineffectiveness under FASB Statement No. 133	17-75
Topic D-109	Determining the Nature of a Host Contract Related to a Hybrid Financial Instrument Issued in the Form of a Share under FASB Statement No. 133	17-76
ASC 825	Financial Instruments	17-77
FSP Issue 00-19-2	Accounting for Registration Payment Arrangements	17-77
ASC 835	Interest	17-81
Topic D-10	Required Use of Interest Method in Recognizing Interest Income	17-81
ASC 860	Transfers and Servicing	17-82
EITF Issue 86-8	Sale of Bad-Debt Recovery Rights	17-82
ASC 942	Financial Services—Depository and Lending	17-83
AcSEC Practice Bulletin-4	Accounting for Foreign Debt/Equity Swaps	17-83
Authoritative Guidance Not Included Separately in the Codification But Incorporated in Another Pronouncement		17-85
FSP FAS-126-1	Applicability of Certain Disclosure and Interim Reporting Requirements for Obligors for Conduit Debt Securities	17-85
FSP FIN-39-1	Amendment of FASB Interpretation No. 39	17-90
Related Chapters in 2011 GAAP Guide Volume II		17-93
Related Chapters in 2011 GAAP Guide Volume I		17-94
Related Chapter in 2011 International Accounting/Financial Reporting Standards Guide		17-94

OVERVIEW

The FASB is involved in a long-term project intended to improve GAAP for financial instruments. Because of the complexity of the issues surrounding financial instruments, the project has been separated into several phases. The project's final output is expected to be broad standards that will assist in resolving financial reporting and

17.04 *Financial Instruments*

other issues about various financial instruments and other related transactions.

The guidance in the following pronouncements, which address the accounting for financial instruments, is discussed in the 2011 *GAAP Guide, Volume I*, Chapter 17, "Financial Instruments."

ASC 825	Disclosures about Fair Value of Financial Instruments (FAS-107)
ASC 825	Exemption from Certain Required Disclosures about Financial Instruments for Certain Nonpublic Entities (FAS-126)
ASC 815	Accounting for Derivative Instruments and Hedging Activities (FAS-133)
ASC 815	Accounting for Certain Derivative Instruments and Certain Hedging Activities (FAS-138)
ASC 815	Accounting for Certain Hybrid Financial Instruments—An Amendment of FASB Statement No. 133 and 140 (FAS-155)
ASC 820	Fair Value Measurements (FAS-157)
ASC 825	The Fair Value Option for Financial Assets and Financial Liabilities—Including an Amendment of FASB Statement No. 115 (FAS-159)
ASC 815; 210	Offsetting of Amounts Related to Certain Contracts (FIN-39)
ASC 210	Offsetting of Amounts Related to Certain Repurchase and Reverse Repurchase Agreements (FIN-41)
ASC 460	Guarantor's Accounting and Disclosure Requirements for Guarantees, Including Indirect Guarantees of Indebtedness of Others (FIN-45)

AUTHORITATIVE GUIDANCE

ASC 310—RECEIVABLES

ETIF Issue 84-19 (Mortgage Loan Payment Modifications) (ASC 310-20-35-13)

OVERVIEW

A mortgagor has five years of payments left on a mortgage. The mortgagor and the lender enter into an agreement, which provides that if the mortgagor increases each of 12 consecutive payments by, for example, 50%, the lender will reduce the remaining principal by a certain percentage. The mortgagor can discontinue the arrangement at any time but will not receive the discount on the principal if fewer than 12 payments were made at the increased amount.

ACCOUNTING ISSUE

The following alternatives were suggested for the lender's accounting for the amount of principal that is forgiven:

- Discount the increased payments using the current interest rate, and recognize a loss based on the assumption that the mortgagor will make increased payments to the maturity of the loan.
- Discount all payments using the current interest rate, and recognize a smaller loss based on the assumption that the mortgagor will make only 12 consecutive increased payments; the remainder of the payments to maturity will be made at the regular amount.
- Recognize the discount on the principal as a loss when the mortgagor has made the required payments.
- Accrue the discount on the principal as a loss pro rata over the 12-month period of increased payments.

EITF CONSENSUS

An expense related to a partial forgiveness should be accrued over a period of increased payments, if it is probable that the borrower will continue making increased payments over the specified period. The Task Force noted that this approach already is used in practice.

DISCUSSION

This transaction differs from the usual loan modification in which a lender modifies the terms of a loan by changing the interest rate or by reducing the principal payable on the loan because the borrower is unable to pay. Rather, in this Issue, for reasons that were not indicated, the mortgagor increases the amount of payments made for 12 consecutive months. The Task Force did not, therefore, treat this situation as a troubled debt restructuring.

EITF Issue 92-5 (Amortization Period for Net Deferred Credit Card Origination Costs) (ASC 310-20-05-3 through 35-4, 6;50-4)

OVERVIEW

A credit card issuer normally charges annual fees to its cardholders. Sometimes, as part of a promotion designed to attract new customers, the issuer waives the annual fee or charges no fee. The issuer incurs certain direct costs of issuing credit cards. In addition, the credit card agreement entered into as part of the promotion generally provides the cardholder with an extended period to repay the outstanding balance on the credit card in the event of cancellation or nonrenewal. If a cardholder does not renew the card after a one-year period, for example, the agreement may allow the cardholder to repay the outstanding balance over an additional period, such as two or three years.

ASC 310 (FAS-91) provides guidance in this area but does not specifically address the amortization of costs associated with credit card originations. The Statement requires that direct loan origination costs be offset against origination fees, with the net amount deferred and recognized as an adjustment to the loan yield.

The Issue applies to the amortization of deferred origination costs on credit cards with fees, without fees, or if fees have been waived for a limited period of time. It does not apply, however, to origination costs for private label credit cards, which are issued by, or on behalf of, an entity for purchases only of that entity's goods or services.

ACCOUNTING ISSUE

Over what period of time should direct credit card origination costs be amortized when the credit card arrangement provides for no fees?

EITF CONSENSUS

- Based on the definition of *Direct Loan Origination Costs* in the ASC *Master Glossary* (paragraph 6 of FAS-91, *Accounting for Nonrefundable Fees and Costs Associated with Originating or Acquiring Loans and Initial Direct Costs of Leases*), a credit card issuer should net credit card origination costs that qualify for deferral against the related credit card fee, if any, and should amortize the net amount on a straight-line basis over the privilege period. If a significant fee is charged, the privilege period is the period over which the cardholder is entitled to use the card. If no significant fee is charged, the privilege period is one year. The significance of the fee should be evaluated based on the relationship of the fee and related costs.

- An entity should disclose its accounting policy, the net amount capitalized at the balance sheet date, and the amortization period of credit card fees and costs for purchased and originated cards.

This Issue applies only to originated credit card accounts, not accounts purchased from third parties. The amortization of a premium, if any, paid on purchases of credit card portfolios is discussed in ASC 310-10-25-7 and 35-52 (EITF Issue 88-20). Some Task Force members questioned whether the consensus in this Issue or the consensus in Issue 88-20 should be used to account for the acquisition of an individual credit card from a third-party originator. The Task Force agreed to discuss that matter as a separate Issue.

SUBSEQUENT DEVELOPMENT

In its discussion of the guidance in ASC 310-20-05-4; 25-18; and 35-8 (Issue 93-1), the Task Force reached a consensus that credit card accounts acquired individually should be accounted for as originations under the guidance in ASC 310 (FAS-91) and ASC 310-20-05-3; 35-4, 35-6; and 50-4 (Issue 92-5) .

DISCUSSION

Three approaches for amortization of direct loan origination costs were proposed: (*a*) over the privilege period, or one year; (*b*) over the repayment period, which may extend beyond the privilege period; or (*c*) over the relationship period, which includes renewal periods.

The FASB staff, who believed that the costs are related to lending activities, noted that according to paragraph 51 of FAS-91 (not in ASC), "a credit card fee represents a payment by the cardholder to obtain the ability to borrow from the lender under predefined conditions."

The Task Force's consensus is based on the first approach. It is consistent with the guidance in ASC 310-20-25-15; 310-20-35-5 (paragraph 10 of FAS-91), which states that "fees that are periodically charged to cardholders shall be deferred and recognized on a straight-line basis over the period the fee entitles the cardholder to use the card." It is also consistent with question 31 of the FASB Special Report, *A Guide to Implementation of Statement 91 on Account-*

ing for Nonrefundable Fees and Costs Associated with Originating or Acquiring Loans and Initial Direct Costs of Leases*, in which the FASB staff repeated the guidance in ASC 310-20-25-15; 310-20-35-5 (paragraph 10 of FAS-91) and stated further that "[r]elated origination costs eligible for deferral should be amortized over the same period on a straight-line basis." Proponents of this approach argued that credit card fees and related costs should be netted and amortized over the same period. Additional arguments for amortization of initiation costs over the privilege period included the fact that this approach is simple, conservative, and it enhances comparability among credit card issuers.

EITF Issue 93-1 (Accounting for Individual Credit Card Acquisitions) (ASC 310-20-05-4; 25-18; 35-8)

OVERVIEW

A credit card issuer can obtain new customer accounts by (*a*) purchasing a portfolio of existing credit card accounts, (*b*) originating the credit card relationship, or (*c*) purchasing individual credit card accounts through a third party. The accounts normally have no outstanding receivable balances at acquisition. (The EITF previously addressed the accounting for the cost associated with a bulk purchase of a credit card portfolio in ASC 310-10-25-7 and 35-52 (EITF Issue 88-20) and internal credit card origination in ASC 310-20-05-3; 35-4, 35-6; and 50-4 (EITF Issue 92-5). Neither Issue provided guidance for situations in which credit card accounts are purchased individually.)

Individual credit card accounts can be obtained three ways:

1. *Direct marketing specialist* The credit card issuer hires a marketing company to solicit new credit card customers and usually pays the specialist a fee for each approved credit card agreement.
2. *Affinity group* The credit card issuer enters into an arrangement with a company or an organization to solicit credit card accounts from their customers or members. This third-party entity is responsible for the solicitation and related costs and sells the approved credit card accounts to the issuer for a fee.
3. *Co-branding* Co-branding is a variation of an affinity group, in which the name of the third party is included on the credit card. The co-branding third party provides additional products and services, such as extended warranties and discounts. In this type of arrangement, the credit card issuer and the third party benefit from increased card usage, an extended cardholder relationship period, and increased sales of the third party's products or services. Whatever the method of acquisition, the credit card issuer incurs a cost in obtaining new accounts.

ACCOUNTING ISSUE

Should a credit card issuer account for acquisitions of individual credit card accounts as purchases in accordance with the guidance in APB-17 and EITF ASC 310-10-25-7 and 35-52 (Issue 88-20), or as self-originations, in accordance with the guidance in ASC 310 (FAS-91) and ASC 310-20-05-3; 35-4, 35-6; and 50-4 (Issue 92-5)?

EITF CONSENSUS

The Task Force reached a consensus that a credit card issuer should:

- Account for credit card accounts acquired individually as originations, in accordance with the guidance in ASC 310 (FAS-91) and ASC 310-20-05-3; 35-4, 35-6; and 50-4 (Issue 92-5).
- Defer amounts paid to third parties to acquire individual credit card accounts, net those amounts against any related credit card fees, and amortize the net amount on a straight-line basis over the privilege period.

The privilege period is the period during which the cardholder is entitled to use the card, if the credit cardholder is charged a significant fee. The privilege period is one year, if there is no significant fee. The significance of the fee is based on the relationship of its amount to the card's acquisition cost.

DISCUSSION

In its deliberations, the Task Force considered alternative methods of accounting for purchases of individual credit card accounts and discussed different criteria to distinguish purchases from self-originations. The Task Force finally adopted the view that all individual credit card account acquisitions should be treated as self-originations; thus, the related costs should be deferred and accounted for in accordance with FAS-91 and EITF Issue 92-5.

Proponents of this view noted that the definition of *Direct Loan Origination Costs* in the ASC, *Master Glossary* (paragraph 6 of FAS-91) addresses this third-party activity as follows: "Direct loan origination costs of a completed loan shall include only (*a*) incremental direct costs of loan origination incurred in transactions with independent third parties for that loan and (*b*) certain costs directly related to specified activities performed by the lender for that loan." Further, it was noted that the third-party relationship in this situation is merely a marketing tool in which the credit card issuer is outsourcing its solicitation and origination activities. The risks and costs are still borne, however, by the credit card issuer. Proponents supported their contention that these credit card accounts are self-originations rather than purchases by arguing that the third party only solicits accounts and acts as an agent for the issuer, and the customer cannot use the credit card until it is issued by the issuer. They also argued that purchases of individual credit card accounts are unlike bulk purchases of existing credit card accounts that may have outstanding balances. In the latter transactions, the credit card issuer must accept the account and issue a credit card.

ASC 320 INVESTMENTS—DEBT AND EQUITY SECURITIES

EITF Issue 96-12 (Recognition of Interest Income and Balance Sheet Classification of Structured Notes) (ASC 320-10-35-38 through 35-43; 55-10 through 55-12, 55-16 through 55-19; 835-10-60-6)

OVERVIEW

The guidance in ASC 320 (FAS-115, *Accounting for Certain Investments in Debt and Equity Securities*) on accounting for debt securities also applies to *structured notes,* which are debt instruments whose cash flows are linked to the movement in one or more indices, interest rates, foreign exchange rates, commodities prices, prepayment rates, or other market variables. Such instruments are issued by enterprises sponsored by the U.S. government, multilateral development banks, municipalities, and private corporations. Interest payments on structured notes may be based on formulas related to the investor's preference for risk and return, and principal payments may be indexed to movements in an underlying market. Structured notes normally include forward or option components, such as caps, calls, and floors, which are not separable or detachable. Consequently, investors that use structured notes to manage financial risks and enhance yield often prefer those debt instruments for administrative reasons over debt securities with fixed interest rates, which may require entering into separate derivatives.

In general, interest income on structured notes is comprised of a stated or coupon interest, acquisition premium or discount amortization, if any, and possible adjustments of the principal based on an index or formula. Because GAAP provide no guidance on interest income recognition for structured notes, some have analogized to the guidance in EITF Issue 86-28 (not in ASC), Issue 89-4 (not in ASC), and ASC 310 (FAS-91).

The following is a list of some common forms of structured notes that are within the scope of this Issue:

- *Index amortizing notes* Principal is repaid based on a predetermined amortization schedule, which is linked to movements in a specific mortgage-backed security or index. Although the investor receives the total principal by the maturity date, it is uncertain when principal payments will be received, because the note's maturity is extended in relation to increasing market interest rates or decreasing prepayment rates. An above-market interest rate is paid on such notes.

- *Inverse floating-rate notes* The coupon rate on such notes changes in an inverse relationship to a specified interest rate level or index.
- *Range bonds* The interest rate on such bonds depends on the number of days a reference rate is between predetermined levels at issuance. No interest or a below-market interest rate is earned when the reference rate is not within the range.
- *Dual index notes* The coupon rate on these notes often is fixed for a short period (the first year) and becomes variable for a longer period. It generally is determined by the spread between two market indices, usually the Constant Maturity Treasury rate and LIBOR.
- *Inflation bonds* The bond's contractual principal is indexed to the inflation rate and its coupon rate is below that for traditional bonds with similar maturity.
- *Equity-linked bear notes* These notes have a fixed coupon rate that is lower than traditional debt. Their principal is guaranteed but may exceed the initial investment based on a decrease in the S&P index.

ACCOUNTING ISSUES

- How should investors in structured notes estimate cash flows that will be received?
- How should changes in cash flow estimates be recognized and measured in interest income?
- Is a held-to-maturity classification permitted for investments in structured notes under the provisions of ASC 320 (FAS-115)?

EITF CONSENSUS

The EITF reached the following consensus positions based on the working group's recommendations:

- Income on structured note securities that are classified as debt securities under the available-for-sale or held-to-maturity categories of ASC 310 (FAS-115) should be measured using the *retrospective interest method.*

Income for a reporting period is measured under the retrospective interest method as the sum of (1) the difference between a security's amortized cost at the end of the period and its amortized cost at the beginning of the period and (2) cash received during the period. A security's amortized cost is based on the present value of estimated future cash flows at an effective yield (the internal rate of return) that equates all past actual and current estimated cash flow streams to the initial investment. If the sum of newly estimated undiscounted cash flows is less than the security's amortized cost, the effective yield is negative. In that case, a zero effective yield is used to compute amortized cost.

All estimates of future cash flows used to determine the effective yield for income recognition under the retrospective interest method either should be based on quoted forward market rates or prices in active markets, if available or should be based on spot rates or prices as of the reporting date if market-based prices are unavailable.

The impairment guidance in ASC 320 (FAS-115) continues to apply to *host contracts* from which embedded derivatives have been separated based on the guidance in ASC 310-20-35-9, 35-10 (paragraphs 12 and 13 of FAS-133) and should be accounted for at fair value.

- Structured notes for which income is recognized using the retrospective method must meet at least one of the following conditions:
  — The note's contractual principal that will be paid at maturity or the original investment is at risk (other than due to a borrower's failure to pay the contractual amounts due). Principal-indexed notes whose principal repayment is based on movements in the S&P 500 index or notes whose principal repayment is linked to certain events or circumstances are examples of these instruments.
  — The note's return on investment varies (other than due to changes in a borrower's credit rating) because either:
    (1) The coupon rate is not stated or a stated coupon rate is not fixed or pre-specified, *and* the variation in coupon rate or the return on investment is not a constant percentage of, or does not move in the same direction as, changes in market-based interest rates or interest rate indices, such as LIBOR or the Treasury Bill Index, or
    (2) A variable or fixed coupon rate is below market interest rates for traditional notes with comparable maturities and a portion of the potential yield depends on the occurrence of future events or circumstances. Inverse floating-rate notes, dual index notes, and equity-linked bear notes are examples of these instruments.
  — The note's contractual maturity is based on a specific index or on the occurrence of specific events or circumstances that cannot be controlled by the parties to the transaction, except for the passage of time or events that cause normal covenant violations. Index amortizing notes and notes whose contractual maturity is based on the price of oil are examples of these instruments.

- The following financial instruments are *not* within the scope of the consensus in this Issue:

  — Mortgage loans or similar debt instruments that are not securities under ASC 320 (FAS-115); traditional bonds convertible into the issuer's stock; multicurrency debt securities; debt securities classified as trading; nonequity high-risk collateralized mortgage obligations and mortgage-backed securities under the scope of Issue 89-4 (not in ASC) and Issue 93-18 (not in ASC); debt securities that participate directly in an issuer's operations, such as participating mortgages; and reverse mortgages.

  — Structured notes that are accounted for as trading securities under ASC 320 (FAS-115), because based on their terms it is reasonably possible that an investor could lose all or substantially all of the investment (other than if a borrower fails to pay all amounts due).

- Entities should determine, based on the provisions of ASC 320 (FAS-115), whether the value of an individual structured note has experienced an other-than-temporary decline below amortized cost and should include the change in earnings.

The Task Force noted that after recognizing an other-than-temporary impairment on a structured note, the entity should consider its collectibility in estimating future cash flows for the purpose of determining the effective yield used in the retrospective interest method calculation of income to be recognized on the note. That is, the entity would no longer assume that the contractual interest and the note's principal would be repaid. For example, if an investor has recognized a $30 other-than-temporary loss on a $100 investment whose fair value has decreased to $70, and the investor expects to collect no more than $80 of the principal at maturity, only $80 of principal should be used in estimating future cash flows for the effective yield calculation.

EFFECT OF ASC 815 (FAS-133)

The impairment guidance in ASC 320 (FAS-115) continues to apply to *host contracts* from which embedded derivatives have been separated based on the guidance in ASC 815-15-25-1, 25-14, 25-26 through 25-29 (paragraphs 12 and 13 of FAS-133) and should be accounted for at fair value.

The consensus on the second Issue is partially nullified by ASC 815 (FAS-133), which requires the separation of certain embedded derivatives from the host contract under the conditions discussed in ASC 815-15-25-1 (paragraph 12 of FAS-133). Those derivatives should be accounted for at fair value under the guidance in ASC 815 (FAS-133). Although they may not be designated as hedging instruments, contracts with embedded derivatives that cannot be reliably identified for separation from their host contracts should be measured at fair value in their entirety. However, the guidance in this Issue (Issue 96-12) should continue to apply to (1) embedded derivatives that are *not* required to be separated under paragraph 12 or the Statement's transition provisions and (2) host contracts that meet any of the three conditions in the first consensus even though their embedded derivatives have been separated under the guidance in ASC 815 (FAS-133). The calculation of the effective yield is not addressed in the Statement.

SUBSEQUENT DEVELOPMENT

In its discussion of the guidance in ASC 310-20-60-1, 60-2; 30-15-5; 320-10-35-38; 55-2; 325-40-05-1, 05-2; 15-2 through 15-9; 25-1 through 25-3; 30-1 through 30-3; 35-1 through 35-13, 35-15, 35-16; 45-1; 55-1 through 55-25; 60-7 (Issue 99-20) (see Chapter 40) at the July 2000 EITF meeting, the Task Force agreed that the guidance in this Issue (Issue 96-12) should apply to the recognition of interest income from beneficial interests in a securitization structure that holds common stocks, because the guidance in ASC 310-20-60-1, 2; 30-15-5; 320-10-35-38; 55-2; 325-40-05-1, 05-2; 15-2 through 15-9; 25-1 through 25-3; 30-1 through 30-3; 35-1 through 35-13, 35-15, 35-16; 45-1; 55-1 through 55-25; 60-7 (Issue 99-20) applies only to securitized financial assets with contractual cash flows, for example, loans, receivables, and guaranteed lease residuals.

DISCUSSION

- The retrospective method is based on the interest method discussed in ASC 310-20-35-26 (paragraph 19 of FAS-91). The working group recommended this method for calculating income on structured notes, whose contractual cash flows are volatile, because it recognizes the effects of differences between actual cash flows and previously estimated cash flows in *each* reporting period. They believed that the volatility in income caused by this method represents the inherent risks of investing in structured notes.

    The effective yield, which initially is calculated for the life of the instrument, is recalculated either from the date of acquisition of the structured note or from the most recent date on which an impairment was recognized under ASC 320 (FAS-115), if actual cash flows at a reporting date are different from anticipated amounts or if estimates for anticipated future cash flows have been revised. The structured note's amortized cost is recalculated based on the newly calculated effective yield—just as if that yield had been used from inception. The change in amortized cost is reported in that period's earnings.

    If the recalculated effective yield is less than zero—because actual past and anticipated future earnings will be insufficient to recover the initial net investment—a *temporary* loss is recognized and an allowance is established. Additional losses or recoveries of previous losses in future periods are charged or credited to the allowance. The allowance should not be reduced to a negative amount, however. It is reduced, but not below zero, for an other-than-temporary impairment loss, and a new cost basis is established.

Under the consensus, a structured note's amortized cost is written down to fair value if an impairment is other than temporary, in accordance with the provisions of ASC 320 (FAS-115). The amount of the writedown is recognized in earnings, except for amounts previously recognized in the allowance. Subsequent recoveries in fair value are not recognized.

- The Issue's scope limitations were influenced by the SEC Observer's concerns that some might apply the recommended treatment to financial instruments that should be accounted for as trading securities—whose changes in fair value are recognized in income. Structured notes that are similar or identical to variable debt instruments accounted for under FAS-91 are outside this Issue's scope.

EITF Issue 98-15 (Structured Notes Acquired for a Specified Investment Strategy) (ASC 320-10-25-19 through 25-20; 40-3; 55-14 through 55-15, 55-21)

OVERVIEW

Structured notes are securities that are issued combined with other structured note securities as a unit or a pair to accomplish a strategic investment result for an investor. Under one strategy, two structured notes with opposite reset positions are purchased. (For example, one month after issuance, the interest rate on Bond A resets from 8% to 1% if ten-year Treasury bond rates decreased by one basis point since the Bond's issuance or to 15% if Treasury rates increased by one basis point. The interest rate on Bond B would reset in the opposite direction.) Each structured note's coupon rate or maturity date is determined shortly after issuance based on the movement of market rates. Although the yields on the two structured notes move in opposite directions after the reset date, the average yield of the two securities generally represents the market yield of the combined instruments at issuance.

ACCOUNTING ISSUE

Should an investor account separately for each structured note security or account for the two securities as a unit?

EITF CONSENSUS

An investor who purchases structured notes for a specific investment strategy should account for the two structured notes as a unit until one of the securities is sold. Thereafter, the remaining security would be accounted for in accordance with the guidance in Accounting Standards Update No. 2009-16 (*Transfer sand Servicing, Topic 860, Accounting for Transfers of Financial Assets*).

In making a judgment as to whether the securities were purchased for a specified investment strategy (not all the indicators are required for the securities to be accounted for under the consensus), the Task Force stated that the following indicators should be used:

1. The securities are related because their fair values will move in opposite directions in response to changes in interest rates on a specified date or after a specified period following issuance. Their fair values may change because of changes in their coupon interest rates or changes in their maturities.
2. The securities are issued simultaneously or they are issued separately but the terms for their remaining lives are as discussed in (1) above.
3. The securities are issued by the same counterparty and/or the same issuer. They may also be issued by different issuers but are structured through an intermediary.
4. The investor's *only* reason for purchasing the two securities is to achieve a specific accounting result, because there would be no valid business purpose for entering into the transactions individually. The investor would not purchase the securities otherwise.

The Task Force noted that the substance of the investment strategy in these transactions is that the investor has purchased one market-based security that results in no gain or loss when the interest rate resets and should be accounted for as such. However, the unit's fair value may change as a result of a change in credit ratings or a change in market rates.

> **OBSERVATION:** ASC 860 (FAS-166), which was issued in 2009, amends the requirements in FAS-140 to require that the guidance in ASC 860-20-30-1 (paragraph 11 of FAS-140), as amended by FAS-166, be followed in accounting for transfers of structured notes that meet the conditions for sale accounting in FAS-140.

SEC OBSERVER COMMENT

The SEC Observer stated that registrants who entered into structured note transactions on or before September 24, 1998, and have not accounted for them as a unit (as required under the consensus) or as trading securities could restate their financial statements to adopt the consensus. If the instruments had been accounted for as a unit, the registrants could disclose in all financial statements issued after September 24, 1998, the effect on income for all periods presented and cumulatively over the life of the instruments. The SEC staff's presumption is that the effect on earnings is de facto material.

ASC 480 DISTINGUISHING LIABILITIES FROM EQUITY

FSP FAS-150-1 (Issuer's Accounting for Freestanding Financial Instruments Composed of More Than One Option or Forward Contract Embodying Obligations under FASB Statement No. 150, *Accounting for Certain Financial Instruments with Characteristics of both Liabilities and Equity*) (ASC 480-10-55-29 through 55-32, 40-42 through 40-52)

Question 1: How does ASC 480-10-25-8 through 25-12 (paragraph 11 of FAS-150) apply to freestanding financial instruments composed of more than one option or forward contract embodying obligations that require or that may require settlement by transfer of assets? An example of this type of financial instrument is a puttable warrant that allows the holder to purchase a fixed number of the issuer's shares at a fixed price that also is puttable by the holder at a specified date for a fixed monetary amount that the holder could require the issuer to pay.

Answer: ASC 480-10-15-3, 15-4 (paragraph 13 of FAS-150) states that the provisions of the statement apply to freestanding financial instruments, including those that are composed of more than one option or forward contract. The guidance in ASC 480-10-25-4 through 25-14 (paragraphs 9 through 12 of FAS-150) applies to a freestanding financial instrument in its entirety. Under the guidance in ASC 480-10-25-8 through 25-12 (paragraph 11 of FAS-150), if a freestanding instrument is composed of a written call option and a written put option, the existence of the call option does not affect the classification. Thus, the puttable warrant is a liability because it includes an obligation indexed to an obligation to repurchase the issuer's shares and may require a transfer of assets. It is a liability even if the repurchase feature is conditional on a defined contingency in addition to the level of the issuer's share price. The warrant is *not* an outstanding share and does *not* meet the exception for outstanding shares in ASC 480-10-25-8 through 25-12 (paragraph 11 of FAS-150) and, unlike the application of ASC 480-10-25-14 (paragraph 12 of FAS-150) does *not* involve making any judgments about whether it is predominant among the entity's obligations or contingencies.

For example, Company X issues a puttable warrant to Investor Y. The warrant allows Investor Y to purchase one equity share at a strike price of $10 on a specified date. The put feature allows Investor Y to put the warrant back to Company X on that date for $2 and to require settlement in cash. If the share price on the settlement date exceeds $12, Investor Y would be expected to exercise the warrant, obligating Company X to issue a fixed number of shares in exchange for a fixed amount of cash. That feature of the financial instrument does *not* result in a liability. However, if the share price is equal to or less than $12, Investor Y would be expected to put the warrant back to Company X and could choose to obligate Company X to pay $2 in cash. That feature does result in a liability, because the financial instrument includes an obligation that is indexed to an obligation to repurchase the issuer's shares and may require a transfer of assets. Therefore, under the guidance ASC 480-10-25-8 through 25-12 (paragraph 11 of FAS-150) Company X would be required to classify the financial instrument as a liability.

Question 2: How does the guidance in ASC 480-10-25-14 (paragraph 12 of FAS-150) apply to freestanding financial instruments composed of more than one option or forward contract that include obligations? For example, a puttable warrant that allows the holder to purchase a fixed number of the issuer's shares at a fixed price that also is puttable by the holder at a specified date for a fixed monetary amount to be paid, at the issuer's discretion, in cash or in a variable number of shares. Does such a financial instrument include an obligation for the issuer that is a liability in accordance with the guidance in ASC 480 (FAS-150)?

Answer: The answer depends on the circumstances. A financial instrument that is composed of more than one option or forward contract including obligations to issue shares must be analyzed to determine whether the obligations under any of the instrument's components have one of the characteristics discussed in ASC 480-10-25-14 (paragraph 12 of FAS-150) and, if so, whether those obligations are predominant relative to other obligations. The analysis involves two steps.

Step 1: Identify any component obligations that, if freestanding, would be liabilities under the guidance in ASC 480-10-25-14 (paragraph 12 of FAS-150) and, also, identify other component obligations of the financial instrument.

Step 2: Assess whether the monetary value of any freestanding components are collectively predominant over the collective monetary value of any other component obligations. If so, the entire financial instrument is accounted for under the guidance in ASC 480-10-25-

14 (paragraph 12). If not, the financial instrument is not included under the scope of ASC 480 (FAS-150).

For example, Company X issues a puttable warrant to Investor Y. The warrant allows Investor Y to purchase one equity share at a strike price of $10 at a specified date. The put feature allows Investor Y to put the warrant back to Company X on that date at $2, and can be settled in fractional shares. If the share price on the settlement date exceeds $12, Investor Y would be expected to exercise the warrant and obligate Company X to issue a fixed number of shares in exchange for a fixed amount of cash. The monetary value of the shares varies directly with changes in the share price above $12. If the share price is equal to or less than $12, Investor Y would most likely put the warrant back to Company X, obligating it to issue a variable number of shares with a fixed monetary value (known at inception) of $2. Thus, at inception, the number of shares that the puttable warrant obligates Company X to issue can vary, and the financial instrument must be examined as described previously. The facts and circumstances are used to make a judgment whether the monetary value of the obligation to issue a number of shares that varies is predominantly based on a fixed monetary amount that is known at inception and, if so, it is a liability under the guidance in ASC 480-10-25-14 (paragraph 12(c) of FAS-150).

In the previous example, if Company X's share price is well below the $10 exercise price of the warrant at inception, the warrant has a short life, and Company X's stock is determined to have low volatility, the circumstances would suggest that the monetary value of the obligation to issue shares is based predominantly on a fixed monetary amount known at inception and the instrument should be classified as a liability.

FSP FAS-150-2 (Accounting for Mandatorily Redeemable Shares Requiring Redemption by Payment of an Amount That Differs from the Book Value of Those Shares, under FASB Statement No. 150, *Accounting for Certain Financial Instruments with Characteristics of both Liabilities and Equity*) (ASC 480-10-45-2A through 45-2B)

Question: Some companies have outstanding shares, all of which are subject to mandatory redemption on the occurrence of events that are certain to occur. Assume that on the date of adoption, the redemption price of the shares is more than the book value of those shares. On the date of adoption, the company would recognize a liability for the redemption price of the shares that are subject to mandatory redemption, reclassifying the amounts previously classified as equity. Any difference between the redemption price on the date of adoption and the amounts previously recognized in equity is reported in income as a cumulative effect transition adjustment loss. The redemption price may be a fixed amount or may vary based on specified conditions. How should the cumulative transition adjustment and subsequent adjustment to reflect changes in the redemption price of the shares be reported if they exceed the company's equity balance?

Answer: The cumulative adjustment amount and any subsequent adjustments to it should be reported as an excess of liabilities over assets (i.e., as a deficit). If the redemption price of the mandatorily redeemable shares is less than the book value of those shares, the excess of that book value over the liability reported for the mandatorily redeemable shares should be reported as an excess of assets over liability (i.e., as equity).

For example, assume that Company X adopts the guidance in ASC 480 (FAS-150) when both the fair value and redemption value of the mandatorily redeemable shares is $20 million and the book value of those shares is $15 million of which $10 million is paid-in capital. On the date that guidance is adopted, the company would recognize a liability of $20 million by transferring $15 million from equity and recognizing a cumulative transition adjustment loss of $5 million. Assume further that net income attributable to the mandatorily redeemable share is $1 million for the year and the fair value of the shares at the end of the year is $21.2 million. No cash dividends are paid. The following is the presentation in the statement of financial position at the end of the year, assuming assets of $26 million and other liabilities of $10 million (all numbers in millions):

Assets	$26,000
Liabilities other than shares	$10,000
Shares subject to mandatory redemption	21,200
Total liabilities	$31,200
Excess of liabilities over assets	(5,200)
Total	$26,000

FSP FAS-150-3 (Effective Date and Transition for Mandatorily Redeemable Financial Instruments of Certain Nonpublic Entities of FASB Statement No. 150, *Accounting for Certain Financial Instruments with Characteristics of both Liabilities and Equity*) (ASC 480-10-65-1)

The FASB directed the staff to issue this FSP to defer the effective date of ASC 480 (FAS-150, *Accounting for Certain Financial Instruments with Characteristics of both Liabilities and Equity*) as it applies to:

- Mandatorily redeemable financial instruments of certain nonpublic entities.
- Certain mandatorily redeemable *noncontrolling* interests.

The FASB also directed the staff to provide guidance on disclosure and transition for those entities.

OVERVIEW

ASC 480 (FAS-150) states that it is effective for mandatorily redeemable financial instruments of nonpublic entities in the first fiscal period beginning after December 15, 2003. Under the guidance in ASC 480-10-25-4, 25-6 (Paragraph 9 of FAS-150) liability classification of mandatorily redeemable financial instruments is required "unless the redemption is required to occur only upon the liquidation or termination of the reporting entity." However, that exception does *not* apply when a subsidiary's financial statements are consolidated with those of its parent. Many entities were concerned about the effect of liability classification and asked that this requirement be changed or delayed in order to give companies time to adapt to the provisions of ASC 480 (FAS-150) and to educate users of their financial statements. Other entities were concerned about whether step acquisition accounting should be applied when mandatorily redeemable *noncontrolling* interests acquired in a purchase business combination are reclassified as liabilities or when they are redeemed. Still others requested a change or delay in the effective date of ASC 480 (FAS-150) because of concern that some implementation issues have not been resolved in time for the adoption of the guidance in ASC 480 (FAS-150) while financial reports are being completed.

FASB STAFF POSITION

- For *nonpublic* entities that are *not* SEC registrants, that is, entities that (*a*) have *not* or will *not* issue debt or equity securities traded in a public market, (*b*) are *not* required to file financial statements with the SEC, or (*c*) do *not* provide financial statements for the purpose of issuing any class of securities in a public market, the guidance in ASC 480 (FAS-150) is effective as follows:
  - *Instruments mandatorily redeemable on fixed dates for fixed amounts or determined by reference to an interest rate index, currency index, or another external index* The classification, measurement, and disclosure provisions of FAS-150 are effective for fiscal periods beginning after December 15, 2004.
  - *All other mandatorily redeemable financial instruments* The classification, measurement, and disclosure provisions of ASC 480 (FAS-150) are deferred *indefinitely* for those instruments until the FASB takes action. During that period, the FASB will reconsider the implementation issues and possibly reconsider the classification and measurement guidance for those instruments concurrently with its ongoing project on liabilities and equity.

Those deferrals do *not* apply to mandatorily redeemable financial instruments issued by SEC registrants, even if they meet the definition for a nonpublic entity in ASC 480 (FAS-150). Registrants should follow the Statement's effective dates and related guidance, which includes the deferral for certain mandatorily *noncontrolling* interests, as applicable.

If an entity is a *nonpublic* entity and *not* an SEC registrant, the deferral in this FSP *does* apply to shares required to be redeemed under related agreements that are issued with a redemption agreement for specific underlying shares that are consequently mandatorily redeemable. However, the requirements in ASC 505-10-15-1; 50-3 through 50-5, 50-11; 470-10-50-5 (FAS-129, *Disclosure of Information about Capital Structure*) continue to apply to such entities. Specifically, disclosure is required about the information in ASC 505-10-50-3 (paragraph 4 of FAS-129), regarding pertinent rights and privileges of various securities outstanding, and the information in ASC 505-10-50-11 (paragraph 8 FAS-129), regarding the amount of redemption requirements for all issues of stock redeemable at fixed or determinable prices on fixed or determinable dates in each of the next five years.

- The effective date of ASC 480 (FAS-150) for certain mandatorily redeemable noncontrolling interests is deferred as follows:
  - For mandatorily redeemable *noncontrolling* interests, the classification and measurement provisions of ASC 480 (FAS-150) are deferred indefinitely until the FASB takes further action if the subsidiary would *not* be required to classify those interests as liabilities under the exception in ASC 480-10-25-4, 25-6 (paragraph 9 of FAS-150) but the parent would have to classify them as liabilities in consolidation.
  - For other mandatorily redeemable *noncontrolling* interests issued before November 5, 2003, the measurement provisions of ASC 480 (FAS-150) are deferred *indefinitely* for a parent in consolidated financial statements and for its subsidiary that issues those instruments until the FASB takes further action. The measurement guidance for redeemable shares and *noncontrolling* interests in ASC 480-10-S99-3; S45-2, S45-3; S35-2; S55-1, S55-4; S30-1, S30-2 (Topic D-98, "Classification and Measurement of Redeemable Securities") should be followed while the deferral of the guidance in ASC 480 (FAS-150) applies. During that time, the FASB will reconsider the implementation issues and possibly reconsider the classification and measurement guidance for those instruments concurrently with its ongoing project on liabilities and equity.

During the deferral period, public entities and nonpublic entities that are SEC registrants should follow the Statement's disclosure requirement in ASC 480-10-50-1, 50-2 (paragraphs 26 and 27) and disclosures required in other applicable pronouncements.

FSP FAS-150-5 (Issuer's Accounting under FASB Statement No. 150 for Freestanding Warrants and Other Similar Instruments on Shares That Are Redeemable) (ASC 480-10-25-9, 25-13, 55-33)

OVERVIEW

The FASB staff issued this FSP at the direction of the FASB and posted the final FSP on the FASB's web site on June 29, 2005. This FSP applies to freestanding financial instruments that are *not* outstanding shares, such as warrants. They are issued with an obligation to repurchase the issuer's equity shares and require or may require settlement by a transfer of assets. Such financial instruments therefore are accounted for as liabilities under the guidance in ASC 480-10-25-9 through 25-12 (paragraph 11 of FAS-150, *Accounting for Certain Financial Instruments with Characteristics of both Liabilities and Equity*). . In ASC 480-10-55-29 through 55-32; 40-42 through 40-52 (FSP FAS-150-1, "Issuer's Accounting for Freestanding Financial Instruments Composed of More Than One Option or Forward Contract Embodying Obligations under FASB Statement No. 150"), there is an example of a warrant that may be put to the issuer at a fixed price immediately after the warrant has been exercised. Constituents have raised the following question.

QUESTION

Does the timing of the redemption feature or the redemption price, which may be at fair value or a fixed amount, affect whether the guidance in ASC 480-10-25-9 through 25-12 (paragraph 11 of FAS-150) should be applied to warrants for shares that can be put to the issuer?

FASB STAFF POSITION

Because freestanding warrants and other similar instruments on shares that are puttable or mandatorily redeemable include obligations to transfer assets, they should be accounted for as liabilities under the guidance in ASC 480-10-25-9 through 25-12 (paragraph 11 of FAS-150) regardless of when they are redeemed or their redemption price.

In ASC 480-10-25-9 through 25-12 (paragraph 11 of FAS-150) the phrase "requires or may require" is used to refer to financial instruments under which an issuer is conditionally or unconditionally obligated to transfer assets. For puttable shares, the issuer would be *conditionally* obligated to transfer assets if the warrant is exercised and the shares are put to the issuer. In the case of mandatorily redeemable shares, the issuer would be *conditionally* obligated to transfer assets if the holder exercises the warrant. In both cases, the warrant should be accounted for as a liability.

EITF Issue 00-4 (Majority Owner's Accounting for a Transaction in the Shares of a Consolidated Subsidiary and a Derivative Indexed to the Noncontrolling Interest in That Subsidiary) (ASC 480-10-55-53 through 55-61; ASC 460-10-60-6)

> **OBSERVATION:** The guidance in ASC 810-10-65-1 (FAS-160), which was issued in December 2007., establishes accounting and reporting standards for a *noncontrolling* interest in a subsidiary and changes the term *minority interest* to *noncontrolling interest*. It does not affect the guidance in this Issue.

OVERVIEW

This Issue addresses the accounting for a scenario in which a parent company is a controlling majority owner of 80% of a subsidiary's equity shares and a minority owner holds 20% of the equity shares. A new owner acquires the minority's 20% interest and simultaneously enters into a derivative contract with the majority owner that is indexed to the subsidiary's equity shares. The form of the derivative may be structured as follows:

- *Derivative 1* The parent has a forward contract to *buy* the minority's 20% interest at a fixed price at a specified future date.
- *Derivative 2* The parent has a call option to *buy* the minority's 20% interest at a fixed price at a specified future date and the minority owner has a put option to *sell* its 20% interest to the parent at the fixed price of the call.
- *Derivative 3* The parent and the minority owner enter into an arrangement referred to as a *total return swap*, which has the following characteristics:
  — The parent agrees to pay the owner of the noncontrolling interest an amount based on the London Interbank Offered Rate (LIBOR) plus an agreed spread and, at the termination date, an amount equal to the net depreciation, if any, of the fair value of the 20% interest since the inception of the swap.
  — The owner of the noncontrolling interest will pay the parent an amount equal to the dividends received on its 20% interest and, at the termination date, an amount equal to the net appreciation, if any, of the 20% interest since the inception of the swap.

The net change in the fair value of the 20% interest at the termination date may be determined based on an appraisal or based on the sales price of the stock.

This Issue applies only to the derivatives discussed above. Further, at the inception of a derivative contract, the parent company must be the majority owner of the subsidiary's outstanding common stock and the subsidiary must be consolidated in the parent's financial statements.

ACCOUNTING ISSUES

1. How should an enterprise that owns a controlling majority ownership interest in a business account for an arrangement in which it enters separately into a derivative transaction with the owner of the noncontrolling interest at the time that individual purchases its interest?

2. How should an enterprise that acquires a controlling majority ownership interest in a business account for an arrangement in which it enters separately into a derivative with the seller (the minority owner) at the same time as it purchases the minority's interest?

3. How should an enterprise that sells a 20% noncontrolling interest of a 100% owned subsidiary to another party account for an arrangement in which the majority owner and the other party enter into the type of derivative transaction described above?

EITF CONSENSUS

OBSERVATION: ASC 480 (FAS-150, *Accounting for Certain Financial Instruments with Characteristics of both Liabilities and Equity*) provides guidance for issuers on the classification and measurement of financial instruments with the characteristics of both liabilities and equity. Financial instruments under the scope of the Statement must be classified as liabilities, or as assets in some situations. Freestanding financial instruments under its scope are *not* permitted to be combined with other freestanding derivatives unless the combination is required under the guidance in ASC 815 (FAS-133) and its related guidance. The guidance in ASC 480 (FAS-150) affects the accounting for Derivatives 1, 2, and 3 as follows:

- *Derivative 1* The accounting discussed in this Issue for this type of derivative is *nullified* by the guidance in ASC 480 (FAS-150), which requires a treatment similar to that in the combined accounting required under the consensus in this Issue. The parent accounts for the transaction as a financing of the noncontrolling interest and consolidates 100% of the subsidiary.

- *Derivative 2* The consensus in this Issue continues to apply to this type of instrument only if the written put option and the purchased call option are embedded in the shares related to the noncontrolling interest and are not mandatorily redeemable. If that is the case, the parent would consolidate 100% of the subsidiary and would allocate to interest expense the stated yield earned under the combination of the derivative and the noncontrolling interest's position (the parent would accrete the financing to the strike price of the forward or option over the period to settlement).

- *Derivative 3* The accounting guidance in this Issue for this type of derivative is *nullified* by the guidance in ASC 480 (FAS-150), which requires that the instrument be accounted for as a liability, or an asset in some circumstances, which is measured initially and thereafter at fair value. A freestanding purchased call on a consolidated subsidiary's shares should be accounted for under the guidance in ASC 810-10-05-7; 25-17, 25-19; 35-1, 35-2; S35-1; 815-10-15-77; S30-2; S35-1; 55-64, 55-65; S99-4 (Issue 00-6, "Accounting for Freestanding Derivative Financial Instruments Indexed to, and Potentially Settled in, the Stock of a Consolidated Subsidiary").

1. In each of the three Issues, Derivatives 1 and 2, the forward or the combination of option contracts, should be considered on a combined basis with the noncontrolling interest and accounted for as a financing of the parent's purchase of the noncontrolling interest. Therefore, the parent consolidates 100% of the subsidiary and allocates to interest expense the stated yield earned under the combination of the derivative and the noncontrolling interest's position (i.e., the parent accretes the financing to the strike price of the forward or option over the period to settlement).

2. In Issue 3, no gain or loss is recognized at the inception of the contract on the parent's "sale" of the noncontrolling interest at the inception of the contract. The same accounting applies to Derivative 2 even if the exercise prices of the put and call options are not equal but do not differ significantly.

3. Derivative 3 should be considered on a combined basis with the noncontrolling interest and accounted for as a financing of the parent's purchase of the noncontrolling interest in the subsidiary. The parent should consolidate 100% of the subsidiary and allocate the stated yield earned on the derivative combined with purchased noncontrolling interest position to interest expense.

4. A parent company that "sells" a noncontrolling interest in a 100% owned subsidiary to another party should not recognize a gain on that "sale" at the inception of the contract.

5. Some members noted that in the situation discussed in this Issue, the parent company retains the risks and rewards of ownership in the noncontrolling interest, even though another party is the noncontrolling interest's legal owner.

6. The Task Force believes that under the circumstances in this Issue, the counterparty to the derivative is financing the parent's purchase of the noncontrolling interest. Therefore, the requirement that the parent account for a purchased non-

controlling interest and a related derivative on a combined basis as a financing results in a presentation of the substance of the transaction.
7. The combined instrument is *not* a derivative under the scope of ASC 815 (FAS-133). The FASB's Derivatives Implementation Group reached a similar conclusion on the combination of two instruments that meet the following criteria:
   a. The transactions are entered into intentionally at the same time,
   b. The transactions are with the same counterparty (or structured through an intermediary),
   c. The transactions are related to the same risk, and
   d. No economic reason or business purpose exists to induce the parties to structure the transactions separately rather than as a single transaction.
8. The consensus positions in this Issue apply to transactions entered into after July 20, 2000.

Topic D-98 (Classification and Measurement of Redeemable Securities) (ASC 480-10-S99-3A)

The SEC Observer stated the views of the SEC staff about the application of Accounting Series Release (ASR) No. 268, *Presentation in Financial Statements of "Redeemable Preferred Stocks."*

SCOPE

Under the guidance in ASR 268, SEC registrants are required to classify outside permanent equity redeemable preferred securities that can be redeemed (*a*) at a fixed or determinable price on a fixed or determinable date, (*b*) at the holder's option, or (*c*) when an event occurs that is not completely under the issuer's control. The SEC staff believes that the above guidance can be applied by analogy to other equity instruments, such as common stock, derivatives instruments, noncontrolling interests if the redemption feature is not considered to be a freestanding option under the scope under the scope of ASC 480-10, equity securities held by and employee stock ownership plan with terms allowing an employee to put the securities to the sponsor for cash or other assets, and redeemable instruments classified in equity granted under a share-based payment arrangement with employees as discussed in ASC 718-10-S99.

The guidance in ASR 268 does *not* apply to the following instruments:

- Freestanding financial instruments that are classified as assets under the guidance in ASC 480-10 or other GAAP;

- Freestanding derivative instruments classified in stockholders' equity under the guidance in ASC 815-40, which applies to embedded derivatives indexed to, and potentially settled in, a company's own stock.
- Equitty instruments subject to registration payment arrangements as defined in ASC 825-20-15-3;
- Share-based payment awards;
- Convertible debt instruments that contain an equity component that is classified separately. A convertible debt instrument may be required to be separated into a liability and an equity component under other GAAP. A convertible debt instrument that is not redeemable at the balance sheet date, but that may become redeemable based on the passage of time or the occurrence of an event is not considered to be redeemable at the balance sheet date;
- Certain redemptions that occur as a result of a liquidation event. However, deemed liquidation events under which a holder is required or permitted to redeem only one or more equity instruments of a specific class for cash or other assets would require the application of ASR 268;
- Certain redemptions covered by proceeds from insurance, for example, an equity instrument that becomes redeemable on the holder's or disability;

CLASSIFICATION

> **OBSERVATION:** ASC 480 (FAS-150, *Accounting for Certain Financial Instruments with Characteristics of both Liabilities and Equity*) provides guidance for issuers on the classification and measurement of financial instruments with the characteristics of both liabilities and equity. Financial instruments under the scope of the Statement must be classified as liabilities, or as assets in some situations, because they represent an issuer's obligations.
>
> The SEC Observer clarified the SEC staff's position regarding the interaction of the staff's guidance on this announcement with the guidance in ASC 480 (FAS-150) when accounting for *conditionally* redeemable preferred shares. The guidance in ASC 480 (FAS-150) does *not* apply to the accounting for such shares if they are conditionally redeemable at a holder's option or when an uncertain event *not* under the issuer's control occurs, because there is no unconditional obligation to redeem the shares by a transfer of assets at a specified or determinable date or when a certain event occurs. The condition is resolved when an uncertain event occurs. Once it becomes certain that such an event will occur, the shares should be accounted for under the provisions of ASC 480 (FAS-150), which requires that the shares be measured at fair value and reclassified as a liability. As a result, stockholders' equity would be reduced by an

equivalent amount with no gain or loss recognition. The reclassification is similar to a redemption of shares by issuing debt. As in the redemption of preferred shares discussed in ASC 260-10-99S-2 (Topic D-42, "The Effect on the Calculation of Earnings per Share for the Redemption or Induced Conversion of Preferred Stock"), when calculating earnings per share, the difference between the fair value of the liability and the carrying amount of the preferred debt at reclassification should be deducted from or added to net earnings available to common shareholders.

The SEC staff believes that an issuer of a redeemable equity security should evaluate separately all the events that could trigger redemption if some of the security's redemption features are not under the issuer's control. A security should be classified outside of permanent equity if *any* event not under the issuer's sole control, regardless of the probability of occurrence, could trigger its redemption. Although a change in classification is not required if an event occurs that would cause a potential ordinary liquidation that would require cash payment only if the company is totally liquidated, the occurrence of events that could cause the redemption of one or more particular classes or types of equity securities would require that those securities be classified outside of permanent equity. The classification of equity securities whose redemption is not solely under the issuer's control should be based on the individual facts and circumstances.

For example, the SEC Observer noted that a redeemable security with a provision that requires the issuer to obtain the approval of the board of directors to call the security may not necessarily be under the issuer's control, because the board of directors may be controlled by the holders of the particular redeemable security. In contrast, classification in permanent equity would continue to be appropriate in a situation in which a preferred stock agreement includes a provision stating that the issuer's decision to sell all or substantially all of the company's assets and a subsequent distribution to common stockholders triggers redemption of the preferred equity security, because the decision to sell all or substantially all of the issuer's assets is solely under the issuer's control. That is, a distribution to common stockholders cannot be *triggered* or required by the preferred stock holders as a result of their representation on the board of directors.

One exception to the requirement in this announcement that should *not* be analogized to other transactions occurs when there is a provision that the equity securities become redeemable as a result of the holder's death or disability. Under this situation, the redemption of the securities would be funded by the proceeds of an insurance policy that is in force and that the issuer intends to and is able to maintain in force. Consequently, the securities continue to be classified in permanent equity.

MEASUREMENT

The SEC staff believes the the initial amount of a redeemable equity security included in temporary equity in accordance with the guidance in ASR 268 should be its fair value on the issue date, except in the following circumstances:

- Share-based payment arrangements with employees. Measure the initial amount recognized in temporary equity based on the instrument's redemption provisions and the proportion of consideration received as employee services
- Employee stock ownership plans. If the cash redemption option is related only to a market value guarantee feature, a registrant's accounting policy for temporary equity may be to present (a) the amount of the total guaranteed market value of the equity securities, or (b) the maximum cash obligation based on the fair value of the underlying equity securities at the balance sheet date.
- Noncontrolling interests. Present in temporary equity the initial carrying amount of a noncontrolling interest in accordance with the guidance in ASC 805-20-30.
- Convertible debt instruments that include a separately classified equity component. Present an amount in temporary equity only if the instrument is currently redeemable or convertible at the issuance date for cash or other assets. If a portion of a component classified as equity is included in temporary equity, present the amount of cash or other assets that would be paid to a holder on conversion or redemption at the issuance date in excess of the component classified as a liability on the issuance date.
- Host equity contracts. Present in temporary equity the initial carrying amount of the host contract in accordance with the guidance in ASC 815-15-30.
- Preferred stock with a beneficial conversion feature or is issued with other instruments. Include in temporary equity the total amount allocated to the instrument in accordance with the guidance in ASC 470-20 *less* the amount of the beneficial conversion feature recognized at the issuance date.

The following are the views of the SEC staff about the subsequent measurement of a redeemable equity instrument subject to the requirements of ASR 268:

- Currently redeemable instrument at the option of the holder. Adjust the amount of the securities redeemable currently to their maximum redemption amount at each balance sheet date. If the maximum amount is contingent on an index or similar variable, calculate the amount in temporary equity based on the existing conditions at the balance sheet date, such as the instrument's current fair value. At each balance sheet date include the amount of dividends *not* currently declared or paid but that will be paid under the redemption features or if their ultimate payment is *not* under the registrant's control. If an instrument is not currently redeemable, an adjustment is unnecessary if it is not probable that the instrument will become redeemable, such as when redemption will occur only based on the passage of time.

- If it is probable that an equity instrument will become redeemable, the SEC staff will not object if either of the following accounting methods are applied consistently for securities that will become redeemable at a future *determinable* date but whose redemption amount is *variable* (e.g., they are redeemable at fair value):

    a. Accrete changes in the redemption value from the date of issuance or when redemption becomes probable (if later) to the security's earliest redemption date using an appropriate method, usually the interest method. Changes in redemption value are considered to be changes in accounting estimates and accounted for, and disclosed, in accordance with the guidance in ASC 250 (FAS-154, *Accounting Changes and Error Corrections*).

    b. Recognize changes in the redemption value (for example, fair value) immediately as they occur and adjust the security's carrying amount to equal the redemption value at the end of each reporting period. Under this method, the end of the reporting period would be viewed as if it were also the security's redemption date.

The following is additional guidance provided by the SEC staff on subsequent measurement under the following circumstances:

- Share based payment arrangements with employees. At each balance sheet date, base the amount included in temporary equity on the instrument's redemption provisions considering the proportion of consideration received in the form of employee services (the pattern of recognition of compensation cost in accordance with the guidance in ASC 718.)
- Employee stock ownership plans. If the cash redemption obligation is related only to a market value guarantee feature, a registrant's accounting policy for temporary equity may be to present (a) the amount of the total guaranteed market value of the equity securities, or (b) the maximum cash obligation based on the fair value of the underlying equity securities at the balance sheet date.
- Noncontrolling interests. Determine the adjustment of the carrying amount in temporary equity after attributing the

subsidiary's net income or a loss according to the guidance in ASC 810-10.

- Convertible debt instruments that include a separately classified equity component. Present an amount in temporary equity only if the instrument is currently redeemable or convertible at the issuance date for cash or other assets. If a portion of a component classified as equity is included in temporary equity, present the amount of cash or other assets that would be paid to a holder on conversion or redemption at the issuance date in excess of the component classified as a liability on the issuance date.

- Fair value option. Redeemable equity instruments included in temporary equity in accordance with the requirements in ASR 268 should not be measured at fair value through earnings instead of applying the SEC staff's measurement guidance. Also see the guidance in ASC 825-10-50-8.

The SEC staff believes that regardless of which of the above accounting methods is used to account for a redeemable equity security, that security's carrying amount should be reduced only to the extent that the registrant had previously increased the security's carrying amount as a result of the application of the guidance in this Topic.

The SEC staff expects registrants to apply the accounting method selected consistently and to disclose the selected policy in the notes to the financial statements. In addition, registrants that elect to accrete changes in redemption value over the period from the date of issuance to the earliest redemption date should disclose the security's redemption value as if it were redeemable.

RECLASSIFICATION INTO PERMANENT EQUITY

If temporary classification of a redeemable equity security is no longer required, its carrying amount should be reclassified from temporary to permanent equity at the date of the occurrence of the event causing reclassification. Prior financial statements should *not* be adjusted. The SEC staff also believes that reversal of previously recorded adjustments to the security's carrying amount would be inappropriate when a reclassification occurs.

DECONSOLIDATION OF A SUBSIDIARY

An entity that deconsolidates a subsidiary recognizes a gain or loss on that transaction in net income based on the measurement guidance in ASC 810-10-40-5 (paragraph 36 of ARB-51, *Consolidated Financial Statements*) , as amended by the guidance in ASC 810-10-65-1 (FAS-160, *Noncontrolling Interests in Consolidated Financial Statements*). The carrying amount of a noncontrolling interest, if any, in the former subsidiary affects that gain or loss calculation. The

SEC staff believes that because adjustments to a noncontrolling interest's carrying amount from the application of the guidance in this SEC staff announcement have not entered into the determination of the entity's net income, the noncontrolling interest's carrying amount should likewise *not* include any adjustments made to the noncontrolling interest as a result of the application of the guidance in this SEC staff announcement. Previous adjustments to the noncontrolling interest's carrying amount from the application of the guidance in this SEC staff announcement should be eliminated by recording a credit to the parent entity's equity.

EARNINGS PER SHARE

Preferred Securities Issued by a Parent or Single Reporting Entity

Increases or decreases in the carrying amount of a redeemable security should be treated like dividends on nonredeemable stock by charging retained earnings, or if no retained earnings exist, by charging paid-in capital, regardless of the method used to account for the security or whether the security is redeemable at a fixed price or at fair value. In calculating earnings per share and the ratio of earnings to combined fixed charges and preferred stock dividends, income available to common stockholders should be reduced or increased as a result of increases or decreases in a preferred security's carrying amount. Guidance related to the accounting at the date of a redemption or induced conversion of a preferred equity security may be found in ASC 260-10- S99-2 (Topic D-42, "The Effect on the Calculation of Earnings per Share for the Redemption or Induced Conversion of Preferred Stock")

Common Securities Issued by a Parent or a Single Reporting Entity

Increases or decreases in the carrying amount of a redeemable security should be treated like dividends on nonredeemable stock by charging retained earnings, or if no retained earnings exist, by charging paid-in capital, regardless of the method used to account for the security or whether the security is redeemable at a fixed price or at fair value. But those increases or decreases in a redeemable common stock's carrying amount should *not* affect income available for common stock holders. The SEC staff believes that in so far as a common shareholder has a contractual right to receive an amount other than the fair value of those shares at redemption, a common shareholder has, in substance, received a different distribution than the other common shareholders. Entities whose capital structures include a class of common stock with dividend rates that differ from those of another class of common shareholders but without senior rights, are required to calculate their earnings per share based on the two-class method discussed in ASC 260-10-45-59A (FAS-128, *Earnings per Share*). As a result, increases or decreases in the carrying amount of a class of common stock that is redeemable at other than fair value should be considered in the calculation of earnings per share using the two-class method. In footnote 8 of this Topic, the SEC staff states that if a common security is redeemable at other than fair value, it is acceptable to allocate earnings under the two-class method using one of the following two methods:

- Treat the total periodic adjustment to the security's carrying amount as a result of the application of the guidance in this Topic like an actual dividend, or
- Treat like an actual dividend only the portion of the periodic adjustment to the security's carrying amount as a result of the application of the guidance in this Topic that represents a redemption in excess of fair value.

The SEC staff does not expect the two-class method to be used in the calculation of earnings per share if a class of common stock is redeemable at fair value, because the dividend distribution to those shareholders does not differ from that made to other common shareholders. The SEC staff believe that common stock redeemable based on a specified formula is considered redeemable at fair value if the formula is intended to equal or reasonably approximate fair value. However, a formula based only on a fixed multiple of earnings or a similar measure would *not* qualify.

The SEC staff also believe that likewise, the two-class method need *not* be used if share-based payment awards in the form of common shares or options or common shares granted to employees are redeemable at fair value. However, the two-class method may still apply to such share-based payment awards under the guidance in ASC 260-10-45-59A (paragraph 60 of FAS-128) and ASC 260-10-45-60, 45-60A through 45-68; 55-24 through 55-30, 55-71 through 55-75 (EITF Issue 03-6, *Participating Securities and the Two-Class Method under Statement No. 128*).

Noncontrolling Interests
In accordance with the guidance in ASC 810-10-45-23 (paragraph 33 of ARB-51, as amended), (a) changes in a parent's ownership interest accounted for by the equity method while a parent retains control of the subsidiary and (b) an adjustment to a noncontrolling interest as a result of the application of the guidance in this SEC staff announcement, have no effect on net income or comprehensive income in the consolidated financial statements. Instead, such adjustments are accounted for like a repurchase of a noncontrolling interest, although they may be recognized in retained earnings rather than in paid-in capital. The SEC staff requires that the above earnings per share guidance for preferred securities and common shares issued by a parent should be applied to noncontrolling interests as follows:

- *Noncontrolling interest in the form of preferred securities.* If a redemption feature of a noncontrolling interest in the form of preferred securities was issued or guaranteed by a parent, an adjustment to the security's carrying amount reduces or increases income available to common stockholders. If not, the adjustment is attributed to the parent and the noncontrolling interest in accordance with the guidance in ASC 260-10-55-64 through 55-67. (paragraph 156 of FAS-128).
- *Noncontrolling interest in the form of common securities.* Adjustments to the carrying amount of a noncontrolling interest issued in the form of common stock to represent a fair value redemption feature do *not* affect earnings per share. However, if a noncontrolling interest was issued in the form of common stock to represent a non-fair value redemption feature, adjustments to the noncontrolling interest's carrying amount affect earnings per share, but the way those adjustments reduce or increase income available to common stockholders may differ. Application of the two-class method is unnecessary if the terms of the redemption feature are fully considered when net income is attributed under the guidance in ASC 810-10-45-21 (paragraph 30 of ARB-51). But if they are not fully considered, the two-class method must be applied at the level of the subsidiary to determine net income available to the parent's common stockholders.

Convertible Debt Instruments that Include a Separately Classified Equity Component

There should be no incremental earnings per share accounting from the application of the SEC staff's guidance in this announcement for convertible debt instruments to the requirements of ASR 268. The earnings per share accounting is addressed in ASC 260-10.

DISCLOSURES

Certain disclosures about redeemable equity instruments are required under the guidance in ASC 268 and SEC Regulation S-X. The SEC staff expects registrants to provide the following additional disclosures in the notes to the financial statements:
- The accounting method used to adjust the amount to be redeemed on a redeemable equity instrument.
- The redeemable amount of an equity instrument as if it were currently redeemable if a registrant chooses to accrete changes immediately in the amount at which a redeemable equity instrument would be redeemed (method b. discussed for equity instruments if it is probable that the equity instrument would be redeemed.)

ASC 815 DERIVATIVES AND HEDGING

FSP FAS-133-1/FIN-45-4 (Disclosures about Credit Derivatives and Certain Guarantees: An Amendment of FASB Statement No. 133 and FASB Interpretation No. 45; and Clarification of the Effective Date of FASB Statement No. 161) (ASC 815-10-65-2)

OVERVIEW

As a result of the expansion of the market in credit derivatives, concerns have been raised that the information about derivative instruments and certain guarantees presented in financial reports do not include an adequate discussion of how potential unfavorable changes in credit risk would affect a reporting entity's financial position, financial performance, and the cash flows of sellers of credit derivatives and certain guarantees. As a result of the issuance of this FSP, (a) the guidance in ASC 815 (FAS-133, *Accounting for Derivative Instruments and Hedging Activities*) has been amended to require that sellers of credit derivatives make such disclosures, including information about derivatives embedded in hybrid instruments, and (b) the guidance in ASC 460-10-05-1, 05-2; 460-10-10-1; 460-10-15-4 through 15-7, 15-9, 15-10; 460-10-25-1 through 25-4; 460-10-30-1 through 30-4; 460-10-35-1, 35-2, 35-4; 460-10-50-2, 50-4 through 50-6, 50-8; 460-10-55-2, 55-3, 55-5 through 55-9, 55-12, 55-13, 55-15 through 55-18, 55-20 through 55-24, 55-28, 55-29; 840-10-25-34; 840-10-60-2, (FIN-45, *Guarantor's Accounting and Disclosure Requirements for Guarantees, Including Indirect Guarantees of Indebtedness of Others*) is amended to require an additional disclosure about the current status of a guarantee's payment and/or performance risk.

FASB STAFF POSITION

Scope

This FSP provides guidance for disclosures about credit derivatives accounted for under the guidance in ASC 815 (FAS-133), hybrid instruments that have embedded credit derivatives, and guarantees accounted for under the scope of ASC 460-10-05-1, 05-2; 460-10-10-1; 460-10-15-4 through 15-7, 15-9, 15-10; 460-10-25-1 through 25-4; 460-10-30-1 through 30-4; 460-10-35-1, 35-2, 35-4; 460-10-50-2, 50-4 through 50-6, 50-8; 460-10-55-2, 55-3, 55-5 through 55-9, 55-12, 55-13, 55-15 through 55-18, 55-20 through 55-24, 55-28, 55-29; 840-10-25-34; 840-10-60-2, (FIN-45).

A credit derivative is defined in this FSP as follows:
A credit derivative is a derivative instrument (a) in which one or more of its underlyings are related to the credit risk of a specified entity (or a group of entities) or an index based on the credit risk of a group of entities and (b) that exposes a seller to potential loss from credit-risk-related events specified in the contract.

The guidance in this FSP applies to credit derivatives, which include credit default swaps, credit spread options, and credit index products, among others. The amendment to ASC 815 (FAS-133) also applies to hybrid instruments that have embedded credit derivatives, such as credit-linked notes.

Amendment to Disclosure Requirements of ASC 815 (FAS-133)

The guidance in this FSP applies to sellers of credit derivatives who are defined as "a party that assume financial risk." That party, which is sometimes called a *writer of a contract*, might be "a guarantor in a guarantee-type contract, and any party that provides the credit protection in an option-type contract, a credit default swap, or any other credit derivative contract." ASC 815 (FAS-133) is amended to require that sellers of credit derivatives disclose information about their credit derivatives and hybrid instruments that have embedded credit derivatives so that users of financial statements can evaluate the possible effect of those financial instruments on their sellers' financial position, financial performance, and cash flows.

A seller of a credit derivative is required to disclose the following information in its balance sheet about each credit derivative or group of similar credit derivatives, even if there is only a remote likelihood that the seller will have to make any payments under the credit derivative. Disclosures for groups of similar derivatives may be presented by (1) separating the information by major types of contracts, such as single-name credit default swaps, traded indexes, other portfolio products, and swaptions, and (2) further separating the information into additional subgroups for major types of referenced/underlying asset classes, such as corporate debt, sovereign debt, and structured finance. The following information should be disclosed:

a. The nature of the credit derivative, including its approximate term; the reason for entering into it; events or circumstance under which a seller would have to perform under a credit derivative; the balance sheet date of the payment/performance risk of a credit derivative, which could be based on either credit ratings issued by an external source or current internal groupings that the seller uses to manage its risk, and if so, how those internal groupings are determined and used to manage risk.

b. The maximum potential amount of undiscounted future payments that a seller could be required to make under a credit derivative that would not be reduced by the effect of amounts, if any, that may possibly be recovered under provisions in the credit derivative providing for recourse or collateralization (see (d) below). If the maximum potential payments under a credit derivative's terms are unlimited, that fact should be disclosed. In addition, a seller that is unable to estimate the maximum potential amount of future payments under a contract should disclose the reasons for the inability to estimate that amount.

c. A credit derivative's fair value as of the balance sheet date.

d. The nature of (1) recourse provisions, if any, that would enable a seller to recover payments made under a credit derivative from a third party, and (2) assets, if any, held as collateral or by a third party that a seller can obtain and liquidate to recover all or a portion of an amount that would be paid under a credit derivative if a payment is triggered by the occurrence of a specified event or condition. If possible, a seller should estimate the approximate portion of the maximum potential amount under a credit derivative that would be expected to be covered by proceeds from the liquidation of those assets. A seller of credit protection should consider the effect of purchased credit protection with identical underlyings in estimating potential recoveries.

A seller of credit derivatives that are embedded in hybrid instruments should disclose the required information for the total hybrid instruments, not solely for the embedded credit derivatives.

Amendment to Disclosure Requirement of ASC 460 (FIN-45)

The disclosures required under the guidance in this FSP are substantially similar to those for guarantors under the guidance in ASC 460-10-50-4 (paragraph 13 of FIN-45), except for the disclosure about the current status of the payment/performance risk of the credit derivative. Therefore, ASC 460-10-50-4 (paragraph 13(a) of FIN-45) is amended by this FSP to require that the current status of a payment/performance risk of a guarantee be disclosed so that similar disclosures will be made for instruments with similar risks and rewards. That is, a guarantor that uses internal groupings to manage its risk is also required to disclose how those groupings are determined and used to manage risk.

EFFECTIVE DATE AND TRANSITION

The provisions of this FSP are effective for interim and annual reporting periods ending after November 15, 2008. In periods after the initial adoption of the guidance in this FSP, comparative disclosures should be made only for periods ending after this FSP's adoption.

EITF Issue 99-2 (Accounting for Weather Derivatives) (ASC 815-45-15-2; 25-1, 25-5, 25-6; 30-1 through 3A; 35-1, 35-2, 35-4, 35-7; 55-1 through 55-8, 55-10, 55-11; 50-1; 460-10-60-15)

OVERVIEW

Weather derivative contracts, which are contracts indexed to climactic or geological variables, are new types of derivatives seen in the market. An increasing number of entities are entering into such contracts for a number of business reasons. Current accounting practices are diverse, because it is unclear whether the contracts should be accounted for under accrual accounting, settlement accounting, or insurance accounting. Some believe that changes in the fair value of those contracts should be recognized in earnings at each reporting date.

Under the guidance in ASC 815 (FAS-133), contracts that are not traded on an exchange are not covered by the Statement if they are settled based on a climactic or geological variable or another physical variable. However, if derivatives settled based on a physical variable eventually become exchange-traded, they will be covered under the guidance in ASC 815 (FAS-133).

Contracts written by insurance companies to compensate their holders for an insurable event that causes the holder to incur a liability or that adversely affects the value of a specific asset or liability for which the holder is at risk are *not* covered by the scope of this Issue.

ACCOUNTING ISSUES

1. How should an entity account for a weather derivative that is nonexchange-traded or forward-based (risk is two-directional)?
2. How should an entity account for a purchased weather derivative that is nonexchange-traded and option-based (risk is one-directional)?
3. How should an entity account for a written weather derivative that is nonexchange-traded and option-based?

EITF CONSENSUS

1. Use the *intrinsic value method* to account for nonexchange-traded, forward-based weather derivatives that are entered into for nontrading purposes. Under that method, the value of the derivative is computed as follows: (*a*) determine the difference between the expected results of an allocation of the cumulative strike price at inception and the actual results during the period; (*b*) multiply that amount by the contract price, such as

dollars per heating degree day; (c) allocate the cumulative strike price based on information from external statistical sources, such as the National Weather Service, to individual periods within the contract's term based on a reasonable expectation at the inception of the term of normal or expected experience under the contract. At interim periods, calculate the intrinsic value of the contract based on the cumulative difference between actual experience and the allocation through that date. The allocation of the cumulative strike price at inception should *not* be adjusted when actual results are known.

2. Amortize the premium paid or due on a nonexchange-traded, option-based weather derivative purchased for nontrading purposes to expense in a rational and systematic manner. Measure the contract at interim balance-sheet dates using the intrinsic value method as discussed above.

3. Account for all weather derivatives entered into for trading or speculative purposes at *fair value* and report subsequent fair value changes in period earnings.

4. Under this Issue, entering into weather derivative contracts for the purpose of earning a profit on an exposure to changes in climactic or geological conditions indicates that an entity may be involved in trading or speculative activities. Judgment based on the relevant facts and circumstances must be used in evaluating whether or when an entity's involvement in weather derivative contracts should be considered a trading or speculative activity. That evaluation should consider the entity's various activities rather than merely considering the terms of the contract. The entity's intent for entering into weather derivative contracts is another consideration. The following factors or indicators should be considered in evaluating whether an operation's (subsidiary, division, or unit) weather derivative contracts are entered into for trading or speculative purposes. Affirmative answers to the questions in Category A are strong indicators that the operation is not engaged in trading activities. Although affirmative answers only to the questions in Category B may indicate that the operation is engaged in trading activities, negative answers to any or all of the questions in either category may not by themselves indicate that the operation is not engaged in trading activities. All available information should be used to reach a conclusion:

   a. Fundamental indicators

      (1) Is the operation's primary business exposed to weather related risk covered by the contracts held?

      (2) Is the volume of weather derivative contracts reasonable in relation to the operation's primary business?

      (3) Is the contract's change in value expected to move in a direction that would mitigate or offset the risk of the underlying exposure?

(4) Does the operation price the contract offers or trades based on externally developed price models?

b. Secondary indicators—management and controls

(1) Are compensation or performance measures or both related to short-term profits on weather derivative contracts?

(2) Do internal communications discuss the operation's business activities in terms of the operation's trading strategy?

(3) Does the operation's business name include the term *trading*?

(4) Are the operation's employees referred to as *traders*?

(5) Are net market positions determined regularly?

(6) Is the operation's infrastructure segregated by back office processing functions and front office trading function as in a trading operation or an investment bank?

(7) Is the operation's infrastructure equipped to determine price and other risks on a real-time basis?

(8) Does the operation manage its activities on a portfolio or book basis?

The Task Force agreed that although it is easier to determine whether an operation is engaged in trading activities when those activities are segregated within the organization or by legal entity, only the portion of an operation that is determined to be engaged in trading activities, based on an evaluation of the indicators discussed above, should be required to account for its activities at fair value. Entities whose trading activities are not segregated from their other activities should identify their trading and nontrading contracts at inception using the above indicators.

The EITF noted that because weather derivative contracts under the scope of this Issue are financial instruments, entities that enter into such contracts should make the required disclosures for financial instruments in ASC 825-10-50-2A, 50-3 through 50-4, 50-8 through 50-23, 50-26; 55-3 through 55-5 (FAS-107).

The Task Force's consensus positions apply to weather derivative contracts entered into after July 22, 1999.

> **OBSERVATION:** Under the guidance in ASC 460 (FIN-45, *Guarantor's Accounting and Disclosure Requirements for Guarantees, Including Indirect Guarantees of Indebtedness of Others*), at the inception of a guarantee, a guarantor is required to recognize a liability for the obligation assumed by issuing the guarantee. Weather derivatives are option-based contracts under which the party receiving the guarantee is paid based on whether a specific event related to the weather does or does not occur at a specified location within a specified time period, such as 20 inches of snow in New York City during the first week of February. Under the guidance in ASC 460 (FIN-45),

which requires that payments be based on a change in an underlying related to an asset or liability of the party to whom the guarantee was given, a weather derivative is *not* a guarantee, because an event related to the weather is not an asset or liability of the party to whom the guarantee was given.

SEC OBSERVER COMMENT

The SEC Observer stated that because weather derivative contracts under the scope of this Issue are financial instruments, the SEC staff believes that registrants should make the disclosures about those contracts required in Item 305 of SEC Regulation S-K, if applicable.

EITF Issue 99-9 (Effect of Derivative Gains and Losses on the Capitalization of Interest) (ASC 815-25-35-14; 55-52; 815-30-35-45)

OVERVIEW

According to the guidance in ASC 835-20 (FAS-34, *Capitalization of Interest Cost*), the purpose of capitalizing interest costs of an acquired asset is to measure cost of interest incurred to finance the asset acquisition that would otherwise not have been incurred. Under that guidance, interest that is eligible for capitalization on qualified assets includes interest on borrowings and obligations with explicit interest rates, interest imputed in accordance with the guidance in ASC 835-30 (APB-21) on certain types of payables, and interest on capital leases. If the specific interest on a new borrowing can be associated with the eligible portion of the asset, that rate should be used for interest capitalization purposes. Otherwise, a weighted average of the rates on borrowings is applied to expenditures not related to specific new borrowings. Interest capitalization during a period is limited to the amount of interest incurred during the period.

This Issue has been raised because there is diversity in practice when the guidance in ASC 835-20 (FAS-34) is applied in connection with the guidance in ASC 815 (FAS-133) to interest costs in a fair value hedge accounting model.

ACCOUNTING ISSUE

Should the interest rate used to capitalize interest costs according with the guidance in ASC 835-20 (FAS-34) on the historical cost of certain assets be the effective yield after gains and losses have been recognized on the effective portion of a derivative instrument that qualifies as a fair value hedge of fixed interest rate debt or should the original effective interest rate on that debt be used?

EITF CONSENSUS

The EITF reached a consensus that an entity that elects to begin amortizing adjustments of the carrying amount of a hedged liability under the guidance in ASC 815-25-55-66 (paragraph 24 of FAS-133) should include those amounts in interest costs used to determine the capitalization rate under the guidance in ASC 835-20 (FAS-34). The Task Force noted that interest costs related to the ineffective portion of a fair value hedge should *not* be included in the capitalization rate.

In the example in ASC 815-25-55-46, 55-48 (paragraphs 115-117 of FAS-133), the entity decides to immediately begin amortizing the adjustments of the carrying amount of the fixed rate debt while the hedge is still in place. If the entity in that example recognizes as interest expense the fair value change attributed to the passage of time, the amounts recognized as expenses in ASC 815-25-55-48 (paragraph 117 of FAS-133) would be eligible for capitalization under FAS-34.

The Task Force also noted that under the guidance in ASC 815 (FAS-133), a gain or loss on the hedging instrument in a cash flow hedge is not permitted to be capitalized as a basis adjustment of the qualifying assets. Under the guidance in ASC 815-30-35-3, 35-4, 35-7, 35-38 through 35-41 (paragraphs 30 and 31 of FAS-133), amounts accumulated in other comprehensive income must be reclassified into earnings in the period in which the forecasted transaction affects earnings. Because an asset's depreciable life coincides with the amortization period of the capitalized interest on the debt, the FASB staff believes that amounts accumulated in comprehensive income that are related to a cash flow hedge of the fluctuations in the variable interest rate on a specific borrowing associated with an asset under construction for which interest costs are capitalized as a cost of that asset should be reclassified into earnings over the depreciable life of the constructed asset.

EITF Issue 00-19 (Accounting for Derivative Financial Instruments Indexed to, and Potentially Settled in, a Company's Own Stock) (ASC 460-10-60-14; 480-10-55-63; 505-10-60-5; 815-10-15-78; 55-52; 15-25-15; 40-05-1 through 05-4, 10, 11,12; 25-1 through 25-5, 25-7 through 25-20, 25-22 through 25-24, 25-26 through 25-35; 25-37 through 25-40; 30-1; 35-1, 35-2, 35-6, 35-8 through 35-13; 40-1, 2; 50-1 through 50-5; 55-1 through 55-18)

> **OBSERVATION:** This Issue is a codification of the EITF's consensus positions reached in Issue 96-13 (not in ASC), Issue 99-3 (not in ASC), and Issue 00-7 (not in ASC) with those reached in its discussions of this Issue.

OBSERVATION: Although EITF Issue 97-8, "Accounting for Contingent Consideration Issued in a Purchase Business Combination," was nullified by the guidance in ASC 805 (FAS-141(R), under the guidance in ASC 805-30-25-6, 25-7 (paragraph 42 of FAS-141(R)), an obligation to pay contingent consideration issued in a business combination is within the scope of this Issue, which is refererred to as one of the sources of guidance for determining whether an acquirer should classify that obligation as a liability or as equity.

OBSERVATION: The guidance in ASC 810-10-45-15 through 45-16; 50-1A; 55j through 55k is an amendment of ARB-51, *Consolidated Financial Statements*, FAS-160 (Noncontrolling Interests in Consolidated Financial Statements—an Amendment of ARB No. 51). That guidance establishes accounting and reporting standards for a *noncontrolling* interest in a subsidiary and changes the term *noncontrolling interest* to *noncontrolling interest*. It does not affect the guidance in this Issue.

OVERVIEW

OBSERVATION: ASC 480-10 (FAS-150) provides guidance for issuers on the classification and measurement of financial instruments with the characteristics of both liabilities and equity. Financial instruments under the scope of the Statement must be classified as liabilities or as assets in some situations.

The guidance in this Issue has been *partially nullified* as follows:

- Free-standing instruments under the scope of ASC 480-10 (FAS-150), such as forward purchase contracts, written put options, and certain other instruments that can be settled with the issuer's equity shares, must be classified as liabilities and measured in accordance with that guidance.

- Nonpublic entities are no longer permitted to classify proceeds from put warrants as equity. In accordance with the provisions ASC 480-10 (FAS-150), a liability should be recognized for a put warrant that includes an obligation to repurchase an issuer's equity shares, or one that is indexed to such an obligation, which requires or may require a transfer of assets. Put warrants that include an obligation to issue a variable number of shares if the value of that obligation is primarily based on (a) a fixed sum of money at inception, (b) variations based on something different than the fair value of the issuer's shares, or (c) variations inversely related to changes in the fair value of the issuer's equity shares are also included under the scope of ASC 480-10 (FAS-150). Put warrants *not* under the scope of ASC 480-10 (FAS-150) should be accounted for under the guidance in this Issue. (See ASC 480-10-55-29 through 55-32; 40-42 through 40-52 (FSP FAS 150-1) for additional guidance on put warrants.)

- The guidance in ASC 480-10 (FAS-150) *nullifies* the requirement under this Issue (which is analogous to the SEC's guidance in ASR-268) that public companies account as temporary equity for the cash redemption amounts of obligations to deliver cash in exchange for the entity's own shares in physical settlements of freestanding financial instruments classified as equity. Such amounts should be classified as liabilities under the guidance in ASC 480-10 (FAS-150) and measured at their fair value or at the present value of the redemption amount, unless the Statement requires a different valuation or other accounting guidance applies.

- The guidance in this Issue continues to apply when financial instruments embedded in other financial instruments that are *not* derivatives in their entirety are evaluated for bifurcation under ASC 815 (FAS-133), such as written put options embedded in nonderivative host contracts, because the guidance in ASC 480-10 (FAS-150) does *not* apply to such financial instruments. That is, an embedded written option that would have been classified in equity under this Issue before the guidance in ASC 480-10 (FAS-150) was issued would continue to be considered an equity instrument when evaluating whether an embedded derivative could be bifurcated under the guidance in ASC 815-15-25-1 (paragraph 12 of FAS-133).

A company may enter into contracts that are indexed to and settled in its own stock for various economic reasons, for example, to hedge share dilution from existing written call options, to hedge the effect of existing written option positions on earnings, to hedge planned future purchases of treasury stock, to hedge a planned future issuance of shares, or to hedge the cost of a business combination. The following are such contracts:

- *Forward sale contract* A contract requiring a company to sell a specific number of its shares of stock at a specific price on a specific future date. For example, a company enters into a contract to sell 500 shares of its common stock at $50 per share on June 30, 20X8. The company has a loss if the market price of the stock is more than $50 per share on that date. Conversely, the company has a gain if the market price of the stock is less than $50 per share on that date.

- *Forward purchase contract* A contract requiring a company to purchase a specific number of shares of its stock at a specific price on a specific future date. For example, a company enters into a contract to purchase 500 shares of its common stock at $50 per share on June 30, 20X8. The company has a gain if the market price of the stock is more than $50 per share on that date. Conversely, the company has a loss if the market price of the stock is less than $50 per share on that date.

- *Purchased put option* A contract giving a company a right to, but not requiring it to, sell a specific number of its shares of stock at a specific price on a specific future date. For example, a company may purchase a right to sell 500 shares of its common stock at $50 per share on June 30, 20X8. The company has a gain if the market price of the stock is less than $50 per share on that date. The contract is worthless if the market price of the stock is more than $50 per share on that date because the company would not exercise the option if it can sell shares for more elsewhere.

- *Purchased call option* A contract giving a company the right to, but not requiring it to, buy a specific number of its shares of stock at a specific price on a specific future date. For example, a company may purchase a right to buy 500 shares of its common stock at $50 per share on June 30, 20X8. The company has a gain if the market price of the stock is more than $50 per share on that date. The contract is worthless if the market price of the stock is less than $50 per share on that date because the company would not exercise the option if it can buy shares for less elsewhere.

- *Written put option* A contract sold by a company giving the holder the right, but not the obligation, to sell to the company a specific number of the company's shares of stock at a specific price on a specific future date. For example, a company may sell put options giving the holder the right to sell to the company 500 shares of its commons tock at $50 per share on June 30, 20X8. If the market price is less than $50, the option will expire unexercised because the holder can buy the shares for less on the open market. The company's gain will be limited to the option premium received.

- *Written call option (and warrant)* A contract sold by a company giving the holder the right, but not the obligation, to purchase a specific number of the company's shares of common stock at a specific price on a specific future date. For example, a company may sell a call option giving the holder the right to purchase 500 shares of the company's common stock at $50 per share on June 30, 20X8. If the market price is less than $50 per share on that date, the option will expire unexercised, because the holder can purchase the shares for less on the option market. The company's gain will be limited to the option premium. If the market price is more than $50 on that date, the holder will exercise the option and the company will have a loss.

Such contracts may be settled as follows:

- *Physical settlement* The buyer delivers the full stated amount of cash and the seller delivers the full stated number of shares.

- *Net share settlement* The party incurring a loss delivers to the party realizing a gain shares equal to the current fair value of the gain.

- *Net cash settlement* The party incurring a loss pays cash to the party realizing a gain in an amount equal to the gain; no shares are exchanged.

The contracts may be freestanding, that is, they are entered into separately from the entity's other financial instruments or equity transactions, or they are entered into with another action, but the contract can be detached legally and exercised separately. Although such contracts may be embedded, that is, be an integral part of a debt security (see ASC 480-10-55-29 through 55-32; 40-42 through 40-52 (EITF Issue 85-9, "Convertible Debt and Debt with Warrants," in Chapter 12, for an example of such a security), the contracts discussed in this Issue are freestanding.

The EITF discussed the initial recognition of written put options in Issue 87-31, which is codified in this Issue. Under that consensus, proceeds received on the sale of written put options were recognized as equity transactions. Changes in the market value of the options were not recognized. Although the consensus in Issue 87-31 did not specify the method of settlement, it is clear that the Task Force expected such transactions would be settled in shares, not in net cash nor based on a choice of settlement in cash or shares. The consensus analogized the transactions to those contemplated under SEC Accounting Series Release (ASR) No. 268 (Presentation in Financial Statements of "Redeemable Preferred Stock"), thus requiring public companies to transfer from permanent equity to temporary equity an amount equal to the redemption price of the common stock, regardless of whether the put options can be exercised immediately or are "in the money" when issued. Under that consensus, permanent equity would not be adjusted until the options are redeemed, exercised, or expire.

Although ASC 470-20 (APB-14), and Issue 86-35 (codified in this Issue), provided guidance on accounting for free-standing written call options or warrants on an entity's own stock, they did not specifically address the accounting for freestanding written call options or warrants that must be settled in either net shares or net cash or that permit the company to choose the method of settlement.

ACCOUNTING ISSUE

How should a company classify and measure freestanding contracts that are indexed to, and potentially settled in, the company's own stock?

EITF CONSENSUS

The Framework for Accounting (the Model)

Scope

The EITF developed a framework of accounting ("the Model"), which only applies to freestanding derivative financial instruments that are indexed to and settled in a company's own stock, such as forward contracts, options, and warrants.

The Model does *not* apply to the accounting for:

- A derivative or a financial instrument if the derivative is embedded in the financial instrument and cannot be detached from it
- Contracts issued to compensate employees or to acquire goods and services from nonemployees *before* performance has occurred (the Issue does apply after performance has occurred)
- Contracts indexed to and settled in a consolidated subsidiary's stock (see Issues 00-4 and 00-6)

Initial and Subsequent Balance Sheet Classification and Measurement

Under the Model, freestanding contracts that are indexed to, and potentially settled in, a company's own stock are classified in the balance sheet based on the concept that contracts that must be settled in net cash are assets or liabilities, and that contracts that must be settled in shares are equity instruments. (See the Observation in a discussion of Issue 00-6 under "EITF CONSENSUS.") It is assumed under the Model that if given a choice between settlement in shares or in cash, a company would choose to settle a contract in its own stock in shares or in net shares, whereas the counterparty would choose to settle the same contract in cash or in net cash. The Model does not apply, however, if the settlement alternatives do not have the same economic value or if one of the settlement alternatives is fixed or has caps or floors. If this is the case, the accounting is based on the instrument's (or combination of instruments') economic substance. If the number of shares a company is required to deliver under a contract is limited in accordance with a net-share settlement alternative, the Model applies even though the settlement alternatives may have different economic values.

Freestanding contracts are measured initially at fair value. At each subsequent balance sheet date before settlement, they are accounted for based on the initial classification and the required or assumed settlement method. For example, if a contract that is classified as an equity instrument gives the company a choice between net share settlement or physical settlement requiring the company to deliver cash, it is assumed that the company would choose to settle the contract in net shares. Conversely, it is assumed that given the choice, the counterparty would require the company to settle the contract by physical delivery of cash.

The contracts are classified based on their economic substance and measured as follows:

1. Contracts Classified as Equity Instruments
    a. *Contracts that require physical settlement in shares or settlement in net shares* Reported in *permanent* equity (see the following discussion on equity instruments classified as temporary equity) and measured initially at fair value. Fair value is not adjusted for subsequent changes for contracts classified in equity.
    b. *Contracts under which the company can choose to settle in (a) its own shares (physical settlement in shares or net share settlement) or in net cash or (b) in net shares or by physical settlement requiring the company to deliver cash* Reported in *permanent* equity and measured initially at fair value, which is not adjusted for subsequent changes. Amounts paid or received for contracts settled in cash are included in contributed capital.
    c. ASR 268 provides guidance by analogy to *public* companies for the transactions discussed in this Issue. Consequently, for the following contracts, which are generally reported in permanent equity, public companies must transfer to *temporary equity* an amount equal to the cash redemption amount in a physical settlement:
        (1) Contracts under which physical settlement in cash is required (for example, the company must buy back its share from the holder of a written put option)
        (2) Contracts under which the company chooses settlement in net cash or by physical settlement requiring the company to deliver cash
        (3) Contracts under which the counterparty can choose to settle in net shares or by physical settlement requiring the company to deliver cash
2. Contracts Classified as Assets or Liabilities
    a. *Contracts that must be settled in net cash* Measured initially and subsequently at fair value.
    b. *Contracts under which a counterparty can choose to settle in net cash or in shares (physical settlement or in net shares)* Measured initially and at fair value.

    Gains and losses on contracts classified as assets or liabilities are reported in income and disclosed in the financial statements. Gains or losses continue to be included in income even if the contract is ultimately settled in shares.

DISCUSSION

- Those who believe that contracts requiring physical settlement in shares should be classified in equity argue that classifying such contracts as assets or liabilities, and thus including gains and losses in income, would be inconsistent with the guidance in ASC 225-10-15-3; 45-1; 225-20-05-1; 250-10-05-5; 45-22, 45-24, 45-28; 50-8 through 50-9; 505-10-25-2 (APB-9) and that in ASC 310-10-45-14; 505-10-45-1 through 45-2; and 850-10-60-4 (EITF Issue 85-1). Such classification also would be inconsistent with the guidance in ASR-268 (Presentation Financial Statements of "Redeemable Preferred Stocks"), which requires an entity to transfer an amount that equals the contracted purchase price of the stock under financial instruments (such as forward purchase contracts and purchased call options) from permanent equity to temporary equity. In addition, a transaction settled in the company's shares was considered to be a classic equity transaction.

- The Task Force agreed that because contracts in which a *company* chooses whether to settle the obligation with the company's shares or in cash are under the company's control, such contracts should be accounted for as equity transactions.

- Contracts that require net cash settlement should be classified as assets or liabilities because the right to receive or pay cash is a future economic benefit or future economic sacrifice that meets the definition of an asset or a liability in CON-6 (Elements of Financial Statements) (not in ASC). In addition, because no shares are exchanged, the transaction does not have the characteristics of an equity transaction, even if the amount of cash to be exchanged is indexed to the price of the company's stock.

- Contracts giving the counterparty the right to demand payment in cash or in shares should be recognized as an asset or a liability because the transaction is not under the company's control. For example, a liability may be incurred if the counterparty demands a cash settlement when a forward contract is in a loss position.

- Proponents of the view that gains and losses on contracts recognized as assets or liabilities should be recognized currently in income argue that ASC 250-10-45-22; 225-10-45-1 (paragraph 17 of APB-9, *Reporting the Results of Operations*) requires that treatment. They believe that because the company does not transfer its shares, the transaction does not qualify for the exemption in ASC 505-10-25-2 (paragraph 28 of APB-9), which states that charges or credits resulting from transactions in the company's capital stock may be excluded from the determination of net income. This is analogous to the view of the majority of the EITF in Issue 86-28 (nullified by FAS-133), that is, that an increase in a contingent payment should be recognized as an expense.

Additional Requirements for Equity Classification

The guidance in ASC 815-10-15-74; 815-15-25-1(paragraphs 11(a) and 12(c) of FAS-133) provides that embedded derivatives indexed to a reporting entity's *own* stock and classified in stockholders' equity should *not* be considered to be derivatives for the purposes of ASC 815 (FAS-133), even if they were freestanding. The EITF reached a consensus that the additional requirements for equity classification discussed in this section do *not* apply under the provisions of ASC 815 (FAS-133) when evaluating whether derivative financial instruments, such as forward contracts, options, or warrants, indexed to a company's own stock that are embedded in a *debt* instrument would be classified in stockholders' equity if they were freestanding.

The Task Force also reached a consensus that the requirements in this Issue used to determine whether an embedded derivative indexed to a company's own stock should be classified in stockholders' equity if it were freestanding do not apply to *conventional convertible debt instruments* if the value of the conversion option can be realized only when the holder exercises that option and receives all of the proceeds in a fixed number of shares or in an equivalent amount of cash, at the issuer's option. Issuers should apply the requirements of this Issue, however, when evaluating whether other embedded derivatives are equity instruments not covered under the scope of ASC 815 (FAS-133).

Equity derivative contracts that include a provision under which a company could be required to settle a contract in net cash should be accounted for as an asset or liability under the Model, *not* as the issuer's equity.

SEC registrants should classify equity contracts as temporary equity in accordance with the SEC's Accounting Series Release (ASR) No. 268 (Presentation in Financial Statements of "Redeemable Preferred Stocks") if the contract includes a provision that could require the issuer to pay cash to the counterparty in a *physical settlement* for the issuer's shares. A contract that permits the counterparty to require a *net cash settlement* should be classified as an *asset* or *liability*. This consensus does *not* require an evaluation of the likelihood that an event causing a cash settlement (net cash or physical) would occur. However, the potential outcome need not be considered when the provisions of ASR-268 are applied if cash payment is required only in the case of the issuer's final liquidation.

A derivative indexed to, and potentially settled in, a company's own stock should be classified in equity *only* if all of the following conditions are met:

- The company is permitted to settle the contract in registered or unregistered shares.
- The company has enough authorized but unissued shares available to settle the contract, after considering all of its other commitments that may require issuing stock during the period the contract is outstanding.
- The contract specifically limits the number of shares to be delivered in a share settlement, even if the contract terminates when the stock price is at a stated trigger price.

- The contract does not require the company to post collateral for any reason.
- The issuer is not required to pay cash to the counterparty if the counterparty has sold the shares initially delivered to it and the proceeds are less than the total amount due.
- The counterparty's rights under a contract are no greater than those of the underlying stock's shareholders.

A company may be required under a contract's provisions to settle in net shares or to physically deliver cash and receive its own shares, such as in a forward purchase contract or a written put option. Therefore, a company that does not control settlement in net shares under the above conditions or the Issues discussed below would continue to account for the contract as an equity instrument. SEC registrants, however, would be required to transfer to temporary equity the amount due in cash on settlement.

The conditions discussed above apply to the following consensus positions:

- A contract that requires an issuer to settle by delivering only registered shares in a net-share or physical settlement, or cash in a net-cash settlement, should be accounted for as an *asset or liability*, because (a) events or actions necessary to deliver registered shares are *not* within the company's control and (b) under the model discussed above, it is assumed that the company will be required to settle in net cash.
- Delivery of unregistered shares in a *private placement* is within a company's control if during the six months before the classification assessment date, the company did not file a statement with the SEC that was later withdrawn (a failed registration statement). However, if the company did have a failed registration during the previous six months, there should be a legal determination as to whether the company can deliver unregistered shares in a settlement in shares or in net shares. A company, therefore, should classify a contract as permanent equity if the company (a) has not had a failed registration statement, (b) is permitted under the contract to deliver unregistered shares to settle a contract in net shares, and (c) meets other conditions in this Issue.
- Settlement in shares or net shares is *not* within a company's control if the shareholders' approval is required to increase the number of authorized shares for such settlement. To control settlement, a company must determine whether it will have a sufficient number of authorized and unissued shares at the date on which a contract's classification is determined. To make this determination, a company should compare (a) the number of authorized but unissued shares, less the number of shares the company could be required to deliver during the contract period to satisfy existing commitments, with (b) the maximum number of shares that the company could be required to deliver in a

net-share or physical settlement under the contract. A company controls settlement in shares if the number of shares in (*a*) is greater than the number of shares in (*b*) and meets the company conditions above. If settlement is *not* under the company's control, the contract should be classified as an *asset* or *liability*.

- If the number of shares a company may need to settle a contract cannot be determined at the classification date, net-share settlement is *not* under the company's control because the company cannot determine whether it has sufficient authorized shares for settlement. If a contract limits the number of shares delivered at the contract's expiration in a net-share settlement, the company *can* determine whether such settlement is within its control by comparing the maximum number of shares needed with the available authorized but unissued shares. That comparison would determine whether a sufficient number of shares is available to settle a contract in net shares after delivering shares to satisfy other existing commitments as well as for top-off or make-whole provisions discussed below.

- A derivative contract must be classified as an *asset* or *liability* if net-share settlement is permitted, but net-cash settlement is *required* if a company does not make timely SEC filings because doing so is not within the company's control.

- If a contract requires net-cash settlement on the occurrence of an event that results in a change of control, the contract should be classified as an *asset* or *liability*, because the occurrence of such an event would not be under the company's control. However, classification in permanent equity would be acceptable if, under a contract's change of control provision, the counterparty can receive or deliver on settlement the same form of consideration as to the shareholders of the security underlying the contract. For example, the counterparty to the contract and the shareholders would both receive cash in the transaction. Further, a contract's classification would not be affected if it includes a provision related to a change in control that specifies that if all stockholders receive the acquiring company's stock, the contract will be indexed to the purchaser's stock (or the issuer's in a business combination accounted for as a pooling of interests).

- A contract that grants a counterparty the rights of a creditor in case the company declares bankruptcy should *not* be classified as equity, unless the contract includes a statement that the counterparty's rights are not senior to the claims of the common shareholders of the underlying stock in case of bankruptcy. However, equity classification would be permitted for a contract that requires net-cash settlement in case of bankruptcy if it is possible to demonstrate that the counterparty's claims in bankruptcy could be settled in net shares or would not have a higher rank in bankruptcy than those of the underlying stock's common shareholders.

- Equity classification is permitted if a contract requires net-cash settlement in case of nationalization, because the counterparty and the underlying stock's common shareholders, who would receive cash as compensation for the expropriated assets, would receive the same form of compensation.

- *Top-off* or *make-whole* provisions are sometimes included in contracts to reimburse a counterparty for losses incurred, or to transfer to the company gains the counterparty recognized on the difference between the value of the contract at the settlement date and the value the counterparty realized in a sale of the securities after the settlement date. A contract that includes such a provision may be classified as equity only if (*a*) the provision can be settled in net shares and (*b*) the maximum number of shares that could be delivered is fixed and is less than the number of available authorized shares after meeting other commitments settled in shares.

- Equity classification is *not* permitted if a contract includes a provision requiring an issuer to post collateral if certain events occur (e.g., a drop in the price of the underlying stock), because the requirement to post collateral is not consistent with the concept of equity. However, equity classification is permitted if the equity securities to be delivered under a contract are placed in trust.

Contract Reclassification

A contract's classification should be reassessed at each balance sheet date. If necessary, a contract should be reclassified as of the date on which an event causing a change in classification has occurred. Contracts may be reclassified an unlimited number of times.

A contract's change in classification should be accounted for as follows:

- A change in the fair value of a contract that is reclassified from permanent or temporary equity to an asset or liability classification should be accounted for as an adjustment to stockholders' equity for the period between the date of the contract's last classification as equity to the date of reclassification to an asset or a liability. In addition, after a contract is reclassified from permanent or temporary equity to an asset or a liability, all changes in the contract's fair value should be recognized in income.

- Conversely, gains or losses recognized in accounting for the fair value of a contract that has been properly classified as an asset or a liability should not be reversed if the contract is reclassified to equity.

- If the total notional amount of a contract that can be partially settled in net shares can no longer be classified in permanent equity, the portion that could be settled in net shares as of the balance sheet date would continue to be classified in permanent equity while the other portion would be reclassified in temporary equity, or as an asset or liability, as appropriate.

If more than one of a company's derivative contracts may be partially settled, and some or all of those contracts are *required* to be partially settled, different methods can be used to determine which contracts, or portions thereof, should be reclassified.

Determining how to partially reclassify such contracts is an accounting policy decision that should be disclosed in accordance with ASC 235-10-05-3 through 05-4, 50-1 through 50-6 (APB-22). However, the reclassification method should be systematic, rational, and consistent. Under acceptable methods, an entity might (*a*) partially reclassify all contracts proportionately, (*b*) reclassify contracts with the *earliest inception* date first, (*c*) reclassify contracts with the *earliest maturity* date first, (*d*) reclassify contracts with the *latest inception* date first, or (*e*) reclassify contracts with the *latest maturity* date first.

Disclosures

The EITF reached a consensus that the following disclosures required under ASC 505-10-15-1; 50-3 through 50-5, 50-11; 470-10-50-5 (FAS-129) apply to *all* contracts under the scope of this Issue:

- For an option or forward contract indexed to the issuer's equity, disclose the forward rate, option strike price, number of issuer's shares to which the contract is indexed, the settlement date or dates of the contract, and whether the issuer accounts for the contract as an asset, a liability, or equity.

- For contracts with terms that *state* alternative settlement methods, disclose the alternatives, including who controls the alternatives and the *maximum* number of shares that *could be required to be issued* to settle a contract with net shares. Under the guidance in ASC 505-10-15-1; 50-3 through 50-5, 50-11; 470-10-50-5 (FAS-129) additional disclosures about actual issuances and settlements that occurred during the accounting period also are required.

- For contracts that *do not* state a fixed or determinable maximum number of shares that may be required to be issued, disclose the fact that an infinite number of shares potentially could be issued to settle the contract.

- Disclose the contract's current fair value for each settlement alternative, denominated in monetary amounts or number of shares, and the effect of changes in the price of the issuer's equity instruments on settlement amounts.

- For equity instruments under this Issue that are classified as temporary equity, disclose the amount of redemption requirements, by issue or combined for all issues, that are redeemable at fixed or determinable prices on fixed or determinable dates in each of the five years after the date of the latest balance sheet presented.
- For contracts classified as assets or liabilities that meet the definition of a derivative under the guidance in ASC 815 (FAS-133), disclose information regarding the objective for holding or issuing those instruments based on the guidance in ASC 815-10-50-1 through 50-5 (paragraph 44 of FAS-133),, as well as the disclosures required in ASC 815-30-50-1 (paragraph 45 of FAS-133), regarding fair value hedges, cash flow hedges, and hedges of net investments in foreign operations.

The Task Force reached a consensus that issuers should disclose information about contract reclassifications in or out of equity during the life of an instrument, the reason for reclassification, and the effect on the issuer's financial statements. In addition, the entity's accounting policy regarding the method used to partially reclassify contracts under this Issue should be disclosed in accordance with with the guidance in ASC 235-10-50-1 through 50-6 (APB-22).

Application Guidance for Specific Instruments

The following guidance represents the Task Force's consensus positions on the application of the Model to the following types of freestanding derivative financial instruments that are indexed to, and potentially settled in, a company's own stock.

1. Forward Sale Contracts, Written Call Options or Warrants, and Purchased Put Options

OVERVIEW

A company enters into a contract to sell a specific number of its shares of common stock to the holder at a specified price on a specified future date. The contract may be settled by delivery of shares to the counterparty (physical settlement), in net shares, in net cash, or based on the company's or counterparty's choice of settlement method.

EITF CONSENSUS

Based on the Model, the contracts are accounted for as follows:

- *Contracts requiring physical settlement in shares or settlement in net shares* The contracts are *equity* instruments recognized in permanent equity and measured initially at fair value. Fair value is not adjusted for subsequent events.

- *Contracts requiring net cash settlement* The contracts are reported as *assets* or *liabilities* and measured initially and subsequently at fair value. Subsequent changes in fair value, if any, are reported in income and disclosed in the financial statements.
- *Contracts giving the company the choice of settlement method*
  — Settlement in net shares or by physical settlement in shares. The contracts are *equity* instruments recognized in permanent equity and measured initially at fair value, which is not adjusted for subsequent changes.
  — Settlement in net shares or net cash, or settlement in net cash or physical settlement in shares. The contracts are *equity* instruments reported in permanent equity and measured initially at fair value, which is not adjusted for subsequent changes. If cash is paid or received in a net cash settlement, that amount is reported in contributed capital.
- *Contracts giving the counterparty the choice of settlement method*
  — Settlement in net shares or by physical settlement in shares. The contracts are *equity* instruments reported in permanent equity and measured initially at fair value, which is not adjusted for subsequent changes.
  — Settlement in net shares or net cash, or settlement in net cash or physical settlement in shares. The contracts are reported as *assets* or *liabilities* and measured initially and subsequently at fair value. Subsequent changes in fair value, if any, are reported in earnings and disclosed in the financial statements. Gains or losses are included in income and disclosed in the financial statements, even if the contract is ultimately settled in shares.

Illustration of the Accounting for a Purchased Put Option Indexed to, and Potentially Settled in, a Company's Own Stock

On 7/15/X5, Preston Company (a public company with a 12/31 year-end) purchases a put option that is indexed to 100 common shares of the company's own stock at $25 per share, when the fair value of the stock is $25 per share. The option expires on 10/13/X5. The option premium is $150. Assume that the price of each common share and the fair value of the option are $23 and $225 on 9/30/X5. The price of each share of common stock on 10/13/X5, the settlement date, is $20. Under the following two scenarios, Preston accounts for the contract at each date as follows: (a) 7/15/X5, (b) 9/30/X5, and (c) 10/13/X5.

Scenario 1: The company can choose to settle in net shares or net cash

(a) At initiation of the contract—7/15/X5

Because the company can choose the method of settlement, the indexed option is an equity transaction.

Additional paid-in capital	$150	
Cash		$150

(b) At interim dates—9/30/X5

Contracts recorded as equity transactions are not adjusted to fair value at interim dates.

(c) At settlement—10/13/X5

The company chooses to settle in net cash. Because the price per share is $20 on the settlement date, the option is worth $500 [($25 − $20) × 100]. The counterparty pays the company $500 to settle the contract.

Cash	$500	
Additional paid-in capital		$500

Scenario 2: The counterparty can choose to settle in net cash or in net shares

(a) At initiation of the contract—7/15/X5

Because the counterparty decides on the method of settlement, the indexed option is recognized as an asset.

Indexed option	$150	
Cash		$150

(b) At interim dates—9/30/X5

The per share price has increased to $23. The company reduces the carrying amount of the option to its fair value of $225 and recognizes a loss of $105 ($330 − $225).

Loss on indexed option	$105	
Indexed option		$105

(c) At settlement—10/13/X5

The counterparty chooses to settle in net shares. Because the price per share is $20 on the settlement date—$5 less than the reference price of $25—the option is worth $500. The company, therefore, had a total gain recognized on settlement is $275 ($500 less the $225 recorded amount of the option).

Treasury stock	$500	
Indexed option		$225
Gain on indexed option		275

SUBSEQUENT DEVELOPMENT

The EITF's Chairman announced at the May 1998 meeting that the SEC Observer stated at the Agenda Committee's meeting that registrants that have entered into forward equity sales transactions after May 1, 1998, should classify those transactions as debt. Such transactions combine the issuance of common stock with a forward contract that requires the issuer to give the holder a guaranteed return.

2. Written Put Options and Forward Purchase Contracts

OVERVIEW

A company enters into a contract under which it agrees to purchase a specified number of the company's shares of common stock at a specified price on a specified future date. The contract may be settled by physical settlement, in net shares, in net cash, or the issuing company or the counterparty may have the right to choose the settlement method. (This discussion also applies to shareholder rights (SHARPs) issued by a company to its shareholders, which give them the right to sell a specified number of common shares to the company for cash.)

EITF CONSENSUS

Based on the Model, the contracts are accounted for as follows:

- *Contracts requiring physical settlement in cash* The contracts are *equity* instruments reported in permanent equity, but because the option writer is required to settle the contract in cash, *public* companies must transfer to temporary equity an amount equal to the redemption amount. The instruments are measured initially at fair value without subsequent adjustment for changes in fair value.

- *Contracts requiring net share settlement* The contracts are equity instruments reported in permanent equity and measured initially at fair value, without subsequent adjustment for changes in fair value.

- *Contracts requiring net cash settlement* The contracts are *liabilities* that are measured initially at fair value and adjusted for changes in fair value, which are reported in earnings and disclosed in the financial statements.

- *Contracts giving the company the choice of settlement method*
  — Settlement in net shares or physical settlement in cash, or settlement in net shares or net cash. The contracts are equity instruments that are reported in permanent equity. The instruments are measured initially at fair value without subsequent adjustment for changes in fair value. Cash paid or received in a physical settlement in cash or a net cash

settlement is recognized in contributed capital. (It is assumed that the company will settle in net shares.)
— Settlement in net cash or by physical settlement in cash. The contracts are *equity* instruments that are reported in permanent equity, but because the option writer is required to settle the contract in cash, *public* companies must transfer to temporary equity an amount equal to the redemption amount. The instruments are measured initially at fair value without subsequent adjustment for changes in fair value. If the contract is ultimately settled in net cash or in net shares, the amount reported in temporary equity is transferred and reported as an addition to permanent equity.
- *Contracts giving the counterparty the choice of settlement method*
- Settlement in net cash or by physical settlement in cash. The contracts are *equity* instruments that are reported in permanent equity, but because the option writer is required to settle the contract in cash, *public* companies must transfer to temporary equity an amount equal to the redemption amount. The instruments are measured initially at fair value without subsequent adjustment for changes in fair value. If the contract is ultimately settled in net cash or in net shares, the amount reported in temporary equity is transferred and reported as an addition to permanent equity.
- Settlement in net cash or net shares, or in net cash or physical settlement in cash. The contracts are liabilities that should be measured at fair value and adjusted for changes in fair value. Gains or losses are included in earnings and disclosed in the financial statements, even if the contract is ultimately settled in shares.

> **OBSERVATION:** Under the provisions of ASC 460-10-05-1, 05-2; 460-10-10-1; 460-10-15-4 through 15-7, 15-9, 15-10; 460-10-25-1 through 25-4; 460-10-30-1 through 30-4; 460-10-35-1, 35-2, 35-4; 460-10-50-2, 50-4 through 50-6, 50-8; 460-10-55-2, 55-3, 55-5 through 55-9, 55-12, 55-13, 55-15 through 55-18, 55-20 through 55-24, 55-28, 55-29; 840-10-25-34; 840-10-60-2 (FIN-45, *Guarantor's Accounting and Disclosure Requirements for Guarantees, Including Indirect Guarantees of Indebtedness of Others*), guarantors are required to recognize a liability at the inception of a guarantee for the obligation assumed. Contracts under the consensus in this Issue that also meet the definition of a guarantee in FIN-45, such as physically settled written puts, are initially valued at fair value, as also required in FIN-45. Although the accounting is *not* affected, the guarantee should be disclosed under the requirements in FIN-45.

DISCUSSION

- A written put option or forward purchase contract that requires settlement in net cash is a liability because it represents an obligation to sacrifice assets in the future. Proponents of this view argued that the transaction should not be recognized in equity because no shares will be exchanged. They also referred to the treatment of purchased options or purchased forward contracts settled in cash. Recognition of gains or losses is based on the view that such recognition is required by ASC 250-10-45-22; 225-10-45-1 (paragraph 17 of APB-9) for items treated as assets or liabilities and is consistent with the Model.

- A written put option that permits the *counterparty* to choose the settlement method should also be recognized as a liability, because the company cannot control whether it will be required to transfer cash to the counterparty. Proponents of this approach also referred to the treatment of purchased put options and purchased forward contracts when the counterparty can choose the method of settlement. Recognition of a gain or loss is based on the view that such recognition is required by ASC 250-10-45-22; 225-10-45-1 (paragraph 17 of APB-9) for items treated as assets or liabilities and is consistent with the Model.

- Written put options giving the *company* the choice of settlement method should be accounted for as equity transactions because the company can choose to settle the option in shares of stock rather than in cash. This consensus conforms to the consensus reached in Issue 87-31 and the Model. The consensus not to recognize gains or losses on such option contracts is also consistent with the consensus in Issue 87-31 (codified in this Issue).

Illustration of the Accounting for the Sale of Written Put Options on an Issuer's Stock That Require or Permit Cash Settlement

On 12/15/X5, Preston Company (a public company with a 12/31 year-end) sells a put option that is indexed to 100 common shares of the company's own stock at a price of $25 per share when the fair value of the stock is $25 per share. The option expires on 3/14/X6. The option premium is $150. Assume that the price of each common share and the fair value of the option is as follows: *(a)* $22 and $330, respectively, on 12/31/X5. The price of each share of common stock on 3/14/X6, the settlement date, is $20.

Under the following two scenarios, Preston accounts for the contract as follows at each date: (a) 12/15/X5, (b) 12/31/X5, and (c) 3/14/X6.

Scenario 1: The company can choose to settle in net cash or by physical settlement in cash.

(a) At initiation of the contract—12/15/X5

Because the company chooses the method of settlement, the indexed option is treated as an equity transaction.

17.62 *Financial Instruments*

Cash	$150		
Additional paid-in capital		$150	

Because the company's stock is publicly traded, the company must transfer to temporary equity an amount equal to 100 shares at the settlement price.

Additional paid-in capital	$2,500		
Cost of settling put options		$2,500	

(b) At year-end—12/31/X5 (interim date)

Contracts recorded as equity transactions are not adjusted to fair value at interim dates.

(c) At settlement of the contract in net shares—3/14/X6

Because the price per share is $20 on the settlement date, the option contract is worth $500 [($25 − $20) × 100]. The company chooses to settle in net cash and pays the counterparty $500 to settle the contract.

Cost of settling put options	$2,500		
Additional paid-in capital		$2,000	
Cash		500	

Scenario 2: The counterparty can choose to settle in net cash or in net shares

(a) At initiation of the contract—12/15/X5

Because the counterparty can choose to settle in net cash or net shares, the option is treated as a liability.

Cash	$150		
Indexed option contract payable		$150	

(b) At year-end—12/31/X5 (interim date)

The per share price of $22 is $3 less than the $25 per share price on settlement. The company adjusts the liability to the option's fair value of $330 and recognizes a loss of $180.

Loss on indexed option contract	$180		
Indexed option contract payable		$180	

(c) At settlement—3/14/X6

The counterparty chooses to settle in net shares. Because the price per share is $20 on the settlement date—$5 less than the reference price of $25—the option is worth $500. The company, therefore, has a total loss of $350 on the contract ($500 less $150 premium). The company settles the contract by delivering 25 shares ($500/$20) to the counterparty to settle the contract. The loss recognized on settlement is $275 ($500 less the $225 recorded liability).

Loss on indexed option contract	$275	
Indexed Option payable	225	
Treasury shares		$500

3. Purchased Call Option

OVERVIEW

A company purchases a call option giving it the right, but not the obligation, to purchase from the option's seller a specific number of the company's shares of common stock at a specified price on a specified future date. The contract may be settled by physical settlement, in net shares, in net cash, or based on the settlement method chosen by the company or the counterparty.

EITF CONSENSUS

Purchased call options are accounted for the same as forward sale contracts, written call options or warrants, and purchased put options as previously discussed.

4. Detachable Stock Purchase Warrants

OVERVIEW

A company issues senior subordinated notes with a detachable warrant giving the holder the right to purchase 5,000 shares of the issuer's stock for $50 per share at any time and the right to require the company to repurchase all or some of the warrants for at least $1,000 per share several months after the notes mature in about five years.

EITF CONSENSUS

The issuer should account for the notes as follows:

- The proceeds should be allocated between the liability for the debt and the warrant. The resulting discount should be amortized over the term of the notes in accordance with the guidance in ASC 835-30 (APB-21).
- The warrants are considered to be, in substance, a debt instrument and are accounted for as a liability, because the

alternatives for settling the warrants do not have the same economic value. The put gives the holder a guaranteed return in cash (5,000 shares × $1,000 = $5,000,000) that significantly exceeds the value of the share settlement (5,000 shares × $ 50 = $ 250,000) without the put at the date of issuance.

DISCUSSION

The EITF's resolution of this Issue in Issue 86-35 (which has been superseded by Issue 96-13) is similar to that in Issue 85-29 (Convertible Bonds with a "Premium Put) (not in ASC, see Chapter 12), which dealt with a "put premium" on convertible bonds. This Issue deals with the balance sheet classification of a detachable stock purchase warrant with a put option at a fixed price. Under the provisions of ASC 470-20-05-2 through 05-6; 25-2 through 25-3, 25-10 through 25-11, 25-13; 30-1 through 30-2; and 505-10-60-3 (APB-14), the proceeds would be allocated between the debt and the warrant. However, the treatment of the warrant as a liability is more appropriate because, based on the economics of the transaction, it is probable that it will be put to the issuer at the fixed price, which substantially exceeds the price of the stock.

5. Put Warrants

OVERVIEW

Put warrants, which generally are issued with debt instruments, combine the characteristics of warrants and put options. They are detachable from the debt and can be exercised under specified conditions by (a) using the warrant feature to acquire the issuer's stock at a specified price, (b) using the put feature to receive cash from the issuer, or (c) using both the warrant and put features to acquire stock and receive cash from the issuer. The put feature may be exercisable only for a specified time period and may expire under certain conditions. The put feature is canceled if the warrant is exercised and, likewise, exercising the put feature cancels the warrant feature. APB-14 requires that a portion of the proceeds from the issuance of debt with detachable warrants be allocated to the warrants.

EITF CONSENSUS

Public companies should report the proceeds from the issuance of put warrants as liabilities because the counterparty has the choice of settling the contract in cash or in shares. In subsequent periods, the put warrants are measured at fair value; changes in fair value are reported in earnings. The consensus in Issue 88-9 (not in ASC) continues to apply to nonpublic companies. (Also see the Observation under "EITF Consensus" in discussion of Issue 00-6.)

6. Contracts with Multiple Settlement Alternatives

- Account as *equity instruments* for contracts under the Model if the contract has several alternatives under which the issuer is required to *receive* net cash when the contract is in a *gain* position, but is required to choose between *paying* in net cash or in net stock when the contract is in a *loss* position.

The Task Force noted that this consensus does not apply if a contract is primarily a purchased option under which the amount of cash that could be received when the contract is in a gain position would significantly exceed the amount that could be paid when the contract is in a *loss* position—for example, if the amount of loss is contractually limited to a small amount. Such contracts should be accounted for as assets or liabilities. (Also see the Observation under "EITF Consensus" in discussion of Issue 00-6 in this Chapter.)

- Account as *assets* or *liabilities* for contracts under the Model, if the contract has several alternatives under which an issuer is required to *pay* net cash when the contract is in a *loss* position, but is required to choose between receiving net cash or net stock when the contract is in a *gain* position.

7. Earnings per Share

A discussion on the effect on earnings per share may be found in Chapter 13, "Earnings per Share."

EITF Issue 02-3 (Issues Involved in Accounting for Derivative Contracts Held for Trading Purposes and Contracts Involved in Energy Trading and Risk Management Activities) (ASC 932-330-35-1; 815-10-45-9)

OVERVIEW

Entities whose business activities involve energy trading contracts and risk management activities can find accounting guidance in the following pronouncements:

- EITF Issue 98-10 (Accounting for Contracts Involved in Energy Trading and Risk Management Activities) (superseded by the guidance in this Issue), required that energy trading contracts be presented at fair value on the balance sheet date. A gross or net income statement presentation of gains or losses related to those contracts is permitted.
- Issue 00-17 (Measuring the Fair Value of Energy-Related Contracts in Applying Issue 98-10) ((superseded by the guidance in this Issue), required that the fair value of energy trading contracts reported in the balance sheet be determined based on the

best available information about the estimated fair values of the *individual* contracts. A contract's initial fair value is its price. Although the EITF decided not to provide guidance on specific measurement methods, the Task Force reached a consensus that *dealer profit*, which is the difference between the bid and ask prices of dealers involved in significant transactions in the market, provides information about current market transactions. That information may be used to estimate changes in the fair value of contracts. Valuation models should be used if information about dealer profit is unavailable.

This Issue was brought before the EITF because some have questioned whether companies should be permitted to report unrealized gains or losses at the *inception* of energy trading contracts if *no* quoted market prices or other current market transactions with similar terms and counterparties exist. The FASB staff believes that the EITF's consensus related to dealer profit indicates that quoted market prices or information about other market conditions is *required* to recognize unrealized gains or losses at the inception of a contract. In addition, the EITF was asked to discuss how the guidance on disclosures in ASC 235-10-05-3 through 05-4; 50-1 through 50-6 (APB-22, *Disclosure of Accounting Policies*) and ASC 205-20-55-80, 55-81; 275-10-05-2 through 05-8; 10-1; 15-3 through 15-6; 50-1, 50-2, 50-4, 50-6 through 50-21, 50-23; 55-1 through 55-19; 60-3; 330-10-55-8 through 55-13; 410-30-55-8 through 55-13; 450-20-50-2; 55-36, 55-37; 460-10-55-27; 605-35-55-3 through 55-10; 740-10-55-219 through 55-222; 932-360-55-15 through 15-19; 958-205-60-1; 605-55-70; 985-20-55-24 through 5-29 (SOP 94-6, "Disclosure of Certain Significant Risks and Uncertainties") applies to energy trading contracts and to suggest additional disclosures.

ACCOUNTING ISSUES

1. Should gains and losses on energy trading contracts be reported gross or net in the income statement?
2. Is recognition of unrealized gains and losses at the inception of an energy trading contract appropriate if no quoted market prices or current market transactions for contracts with similar terms exist?
3. What information should companies be required to disclose about energy trading activities?

EITF CONSENSUS

1. The guidance in Issue 98-10 (Accounting for Contracts Involved in Energy Trading and Risk Management Activities) should be rescinded. The EITF reached this consensus because Issue 98-10 permitted fair value accounting for contracts that did not have a ready market with readily available prices. As a result of this

consensus, fair value accounting is permitted only for contracts that are accounted for as derivatives under the provisions of ASC 815 (FAS-133, *Accounting for Derivative Instruments and Hedging Activities*).

2. Realized and unrealized gains or losses should be presented on a *net* basis for *all* securities accounted for as *derivatives* under the provisions of ASC 815 (FAS-133) that are part of a trading activity or held for trading purposes. To clarify the meaning of *trading purposes*, the FASB staff observed that whether derivatives are held for trading purposes depends on an issuer's or holder's intent as discussed in ASC 320-10-25-1 (paragraph 12(a) of FAS-115)—that is, whether the instruments are bought and sold frequently to produce profits on short-term price differences. Members noted that other commodity derivatives, such as gold, are presented net in the financial statements.

SUBSEQUENT DEVELOPMENTS

- At its November 2002 meeting, the EITF agreed to include the FASB staff's clarification of the guidance in the ASC, *Master Glossary* (paragraph 540 of FAS-133) regarding the determination of fair value when a quoted market price is unavailable. The FASB staff believes that the price used in a transaction is the best information available on which to estimate the fair value of a transaction at the inception of an arrangement if there are *no* (*a*) *quoted* market prices in an active market, (*b*) *observable* prices of other current market transactions, or (*c*) other *observable data* to use in making a valuation. Consequently, unrealized gains or losses should be recognized on derivative instruments only if the fair value of an instrument can be obtained from quoted market prices in active markets, from observable evidence of comparable market transactions, or based on valuation techniques using observable market data.

- This Issue rescinds Issue 98-10 and prohibits mark-to-market accounting for energy trading contracts that are not derivative instruments under the guidance in ASC 815 (FAS-133). In addition, the EITF reached a consensus that gains and losses on all derivative instruments under the guidance in ASC 815 (FAS-133) that are held for trading purposes should be presented *net* in the income statement, regardless of the method of settlement. Some have questioned whether the guidance regarding the meaning of *trading purposes* in the context of that consensus contradicts the hedge criteria in ASC 815 (FAS-133), so that a derivative held for trading purposes could not be designated as a hedge. The FASB staff reported that the EITF's agenda committee considered that question and concluded that the clarification regarding the meaning of *trading purposes* was not intended to limit the designation of a derivative as a hedge under the provisions of ASC 815 (FAS-133). The EITF agreed that a derivative held for trading purposes may be designated *prospectively* as a hedge if it meets all the related requirements in ASC 815 (FAS-133).

> **OBSERVATION:** Derivatives and other financial instruments accounted for under the guidance in ASC 815 (FAS-133) should be measured at fair value on initial recognition and in subsequent periods under the guidance in ASC 820-10 (FAS-157). The provisions of ASC 820-10 (FAS-157), should be applied *retrospectively* in the year in which FAS-157 is first applied to a financial instrument that was measured at fair value when initially recognized under the provisions of ASC 815 (FAS-133) using the transaction price in accordance with the FASB staff's guidance, which clarified the guidance in the ASC, *Master Glossary* (paragraph 540 of FAS-133) regarding the determination of fair value when a quoted market price is unavailable.

SEC OBSERVER COMMENT

The SEC Observer stated that the EITF's consensus prohibiting mark-to-market accounting for energy trading contracts that are not derivatives also applies to brokers and dealers in securities, because the AICPA's audit and accounting guide applicable to those entities does not provide for specialized accounting in that area.

The SEC Observer also reminded registrants about the required disclosures in Item 303 of Regulations S-K and S-B, which addresses the requirements for Management's Discussion and Analysis, and the guidance in Financial Reporting Release (FRR) 61.

EITF Issue 03-11 (Reporting Realized Gains and Losses on Derivative Instruments That Are Subject to FASB Statement No. 133, *Accounting for Derivative Instruments and Hedging Activities*, and Not "Held for Trading Purposes" as Defined in EITF Issue No. 02-3, "Issues Involved in Accounting for Derivative Contracts Held for Trading Purposes and Contracts Involved in Energy Trading and Risk Management Activities") (ASC 815-10-55-62)

OVERVIEW

During its discussion of the guidance in ASC 932-330-35-1; 815-10-45-9 (Issue 02-3, "Issues Involved in Accounting for Derivative Contracts Held for Trading Purposes and Contracts Involved in Energy Trading and Risk Management Activities"), the EITF reached a consensus that *all* derivatives instruments held for trading purposes that are accounted for under the provisions of ASC 815 (FAS-133, *Accounting for Derivative Instruments and Hedging Activities*) should be reported *net* in the income statement, regardless of whether or not they are settled physically.

ACCOUNTING ISSUE

Should realized gains and losses on contracts *not* held for trading purposes (as defined in ASC 932-330-35-1; 815-10-45-9 (Issue 02-3)) that are accounted for as derivatives under the guidance in ASC 815 (FAS-133) be reported gross or net in the income statement, regardless whether the derivative is designated as a hedging instrument?

EITF CONSENSUS

The EITF reached a consensus that:

- Judgment based on the facts and circumstances, considering the context of the entity's various activities rather than solely on the terms of the contract, should be used to determine whether realized gains and losses on *physically* settled derivative contracts *not* held for trading purposes should be reported in the income statement gross or net; and

- The economic substance of the transaction, the guidance in ASC 845-10 (APB-29, *Accounting for Nonmonetary Transactions*) for nonmonetary exchanges, and the gross versus net reporting indicators in ASC 605-45-05-1, 05-2; 15-3 through 15-5; 45-1, 45-2, 45-4 through 45-14, 45-6 through 45-18; 50-1; 55-2, 55-3, 55-5, 55-6, 55-8, 55-9, 55-11 through 55-14, 55-16, 55-18, 55-20, 55-22, 55-24, 55-25, 55-27 through 55-31, 55-33, 55-34, 55-36 through 55-38, 55-40 through 55-45 (Issue 99-19, "Reporting Revenue Gross as a Principle versus Net as an Agent"), should also be considered in that decision.

The FASB ratified this consensus at its August 13, 2003, meeting.

EITF Issue 07-5 (Determining Whether an Instrument (or Embedded Features) Is Indexed to an Entity's Own Stock) (ASC 718-10-60-1B; 815-10-65-3; 40-15-5 through 15-8; 55-26 through 55-48)

OVERVIEW

Under the guidance in ASC 815-10-15-74 (paragraph 11(a) of FAS-133, *Accounting for Derivative Instruments and Hedging Activities*), a freestanding contract, such as a stock purchase warrant, that is (1) indexed to its own stock *and* (2) classified in an entity's balance sheet as equity is *not* be considered to be a derivative.

Although under the guidance in ASC 815-15-25-1 (paragraph 12 of FAS-133), a derivative instrument embedded in a host contract must be separated and accounted for separately as a derivative, under the guidance in ASC 815-15-25-1 (paragraph 12(c) of the Statement), an embedded instrument's terms must be the same as those of the host instrument in order for that instrument to be accounted for separately as a derivative. Therefore, an embedded derivative that meets the exception in ASC 815-10-15-74 (paragraph 11(a) of FAS-133) would *not* be separated from its host instrument and accounted for as a derivative.

The purpose of this Issue is to develop guidance on how to determine whether an instrument or an embedded feature is indexed to an entity's own stock, which is the first part of the exception in ASC 815-10-15-74 (paragraph 11(a) of FAS-133). However, this Issue does *not* address the second requirement in ASC 815-10-15-74 (paragraph 11(a) of FAS-133) (i.e., whether an instrument or an embedded feature that has the characteristics of a derivative, as discussed in ASC 815-10-15-83, 15-85, 15-88, 15-89, 15-92 through 15-96, 15-99, 15-100, 15-110, 15-119, 15-120, 15-128, 440-10-60-10 (paragraphs 6 through 9 of FAS-133), is classified in an entity's stockholder's equity or would be classified that way if it were a freestanding instrument) because other authoritative accounting guidance, including that in ASC 460-10-60-14; 480-10-55-63; 505-10-60-5; 815-10-15-78; 55-52; 15-25-15; 40-05-1 through 05-4, 05-10, 05-11, 05-12; 25-1 through 25-5, 25-7 through 25-20, 25-22 through 25-24, 25-26 through 25-35; 25-37 through 25-40; 30-1; 35-1, 35-2, 35-6, 35-8 through 35-13; 40-1, 40-2; 50-1 through 50-5; 55-1 through 55-18 (Issue 00-19, "Accounting for Derivative Financial Instruments Indexed to, and Potentially Settled in, a Company's Own Stock") and ASC 815-40-25-41, 42 (Issue 05-2, "The Meaning of 'Conventional Convertible Debt Instrument' in Issue No. 00-19) address that question.

The purpose of the guidance in this Issue is help users to evaluate whether certain freestanding instruments that do *not* have all of the characteristics of a derivative under the guidance in ASC 815 (FAS-133), but are potentially settled in an entity's own equity shares, should be accounted for under the guidance in Issue 00-19. For example, a physically settled forward contract to issue an entity's own equity shares for cash does *not* meet the net settlement characteristic of a derivative discussed in ASC 815-10-15-83, 15-85, 15-88, 15-89, 15-92 through 15-96, 15-99, 15-100, 15-110, 15-119, 15-120, 15-128, 440-10-60-10 (paragraphs 6(c) and 9 of FAS-133) if the underlying equity shares are *not* readily convertible to cash. However, if that forward contract is *not* considered to be indexed to an entity's own stock, the contract would *not* be accounted for under the guidance in ASC 460-10-60-14; 480-10-55-63; 505-10-60-5; 815-10-15-78; 55-52; 15-25-15; 40-05-1 through 05-4, 05-10, 05-11, 05-12; 25-1 through 25-5, 25-7 through 25-20, 25-22 through 25-24, 25-26 through 25-35; 25-37 through 25-40; 30-1; 35-1, 35-2, 35-6, 35-8 through 35-13; 40-1, 40-2; 50-1 through 50-5; 55-1 through 55-18 (Issue 00-19), which applies only to instruments indexed to, and potentially settled in, an issuer's own stock.

The guidance in this Issue should be applied to a unit of accounting based on the requirements in other U.S. generally accepted accounting principles (GAAP). That is, an issuer that had issued two freestanding financial instruments should apply the guidance in this Issue separately to each instrument if that treatment is required under other GAAP. However, an issuer that had issued two freestanding financial instruments would apply the guidance in this Issue to a *single combined* financial instrument if under other GAAP, the two instruments must be *linked* and accounted for as one financial instrument.

EITF CONSENSUS

The EITF reached the following consensus positions.

Scope

The guidance in Issue 07-5 applies to: (1) freestanding financial instruments or embedded features with all of the characteristics of derivatives in ASC 815-10-15-83, 15-85, 15-88, 15-89, 15-92 through 15-96, 15-99, 15-100, 15-110, 15-119, 15-120, 15-128, 440-10-60-10 (paragraphs 6 through 9 of FAS-133) when determining whether those instruments qualify for the first part of the scope exception in ASC 815-10-15-74 (paragraph 11(a) of FAS-133); and (2) freestanding financial instruments that are potentially settled in an entity's own stock, regardless of whether they have all of the characteristics of a derivative in ASC 815-10-15-83, 15-85, 15-88, 15-89, 15-92 through 15-96, 15-99, 15-100, 15-110, 15-119, 15-120, 15-128, 440-10-60-10 (paragraphs 6 through 9 of FAS-133), when determining whether an instrument should be accounted for under the guidance in ASC 460-10-60-14; 480-10-55-63; 505-10-60-5; 815-10-15-78; 55-52; 15-25-15; 40-05-1 through 05-4, 05-10, 05-11, 05-12; 25-1 through 25-5, 25-7 through 25-20, 25-22 through 25-24, 25-26 through 25-35; 25-37 through 25-40; 30-1; 35-1, 35-2, 35-6, 35-8 through 35-13; 40-1, 40-2; 50-1 through 50-5; 55-1 through 55-18 (Issue 00-19).

This Issue does *not* apply to share-based payment awards under the scope of ASC 718 (FAS-123(R), Revised December 2004, *Share-Based Payment*), when determining whether those instruments are classified as liability awards or equity awards under the guidance in ASC 718 (FAS-123(R). However, because equity-linked financial instruments issued to investors in order to establish a market-based measure of the fair value of employee options at the grant date are *not* covered under the guidance in ASC 718 (FAS-123(R), the guidance in this Issue applies when determining whether an instrument or an embedded feature: (1) is indexed to an entity's own stock; or (2) should be accounted for under the guidance in ASC 460-10-60-14; 480-10-55-63; 505-10-60-5; 815-10-15-78; 55-52; 15-25-15; 40-05-1 through 05-4, 05-10, 05-11, 05-12; 25-1 through 25-5, 25-7 through 25-20, 25-22 through 25-24, 25-26 through 25-35; 25-37 through 25-40; 30-1; 35-1, 35-2,

35-6, 35-8 through 35-13; 40-1, 40-2; 50-1 through 50-5; 55-1 through 55-18 (Issue 00-19).

Accounting Issue

How should an entity determine whether an equity-linked financial instrument or an embedded feature is indexed to the entity's own stock?

Recognition

For accounting purposes, the financial instruments discussed in this Issue are always considered to have been issued, except when parties to a business combination exchange contingently exercisable options (i.e., lock-up options) to purchase the other entity's equity securities at favorable prices in order to encourage a merger's completion. Under the terms of such options, if a specified event interferes with a merger's completion, it may trigger the exercise of those options. However, such options are *not* exercised and expire if a merger is completed as planned. For accounting purposes, lock-up options are *not* considered to have been issued. The guidance in this paragraph applies to both the issuer and the holder of instruments under the scope of this Issue.

An "exercise contingency," as the term is used in this Issue, is a provision that gives the right to an entity or its counterparty to exercise an equity-linked financial instrument or an embedded feature based on changes in an "underlying," which is defined in ASC 815 (FAS-133) as a specific interest rate, security price, commodity price, foreign exchange rate, index of prices or rates, or other variable, such as a requirement that a specific event should or should *not* occur. For example, an instrument may include a provision that accelerates an entity's or counterparty's ability to exercise an instrument or a provision that extends the time period during which an entity or its counterparty can exercise an instrument. Both are exercise contingencies. An exercise contingency that would result in an adjustment to an instrument's strike price or to the number of shares used to calculate the amount of a settlement should be evaluated under Step 1 (below) and the potential adjustment of the settlement amount should be evaluated under Step 2 (below).

The EITF reached a consensus that the following two-step approach should be used to determine whether an equity-linked financial instrument or an embedded feature is indexed to an entity's own stock:

- *Step 1.* Evaluate the instrument's contingent exercise provisions, if any. A financial instrument or an embedded feature that is subject to an exercise contingency may be considered to be indexed to an entity's own stock if the index triggering the instrument's contingent exercise provisions is *not* based on:

(1) an observable market, except for the market for the issuer's stock, if applicable; or (2) an observable index, except for one that is calculated or measured exclusively by referring to the issuer's own operations, such as its sales revenues; earnings before interest, taxes, depreciation, and amortization (EBITDA); net income; or total equity. Proceed to Step 2 if (as a result of the evaluation in Step 1) an instrument is *not* prohibited from being considered to be indexed to an entity's own stock.

- *Step 2.* Evaluate the instrument's settlement provisions. An instrument should be considered to be indexed to an entity's own stock if the amount of the settlement will be equal to the difference between the fair value of a *fixed* number of the entity's equity shares and a *fixed* monetary amount or a *fixed* amount of a debt instrument issued by the entity. For example, an issued share option that gives a counterparty the right to buy a *fixed* number of the issuer's shares for a *fixed* price or for a *fixed* stated principal amount of a bond to be issued by the entity should be considered to be indexed to the issuing entity's own stock.

If an instrument's strike price or the number of shares used to calculate the amount to settle may be adjusted under an instrument's provisions, they are *not* fixed—regardless of the probability that an adjustment will occur or whether an adjustment is under the entity's control. However, an instrument or an embedded feature whose strike price or number of shares used to calculate the settlement amount are *not* fixed may still be considered to be indexed to an entity's own stock if inputs to the fair value of a "fixed-for-fixed" forward or option on equity shares are the only variables that could affect the amount of a settlement, which is equal to the difference between the price of a *fixed* number of equity shares and a *fixed* strike price. Such fair value inputs may include an entity's stock price and additional variables, such as: (1) the instrument's strike price; (2) its terms; (3) expected dividends or other dilutive activities; (3) stock borrow cost; (4) interest rates; (5) stock price volatility; (6) an entity's credit spread; and (7) an entity's ability to maintain a standard hedge position in the underlying shares. The determination and adjustments of the settlement amount, including a determination of an entity's ability to maintain a standard hedge position must be commercially reasonable.

Nevertheless, an instrument or an embedded feature should *not* be considered to be indexed to an entity's own stock if the *calculation* of the amount at which a fixed-for-fixed option or forward on equity shares would be settled: (1) is affected by variables that are *not* pertinent to the option's or forward contract's pricing; (2) include variables other than those used to determine the forward's or option's fair value; or (3) includes a feature, such as a leverage factor, that increases the instrument's exposure to the additional variables related to fair value inputs discussed above in a manner that is inconsistent with a fixed-for-fixed forward or option on equity shares.

The following two types of provisions related to equity-linked financial instruments also should *not* prevent an instrument from being considered to be indexed to an entity's own stock:

1. Provisions permitting adjustments that would neutralize the effects of events that may cause stock price irregularities. For example, provisions that adjust a financial instrument's terms to offset a net gain or loss incurred by an instrument's holder as a result of differences between changes in: (1) the fair value of an equity-linked instrument; and (2) the fair value of an offsetting hedge position in the underlying shares caused by a merger announcement or a similar event.
2. Provisions that enable an entity to unilaterally modify a financial instrument's terms at any time, as long as that modification benefits the counterparty. An issuer's ability to reduce the conversion price of a convertible debt instrument at anytime to induce conversion is an example of such a provision.

Strike Price Denominated in a Foreign Currency

An issuer of an equity-linked financial instrument having a strike price denominated in a functional currency that differs from the issuer's is exposed to changes in currency exchange rates. If the strike price of an equity-linked financial instrument is valued in a currency other than the issuer's functional currency, including a conversion option that is embedded in a convertible debt instrument valued in a currency other than the issuer's functional currency, an equity-linked financial instrument would *not* be considered to be indexed to the issuing entity's own stock. However, the currency in which the underlying shares trade does *not* affect the determination of whether an equity-linked instrument is indexed to an entity's own stock.

Transition

The guidance in this Issue should be applied in financial statements issued for fiscal years that begin after December 15, 2008, and interim periods in those fiscal years. Early adoption is *not* permitted if an entity previously adopted an alternative accounting policy.

When the guidance in this Issue is adopted, it should be applied as follows to outstanding instruments as of the beginning of the fiscal year of initial application:

- Recognize the cumulative effect of a change in accounting principle as an adjustment to the opening balance of retained earnings or other appropriate components of equity or net assets in the balance sheet for that fiscal year and present it separately. That adjustment is the difference between: (1) the amounts recognized in the balance sheet *before* the guidance in this issue is first applied; and (2) the amounts recognized in the balance sheet when the guidance in this Issue is first applied.

- Determine the amounts recognized in the balance sheet as a result of the initial application of the guidance in this Issue based on the amounts that would have been recognized if the guidance if the guidance in this Issue had been applied from the instrument's issuance date.
- Reclassify to shareholders' equity the carrying amount of a liability (i.e., its fair value at the adoption date) for an embedded conversion option in a convertible debt instrument that previously had been bifurcated if the conversion option no longer meets the criteria for bifurcation in ASC 815 (FAS-133) when the guidance in this Issue is first applied. However, continue amortizing a debt discount, if any, that was recognized when the conversion option was first separated from the convertible debt instrument.

The guidance regarding contingent options in a business combination and the guidance in Step 1 should *not* result in a transition adjustment when the guidance in this Issue is effective because that guidance was brought forward from Issue 01-6 (not in ASC), which is nullified by the guidance in this Issue. In addition, the transition disclosures in ASC 250-10-50-1,through 50-3, (paragraphs 17 and 18 of FAS-154, *Accounting for Accounting Changes and Error Corrections*) should be presented.

FASB RATIFICATION

The FASB ratified the EITF's consensus positions on Issue 07-5 at its June 25, 2008, meeting.

Topic D-102 (Documentation of the Methods Used to Measure Hedge Ineffectiveness under FASB Statement No. 133) (ASC 815-20-25-3)

This announcement clarifies the guidance in ASC 815 (FAS-133) related to the required documentation at the beginning of fair value, cash flow, and net investment hedges. According to the FASB staff, ASC 815-20-25-3 (paragraphs 20(a), 28(a), and 62 of FAS-133) and ASC 815-30-35-11 through 35-32; 55-91 through 55-93 (Issue No. G7 of the *Guide to Implementation of Statement 133 on Accounting for Derivative Instruments and Hedging Activities*) require formal documentation, at the beginning of a hedge, about the hedging relationship, and the entity's risk management objective for entering into the hedge. The following information is required:

- The hedging instrument
- The hedged item or transaction
- The nature of the hedged risk

- The method used to retrospectively and prospectively evaluate whether the hedging instrument will be effective
- The method to be used to measure hedge ineffectiveness (including when the change in fair value method discussed in Issue G7 of the Implementation Guide is used)

Topic D-109 (Determining the Nature of a Host Contract Related to a Hybrid Financial Instrument Issued in the Form of a Share under FASB Statement No. 133) (ASC 815-10-S99-3)

At the EITF's March 15, 2007, meeting, the SEC Observer announced the position of the SEC staff related to an entity's determination whether a host contract related to a hybrid financial instrument issued in the form of a share is considered to be a debt instrument or an equity instrument when an embedded derivative is evaluated under the guidance in ASC 815-15-25-1 (paragraph 12(a) of (FAS-133, *Accounting for Derivative Instruments and Hedging Activities*).

SCOPE

This announcement applies only to the determination stated above. It is *not* intended to address when an embedded derivative (or multiple embedded derivatives) should be separated from the host contract under the guidance in ASC 815 (FAS-133) or the accounting under ASC 815 (FAS-133) if a separation is required. ASC 815 (FAS-133) provides guidance on such matters.

SEC STAFF POSITION

The SEC staff believes that in accordance with the guidance in ASC 815-15-25-1 (paragraph 12 of FAS-133) (1), an entity should consider the host instrument's economic characteristics and risks in determining whether a host contract related to a hybrid financial instrument issued in the form of a share is considered to be a debt instrument or an equity instrument. When evaluating the features of an embedded derivative under the guidance in ASC 815-15-25-1a (paragraph 12a of FAS-133), the economic characteristics and risks of the host contract should be considered based on *all* of the hybrid instrument's stated or implied substantive terms and features. Although a host contract's economic characteristics and risks should *not* be determined based on whether a single term or feature does or does not exist, a single term or feature may be considered more significant. Judgment based on an evaluation of *all* of the relevant terms and features is required to determine whether the host contract in this situation should be considered a debt instrument or an equity instrument.

ASC 825 FINANCIAL INSTRUMENTS

FSP Issue 00-19-2 (Accounting for Registration Payment Arrangements) (ASC 825-20-05-1; 15-1 through 15-5; 25-2, 25-3; 30-1, 30-4, 30-5; 35-1; 50-1, 50-2; 55-2 through 55-8, 55-10 through 55-14; 815-10-25-16; 40-25-21, 25-43; 470-20-30-23)

OVERVIEW

An entity may issue equity shares, warrants, or debt instruments that are conditional on a *registration payment arrangement,* which has the following characteristics:

- The agreement states that the issuer agrees to try to use its "best efforts" or apply "commercially reasonable efforts" to (*a*) file a registration statement for the resale of specified financial instruments or equity shares that will be issued when specified financial instruments are exercised or converted and to have the Securities and Exchange Commission (SEC) or another securities regulator (if the registration statement is filed in a foreign jurisdiction) declare the registration statement effective within a specified grace period, and (*b*) to maintain the registration statement's effectiveness for a specified time period or indefinitely.

- The issuer must transfer consideration, which may be significant, to the counterparty if the issuer fails to take those actions within the grace period or the registration statement's effectiveness is not maintained. The consideration may be required to be transferred in a lump sum of cash or in periodic cash payments, equity instruments, or as adjustments to the financial instrument conditional to the registration payment arrangement.

This FSP addresses the accounting under such arrangements for financial instruments that are accounted for under the guidance in ASC 460-10-60-14; 480-10-55-63; 505-10-60-5; 815-10-15-78; 55-52; 15-25-15; 40-05-1 through 05-4, 05-10, 05-11, 05-12; 25-1 through 25-5, 25-7 through 25-20, 25-22 through 25-24, 25-26 through 25-35; 25-37 through 25-40; 30-1; 35-1, 35-2, 35-6, 35-8 through 35-13; 40-1, 40-2; 50-1 through 50-5; 55-1 through 55-18 (Issue 00-19, "Accounting for Derivative Financial Instruments Indexed to, and Potentially Settled in, a Company's Own Stock").

FASB STAFF POSITION

The guidance in this FSP applies to:

- Issuers' accounting for registration payment arrangements having the characteristics discussed in the Overview, regardless of

whether the arrangement is included as a provision of a financial instrument or other agreement or is issued as a separate agreement.
- Arrangements under which an issuer is required to obtain or maintain a listing on a stock exchange, instead of, or in addition to, obtaining or maintaining an effective registration statement, as long as the registration payment arrangement has the characteristics discussed in the Overview.

This FSP's guidance does *not* apply to:
- Contracts that are *not* registration payment arrangements that have the characteristics discussed in the Overview, such as a building contract with a provision that requires a contractor to obtain a certificate of occupancy by a specific date or pay a penalty every month until it is obtained.
- Arrangements requiring registration or listing of convertible debt instruments or convertible preferred stock if the form of consideration that would be transferred to a counterparty is an adjustment to the conversion ratio. (See ASC 470-20-05-7 through 05-08; 25-4 through 25-5; 30-3, 30-6, 30-8, 30-10, 30-15; 35-2 through 35-3, 35-7; 40-2 through 40-3; 55-30 through 55-33, 55-35 through 55-38, 55-45 through 55-48, 55-50 through 55-52, 55-54 through 55-54A, 55-56 through 55-58, 55-60 through 55-60A, 55-62 through 55-66, 55-69; 505-10-50-8 (EITF Issues 98-5, "Accounting for Convertible Securities with Beneficial Conversion Features or Contingently Adjustable Conversion Ratios") and ASC 260-10-50-1; 470-20-25-8, 25-9, 25-20; 30-1, 30-5, 30-7, 30-9, 30-10, 30-12, 30-13, 30-16 through 30-21; 35-1, 35-4, 35-7 through 35-10; 40-1, 40-4; 45-1; 55-11, 55-12, 55-14 through 55-17, 55-19 through 55-21, 55-23, 55-24, 55-26, 55-27; 505-10-50-7 (Issue 00-27, "Application of Issue No. 98-5 to Certain Convertible Instruments") for accounting guidance.)
- Arrangements in which an observable market, other than the market for the issuer's stock, or an observable index must be consulted to determine the amount of consideration that should be transferred to a counterparty, for example, if consideration transferred to a counterparty when an issuer cannot obtain an effective registration statement is determined based on the price of a commodity.
- Arrangements in which the financial instrument or instruments conditional on the registration payment arrangement are settled when consideration is transferred, for example, if a warrant can be put to the issuer when an effective registration statement is not declared within the grace period for the resale of equity shares that would be issued when the warrant is exercised.

Recognition and Measurement

The FSP provides the following recognition and measurement guidance:

- A contingent obligation to make future payments or to transfer consideration in another manner under a registration payment arrangement should be recognized and measured *separately* in accordance with the guidance in ASC 450 (FAS-5, Accounting *for Contingencies*) and ASC 450-20 (FIN-14, *Reasonable Estimation of the Amount of a Loss*).

- A financial instrument conditional on a registration payment arrangement should be recognized and measured in accordance with other guidance in generally accepted accounting principles, such as ASC 835-30 (APB-21, *Interest on Receivables and Payables*), ASC 815 (FAS-133, *Accounting for Derivative Instruments and Hedging Activities*), and ASC 825-20-05-1; 15-1 through 15-5; 25-2, 25-3; 30-1, 30-4, 30-5; 35-1; 50-1, 50-2; 55-2 through 55-8, 55-10 through 55-14; 815-10-25-16; 40-25-21, 25-43; 470-20-30-23 (EITF Issue 00-19), without considering the contingent obligation to transfer consideration under a registration payment arrangement. In other words, the registration payment arrangement should be recognized and measured separately from the financial instrument conditional on the arrangement.

- A contingent liability under a registration payment arrangement should be included in the allocation of proceeds for a related financing transaction in accordance with the measurement guidance in ASC 450 (FAS-5) if it is *probable* that consideration under a registration payment arrangement will be transferred. The guidance in other applicable GAAP should be applied to allocate the remaining proceeds to financial instruments issued along with the registration payment arrangement. For example, after a liability for a registration payment arrangement has been recognized and measured under the guidance in ASC 450 (FAS-5), the remaining proceeds of a debt instrument and a warrant classified as equity that are issued along with the registration payment arrangement would be allocated based on their relative fair values of the debt and the warrant under the guidance in ASC 470-20-25-2, 25-3 (paragraph 16 of APB-14, *Accounting for Convertible Debt and Debt Issued with Stock Purchase Warrants*). Under this allocation method, a financial instrument issued along with a registration payment arrangement might initially be measured at a discount to its principal amount. To determine whether a convertible instrument includes a beneficial conversion feature under the guidance in ASC 470-20-05-7 through 05-08, 25-4 through 25-5, 30-3, 30-6, 30-8, 30-10, 30-15, 35-2 through 35-3, 35-7, 40-2 through 40-3, 55-30 through 55-33, 55-35 through 55-38, 55-45-through 55-48, 55-50 through 55-52, 55-54 through 55-54A, 55-56 through 55-58, 55-60 through 55-

60A, 55-62 through 55-66, 55-69; ASC 505-10-50-8 (EITF Issue 98-5) and ASC 260-10-50-1; 470-20-25-8, 25-9, 25-20; 30-1, 30-5, 30-7, 30-9, 30-10, 30-12, 30-13, 30-16 through 30-21; 35-1, 35-4, 35-7 through 35-10; 40-1, 40-4; 45-1; 55-11, 55-12, 55-14 through 55-17, 55-19 through 55-21, 55-23, 55-24, 55-26, 55-27; 505-10-50-7 (Issue 00-27), an entity should use the effective conversion price based on the proceeds allocated to the convertible instrument to calculate the embedded conversion option's intrinsic value, if any.

- If it becomes probable that consideration will be transferred under a registration payment arrangement or if the amount of a previously recognized contingent liability increases or decreases in a subsequent period, the initial recognition of the contingent liability or the change in the amount of a previously recognized contingent liability should be recognized as income.

- An issuer's share price at the reporting date should be used to measure a contingent liability under ASC 450 (FAS-5), if:
  — The entity would be required to deliver shares under a registration payment arrangement,
  — It is probable that consideration will be transferred, and
  — It is possible to reasonably estimate the number of shares that will be delivered.

DISCLOSURES

In addition to the required disclosures under other applicable GAAP, an issuer of a registration payment arrangement is required to disclose the following information about each registration payment arrangement or each group of similar arrangements, even if there is only a *remote* likelihood that the issuer will be required to transfer consideration under an arrangement:

- The features of a registration payment arrangement, including its term, the financial instrument conditional on the arrangement, and the events or circumstances under which an issuer would be required to transfer consideration.

- Settlement alternatives, if any, stated in a registration payment arrangement, including the party controlling the settlement alternatives.

- The maximum potential undiscounted amount of consideration that an issuer would be required to transfer under a registration payment arrangement, including the maximum number of shares that may be required to be issued or, if applicable, that the potential amount of the consideration to be transferred is *unlimited*.

- The current carrying amount of an issuer's liability under a registration payment arrangement and the income statement classification of gains or losses, if any, as a result of changes in that liability's carrying amount.

AMENDMENTS TO OTHER PRONOUNCEMENTS

This FSP amends the following guidance:

- ASC 815-10-15-82 (FAS-133, paragraph 10(j)). The following guidance has been added:
  Registration payment arrangements. Registration payment arrangements within the scope of FSP EITF 00-19-2 (Accounting for Registration Payment Arrangements) are not subject to the requirements of this Statement. The exception in this subparagraph applies to both (a) the issuer that accounts for the arrangement pursuant to FSP EITF 00-19-2 and (b) the counterparty.
- ASC 480-10-15-7 (FAS-150, paragraph 17A). the following guidance has been added:
  This Statement does not apply to registration payment arrangements within the scope of FSP EITF 00-19-2 (Accounting for Registration Payment Arrangements).
- ASC 460-10-15-7 (FIN-45, paragraph 6(g)). The following guidance has been added: A registration payment arrangement within the scope of FSP EITF 00-19-2 (Accounting for Registration Payment Arrangements).

ASC 835   INTEREST

Topic D-10 (Required Use of Interest Method in Recognizing Interest Income) (ASC 835-30-55-2)

Because ASC 310-20 (FAS-91) discusses the application of the interest method to nonrefundable loan fees and costs, not to interest income, some have questioned whether the interest method must be used to determine interest income. Specifically, the FASB staff was asked whether methods other than the interest method, such as the rule of 78s, sum of the years' digits, and straight-line methods, could be used to determine interest income, even if the results would differ materially from those based on the interest method. The Task Force Chairman stated that the FASB staff believes that using the interest method to recognize interest income is required by GAAP unless alternative methods result in amounts that do not differ materially from those based on the interest method.

ASC 860 TRANSFERS AND SERVICING

EITF Issue 86-8 (Sale of Bad-Debt Recovery Rights) (ASC 860-10-55-13)

OVERVIEW

A financial institution and another party enter into an agreement in which the financial institution sells the other party the right to receive the first $5 million collected on loans that had been previously written off by the financial institution. The other party (the buyer) pays the financial institution $5 million for that right and will receive a specified market rate of interest annually on $5 million reduced by loans recovered. The agreement continues until the buyer has recovered the $5 million. The buyer has no recourse to the financial institution and can use its own efforts to recover on the loans if dissatisfied with the financial institution's collection results.

ACCOUNTING ISSUES

Should the transaction be accounted for as:

- A sale of recovery rights and recognize a gain at the date of the transaction?
- A recovery of loans previously written off and recognized as a credit to the loan loss allowance?
- A borrowing secured by the potential recovery rights and recognized as a liability?
- A secured borrowing with the amount of proceeds received from the buyer considered in computing the current year's loan-loss provision?

EITF CONSENSUS

The transaction is a secured borrowing. The Task Force did not, however, reach a consensus on whether proceeds received from a buyer should be considered in the current year's loan loss provision.

DISCUSSION

The following arguments supported the Task Force's consensus that the transaction is a secured borrowing:

- The transaction is similar to a nonrecourse financing or a funded guarantee.

- The buyer's stated annual return is more like a return on a financing transaction than a return on an equity transaction, because the buyer has no reward beyond recovery of the principal and interest.
- The buyer has no risk because, based on the institution's experience, the buyer will cover the principal and interest.
- The financial institution does not sell the buyer a right to recoveries on specific loans.
- Loans written off continue to be controlled by the financial institution, which has the incentive to make recoveries and limit the amount of interest paid.

ASC 942 FINANCIAL SERVICES—DEPOSITORY AND LENDING

AcSEC Pratice Bulletin No. 4 (Accounting for Foreign Debt/ Equity Swaps) (ASC 942-310-05-3; 25-2; 30-1 through 30-3; 35-5 through 35-7; 55-1)

BACKGROUND

Certain foreign countries, particularly those with rapidly developing economies, may experience periodic financial difficulties. These financial difficulties may call into question the ability of these countries to service debt that they have issued. As a method of dealing with these financial difficulties, foreign countries experiencing financial difficulties may permit U.S. lending institutions to convert dollar-denominated debt, issued by these same countries, into approved local equity investments.

These foreign debt/equity swaps are generally structured as follows. First, holders of the U.S. dollar-denominated debt are credited with an amount of the local currency approximately equal to the amount of the outstanding debt. This conversion is performed at the official exchange rate, with a discount from the exchange rate imposed as a transaction fee. Second, the local currency so credited to the lender must be used to make an approved equity investment—the currency can be used for no other purpose. Third, capital usually cannot be repatriated for several years. In some cases, it may be permissible to sell the investment. However, the proceeds from such a sale are generally subject to the same repatriation restrictions.

STANDARDS

These types of foreign debt/equity swaps represent the exchange of a monetary asset for a nonmonetary asset. The transaction should be measured at its fair value on the date it is agreed to by both parties. Determining fair value for these types of transactions can be challenging. In some cases, the fair value of the equity investment received is unclear, and the fair value of the debt surrendered may be equally difficult to determine. It is not unusual for debt of foreign countries experiencing financial difficulty to be thinly traded.

Regarding the fair value of the exchange, both the secondary market value of the loan surrendered and the fair value of the equity investment/net assets received should be considered. The following factors should be considered in determining the fair value of the equity investment/net assets received:

- Similar transactions for cash
- Estimated cash flows from the equity investment or net assets received
- Market value (if available) of similar equity investments
- Currency restrictions affecting (a) dividends, (b) the sale of the investment, or (c) the repatriation of capital

If the fair value of the equity investment/net assets received is less than the recorded amount of the loan, the resulting difference should be reflected in income as a loss at the time the transaction is consummated. The amount of any resulting loss recognized is to be charged against the allowance for loan losses. This treatment is not affected even if some portion of the loan loss may have been due to changes in the interest rate environment (i.e., the fair value of the loan had declined due to an increase in interest rates). It is assumed that the causal factor leading to the debt/equity swap, which precipitates the loss, is the adverse financial condition of the foreign debtor.

Illustration of Loss on Debt/Equity Swap

Countries Bank, Inc., has a long-term $10 million dollar-denominated loan outstanding to the Mexican government. As a result of adverse financial conditions, the Mexican government is having difficulty making payments on the above loan. The Mexican government and Countries Bank have agreed to enter into a debt/equity swap. At the current exchange rate, 1 peso equals $.125; however, as a transaction fee, the exchange rate used for the swap is $.126. Therefore, Countries Bank receives 79,365,000 pesos in exchange for the $10 million of dollar-denominated debt (Countries Bank would have received 80 million pesos if the official exchange rate had been used; the difference is a transaction fee). Countries Bank will use these proceeds to purchase 50,000 shares of MexPower, a state-owned utility. MexPower is not publicly traded; however, a third party recently paid 140 million pesos for a 10% stake in MexPower (100,000 shares). The secondary market for the dollar-denominated debt issued by the Mexican government is thinly traded. Therefore, the fair value of this swap transaction will be measured by the fair value of the shares of MexPower received. Based on the recent cash transaction, the fair value of the MexPower shares received by Countries Bank is estimated to be 70 million pesos. In U.S. dollars, the fair value of Countries

Bank's MexPower stake is $8.75 million (70 million pesos × .125). Therefore, Countries Bank will recognize a $1.25 million loss on this debt/equity swap ($10 million − $8.75 million).

OTHER ISSUES

With the exception of a discount from the official exchange rate imposed as a transaction fee, all other costs and expenses associated with the swap are to be charged to income as incurred. Any discount from the official exchange rate has the effect of reducing the fair value of the equity investment received by the lender; therefore, such a discount is considered in determining the amount of any loss recognized by the lender as a result of the swap.

Given the subjective nature of the valuation process, the fair value of the equity investment/net assets received might exceed the carrying amount of the loan. This apparent gain (or recovery of previous losses recognized on the loan) should not be recognized until the equity investment/net assets received are converted into unrestricted cash or cash equivalents.

A particular lender may have loans outstanding to a number of financially troubled countries. A loss recognized in a foreign debt/equity swap would be one piece of evidence suggesting that the allowance for loan losses, relating to loans outstanding to other financially distressed countries, should be increased.

AUTHORITATIVE GUIDANCE NOT INCLUDED SEPARATELY IN THE CODIFICATION BUT INCORPORATED IN ANOTHER PRONOUNCEMENT

FSP FAS-126-1 (Applicability of Certain Disclosure and Interim Reporting Requirements for Obligors for Conduit Debt Securities)

OVERVIEW

Conduit municipal bonds are issued by a governmental entity, that is, a state or a unit of a local government or an agency or instrumentality of a state or local government, to raise funds in the capital markets. Governmental entities issue conduit municipal bonds for the use of private parties, not for their own use, and are permitted to do so under the Internal Revenue Code only for use by (*a*) certain not-for-profit entities, such as hospitals, museums, and libraries, and (*b*) for-profit entities, such as industrial revenue or development bonds issued for a specific allowed purpose. Once the bonds have been issued, the governmental entity usually has *no* liability or ongoing involvement with those bonds. The governmental entity is listed as the issuer in the *initial* bond offering with the conduit bond obligor and the party that receives the proceeds from the sale of the conduit debt security is listed as the obligated party. No information about the governmental entity's operating results is included in the initial offering or future filings. The conduit bond obligor makes all interest and principal payments and is responsible for all future financial reporting.

The FASB staff has received questions as to whether a conduit bond obligor for conduit debt securities that are traded on a domestic or foreign stock exchange or an over-the-counter market, including local or regional markets (a public market), meets the definition of a *public entity*.

The definition of a *public entity* is clarified in this FSP to include entities that are conduit bond obligors for conduit debt securities traded in a public market. The guidance related to public entities in the following pronouncements is amended by this FSP: ASC 270-10 (APB-28, *Interim Financial Reporting*); ASC 932-235-55-1 through 55-7 (FAS-69, *Disclosures about Oil- and Gas-Producing Activities*); ASC 740 (FAS-109, *Accounting for Income Taxes*); ASC 825-10-50-3 through 50-7 (FAS-126, *Exemption from Certain Required Disclosures about Financial Instruments for Certain Nonpublic Entities*); ASC 280-10 (FAS-131, *Disclosures about Segments of an Enterprise and Related Information*); ASC 715-20 (FAS-132(R), *Employers' Disclosures about Pensions and Other Postretirement Benefits*); ASC 805 (FAS-141(R), *Business Combinations*); and ASC 954 (AICPA Audit and Accounting Guides, *Health Care Organizations* and *Not-for-Profit Organizations*.

FASB STAFF POSITION

A conduit bond obligor for conduit debt securities traded in a public market, such as a domestic or foreign stock exchange market or an over-the-counter market, including local or regional markets, meets the definition of a public entity or enterprise. All individual bond obligors participating in a pooled conduit debt security are included in the definition of a conduit bond obligor. This FSP amends the definition of a public entity in (See ASC references in paragraph above) APB-28, FAS-69, FAS-109, FAS-126, FAS-131, FAS-132, and FAS-141 to include conduit bond obligors. This FSP does *not* affect the definition of a public entity in other authoritative accounting pronouncements that are not specifically amended.

AMENDMENTS

The affected pronouncements are amended as follows:

- ASC, *Master Glossary* (APB-28, footnote 1 to paragraph 6), which provides a definition of a publicly traded company. Add the following at the end of the first sentence:

or any company that is a conduit bond obligor for conduit debt securities that are traded in a public market (a domestic or foreign stock exchange or an over-the-counter market, including local or regional markets). Additionally,

Add the following additional paragraph:

Conduit debt securities refers to certain limited-obligation revenue bonds, certificates of participation, or similar debt instruments issued by a state or local governmental entity for the express purpose of providing financing for a specific third party (the conduit bond obligor) that is not a part of the state or local government's financial reporting entity. Although conduit debt securities bear the name of the governmental entity that issues them, the governmental entity often has no obligation for such debt beyond the resources provided by a lease or loan agreement with the third party on whose behalf the securities are issued. Further, the conduit bond obligor is responsible for any future financial reporting requirements.

ASC, Master *Glossary* (FAS-69, footnote 2 to paragraph 1), which provides a definition of a publicly traded company . Insert the following after the end of the sentence in (a) and change (b) to (c):

(b) that is a conduit bond obligor for conduit debt securities that are traded in a public market (a domestic or foreign stock exchange or an over-the-counter market, including local or regional markets),

Add the following additional paragraph:

Conduit debt securities refers to certain limited-obligation revenue bonds, certificates of participation, or similar debt instruments issued by a state or local governmental entity for the express purpose of providing financing for a specific third party (the conduit bond obligor) that is not a part of the state or local government's financial reporting entity. Although conduit debt securities bear the name of the governmental entity that issues them, the governmental entity often has no obligation for such debt beyond the resources provided by a lease or loan agreement with the third party on whose behalf the securities are issued. Further, the conduit bond obligor is responsible for any future financial reporting requirements.

(ASC, *Master Glossary*). FAS-109, paragraph 289 (Glossary) Insert the following into the definition of **Nonpublic enterprise** after the end of the sentence in (a) and change (b) to (c) in the remaining paragraph:

(b) that is a conduit bond obligor for conduit debt securities that are traded in a public market (a domestic or foreign stock exchange or an over-the-counter market, including local or regional markets), or (c)

Add the following additional paragraph:

Conduit debt securities refers to certain limited-obligation revenue bonds, certificates of participation, or similar debt instruments issued by a state or local governmental entity for the express purpose of providing financing for a specific third party (the conduit bond obligor) that is not a part of the state or local government's financial reporting entity. Although conduit debt securities bear the name of the governmental entity that issues them, the governmental entity often has no obligation for such debt beyond the resources provided by a lease or loan agreement with the third party on whose behalf they are issued. Further, the conduit bond obligor is responsible for any future financial reporting requirements.

ASC, *Master Glossary* (FAS-109, paragraph 289 (Glossary) Insert the following into the definition of **Public enterprise** after the end of the sentence in (a) and change (b) to (c) in the remaining paragraph:

(b) that is a conduit bond obligor for conduit debt securities that are traded in a public market (a domestic or foreign stock exchange or an over-the-counter market, including local or regional markets), or (c)

Add the following additional paragraph:

Conduit debt securities refers to certain limited-obligation revenue bonds, certificates of participation, or similar debt instruments issued by a state or local governmental entity for the express purpose of providing financing for a specific third party (the conduit bond obligor) that is not a part of the state or local government's financial reporting entity. Although conduit debt securities bear the name of the governmental entity that issues them, the governmental entity often has no obligation for such debt beyond the resources provided by a lease or loan agreement with the third party on whose behalf they are issued. Further, the conduit bond obligor is responsible for any future financial reporting requirements.

ASC, *Master Glossary* (FAS-126, paragraph 3). Insert the following after the end of the sentence in (a) and change (b) to (c), and (c) to (d) in the remaining paragraph:

(b) that is a conduit bond obligor for conduit debt securities[a] that are traded in a public market (a domestic or foreign stock exchange or an over-the-counter market, including local or regional markets), (c), (d), (b), or (c).

Add the following paragraph as footnote a:

Conduit debt securities refers to certain limited-obligation revenue bonds, certificates of participation, or similar debt instruments issued by a state or local governmental entity for the express purpose of providing financing for a specific third party (the conduit bond obligor) that is not a part of the state or local government's financial reporting entity. Although conduit debt securities bear the name of the governmental entity that issues them, the governmental entity often has no obligation for such debt beyond the resources provided by a lease or loan agreement with the third party on whose behalf the securities are issued. Further, the conduit bond obligor is responsible for any future financial reporting requirements.

- ASC, *Master Glossary* (FAS-131, Paragraph 9). In the second sentence, insert "or are conduit bond obligors for conduit debt securities[1a]" between "equity securities" and "that." In the penultimate sentence insert: "(regardless of whether the entity meets the definition of a public entity as defined above)" between "organizations" and "or." Add the following paragraph as footnote 1a:

Conduit debt securities refers to certain limited-obligation revenue bonds, certificates of participation, or similar debt instruments issued by a state or local governmental entity for the express purpose of providing financing for a specific third party (the conduit bond obligor) that is not a part of the state or local government's financial reporting entity. Although conduit debt securities bear the name of the governmental entity that issues them, the governmental entity often has no obligation for such debt beyond the resources provided by a lease or loan agreement with the third party on whose behalf the securities are issued. Further, the conduit bond obligor is responsible for any future financial reporting requirements.

- ASC, *Master Glossary* (FAS-132, paragraph E1 (Glossary). After (a) add "(b) that is a conduit bond obligor for conduit debt securities that are traded in a public market (a domestic or foreign stock exchange or an over-the-counter market, including local or regional markets), (c), (d), (b), or (c)"

Conduit debt securities refers to certain limited-obligation revenue bonds, certificates of participation, or similar debt instruments issued by a state or local governmental entity for the express purpose of providing financing for a specific third party (the conduit bond obligor) that is not a part of the state or local government's financial reporting entity. Although conduit debt securities bear the name of the governmental entity that issues them, the governmental entity often has no obligation for such debt beyond the resources provided by a lease or loan agreement with the third party on whose behalf the securities are issued. Further, the conduit bond obligor is responsible for any future financial reporting requirements.

- ASC, *Master Glossary* (FAS-141, paragraph F1 (Glossary). In the first sentence of the definition of a **Public business enterprise**, insert "or is a conduit bond obligor for conduit debt securities" between "equity securities" and "that." At the end of that paragraph delete the parenthetical. Add the following paragraph to that definition:

  Conduit debt securities refers to certain limited-obligation revenue bonds, certificates of participation, or similar debt instruments issued by a state or local governmental entity for the express purpose of providing financing for a specific third party (the conduit bond obligor) that is not a part of the state or local government's financial reporting entity. Although conduit debt securities bear the name of the governmental entity that issues them, the governmental entity often has no obligation for such debt beyond the resources provided by a lease or loan agreement with the third party on whose behalf the securities are issued ASC, *Glossary*; 280-20-15-3 (FAS-131, *Disclosure about Segments of an Enterprise and Related Information*, paragraph 9). Further, the conduit bond obligor is responsible for any future financial reporting requirements.

FSP FIN-39-1 (Amendment of FASB Interpretation No. 39)

OVERVIEW

This FASB Staff Position (FSP) addresses the following two questions related to the guidance in ASC 210-20 and ASC 815-10 (FASB Interpretation No. 39, *Offsetting of Amount Related to Certain Contracts*):

1. Under the guidance in ASC 815-10-45-3 (paragraph 3 of FIN-39), the term *contractual contracts* is defined as "those whose obligations or rights depend on the occurrence of some specified future event that is not certain to occur and that could change the timing of the amounts or the instruments to be received, delivered, or exchanged." The question addressed in this FSP is whether the definition of a

conditional contract would apply to a contract whose obligations or rights depend exclusively on the occurrence of a default or termination.

2. Under the guidance in ASC 210-20-45-1 (paragraph 5 of FIN-39), the right of setoff exists if four conditions are met. One of those conditions, which is stated in ASC 210-20-45-1 (paragraph 5(c)), is that "[t]he reporting party intends to set off." However, under the guidance in ASC 815-10-45-5 (paragraph 10 of FIN-39), a reporting entity is permitted to offset fair value amounts recognized for derivative instruments that are executed with the same counterparty under a master netting arrangement *without* applying the condition in ASC 210-20-45-1 (paragraph 5(c) of FIN-39). Constituents have asked whether a reporting entity that had met the conditions in ASC 210-20-45-1 (paragraphs 5(a), 5(b), and 5(d) of FIN-39) and had an accounting policy to offset the fair values of derivative instruments executed with the same counterparty under a master netting agreement could offset a receivable or a payable recognized when a payment or cash collateral is received against derivative instruments recognized at fair value that had been offset under the same master netting arrangement according to the guidance in ASC 815-10-45-5 (paragraph 10 of FIN-39). Further, under the terms of those master netting arrangements, the entity in a net asset position under the netting arrangement is granted the right to require the counterparty to provide cash collateral, which the entity would recognize as an asset and as a payable for the obligation to return the cash collateral. The counterparty, which would pay the cash collateral, would recognize a receivable for the right to reclaim the cash collateral.

FASB STAFF POSITION

The following are amendments to the guidance in ASC 210-20 and ASC 815-10 (FIN-39) (added text is underlined and deleted text is struck out):

Summary Beginning in the third sentence:

It also addresses the applicability of that general principle to derivative instruments forward, interest rate swap, currency swap, option, and other conditional or exchange contracts and clarifies the circumstances in which it is appropriate to offset amounts recognized for those instruments contracts in the statement of financial position. In addition, it permits offsetting of fair value amounts recognized for multiple derivative instruments forward, interest rate swap, currency swap, option, and other conditional or exchange contracts executed with the same counterparty under a master netting arrangement and fair value amounts recognized for the right to reclaim cash collateral (a receivable) or the obligation to return cash collateral (a payable) arising from the same master netting arrangement as the derivative instruments.

ASC 815-10-45-3 *(Paragraph 3)* First sentence: "The contracts described in paragraphs 1 and 2 are often referred to as derivative instruments."[1a]
The remainder of paragraph 3 is deleted.

[1a] The term *derivative instruments* is defined in FASB Statement No. 133,*Accounting for Derivative Instruments and Hedging Activities,* and related implementation guidance. For purposes of this Interpretation, derivative instruments include those that meet the definition of a derivative instrument but are not included in the scope of Statement 133.

Heading for ASC 815.10.45-4, 5 (Paragraphs 8–10 and footnote 5)
Applicability to Derivative Instruments Forward, Interest Rate Swaps, Currency Swaps, Option, and Other Conditional or Exchange Contracts
ASC 815-10-45-4 (paragraph 8) is unchanged, and paragraph 9 and footnote 4 are deleted. The following are the amendments to ASC 815-10-45-5 (paragraph 10) and new footnote 5:

10. Without regard to the condition in paragraph 5(c), a reporting entity may offset *fair value amounts* recognized for derivative instruments and fair value amounts5 recognized for the right to reclaim cash collateral (a receivable) or the obligation to return cash collateral (a payable) arising from derivative instrument(s) recognized at fair value forward, interest rate swap, currency swap, option, and other conditional or exchange contracts executed with the same counterparty under a master netting arrangement may be offset. The fair value recognized for some contracts may include an accrual component for the periodic unconditional receivables and payables that result from the contract; the accrual component included therein may also be offset for contracts executed with the same counterparty under a master netting arrangement.The reporting entity's choice to offset or not must be applied consistently. A master netting arrangement exists if the reporting entity has multiple contracts whether for the same type of derivative instrument conditional or exchange contract or for different types of derivative instrument contracts, with a single counterparty that are subject to a contractual agreement that provides for the net settlement of all contracts through a single payment in a single currency in the event of default on or termination of any one contract. Offsetting the fair values recognized for forward, interest rate swap, currency swap, option, and other conditional or exchange contracts outstanding with a single counterparty results in the net fair value of the position between the two counterparties being reported as an asset or a liability in the statement of financial position.

[5] Solely as it relates to the right to reclaim cash collateral or the obligation to return cash collateral, fair value amounts include amounts that approximate fair value. This footnote should not be analogized to for any other asset or liability.

ASC 815-10-45-6 (paragraph 10A) and ASC 815-10-50-7, 50-8 (paragraph (10B) The following paragraphs are added:

10A. A reporting entity shall make an accounting policy decision to offset fair value amounts pursuant to paragraph 10 of this Interpretation. The reporting entity's choice to offset or not must be applied consistently. A reporting entity shall not offset fair value amounts recognized for derivative instruments without offsetting fair value amounts recognized for the right to reclaim cash collateral or the obligation to return cash collateral. A reporting entity that makes an accounting policy decision to offset fair value amounts recognized for derivative instruments pursuant to paragraph 10 but determines that the amount recognized for the right to reclaim cash collateral or the obligation to return cash collateral is not a fair value amount shall continue to offset the derivative instruments.

10B. A reporting entity's accounting policy to offset or not offset in accordance with this Interpretation shall be disclosed. A reporting entity shall disclose the amounts recognized at the end of each reporting period for the right to reclaim cash collateral or the obligation to return cash collateral as follows:

a. A reporting entity that has made an accounting policy decision to offset fair value amounts shall separately disclose amounts recognized for the right to reclaim cash collateral or the obligation to return cash collateral that have been offset against net derivative positions in accordance with this Interpretation. A reporting entity that has made an accounting policy decision to offset fair value amounts is not permitted to offset amounts recognized for the right to reclaim cash collateral or the obligation to return cash collateral against net derivative positions if those amounts (1) were not fair value amounts or (2) arose from instruments in a master netting arrangement that are not eligible to be offset. A reporting entity shall separately disclose amounts recognized for the right to reclaim cash collateral or the obligation to return cash collateral under master netting arrangements that have not been offset against net derivative positions.

b. A reporting entity that has made an accounting policy decision to not offset fair value amounts shall separately disclose the amounts recognized for the right to reclaim cash collateral or the obligation to return cash collateral under master netting arrangements.

RELATED CHAPTERS IN 2011
GAAP GUIDE, VOLUME II

Chapter 4, "Balance Sheet Classification and Related Display Issues"
Chapter 13, "Convertible Debt and Debt with Warrants"
Chapter 38, "Stock Compensation"

RELATED CHAPTERS IN 2011
GAAP GUIDE, VOLUME I

Chapter 3, "Balance Sheet Classification and Related Display Issues"
Chapter 9, "Convertible Debt and Debt with Warrants"
Chapter 17, "Financial Instruments"
Chapter 43, "Stock-Based Payments"

RELATED CHAPTER IN 2011
INTERNATIONAL ACCOUNTING/FINANCIAL REPORTING STANDARDS GUIDE

Chapter 16, "Financial Instruments"

CHAPTER 18
FOREIGN OPERATIONS AND EXCHANGE

CONTENTS

Overview	18.02
Authoritative Guidance	
ASC 320 Investments—Debt and Equity Securities	18.03
EITF Issue 96-15 Accounting for the Effects of Changes in Foreign Currency Exchange Rates on Foreign-Currency-Denominated Available-for-Sale Debt Securities	18.03
ASC 815 Derivatives and Hedging	18.05
EITF Issue 86-25 Offsetting Foreign Currency Swaps	18.05
ASC 830 Foreign Currency Matters	18.06
EITF Issue 87-12 Foreign Debt-for-Equity Swaps	18.06
EITF Issue 92-4 Accounting for a Change in Functional Currency When an Economy Ceases to Be Considered Highly Inflationary	18.07
EITF Issue 92-8 Accounting for the Income Tax Effects under FASB Statement No. 109 of a Change in Functional Currency When an Economy Ceases to Be Considered Highly Inflationary	18.11
EITF Issue 01-5 Application of FASB Statement No. 52 to an Investment Being Evaluated for Impairment That Will Be Disposed Of	18.12
Topic D-12 Foreign Currency Translation—Selection of Exchange Rate When Trading Is Temporarily Suspended	18.13
Topic D-55 Determining a Highly Inflationary Economy under FASB Statement No. 52	18.14

18.02 *Foreign Operations and Exchange*

Topic D-56	Accounting for a Change in Functional Currency and Deferred Taxes When an Economy Becomes Highly Inflationary	18.14
ASC 946-830	Financial Services—Investment Companies	18.15
SOP 93-4	Foreign Currency Accounting and Financial Statement Presentation for Investment Companies	18.15
Related Chapters in 2011 GAAP Guide, Volume II		18.24
Related Chapters in 2011 GAAP Guide, Volume I		18.24
Related Chapter in 2011 International Accounting/Financial Reporting Standards Guide		18.24

OVERVIEW

There are two major areas of foreign operations:

1. Translation of foreign currency financial statements for purposes of consolidation, combination, or reporting on the equity method (one-line consolidation)
2. Accounting and reporting of foreign currency transactions, including forward exchange contracts

The following pronouncements, which provide GAAP for foreign operations and exchange, are discussed in the 2011 *GAAP Guide, Volume I,* Chapter 18, "Foreign Operations and Exchange":

ASC 830	Foreign Currency Translation (FAS-52)
ASC 830	Accounting for Translation Adjustments upon Sale of Part of an Investment in a Foreign Entity (FIN-37)

AUTHORITATIVE GUIDANCE

ASC 320 Investments—Debt and Equity Securities

EITF Issue 96-15 (Accounting for the Effects of Changes in Foreign Currency Exchange Rates on Foreign-Currency-Denominated Available-for-Sale Debt Securities) (ASC 320-10-35-36 through 35-37; 830-20-35-6 through 35-7)

OVERVIEW

The *available-for-sale* (AFS) category of securities was established in ASC 320-10 (FAS-115). Unrealized holding gains or losses on securities in that category are reported in a separate component of stockholders' equity and recognized in income when realized.

This Issue addresses the accounting for available-for-sale securities denominated in a foreign currency. Under the guidance in ASC 830-20-35-1 (paragraph 15 of FAS-52), foreign currency transaction gains or losses occur when *monetary* assets and liabilities are denominated in a currency other than the entity's functional currency and the exchange rate between the currencies changes. Some have questioned whether available-for-sale debt securities should be considered to be non-monetary with no recognition of gains and losses on remeasurement, because such securities, which are not held to maturity, are carried at fair value, so their amounts are not fixed. Gains or losses on hedges of net investments in foreign entities and hedges of identifiable foreign currency commitments also are exempted from recognition in earnings under the guidance in ASC 830-20-35(a) (paragraph 20 of FAS-52).

A change in the fair value of available-for-sale (AFS) debt securities denominated in a foreign currency consists of the following two components: (*a*) a change in the market price of the security in the local currency as a result of such factors as changes in interest rates and credit risk and (*b*) a change in exchange rates between the local currency and the entity's functional currency.

ACCOUNTING ISSUE

Should both components of a change in the fair value of available-for-sale debt securities be reported in a separate component of stockholders' equity, or should the component related to the change in exchange rates (component b) be reported in earnings as a foreign currency transaction gain or loss, with changes due to other factors (component a) reported in stockholders' equity?

EITF CONSENSUS

Entities should report both components of a change in the fair value of foreign-currency-denominated available-for-sale debt securities in other comprehensive income in accordance with the guidance in ASC 220 (FAS-130).

The Task Force noted that based on the guidance in ASC 320 (FAS-115) and Topic D-44 (not in ASC), changes in market interest rates and foreign exchange rates since acquisition should be considered when determining whether an AFS debt security denominated in a foreign currency has experienced an other-than-temporary impairment.

EFFECT OF ASC 815 (FAS-133)

The guidance in Issue 1 is not affected by the guidance in ASC 815 (FAS-133), which applies only to AFS debt securities that are designated in fair value hedging relationships. The EITF's consensus on the second Issue was nullified in ASC 815-10-25-71 (paragraph 38 of FAS-133), because ASC 815 (FAS-133) prohibits hedging an AFS debt security with a foreign-currency-denominated liability. In addition, a gain or loss on a currency derivative in a fair value hedge of an AFS security is reported in earnings under the guidance in ASC 815 (FAS-133), instead of in other comprehensive income as required under the consensus, together with the gain or loss on the AFS security related to changes in the foreign currency's exchange value.

Illustration of a Change in Market Value of an Available-for-Sale Debt Security Denominated in a Foreign Currency

On 7/1/X6, a company whose functional currency is the U.S. dollar acquires a debt security denominated in a foreign currency (FC) and classifies it as available for sale. How would the company compute the change in market value at 9/30/X6?

At 7/1/X6
- Purchase price = FC500
- Exchange rate = $2.50 per FC1
- Historical cost basis = $1,250

At 9/30/X6
- Fair market value = FC600
- Exchange rate = $2.00 per FC1
- U.S. dollar fair market value = $1,200

Components of the Change in Market Value at 9/30/X6

(a) Change in market value   Change in fair market value at historical exchange rate

  (FC600 − FC500) × $2.50 $250

(b) Effect of exchange rates   Current fair market value less historical cost basis plus change in fair market value at historical exchange rates

  (FC600 × $2.00) − ($1,250 + $250)   (300)
  Net effect   ($ 50)

ASC815 Derivatives and Hedging

EITF Issue 86-25 (Offsetting Foreign Currency Swaps) (ASC 815-10-45-2)

OVERVIEW

A Company has entered into a debt agreement with principal and interest payable in a foreign currency. The company's functional currency is the U.S. dollar. To avoid fluctuations in the value of the debt resulting from changes in exchange rates, the company enters into a currency swap contract under which periodically it will receive foreign currency equivalent to its principal and interest payments on the debt (which is denominated in the foreign currency) for which the company will pay a stipulated amount in U.S. dollars. The swap thus creates a foreign currency receivable and a U.S. dollar payable. If the terms of the swap contract require settlement only of the net change in the contract value, the company calculates and recognizes that amount at each balance sheet date. Some believe, as a result of these transactions, the U.S. dollar debt replaces the foreign currency debt.

ACCOUNTING ISSUE

How should the effect of a change in exchange rates on a foreign currency swap contract be displayed in the balance sheet?

EITF CONSENSUS

The EITF reached a consensus that the effect of a change in exchange rates (the difference between the accrued receivable and payable) on a foreign currency swap should *not* be netted against foreign currency debt, because a swap and debt are unrelated transactions without the legal right of setoff ASC 220 (see FIN-39).

ASC 830 Foreign Currency Matters

EITF Issue 87-12 (Foreign Debt-for-Equity Swaps) (ASC 830-20-55-1 through 55-3)

OVERVIEW

In a foreign debt-for-equity swap, a U.S. company that has a subsidiary in Mexico purchases a U.S. dollar-denominated loan in the secondary market at less than the loan's face amount. The loan is due from the Mexican government or an entity operating in Mexico. The company in turn enters into an agreement to sell the loan to the Mexican government for an amount denominated in Mexican pesos that exceeds the amount the company paid for the loan. Under the agreement, which is designed to keep the pesos within Mexico's economy, the company must invest the proceeds in its subsidiary, which is required to use the proceeds for a specified purpose, such as capital expenditures. When the Mexican government purchases the loan, it transmits the pesos directly to the subsidiary, which issues capital stock to the U.S. parent. The agreement restricts the U.S. parent from redeeming the shares, receiving dividends on those shares, or selling the shares within Mexico for a stated period of time. For example, a U.S. company purchases a loan with remaining principal of $15 million for $7.5 million. The Mexican government purchases the loan from the company for $11 million in pesos translated at the official exchange rate, which the company invests in its Mexican subsidiary and receives stock.

ACCOUNTING ISSUE

How should the U.S. company report in its consolidated financial statements the difference between the amount paid to purchase the dollar-denominated loan and the local currency proceeds from the sale of the loan invested in its foreign subsidiary?

EITF CONSENSUS

Note: ASC 805 (FAS-141(R), Business Combinations) was issued in December 2007 to replace FAS-141. It provides guidance on accounting for a bargain purchase, which was previously referred to as negative goodwill.

The excess proceeds in local currency from the sale of a loan translated at the official exchange rate over the cost to purchase the loan should be reported as follows in the parent company's consolidated financial statements:

- Reduce the basis of long-lived assets acquired or constructed under the agreement.
- Reduce the carrying amounts of existing long-lived assets other than goodwill by a corresponding amount, if the agreement does not specifically require the acquisition or construction of long-lived assets, or if the excess is greater than the cost of such assets.

The excess should be applied first to fixed assets with the longest remaining lives until they have been reduced to zero. A remainder, if any, after the carrying amounts of all fixed assets have been reduced to zero should be reported as a bargain purchase as required in ASC 805-30 (FAS-141(R)).

The Task Force also agreed that that the consensus also applies to a debt-to-equity swap of a foreign branch that has (1) an accumulated deficit and no significant assets or liabilities other than the local currency debt, and (2) used the proceeds from the foreign debt-for-equity currency swap to extinguish the debt. The excess should be reported as a bargain purchase as required in ASC 805-30 (FAS-141(R)).

DISCUSSION

Because the excess in a foreign debt-for-equity swap does not result from a change in exchange rates, it does not meet the criteria to be reported as a transaction gain or loss or a translation adjustment under the provisions of FAS-52 (Foreign Currency Translation). The issue here was whether the U.S. company should report the excess of the proceeds invested in the subsidiary over the purchase price of the loan in income in its consolidated financial statements. Proponents of the consensus argued that because the foreign government required the company to invest the total proceeds in the subsidiary and restricted its use of the proceeds, the earnings process was not complete. Any excess that cannot be identified with assets is accounted for similarly to an unallocated excess in a purchase method business combination, which would be reported as a bargain purchase.

EITF Issue 92-4 (Accounting for a Change in Functional Currency When an Economy Ceases to Be Considered Highly Inflationary) (ASC 830-10-45-1 through 45-5; 55-13 through 55-14)

OVERVIEW

Company A has a subsidiary operating in an economy that was considered highly inflationary during the previous five years. A *highly inflationary economy* is defined in ASC 830 (FAS-52) as one that has experienced a cumulative inflation rate of 100% or more for the most recent three-year period. In accordance with the guidance in ASC 830 (FAS-52), the subsidiary used Company A's reporting currency rather than the local (foreign) currency as its functional currency. Based on the criteria in ASC 830 (FAS-52), except for the inflationary environment, the subsidiary would have used the local currency as its functional currency. In 20X6, the inflation rate had declined sufficiently that the cumulative rate for the three most recent years was less than 100%; the economy was no longer considered highly inflationary. Accordingly, Company A decided to use the local currency as the subsidiary's functional currency.

> **OBSERVATION:** When the local currency is not the functional currency, the subsidiary's statements must be **remeasured** into the functional currency using **current** exchange rates for monetary items and **historical** exchange rates (exchange rate at acquisition) for nonmonetary items. When the local currency is also the functional currency, all assets and liabilities are **translated** at current exchange rates.

ACCOUNTING ISSUE

How should an entity account for a change in a subsidiary's functional currency from the reporting currency to the local currency solely because the economy in which the subsidiary operates is no longer considered to be highly inflationary?

EITF CONSENSUS

The EITF reached a consensus in ASC 830-10-45-9 through 45-10 (paragraph 46 of FAS-52), which provides guidance on the treatment of a change in functional currency from the reporting currency to the local currency, does not apply to situations in which the functional currency changes solely because the economy has ceased to be highly inflationary. The functional currency bases of nonmonetary assets and liabilities should be restated at the date of change by translating reporting currency amounts into the local currency at their current exchange rates. Those translated amounts become the new accounting bases for the nonmonetary assets and liabilities in the entity's new functional currency (the local currency).

The Task Force also noted that the difference between the new accounting bases in the functional currency and their tax bases in that currency is considered a temporary difference under ASC 740 (FAS-109). The guidance in ASC 830-740-25-2; 45-2 (EITF Issue 92-8, which is discussed below) addresses how related deferred taxes should be recognized.)

DISCUSSION

The issue arose because in cases in which the local currency becomes the functional currency, the bases of nonmonetary assets and liabilities must be established in the new functional currency (local currency). Those functional currency bases are then translated into the reporting currency at current rates in accordance with ASC 830 (FAS-52). The following two methods were suggested for determining the bases of nonmonetary assets and liabilities in the newly established functional currency:

Method 1   The historical bases in the *local currency* become the functional currency bases for nonmonetary items.

Method 2   Historical bases in the *reporting currency* are translated into the local currency at current rates to establish the new functional currency bases for nonmonetary items. (The Task Force adopted this method in its consensus.)

Illustration of Two Methods Considered for Determining New Functional Currency Bases of Nonmonetary Items

- Company A's Subsidiary F operated in a highly inflationary economy from 1/1/X1 to 12/31/X5.
- On 1/1/X2, Subsidiary F purchased equipment costing LC10,000 (local currency) with a useful life of 20 years.
- On 1/1/X6, the economy in which Subsidiary F operated ceased to be considered highly inflationary. As of this date, under the consensus, a new functional currency basis needs to be established.
- The exchange rates used in this illustration are as follows:

1/1/X2	$1 = LC2
1/1/X6	$1 = LC10
19X6 average	$1 = LC11
12/31/X6	$1 = LC12

On 12/31/X5, the equipment has a net book value of LC8,000 (LC10,000 less accumulated depreciation of LC2,000) in Subsidiary F's financial statements. The equipment is presented in Company A's financial statements at a net book value of $4,000 [$5,000 original remeasured cost (LC10,000 × $1/LC2) less $1,000 accumulated depreciation].

Effect of Using Methods 1 and 2

Method 1

Net book value in local currency	LC8,000
Current exchange rate	LC10 to $1

18.10 Foreign Operations and Exchange

Translation at current rate—	
New reporting currency basis	$800
Prior reporting currency basis	$4,000
Cumulative translation adjustment	$3,200

Method 2 (Adopted in the Consensus)

Reporting currency basis	$4,000
Translation back to local currency at current rate	LC10 to $1
New local currency basis	LC40,000

Comparison of Methods

	Method 1	Method 2
Local currency basis	LC8,000	LC40,000
Reporting currency basis	$800	$4,000
Prior reporting currency basis	$4,000	$4,000
Adjustment to cumulative Translation adjustments account	$3,200	0

Effect on 20X6 Earnings

	Method 1	Method 2
Book value 1/1/X6	$800	$4,000
20X6 depreciation expense		
Functional currency basis	LC8,000	LC40,000
Remaining useful life	16 years	16 years
Depreciation in LC	500	2,500
Average exchange rate	LC11 to $1	LC11 to $1
Depreciation expense	$45	$227
Book value 12/31/X6	$755	$3,773

The principal argument for Method 2 was that it is stated in the discussion in paragraphs 102 through 109 of FAS-52 (*Note:* Paragraphs 102 through 108 are not included in the Codification; paragraph 109 is in ASC 830-10-45-13) that financial information presented in the local currency of a highly inflationary economy is not meaningful, because the local currency is too unstable to provide a reliable measurement of an entity's financial position and results of operations. Accordingly, the reporting currency provides a better basis for establishing the new measurement basis of nonmonetary assets and liabilities. In the same vein, opponents to Method 1 argued that using the historical local currency basis would deem the local currency a reliable measuring unit during a highly inflationary period, thus reintroducing the effects of inflation and negating the intent of FAS-52.

EITF Issue 92-8 (Accounting for the Income Tax Effects under FASB Statement No. 109 of a Change in Functional Currency When an Economy Ceases to Be Considered Highly Inflationary) (ASC 830-740-25-2; 45-2)

OVERVIEW

When applying the consensus in ASC 830-740-25-2, 45-2 (Issue 92-4), the functional currency bases of nonmonetary assets generally will exceed their local currency tax bases. This difference represents a temporary difference under the guidance in ASC 740 (FAS-109, Accounting for Income Taxes), for which a deferred tax liability normally must be recognized.

ACCOUNTING ISSUE

Should an entity account for the income tax effects of a change in functional currency when an economy ceases to be considered highly inflationary by charging income tax expense or the cumulative adjustments component of shareholders' equity?

EITF CONSENSUS

The EITF reached a consensus that when an economy ceases to be considered highly inflationary, deferred taxes associated with a temporary difference resulting from a change in functional currency should be presented as an adjustment to the cumulative translation adjustments component of shareholders' equity.

> **OBSERVATION:** ASC 830 (FAS-52) has been amended by ASC 220 (FAS-130) to require that translation adjustments be reported in other comprehensive income. Therefore, deferred taxes would be recognized in other comprehensive income. It does not change the reporting for accumulated translation adjustments that are reported in a separate component of equity until the foreign investment is sold or liquidated.

DISCUSSION

The EITF's consensus is supported by the following arguments:
- Differences between the local currency tax bases of nonmonetary assets and their financial reporting currency bases result from inflation in a highly inflationary economy. Proponents refer to paragraph 119 of FAS-109 (not in ASC), which states that it is inappropriate to recognize the difference between the foreign currency equivalent of the U.S. dollar cost of nonmonetary assets and their local tax bases as a temporary difference in calculating

deferred taxes while an economy is highly inflationary, because that would result in recognition of deferred taxes on exchange gains and losses not recognized in the financial statements under FAS-52. They believe that the same rationale should be used if the functional currency is changed from the reporting currency to the local currency in cases in which the local economy is no longer considered highly inflationary. Although deferred taxes must be provided for that difference, they should be charged to the cumulative translation adjustments component because they are related to the net investment in the foreign entity.

- The guidance in ASC 830-10-45-9, 45-10 (paragraph 46 of FAS-52), which requires charging the effect of a change in functional currency to the cumulative translation adjustments account, should be applied to this situation by analogy. The EITF did not adopt the approach in ASC 740-10-50-10 (paragraph 46 of FAS-109) in their consensus in ASC 830-10-45-9 through 45-10 (Issue 92-4) because they believed that it does not apply to a change in functional currency when an economy ceases to be highly inflationary. Nevertheless, proponents argued that the effect on net income should not differ based on the reason for changing the functional currency.

- The deferred tax effects discussed in this Issue are not caused by an economic effect on the entity when a foreign economy ceases to be considered highly inflationary, but rather by the results of the consensus in ASC 830-10-45-9 through 45-10 (Issue 92-4) and the difference between the way basis differences are normally treated under in the guidance ASC 740 (FAS-109) and those caused by highly inflationary economies. Opponents of recognition in income argued that it would be difficult to explain to users why such a change should result in a charge to income.

EITF Issue 01-5 (Application of FASB Statement No. 52 to an Investment Being Evaluated for Impairment That Will Be Disposed Of) (ASC 830-30-45-13 through 45-15)

OVERVIEW

Under the provisions of ASC 830 (FAS-52, Foreign Currency Translation), translation adjustments that result when a foreign entity's financial statements are translated into a parent company's or an investor's reporting currency are reported separately from the entity's earnings in other comprehensive income. Foreign currency translation adjustments (CTA) that are accumulated in other comprehensive income are reclassified to income only when they are realized if the investment in the foreign entity is sold or is substantially or completely liquidated. This Issue does not apply to foreign investments that are held for use or to transactions related to foreign investments in which CTA will not be reclassified when the transaction is consummated.

ACCOUNTING ISSUES

- Should an entity include CTA in the carrying amount of its investment in evaluating the impairment of an *equity* method investment in a foreign entity that has committed to a plan to dispose of an investment that will result in the reclassification of CTA to earnings?
- Should an entity include CTA in the carrying amount of its investment in evaluating the impairment of a *consolidated* investment in a foreign entity that has committed to a plan to dispose of an investment that will result in the reclassification of CTA to earnings?
- Should an entity that has committed to a plan to dispose of a net investment in a foreign operation (accounted for as an equity investment or as a consolidated subsidiary) include the portion of CTA representing a gain or a loss from an effective hedge of that net investment in the carrying amount of the investment when evaluating the investment for impairment?

EITF CONSENSUS

The EITF reached a consensus that when evaluating the impairment of a foreign investment, an entity that has committed to a plan to dispose of an equity method investment in a foreign operation or a consolidated foreign subsidiary should *include* in the investment's carrying amount (1) foreign currency translation adjustments that will be reclassified to earnings on the foreign entity's disposal and (2) the portion of CTA related to a gain or loss from an effective hedge of the entity's net investment in the foreign operation.

Topic D-12 (Foreign Currency Translation—Selection of Exchange Rate When Trading Is Temporarily Suspended) (ASC 830-30-55-1)

The FASB staff discussed an inquiry from a U.S. company, which had a significant subsidiary in Israel, about the appropriate exchange rate for translating financial statements at year-end. In this case, foreign currency trading was suspended between December 30, 1988, and January 2, 1989. The Israeli government had announced on December 30 that the Israeli shekel, which traded at 1.68 shekel to $1 on December 29, would be devalued on January 2. Although trading resumed on January 2, the new exchange rate of 1.81 shekel to $1 was not established until January 3, 1989. The issue was how to select an exchange rate for year-end reporting when trading is temporarily suspended.

The FASB staff announced that, based on the guidance in ASC 830-30-45-9 (paragraph 26 of FAS-52), the exchange rate on January 3, 1989, would be appropriate for translating the year-end financial statements. ASC 830-30-45-9 (paragraph 26 of FAS-52) states that " [i]f exchangeability between two currencies is *temporarily* lacking at the transaction date or balance sheet date, the first subsequent rate at which exchanges could be made shall be used for purposes of this Statement." [Emphasis added.] The FASB staff noted that the SEC staff agrees with that guidance.

Topic D-55 (Determining a Highly Inflationary Economy under FASB Statement No. 52) (ASC 830-10-45-12; 55-24 through 55-26)

The FASB staff made an announcement interpreting the guidance in ASC 830 (FAS-52) on how to determine whether an economy is highly inflationary. It is stated in ASC 830-10-45-11 (paragraph 11 of FAS-52) that an economy is highly inflationary if its cumulative inflation rate is 100% or more over a three-year period. The role of judgment in making that determination is discussed in ASC 830-10-45-13 (paragraphs 104 and 109 of FAS-52).

The FASB staff believes that an economy should always be considered highly inflationary if the cumulative inflation rate for the previous three-year period exceeds 100%. However, the staff gave the following examples in which historical trends and other factors would be considered to determine whether an economy is highly inflationary if the cumulative inflation rate is *less* than 100%:

- An economy would continue being considered highly inflationary if it was so in the past, even though its cumulative three-year inflation rate is close to but less than 100% as a result of a decrease in the rate during the last one or two years, unless evidence suggests that the drop is not temporary.
- An economy that was highly inflationary in the prior year should *not* be considered highly inflationary in the current year, if its cumulative three-year inflation rate is close to but less than 100%, even though the inflation rate was very high in one isolated year, which was atypical in comparison to the economy's historical inflation rates and the rate in the current year.

The SEC Observer stated that this guidance should be applied to investments in Mexico and that registrants are expected to apply it to reporting periods beginning after December 31, 1996.

Topic D-56 (Accounting for a Change in Functional Currency and Deferred Taxes When an Economy Becomes Highly Inflationary) (ASC 830-10-45-10, 45-16)

The FASB staff announced that a change in the functional currency of an economy that is determined to be highly inflationary in accordance with the provisions in ASC 830 (FAS-52) should be accounted for based on the guidance in ASC 830-10-45-9, 45-10 (paragraph 46 of FAS-52). According to that guidance "translation adjustments for prior periods should not be removed from equity and the translated amounts for nonmonetary assets at the end of the prior period become the accounting basis for those assets in the period of the change and subsequent periods."

The FASB staff also announced its view on the recognition of deferred tax benefits when the functional currency changes to that of the reporting entity. Under ASC 740-10-25-3 (paragraph 9f of FAS-109), recognition of deferred tax benefits is not permitted for assets and liabilities indexed for tax purposes, if those assets are remeasured into the reporting currency using historical exchange rates. Consequently, no deferred tax benefits should be recognized as a result of tax indexing that occurs after a functional currency becomes the reporting currency until those benefits are realized on the tax return. Nevertheless, deferred tax benefits that are recognized before the functional currency changes to the reporting currency should be eliminated only when the related indexed amounts are realized as deductions for tax purposes.

ASC 946-830 Financial Services—Investment Companies

SOP 93-4 (Foreign Currency Accounting and Financial Statement Presentation for Investment Companies) (ASC 946-830-05-1 through 05-2; 50-1 through 50-4; 55-1 through 55-8, 55-10 through 55-16; 45-1 through 45-5, 45-7 through 45-12, 45-14, 45-22 through 45-23, 45-25 through 45-29, 45-31, 45-34 through 45-39)

BACKGROUND

A number of U.S. investment companies offer closed-end single-country funds (e.g., the Germany Fund). These funds typically adopt the U.S. dollar as their functional currency, even though many of the transactions of the fund are denominated in a different currency (e.g., the mark for the Germany Fund). The U.S. dollar is typically adopted as the functional currency because sales, redemptions, and dividends are paid to shareholders in U.S. dollars.

This pronouncement is designed to provide guidance to investment companies in computing and reporting foreign currency gains and losses in two types of investment transactions: (1) transactions involving securities denominated in or expected to be settled in a currency other than the U.S. dollar, and (2) investments in a currency other than the U.S. dollar. This Statement also provides guidance in handling other transactions (e.g., receivables and payables) denominated in a currency other than the U.S. dollar.

STANDARDS

Scope

The provisions of this pronouncement apply to all investment companies subject to the provisions of ASC 946-830, Financial Services-Investment Companies (AICPA Audit and Accounting Guide, *Audits of Investment Companies*). If a single-country fund invests in a country that is classified as "highly inflationary" in accordance with the guidance in ASC 830-10-45-11 (paragraph 11 of FAS-52), the measurement and disclosure guidelines in this pronouncement may not apply.

> ☞ **PRACTICE POINTER:** This pronouncement does not specify the measurement and disclosure guidelines to follow if a single-country fund invests in a country classified as "highly inflationary." However, it seems reasonable to adapt the guidance on "highly inflationary" economies discussed in ASC 830 (FAS-52, Foreign Currency Translation) to the accounting for the single-country fund.

General Conclusions

The following conditions can give rise to a foreign currency gain or loss:

- The value of securities held, based on current exchange rates, differs from the securities cost.
- The amount of a receivable or payable at the transaction date differs from the amount ultimately received or paid upon settlement, or differs from the amount receivable or payable at the reporting date based on current exchange rates.
- The amount of interest, dividends, and withholding taxes at the transaction date differs from the amount ultimately received or paid, or differs from the amount receivable or payable at the reporting date based on current exchange rates.
- Expenses accrued at the transaction date(s) differ from the amount ultimately paid, or differ from the amount payable at the reporting date based on current exchange rates.
- Forward exchange contracts or foreign exchange futures contracts need to be marked to market.

All of these conditions result from changes in the exchange rate between the U.S. dollar and the foreign currency applicable to the fund. Before the settlement date of the transaction, a revaluation of securities, receivables, payables, etc., is classified as an unrealized gain or loss. When the transaction is settled (the cash flow occurs), the gain or loss is realized.

Differences between the amounts that were originally recorded and the amounts at which transactions are settled, or the amounts at which unsettled transactions are measured on the reporting date (based on the current exchange rate), are a function of changes in the exchange rate and changes in market prices. In recording the original transaction, the transaction at settlement, and the unsettled transaction at a reporting date, the reporting currency is used (i.e., typically the U.S. dollar).

The two components of gain/loss identified in the previous paragraph (changes in exchange rates and changes in market prices) must be separately identified, computed, and reported for all transactions other than for investments. Entities can choose to separately disclose the two components of gain/loss for investment transactions, or to combine these two elements.

Investments—Purchased Interest

Interest-bearing securities are often purchased between coupon dates. Accrued interest since the last coupon date is included in the purchase price of the security. The purchaser is to recognize this accrued interest as interest receivable, measured on the basis of the spot exchange rate on the transaction date. If a reporting date intervenes before the purchased interest is received, the interest receivable is measured at the reporting date on the basis of the spot exchange rate on that date. After the settlement date, interest is to be accrued on a daily basis using each day's spot exchange rate. If the exchange rate is relatively stable, however, interest can be accrued either weekly or monthly.

Illustration of the Accrual of Interest—Stable Exchange Rate

New Millennium Foreign Fund, a single-country closed-end fund, purchases an investment grade corporate bond for 1,000,000FC on December 1, 20X4. The interest rate is 8%, and the investment is purchased at face value. The semiannual interest payment dates are September 1 and March 1. The exchange rate at December 1, 20X4, is $.58 per FC. This transaction would be recorded at December 1, 20X4 (in the fund's functional currency, the U.S. dollar), as follows:

Investment in Corporate Debt (1,000,000 × $.58) $580,000

Interest Receivable (1,000,000 × .08 × 3/12 × $.58)   11,600

    Cash $591,600

The exchange rate is relatively stable during December. New Millennium will accrue interest at December 31, 20X4, using the average exchange rate for December ($.57 per FC). The appropriate journal entry is as follows:

Interest Receivable (1,000,000 × .08 × 1/12 × $.57) $3,800

    Interest Income $3,800

Investments—Marking to Market

As discussed previously, due to changes in both exchange rates and market values, the market value of a security at a valuation date (a reporting date) may differ from the amount at which the security was originally recorded on the transaction date. The two components of any unrealized gain or loss on securities *do not* have to be separately reported. However, the guidance in this pronouncement indicates that in many cases such separate reporting would provide valuable information to users of the fund's financial statements.

The two components—changes in exchange rates and changes in market prices—of any unrealized gains or losses can be computed as follows:

Unrealized foreign currency gain or loss

(Cost in foreign currency × Valuation date spot rate)
− Cost in functional currency

Unrealized market value appreciation or depreciation

(Market value in foreign currency
− Original cost in foreign currency)
× Valuation date spot rate

In the above computations, weekly or monthly average exchange rates can be used if daily fluctuations in exchange rates are not significant. Also, if an entity holds a short-term security that is being carried at amortized cost, amortized cost should be substituted for market value in the above formulas.

Illustration of the Computation of Unrealized Gain

The New Millennium Foreign Fund purchases 1,000 shares of WMB Motors on December 1, 20X4, at a price of 40FC per share. The exchange rate on December 1, 20X4, is $.58 per FC. On December 31, 20X4, the market price of WMB Motors is 41FC per share, and the average exchange rate during December was $.57 (the exchange rate was relatively stable during the month). The two components of the unrealized gain recognized by New Millennium would be computed as follows:

Unrealized foreign currency gain or loss

(1,000 shares × 40FC per share × $.57)
− (1,000 shares × 40FC per share × $.58) = ($400)

Unrealized market value appreciation or depreciation

[(1,000 shares × 41FC per share)
− (1,000 shares × 40FC per share)] × $.57 = $570

PROOF:

>(1,000 shares × 41FC per share × $.57)
>− (1,000 shares × 40FC per share × $.58) = $170

This proof is based on the following formula: (Market value in foreign currency × Valuation date spot rate) − (Cost in foreign currency × Transaction date spot rate)

Investments—Sale

A realized gain or loss on a security sale has two components: a realized exchange gain or loss and a realized market gain or loss. However, separately computing and displaying these two components is *optional*. If the entity chooses to report both pieces of the realized gain or loss, these amounts would be computed as follows:

Realized foreign currency gain or loss

>(Cost in foreign currency × Sale date spot rate)
>− Cost in functional currency

Realized market gain or loss

>(Sale proceeds in foreign currency
>− Original cost in foreign currency)
>× Sale date spot rate

Upon the sale of securities, a receivable is recorded based on the exchange rate on the trade date. Any change in the exchange rate between the trade date and the settlement date will be recognized as a gain or loss when the trade is settled.

Investments—Sale of Interest

An entity may sell an interest-bearing security between coupon dates. The difference between the recorded interest receivable and the foreign currency received, translated into the functional currency at the current exchange rate, represents a realized gain or loss.

Income—Interest

Interest on a security denominated in a foreign currency is to be accrued daily. First the interest is measured in the foreign currency, and then it is converted into the functional currency using the daily spot exchange rate. If the exchange rate is relatively stable, this calculation can be based on the average weekly or monthly exchange rate.

Interest receivable, which includes both accrued interest and purchased interest, is initially measured in the foreign currency. At the valuation date (which may be daily), the receivable is converted into the functional currency using the current exchange rate. The difference between the interest receivable, converted at the spot exchange date on the valuation date, and interest accrued in the foreign currency is the unrealized foreign currency gain or loss.

Income—Accretion and Amortization

Bonds are often purchased at a premium or a discount. Any such premium or discount should initially be amortized daily on a foreign currency basis. At maturity, the carrying value of the bond in the foreign currency will equal the foreign currency proceeds received. However, in most cases there will be a realized foreign currency gain or loss.

The purchase price of the bond, at the trade date, is converted into the entity's functional currency using that day's exchange rate. Daily amortization of discount or premium, in the entity's foreign currency, is converted into functional currency using the daily exchange rate (again, if exchange rates are relatively constant, a weekly or monthly average rate can be used). The sum of the purchase price of the bond (converted into functional currency on the trade date) plus (minus) amortization of the discount (premium) over the life of the bond (converted into functional currency at periodic spot rates) will produce the carrying value of the bond in the entity's functional currency. The proceeds received upon the expiration of the bond (its face value in foreign currency) is to be converted into the entity's functional currency using the exchange rate in effect on the maturity date. In most cases, the proceeds in functional currency will differ from the carrying value of the bond in functional currency. This is what gives rise to a foreign currency gain or loss.

Illustration of the Computation of a Foreign Currency Gain—Bond Expiration

The New Millennium Germany Fund purchased a 25,000,000 mark bond on October 1, 20X4, at 97%. The exchange rate on this date was $.56 per mark. The carrying value of this bond in U.S. dollars, the functional currency, on October 1, 20X4, is $13,580,000 (25,000,000 marks × 97% × $.56). Over the remaining life of this bond, New Millennium must amortize the discount of 750,000 marks. Based on the spot rates in effect when this discount was amortized, the functional currency amount of the discount amortization was $412,500. The spot exchange rate is $.59 on the bond's due date. Therefore, on the bond's due date the New Millennium Germany Fund will receive 25,000,000 marks, which is convertible into $14,750,000 (25,000,000 marks × $.59). The carrying value of the bond in U.S. dollars is $13,992,500 ($13,580,000 + $412,500). Therefore, New Millennium would have a realized foreign currency gain of $757,500.

Dividends

Dividend income on securities denominated in a foreign currency is to be recognized on the ex-dividend date. The amount of the dividend in foreign currency is to be converted into functional currency using the exchange rate on that date (DR, Dividend Receivable; CR, Dividend Income). The related Dividend Receivable account is to be translated daily at the spot exchange rate; differences that arise as a result of this process are unrealized gains or losses. When the dividend is received, the unrealized gain or loss account is reclassified as realized gain or loss.

Withholding Tax

In some cases, taxes are withheld from investment and dividend income at the source. These withheld amounts may or may not be reclaimable by the fund. If the tax withheld is not reclaimable, it should be accrued on each income recognition date if the tax rate is fixed and known. If the tax withheld is reclaimable, it should be recorded as a receivable and not as an expense. If the tax rate is not known or estimable, the expense (when the tax is not reclaimable) or the receivable (when the tax is reclaimable) is recorded on the date the (net) investment income is received. When the net investment income is received, the realized foreign currency gain or loss is computed on the gross income receivable and the accrued tax expense.

Expenses

Expenses should be accrued as incurred and translated into the functional currency using the exchange rate on the day the expense is incurred. The difference between the expense accrued in the functional currency and the related foreign currency accrued expense balance (a liability) translated into the functional currency using the exchange rate on the valuation date is the unrealized foreign currency gain or loss. When the expense is paid, the unrealized foreign currency gain or loss is reclassified as a realized gain or loss.

Receivables and Payables

Receivables and payables typically arise to record items of income and expense and to record the purchase or sale of securities. At each valuation date, all receivables and payables should be translated into the functional currency using the exchange rate on the valuation date. In most cases, there will be a difference between the amount of the receivable or payable translated at the valuation date and the functional currency amount that was recorded at various spot rates for income or expense items (or for purchases and sales of securities on different dates). This difference is an unrealized gain or loss. When a receivable or payable is settled, the difference between the amount received or paid (in functional currency) and the functional currency amount that was recorded at various spot rates for income or expense items (or for purchases and sales of securities on different dates) is a realized gain or loss.

Illustration of the Computation of a Foreign Currency Loss—Payables

The New Millennium Foreign Fund incurs the following expenses during December 20X4: 10,000FC on 12/7; 11,000FC marks on 12/14; 12,000FC on 12/21; and 13,000FC on 12/28. The spot exchange rates on these dates are $.55, $.59, $.57, and $.58, respectively. Therefore, the functional currency value of these expenses is $26,370 [(10,000FC × $.55) + (11,000FC × $.59) + (12,000FC × $.57) + (13,000FC × $.58)]. The exchange rate on December 31, 20X4, is $.58. Also, these expenses represent the December 31, 20X4, accrued expense balance. New Millennium's accrued expense balance, in its functional currency, is $26,680 at year-end. Therefore, New Millennium would have an unrealized (the liability is not yet settled) foreign currency loss of $310 ($26,680−$26,370).

Cash

Receipts of foreign currency (cash) are to be treated as if a foreign currency denominated security had been purchased. The foreign currency received is to be converted into the functional currency using the exchange rate on the day the cash is received. Every disbursement of foreign currency is to be treated as if a security had been sold. The functional equivalent of the foreign currency disbursed is to be credited (using specific identification, FIFO, or average cost to determine the amount of the functional currency to be released).

The acquisition of foreign currency does not result in a gain or loss. However, the disposition of foreign currency typically does result in a gain or loss. The gain or loss is measured as the difference between the functional currency equivalent on the date the foreign currency was acquired and the functional currency equivalent on the date the foreign currency is disbursed.

The functional currency equivalent of foreign currency held is to be computed on each valuation date. Any difference between this amount and the functional currency equivalent of the foreign currency on the date it was acquired is an unrealized gain or loss.

Forward Exchange Contracts

A *forward exchange contract* is an agreement between two parties to exchange two currencies at a specified rate on a specified date in the future. If a fund enters into a forward exchange contract, the contract is to be initially recorded at the forward rate and marked to market on a daily basis.

Unrealized gain or loss on these contracts is computed as follows: the foreign currency amount valued at the valuation date forward rate minus the amount to be received or paid at the settlement date. On the settlement date, the unrealized gain or loss is reclassified as realized gain or loss.

Financial Statement Presentation

A section of the Statement of Operations is titled "Realized and Unrealized Gain (Loss) from Investments and Foreign Currency." This section follows the presentation of investment income and investment expenses. All foreign currency gains and losses should be reported in this section. Gains or losses from non-investment transactions would have their own line item in the Statement: "Foreign currency transactions" (with separate line items for realized and unrealized gains and losses). If foreign currency gains and losses from investment transactions are computed separately, these amounts would be included in the line item "Foreign currency transactions" as well. If foreign currency gains and losses from investment transactions are not computed separately, they would be aggregated with market gains or losses from investment transactions and reported in the line item "Investments."

The Statement of Assets and Liabilities and the Statement of Changes in Net Assets should reflect the same unrealized and realized gain and loss components. It is permissible to combine (*a*) net realized gains and losses from investments with net realized gains and losses from foreign currency transactions and (*b*) net unrealized appreciation (depreciation) on investments with the net unrealized appreciation (depreciation) on the translation of assets and liabilities in foreign currencies.

The notes to the financial statements should disclose the entity's policy regarding the treatment of unrealized and realized gains or losses from investments. Otherwise these amounts do not have to be separately disclosed; however, such disclosure may provide useful information to financial statement users.

Certain taxes on foreign source income are not reclaimable. To the extent such taxes exist, the relevant amount should be deducted from the related amount of income. Either this reduction in the income amount is shown parenthetically on the face of the income statement or else a contra-account (to the income item) should be presented on the face of the income statement. Taxes that are based on the aggregate income or capital gains of the investment company are to be treated in a manner similar to income taxes.

Other Issues

Investing in foreign securities poses a number of risks. In addition to the foreign currency risks already discussed, risks related to liquidity, size, and valuation need to be monitored by management and considered for disclosure. Some foreign markets are illiquid. Therefore, quoted market prices may not necessarily be indicative of net realizable value. Some foreign markets are relatively small, and a fund may hold an investment that represents a sizable stake in the overall market. In these cases, quoted market prices may not be indicative of net realizable value. For the reasons previously discussed, determining the proper valuation of securities is sometimes subjective. The fund's board of directors has the ultimate responsibility for determining the fair values of securities.

RELATED CHAPTERS IN 2011
GAAP GUIDE, VOLUME II

Chapter 20, "Income Taxes"
Chapter 25, "Investments in Debt and Equity Securities"

RELATED CHAPTERS IN 2011
GAAP GUIDE, VOLUME I

Chapter 18, "Foreign Operations and Exchange"
Chapter 21, "Income Taxes"
Chapter 28, "Investments in Debt and Equity Securities"

RELATED CHAPTER IN 2011
INTERNATIONAL ACCOUNTING/FINANCIAL
REPORTING STANDARDS GUIDE

Chapter 17, "Foreign Currency Translation"

CHAPTER 19
IMPAIRMENT OF LONG-LIVED ASSETS

CONTENTS

Overview		19.01
Authoritative Guidance		
ASC 310 Receivables		19.03
FSP FAS-144-1	Determination of Cost Basis for Foreclosed Assets under FASB Statement No. 15, *Accounting by Debtors and Creditors for Troubled Debt Restructurings*, and the Measurement of Cumulative Losses Previously Recognized under Paragraph 37 of FASB Statement No. 144, *Accounting for the Impairment or Disposal of Long-Lived Assets*	19.03
ASC 350 Intangibles, Goodwill, and Other		19.05
EITF Issue 02-7	Unit of Accounting for Testing Impairment of Indefinite-Lived Intangible Assets	19.05
ASC 360 Property, Plant, and Equipment		19.08
EITF Issue 95-23	The Treatment of Certain Site Restoration/Environmental Exit Costs When Testing a Long-Lived Asset for Impairment	19.08
Related Chapter in 2011 GAAP Guide, Volume II		19.11
Related Chapters in 2011 GAAP Guide, Volume I		19.11
Related Chapters in 2011 International Accounting/Financial Reporting Standards Guide		19.11

OVERVIEW

Recognition of impairment of assets generally is required when events and circumstances indicate that the carrying amount of those assets will not be recovered in the future. For long-lived plant and identifiable intangible assets that are to be held and used, impairment is indicated when the carrying amount of the asset exceeds the undiscounted future cash flows expected from the asset. For similar assets that are to be disposed of, an impairment loss is recognized when the carrying amount exceeds its net realizable value or its fair value less cost to sell.

The following pronouncements, which provide GAAP for recognizing impairment of long-lived assets, are discussed in the 2011 *GAAP Guide, Volume 1,* Chapter 20, "Impairment of Long-Lived Assets":

ASC 360	Accounting for the Impairment or Disposal of Long-Lived Assets (FAS-144)
ASC 410	Accounting for Conditional Asset Retirement Obligations (FIN-47)

AUTHORITATIVE GUIDANCE

ASC 310 Receivables

FSP FAS-144-1 (Determination of Cost Basis for Foreclosed Assets under FASB Statement No. 15, *Accounting by Debtors and Creditors for Troubled Debt Restructurings*, and the Measurement of Cumulative Losses Previously Recognized under Paragraph 37 of FASB Statement No. 144, *Accounting for the Impairment or Disposal of Long-Lived Assets*) (ASC 310-40-4-10; 35-11; 55-13 through 55-15)

Question: When a long-lived asset is accounted for under the guidance in FAS-144 after foreclosure, should a valuation allowance related to the loan that was collateralized by that long-lived asset be carried over as a separate element of the asset's cost basis?

Answer: No. When a loan is foreclosed, the lender receives the long-lived asset collateralizing the loan in full satisfaction of the receivable. As required in FASB Accounting Standards Codification™ (ASC) 310-40-40-3 (paragraph 28 of FAS-15, Accounting by Debtors and Creditors for Troubled Debt Restructurings), ,the asset that collateralized the loan must be measured at its fair value less selling costs, which measurement becomes its new cost basis. After foreclosure, when the asset is accounted for under the provisions of ASC 360 (FAS-144), the valuation allowance related to the loan before foreclosure should not be carried over to the long-lived asset's cost basis because under the guidance in ASC 360-10-35-40 (paragraph 37 of FAS-144) the amount of gain that can be recognized on a long-lived asset is limited to the amount of cumulative impairment losses recognized and measured under the guidance in ASC 360 (FAS-144). *Loan losses* previously measured and recognized under the guidance in ASC 450 (FAS-5, Accounting for Contingencies), ASC 310 (FAS-15, and FAS-114,Accounting by Creditors for Impairment for a Loan) do not enter into the calculation of the impairment of an asset's value under the guidance in ASC 360 (FAS-144).

For example, a lender has a $100,000 loan receivable, which is collateralized by a long-lived asset with a fair value of $80,000 and estimated selling costs of $6,000 at the date on which the lender determines that foreclosure is probable. One month later, when the asset is foreclosed, the fair value of the collateral is unchanged. Based on the guidance in ASC 310-40-05-8; 310-10-35-16 through 35-17 (paragraph 8 of FAS-114), the lender's *loan impairment* loss at the foreclosure date is measured at $26,000, based on the difference between the loan receivable ($100,000) and the fair value of the collateral ($80,000) less selling costs ($6,000). At that date, the new cost basis of the long-lived asset received in full satisfaction of the receivable also is measured at $74,000 under the guidance in ASC 310 (FAS-15). Three months later when the asset is tested for

19.04 *Impairment of Long-Lived Assets*

impairment under the guidance in ASC 360 (FAS-144), its value has declined to $70,000 with estimated selling costs at $4,000. Under the provisions of ASC 360 (FAS-144), the lender recognizes an $8,000 asset impairment loss [($80,000−$6,000)−($70,000−$4,000)]. When the asset is sold six months later, its fair value has increased to $84,000, less $7,000 in selling costs. Although the asset's fair value has increased by $11,000 [($84,000−$7,000)−($70,000−$4,000)], the lender can recognize only a gain of $8,000, which is the amount of the asset's impairment loss previously recognized under the guidance in ASC 360 (FAS-144). The $26,000 loan impairment loss on foreclosure is *not* included in measuring the cumulative losses recognized under the guidance in ASC 360 (FAS-144).

ASC 350 Intangibles, Goodwill, and Other

EITF Issue 02-7 (Unit of Accounting for Testing Impairment of Indefinite-Lived Intangible Assets) (ASC 350-30-35-21 through 35-28, 35-30 through 35-32, 35-34 through 35-35, 35-37 through 35-38)

> **OBSERVATION:** ASC 805 (FAS-141(R)) replaces FAS-141, but does not affect the guidance in this issue.

OVERVIEW

Under the provisions of ASC 350 (FAS-142, Goodwill and Other Intangible Assets), intangible assets that are not required to be amortized must be evaluated for impairment at least annually. If an intangible asset's carrying amount exceeds its fair value, an impairment loss should be recognized. Recognized losses should not be restored in the future.

The EITF has been asked to provide guidance regarding the unit of accounting to be used when evaluating the impairment of intangible assets with indefinite lives. That is, (*a*) whether identical or similar indefinite-lived intangible assets may be combined for the purpose of testing impairment, for example, contiguous easements that were purchased in separate transactions but that are used as one asset, and (*b*) whether different indefinite-lived intangible assets, for example, a trade name and an easement, may be tested for impairment on a combined basis.

ACCOUNTING ISSUE

What unit of accounting should be used when testing indefinite-lived intangible assets for impairment under the guidance in ASC 350-30-35-18 through 35-20 (paragraph 17 of FAS-142)?

EITF CONSENSUS

The EITF reached a consensus that acquired or internally developed *intangible* assets with indefinite lives that have been separately recognized and are inseparable from each other because they are operated as a single unit should be combined in one accounting unit when testing impairment. Judgment, depending on the relevant facts and circumstances, is required to determine whether several such intangible assets are inseparable. Although the indicators discussed below should be considered in making that determination, they should not be considered to be presumptive or determinative.

Indicators that two or more indefinite-lived intangible assets should be combined as a single unit of accounting when testing for impairment

- The assets were purchased to construct or improve a single asset and will be used together.
- The assets would have been recognized as one asset if they had been acquired at the same time.
- The assets represent the highest and best use when considered as a group, because (a) it is unlikely that a substantial portion of the assets would be sold separately or (b) if a substantial portion of the assets were sold individually, the fair value of the remaining assets as a group would be significantly lower.
- The company's marketing or branding strategy indicates that the assets are complementary, as that term is used in ASC 805-20-55-18 (paragraph A34 of FAS-141(R)).

Indicators that two or more indefinite-lived intangible assets should not be combined as a single unit of accounting for impairment testing purposes

- The assets generate cash flows independently of one another.
- Each asset is likely to be sold separately. Previous separate sales of such assets are an indicator that combining them is not appropriate.
- The entity has a plan or is considering one to dispose of one or more of those assets separately.
- The assets are used exclusively by different asset groups referred to in ASC 360 (FAS-144).
- Economic and other factors that might limit the useful economic life of one of the assets would not necessarily be the same for other assets combined in the unit of accounting.

The EITF noted the following about the unit of accounting used to test indefinite-lived intangible assets for impairment:

- Indefinite-lived intangible assets should be in a separate unit of accounting, not tested with goodwill or finite-lived assets.
- A unit of accounting cannot consist of indefinite-lived assets that together represent a business.
- A unit of accounting may consist of indefinite-lived intangible assets presented in the separate financial statements of consolidated subsidiaries. Consequently, a loss recognized in consolidated financial statements may differ from total impairment losses, if any, recognized in the subsidiaries' separate financial statements.
- A unit of accounting and associated fair value used to test impairment of indefinite-lived intangible assets contained in a

single reporting unit also should be used to measure a goodwill impairment loss in accordance with the guidance in ASC 350-20-35-9 through 13 (paragraph 20 of FAS-142).

- If, because of a change in the way its intangible assets are used, a company combines those assets with assets that were previously tested separately for impairment to constitute a unit of accounting for the purpose of testing for impairment, the assets that were accounted for separately should be tested for impairment in accordance with the guidance in ASC 350-30-35-18 through 20 (paragraph 17 of FAS-142) before they are combined as a unit of accounting.

ASC 360 Property, Plant, and Equipment

EITF Issue 95-23 (The Treatment of Certain Site Restoration/Environmental Exit Costs When Testing a Long-Lived Asset for Impairment) (ASC 360-20-60-1; 55-2 through 55-6, 55-8, 55-13 through 55-18)

OVERVIEW

This Issue addresses the accounting for environmental exit costs that have not been recognized for accounting purposes and that are incurred when operations cease (even if the asset is retained) or if the asset is sold or abandoned. Such costs can include an environmental audit or assessment; a feasibility study or other assessment; actual remediation and/or site restoration; monitoring activities; legal costs; costs to change permits or licenses; costs related to equipment shutdown; and fines and penalties. An entity may incur environmental exit costs if certain assets are sold, abandoned, or cease operations. Funds for such costs may not be expended for some time if the costs are not incurred until the end of the asset's life or if the costs are deferred indefinitely, because the asset has not been sold or abandoned.

The EITF was asked to discuss the treatment of such costs. Under the provisions of ASC 360 (FAS-144, Accounting for the Impairment or Disposal of Long-Lived Assets), which has superseded FAS-121 (not in ASC), future cash flows from using or eventually disposing of an asset must be estimated when the recovery of the asset's carrying amount is reviewed because events or changes in circumstances suggest that it may be impaired. An impairment loss is recognized based on the asset's fair value if its carrying amount exceeds the sum of the asset's expected undiscounted future cash flows, excluding interest charges.

The environmental exit costs considered in this Issue generally are not accrued over the life of the asset, and it is unclear whether those costs should be included in undiscounted future cash flows used in the impairment calculation. Because such costs might not be incurred for many years, the amount would be small on a discounted basis but might be very large on an undiscounted basis. Consequently, including such costs in the undiscounted cash flow test would result in more frequent measurement of asset impairment and asset revaluation to fair value. (See the Subsequent Development section.)

ACCOUNTING ISSUE

Should undiscounted expected future cash flows used to test the recoverability of the carrying amount of a long-lived asset under the guidance in ASC 360 (FAS-144) include exit costs related to environmental matters that may be incurred if a long-lived asset is sold, abandoned, or ceases operations?

EITF CONSENSUS

> **OBSERVATION:** ASC 410 (FAS-143, Accounting for Asset Retirement Obligations) provides guidance for the initial recognition and measurement of asset retirement obligations and subsequent accounting for such obligations. It applies to all *legal* obligations related to the retirement of tangible long-lived assets and requires that the fair value, if estimable, of such obligations be recognized in the period in which the liability is incurred. If the fair value is not estimable at that time, recognition is required when a reasonable estimate of fair value can be made. The EITF's consensus related to liabilities that have not been recognized has been partially nullified by the guidance in ASC 410 (FAS-143).

At the June 2002 meeting, the EITF agreed to modify the consensus positions reached in this Issue based on the guidance in (*a*) ASC 360 (FAS-144) and (*b*) ASC 410 (FAS-143), as follows:

- The guidance in ASC 410 (FAS-143) nullifies the original consensus that future cash flows for environmental exit costs that have been *recognized* as a liability be excluded from undiscounted expected future cash flows used to test an asset's recoverability under the guidance in ASC 360 (FAS-144), even though under the guidance in ASC 410 (FAS-143) future cash flows for a liability that has been recognized for an asset's retirement obligation should be excluded from undiscounted cash flows used to test the asset for recoverability.

- The guidance in ASC 360 (FAS-144) affects the EITF's consensus position regarding management's intent for an asset by requiring that the likelihood of possible outcomes be considered if (*a*) a range of possible future cash flows is estimated or (*b*) management intends to recover an asset's carrying amount by alternative means instead of by selling or abandoning the asset, or ceasing its operations.

The FASB staff developed examples of situations in which environmental exit costs either would be included in or excluded from undiscounted cash flows, based on management's intent for the asset. Environmental exit costs would be *included* in the ASC 360 (FAS-144) recoverability test in the following situations:

- The asset's useful life is expected to be limited because of actual or expected technological advances, contractual provisions, or regulatory restrictions, and management intends to sell, abandon, or close the asset at the end of its useful life and will incur environmental exit costs in doing so.

- Although management expects the asset to become profitable in the future, the asset has a negative cash flow from operations in the current period, and a forecast or projection anticipates continuing losses. Management is uncertain whether it can continue funding future cash outflows until the asset begins generating net cash inflows. Under a forced liquidation, management would have to sell, abandon, or close the asset and would incur environmental exit costs.
- Management's intent to sell or abandon the asset in the future will result in remediation costs to conform with applicable laws or regulations.

Environmental exit costs would be *excluded* from undiscounted expected future cash flows in the following situations:

- The asset has an indefinite useful life; management intends to operate the asset indefinitely and has the ability to do so; and based on all available information the asset will continue to be profitable. Expected future cash flows for repair, maintenance, and capital expenditures required to obtain future cash flows would be included in the recoverability test under the guidance in ASC 360 (FAS-144), however.
- Management intends to operate the asset at least during its remaining depreciable life. Total undiscounted future cash flows expected from operating the asset during that period exceed its carrying amount, including related goodwill, and there is no reason for management to believe that disposal of the asset would result in a net cash outflow.
- Environmental exit costs related to an asset that has a finite life would be incurred only if it is sold or abandoned. To avoid the cost of remediating the asset, management intends to close the asset permanently at the end of its useful life or to idle it by reducing production to a minimal level. The recoverability test should consider the entity's assumptions for the use of the asset. Expected future cash flows required to (*a*) maintain or protect the asset after it has been closed or (*b*) to fund losses incurred after the asset has been idled should nevertheless be included in the recoverability test under the guidance in ASC 360 (FAS-144).
- Management expects to sell the asset in the future without incurring environmental exit costs. The effect of environmental exit costs on the asset's fair value should be considered in estimating net proceeds from a future sale to be used in the recoverability test under the guidance in ASC 360 (FAS-144).

DISCUSSION

The EITF based its consensus on the premise that the environmental exit costs discussed in this Issue generally are not accrued over the life of the asset, either because they are considered avoidable or because in some jurisdictions, they are considered deferrable indefinitely as long as the asset is in operation or is not sold or abandoned, even if its operations cease. The Task Force thus agreed that the trigger should be based on management's plans for the asset. However, management's intention to operate an asset indefinitely or to idle it, but not sell or abandon it, would have to be supported by cash flow estimates demonstrating an entity's ability to do so.

The FASB staff's scenarios—under which exit costs would be included or excluded from the calculation under the provisions of ASC 360 (FAS 144)—are intended to provide facts and circumstances for the application of the consensus, but they also provide some specific guidance. For example, the second and fourth situations—under which environmental exit costs would *not* be included in undiscounted cash flows—nevertheless specify certain costs that *would be included* in the recoverability test under the guidance in ASC 360 (FAS-144).

RELATED CHAPTER IN 2011
GAAP GUIDE, VOLUME II

Chapter 12, "Contingencies, Risks, and Uncertainties"

RELATED CHAPTERS IN 2011
GAAP GUIDE, VOLUME I

Chapter 8, "Contingencies, Risks, and Uncertainties"
Chapter 20, "Impairment of Long-Lived Assets"

RELATED CHAPTERS IN 2011
INTERNATIONAL ACCOUNTING/FINANCIAL REPORTING STANDARDS GUIDE

Chapter 5, "Accounting Policies, Changes in Accounting Estimates, and Errors"
Chapter 16, "Financial Instruments"
Chapter 19, "Impairment of Assets"
Chapter 21, "Intangible Assets"
Chapter 26, "Non-Current Assets Held for Sale and Discontinued Operations"
Chapter 27, "Property, Plant, and Equipment"

CHAPTER 20
INCOME TAXES

CONTENTS

Overview		20.03
Authoritative Guidance		
ASC 350 Intangibles—Goodwill and Other		20.04
EITF Issue 02-13	Deferred Income Tax Considerations in Applying the Goodwill Impairment Test in FASB Statement No. 142, *Goodwill and Other Intangible Assets*	20.04
ASC 718 Compensation—Stock Compensation		20.06
EITF Issue 06-11	Accounting for Income Tax Benefits of Dividends on Share-Based Payment Awards	20.06
ASC 740 Income Taxes		20.08
FSP FAS-109-1	Application of FASB Statement No. 109, *Accounting for Income Taxes*, to the Tax Deduction on Qualified Production Activities Provided by the American Jobs Creation Act of 2004	20.08
FSP FIN-48-1	Definition of *Settlement* in FASB Interpretation No. 48	20.09
EITF Issue 87-8	Tax Reform Act of 1986: Issues Related to the Alternative Minimum Tax	20.12
EITF Issue 91-8	Application of FASB Statement No. 96 to a State Tax Based on the Greater of a Franchise Tax or an Income Tax	20.14
EITF Issue 93-13	Effect of a Retroactive Change in Enacted Tax Rates That Is Included in Income from Continuing Operations	20.17
EITF Issue 93-17	Recognition of Deferred Tax Assets for a Parent Company's Excess Tax Basis in the Stock of a Subsidiary That Is Accounted for as a Discontinued Operation	20.19

20.02 *Income Taxes*

EITF Issue 94-10	Accounting by a Company for the Income Tax Effects of Transactions among or with Its Shareholders under FASB Statement No. 109	**20.21**
EITF Issue 95-9	Accounting for Tax Effects of Dividends in France in Accordance with FASB Statement No. 109	**20.24**
EITF Issue 95-10	Accounting for Tax Credits Related to Dividend Payments in Accordance with FASB Statement No. 109	**20.26**
EITF Issue 95-20	Measurement in the Consolidated Financial Statements of a Parent of the Tax Effects Related to the Operations of a Foreign Subsidiary That Receives Tax Credits Related to Dividend Payments	**20.28**
EITF Issue 98-11	Accounting for Acquired Temporary Differences in Certain Purchase Transactions That Are Not Accounted for as Business Combinations	**20.30**
EITF Issue 05-8	Income Tax Consequences of Issuing Convertible Debt with a Beneficial Conversion Feature	**20.35**
Topic D-30	Adjustment Due to Effect of a Change in Tax Laws or Rates	**20.37**
Topic D-31	Temporary Differences Related to LIFO Inventory and Tax-to-Tax Differences	**20.37**
Topic D-32	Intraperiod Tax Allocation of the Tax Effect of Pretax Income from Continuing Operations	**20.38**
FIG-FAS 109	A Guide to Implementation of Statement 109 on Accounting for Income Taxes	**20.38**
ASC 805 Business Combinations		**20.45**
EITF Issue 86-9	IRC Section 338 and Push-Down Accounting	**20.45**
ASC 830-740 Foreign Currency Matters—Income Taxes		**20.46**
EITF Issue 93-9	Application of FASB Statement No. 109 in Foreign Financial Statements Restated for General Price-Level Changes	**20.46**

EITF Issue 93-16 Application of FASB Statement No. 109 to Basis Differences within Foreign Subsidiaries That Meet the Indefinite Reversal Criterion of APB Opinion No. 23	20.48
Related Chapters in 2011 GAAP Guide, Volume II	20.50
Related Chapters in 2011 GAAP Guide, Volume I	20.51
Related Chapters in 2011 International Accounting/Financial Reporting Standards Guide	20.51

OVERVIEW

The tax consequences of many transactions recognized in the financial statements are included in determining income taxes currently payable in the same accounting period. Sometimes, however, tax laws differ from the recognition and measurement requirements of financial reporting standards. Differences arise between the tax bases of assets or liabilities and their reported amounts in the financial statements. These differences are called *temporary differences* and they give rise to deferred tax assets and liabilities.

Temporary differences ordinarily reverse when the related asset is recovered or the related liability is settled. A *deferred tax liability* or *deferred tax asset* represents the increase or decrease in taxes payable or refundable in future years as a result of temporary differences and carryforwards at the end of the current year.

The objectives of accounting for income taxes are to recognize:

- The amount of taxes payable or refundable for the current year.
- The deferred tax liabilities and assets that result from future tax consequences of events that have been recognized in the enterprise's financial statements or tax returns.

The following pronouncements, which provide GAAP for accounting for income taxes, are discussed in the 2011 *GAAP Guide Volume I*, Chapter 21, "Income Taxes":

ASC 740	Accounting for the "Investment Credit" (APB-2)
ASC 740	Accounting for the "Investment Credit" (APB-4)
ASC 740; ASC 210	Paragraph 6, Tax Allocation Accounts—Discounting Paragraph 7, Offsetting Securities against Taxes Payable (APB-10; 605)
ASC 740; ASC 942	Accounting for Income Taxes—Special Areas (APB-23)
ASC 740	Accounting for Income Taxes (FAS-109)
ASC 740	Accounting for Income Taxes in Interim Periods (FIN-18)

AUTHORITATIVE GUIDANCE

ASC 350 Intangibles—Goodwill and Other

EITF Issue 02-13 (Deferred Income Tax Considerations in Applying the Goodwill Impairment Test in FASB Statement No. 142, *Goodwill and Other Intangible Assets*) (ASC 350-20-35-7, 35-25, 35-27, 35-20, 35-21; 55-10 through 55-16, 55-18 through 55-23)

OVERVIEW

ASC 350 (FAS-142, Goodwill and Other Intangible Assets) has drastically changed the way companies account for goodwill acquired in a business combination. Under FAS-142, an entity must allocate goodwill acquired in a business combination to one or more reporting units. In addition, corporate assets and liabilities also must be allocated to reporting units if (*a*) an asset is employed or a liability is related to a reporting unit's operations, and (*b*) the asset or liability will be taken into account in determining the reporting unit's fair value.

FAS-142 requires that goodwill be tested for impairment at the reporting level at least annually using the following procedure: (1) a reporting unit's fair value is compared to its carrying amount to determine whether the carrying amount exceeds its fair value (an excess, if any, may be a goodwill impairment), and (2) the *implied* fair value of goodwill, which is determined in the same way as the measurement of goodwill in a business combination under the provisions of ASC 805 (FAS-141(R), Business Combinations), an acquisition of a business, or a nonprofit activity acquired by a not-for-profit entity under the guidance in ASC 958-805 (FAS-164), which is compared with the carrying amount of goodwill. (FAS-141(R), revised 2007, replaces FAS-141.)

ACCOUNTING ISSUES

1. In estimating a reporting unit's fair value, should it be assumed that it would be bought or sold in a nontaxable rather than in a taxable transaction?
2. Should deferred income taxes be included in a reporting unit's carrying amount when comparing the reporting unit's fair value to its carrying amount?
3. When measuring deferred tax assets and liabilities for the purpose of determining the implied fair value of a reporting unit's

goodwill for the ASC 350 (FAS-142) goodwill impairment test, should an entity use the existing income tax bases or assume new income tax bases for a reporting unit's assets and liabilities?

EITF CONSENSUS

The EITF reached the following consensus positions:

1. Judgment based on the relevant facts and circumstances should be used in determining whether the fair value of a reporting unit should be estimated based on the assumption that the unit could be bought or sold in a nontaxable transaction rather than in a taxable transaction. That decision should be made on a case-by-case basis by considering whether (*a*) the assumption is consistent with those that others in the marketplace would include in fair value estimates, (*b*) the assumed structure is practicable, and (*c*) the assumed structure provides a seller with the highest economic value for the reporting unit, including consideration of related tax implications. Members noted that in determining whether a nontaxable transaction is practicable, an entity should consider whether the reporting unit could be sold in a nontaxable transaction; and whether the entity's ability to treat a sale as a nontaxable transaction would be impeded by income tax laws and regulations or corporate governance requirements.

2. Deferred income taxes should be included in a reporting unit's carrying amount for Step 1 of the (FAS-142) goodwill impairment test, regardless of the tax structure (taxable or nontaxable) on which the reporting unit's fair value will be determined based on an assumption that it would be bought or sold in a taxable or nontaxable transaction.

The income tax bases of a reporting unit's assets and liabilities inherent in the tax structure (taxable or nontaxable) assumed in an entity's estimate of the reporting unit's fair value in Step 1 of the impairment test should be used in determining the implied fair value of the reporting unit's goodwill in Step 2 of the impairment test. If a *nontaxable* transaction is assumed, the entity's existing income tax bases should be used. *New* income tax bases should be used if a *taxable* transaction is assumed. The EITF noted that in Step 2 of the test, the implied fair value of a reporting entity's goodwill is determined in the same way as the amount of goodwill recognized in a business combination under the guidance in ASC 805-30-30-5 (paragraph 38 of FAS-141(R)). This method is also used to determine the amount of goodwill recognized in an acquisition of a business or the acquisition of a nonprofit activity by a not-for-profit entity under the guidance in ASC 958-805 (FAS-164).

ASC 718 Compensation—Stock Compensation

EITF Issue 06-11 (Accounting for Income Tax Benefits of Dividends on Share-Based Payment Awards) (ASC 718-740-45-8 through 45-12, 45-5(a)1; 65-1)

OVERVIEW

A share-based payment arrangement may include a "dividend protection" provision under which employees may be entitled to receive, for example, (a) dividends or dividend equivalents on *nonvested* equity shares and *nonvested* equity share units during the vesting period, (b) payments equal to dividends on equity shares underlying an outstanding option, or (c) exercise price reductions of share options based on dividends paid on the underlying equity shares while an option is outstanding.

Under the guidance in ASC 718 (FAS-123(R)), employers charge the payment of dividends or dividend equivalents to employees on nonvested shares to retained earnings, but in some cases, those amounts are treated as deductible compensation cost for income tax purposes. The FASB staff has received questions regarding the accounting for income tax benefits related to the dividend payments discussed above.

SCOPE

The guidance in this Issue applies to share-based payment arrangements with dividend protection features under which employees have a right receive: (1) dividends or dividend equivalents during the vesting period on awards of nonvested shares and nonvested share units, all of which are classified as equity; or (2) equity share options until the awards are exercised. Some entities have been treating those dividends, nonvested equity units, and outstanding equity share options as deductible compensation for income tax purposes while charging those dividends to retained earnings under the provisions in ASC 718 (FAS-123(R), Share-Based Payment (Revised December 2004)), thus providing employers with an income tax deduction.

ACCOUNTING ISSUE

How should an entity recognize an income tax benefit it receives on dividends or dividend equivalents that are: (1) paid to employees that hold nonvested shares, nonvested share units, or outstanding share options, all of which are classified as equity; and (2) charged to retained earnings under the provisions of ASC 718 (FAS-123(R))?

EITF CONSENSUS

The EITF reached a consensus position that:

- Additional paid-in capital should be *increased* by an amount equal to a *realized* income tax benefit from dividends or dividend equivalents that have been charged to retained earnings and paid to employees for nonvested equity shares, nonvested equity share units, and outstanding equity share options that are classified as equity.
- The amount recognized in additional paid-in capital should be included in a pool of *excess tax benefits* available to absorb potential future tax deficiencies on share-based payment awards discussed in ASC 718-740-35-5 (paragraphs 62 and 63 of FAS-123(R)).

To reach that consensus, the EITF took into account the fact that such dividends or dividend equivalents paid to employees for nonvested equity shares, nonvested equity share units, and outstanding equity share options that are charged to retained earning may result in a tax deduction *before* the related tax benefit has actually been realized because, for example, an employer may have a net operating loss carryforward. According to the guidance in ASC 718-740-25-10 (footnote 82 of FAS-123(R)), an entity would *not* recognize an income tax benefit until income taxes payable have been reduced by the deduction. Consequently, *unrealized* income tax benefits from dividends on employee share-based payment awards should *not* be included in the pool of excess tax benefits available to absorb tax deficiencies on share-based payment awards.

Under the guidance in ASC 718 (FAS-123(R)), dividend equivalents paid to employees for nonvested equity shares, nonvested equity share units, and outstanding equity share options related to awards that are expected to vest are charged to retained earnings. Dividends and dividend equivalents related to awards that are *not* expected to vest are recognized as compensation cost. If an entity changes its estimates of forfeitures or actual forfeitures vary from previous estimates, dividends and dividend equivalents are reclassified between retained earnings and compensation cost in a subsequent period. An entity's pool of excess tax benefits available to absorb tax deficiencies would increase or decrease as a result of adjustments to additional paid-in capital by an amount that matches the amount of reclassifications between retained earnings and compensation cost. Further, if an entity's estimated forfeitures increase or actual forfeitures are greater than estimated, the amount of tax benefits from dividends that have been reclassified from additional paid-in capital to the income statement to reduce income tax expense or to increase an entity's income tax benefit should be restricted to the amount of the entity's pool of excess tax benefits available to absorb deficiencies on the date on which a reclassification occurs.

FASB RATIFICATION

The FASB ratified the consensus positions in this Issue at its June 27, 2007 meeting.

ASC 740 Income Taxes

FSP FAS-109-1 (Application of FASB Statement No. 109, *Accounting for Income Taxes*, to the Tax Deduction on Qualified Production Activities Provided by the American Jobs Creation Act of 2004) (ASC 740-10-55-27 through 55-30, 55-146 through 55-148)

OVERVIEW

Under the American Jobs Creation Act (the Job Act), which was signed into law on October 22, 2004, employers will be able to deduct up to 9% of (1) income from qualified production activities, as defined in the Job Act or (2) taxable income after the deduction for net operating loss carryforwards, if any, whichever is less. Up to 50% of W-2 wages paid by an employer qualify for the deduction. The FASB directed the FASB staff to provide guidance on the application of FAS-109 (Accounting for Income Taxes) in accounting for this deduction.

QUESTION

Should the tax deduction related to income from qualified production activities be accounted for under FAS-109 as a special deduction or as a tax-rate reduction?

FASB STAFF POSITION

The FASB staff believes that the characteristics of the Job Act's deduction for qualified production activities are similar to the special deductions illustrated in paragraph 231 of FAS-109 (FASB Accounting Standards Codification™ (ASC) 740-10-25-37) because this deduction depends on the performance of specific activities and the level of wages in the future. Consequently, the deduction under the Job Act should be accounted for as a special deduction under the provisions of FAS-109. The FASB staff also noted that an entity should take this special deduction into account in (1) measuring deferred taxes if graduated taxes are a significant factor and (2) determining whether a valuation allowance is required in accordance with paragraph 232 of FAS-109 (ASC 740-10-25-37).

EFFECTIVE DATE AND TRANSITION

FSP FAS-109-1 is effective as of December 21, 2004, which is the date it was posted on the FASB's web site. Entities that have recognized the deduction for qualified production activities as a tax rate reduction should restate their financial statements in accordance with paragraph 27 of APB-20 (Accounting Changes), to present the deduction as a special deduction under the provisions of paragraphs 231 and 232 of FAS-109 (ASC 740-10-25-37).

FSP FIN-48-1 (Definition of *Settlement* in FASB Interpretation No. 48) (ASC 740-10-25-9)

OVERVIEW

The FASB directed the FASB staff to draft this FSP, which amends the guidance in FIN-48 (Accounting for Uncertainty in Income Taxes), because constituents have asked the staff whether an entity may recognize a tax benefit that it previously had decided should not be recognized if the only change that has occurred is the completion of a tax authority's examination or audit. Constituents have also asked for clarification of the following information in FIN-48:

- The meaning of the term *ultimate settlement* in paragraph 8 of the Statement (ASC 740-10-30-7);
- The meaning of the terms *ultimately settled* and *negotiation* in paragraph 10(b) (ASC 740-10-40-3);
- The concept stated in paragraph 12 (ASC 740-10-35-2) that "a tax position need not be legally extinguished and its resolution need not be certain to subsequently recognize or measure the position."

This FSP amends the guidance in FIN-48 by clarifying that a taxing authority's examination effectively could result in the settlement of a tax position. Judgment is required in determining whether a tax position is effectively settled, because examinations occur in different ways. That determination should be made separately for each individual tax position, but an entity may conclude that all its tax positions in a specific tax year have effectively been settled.

FASB STAFF POSITION

In applying the guidance in paragraph 10(b) of FIN-48 (ASC 740-10-40-3), the benefit of a tax position should be recognized when it is considered to be effectively settled. All of the following conditions should be valuated to determine whether an effective settlement has occurred:

- The taxing authority's examination procedures have been completed, including all appeals and administrative reviews related to the tax position that the taxing authority is required or expected to perform;
- The entity does *not* intend to appeal or litigate any aspect of the tax position included in the completed examination;

- Assuming that the taxing authority has full knowledge of all the relevant information, the entity believes that the possibility that the taxing authority would reexamine any aspect of the tax position is remote based on the taxing authority's commonly understood policy on reopening closed examinations and the tax position's specific circumstances.

Further, to be considered effectively settled through examination, the taxing authority need not have specifically reviewed or examined the tax position in the tax years under examination. Nevertheless, a tax position's effective settlement as a result of an examination does not mean that it is an effective settlement of a similar or identical tax position that has *not* been examined.

If at a later date, an entity becomes aware that a tax position that it had considered effectively settled may be examined or reexamined, the entity should reevaluate the tax position in accordance with the guidance in ASC 740 (FIN-48), because the tax position should no longer be considered to be effectively settled.

Based on information obtained during the examination process, an entity may change its judgment about the technical merits of a tax position and wish to apply that view to similar tax positions taken in other periods. However, an entity should not change its judgment about the technical merits of a tax position in other periods based exclusively on the conditions for effective settlement stated above.

A number of changes are made to the terms *ultimate settlement* or *ultimately settled,* in ASC 740 (FIN-48) to conform to the guidance in the FSP. The term *effectively settled* replaces the term *ultimately settled* when it is used in the Interpretation to describe recognition. Likewise, the terms *settlement* or *settled* replace the terms *ultimate settlement* or *ultimately settled* when they are used in the Interpretation to describe measurement.

EFFECTIVE DATE AND TRANSITION

The guidance in this FSP should be applied when the guidance in ASC 740 (FIN-48) is initially adopted. If an entity's application of the guidance in FIN-48 is consistent with the provisions of this FSP, the entity would continue to apply the provisions in this FSP from the date of its initial application of FIN-48. Entities whose application of the guidance in FIN-48 has not been consistent with the provisions of this FSP are required to *retrospectively* apply the FSP's provisions to the date on which the guidance in FIN-48 was initially adopted.

Alternative View

Edward Trott, a member of the FASB, believes that constituents have asked for a clarification of the term *ultimately settled* in ASC 740-10-40-3 (paragraph 10(b) of FIN-48) because they believe that unless the tax laws or regulations have changed or there is a change because of litigation, a taxing authority's examination of tax returns or other actions do not provide new information that should be considered in deciding whether the criteria for recognition have been met or continue to be met as discussed in paragraphs 10(a), 11, and 12 (ASC 740-10-40-2) of the Interpretation. Mr. Trott believes that a taxing authority's examination or other actions do provide new information that should be considered. In addition, he believes that more possible tax law sources exist than those listed parenthetically in paragraph 7(b) of FIN-48 (ASC 740-10-25-7) for illustrative purposes.

Mr. Trott believes that constituents can make their decision based on the following information and should be able to determine which positions have been examined by a taxing authority:

- If a taxing authority examines a tax position and proposes *no* adjustment, there is significant evidence that the taxing authority accepts the position based on its technical merits.
- If a taxing authority proposes an adjustment, there is significant evidence that the taxing authority does *not* accept the tax position.
- If a taxing authority decides not to propose an adjustment for one tax position in exchange for the taxpayer's agreement to a change in another tax position, there is little evidence on which to analyze the first position.
- *No* new evidence is obtained if a tax position is *not* examined.

Mr. Trott disagrees with the guidance related to the term *effectively settled*, because he believes that it is inappropriate to treat unexamined positions as effectively settled based on the "closing of a tax year" if a taxing authority can reopen and examine additional positions.

Under the FSP's guidance, an entity is required to estimate the probability for each uncertain tax position that the taxing authority will examine or reexamine the position in the future. If an entity determines that the probability is remote, the position is considered to be settled resulting in the recognition of previously unrecognized benefit. Donald Young, another member of the FASB, believes that this accounting treatment under the FSP's definition of *settlement* may directly cause tax positions to be reopened, because under the guidance in paragraph 21(d) of FIN-48 (ASC 740-10-50-15), an entity is required to disclose an estimate of the amount or range of unrecognized tax benefits that it is reasonably possible will be recognized in the next 12 months. Consequently, if an entity's tax positions are examined or reexamined as a result of that disclosure, the entity's judgment that this occurrence is remote would be invalidated.

Mr. Young believes that the following approach should be developed:

- Define tax settlements as an accounting policy decision that should be disclosed
- Provide alternative disclosure for uncertain tax positions if disclosure is likely to undermine a preparer's tax positions.

Mr. Young believes that this FSP is not consistent with his view that accounting standards should be neutral in their potential to cause conflict between preparers and taxing authorities.

EITF Issue 87-8 (Tax Reform Act of 1986: Issues Related to the Alternative Minimum Tax) (ASC 740-10-25-43; 35-48 through 35-52)

OVERVIEW

Under the Tax Reform Act of 1986 (the Act), an entity computes its federal income tax liability based on the regular tax system or on the alternative minimum tax (AMT) system, whichever tax amount is greater. An entity may earn an AMT credit for tax paid under the AMT system that exceeds the amount that would have been paid under the regular tax system. An AMT credit can be carried forward indefinitely to reduce the regular tax in future years, but not below the AMT for that year.

ACCOUNTING ISSUES

1. Should the AMT system be considered a separate but parallel tax system that can generate a credit for use in future years, or should the AMT amount paid in excess of the regular tax that results in an AMT credit be considered a prepayment of the regular tax in a future year?
10. Should leveraged lease calculations consider the effect of the AMT on cash flows and, if so, how? (Discussed in Chapter 26, "Leases.")

(The consensus positions on Issues 2 through 9 and 11 were nullified by FAS-109.)

EITF CONSENSUS

The EITF reached a consensus that the AMT system should be considered a separate but parallel tax system that may result in a tax carryforward. Because the AMT credit can only be used to reduce regular tax in excess of AMT in a future year, it should not be considered a prepayment of the regular tax in a future year.

SUBSEQUENT DEVELOPMENT

Paragraph 19 of FAS-109 (ASC 740-10-30-10) states that, for federal tax purposes, the applicable tax rate is the regular tax rate. The applicable tax rate in other jurisdictions is determined based on the tax law after considering any interaction between the two systems. A deferred tax asset is recognized for AMT carryforwards in accordance with the Statement's requirements for the computation of deferred tax assets and the provision of a valuation allowance.

DISCUSSION

The EITF's consensus to treat the AMT as a separate tax system was based on the fact that the AMT system included many items considered to be "permanent" tax differences under the provisions of APB-11, which was the authoritative pronouncement on accounting for income taxes at the time this Issue was discussed. Task Force members argued that because the AMT credit could be carried forward only to offset the regular tax in excess of the AMT in future years, its realizability was not assured and amounts that would otherwise be excluded from taxation would be taxed under the AMT system.

Under FAS-109, the AMT credit is treated as a deferred tax asset that may require a valuation allowance. To simplify the calculation of deferred taxes, FAS-109 requires the recognition of deferred taxes for regular tax temporary differences at the enacted regular tax rate. Thus, an entity that can offset taxable differences with tax-deductible differences can realize the tax benefit at the regular tax rate. However, if an entity expects to be taxed indefinitely under the AMT system, has no reversals available, and must use regular tax-deductible differences against future taxable income, it may need to establish a valuation allowance to reduce its deferred tax asset to an amount that is realizable under the AMT system. In addition, under the provisions of FAS-109, an entity's deferred tax liability may build up beyond an amount that can be reversed, because deferred taxes continue to be provided on deferred tax liabilities at the regular rate, which exceeds the AMT rate. Nevertheless, an entity that continues paying taxes based on the AMT system will eventually have a deferred tax asset from AMT credit carryforwards sufficient to reduce the deferred tax liability to the AMT rate applied to AMT differences. Because of these anomalous results, some now believe that the AMT credit is a prepayment of regular taxes.

EITF Issue 91-8 (Application of FASB Statement No. 96 to a State Tax Based on the Greater of a Franchise Tax or an Income Tax) (ASC 740-10-55-26, 55-140 through 55-144; 15-4; 05-5)

OVERVIEW

The state of Texas revised its corporate franchise tax in August 1991 to include a tax on income apportioned to Texas. The tax is based on federal taxable income and became effective January 1, 1992. The corporate tax is computed as follows:

- 0.25% of net taxable capital at the beginning of the year, *or*
- 4.5% of net earned surplus (a term used in the Texas tax code to refer to federal taxable income apportioned to Texas), whichever is greater.

ACCOUNTING ISSUE

What portion of the tax is based on income, and how should deferred taxes be calculated under FAS-96?

EITF CONSENSUS

- The amount of computed Texas tax that exceeds the tax based on capital in a given year is considered an income tax. Under FAS-109, recognize a deferred tax liability for temporary differences that will reverse in future years in which annual taxable income is expected to be more than 5.5% (.25% of net taxable capital divided by 4.5% of taxable income) of expected net taxable capital. Companies applying the consensus should refer to paragraph 236 of FAS-109 (ASC 740-10-55-138) for guidance on whether it is necessary to prepare a detailed analysis of the net reversals of temporary differences in each future year.

   > **OBSERVATION:** The consensus, which was reached before the issuance of FAS-109, required companies that had adopted FAS-96 to schedule temporary differences and to recognize a deferred tax liability related to the excess of tax payable based on income on net reversals of temporary differences in each future year over the tax based on capital at the end of each future year for which deferred taxes were calculated. The scheduling requirement in FAS-96 was not carried forward to FAS-109, which was issued in February 1992 and which superseded that Statement.

- Adjust the balance of a deferred tax liability or asset in the period of enactment for the effect of a change in tax law, and include the effect in income from continuing operations in that period. In this case, an adjustment was required in the first reporting period that included August 1991.
- Accrue the portion of the current tax liability that is based on income and charge to income in the period in which income is earned. Recognize the portion of the deferred tax liability that is related to temporary differences as of the balance sheet date for temporary differences existing as of that balance sheet date. The deferred tax liability or asset should be adjusted for the effect of changes in tax laws in the period in which the change is enacted with the effect included in income from continuing operations.

The Task Force's discussion implied that the recommended accounting would apply to other states with the same state tax structures.

DISCUSSION

Because it was unclear as to which portion of the tax under the Texas statute was based on income, the Task Force considered and supported the following approach: The portion related to income is equal to 4.5% of income that exceeds 5.5% (.05555) of capital (.0025/.045 = .05555). Deferred income taxes are calculated only on the excess.

The Task Force supported this approach, because they believed that it was similar to the approach used in AICPA Accounting Interpretation 24 of APB-11, which was issued in 1972 to address an Ohio corporate tax law that was based on capital and income, and that was similar to the Texas law. The Interpretation considered the portion of the tax related to income to be an additional tax, which should be accrued in the year the income was earned. Under this approach, deferred taxes should be recognized only on the amount that the tax on income exceeds the tax on capital.

The following illustration demonstrates how to apply the consensus under which only a portion of the state tax is considered an income tax and deferred taxes are recognized only for temporary differences that will reverse in future years in which net taxable income will exceed net taxable capital. To determine whether a deferred tax liability should be established, it is necessary to estimate net taxable capital and net taxable income in future years based on a consideration of enacted tax rates and future transactions.

20.16 *Income Taxes*

Illustration of the Calculation of Texas State Tax and Deferred Tax Liability

- Company A is a Texas corporation whose business is conducted only in Texas.
- The company's net taxable income in 20X5 is $75,000, and net taxable income is expected to be $100,000 and $50,000 in 20X6 and 20X7, respectively.
- Company A has taxable temporary differences of $100,000 in 20X5 that are expected to reverse as follows: $75,000 in 20X6 and $25,000 in 20X7.
- Net taxable capital is $1,075,000 in 20X5 and is estimated to be $1,171,625 in 20X6 and $1,217,125 in 20X7.
- The following computation of the deferred tax liability for state franchise taxes at the end of 20X5 ignores the effects of federal income taxes.

State Franchise Tax—20X5

Tax based on net taxable capital (.0025 × $1,075,000) = $2,687
Tax based on net taxable income (.045 × $75,000) = $3,375

In 20X5, Company A's state franchise tax of $3,375 is based on net taxable income. Based on the consensus, that tax consists of the following components:

Tax related to net taxable capital (.0025 × $1,075,000) $2,687
Tax related to net taxable income
[$75,000 − (.05555 × $1,075,000) = .045 × $15,283]   688*

Total tax $3,375

*If the franchise tax payable is based on net taxable income, a simpler method of determining the amount related to income is to calculate the difference between the tax based on net taxable capital and the tax based on net taxable income.

Income tax expense in 20×5 is $688, the amount related to net taxable income.

Estimated State Franchise Tax—20×6

Tax based on net taxable capital (.0025 × $1,171,625) = $2,929
Tax based on net taxable income (.045 × $100,000) = $4,500

The deferred tax liability on the $75,000 taxable temporary difference expected to reverse in 20X6 would be (.045 × $75,000) $3,375, but based on the consensus, the amount is limited to $1,571, the excess of net taxable income over net taxable capital ($4,500 X $2,929).

Estimated State Franchise Tax—20X7

Tax based on net taxable capital (.0025 × $1,217,125)   = $3,043
Tax based on net taxable income (.045 × $50,000)   = $2,250

No deferred tax liability is recognized for the $50,000 of temporary tax differences expected to reverse in 20X7, because the tax based on net taxable capital exceeds the tax based on net taxable income.

EITF Issue 93-13 (Effect of a Retroactive Change in Enacted Tax Rates That Is Included in Income from Continuing Operations) (ASC 740-10-25-48)

OVERVIEW

The Omnibus Budget Reconciliation Act of 1993 (OBRA) was enacted on August 10, 1993. OBRA increased the top corporate tax rate from 34% to 35% retroactively to January 1, 1993. Paragraph 27 of FAS-109 (ASC 740-10-35-4; 45-15) requires adjusting deferred tax liabilities and assets for the effect of a change in tax rates and including the adjustment in income from continuing operations in the period that includes the date the new tax law was enacted.

ACCOUNTING ISSUES

1. If an enacted change in tax rates has a retroactive effective date, how should the tax effect on current and deferred tax assets and liabilities be measured on the date of enactment?

2. How should the reported tax effect among items not included in income from continuing operations, such as discontinued operations, extraordinary items, cumulative effects of changes in accounting principles, and items charged or credited directly to shareholders' equity, be measured and recognized?

EITF CONSENSUS

- The tax effect of a retroactive change in enacted tax rates on current and deferred tax assets and liabilities should be measured on the date of enactment (August 10, 1993), based on temporary differences and currently taxable income existing at the date of enactment. The cumulative tax effect should be included in income from continuing operations.

- An entity should measure the reported tax effect of items not included in income from continuing operations, such as discontinued operations, extraordinary items, cumulative effects of changes in accounting principles, and items charged or credited directly to shareholders' equity, that occurred during the current fiscal year but before the date of enactment based on the enacted rate at the time the transaction was recognized for financial reporting purposes. The tax effect of a retroactive change in enacted tax rates on current or deferred tax assets and liabilities related to such items should be included in income from continuing operations in the period in which the change was enacted.

Illustration Using EITF Issue 93-13 Consensus

Income from January 1, 19X3, through August 9, 19X3

Pretax income from continuing operations	$5,000,000
Pretax income from extraordinary gain on June 30, 19X3	500,000
Total pretax income on August 9, 19X3	$5,500,000

Temporary differences

Balance on January 1, 19X3	$8,000,000
Extraordinary gain on June 30, 19X3	500,000
Balance on August 10, 19X3	$8,500,000

Total 19X3 tax expense

Current ($5,000,000 × .35)	$1,750,000
Deferred [($8,500,000 × .35) − ($8,000,000 × .34)]	255,000
Total 19X3 tax expense	$2,005,000

Allocation of 19X3 tax expense

Continuing operations

Current	$1,750,000
Rate change ($8,500,000 × .01)	85,000

Extraordinary item

Tax effect on extraordinary gain ($500,000 × .34)	170,000
Total 19X3 tax expense	$2,005,000

Effect of change in rates enacted August 10, 19X3

Increase in tax on income from continuing operations ($5,000,000 × .01)	$ 50,000
Increase in tax on balance of temporary differences on August 10, 19X3 ($8,500,000 × .01)	85,000
Adjustment included in continuing operations in period of enactment	$ 135,000
Tax adjustment allocated to extraordinary gain in period of enactment*	0

*The tax adjustment is included in the rate change on $8,500,000, which is allocated to continuing operations.

DISCUSSION

Paragraph 27 of FAS-109 (ASC 740-10-45-15) requires including the deferred tax effects of changes in tax laws or rates in income from continuing operations in the period that includes the enactment date. The EITF decided to measure the effect of a retroactive change in enacted tax rates on current and deferred tax assets and liabilities based on the balance of temporary differences at the date of enactment rather than on the balance at the beginning of the year, because they believed that such an approach conforms with the requirements of paragraph 27 (ASC 740-10-45-15). Proponents of this view also believed that remeasurement of items not included in income from continuing operations that originated before the enactment date using the newly enacted tax rates would be tantamount to backward tracing of tax rates and would violate the intent of FAS-109.

EITF Issue 93-17 (Recognition of Deferred Tax Assets for a Parent Company's Excess Tax Basis in the Stock of a Subsidiary That Is Accounted for as a Discontinued Operation) (ASC 740-30-25-10)

OVERVIEW

A company decides to sell a subsidiary, which can be accounted for and reported as a discontinued operation under the requirements of APB-30. It is expected that the subsidiary's operations will break even between the date the company decides to dispose of the subsidiary (the measurement date) and the disposal date, and the company expects no pretax gain or loss on the disposal. Because the company's tax basis in the subsidiary's stock exceeds its basis in the subsidiary for financial reporting, the decision to sell the subsidiary makes it more likely than not that the deductible temporary difference will reverse in the near future and the company will realize the deferred tax asset.

ACCOUNTING ISSUE

Should the company recognize a deferred tax asset at the measurement date in accordance with paragraph 34 of FAS-109 (ASC 740-30-25-9), or should the company defer recognition of the tax benefit until disposal in accordance with paragraph 15 of APB-30 (Paragraph 15 has been superseded by the guidance in FAS-144)?

EITF CONSENSUS

The EITF reached a consensus that a tax benefit should be recognized for the excess of the entity's outside tax basis over its financial reporting basis in the subsidiary in accordance with the guidance in paragraph 34 of FAS-109 (ASC 740-30-25-9), when it becomes apparent that the temporary difference will reverse in the foreseeable future. The Task Force noted that this criterion should also be applied to situations in which the financial reporting basis exceeds the company's outside tax basis in its investment in the subsidiary by recognizing a deferred tax liability.

DISCUSSION

Paragraph 34 of FAS-109 (ASC 740-30-25-9) states that "[a] deferred tax asset shall be recognized for an excess of the tax basis over the amount for financial reporting of an investment in a subsidiary or corporate joint venture that is essentially permanent in duration only if it is apparent that the temporary difference will reverse in the foreseeable future." In contrast, paragraph 15 of APB-30, which has been superseded by the guidance in FAS-144, stated that: "If a loss is expected from the proposed sale or abandonment of a segment, the estimated loss should be provided for at the measurement date. If a gain is expected, it should be recognized when realized, which ordinarily is the disposal date." (Footnote omitted.)

This Issue was raised because it was unclear whether, under the circumstances discussed in the Overview, an entity should follow the guidance in FAS-109 and recognize the tax benefit when deciding to dispose of a segment of a business or whether it should wait until a gain is realized on disposal, as required in APB-30. Proponents of recognition of a tax benefit on the measurement date believed that the approach to recognition of a tax *benefit* should differ from that in APB-30 because the focus of the authoritative literature on income taxes has changed since APB-30 was issued. APB-11, which had an income statement focus, provided authoritative guidance when APB-30 was issued. Under that Opinion's deferred method of interperiod tax allocation, basis differences for tax and financial reporting purposes would not have been identified in determining income tax expense or benefit until the date of disposal. However, under FAS-109's asset/liability method, which focuses on the balance sheet, such basis differences are considered.

EITF Issue 94-10 (Accounting by a Company for the Income Tax Effects of Transactions among or with Its Shareholders under FASB Statement No. 109) (ASC 740-10-45-21; 740-20-45-11)

OVERVIEW

Under U.S. tax laws, the following transactions among shareholders or between a company and its shareholders may have tax consequences.

Transactions that result in a change in expectations about the future realization of deferred tax assets If the ownership of more than 50% of a company's stock changes within a certain time period, the company may be prohibited from using an existing net operating loss (NOL) carryforward or the amount available to offset future income may be limited. Consequently, the NOL deferred tax asset would have to be written off or a valuation allowance, which was not previously required, would have to be recognized to reduce the deferred tax asset. The following are examples of such transactions:

- An investor purchases more than 50% of the shares in the open market and consolidates the company but does not use push-down accounting for financial reporting purposes.
- The company converts debt into equity in a troubled debt restructuring.

Transactions that result in changes in tax bases of an entity's assets or liabilities for tax purposes

- One hundred percent of a company's shares are purchased by a privately held company. The company accounts for the transaction as a purchase business combination and consolidates the subsidiary, but because it is a private company it need not push down the fair value of the assets to the subsidiary. The company, however, adjusts the bases of the subsidiary's assets and liabilities for tax purposes.
- A company merges with another company and accounts for the business combination as a pooling of interests. The entity treats the transaction as a purchase of assets for tax purposes.

This Issue does not apply to transactions among or with a subsidiary's minority shareholders or to transactions with shareholders requiring a change in a company's tax status (for example, a change from a nontaxable S corporation to a taxable C corporation).

ACCOUNTING ISSUES

1. Should an entity charge changes in the *valuation allowance* as a result of transactions among or with shareholders to the income statement or directly to equity?
2. Should write-offs of deferred tax assets that result from transactions among or with shareholders be charged to the income statement or directly to equity?
3. Should the tax effects of changes in the *tax bases of assets (and liabilities)* that result from transactions among or with shareholders be charged (or credited) to the income statement or directly to equity?
4. Should a subsequent reduction in the valuation allowance that was initially established when deferred tax assets were created from changes in the tax bases of assets and liabilities in transactions among or with shareholders be credited to income or directly to equity?

EITF CONSENSUS

1. Changes in the *valuation allowance* caused by changes in expectations about the realization of deferred tax assets that result from transactions among or with shareholders should be included in the *income statement*.
2. Write-offs of preexisting deferred tax assets that will not be realized that result from a transaction with or among an entity's shareholders should be included in the *income statement*.
    The Task Force observed that the net effect is the same whether a deferred tax asset is eliminated or the valuation allowance is increased to equal 100% of the related deferred tax asset.
3. The tax effects of all changes in the *tax bases of assets and liabilities* that result from transactions among or with shareholders should be included *in equity*. Also included in equity is the effect of a valuation allowance initially required on the recognition of deferred tax assets because of changes in the tax bases of assets and liabilities from transactions with or among shareholders.
4. Changes in the valuation allowance initially required on the recognition of deferred tax assets that result from changes in the tax bases of assets and liabilities because of transactions with or among shareholders should be included in the *income statement* in subsequent periods.

DISCUSSION

The FASB staff asked the Task Force to develop a framework that could be used to categorize the tax effects of transactions among shareholders and between a company and its shareholders in a consistent manner.

1. Proponents of recognizing changes in the valuation allowance as a result of an entity's transactions with shareholders or among shareholders in the income statement argued that the model for intraperiod tax allocation in FAS-109 (Accounting for Income Taxes) generally requires allocating the tax expense or benefit to income from continuing operations, unless the incremental portion of the tax expense or benefit is not directly related to continuing operations. Because there is no pretax charge or credit to equity for transactions among shareholders, the tax expense or benefit would not be allocated to equity under FAS-109. Further, they argued that changes in the valuation allowance as a result of an entity's transactions with shareholders are only indirectly related to the equity transaction, such as an initial public stock offering. The effects of the change should, therefore, also be included in the income statement.

2. Proponents of this view believed that the treatment of a write-off of a deferred tax asset should be the same as that for an increase in the valuation allowance in Issue 1, because the end result is the same. In both cases, the company expects that a deferred tax asset will not be realized because of a transaction with or among shareholders.

3. The rationale for charging equity with the tax effects of changes to the tax bases of assets and liabilities as a result of transactions with or among shareholders is that such transactions are similar to a taxable business combination accounted for as a pooling of interests, which is discussed in paragraph 272 of FAS-109. (ASC 740-10-25-3, 25-18) The Statement provides that the deferred tax consequences of temporary differences resulting from an increase in the tax basis of assets in the transaction be recognized in equity. Proponents of this view believe that a taxable pooling does not differ from other transactions among shareholders that result in a change in the tax bases of assets and liabilities.

4. Proponents of this view also refer to paragraph 272 of FAS-109 (ASC 740-10-25-3, 25-18), which requires that tax benefits resulting from increases in the tax bases of assets after the date of a taxable business combination should be recognized in the income statement.

EITF Issue 95-9 (Accounting for Tax Effects of Dividends in France in Accordance with FASB Statement No. 109) (ASC 740-10-55-73, 55-74; 15-4)

OVERVIEW

To eliminate double taxation on dividends at the shareholder level, French shareholders who receive dividends from French corporations automatically receive a tax credit for taxes paid by the corporation under that country's integrated tax system. To achieve such integration, when a French corporation distributes dividends to its shareholders, it is required to pay a tax known as *precompte mobilier* (precompte), which is equal to the tax credit available to shareholders (50% of the dividend received) but is limited to the difference between the tax calculated by applying the regular corporate tax rate (currently, 33%) to the dividend declared and taxes already paid by the corporation on the income distributed to shareholders. However, taxes previously paid on income retained for five years or longer are not considered in this calculation. An example of a precompte calculation is as follows:

Income Distributed within Five Years		Income Distributed after Five Years	
Corporate Taxation When Income Is Earned			
Taxable income	€600,000	Taxable income	€600,000
Corporate tax	(200,000)	Corporate tax	(200,000)
Available for dividends	€400,000	Available for dividends	€400,000
Corporate Taxation When Income Is Distributed			
Earnings to be distributed	€400,000	Earnings to be distributed	€400,000
Precompte*	0	Precompte*	(133,000)
Amount distributed	€400,000	Amount distributed	€267,000
Shareholder Taxation			
Cash dividend	€400,000	Cash dividend	€267,000
Imputed amount for corporate tax paid (50% of dividend)	200,000	Imputed amount for corporate tax paid (50% of dividend)	133,000
Taxable income	€600,000	Taxable income	€400,000
Shareholder tax rate**	60%	Shareholder tax rate**	60%

Tax liability before credit	360,000	Tax liability before credit	240,000
Tax credit (50% of dividend)	(200,000)	Tax credit (50% of dividend)	(133,000)
Tax payable by shareholder	160,000	Tax payable by shareholder	107,000
Net dividend to shareholder (€400,000 − €160,000)	€240,000	Net dividend to shareholder (€267,000 − €107,000)	€160,000

* Precompte paid by the corporation on distribution equals the regular corporate tax rate applicable to the amount distributed (€€400,000 × .33) less corporate taxes previously paid on that amount. The credit for previously paid corporate taxes is unavailable if earnings are not distributed within five years. The precompte is equal to zero in this example, because earnings are distributed within five years and the corporate rate on distributions is the same as the regular corporate tax previously paid on earnings.

** A 60% shareholder tax rate is assumed.

ACCOUNTING ISSUE

Should a distributing corporation record a tax assessed on dividends distributed to shareholders, such as the French precompte tax, as (*a*) an income tax recorded as tax expense or (*b*) a withholding tax for shareholders receiving dividends that would be recorded in equity and included in dividends paid?

EITF CONSENSUS

The EITF reached a consensus that a tax such as precompte is a withholding tax that should be included with the dividend and recorded in equity in the corporation's *separate* financial statements if both of the following conditions are met:

- The corporation is required to pay the tax only if a dividend is distributed to shareholders and the corporation's future income taxes are not reduced by that tax.
- Recipients of dividends receive (*a*) a credit for at least the amount of corporate taxes paid on amounts distributed that can be used to reduce taxes due, regardless of the recipient's tax status, or (*b*) a refund (if the shareholder's marginal tax rate is less than 33% or a foreign shareholder with ownership in excess of 5%-15% is from a country having a tax treaty with France).

DISCUSSION

The Task Force based its consensus on the arguments that the precompte is considered a withholding tax under the French tax system and that a corporation incurs this tax only when it distributes earnings. Although the precompte is equal to the tax credit available to shareholders to avoid double taxation, which is 50% of the dividend received, it cannot exceed the difference between the regular tax on the dividend paid and the amount previously paid by the corporation on that income. Thus, if a corporation is taxed at less than the 33% rate, the tax credit received by shareholders would be overstated. Through the precompte, the excess is withheld at the source, rather than by reducing the tax payer's credit. That approach treats all dividends in the same manner and is more convenient administratively. Another argument to support the view that the precompte is a withholding tax is that shareholders can receive a refund on overpayments of the tax.

It was noted during the Task Force's discussions that this treatment would only be appropriate in the freestanding financial statements of a French company. In consolidation, the withholding tax could not be charged to equity, but would be recognized as an expense and charged to the subsidiary's retained earnings.

EITF Issue 95-10 (Accounting for Tax Credits Related to Dividend Payments in Accordance with FASB Statement No. 109) (ASC 740-10-25-39, 25-40; 30-14)

OVERVIEW

In certain foreign jurisdictions, such as Germany, corporate income tax rates depend on whether the income is distributed to shareholders. In Germany, undistributed profits are taxed at a 45% rate, but distributed income is taxed at a 30% rate. If a corporation pays dividends from undistributed income that was taxed at the undistributed rate, it receives a tax credit or tax refund for the difference between (a) the tax calculated at the *undistributed rate* effective in the year the income was earned for tax purposes and (b) the tax calculated at the *distributed rate* effective in the year in which a dividend was paid. Germany also has an integrated tax system, under which shareholders are taxed on the pretax dividend and receive a credit for taxes previously paid by the corporation on that income. For example:

Corporate Tax before Distribution	
Taxable income	€500,000
Corporate tax (45%)	(225,000)
Retained earnings	275,000

Corporate Tax at Distribution	
Retained earnings	€275,000
Tax credit received on distribution	
[500,000 × (45% − 30%)]	75,000
Tax basis of dividend declared	350,000
Withholding tax (25%)	(87,500)
Cash distributed to shareholder	€262,500

Shareholder Taxation

Cash received	€262,500
Tax withheld	87,500
	350,000
Add: Net corporate tax paid (30%)	150,000
Taxable income	500,000
Tax rate (maximum individual rate)	53%
Tax liability before credits	265,000
Tax credit for corporate tax	(150,000)
Credit for withholding tax	(87,500)
Net tax due	€27,500
Net cash to shareholder (262,500DM − 27,500DM)	€235,000

Because German companies are permitted to consider dividends declared from the current year's earnings and paid in a subsequent year in the tax provision, a blended tax rate between 45% and 30% is used. Some German companies also use a blended rate when calculating deferred tax assets and liabilities. Others use the undistributed rate and recognize the effect of the tax credit, which has no time limit, in the period in which dividends are paid. The effective tax rate for that year would be less than 30% to the extent that distributions are greater than earnings in that year.

> **OBSERVATION:** This Issue applies only to the accounting in the German entity's separate financial statements. See the discussion below in Issue 95-20 for a discussion of the accounting in the consolidated financial statements.

ACCOUNTING ISSUE

Should a corporate entity recognize in its separate financial statements a deferred tax asset for the tax benefit of future tax credits that will be realized when it distributes income that was previously taxed at the undistributed rate (thus measuring the tax effect of temporary differences at the distributed rate), or should the entity recognize the tax credit in the period in which it is realized on the tax return (thus measuring the tax effects of temporary differences at the undistributed tax rate)?

EITF CONSENSUS

The EITF reached the following consensus on the accounting in the *separate* financial statements of a foreign entity for tax benefits of future tax credits:

- A corporate entity paying dividends subject to a tax credit should *not* recognize a deferred tax asset for tax benefits related to future tax credits that it will realize when it distributes income that was previously taxed.
- The entity should reduce income tax expense in the period that these tax credits are included in the entity's tax return.

Consequently, the tax effects of temporary differences should be measured using the *undistributed* tax rate.

DISCUSSION

The approach supported by the Task Force is similar to the one discussed in paragraphs 231 and 232 of FAS-109 (Accounting for Income Taxes) (ASC 740-10-25-37) for a special deduction, under which tax expense is recognized in the current period based on an estimate of the liability reported for tax purposes. The tax provision is reduced in the period in which the tax credit is realized for tax purposes. Proponents of this view argued that this approach avoids an overstatement of net assets by anticipating a refund that will occur only if earnings are distributed. The declaration and payment of dividends is the event that would trigger the recognition of a deferred tax asset in this Issue. Proponents also argued that because the company must distribute cash to realize the tax credits, a potential credit does not represent an asset that would be available to the entity's general creditors and that would be reported for an extended time period if the entity does not pay dividends. Another argument to support this view was that under FAS-109, deferred tax assets are recognized only for future deductible temporary differences and for tax credit and loss carryforwards; the tax credit in this Issue is not a basis difference or a carryforward.

> **OBSERVATION:** Under the Task Force's consensus, entities with net operating loss carryforwards would recognize the deferred asset at the 45% undistributed rate.

EITF Issue 95-20 (Measurement in the Consolidated Financial Statements of a Parent of the Tax Effects Related to the Operations of a Foreign Subsidiary That Receives Tax Credits Related to Dividend Payments) (ASC 740-10-25-41)

OVERVIEW

See the Overview to Issue 95-10. The EITF's consensus in Issue 95-10, which only applies to the accounting in the foreign entity's separate financial statements, states that a deferred tax asset should not be recognized for the tax benefits of future tax credits that will be realized when earnings taxed at the undistributed tax rate are subsequently distributed to shareholders. Thus, the tax effects of temporary differences would be measured at the undistributed tax rate in a foreign subsidiary's separate financial statements. This Issue applies to the accounting in the parent's consolidated financial statements.

ACCOUNTING ISSUE

Should the tax effects related to the operations of a foreign subsidiary eligible to receive a tax credit for dividends paid be measured based on the undistributed or distributed tax rate of the applicable foreign jurisdiction in the consolidated financial statements of a parent company that has not taken advantage of the exception in APB-23 for foreign unremitted earnings?

EITF CONSENSUS

- The *distributed* rate should be used to measure a future tax credit that will be received when dividends are paid. The deferred tax effects related to a foreign subsidiary's operations should be measured at the distributed rate in a parent company's consolidated financial statements if the entity does not apply the exception for foreign unremitted earnings in APB-23.
- The undistributed rate should be used in a parent company's consolidated financial statements to the extent that deferred taxes have not been provided for unremitted earnings as a result of the application of the exception in APB-23.

DISCUSSION

Proponents of using the distributed rate in the parent's consolidated financial statements noted that, in this Issue, the transfer of cash is within the entity, while dividends discussed in Issue 95-10 would be paid to outside shareholders. An argument supporting the distributed rate was that a corporation's income will eventually be distributed to its shareholders for whose benefit it is earned. In addition, the tax credit is available to German corporations for an unlimited time once income has been taxed at the undistributed rate. When a dividend is distributed to the parent by a German subsidiary, the tax credit will be realized at the distributed rate. Some proponents of this view also analogized the distributed tax rate to the regular tax system and the undistributed tax rate to the alternative tax system as used in the discussion of the recognition of a deferred tax asset for alternative minimum tax credit carryforwards in paragraph 9 of FAS-109 (ASC 740-10-25-3).

EITF Issue 98-11 (Accounting for Acquired Temporary Differences in Certain Purchase Transactions That Are Not Accounted for as Business Combinations) (ASC 740-10-25-50, 25-51; 45-22 through 25-24; 52-55; S25-1; S99-3; 55-171 through 55-201, 55-203, 55-204, 55-76)

OVERVIEW

Paragraph 16 of FAS-109 (ASC 740-10-25-29) provides that a deferred tax liability or deferred tax asset be recognized for all temporary differences between the reported amount of an asset or liability and its tax basis. Paragraph 30 of the Statement (ASC 805-740-25-3) provides specific guidance for the accounting of deferred taxes in business combinations. FAS-109 provides that when the assigned values of assets and liabilities acquired in a purchase business combination differ from their tax bases, the acquiring entity should recognize a deferred tax liability or a deferred tax asset, or both, for those differences. Deferred tax assets and deferred tax liabilities recognized as a result of a purchase business combination are included in the calculation of the purchase price of the acquisition (paragraph 260 of FAS-109) (ASC 805-740-55-3), rather than in income of the period in which the combination occurred.

This Issue has been raised because FAS-109 does not provide guidance on how to account for a deferred tax asset or deferred tax liability that results from the purchase of a single asset that is *not* a business combination. The Issue applies to the following four types of transactions:

1. A company imports an asset into a foreign jurisdiction. The asset costs $100 but its tax basis is reduced to $80 as a result of a penalty imposed by the jurisdiction on imported goods.

2. A foreign jurisdiction is encouraging companies in certain industries to purchase certain kinds of equipment. A company purchases an asset that costs $100, but its tax basis has been increased to $150. The additional tax deduction cannot be recaptured on sale of the asset.

3. A subsidiary of a U.S. company acquires a shell company that has no assets to take advantage of its net operating losses (NOLs). The NOLs are acquired at a discount from their undiscounted face value. For example, NOLs with a $5 million deferred tax benefit are acquired for $2 million.

4. Corporate taxpayers in a foreign country can elect to step up the tax basis of certain fixed assets to fair value if they immediately pay the authorities 3% of the step-up. A company would make this election if it believes it's likely that it will use the additional deductions (at a 35% tax rate) to reduce future taxable income

and the current payment is justified by the timing and amount of future tax savings.

ACCOUNTING ISSUES

1. How should an entity account for the tax effect of the acquisition of assets not in a business combination if the acquisition cost and tax basis differ?
2. How should an entity account for a net-tax benefit as a result of the purchase of future tax benefits from a nongovernmental third party that is not a taxing authority?
3. How should an entity account for all direct transactions with a government acting as a taxing authority?

EITF CONSENSUS

> **OBSERVATION:** In December 2007, the FASB replaced FAS-141 with FAS-141(R), which amends the guidance for business combination in paragraphs 30 and 266 of FAS-109 (ASC 805-740-25-12; 805-740-30-3). In addition, FAS-109 and FIN-48 have been amended to require that changes in valuation allowances and income tax uncertainties made as a result of events and circumstances that occurred after the acquisition date be recorded (a) as an increase or a decrease in income tax expense, or (b) in accordance with the guidance in FIN-48 for uncertainties.

1. The carrying amount of an asset acquired individually, not in a business combination, should be adjusted for the tax effect resulting from the difference between the acquisition cost of the asset and its tax basis. The Task Force agreed that the asset's assigned value and the related deferred tax asset or liability should be recognized using the simultaneous equations method, which is illustrated in Question 15 of the FASB Special Report, *A Guide to Implementation of Statement 109 on Accounting for Income Taxes: Questions and Answers*. The consensus should be applied as follows:
    a. Recognize (1) a *financial asset* at its fair value, (2) an *acquired asset held for disposal* at fair value less cost to sell, and (3) deferred tax assets as required in FAS-109.
    b. Allocate the excess of amounts assigned to acquired assets over the amount paid pro rata to reduce the assigned values of acquired noncurrent assets, except those discussed in (a) above. If noncurrent assets have been reduced to zero, classify a remainder, if any, as a deferred credit, which is not a temporary difference under FAS-109.
    c. Adjust the purchase price in accordance with paragraph 266 of FAS-109 (ASC 805-740-30-3), as amended by

FAS-141(R), for a reduction in the acquiring company's valuation allowance directly related to the asset acquisition. After the acquisition, account for an acquired valuation allowance in accordance paragraphs 30 and 30A of FAS-109 (ASC 805-740-25 through 3, 4; 45-2), as amended by FAS-141(R).
- d. Amortize to income tax expense deferred credits resulting from the application of the consensus in proportion to the tax benefits realized by recognizing those deferred credits, which should not be classified as deferred tax liabilities or offset against deferred tax assets.
- e. Subsequent to the acquisition, account for the effect of the adjustments as follows: (1) recognize in continuing operations as part of income tax expense, if it is more likely than not that some or all of the acquired deferred tax asset will not be realized, and (2) offset against income tax expense the proportionate share of any unamortized balance of the deferred credit.
- f. Account for income tax uncertainties that exist at the acquisition date in accordance with FIN-48, as amended by FAS-141(R).

2. An entity purchasing future tax benefits from a nongovernmental third party should account for the net tax benefit using the same model as discussed above in the first consensus.
3. Recognize in income transactions directly between a taxpayer and a governmental entity acting in its capacity as a taxing authority, in a manner similar to the accounting for changes in tax laws, rates, or other tax elections under FAS-109.

The Task Force noted that no deferred tax asset should be recognized for an increase in basis if the step-up in tax basis is related to previously nondeductible goodwill, except if the amount of newly deductible goodwill is more than the balance of the nondeductible goodwill.

In addition, the Task Force noted that the prohibition in paragraph 9e of FAS-109 (ASC 740-10-25-3) against the recognition of a deferred tax asset for the difference between the basis of assets in the buyer's tax jurisdiction and the reported cost of those assets in the consolidated financial statements also applies to intercompany purchases of tax benefits by one member of a consolidated entity from another member.

SEC OBSERVER COMMENT

The SEC Observer reported that unless the SEC staff clearly understands the specific fact pattern, the staff would object if the consensus in this Issue were used to adjust the basis of acquired assets in situations other than those discussed in the following examples.

Illustrations of the Consensus on Accounting for Temporary Differences in Certain Purchases That Are Not Accounted for as Business Combinations

Example 1—Tax basis exceeds purchase price

A. A company purchases a building for $500,000 in a foreign jurisdiction that permits tax deductions to exceed the cost of the asset. The tax basis of the building is $600,000 and the tax rate is 40%. The additional tax deduction is not recaptured when the asset is sold.

The following simultaneous equations should be used to determine the amounts at which to recognize the building and the deferred tax asset:

FBB = Final Book Basis
CPP = Cash Purchase Price
DTA = Deferred Tax Asset

To determine the amount of the building's FBB:

FBB − (Tax Rate × (FBB − Tax Basis)) = CPP
FBB − (.40 × (FBB − $600,000)) = $500,000
FBB = $433,333

To determine the amount of DTA:

(Tax Basis − FBB) × Tax Rate = DTA
($600,000 − $433,333) × .40 = DTA
DTA = $66,667

The company would make the following entry for the transaction:

Building	$433,333	
Deferred Tax Asset	66,667	
Cash		$500,000

B. The same situation as in A above, but the purchase price is $250,000 and the tax basis is $1,000,000.

Use the formulas above to calculate the FBB and DTA.

FBB = ($250,000)

Because FBB is a negative amount, zero is used for FBB in the second equation.

DTA = $400,000

When recording the transaction, the difference between the deferred tax asset and the amount of cash paid to acquire the building is recognized as a deferred credit as follows:

Building	$0	
Deferred tax asset	$400,000	
Deferred credit		$150,000
Cash		$250,000

20.34 *Income Taxes*

C. In this example the acquisition of a financial asset results in a deferred credit. Company X acquires the stock of Company Y for $900,000. Company Y's principal asset is a marketable equity security with a fair value of $750,000 and a tax basis of $1,250,000. The tax rate is 40%. The acquisition of Company Y's stock is accounted for as an asset acquisition, not a business combination, because Company Y has no operations.

In recording this transaction, the acquired financial asset is recognized at its fair value and the deferred tax asset is calculated based on the guidance in FAS-109. A deferred credit is recognized for the difference between the total of the fair value of the stock plus the amount of the deferred asset and the amount paid for the stock.

Marketable equity security	$750,000	
Deferred tax asset ($500,000 × .40)	200,000	
Deferred credit		$ 50,000
Cash		900,000

D. In this example, Company Z acquires future tax benefits by purchasing the net operating loss carryforwards (NOLs) of Company P, which is a shell company without operations. The shell entity is acquired for $7 million, which is substantially less than the $15 million gross amount of the deferred tax asset for the NOLs. It is more likely than not that the deferred tax asset will be realized. The tax rate is 40%.

In recording the transaction, Company Z recognizes the deferred tax asset at its gross amount and records a deferred credit for the amount by which the deferred tax asset exceeds the amount paid.

Deferred tax asset	$15,000,000	
Deferred credit		$8,000,000
Cash		7,000,000

Example 2—Purchase price exceeds tax basis

A company in a foreign jurisdiction imports a machine, which costs $25,000. Its tax basis is reduced, however, to $20,000, because the jurisdiction imposes a 20% penalty on imported goods. A deferred tax liability has to be recognized for the temporary difference related to the machine. The tax rate is 40%.

The amount of the machine's final book basis (FBB) and the deferred tax liability (DTL) are calculated by the simultaneous equations used in Example 1.

FBB − .40 × (FBB − $20,000) = $25,000

FBB = $28,333

($28,333 − $20,000) .40 = DTL
DTL = $3,333

The company recognizes the following amount:

Machine	$28,333	
Deferred tax liability		$3,333
Cash		25,000

Example 3—A transaction with a governmental taxing authority

Under the tax laws of country X, Company A decides to step up the tax basis of fixed assets with a current tax basis of $4 million to their $8 million fair value. To do so, the company must pay the government $200,000, which is 5% of the $4 million step-up. The company believes that at its 40% tax rate, it is likely that it will be able to use the additional deductions from the stepped up tax basis of certain fixed assets, which would justify the $80,000 payment.

Company A would record the tax effects of the transaction as follows:

Deferred tax asset ($4 million × .4)	$1,600,000	
Deferred income tax benefit		$1,400,000
Cash		200,000

EITF Issue 05-8 (Income Tax Consequences of Issuing Convertible Debt with a Beneficial Conversion Feature) (ASC 740-10-55-51)

OVERVIEW

Under the guidance in ASC 470-20 (APB-14, Accounting for Convertible Debt and Debt Issued with Stock Purchase Warrants), nondetachable conversion features of convertible securities are not accounted for separately. However, under the guidance in EITF Issue 00-27 (Application of Issue 98-5 to Certain Convertible Instruments), a nondetachable conversion feature of a convertible debt security that is "in-the-money" should be accounted separately, because it is considered a beneficial conversion feature that is recognized and measured separately by allocating a portion of the proceeds equal to the intrinsic value of the conversion feature to additional paid-in capital. At the commitment date, as defined in EITF Issue 00-27 (see chapter 12), the intrinsic value of the beneficial conversion feature is calculated as the difference between the conversion price and the fair value of the common stock or other securities into which the security can be converted multiplied by the number of shares into which the security can be converted. A convertible security is recognized at par if no discount or premium is associated with it at issuance and a discount is recognized for the amount allocated to additional paid-in capital. A convertible instrument's debt discount should be accreted from the instrument's issuance date to a stated redemption date or through the earliest conversion date if the instrument does not have a stated redemption date as discussed in EITF Issue 00-27. Under the U.S. Federal Income Tax Code, a convertible debt security's tax basis equals the total proceeds received when the debt is issued.

ACCOUNTING ISSUES

1. Does the issuance of convertible debt with a beneficial conversion feature result in a basis difference when applying the guidance in ASC 740 (FAS-109, Accounting for Income Taxes)?
2. If issuance of convertible debt with a beneficial conversion feature results in a basis difference, is that difference a temporary difference under the guidance in ASC 740 (FAS-109)?
3. If issuance of convertible debt with a beneficial conversion feature results in a temporary difference under the guidance in ASC 740 (FAS-109), should a deferred tax liability for the temporary difference of the convertible debt be recognized as an adjustment to additional paid-in capital or by recognizing a deferred charge by analogy to the accounting model in Example 4 of Issue 98-11 (Accounting for Acquired Temporary Differences in Certain Purchase Transactions That Are Not Accounted for as Business Combinations) (see the Issue in this chapter)?

EITF CONSENSUS

The EITF reached the following consensus positions:

1. Convertible debt issued with a beneficial conversion feature results in a basis difference when the guidance in ASC 740 (FAS-109) is applied. The EITF noted that by recognizing a beneficial conversion feature, two separate instruments, a debt instrument and an equity instrument, are created for financial reporting purposes and are accounted for as a single debt instrument under the Federal Income Tax Code. As a result, the debt instrument's book basis and tax basis differ.
2. The basis difference resulting from the issuance of convertible debt with a beneficial conversion feature should be treated as a temporary difference under the guidance in ASC 740 (FAS-109). This consensus is consistent with the definition of a temporary difference in FAS-109 because the amount recognized as a liability for the difference between the book basis and the tax basis of debt with a beneficial conversion feature becomes taxable when the liability's reported amount is settled.
3. Deferred taxes recognized for a temporary difference of debt with a beneficial conversion feature should be recognized as an adjustment of additional paid-in capital. The EITF noted that because additional paid-in capital was adjusted for the basis difference created when the beneficial conversion feature of the convertible debt was recognized, additional paid-in capital should be adjusted when the deferred tax liability caused by the basis difference is established in accordance with the guidance in ASC 740-20-45-11 (paragraph 36(c) of FAS-109 that

requires an adjustment to be made to "the related components of shareholders' equity."

FASB RATIFICATION

The FASB ratified the consensus positions in this Issue at its September 28, 2005, meeting.

Topic D-30 (Adjustment Due to Effect of a Change in Tax Laws or Rates) (ASC 740-10-45-18; 25-47)

The discussion at the March 1993 EITF meeting dealt with questions received by the FASB staff on proposed changes in tax rates, which were eventually enacted on August 10, 1993, retroactive to January 1, 1993. The questions dealt with when such a change should be recognized, especially when a company is adopting a new accounting standard at the same time. In addition to referring to the requirements of ASC 740-10-35-4 (paragraph 27 of FAS-109), the FASB staff stated that the effect of a change in tax rates should be recognized on the date it is enacted. Thus, if a company adopts a new accounting standard before the date of enactment, the cumulative effect of adopting that standard would not include the change in tax rates, which would be recognized in income from continuing operations in the period of enactment, even if the change in tax rates is retroactive to the date on which a new standard was adopted.

Topic D-31 (Temporary Differences Related to LIFO Inventory and Tax-to-Tax Differences) (ASC 740-10-55-50; 25-31)

At the March 1993 EITF meeting, the FASB staff discussed the following responses to inquiries related to LIFO temporary differences:

- A deferred tax liability should be recognized in accordance with FAS-109 for LIFO inventory temporary differences resulting from excess financial reporting basis over tax basis.
- A deferred tax liability should be recognized for LIFO inventory belonging to a parent company or its subsidiary even if that temporary difference is not "settled" because the subsidiary will be sold before that difference reverses.

Paragraph 72 of FAS-96 required recognition of a tax benefit for the difference between (1) the tax basis of a parent company in an acquired company's stock and (2) the acquired company tax basis of its net assets. Such differences are referred to as *tax-to-tax* differences. Although that requirement was eliminated in ASC 740 (FAS-109), the FASB staff was asked whether recognition of a deferred tax asset for a tax-to-tax difference is *permitted*. The staff responded that under ASC 740 (FAS-109), deferred tax assets may be recognized *only* for deductible temporary differences and carryforwards, which are book-tax differences.

Topic D-32 (Intraperiod Tax Allocation of the Tax Effect of Pretax Income from Continuing Operations) (ASC 740-10-55-53; 25-31)

In response to several inquiries about *intraperiod* tax allocation, the FASB staff stated at the July 1993 EITF meeting that ASC 740 (FAS-109) generally requires determining the tax effect of pretax *income* from continuing operations without considering the tax effect of items not included in continuing operations. For example, an entity has income from continuing operations of $1,000 and a loss from discontinued operations of $1,000 in the current year. The entity also has a $2,000 net operating loss carryforward from a previous year. The deferred tax asset is zero, because it is offset by a valuation allowance that has not been reduced during the year. According to the FASB staff, tax expense from continuing operations should be offset by the loss carryforward with no tax benefit allocated to the loss from discontinued operations.

The staff noted, however, that the guidance in ASC 740-20-45-7 (paragraph 140 of FAS-109) is an exception to the Statement's approach to intraperiod tax allocation. Under the approach discussed in that paragraph, items not included in income from continuing operations in the current year are considered, nevertheless, in calculating the amount of tax benefit that results from a *loss* from continuing operations and that should be allocated to continuing operations. The Board made that exception for consistency with the Statement's approach, under which the tax consequences of future taxable income are considered in evaluating whether deferred tax assets are realizable.

FIG-FAS 109 (A Guide to Implementation of Statement 109 on Accounting for Income Taxes) (ASC 740-10-25-34; 50-4; 55-2 through 55-6, 55-15 through 55-22, 55-25, 55-40, 55-41, 55-48, 55-59 through 55-65, 55-79, 55-80, 55-163, 55-164, 55-168, 55-169, 55-213 through 55-216; 740-20-55-1 through 55-7; 942-740-35-1 through 35-3; 942-852-55-2 through 55-6; 855-10-60-2)

BACKGROUND

The FASB has provided the following guidance in an Implementation Guide to address some of the most frequently asked questions about the implementation of ASC 740 (FAS-109).

STANDARDS

Scheduling

Question 1: When is it necessary to schedule reversal patterns of existing temporary differences?

Answer: Scheduling individual years in terms of reversals of temporary differences is required under ASC 740 (FAS-109) in the following circumstances:

- Deferred taxes that do not relate to a specific asset or liability are classified as current or noncurrent based on the timing of their reversal.
- When deferred tax assets are recognized without consideration of offsetting, after which an assessment is required concerning the need for a valuation allowance. The timing of reversal of temporary differences may be an important consideration in determining the need for and amount of a valuation allowance on deferred tax assets.
- When tax rate changes are phased in, which will often require scheduling.

In scheduling the reversal of temporary differences, consistency and minimizing complexity are particularly important considerations. The same methods should be used for all temporary differences in a particular category for a particular tax jurisdiction.

Question 2: ASC 740 (FAS-109) states that future originating temporary differences for existing depreciable assets and their subsequent reversals are a factor in assessing the likelihood of future realization of a tax benefit of deductible temporary differences and carry forwards. Should future originating and reversing temporary differences always be scheduled for purposes of determining the need for a valuation allowance for deferred tax assets related to existing deductible temporary differences and carryforwards?

Answer: Not necessarily. There are four possible sources of taxable income to support the realizability of deferred tax assets. When it can easily be demonstrated that future taxable income will be sufficient, scheduling is generally not necessary. However, if reversal of taxable temporary differences is the basis for a realization assumption for deferred tax assets, the timing of reversal is important and may require scheduling.

Question 3: Does ASC 740 (FAS-109) require separate deferred tax computations for each state or local tax jurisdiction?

Answer: As a general rule, the answer is "yes," if there are significant differences between the tax laws of the different jurisdictions involved. In the United States, however, many state and local income taxes are based on U.S. federal income tax, and aggregate computations of deferred tax assets and liabilities may be appropriate.

Question 4: An enterprise may have a basis under the tax law for claiming certain deductions (e.g., repair expense) on its income tax return. It may have recognized a liability (including interest) for the probable disallowance of that deduction that, if disallowed, would be capitalized for tax purposes and deductible in future years. How should an item like this be considered in the scheduling of future taxable or deductible differences?

Answer: If expenses are disallowed, taxable income of that year is higher, which provides a source of taxable income for purposes of assessing the need for a valuation allowance for deductible temporary differences. Taxable income after the year of disallowance will be lower because of annual deductions attributable to those capitalized amounts. A deductible amount for the accrued interest is scheduled for the future year in which that interest is expected to be deductible (i.e., when the underlying issues are expected to be settled with the tax authority).

Question 5: A change in tax law may require a change in accounting method for tax purposes (e.g., the uniform cost capitalization rules required by the Tax Reform Act of 1986). For calendar-year taxpayers, inventories on hand at the beginning of 1987 are revalued under the new rules, and the initial catch-up adjustment is deferred and taken into taxable income over not more than four years. Does the deferral of the initial catch-up adjustment for a change in accounting method for tax purposes give rise to a temporary difference?

Answer: Yes. The uniform cost capitalization rules initially resulted in two temporary differences—one related to the additional amounts initially capitalized into inventory for tax expense and one related to the deferred income for tax purposes that results from the initial catch-up adjustment.

Question 6: The Omnibus Budget Reconciliation Act of 1987 requires family-owned farming businesses to use the accrual method of accounting for tax purposes. The initial catch-up adjustment to change from the cash method to the accrual method is deferred and included in taxable income if the business ceases to be family-owned. It also is included in taxable income if gross receipts from farming activities in future years drop below certain 1987 levels. Does the deferral of the initial catch-up adjustment for that change in accounting method for tax purposes give rise to a temporary difference?

Answer: Yes. The entire amount of the catch-up adjustment is a temporary difference.

Question 7: State income taxes are deductible for U.S. federal income tax purposes. Does a deferred state income tax liability or asset give rise to a temporary difference for purposes of determining a deferred U.S. federal income tax liability or asset?

Answer: Yes. A deferred state income tax liability or asset gives rise to a temporary difference for purposes of determining deferred taxes for U.S. federal income tax purposes.

Recognition and Measurement

Question 8: The temporary difference for the "base-year tax reserve" of a savings and loan association is one of the exceptions to comprehensive recognition of deferred taxes under the guidance in ASC 740 (FAS-109). If a deferred tax liability is not recognized for that temporary difference, should a savings and loan association anticipate future percentage-of-taxable-income (PTI) bad-debt deductions in determining the deferred tax liability for other types of temporary differences?

Answer: No. Deferred tax assets and liabilities for temporary differences are measured based on enacted tax rates expected to apply to taxable income when the deferred tax asset or liability is expected to be realized or settled. For the same reason that other special deductions may not be anticipated, it is not permissible to reduce a deferred tax liability by anticipating future PTI bad-debt reductions.

Question 9: An enterprise charged losses directly to contributed capital in a quasi-reorganization. At that time, the deferred tax asset for the enterprise's deductible temporary differences and carryforwards was offset by a valuation allowance. Part of those deductible temporary differences were related to losses that were included in determining income in prior years, and the remainder were attributable to losses that were charged directly to contributed capital. When recognized by reducing or eliminating the valuation allowance, how should the tax benefit of such deductible temporary differences and carryforwards be reported?

Answer: All unrecognized tax benefits of deductible temporary differences and carryforwards that existed at the time of a quasi-reorganization (except as provided in ASC 852-740-45-3 (FAS-109), par. 39) should be reported as a direct addition to contributed capital when recognized at a date after the quasi-reorganization. ARB-43, Chapter 7 (Capital Accounts), indicates that the benefit of an operating loss or tax credit carryforward that existed at the date of a quasi-reorganization should not be included in the determination of income of the "new" enterprise, regardless of whether they were charged to income before the quasi-reorganization or were charged directly to contributed capital as part of the quasi-reorganization. A charge to income is appropriate only if, subsequent to a quasi-reorganization, the enterprise determines that due to a change in circumstances it should recognize or increase a valuation allowance to reduce the tax benefits that were recognized in recording the quasi-reorganization.

Question 10: Some enterprises have credited a net gain directly to contributed capital at the date of a quasi-reorganization. Does the answer to Question 9 change for those enterprises?

Answer: No. The accounting for any subsequently recognized tax benefit of deductible temporary differences and carryforwards that exist at the time of a quasi-reorganization should not change based on whether gains were credited or losses charged directly to contributed capital.

Change in Tax Status

Question 11: What disclosure is required if a change in an enterprise's tax status becomes effective after year-end but before financial statements are issued?

Answer: This change should not be reflected in the financial statements of the previous year, but disclosure should include the change in the enterprise's tax status for the following year and the effects of that change, if material.

Question 12: Should an enterprise that changes from taxable C corporation status to nontaxable S corporation status eliminate its entire U.S. federal deferred tax liability?

Answer: The enterprise should continue to recognize a deferred tax liability to the extent that it would be subject to a corporate-level tax on net unrealized "built-in gains."

Illustration of Change in Tax Status

Company M's assets are as followed when its S corporation election becomes effective:

	Tax Basis	Reported Amount	Temporary Difference	Built-In Gain (Loss)
Marketable Securities	$100	$ 80	$(20)	$(8)
Inventory	50	100	50	20

If the enterprise has no tax loss or tax credit carryforwards available to offset the built-in gain and if marketable securities and inventory will both be sold in the same year, the $20 built-in gain on the inventory is offset by the $8 built-in loss on the marketable securities, and the $12 difference would be shown as a deferred tax liability.

Business Combinations

Questions 13–17a to c were nullified by the guidance in FAS-141(R).

Disclosure

Question 18: ASC 740 (FAS-109) requires disclosure of the significant components of income tax expense attributable to continuing operations. Should the total of the amounts disclosed for the components of tax expense equal the amount of income tax expense that is reported in the statement of earnings? Should the amounts for current and deferred tax expense be disclosed before or after reduction for the tax benefit of operating loss carryforwards and tax credits?

Answer: The total of the amounts disclosed for the components of tax expense should be the amount of tax expense reported in the statement of earnings for continuing operations. Separate disclosure is required of (*a*) the tax benefit of operating loss carryforwards and (*b*) tax credits and tax credit carryforwards that were recognized.

Allocation of Tax Expense

Question 19: How should income tax expense be allocated between pretax income from continuing operations and other items when the enterprise has temporary differences?

Answer: The guidance in ASC 740 (FAS-109) states that the amount of income tax expense or benefit allocated to continuing operations is the tax effect of pretax income or loss from continuing operations that occurred during the year (subject to certain adjustments). Income tax expense allocated between pretax income from continuing operations and other items should include deferred taxes.

Questions 20 and 21 are deleted because the effective date of FAS-109 has passed.

Tax-Planning Strategies

Question 25: The guidance in ASC 740 (FAS-109) indicates that tax-planning strategies include elections for tax purposes. What are some examples of those elections?

Answer: Examples are as follows:

- Election to file a consolidated tax return
- Election to claim either a deduction or a tax credit for foreign taxes paid

- Election to forego carrying an operating loss back and only carry that loss forward

Question 26: An enterprise might identify several qualifying taxplanning strategies that would either reduce or eliminate the need for a valuation allowance for its deferred tax assets. May the enterprise recognize the effect of one strategy in the current year and postpone recognition of the effect of the other strategies to a later year?

Answer: No. The enterprise should recognize the effect of all tax-planning strategies that meet the criteria of ASC 740 (FAS-109) in the current year.

Illustration of Multiple Tax Planning Strategies

Amber Co. has determined that its allowance on deferred tax assets should be $60,000, without regard to tax-planning strategies. The company has identified two income tax-planning strategies that would reduce its allowance on deferred tax assets by $10,000 (Strategy 1) and by $15,000 (Strategy 2), respectively. Both qualify as tax-planning strategies under FAS-109. Amber cannot recognize the effect of only Strategy 1 or only Strategy 2 but, rather, must recognize the impact of both and report an allowance on deferred tax assets of $35,000 [$60,000 − ($10,000 + $15,000)].

Question 27: Because the effects of known qualifying tax strategies must be recognized, is management required to make an extensive effort to identify all tax-planning strategies that meet the criteria for tax-planning strategies?

Answer: Management is required to make a reasonable effort to identify significant tax-planning strategies. If evidence indicates that other sources of taxable income will be adequate to eliminate the need for a valuation allowance, consideration of tax-planning strategies is not required.

Question 28: Under current U.S. federal income tax law, approval of a change from taxable C corporation status to nontaxable S status is automatic if the enterprise meets the criteria for S corporation status. If an enterprise meets those criteria but has not changed to S corporation status, would a strategy to change to nontaxable S corporation status be a qualifying tax-planning strategy that would permit an enterprise to not recognize deferred taxes?

Answer: No. The effect of a change in tax status should be recognized on the date when the change in tax status occurs.

ASC 805 Business Combinations

EITF Issue 86-9 (IRC Section 338 and Push-Down Accounting) (ASC 805-50-05-8; 15-8, 15-9; 25-3, 25-13)

OVERVIEW

As a result of the Tax Equity and Fiscal Responsibility Act of 1982, a company can step up an acquired company's tax basis by making such an election rather than changing its legal form through a liquidation, corporate reorganization, or statutory merger. In addition, some companies also have justified a "push down" of the acquiring company's basis to the subsidiary for financial reporting purposes. One advantage of push-down accounting is that it conforms balances for both tax and financial reporting purposes.

ACCOUNTING ISSUES

- Should push-down accounting be required if (*a*) the acquired company is neither an SEC registrant nor a party to the transaction effecting the change in ownership, (*b*) a step-up in basis is elected, and (*c*) it is not essential to retain the old basis?
- If the acquiring company's basis for financial reporting is not pushed down to the financial statements of the acquired company, which one of the following methods is preferable for allocating the consolidated tax provision:
  —Modifying the intercorporate tax allocation agreement so that taxes are allocated to the acquired company using its preacquisition tax basis?
  —Crediting the tax benefit from the step-up in the acquired company's tax basis to its capital surplus when realized?
  —Crediting the tax benefit to the acquired company's income as a permanent difference when realized?

EITF CONSENSUS

- Companies that are not SEC registrants are not required to use push-down accounting.
- Any one of the three methods may be used to allocate the consolidated tax provision, with appropriate disclosure.

SUBSEQUENT DEVELOPMENT

Although paragraph 40 of FAS-109 (Accounting for Income Taxes) (ASC 740-10-30-28), which was issued in February 1992, does not require a specific method of tax allocation for the separate financial statements of members of a group filing a consolidated tax return, it does require that the method of allocation be systematic, rational, and consistent with the principles established in the Statement. Those criteria are met if current and deferred taxes are allocated to members of the consolidated group as if they are separate tax payers. Footnote 10 notes that as a result of that method of allocation, the total of allocated amounts may not equal the consolidated amount. (Also see Issue 94-10).

DISCUSSION

The Task Force did not reach a consensus on which of the three methods in Issue 2 would be preferable. Under methods (a) and (b), the acquired company would have to continue using its preacquisition tax records, which predate the step-up in tax basis, only for the purpose of allocating the consolidated tax provision. An argument against method (a) was that it makes the tax allocation artificial. The tax benefit under method (b) is treated as a constructive dividend, which some argued is rare. Under method (c), a so-called double dip exists; that is, if the old basis is maintained for financial reporting purposes, the acquired company's results of operations do not recognize the acquiring company's higher asset basis and consequent higher depreciation in pre-tax income, but the increased tax benefit from the step up in tax basis is recognized.

ASC 830-740 Foreign Currency Matters—Income Taxes

EITF Issue 93-9 (Application of FASB Statement No. 109 in Foreign Financial Statements Restated for General Price-Level Changes) (ASC 830-740-25-4, 25-5; 30-1, 30-2; 55-1 through 55-3)

OVERVIEW

Company M, which is located in a country with a highly inflationary economy, prepares price-level-adjusted financial statements in accordance with U.S. GAAP that present changes in the local currency's general purchasing power. In addition, the tax bases of Company M's assets and liabilities are indexed to consider the effects of inflation. Because the adjustments may not be the same for tax and financial statement purposes, the financial reporting and tax bases of assets and liabilities may differ.

Under FAS-109, the difference between an asset and liability's financial reporting basis and tax basis is a temporary difference that generally requires the provision of deferred taxes. However, paragraph 9f of the Statement (ASC 740-10-25-3) prohibits recognizing a deferred tax liability or asset for differences related to the bases of assets or liabilities that are remeasured under the provisions of FAS-52 from the local currency used in the country in which the entity operates to the functional currency at historical exchange rates and that result from changes in exchange rates or from indexing for tax purposes. FAS-109 states that to do so would result in recognition of deferred taxes on exchange gains or losses not recognized for financial reporting purposes.

Because of that prohibition in paragraph 9f of FAS-109 (ASC 740-10-25-3), it was unclear whether deferred taxes should be provided for differences in the bases of assets and liabilities that occur as a result of tax indexing when comprehensive, general price-level-adjusted financial statements are prepared using the guidance in APB-3.

ACCOUNTING ISSUES

1. Should paragraph 9f of FAS-109 (ASC 740-10-25-3) apply to temporary differences between the bases of assets and liabilities for financial reporting in general price-level-adjusted financial statements and their indexed tax bases?
2. If paragraph 9f (ASC 740-10-25-3) does not apply, how should deferred income tax expense or benefit for the year be determined?

EITF CONSENSUS

1. Paragraph 9f (ASC 740-10-25-3) should not apply to general price-level-adjusted financial statements. Temporary differences in financial statements restated for general price-level changes using end-of-current-year units of purchasing power should be calculated based on the difference between the indexed tax basis amounts of assets and liabilities and the related amounts reported in general price-level-adjusted financial statements.
2. The deferred tax expense or benefit should be calculated as the difference between (a) the deferred tax asset or liability reported at the end of the current year based on the above calculation and (b) the deferred tax asset or liability reported at the end of the prior year remeasured in end-of-current-year units of purchasing power. Remeasurement of deferred tax assets and liabilities at the end of the prior year should be reported with the remeasurement of all other assets and liabilities as a restatement of beginning equity.

Illustration Using EITF Issue 93-9 Consensus

Assumptions

- Company M has land that was purchased in 20X0 for FC10,000 (local currency).

- The general price-level-adjusted financial reporting amount of the land at December 31, 20X4, is CFC48,384 (current purchasing power units).
- The indexed basis for tax purposes at December 31, 20X4, is CFC36,456.
- The enacted tax rate is 50%.
- Company M has a taxable temporary difference of CFC11,928 (CFC48,384 − CFC36,456) at December 31, 20X4.
- The related deferred tax liability in current purchasing power units at December 31, 20X4, is CFC5,964 (CFC11,928 × .5).
- During 20X5, general price levels increased by 40% and indexing for tax purposes was 30%.
- The following is the calculation of the deferred tax liability and deferred tax expense at December 31, 20X5:

	20X5
Land—financial reporting basis (CFC48,384 × 1.4)	CFC67,738
Land—tax basis (CFC36,456 × 1.3)	CFC47,393
Taxable temporary difference	CFC20,345
Tax rate	× .5
Deferred tax liability, end of year	CFC10,173
Deferred tax liability restated, at beginning of year (CFC5,964 × 1.4)	CFC 8,350
Deferred tax expense for 20X5	CFC 1,823

Company M should report CFC2,386 (CFC8,350 − CFC5,964) as a restatement of beginning equity for 20X5.

EITF Issue 93-16 (Application of FASB Statement No. 109 to Basis Differences within Foreign Subsidiaries That Meet the Indefinite Reversal Criterion of APB Opinion No. 23) (ASC 830-740-25-6 through 25-8; 740-30-25-17)

OVERVIEW

Under the guidance in ASC 740 (FAS-109) and ASC 740 (APB-23), as amended, entities do not recognize a deferred tax liability on temporary differences related to the financial reporting and tax bases of investments in foreign subsidiaries or foreign joint ventures that are not expected to reverse in the foreseeable future. Such differences are referred to as outside basis differences. However, foreign subsidiaries may have other temporary differences, referred to as inside basis differences, that also may not reverse in the foreseeable future.

In this particular situation, an Italian subsidiary of a U.S. company uses the Italian lira as its functional currency. The tax basis of the company's fixed assets has been increased to compensate for the effects of inflation, and an equivalent amount has been credited to an account referred to as "revaluation surplus," which is a component of equity established for tax purposes. That amount becomes taxable only if the Italian entity is liquidated or if earnings associated with the revaluation surplus are distributed. Because that amount would not be taxable if the asset is sold, the tax related to the surplus may be deferred indefinitely. However, for discussion purposes, the EITF assumed that there was no strategy within the entity's control under which it could avoid triggering the tax on the revaluation surplus if it were to realize the carrying amounts of its assets and transfer the net assets to its shareholders.

ACCOUNTING ISSUES

1. Should the indefinite reversal criterion in APB-23, as amended by FAS-109, apply only to outside basis differences, or should it also apply to the revaluation surplus related to inside basis differences of foreign subsidiaries in the consolidated financial statements of the U.S. parent and its foreign subsidiaries?
2. If the indefinite reversal criterion does not apply to inside basis differences, how should the provisions of FAS-109 be applied?

EITF CONSENSUS

1. The indefinite reversal criterion in APB-23, as amended, does not apply to a revaluation surplus related to *inside* basis differences of foreign subsidiaries. A deferred tax liability should be provided on the balance of the revaluation surplus.

    The Task Force analogized their consensus to paragraph 15 of FAS-109 (ASC 740-10-05-10), which discusses temporary differences that have balances only on the income tax balance sheet and that cannot be related to specific assets or liabilities in the financial statements. Deferred taxes are nevertheless provided for such differences, which will result in taxable or deductible amounts in the future. Similarly, based on Italian law, a revaluation surplus related to inside basis differences will be taxable in the future and thus qualifies as a temporary difference, even though it is a component of equity for tax purposes. In addition, the Task Force observed that paragraph 31 of FAS-109 (ASC 740-10-25-3) specifically limits the indefinite reversal criterion in APB-23, as amended, to the situations discussed in that paragraph and prohibits applying it by analogy to other types of temporary differences.

2. Entities should recognize a deferred tax liability for inside basis differences that originated in fiscal years beginning *after* December 15, 1992. Therefore, recognition of a deferred tax

liability is not required for existing inside basis differences that originated in fiscal years beginning *before* December 16, 1992 and for which no deferred tax liability was recognized on adoption of FAS-109. However, the information required in paragraph 44 of FAS-109 (ASC 942-740-50-1) should be disclosed in those situations.

DISCUSSION

1. Although the primary argument against extending the indefinite reversal criterion in ASC 740 (APB-23), as amended, to inside basis differences is based on the prohibition in ASC 740-30-15-4 (paragraph 31 of FAS-109) against analogizing it to other temporary differences, there are other relevant arguments. One is based on the discussion in paragraph 170 of FAS-109 (not in ASC). Before ASC 749 (FAS-109) was issued, the rationale under APB-23 for not recognizing deferred tax liabilities for certain temporary differences was related to management's ability to control the timing of events that would cause the temporary difference to reverse and result in a taxable amount in the future. The FASB decided that management's ability to determine when a liability would be settled in the future does not contradict the fact that a liability exists in the current year.

   Another relevant argument against extending the indefinite reversal criterion to inside basis differences of foreign subsidiaries of U.S. corporations is that the treatment of temporary differences in the financial statements of those entities and in the U.S. GAAP financial statements of foreign entities that are not subsidiaries of U.S. corporations would differ. The latter are not exempt from the recognition of deferred taxes under APB-23, as amended.

2. The Task Force's consensus on the effective date and transition is similar to the prospective approach for the provision of deferred taxes on temporary differences related to bad-debt reserves of U.S. savings and loan associations and policyholders' surplus of stock life insurance companies, which are no longer included under the provisions of APB-23, as amended.

RELATED CHAPTERS IN 2011
GAAP GUIDE, VOLUME II

Chapter 6, "Business Combinations"
Chapter 21, "Intangible Assets"

RELATED CHAPTERS IN 2011
GAAP GUIDE, VOLUME I

Chapter 4, "Business Combinations"
Chapter 21, "Income Taxes"
Chapter 23, "Intangible Assets"

RELATED CHAPTERS IN 2011
INTERNATIONAL ACCOUNTING/FINANCIAL REPORTING STANDARDS GUIDE

Chapter 10, "Consolidated Financial Statements"
Chapter 20, "Income Taxes"
Chapter 22, "Interim Financial Reporting"
Chapter 25, "Leases"
Chapter 27, "Property, Plant, and Equipment"
Chapter 28, "Provisions, Contingent Liabilities, and Contingent Assets"

CHAPTER 21
INTANGIBLE ASSETS

CONTENTS

Overview		21.01
Authoritative Guidance		
ASC 310 Receivables		21.03
EITF Issue 88-20	Difference between Initial Investment and Principal Amount of Loans in a Purchased Credit Card Portfolio	21.03
ASC 350 Intangibles—Goodwill and Other		21.04
FSP FAS-142-3	Determination of the Useful Life of Intangible Assets	21.04
EITF Issue 08-7	Accounting for Defensive Intangible Assets	21.07
ASC 932-350 Extractive Activities—Oil and Gas		21.09
FSP FAS-142-2	Application of FASB Statement No. 142, *Goodwill and Other Intangible Assets,* to Oil- and Gas-Producing Entities	21.09
Related Chapter in 2011 GAAP Guide, Volume I		21.10
Related Chapters in 2011 International Accounting/Financial Reporting Standards Guide		21.10

OVERVIEW

Intangible assets are long-lived assets used in the production of goods and services. They are similar to property, plant, and equipment except for their lack of physical properties. Examples of intangible assets include copyrights, patents, trademarks, and goodwill. Under the provisions of ASC 350, Intangibles—Goodwill and Other (FAS-142, Goodwill and Other Intangible Assets), intangible assets with finite useful lives are subject to amortization over their estimated useful lives. Intangible assets with indefinite useful lives are not amortized, but they are periodically evaluated for impairment. If the intangible asset is impaired, an impairment loss is recorded as the difference between the carrying amount of the asset and the asset's fair value.

The following pronouncements, which provide GAAP for intangible assets, are discussed in the 2011 *GAAP Guide, Volume I,* Chapter 23, "Intangible Assets."

ASC 805 Business Combinations (FAS-141(R))

ASC 350 Intangibles—Goodwill and Other (FAS-142)

AUTHORITATIVE GUIDANCE

ASC 310 Receivables

EITF Issue 88-20 Difference between Initial Investment and Principal Amount of Loans in a Purchased Credit Card Portfolio (ASC 310-10-25-7; 35-52)

OVERVIEW

An entity has purchased a credit card portfolio for an amount of cash that exceeds the balance of the credit card receivables.

Question 33 of the FASB Implementation Guide on FAS-91 (not in ASC) discussed the period over which a financial institution should amortize a premium paid to acquire a credit card portfolio from another financial institution for cash. The Implementation Guide stated that based on guidance in ASC 310-20-35-15; 25-22 (paragraph 15 of FAS-91), which states that the difference between the amount paid to acquire a loan (initial investment) and the loan's principal amount at acquisition should be recognized over the life of the loan as a yield adjustment. The financial institution should defer and amortize the premium on a straight-line basis over the period the cardholders are entitled to use their cards.

The FASB staff asked the EITF to address this Issue because the guidance in Question 33 was being interpreted in different ways in practice.

ACCOUNTING ISSUES

1. Should the difference (premium) between the amount an entity pays to purchase credit card loans and the sum of the balances of the receivables at the date of purchase be allocated between the loans acquired and identifiable intangible assets acquired, if any?
2. Over what period should an entity amortize amounts allocated to loans and identifiable intangible assets acquired?

EITF CONSENSUS

The EITF reached the following consensus positions:

1. The difference (premium) between the amount an entity pays to purchase a credit card portfolio, including the cardholder relationships, and the sum of the balances of the credit card loans at the date of purchase should be allocated between the credit cardholder relationships acquired and loans acquired. (See discussion of the effect of FAS-140.)

2. The portion of the premium related to credit cardholder relationships is an identifiable intangible asset and should be amortized over the period of estimated benefit under the provisions of ASC 350 (FAS-142). The portion allocated to the loans should be amortized over the life of the loans in accordance with the guidance in ASC 310 (FAS-91). Task Force members noted that the determination of the life of a credit card loan should consider whether the terms of the agreement permit the loan's repayment period to continue after the expiration date of the credit card if the card is not renewed.

> **OBSERVATION:** Under the guidance in ASC 350 (FAS-142), which superseded APB-17, intangible assets should be amortized over their useful lives, unless the life of the intangible asset is considered to be indefinite.

EFFECT OF ASC 860 (FAS-140)

Under the guidance in ASC 860, Transfers and Servicing (FAS-140, as amended by FAS-166, Accounting for Transfers of Financial Assets), the consensus position in Issue 1, that the difference between the amount paid to purchase credit card loans and the sum of the balances of the receivables at the purchase date should be allocated between the credit cardholder relationships and the loans acquired, is unaffected if the conditions for treatment as a sale in ASC 860-10-40-4 through 40-5 and 55-68A (paragraph 9 of FAS-140) exist. ASC 860-20-30-1 (Paragraph 11) provides that assets obtained and liabilities incurred by a transferee should be measured and recognized at fair value. The subsequent measurement issues discussed in Issue 2 are not addressed in ASC 860 (FAS-140, as amended by FAS-166) and therefore do not affect the EITF's consensus position on the amortization of credit cardholder relationships.

ASC 350 Intangibles—Goodwill and Other

FSP FAS-142-3 (Determination of the Useful Life of Intangible Assets) (ASC 350-30-50-4 through 50-5; 55-1(c); 65-1; 275-10-50-15A)

OVERVIEW

When the EITF considered providing guidance on Issue No. 03-9 (Determination of the Useful Life of Renewable Intangible Assets under FASB Statement No. 142) (removed from EITF's agenda), one of the problems that the EITF faced was that the guidance in ASC

350 (FAS-142, Goodwill and Other Intangible Assets), which addresses the determination of the useful life of a renewable intangible asset, was inconsistent with the guidance in ASC 805 (FAS-141 (R), Business Combinations), which addresses the period of expected cash flows used to measure an asset's fair value. Because of that inconsistency in the FASB's literature, the EITF decided to remove Issue 03-9 from its agenda and asked the FASB to address the inconsistent guidance in ASC 805 (FAS-141 and ASC 305 (FAS-142).

Under the guidance in ASC 350-30-35-3 (paragraph 11(d) of FAS-142), "legal, regulatory, or contractual provisions that enable renewal or extension of the asset's legal or contractual life without substantial cost" must be considered, but only if renewal or extension of an asset's useful life is supported by evidence and can be achieved without "material modifications of the existing terms and conditions."

The problem is that the useful life of an intangible asset recognized under the guidance in ASC 350 (FAS-142) frequently differs from the period of expected cash flows used to measure the asset's fair value under the guidance in ASC 805 (FAS-141) if the underlying arrangement includes terms related to the renewal or extension of the asset's useful life (i.e., the useful life of an asset accounted for under the guidance in ASC 350 (FAS-142(R) is usually shorter than the expected period of cash flows under the guidance in FAS-141 (R)). That difference may occur, especially if material modifications are required for renewal or extension of a long-lived intangible asset's useful life, even though the likelihood of renewal or extension is high. The FASB was asked to consider whether the difference between an intangible asset's useful life and the period of expected cash flows used to measure its fair value is justified. This FSP does *not* provide guidance for the *initial measurement* of recognized intangible assets, the *amortization method* to be used, and the accounting for costs incurred to renew or extend a recognized intangible asset's term.

FASB STAFF POSITION

The guidance in this FSP applies to recognized intangible assets accounted for under the guidance in ASC 350 (FAS-142), regardless of how they were acquired.

Subsequent Measurement—Determining Useful Life

To determine the useful life of a recognized intangible asset, an entity is required to develop assumptions about the renewal or extension of an arrangement based on its own historical experience related to the renewal or extension of similar arrangements, which should be adjusted for entity-specific factors discussed in ASC 350-30-35-3 (paragraph 11 of FAS-142). An entity that has no historical experience should consider assumptions that other participants in the market would use about an arrangement's renewal or extension that are (1) consistent with the asset's highest and best use and (2) adjusted for factors in ASC 350-30-35-3 (paragraphs 11(a) through 11(f) of FAS-142) that specifically apply to the entity.

Under the guidance in ASC 350-30-35-3 (paragraph 11(d) of FAS-142), an entity is currently not permitted to base its assumptions on its own past experience related to the renewal or extension of an arrangement if it is likely that doing so would require incurring a substantial cost or making material modifications to an arrangement, because of a concern that entities might lengthen the useful lives of intangible assets inappropriately. The FASB staff believes that the guidance related to the fair value measurement of intangible assets and the requirement to test intangible assets for impairment along with the FSP's disclosure requirements would reduce that concern. The guidance in this FSP amends the guidance in ASC 350-30-35-3 (paragraph 11(d) of FAS-142) to permit an entity to base its assumptions on its own past experience even if it would result in a substantial cost or would require material modifications to the arrangement.

Entities that measure a recognized intangible asset's fair value by the *income approach* should determine the asset's useful life for amortization purposes by considering the period of expected cash flows used to measure the intangible asset's fair value adjusted for the entity's specific circumstances in accordance with the guidance in ASC 350-30-35-3 (paragraphs 11(a) to 11(f) of FAS-142). Those factors include, but are not limited to, an entity's expected use for the asset and its past experience in renewals and extensions of such arrangements.

If the useful life of a recognized intangible asset differs from the expected cash flows used to measure the asset's fair value, it is usually because the assumptions used by the entity to measure the asset's fair value are specific to the entity and thus differ from those used by other entities in the market to determine the asset's price. In that case, the entity should use its own assumptions because its amortization of a recognized intangible asset should be based on the period over which the asset will contribute, directly or indirectly, to the entity's future cash flows.

DISCLOSURES

Entities are required to disclose information about recognized intangible assets that would help users of financial statements to determine how the entity's intent or ability to renew or extend an arrangement affects the entity's expected cash flows associated with the asset.

Entities are required to disclose the following information, if applicable, in addition to the disclosures required in ASC 350-20-50-1 through 50-2 (paragraphs 44 and 45 of FAS-142):

- The accounting policy for costs incurred to renew or extend a recognized intangible asset's term;
- For each class of major intangible assets, the weighted-average period at acquisition or renewal before the next explicit or implicit renewal or extension;
- If renewal or extension costs are capitalized, the total cost incurred to renew or extend the term of a recognized intangible asset disclosed by major class of intangible assets for each period for which a balance sheet is presented.

The criterion in ASC 275-10-50-8 (paragraph 13(b) of AICPA Statement of Position (SOP) 94-6, Disclosure of Certain Significant Risks and Uncertainties)), which provides guidance on when an entity should disclose information about an estimate, has been met if the effect of a change in either an intangible asset's (a) useful life, or (b) the expected likelihood of its renewal or extension would be material to the financial statements, either individually or in total by major class of intangible assets.

EFFECTIVE DATE AND TRANSITION

The guidance in this FSP is effective for financial statements issued for fiscal years that begin after December 15, 2008, and interim periods in those fiscal years. Early adoption is *not* permitted.

The FSP's guidance related to the determination of a recognized intangible asset's useful life should be applied *prospectively* to intangible assets acquired *after* the effective date. The disclosure requirements should be applied *prospectively* to intangible assets *recognized* as of and *after* the effective date.

EITF Issue 08-7 (Accounting for Defensive Intangible Assets) (ASC 350-30-15-5; 25-5; 35-5A through 35-5B; 55-1 through 55-1B, 55-28H through 55-28I, 55-28K through 55-28L, 65-2)

OVERVIEW

A "defensive asset" or "locked-up asset" is an intangible asset that has been acquired in a business combination or in an asset acquisition that an entity does *not* intend to actively use but intends to keep others from using it. Although the entity does not actively use the asset, its existence probably increases the value of other assets owned by the acquiring entity. In the past, entities have attributed little or no value to acquired intangible assets that they did not intend to actively use, regardless of whether they might have been actively used by another acquirer.

However, as a result of the issuance of ASC 805 (FAS-141(R) and ASC 820, Fair Value Measurements and Disclosures (FAS-157, Fair

Value Measurements) intangible assets must be recognized at a value that represents an asset's *highest and best use* based on assumptions about other entities in the market. When those Statements become effective, entities will generally assign a greater value to defensive intangible assets than they previously would have assigned under the guidance in ASC 805 (FAS-141(R), Business Combinations). Consequently, constituents have asked how defensive assets should be accounted for after their acquisition, including the assignment of an estimated useful life.

SCOPE

Issue 08-7 applies to all acquired intangible assets that an entity does *not* intend to use actively but intends to hold to keep competitors from gaining access to those assets, except if an intangible asset is used in research and development activities, which are accounted for in accordance with ASC 350-30-35-15 through 35-17A (paragraph 16 of FAS-142, Goodwill and Other Intangible Assets). Whether an asset is a defensive asset depends on the entity's intentions for its use. The accounting for such assets may change if an entity decides to begin to actively use the asset.

The identification of market participants, market participants' assumptions, or valuation issues related to defensive intangible assets are not discussed in this Issue.

EITF CONSENSUS

The EITF reached the following consensus positions:

Recognition. A defensive intangible asset should be accounted for as a separate unit of accounting and should not be included in the cost of an entity's existing intangible assets because defensive intangible assets are identified separately.

Subsequent measurement. A defensive asset's benefit to an entity that holds it is represented by the direct or indirect cash flows that result from preventing others from realizing value from that asset. The useful life assigned to a defensive intangible asset, in accordance with the guidance in ASC 350-30-35-1 through 35-3 (paragraph 11 of FAS-142) should represent an entity's consumption of the expected benefits related to the asset by estimating the period over which the asset's fair value will diminish. That period is a surrogate for the period over which an entity expects that the defensive asset will contribute indirectly to the entity's future cash flows.

Defensive intangible assets rarely have an indefinite useful life because their fair value generally diminishes over time due to a lack of market exposure or as a result of competitive or other factors. In addition, an acquired intangible asset that meets the definition of a defensive intangible asset cannot be considered as immediately abandoned.

TRANSITION

The guidance in this Issue is effective for intangible assets acquired on or after the beginning of the first annual reporting period beginning on or after December 15, 2008.

FASB RATIFICATION

The FASB ratified the EITF's consensus positions at its November 24, 2008, meeting.

ASC 932-350 Extractive Activities—Oil and Gas

FSP FAS-142-2 (Application of FASB Statement No. 142, Goodwill and Other Intangible Assets, to Oil- and Gas-Producing Entities) (ASC 932-350-50-12)

QUESTION

Does the scope exception, related to ASC 932 (FAS-19, Financial Accounting and Reporting by Oil and Gas Producing Companies) in ASC 350-10-15-4 (paragraph 8(b) of FAS-142, Goodwill and Other Intangible Assets) apply to the balance sheet classification of and disclosures about drilling and mineral rights of oil- and gas-producing entities?

FASB STAFF POSITION

The FASB staff believes that the scope exception in ASC 350-10-15-4 (paragraph 8(b) of FAS-142) applies to the balance sheet classification of and disclosures about drilling and mineral rights of oil- and gas-producing entities that account for their operations under the provisions of ASC 932 (FAS-19).

Because the accounting framework of ASC 932 (FAS-19) is based on the level of an oil- or gas-producing entity's established reserves, rather than on whether its assets are accounted for as tangible or intangible assets, the FASB staff believes that the scope exception in ASC 350-10-15-4 (paragraph 8(b) of FAS-142) also applies to the disclosure provisions for drilling and mineral rights of oil- and gas-producing entities. The FASB staff noted, however, that, if they choose, entities are permitted to provide information about their drilling and mineral rights in addition to the information required to be disclosed under the provisions of ASC 932-235 (FAS-69, Disclosures about Oil- and Gas-Producing Activities).

The conclusion in this FSP should *not* be applied analogously to other items included in ASC 350-10-15-4 (paragraph 8 of FAS-142).

RELATED CHAPTER IN 2011
GAAP GUIDE, VOLUME I

Chapter 23, "Intangible Assets"

RELATED CHAPTERS IN 2011
INTERNATIONAL ACCOUNTING/FINANCIAL REPORTING STANDARDS GUIDE

Chapter 7, "Business Combinations"
Chapter 14, "Equity Method"
Chapter 19, "Impairment of Assets"
Chapter 21, "Intangible Assets"
Chapter 27, "Property, Plant, and Equipment"
Chapter 31, "Segment Reporting"

CHAPTER 22
INTEREST ON RECEIVABLES AND PAYABLES

CONTENTS

Overview	22.01
Authoritative Guidance	
ASC 470 Debt	22.02
EITF Issue 86-15 Increasing-Rate Debt	22.02
ASC 932-835 Extractive Activities—Oil and Gas—Interest	22.05
AIN-APB-21 Interest on Receivables and Payables: Accounting Interpretations of APB Opinion No. 21	22.05
Related Chapter in 2011 GAAP Guide, Volume I	22.05
Related Chapters in 2011 International Accounting/Financial Reporting Standards Guide	22.05

OVERVIEW

Business transactions often involve the exchange of cash or other assets for a note or other instrument. When the interest rate on the instrument is consistent with the market rate at the time of the transaction, the face amount of the instrument is assumed to be equal to the value of the other asset(s) exchanged. An interest rate that is different from the prevailing market rate, however, implies that the face amount of the instrument may not equal the value of the other asset(s) exchanged. In this case, it may be necessary to impute interest that is not stated as part of the instrument, or to recognize interest at a rate other than that stated in the instrument.

The following pronouncement, which provides guidance for the recognition of interest on receivables and payables, is discussed in the 2011 *GAAP Guide, Volume I,* Chapter 25, "Interest on Receivables and Payables."

    ASC 835   Interest on Receivables and Payables (APB-21)

AUTHORITATIVE GUIDANCE

ASC 470 Debt

Issue 86-15 (Increasing-Rate Debt) (ASC 470-10-35-1 through 35-2; 45-7 through 45-8; 835-10-60-9)

OVERVIEW

Increasing-rate debt is a financial instrument consisting of notes that mature three months from the original issue date, for example, and that can be extended at the issuer's option for another period of the same duration at each maturity date, but not for longer than five years from original issuance, for example. The interest rate on the notes increases each time their maturity is extended.

ACCOUNTING ISSUES

1. How should an issuer determine interest expense on increasing-rate debt, and what maturity date should be used in that determination?
2. Over what period should debt-issue costs be amortized?
3. How should an issuer account for an excess interest accrual if interest expense is determined by the interest method and the debt is paid earlier than estimated, and should any of it be classified as extraordinary?
4. How should the note be classified in the balance sheet? (Discussed in Chapter 4, "Balance Sheet Classification and Related Display Issues.")

EITF CONSENSUS

The EITF reached the following consensus positions:

1. An issuer should determine periodic interest expense on increasing-rate debt by the interest method based on an estimate of the outstanding term of the debt. That estimate should consider the issuer's plans, ability, and intent to service the debt.
2. An issuer should amortize debt-issue costs over the same period used in determining the periodic interest cost.
3. If the issuer repays the debt at par before its estimated maturity date, interest expense should be adjusted for excess accrued interest, if any. Such an adjustment should not be considered an extraordinary item.

EFFECT OF ASC 815 (FAS-133)

Provisions that extend the term of a debt instrument should be analyzed to determine whether they represent a derivative that should be accounted for separately under the guidance in FAS-133. Therefore, the consensus in Issue 1 may be partially nullified. [See ASC 815-15-05-1, 25-1, 25-14, 35-2A (paragraph 12 of FAS-133, FASB Accounting Standards Codification for guidance as well as ASC 815-10-15-104 (Statement 133 Implementation Issue No. A13, Whether Settlement Provisions That Require a Structured Payout Constitute Net Settlement under Paragraph 9(a))

> **OBSERVATION:** The guidance in ASC 815 (FAS-133) has been amended by the guidance in ASC 815-15-25-4 through 25-5 (FAS-155, Accounting for Certain Hybrid Financial Instruments), which permits an entity to elect to measure at their fair value certain hybrid financial instruments with embedded derivatives that otherwise would have to be bifurcated. If an entity elects to measure an entire hybrid instrument at its fair value, that financial instrument *cannot* be used as a hedging instrument in hedging relationship under the guidance in ASC 815 (FAS-133).

DISCUSSION

The discussion in ASC 835-30 (APB-21) on accounting for a note issued for cash only does not address the issue of a changing interest rate. Under the guidance in ASC 835-30-25-4 (paragraph 11 of APB-21), the presumption that the present value of a note issued for cash only is the same as the cash proceeds. The interest rate would normally not be adjusted on such a note unless the cash proceeds differed from the note's face amount.

Various approaches were suggested to resolve the Issue. One approach analogized to ASC 840-20 (FTB 85-3, Accounting for Operating Leases with Scheduled Rent Increases), which provides accounting guidance for operating leases with scheduled rent increases during a noncancelable lease term. The Technical Bulletin states that rental expense may be recognized on other than a straight-line basis if another basis is rational and systematic and better represents the time pattern over which the property is used.

The EITF's consensus seems to be based on an approach that considers the notes to be long-term rather than short-term notes. Under that approach, a level rate is determined based on an estimate of the term of the notes. One problem with that approach is that the issuer has to estimate the period over which the notes will be outstanding. Some argued that the issuer would have an incentive to repay the notes as soon as possible, because each time they are renewed the interest rate escalates. By taking a long-term approach, the issuer's estimated interest cost would represent applicable interest rates over the next several quarters. Because the rates will exceed the initial interest rate on the notes, a debt discount should be recognized and amortized over the estimated term of the notes.

Although the resolution of Issue 1 is based on a long-term approach, this consensus does not affect the balance sheet classification of the notes, which depends on the source of repayment. (See discussion in Chapter 4, "Balance Sheet Classification and Related Display Issues.")

SUBSEQUENT DEVELOPMENT

ASC 340-10-S99-2 (SEC Staff Accounting 2.A.6, Question 2 (Debt Issue Costs in Conjunction with a Business Combination)), which was issued in March 1988, states the view of the SEC staff that the Task Force's consensus should be followed in accounting for "bridge financing" that consists of increasing-rate debt.

ASC 932-835 Extractive Activities—Oil and Gas—Interest

AIN-APB-21 (Interest on Receivables and Payables: Accounting Interpretations of APB Opinion No. 21) (ASC 932-835-25-2)

BACKGROUND

ASC 932-835-25-2 (AIN-APB-21) provides implementation guidance for ASC 835-30 (APB-21).

STANDARDS

Question: Under the guidance in ASC 835-30 (APB-21) interest must be imputed for some rights to receive or to pay money on fixed or determinable dates. For example, a pipeline company may make an advance payment to encourage exploration. The intent is for this advance payment to be satisfied by the delivery of future production. However, if future production is not sufficient to discharge the amount of the advance payment, there is an obligation to pay cash to settle the obligation. Does the guidance in ASC 835-30 (APB-21) apply to such advances?

Answer: No. The guidance in ASC 835-30 (APB-21) does *not* apply to amounts that will not be repaid in the future, but rather to amounts that will be applied to the purchase price of property, goods, or services. The advance described above fits this exclusion even though there is an obligation to pay cash if future production is not sufficient to settle the liability.

RELATED CHAPTER IN 2011 *GAAP GUIDE, VOLUME I*

Chapter 25, "Interest on Receivables and Payables"

RELATED CHAPTERS IN 2011 *INTERNATIONAL ACCOUNTING/FINANCIAL REPORTING STANDARDS GUIDE*

Chapter 6, "Borrowing Costs"
Chapter 27, "Property, Plant, and Equipment"

CHAPTER 23
INTERIM FINANCIAL REPORTING

CONTENTS

Overview	23.01
Authoritative Guidance	
ASC 330 Inventory	23.02
EITF Issue 86-13 Recognition of Inventory Market Declines at Interim Reporting Dates	23.02
ASC 740-270 Income Taxes —Interim Reporting	23.03
FTB 79-9 Accounting in Interim Periods for Changes in Income Tax Rates	23.03
Related Chapter in 2011 GAAP Guide, *Volume I*	23.03
Related Chapters in 2011 International Accounting/Financial Reporting Standards Guide	23.03

OVERVIEW

Interim financial reports may be issued quarterly, monthly, or at other intervals, and may include complete financial statements or summarized data. In addition, they usually include the current interim period and a cumulative year-to-date period, or last 12 months to date, with comparative reports on the corresponding periods of the immediately preceding fiscal year.

The following pronouncement, which provides GAAP for interim financial statements, is discussed in the 2011 *GAAP Guide, Volume I*, Chapter 26, "Interim Financial Reporting."

    ASC 270   Interim Financial Reporting (APB-28)

AUTHORITATIVE GUIDANCE

ASC 330 Inventory

EITF Issue 86-13 (Recognition of Inventory Market Declines at Interim ReportingDates) (ASC 330-10-55-2)

OVERVIEW

A company has inventory whose market price has declined below its cost in an interim period. Although economic projections indicate that prices will not recover in the near term, there is considerable uncertainty about the accuracy of such projections.

ACCOUNTING ISSUE

Should a company account for a decline in the market price of its inventory below cost during an interim period if it is uncertain whether the market price will recover in the near term?

EITF CONSENSUS

The EITF reached a consensus that under the provisions of ASC 270 (APB-28), the value of inventory should be reduced to the lower of cost or market during an interim period unless (1) there is strong evidence that market prices will recover before the inventory is sold or that (2) inventory accounted for by the LIFO method will regain its value by year-end. Task Force members noted that unless a decline in market prices is the result of seasonal price fluctuations, the value of the inventory generally should be reduced.

DISCUSSION

One of the then Big Eight firms had raised this Issue in an attempt to clarify the language in ASC 270-20-45-6 (paragraph 14c of APB-28, Interim Financial Reporting) related to the recognition of market declines in interim periods if there is a *reasonable* expectation that prices will recover in the fiscal year. It states that *"[t]emporary* market declines need not be recognized at the interim date since no loss is expected to be incurred in the fiscal year." Their inquiry referred to SEC SAB-59 (Views on Accounting for Noncurrent Marketable Equity Securities), which states that the SEC staff does not believe that the term *other than temporary*, as used by the FASB in FAS-12, which was superseded by the guidance in ASC 320 (FAS-115, Accounting for Certain Investments in Debt and Equity Securities), should be interpreted to mean *permanent impairment* as used elsewhere in accounting practice. The EITF's consensus on this Issue appears to indicate that the Task Force was unwilling to interpret the language in ASC 270 (APB-28) to mean anything other than what it says, and that positive evidence of recovery is necessary to avoid a write-down rather than uncertainty that the decline will be permanent

ASC 740-270 Income Taxes —Interim Reporting

FTB 79-9 (Accounting in Interim Periods for Changes in Income Tax Rates) (ASC 740-270-55-51)

BACKGROUND

Federal tax rates may change, raising questions about how a company with a fiscal year other than the calendar year should account for the change in interim periods.

STANDARDS

Question: How should a company with a fiscal year other than a calendar year account during interim periods for the reduction in the corporate tax rate resulting from the Revenue Act of 1978?

Answer: Under the guidance in ASC 740-270-55-50 (paragraph 24 of FIN-18, Accounting for Income Taxes in Interim Periods), the effects of a change in tax rate should be considered in a revised annual effective tax rate calculation in the same way that the change will be applied to the company's taxable income for the year. The revised annual tax rate would then be applied to pretax income for the year-to-date at the end of the current interim period.

> **OBSERVATION:** While this technical bulletin refers specifically to a reduction in tax rate in 1978, it appears to apply to any change in federal tax rate.

RELATED CHAPTER IN 2011 GAAP GUIDE, VOLUME I

Chapter 26, "Interim Financial Reporting"

RELATED CHAPTERS IN 2011 INTERNATIONAL ACCOUNTING/FINANCIAL REPORTING STANDARDS GUIDE

Chapter 5, "Accounting Policies, Changes in Accounting Estimates, and Errors"

23.04 *Interim Financial Reporting*

Chapter 20, "Income Taxes"
Chapter 22, "Interim Financial Reporting"
Chapter 23, "Inventories"
Chapter 31, "Segment Reporting"

CHAPTER 24
INVENTORY

CONTENTS

Overview	24.01
Authoritative Guidance	
ASC 330 Inventory	24.03
EITF Issue 86-46 Uniform Capitalization Rules for Inventory under the Tax Reform Act of 1986	24.03
ASC 810 Consolidation	24.04
PB-2 Elimination of Profits Resulting from Intercompany Transfers of LIFO Inventories	24.04
ASC 930 Extractive Industries—Mining—Inventory	24.05
EITF Issue 04-6 Accounting for Stripping Costs Incurred during Production in the Mining Industry	24.05
Related Chapter in 2011 GAAP Guide, Volume II	24.07
Related Chapters in 2011 GAAP Guide Volume I	24.07
Related Chapters in 2011 International Accounting/Financial Reporting Standards Guide	24.07

OVERVIEW

An entity's preparation of financial statements requires careful determination of the value of its inventory. Usually, that amount is presented as a current asset in the balance sheet and is a direct determinant of cost of goods sold in the income statement; as such, it has a significant effect on the amount of net income. When the matching principle is applied in determining net income, the valuation of inventories is of primary importance.

The following pronouncements, which provide GAAP for the measurement of inventories, are discussed in the 2011 *GAAP Guide, Volume I*, Chapter 27, "Inventory":

ASC 270 and ASC 740	Interim Financial Reporting (APB-28)
ASC 330	Inventory Pricing (ARB-43, Chapter 4)
ASC 730	Accounting for Research and Development Costs (FAS-2)
ASC 250 and ASC 330	Accounting Changes Related to the Cost of Inventory (FIN-1)

OBSERVATION: See Chapter 28, "Nonmonetary Transactions," for a discussion of EITF Issue 04-13 (Accounting for Purchases and Sales of Inventory with the Same Counterparty).

AUTHORITATIVE GUIDANCE

ASC 330 Inventory

EITF Issue 86-46 (Uniform Capitalization Rules for Inventory under the Tax Reform Act of 1986) (ASC 330-10-55-3 through 55-4)

OVERVIEW

Under the Tax Reform Act of 1986, manufacturers of products and wholesalers and retailers of goods for resale are required to capitalize certain direct costs and a portion of indirect costs related to the inventory produced or acquired for resale. Examples of such costs are excess tax depreciation over depreciation for financial reporting purposes, warehousing costs, insurance premiums, certain personnel costs, and costs related to accounting and data services operations for inventory. Previously, such costs were charged to expense for financial reporting and tax purposes.

ACCOUNTING ISSUES

- Are the types of costs required to be allocated to inventories for tax purposes capitalizable for financial reporting purposes under generally accepted accounting principles?
- If so, would a new costing method be a preferable method for justifying a change in accounting method?

EITF CONSENSUS

The EITF reached a consensus that it may not be preferable or appropriate to capitalize costs for reporting purposes that are capitalizable for tax purposes. The Task Force indicated, however, that some costs capitalized for tax purposes also may qualify to be capitalized for financial reporting purposes, depending on such factors as the nature of the entity's operations and industry practice. An entity should decide whether to capitalize or expense such costs based on an analysis of the individual facts and circumstances.

Discussion

The Issue was brought before the EITF because of concerns about the burden to companies of maintaining separate inventory records for financial and tax reporting purposes. However, as discussed in Chapter 7, "Capitalization and Expense Recognition Concepts," only costs having a future economic benefit to the entity may be capitalized. The Task Force's comment on the possibility that some costs capitalized for tax purposes also may be capitalizable for reporting purposes leaves room for judgment based on the specific circumstances.

ASC 810 Consolidation

PB-2 (Elimination of Profits Resulting from Intercompany Transfers of LIFO Inventories) (ASC 810-10-55-2 through 55-4)

BACKGROUND

AcSEC issued PB-2 as a reminder concerning inventory transfers between or from LIFO pools, either within a company or between subsidiaries or divisions of a reporting entity. A LIFO liquidation or decrement occurs when the number of units (or total base year cost if the dollar-value LIFO method is used) in a LIFO pool is less at the end of the year than at the beginning of the year, causing prior-year costs, rather than current-year costs, to be charged to current-year income.

STANDARDS

According to the guidance in ASC 810 (ARB-51, Consolidated Financial Statements), the purpose of consolidated financial statements is to present the results of operations and the financial position of the parent company and its subsidiaries as if the group were a single company. Intercompany profits on assets remaining within the group should be eliminated in the preparation of consolidated financial statements so that the results of operations and financial position are not affected by inventory transfers within the reporting entity. Inventory transferred between or from LIFO pools may cause LIFO inventory liquidations that could affect the amount of intercompany profit to be eliminated.

Different approaches are used to eliminate such profit in the preparation of consolidated financial statements. The AICPA's Accounting Standards Executive Committee (AcSEC, now known as the AICPA's Financial Reporting Executive Committee) believes that each reporting entity should adopt an approach that, if consistently applied, defers reporting intercompany profits from transfers within a reporting entity until those profits are realized by the reporting entity through sales outside the consolidated group of entities. The approach selected should be one that is suited to the circumstances of the reporting entity.

ASC 930-330 Extractive Activities—Mining—Inventory

EITF Issue 04-6 (Accounting for Stripping Costs Incurred during Production in the Mining Industry) (ASC 930-10-15-2; 930-330-05-1; 25-1)

OVERVIEW

Mining entities remove waste materials from a mine in order to extract ore from the ground. The costs of removing waste materials from a mine are referred to in the mining industry as stripping costs. Those costs may be incurred while a mine is under development, as preproduction stripping costs, and after production has begun, as post-production stripping costs. Mining entities generally capitalize stripping costs during the development stage as a component of a mine's depreciable cost, which includes costs related to building, developing, and constructing the mine. Amortization of costs related to preproduction begins when production begins and continues over the mine's productive life. A mine's production phase is defined in this Issue as the period when production begins and revenue is earned from the sale of minerals, regardless of the level of production. Because of a lack of authoritative literature on the accounting for stripping costs after production has begun, there has been diversity in practice in accounting for those costs. Some entities have been expensing those costs, others have been deferring them, and still others have been capitalizing and amortizing stripping costs during production.

ACCOUNTING ISSUE

How should entities in the mining industry account for stripping costs?

EITF CONSENSUS

The EITF reached a consensus that stripping costs incurred by mining entities involved in finding and removing wasting natural resources, other than oil- and gas-producing entities accounted for under the guidance in ASC 932 (FAS-19, Financial Accounting and Reporting by Oil and Gas Producing Companies), are variable production costs. Those costs should be included in the costs of inventory produced during the period in which the stripping costs were incurred. This consensus does *not* apply to the accounting for stripping costs incurred during a mine's *pre-production phase*.

FASB RATIFICATION

The FASB ratified the EITF's consensus in this Issue at its March 30, 2005, meeting.

SUBSEQUENT DEVELOPMENT

At its meeting on June 15-16, 2005, the EITF reached a consensus to modify the Issue in two ways:

1. Clarify that the term "inventory produced" as used in this Issue means "inventory extracted."
2. In view of the issuance of ASC 250 (FAS-154, Accounting Changes and Error Corrections), a cumulative effect of a change in accounting principle recognized when applying the transition guidance in this Issue should be included in the opening balance of retained earnings rather than in the income statement. Entities that have already adopted the consensus in this Issue and recognized the cumulative effect of a change in accounting principle in the income statement, however, should *not* follow this revised transition guidance.

The FASB ratified this consensus at its June 29, 2005, meeting.

At the March 16, 2006, EITF meeting, a member of the FASB staff reported that Task Force members had been contacted by e-mail regarding proposed editorial changes made by the FASB staff to the definition of the *production phase* in the FASB Accounting Standards Codification™ (ASC), *Glossary* (*EITF Abstracts*, paragraph 4 of Issue 04-6). The EITF did not object to the proposed changes, which are intended to clarify the definition of a mine's *production phase*. At its January 11, 2006 meeting, the FASB ratified the following revised definition in ASC 930-330-25-1 (paragraph 4 of EITF Issue 04-6 in *EITF Abstracts*):

> The production phase of a mine is deemed to have begun when saleable minerals are extracted (produced) *from an ore body*, regardless of the level of production (or revenues). However, the production phase does not commence with the removal of de minimis saleable mineral material that occurs in conjunction with the removal of overburden or waste material for the purpose of obtaining access to an ore body.

AICPA AcSEC Practice Bulletins

RELATED CHAPTER IN 2011 GAAP GUIDE, VOLUME II

Chapter 11, "Consolidated Financial Statements"

RELATED CHAPTERS IN 2011 GAAP GUIDE, VOLUME I

Chapter 7, "Consolidated Financial Statements"
Chapter 27, "Inventory"

RELATED CHAPTERS IN 2011 INTERNATIONAL ACCOUNTING/FINANCIAL REPORTING STANDARDS GUIDE

Chapter 3, "Presentation of Financial Statements"
Chapter 5, "Accounting Policies, Changes in Accounting Estimates, and Errors"
Chapter 6, "Borrowing Costs"
Chapter 7, "Business Combinations"
Chapter 9, "Changing Prices and Hyperinflationary Economies"
Chapter 10, "Consolidated Financial Statements"
Chapter 11, "Construction Contracts"
Chapter 22, "Interim Financial Reporting"

CHAPTER 25
INVESTMENTS IN DEBT AND EQUITY SECURITIES

CONTENTS

Overview		25.02
Authoritative Guidance		
ASC 320 Investments—Debt and Equity Securities		25.03
FSP FAS-115-1 and FAS 124-1	The Meaning of Other-Than-Temporary Impairment and Its Application to Certain Investments	25.03
EITF Issue 96-10	Impact of Certain Transactions on the Held-to-Maturity Classification under FASB Statement No. 115	25.04
EITF Issue 96-11	Accounting for Forward Contracts and Purchased Options to Acquire Securities Covered by FASB Statement No. 115	25.06
Topic D-41	Adjustments in Assets and Liabilities for Holding Gains and Losses as Related to the Implementation of FASB Statement No. 115 (Subtopic 320-10)	25.11
Topic D-51	The Applicability of FASB Statement No. 115 to Desecuritizations of Financial Assets	25.13
FIG-FAS 115	A Guide to Implementation of Statement 115 on Accounting for Certain Investments in Debt and Equity Securities	25.14
SOP 90-3	Definition of the Term *Substantially the Same for Holders of Debt Instruments*, as Used in Certain Audit Guides and a Statement of Position	25.31
ASC 942-320 Financial Services—Depository and Lending—Debt and Equity Securities		25.33
Topic D-39	Questions Related to the Implementation of FASB Statement No. 115	25.33

Authoritative Guidance not Included Separately in the Codification but Incorporated with Other Guidance on the Subject

FSP FAS 115-2 and FAS 124-2	Recognition and Presentation of Other-Than-Temporary Impairments	**25.34**
Related Chapter in 2011 GAAP Guide Volume I		**25.43**
Related Chapters in 2011 International Accounting/Financial Reporting Standards Guide		**25.43**

OVERVIEW

The primary issue in accounting and reporting for debt and equity investments is the appropriate use of market value.

The following pronouncements, which provide GAAP for various types of investments, are discussed in the 2011 *GAAP Guide, Volume I*, Chapter 28, "Investments in Debt and Equity Securities."

ASC 320   Accounting for Certain Investments in Debt and Equity Securities (FAS-115)

ASC 820   Fair Value Measurements (FAS-157)

ASC 825   The Fair Value Option for Financial Assets and Financial Liabilities—Including an Amendment of FASB Statement No. 115 (FAS-159)

ASC 320 (FAS-115, Accounting for Certain Investments in Debt and Equity Securities) addresses accounting and reporting for (*a*) investments in equity securities that have readily determinable fair values and (*b*) all investments in debt securities. It requires that these securities be classified in three categories and accounted for as follows:

Classification	*Accounting Treatment*
Held-to-maturity Debt securities with the intent and ability to hold to maturity	Amortized cost
Trading securities Debt and equity securities bought and held primarily for sale in the near term	Fair value, with unrealized holding gains and losses included in earnings
Available-for-sale Debt and equity securities not classified as held-to-maturity or trading	Fair value, with unrealized holding gains and losses excluded from earnings and reported in other comprehensive income.

AUTHORITATIVE GUIDANCE

ASC 320   Investments—Debt and Equity Securities

FSP FAS-115-1 and FAS-124-1 (The Meaning of Other-Than-Temporary Impairment and Its Application to Certain Investments) (ASC 320-10-15-7; 35-17, 35-20, through 35-30, 35-32A through 35-35A; 35-45-8A through 35-9A; 50-6 through 50-8B; 55-22 through 55-23)

OVERVIEW

In September 2004, the FASB directed the staff to issue proposed FASB Staff Position (FSP) EITF 03-1-a (Implementation Guidance for the Application of Paragraph 16 of EITF Issue No. 03-1) in response to a request from the Emerging Issues Task Force (EITF) for implementation guidance on its consensus in Issue 03-1 (The Meaning of Other-Than-Temporary Impairment and its Application to Certain Investments), which does not provide guidance for investments accounted for under the equity method. Most of the respondents to the proposal asked the EITF to rescind its consensus in Issue 03-1.

This FSP provides guidance on how to determine when an investment is considered impaired, whether the impairment is other than temporary, and how to measure an impairment loss. It also provides guidance on the recognition of other-than-temporary impairment and requires certain disclosures about unrealized losses that have not been recognized as other-than-temporary impairments. As a result of the issuance of this FSP, certain provisions of ASC 320 (FAS-115, Accounting for Certain Investments in Debt and Equity Securities), ASC 958-320 (FAS-124, Accounting for Certain Investments Held by Not-for-Profit Organizations), and ASC 323 (APB-18, The Equity Method of Accounting for Investments in Common Stock) are amended.

SCOPE

The guidance in this FSP applies to investments in:

- Debt and equity securities under the scope of ASC 320 (FAS-115).
  - All equity securities held by insurance companies, in accordance with the guidance in paragraph 127(b) of FAS-115 (not in ASC).
  - An investment should be evaluated for impairment based on its form (e.g., a mutual fund that primarily invests in debt securities should be evaluated for impairment as an equity security).

25.04 *Investments in Debt and Equity Securities*

—Investments that meet the criteria in ASC 815-15-25-1 (paragraph 12 of FAS-133, Accounting for Derivative Instruments and Hedging Activities), which should be bifurcated with the host instrument and the embedded derivative accounted for separately. The guidance in this FSP should be applied to host instruments under the scope of this FSP.

- Debt and equity securities under the scope of ASC 958-320 (FAS-124) held by investors that report a "performance indicator" as defined the AICPA Accounting and Audit Guide, *Health Care Organizations*.
- Equity securities *not* under the scope of FAS-115 or FAS-124 and not accounted for under the equity method in ASC 323 (APB-18) and related interpretations (i.e., cost-method investments).

FASB STAFF POSITION

This FSP affects the guidance in Issue 03-1 as follows:

- Nullifies the application guidance related to the evaluation of whether an impairment is other-than-temporary.
- Carries forward the Issue's guidance related to the determination whether a cost method investment is impaired.
- Carries forward the disclosure requirements for investments in an unrealized loss position for which other-than-temporary impairments have *not* been recognized and for cost method investments.

The FSP supersedes the guidance in Topic D-44 (Recognition of Other-Than-Temporary Impairment upon the Planned Sale of a Security Whose Cost Exceeds Fair Value).

> **OBSERVATION:** The guidance in FSP FAS-115-1 and FSP FAS-124-1 also supersedes the guidance in FSP Issue 03-1-1 (Effective Date of Paragraphs 10–20 of EITF Issue No. 03-1 (The Meaning of Other-Than-Temporary Impairment and Its Application to Certain Investments)).

EITF Issue 96-10 (Impact of Certain Transactions on the Held-to-Maturity Classification under FASB Statement No. 115) (ASC 320-10-25-18)

OVERVIEW

Until the issuance of FAS-125 on June 30, 1996, which was superseded by ASC 860 (FAS-140 as amended by FAS-166), certain transactions, such as wash sales and bond swaps, which involve securities classified as held-to-maturity under the provisions of ASC 320 (FAS-115), were not accounted for as sales, because the transferor intended to reacquire the same or substantially the same securities in the future. Under current guidance, however, sales recognition is required if control of a security has been transferred to another entity, unless a concurrent contract to repurchase the security exists. Wash sales and certain bond swaps that do not involve the issuer are accounted for as sales, therefore, under that pronouncement.

Although ASC 320 (FAS-115) lists changes in circumstances that would result in a change of intent to hold a security to maturity without calling into question the entity's intent to hold other debt securities to maturity, it does not discuss the effect of exchanges not accounted for as sales.

ACCOUNTING ISSUE

Are certain transactions related to held-to-maturity securities that are not accounted for as sales (such as wash sales and bond swaps) inconsistent with the entity's previously stated intent to hold those securities to maturity, and do such transactions therefore call into question the entity's intent to hold other debt securities to maturity?

EITF CONSENSUS

The EITF reached a consensus that if a transaction, such as a wash sale or bond swap, involving held-to-maturity securities is *not accounted for as a sale*, the transaction is not inconsistent with the entity's previously stated intent to hold the security to maturity and, therefore, would *not* call into question the entity's intent to hold other debt securities to maturity.

> **OBSERVATION:** ASC 860-10-40-5 (paragraph 9 of FAS-140), which requires that a wash sale or swap be accounted for as a sale, partially nullifies the guidance in this Issue. Unless there is a concurrent contract to repurchase or redeem the transferred financial assets from the transferee, the transferor does not continue to have effective control over the transferred assets. However, the consensus would apply to other transactions not accounted for as sales under ASC 860 (FAS-140), such as the desecuritization of securities discussed in Topic D-51. This Issue was not reconsidered in ASC 860 (FAS-140), which superseded FAS-125. Additional guidance on wash sales may be found in ASC 860-10-55-57 (paragraph 99 of FAS-140).

The Task Force observed, however, that the entity's intent to hold other debt securities to maturity would be called into question if the entity does not hold to maturity the debt instrument received or retained as a result of the transaction.

DISCUSSION

The Task Force's consensus is based on the view that a transaction that is not accounted for as a sale should not be considered a sale when applying the provisions of ASC 320 (FAS-115). Proponents of this view argued that a sale has not occurred because the entity is in the same economic position as before the wash sale or swap occurred; the risks and benefits of ownership are not transferred when an entity receives substantially the same security as the security transferred.

EITF Issue 96-11 (Accounting for Forward Contracts and Purchased Options to Acquire Securities Covered by FASB Statement No. 115) (ASC 320-10-55-5; 815-10-15-141, 15-142; 25-17; 30-5; 35-5; 50-9)

OVERVIEW

The EITF discussed a transaction in which an entity enters into forward contracts or purchased options to acquire securities that will be accounted for under ASC 320 (FAS-115). (FAS-115 does *not* cover the accounting for forward contracts or options on debt securities.) The forward contracts, purchased options, and underlying securities are denominated in the same currency as the entity's functional currency. A period of time elapses between the date the forward contracts are entered into or the options are purchased and the acquisition date of the underlying securities. This Issue only applies to transactions that involve physical settlement of the securities.

ACCOUNTING ISSUE

How should an entity account for forward contracts and purchased options having no intrinsic value at acquisition that are entered into to purchase securities that will be accounted for under ASC 320 (FAS-115) during the time the forward contract or option is outstanding and when the securities are acquired?

EITF CONSENSUS

The EITF reached a consensus that an entity entering into forward contracts and purchased options with no intrinsic value at acquisition in order to acquire securities that will be accounted for under ASC 320 (FAS-115) should designate the forward contracts or options at inception as held-to-maturity, available-for-sale, or trading securities and account for them based on the guidance for the applicable category in ASC 320 (FAS-115).

OBSERVATION: The guidance in the above paragraph has been partially nullified by the guidance in ASC 815 (FAS-133, Accounting for Derivative Instruments and Hedging Activities). See the section on the "Effect of FAS-133" below for additional information.

The Task Force observed that an entity's accounting policy for the premium paid to acquire an option classified as held-to-maturity or available-for-sale should be disclosed.

After inception, the consensus should be applied to the three categories of securities as follows:

1. **Held-to-maturity**
   a. Recognize *no* changes in the fair value of the forward contract or purchased option; recognize a loss in earnings, however, if a decline in the fair value of the underlying securities is other than temporary.
   b. Record debt securities purchased under a forward contract at the forward contract price on the settlement date.
   c. Record debt securities purchased by exercising an option at the option strike price plus the option premium's remaining carrying amount, if any.
   d. Record a debt security purchased in the market at its market price plus the option premium's remaining carrying amount, if any, if the option to purchase the security expired worthless.

If a purchased option expires worthless, an entity's intent to hold other debt securities to maturity would be called into question if the entity does not purchase the same securities in the market. Further, if the entity does not take delivery under a forward contract, its intent would also be questionable.

2. **Available-for-sale**
   a. Recognize changes in the fair value of a forward contract or purchased option as part of the ASC 320 (FAS-115) separate component of shareholders' equity as they occur; recognize a loss in earnings, however, if a decline in the fair value of the underlying securities is other than temporary.
   b. Record securities purchased under a forward contract at their fair values on the settlement date.
   c. Record securities purchased by exercising an option at the option strike price plus the fair value of the option at the exercise date.
   d. Record the purchase of the same security in the market at its market price plus the option premium's remaining carrying amount, if any, if the option to purchase a security expired worthless.

3. **Trading**

   a. Recognize changes in the fair value of a forward contract or purchased option in earnings as they occur.

   b. Record securities purchased under a forward contract or by exercising an option at the fair value of the securities at the settlement date.

   OBSERVATION: Because ASC 220 (FAS-130, Reporting Comprehensive Income) requires that unrealized gains and losses on available-for-sale securities be reported in other comprehensive income, changes in the fair value of forward contracts or purchased options would be reported in that manner. Accumulated changes in value continue to be reported in a separate component of equity.

EFFECT OF ASC 815 (FAS-133)

The forward contracts and purchased options discussed in this Issue meet the definition of a derivative in ASC 815 (FAS-133) if the assets related to the underlying to the derivatives are convertible to cash. Contracts that permit net settlement would be accounted for in the same manner. Forward contracts and purchased options that are derivatives should be recognized as assets or liabilities and accounted for at fair value in accordance with the guidance in ASC 815 (FAS-133). However, the existing consensus continues to apply to forward contracts and purchased options that do not meet the definition of a derivative in ASC 815 FAS-133) and involve the acquisition of securities accounted for under the provisions of ASC FAS-115).

DISCUSSION

The Task Force's consensus follows the *trade date accounting approach* used in ASC 320 (FAS-115), under which the effect of a transaction is recognized when it occurs. That is, unrealized gains or losses are recognized when incurred rather than when the security is recorded—as would be the case under a settlement approach.

Illustration of Accounting for Forward Contracts and Purchased Options to Acquire Securities Covered by FAS-115

Example 1

On December 1, 20X5, Rolling Ridge Realty Corp., a company with a 12/31 year-end, entered into a forward purchase contract to purchase a debt security on February 28, 20X6, at $5,000. The forward purchase contract has no cost. Assume that on December 31, 20X5, the fair value of the debt security declined to $4,500, but the decline is *not* considered to be other than temporary. The fair value of the debt security was $4,000 on the settlement date. The company should account for the transaction as follows if the debt security is classified as (a) held-to-maturity, (b) available-for-sale, or (c) trading:

(a) Held-to-maturity

December 1, 20X5

A forward contract having no cost is not recognized.

December 31, 20X5

A change in the fair value of the forward contract is not recognized.

February 29, 20X6

The debt security is recognized at the forward contract price on the settlement date.

Debt security	$5,000	
Payable		$5,000

(b) Available-for-sale

December 1, 20X5

A forward contract having no cost is not recognized.

December 31, 20X5

A decline in the fair value of the forward contract is recognized in a separate component of equity and also is reported in comprehensive income in the financial statements.

Equity (separate component)	$500	
Payable		$500

February 29, 20X6

A debt security purchased under a forward contract is recognized at the fair value of the underlying security at the settlement date.

Debt security	$4,000	
Loss on forward contract	1,000	
Payable		$4,500
Equity (separate component)		500

(c) Trading

December 1, 20X5

A forward contract having no cost is not recognized.

December 31, 20X5

A decline in the fair value of the forward contract is recognized in earnings.

Loss on forward contract	$500	
Payable		$500

February 29, 20X6

A debt security purchased under a forward contract is recognized at the fair value of the security on the settlement date.

Debt security	$4,000	
Loss on forward contract	500	
Payable		$4,500

Example 2

On December 1, 20X5, Rolling Ridge Realty Corp., a company with a 12/31 year-end, purchases an option at a $50 premium to purchase a debt security at $5,000. The option, which has no intrinsic value at acquisition, expires on February 29, 20X6. Assume that the price of the debt security and the fair value of the option are as follows: (a) $5,100 and $100, respectively, on December 31, 20X5, and (b) $5,200 and $200, respectively, on February 29, 20X6, the settlement date.

The company should account for the transaction as follows if the debt security is classified as (a) held-to-maturity, (b) available-for-sale, or (c) trading:

(a) Held-to-maturity

December 1, 20X5

The cost of the option is recognized as an asset.

Option	$50	
Cash		$50

December 31, 20X5

A change in the fair value of the option is not recognized.

February 29, 20X6

On the settlement date, the debt security is recognized at the strike price plus the cost of the option.

Debt security	$5,050	
Payable		$5,000
Option		50

(b) Available-for-sale

December 1, 20X5

The cost of the option is recognized as an asset.

Option	$50	
Cash		$50

December 31, 20X5

An unrealized increase in the fair value of the option is recognized in a separate component of equity and also is reported in comprehensive income in the financial statements.

Option	$50	
Equity (separate component)		$50

February 29, 20X6

On settlement, the debt security is recognized at the option strike price plus the fair value of the option on the exercise date.

Debt security	$5,200	
Equity (separate component)	50	
Payable		$5,000
Option		100
Gain on option		150

(c) Trading

December 1, 20X5

The option is recognized as an asset.

Option	$50	
Cash		$50

December 31, 20X5

An increase in the fair value of the option is recognized in earnings.

Option	$50	
Gain on option		$50

February 29, 20X6

On settlement, the debt security is recognized at its fair value.

Debt security	$5,200	
Payable		$5,000
Option		100
Gain on option		100

Topic D-41 (Adjustments in Assets and Liabilities for Holding Gains and Losses as Related to the Implementation of FASB Statement No. 115 (Subtopic 320-10)) (ASC 320-10-S35-1; S99-2)

The SEC staff has been asked about the adjustment of certain assets and liabilities, such as noncontrolling interests, certain life insurance policyholder liabilities, deferred acquisition costs, amortized using the gross-profits method, or and intangible assets acquired in business combination with a corresponding adjustment to other comprehensive income when unrealized holding gains and losses from securities held as available-for-sale are recognized in comprehensive income. In other words, whether an entity should adjust the carrying amounts of those assets and liabilities to the amount at which they would have been reported if those unrealized gains and losses had been realized.

The SEC observer analogized to ASC 740-20-45-11 (paragraph 36b of FAS-109), which discusses the classification of deferred tax effects of unrealized holding gains and losses reported in comprehensive income. Under that guidance, entities are required to report the tax effects of those gains and losses as charges or credits to other comprehensive income. In other words, by recognizing unrealized holding gains and losses in equity, temporary differences may be created. Deferred differences would be recognized for those temporary differences and their effect would be reported in accumulated other comprehensive income with the related unrealized holding gains and losses. Consequently, deferred tax assets and liabilities must be recognized for temporary differences related to unrealized holding gains and losses, but their corresponding charges or credits are reported in other comprehensive income as charges or credits to income in the income statement.

By analogy to ASC 740-20-45-11 (paragraph 36b of FAS-109), the SEC staff believes that registrants should adjust certain assets and liabilities, such as noncontrolling interests, certain life insurance policyholder liabilities, deferred acquisition costs amortized using the gross-profits method, and intangible assets related to the acquisition of insurance contracts in a business combination that are amortized using the gross-profits method for unrealized holding gains or losses from securities classified as available-for-sale if such adjustments would have been made had the gains or losses actually been realized. Corresponding credits or charges should be made to other comprehensive income. Assets should be adjusted at subsequent balance sheet dates through valuation allowances.

Liabilities, such as certain policyholder liabilities should be adjusted if an insurance policy requires the holder to be charged or credited for a portion or all of the realized gains or losses of specific securities classified as available-for-sale. In addition, assets that are amortized using the gross-profits method, such as deferred acquisition costs accounted for under the guidance in ASC 944-30-35-4 (paragraph 22 of FAS-97) and certain intangible assets as a result of insurance contracts acquired in a business combination should be adjusted to show the effects that would have been recognized if unrealized gains or losses had actually been realized. However, capitalized acquisition costs related to such insurance contracts under the scope of ASC 944-30-35-4 (paragraph 22 of FAS-97) should not be adjusted for unrealized gains or losses unless there would have been a "premium deficiency" if the gain or loss had been realized.

The guidance in this SEC staff announcement should not affect reported net income.

Topic D-51 (The Applicability of FASB Statement No. 115 to Desecuritizations of Financial Assets) (ASC 320-10-25-18; 860-10-55-34, 55-74)

The FASB staff made the following announcements about the applicability of ASC 320 (FAS-115) to the accounting for the desecuritization of financial assets: the process by which securities are broken down into their underlying loans or other financial assets.

- The FASB staff addressed the accounting for desecuritizations by analogizing to ASC 860-10-40-5 (paragraph 9 of FAS-140), which addressed the accounting for the securitization of financial assets. The paragraph states that a transfer of financial assets over which the transferor surrenders control should be accounted for as a sale if consideration (other than a beneficial interest in the transferred assets) has been received. (In contrast, sales accounting is not appropriate for a transaction transferring securities or a beneficial interest in a securitized pool of financial assets in which the only consideration received by the transferor is the financial assets underlying the securities or the beneficial interest in the transferred securities.) The FASB agreed that this approach should be used for desecuritizations in general.

- The FASB staff believes that the guidance in EITF Issue 96-10 on the effect of the held-to-maturity classification of wash sales and bond swaps also should apply to desecuritizations that are not accounted for as sales. Issue 96-10 states that an entity's intent to hold to maturity other debt securities under FAS-115 is not called into question if the entity holds to maturity securities received or retained in a wash sale or bond swap transaction not accounted for as a sale. Similarly, the FASB staff believes that an entity's intent to hold other debt securities to maturity should not be called into question if an entity that transfers beneficial interests classified as held-to-maturity in a desecuritization transaction not accounted for as a sale holds to maturity the financial assets received or retained in the desecuritization.

This announcement applies *prospectively* to desecuritizations entered into after July 18, 1996.

> **OBSERVATION:** The provisions of paragraph 9 of FAS-125 have been carried forward to ASC 860-10-40-5 (FAS-140) unchanged.

FIG FAS-115 (A Guide to Implementation of Statement 115 on Accounting for Certain Investments in Debt and Equity Securities) (ASC 320-10-15-2, 15-5; 25-1, 25-5, 25 through 25-8, 25-10, 25-12 through 25-13, 25- 16 through 18; 30-3 through 30-4; 35-6 through 35-9, 35-13, 35-15 through 35-16, 35-18, 35-32 through 35-33; 40-1 through 45-7, 45-12; 50-12 through 50-14; 55-2 through 55-6, 55-8 through 55-9, 55-24 through 55-25; 323-30-60-2; 958-320-15-4, 15-6; 55-2 through 55-3, 60-1)

BACKGROUND

FIG FAS-115, reported on in this section, includes responses to 60 specific questions regarding the application of ASC 320 (FAS-115).

STANDARDS

Scope

Question 1: Does ASC 320 (FAS-115) apply to a loan that has been insured, such as a loan insured by the Federal Housing Administration, or to a conforming mortgage loan?

Answer: No. ASC 320 (FAS-115) applies only to debt securities, including debt instruments that have been securitized. A loan is not a debt security until it has been securitized.

Question 2: For a loan that was restructured in a troubled debt restructuring involving a modification of terms, does ASC 320 (FAS-115) apply to the accounting by the creditor (i.e., investor) if the restructured loan meets the definition of a *security* in ASC 320 (FAS-115)?

Answer: Yes. ASC 320 (FAS-115) applies to all debt securities. See FAS-125 (Accounting for Transfers and Servicing of Financial Assets and Extinguishments of Liabilities); FTB 94-1 (Application of Statement 115 to Debt Securities Restructured in a Troubled Debt Restructuring); and EITF Issue 94-8 (Accounting for Conversion of a Loan into a Debt Security in a Debt Restructuring) for further guidance on this general topic.

Question 3: Are options on securities covered by ASC 320 (FAS-115)?

Answer: In some cases. An investment in an option on an equity interest is covered by ASC 320 (FAS-115) if the option has a fair value that is "currently available on a securities exchange." An equity interest includes any security that gives the holder the right to acquire (e.g., warrants, rights, calls) or to sell (e.g., puts) an ownership interest in an enterprise at a fixed or determinable price. ASC 320 (FAS-115) does not cover written options, cash-settled options on equity securities, options on equity-based indexes, or options on debt securities.

Question 4: What accounting literature addresses the accounting for equity securities that do not have readily determinable fair values?

Answer: ASC 323 (APB-18, The Equity Method of Accounting for Investments in Common Stock) provides guidance in accounting for equity securities that do not have readily determinable fair values. If the investment does not qualify for treatment under the equity method (i.e., typically less than a 20% ownership stake), the investment is accounted for using the cost method. Investments accounted for using the cost method are to be adjusted to reflect other-than temporary declines in fair value. [There is an exception to this general requirement for investments made by insurance companies—see ASC 944 (FAS-60, Accounting and Reporting by Insurance Enterprises)]. There is currently no authoritative guidance as to the accounting for options and warrants in the absence of a readily determinable fair value.

Question 5: An entity invests in a limited partnership interest (or a venture capital company) that meets the definition of an *equity security* but does not have a readily determinable fair value. That is, it does not have a fair value per unit that is "currently available on a securities exchange" under paragraph 3a or a "fair value per share (unit) [that] is determined and published and is the basis for current transactions" under paragraph 3c. However, substantially all of the partnership's assets consist of investments in debt securities or equity securities that have readily determinable fair values. Is it appropriate to "look through" the form of an investment to determine whether ASC 320 (FAS-115) applies?

Answer: No, an entity should not "look through" its investment to the nature of the securities held by an investee. Therefore, given the lack of a readily determinable market value in this case, ASC 320 (FAS-115) would not apply. Guidance in accounting for limited partnership investments can be found in EITF Topic D-46 (Accounting for Limited Partnership Investments).

Securities Classified as Held-to-Maturity

Question 6: Does ASC 320 (FAS-115) apply to certificates of deposit (CDs) or guaranteed investment contracts (GICs)?

Answer: It depends on whether the CD or GIC meets the definition of a *security*. The definition of a *security* in ASC 320 (FAS-115) was modeled after the Uniform Commercial Code definition. Most CDs and GICs would not be classified as securities under this definition; however, certain jumbo CDs and GICs might qualify as securities.

Question 7: Are short sales of securities (sales of securities that the seller does not own at the time of the sale) covered by ASC 320 (FAS-115)?

Answer: No. A short sale gives rise to an obligation to deliver securities. Short sales are not investments and therefore do not fall under the ASC 320 (FAS-115) purview. Various AICPA Industry Audit Guides require obligations due to short sales to be periodically adjusted to market value. Changes in the underlying obligation are reflected in earnings as they occur.

Question 8: If, subsequent to the purchase of equity securities, an investor enters into an arrangement that limits its ability to sell the securities, would the shares be considered "restricted" under footnote 2 to paragraph 3?

Answer: No. Restrictions on the sale of stock, as contemplated by ASC 320 (FAS-115), refer to governmental or contractual restrictions. Presumably these types of restrictions would exist at the time the security was purchased.

Question 9: Does ASC 320 (FAS-115) apply to preferred stock that is convertible into marketable common stock?

Answer: If the convertible preferred stock is redeemable (either on a fixed date or at the option of the holder), it would be classified as a debt security. Therefore, ASC 320 (FAS-115) would apply even if the preferred stock did not have a readily determinable fair value. A convertible preferred stock that is not redeemable would be subject to the provisions of ASC 320 (FAS-115) only if the preferred stock (now treated as an equity security) has a readily determinable fair value.

Question 10: Does ASC 320 (FAS-115) apply to financial statements issued by a trust?

Answer: It depends. ASC 320 (FAS-115) applies if the trust does not report all of its investments at fair value. Some trusts record all investments at fair or market value, with any resulting changes reflected in income or in the change in net assets. ASC 320 (FAS-115) does not apply in such cases.

Question 11: Paragraph 6 (ASC 320-20-35-5) states, "At each reporting date, the appropriateness of the [security's] classification shall be reassessed." If paragraph 6 (ASC 320-20-35-5) requires an enterprise to reassess its classification of securities, why do transfers or sales of held-to-maturity securities for reasons other than those specified in paragraphs 8 and 11 (ASC 320-10-25-6, 25-9, 25-14) call into question ("taint") an enterprise's intent to hold other debt securities to maturity in the future?

Answer: The point of paragraph 6 (ASC 320-20-35-5) is primarily to require a periodic evaluation of an entity's ability to hold a security to maturity. An enterprise's intent to hold a security to maturity should not change; however, the ability of the enterprise to hold the security to maturity may change. Also, while an entity may initially classify a debt security as available-for-sale, subsequent developments may indicate that the entity has the ability to hold the securities to maturity. Assuming management intends to hold the debt securities to maturity, the investment would be reclassified from the available-for-sale portfolio to the held-to-maturity portfolio.

Question 12: What are the consequences of a sale or transfer of held-to-maturity securities for a reason other than those specified in ASC 320-10-25-6, 25-9, and 25-14 (paragraphs 8 and 11 of FAS-115)? In other words, what does it mean to "call into question [the entity's] intent to hold other debt securities to maturity in the future"?

Answer: A sale or transfer of held-to-maturity securities for a reason other than those specified in ASC 320-10-25-6, 25-9, and 25-14 (paragraphs 8 and 11 of FAS-115) calls into question the appropriateness of continuing to classify any debt securities as held-to-maturity. If the sale represents a material contradiction of the entity's stated intent to hold securities to maturity, any remaining securities classified as held-to-maturity would need to be reclassified as available-for-sale. Also, if a pattern of sales of held-to-maturity securities has occurred, any remaining securities classified as held-to-maturity would need to be reclassified. The reclassification would occur in the reporting period in which the sale occurred.

Question 13: If a sale or transfer of a security classified as held-to-maturity occurs for a reason other than those specified in ASC 320-10-25-6, 25-9, and 25-14 (paragraphs 8 and 11 of FAS-115), does the sale or transfer call into question ("taint") the enterprise's intent about only the same type of securities (e.g., municipal bonds) that were sold or transferred, or about all securities that remain in the held-to-maturity category?

Answer: All securities that remain in the held-to-maturity category would be tainted.

Question 14: If held-to-maturity securities are reclassified to available-for-sale because sales occurred for reasons other than those specified in ASC 320-10-25-6, 25-9, and 25-14 (paragraphs 8 and 11 of FAS-115), what amount of time must pass before the enterprise can again classify securities as held-to-maturity?

Answer: This is a matter of judgment. The key issue is whether circumstances have changed sufficiently for management to assert with a greater degree of credibility that it has the intent and ability to hold the debt securities to maturity.

> **PRACTICE POINTER:** No specific guidance is provided on the length of time that must pass before an enterprise can again

classify securities as held-to-maturity when it had previously sold held-to-maturity securities for reasons other than those specified in ASC 320-10-25-6, 25-9, and 25-14 (paragraphs 8 and 11 of FAS-115)). At a minimum, the reasons why management previously sold held-to-maturity securities must have changed. For example, if management previously sold held-to-maturity securities due to a cash shortage brought about by the enterprise's deteriorating financial condition, the financial condition and cash position of the enterprise must have substantially improved. Or, if held-to-maturity securities were sold in the past due to a shortage of capital, the enterprise must have obtained or have ready access to the capital it is likely to need in the future.

In addition, it would seem reasonable for at least one year to pass before an enterprise could again classify securities as held-to-maturity when it had previously sold held-to-maturity securities for reasons other than those specified in ASC 320-10-25-6, 25-9, and 25-14 (paragraphs 8 and 11 of FAS-115). Finally, a change in top management—particularly financial management—may allow management to credibly assert that it has the intent to hold debt securities to maturity. The ability of the entity to hold such securities to maturity even after new management is hired would still need to be assessed.

Question 15: Is it consistent with ASC 320 (FAS-115) to have a documented policy to initially classify all debt securities as held-to-maturity but then automatically transfer every security to available-for-sale when it reaches a predetermined point before maturity (e.g., every held-to-maturity security will be transferred to available-for-sale 24 months before its stated maturity) so that an entity has the flexibility to sell securities?

Answer: No. Such a policy would suggest that the entity does not have the intent and ability to hold the security to maturity.

Question 16: May securities classified as held-to-maturity be pledged as collateral?

Answer: Yes. However, the entity must believe that it will be able to satisfy the liability and thereby recover unrestricted access to the debt security that is serving as collateral for the borrowing. However, if sale accounting per ASC 860 (FAS-140, Accounting for Transfers and Servicing of Financial Assets and Extinguishments of Liabilities) is applied, the securities pledged may not be treated as held-to-maturity.

Question 17: May held-to-maturity securities be subject to a repurchase agreement (or a securities lending agreement)?

Answer: Yes, if the repurchase agreement is accounted for as a secured borrowing. The entity must intend and expect to repay the borrowing and thereby recover unrestricted access to the debt security that is serving as collateral for the borrowing.

Question 18: May convertible debt securities be classified as held-to-maturity?

Answer: Although such treatment is not specifically prohibited, classifying convertible debt securities as held-to-maturity generally would be inappropriate. Convertible debt securities generally carry a lower interest rate than standard debt securities. However, the holder of a debt security stands to profit from the conversion feature if the common stock of the entity issuing the convertible security rises in value. It is implausible to suggest that an entity would not avail itself of such a profit opportunity because it characterized securities as held-to-maturity. If an entity exercises a conversion feature on a security being treated as held-to-maturity, it will call into question the appropriateness of classifying any other securities as held-to-maturity.

Question 19: May a callable debt security be classified as held-to-maturity?

Answer: Yes. The debt instrument's maturity date is viewed as being accelerated if an issuer exercises its call provision. The issuer's exercise of a call feature in no way invalidates the holder's treatment of the security as held-to-maturity. However, per ASC 860 (FAS-140, Accounting for Transfers and Servicing of Financial Assets and Extinguishments of Liabilities), some callable debt securities may not qualify for treatment as held-to-maturity securities. More specifically, this limitation applies to a callable debt security purchased at a significant premium if that security can be prepaid or otherwise settled in such a way that the holder would not recover its full investment.

Question 20: May a puttable debt security be classified as held-to-maturity?

Answer: Yes, if the entity has the intent and ability to hold the puttable debt security to maturity. If the entity exercises the put feature, it will call into question the appropriateness of classifying any other debt securities as held-to-maturity. In addition, some puttable debt securities may not qualify for held-to-maturity treatment per ASC 860-20-35-2 (paragraph 14 of FAS-140, Accounting for Transfers and Servicing of Financial Assets and Extinguishments of Liabilities).

Question 21: The Federal Financial Institutions Examination Council (FFIEC) Policy Statement, "Supervisory Policy Statement on Securities Activities," issued in December 1991 and adopted by the respective regulators, identifies criteria for determining when a mortgage derivative product should be considered a "high-risk mortgage security." In certain situations, regulators can direct institutions to sell high-risk mortgage securities. If a mortgage derivative product (held by a regulated institution) is not a high-risk mortgage security at purchase but could later become a high-risk mortgage security before maturity due to a change in market interest rates and the related change in the security's prepayment risk, can it be classified at acquisition as a held-to-maturity security under ASC 320 (FAS-115)?

Answer: The entity should consider the divestiture policy of its particular regulator in deciding whether it can support classifying this type of debt instrument as held-to-maturity. Additional guidance is provided in EITF Topic D-39 (Questions Related to the Implementation of ASC 320 (FAS-115)).

Question 22: May a mortgage-backed interest-only certificate be classified as held-to-maturity?

Answer: No. ASC 860 (FAS-140, Accounting for Transfers and Servicing of Financial Assets and Extinguishments of Liabilities) amends ASC 320 (FAS-115) to prohibit held-to-maturity accounting for interest-only strips.

Question 23: If an enterprise holds a debt security classified as held-to-maturity, and that security is downgraded by a rating agency, would a sale or transfer of that security call into question the entity's intent to hold other debt securities to maturity in the future?

Answer: No. A downgrade by a rating agency is an example of a significant deterioration in the issuer's creditworthiness. A sale or transfer that results from such a deterioration does not "taint" the remaining held-to-maturity portfolio (see ASC 320-10-25-6 (FAS-115, paragraph 8a)).

Question 24: What constitutes a "major" business combination or a "major" disposition under ASC 320-10-25-6 (paragraph 8c of FAS-115)?

Answer: ASC 320-10-25-6 (paragraph 8c of FAS-115) permits the sale or transfer of held-to-maturity securities as part of a "major" business combination or "major" disposition if necessary to maintain the enterprise's existing interest rate risk position or credit risk policy. However, ASC 320 (FAS-115) does not define what constitutes a "major" business combination or disposition. The Statement does state that the sale of a component of an entity qualifies as a major disposition. The purchase or sale of a large pool of financial assets or liabilities would not constitute a major business combination or disposition. In addition, the sale of held-to-maturity securities to fund a business combination is not permitted.

Question 25: Is it consistent with ASC 320 (FAS-115) to reassess the classification of held-to-maturity securities concurrent with or shortly after a major business combination accounted for as a purchase?

Answer: Yes, provided that a sale or transfer of held-to-maturity securities is necessary to maintain the enterprise's existing interest rate risk position or credit risk policy. Some of the acquiring enterprise's held-to-maturity securities may need to be transferred or sold because of the nature of the liabilities assumed.

Question 26: May securities classified as held-to-maturity be sold under the exception provided in ASC 320-10-25-6 (paragraph 8c of FAS-115) in anticipation of or otherwise prior to a major business combination or disposition without calling into question the enterprise's intent to hold other debt securities to maturity in the future?

Answer: No. Any such transfers or sales should occur at the same time as or after the business combination or disposition.

Question 27: ASC 320-10-25-12 (paragraph 74 of FAS-115) states that "necessary transfers or sales should occur concurrent with or shortly after the business combination or disposition." How long is *shortly*?

Answer: ASC 320 (FAS-115) does not define *shortly*. However, as time elapses it becomes increasingly difficult to justify that any sale or transfer of held-to-maturity securities was necessitated by the combination or disposition, and not by other events and circumstances.

Question 28: If a regulator directs a particular institution (rather than all institutions supervised by that regulator) to sell or transfer held-to-maturity securities (e.g., to increase liquid assets), are those sales or transfers consistent with ASC 320-10-25-6 (paragraph 8d of FAS-115)?

Answer: No. The exception provided in ASC 320-10-25-6 (paragraph 8d of FAS-115) pertains only to a change in regulations affecting all entities affected by the legislation or regulator. However, this type of sale does not necessarily "taint" the remainder of the held-to-maturity portfolio. A forced sale by a regulator may qualify as an event that is isolated, nonrecurring, and unusual, and that could not have been reasonably anticipated (see ASC 320-10-25-6 (FAS-115, paragraph 8 and Question 32).

Question 29: Is a sale of held-to-maturity securities in response to an unsolicited tender offer from the issuer consistent with ASC 320-10-25-6 (paragraph 8 of FAS-115)?

Answer: No. Such a sale does not fall under one of the specific exceptions outlined in ASC 320-10-25-6 (paragraphs 8a through 8f of FAS-115) It also does not qualify as an event that is isolated, nonrecurring, and unusual, and that could not have been reasonably anticipated. Therefore, if held-to-maturity securities are sold in response to the tender offer, the remaining held-to-maturity portfolio is tainted.

Question 30: Is it consistent with ASC 320 (FAS-115) for an insurance company or other regulated enterprise to classify securities as held-to-maturity and also indicate to regulators that those securities could be sold to meet liquidity needs in a defined interest rate scenario whose likelihood of occurrence is reasonably possible but not probable?

Answer: No. Stating that held-to-maturity securities could be sold if a particular interest-rate environment developed is inconsistent with management's intent and ability to hold these securities to maturity.

Question 31: Is it ever appropriate to apply the exceptions in paragraphs 8a through 8f (ASC 320-10-25-6) to situations that are similar, but not the same?

Answer: No. The exceptions outlined in ASC 320-10-25-6 (paragraphs 8a through 8f of FAS-115) are quite specific by design. They should not be extended to similar fact patterns. Paragraph 8 of FAS-115 (ASC 320-10-25-6) does permit a general exception to the requirement for holding held-to-maturity securities to maturity. That is, held-to-maturity securities can be sold in response to an event that is isolated, nonrecurring, and unusual, and that could not have been reasonably anticipated.

Question 32: What constitutes an event that is "isolated, nonrecurring, and unusual...that could not have been reasonably anticipated" as described in ASC 320-10-25-6 (paragraph 8 of FAS-115)?

Answer: This general exception provision involves four elements. Three of these elements are as follows: (1) Was the event isolated? (2) Was the event nonrecurring? (3) Was the event unusual? The fourth element pertains to the extent that the event could have been reasonably anticipated. Very few events will meet all four of these conditions. In general, the types of events that would qualify are extremely remote disaster scenarios. For example, a run on a bank or on an insurance company would qualify.

Question 33: Paragraph 11b of FAS-115 (ASC 320-10-25-14) allows a sale of a held-to-maturity security to be considered a maturity when the enterprise has collected a substantial portion (at least 85%) of the principal outstanding at acquisition due to scheduled payments on a debt security payable in equal installments (that comprise both principal and interest) over its term. What types of securities would typically qualify or not qualify for this exception?

Answer: This exception applies to (*a*) debt securities that are payable in equal installments, comprising both principal and interest, and (*b*) variable rate debt securities that would be payable in equal installments if there were no change in interest rates. It does not apply to debt securities for which the principal payment is level and the interest amount is based on the outstanding principal balance.

Securities Classified as Trading and as Available-for-Sale

Question 34: How often must sales occur for an activity to be considered "trading"?

Answer: ASC 320 (FAS-115) describes trading securities as securities that will be held for only a short period of time or that will be sold in the near term. Securities that management intends to hold for only hours or days must be classified as trading securities. However, securities that will be held for a longer period of time are not precluded from being classified as trading securities.

Question 35: If an enterprise acquires a security without intending to sell it in the near term, may the enterprise classify the security in the trading category?

Answer: Yes. In general, securities classified as trading will be held for a short period of time or will be sold in the near term. This general requirement is not an absolute. However, the decision to classify a security as trading is to be made at the time the security is acquired. Transfers of securities into or out of the trading category should be rare.

Question 36: If an enterprise decides to sell a security that has been classified as available-for-sale, should the security be transferred to trading?

Answer: No. Securities that will mature within one year or that management intends to sell within one year should not automatically be transferred into the trading category. Similarly, if an entity decides to sell a held-to-maturity security (in response to one of the conditions outlined in ASC 320-10-25-6 (paragraph 8 of FAS-115), such security should not be reclassified as available-for-sale or trading. Refer to ASC 320-10-50-9 and 50-10 (paragraphs 21 and 22 of FAS-115) for mandated disclosures relating to the sale.

Question 37: What should be the initial carrying amount under ASC 320 (FAS-115) of a previously nonmarketable equity security that becomes marketable (i.e., due to a change in circumstances, it now has a fair value that is readily determinable)?

Answer: In general, the basis for applying the provisions of ASC 320 (FAS-115) should be the security's cost. However, if the change in marketability provides evidence that an other-than-temporary impairment has occurred, the impairment loss should be recognized and the writedown recorded prior to applying ASC 320 (FAS-115). (This treatment assumes that the nonmarketable security had not been accounted for using the equity method.)

Question 38: What should be the initial carrying amount under ASC 320 (FAS-115) of a marketable equity security that should no longer be accounted for under the equity method (e.g., due to a decrease in the level of ownership)?

25.24 *Investments in Debt and Equity Securities*

Answer: The initial carrying amount of the security should be the previous carrying amount of the investment.

Changes in Fair Value—Reporting

Question 39: How is a sale of an available-for-sale security recorded?

Answer: In general, cash or a receivable account should be debited for the amount of the proceeds, and the investment account should be credited for its fair value (i.e., its selling price). Any unrealized gain or loss relating to the investment being sold (recorded in comprehensive income) is reversed into earnings. Deferred tax accounts that relate to any unrealized gain or loss are also adjusted. This general procedure needs to be modified if the entity has not yet recorded all changes in the value of the security being sold (some entities record these changes only at reporting dates), or if a write-down for an other-than-temporary impairment has already been recorded.

Illustration of Sale of Available-for-Sale Securities

Pluto Enterprises purchases 1000 shares of Venus, Inc., common stock for $10 per share on April 1, 20X5. Pluto accounts for these securities as available-for-sale securities. The fair value of Venus' stock at December 31, 20X5, is $12 per share. Therefore, in Pluto's December 31, 20X5, balance sheet, its investment in the Venus securities would be recorded at $12,000. A $2,000 unrealized gain would be recorded in the stockholders' equity section of Pluto. Pluto's effective tax rate is 34%. Pluto sells these shares on June 30, 20X6, at $7 per share. Pluto adjusts the carrying value of securities only at year-end. The journal entry to record the sale would be as follows:

Cash (1,000 shares × $7 per share)	$7,000	
Unrealized gain	2,000	
Deferred tax liability ($2000 × 34%)	680	
Loss on sale of securities	3,000	
Available-for-sale securities		$12,000
Income tax expense		680

Question 40: How is a sale of a trading security recorded?

Answer: For trading securities, changes in fair value are recorded as they occur. Therefore, in most cases, the entry is to debit cash (or a receivables account) for the proceeds received, and to credit the trading securities account for the fair value of the securities sold (i.e., the selling price of the securities). This procedure must be modified if, for example, changes in the fair value of securities are recorded at the end of the day. Also, for those entities not taxed on a marked-to-market basis, the deferred tax accounts would be adjusted.

Question 41: If a derivative instrument is used to hedge a security classified as available-for-sale, may changes in the fair value of the derivative instrument also be recorded in the separate component of shareholders' equity?

Answer: Yes. ASC 320 (FAS-115) does not change the accounting for derivative instruments used to hedge a security. Generally, while the hedge contract is open, changes in the value of the contract are recorded in other comprehensive income. Subsequently, but no later than when the derivative contract is closed, any resulting gain or loss is treated as an adjustment to the cost basis of the security. In the case of a debt security, any such gain or loss is amortized over the remaining life of the debt security as an adjustment to its yield.

Question 42: If an interest rate swap is used to change the interest rate characteristics of an available-for-sale security from a fixed rate to a floating rate or vice versa may the accounting described in paragraph 115 be applied?

Answer: Yes. The phrase "used to hedge" encompasses the above transaction.

Transfer of Securities between Category Type

Question 43: When securities are transferred from available-for-sale to held-to-maturity or vice versa, is the subsequent amortization of a premium or discount based on the amortized cost of the security or on its fair value at the date of transfer?

Answer: The answer to this question depends on whether the transfer is from the available-for-sale category to the held-to-maturity category, or vice versa.

In the case of *transfer from available-for-sale to held-to-maturity*, the difference between the par value of the debt security that is transferred and its fair value on the date of transfer is accounted for as a yield adjustment in accordance with the provisions of ASC 310 (FAS-91, Accounting for Nonrefundable Fees and Costs Associated with Originating or Acquiring Loans and Initial Direct Costs of Leases). The fair value of the debt security on the date of transfer, adjusted for subsequent amortization, serves as the security's amortized cost basis for required disclosures.

In the case of *transfer from held-to-maturity to available-for-sale*, the amortized cost of the security in the held-to-maturity portfolio is transferred to the available-for-sale portfolio for purposes of determining future amortization. In addition, the amortized cost of the security is used for comparing the cost of the security with its fair value (for the purpose of computing unrealized gain or loss) and for disclosure purposes.

Question 44: ASC 320-10-35-10 and 35-12 (paragraph 15 of FAS-115) indicates that for transfers involving the trading category, the unrealized holding gain or loss should be recognized in earnings. How should the gain or loss be classified on the income statement?

Answer: Unrealized gains or losses that have accumulated before the transfer date should be recognized in the income statement when securities are transferred into the trading category. Such gains or losses are recognized in a manner consistent with how realized gains and losses for the category from which the security being transferred are treated.

Question 45: How is a transfer from available-for-sale to held-to-maturity accounted for?

Answer: The following are some of the salient points in transferring a security from available-for-sale to held-to-maturity:

1. Any unrealized holding gain or loss is combined with any unamortized premium or discount. This aggregate figure serves as the "adjusted" discount or premium, which is the amount that is amortized against income in the future. The net effect is to state the security at its fair value on the date of transfer.

2. The adjusted discount or premium is amortized to income over the remaining life of the debt security.

3. Any unrealized holding gain or loss (reflected in stockholders' equity) on the transfer date is amortized to income over the remaining life of the debt security.

4. The net effect of steps 2 and 3 is that only the unamortized discount or premium (on the transfer date) from the original par value of the debt security is reflected in income over the remaining life of the debt security.

5. Future changes in the fair value of the debt security are ignored, because the security is now classified as held-to-maturity.

Illustration of Transferring a Security from Available-for-Sale to Held-to-Maturity

Sonic, Inc., has a $1,000 par value bond that it acquired at $1,100 on January 1, 20X4. The bond has a ten-year life. During 20X4, $10 of the bond premium would be amortized. The bond is originally accounted for as available-for-sale. On December 31, 20X4, the fair value of the bond is $1,180. Therefore, at December 31, 20X4, Sonic would have $90 of unrealized gain in stockholders' equity. The $90 of unrealized gain plus the $90 of unamortized premium has the effect of stating the bond at its fair value, $1,180.

On January 1, 20X5, Sonic transfers this debt security into its held-to-maturity category. On the date of transfer, the adjusted bond premium is $180 ($90 of original unamortized premium and the $90 unrealized gain). The remaining life of the debt security is nine years. Each year for the next nine years, Sonic will amortize $20 of the bond investment premium. This has the effect of reducing income. Sonic also will amortize the unrealized gain that existed on the date of transfer at the rate of $10 per year ($90/9 years). This has the effect of increasing income. The net effect of both amortization entries is a reduction in Sonic's income of $10 per year for the next nine years (the remaining life of the bond). This amount, $10, is equal to what would be amortized based on the original unamortized bond premium.

Impairment

Question 46: ASC 320-10-30-18; ASC 320-10-45-9 (paragraph 16 of FAS-115) provides an example of when a decline in the fair value of a debt security is other than temporary. What other factors indicate that impairment is other than temporary? How is an equity security evaluated for other-than-temporary impairment?

Answer: ASC 320-10-30-18; ASC 320-10-45-9 (paragraph 16 of FAS-115) specifically mentions a decline in the issuer's-creditworthiness as an indication of an other-than-temporary impairment. In addition, an impairment may need to be recognized if a debt security will be disposed of before its maturity date and if its value has declined due to an increase in interest rates or a change in foreign exchange rates. Additional guidance can be found in SAB-59 (Accounting for Noncurrent Marketable Equity Securities) and AU Section 332 (Long-Term Investments).

Question 47: Should an enterprise recognize an other-than-temporary impairment when it decides to sell a specific available-for-sale debt security at a loss shortly after the balance sheet date?

Answer: In most cases, yes. A loss should be recognized if the enterprise does not expect the fair value of the security to recover before the planned sale date. The loss resulting from an other-than-temporary impairment is to be recorded in the period in which the decision to sell the security was made, not in the period when the actual sale occurs.

Question 48: May a valuation allowance be used to recognize impairment on securities subject to ASC 320 (FAS-115)?

Answer: No. A general allowance for unidentified impairments in an overall portfolio is inappropriate. Other-than-temporary impairments are to be evaluated on a security-by-security basis. When such an impairment is identified, the related security is to be written down to this reduced value, which serves as the security's cost basis going forward. Such a write-down is recognized in earnings when it occurs.

Question 49: After an other-than-temporary impairment has been recognized on an available-for-sale security, how should subsequent recoveries be accounted for?

Answer: After an other-than-temporary impairment in value is recognized, a security's new cost basis is not to be changed due to subsequent recoveries in the fair value of the security. Unrealized gains or losses are computed by a comparison of the security's new cost basis with the fair value of the security. However, a recovery in the fair value of the security is not to be recognized in earnings until the security is sold.

Question 50: EITF Issue 89-4 (Accounting for a Purchased Investment in a Collateralized Mortgage Obligation Instrument or in a Mortgage-Backed Interest-Only Certificate) provides guidance on recognizing impairment for certain types of securities. Does ASC 320 (FAS-115) supersede that guidance?

Answer: Yes. EITF Issue 89-4 measured impairment by referring to undiscounted cash flows. The focus of ASC 320 (FAS-115) in measuring impairment is on fair value. Refer to EITF Issue 93-18 (Recognition of Impairment for an Investment in a Collateralized Mortgage Obligation Instrument or in a Mortgage-Backed Interest-Only Certificate) for additional information.

Presentation of Financial Statements and Disclosure

Question 51: Must the statement of cash flows show purchases, sales, and maturities of securities reported as cash equivalents?

Answer: No. ASC 320 (FAS-115) does not change the portion of FAS-95 (Statement of Cash Flows) that permits cash equivalents to be shown as a net change within the statement of cash flows. However, ASC 320 (FAS-115) does require the disclosure of the amortized cost and fair values of cash equivalents, shown separately by major security type. In addition, a note should explain what portion of each category of securities is shown as cash equivalents in the statement of financial position and the statement of cash flows.

Question 52: Must the disclosures required in ASC 320-10-50-1 through 50-3, 50-5, 50-9 through 50-10 (paragraphs 19 through 22 of FAS-115) be included in interim financial statements?

Answer: Only if a complete set of financial statements is presented at an interim-period date. If the interim financial statements are limited to summary financial information, per the requirements of APB-28 (Interim Financial Reporting), the above-mentioned disclosure requirements of ASC 320 (FAS-115) are not required.

Question 53: Paragraph 21e of FAS-115 (ASC 320-10-50-9) requires disclosure of the change in the net unrealized holding gain or loss on trading securities that has been included in earnings during the period. How is that amount calculated?

Answer: Paragraph 21e of FAS-115 (ASC 320-10-50-9) requires the disclosure of gains or losses recognized in income during the period that resulted from trading securities still held at the end of the period.

Illustration of Disclosing Unrealized Gains and Losses

Rutledge, Inc., reports $100,000 of net gains and losses from trading securities in its 20X5 income statement. Of this amount, $80,000 resulted from securities that were sold during 20X5. Therefore, to satisfy the disclosure requirement of paragraph 21e (ASC 320-10-50-9), Rutledge would disclose that $20,000 of gains recognized during 20X5 pertain to trading securities still held at December 31, 20X5.

Deferred Tax Implications

Question 54: If an enterprise recognizes a deferred tax asset relating only to a net unrealized loss on available-for-sale securities and at the same time concludes that it is more likely than not that some or all of that deferred tax asset will not be realized, is the offsetting entry to the valuation allowance reported in other comprehensive income related to the unrealized loss under ASC 320 (FAS-115) or as an item in determining income from continuing operations?

Answer: The offsetting entry to the valuation allowance would be reported as a component of other comprehensive income. This is because the valuation allowance is directly related to the unrealized loss on the available-for-sale securities.

Question 55: An enterprise has recognized a deferred tax asset relating to other deductible temporary differences in a previous fiscal year and at the same time has concluded that no valuation allowance was warranted. If in the current year the enterprise recognizes a deferred tax asset relating to a net unrealized loss on available-for-sale securities that arose in the current year and at the same time concludes that a valuation allowance is warranted, is the offsetting entry reported in the ASC 320 (FAS-115) component of other comprehensive income or as an item in determining income from continuing operations?

Answer: Management needs to determine the extent to which the valuation allowance directly pertains to the unrealized loss on available-for-sale securities. The offsetting entry is reported in the ASC 320 (FAS-115) component of other comprehensive income only to the extent that the valuation allowance pertains to the available-for-sale securities.

Question 56: If an enterprise does not need to recognize a valuation allowance at the same time that it establishes a deferred tax asset relating to a net unrealized loss on available-for-sale securities, but in a subsequent fiscal year concludes that it is more likely than not that some or all of that deferred tax asset will not be realized, is the

25.30 *Investments in Debt and Equity Securities*

offsetting entry to the valuation allowance reported in the ASC 320 (FAS-115) component of other comprehensive income or as an item in determining income from continuing operations?

Answer: The offsetting entry should be included as an item in determining income from continuing operations.

Question 57: An enterprise recognizes a deferred tax asset relating to a net unrealized loss on available-for-sale securities and at the same time concludes that a valuation allowance is warranted. In a subsequent fiscal year the enterprise makes a change in judgment about the level of future years' taxable income such that all or a portion of that valuation allowance is no longer warranted. Is the offsetting entry reported in the ASC 320 (FAS-115) component of other comprehensive income or as an item in determining income from continuing operations?

Answer: The entry to record the reversal in the valuation allowance account should be recorded as an item in determining income from continuing operations. This is the case even though the original entry was to the ASC 320 (FAS-115) component of other comprehensive income. However, if the entity generates taxable income in the current year that can utilize the benefit of the deferred tax asset (rather than a change in judgment about future years' taxable income), the reduction of the valuation allowance account is allocated to that taxable income. See ASC 740-10-45-20; 740-20-45-20; 225-20-60-2; 740-20-45-2, 45-3, 45-5, 45-8, 45-11, and 45-12, 45-14; and 740-20-05-2 (paragraphs 26 and 35 through 38 of FAS-109 (Accounting for Income Taxes) for additional information.

Methods of Determining Fair Value

Question 58: If a company has a significant investment in a particular security and believes that an attempt to sell the entire investment at one time would significantly affect the security's market price, should the size of the investment be considered in determining the fair value of the security?

Answer: No. If a quoted market price is available, fair value is determined by multiplying the number of shares held by the market price per share.

Question 59: How should an enterprise determine the fair value of a debt security when quoted market prices are not available?

Answer: In the absence of market prices, estimates of fair value should consider existing prices for similar debt instruments and the results of various valuation techniques. Valuation techniques include (*a*) discounting cash flows from the debt security using a discount rate commensurate with the risks involved, (*b*) option pricing models, (*c*) matrix pricing, (*d*) option-adjusted spread models, and (e) fundamental analysis. See paragraph 111 of ASC 320 (FAS-115) for additional guidance.

SOP 90-3 (Definition of the Term *Substantially the Same for Holders of Debt Instruments*, as Used in Certain Audit Guides and a Statement of Position) (ASC 860-10-55-35, 40-24)

BACKGROUND

Banks and other financial institutions will sometimes sell investment securities with the intent to reacquire either the same or similar securities. These actions are often tax-motivated. The accounting issue is whether these transactions are a sale or a borrowing. The AICPA's *Bank Audit Guide* provides that no sale has occurred when the proceeds from the sale of a debt security are immediately reinvested in identical or similar securities. If a period of time elapses between the sale and subsequent investment, the critical factor is whether the bank was at risk for a reasonable period of time to warrant recognition as a sale. What constitutes a reasonable period of time for sale recognition depends on the nature of the underlying security; securities that are sold and then subsequently repurchased within a short period of time might still qualify for sale treatment if the price of the underlying debt instrument is volatile.

SOP 90-3 addresses whether two debt instruments are substantially the same. This guidance is designed to help classify various types of repurchase agreements as a sale or as a financing. For example, an entity may sell a debt instrument with an agreement to repurchase another debt instrument. If the debt instrument to be repurchased is substantially the same as the debt instrument that was sold, the transaction would be treated as a financing. Otherwise, the transaction would be treated as a sale.

STANDARDS

Scope

SOP 90-3 pertains to the sale and purchase, or the exchange, of debt instruments between two entities that both hold the debt instrument as an asset. The term *debt instrument* is defined broadly, including those instruments traditionally viewed as securities and those not classified as such. The debt instruments encompassed by SOP 90-3 include notes, bonds, debentures, money market instruments, certificates of deposit, mortgage loans, commercial loans, commercial paper, and mortgage-backed certificates. SOP 90-3 does not apply in circumstances where an entity originates or acquires a whole loan mortgage and then exchanges the loan for a participation certificate issued by a government-sponsored enterprise or agency (e.g., FHLMC, FNMA, or GNMA). However, exchanges of participation certificates are included within the purview of SOP 90-3.

Because SOP 90-3 was issued before March 15, 1992 (the effective date of SAS-69), entities that were using a different approach for determining whether two debt instruments were substantially the same prior to the release of SOP 90-3 need not change the approach they were using. This provision is referred to as the grandfather clause of SAS-69.

Conclusions

For debt instruments to be classified as substantially the same, all of six criteria must be met. This has the practical effect of making it quite difficult for two debt instruments to be viewed as substantially the same. The six criteria that must be met in order for two debt instruments to be classified as substantially the same are as follows:

1. The debt instruments must have the same primary obligor. However, if the debt instrument is guaranteed by a sovereign government, a central bank, or a government-sponsored enterprise or agency thereof, the debt must be guaranteed by the same party. Also, the terms of the guarantee must be identical.

2. Each debt instrument must be identical in form and type so that all provide the same risks and rights to their holders. For example, the following types of exchanges would not meet this criterion: (a) GNMA I securities for GNMA II securities, (b) loans to foreign debtors that are otherwise the same except for different U.S. foreign tax credits, and (c) commercial paper for redeemable preferred stock.

3. Each debt instrument must carry the same contractual interest rate.

4. In general, the debt instruments must have the same maturity. In the case of mortgage-backed pass-through and pay-through securities, the mortgages underlying the securities must have similar remaining weighted average maturities that result in approximately the same market yield. For example, an exchange of GNMA securities that have a high prepayment record for GNMA securities with a low prepayment record would not meet this criterion.

5. Mortgage-backed pass-through or pay-through securities must be collateralized by a similar pool of mortgages, such as single-family residential mortgages.

6. In general, each debt instrument must have the same unpaid principal amount. In the case of mortgage-backed pass-through or pay-through securities, the aggregate principal amounts of the mortgage-backed securities given up and the mortgage-backed securities reacquired must be within the accepted

"good delivery" standard for the type of mortgage-backed security involved. These specific standards are promulgated by the Public Securities Association and are discussed in *Uniform Practices for the Clearance and Settlement of Mortgage-Backed Securities and Other Related Securities.*

Illustration of Applying Criteria

First Interstate Bank of Texas transfers its portfolio of mortgage-backed pass-through securities for a similar portfolio held by First Virginia Bank. At issue is whether this transfer of debt instruments would represent the transfer of instruments that are substantially the same.

Assume that criteria 2-4 and 6 are met. Criterion 5 also is met—both sets of mortgage-backed securities are collateralized by a similar pool of mortgages: single-family residential mortgages. However, criterion 1, which requires the debt instruments to have the same primary obligor, is not met; there is a different set of primary obligors on First Interstate's loans than on First Virginia's loans. Therefore, this transfer does not represent the transfer of debt instruments that are substantially the same.

ASC 942-320 Financial Services—Depository and Lending—Debt and Equity Securities

Topic D-39 (Questions Related to the Implementation of FASB Statement No. 115) (ASC 942-320-55-1, 55-2)

The FASB staff reported on the following responses to inquiries on the application of ASC 320 (FAS-115):

- The Statement applies to all debt instruments that meet the definition of a security—even those that had been reported as loans or cash equivalents in the balance sheet. For example, mortgage loans securitized as Ginnie Maes but reported as loans in the Call Report would be considered debt securities and subject to the provisions of ASC 320 (FAS-115). The same applies to Brady bonds, which were issued to financial institutions by foreign governments such as Mexico and Venezuela to help those developing countries restructure their debt to the financial institutions. Although the FASB was asked to amend ASC 320 (FAS-115) to exclude Brady bonds from its scope, the Board decided not to do so.

  The FASB subsequently issued FTB 94-1 (Application of Statement 115 to Debt Securities Restructured in a Troubled Debt Restructuring) to clarify that a loan restructured in a

25.34 *Investments in Debt and Equity Securities*

troubled debt restructuring that involves a modification of terms falls under the scope of ASC 320 (FAS-115) if it meets the definition of a security.

- A policy statement issued by the Federal Financial Institutions Examination Council (FFIEC) in December 1991 identified criteria for determining when FDIC-insured banks and savings institutions should consider mortgage derivative products to be *high-risk mortgage securities* that should be disposed of. In response to inquiries about the classification of such securities, the FASB staff announced that mortgage derivative products should not be classified as held-to-maturity if they could become high-risk securities as a result of subsequent changes in market interest rates and changes in the security's related prepayment risk. This announcement was later withdrawn by the FASB staff, because the FFIEC clarified its policy statement in a memorandum, which was issued in final form on August 8, 1994, to the effect that the existence of the bank examiners' authority to ask institutions to dispose of high-risk securities should not preclude institutions from classifying as held-to-maturity securities that are non-high-risk when acquired and when the institution has the ability and intent to hold such securities to maturity. The EITF agreed that a financial institution that transfers available-for-sale securities into the held-to-maturity category in response to the FFIEC's final memorandum should do so at the security's fair value at the time of transfer. The transfer should be accounted for in accordance with the provisions of ASC 320-20-35-10 (paragraph 15d of FAS-115).

AUTHORITATIVE GUIDANCE NOT INCLUDED SEPARATELY IN THE CODIFICATION BUT INCORPORATED WITH OTHER GUIDANCE ON THE SUBJECT

FAS 115-2 and FAS 124-2 (Recognition and Presentation of Other-Than-Temporary Impairments)

OVERVIEW

Under U.S. generally accepted accounting principles an entity holding an investment in a debt or equity security, such as an available-for-sale or held-to-maturity security for which changes in fair value are not regularly recognized in earnings, is required to determine whether that investment's value has been impaired. An investment's value is considered to be impaired if its fair value is less than its amortized cost basis. In that case, the entity is required to recognize an other-than-temporary impairment of the security. The guidance in this FSP amends current guidance on the manner in which an other-than-temporary impairment of a debt security is recognized and provides additional guidance for the presentation and disclosure of such an impairment for debt and equity securities.

FASB STAFF POSITION

Scope

This FSP provides guidance for the recognition of other-than-temporary impairment of debt securities classified as available-for-sale and held-to-maturity, which are accounted for in accordance with the guidance in (a) ASC 320 (FAS-115 (Accounting for Certain Investments in Debt and Equity Securities);(b) FSP FAS 115-1 and FAS 124-1 (The Meaning of Other-Than-Temporary Impairment and Its Application to Certain Investments) (ASC 320-10-15-7; 320-10-35-17; 320-10-35-20 through 35-30; 320-10-35-32A through 35-35A; 320-10-45-8A, 45-9A; 320-10-50-6 through 50-8B; 320-10-55-21A through 55-23; 325-20-35-2; 325-20-50-1; 325-40-65-1; 958-325-15-35-8, 35-10 through 35-11, 35-13); (c) EITF Issue 99-20 (Recognition of Interest Income and Impairment on Certain Investments) (ASC 310-20-60-1, 60-2; 310-30-15-5; 320-10-35-38; 320-10-55-2; 325-40-05-1, 05-2; 325-40-15-2 through 15-9; 325-40-25-1 through 25-3; 325-40-30-1 through 30-3; 325-40-35-1 through 35-13, 35-15, 35-16; 325-40-45-1; 325-40-55-1 through 55-25; 325-40-60-7) as amended by FSP EITF 99-20-1 (Amendments to the Impairment Guidance of EITF Issue No. 99-20) (325-40-65-1); (d) AICPA Statement of Position (SOP) 03-3 (Accounting for Certain Loans or Debt Securities in a Transfer)(ASC 310-10-50-18; 310-30-05-2, 05-3; 310-30-15-1 through 15-4, 15-6 through 15-10; 310-30-25-1; 310-30-30-1; 310-30-35-2, 35-3, 35-5, 35-6, 35-8 through 35-15; 310-30-40-1; 310-30-45-1; 310-30-50-1 through 50-3; 310-30-55-2, 55-5 through 55-29; 310-30-60-3).

In this FSP's discussion of debt securities accounted for under the scope of ASC 958-320 (FAS-124, Accounting for Certain Investments Held by Not-for-Profit Organization) that are held by entities that report a "performance indicator," as defined in the AICPA Accounting and Audit Guide, *Health Care Organizations*, that term will be used instead of "earnings," and the term "outside the performance indicator" will be used instead of "comprehensive income."

The guidance on presentation and disclosure in this FSP applies to *debt* and *equity* securities subject to the disclosure requirements of ASC 320 (FAS-115) and FSP FAS 115-1 and FAS 124-1 (see ASC reference above).

Recognition

The following guidance applies if a debt security's fair value is *less* than its amortized cost basis at the balance sheet date:

- An entity should determine whether an impairment is other than temporary if, at the balance sheet date, a debt security's fair value is less than its amortized cost basis, which includes adjustments for accretion, amortization, cash collection, previous recognition in earnings of other-than-temporary impairments (less cumulative-effect-adjustments, if any, recognized in accordance with guidance discussed below for the adoption of this FSP), and adjustments related to the accounting for fair value hedges.
- An other-than-temporary impairment should be considered to have occurred if an entity has decided to sell such a debt security.
- If an entity decides *not* to sell such a security, available evidence should be considered to determine whether it is *more likely than not* that the entity will be required to sell such a security before its amortized cost basis has been recovered. For example, an entity may be forced to sell a security to meet cash flow or working capital requirements, or to meet contractual or regulatory obligations. If the security is sold before it is more likely than not that the security's amortized cost basis will be recovered, an other-than-temporary impairment should be considered to have occurred.
- An entity that does *not* intend to sell a debt security but also does *not* expect that the total amount of the security's amortized cost basis will be recovered should consider that an other-than-temporary impairment of the security has occurred. To determine whether the debt security's total amortized cost will be recovered, the present value of cash flows that the entity expects to collect from the security should be compared to the security's amortized cost basis. If the present value of cash flows to be collected is *less* than the security's amortized cost basis, a credit loss exists and the security's total amortized cost basis will *not* be recovered. Therefore, an other than temporary impairment should be considered to have occurred.

An entity should use its best estimate of the present value of cash flows expected to be collected from a debt security to determine whether a credit loss on the security has occurred. To estimate that amount, an entity may use the guidance for the measurement of an impairment based on the present value of expected future cash flows in paragraphs 12 through 16 of FAS-114 (Accounting by Creditors for Impairment of a Loan) (ASC 310, *Receivables*; 310-10-35-21, 35-22, 35-24 through 35-26, 35-28, 35-37; 310-10-50-15; 310-30-30-2; 310-40-35-12) under which the expected cash flows are discounted at the effective interest rate inherent in the security at the acquisition date. Guidance for that calculation is provided in Paragraph 14 of FAS-114 (ASC 310-35-25 and 35-28; 310-30-30-2; 310-40-35-12).

To determine the present value of cash flows expected to be collected from debt securities that are beneficial interests in securitized financial assets accounted for under the guidance in EITF Issue 99-20 (see ASC reference above), as amended by FSP EITF 99-20-1 (see ASC reference above), the guidance in ASC 310-40-35-4 (paragraph 12b of Issue 99-20, as amended), should be considered in determining whether cash flows expected to be collected based on previous projections have decreased. That is, at the current financial reporting date, estimated cash flows should be discounted at a rate that equals the current yield used to accrete the beneficial interest. Furthermore, in debt securities accounted for in accordance with the guidance in SOP 03-3 (see ASC reference above), the guidance in the SOP should be considered in estimating the present value of cash flows expected to be collected from such debt securities. An estimate of the present value of cash flows expected to be collected on asset-backed securities should take into account a decrease in the collection of expected cash flows that has occurred as a result of increased prepayments on the underlying assets.

The following factors, among others, should be considered in determining whether a credit loss exists and the period over which the debt security is expected to recover:

- The length of time and amount by which the security's fair value has been less than its amortized cost basis;
- Unfavorable conditions related to the security, an industry, or a geographic area, such as changes in an issuer's financial condition, changes in technology, the discontinuance of a segment of a business that may affect the issuer's or the security's underlying loan obligors future earnings potential, or changes in the quality of a credit enhancement (guarantee);
- The historical and implied volatility of a security's fair value;
- A debt security's payment structure, such as the nontraditional loan terms discussed in ASC 825-10-55-1 through 55-2; 310-10-50-25 (FSP SOP 94-6-1 (Terms of Loan Products That May Give Rise to a Concentration of Credit Risk)) and the likelihood that the issuer will be able to make payments that increase in the future;
- The security's issuer's failure to make scheduled interest or principal payments;
- Changes in a rating agency's rating of a security; and
- Recoveries or additional reductions in a security's fair value after the balance sheet date.

In determining whether there has been an other-than-temporary impairment of a debt security, all of the available information related to the security's collectibility should be considered, including information about past events, current conditions, and reasonable and supportable forecasts, which are useful in estimating cash flows expected to be collected. A security's remaining payment terms, prepayment speeds, issuer's financial condition, expected defaults, and value of underlying collateral, if any, also should be considered, as well as industry analyst reports and forecasts, sector credit ratings, and other market information related to a security's collectibility. Additional considerations include how other credit enhancements affect a security's expected performance, the current financial condition of a security's guarantor if the security is *not* a separate contract, as discussed in ASC 320-10-35-23 (paragraph 8 of FSP FAS 115-1 and FAS-124-1), and whether estimated losses on loans underlying a security can be absorbed by subordinated interests.

Because a security's remaining payment terms should differ significantly from the terms in prior periods, an entity should consider whether a security backed by loans that are currently performing will continue to perform when future required payments (e.g., balloon payments) increase. How the value of any collateral would affect a security's expected performance is another consideration. A decline in the fair value of collateral should be evaluated to determine its effect on the collectibility of a balloon payment.

Determining the amount of an other-than-temporary impairment recognized in earnings and other comprehensive income

An other-than-temporary impairment should be recognized as follows:

- An entity should recognize an other-than-temporary impairment on a debt security in earnings for the total difference between the investment's amortized cost basis and its fair value at the balance sheet if the entity intends to sell the security or more likely than not will be required to do so before it has recovered the investment's amortized cost basis less a credit loss incurred in the current period, if any. The factors discussed above for determining whether a credit loss exists should be considered in evaluating whether it is more likely than not that an entity will be required to sell a security before its amortized cost basis less a credit loss in the current period, if any, will be recovered.

- An entity should separate an other-than-temporary impairment on a debt security into two segments and account for them as follows: (a) the amount related to a credit loss should be recognized in earnings and (b) the amount related to all other factors should be recognized in other comprehensive income net of applicable taxes, if the entity does *not* intend to sell a debt security and it is *not* more likely than not that the entity will be required to sell the security before it has recovered its amortized cost basis less a credit loss incurred in the current period, if any.

A debt security's new amortized cost basis, which should *not* be adjusted for future recoveries in fair value, consists of its previous amortized cost basis reduced by the other-than-temporary impairment recognized in earnings. That amount should be adjusted for accretion and amortization.

Accounting for debt securities after an other-than-temporary impairment
After an other-than-temporary impairment of a debt security has been recognized, a debt security should be accounted for as if it had been purchased on the measurement date of the debt security's new amortized cost basis discussed above. The difference between the new amortized cost basis of a debt security for which an other-than-temporary impairment has been recognized in earnings and cash flows expected to be collected should be accreted as interest income in accordance with existing guidance. Estimates of the present value of cash flows expected to be collected over the life of a debt security should continue to be made. Entities accounting for debt securities under the guidance in EITF Issue 99-20, as amended (see above for ASC references) should account for changes expected to be collected in accordance with the guidance in that pronouncement. If, based on a subsequent evaluation of all other debt securities, an entity experiences a significant increase in the cash flows expected to be collected or, if actual cash flows significantly exceed expected cash flows, such changes should be accounted for based on the guidance in SOP 03-3 (see ASC reference above) even if the debt security would not otherwise be under the SOP's scope. This FSP does not provide guidance on when a debt security's holder would put it on nonaccrual status or on the manner of reporting subsequent income on a nonaccrual debt security.

Debt securities classified as available-for-sale. Subsequent increases or decreases in the fair value of available-for-sale securities, other than an additional other-than-temporary impairment, should be included in other comprehensive income.

Debt securities classified as held-to-maturity. An amount of other-than-temporary impairment recognized in comprehensive income for a security classified as held-to-maturity should be accreted from other comprehensive income to the debt security's amortized cost basis *prospectively* over the security's remaining life based on the amount and timing of future estimated cash flows. The accretion should increase security's carrying value and should continue until the security is sold, matures, or an additional other-than-temporary impairment is recognized in earnings. If the security is sold, ASC 320-10-25-4, 25-6, 25-8, 25-14, 25-18; 320-10-50-11 (paragraphs 8 through 11 of FAS-115) provide guidance on the effect of changes in circumstances that would *not* call into question an entity's intent to hold other debt securities to maturity in the future.

Presentation

An entity should present the total amount of other-than-temporary impairment in the income statement and a reduction of that amount by the portion of the other-than-temporary impairment that is recognized in other comprehensive income in the period in which the entity determines that the decline of the value of a security below its amortized cost basis is other than temporary. Amounts recognized in comprehensive income that are related to held-to-maturity and available-for-sale debt securities for which a portion of an other-than-temporary impairment has been recognized in earnings should be presented separately in the financial statements as part of the financial statement presentation of the components of other comprehensive income.

Disclosures

To help users to understand the types of available-for-sale and held-to-maturity debt and equity securities held, an entity should disclose in its interim and annual financial statements information about investments in an unrealized loss position for an other-than-temporary impairment that has or has not been recognized. In addition, information that helps users to understand the reason that a portion of an other-than-temporary impairment of a debt security was *not* recognized in earnings and the methods and significant inputs used to calculate the portion of the total other-than-temporary impairment recognized in earnings also should be disclosed.

To make the information accessible to users, an entity should identify major types of securities consistent with how it manages and measures its securities based on their nature and risks. To determine whether disclosure for a particular type of security is necessary and whether to provide further detail about a security, its activity or business sector, vintage, geographic concentration, credit quality, or economic characteristic should be considered. A financial institution (i.e., banks, savings and loan associations, savings banks, credit unions, finance companies, and insurance companies) should, at a minimum, include the following major security types in its compliance with the disclosure requirements in ASC 320-10-50-1B, 50-2, and 50-5 (paragraph 19 of FAS-115):

- Equity securities, separated by industry type, company size, or investment objective;
- Debt securities issued by the U.S. Treasury and other U.S. government corporations and agencies;
- Debt securities issued by states of the United States and political subdivisions of the states;
- Debt securities issued by foreign governments;

- Corporate debt securities;
- Collateralized debt obligations; and
- Other debt obligations.

The amortized cost basis of securities classified as available-for-sale or held-to-maturity should be disclosed by major type of security in accordance with the guidance in FAS-115 (ASC 320) as of the date of each interim or annual reporting period for which a balance sheet is presented. All disclosures required in FAS-115 (ASC 320) should also be presented quarterly.

The information required by FSP FAS 115-1 and FAS 124-1 (see ASC references above) should be disclosed by major type of security for each interim and annual reporting period presented. In addition, the information required in ASC 320-10-50-6 through 50-8 (paragraph 7 of FSP 115-1 and FAS-124-1) also should be presented for debt securities for which an other-than-temporary impairment was recognized and only the amount related to a credit loss was recognized in earnings. The method and significant inputs used to measure the amount related to a credit loss that was recognized in earnings should be disclosed by major type of security in periods in which a debt security's other-than-temporary impairment was recognized and only the credit loss was recognized in earnings. Significant inputs include performance indicators of the underlying assets in the security, among others, such as default rates, delinquency rates, and percentage of nonperforming assets, as well as loan to collateral value ratios, third-party guarantees, current levels of subordination, vintage, geographic concentration, and credit ratings.

The following is the minimum amount of information about credit losses recognized in earnings according to the guidance in this FSP that should be presented in a table for each interim and annual period rolling forward:

- The beginning balance of credit losses on debt securities held at the beginning of the period for which a portion of an other-than-temporary impairment was recognized in other comprehensive income;
- Additions for the amount related to the credit loss for which an other-than-temporary impairment was *not* previously recognized;
- Reductions for securities sold during the period (realized);
- Reductions for securities in which the amount previously was recognized in earnings because the entity intended to sell the security or it was more likely than not that the entity would be required to sell the security before recovering its amortized cost basis;
- Increases to the amount related to a credit loss for which an other-than-temporary impairment was previously recognized if an entity does *not* intend to sell the security and it is *not*

more likely than not that the entity will be required to sell the security before its amortized cost basis has been recovered;
- Reductions for increases in cash flows expected to be collected that are recognized over a security's remaining life; and
- The ending balance of the amount related to credit losses on debt securities held at the end of the period for which a portion of an other-than-temporary impairment was recognized in other comprehensive income.

Effective date and transition. This FSP is effective for interim and annual reporting periods ending after June 15, 2009, but early adoption is permitted for periods ending *after* March 15, 2009. An entity that elects early adoption of FSP FAS-157-4 (Determining Fair Value When the Volume and Level of Activity for the Asset or Liability Have Significantly Decreased and Identifying Transactions That Are Not Orderly) (ASC 820-10-65-4), or FSP FAS 107-1 and APB 28-1 (Interim Disclosures about Fair Value of Financial Instruments) (ASC 825-10-65-1), also must early adopt the guidance in this FSP. Likewise, an entity that elects to early adopt this FSP must early adopt the guidance in FSP FAS 157-4 (ASC 820-10-65-4). Disclosures for earlier periods presented for comparative purposes at initial adoption are not required. After initial adoption of the guidance in this FSP, comparative disclosures are required only for periods ending after this FSP's initial adoption.

The guidance in this FSP should be applied to existing and new investments held as of the beginning of the interim period of adoption, that is, April 1, 2009, if adopted for periods ending after June 15, 2009. An entity should recognize a cumulative effect of initially applying the guidance in this FSP as an adjustment to the opening balance of retained earnings and a corresponding adjustment to accumulated other comprehensive income if, at the beginning of the interim period in which this FSP's guidance is adopted, the entity holds debt securities for which it had previously recognized an other-than-temporary impairment and, after considering the guidance in this FSP, it does not intend to sell those securities and it is *not* more likely than not the securities will have to be sold before their amortized cost basis has been recovered. To calculate the cumulative effect on retained earnings, the present value of cash flows expected to be collected determined in accordance with the method discussed in this FSP should be compared to the debt security's amortized cost basis as of the beginning of the interim period in which this FSP's guidance is adopted. The cumulative-effect adjustment should include the related tax effects. The discount rate used to calculate the present value of cash flows expected to be collected should be the rate in effect before any other-than-temporary impairments are recognized, not a rate adjusted to include those impairments.

The amount of the cumulative-effect adjustment before taxes should be used to adjust the amount of the amortized cost basis of a security for which an other-than-temporary impairment was previously recognized. The difference between the new amortized cost basis and the cash flows expected to be collected should be accreted as interest income in accordance with existing guidance. Disclosures about changes in accounting principles required by the guidance in ASC 250 (FAS-154,Accounting Changes and Error Corrections) should be provided in the period in which this FSP's guidance is adopted.

RELATED CHAPTER IN 2011
GAAP GUIDE LEVEL I

Chapter 28, "Investments in Debt and Equity Securities"

RELATED CHAPTERS IN 2011
INTERNATIONAL ACCOUNTING/FINANCIAL REPORTING STANDARDS GUIDE

Chapter 3, "Presentation of Financial Statements"
Chapter 10, "Consolidated Financial Statements"
Chapter 14, "Equity Method"
Chapter 16, "Financial Instruments"
Chapter 17, "Foreign Currency Translation"
Chapter 24, "Investment Property"

CHAPTER 26
LEASES

CONTENTS

Overview		26.04
Authoritative Pronouncements		
ASC 840 Leases		26.06
FSP FAS-13-1	Accounting for Rental Costs Incurred during a Construction Period	26.06
FTB 79-10	Fiscal Funding Clauses in Lease Agreements	26.07
FTB 79-14	Upward Adjustment of Guaranteed Residual Values	26.07
FTB 79-15	Accounting for Loss on a Sublease Not Involving the Disposal of a Segment	26.08
FTB 79-16(R)	Effect of a Change in Income Tax Rate on the Accounting for Leveraged Leases	26.08
FTB 85-3	Accounting for Operating Leases with Scheduled Rent Increases	26.09
FTB 88-1	Issues Relating to Accounting for Leases	26.10
Sale-Leaseback Transactions		26.13
EITF Issue 86-17	Deferred Profit on Sale-Leaseback Transaction with Lessee Guarantee of Residual Value	26.13
EITF Issue 88-21	Accounting for the Sale of Property Subject to the Seller's Preexisting Lease	26.15
EITF Issue 89-16	Consideration of Executory Costs in Sale-Leaseback Transactions	26.19
EITF Issue 90-14	Unsecured Guarantee by Parent of Subsidiary's Lease Payments in a Sale-Leaseback Transaction	26.21
EITF Issue 90-20	Impact of an Uncollateralized Irrevocable Letter of Credit on a Real Estate Sale-Leaseback Transaction	26.22

26.02 *Leases*

EITF Issue 93-8	Accounting for the Sale and Leaseback of an Asset That Is Leased to Another Party	**26.23**
EITF Issue 97-10	The Effect of Lessee Involvement in Asset Construction	**26.25**
EITF Issue 99-13	Application of Issue No. 97-10 and FASB Interpretation No. 23 to Entities That Enter into Leases with Governmental Entities	**26.34**
Leveraged Leases		**26.36**
EITF Issue 85-16	Leveraged Leases: Real Estate Leases and Sale-Leaseback Transactions, Delayed Equity Contributions by Lessors	**26.36**
EITF Issue 86-43	Effect of a Change in Tax Law or Rates on Leveraged Leases	**26.38**
Tax-Related Matters		**26.39**
EITF Issue 86-33	Tax Indemnifications in Lease Agreements	**26.39**
EITF Issue 87-8	Tax Reform Act of 1986: Issues Related to the Alternative Minimum Tax	**26.41**
EITF Issue 89-20	Accounting for Cross Border Tax Benefit Leases	**26.43**
Other Matters		**26.45**
EITF Issue 92-1	Allocation of Residual Value or First-Loss Guarantee to Minimum Lease Payments in Leases Involving Land and Building(s)	**26.45**
EITF Issue 95-17	Accounting for Modifications to an Operating Lease That Do Not Change the Lease Classification	**26.47**
EITF Issue 96-21	Implementation Issues in Accounting for Leasing Transactions Involving Special-Purpose Entities	**26.49**
EITF Issue 97-1	Implementation Issues in Accounting for Lease Transactions, Including Those Involving Special-Purpose Entities	**26.54**
EITF Issue 98-9	Accounting for Contingent Rent	**26.57**

EITF Issue 00-11	Lessors' Evaluation of Whether Leases of Certain Integral Equipment Meet the Ownership Transfer Requirements of FASB Statement No. 13	**26.60**
EITF Issue 01-8	Determining Whether an Arrangement Is a Lease	**26.62**
EITF Issue 01-12	The Impact of the Requirements of FASB Statement No. 133, *Accounting for Derivative Instruments and Hedging Activities,* on Residual Value Guarantees in Connection with a Lease	**26.66**
EITF Issue 05-6	Determining the Amortization Period for Leasehold Improvements Purchased after Lease Inception or Acquired in a Business Combination	**26.68**
EITF Issue 08-3	Accounting by Lessees for Maintenance Deposits under Lease Agreements	**26.70**
Topic D-24	Sale-Leaseback Transactions with Continuing Involvement	**26.72**
FTB 79-12	Interest Rate Used in Calculating the Present Value of Minimum Lease Payments	**26.72**

Authoritative Guidance not Included Separately in the Codification but Incorporated with Other Guidance on the Subject

FSP FIN-46(R)-4	Technical Correction of FASB Interpretation No. 46, *Consolidation of Variable Interest Entities* (revised December 2003), Relating to Its Effects on Question No. 12 of EITF Issue No. 96-21, *Implementation Issues in Accounting for Leasing Transactions Involving Special-Purpose Entities*	**26.73**
FSP FAS-13-2	Accounting for a Change in the Timing of Cash Flows Relating to Income Taxes Generated by a Leveraged Lease Transaction	**26.74**
EITF Issue 87-7	Sale of an Asset Subject to a Lease and Nonrecourse Financing: "Wrap Lease Transactions"	**26.77**
Topic D-8	Accruing Bad-Debt Expense at Inception of a Lease	**26.78**

26.04 *Leases*

Related Chapters in 2011 GAAP Guide, Volume II	**26.79**
Related Chapters in 2011 GAAP Guide, Volume I	**26.79**
Related Chapters in 2011 International Accounting/Financial Reporting Standards Guide	**26.79**

OVERVIEW

A *lease* is an agreement that conveys the right to use property, usually for a specified period. Leases typically involve two parties: the owner of the property (lessor) and the party contracting to use the property (lessee). Because of certain tax, cash flow, and other advantages, leases have become an important alternative to the outright purchase of property by which companies (lessees) acquire the resources needed to operate.

Leases include agreements that, while not nominally referred to as leases, have the characteristic of transferring the right to use property (e.g., heat supply contracts), and agreements that transfer the right to use property even though the contractor may be required to provide substantial services in connection with the operation or maintenance of the assets.

The term *lease*, as used in promulgated GAAP, does *not* include the following:

- Agreements that are contracts for services that do not transfer the right to use property from one contracting party to another
- Agreements that concern the right to explore for or exploit natural resources such as oil, gas, minerals, and timber
- Agreements that represent licensing agreements for items such as motion picture films, plays, manuscripts, patents, and copyrights

A central accounting issue associated with leases is the identification of those leases that are treated appropriately as sales of the property by lessors and as purchases of the property by lessees (*capital leases*). Those leases that are not identified as capital leases are called *operating leases* and are not treated as sales by lessors and as purchases by lessees. Rather, they are treated on a prospective basis as a series of cash flows from the lessee to the lessor.

Guidance related to the accounting for leases is provided in the largest number of authoritative accounting pronouncements of any single subject in the accounting literature. The following pronouncements, which explain, interpret, or amend FAS-13 (Accounting for Leases), are discussed in the 2010 *GAAP Guide, Volume I*, Chapter 29, "Leases":

ASC 840	Accounting for Leases (FAS-13)
ASC 840	Changes in the Provisions of Lease Agreements Resulting from Refundings of Tax-Exempt Debt (FAS-22)
ASC 840	Inception of the Lease (FAS-23)
ASC 840	Accounting for Sales with Leasebacks (FAS-28)
ASC 840	Determining Contingent Rentals (FAS-29)
ASC 310	Accounting for Nonrefundable Fees and Costs Associated with Originating or Acquiring Loans and Initial Direct Costs of Leases (FAS-91)
ASC 840	Accounting for Leases: • Sale-Leaseback Transactions Involving Real Estate • Sales-Type Leases of Real Estate • Definition of the Lease Term • Initial Direct Costs of Direct Financing Leases (FAS-98)
ASC 470	Rescission of FASB Statements No. 4, 44, and 64, Amendment of FASB Statement No. 13, and Technical Corrections (FAS-145)
ASC 840	Lessee Guarantee of the Residual Value of Leased Property (FIN-19)
ASC 840	Accounting for Leases in a Business Combination (FIN-21)
ASC 840	Leases of Certain Property Owned by a Governmental Unit or Authority (FIN-23)
ASC 840	Leases Involving Only Part of a Building (FIN-24)
ASC 840	Accounting for Purchase of a Leased Asset by the Lessee during the Term of the Lease (FIN-26)
ASC, *Glossary*	Accounting for a Loss on a Sublease (FIN-27)

AUTHORITATIVE PRONOUNCEMENTS

ASC 840 Leases

FSP FAS-13-1 (Accounting for Rental Costs Incurred during a Construction Period) (ASC 840-20-25-10, 25-11; 840-20-45-1)

Under some operating leases for land and buildings, a lessee may be able to control the leased property even *before* beginning its operations or beginning to pay rent under a lease's terms. A lessee usually uses a leased asset during that period to construct an asset, such as leasehold improvements. A lessee begins its operations *after* construction is completed and it is then that the lessee begins paying rent under the lease's terms. However, under some leases, a lessee may be required to begin paying rent as soon as the lessee controls the property.

ASC 840-10-55-45, 55-46; 840-20-25-3 through 7, 55-1 through 3; ASC 840-30-55-14, 55-19, 55-20; ASC 840-40-55-17 through 21 (FASB Technical Bulletin (FTB) 88-1, Issues Relating to Accounting for Leases) requires that rental costs related to operating leases be allocated on a straight-line basis over the term of a lease beginning on the date that a lessee is given control of a leased property, in accordance with the guidance in ASC 840 (FAS-13, Accounting for Leases) and ASC 840-20-25-2 (FTB 85-3, Accounting for Operating Leases with Scheduled Rent Increases). For example, a lessee enters into an operating lease on January 1, 2005, and is given control of the leased property on that date for the purpose of constructing leasehold improvements. The lessee expects to begin its operations on July 1, 2005, and, therefore, must begin paying rent on that date. In this case, the lessee would begin *allocating* rental costs on January 1, 2005, on a straight-line basis over the term of the lease.

The question addressed is whether a lessee is permitted to *capitalize* rental costs related to ground and building operating leases that are incurred during a construction period.

FASB STAFF POSITION

A lessee's right to use a leased asset during the construction period or thereafter does *not* differ. Therefore, rental costs incurred on ground or building operating leases during and after the construction period should be accounted for in the same the same manner (i.e., they should be recognized as rental expense and included in income from continuing operations). Rental costs should be allocated over the lease term based on the guidance in ASC 840 (FAS-13) and ASC 840-20-25-2 (FTB 85-3). However, the guidance in this FSP does *not* affect the application of the maximum guarantee test in ASC 460-10-60-28, 60-29, 60-31; 840-40-05-5; 15-5; 25-4; 35-3;

55-2 through 55-6, 55-8, 55-9 through 55-16; S55-2; S99-2 (EITF Issue 97-10, The Effect of Lessee Involvement in Asset Construction).

This FSP amends the guidance in paragraph 6 of EITF Issue 97-10 by deleting the phrase "consistent with GAAP" at the end of that paragraph.

FASB Technical Bulletins

FTB 79-10 (Fiscal Funding Clauses in Lease Agreements) (ASC 840-10-25-3)

BACKGROUND

Fiscal funding clauses are frequently found in lease agreements in which the lessee is a governmental entity. The clause generally provides for the lease to be cancelable if the legislature or other funding authority does not appropriate the funds necessary for the governmental unit to fulfill its obligations under the lease agreement.

STANDARDS

Question: What effect, if any, does the existence of a fiscal funding clause in a lease agreement have on the classification of the lease in accordance with ASC 840 (FAS-13, Accounting for Leases)?

Answer: The existence of a fiscal funding agreement in a lease necessitates an assessment of the probability that the lease will be canceled through the existence of the fiscal funding agreement. If the likelihood of this occurring is assessed as being remote, the lease is considered noncancelable. If the probability is considered other than remote, the lease is considered cancelable and, therefore, is classified as an operating lease.

> ☞ **PRACTICE POINTER:** The term *remote* is used in this pronouncement in the same manner as in ASC 450 (FAS-5, Accounting for Contingencies) (i.e., the chance of the future event or events occurring is slight).

FTB 79-14 (Upward Adjustment of Guaranteed Residual Values) (ASC 840-30-35-25)

BACKGROUND

Under the guidance in ASC 840 (FAS-13), a lessor is required to periodically review the estimated residual value of sales-type, direct-financing, and leveraged leases. ASC 840 (FAS-13) also prohibits an upward adjustment in residual values.

STANDARDS

Question: Does the prohibition of upward adjustments of estimated residual values in ASC 840 (FAS-13) also apply to upward adjustments that result from renegotiations of the guaranteed portions of residual values?

Answer: The prohibitions against upward adjustments of residual values of leased assets under the guidance in ASC 840 (FAS-13) are equally applicable to the guaranteed portion of the residual values. If a lease initially transferred substantially all of the risks and rewards of ownership of the leased property to the lessee, it is not reasonable that the lessor could subsequently increase the benefits that were accounted for as having been retained initially.

FTB 79-15 (Accounting for Loss on a Sublease Not Involving the Disposal of a Segment) (ASC 840-20-25-15; 840-30-35-13)

BACKGROUND

The general principle of recognizing loss on transactions is well established, and extends to contracts that are expected to result in a loss. ASC 840 (FAS-13), however, does not specifically refer to the recognition of a loss on a lease contract.

STANDARDS

Question: Should a loss on a sublease not involving a disposal of a segment be recognized, and how is that loss determined?

Answer: If costs expected to be incurred on an operating sublease exceed anticipated revenue on the sublease, the sublessor should recognize a loss. Similarly, a loss should be recognized on a direct financing sublease if the carrying amount of the investment in the sublease exceeds (1) the total of rentals expected to be received and (2) the property's estimated residual value. An exception to this requirement exists if the lessor's tax benefits from the transactions are sufficient to offset that loss.

FTB 79-16(R) (Effect of a Change in Income Tax Rate on the Accounting for Leveraged Leases) (ASC 840-30-35-41; 50-6)

BACKGROUND

When an important assumption changes, a recalculation of the rate of return and allocation of income is required under the guidance in ASC 840 (FAS-13) from the inception of the lease. The change in the recalculated balances of net investment is recognized as a gain or loss in the year in which the assumption is changed.

STANDARDS

Question: What effect, if any, does a change in income tax rate have on accounting for leveraged leases under the guidance in ASC 840 (FAS-13)?

Answer: The lessor's income tax rate is an important assumption in accounting for a leveraged lease. Accordingly, the effect of a change in income tax rate should be recognized in the first accounting period ending on or after the date on which the legislation affecting the change becomes law. If such a change results in a significant variation in the normal relationship between income tax expense and pretax accounting income, the reasons for that variation should be disclosed if they are not otherwise apparent, in accordance with paragraph 47 of FAS-109 (Accounting for Income Taxes) (ASC 740-10-50-12 through 50-14).

FTB 85-3   (Accounting for Operating Leases with Scheduled Rent Increases) (ASC 840-20-25-2)

BACKGROUND

The guidance in ASC 840 (FAS-13) specifies that rent income generally should be recognized by lessors and lessees as it becomes receivable or payable. If the rental payments vary from a straight-line pattern, the income or expense should be recognized on a straight-line basis unless another systematic and rational method is more representative of the time pattern in which the benefit from use of the asset was diminished (lessor) or received (lessee). It has been suggested that, under certain circumstances, rentals should be recognized on a basis that is neither straight-line nor representative of the time pattern of the physical use of the asset. Examples of situations in which another pattern of recognition might be appropriate are (*a*) rent reductions in the early periods to induce the lessee to sign the lease and (*b*) scheduled rent increases that anticipate inflation.

STANDARDS

Question: If an operating lease includes a scheduled rent increase, is it ever appropriate for lessees and lessors to recognize rent expense or income on a basis other than straight-line?

Answer: The effects of scheduled rent increases, which are included in the calculation of the minimum lease payments, should be recognized on a straight-line basis over the lease term, unless some other systematic and rational allocation basis is more representative of the time pattern in which the leased property is used. Factors such as the time value of money, anticipated inflation, and expected future revenues to allocate scheduled rent increases are inappropriate, because they do not relate to the time pattern of the physical use of the leased asset. These factors may affect the amount of rent, however, if they affect the amount of contingent rentals that are not part of the minimum lease payment amount.

FTB 88-1 (Issues Relating to Accounting for Leases) (ASC 840-10-55-45, 55-46; 840-20-25-3 through 7, 55-1 through 3; 840-30-55-14, 55-19, 55-20; 840-40-55-17 through 21)

BACKGROUND

FTB 88-1 responds to five questions with regard to lease accounting in the following areas:

- Time pattern of the physical use of the property in an operating lease
- Lease incentives in an operating lease
- Applicability of leveraged lease accounting to existing assets of the lessor
- Money-over-money lease transactions
- Wrap lease transactions

STANDARDS

Question 1: For operating leases that include scheduled rent increases designated to accommodate the lessee's projected physical use of the property, how should the rental payment obligation be recognized by the lessee and the lessor in accordance with the guidance in ASC 840 (FAS-13)?

Answer: Both the lessee and the lessor should recognize the lease payments as follows:

- If rent escalates in contemplation of the lessee's physical use of the leased property, but the lessee takes possession of or controls the physical use of the property at the beginning of the lease term, all rent payments (including the escalated payments) should be recognized as rental expense (by the lessee) or revenue (by the lessor) on a straight-line basis.
- If rent escalates under a master leasing agreement because the lessee gains access to and control over additional leased property at the time of the escalation, the escalated rents should be considered rental expense (by the lessee) or revenue (by the lessor) attributed to the additional leased property and should be recognized in proportion to the relative fair value of the additional property.

Illustration of an Operating Lease with Scheduled Rent Increases

Reeve & Sons is a construction company. Reeve leases a number of pieces of heavy equipment on 1/1/20X4 by entering into a ten-year operating lease. The fair value of this equipment is $600,000 at lease inception, and the yearly lease payment is $50,000. In addition, Reeve's yearly lease payment will increase to $100,000 on 1/1/20X9. On 1/1/20X9, Reeve will also gain access to and control over additional leased property. This additional leased property has a fair value of $300,000 on 1/1/20X4.

Reeve will recognize rental expense of approximately $58,333 during the years 20X4–20X8, and approximately $91,667 during the years 20X9–20Y3. These amounts are computed as follows:

Absolute (relative) fair value of equipment Reeve gains access to on 1/1/20X4	$600,000 (66.67%)
Absolute (relative) fair value of equipment Reeve gains access to on 1/1/20X9	$300,000 (33.33%)
Total lease payments over the ten-year lease	$750,000 [($50,000 × 5) + ($100,000 × 5)]
Portion of $100K annual lease payment from X9–Y3 attributable to the additional leased property	$33,334 ($100K × .3333, rounded)
Total lease payments attributable to the additional leased property	$167,667 ($33,334 × 5, rounded)
Total lease payments attributable to the original leased property	$583,333 [$750K − $167.667K]
Portion of lease payment attributable to original leased property, X4–Y3	$58,333 ($583,333 / 10)
Lease expense recognized, X4–X8	$58,333
Lease expense recognized, X9×Y3	$91,667 ($58,333 + $33,334)

Question 2: For operating leases that include an incentive for the lessee to sign (e.g., up-front cash payment to the lessee), should the lessee or lessor ever recognize rental expense or revenue other than on a straight-line basis?

Answer: Incentive payments to the lessee represent reductions in rent expense by the lessee and rental revenue to the lessor. They should be recognized on a straight-line basis over the lease term.

Question 3: For a lease to be classified as direct financing, the cost or carrying amount, if different, and the fair value of the asset must be the same at the inception of the lease. For a lease to qualify for leveraged lease accounting, it must be a direct financing lease. How does the lessor apply these requirements to leasing an asset that the lessor has owned and previously placed in service?

Answer: The carrying amount of an asset previously placed in service may not be significantly different from its fair value, but the two are not likely to be the same. Therefore, leveraged lease accounting is not appropriate, other than when an asset to be leased is acquired by the lessor. Any write-down to the existing asset's fair value in contemplation of leasing the asset precludes the transaction from being accounted for as a leveraged lease.

Question 4: An enterprise manufactures or purchases an asset, leases the asset to a lessee, and obtains nonrecourse financing in excess of the asset's cost using the leased asset and the future lease rentals as collateral (referred to as a money-over-money lease transaction). Should the enterprise ever recognize any of the amount by which the cash received plus the present value of any estimated residual retained exceeds the carrying amount of the leased asset as profit on the transaction at the beginning of the lease term? If not, how should the lessor account for the transaction?

Answer: Other than recognizing manufacturer's or dealer's profit in a sales-type lease, an enterprise should never recognize as income the proceeds from the borrowing in a money-over-money lease at the beginning of the lease term. The enterprise should account for the transaction as (1) the manufacture or purchase of an asset; (2) the leasing of the asset under an operating, direct financing, or sales-type lease; and (3) the borrowing of funds. The asset and the liability for the nonrecourse financing should not be offset in the statement of financial position unless a legal right of setoff exists.

Question 5: A lessor purchases an asset, leases it to a lessee, obtains nonrecourse financing using the lease rentals or the lease rentals and the asset as collateral, sells the asset and the nonrecourse debt to a third-party investor, and leases the asset back while remaining the principal lessor under the original lease (referred to as a wrap-lease transaction). How should the enterprise account for this transaction?

Answer: If the leased asset is real estate, the guidance in ASC 840-40-05-9 through 05-10, 15-4, 15-9 through 15-10, 25-9 through 25-14, 25-17, 50-1 through 50-2, 55-36, 55-49 through 55-77; ASC 980-840-25-1 through 25-3, 35-1 through 35-2 FAS-98) applies to the sale-leaseback transaction. If the property is not real estate, the enterprise should account for the transaction as a sale-leaseback transaction in accordance with ASC 840 (FAS-13).

Sale-Leaseback Transactions

EITF Issue 86-17 (Deferred Profit on Sale-Leaseback Transaction with Lessee Guarantee of Residual Value) (ASC 460-10-55-17; 60-32; 840-40-55-26 through 55-28)

OVERVIEW

A seller-lessee in a sale-leaseback transaction guarantees to the buyer-lessor that the residual value will be a stipulated amount at the end of the lease term. The lease agreement stipulates that the seller-lessee will indemnify the buyer-lessor for a deficiency, if any, in the property's residual value up to a specified amount. The lease does not meet any of the criteria for a capital lease in paragraph 7 of FAS-13 (ASC 840-10-25-1); hence, it is classified as an operating lease. More than a minor portion of the property, but less than substantially all, is covered by the leaseback.

ACCOUNTING ISSUES

If a residual value guarantee affects the determination of profit on a sale-leaseback transaction in accordance with ASC 840-40-25-4 through 25-5, 35-4, 55-79 through 55-80, 55-82 through 55-84, 55-86 through 55-88, 55-90 through 55-92, 55-94 (FAS-28), should a seller-lessee use the gross amount or the present value of the guarantee in making that calculation?

EITF CONSENSUS

The EITF reached a consensus that a seller-lessee should defer profit equal to the present value of the periodic rents plus the *gross* amount of the guarantee at the date of sale and account for the components as follows:

- Defer profit equal to the gross amount of the guarantee until the guarantee is resolved at the end of the lease term.
- Amortize profit equal to the present value of the periodic rents in proportion to total gross rental expense over the lease term.

> **OBSERVATION:** This consensus applies only to sale-leasebacks *other than* real estate as a result of the issuance of FAS-98, which specifically applies to sale-leaseback transactions involving real estate. FAS-98 applies the provisions in FAS-66, which precludes sale-leaseback accounting if the seller-lessee has any kind of continuing involvement with the property, such as a guarantee of the buyer's investment.

SEC OBSERVER COMMENT

The SEC Observer stated that the SEC staff is concerned about sales recognition in transactions that include a repurchase option. Important criteria to be considered, individually and in the aggregate, in determining whether such transactions qualify as sales include: the buyer's initial and continuing investment, the seller's continuing involvement with the property, repurchase options at other than fair value at the exercise date, seller's residual guarantees, and other evidence that indicates that the seller has not passed the risks and rewards of ownership to the buyer. Registrants should consider *all* the terms of the transaction. In addition, those comments apply to transactions that have a material income statement or balance sheet effect. (The SEC Observer's concerns about sales recognition in sale-leaseback transactions of real estate were resolved by the issuance of FAS-98, as discussed above.)

Illustration of Calculation of Profit at the Sale Date and Amortization of Deferred Profit

Assumptions

Sales price of property	$150,000
Seller's basis in the property	$ 50,000
Annual rent (payable at beginning of year)	$ 16,000
Maximum amount of guarantee	$ 27,000
Leaseback term	5 years
Incremental borrowing rate	12% per year
Date of sale	12/31/X4

Profit to Be Recognized at Date of Sale

Sales price	$150,000
Less: Basis in property	50,000
Profit on sale	$100,000
Present value of annual rents	$ 64,598
Residual value guarantee—Gross amount	27,000
Profit to be deferred	$ 91,598
Profit to be recognized at date of sale	$ 8,402

Amortization of Deferred Profit

Total deferred profit at 12/31/X4	$ 91,598
	$.8074

$\dfrac{\text{Present value of total rent at date of sale}}{\text{Total annual rents}}$	$\dfrac{\$\,64{,}598}{80{,}000} =$	amortized for each $1 of rent
Annual amortization of deferred profit:	$\$16{,}000 \times .8074 = \$12{,}918$	
Deferred profit at 12/31/X9	$\$\,27{,}000$	

DISCUSSION

Although the guidance in ASC 840-40-25-4 through 25-5, 35-4, 55-79 through 55-80, 55-82 through 55-84, 55-86 through 55-88, 55-90 through 55-92, 55-94 (FAS-28) is clear that a seller-lessee should defer profit on a sale-leaseback transaction equal to the present value of the minimum lease payments over the lease term and that such an amount should be amortized in proportion to rental expense over the lease term, it is unclear whether that amount should include a guaran-tee. In addition, even if the guarantee is included in deferred profit, it is unclear whether it should be included at its gross amount or at its present value. Those who supported including the guarantee at its gross amount, rather than reducing it to its present value, argued that because a guarantee is a contingent gain that is not resolved until the end of the lease term, it should not result in additional profit recognition at the inception of the lease term. Under ASC 450 (FAS-5), a contingent gain is not recognized until realized.

EITF Issue 88-21 (Accounting for the Sale of Property Subject to the Seller's Preexisting Lease) (ASC 840-40-55-37 through 55-41)

OVERVIEW

A lessee of all or a portion of a property also may own an interest in that property. This might occur if, for example, the lessee has an investment in a partnership that owns the leased property. The lessee might have acquired the equity interest at or near the time the lease agreement was consummated.

The existence of both an operating lease and an equity interest in the property raises a question about whether a gain should be recognized if a lessee sells its equity interest in the property (or the partnership sells the property), but the lessee continues to lease the property under a preexisting operating lease. The question arises because a portion of the gain is deferred in other transactions in which owned property is sold and leased back.

ACCOUNTING ISSUES

1. Should the sale of the lessee's equity interest in the property be accounted for as a sale-leaseback transaction?
2. Should the amount of profit to be deferred be affected by the seller-lessee's prior ownership interest in the property?
3. Should the guidance in ASC 840-40-05-9 through 05-10, 15-4, 15-9 through 15-10, 25-9 through 25-14, 25-17, 50-1 through 50-2, 55-36, 55-49 through 55-77; ASC 980-840-25-1 through 25-3, 35-1 through 35-2 (FAS-98) apply to transactions involving real estate or real estate and equipment if the seller-lessee vacates and intends to sublease the property or exercises a renewal option subject to provisions in the preexisting lease?
4. Should FAS-98 apply to transactions that involve property under the scope of that Statement if the preexisting lease is between parties under the seller's common control?

EITF CONSENSUS

1a. A sale of an equity interest in a leased property should be accounted for as a sale-leaseback if the lease is modified in connection with the sale, excluding insignificant modifications.

1b. The provisions of ASC 840-40-05-9 through 05-10, 15-4, 15-9 through 15-10, 25-9 through 25-14, 25-17, 50-1 through 50-2, 55-36, 55-49 through 55-77; ASC 980-840-25-1 through 25-3, 35-1 through 35-2 (FAS-98) should be followed for transactions in paragraph 1a and for all transactions that involve real estate and real estate with equipment if the preexisting lease was entered into *after* June 30, 1988, the Statement's effective date.

1c. Profit on a sales transaction in which the preexisting lease is not modified significantly should be deferred and amortized into income in accordance with the provisions of ASC 840-40-25-4 through 25-5, 35-4, 55-79 through 55-80, 55-82 through 55-84, 55-86 through 55-88, 55-90 through 55-92, 55-94 (FAS-28).

1d. The provisions of ASC 976-605-25-4, 25-1 through 25-2, 25-6, 25-8 through 25-9, 25-11 through 25-12, 30-1 through 30-4, 35-1, 55-1 through 55-11, 55-13 through 55-14; ASC 976-10-15-1 through 15-4; ASC 976-310-30-1, 35-1, 40-1, 50-1; 976-330-50-1; 976-705-30-1; ASC 360-20-15-10, 15-1 through 15-2, 40-3 through 40-5, 40-7 through 40-10, 40-13, 40-18 through 40-31, 40-33 through 40-34, 40-36 through 40-38, 40-40 through 40-50, 40-56 through 40-64, 55-1 through 55-2, 55-7 through 55-17, 55-19 through 55-21, 55-23 through 55-34, 55-36 through 55-38, 55-40 through 55-54, 55-61 through 55-64; ASC 360- ASC 460-10-60-3; ASC 840-10-25-60 FAS-66) should be followed for all transactions involving real estate. If the guidance in FAS-98 (see ASC references above) does not

apply, continuing involvement in the preexisting lease is not considered in determining whether to recognize a sale.
2. The seller's prior ownership percentage in the property should not affect the calculation of the amount of deferred profit, *regardless* of lease modifications.
3. The accounting for the transaction should not be affected by the seller-lessee's exercise of (a) a sublease provision contained in the preexisting lease or (b) a renewal option for a period within the original lease term, as defined in paragraph 5f of FAS-13. However, the EITF considered a renewal option for a period not part of the original lease term to constitute a new lease. The guidance in ASC 840-40-05-9 through 05-10, 15-4, 15-9 through 15-10, 25-9 through 25-14, 25-17, 50-1 through 50-2, 55-36, 55-49 through 55-77; ASC 980-840-25-1 through 25-3, 35-1 through 35-2 (FAS-98) applies to such transactions. For example, if a lease has an initial term of ten years and a bargain renewal for an additional five years, the original minimum lease term would be 15 years, and the exercise of the renewal option would not affect the accounting. If, however, the renewal option were a fair value rental option, the minimum lease term would be ten years, and the exercise of the renewal would make the transaction subject to the provisions of FAS-98 (see ASC references above).
4. A lease between parties under common control is not a preexisting lease for the purpose of these consensus positions. The guidance in ASC 840-40-05-9 through 05-10, 15-4, 15-9 through 15-10, 25-9 through 25-14, 25-17, 50-1 through 50-2, 55-36, 55-49 through 55-77; ASC 980-840-25-1 through 25-3, 35-1 through 35-2 (FAS-98) thus applies to such transactions, with one exception. If the guidance in ASC 980, Regulated Operations (FAS-71) applies—that is, if one of the parties to the lease is a regulated enterprise and the lease has been approved by the appropriate regulatory agency—a lease between parties under common control is treated as a preexisting lease.

DISCUSSION

1a. The transaction discussed in this Issue deals with the sale of property that was leased by the seller *before* the sale and will continue to be leased by the seller after the sale. The transaction differs from a normal sale-leaseback transaction described in paragraph 6 of FAS-98 (ASC 840-40-15-9), in which "separate sale and leaseback agreements...are consummated at or near the same time." Thus, the Task Force focused on the status of the preexisting lease in determining whether such transactions should be recognized as sales or as sale-leasebacks. The Task Force's consensus—that the transaction is a sale-leaseback rather than a sale if the preexisting lease undergoes significant modification in conjunction with the sales transaction—represents the view that a significant modification to a preexisting lease is the same as negotiating a new lease with the buyer-lessor.

1b. The EITF's original consensus on this Issue required that only transactions in which the preexisting lease was modified in conjunction with the sale and that involve real estate or real estate with equipment be accounted for as sale-leasebacks subject to the requirements in ASC 840-40-05-9 through 05-10, 15-4, 15-9 through 15-10, 25-9 through 25-14, 25-17, 50-1 through 50-2, 55-36, 55-49 through 55-77; ASC 980-840-25-1 through 25-3, 35-1 through 35-2 (FAS-98). The FASB staff subsequently asked the EITF to amend that consensus, however, to require that FAS-98 (see ASC references above) apply to all such transactions in which the preexisting lease was entered into after June 30, 1988 (the Statement's effective date). That request was based on the concern that ignoring continuing involvement in a preexisting lease that has not been modified could result in sales recognition on transactions that did not transfer the risks and rewards of ownership to the buyer. Under FAS-98 (see ASC references above), a seller-lessee's continuing involvement in the sale and in the lease would be evaluated separately in considering the transfer of the risks and rewards of ownership. Transactions involving property outside the scope of FAS-98 (see ASC references above) would be governed by the sale-leaseback provisions in ASC 840-40-25-4 through 25-5, 35-4, 55-79 through 55-80, 55-82 through 55-84, 55-86 through 55-88, 55-90 through 55-92, 55-94 (FAS-28).

1c. Although the Task Force believed that a transaction in which an unmodified preexisting lease negotiated with a party other than the buyer of the lessee's interest in the property is not a sale-leaseback transaction, they argued that profit related to the remaining lease payments should be deferred and accounted for based on the guidance in FAS-28 (see ASC references above).

1d. If the lease has not been modified and sale-leaseback accounting is not required, the provisions in ASC 976-605-25-4, 25-1 through 25-2, 25-6, 25-8 through 25-9, 25-11 through 25-12, 30-1 through 30-4, 35-1, 55-1 through 55-11, 55-13 through 55-14; ASC 976-10-15-1 through 15-4; ASC 976-310-30-1, 35-1, 40-1, 50-1; 976-330-50-1; 976-705-30-1; ASC 360-20-15-10, 15-1 through 15-2, 40-3 through 40-5, 40-7 through 40-10, 40-13, 40-18 through 40-31, 40-33 through 40-34, 40-36 through 40-38, 40-40 through 40-50, 40-56 through 40-64, 55-1 through 55-2, 55-7 through 55-17, 55-19 through 55-21, 55-23 through 55-34, 55-36 through 55-38, 55-40 through 55-54, 55-61 through 55-64; ASC 360- ASC 460-10-60-3; ASC 840-10-25-60 FAS-66) should be followed in all cases to account for sales that involve real estate. However, the decision whether to recognize a sale under the provisions of that Statement should ignore the preexisting lease and related continuing involvement, if any, if the preexisting lease was entered into before June 30, 1988, and the provisions of FAS-98 (see ASC references above) do not apply.

2. Some had argued that a seller-lessee should be required to defer profit only to the extent of its previous ownership percentage in the property. Opponents of that view argued that the amount deferred should be equivalent to the lessee's maximum exposure, as required in paragraph 25 of FAS-66 (ASC 360-20-40-37) for real estate transactions. FAS-28 (see ASC references above) requires deferred profit to be the lesser of the present value of the seller-lessee's remaining minimum lease payments or the seller-lessee's share of the profit. The SEC Observer stated that the SEC staff would expect profit to be deferred using that approach.

3. Those who believed that a sublease does not modify the original lease and thus should not result in sale-leaseback accounting argued that subleasing is a common lease provision. Although subleasing is prohibited under the guidance in ASC 840-40-05-9 through 05-10, 15-4, 15-9 through 15-10, 25-9 through 25-14, 25-17, 50-1 through 50-2, 55-36, 55-49 through 55-77; ASC 980-840-25-1 through 25-3, 35-1 through 35-2 (FAS-98), which considers it to be a guarantee to the buyer, they argued that a sublease under a preexisting lease continues the seller's commitment under the existing lease and does not constitute a guarantee. Further, if subleasing is not considered a modification of the lease before the sale, it should not be considered as such after the sale and FAS-98 (see ASC references above) should not apply.

4. The consensus related to the modification of the preexisting lease should not apply to transactions in which the seller and the lessee are under common control, because the parties are not independent and the preexisting lease is not considered an arm's-length transaction.

EITF Issue 89-16 (Consideration of Executory Costs in Sale-Leaseback Transactions) (ASC 840-40-30-5, 30-6)

OVERVIEW

Executory costs on a lease include such items as maintenance, insurance, and taxes. Those costs may be included in each rental payment, paid separately by the seller-lessee, or paid by the buyer-lessor and billed to the seller-lessee.

Although minimum lease payments, as defined in paragraph 5j(i) of FAS-13 (ASC 840-10-25-6), include executory costs but exclude such costs if they are paid separately, minimum lease payments exclude executory costs in certain lease calculations. For example, executory costs are excluded from minimum lease payments when determining lease classification or in accounting for capital, sales-type, or direct financing leases.

Under the guidance in ASC 840-40-25-4 through 25-5, 35-4, 55-79 through 55-80, 55-82 through 55-84, 55-86 through 55-88, 55-90 through 55-92, 55-94 (FAS-28) profit equal to the present value of minimum lease payments in certain sale-leasebacks should be deferred. The Statement is silent, however, on whether executory costs should be included or ex-cluded from minimum lease payments when making that calculation.

ACCOUNTING ISSUE

Should minimum lease payments include or exclude executory costs for the purpose of calculating deferred profit in a sale-leaseback transaction?

EITF CONSENSUS

The EITF reached a consensus that executory costs should be excluded from minimum lease payments in calculating deferred profit in a sale-leaseback transaction, regardless of how executory costs are paid or whether the lease is a capital or operating lease.

DISCUSSION

The accounting for executory costs in a sale-leaseback transaction is a significant issue, because executory costs can be as high as 30% of the cost of a long-term lease. Because a sale-leaseback transaction is viewd under the guidance in ASC 840-40-25-4 through 25-5, 35-4, 55-79 through 55-80, 55-82 through 55-84, 55-86 through 55-88, 55-90 through 55-92, 55-94 (FAS-28) as if it were in substance a financing of the seller's future use of the property as a lessee, it provides that no profit be recognized on amounts related to the financing aspect of the transaction. Proponents of excluding executory costs from the deferred profit calculation in all sale-leasebacks argued that executory costs included in lease payments are the lessee's best estimate of property-related costs paid by the lessor and are not related to the financing portion of a sale-leaseback. They also argued that it would be inconsistent to exclude executory costs from the calculation of deferred profit if the lessee pays those costs directly or when there is a capital lease, but to include them when they are included in lease payments or when there is an operating lease.

EITF Issue 90-14 (Unsecured Guarantee by Parent of Subsidiary's Lease Payments in a Sale-Leaseback Transaction) (ASC 460-10-60-26, 60-27; 840-40-25-15, 25-16)

OVERVIEW

A wholly owned subsidiary enters into a sale-leaseback transaction for a building. In connection with the sale-leaseback, the buyer-lessor requires the subsidiary's parent to guarantee the subsidiary's obligations under the lease. Under the guidance in ASC 840-40-05-9 through 05-10, 15-4, 15-9 through 15-10, 25-9 through 25-14, 25-17, 50-1 through 50-2, 55-36, 55-49 through 55-77; ASC 980-840-25-1 through 25-3, 35-1 through 35-2 (FAS-98) the use of sale-leaseback-accounting is prohibited when there is continuing involvement with a real estate property other than a normal leaseback involving the active use of the property by the seller-lessee. A guarantee is one example of continuing involvement mentioned in FAS-98 (see ASC references above). Except for the lease guarantee, the transaction meets all the requirements for sale-leaseback accounting under FAS-98 (see ASC references above).

ACCOUNTING ISSUE

If one member of a consolidated group guarantees another member's lease payments in a sale-leaseback of real estate, can the transaction be accounted for as a sale-leaseback in the seller-lessee's separate financial statements and in the entity's consolidated financial statements?

EITF CONSENSUS

The EITF reached the following consensus about the effect of unsecured guarantees of lease obligations of one member of a consolidated group by another member of the consolidated group:

- Sale-leaseback accounting is *not* precluded in the consolidated financial statements if one member of a consolidated group guarantees the lease payments of another member of that group. The Task Force's consensus was based on the rationale that an entity's unsecured guarantee of its own lease does not provide a lessor with additional collateral, except if the lessee declares bankruptcy. Thus, such a guarantee does not constitute continuing involvement that would preclude sale-leaseback treatment under the guidance in ASC 840-40-05-9 through 05-10, 15-4, 15-9 through 15-10, 25-9 through 25-14, 25-17, 50-1 through 50-2, 55-36, 55-49 through 55-77; ASC 980-840-25-1 through 25-3, 35-1 through 35-2 (FAS-98).
- Sale-leaseback accounting *is precluded*, however, in the sellerlessee's separate financial statements, because an unsecured

guarantee of the seller-lessee's lease payments by another member of the consolidated group provides the buyer-lessor with additional collateral that reduces the risk of loss and thus constitutes a form of continuing involvement.

DISCUSSION

It appears that the EITF's consensus was influenced by background materials that discussed a legal opinion on the weight of an entity's unsecured guarantee of its leaseback obligation. The legal opinion stated that such a guarantee does not improve a lessor's status as a creditor over any other general creditor when trying to recover from the lessee for nonpayment and does not create greater rights for the lessor. In fact, it was believed to be redundant and unnecessary. In reaching its consensus, the EITF viewed the guarantee of any member of a consolidated group of an obligation of another member of that group as essentially equivalent to a guarantee of the consolidated entity's own obligation and therefore as nonsubstantive in the consolidated financial statements. Some also contended that the guarantee does not create an additional obligation to the consolidated entity. However, such a guarantee would constitute continuing involvement in the seller-lessee's separate financial statements, because the guarantee is considered to be from a party outside that entity and therefore substantive.

EITF Issue 90-20 (Impact of an Uncollateralized Irrevocable Letter of Credit on a Real Estate Sale-Leaseback Transaction) (ASC 460-10-60-33; 840-40-25-14)

OVERVIEW

A buyer-lessor may require a seller-lessee to provide an irrevocable letter of credit to secure all or a portion of the lease payments in connection with a sale-leaseback of real estate. If the seller-lessee pledges assets as collateral for the letter of credit, sale-leaseback accounting for the transaction is precluded under the guidance in ASC 840-40-05-9 through 05-10, 15-4, 15-9 through 15-10, 25-9 through 25-14, 25-17, 50-1 through 50-2, 55-36, 55-49 through 55-77; ASC 980-840-25-1 through 25-3, 35-1 through 35-2 (FAS-98), because there is continuing involvement. It is unclear, however, whether an *uncollat-eralized* letter of credit would constitute continuing involvement.

ACCOUNTING ISSUE

Does the existence of an uncollateralized, irrevocable letter of credit preclude sale-leaseback accounting for a transaction that otherwise would qualify?

EITF CONSENSUS

The EITF reached a consensus that sale-leaseback accounting is not precluded, because an uncollateralized, irrevocable letter of credit is not a form of continuing involvement under the provisions of FAS-98 (see ASC references above). Although a lessee is not precluded from accounting for a transaction as a sale-leaseback under the provisions of FAS-98 while providing an independent third-party guarantee of the lease payments, such transactions should be analyzed carefully to ensure that they are uncollateralized in form and substance. For example, the EITF would consider a financial institution's right to offset amounts on deposit against payments on the letter of credit to be a form of collateral and, therefore, continuing involvement that would preclude sale-leaseback accounting.

DISCUSSION

The following arguments were made in support of sale-leaseback accounting:

- An uncollateralized letter of credit does not increase the lessee's commitment beyond the obligation to pay rent. It is not a guarantee of return of the buyer's investment.
- A buyer-lessor could achieve almost the same protection by purchasing a surety bond to secure the lease payments. The lessee would not be involved in that transaction and sale-leaseback accounting would not be precluded. If an equivalent level of security could be achieved without the seller-lessee's consent, the seller-lessee is not providing additional collateral or a guarantee by obtaining an uncollateralized letter of credit.
- Letters of credit and lease guarantees are only promises to pay obligations under a lease agreement. If the seller-lessee has provided a letter of credit and subsequently defaults on the lease payments, the seller-lessee has the same unsecured obligation, but to another party.

EITF Issue 93-8 (Accounting for the Sale and Leaseback of an Asset That Is Leased to Another Party) (ASC 840-40-55-22 through 55-24)

OVERVIEW

Company A sells equipment to Company B and then leases it back from Company B. The sale and leaseback of the asset is subject to an operating lease and is intended to be leased by Company A to another entity under an operating lease. Company A has thus become a seller, lessee, and sublessor. The question here addresses the accounting treatment of a sale-leaseback transaction in which the seller-lessee retains substantial risks of ownership in the property through the terms of the leaseback.

ACCOUNTING ISSUE

Should a sale-leaseback transaction in which the seller-lessee retains substantial risks of ownership in the property through the leaseback be accounted for as a borrowing or as a sale-leaseback transaction, if property outside the scope of the guidance in ASC 840-40-05-9 through 05-10, 15-4, 15-9 through 15-10, 25-9 through 25-14, 25-17, 50-1 through 50-2, 55-36, 55-49 through 55-77; ASC 980-840-25-1 through 25-3, 35-1 through 35-2 (FAS-98) is subject to an operating lease, is subleased, or is intended to be subleased by the seller-lessee to a third party at the time of the sale?

EITF CONSENSUS

The EITF reached a consensus that a seller-lessee should account for the above transactions as a sale-leaseback in accordance with paragraphs 32 and 33 of FAS-13 (ASC 840-40-25-2, 25-3), as amended. Thus, a seller-lessee should recognize a sale, remove the asset from the balance sheet, and classify the leaseback in accordance with paragraph 6 of FAS-13 (ASC 840-10-25-43). Any gain on the transaction should be recognized or deferred and amortized in accordance with paragraph 33 of FAS-13 (ASC 840-40-25-3), as amended.

DISCUSSION

Paragraph 21 of FAS-13 (ASC 840-20-40-3) states that "the sale of property subject to an operating lease, or of property that is leased by or intended to be leased by the third-party purchaser to another party, shall not be treated as a sale if the seller or any party related to the seller retains substantial risks of ownership of the leased property. A seller may by various arrangements assure recovery of the investment by the third-party purchaser in some operating lease transactions and thus retain substantial risks in connection with the property." This issue was raised because it was unclear whether and how the provisions of paragraph 21 (ASC 840-20-40-3, 4) apply to sale-leaseback transactions that include assets under an operating lease or that are intended to be subleased by the seller-lessee to another party.

Under one view, the provisions of paragraph 21 (ASC 840-20-40-3, 40-4) and of paragraphs 32 and 33 of FAS-13 (ASC 840-40-25-2, 25-3) do not apply to the same transactions. That is, transactions that do not qualify as sale-leasebacks under the definition in paragraph 32 (ASC 840-40-25-2) of FAS-13, as amended, fall under the provisions of paragraph 21 (ASC 840-20-40-3, 40-4) and are accounted for as borrowings in accordance with the provisions of paragraph 22 (ASC 840-20-35-4). Paragraph 33 (ASC 840-40-25-3) would apply to the accounting for transactions that qualify as sale-leaseback transactions. This view, referred to as the "mutually exclusive" approach, represented predominant practice.

Under a second view, referred to as the "sequential approach," the provisions of paragraphs 21, 32, and 33 (ASC 840-20-40-3, 40-4; 840-40-25-2, 25-3) do apply to the same transactions. Following this approach, the provisions of a sale-leaseback agreement of property subject to an operating lease or intended to be subleased to an unrelated party after the sale-leaseback are evaluated to determine whether the transaction qualifies for sales recognition under the provisions of paragraph 21 (ASC 840-20-40-3, 40-4). Transactions that do not are accounted for as borrowings under paragraph 22 (ASC 840-20-35-4).

Although unstated, the Task Force's consensus indicates support for the mutually exclusive approach, which applies only the provisions of paragraphs 32 and 33 of FAS-13 (ASC 840-40-25-2, 25-3), as amended, in accounting for a sale-leaseback transaction of property other than real estate that is subject to an operating lease or a sublease of the property.

EITF Issue 97-10 (The Effect of Lessee Involvement in Asset Construction) (ASC 460-10-60-28, 60-29, 60-31; 840-40-05-5; 15-5; 25-4; 35-3; 55-2 through 55-6, 55-8, 55-9 through 55-16; S55-2; S99-2)

OVERVIEW

This Issue addresses the effect of a lessee's involvement in the construction of an asset by discussing a build-to-suit lease transaction in which a lessee is actively involved with an asset's construction and may assume some or all of the construction risk. The property may be owned by a developer, a Real Estate Investment Trust (REIT), or an institutional investor. Frequently, a securitization entity is established to hold the real estate and becomes the owner-lessor of the property. The SPE's activities include constructing, owning, and leasing the land and buildings to the lessee. Because the SPE is sufficiently capitalized by third-party investors, the SPE does not meet condition 3 in Issue 90-15 and the lessee is not required to consolidate the SPE.

Although the lessee may be actively involved in the asset's construction by entering into an agreement with the owner-lessor to act as the construction manager or general contractor, the owner-lessor retains title to the land and improvements during construction and during the lease period. Sometimes, an affiliate of the lessee enters into a fixed-price construction contract to perform those duties. The lessee leases the property from the owner-lessor when construction is completed. Some have questioned whether a lessee is, in substance, the owner of the project rather than an agent for the owner-lessor if the lessee assumes some or all of the following obligations during the construction period:

- Makes lease payments before construction is completed
- Guarantees construction debt or provides financing, directly or indirectly
- Assumes primary or secondary obligation on construction contracts
- Acts as an agent for the owner-lessor in the construction, financing, or sale of the asset
- Acts as a developer or in the capacity of a general contractor
- Assumes the obligation to purchase the asset if construction is not completed by a specific date
- Assumes the obligation to fund cost overruns

Those who believe that a lessee who assumes the above obligations during the construction period becomes the owner of the project argue that the lessee is clearly a party to a sale-leaseback transaction covered the guidance in ASC 840-40-05-9 through 05-10, 15-4, 15-9 through 15-10, 25-9 through 25-14, 25-17, 50-1 through 50-2, 55-36, 55-49 through 55-77; ASC 980-840-25-1 through 25-3, 35-1 through 35-2 (FAS-98) when the asset is complete. Under that guidance a transaction must meet certain conditions for the lessee to recognize a sale and derecognize the real estate when construction has been completed and the lease term has begun. If the conditions in FAS-98 (see ASC references above) are not met, the lessee must account for the transaction under the provisions of ASC 840 (FAS-13 as amended by ASC 840-40-25-4 through 25-5, 35-4, 55-79 through 55-80, 55-82 through 55-84, 55-86 through 55-88, 55-90 through 55-92, 55-94 (FAS-28). Those who believe that the transaction does not fall under the provisions of FAS-98 argue that the lessee is acting as an agent for the owner-lessor or working as a general contractor.

Although the EITF discussed the Issue in terms of the construction of a build-to-suit real estate project, the Task Force agreed that the consensus in this Issue applies to all projects involving the construction of an asset, such as a project to build or lease a ship. However, the consensus would not apply if a lessee's (or a party that has an option to become a lessee) maximum obligation, including guaranteed residual values, is only a minor amount (as defined in ASC 840-40-25-4 through 25-5, 35-4, 55-79 through 55-80, 55-82 through 55-84, 55-86 through 55-88, 55-90 through 55-92, 55-94 (FAS-28)) relative to the asset's fair value.

ACCOUNTING ISSUE

How should an entity involved in the construction of an asset it plans to lease when completed determine whether it should be considered the owner of the asset while the asset is under construction?

OBSERVATION: See the guidance in FSP FAS-13-1.

EITF CONSENSUS

1. A lessee that has *substantially* all of the construction period risks should be considered the owner of a real estate project during the construction period and should follow the guidance in FAS-98. A 90% *maximum guarantee test* similar to the recovery-of-investment test discussed in paragraph 7d of FAS-13 (ASC 840-10-25-1) should be used to evaluate whether a lessee has substantially all of the risks during the construction period. All payments associated with the construction project that the lessee is obligated to or can be required to make are included in the lessee's maximum guarantee.

The following are some items that should be included in the lessee's maximum guarantee, unless modified by other consensus positions in this Issue:

  a. Lease payments on a "date certain" lease that must be made whether or not the project is complete
  b. Construction financing guarantees, which can be made only to the owner-lessor (See paragraph 2(d) below.)
  c. Existing equity investments in the owner-lessor or in a party related to the owner-lessor or an obligation to make such investments
  d. Existing loans or advances (or an obligation to makes loans or advances) to the owner-lessor or a party related to the owner-lessor
  e. Payments made in the capacity of developer, general contractor, or construction manager or agent that are reimbursed more infrequently than normal or customary in the real estate construction industry for transactions with parties not involved in the project in any other capacity
  f. Payments as the primary or secondary obligor for project costs under construction contracts
  g. Obligations as a result of the lessee's activities in the capacity of developer or general contractor
  h. An obligation to purchase the real estate project under any circumstances
  i. An obligation to pay for construction cost overruns
  j. An obligation to pay to the lessor, or on behalf of the lessor, rent or fees, such as transaction costs, during the construction period
  k. Payments that may be made for indemnities or guarantees to the owner-lessor

A lessee is considered to have substantially all of the construction period risks and to be the owner of the real estate project during the construction period, if it is determined at the inception of the lease or the date on which the parties agree to the terms of the construction arrangement, whichever is earlier, that the lessee could be required under the governing documents to pay at least 90% of the project's total costs (other than the costs of land acquisition) under any circumstances at any time during the construction period. Although the evaluation of whether the lessee is the owner of the construction project should be made only once, it is necessary to determine whether, at each point during the construction period, the *sum* of the following *two* amounts is *less* than 90% of the total costs incurred on the project to date, other than the costs of acquiring the land:

1. The accreted value of the lessee's previous payments, if any
2. The present value of the maximum amount the lessee can be required to pay as of that point in time, regardless of whether construction is complete

If the test is not met, the lessee is considered to be the real estate project's owner during construction. A lessee is permitted to guarantee an amount that does not exceed the acquisition cost of the land without being considered the owner-lessor of the property, but any unused portion of that guarantee may not be used to cover a shortfall in the guarantee of total project costs. To accrete and discount the cash flows in this calculation, the lessee should use (*a*) the interest rate used to discount the lease payments for lease classification purposes, if it is known, or (*b*) the construction borrowing rate. The probability that a lessee will be required to make such payments is *not considered in the maximum guarantee test.*

2. A lessee would be considered the owner of a real estate project even if the present value of the maximum guarantee is *less than* 90% of the project's total costs under the following conditions:

   a. The lessee or any party related to the lessee associated with the construction project makes or is required to make on behalf of the lessee an equity investment in the owner-lessor that would be considered in substance an investment in real estate according to FAS-66, which includes examples of equity investments that are in substance real estate. (Also see Question 10 of Issue 96-21, which states that the fair value of an option is a soft cost.) The following provide guidance on loans made by the lessee during construction that in substance are considered to be investments in a real estate project: Practice Bulletin 1, Exhibit I; SAB-71; and EITF Issue 84-4.

   b. The lessee must pay directly, instead of through rent payments under the lease, for project costs other than

(1) Costs reimbursed under a contract (as discussed under the first consensus above),

(2) Preexisting environmental risks with a remote risk of loss, or

(3) Costs of normal tenant improvements, except for the following:

  (a) Costs of structural elements, even if those costs were incurred specifically for the lessee

  (b) Equipment that would be a necessary improvement for any lessee, such as the costs of elevators, air conditioning systems, or electrical wiring

  (c) Amounts included in the project's original budget that the owner-lessor agreed to pay for on the date the contract was negotiated, regardless of the character of those costs

c. The lessee indemnifies the owner-lessor or its lenders for preexisting environmental risks for which the risk of loss is more than remote. The guidance in the response to Question 1 of EITF Issue 97-1 should be followed for indemnification of environmental risks.

d. The lessee provides indemnities or guarantees to parties other than the owner-lessor or agrees to indemnify the owner-lessor for costs as a result of claims for damages made by third parties. This excludes certain environmental costs discussed in 2(b) above (see consensus 2(a) in Issue 97-1) and claims made by third parties as a result of the lessee's own actions or lack of action while possessing or controlling the construction project. (See the discussion below on the maximum guarantee test, which should include any indemnification of or guarantee to the owner-lessor against third-party claims related to completion of construction. For example, a lessee is not permitted to provide indemnities or guarantees for acts not under the lessee's control, such as condemnation proceedings or casualties.) A lessee who acts in the capacity of a general contractor is responsible for the actions or failure to act of its subcontractors.

e. The lessee takes title to the real estate during the construction period or provides supplies or other materials used in the construction other than those purchased after the lease term began (or the date of the construction agreement, whichever is earlier) that can be reimbursed as discussed above. Materials provided by the lessee are considered "hard costs," which are discussed in the response to Question 10 of EITF Issue 96-21.

26.30 *Leases*

    f. The lessee (i) owns the land but does not lease it or (ii) leases the land but does not sublease it (or provides an equivalent interest in the land, such as a long-term easement) to the owner-lessor before construction begins. A lessee's sale of the land to the owner-lessor must occur before construction begins. If that transaction occurs and the lessee subsequently leases the land back with improvements, the sale of the land would be accounted for under the requirements of ASC 840-40-05-9 through 05-10, 15-4, 15-9 through 15-10, 25-9 through 25-14, 25-17, 50-1 through 50-2, 55-36, 55-49 through 55-77; ASC 980-840-25-1 through 25-3, 35-1 through 35-2 (FAS-98), even if that guidance would not apply to the lease or the improvements under this consensus.

3. A lessee involved in transactions discussed in this Issue should defer its profit, if any, realized during construction—for example, from rental income received under a ground lease or from fees for construction or development services—and amortize it to income based on the guidance in EITF Issue 86-17. As provided in ASC 840 (FAS-13), the numerator in the maximum guarantee test should not be reduced for deferred gains, if any.
4. The consensus positions in this Issue also should be used to determine whether an entity is the owner of a project during the construction period if the entity has an option to or is required to lease the asset after construction is completed.

> **OBSERVATION:** The consolidation of variable interest entities by an entity that absorbs a majority of a variable entity's expected losses or has the right to receive a greater part of the variable entity's expected residual returns or both is discussed in ASC 810 (FIN-46(R), Consolidation of Variable Interest Entities, as amended by ASC 810 (FAS-167). Under that guidance, an entity that has a variable interest or a combination of interests in a variable interest entity that gives it a controlling financial interest in that entity is required to consolidate the variable interest entity in its financial statements. ASC 810-10-25-38 through 25-38G and ASC 810-10-05-10 (paragraphs 14 through 14G of FIN 46(R)) provide guidance for determining whether an entity has a controlling financial interest in a variable interest entity. The Interpretation applies to many entities involved in the type of leasing arrangements discussed in this Issue.

APPLICATION GUIDANCE

The Task Force provided the following application guidance on the maximum guarantee test:

1. The maximum guarantee test should *include* the following:
   a. Amounts the lessee or any party related to the lessee has invested or is required to invest in the lessor, or any party

related to the lessor, except for investments discussed in 2(a) above.

b. Loans and advances (including time deposits) the lessee or any party related to the lessee has made or is required to make to the lessor, or any party related to the lessor, except for loans that are in substance investments in the project.

c. The maximum amount of project costs the lessee has paid or is required to pay in its capacity as a developer, general contractor, or construction manager/agent that are reimbursed less frequently than is normal or customary. For example, a lessee may be required to make such payments if the project's owner-lessor lacks the funds or a committed line of credit to make the reimbursements. The line of credit would not be considered to be committed if it is possible the lessee would not be reimbursed because the loan agreement, agency agreement, or other document related to the transaction permits the lender to withhold funds for any reason other than the owner-lessor's or its agent's misappropriation of funds or willful misconduct.

d. Guarantees or commitments made to the owner-lessor by a party related to the lessee as if they were made by the lessee, unless all the parties are under common control, for example, if the lessee is a private company controlled by a shareholder who also owns the lessor.

e. The maximum amount of indemnities or guarantees made to the owner-lessor against claims related to construction completion made by third parties, regardless of the probability that such claims will be asserted.

f. Lease payments made under a date-certain lease regardless of whether construction is complete or the lessee is required to make rent prepayments. Those amounts should also be included in determining the lease classification and accounted for according to the guidance in the response to Question 4 of Issue 96-21.

g. The maximum amount of all contingent obligations, regardless of the probability of occurrence, including the following:

   (1) Guarantees and indemnities to the lessor that are assumed by the lessee

   (2) Obligations resulting directly or indirectly from the lessee's inability to complete the project on time, for example, if noncompletion is considered a default under the lease agreement

2. The maximum guarantee test should *exclude* the following:
    a. Contingent obligations assumed by a lessee that are related to
        (1) Permitted environmental indemnities discussed in 2(b) above
        (2) Indemnities for permitted third-party damage claims paid to the owner-lessor as discussed in 2(d) above, except for claims caused directly or indirectly by the lessee's failure to complete construction or to complete it by a specified date (for example, a lender's request for accelerated payments on construction financing)
        (3) An owner-lessor's claims related to a lessee's fraud, misapplication of funds, illegal acts, or willful misconduct
        (4) A lessee's bankruptcy, but only if, based on the facts and circumstances existing on the date the construction contract was entered into, it is reasonable to assume that a bankruptcy will not occur during the expected construction term
    b. Land acquisition costs, regardless of the land's value in relation to the project's overall value. However, in accordance with GAAP, total project costs should *include* land carrying costs, such as interest or ground rentals incurred during construction.
3. The following is other guidance related to the maximum guarantee test:
    a. A lessee is considered to be a construction project's owner if the lessee pays transaction costs, which a lessor would not capitalize under GAAP, to or on behalf of a lessor at the time the construction arrangement is entered into, for example, a facility fee paid to establish a master lease. Such payments would be in excess of total project costs incurred to that point in time, which are used in computing the maximum guarantee. Total project costs include only amounts related to the project that would be capitalized by an owner-lessor under GAAP and other costs related to the project that are paid to third parties other than lenders or owners, such as cancellation fees payable to subcontractors if the project is canceled before completion. Total project costs also specifically *exclude* imputed yield on equity in the project.
    b. A lessee would be considered the owner of a project if the lessee has an unlimited obligation to cover costs over a certain amount, for example, if a lessee acting as a general contractor enters into a fixed-price contract, because the lessee's maximum guarantee would exceed 90% of total project costs.

c. Payments a lessee is required to make as a result of *cost overruns* should be considered carefully. For example, as stated above, a lessee that pays for project costs and is not reimbursed by the owner-lessor would be considered the project's owner during construction. Nevertheless, a lessee is not automatically deemed to be the project's owner during construction because lease payments are made during construction, but should *include* those amounts in the maximum guarantee test and lease classification test.

d. A lessee's payments during construction for *tenant improvements* should also be considered carefully. The maximum guarantee and lease classification tests would not be affected if such payments are for normal tenant improvements, as discussed in 2(a) above. However, payments for other tenant improvements, such as those originally included in amounts that would be paid by the lessor, would be accounted for the same as cost overruns.

e. All alternatives available to the owner-lessor if the lessee is deemed to be in default of the construction period agreement should be considered when the lessee performs the maximum guarantee test. The lessee should select the alternative with the highest cost as a percentage of total project costs. For example, the owner-lessor may be able to (*a*) trigger the lessee's maximum guarantee payment by selling the uncompleted project or (*b*) activate the lease and enforce its rights under the lease.

SEC OBSERVER COMMENT

The SEC Observer stated that the SEC staff believes that under 2a above, a lessee's loan to a lessor should be treated as an ADC arrangement under PB-1, Exhibit I, if the lessee can participate in residual profit. The staff further believes that a lessee that has an option to purchase a leased asset at a fixed price would be considered to be entitled to participate in expected residual profit. Under the Practice Bulletin, a loan is, in substance, an investment if the lessee is expected to receive more than 50% of the residual profit. The classification of the loan depends on the circumstances if the lender/lessee receives 50% or less of the residual profit. A borrower that has a substantial investment in a project not funded by the lender under the guidance in FAS-66 may classify the borrowing as a loan. A lessee would also be considered the owner of the leased asset if the lessor is a special-purpose entity and the lease gives the lessee a fixed-price option to purchase the property or a remarketing agreement under which the lessee receives the majority of the sales proceeds in excess of the leased asset's original cost.

DISCUSSION

Those who supported using a *maximum guarantee test*, which is computed in a similar manner to the 90% recovery-of-investment test in ASC 840 (FAS-13), believed that all payments a lessee is obligated to or can be required to make during the construction period should be considered to be comparable to lease payments, which are included in the minimum lease payment calculation. The working group argued that because in many build-to-suit transactions, the project's financing is the owner's only significant contribution to the project, a lessee that must provide the financing should be considered the project's owner. They believed that the same reasoning should be applied to a lessee's equity investments in a project. Proponents of this view argued that such payments are the same as a lessee's residual value guarantees discussed in ASC 840 (FAS-13). Accordingly, if as a result of loans, guarantees, or other contingent obligations, the present value of the amount for which a lessee is at risk exceeds 90% of total project costs, the lessee should be considered the owner of the project during the construction period. However, the Task Force believed the calculation should exclude contingent rental payments and payments related to certain environmental risks and default covenants related to nonperformance, which are discussed in Questions 1 and 2 of EITF Issue 97-1.

EITF Issue 99-13 (Application of Issue No. 97-10 and FASB Interpretation No. 23 to Entities That Enter into Leases with Governmental Entities) (ASC 840-40-15-2)

OVERVIEW

The EITF reached a consensus in Issue 97-10 that a lessee who is involved with a property during the construction period may be considered the owner of the property for financial reporting purposes depending on the circumstances. For example, a lessee that guarantees the construction debt during the construction period is automatically deemed to be the owner of the property.

Although Issue 97-10 was initially intended to apply to the private sector, some have questioned whether it also should apply to projects involving major real estate improvements funded by governmental entities, such as airports and other transit facilities. A governmental entity generally finances such projects by issuing tax-exempt bonds that are repaid from rental payments made by lessees. The lessee, such as an airline, is usually the general contractor of the project and is reimbursed by the bond trustee for costs incurred during the project.

Questions have been raised about the accounting literature that applies to such transactions. Some believe that depending on the arrangement, a lessee involved in the construction of such a project may be required to account for the property under Issue 97-10. Some projects may be accounted for as financings or as deposits under the guidance in ASC 840-40-05-9 through 05-10, 15-4, 15-9 through 15-10, 25-9 through 25-14, 25-17, 50-1 through 50-2, 55-36, 55-49 through 55-77; ASC 980-840-25-1 through 25-3, 35-1 through 35-2 (FAS-98), in which case the transactions need not be accounted for under the leasing literature. In addition, ASC 840 (FAS-13) and ASC 840-10-25-25 (FIN-23) require that leases meeting certain criteria must be accounted for as operating leases.

ACCOUNTING ISSUE

Should the scope of Issue 97-10 exclude projects that involve the construction and lease of properties owned by governmental entities that would be accounted for as operating leases under the provisions in ASC 840-10-25-25 (FIN-23)?

EITF CONSENSUS

Government-owned properties under construction that will be leased by others after completion should be included in the scope of Issue 97-10. That is, a lessee that has substantially all of the risk during the construction period, as defined in Issue 97-10, should be considered the property's owner for accounting purposes. FAS-98 would apply to a subsequent sale-leaseback.

> **OBSERVATION:** Under the provisions of ASC 460 (FIN-45, Guarantor's Accounting and Disclosure Requirements for Guarantees, Including Indirect Guarantees of Indebtedness to Others), a guarantor is required to recognize a liability for the obligation assumed by issuing the guarantee. ASC 460 also provides guidance on appropriate disclosures that should be made by a guarantor.
> The consolidation of variable interest entities by an entity that absorbs a majority of a variable entity's expected losses or has the right to receive a greater part of the variable entity's expected residual returns or both is discussed in ASC 810 (FIN-46(R), Consolidation of Variable Interest Entities, as amended by FAS-167). Under the guidance in ASC 810, an entity that has a variable interest or a combination of interests in a variable interest entity that gives it a controlling financial interest in that entity is required to consolidate the variable interest entity in its financial statements. ASC 810-10-25-38 through 25-38G and ASC 810-10-05-10 (paragraphs 14 through 14G of FIN 46(R)) provide guidance for determining whether an entity has a controlling financial interest in a variable interest entity.
> Under the guidance in ASC 810 (FIN-46(R), as amended by FAS-167), an entity is not required to consolidate a governmental organization and generally is not required to consolidate a

financing entity that has been established by a governmental organization.

SEC OBSERVER COMMENT

Airlines and other registrants affected by this Issue that have applied the guidance in Issue 97-10 in the proper manner are *not* permitted to change their prior accounting and adopt the consensus in Issue 99-13 in a later period.

Leveraged Leases

EITF Issue 85-16 (Leveraged Leases: Real Estate Leases and Sale-Leaseback Transactions, Delayed Equity Contributions by Lessors) (ASC 840-30-55-15, 55-16)

OVERVIEW

Accounting for Real Estate Leases and Sale-Leaseback Transactions as Leveraged Leases This issue dealt with whether leases and sale-leaseback transactions involving real estate may be accounted for as leveraged leases. During its discussion of Issue 85-16 the EITF reached a consensus that leveraged lease accounting is permitted for leases of real estate, but did not address the issue of leveraged lease accounting for sale-leaseback transactions. The guidance in ASC 840-40-05-9 through 05-10, 15-4, 15-9 through 15-10, 25-9 through 25-14, 25-17, 50-1 through 50-2, 55-36, 55-49 through 55-77; ASC 980-840-25-1 through 25-3, 35-1 through 35-2 (FAS-98), which was issued in May 1988, amends paragraph 26a(ii) of FAS-13 to permit leveraged lease accounting for real estate leases and real estate sale-leaseback transactions that meet certain criteria.

Accounting for Delayed Equity Contributions by Lessors Lessors finance leveraged leases of real estate and equipment with debt that is nonrecourse to the general credit of the lessor as required under paragraph 42c of FAS-13. Rental payments in leveraged lease transactions usually are equal to or greater than payments to service the nonrecourse debt. Depreciation deductions in typical leveraged lease transactions exceed the net amount of rental income and interest expense and provide lessors with tax savings during the early periods of the lease term. Lessors thus recover equity investments quickly. Excess cash accumulated in the middle periods of a leveraged lease's term is used in later periods to pay for taxes due on amounts deferred in earlier periods.

When this Issue was discussed in 1985, some leveraged lease transactions were being structured so that the lessee began making payments from one to two years after the inception of the lease, thus obligating the lessor to make up the deficiency between rent payments and debt service during that period. In such cases, the lessor agreed, in the lease agreement or in a separate binding agreement, to service the nonrecourse debt with equity contributions limited to a specific amount during the period. Such contributions, which are referred to as *delayed equity investments*, were limited to the specified amount and could be measured at the inception of the lease. Although the debt was nonrecourse to the lessor, long-term creditors frequently had recourse to the lessors' general credit for debt service contributions.

ACCOUNTING ISSUES

The EITF considered the following issues related to accounting for delayed equity contributions by lessors:

1. Does paragraph 42c of FAS-13 (ASC 840-10-25-43) preclude leveraged lease accounting if a delayed equity investment is considered to be recourse debt?
2. If leveraged lease accounting is not precluded, should the lessor recognize a liability for the delayed equity investment at the inception of the lease?

EITF CONSENSUS

The EITF reached the following consensus positions related to accounting for delayed equity contributions by lessors:

1. Leveraged lease accounting is not precluded if a delayed equity investment is considered to be recourse debt, because such debt does not contradict the notion of nonrecourse debt under paragraph 42c of FAS-13 (ASC 840-10-25-43).
2. The lessor should recognize a liability for the present value of the obligation at the inception of the lease. The liability increases the lessor's net investment on which the lessor's pattern of income recognition is based. It was noted that although an increase in the net investment would result in additional income, the accrual of interest on the liability would offset that amount.

DISCUSSION

Proponents of leveraged lease accounting argued that a delayed equity investment is part of the lessor's initial investment and does not differ in substance from debt incurred to finance the initial investment. Although the lessor uses such contributions to service the debt, the agreement limits the lessor's payments, which are measurable at the inception of the lease. Further, they noted that based on the economics of the transaction, leveraged lease accounting should not be precluded if the substantial leverage criterion in paragraph 42c (ASC 840-10-25-43) has been met and the transaction conforms with the investment phases stipulated in paragraph 42d of FAS-13 (ASC 840-10-25-43). Those who supported this view also believed that the lessor should recognize a liability for the commitment to make payments on the debt and increase the investment in the leveraged lease at the inception of the lease.

EITF Issue 86-43 (Effect of a Change in Tax Law or Rates on Leveraged Leases) (ASC 840-30-S35-1; S99-2)

OVERVIEW

ASC 840-30-35-38 and 35-39 (paragraph 46 of FAS-13, as interpreted by FTB 79-16 (as revised), requires recalculating the total net income from a leveraged lease as well as the rate of return and the income allocation to years in which the investment had a positive balance from the inception of the lease if there is a change in an important assumption. Because the tax rate is considered an important assumption, lessors under leveraged leases are required to recalculate such leases and recognize an adjustment as a result of the Tax Reform Act of 1986, which changed corporate tax rates.

ACCOUNTING ISSUE

How should a lessor under a leveraged lease calculate and recognize an adjustment, if any, as a result of a change in tax rates?

EITF CONSENSUS

The EITF reached a consensus that under the requirements in ASC 840-30-35-38 and 35-39 (paragraph 46 of FAS-13, as amended by FTB 79-16(R), a lessor should:

- Recalculate all components of a leveraged lease from the inception of the lease based on the revised *after-tax* cash flows resulting from a change in tax law, including revised tax rates and the repeal of the investment tax credit.
- Include the difference between the originally recognized amount and recalculated amounts in income in the year in which the tax law is enacted.

SEC OBSERVER COMMENT

The SEC Observer noted that the ratio of earnings to fixed assets as calculated may be distorted as result of the recommended accounting. For example, a favorable after-tax effect might consist of an unfavorable adjustment to pretax income that is more than offset by a favorable adjustment to income tax expense. If so, notwithstanding the overall favorable effect, there would be a negative effect on the ratio as calculated based on the instructions to Item 503(d) of Regulation S-K, because the "earnings" component of the ratio is based on pretax income.

The SEC Observer also stated that the SEC staff expects registrants to report the cumulative effect on pretax income and income tax expense as a separate line item in the income statement. The SEC staff would not object if registrants excluded an unfavorable pretax adjustment from the "earnings" component of the ratio if the after-tax effect is favorable and (1) the exclusion is adequately identified and explained in all disclosures related to the ratio and (2) there is supplemental disclosure of the ratio as calculated in accordance with the applicable instructions.

DISCUSSION

Some had suggested an alternative approach under which the deferred tax liability for cumulative unreversed timing differences would be calculated using the new tax rates, and deferred tax credits associated with leveraged leases would be adjusted to that amount. Pretax income or the investment tax credit previously recognized would not be adjusted. The EITF's consensus indicates that the Task Force decided to follow a literal interpretation of the requirement in paragraph 46 of FAS-13 (ASC 840-30-35-38, 35-39) rather than an approach for which there was no basis in ASC 840 (FAS-13).

> **OBSERVATION:** See the consensus on Issue 87-8 (Tax Reform Act of 1986: Issues Related to the Alternative Minimum Tax) in which the Task Force reached a consensus that leveraged lease computations should include assumptions about the effect of the alternative minimum tax.

Tax-Related Matters

EITF Issue 86-33 (Tax Indemnifications in Lease Agreements) (ASC 460-10-55-23A; 840-10-25-10, 25-11, 25-53; 50-3)

OVERVIEW

In anticipation of the Tax Reform Act of 1986, some lessors were including tax indemnification clauses in lease agreements that would require a lessee to indemnify the lessor, on an after-tax basis, for tax benefits lost as a result of changes in tax laws. The tax law changes contemplated at the time included the retroactive elimination of the investment tax credit (ITC) and significant reductions in tax rates.

ACCOUNTING ISSUE

Should lessors and lessees account for tax indemnification payments as (1) contingent rent, (2) replacement of tax benefits, (3) ratably as income/expense, or (4) a revision of the lease?

> **OBSERVATION:** Under the provisions of FIN-45 (Guarantor's Accounting and Disclosure Requirements for Guarantees, Including Indirect Guarantees of Indebtedness to Others), a guarantor is required to recognize a liability for the obligation assumed by issuing the guarantee. The Interpretation also provides guidance on appropriate disclosures that should be made by a guarantor. The lessee, who is the guarantor in this Issue, is required to recognize a liability for the indemnification agreement at the inception of the lease in accordance with paragraph 3(c) of FIN-45 (ASC 460-10-15-4) and to measure the liability at the fair value of the obligation under the indemnification agreement.

EITF CONSENSUS

The EITF reached a consensus that, although tax indemnification payments may appear to meet the definition of a contingent rental in ASC 840 (FAS-13) as amended by ASC 840-10-55-38 through 55-39 (FAS-29), they are not the type of payments normally expected to occur under continuing rent provisions. Because they can be closely associated with specific aspects of the tax law, such payments should be accounted for in a manner that recognizes that association. The transaction should not affect the lease's original classification.

Lessors should allocate tax indemnification payments into amounts associated with (1) the lost investment tax credit and (2) all other tax effects. Those amounts should be accounted for as follows:

- Account for the amount attributed to the ITC based on the lessor's method of accounting for the ITC. That is, recognize payments related to the ITC in the income statement in the same period as the ITC would have been recognized. The EITF did not, however, discuss how to classify such payments in the income statement.
- Account for amounts related to all other tax effects consistent with the lease classification as follows:

    —Capital lease: Adjust the lessor's investment.

    —Operating lease: Recognize ratably over the lease term.

Lessees should account for tax indemnification payments as follows:

- Operating lease: Recognize as additional expense ratably over the remaining lease term, regardless of when payments are made. This treatment is consistent with the accounting for

nonlevel rents under the guidance in ASC 840 (FAS-13) and FTB 85-3.
- Capital lease: Adjust the basis of the leased asset.

DISCUSSION

Those who supported accounting for tax indemnification payments as the replacement of tax benefits, rather than by one of the other methods suggested, argued that this method is the most equitable for both lessors and lessees. It is consistent with the economics of the transaction and allows the parties to continue accounting for the lease without revising the agreement. Under this method, lessees can expense the additional payments over the term of the lease rather than accruing the total amount, as would be required under the contingent rent method. Supporters argued that payments should be attributed to the period during which the leased property is used.

EITF Issue 87-8 (Tax Reform Act of 1986: Issues Related to the Alternative Minimum Tax) (ASC 740-10-25-43; 840-30-35-48 through 35-52)

OVERVIEW

Under the Tax Reform Act of 1986 (the Act), an entity computes its federal income tax liability based on the regular tax system or on the alternative minimum tax (AMT) system, whichever tax amount is greater. An entity may earn an AMT credit for tax paid under the AMT system that exceeds the amount that would have been paid under the regular tax system. An AMT credit can be carried forward indefinitely to reduce the regular tax in future years, but not below the AMT for that year.

ACCOUNTING ISSUE

Should leveraged lease calculations consider the effect of the AMT on cash flows and if so, how? (Issue 1 is discussed in Chapter 20, "Income Taxes." Consensus positions on Issues 2-9 and 11 have been nullified.)

EITF CONSENSUS

The EITF reached a consensus that an entity's leveraged lease tax computations should include assumptions about the effect of the AMT by considering the entity's overall tax position. Paragraph 46 of FAS-13 (ASC 840-30-35-38, 35-39) requires entities involved in leveraged leases to evaluate annually important assumptions that affect total net income from the lease. If total after-tax net income changes as a result of a change in tax assumptions, the lessor should:

- Recalculate the rate of return on the leveraged lease from inception,
- Adjust accounts that constitute the lessor's net investment, *and*
- Recognize a gain or loss in the year in which an assumption is changed.

However, if an entity's tax position changes frequently between the AMT and the regular tax, such recomputation is not required unless there is an indication that the original assumptions about total after-tax income are no longer valid. In that case, the entity should revise the leveraged lease computations in any period in which total net income from the leveraged lease changes because of the effect of the AMT on the lease's cash flows.

According to paragraph 44 of FAS-13 (ASC 840-30-35-33 through 35-35), a lessor is required to allocate income from a leveraged lease among years in which the net investment in the leveraged lease is positive based on projected after-tax cash flows at the inception of the lease. Important assumptions in a leveraged lease calculation include the lessor's income tax rate and the amount of taxes paid or tax benefits received. A difference, if any, between AMT depreciation and tax depreciation assumed in the leveraged lease calculation or between income recognition for financial reporting and AMT income could—depending on the lessor's overall tax situation—result in AMT or utilization of AMT credits. An AMT payment or use of an AMT credit could change total cash flows from the leveraged lease and affect the lessor's income recognition.

DISCUSSION

Two methods were proposed for evaluating the effect of the AMT on cash flows in a leveraged lease. Under the first approach, the effects of the AMT on leveraged leases would have been analyzed on a lease-by-lease basis. Such an approach viewed leveraged leases separately and would have ignored the entity's overall tax position. Under the second approach, which was the basis for the EITF's consensus, the effect of the AMT would be analyzed considering the lessor's overall tax position. The argument for that approach was that accounting for leveraged leases is based on the concept of after-tax cash flows. The leveraged lease calculation treats projected tax benefits received or taxes paid as receipts or disbursements for the purpose of income recognition. Although the tax consequences of a leveraged lease may not be otherwise affected by the AMT, they could be affected by other preference items included in the lessor's income. Thus, the lessor's anticipated overall tax position should be included in the leveraged lease's tax assumptions, which should be reviewed annually.

EITF Issue 89-20 (Accounting for Cross Border Tax Benefit Leases) (ASC 840-40-55-29 through 55-34)

OVERVIEW

Sale-leaseback transactions can be arranged so that both the seller-lessee and the buyer-lessor are entitled to tax deductions for the same depreciable asset. To accomplish this, the seller-lessee and the buyer-lessor must be located in different countries whose income tax laws differ as to which party is entitled to the deduction for a depreciable asset.

A typical example involves a U.S. company as the seller-lessee and a foreign investor as the buyer-lessor. The transaction usually is structured as follows:

- A U.S. company purchases equipment costing $500,000 from a manufacturer and thus obtains title and tax benefits to be used in filing its U.S. taxes.

- The U.S. company, also a manufacturer, enters into a conditional sales agreement with a foreign investor; under the agreement, it sells the equipment to the foreign investor for $500,000. The agreement enables the foreign investor to claim ownership of the equipment in its own country, thus obtaining certain tax benefits in that foreign country.

- To retain its U.S. tax benefits, the U.S. company enters into a financing lease for tax purposes. The lease contains a bargain purchase option and a penalty at the end of the lease term that virtually assures the exercise of the purchase option. The present value of the lease payments, including the bargain purchase option, is $460,000.

- The lease also calls for the lessee to place $460,000 with a third-party trustee who makes future lease payments unless the trustee becomes insolvent.

- In a sale-leaseback, the U.S. company nets $40,000, the excess of the sales proceeds ($500,000) over the payment to the trustee ($460,000).

- The U.S. company agrees to indemnify the foreign investor only for a loss of tax benefits as a result of certain events such as the sale, loss, or destruction of the equipment or bankruptcy of the U.S. company, which can settle the obligation by buying a letter of credit from a bank in favor of the foreign investor.

There are two views on the accounting for the $40,000 retained by the U.S. company. Some view the net proceeds as income that should be recognized immediately. Others view the net proceeds as an adjustment of the cost of the equipment or as deferred income.

ACCOUNTING ISSUE

Should net proceeds retained by the U.S. company (seller-lessee) in a tax benefit sale-leaseback transaction be reported as income immediately or deferred and amortized to income?

EITF CONSENSUS

> **OBSERVATION:** Under the provisions of ASC 460 (FIN-45), a guarantor is required to recognize a liability for the obligation assumed by issuing the guarantee. The Interpretation also provides guidance on appropriate disclosures that should be made by a guarantor. ASC 460 (FIN-45) *partially nullifies* the consensus in this Issue, because the foreign entity's payment to the U.S. company is for both the transfer of tax benefits and an agreement to indemnify that entity or a third party for a loss of the tax benefits under certain circumstances. Therefore, in accordance with the requirements of ASC 460 (FIN-45), the U.S. company should recognize a liability at the inception of the transaction at the fair value of the indemnification agreement.
>
> The consolidation of variable interest entities by an entity that absorbs a majority of a variable entity's expected losses or has the right to receive a greater part of the variable entity's expected residual returns or both is discussed in ASC 810 (FIN-46(R), Consolidation of Variable Interest Entities, as amended by FAS-167). Under the guidance in ASC 810, an entity that has a variable interest or a combination of interests in a variable interest entity that gives it a controlling financial interest in that entity is required to consolidate the variable interest entity in its financial statements. ASC 810-10-25-38 through 25-38G and ASC 810-10-05-10 (paragraphs 14 through 14G of FIN 46(R)) provide guidance for determining whether an entity has a controlling financial interest in a variable interest entity.

The EITF reached a consensus that the net proceeds should be accounted for based on the individual facts and circumstances. However, immediate recognition is not appropriate if there is more than a remote possibility of a loss as a result of contingencies, such as indemnification clauses.

DISCUSSION

The EITF's consensus indicates that there was no straightforward solution to this Issue. Those who supported immediate income recognition of the net proceeds retained in the transaction believed that the sale of the ownership right to U.S. tax benefits to an entity in a foreign tax jurisdiction was consummated and income was earned when the transaction was closed. They argued that the economic substance for the various components of the transaction is related only to the sale of tax benefits. Others argued, however, that income recognition is not assured when the transaction is consummated, if there is an agreement to indemnify the foreign investor for the loss of tax benefits as a result of certain events. Such an agreement creates a contingency that must be evaluated for the probability of loss under the provisions of ASC 450 (FAS-5).

Other Matters

EITF Issue 92-1 (Allocation of Residual Value or First-Loss Guarantee to Minimum Lease Payments in Leases Involving Land and Building(s)) (ASC 460-10-60-19; 840-10-25-21, 25-22)

OVERVIEW

Real estate leases for land and buildings often include a clause guaranteeing the property's residual value (guarantee) that transfers some risks to the lessee and ensures that the lessor will receive an appropriate return of and on the investment in the property. ASC 850-10-55-15 (paragraph 5j(i) of FAS-13) requires including a guarantee in minimum lease payments in determining whether to classify a lease as an operating or a capital lease.

ASC 840-10-25-1 (paragraph 7 of FAS-13) provides that a lease should be treated as a capital lease if any of the following criteria is met:

- Ownership of the property is transferred to the lessee by the end of the lease term.
- The lease contains a bargain purchase option.
- The lease term is 75% or more of the estimated economic life of the leased property.
- The present value of minimum lease payments (as defined) is 90% or more of the estimated fair value of the leased property.

FAS-13 distinguishes between real estate leases involving only land and those that involve land and buildings for the purpose of lease classification. Paragraph 25 (ASC 840-10-25-55-59), which applies to leases of land only, classifies a lease as a capital lease if it meets one of the criteria in paragraphs 7a and 7b (ASC 840-10-25-1). Thus, a guarantee, which is a component of minimum lease payments and is considered in the calculation in paragraph 7d (ASC 840-10-25-1), is excluded from the calculation in determining the lease classification of land.

Under the provisions of paragraph 26 (ASC 840-10-25-38), a lease involving land and buildings should be classified and accounted for as a capital lease if either criterion (*a*) or criterion (*b*) is met. If neither of those criteria is met, and the fair value of the land is less than 25% of the total value of the leased property at inception of the lease, paragraph 26b(i) (ASC 840-10-25-38) provides that the land and building be considered as a unit and treated essentially the same as a building.

However, if the fair value of the land is greater than 25% of the total fair value of the property at inception of the lease, paragraph 26b(ii) of FAS-13 (ASC 840-10-25-38) requires that the land and building be evaluated *separately* in applying paragraphs 7c and 7d (ASC 840-10-25-1) to determine whether to classify the building as an operating or capital lease. Because a guarantee is not considered in the classification of land only, as discussed above, a literal interpretation of paragraph 26b(ii) of FAS-13 (ASC 840-10-25-38) would included a guarantee solely in minimum lease payments attributed to the building in this separate evaluation.

Some questioned this interpretation of the treatment of the guarantee in an economic environment in which land may no longer retain its value. A literal interpretation of paragraph 26b(ii) (ASC 840-10-25-38) often provides anomalous results. For example, if a guarantee equals or exceeds the building's fair value, a separate evaluation of the land and building may indicate that the lessee should classify the lease on the building as a capital lease; an evaluation of the land and building as a unit would result in an operating lease classification. Consequently, the following alternative methods have been used in practice:

- Allocating the guarantee to the land and the building in proportion to their relative fair values.
- Allocating the guarantee to the building in proportion to its fair value at inception of the lease and the remainder to the land.
- Allocating the total amount of the guarantee to the building.

ACCOUNTING ISSUE

How should a guarantee be treated when applying the criterion in paragraph 7d of FAS-13 (ASC 840-10-25-1) to a real estate lease involving land and a building if the fair value of the land is 25% or more of the total fair value of the leased property?

EITF CONSENSUS

The EITF reached a consensus that the literal interpretation of paragraph 26b(ii) (ASC 840-10-25-1) should be followed. Thus, the lessee and the lessor should determine the amount of annual minimum lease payments to be attributed to the portion of the lease related to the land by multiplying the lessee's incremental borrowing rate by the fair value of the land. The remaining minimum lease payments, including the full amount of the guarantee, should be attributed to the portion of the lease related to the building.

> **OBSERVATION:** The embedded guarantee discussed in this Issue is not a derivative under the provisions of FAS-133.

DISCUSSION

Under the model followed in FAS-13, the value of land does not depreciate and therefore does not require a guarantee.

EITF Issue 95-17 (Accounting for Modifications to an Operating Lease That Do Not Change the Lease Classification) (ASC 840-20-55-4 through 55-6)

OVERVIEW

An operating lease on real estate is modified before the lease term expires by shortening the lease term and increasing lease payments during that period. As a result, lease payments exceed comparable market rents. The lease classification is unaffected by this modification, which involves no other changes to the lease.

ACCOUNTING ISSUE

Should the amount of lease payments under a modified lease that exceeds the amount of lease payments that would have been required during the shortened lease period under the original lease be considered a modification of future lease payments, or is the excess, in substance, a termination penalty?

EITF CONSENSUS

The EITF reached the following consensus positions:

- Lease payments under a modified lease that exceed payments that would have been required during the shortened lease period under the original lease should be accounted for as follows, based on the relevant facts and circumstances:
  - Excess payments considered to be a modification of future lease payments should be accounted for prospectively over the modified lease term.
  - Excess payments considered to be, in substance, a termination penalty should be charged to income in the period of the modification.

  The following factors should be considered in determining the nature of the modification:
  - *The relationship of the modified lease term to the remaining term on the original lease* The likelihood that the excess is a termination penalty is increased the shorter the term of the modified lease is in comparison to the remaining original lease term.
  - *The difference between the modified lease payments and market rents* The likelihood that the excess is a modification of future

lease payments is increased the closer the amount of modified lease payments is to market rentals for comparable property.
- The charge to income for an increase in lease payments considered to be a *termination penalty* is calculated as the amount by which modified lease payments exceed required lease payments under the original lease for the shortened period. Actual or discounted amounts may be recognized consistent with the entity's accounting policy and should be disclosed in accordance with APB-22, if material.

Illustration of the Accounting for Modifications on an Operating Lease That Do Not Change the Lease Classification

Morningstar, Inc. has a lease for office space that expires on February 28, 20X9, with monthly rental payments of $10,000. On February 20, 20X6, Morningstar and the lessor agree to modify the lease term: it will terminate on February 28, 20X7, with modified monthly lease payments of $18,000 as of March 1, 20X6. Monthly rentals for comparable space are $12,000.

Morningstar should account for the modification in the lease by recognizing a termination penalty of $96,000 [($18,000 − $10,000) × 12 months] in income in the quarter ended March 31, 20X6. The excess payments are considered a termination penalty because (*a*) the shortened lease term of 12 months is only one third of the remaining lease term of 36 months, and (*b*) the modified monthly rental payment of $18,000 exceeds market rents by 50%.

DISCUSSION

This Issue was raised because of the lack of guidance in FAS-13 for such lease modifications. Proponents of accounting for the excess payments prospectively as a modification of future lease payments believed that paragraph 9 of FAS-13 (ASC 840-10-35-4) requires that approach if the lease classification is unchanged. They also believed that the excess lease payments do not qualify for immediate recognition as a termination penalty, because they are associated with continuing operations and thus do not qualify for accrual as an exit cost under the consensus in EITF Issue 94-3, because the activity is not terminated. Conversely, those who believed the excess payments represent a termination penalty argue that the entity receives no future benefit from those payments. They believe that the modification of a lease to a shorter term is analogous to a termination or exit activity.

The views of the Task Force on this Issue were mixed. Many members believed that the excess payments should be accounted for as a cost of canceling a portion of the lease term and recognized currently as an exit cost. One member suggested another approach, under which termination costs would equal the excess of the present value of rents under the modified lease over rents on the original lease. The Task Force was unable to decide, however, whether such costs represent an exit cost in all situations. As a result, the Task Force concluded that neither approach may be applicable to all situations and tentatively decided to account for such costs prospectively or in the current period, based on the facts and circumstances.

EITF Issue 96-21 (Implementation Issues in Accounting for Leasing Transactions Involving Special-Purpose Entities) (840-10-25-6, 25-8, 25-12, 25-13; 840-20-30-1; 35-1; 840-40-55-42 through 55-47; 958-810-25-9; 55-7 through 55-16; 958-840-55-2 through 55-3; 460-10-60-24)

> **OBSERVATION:** ASC 810-10 (FIN-46(R), Consolidation of Variable Interest Entities), which has been amended by FAS-167, requires the consolidation of variable interest entities by an entity that absorbs a majority of a variable entity's expected losses or has the right to receive a greater part of the variable entity's expected residual returns or both. Because the consensuses reached in Questions 1 through 3, 5, and 7 through 9 are related to the implementation of the first and third conditions of Issue 90-15 (Impact of Substantive Lessors, Residual Value Guarantees, and Other Provisions in Leasing Transactions), which was *nullified* by FIN-46 (R), those questions and all but the first sentence in the response to Question 6 also have been nullified by the Interpretation. This Issue has been updated for the amendments in FAS-167.

OVERVIEW

The consensus in EITF Issue 90-15 requires a lessee to consolidate in its financial statements the assets, liabilities, results of operations, and cash flows of a securitization entity that is established for the construction and subsequent lease of an asset if *all* of the following conditions exist:

1. Substantially all of the securitization entity's activities are related to assets that are leased to one lessee.
2. The lessee is expected to have, directly or indirectly, the substantive residual risks, substantially all the residual rewards of the leased asset(s), and the obligation related to the underlying securitization entity debt as a result of the following:
   a. The lease agreement
   b. A residual value guarantee (for example, the lessee assumes losses above a given amount)
   c. A guarantee of the securitization entity's debt
   d. The lessee has the option to purchase the leased asset at a fixed price or a defined price other than fair value at the exercise

date. (Alternatively, the lessee may be entitled to proceeds from a sale of the leased asset exceeding a stated amount.)
3. The securitization entity's owner(s) of record has not made a substantive residual equity investment that is at risk during the entire lease term.

Under the consensus in Issue 90-15, the lessee should begin consolidating the securitization entity at the inception of the lease (the date of the lease or written commitment), as defined in FAS-13 and amended by FAS-23, rather than at the beginning of the lease term.

Questions had arisen about the application of conditions 1 and 3 of Issue 90-15; questions also had arisen about leasing transactions involving securitization entities that can affect other leasing transactions not involving securitization entities. In essence, the EITF was asked to develop implementation guidance for determining the present value of minimum lease payments at the beginning of the lease term, as discussed in paragraph 7d of FAS-13 (ASC 840-10-25-1), and about the sale-leaseback provisions of FAS-98. In response, the EITF appointed a working group, which recommended the guidance adopted by the EITF in the consensus positions on the following questions and answers.

Question 4—Lessee Payments Made before the Beginning of the Lease Term

OVERVIEW

Lessees may sometimes be required to make payments (known as construction period lease payments) to the lessor before construction is completed and the lease term has begun in build-to-suit transactions.

ACCOUNTING ISSUES

1. Should construction period lease payments be included in the minimum lease payments when applying the 90% of fair value recovery test specified in paragraph 7d of FAS-13 (ASC 840-10-25-1)?
2. How should a lessee account for such payments if the lease is classified as an operating lease?

EITF CONSENSUS

1. Payments made before the lease term begins should be considered to be part of the minimum lease payments, and they should be included in the 90% test at their future value at the beginning of the lease term. The interest rate used to compute the future value of payments to be made before the beginning of the lease term should be the same as that used to discount lease payments to be made during the lease term.

2. If a lease is classified as an operating lease, lease payments made before the lease term begins should be accounted for as prepaid rent and included in total rent costs, which generally should be allocated on a straight-line basis over the term of the lease, in accordance with FTB 88-1 (Issues Relating to Accounting for Leases).

Question 6—Fees Paid to a securitization entity's Owners

OVERVIEW

Under some lease agreements, a lessee is required to pay the securitization entity's owner certain fees, which are referred to as structuring or administrative fees, for arranging the lease.

ACCOUNTING ISSUE

How should the lessee and the securitization entity account for structuring or administrative fees paid to the securitization entity's owner of record?

EITF CONSENSUS

A lessee should include such fees in the minimum lease payments—but not in the fair value of the property—for the purpose of applying the 90% test in paragraph 7d of FAS-13 (ASC 840-10-25-1).

DISCUSSION

Only payments from GAAP earnings or previously undistributed earnings can be considered a return *on* investment.

Question 10—Costs Incurred by Lessees before Entering into a Lease

OVERVIEW

In build-to-suit lease transactions, a lessee sometimes incurs certain development costs before entering into a lease with a developer-lessor. The costs may be soft costs, such as architectural fees and zoning fees, or hard costs, such as site preparation and construction costs.

ACCOUNTING ISSUE

What kinds of costs (and in what amount) can a lessee incur before entering a lease agreement without being considered the owner of the property and therefore subject to the requirements of ASC 840-40-05-9 through 05-10, 15-4, 15-9 through 15-10, 25-9 through 25-14, 25-17, 50-1 through 50-2, 55-36, 55-49 through 55-77; ASC 980-840-25-1 through 25-3, 35-1 through 35-2 (FAS-98) for sale-leaseback transactions?

EITF CONSENSUS

A lessee that begins construction activities should recognize construction in progress as an asset and account for it under the provisions of FAS-98, as discussed in Question 11 below. Construction activities are deemed to have begun if any of the following have occurred:

- The lessee has begun construction (broken ground).
- The lessee has incurred hard costs, whether those costs are insignificant or not to the fair value of the property to be constructed.
- The lessee has incurred soft costs that amount to more than 10% of the expected fair value of the leased property. In a build-to-suit lease, soft costs would include the fair value of the lessee's option to acquire real property that is transferred to the securitization entity. Off-balance-sheet purchase commitments at market would not be included, however.

DISCUSSION

A lessee that is involved in more than an insignificant aspect of the construction process and has incurred hard costs or significant soft costs on a project assumes the risks of ownership.

Question 11—Accounting under FAS-98 for Construction-in-Process Transferred to a Securitization Entity

OVERVIEW

A lessee begins construction activities, as discussed in Question 10, and subsequently transfers the property to a securitization entity in a transaction deemed to be within the scope of ASC 840-40-05-9 through 05-10, 15-4, 15-9 through 15-10, 25-9 through 25-14, 25-17, 50-1 through 50-2, 55-36, 55-49 through 55-77; ASC 980-840-25-1 through 25-3, 35-1 through 35-2 (FAS-98).

ACCOUNTING ISSUE

How should the lessee apply the provisions of FAS-98 to the transaction?

EITF CONSENSUS

The transaction would be evaluated as a sale-leaseback under the provisions of FAS-98, because the lessee is considered the owner of the project. The lessee should account for the property as follows:

- Recognize a sale and profit or loss if the transaction qualifies as a sale under the provisions of ASC 840-40-25-4 through 25-5, 35-4, 55-79 through 55-80, 55-82 through 55-84, 55-86 through 55-88, 55-90 through 55-92, 55-94 (FAS-28), ASC 976-605-25-4, 25-1 through 25-2, 25-6, 25-8 through 25-9, 25-11 through 25-12, 30-1 through 30-4, 35-1, 55-1 through 55-11, 55-13 through 55-14; ASC 976-10-15-1 through 15-4; ASC 976-310-30-1, 35-1, 40-1,50-1; 976-330-50-1; 976-705-30-1; ASC 360-20-15-10, 15-1 through 15-2, 40-3 through 40-5, 40-7 through 40-10, 40-13, 40-18 through 40-31, 40-33 through 40-34, 40-36 through 40-38, 40-40 through 40-50, 40-56 through 40-64, 55-1 through 55-2, 55-7 through 55-17, 55-19 through 55-21, 55-23 through 55-34, 55-36 through 55-38, 55-40 through 55-54, 55-61 through 55-64; ASC 360- ASC 460-10-60-3; ASC 840-10-25-60 (FAS-66), and ASC 840-40-05-9 through 05-10, 15-4, 15-9 through 15-10, 25-9 through 25-14, 25-17, 50-1 through 50-2, 55-36, 55-49 through 55-77; ASC 980-840-25-1 through 25-3, 35-1 through 35-2 (FAS-98).

- Continue reporting construction-in-progress as an asset and recognize proceeds received from the securitization entity as a liability; if the transaction does *not* qualify for sale-leaseback accounting, the lessee would:

    —Report additional amounts spent by the securitization entity on construction as construction-in-progress and as a liability to the securitization entity.

    —Depreciate the property after the property is placed in service and account for the lease payments as debt service on the liability.

Question 12—Interest-only Payments

OVERVIEW

Rental payments on real estate leases that involve a securitization entity often consist of the total interest on the securitization entity's debt plus a return on the securitization entity's equity. The lessee also frequently guarantees that the value of the property will be a specified amount at the end of the lease term. The lease is classified as an operating lease, because the present value of the minimum lease payments, including the maximum deficiency under the residual value guarantee that the lessee is required to pay, does not meet the 90% test under paragraph 7d of FAS-13 (ASC 840-10-25-1).

ACCOUNTING ISSUE

How should a lessee account for an interest-only lease that otherwise qualifies as an operating lease?

EITF CONSENSUS

> **OBSERVATION:** Under the provisions of ASC 460 (FIN-45, Guarantor's Accounting and Disclosure Requirements for Guarantees, Including Indirect Guarantees of Indebtedness to Others), a guarantor is required to recognize a liability for an obligation assumed by issuing a guarantee. The Interpretation also provides guidance on appropriate disclosures that should be made by a guarantor. The consensus in this Issue is *partially nullified* by the Interpretation, because, under the guidance in ASC 460 (FIN-45), a guarantor-lessee is required to recognize the fair value of a residual value guarantee at the inception of a lease even though the likelihood that a deficiency will occur is *not* probable at that time. However, depending on the guarantor-lessee's accounting policy for subsequent payments, that requirement may not affect the guarantor-lessee's earnings for each reporting period over the lease term if no payments for a deficiency are due under the guarantee. The guidance in the response to Question 12 on a guarantor-lessee's accrual for a contingent loss under a guarantee continues to apply, because the Interpretation does *not* address that matter.

The lessee should recognize rent expense on a straight-line basis, in accordance with paragraph 15 of FAS-13 (ASC 840-20-25-1). Payments related to a deficiency would not be included in that calculation until it becomes probable that the value of the property at the end of the lease term will be less than the guaranteed amount (even though the maximum deficiency under the residual value guarantee is included in minimum lease payments for the 90% test). When a deficiency becomes probable, the lessee should accrue the amount of the expected deficiency and recognize it on a straight-line basis over the remainder of the lease term. The deficiency must be accrued even if the lessee expects to exercise a purchase or renewal option at the end of the lease term.

EITF Issue 97-1 (Implementation Issues in Accounting for Lease Transactions, Including Those Involving Special-Purpose Entities) (ASC 450-20-60-16; 460-10-60-23; 840-10-05-7, 05-8; 25-12, 25-14; 840-40-15-2; 25-13; 958-840-55-4)

OVERVIEW

Issue arose because the guidance in ASC 840 (FAS-13), which requires lessees to classify leases as operating or capital leases, does not address the effect of certain lease provisions on a lessee's balance sheet classification. Specifically, it addresses questions related to a lessee's balance sheet classification of leases that (1) require a lessee to accept responsibility for certain risks that are normally the responsibility of the property's legal owner, such as environmental contamination that occurred before the inception of the lease, or (2) include default covenants for nonperformance—for example, if the lessee does not maintain certain financial ratios. The lessor may have the right under such provisions to require the lessee to acquire the property or to pay the lessor.

An additional question addressed in this Issue, which was not addressed in Issue 90-15 or Issue 96-21, is related to a securitization entity's computation of depreciation in determining GAAP earnings when a lessee meets condition (2) of Issue 90-15.

Questions 1 and 2 apply to all leasing transactions. Question 3 applies only to leasing transactions in which the lessor is a securitization entity.

> **OBSERVATION:** Under the provisions of ASC 460 (FIN-45), a guarantor is required to recognize a liability for an obligation assumed by issuing a guarantee. The Interpretation also provides guidance on appropriate disclosures that should be made by a guarantor. If a guarantee or indemnification included in an *operating lease* meets any of the characteristics in ASC 460-10-15-4 (paragraph 3 of the Interpretation), the lessee may be required to recognize a liability at the inception of the lease. The disclosure requirement in FIN-45 also would apply to the guarantee. Capital leases accounted for under the guidance in ASC 840 (FAS-13, Accounting for Leases) are excluded from the scope of the Interpretation.
>
> ASC 819-19 (FIN-46(R), Consolidation of Variable Interest Entities), which has been amended by FAS-167, requires the consolidation of variable interest entities by an entity that absorbs a majority of a variable interest entity's expected losses or has the right to receive a greater part of the variable interest entity's expected residual returns or both. Because the guidance in Issue 90-15 (Impact of Substantive Lessors, Residual Value Guarantees, and Other Provisions in Leasing Transactions) has been nullified by ASC 810-10 (FIN-46(R)), Question 3 in this Issue, which discussed the implementation of the conditions in Issue 90-15, consequently also has been nullified. This Issue has been updated for the amendments in FAS-167.

Question 1—Lessee's Responsibility for Environmental Risk

OVERVIEW

A lease requires the lessee to indemnify the lessor or the lessor's lender against loss or damage from the lessee's environmental contamination during the term of the lease and for environmental contamination that occurred before the inception of the lease. Instead of requiring indemnification, the lease may require the lessee to acquire the property.

ACCOUNTING ISSUE

How should a lease with such provisions be classified in a lessee's balance sheet?

EITF CONSENSUS

- Lease provisions requiring indemnification for a lessee's environmental contamination during the term of the lease do not affect the lessee's balance sheet classification of the lease.
- A lessee required under the terms of a lease to indemnify the lessor or its lender for environmental contamination that existed before the lease term should at the inception of the lease term evaluate the likelihood of a loss (without recoveries from third parties) based on enacted environmental laws and existing regulations and policies and whether the lessee may be considered the owner of the property.
    —If the likelihood of a loss is remote, the lessee would not be considered the owner of the property.
    —If the likelihood of a loss is at least reasonably possible (according to FAS-5), the lessee should account for the lease in accordance with the sale-leaseback provisions of FAS-98 as if the lessee had purchased, sold, and leased back the property.

DISCUSSION

When a lessee agrees to pay for remediation of environmental contamination that occurred before the term of the lease, the lessee is taking on a risk of ownership of a property, which is beyond the responsibility of a lessee. The lessee reflects that additional risk by classifying the lease as a capital rather than as an operating lease.

Question 2—Non–Performance-Related Default Covenants

OVERVIEW

A lease contains default provisions unrelated to the lessor's use of the property, such as financial covenants that require the lessee to maintain certain financial ratios. To remedy default, the lessee may be required to make a payment to the lessor or acquire the property.

ACCOUNTING ISSUE

How should a lessee classify a lease containing a default provision that is unrelated to the lessee's performance on the lease?

EITF CONSENSUS

1. The classification of a lease containing a default provision is unchanged if it meets *all* the following conditions:

    a. The default covenant is customary in financing arrangements.

    b. The occurrence of default can be determined objectively (acceleration clauses would not meet this condition).

    c. Default would be determined based on specific criteria that apply only to the lessee and its operations.

    d. Based on the facts and circumstances existing at the inception of the lease, it is reasonable to assume that default will not occur.

    Recent trends in the lessee's operations should be considered in applying condition d. If one of the above conditions is absent, the lessee should include the maximum required payment under the default covenant in the amount of minimum lease payments when applying paragraph 7d of FAS-13 (ASC 840-10-25-1).

2. A lease with a default provision that is part of a sale-leaseback transaction and thus covered by the provisions of FAS-98 should be accounted for by the deposit method or as a financing transaction based on the guidance in FAS-66, regardless of whether all the conditions in (1) above are met. This is so because a default remedy that allows the buyer-lessor to require the lessee to acquire the property violates the continuing involvement criteria in FAS-98. That default remedy is equivalent to a purchase option under which the seller-lessee can compel the buyer-lessor to sell back the property, for example, by missing scheduled lease payments to the lessor.

DISCUSSION

If all the conditions in (1) above are met, the default payment is not included in the minimum lease payments, because there is no indication of impending default and the lessor would not have a right to the payment until default. Also, under those circumstances there is no indication that the default provision is in substance a purchase option.

EITF Issue 98-9 (Accounting for Contingent Rent) (ASC 840-10-25-35; 40-1; 50-5; 450-20-60-15; 450-30-60-5)

OVERVIEW

Under some lease agreements, a lessee may be required to pay the lessor a contingent amount in addition to a fixed monthly rental payment. Contingent rental payments are usually related to the lessee's use of the property and may be based on machine hours of use or on sales volume during the lease term. For example, a manufacturer may be required to pay contingent rent of $1 per machine hour over 600,000 machine hours per year. Paragraph 11 of FAS-29 defines *contingent rent* as "[t]he increases or decreases in lease payments that result from changes occurring subsequent to the inception of the lease in the factors (other than the passage of time) on which lease payments are based...." It states further that contingent rental payments should *not* be included in minimum lease payments.

The EITF was asked to address this Issue, because some lessors and lessees have been accruing amounts related to contingent rent in interim periods based on estimates of the final amount while others wait for recognition until the actual amount has been determined.

ACCOUNTING ISSUES

1. How should a *lessor* account in interim periods for contingent rental revenue that is based on future specified targets to be met by the lessee during the lessor's fiscal year?
2. How should a *lessee* account in interim periods for contingent rental expense that is based on future specified targets to be met during the lessee's fiscal year?

EITF CONSENSUS

1. At the May 1998 meeting, the EITF reached a consensus that a *lessor* should not recognize contingent rental *revenue* in interim periods until the lessee has met specified targets that trigger contingent rental income.

    At the November 1998 meeting, the Task Force reconsidered its consensus but was unable to agree whether lessors should be required to defer recognition of contingent rental income until the lessee has met a specific target that triggers the payment of contingent rent or whether contingent rental income should be accrued before the lessee has reached the target if it is probable that the target would be reached. The SEC Observer stated that the SEC staff strongly believes that lessors should defer recognition of contingent rental income until after the specified target has been reached.

    The Task Force agreed to withdraw its consensus on lessors' accounting for contingent rental income in interim periods as a result of the Task Force's mixed views on the subject and because the SEC staff is considering the issuance of a Staff Accounting Bulletin on revenue recognition. The Task Force also agreed that lessors that changed their accounting for contingent rental income based on the consensus reached at the May 1998 meeting are permitted to continue following that consensus for fiscal years ending after November 19, 1998, or they can return to the accounting for contingent rental income used before making the change. Lessors whose accounting was consistent with the May consensus, and therefore did not need to change, should continue using that accounting. In essence, the Task Force would like lessors to follow a method of accounting for contingent rental income that is consistent with that followed in the prior fiscal year or the method followed after the May 1998 consensus.

The Task Force also decided that lessors should disclose their accounting policy for contingent rental income. A lessor that accrues contingent rental income before the lessee has reached a specified target should also disclose the effect on rental income if the lessor previously had been deferring contingent rental income until a specified target was reached.

2. At the May 1998 meeting, the EITF reached a consensus that a *lessee* should accrue contingent rental *expense* in interim periods before achieving the specified target that triggers contingent rental expense if it is *probable* that the target will be met by the end of the fiscal year.

At the September 1998 meeting, the Task Force withdrew that consensus and reached a new consensus that a lessee should recognize contingent rental expense in annual periods and interim periods before having reached specified targets that trigger contingent rental expense if it is *probable* that the target will be reached. If at any time thereafter it becomes probable that a specified target will *not* be reached, the lessee should reverse the expense into income.

The Task Force also agreed that lessees that did not accrue contingent rental expense in interim periods before September 24, 1998, because it was not probable under the previous consensus that the lessee would meet the target by its fiscal year-end, should make such accruals as of September 25, 1998, if it is probable that the target will be attained. Or, the lessee could report the information for interim periods retroactively under this consensus in a similar manner to a cumulative effect of a change in accounting principle under the guidance in ASC 250, Accounting Changes and Error Corrections..

SUBSEQUENT DEVELOPMENT

The SEC has issued SAB-101 (Revenue Recognition in Financial Statements), which applies to the accounting by lessors. It provides that contingent rental income *accrues* when changes in the factors on which contingent lease payments are based actually occur (for example, when a lessee's sales volume reaches an amount that triggers contingent rental income). Because it is inappropriate to recognize revenue based on a probability that an event will occur, contingent rental income should be recognized only in the period in which the contingency is resolved.

SEC OBSERVER COMMENT

All registrants are expected to apply the requirements of SAB-101. The SEC staff expects registrants that have not already done so to apply this accounting by reporting a change in accounting principle in accordance with the guidance in ASC 250, no later than in the first fiscal quarter of a fiscal year that begins after December 15, 1999.

Illustration of a Lessee's Recognition of Contingent Rental Expense in Interim Periods

Barr Stationary and Supplies, Inc., a retail store, has a 3/31 year-end. The company has entered into a three-year lease at a new location beginning 1/1/X8. The lease specifies a monthly rental of $10,000. In addition, at the end of each year during the term of the lease, the company is obligated to pay the lessor an additional $1,000 rent for each month the company's revenues were equal to or exceeded $50,000 and if the company's total annual sales revenues during that year of the lease were at least $600,000 or more. During the past three years, Barr's monthly revenues ranged between $50,000 and $60,000.

Barr moved into its new location on 2/15/X8. Revenues during January 20X8 were $35,000. Revenues during February were $35,000. Because it was not probable that Barr would meet its monthly target in March, no contingent rental income was accrued for the last quarter of 20X8. Therefore, Barr will accrue contingent rent expense in interim periods beginning in the first quarter of fiscal 20X9.

EITF Issue 00-11 (Lessors' Evaluation of Whether Leases of Certain Integral Equipment Meet the Ownership Transfer Requirements of FASB Statement No. 13) (ASC 840-10-25-46, 25-48 through 25-50)

OVERVIEW

FIN-43 provides that lease transactions involving integral equipment, as defined in the Interpretation, are considered to be leases of real estate. Under paragraph 7a of FAS-13 (ASC 840-10-25-1), as amended by FAS-98, classification as a sales type lease requires that *ownership* of the property be transferred to the lessee by the end of the lease term.

Article 2 of the Uniform Commercial Code (UCC) provides guidelines to be used in determining whether title to personal property has passed. However, unlike transfers of real property, which are recorded in accordance with state law as evidence that ownership has been transferred, there is no system under which title to personal property is recorded. Consequently, questions have been raised about how to provide evidence of a transfer of ownership in integral equipment (without a transfer of the real property) to a lessee by the end of the lease term.

ACCOUNTING ISSUES

1. Should integral equipment under a lease be evaluated as real estate in accordance with FAS-13?
2. If so, how should the requirement in paragraph 7(a) (ASC 840-10-25-1) regarding the transfer of ownership be evaluated when there is no statutory registration system for leased integral equipment?

EITF CONSENSUS

The EITF reached the following consensus positions:

1. Equipment subject to a lease that is attached to real property (integral equipment) should be evaluated as real estate using the guidance in FAS-13 (Accounting for Leases), as amended by FAS-98 (Accounting for Leases).
2. Absent a statutory system of title registration to integral equipment, the requirement in paragraph 7(a) of FAS-13 (ASC 840-10-25-1) that ownership to equipment be transferred to a lessee by the end of the lease term is met if, under the lease agreement, the lessor is required to deliver the necessary documents (including a bill of sale, if applicable) that will release the integral equipment from the lease and will transfer ownership of the equipment to the lessee. The requirement in paragraph 7(a) (ASC 840-10-25-1) would also be met if an agreement requires a nominal payment on the transfer of ownership. However, the requirement in paragraph 7(a) (ASC 840-10-25-1) would *not* be met if a lease agreement requires a lessee to make a payment to the lessor, regardless of the amount, for a transfer of ownership to occur, because that requirement would be considered a *purchase option*.

EFFECTIVE DATE

This Issue applies to leases that begin after July 19, 2001, and leases modified after that date if they are considered new agreements under the guidance in paragraph 9 of FAS-13 (ASC 840-10-35-4). Companies that modify their lease agreements by changing their classification should *disclose* the effect of the change on the balance sheet and the income statement as if the leases had been classified in accordance with this guidance from the inception of the original lease.

EITF Issue 01-8 (Determining Whether an Arrangement Is a Lease) (ASC 840-10-15-3 through 15-6, 15-10 through 15-20; 35-2, 35-3, 55-26, 55-30 through 55-37; 840-20-25-9, 25-22; 40-2, 40-6; 840-30-25-4; 30-5; 40-2, 40-3, 40-6; 440-10-25-1, 25-3; 815-10-15-79)

OVERVIEW

During its discussion of Issue 98-10 (Accounting for Contracts Involved in Energy Trading and Risk Management Activities), which requires that energy contracts and related contracts be accounted at fair value, the EITF noted that some transportation contracts and other energy-related contracts may be lease transactions that should be accounted for based on the substance of the specific contract in accordance with the guidance in FAS-13. The EITF made the same statement regarding the treatment of certain energy-related contracts as leases during its discussion of Issue 00-17 (Measuring the Fair Value of Energy-Related Contracts in Applying Issue 98-10). However, the EITF decided to expand the scope of the Issue to provide guidance that would apply to *all* kinds of arrangements that may be leases.

ACCOUNTING ISSUE

How should an entity determine whether an arrangement is a lease that should be accounted for under the guidance in FAS-13?

EITF CONSENSUS

The EITF reached a consensus that the determination of whether an arrangement contains a lease should be based on the substance of an arrangement, using the definition of a lease in paragraph 1 of FAS-13 (ASC, *Glossary*). Paragraph 1 states that a lease is an agreement that transfers from one party to another the *right to use* property, plant, or equipment—that is, land or *depreciable* assets—usually for a stated period of time. The following guidance should be used to determine whether an arrangement contains a lease under the provisions of FAS-13.

Application Guidance

The determination as to whether or not an arrangement includes a lease under FAS-13 should be made in accordance with the following application guidance:

1. Under FAS-13, the phrase *property, plant, and equipment* refers only to land and *depreciable* assets. Therefore, any inventory, as well as minerals, precious metals, or other natural resources—all of which are *not* depreciable assets—cannot be subject to a

lease under the definition of a lease in FAS-13. Similarly, intangible assets, such as motion picture film licensing rights and rights to minerals, precious metals, or other resources, which are amortized or depleted but not depreciated, would *not* qualify for lease accounting.

2. Although an arrangement may explicitly refer to a transfer of specific property, plant, or equipment, it contains a lease only if the transferred property, plant, or equipment—*not* other available property, plant, or equipment—is used to fulfill the purpose of the arrangement.

3. An arrangement qualifies as a lease even if the property, plant, or equipment is *not* explicitly identified, if the owner/seller owns or leases only one asset with which the obligation can be fulfilled and it is not possible for the owner/seller to fulfill its obligation with alternative property, plant, or equipment.

4. Lease accounting is permitted (*a*) if an owner/seller has the right to substitute other property, plant, or equipment because the owner/seller has a warranty obligation under the arrangement, (*b*) until a substitution occurs, if an owner/seller has an obligation or the ability, which may be contingent, to substitute other property, plant, or equipment for any reason on or after a specified date.

5. An arrangement transfers the *right to use* property, plant, or equipment if a purchaser/lessee has the right to control how the property, plant, or equipment is used. A right to use has been transferred if a purchaser/lessee is able to, or has the right to do, any one of the following:

    a. Operate the property, plant, or equipment or instruct others to do so at will during the time the purchaser/lessee obtains and controls more than a minor amount of the property, plant, or equipment's output or other function,

    b. Control physical access and obtain and control more than a minor amount of the property, plant, or equipment's output or other function, or

    c. Take the output produced or other function of the property, plant, or equipment during the term of the arrangement and if, based on the facts or circumstances, it is a remote possibility that other parties will take more than a minor amount of the output or other function of the property, plant, or equipment. The price paid per unit of output does not equal the current market price per unit at the time the output is delivered.

Reevaluating an Arrangement

1. A judgment as to whether an arrangement includes a lease should be made at the inception of an arrangement based on all of the facts and circumstances. That judgment should

be reevaluated under the application guidance in this Issue, including the remaining term of the arrangement, based on the facts and circumstances at the reevaluation date under the following circumstances:

a. *Contractual terms change* The arrangement should be reevaluated under the application guidance in this Issue unless a change is due to a renewal or extension of the arrangement.

b. *A renewal option or an extension of the arrangement is exercised* Only the renewal or extension period of an arrangement should be reevaluated if the original terms of an arrangement are not modified. The accounting for the remaining term of the arrangement should not be modified. Exercising a renewal option included in the *lease term*, as defined in paragraph 5f of FAS-13 (ASC, *Glossary*), as amended, is not considered a renewal that requires a reevaluation under the application guidance in this Issue.

c. *Dependence on specific property, plant, or equipment exists* An arrangement should be reevaluated prospectively to determine whether it contains a lease if there is a change in the position as to whether or not fulfillment depends on specified property, plant, or equipment.

d. *There is a physical change of specific property, plant, or equipment* An arrangement should be reevaluated prospectively to determine whether it includes a lease if a physical change in specified property, plant, or equipment occurs. For example, replacement of a machine specified in the original arrangement with increased production capacity would require a reevaluation. However, a physical change of property, plant, or equipment that does not affect the productivity of the property, plant, or equipment specified in the original arrangement does not require such a reevaluation.

2. The following guidance should be applied to account for an arrangement if its classification, or that of a portion of the arrangement, changes, because a modification or another change in the arrangement discussed previously causes the arrangement to be classified as a lease or ends its classification as a lease:

a. *A supply arrangement becomes an operating lease for a Purchaser/ Lessee* A recognized asset for a purchase contract, such as a prepaid asset or a derivative, should be considered part of minimum lease payments and recognized initially as prepaid rent. A recognized liability for a purchase contract, such as a payable or a derivative, should be considered a reduction of minimum lease payments and recognized initially as a lease payable.

b. *A supply arrangement becomes an operating lease for a Seller/ Lessor* A recognized liability for a sales contract, such as deferred revenue or a derivative, should be part of minimum lease payments and recognized initially as deferred rent. A recognized asset for a sales contract, such as a receivable or a derivative, should be considered a *reduction* of minimum lease payments and recognized initially as a lease receivable if the asset can be recovered from future receipts.

c. *A supply arrangement becomes a capital lease for a Purchaser/Lessee* A recognized asset or liability for the purchase contract, such as a prepaid asset, a payable, or a derivative should be included in the basis of the leased asset or lease obligation.

d. *A supply arrangement becomes a sales-type lease for a Seller/Lessor* The property, plant, or equipment should be derecognized, and an asset or liability for the supply arrangement, if any, should be recognized in earnings as an adjustment of minimum lease payments if the criteria for treatment as a sale in paragraph 8 of FAS-13 (ASC 840-10-25-43) or other applicable literature, such as FAS-66, are met. Otherwise, a recognized asset or liability for the supply arrangement, if any, should be considered a reduction of, or part of, minimum lease payments and the lease should be recognized in accordance with the guidance in ASC 840 (FAS-13.

e. *An operating lease becomes a supply arrangement for a Purchaser/Lessee* Previously recognized prepaid rent or rent payable, if any, should be recognized initially as an asset or a liability related to the purchase contract.

f. *An operating lease becomes a supply arrangement for a Seller/Lessor* Previously recognized deferred rent or rent receivable, if any, should be recognized initially as a liability or an asset related to the sales contract, subject to a recoverability test.

g. *A capital lease becomes a supply arrangement for a Purchaser/Lessee* Property, plant, or equipment based on the guidance in ASC 976-605-25-4, 25-1 through 25-2, 25-6, 25-8 through 25-9, 25-11 through 25-12, 30-1 through 30-4, 35-1, 55-1 through 55-11, 55-13 through 55-14; ASC 976-10-15-1 through 15-4; ASC 976-310-30-1, 35-1, 40-1, 50-1; 976-330-50-1; 976-705-30-1; ASC 360-20-15-10, 15-1 through 15-2, 40-3 through 40-5, 40-7 through 40-10, 40-13, 40-18 through 40-31, 40-33 through 40-34, 40-36 through 40-38, 40-40 through 40-50, 40-56 through 40-64, 55-1 through 55-2, 55-7 through 55-17, 55-19 through 55-21, 55-23 through 55-34, 55-36 through 55-38, 55-40 through 55-54, 55-61 through 55-64; ASC 360- ASC 460-10-60-3; ASC 840-10-25-60 (FAS-66) should be derecognized if a leased asset is real estate, including integral equipment. Leased property, plant, or equipment, and the related lease obligation, other than real estate, including integral equipment, should be derecognized. Before a sale is recognized, an asset subject to a capital lease should be evaluated for impairment under the guidance in ASC 360-10 (FAS-144, Accounting for the Impairment or Disposal of Long-Lived Assets). The terms of the changes in the arrangement that cause a reevaluation must be considered. After an asset is reduced for impairment, if any, any difference between the capital lease asset and the obligation is recognized initially as an asset or a liability associated with a supply arrangement.

h. *A direct-financing lease or a sales-type lease becomes a supply arrangement for a Seller/Lessor* Property, plant, or equipment should be recognized at the lower of (1) its original cost, (2) its current fair value, or (3) the lease receivable's current carrying amount.

Multiple-Element Arrangements That Include a Lease

A purchaser and a supplier to the lease element of an arrangement should apply the classification, recognition, measurement, and disclosure requirements of ASC 840 (FAS-13) if the arrangement includes a lease and related executory costs as well as other nonlease elements. Elements of an arrangement not under the scope of ASC 840 (FAS-13) should be accounted for in accordance with other applicable GAAP. When applying the guidance in ASC 840 (FAS-13), payments and other consideration required under an arrangement should be separated at the inception of an arrangement or when it is reevaluated into (*a*) payments for the lease, including related executory costs and profits, and (*b*) payments for other services based on the guidance in EITF Issue 08-1, which supersedes the guidance in EITF Issue 00-21.

EITF Issue 01-12 (The Impact of the Requirements of FASB Statement No. 133, *Accounting for Derivative Instruments and Hedging Activities*, on Residual Value Guarantees in Connection with a Lease) (ASC 840-10-15-20; 815-10-15-80, 15-81; 460-10-60-20)

OVERVIEW

The EITF has been asked to resolve the scope overlap between ASC 815 (FAS-133, Accounting for Derivative Instruments and Hedging Activities) and ASC 840 (FAS-13, Accounting for Leases) regarding the accounting for residual value guarantees (*a*) for transactions accounted for under the guidance in ASC 840 (FAS-13), (*b*) that meet the definition of a derivative in ASC 815 (FAS-133), and (*c*) that are either not explicitly excluded from the scope of ASC 815 (FAS-133) or do not meet one of the Statement's scope exceptions. Although the guidance in ASC 815 (FAS-133) did not amend the guidance in ASC 840 (FAS-13), it does not exclude residual value guarantees included in lease transactions, except as provided in ASC 815-10-15 (paragraph 10(f) of FAS-133). The scope overlap does not apply, however, to third-party guarantors' accounting for obligations related to residual guarantees or to contracts not accounted for under the scope of the guidance in ASC 840 (FAS-13).

Under the guidance in ASC 840 (FAS-13), both lessees and lessors are required to account for residual value guarantees based on the stated amount of a guarantee, not based on an estimated deficiency that has to be made up by a lessee or an independent third-party guarantor, or both. In a sales-type lease or a direct financing lease, a *lessor* includes the guaranteed and unguaranteed portions of a leased property's residual value in its gross investment. The lessor accretes the present value of its investment on the interest method to the lease's future value over the term of the lease. Although a lessor must adjust the estimated residual value of a leased property for other-than-temporary losses that occur during the lease term, the existence of a residual value guarantee precludes the lessor from recognizing a loss (up to the amount of the guarantee) in the residual value of the leased property if it is probable that the guarantor will perform.

The requirement in ASC 840 (FAS-13) that a *lessee* include in its minimum lease payments the stated amount of a residual value guarantee that will be realized by a lessor affects the lessee's lease classification tests and the amount capitalized and recognized as an obligation in a capital lease.

A residual value guarantee that meets the definition of a derivative in ASC 815 (FAS-133) would be accounted for at fair value with changes in value recognized in periodic earnings.

ACCOUNTING ISSUES

1. How should the scope overlap between ASC 840 (FAS-13) and ASC 815 (FAS-133) regarding residual value guarantees be resolved?
2. Should third-party residual value guarantors account for residual value guarantees under the requirements in ASC 815 FAS-133)?

EITF CONSENSUS

1. The EITF agreed *not* to proceed further on this Issue, because (1) the difficulty of resolving it and (2) the few constituents that would benefit if the Issue were resolved do not justify the cost of additional work on the Issue.
2. The EITF reached a consensus that the guidance in ASC 815 (FAS-133) may apply to residual value guarantees made by third-party residual value guarantors. Although such contracts

may be excluded from the scope of ASC 815 (FAS-133) under several of its scope exceptions, the EITF noted that third-party residual value guarantors should consider the guidance in ASC 815 (FAS-133) for *all* residual value guarantees to determine whether the guarantees are derivatives or whether they qualify for one of the Statement's scope exceptions.

> **OBSERVATION:** Under the provisions of ASC 460 (FIN-45), a guarantor is required to recognize a liability for the obligation assumed by issuing a guarantee. The Interpretation also provides guidance on appropriate disclosures that should be made by a guarantor. FIN-45 does *not* apply to residual value guarantees related to capital leases accounted for under the guidance in ASC 840 (FAS-13). In addition, residual value guarantees accounted for as derivative instruments under the guidance in ASC 815 (FAS-133, Accounting for Derivative Instruments and Hedging Activities) also are exempted from the Interpretation's initial measurement and recognition requirements, but its disclosure requirements do apply. Although the consensuses reached in this Issue are *not* affected by the provisions of ASC 460 (FIN-45), the requirements related to initial recognition, initial measurement, and disclosure would apply to guarantees described in this Issue that do *not* qualify for the exceptions.

EITF Issue 05-6 (Determining the Amortization Period for Leasehold Improvements Purchased After Lease Inception or Acquired in a Business Combination) (ASC 840-10-35-6 through 35-9; 805-20-35-6)

OVERVIEW

A *lease term* is defined in paragraph 5(f) of FAS-13 (Accounting for Leases) (ASC, *Glossary*) as a predetermined period of time during which a lessee cannot cancel the lease as well as periods of time covered by bargain renewal options or periods during which renewal is reasonably assured because the lessee would incur a large penalty if the lease is not renewed. Paragraph 11(b) of FAS-13 (ASC 840-30-35-1) states that assets, such as leasehold improvements, under capital leases that do not transfer ownership of those assets to the lessee and do not contain a bargain renewal option should be amortized over the assets' useful life or a period limited to the term of the lease, whichever is shorter. Although FAS-13 does not discuss the amortization of leasehold improvements under capital leases, practitioners analogize to the guidance in paragraph 11(b) (ASC 840-30-35-1) for operating leases, because as in capital leases, a lessee will not control the use of leasehold improvements if there is no assurance that the lease will be renewed.

Some practitioners have questioned whether the amortization period of leasehold improvements acquired a period of time after the beginning of the lease term can extend beyond the lease term. Paragraph 9 of FAS-13 (ASC 840-10-35-4) provides that the term of a lease for purposes of lease classification cannot be changed unless (*a*) a lease's provisions are modified so that the lease is considered a new agreement or (*b*) a lease is extended or renewed beyond the existing lease term.

The same question has been raised regarding the amortization of leasehold improvements acquired as a result of the assumption of existing lease agreements in a business combination, i.e., whether leasehold improvements acquired in a business combination can be amortized over a period that extends beyond the term determined at the inception of a lease by the acquired entity. Under the guidance in paragraphs 12 and 13 of FIN-21 (Accounting for Leases in a Business Combination) (ASC 840-10-35-5), the acquiring entity is required to retain the lease classification used by the acquired entity, unless one of the conditions in paragraph 9 of FAS-13 (ASC 840-10-35-4) has been met.

ACCOUNTING ISSUES

1. What period should be the amortization period for leasehold improvements acquired in a business combination?
2. What period should be the amortization period for leasehold improvements in operating leases that were *not* considered at the beginning of a lease term but purchased a significant period of time after the inception of the lease?

EITF CONSENSUS

The EITF reached the following consensus positions:

1. Leasehold improvements acquired in a business combination should be amortized over (*a*) the useful life of the assets or (*b*) the term that includes required lease periods and renewals that are "reasonably assured," as defined in paragraph 5 of FAS-13 (ASC, *Glossary*), at the acquisition date, whichever is shorter.
2. Leasehold improvements *not* considered at or near the beginning of a lease and placed in service a significant period of time after the lease's inception should be amortized over (*a*) the assets' useful life or (*b*) a term that includes required lease periods and renewals that are "reasonably assured," as defined in paragraph 5 of FAS-13 (ASC, *Glossary*), at the date the leasehold improvements are purchased, whichever is shorter.

The EITF discussed but was not asked to reach a consensus as to whether the amortization period for existing leaseholds should be reevaluated after its initial determination. The EITF asked its Agenda Committee to consider whether this issue should be discussed separately.

SUBSEQUENT DEVELOPMENT

At its September 15, 2005, meeting, the EITF agreed to clarify that the consensus positions in this Issue do not apply to preexisting leasehold improvements and should not be used to justify a reevaluation of the amortization period of preexisting leasehold improvements for additional renewal periods when new leasehold improvements that were not considered before are placed into service significantly after the beginning of a lease term.

The FASB ratified the modification of the consensus at its September 28, 2005, meeting.

EITF Issue 08-3 (Accounting by Lessees for Maintenance Deposits under Lease Agreements) (ASC 840-10-05-9A through 05-9C; 25-39A, 25-39B; 35-9A; 65-1)

OVERVIEW

Under the terms of certain agreements for leased *equipment* the lessee is required to repair and maintain the leased asset during the lease term. To protect a lessor if a lessee does *not* properly maintain the leased equipment, some lease agreements include a requirement that the lessee give the lessor a deposit, which is commonly referred to as a "maintenance reserve" or "supplemental rent." Usually, the deposit is calculated based on a performance measure, such as the number of hours a leased asset has been used. Under the terms of the lease, the lessor must use the deposit to reimburse the lessee, up to the amount of the deposit, for costs incurred for maintenance activities that the lessee is contractually obligated to perform under the lease agreement.

If at the end of the lease term of some agreements the deposit exceeds the total cumulative cost of maintaining the equipment over the lease term, the lessor is required to return the remainder of the deposit to the lessee. Lessees generally account for such refundable maintenance deposits as deposits. However, under the terms of other lease agreements, at the end of the lease term, the lessor is permitted to retain an excess of a deposit, if any, over the lessee's maintenance expenditures if the lessee has not performed the required maintenance activities. There is diversity in practice in the way that lessees account for the portion of a deposit that has *not* been refunded.

Under some contracts, the lessee is required to return the leased asset in a certain condition at the end of the lease term. In that case, a lessee should consult other generally accepted accounting principles (GAAP) to determine when and whether to recognize a liability related to that requirement.

ACCOUNTING ISSUE

How should lessees account for maintenance deposits?

SCOPE

Issue 08-3 addresses a lessee's accounting for a maintenance deposit under an arrangement providing that the remainder of the deposit will be refunded only if the lessee has performed specified maintenance activities. Issue 08-3 does *not* apply to a lessee's payments to a lessor that are *not* substantively and contractually related to the maintenance of a leased asset. At the inception of a lease, a lessee that determines that it is *less than probable* (as defined in paragraph 25 of CON-6 (Elements of Financial Statements—a Replacement of FASB Concepts Statement No. 3 (incorporating an amendment of FASB Concepts Statement No. 2)) that the lessor will return to the lessee the total amount of payments as a reimbursement of maintenance activities, the lessee should consider that fact in determining the portion of each payment that is not accounted for under the scope of Issue 08-3.

RECOGNITION

The EITF reached a consensus that lessees should account for maintenance deposits under the scope of Issue 08-3 as deposit assets. After the inception of a lease agreement, a lessee should continue to evaluate the probability that the lessor will return the deposit to the lessee through reimbursements for the costs of maintenance activities incurred by the lessee. A lessee should recognize a deposit as additional expense if it is determined that it is less than probable that the lessor will return the deposit. A lessee should expense or capitalize the cost of maintenance activities when the underlying maintenance is performed in accordance with its accounting policy for maintenance activities.

EFFECTIVE DATE AND TRANSITION

The EITF reached a consensus that Issue 08-3 should be effective for financial statements issued for fiscal years that begin after December 15, 2008, and interim periods in those fiscal years. An entity that has previously adopted a different accounting policy is prohibited from early application of the consensus in Issue 08-3.

The effect of a change in accounting principle should be recognized as of the beginning of the fiscal year in which the consensus is first applied for all arrangements that exist at the effective date. A cumulative effect adjustment as result of a change in accounting principle, which is the difference between amounts recognized in the balance sheet before and after the application of the consensus in Issue 08-3, should be recognized in the opening balance of retained earnings, or in other appropriate components of equity or net assets in the balance sheet for that fiscal year, and should be presented separately. Presentation of the transition disclosures in paragraphs

17 and 18 of FAS-154 (Accounting Changes and Error Corrections) (ASC 250-10-50-1 through 50-3) is required.

FASB RATIFICATION

The FASB ratified the EITF's consensus at its June 25, 2008, meeting.

Topic D-24 (Sale-Leaseback Transactions with Continuing Involvement) (ASC 840-25-18; 55-48)

The FASB staff discussed its responses to the following questions on the accounting for sale-leaseback transactions in which the seller has a continuing involvement with the property:

- Sale-leaseback accounting is precluded in transactions in which the seller retains a partial ownership in the property.
- Sale-leaseback accounting is precluded if the seller-lessee can require the buyer-lessor to refinance debt related to the property and pass the interest savings to the seller-lessee in the form of reduced leaseback payments. Sale-leaseback accounting is *permitted*, however, if leaseback payments, which are considered contingent rentals under the provisions of paragraph 8 of FAS-98 (ASC, *Glossary*), change because they are indexed to an interest rate.

FTB 79-12 (Interest Rate Used in Calculating the Present Value of Minimum Lease Payments) (ASC, *Glossary*—Incremental Borrowing Rate)

BACKGROUND

FAS-13 requires the lessee to use its incremental borrowing rate (or the lessor's implicit interest rate in certain circumstances) in calculating the minimum lease payments. The *incremental borrowing rate* is defined as the rate the lessee would have incurred to borrow over a similar term the funds necessary to purchase the leased asset.

STANDARDS

Question: Is a lessee permitted to use its secured borrowing rate to calculate the present value of minimum lease payments in accordance with ASC 840 (FAS-13)?

Answer: FAS-13, paragraph 5l (not in ASC), does not preclude the lessee from using its secured borrowing rate as its incremental borrowing rate if that rate is determinable, reasonable, and consistent with the financing that would have been used in the circumstances surrounding the lease.

AUTHORITATIVE GUIDANCE NOT INCLUDED SEPARATELY IN THE CODIFICATION BUT INCORPORATED WITH OTHER GUIDANCE ON THE SUBJECT

FSP FIN-46(R)-4 (Technical Correction of FASB Interpretation No. 46, *Consolidation of Variable Interest Entities* (revised December 2003), Relating to Its Effects on Question No. 12 of EITF Issue No. 96-21, *Implementation Issues in Accounting for Leasing Transactions Involving Securitization Entities*) (ASC 810)

The FASB directed the FASB staff to issue this FSP to correct an erroneous statement in FIN-46(R) (Consolidation of Variable Interest Entities) (revised December 2003) regarding the Interpretation's effect on the EITF's consensus on Question 12 of Issue 96-21 (Implementation Issues in Accounting for Leasing Transactions Involving Securitization Entities).

The EITF's consensus on Question 12 of Issue 96-21 provides guidance to lessees on accounting for guarantees of the residual value of leased properties accounted for as operating leases. The guidance in Question 12, other than that regarding the timing of a guarantor-lessee's accrual for a contingent loss under the guarantee, was nullified by the guidance in FIN-45 (Guarantor's Accounting and Disclosure of Requirements for Guarantees, Including Indirect Guarantees of Indebtedness of Others). Appendix F of FIN-46(R) states that the Interpretation nullifies the entire consensus on Question 12. However, that statement is erroneous because FIN-46(R) nullifies only the application of the consensus in Question 12 to guarantor-lessees that are the primary beneficiaries of lessors that are variable interest entities. The guidance in Question 12 regarding the timing of a guarantor-lessee's accrual of a contingent loss under a guarantee continues to apply to guarantor-lessees that are *not* the primary beneficiaries of lessors under FIN-46(R).

EFFECTIVE DATE AND TRANSITION

The effective date and transition provisions of FIN-46(R) apply to the guidance in this FSP, which also has been incorporated in Appendix F of the Interpretation.

FSP FAS-13-2 (Accounting for a Change in the Timing of Cash Flows Relating to Income Taxes Generated by a Leveraged Lease Transaction)

OVERVIEW

Leveraged lease transactions usually produce favorable cash flows for lessors. Additionally, they provide lessors with a significant portion of their expected return. A lessor in a leveraged lease transaction is usually considered to be the asset's owner for income tax purposes. Therefore, the lessor can depreciate the asset for income tax purposes and accelerate tax deductions related to the asset's depreciation. As a result, for tax purposes, a lessor's rental income from a leveraged lease is usually *less* than its accelerated deductions of tax depreciation and interest expense on nonrecourse debt during a leveraged lease's early years. The nonrecourse financing and the favorable tax cash flows that a lessor enjoys during those years enable the lessor to recover its investment and to use the funds temporarily to obtain additional income. Nevertheless, during a lease's later years, a lessor must expend cash because (a) taxable income from the lease no longer is reduced by accelerated depreciation and interest expense deductions and (b) a larger amount of the principal on the nonrecourse debt is being repaid.

Under paragraph 44 of FAS-13 (Accounting for Leases) (FASB Accounting Standards Codification (ASC) 840-30-35-33), a lessor in a leveraged lease must recognize income at a level rate of return on its net investment during periods in which its net investment, as defined in paragraph 43 of FAS-13 (ASC 840-30-35-33), is a positive amount. Consequently, the timing of income recognition from a leveraged lease is affected by the timing of income tax cash flows generated by that lease. Lessors generally allocate disproportionally more (less) income from a leveraged lease to the lease's earlier (later) periods because the tax benefits on such leases are often realized in the early periods of the lease term.

The Internal Revenue Service (IRS) has challenged the ability of some lessors to accelerate the timing of tax deductions and the amounts of those deductions in certain leveraged lease transactions—known as Lease In-Lease Out (LILO) and Sale In-Sale Out (SILO) transactions. Rather than be subject to court action, some lessors with LILO transactions have settled with the IRS. Some lessors in SILO transactions may also settle with the IRS if and when they are challenged by the IRS. As a result of the settlements, lessors have had to make significant changes to the timing and realization of tax benefits on leveraged leases; some have been assessed interest and penalties. Although changes in the timing of the realization of tax benefits and of estimated after-tax cash flows from leveraged leases affect the timing of income recognition from those leases and reduce the overall expected rate of return, they do *not* change an entity's estimated total income. In practice, an assessment of interest and penalties, which would change total net income from a leveraged lease, has been excluded from the recalculation of a lease's cash flows; the FASB has not opposed that treatment.

Under the requirements of paragraph 46 of FAS-13 (ASC 840-30-35-38), which provides accounting guidance for circumstances in which a change in an important assumption changes estimated total net income from a lease, a lessor is required to use the method discussed in paragraph 44 of FAS-13 (ASC 840-30-35-33) to recalculate the rate of return and the allocation of income to positive investment years from the inception of the lease based on the revised assumption. Paragraph 46 (ASC 840-30-35-38) does *not* require, however, that a leveraged lease be recalculated if only the *timing* of estimated cash flows related to *income taxes* generated by the lease changes because an important assumption has been revised. Therefore, questions have been raised as to whether a lessor in a leveraged lease transaction should be required to recognize the effects of a change or projected change in the timing of cash flows related to income taxes generated by the lease and, if so, how those effects should be accounted for.

FASB STAFF POSITION

The following guidance applies to all transactions classifies as leveraged leases in accordance with FAS-13:

- The timing of cash flows related to income taxes generated by a leveraged lease is an important assumption that affects periodic income recognized by a lessor for the lease. Therefore, a change or projected change in the timing of cash flows related to income taxes generated by a leveraged lease should be accounted for in accordance with the guidance in paragraph 46 of FAS-13 (ASC 840-30-35-38).

- Under the guidance in paragraph 46 of FAS-13 (ASC 840-30-35-41), a lessor should review the projected timing of income tax cash flows generated by a leveraged lease transaction *annually*, or more frequently, if the occurrence of an event or a change in circumstances indicates that a change in timing has occurred or is expected to occur.

- If the projected timing of income tax cash flows generated by a leveraged lease is revised during the term of a leveraged lease, the rate of return and the allocation of income to positive investment years should be recalculated from the inception of the lease in accordance with the method discussed in paragraph 44 of FAS-13 (ASC 840-30-35-33).

- A lessor should update all the assumptions used to calculate total periodic income on a leveraged lease, including actual cash flows up to the recalculation date and projected cash flows after that date.

- A lessor that expects to settle with a taxing authority should include in cash flows after the recalculation date (*a*) projected cash flows between the recalculation date and the date of a projected settlement, if any, and (*b*) a projected amount of the settlement at the projected settlement date.
- Interest or penalties should *not* be included in the recalculation of cash flows from a leveraged lease.
- For the purpose of applying this FSP, the actual cash flows of a leveraged lease should *not* include advance payments and deposits made to a taxing authority; those amounts should be included in a projected amount of a settlement.
- Accounts that comprise the net investment balance should be adjusted to conform to the recalculated balances with the change in the net investment recognized as a gain or a loss in the year in which an assumption has changed.
- A recognized pretax gain or loss should be included in income from continuing operations *before* income taxes in the same line item in which income from a leveraged lease is recognized.
- The tax effect of a recognized gain or loss should be included in the income tax line item.

Illustration of Presentation of Advance Payments and Deposits When a Leveraged Lease Is Recalculated

The lessor has concluded that its original position on the tax return would meet the "more-likely-than-not" threshold stated in FIN-48 (Accounting for Uncertainty in Income Taxes) and that its estimate for the projected LILO settlement is consistent with the measurement guidance in FIN-48.

To account for an advance, on October 1, 2006, the lessor:

- Pays a $30,000 advance to the taxing authority, $12,000 of which is related to issues as a result of a LILO transaction.
- Changes its assumptions about the timing of tax cash flows and projects that it will settle with the IRS on December 1, 2008, with a $150,000 payment, $60,000 of which would be related to the LILO transaction.

On December 1, 2008, the lessor recalculates its cash flow from the leveraged lease and presents $60,000 in its financial statements as a projected cash *outflow*.

The guidance is this FSP applies only to changes or projected changes in the timing of income taxes directly related to leveraged lease transactions requiring recalculation of the leveraged lease, such as timing changes caused by:

- An interpretation of a tax law.
- A change in a lessor's assessment of the likelihood of prevailing in a taxing authority's challenge of its accounting for LILO and SILO transactions.

- A change in a lessor's expectations about a settlement with a taxing authority that would change the timing or projected timing of tax benefits generated by a leveraged lease.

Consistent with the guidance in Issue 10 of EITF Issue 87-8 (Tax Reform Act of 1986: Issues Related to the Alternative Minimum Tax), it would *not* be appropriate to recalculate a leveraged lease as a result of a change in timing directly related to an alternative minimum tax (AMT) credit or a lessor's insufficient taxable income, because that timing change would *not* be directly related to the leveraged lease. Further, as stated in Issue 87-8, a recalculation is necessary only if there is an indication that previous assumptions about *total* after-tax net income from a lease are no longer valid.

A lessor's tax positions should be presented in its initial calculation or subsequent recalculations based on the recognition, derecognition, and measurement criteria in ASC 740 (FIN-48). The decision that a tax position no longer meets those criteria in ASC 740 (FIN-48) should be based on the individual facts and circumstances.

EITF Issue 87-7 (Sale of an Asset Subject to a Lease and Nonrecourse Financing: "Wrap Lease Transactions")

OVERVIEW

In a *wrap lease transaction*, a lessor leases an asset to a lessee and obtains financing from a financial institution collateralized by the asset and the lease receivable. At the same time or shortly thereafter, the lessor sells the asset subject to the lease and the nonrecourse financing to a third party and leases the asset back, thus remaining the principal lessor with the user of the asset. The lessor receives cash and a note receivable from the buyer of the asset, but may retain an interest in the residual value of the leased asset and remarketing rights.

ACCOUNTING ISSUES

1. How should a lessor account for cash proceeds from a wrap lease transaction?
2. Should the lessor recognize an asset for the interest retained in the residual value of the asset and recognize income in the period of the transaction?
3. How should a lessor account for fees for remarketing the asset at the end of the lease term?

EITF CONSENSUS

1. The Task Force was unable to reach a consensus on how the lessor should account for income from proceeds from a wrap lease transaction, except for proceeds for remarketing rights, as

discussed in issue 3 below. Although there was no consensus, a majority of the Task Force agreed that wrap lease transactions should be accounted for as sale-leaseback transactions. (See discussion below.)

2. The lessor should recognize an asset for an interest retained in the residual value of the leased asset.

3. The lessor should separate revenue associated with future remarketing rights from other proceeds received in the transaction. That revenue should be deferred and recognized in income at the time the lessor performs the remarketing services.

SEC OBSERVER COMMENT

The Task Force discussed without reaching a consensus whether a lessor should remove nonrecourse debt from the financial statements after selling the leased asset. The SEC Observer stated that footnote 1 of SAB-70 states that debt should not be removed from the balance sheet if the lessor retains a residual interest in the asset.

DISCUSSION

1. The FASB issued FTB 88-1 (Issues Relating to Accounting for Leases) at the end of 1988. This FTB provides guidance on accounting for wrap lease transactions and resolves the first issue discussed above.

2. Recognition of an asset for the retained residual was supported for a number of reasons. Some saw no difference in the residual before and after the sale and thus believed that it should continue being recognized as an asset. Others referred to ASC 360-10-25-3 (paragraph 4 of FTB 86-2), which requires recognizing an asset for an acquired interest in the residual value of a leased asset "at the amount of cash disbursed, the fair value of other consideration given, and the present value of liabilities assumed at the date the right is acquired." Those proponents also noted that the existence of an asset is corroborated by ASC 840-30-35-53 (paragraph 10 of the FTB).

3. Those who supported deferring remarketing fees until the service was performed argued that the fees are not earned until that time. They also referred to the AICPA Issues Paper, *Accounting by Lease Brokers*, which required unbundling remarketing fees and recognizing them separately from other cash proceeds.

Topic D-8 (Accruing Bad-Debt Expense at Inception of a Lease)

The FASB staff reconfirmed that, as stated in paragraph 44 of FAS-91 (not in ASC), lessors should not accrue bad debts at the inception of a lease and offset them against unearned income. Rather, bad debts should be recognized based on the provisions for loss recognition in ASC 450 (FAS-5).

RELATED CHAPTERS IN 2011
GAAP GUIDE, VOLUME II

Chapter 4, "Balance Sheet Classification and Related Display Issues"
Chapter 20, "Income Taxes"
Chapter 33, "Real Estate Transactions"
Chapter 35, "Results of Operations"

RELATED CHAPTERS IN 2011
GAAP GUIDE, VOLUME I

Chapter 3, "Balance Sheet Classification and Related Display Issues"
Chapter 21, "Income Taxes"
Chapter 29, "Leases"
Chapter 37, "Real Estate Transactions"
Chapter 40, "Results of Operations"

RELATED CHAPTERS IN 2011
INTERNATIONAL ACCOUNTING/FINANCIAL REPORTING STANDARDS GUIDE

Chapter 3, "Presentation of Financial Statements"
Chapter 7, "Business Combinations"
Chapter 10, "Consolidated Financial Statements"
Chapter 16, "Financial Instruments"
Chapter 21, "Intangible Assets"
Chapter 25, "Leases"
Chapter 27, "Property, Plant, and Equipment"
Chapter 29, "Related Party Disclosures"

CHAPTER 27
LONG-TERM CONSTRUCTION CONTRACTS

CONTENTS

Overview	27.01
Authoritative Guidance	
ASC 605 Revenue Recognition	27.02
SOP 81-1 Accounting for Performance of Construction-Type and Certain Production-Type Contracts	27.02
Related Chapter in 2011 GAAP Guide, Volume I	27.08
Related Chapters in 2011 International Accounting/Financial Reporting Standards Guide	27.08

OVERVIEW

Long-term construction contracts present a difficult financial reporting problem primarily because of their large dollar amounts and their relatively long duration (i.e., they span more than one accounting period, sometimes beginning and ending several years apart). GAAP in the area of revenue recognition for long-term construction contracts deal with this situation by permitting two methods—the *percentage-of-completion method* and the *completed-contract method*. The percentage-of-completion method is appropriate in situations in which reliable estimates of the degree of completion are possible, in which case a pro rata portion of the income from the contract is recognized in each accounting period covered by the contract. If reliable estimates are not available, the completed-contract method is used, in which income is deferred until the end of the contract period.

The following pronouncement, which is the source of GAAP for long-term construction contracts, is discussed in the 2011 *GAAP Guide, Volume I*, Chapter 30, "Long-Term Construction Contracts":

    ASC 605   Long-Term Construction-Type Contracts (ARB-45)

AUTHORITATIVE GUIDANCE

ASC 605 Revenue Recognition

SOP 81-1 (Accounting for Performance of Construction-Type and Certain Production-Type Contracts) (ASC 605-35-05-1, 05-2, 05-4 through 05-6, 05-8 through 05-11, 05-13; 15-6; 25-1 through 25-50, 25-54 through 25-88, 25-90 through 25-98; 45-1 through 45-2; 50-1 through 50-10, 55-1; 210-10-60-2; 460-1-60-10; 910-20-25-5; 912-20-25-1)

BACKGROUND

SOP 81-1 provides guidance on the application of GAAP in accounting for the performance of contracts for which the customer provides specifications for any of the following:

- Construction of facilities
- Production of goods
- Provision of related services

In the current business environment, there are many types of contracts, ranging from relatively simple to highly complex and from short-term to long-term. These contracts are used in many industries for construction, production, and provision of a broad range of goods and services. At the time SOP 81-1 was written, existing GAAP for these types of contracts were not stated in sufficient detail for the scope of activities to which they were applied. The objective of this SOP was to provide the required guidance.

The basic accounting issue for contract accounting is the point(s) at which revenue should be recognized as earned and costs should be recognized as expenses. This may involve the allocation of revenues and expenses of relatively long-term events over relatively short-term accounting periods. This allocation process often requires estimates to deal with the uncertainties inherent in the performance of contracts.

ASC 605 (ARB-45) describes two generally accepted methods of accounting for long-term construction contracts:

1. *Percentage-of-completion* Recognizes income as work progresses on the contract
2. *Completed-contract* Recognizes income only when the contract is completed

The units-of-delivery method, which is a modification of the percentage-of-completion method, recognizes revenue on a contract as deliverable products are completed.

The following three key estimates are required to account for long-term construction contracts:

1. The extent of progress toward completion
2. Contract revenues
3. Contract costs

☛ **PRACTICE POINTER:** The Committee on Accounting Procedures indicates that when estimates of costs to complete the contract and the extent of progress toward completion are reasonably dependable, the percentage-of-completion method is preferable. When these estimates are unreliable, the completed-contract method is required. The two methods are not considered alternatives for the same circumstances.

STANDARDS

The guidance in SOP 81-1 applies to the accounting for contracts performed. It is not limited to long-term contracts, nor is it limited to construction contracts. Contracts covered are binding agreements between a buyer and a seller in which the seller agrees, for compensation, to perform a service to the buyer's specifications. These contracts are legally enforceable agreements. Performance often will extend over long periods, and the seller's right to receive payment depends on performance in accordance with the agreement. Contracts that are under the scope of this SOP include the following:

- Construction industry contracts (e.g., general building and heavy earthmoving)
- Contracts to design and build ships and transport vessels
- Contracts to design, develop, manufacture, or modify complex aerospace or electronic equipment
- Contracts for construction consulting services
- Contracts for services performed by architects, engineers, or architectural or engineering design firms

☛ **PRACTICE POINTER:** Although not contemplated at the time SOP 81-1 was written, in certain situations, its guidance also applies to contracts to design and deliver computer software products. See the discussion of SOP 97-2 (Software Revenue Recognition) in Chapter 10 for additional details related to when contract accounting is appropriate.

Contracts under the scope of SOP 81-1 may be classified into four broad types based on their pricing method:

1. *Fixed-price or lump-sum* An agreement to perform all acts under the contract for a stated price

27.04 *Long-Term Construction Contracts*

2. *Cost-type (including cost-plus)* An agreement to perform under a contract for a price to be determined on the basis of a defined relationship to the costs to be incurred
3. *Time-and-material* An agreement to perform all acts required under the contract for a price based on fixed hourly rates for some measure of the labor hours required
4. *Unit-price* An agreement to perform all acts required under the contract for a specified price for each unit of output

The term *contractor* refers to a person or entity that enters into a contract to construct facilities, produce goods, or render services to the specifications of a buyer as a general or prime contractor, as a subcontractor, or as a construction manager. The term *profit center* refers to the unit for the accumulation of revenues and costs and the measurement of income. Revenues, costs, and income are usually determined for a single contract, but under specified circumstances they may be determined for a combination of two or more contracts, a segment of a contract, or a group of combined contracts.

Basic Accounting Policy

The percentage-of-completion method and the completed-contract method constitute the basic accounting policy decision within GAAP. As stated previously, the determination of which is preferable depends on a careful evaluation of circumstances, and the two methods are not alternatives for the same situation. The basic policy followed should be disclosed in a note to the financial statements.

The use of the percentage-of-completion method depends on the ability to make reasonably dependable estimates of the extent of completion, contract revenues, and contract costs. The percentage-of completion method is preferable as an accounting policy in circumstances where these estimates can reasonably be made. Entities with significant contracting operations generally have the ability to produce reasonably reliable estimates and, accordingly, the percentage-of-completion method is preferable in most circumstances. In some circumstances, estimating the final outcome of a contract may be impractical except to assure that no loss will be incurred. In this case, the contractor should use a zero estimate of profit, and equal amounts of revenues and costs should be recognized until results can be estimated more precisely.

The completed-contract method recognizes income only when the contract is completed or substantially completed. During the period of performance, billings and costs are accumulated on the balance sheet as inventory, but no profit or income is recorded until the contract is complete or substantially complete. The completed-contract method is appropriate when reasonably dependable estimates of the extent of completion, contract revenues, and/or contract costs cannot be made, or when the contractor's financial position and results of operations would not vary materially from those resulting from the use of the percentage-of-completion method. When there is assurance that no loss will be incurred on a contract, the percentage-of-completion method based on a zero profit margin is preferable until more precise estimates can be made.

Profit Center

The basic assumption is that each contract is a profit center for revenue recognition, cost accumulation, and income measurement. A group of contracts may be so closely related, however, that they are effectively parts of a single project with an overall profit margin. In these circumstances, consideration should be given to combining the contracts for purposes of profit recognition.

Contracts may be combined for accounting purposes when the following criteria are met:

- They are negotiated as a package in the same economic environment with an overall profit margin.
- They constitute in essence an agreement to do a single project.
- They require closely interrelated construction activities with common costs.
- They constitute in substance an agreement with a single customer.

A single contract or a group of contracts that otherwise meet the test for combining may include several elements or phases, each of which was negotiated separately without regard to the performance of the others. A contract may be segmented for accounting purposes if the following steps were taken and are documented and verifiable:

- The contractor submitted bona fide proposals on the separate components of the project and on the entire project.
- The customer had the right to accept the proposals either on the separate components of the project or on the entire project.
- The aggregate amount of the proposal on the separate components approximated the amount of the proposal on the entire project.

Measuring Progress on Accounts

Some methods used in practice measure progress toward completion in terms of costs, others in terms of units of work, and others in terms of value added. All are acceptable in appropriate circumstances. The method or methods selected should be applied consistently.

Several approaches can be described as based on input measures. These methods are based on costs and on other efforts expended. An example is the efforts-expended approach, in which a measure of work, such as labor hours, machine hours, or materials quantities, is used as a measurement of the extent of progress. Output methods, on the other hand, measure progress in terms of results achieved. Estimating the extent of progress toward completion based on units completed is an example of an output method.

Income Determination—Revenue Elements

The major factors that must be considered in determining total estimated revenues are the basic contract price, contract options and additions, change orders, and claims.

Basic Contract Price

The estimated revenue from a contract is the total amount that a contractor expects to realize from the contract. It is determined primarily by the terms of the contract. The contract may be relatively fixed or highly variable and, as a result, subject to a great deal of uncertainty. One problem peculiar to cost-type contracts is the determination of reimbursable costs that should be reflected as revenue.

Contract Options and Additions

An option or an addition to an existing contract is treated as a separate contract in any of the following circumstances:

- The product or service to be provided differs significantly from the product or service provided under the original contract.
- The price of the new product or service is negotiated without regard to the original contract and involves different economic judgments.
- The product or service to be provided under the exercise option or amendment is similar to that under the original contract, but the contract price and anticipated contract cost relationship are significantly different.

If none of these circumstances is present, the option or addition may be combined with the original contract for purposes of revenue recognition.

Change Orders

Change orders are modifications of an original contract that effectively change the provisions of the contract without adding new provisions. Change orders may have a significant impact on the amount of contract revenue to be recognized.

Claims

Claims are amounts in excess of the agreed contract price that a contractor seeks to collect from customers or others as a result of customer-caused delays, errors in specifications and designs, contract terminations, change orders in dispute, and other similar causes. Recognition of such claims is appropriate only if it is probable that the claim will result in additional contract revenue and if the amounts can be reliably estimated.

Income Determination—Cost Elements

At any point in the contract, estimated contract costs consist of two components: costs incurred to date and estimated costs to complete the contract. Costs incurred to date generally can be determined with reasonable certainty, depending on the adequacy and effectiveness of the cost accounting system. Estimating the costs to complete the contract generally involves greater uncertainty.

Contract costs are accumulated in the same manner as inventory and are charged to operations as the related revenue from the contract is recognized. General principles for accounting for production costs are as follows:

- All direct costs (e.g., materials, labor, subcontracting costs) are included in contract costs.
- Indirect costs allocable to all contracts, such as indirect labor, contract supervision, tools and equipment, and supplies, may be allocated to contracts as indirect costs if otherwise allowable under GAAP.
- General and administrative costs ordinarily should be charged to expense, but may be included as contract costs under certain circumstances.
- Selling costs are generally excluded from contract costs.
- Costs under cost-type contracts are charged to contract costs in conformity with GAAP in the same manner as costs under other types of contracts.
- In computing estimated gross profit or in providing for losses on contracts, estimates of costs to complete should reflect all the types of costs included in contract costs.
- Inventoriable costs should not be carried at amounts that, when added to the estimated costs to complete, are greater than the estimated realizable value of the contract.

Estimating the costs to complete a contract should result from the following:

- Systematic and consistent procedures that are correlated with the cost accounting system to provide a basis for periodically comparing actual and estimated amounts
- Quantities and prices of all significant elements of costs
- Estimation procedures that include the same elements of cost that are included in actual accumulated costs
- The effects of future wage and price escalations
- Periodic review and revision, as appropriate, to reflect new information

Revised Estimates

Adjustments to the original estimates of the total contract revenue, total contract cost, and extent of progress toward completion may be required as work progresses under the contract and as experience is gained. Such revisions should be accounted for by the cumulative catch-up method in accordance with APB-20 (Accounting Changes).

Provisions for Anticipated Losses

When current estimates indicate that the total contract revenues and costs will result in a loss, a provision of the entire loss on the contract should be made. This is true for both the percentage-of-completion method and the completed-contract method. A provision for loss should be made in the accounting period in which it becomes evident.

A provision for a loss on a contract should be shown separately as a liability on the balance sheet—unless related costs are accumulated in the balance sheet, in which case the loss provision may be offset against the related accumulated costs. In a classified balance sheet, a provision shown as a liability should be classified as a current liability.

RELATED CHAPTER IN 2011
GAAP GUIDE, VOLUME I

Chapter 30, "Long-Term Construction Contracts"

RELATED CHAPTERS IN 2011
INTERNATIONAL ACCOUNTING/FINANCIAL REPORTING STANDARDS GUIDE

Chapter 5, "Accounting Policies, Changes in Accounting Estimates, and Errors"
Chapter 11, "Construction Contracts"
Chapter 18, "Government Grants and Government Assistance"
Chapter 23, "Inventories"
Chapter 30, "Revenue"

CHAPTER 28
NONMONETARY TRANSACTIONS

CONTENTS

Overview	**28.01**
Authoritative Guidance	
ASC 605 Revenue Recognition	**28.02**
EITF Issue 99-17 Accounting for Advertising Barter Transactions	**28.02**
ASC 845 Nonmonetary Transactions	**28.04**
EITF Issue 93-11 Accounting for Barter Transactions Involving Barter Credits	**28.04**
EITF Issue 01-2 Interpretations of APB Opinion No. 29	**28.06**
EITF Issue 04-13 Accounting for Purchases and Sales of Inventory with the Same Counterparty	**28.18**
Related Chapter in 2011 GAAP Guide, Volume I	**28.21**
Related Chapters in 2011 International Accounting/Financial Reporting Standards Guide	**28.21**

OVERVIEW

As a general rule, GAAP require that exchanges be recorded based on the fair value inherent in the transaction. This applies to both monetary and nonmonetary transactions. Certain exceptions exist, however, for nonmonetary transactions. Different accounting bases may be required for these transactions, depending on the unique characteristics of the exchange transaction.

The following pronouncements, which provide guidance on accounting for nonmonetary transactions, are discussed in the 2010 *GAAP Guide, Volume I,* Chapter 32, "Nonmonetary Transactions":

    ASC 845   Accounting for Nonmonetary Transactions (APB-29)

    ASC 605   Accounting for Involuntary Conversions of Nonmonetary Assets to Monetary Assets (FIN-30)

AUTHORITATIVE GUIDANCE

ASC 605 Revenue Recognition

EITF Issue 99-17 (Accounting for Advertising Barter Transactions) (ASC 605-20-25-14 through 25-18, 50-1)

OVERVIEW

A number of Internet companies have been entering into barter transactions with other Internet companies under which two companies advertise each others' products or services on their respective web sites without additional compensation. The transactions have no affect on net income or cash flow from operations because the companies generally account for the transactions by recognizing equal amounts of barter advertising revenue and barter advertising expense in their income statements.

Some are concerned that this accounting does not conform with current guidance on the recognition of revenues and expenses in Statement of Financial Accounting Concepts No. 6 (not in ASC), guidance on accounting for nonmonetary transactions in ASC 845 (APB-29) and EITF Issue 01-2 (see Issue below), and guidance on accounting for barter transactions in EITF Issue 87-10 (not in ASC) (The guidance in Issue 87-10 referred to the guidance in FAS-53, which has been superseded by FAS-139. FAS-139 states that entities that have used the guidance in FAS-53 should follow the guidance in ASC 210-10-60-1; 430-10-60-1; 460-10-60-38; 855-10-60-3; 926-10-15-2, 15-3; 20-05-1; 25-1 through 25-9; 35-1 through 35-9, 35-11 through 35-18; 40-1 through 40-4; 45-1; 50-1 through 50-5; 55-1 through 55-15; 926-230-45-1; 926-330-35-12; 926-405-25-1 through 25-6; 35-1; 50-1, 50-2; 55-1 through 55-6; 926-430-25-1, 25-2; 926-605-25-1 through 25-21; 25-23 through 25-31; 50-1; 55-1 through 55-13; 926-705-25-1, 25-2; 926-720-25-1 through 25-3; 50-1; 926-835-25-1; 926-845-25-1; 926-855-35-1 (SOP-002, Accounting by Producers and Distributors of Films) and EITF Issue 93-11 (see below). Further, some contend that recognition of barter advertising revenue that results in no income or cash flows may mislead investors who use information about revenues to evaluate companies that have net operating *losses* and net cash *outflows*. The scope of this Issue is *not* limited to Internet companies.

ACCOUNTING ISSUE

Should revenues and expenses related to nonmonetary exchanges involving barter transactions of advertising be recognized at the readily determinable fair values of the advertising provided or received in the exchange?

EITF CONSENSUS

- Revenues and expenses related to advertising barter transactions should be recognized at their fair value only if the fair value of the advertising provided to the counterparty can be determined based on the entity's own known amount of cash received for similar advertising from other buyers that are unrelated to the counterparty in the current barter transaction. A swap of offsetting consideration between the parties to the barter transaction, such as exchanging checks for the same amount, does not provide evidence of the fair value of the barter transaction. If the fair value of an advertising barter transaction cannot be determined based on the above, the transaction should be recognized based on the carrying amount of the advertising provided to the counterparty, which most likely will be zero.
- An entity's historical practice of receiving cash or marketable securities for similar advertising provided should be based on a period no longer than six months before the current barter transaction. A shorter and more representative period should be used if as a result of economic changes, similar transactions that occurred during the previous six months are not representative of the fair value of the advertising provided. Cash transactions that occur after advertising was provided in a barter transaction should not be used to determine the fair value of the advertising provided in the barter transaction (i.e., no look back is permitted to value previous barter transactions).
- Advertising provided for cash may be considered to be similar to advertising provided in a barter transaction if the cash transaction was in the same medium and used the same advertising vehicle, such as the same publication, same web site, or the same broadcast channel, as the barter transaction. Further, the characteristics of advertising provided for cash and that provided in a barter transaction should be reasonably similar in the following respects:
  - Circulation, exposure, or saturation in an intended market
  - Timing in terms of time of day, day of week, daily, weekly, 24 hours a day/7 days a week, and the season
  - Prominence in terms of page on web site, section of periodical, location on page, and size of advertisement
  - Demographics of readers, viewers, or customers
  - Length of time advertising will be shown
- The quantity or volume of advertising provided in a past cash or near-cash transaction that meets the criteria in this Issue can be used as evidence of fair value for a subsequent barter transaction only if the latter provides an equal quantity or volume of advertising. That is, a past cash transaction can be used as

evidence for the recognition of revenue on a barter transaction only up to the dollar amount of the cash transaction. In addition, a cash transaction that has been used to support an equivalent quantity and dollar amount of barter revenue, within the limits of this Issue, cannot be used as evidence of fair value of other barter transactions.

- The amount of revenue and expense recognized from advertising barter transactions should be disclosed for each income statement period presented. Entities providing advertising in barter transactions that do not qualify for recognition at fair value under this Issue should disclose for each income statement period presented the volume and type of advertising provided and received, such as the number of equivalent pages, number of minutes, or the overall percentage of advertising volume.

- The consensus should be applied prospectively to transactions after January 20, 2000, or as a change in accounting principle based on the provisions in APB-20 and FAS-3.

ASC 845 Nonmonetary Transactions

EITF Issue 93-11 (Accounting for Barter Transactions Involving Barter Credits) (ASC 845-10-05-10; 15-11; 30-17 through 30-20)

OVERVIEW

Entities sometimes exchange nonmonetary assets—equipment, for example—for barter credits. Such transactions may be entered into by the parties to the transaction directly, or the transactions may be arranged by a barter company whose business is to match buyers with sellers.

Companies can use barter credits obtained in an exchange to purchase goods or services, such as advertising time, from the other party to the transaction, the barter company, or members of the barter company's exchange network. A barter contract may specify the goods and services that may be purchased, which can be limited to those available from the barter exchange network. Some barter transactions also require a payment of cash in addition to barter credits. Barter credits may expire on a specific date.

ACCOUNTING ISSUES

1. Should exchanges of nonmonetary assets for barter credits be accounted for in accordance with the provisions of ASC 845 (APB-29)?

2. If so, how should a gain or loss, if any, be determined and recognized?

EITF CONSENSUS

1. The provisions of ASC 845 (APB-29) apply to exchanges of nonmonetary assets for barter credits.
2. Gain or loss on an exchange should be determined and recognized as follows:
   a. Before recording the barter transaction:
      (1) Recognize an impairment loss, if the fair value of a nonmonetary asset to be exchanged is less than its carrying amount.
      (2) Measure impairment as the excess of the asset's carrying amount over its fair value. ASC 470-60-35-2 (paragraph 13 of FAS-15, Accounting by Debtors and Creditors for Troubled Debt Restructurings) provides guidance on estimating fair value.

      OBSERVATION: ASC 360 (FAS-144, Accounting for the Impairment or Disposal of Long-Lived Assets), which superseded FAS-121 (Accounting for the Impairment of Long-Lived Assets and for Long-Lived Assets to Be Disposed Of), provides guidance on the measurement and recognition of the impairment of long-lived assets and on the accounting for long-lived assets to be disposed of.

      (3) Recognize impairment of an asset or contractual right exchanged that is not reported in the balance sheet, such as an operating lease, if the transferor remains the primary obligor on the related liability. Measure impairment as the excess of remaining lease costs (total of discounted rental payments and unamortized leasehold improvements) over the discounted amount of sublease rentals for the remaining term of the lease.
      (4) Estimate fair value based on the asset to be exchanged, not on the barter credits to be received.
   b. Report the barter transaction as follows:
      (1) Assume that the fair value of the nonmonetary asset exchanged is more clearly evident than the fair value of the barter credits received and that barter credits should be reported at the fair value of the asset exchanged. This assumption may be overcome if:
         (a) The barter credits can be converted into cash in the near future as evidenced by past transactions, *or*

(b) Independent quoted market prices can be used to determine the fair value of items to be received in exchange for barter credits.

(2) Assume that the nonmonetary asset's fair value does not exceed its carrying amount unless persuasive evidence supports a higher value.

(3) Recognize an impairment loss on barter credits if after the exchange it becomes apparent that:

(c) The remaining value of the barter credits is less than their carrying amount.

(d) It is probable that the entity will not use some, or all, of its barter credits before they expire.

DISCUSSION

Some Task Force members initially believed that the guidance in APB-29 was adequate and no further clarification was necessary. However, because of concerns that barter transactions were being used to defer losses that should have been recognized before the exchange, the Task Force's consensus requires an evaluation of (1) the impairment of the nonmonetary asset exchanged and (2) loss recognition prior to the exchange, if the fair value of the nonmonetary asset to be exchanged for barter credits is less than its carrying amount.

The Task Force's consensus requiring the presumption that the fair value of the nonmonetary asset exchanged be more clearly evident than the fair value of barter credits was reached in response to concerns about the objectivity of the valuation of barter credits. The barter industry strongly opposed that consensus; it argued that it is easier to value barter credits than, for example, obsolete inventory. The Task Force did provide, however, that valuation based on the fair value of barter credits would be permitted if an entity could provide evidence of its ability to convert barter credits for cash in the near future.

EITF Issue 01-2 (Interpretation of APB Opinion No. 29)
ASC 845-10-05-11 through 05-12; 15-12 to 15-17, 15-20; 25-3, 25-6 through 25-11; S30-2; 30-12 through 30-14, 30-21 through 30-27; 55-2, 55-28, 55-30 through 55-37; 60-3; S99-3; 810-10-55-1A)

OVERVIEW

OBSERVATION: The FASB issued FAS-153 (Exchanges of Nonmonetary Assets—An amendment of APB Opinion No. 29) (not listed separately in ASC) in December 2005. The exception from fair value measurement for nonmonetary exchanges of similar productive assets in ASC 845 (APB-29) has been eliminated by the Statement and replaced with an exception from fair value measurement for nonmonetary exchanges that do not have commercial substance. As a result, the consensus position in Issues 1(b), 1(c), 2 through 5, and 7 have been nullified by the guidance in FAS-153; however, the SEC Observer's comments during the discussion of Issue 1(b) continue to apply to SEC registrants. Issue 6 applies only to exchanges of *nonfinancial* assets exchanged for a noncontrolling ownership interest in another entity if the exchange is required to be accounted for at fair value. Issues 10(a) and 10(b) continue to apply if an entity is involved in a real estate exchange that meets the following conditions: (1) the exchange includes boot that is at least 25% of the fair value of the exchange and (2) the exchange meets one of the conditions in ASC 845-10-30-3 (paragraph 20 of APB-29). FAS-153 does not affect the consensus positions in Issues 8(a), 8(b), 9, 11, and 12.

ASC 845 (APB-29, Nonmonetary Transactions) established broad guidance on accounting for nonmonetary transactions. Since its issuance in May 1973, many questions have been raised about its application under various circumstances. The EITF has addressed those questions in the following Issues (the consensus positions of which are codified and reconciled by Issue 01-2):

- Issue 86-29 (Nonmonetary Transactions: Magnitude of Boot and the Exceptions to the Use of Fair Value)
- Issue 87-17 (Spinoffs or Other Distributions of Loans Receivable to Shareholders)
- Issue 87-29 (Exchange of Real Estate Involving Boot)
- Issue 89-7 (Exchange of Assets or Interest in a Subsidiary for a Noncontrolling Equity Interest in a New Entity)
- Issue 96-2 (Impairment Recognition When a Nonmonetary Asset Is Exchanged or Is Distributed to Owners and Is Accounted for at the Asset's Recorded Amount)
- Issue 96-4 (Accounting for Reorganizations Involving a Non-Pro Rata Split-off of Certain Nonmonetary Assets to Owners)
- Issue 98-7 (Accounting for Exchanges of Similar Equity Method Investments)
- Issue 00-5 (Determining Whether a Nonmonetary Transaction Is an Exchange of Similar Productive Assets)

Because some guidance has been modified by the Task Force's consensus positions in Issue 98-3 (Nullified by ASC 805 (FAS-141 (R)), Issue 00-5, and by the positions stated by the SEC Observer and the SEC staff's interpretations of previous guidance on nonmonetary transactions, the Task Force reached a consensus at the April 2001 meeting to codify those Issues as well as certain positions expressed by the SEC staff during the discussions of Issue 98-3.

The Task Force also reached a consensus at the April 2001 meeting that the following Issues, which address narrow fact patterns, should continue to be presented as separate Issues:

- Issue 93-11 (Accounting for Barter Transactions Involving Barter Credits)
- Issue 99-17 (Accounting for Advertising Barter Transactions)

The EITF also reached a consensus that the consensus positions reached in Issues 1 through 6, below, do not apply to the following transactions, which are addressed in other pronouncements:

- Transfers between a joint venture (as defined in ASC 323; ASC 325 (APB-18), but not limited to corporate entities) and its owners
- Contributions of real estate in exchange for an unconsolidated real estate investment (accounted for under ASC 970-323 (SOP 78-9))
- Transfers of real estate in exchange for nonmonetary assets other than real estate (accounted for under ASC 360 (FAS-66))
- Transfers of assets used in oil- and gas-producing activities (proved and unproved properties) in exchange for other assets also used for those activities (accounted for under ASC 932-360-40-7 (paragraph 44(a) of FAS-19))

ACCOUNTING ISSUES

Exchanges of Similar Productive Assets

> **OBSERVATION:** The FASB has issued ASC 805 (FAS-141(revised 2007) (FAS-141(R)), to replace FAS-141, which superseded the guidance in APB Opinion No.16. FAS-141(R) nullifies the guidance in EITF Issue 98-3 and clarifies in ASC 805-10-55-2 (paragraph A2(a)) that an exchange of a business for a business should be accounted for as a business combination.

The Issues discussed below address the accounting for exchanges of similar productive assets. ASC 845 (APB-29) provides that, generally, exchanges of nonmonetary assets should be recognized at the fair value of the assets exchanged. Such exchanges result in gain or loss recognition on the transaction. However, that guidance is modified in ASC 845-10-30-4 (paragraph 21(b) of APB 29), which applies to exchanges of productive assets for similar productive assets that should be accounted for at the historical cost of the asset given up.

Some believe that reciprocal exchanges of groups of assets (referred to here as *operating assets*)—such as radio stations, cable systems, and hotels—for similar assets are business combinations and should be accounted for based on the guidance in ASC 805 (FAS-141 (R), Business Combinations). This Issue applies only to transactions in which each party relinquishes complete control of the assets given up and acquires complete control of the assets received. It does not apply to partial exchanges or exchanges of common stock.

> Issue 1a. was nullified by the guidance in FAS-141(R). Issues 1b. and 1c. were nullified by the guidance in FAS-153, which eliminates the fair value measurement exception for nonmonetary exchanges of similar productive assets provided in APB-29. However, the statement provides an exception from fair value measurement for nonmonetary exchanges that lack commercial substance.

2. Should certain criteria, such as the same general type, same function, employed in the same line of business, be applied only to certain transactions?

This issue and issues 3, 4, and 5 were nullified by the guidance in FAS-153. (See Issue 1A.)

6. If a nonmonetary exchange is required to be accounted for at fair value, should a full or partial gain be recognized if Entity A transfers its ownership in a controlled productive asset or assets to Entity B in exchange for a noncontrolling ownership interest in Entity B?

Exchange of Product or Property Held for Sale for Productive Assets

> Issue 7 was nullified by the guidance in FAS-153. (See Issue 1A.)

Exchanges Involving Monetary Consideration

8a. How much monetary consideration in a nonmonetary exchange would cause an entire transaction to be accounted for as a monetary exchange, which is not under the scope of ASC 845 (APB-29)?

8b. Is full or partial gain recognition appropriate in a monetary exchange (accounted for at fair value) if Entity A transfers its ownership in a controlled asset or group of assets to Entity B in exchange for a noncontrolling ownership interest in Entity B?

9. Should the amount of a gain realized in the exchange discussed below exceed the amount that would be computed based on the guidance in Issue 8(b)?

Exchanges of Real Estate Involving Monetary Consideration

10a. Does ASC 360 (FAS-66) apply to an exchange of similar real estate not covered under the guidance in ASC 845 (APB-29), because the transaction involves sufficient boot for the exchange to be considered monetary under the consensus in Issue 8(a)?

10b. If applicable, how should the guidance in ASC 360 (FAS-66) be applied?

Nonreciprocal Transfers to Owners

Spinoffs or Other Distributions to Shareholders

11. Should an enterprise report a distribution to shareholders of a subsidiary that holds loans receivable as a spinoff or at fair value as a dividend-in-kind if the book value (the recorded investment in the receivable or its carrying amount) of the loan receivable exceeds the receivable's fair value, and how should the recipients account for the transaction?

Reorganizations Involving a Non-Pro Rata Split-off of Certain Nonmonetary Assets to Owners

12. Should a non-pro rata split-off of all or a significant segment of a business in a corporate reorganization plan be accounted for at historical cost or at fair value?

Issues Related to Impairment

Issues 13a and 13b were resolved by the guidance in ASC 360 (FAS-144).

EITF CONSENSUS

Exchanges of Similar Productive Assets

> **OBSERVATION:** FAS-141(R), *Business Combinations*, which was issued in December 2007 to replace FAS-141, provides that an exchange of a business for another business should be accounted for as a business combination. The FASB also issued ASC 810-10-65-1 (FAS-160, *Noncontrolling Interests in Consolidated Financial Statements—an Amendment of ARB No. 51)*, in December 2007 to amend the guidance in ARB-51, *Consolidated Financial Statements*. The guidance in FAS-160 requires that an acquisition of a noncontrolling interest in a controlled subsidiary be accounted for as an equity transaction, thus replacing the guidance in FAS-141 that required entities to account for such transactions by the purchase method.

> **OBSERVATION:** Issues 1b and 1c have been nullified by the guidance in FAS-153 (Exchanges of Nonmonetary Assets). Under the Statement's guidance, the fair value measurement exception for nonmonetary exchanges of similar productive assets discussed in ASC 845 (APB-29) (Accounting for Nonmonetary Transactions) is eliminated and replaced by an exception for the measurement of fair value of nonmonetary assets that have no commercial substance. However, the SEC Observer's comments during the EITF's discussion of issue 1b continue to apply for SEC registrants. Issue 1a has been nullified by the guidance in FAS-141(R).

The EITF reached a consensus on issue 6 that if the fair value of a transferred asset is less than its carrying value, the difference should be recognized as a *loss*. If the fair value of a transferred asset is greater than its carrying value, a *gain* for the difference should be recognized if the entity uses the cost method to accounts for the ownership received. A *partial gain* should be recognized if the equity method is used to account for the ownership interest received. That amount should be calculated using the cost method reduced by a portion of the gain that is related to an economic interest retained in the transferred asset based on the guidance in paragraph 20 of APB-29 (ASC 845-10-30-3). For example, for a transferred asset with a fair value of $500,000 whose carrying value was $200,000 and for which a 20% economic interest is retained, the calculation would be $500,000 − $200,000 = $300,000 × .2 = $60,000. The gain would be $300,000 − $60,000 = $240,000.

> **OBSERVATION:** As a result of the issuance of FAS-153 (Exchanges of Nonmonetary Assets—An Amendment of APB No. 29), (a) the scope of ASC 845 (APB 29) has been amended to exclude transfers of assets to an entity in exchange for an equity interest in that entity and (b) ASC 860 (FAS 140, Accounting for Transfers of Financial Assets and Extinguishments of Liabilities—A Replacement of FASB 125, as amended by FAS-166)) has been amended so that its provisions now apply to transfers of equity method investments. Because ASC 845 (APB-29) (as amended by FAS-153) and ASC 860 (FAS-140) do not provide guidance on accounting for transfers of nonfinancial assets in exchange for other assets, the guidance in this Issue continues to apply to transfers of *nonfinancial* assets in exchange for *noncontrolling* assets in other entities if an exchange is accounted for at fair value.

> **OBSERVATION:** ARB-51, as amended by FAS-160, provides guidance to a parent company on the accounting for a subsidiary's deconsolidation. If Entity A transfers a subsidiary to Entity B in exchange for a *noncontrolling* interest in Entity B, Entity A should account for a gain or loss on the exchange of its *controlling* interest in the subsidiary in accordance with the guidance in ARB-51.

Exchanges Involving Monetary Consideration

8a. If an exchange of nonmonetary assets that would normally be recognized at historical cost includes boot, it should be accounted for as follows:

(1) As a monetary exchange at fair value by both parties if boot is significant (i.e., at least 25% of the fair value of the exchange).

(2) If boot is less than 25% of the fair value of an exchange, the recipient of boot should follow the guidance on pro rata gain recognition in paragraph 22 of APB-29 (ASC 845-10-30-6); the payer of boot does *not* recognize a gain. Fair value should be used only if it can be measured satisfactorily.

The Task Force's consensus that transactions in which boot is significant (25% or more of the fair value of exchange) should be accounted for as monetary transaction by both parties follows the view of the two members of the APB who dissented on Opinion 29, because of the pro rata revenue recognition requirement in paragraph 23 of the Opinion (ASC 845-10-30-10). The dissenters believed that it is illogical to realize a portion of the value of an asset exchanged for a similar nonmonetary transaction that should be accounted for at fair value with gain or loss recognition. In adopting that approach, the Task Force established 25% as a threshold for determining significance.

8b. A full or partial gain in a monetary exchange should be accounted for according to the guidance in Issue 6. This consensus applies to exchange transactions committed to after April 19, 2001. That is, a commitment exists if the parties to the exchange have signed a binding, written agreement that specifies the agreement's principal provisions. A preliminary agreement does not qualify as a commitment for the purpose of this consensus if the principal provisions have not yet been negotiated, or are subsequently changed.

> **OBSERVATION:** The EITF clarified the scope of this Issue. That is, the consensus positions in Issues 8 and 9 do *not* apply to transfers between joint ventures and their owners. Further, exchanges involving transfers of real estate that include monetary consideration do not fall under the scope of Issues 8(b) and 9. FAS-66 and Issue 10 of Issue 01-2 provide guidance for such transactions.

9. The EITF reached the consensus in this Issue based on the following facts:
    a. Company A transfers equipment with a book basis of $100 and an appraised value of $400 to Company C, which is a newly created subsidiary of Company B, an entity previously unrelated to Company A.
    b. Company B transfers $60 to Company C.
    c. Simultaneously with the exchange, Company C borrows $300 with recourse only to the equipment.
    d. In exchange for the transferred equipment, Company A receives shares of Company C representing a 40% interest and $360 in cash.
    e. Company A will account for the transaction by the equity method.
    f. The monetary consideration received exceeds the fair value of the portion of the surrendered asset sold in the exchange.
    g. Company A does not control Company C after the transfer.

The EITF reached a consensus that if Company A has no actual or implied financial or other commitment to support Company C's operations, it should recognize a gain of $260 ($240 fair value [$400 appraisal value × .6] less $60 [$100 cost × .6] plus $80 additional gain related to the negative investment [$40 remaining cost of equipment sold *less* $120 excess cash over $240 fair value of 60% of equipment]). The EITF noted that gain recognition would be affected by the specific facts and circumstances of a transaction. The SEC Observer agreed with the EITF's comment and stated that a gain should not be recognized if there is significant uncertainty about its realization or if a transferor has an actual or implied commitment to support the new entity's operations in any way (see SAB-81).

Exchanges of Real Estate Involving Monetary Consideration

10. This Issue was raised with the EITF because the guidance in ASC 360 (FAS-66) on exchanges of real estate assets appeared to conflict with the EITF's consensus in Issue 8(a) above. Specifically, ASC 360-20-15-10 (paragraph 1 of FAS-66) states that its provisions do not apply to exchanges of real estate for other real estate, which are covered by the provisions of ASC 845 (APB-29), while the EITF's consensus in Issue 8(a) states that all exchanges that include boot equivalent to 25% or more of the fair value of nonmonetary assets exchanged should be accounted for as monetary exchanges.

    It is clear that under the consensus in Issue 8(a) a party receiving boot in an exchange of similar real estate in which boot is less than 25% of the exchange would follow the guidance in ASC 845-10-30-6 (paragraph 22 of APB-29) for pro rata gain recognition. The party paying boot would not recognize a gain.

    However, if boot is more than 25% of the fair value of the exchange and fair value can be measured satisfactorily, Issue 8(a) requires both parties account at fair value for exchanges of (*a*) real estate held for sale in the ordinary course of business for real estate sold in the same line or business or (*b*) real estate not held for sale in the ordinary of business for similar real estate. As a result, it was unclear whether and how such transactions should be recorded under the provisions of ASC 360 (FAS-66).

10a. The EITF reached a consensus that an exchange of similar real estate with boot equivalent to 25% or more of the fair value of an exchange that is considered to be a monetary exchange under the consensus in Issue 8(a) should be allocated between the monetary and nonmonetary components of the transaction based on the relative fair values of the real estate assets exchanged at the time of the transaction. A Task Force member noted that ASC 360-20-15-2 through 15-3, 15-10; 55-4 through

28.14 *Nonmonetary Transactions*

55-5 (FIN-43) provides guidance for real estate assets. (Also see the "Observation" under "Overview" in Issue 01-2.)

10b. The party *receiving* boot should account for (*a*) the *monetary portion* under the guidance in ASC 360 (FAS-66) as a sale of an interest in the underlying real estate and (*b*) the *nonmonetary portion* under ASC 845-10-30-4 (paragraph 21 of APB-29) at the historical cost of the monetary asset given up. The party *paying* boot should account for (*a*) the *monetary portion* as an acquisition of real estate and (*b*) the *nonmonetary portion* under ASC 845-10-30-4 (paragraph 21 of APB-29). (Also see the "Observation" under "Overview" in Issue 01-2.)

Illustration of Accounting for an Exchange of Real Estate with Boot

Company A transfers real estate with a fair value of $500,000 and a net book value of $100,000 to Company B for $120,000 in cash, a note for $100,000, and real estate having a fair value of $280,000 and a net book value of $240,000. The initial investment requirement for full accrual profit recognition under FAS-66 is 20%. The terms of the note from Company B satisfy the continuing investment provisions necessary to apply the full accrual method. Interest on the note, which is considered fully collectible, is at a market rate. The fair values of the real estate transferred by both parties are readily determinable and realizable at the date of the exchange. Neither party has any continuing involvement with the real estate exchanged.

Allocation to Monetary and Nonmonetary Portions

Monetary portion:

$$\frac{\text{Total monetary consideration}}{\text{Total fair value of the exchange}} = \frac{\$220{,}000}{\$500{,}000} = 44\%$$

The monetary portion of the exchange is $120,000 in cash and a note for $100,000.

Nonmonetary portion:

$$\frac{\text{Fair value of real estate exchanged}}{\text{Total fair value of the exchange}} = \frac{\$280{,}000}{\$500{,}000} = 56\%$$

The nonmonetary portion of the exchange is real estate with a fair value of $500,000 for similar real estate with a fair value of $280,000 ($500,000 × .56).

Company A (Receiver of boot)

Because the monetary portion of $120,000 in cash (more than 20% of the total consideration) and the $100,000 note meet the requirements for the buyer's initial and continuing investment, full accrual profit recognition is permitted on the monetary portion under FAS-66. Company A would recognize a gain as follows:

Monetary consideration	$220,000
Less: Company A's book value ($100,000) × .44	44,000
Profit recognized	$176,000

No gain is recognized on the nonmonetary portion, because two similar assets are exchanged. The basis for the new asset is as follows:

Net book value of real estate exchanged	$100,000
Pro rata portion of net book value retired ($100,000 × .44)	44,000
	$ 56,000

Company B (Payer of boot)

Company B accounts for the monetary portion of the exchange at the amount of boot, $220,000, which represents an acquisition of real estate. No gain is recognized on the nonmonetary portion, because two similar assets are exchanged. The basis for the new asset is as follows:

Net book value of real estate exchanged	$240,000
Boot	220,000
	$460,000

This was a difficult issue for the Task Force to resolve because of the conflict in the accounting literature. The guidance in ASC 360 (FAS-66) excludes exchanges of real estate from its scope, because it considers them to be nonmonetary transactions, whereas Issue 86-29 (codified here in Issue 8(a) above), which established uniform guidance for transactions that include boot, stated that all exchanges that include boot equal to 25% or more of the fair value of the exchange are monetary transactions. In trying to resolve this Issue, the FASB staff suggested, and the Task Force agreed, that transactions involving real estate should be accounted for based on the provisions of ASC 360 (FAS-66) for profit recognition.

The Task Force found it difficult, however, to apply the profit recognition criteria in ASC 360 FAS-66) to transactions in which consideration consists of monetary assets and real estate. Specifically, ASC 360 (FAS-66) uses a cookbook-like approach, under which a seller of real estate (the receiver of boot, in this case) cannot recognize profit on the full accrual method unless the transaction meets the initial and continuing investment criteria. The initial investment criterion is met if cash is equal to a prescribed percentage of the purchase price, and the continuing investment criterion is met if the buyer demonstrates an economic commitment to meet its obligation. For example, a mortgage from a third party satisfies the continuing investment requirement. Essentially, the emphasis is on conversion to cash. Hence, real estate received does not fulfill the continuing investment criterion unless it is converted to cash.

As a compromise, the Task Force ultimately reached the consensus that allocates the transaction into a monetary and a nonmonetary component, because of the difficulty of applying the provisions in ASC 360 (FAS-66) to the real estate included in the exchange.

Nonreciprocal Transfers to Owners

11. A company forms a subsidiary to which it transfers loans receivable having a book value that exceeds their fair value. The parent company then distributes stock in the subsidiary to the parent's stockholders.

The EITF reached a consensus that both the company distributing the shares and the recipients of the shares should record the transaction at fair value.

The Task Force noted that the transaction should be considered a dividend-in-kind rather than a spinoff because the subsidiary does not meet the definition of a business in Issue 98-3. Paragraph 23 of APB-29 (ASC 845-10-30-10) states that dividends-in-kind are nonreciprocal transfers of nonmonetary assets. Such transactions are accounted for at fair value if the fair value of the nonmonetary asset distributed can be measured objectively and the distributing entity can realize the value in a sale at or near the time of distribution.

SEC Staff Accounting Bulletin (SAB) No. 82 (Certain Transfers of Nonperforming Assets; Disclosures of the Impact of Assistance from Federal Financial Institutions Regulatory Agencies), issued in July 1989, supports the Task Force's consensus.

Accounting for Reorganizations Involving a Non-Pro Rata Split-off of Certain Nonmonetary Assets to Owners

12. Companies sometimes distribute to shareholders some or all of their shares in a subsidiary in exchange for some or all of the shares hold by the subsidiary's shareholders in the parent company. If a significant portion of a subsidiary's stock is distributed, some consider such a transaction to be an acquisition of treasury stock, while others believe it is a corporate reorganization or liquidation, commonly referred to as a spinoff, split-off, or split-up. Under federal income tax law, a *split-off* is a parent company's exchange of its stock in a subsidiary for stock held by shareholders in the parent company. Distributions are said to be pro rata when shareholders participate on an equal basis in the exchange of the parent company's shares for those of the subsidiary in a split-up or split-off.

The basic principle of APB-29 is that nonmonetary transactions should be accounted for based on the fair value of the assets exchanged. Paragraph 23 of ABP-29 (ASC 845-10-30-10), which addresses nonreciprocal transfers of nonmonetary assets to owners, provides an exception to the basic principle by requiring that distributions of nonmonetary assets to owners in a "spinoff or *other form of reorganization or liquidation* or in a plan that is in substance the rescission of a prior business combination" (emphasis added) should be accounted for at historical cost.

This Issue has been raised because it is unclear as to whether the reference in paragraph 23 (ASC 845-10-30-10) to an "other form of reorganization or liquidation" applies to distributions to owners in transactions known as *split-ups* or *split-offs*, in which the parent company distributes shares in a subsidiary to its stockholders in exchange for shares held in the parent company. If it applies, such transactions would also be accounted for at historical cost. Some believe, however, that non-pro rata split-ups or split-offs should be accounted for based on the fair value of the assets distributed in the exchange, because the second sentence of paragraph 23 (ASC 845-10-30-10) refers only to pro rata distributions.

The Issue primarily relates to situations in which there is a potential gain, and the fair value of the nonmonetary asset distributed is objectively measurable and would be realized by the distributing entity if the asset were sold at or near the time of distribution.

The EITF reached a consensus that:

a. A non-pro rata split-off of a segment of a business in a corporate reorganization plan should be accounted for at *fair value*.

b. A split-off of a targeted business in which shares are distributed on a pro rata basis to the holders of a targeted entity's stock should be accounted for at *historical cost*. However, a split-off in which the targeted stock was created with the intent to subsequently split-off the targeted business should be accounted for at fair value because the Task Force believes the two steps constitute one transaction.

Proponents of the first part of the consensus argued that the first sentence of paragraph 23 (ASC 845-10-30-10) of APB-29 creates an exception to the general principle of APB-29, which only applies to nonreciprocal distributions of nonmonetary assets to owners in a spinoff or other form of reorganization, liquidation, or in a rescission of a prior business combination. They argued further that the second sentence limits the exception to pro rata distributions to owners and that a non-pro rata split-off is, in fact, an acquisition or redemption of capital stock, regardless of the nonmonetary asset exchanged. They noted that a non-pro rata split-off should be accounted for at fair value, because paragraph 18 of APB-29 (ASC 845-10-30-1) specifically requires that type of treatment when a company acquires or redeems its shares by distributing nonmonetary assets. Some Task Force members noted that a majority of non-pro rata split-offs have been accounted for at fair value. The Task Force's consensus that the distribution of targeted stock only to that stock's holders should be accounted for at historical cost is based on the view that such a distribution is a pro rata distribution, because it applies to all of the owners of a specific class of common stock. The Task Force added the prohibition against the creation of targeted stock and immediate distribution of that stock to shareholders to prevent abusive transactions that would circumvent the consensus on non-pro rata distributions.

Illustration of the Accounting for a Non-Pro Rata Split-Off of Certain Nonmonetary Assets to Owners

AML Corp. decides to split-off its ownership in its subsidiary, WHS, Inc., on a non-pro rata basis by offering to exchange its holdings of 100,000 shares in WHS for 50,000 AML shares. AML's recorded investment in WHS is $4,000,000. Shares in WHS traded on a recognized public exchange at $50 per share on March 31, 20X6—the date of the transaction. Shares in AML traded at $80 on March 31, 20X6.

AML should account for the transaction at the fair value of the asset distributed, which is $50 per share on March 31, 20X6. AML should make the following journal entry to account for the split-off:

Treasury stock	$5,000,000	
Investment in WHS		$4,000,000
Gain on split-off		$1,000,000

SEC OBSERVER COMMENT

In Issue 98-3, the SEC Observer stated that registrants are required to account for exchanges of consolidated businesses at fair value under the provisions of ASC 805 (FAS-141 (R)), even if they are in the same line of business.

In addition, the SEC staff believes that all exchanges of consolidated businesses for nonmonetary assets should be accounted for under the provisions of ASC 805 (FAS-141(R)), even if the nonmonetary assets acquired are equity method investments. The staff believes, however, that a gain need not be recognized in an exchange of a consolidated business for a joint venture unless it includes cash or near cash consideration. The SEC Observer noted that the guidance in SAB-48 (Transfers of Nonmonetary Assets by Promoters or Shareholders), as modified by SAB-97 (Business Combinations Prior to an Initial Public Offering and Determination of the Acquiring Corporation), continues to apply. Exchanges of assets, such as radio stations and cable systems, should be accounted for based on the facts and circumstances and should consider the definition of a business in Issue 98-3.

EITF Issue 04-13 (Accounting for Purchases and Sales of Inventory with the Same Counterparty) (ASC 845-10-05-8; 15-6 through 15-9; 25-4 through 25-5; 30-15-6; 45-1; 50-3; 55-10, 55-12 through 55-17, 55-19 through 55-22, 55-24 through 55-26)

OVERVIEW

Companies sometimes enter into transactions to buy inventory from and sell inventory in the form of raw materials, work-in-process

(WIP), or finished goods to companies in the same line of business. Such purchase and sale arrangements may be structured under a single contract or under separate contracts.

Issue 04-13 does *not* apply to inventory purchases and sales arrangements (*a*) accounted for as derivatives under the guidance in ASC 815 (FAS-133, Accounting for Derivative Instruments and Hedging Activities) or (*b*) related to exchanges of software or exchanges of real estate. No guidance is provided as to whether transactions reported at fair value qualify for revenue recognition.

ACCOUNTING ISSUES

- For the purpose of determining the effect of ASC 845 (APB-29, Accounting for Nonmonetary Transactions) on sale and purchase transactions of inventory with the same entity in the same line of business, under what circumstances should two or more inventory exchange transactions be considered to be one transaction?
- Are there circumstances under which nonmonetary exchanges of inventory in the same line of business should be recognized at fair value?

EITF CONSENSUS

The EITF reached the following consensus positions:

- For the purpose of determining the effect of ASC 845 (APB-29) on sale and purchase transactions of inventory between two parties in the same line of business, two or more such transactions should be combined and accounted for as one transaction, because the EITF believes that purchase and sale transactions between the same two parties are entered into in contemplation of one another. The same guidance applies if an inventory transaction, such as a sale to a counterparty, legally depends on the performance of another inventory transaction, such as a purchase from the same counterparty.

An inventory transaction that does *not* legally depend on the performance of another inventory transaction should be evaluated based on the following factors, which are *not* determinative individually or all-inclusively, to determine whether those transactions were entered into in contemplation of one another:

— *The counterparties have a specific legal right of offset related to the inventory purchase and sale transactions.* The ability to offset transactions indicates there is a connection between them. This indicates that transactions my have been entered into separately, actually were entered into in contemplation of one another. This indicator is more important for net settlement provisions

related to specific inventory transactions identified by the counterparties that for those that are netted as part of a master netting agreement for all the transactions between the counterparties.
— *The counterparties have entered into the inventory purchase and sale transactions at the same time.* This indicates that the transactions were entered into in contemplation of one another. If an entity enters into a sale transaction with a counterparty and the counterparty may, but is not obligated to, deliver an agreed amount of inventory, the two transactions are considered to have been entered into in contemplation of one another the more certain it becomes that the counterparty will deliver the agreed amount of inventory.
— *The terms of inventory sale and purchase transactions between two counterparties are at off-market rates at the inception of the agreement.* Inventory transactions entered into under such terms indicate they are related to one another, and have been entered into in contemplation of another inventory transaction between the counterparties. This indicator is more important if the products' market prices are readily determinable than if the prices for those products are more flexible.

In addition, the EITF agreed that separate invoices and an exchange of offsetting cash payments is not a factor that should be considered in determining whether two or more inventory transactions with the same counterparty should be considered to be a single exchange transaction.

— *Nonmonetary* exchange transactions of finished goods inventory for raw materials or WIP inventory in the same line of business are *not* exchange transactions that have commercial substance in accordance with ASC 845-10-30-3 (paragraph 20(b) of APB-29), as amended by FAS-153, (Exchanges of Nonmonetary Assets). A transaction should be accounted for at *fair value*, however, if (*a*) its fair value can be determined within reasonable limits and (*b*) the transaction has commercial substance. All other nonmonetary exchanges of inventory in the same line of business, such as an exchange of raw materials or WIP inventory for raw materials, WIP, finished goods inventory, or finished goods inventory for finished goods inventory, should be recognized at the *carrying amount* of the transferred inventory.

For the purpose of this Issue, inventory should be classified by type, that is, as raw materials, WIP, or finished goods, in the same manner as it would be classified in the entity's external financial reports. Entities should disclose the amount of revenue and costs or gains and losses related to inventory exchanges recognized at fair value.

The guidance in this issue should be considered if a transaction includes boot.

FASB RATIFICATION

The FASB ratified the consensus positions in this Issue at its September 28, 2005, meeting.

RELATED CHAPTER IN 2011
GAAP GUIDE, VOLUME I

Chapter 32, "Nonmonetary Transactions"

RELATED CHAPTERS IN 2011
INTERNATIONAL ACCOUNTING/FINANCIAL REPORTING STANDARDS GUIDE

Chapter 19, "Impairment of Assets"
Chapter 23, "Inventories"
Chapter 24, "Investment Property"
Chapter 27, "Property, Plant, and Equipment"

CHAPTER 29
PENSION PLANS—EMPLOYERS

CONTENTS

Overview		29.02
Authoritative Guidance		
ASC 715 Compensation—Retirement Benefits		29.03
FIG-FAS-87	A Guide to Implementation of Statement 87 on Employers' Accounting for Pensions: Questions and Answers	29.03
Issue 88-1	Determination of Vested Benefit Obligation for a Defined Benefit Pension Plan	29.28
EITF Issue 90-3	Accounting for Employers' Obligations for Future Contributions to a Multiemployer Pension Plan	29.31
EITF Issue 03-2	Accounting for the Transfer to the Japanese Government of the Substitutional Portion of Employee Pension Fund Liabilities	29.32
EITF Issue 03-4	Accounting for "Cash Balance" Pension Plans	29.35
Topic D-27	Accounting for the Transfer of Excess Pension Assets to a Retiree Health Care Benefits Account	29.37
Topic D-36	Selection of Discount Rates Used for Measuring Defined Benefit Pension Obligations and Obligations of Postretirement Plans Other Than Pensions	29.37
Related Chapters in 2011 GAAP Guide, Volume II		29.38
Related Chapters in 2011 GAAP Guide, Volume I		29.38
Related Chapters in 2011 International Accounting/Financial Reporting Standards Guide		29.38

OVERVIEW

GAAP for employers' accounting for pension plans focus on the determination of annual pension expense (identified as net periodic pension cost) and the presentation of an appropriate amount of pension liability in the statement of financial position. Net periodic pension cost has often been viewed as a single homogeneous amount, but it actually consists of several components that present different aspects of an employer's financial arrangements, as well as the cost of benefits earned by employees.

In applying principles of accrual accounting for pension plans, the FASB emphasizes three fundamental features:

1. *Delayed recognition* Changes in the pension obligation and changes in the value of pension assets are recognized not as they occur, but systematically and gradually over subsequent periods.

2. *Net cost* The recognized consequences of events and transactions affecting a pension plan are reported as a single net amount in the employer's financial statements. This approach results in the aggregation of items that would be presented separately for any other part of the employer's operations: the compensation cost of benefits, the interest cost resulting from deferred payment of those benefits, and the results of investing pension assets.

3. *Offsetting* Pension assets and liabilities are shown net in the employer's statement of financial position, even though the liability has not been settled. The assets may still be controlled and substantial risks and rewards associated with both are clearly borne by the employer.

The following pronouncements are discussed in the 2011 *GAAP Guide, Volume I,* Chapter 33, "Pension Plans":

ASC 715	Employers' Accounting for Pensions (FAS-87)
ASC 715	Employers' Disclosures about Pensions and Other Postretirement Benefits—An Amendment of FASB Statements No. 87, 88, and 106 (FAS-132(R))
ASC 715; ASC 958	Employers' Accounting for Defined Benefit Pension and Other Postretirement Plans—An Amendment of FASB Statements No. 87, 88, 106, and 132(R) (FAS-158)

AUTHORITATIVE GUIDANCE

ASC 715 Compensation—Retirement Benefits

FIG-FAS-87 A Guide to Implementation of Statement 87 on Employers' Accounting for Pensions: Questions and Answers (ASC 715-20-50-1, 50-8; 715-30-15-4; 35-5, 35-15 through 35-16, 35-20, 35-23, 35-31, 35-39, 35-42, 35-46 through 35-49, 35-61, 35-69, 35-84 through 35-85; 55-3 through 55-5, 55-8 through 55-15, 55-17 through 55-22, 55-24 through 55-33, 55- 35 through 55-43, 55-46 through 55-51, 55-53 through 55-61, 55-63 through 55-64, 55-66 through 55-67, 55-88, 55-90, 55-108, 55-110 through 55-120, 55-122 through 55-127; 715-55-60-2; ASC 740-10-60-1; ASC 958-715-55-2; ASC 980-715-55-2 through 55-8, 55-10 through 55-25; 330-10-55-5 through 55-7)

OVERVIEW

The following Implementation Guide is based on the guidance in FSP FAS-158-1 (not listed separately in ASC), which superseded the previous Implementation Guide for FAS-87 (A Guide to Implementation of Statement 87 on Employers' Accounting for Pensions), and was carried over into ASC 715 (FAS-87) as Appendix E.

FAS-87—APPENDIX E

Question E1: This question has been deleted.

Question E2: Does this Statement apply to a non-U.S. pension plan that provides death and disability benefits that are greater than the incidental death and disability benefits allowed in U.S. tax-qualified pension plans?

Answer: Yes, if the non-U.S. pension plan is in substance similar to a U.S. plan.

Question E3: This question has been deleted.

Question E4: How should an employer with regulated operations account for the effects of applying this Statement for financial reporting purposes if another method of accounting for pensions is used for determining allowable pension cost for rate-making purposes?

Answer: This Statement applies to an employer with regulated operations. However, ASC 980 (FAS-71, Accounting for the Effects of Certain Types of Regulation) may require that an asset or liability be recorded for the difference between net periodic pension cost recognized under this Statement and pension cost allowed for rate-making purposes. If an entity is subject to the provisions of ASC 980 (FAS-71), an asset is recognized if the provisions of ASC 980-320-25-1 (paragraph 9 of FAS-71) are met. Also, a liability is recognized if the conditions of ASC 980-405-25-1 (paragraph 11b of FAS-71) are met.

Exceptions to the General Rule

For entities subject to ASC 980 (FAS-71), an asset is generally recognized when net periodic pension cost under this Statement exceeds pension cost allowable for rate-making purposes ASC 980-320-25-1 (FAS-71, paragraph 9) . However, the criteria of ASC 980-320-25-1 (paragraph 9) would not be met if (1) it is probable that the regulator will soon adopt this Statement for rate-making purposes and (2) it is *not* probable that the regulator will permit the entity to recover the difference between pension costs under the guidance in this Statement and pension costs allowable by the regulator, before the regulator adopts the approach in this Statement.

For entities subject to the requirements in ASC 980 (FAS-71), a liability generally is recognized when net periodic pension cost under the guidance in this Statement is less than pension cost allowable for rate-making purposes ASC 980-405-25-1 (FAS-71, paragraph 11b). However, the criteria in ASC 980-405-25-1 (paragraph 11b) would not be met if (1) it is probable that the regulator will soon adopt the guidance in this Statement for rate-making purposes, (2) the regulator will not hold the employer responsible for the costs that were intended to be recovered by the current rates and that have been deferred by the change in method, *and* (3) the regulator will provide revenue to cover these same costs when they are ultimately recognized under the provisions of this Statement.

A regulator cannot eliminate a liability even if it was *not* imposed by its actions. Therefore, regulation does not affect the need to recognize the underfunded status of a defined benefit pension plan under the guidance in ASC 980-470-40-1 through 40-2 (paragraphs 35 and 36 of this Statement).

Question E5: If an employer has a pension plan that also provides postemployment health care benefits, should the guidance in this Statement apply to those benefits?

Answer: No. ASC 715 (FAS-106, Employers' Accounting for Postretirement Benefits Other Than Pensions) provides guidance in accounting for postemployment health care benefits.

Question E6: Does footnote 4 of this Statement (which states that "the interest cost component of net periodic pension cost shall not be considered to be interest for purposes of applying FAS-34 (Capitalization of Interest Cost))" proscribe the capitalization of the interest cost component of net periodic pension cost when employee compensation is capitalized as part of the cost of inventory or other assets?

Answer: No. Net periodic pension cost, including the interest element included in that amount, is viewed as an element of employee compensation. If it is appropriate to capitalize employee compensation as part of the cost of inventory or as part of a self-constructed asset, the entire amount of net periodic pension cost is included in making this computation.

Question E7: May an employer have net periodic pension cost that is a net credit (i.e., net periodic pension income)?

Answer: Yes. The computation of net periodic pension cost involves the combination of elements that are both expenses/losses and revenues/gains. The revenues/gains components (e.g., return on plan assets, amortization of a transition asset) of the pension cost computation may exceed the expense/loss portion of the computation of net periodic pension cost.

> ☛ **PRACTICE POINTER:** In an environment of low interest rates and high stock market returns, many employers with a defined benefit pension plan may report net periodic pension credits. Low interest rates correspond with a reduction in the interest cost component of net periodic pension cost, and high stock market returns often correspond with a high realized return on plan assets.

Question E8: If an employer has net periodic pension cost that is a net credit (i.e., net periodic pension income), how should that be treated if employee compensation is capitalized as part of the cost of inventory or other assets?

Answer: The portion of net periodic pension income that is capitalized as part of the cost of an asset would serve to reduce the applicable asset's cost.

Question E9: If an employer sponsoring a pension plan that is overfunded has net periodic pension cost that is a net credit (i.e., net periodic pension income) and the employer makes no contribution to the pension plan because it cannot currently deduct the amount for tax purposes, is the difference between net periodic pension income and the tax deductible amount a temporary difference as discussed in paragraphs 10 through 11 of FAS-109 (ASC 740-10-25-18, 19, 20)? If it is a temporary difference, when and how will it reverse?

Answer: Yes. A difference between the net periodic pension income and the tax deductible expense would create a temporary difference (i.e., the financial reporting basis of the pension liability or asset would differ from its tax basis). The temporary difference may reverse in the future when net periodic pension cost exceeds amounts funded (the pension plan may not be overfunded indefinitely). Alternatively, if the pension plan continues to be overfunded for an extended period of time, the employer may terminate the plan and capture the excess assets. In this case, the gain for accounting purposes would be less than the taxable amount.

Question E10: If transferable securities issued by the employer are included in plan assets, should the measurement of plan assets also include the interest accrued but not yet received on those securities?

Answer: Yes. Amounts accrued by the employer but not yet paid to the plan (which are to be excluded from plan assets per ASC 980-605-50-1 (paragraph 19 of FAS-71) are related to the recognized pension lia-bility.

Question E11: If an employer has a nonqualified pension plan (for tax purposes) that is funded with life insurance policies owned by the employer, should the cash surrender value of those policies be considered plan assets for purposes of applying this Statement?

Answer: Not if the employer is the owner or beneficiary of the life insurance policies. The applicable accounting treatment for those policies is specified in ASC 325-30-15-3 through 15-3; 35-2 through 35-2; 25-1; 05-3 through 05-5 (FTB 85-4, Accounting for Purchases of Life Insurance).

Question E12: If the actual return on plan assets for a period is a component of net periodic pension cost, how does the expected return on plan assets affect the determination of net periodic pension cost?

Answer: When the current year's net periodic pension cost is computed, both the actual return on plan assets and any difference between this actual return and the expected return are considered. The difference (a net gain or loss) between the actual return on plan assets and the expected return on assets is recognized in other comprehensive income in the period in which it occurs. The net result of this treatment is that the expected return on plan assets is included in the computation of the current year's net periodic pension cost. The total of the amount recognized in other comprehensive income and the actual return on plan assets equals the expected return on plan assets. Future net periodic pension cost is affected through the amortization of the net gain or loss recognized in other comprehensive income.

Illustration of Return on Asset Component of Net Periodic Pension Cost

As of January 1, 20X8, GAF, Inc., has pension plan assets of $500,000. The expected return on plan assets for 20X4 is 10%. Contributions and benefit payments during the year were both $100,000. At December 31, 20X8, plan assets are $600,000. Service cost is $100,000 and interest cost is $80,000. GAF has no other components of net periodic pension cost. GAF would compute net periodic pension cost as follows:

Service cost	$100,000
Interest cost	80,000
Actual return on plan assets	(100,000)
Net gain recognized in other comprehensive income	50,000
Net periodic pension cost	$130,000

Question E13: If an employer has a substantive commitment to have a formula greater than the pension plan's written formula, how should the difference between the effects of a retroactive plan amendment that was anticipated as part of that substantive commitment and the effects of the actual retroactive plan amendment be accounted for?

Answer: The accounting depends on whether the difference results from an intended modification of the formula for which there is a substantive commitment. If it does, then the accounting should follow the guidance in ASD 980-250-55-1 (paragraphs 24 through 28 of FAS-71) for a retroactive plan amendment. If it does not, the difference is a gain or loss and should be accounted for in accordance with the provisions of paragraphs 29 through 34 ASC 980-350-35-1 through 35-2; 980-250-55-3; 980-340-55-2 through 55-3) (paragraphs 29 through 34 of FAS-71)..

Question E14: Once a schedule of amortization of prior service cost from a specific retroactive plan amendment has been established, should that schedule remain the same or is it subject to revision on a periodic basis?

Answer: An amortization schedule of prior service cost should be revised only if one of three conditions occurs: (1) the pension plan is curtailed, (2) events indicate that the period for which the employer will receive benefits from a retroactive plan benefit is shorter than initially estimated, or (3) the future economic benefits have been impaired. The amortization schedule should not be revised because of variances in the expected service lives of employees. Finally, this Statement specifically proscribes reducing the length of such an amortization schedule (i.e., under no circumstances can prior service cost be recognized in net periodic pension cost more slowly than originally planned).

Question E15: In a business combination that is accounted for by the purchase method under the guidance in ASC 805 FAS-141(R) (Business Combinations), if the acquiring employer includes the employees of the acquired employer in its pension plan and grants them credit for prior service (the acquired employer did not have a pension plan), should the credit granted for prior service be treated as prior service cost and recognized in other comprehensive income or treated as part of the cost of the acquisition?

29.08 *Pension Plans—Employers*

Answer: It depends. If the selling entity requires that prior service credit be granted as a condition of the acquisition, the prior service credit granted would be treated as part of the cost of the acquisition; the offsetting debit is an adjustment to goodwill. In all other cases, the granting of prior service credit is treated as a retroactive plan amendment. Prior service cost is recognized in other comprehensive income and amortized under the guidance in ASC 980-250-55-1 (paragraphs 24–27 of FAS-71).

Question E16: In determining the periods for (*a*) amortization of prior service cost included in accumulated other comprehensive income, (*b*) minimum amortization of net gain or loss included in accumulated other comprehensive income, or (*c*) amortization of the transition asset or obligation remaining in accumulated other comprehensive income ASC 715 (FAS-87), is it necessary to include the service periods of employees who are expected to receive only a return of their contributions (plus interest, if applicable) to a contributory defined benefit pension plan in determining the future service periods of employees who are expected to receive benefits under that pension plan?

Answer: No. Only the expected future service periods of employees who are expected to receive a benefit provided by the employer need to be included.

Question E17: Are the service periods of employees who are expected to terminate before their benefits are vested included in the determination of the average remaining service period of employees who are expected to receive benefits under the pension plan?

Answer: No. Only the expected service periods of employees who are expected to receive benefits under the pension plan need to be included.

Question E18: Is there a specific threshold for determining if a pension plan has "almost all" inactive participants for purposes of selecting the amortization period for certain components of net periodic pension cost?

Answer: No. Judgment is required for determining whether "almost all" of a pension plan's participants are inactive.

Question E19: May an employer adopt an accounting policy to immediately recognize as a component of net periodic pension cost the cost of all plan amendments that grant increased benefits for services rendered in prior periods (prior service cost)?

Answer: No. Under the guidance in ASC 715 (FAS-87), an entity is not permitted to adopt an accounting policy under which the cost of *all* plan amendments granting increased benefits for services performed in prior periods would be recognized immediately as a component of net periodic pension cost. Prior service cost should be recognized immediately in other comprehensive income, unless based on an evaluation of the facts and circumstances, an employer does *not* expect to receive a future economic benefit from the retroactive plan amendment.

Question E20: If an employer has a history of granting retroactive plan amendments every three years, should the resulting prior service costs be amortized over a three-year period?

Answer: This decision needs to be made on a case-by-case basis after the applicable facts and circumstances are considered. If it is determined that future economic benefits that result from a plan amendment will last for example, for only three years, it would be appropriate to amortize prior periodic cost included in accumulated comprehensive income over a three-year period. That is, if employees become accustomed to a retroactive increase in plan benefits every three years, the expected future economic benefits may not continue if this pattern is broken.

Question E21: If an employer grants a retroactive plan amendment that reduces the projected benefit obligation (a negative retroactive plan amendment), what method should be used to reduce prior service cost included in accumulated comprehensive income when several prior retroactive plan amendments in the aggregate have resulted in prior service costs in accumulated comprehensive income that exceed the effects of the negative retroactive plan amendment?

Answer: Unless a negative retroactive plan amendment can be specifically related to a prior retroactive plan amendment, it is acceptable to apply any systematic and rational method (e.g., last-in, first-out; first-in, first-out; pro rata) in a consistent manner.

Question E22: If an employer amends a pension plan to delete a provision that a percentage of the employee's accumulated benefits be paid to the employee's spouse if the employee dies before reaching a specified age, should the reduction in benefits be accounted for as a retroactive plan amendment?

Answer: Yes. This is an example of a negative retroactive plan amendment.

Question E23: This question has been deleted.

Question E24: Should the amount and timing of pension plan contributions and benefit payments expected to be made during the year be considered in determining the expected return on plan assets for that year?

Answer: Yes. The expected return on plan assets should consider the asset amounts that will be available for investment purposes during the year, including new contributions made.

29.10 Pension Plans—Employers

Question E25: This question has been deleted.

Question E26: May an employer that has several pension plans with similar plan assets use different asset valuation methods to determine the market-related value of those plan assets?

Answer: Ordinarily not, especially since one objective of this Statement is to enhance the comparability of pension plan information. However, different asset valuation methods may be appropriate if they reflect underlying differences in the pension plans' inherent facts and circumstances.

Question E27: Is there a limitation on the number of classes into which plan assets may be divided for purposes of selecting asset valuation methods for determining the market-related value of plan assets?

Answer: No. However, the method selected for each asset class should be appropriate for recognizing changes in the fair value of assets in a systematic and rational manner over a period not to exceed five years. Asset valuation methods adopted should be applied consistently within each class, and the method used to divide assets into different classes should be applied consistently.

Question E28: Is the following an acceptable asset valuation method for determining the market-related value of plan assets? The market-related value of plan assets is determined with a total return-on-plan asset component consisting of three layers:

1. An expected return-on-plan asset component based on the beginning-of-year market-related value of plan assets, cash flow during the year, and the expected long-term rate of return on plan assets

2. An amount equal to the change in the accumulated benefit obligation that resulted from any change during the year in the assumed discount rates used to determine the accumulated benefit obligation (The amount is reduced pro rata if plan assets are less than the accumulated benefit obligation.)

3. A variance component equal to a percentage (e.g., 20% if a five-year averaging period is used) of the difference between the actual return on plan assets based on the fair values of those plan assets and the expected return on plan assets derived from components (1) and (2)

Answer: No. Factor (2), the change in the accumulated benefit obligation resulting from changes in the assumed discount rate, is unrelated to changes in the fair value of plan assets. Only changes in the fair value of plan assets between various dates can be considered in computing the market-related value of plan assets.

Question E29: How does the use of a market-related value of plan assets affect the determination of net periodic pension cost?

Answer: The use of a market-related value of plan assets affects the determination of net periodic pension cost in two ways. First, the expected return on plan assets is based on the market-related value of plan assets (not based on the fair value of plan assets). Second, to the extent that gains and losses based on the fair value of plan assets are not yet reflected in the market-related value of plan assets, such amounts are excluded from the net gain or loss included in accumulated other comprehensive income that is subject to amortization in the following period.

Illustration of the Effect on Net Periodic Pension Cost of Using the Market-Related Value of Plan Assets

Touchstone Enterprises has pension plan assets with a fair value and FAS-87 market-related value of $10 million on 1/1/20X4. Touchstone expects a 10% return on pension plan assets. The actual return during 20X4 was $2 million. Touchstone's pension contributions and benefit payments were both $800,000 during 20X4. Touchstone adjusts the market-related value of plan assets for differences between the expected and actual return on assets over 5 years. Therefore, the expected return on plan assets in 20X5 is $1,120,000, computed as follows:

Plan assets (both at fair value and market-related value) at 1/1/20X4		$10,000,000
Contributions		800,000
Benefit payments		(800,000)
Actual return on plan assets	$2,000,000	
Expected return on plan assets	(1,000,000)	1,000,000
Difference	$1,000,000	
Amortization of difference over 5 years		200,000
Plan assets at market-related value at 1/1/20X5		$11,200,000
Expected return on plan assets during 20X5 at 10%		$ 1,120,000

Question E30: This question has been deleted.

Question E31: If all or almost all of a pension plan's participants are inactive due to a temporary suspension of the pension plan (i.e., for a limited period of time, employees will not earn additional defined benefits), should the minimum amortization of net gain or loss included in accumulated other comprehensive income be determined based on the average remaining life expectancy of the temporarily inactive participants?

Answer: No. The amortization period should be based on the average remaining service period of temporarily inactive participants who are expected to receive benefits under the pension plan.

Question E32: If all employees covered by a pension plan are terminated but not retired, should the minimum amortization of a net gain or loss included in accumulated comprehensive income be determined based on the average remaining life expectancy of the inactive participants?

Answer: Yes.

Question E33: May an employer immediately recognize gains and losses as a component of net periodic pension cost instead of recognizing them in accumulated other comprehensive income?

Answer: Yes. However, the following three conditions must be met: (1) the method must be used consistently, (2) the method must be applied to *all* gains and losses (on both plan assets and pension plan obligations), and (3) the method used is disclosed based on the guidance in paragraph 5(o) of FAS-132(R) (ASC 715-20-50-1).

Questions E34–E43: These questions have been deleted.

Question E44: If a career-average-pay pension plan has a formula that provides pension benefits equal to 1% of each year's salary for that year's service and if prospective (flat-benefit) plan amendments are granted every three years as part of union negotiations (e.g., a negotiated increase may provide that additional benefits of $360 per year are earned for each of the following three years of service), should the projected unit credit method be used for both the career-average-pay and the flat-benefit portions of the pension benefits provided under the pension plan?

Answer: No. The projected unit credit method should be used to apportion the career-average-pay portion of the plan to the expected service period of active employees. The unit credit method should be used for the flat-benefit portion of the plan.

Question E45: If an employer has a pension plan that provides a pension benefit of 1% of final pay for each year of service up to a maximum of 20 years of service and final pay is frozen at year 20, should the employer attribute the total projected benefits under the pension plan for an employee over the employee's expected service period even if that service period is anticipated to exceed the 20-year limitation?

Answer: No. If a pension plan attributes all of its prospective benefits over a 20-year time period, the service cost component should be recognized over this time period even if the employee is expected to work beyond 20 years. Note, however, that interest cost would continue to accrue on the projected benefit obligation beyond 20 years.

Question E46: Would the answer to the question in paragraph E45 be different if the pension plan's formula provided a pension benefit of 1% of final pay for each year of service up to a maximum of 20 years of service and final pay was not frozen at year 20?

Answer: No. The only difference is that a liability gain or loss will exist beyond year 20 if future experience regarding employee pay levels differs from that which was assumed.

Question E47: How should an employer determine the accumulated and projected benefit obligations if a pension plan has more than one formula and an employee's pension benefits are determined based on the formula that provides the greatest pension benefit at the time the employee terminates or retires (For example, if the employee terminates in year 10, the pension plan's flat-benefit formula provides a greater pension benefit than does the pension plan's pay-related formula; however, if the employee terminates in year 11, the pension plan provides that same employee with a greater benefit under its pay-related formula than under its flat-benefit formula.)

Answer: A pension plan that uses more than one formula may not assign the same benefit for each year of service. Therefore, the employer may need to use an attribution approach that does not assign the same level of benefits for each year of service. In calculating the accumulated benefit obligation, the employer should choose the formula that produces the greatest liability amount based on service rendered to date. Since the accumulated benefit obligation (ABO) cannot exceed the projected benefit obligation (PBO), the calculated PBO for service already rendered must equal or exceed the ABO. For service not yet rendered, the PBO should be calculated using the formula that results in the largest measure of the liability. A number of illustrations of these concepts are included in FIG-FAS 87. One illustration adapted from FIG-FAS 87 appears below.

Illustration of Attribution with Multiple Formulas

FRW, Inc., has a pension plan that uses two benefit formulas. The plan benefit that participants will receive is the larger of the amounts computed by each of the two formulas. Formula A provides a flat benefit of $900 for each of the first 20 years of an employee's service, with no pension benefits earned for service beyond 20 years. Formula B provides a benefit equal to 1% of final pay for each year of service.

29.14 Pension Plans—Employers

An employee starts at a salary of $21,000 in year 1 and receives a $2,000 increase in salary for each year of service. (For purposes of simplicity, the accumulated and projected benefit obligations are expressed in terms of the annual pension benefits that begin when the employee retires.) This employee of FRW is expected to retire at the end of year 30 with a final salary of $79,000. Formula A would provide an annual pension benefit of $18,000 for 30 years of service ($900 in each of the first 20 years of service and no additional benefits for any service beyond 20 years). Formula B would provide a pension benefit of $23,700 for 30 years of service (30 × 1% × $79,000, or $790 for each year of service). Under Formula A, $900 of service cost is attributed to each of the first 20 years of service; no service cost is attributed to employee service beyond 20 years. Under Formula B, $790 of service cost is attributed to each of the 30 expected years of employee service.

At the end of year 20, the ABO and the PBO under Formula A, both $18,000, exceed the comparable amounts computed under Formula B. For example, the PBO under Formula B at the end of 20 years is $15,800 (20 × 1% × $79,000). Therefore, at the end of year 20, both the ABO and the PBO are measured using Formula A. However, by the end of year 30, the benefit under Formula B, $23,700, will exceed the benefit under Formula A, still $18,000 because no benefits are earned under Formula A after 20 years. Therefore, additional pension benefits of $570 [($23,700 − $18,000) / 10] are attributed to years 21–30.

The accumulated and projected benefit obligations for years 1–30 are as follows:

Year	ABO	PBO
1–19	—[a]	—[a]
20	$18,000[a]	$18,000[a]
21	18,000[a]	18,570[b]
22	18,000[a]	19,140[b]
23	18,000[a]	19,710[b]
24	18,000[a]	20,280[b]
25	18,000[c]	20,850[b]
26	18,460[c]	21,420[b]
27	19,710[c]	21,990[b]
28	21,000[c]	22,560[b]
29	22,330[c]	23,130[b]
30	23,700[b]	23,700[b]

[a]$900 × years of service, not to exceed 20 years (Formula A)

[b]Formula A benefits earned through year 20 plus attribution of additional projected benefits under Formula B (for years 21–30 of employee service) in proportion to the number of completed years of service compared to the number of years of service that are expected to be completed for the period during which Formula B is applied. Although no additional pension benefits are "earned" in years 21 and 22, because

the PBO in those years is less than $18,000 ($16,590 at end of year 21 and $17,380 at end of year 22), $570 of pension benefits is attributed to each of those years of service based on the total incremental pension benefits for years 21–30 ($5,700/10 years).

(c)Computed as 1% of the end-of-year salary times the number of years worked. For example, in year 29, 1% of $77,000 times 29 years is $22,330; in year 30, 1% of $79,000 times 30 years is $23,700.

Question E48: Can a pension plan have an accumulated benefit obligation that exceeds the projected benefit obligation?

Answer: No. The projected benefit obligation must always equal or exceed the accumulated benefit obligation.

Question E49: How is the projected benefit obligation attributed to a qualified pension plan (for tax purposes) and an excess benefit (top hat) pension plan during an employee's service period if the employee is expected to receive a pension benefit under the excess benefit pension plan (i.e., the employee's pension benefit at retirement is expected to exceed the Section 415 limitations of the U.S. Internal Revenue Code)?

Answer: The projected benefit obligation should be attributed to the qualified pension plan (for tax purposes) until the Section 415 limitations are reached. Thereafter, any incremental pension benefits are attributed to the excess benefit plan. The following example illustrates this computation.

Illustration of Attribution of the Projected Benefit Obligation to a Qualified Pension Plan and an Excess Benefit Pension Plan

The pension plan formula of SBS, Inc., provides for an annual pension benefit of 1.5% of final salary for each year of service. Employee Jones has a beginning salary of $400,000, receives increases of $30,000 per year, and retires at the end of 21 years at a salary of $1,000,000. Section 415 will permit annual pension benefit payments of $200,000 for all the years Jones will receive benefit payments.

Attribution of the accumulated and projected benefit obligations is shown in the following table. Rather than being calculated, the actuarial present value of the accumulated and projected benefit obligations are expressed in terms of the benefit that Jones is expected to receive upon retirement.

29.16 Pension Plans—Employers

		Total		Qualified Pension Plan		Excess Benefit Pension Plan	
Year of Service	Salary	ABO	PBO	ABO	PBO	ABO	PBO
1	$400,000	$6,000	$15,000	$6,000	$15,000		
2	430,000	12,900	30,000	12,900	30,000		
3	460,000	20,700	45,000	20,700	45,000		
4	490,000	29,400	60,000	29,400	60,000		
5	520,000	39,000	75,000	39,000	75,000		
6	550,000	49,500	90,000	49,500	90,000		
7	580,000	60,900	105,000	60,900	105,000		
8	610,000	73,200	120,000	73,200	120,000		
9	640,000	86,400	135,000	86,400	135,000		
10	670,000	100,500	150,000	100,500	150,000		
11	700,000	115,500	165,000	115,500	165,000		
12	730,000	131,400	180,000	131,400	180,000		
13	760,000	148,200	195,000	148,200	195,000		
14	790,000	165,900	210,000	165,900	200,000		$10,000
15	820,000	184,500	225,000	184,500	200,000		25,000
16	850,000	204,000	240,000	200,000	200,000	$4,000	40,000
17	880,000	224,400	255,000	200,000	200,000	24,400	55,000
18	910,000	245,700	270,000	200,000	200,000	45,700	70,000
19	940,000	267,900	285,000	200,000	200,000	67,900	85,000
20	970,000	291,000	300,000	200,000	200,000	91,000	100,000
21	1,000,000	315,000	315,000	200,000	200,000	115,000	115,000

Question E50: If a pension plan's formula provides an annual pension benefit equal to 1% of each year's salary (i.e., the formula does not base pension benefits for the current year on any future salary level), should the projected unit credit method be used to attribute the service cost component of net periodic pension cost over employees' service periods?

Answer: Yes. This pension plan benefit is based on the level of employee pay. As such, it is in essence a career-average-pay pension plan. This Statement requires the use of the projected unit credit method for pay-related pension plans.

Question E51: What is intended by the fourth sentence of paragraph 143 of FAS-87 (not in ASC) which states the following: "The Board perceives a difference between an employer's promise to pay a benefit of 1% of an employee's final pay and a promise to pay an employee a fixed amount that happens to equal 1% of the employee's current pay"? Is the Board referring to a career-average-pay pension plan in the latter part of the sentence?

Answer: No. The intended distinction is between a final-pay pension plan (discussed in the first half of the sentence) and a flat-benefit pension plan (discussed in the latter half of the sentence).

Question E52: What constitutes a substantive commitment requiring recognition of pension benefits beyond those defined in the pension plan's written formula?

Answer: Paragraph 41 (ASC 715-30-35-34) states, "[I]n some situations a history of regular increases in non-pay-related benefits or benefits under a career-average-pay plan and other evidence may indicate that an employer has a present commitment to make future amendments and that the substance of the plan is to provide benefits attributable to prior service that are greater than the benefits defined by the written terms of the plan." In the determination of whether such a "substantive commitment" exists, all the facts and circumstances surrounding the pension plan should be carefully considered. Actions of the employer, including communications to employees, should be considered. A history of regular plan amendments is not enough, by itself, to demonstrate a substantive commitment. However, if the employer has a history of regular plan amendments, prior service cost should be amortized more quickly than might normally be the case (see paragraph 27 (ASC 715-30-35-14)).

Question E53: Should an employer's accounting for its pension plan anticipate a retroactive plan amendment that is not part of a series of retroactive plan amendments necessary to effect a substantive commitment to have a formula greater than its written form?

Answer: No.

Question E54: Is it always necessary for assumed compensation levels to change each time assumed discount rates (and expectations of future inflation rates inherently contained in the assumed discount rates) change?

Answer: No. This Statement requires that assumed discount rates and compensation levels consider the same future economic conditions. However, it does not suggest that these future economic conditions—for example, inflation—will affect discount rates and compensation levels in exactly the same way, or to the same extent.

Question E55: May an employer determine a range of discount rates each year based, for example, on the Pension Benefit Guaranty Corporation's interest rates and high-quality bond rates and continue to use the prior year's assumed discount rates as long as those rates fall within the range?

Answer: No. On a yearly basis the employer should make its best estimate of what discount rate most closely approximates the rate

29.18 Pension Plans—Employers

inherent in the price at which the pension benefit obligation could be effectively settled. For example, this rate might be the interest rate inherent in annuity contracts or the interest rate on high-quality bonds.

Question E56: May an employer determine a range of discount rates as described in the question in paragraph E55 and then arbitrarily select the assumed discount rates from within that range?

Answer: No. The employer should make its best estimate of the discount rate consistent with effectively settling the pension benefit obligation. This process should be performed yearly.

Question E57: If an employer changes its basis of estimating assumed discount rates, for example, by using high-quality bond rates for one year and annuity rates for the following year, is that a change in method of applying an accounting principle?

Answer: No. This type of change would be viewed as a change in estimate. The decision to use a particular methodology in one year (e.g., the interest rate on high-quality bonds versus the interest rate inherent in annuity contracts) does not obligate the entity to continue using that approach in future years. The objective is to use a method that produces a discount rate that most closely approximates the rate inherent in the price at which the pension obligation could be effectively settled. However, if the facts and circumstances have not changed from the prior year, it generally would be inappropriate to change the method of selecting the discount rate. For example, an entity may historically have determined the discount rate by reference to the high-quality bond rate. Absent a change in circumstances that suggests this method does not produce the most appropriate measure of the discount rate at which the pension benefit obligation could be effectively settled, it should be used consistently from one year to the next.

Question E58: If a pension plan has a bond portfolio that was dedicated at a yield significantly higher or lower than current interest rates, may the historical rates of return as of the dedication date be used in discounting the projected and accumulated benefit obligations to their present value?

Answer: No. It would be acceptable to consider current rates of return on high-quality fixed-income investments. The use of historical rates of return is not permitted.

Question E59: May the assumed discount rates used to discount the vested, accumulated, and projected benefit obligations be different?

Answer: Yes, if the circumstances justify different discount rates. For example, different discount rates may be appropriate for active and retired employees because of differences in the maturity and duration of expected pension benefits. However, the discount rate used to value pension benefits maturing in any particular year should not differ, regardless of whether the obligation is presently classified as vested, accumulated, or projected.

Question E60: This question has been deleted.

Question E61: Because a current settlement of the portion of the projected benefit obligation that relates to future compensation levels is unlikely, may an employer use those interest rates implicit in current prices of annuity contracts to determine the accumulated benefit obligation, and use interest rates expected to be implicit in future prices of annuity contracts to determine the pension obligation in excess of the accumulated benefit obligation?

Answer: No. This Statement requires the selection of a discount rate consistent with the rate inherent in the price at which the pension obligation could be effectively settled currently. An employer would not purchase an annuity contract to cover pension benefits based on future compensation levels, and an insurance company would not write such a contract without charging for the additional risk it would be assuming. However, this fact is irrelevant for selecting the appropriate discount rate. When interest rates on annuity contracts are discussed in the Statement, one approach is presented for determining the appropriate discount rate for valuing the pension plan benefit obligation. (Another approach is the interest rate on high-quality fixed-income investments.) The objective is *not* to determine the price an insurance company would charge for assuming the employer's obligation. Rather, the rates implicit in the current prices of annuity contracts might serve as a useful measure of the appropriate discount rate for valuing the pension plan obligation.

Question E62: Should the expected return on future years' contributions to a pension plan be considered in determining the expected long-term rate of return on plan assets?

Answer: No. The expected long-term rate of return on plan assets should be limited to the return expected on existing plan assets and on contributions received during the current year.

Question E63: Should changes under existing law in benefit limitations (such as those currently imposed by Section 415 of the U.S. Internal Revenue Code) that would affect benefits provided by a pension plan be anticipated in measuring the service cost component of net periodic pension cost and the projected benefit obligation?

Answer: Yes. Changes in existing pension law that would affect benefits provided should be considered in measuring service cost and the projected benefit obligation if such changes in laws have already been enacted. Possible changes to law should not be anticipated.

Question E64: If Section 415 of the U.S. Internal Revenue Code is incorporated by reference into a pension plan's formula, thereby limiting certain participants' accumulated benefits, should determination of the pension plan's accumulated benefit obligation reflect the current limitation if (*a*) the pension plan's formula requires automatic increases in accumulated benefits as each change in the limitation under existing law occurs and (*b*) future service is not a prerequisite for participants to receive those increases?

Answer: No. The calculation of the accumulated benefit obligation should reflect those increases in the limitation under existing law that would be consistent with the pension plan's other assumptions. This result presupposes that the employee does not have to render any additional service to be eligible for these benefits. However, if an employee would not automatically receive these benefit increases upon retiring or terminating his or her service, the accumulated benefit obligation should be calculated based on the Section 415 limitation as it currently exists.

Question E65: If an actuarial valuation is made as of a pension plan's year-end and that date precedes the date of the employer's fiscal year-end statement of financial position, is it always necessary to have another actuarial valuation made as of that date?

Answer: No. This Statement requires that the projected benefit obligation reflect the actuarial present value of benefits attributed to employee service rendered before the date of the employer's year-end statement of financial position, with limited exceptions. Actuarial assumptions for turnover, mortality, discount rates, etc., should be appropriate for the date of the employer's fiscal year-end statement of financial position. However, it may be possible to measure the projected benefit obligation at the date of the employer's year-end statement of financial position, with limited exceptions, with a sufficient degree of reliability based on rolling forward the earlier actuarial valuation of the PBO. In such a case, a new actuarial valuation is not required. This situation is analogous to taking a physical inventory before year-end and rolling the inventory balance forward to the financial statement date.

Question E66: How should net periodic pension cost for the year be determined if it is necessary to have an actuarial valuation as of the date of the employer's fiscal year-end (e.g., December 31) in addition to the actuarial valuation as of the pension plan's preceding year-end (e.g., June 30)?

Answer: Measurement of net periodic pension cost should be based on the most recent measurements of plan assets and obligations. If two actuarial measurements are completed during the year, net periodic pension cost should be the sum of two separate six-month periods (in the case above, January 1-June 30 and July 1-December 31). Net periodic pension cost for the first six months (latter six months) would be determined as of the preceding December 31 (the preceding June 30).

Question E67: If an employer that has a December 31 financial report date and measures its plan assets and obligations as of an interim date during its fiscal year (e.g., because of a significant retroactive plan amendment), should net periodic pension cost for the subsequent interim periods be based on those measurements?

Answer: Yes. Net periodic pension cost should be based on the most recent measurement of plan assets and obligations that is available. Paragraph 53 (ASC 715-30-35-68) states, "[M]easurements of net periodic pension cost for both interim and annual financial statements shall be based on the assumptions used for the previous year-end measurements unless more recent measurements of both plan assets and obligations are available...."

Question E68: Under the circumstances described in Question 67, should net periodic pension cost for the preceding interim periods be adjusted?

Answer: No.

Question E69: If an employer uses a measurement date of December 31 but does not complete the actual measurements until some time later in the year—for example, in January—should the determination of the pension obligations be based on the assumed discount rates and other actuarial assumptions as of January?

Answer: No. The employer should use the actuarial assumptions that were appropriate as of the measurement date of December 31.

Questions E70–E72: These questions have been deleted.

Question E73: This question has been moved to paragraph E88A.

Questions E74–E78: These questions have been deleted.

Question E79: Should the assumptions disclosed be as of the beginning or ending measurement date?

Answer: They should be as of the year-end measurement date.

Question E80: If an employer combines several of its pension plans and the assets of each predecessor pension plan are available to satisfy the previously existing obligations of the other, how should the combined pension plan be accounted for?

Answer: Except for prior service costs included in accumulated other comprehensive income, the fair value of pension plan assets and the actuarial present value of pension plan obligations (vested, accumulated, and projected) should be combined and reported as a single amount. Net gain or loss included in accumulated other comprehensive income, transition assets and liabilities included in accumulated other comprehensive income, and unrecognized prior service cost included in accumulated other comprehensive income are treated as follows:

Item	Combination Treatment	Amortization Treatment
Aggregate net gain/loss included in accumulated other comprehensive income	Aggregate amounts from previously separate pension plans	Amortize using the average remaining service period of the combined employee group
Transition asset/liability of separate pension plans remaining in accumulated other comprehensive income	Aggregate amounts from previously remaining amortization	Amortize using a weighted average of periods previously used by the separate pension plans
Prior service cost included in accumulated other comprehensive income of each pension plan	Not aggregated	Amortize separately, as previously determined, based on specific employee groups covered

Illustration of Combining Two Plans

TELWIN, Inc., has two separate pension plans, Plan A and Plan B, that it plans to combine into one plan on December 31, 20X4. TELWIN adopted the provisions of FAS-87 for the year ended December 31, 20Y0. Relevant details about each separate pension plan and about how the combination would be effected follow.

Prior to Combination of Plan A and Plan B

	Plan A	Plan B
Assumptions:		
Weighted-average discount rate	11%	10.5%
Expected long-term rate of return on plan assets	12%	12%

	Plan A	Plan B
Average remaining service period	20 years	13 years
Average remaining service period at date of initial application of FAS-87	20 years	13 years
Number of employees as of December 31, 20X4, expected to receive benefits under the pension plan	400	550
Amortization Method:		
Prior service cost	Straight-line amortization over average remaining service period of employees expected to receive benefits (20 years)	Straight-line amortization over average remaining service period of employees expected to receive benefits (13 years)
Projected benefit obligation	$(1,004)	$(1,280)
Plan assets at fair value	1,608	410
Funded status and recognized asset/liability	$ 604	$ (870)
Amounts recognized in accumulated other comprehensive income:		
Net (gain) loss	(228)	82
Prior service cost (credit)	240	642
Prepaid pension cost	$ 12	$ 724

After Combination of Plan A and Plan B

	Combined Plan AB
Assumptions:	
Weighted-average discount rate	10.6%[a]
Expected long-term rate of return on plan assets	12%[b]
Average remaining service period	15.95 years[c]
Number of employees as of December 31, 20X4, expected to receive benefits under the pension plan	950
Amortization method:	
Prior service cost	The existing prior service costs of Plan A and Plan B continue to be amortized separately. The amortization bases used prior to the combination continue to apply.

29.24 *Pension Plans—Employers*

	Combined Plan AB
Net gain or loss	Minimum amortization specified in paragraph 32 (ASC 715-30-35-24) (average remaining service period is 15.95 years[d])

[a] The weighted-average assumed discount rate reflects the rate at which the pension obligation could be effectively settled. (This illustration assumes that 10.6% is the appropriate discount rate. The discount rate is calculated without reference to either of the discount rates on the previously separate plans.)

[b] There is no change in the expected long-term rate of return on plan assets, because both Plan A and Plan B assume the same rate of return.

[c] The average remaining service period of employees who are expected to receive benefits under the pension plan is weighted by the number of covered employees from each group. This calculation is performed as follows: (20 years × 400/950) + (13 years × 550/950) = 15.95 years. The remaining service period should be the same when a new calculation is made for the combined group.

[d] The amortization period for the remaining unrecognized net obligation existing at the date of initial application of FAS-87 is determined by weighting (1) the average *remaining* amortization period for each plan and (2) the *absolute value* of the remaining unrecognized net asset or net obligation existing at the date FAS-87 was adopted. In this example, the calculation is as follows: [(20 years − 5 years) × 40/540] + [(15 years − 5 years) × 500/540] = 10.4 years (rounded).

	Combined Plan AB
Projected benefit obligation	$(2,284)
Plan assets at fair value	$ 2,018
Funded status and recognized asset/ liability	$ (266)
Amounts recognized in accumulated other comprehensive income:	
Net (gain) loss	(146)
Prior service cost (credit)	882
Prepaid pension cost	$ 736

Question E81: If an employer divides a pension plan into two or more separate pension plans after the date of initial application of this Statement, how should (*a*) the transition asset or obligation remaining in accumulated other comprehensive income, (*b*) net gain or loss, if any, included in accumulated other comprehensive income, and (*c*) prior service included in accumulated other comprehensive income cost, if any, allocated to each of the separate plans based on the applicable individuals included in the employee groups covered?

Answer: An employer should allocate the transition asset or obligation remaining in accumulated other comprehensive income and the net gain or loss included in accumulated other comprehensive income the respective pension plans in proportion to the projected benefit obligation of the surviving plans. Prior service costs included in accumulated other comprehensive income should be allocated to the surviving pension plans based on the applicable individuals in the employee groups covered.

Question E82: Are annuity contracts defined differently in this Statement and ASC 715-30 (FAS-88)? If so, how are the definitions different, and why?

Answer: Yes. Settlement accounting under the guidance in ASC 715-30 (FAS-88) does not apply if annuity contracts are purchased from an enterprise that is controlled by the employer. Therefore, if an employer purchases annuity contracts from an enterprise that is controlled by the employer, no settlement gain or loss is recognized on the transaction. Under this statement, pension benefits covered by annuity contracts purchased from a non-captive insurer are to be excluded from the projected benefit obligation and from plan assets. The net effect of the above is that no settlement gain or loss is recognized if annuity contracts are purchased from an entity controlled by the employer; however, unless these annuity contracts are purchased from a captive insurer, the pension benefits covered by the contracts are excluded from the PBO and from plan assets. Disclosure is required of the appropriate amount of annual benefits covered by annuity contracts issued by an employer and related entities.

Question E83: Is a guaranteed investment contract (GIC) an annuity contract?

Answer: No. All a GIC does is transfer investment risk to the insurer. In an annuity contract, the insurer assumes an unconditional legal obligation to provide specified pension benefits to specific individuals.

Question E84: If a GIC is not considered an annuity contract, how should an employer value the contract if it has a specified maturity date and there is no intent to liquidate the contract before that date?

Answer: The GIC should still be valued at its fair value on a yearly basis even if the employer has no intent to liquidate the contract before its maturity date. The employer may estimate the fair value of the GIC by looking to current interest rates on similar debt securities of comparable risk and duration.

Question E85: Should the market value adjustment in an immediate participation GIC be considered in determining its fair value?

Answer: Yes. The contract value adjusted for any such market value adjustment represents the contract's cash surrender value. In some cases an immediate participation GIC can be converted into an annuity contract. In these cases the conversion value of the contract is relevant in estimating the contract's fair value.

Question E86: A not-for-profit organization has a defined benefit pension plan that covers employees at the national level and in all local chapters. If (a) each chapter is required to contribute to the pension plan based on a predetermined formula (e.g., on a percentage-of-salary basis), (b) plan assets are not segregated or restricted on a chapter-by-chapter basis, and (c) the pension obligations for a chapter's employees are retained by the pension plan if a chapter withdraws from the pension plan, as opposed to being allocated to the withdrawing chapter, should that arrangement be accounted for as a single-employer pension plan or as a multiemployer pension plan?

Answer: The not-for-profit organization should account for the pension plan as a single-employer plan in its consolidated financial statements. However, each of the separate chapters should account for the plan as a multiemployer plan in its individual financial statements. Each chapter should recognize its required yearly contribution, whether fully funded or not, as net periodic pension cost. If the yearly contribution is not fully funded, the local chapter would need to record a liability. Each local chapter must make the disclosures required in paragraph 69 of this Statement and the required related-party disclosures of ASC 850-10 (FAS-57, Related Party Disclosures) (if applicable).

Question E87: Does the answer to the previous question also apply to a similar parent subsidiary arrangement if each subsidiary issues separate financial statements?

Answer: Yes. The parent would account for the pension plan as a single-employer plan in the consolidated financial statements. Each subsidiary would account for the plan as a multiemployer plan in its individual financial statements.

Question E88: Should the pension asset or pension liability recognized by the acquiring employer be separately amortized to income in periods subsequent to the acquisition?

Answer: No. Any such pension asset or liability should not be separately amortized. However, a pension asset or liability recognized by the acquiring employer will be affected by the accounting for the pension plan in future periods.

Question E88a: If an employer has (a) a qualified pension plan (for tax purposes) and (b) a nonqualified pension plan (which pays pension benefits in excess of the maximum allowed for the qualified pension plan by Section 415 of the U.S. Internal Revenue Code—an excess benefit [top-hat] pension plan) and the plans cover the same employees, may those pension plans be considered in substance a single pension plan under this Statement?

Answer: No. In most cases a qualified pension plan (for tax purposes) is legally prohibited from using its assets to pay benefits of an excess benefit pension plan. Therefore, in the situation described above, each plan would be accounted for separately. The fact that the employer could (*a*) contribute less to the qualified plan and use any savings to pay benefits under the excess benefit plan or (*b*) terminate the qualified plan and use the assets that revert to it to pay benefits under the excess plan does not, in itself, indicate that the two pension plans should be combined.

Questions E89–E106: These questions have been deleted.

Question E107: If a pension plan curtailment occurs that causes almost all of the pension plan's participants to become inactive, should the employer continue to amortize any transition asset or obligation remaining in accumulated other comprehensive income using the same amortization period determined at that date of initial application of this Statement?

Answer: An employer should continue amortizing a transition asset or obligation, if any, that remains in accumulated other comprehensive income, which is the amount that remains after the employer accounts for the curtailment as required under the guidance in paragraphs 12 and 13 of FAS-88 (ASC 715-30-35-92, 93), based on the same amortization period that was determined on the date that this Statement was initially applied.

EITF Issue 88-1 (Determination of Vested Benefit Obligation for a Defined Benefit Pension Plan) (ASC 715-20-S50-1; S99-2; 30-35-40 through 35-41)

OVERVIEW

A projected benefit obligation (PBO) is defined in paragraph 264 of FAS-87 (ASC, *Glossary*) as "the actuarial present value as of a date of all benefits attributed by the pension benefit formula to employee service rendered prior to that date." The only difference between a PBO and an accumulated benefit obligation (ABO) is that the PBO considers assumptions about future compensation levels. The PBO and the ABO are both affected by the vested benefit obligation (VBO), which is the actuarial present value of benefits for which an employee is entitled to receive a pension currently or in the future without the requirement for continued employment.

Under some defined benefit pension plans, such as foreign plans, most or all of the benefits to which an employee is entitled upon termination is based on service to date. If the employee is terminated, the vested benefit would be payable to the employee immediately or indexed for inflation, if it were payable at a future date. For example, the Italian severance pay statute usually requires that the accrued benefit paid to an employee on separation be based on service to date. The undiscounted value of the amount paid immediately would be greater than the actuarial present value of the benefits the employee has a right to receive based on service to date. Similarly, legislation in the United Kingdom requires that deferred vested benefits of terminated employees be revalued from the separation date to the normal retirement age. In that situation, the VBO based on termination at the measurement date could be greater than the ABO if the calculation of the ABO considers the statutory revaluation only after the employee's expected termination date.

The difficulty in applying ASC 715 (FAS-87) to such plans is in determining whether the VBO should be calculated based on the presumption that the employee is terminated immediately (Approach 1) or the employee continues to provide service to the termination or retirement date with the maximum amount discounted to its present value (Approach 2). If the VBO exceeds the PBO, the ABO, or both in Approach 1, these amounts would have to be adjusted.

ACCOUNTING ISSUE

Should the VBO be the actuarial present value of the vested benefits to which an employee is entitled, based on service to date as if the employee were separated immediately (Approach 1), or to which an employee is currently entitled, based on the employee's expected separation or retirement date (Approach 2)?

EITF CONSENSUS

The EITF reached a consensus that the VBO may be based on either approach for situations that are not specifically considered in ASC 715 (FAS-87), in which the facts and circumstances are analogous to those discussed above.

A FASB staff representative reported that when responding to technical inquiries, the FASB staff recommended that the VBO be determined using Approach 1, because the staff believed that the VBO is not contingent on future service under that approach. Several Task Force members believed that Approach 2 is more consistent with the intent of ASC 715 (FAS-87), because the Statement measures pension obligations based on actuarial expectations.

SEC STAFF COMMENT

The SEC Observer noted that registrants should disclose the method used.

DISCUSSION

The following is the rationale for the two approaches.

Approach 1 Vested benefits are defined in paragraph 264 of FAS-87 (ASC, *Glossary*) as "benefits for which the employee's right to receive a *present* or future pension benefit is no longer contingent on remaining in the service of the employer." (Emphasis added.) Those who supported this approach argued that the *present* benefit that the employee is entitled to should be measured at the *present* time. They believed that the value of the vested benefit is the actuarial value at the present, which should not be discounted. Supporters also believed that the employer's liability for the VBO should be based on the concept that it is a measure of the employer's obligation if the plan were discontinued. Proponents believed that if the vested benefit is an obligation, it should not be discounted to a lesser amount than the employer's current obligation. Rather, it should be measured based on service to date using the plan's benefit formula. They argued further that discounting the obligation assumes that the employee will perform future services for the employer. That conflicts with the definition of vested benefits, which do not depend on future services. Others argued for measuring the obligation at its current value, because some plans permit employees to take advances against their vested benefits while still employed.

Approach 2 Proponents of this approach noted that the PBO, ABO, and VBO are defined in FAS-87 in terms of actuarial present value, which is based on estimates of death, disability, withdrawal, or retirement in determining the probability and timing of payment. That amount is discounted from the expected payment date to the present. Others argued that even if the VBO under Approach 1 were greater than the PBO or the ABO or both, those amounts need not be adjusted, because they believed that the VBO does not represent a minimum value for the ABO and the PBO.

The EITF's background papers discussed the application of the two approaches to the Italian Termination Indemnity Plan and the U.K. Plan as follows:

Italian Termination Indemnity Plan Under the Italian plan, an employee's benefit generally is paid on termination. The amount equals a total of the following: (*a*) the prior year's balance, (*b*) the prior year's balance times 75% of the increase in the consumer price index, plus 1.5%, and (*c*) one month service accrual for the current year.

Under Approach 1, the VBO must equal the balance payable to the employee on immediate separation. The VBO will usually be greater than the PBO, which discounts the benefits of expected payment. If so, the PBO is adjusted so the two amounts are equal. As a result, net periodic pension cost equals the change in the balance of the VBO and PBO from the beginning to the end of the year, adjusted for payments to employees actually terminated during the year. This method is the same as the method by which pension costs were measured before the issuance of ASC 715 (FAS-87). If the PBO is greater than the VBO, net periodic pension cost is based on the PBO and the usual application of ASC 715 (FAS-87).

Under Approach 2, the VBO is calculated by projecting out to the date when benefits to which the employee is currently entitled would be paid and discounting that amount to the present. The VBO would thus be the same as the usual calculation of the PBO. ASC 715 (FAS-87) would be applied as for U.S. plans.

U.K. Plan Under government regulations in the U.K., an employee who reaches a certain age is entitled to a guaranteed minimum pension of a specified amount based on salary and service to date. Legislation enacted near the time this Issue was discussed required that benefits for an employee's services after the date of the legislation be revalued from the date of separation to the normal retirement date based on changes in price indices. Some plans were amended to provide such increases for all of an employee's service. Consequently, the VBO often would be greater than the ABO when vested benefits are revalued. Because the PBO includes salary escalation, it would still be greater than the VBO.

Under Approach 1, the ABO would have to be adjusted to equal the VBO, because the ABO should not be less than the benefit to which an employee is currently entitled.

Under Approach 2, the VBO would be measured based on the discounted value of the benefit receivable at the date of expected separation. It would not exceed the ABO and would not require adjustment.

Although periodic pension cost is unlikely to be affected by the different ABO amounts under the two approaches, the minimum liability as calculated under FAS-87 could be affected.

EITF Issue 90-3 (Accounting for Employers' Obligations for Future Contributions to a Multiemployer Pension Plan) (ASC 715-80-55-2)

OVERVIEW

A multi employer pension plan is a pension plan established by two or more unrelated entities to provide pension benefits to employees of those participating employers. To qualify as a multiemployer plan, assets contributed by employers are not segregated into separate accounts and may be used by the multiemployer plan to provide pension benefits to any employer's employees. All employers share in the plan's gains and losses.

When an employer enters a plan initially or elects to improve employees' pension benefits, the employer must sign a written agreement and make an unconditional promise to make certain future contributions to the plan. The contributions will be used to liquidate the past service cost associated with initiating the plan or increasing benefits. In return, the plan agrees unconditionally to pay pension benefits to the employer's employees covered under the plan.

ACCOUNTING ISSUE

Should an employer recognize a liability to a multiemployer plan for the total amount of future payments related to prior service cost, as required under an agreement executed when an employer begins participating in a multiemployer plan or increases benefits to employees under the plan?

EITF CONSENSUS

The EITF reached a consensus that an employer that agrees to make future contributions to a multiemployer plan to liquidate prior service cost associated with initiating a defined benefit pension plan or increasing its benefits is not required to recognize a liability for more than unpaid contributions that are due. The consensus was based on the guidance in paragraph 68 of FAS-87 (not in ASC).

DISCUSSION

In discussing the accounting for single-employer defined benefit pension plans, ASC 715-30-35-10 (paragraph 24 of FAS-87) provides guidance on how to account for prior service cost related to initiation of a plan and plan amendments that provide for increased benefits based on prior service. It states that related costs should be recognized over the future service periods of active employees when a plan is amended who are expected to benefit under the plan.

This Issue was brought to the EITF because of diversity in views on the timing of recognition of prior service costs under an agreement in a multiemployer defined benefit plan. Such agreements provide that an employer has an "unconditional obligation" to make future installment payments for past service costs, and the plan has an unconditional obligation to make future benefit payments to participants. The problem was that although ASC 715-30-35-10 (paragraph 24 of FAS-87) provides for delayed recognition of prior service costs, the discussion of multiemployer plans in ASC 715-80-05-1 (paragraphs 67 to 70 of FAS-87), does not specifically address the recognition of such costs. Some believed that an employer participating in a multiemployer plan should recognize a liability for the total obligation under the employer's agreement with the multiemployer plan. Proponents of recognition argued that the delayed recognition concept in ASC 715 (FAS-87) does not apply to multiemployer plans, because of the bilateral agreement between the parties.

Opponents of immediate recognition of the total liability for prior service costs at the date of the agreement argued that a multiemployer plan does not differ from other defined benefit pension plans and that the agreement provides for a bilateral unconditional obligation to comply with federal pension laws. In addition, they argued that ASC 715 (FAS-87) did not intend to change previous practice for multiemployer pension plans under which a prior service liability was not accrued.

Paragraph 68 of FAS-87 (not included in ASC) states that "an employer participating in a multiemployer plan shall recognize as net pension cost the required contribution for the period and shall recognize as a liability any contributions due and unpaid." The EITF's interpretation of the paragraph in its consensus implies that the Task Force believes that the delayed recognition of prior service cost also applies to multiemployer plans.

EITF Issue 03-2   Accounting for the Transfer to the Japanese Government of the Substitutional Portion of Employee Pension Fund Liabilities (ASC 715-20-50-10; 30-55-70 through 55-78, 55-171)

OVERVIEW

Many large Japanese corporations have Employee Pension Fund (EPF) plans that are defined benefit pension plans established under the Japanese Welfare Pension Insurance Law (JWPIL). Those plans consist of the following:

- A substitutional portion based on the part of the old-age pension benefits set by JWPIL based on pay (similar to social security benefits).

- A corporate portion based on a contributory defined benefit pension arrangement established by employers with benefits based on a formula determined by each employer and its EPF.

Corporations that have an EPF—and their employees—need not contribute to Japanese Pension Insurance (JPI), which would be required if the substitutional portion of the benefit were not funded through the EPF. As a result, the corporate and substitutional benefits are paid to retired beneficiaries out of the EPF's assets. All of an EPF's assets are invested and managed as a single portfolio and are not separately segregated to the substitutional and corporate portions. The percentage of the substitutional portion relative to the total EPF is not predetermined and varies by employer.

In June 2001, the JWPIL was amended to allow employers and their EPFs to separate the substitutional portions of their pension plans and transfer the obligations and related assets to the government. The separation process will be completed in four phases. After completion of that process, employers and their EPFs will be released from making further payments of the substitutional portion to beneficiaries. In addition, employers and their employees will be required to contribute periodically to the JPI; the Japanese government will be responsible for making all benefit payments earned under JWPIL. The remaining part of the EPF will be a corporate defined benefit plan (CDBP), which employers will be able to transfer to a defined contribution plan.

ACCOUNTING ISSUE

How should Japanese companies that report on U.S. securities exchanges and consequently account for EPFs as single-employer defined benefit plans using a single-plan approach account for (a) the separation of the substitutional portion of the benefit obligation of an EPF from the corporate portion and (b) the transfer of the substitutional portion and related assets to the Japanese government?

EITF CONSENSUS

The EITF reached a consensus that when a transfer to the Japanese government of the substitutional portion of the pension benefit obligation and the related assets (phase 4) has been completed, employers should account for that process as the conclusion of a single settlement transaction consisting of a series of steps. This consensus applies only to this specific situation.

The consensus should be applied as follows:

- A transaction should be accounted for as a settlement when it is complete, that is, when the total substitutional portion of the benefit obligation has been eliminated because a sufficient

29.34 *Pension Plans—Employers*

amount of assets to complete the separation process have been transferred to the Japanese government.

- In accordance with the guidance in ASC 715-30 (FAS-88, Employers' Accounting for Settlements and Curtailments of Defined Benefit Pension Plans and for Termination Benefits), immediately before the separation, the total projected benefit obligation should be remeasured at fair value, including the effects of changes in actuarial assumptions (such as expected future salary increases), if any, and actual experience since the previous measurement date. This remeasurement should include only benefits earned under the substitutional arrangement *before* the government accepts responsibility for all substitutional payments.

- A settlement of the substitutional portion of the obligation should be accounted for as follows:

    —Recognize as a gain or loss on settlement a proportionate amount of the ASC 715 (FAS-87) net gain or loss included in accumulated other comprehensive income related to the total EPF as a gain or loss on settlement.

    —Determine the proportionate amount of the net gain or loss that should be recognized based on the proportion of the projected benefit obligation settled to the total projected benefit obligation, but exclude previously accrued salary progression from that calculation.

    —After separation, continue accounting for the EPF's remaining assets and obligation as well as for both prior-service costs included in accumulated other comprehensive income and gains and losses, if any, in accordance with the guidance in ASC 715 (FAS-87) and ASC 715-20 (FAS-158).

    —Account for and disclose the difference between the settled obligation and the assets transferred to the government, which were determined based on the government's formula, as a subsidy from the government separately in accordance with generally accepted accounting principles.

    —In accordance with this consensus, account for and disclose the derecognition of previously accrued salary progression at the time of settlement *separately* from the government's subsidy.

    OBSERVATION: Under the guidance in ASC 715-30 (FAS-158, Employers' Accounting for Defined Benefit Pension and Other Postretirement Plans—An Amendment of FASB Statements No. 87, 88, 106, and 132(R)), employers are required to recognize in the financial statements the full amount of obligations related to single-employer defined benefit pension plans, retiree health care, and other postretirement plans.

Minimum pension liability adjustments are eliminated under the Statement. Gains or losses, prior service costs or credits, and transition assets and obligations must be recognized in accumulated other comprehensive income if they have not yet been recognized as components of net periodic benefit cost.

FASB RATIFICATION

The FASB ratified the EITF's consensus in this Issue at its February 5, 2003, meeting.

EITF Issue 03-4 (Accounting for "Cash Balance" Pension Plans) (ASC 715-30-15-3; 35-71, 35-72)

OVERVIEW

A survey conducted in 2002 indicated that 32 of the Fortune 100 companies have changed their traditional defined benefit plans to cash balance plans. The IRS defines a cash balance plan as follows:

> A defined benefit plan that defines benefits for each employee by reference to the employee's hypothetical account. An employee's hypothetical account is determined by reference to hypothetical allocations of contributions and earnings to an employee's account under a defined contribution plan.

The benefits in most cash balance plans are reported to employees as accumulated cash balances. Although most plans offer members the option to receive a lump-sum distribution of the account balance in settlement of the full obligation, to maintain a plan's tax-qualified status, such plans are required to offer members the option to receive their benefits in the form of a life annuity. The IRS requires that cash balance plans are funded similar to defined benefit plans, but employers report the benefits to employees as principal credits and interest credits as in 401(k) plans and other defined contribution plans. Nevertheless, cash balance plans have some features of defined benefit plans, such as the option of a life annuity, interest credits not based on plan assets' performance, joint and survivor options, and grandfathered or transitional defined benefit formulas. The existence of prior-service costs, deferred gains or losses, and an inability to divide the assets into defined contribution and defined benefit components makes it impractical to account for cash balance plans as defined contribution plans. Further, most employers classify cash balance plans as defined benefit plans, because (*a*) under the IRS definition of a defined contribution plan, employers are required to report individual funded account balances, and (*b*) according to ASC 715 (FAS-87), a plan is a defined benefit plan if it is *not* a defined contribution plan.

ACCOUNTING ISSUE

- Should a cash balance pension plan be considered a defined benefit plan or a defined contribution plan when applying the provisions of ASC 715 (FAS-87)?
- What is the appropriate pattern of accruals for defined benefit plans that are cash balance pension plans?

EITF CONSENSUS

The EITF reached the following consensus positions:

1. For the purpose of applying ASC 715 (FAS-87, Employers' Accounting for Pensions), cash balance pension plans, which provide a pension benefit in the form of an account balance based on principal credits and interest credits over time, are considered to be *defined benefit pension plans*. The EITF reached this consensus based on the following characteristics of cash balance plans:

    a. The amount of the pension benefit to be received is defined as a function of principal credits based on salary and future interest credits at a stated rate.

    b. Over time, an employer must fund amounts that can accumulate to the actuarial present value of the benefit due at the time of distribution to each participant based on the plan's terms.

    c. Individual account balances are determined based on a hypothetical account rather than on specific assets, and the benefit depends on an employer's promised interest that will be credited, not based on an actual return on a plan's assets. Under the guidance in ASC 715 (FAS-87), any plan that is not a defined contribution plan is considered to be a defined benefit plan.

    d. An employer's contributions to a cash balance plan trust and the earnings on the invested assets are *not* related to the principal and interest credited to the hypothetical accounts.

2. Because the benefit promise in a cash balance arrangement is not pay related, using the projected unit credit method is *not* appropriate and therefore *not* required in measuring the benefit obligation and annual cost of benefits under FAS 715 (FAS-87). Cost attribution should be based on the traditional unit credit method.

The EITF noted that consensus positions reached in this Issue apply specifically to the plan discussed here. To determine whether *cash balance* plans with other characteristics or other types of defined benefit plans are pay related and the benefit attribution approach that should be used, the specific features of those benefit arrangements should be evaluated.

FASB RATIFICATION

The FASB ratified the consensus positions at its May 28, 2003, meeting.

Topic D-27 (Accounting for the Transfer of Excess Pension Assets to a Retiree Health Care Benefits Account) (ASC 715-30-35-73)

Under the Revenue Reconciliation Act of 1990 (the Act), an employer can transfer excess pension assets of a defined benefit pension plan (other than a multiemployer plan) to a health care benefits account that is part of the pension plan without including that amount in gross taxable income and without incurring penalties. The Act provides that such transfers be made beginning after December 31, 1990, and before the employer's 1996 tax year, and that amounts transferred not exceed the amount reasonably expected to be paid for "qualified current retiree health liabilities." Transfers are limited to one per year.

The FASB staff announced that such transfers should be recognized as a negative contribution or withdrawal from the pension plan and a positive contribution to the retiree health care plan. The transfer does not result in a gain or loss.

Topic D-36 (Selection of Discount Rates Used for Measuring Defined Benefit Pension Obligations and Obligations of Postretirement Plans Other Than Pensions) (ASC 715-20-S55-1; S99-1)

The SEC Observer announced that registrants should use the guidance in paragraph 186 of FAS-106 (Employers' Accounting for Postretirement Benefits Other Than Pensions) (not included in ASC) to select the discount rate for measuring the pension benefit obligation in a defined benefit pension plan. That paragraph states in part that "the objective of selecting assumed discount rates to measure the single amount that, if invested at the measurement date in a portfolio of high-quality debt instruments, would provide the necessary future cash flows to pay the accumulated benefits when due."

When the SEC Observer made this announcement in September 1993, interest rates had declined to the lowest level in more than a decade. The SEC Observer stated that the staff expects that discount rates used by registrants at each measurement date to measure obligations for pension benefits and postretirement benefits other than pensions would reflect the current level of interest rates. He stated that the SEC staff suggests that high-quality, fixed-income debt securities are those that receive one of the two highest ratings from a recognized ratings agency, such as a rating of Aa or higher from Moody's Investors Service, Inc.

RELATED CHAPTERS IN 2011
GAAP GUIDE, VOLUME II

Chapter 30, "Pension Plans—Settlements and Curtailments"
Chapter 32, "Postemployment and Postretirement Benefits Other Than Pensions"

RELATED CHAPTERS IN 2011
GAAP GUIDE, VOLUME I

Chapter 33, "Pension Plans"
Chapter 34, "Postemployment and Postretirement Benefits Other Than Pensions"

RELATED CHAPTERS IN 2011
INTERNATIONAL ACCOUNTING/FINANCIAL
REPORTING STANDARDS GUIDE

Chapter 7, "Business Combinations"
Chapter 13, "Employee Benefits"
Chapter 16, "Financial Instruments"
Chapter 22, "Interim Financial Reporting"

CHAPTER 30
PENSION PLANS—SETTLEMENTS AND CURTAILMENTS

CONTENTS

Overview		30.02
Authoritative Guidance		
ASC 715 Compensation—Retirement Benefits		30.03
FSP FAS-146-1	Evaluating Whether a One-Time Termination Benefit Offered in Connection with an Exit or Disposal Activity Is Essentially an Enhancement to an Ongoing Benefit Arrangement	30.03
FIG FAS-88	Guide to Implementation of Statement 88 on Employers' Accounting for Settlements and Curtailments of Defined Benefit Pension Plans and for Termination Benefits	30.04
EITF Issue 91-7	Accounting for Pension Benefits Paid by Employers after Insurance Companies Fail to Provide Annuity Benefits	30.31
EITF Issue 05-5	Accounting for Early Retirement or Postemployment Programs with Specific Features (Such as Terms Specified in Altersteilzeit Early Retirement Arrangements)	30.32
Related Chapters in 2011 GAAP Guide, Volume II		30.34
Related Chapters in 2011 GAAP Guide, Volume I		30.34
Related Chapters in 2011 Reporting International Accounting/ Financial Reporting Standards Guide		30.34

OVERVIEW

A *settlement of a pension plan* is an irrevocable action that relieves the employer (or the plan) of primary responsibility for an obligation and eliminates significant risks related to the obligation and the assets used to effect the settlement. Examples of transactions that constitute a settlement include (*a*) making lump-sum cash payments to plan participants in exchange for their rights to receive specified pension benefits and (*b*) purchasing nonparticipating annuity contracts to cover vested benefits.

A *curtailment* is a significant reduction in, or an elimination of, defined benefit accruals for present employees' future services. Examples of curtailments are (*a*) termination of employees' services earlier than expected, which may or may not involve closing a facility or discontinuing a segment of a business, and (*b*) termination or suspension of a plan so that employees do not earn additional defined benefits for future services.

The following pronouncements, which are the sources of GAAP for pension plans—settlements and curtailments–are discussed: in the 2011 *GAAP Guide Volume I*, Chapter 33, "Pension Plans":

ASC 715	Employers' Accounting for Settlements and Curtailments of Defined Benefit Pension Plans and for Termination Benefits (FAS-88)
ASC 715	Employers' Disclosures about Pensions and Other Postretirement Benefits—An Amendment of FASB Statements No. 87, 88, and 106 (FAS-132(R))
ASC 715; ASC 958	Employers' Accounting for Defined Benefit Pension and Other Postretirement Plans—An Amendment of FASB Statements No. 87, 88, 106, and 132(R) (FAS-158)

AUTHORITATIVE GUIDANCE

ASC 715 Compensation—Retirement Benefits

FSP FAS-146-1 (Evaluating Whether a One-Time Termination Benefit Offered in Connection with an Exit or Disposal Activity Is Essentially an Enhancement to an Ongoing Benefit Arrangement) (ASC 715-30-60-4; 420-10-55-1, 55-16, 55-19)

Question: Under what circumstances are additional termination benefits offered in connection with an exit or disposal activity considered, in substance (*a*) enhancements to an ongoing benefit arrangement and, therefore, subject to the provisions of ASC 715 (FAS-87, Employers' Accounting for Pensions), ASC 715 (FAS-88, Employers' Accounting for Settlements and Curtailments of Defined Benefit Pension Plans and for Termination Benefits), ASC 715 (FAS-106, Employers' Accounting for Postretirement Benefits Other Than Pensions), and ASC 712 (FAS-112, Employers' Accounting for Postemployment Benefits), or (*b*) one-time termination benefits subject to the guidance in ASC 420 (FAS-146, Accounting for Costs Associated with Exit or Disposal Activities)?

Answer: Certain companies offer postretirement (e.g., pension and health care) and other postemployment benefits to employees under the terms of an ongoing employee benefit plan. Those types of benefit plans are accounted for under the terms discussed in ASC 715 (FAS-87, FAS-88, and FAS-106), and ASC 712 (FAS-112). The issue is whether a one-time termination benefit should be accounted for under the terms discussed in ASC 715 (FAS-87, FAS-88, and FAS-106), or ASC 712 (FAS-112) or under the terms of ASC 420 (FAS-146). The guidance in ASC 715 (FASB Statements No. 87, 88, 106), or ASC 712 (FAS-112), applies if an additional termination benefit amends the terms of an existing pension, other postretirement, or postemployment benefit arrangement. For example, if a company has an employee benefit plan providing that employees who are terminated for reasons other than cause will receive one week of salary for every year of service, the provisions of ASC 712 (FAS-112) would apply if, as part of an exit or disposal activity, that plan is revised to provide that each involuntarily terminated employee will receive *two* weeks of salary for every year of service, and the revised terms of the employee benefit plan would apply to future exit or disposal activities. If, however, the terms of the ongoing employee benefit arrangement are *not* revised, and an additional termination benefit only applies to an exit or disposal activity that occurs in the current year, the provisions of ASC 420 (FAS-146) would apply.

The guidance in this FSP is effective for exit or disposal activities initiated in interim or annual reporting periods beginning after

September 15, 2003. However, an entity may elect to report the change in accounting as a cumulative-effect adjustment in accordance with APB-20 (Accounting Changes) for exit activities initiated after December 31, 2002, which is the original effective date of FAS-146.

FIG FAS-88 Guide to Implementation of Statement 88 on Employers' Accounting for Settlements and Curtailments of Defined Benefit Pension Plans and for Termination Benefits (ASC 715-20-45-4; 30-15-7; 25-9, 25-11; 25-35-22, 25-75, 25-81, 25-82, 25-84, 25-95; 55-52, 55-92, 55-130 through 55-137, 55-140, 55-142 through 55-168, 55-170 through 55-184, 55-186 through 55-197, 55-201, 55-208, 55-217 through 55-219, 55-221, 55-226 though 55-230, 55-237 through 55-238, 55-241 through 55-246, 55-248 through 55-249, 55-251 through 55-252; 60-5, 60-8; 740-10-55-75; 845-10-55-1, 55-3 through 55-9; 205-20-60-5; 712-2-10-05-2; 25-1)

OVERVIEW

The following FASB Implementation Guide (FIG) is based on the guidance in FSP FAS-158-1, which superseded the guidance in the Implementation Guide for FAS-88 (A Guide to Implementation of Statement 88 on Employers' Accounting for Settlements and Curtailments of Defined Benefit Pension Plans and for Termination Benefits) that consisted of questions and answers developed by the FASB staff in response to inquiries from constituents. However, the guidance below, which was included in the Implementation Guide, was carried over into ASC 715 (FAS-88) as Appendix C.

FAS-88—APPENDIX C

STANDARDS

Question C1: Should an employer recognize a settlement gain or loss in the period in which all of the following occur: (*a*) the employer decides to terminate a defined benefit pension plan and establish a successor pension plan, (*b*) a nonparticipating annuity contract for the vested benefits of all plan participants is purchased but can be rescinded if certain regulatory approvals for the termination of the pension plan are not obtained, and (*c*) it is determined that the regulatory approvals are probable?

Answer: No. ASC 715 (FAS-88) specifies three criteria that define when a pension plan settlement has occurred. A *settlement* is defined as a transaction that (1) is irrevocable, (2) relieves the employer (or the pension plan) of the primary responsibility for a pension plan obligation, and (3) eliminates significant risks related to the pension plan obligation and plan assets used to effect the settlement. In the situation described above, an irrevocable transaction has not occurred. The probability that an irrevocable action will be completed is not relevant.

Question C2: If an employer decides in 20X4 to terminate its pension plan, withdraw excess plan assets, and establish a successor pension plan but is unable to effect the transactions (which include the settlement of the vested benefit obligation) until regulatory approval is obtained, does the purchase of nonparticipating annuity contracts in January 20X5 (after regulatory approval has been obtained and before issuance of the 20X4 financial statements) require adjustment of the 20X4 financial statements?

Answer: No. As discussed in the answer to the question in paragraph C1, a *settlement* is defined as a transaction that (1) is irrevocable, (2) relieves the employer (or the pension plan) of the primary responsibility for a pension plan obligation, and (3) eliminates significant risks related to the pension plan obligation and plan assets used to effect the settlement. All three of these criteria are not met until January 20X5. However, the employer would need to disclose its plans to terminate the pension plan and its receipt of the required regulatory approvals in January 20X5.

Question C3: If plan participants have agreed to accept lump-sum cash payments in exchange for their rights to receive specified pension benefits and the amounts of the payments have been fixed, may a settlement gain or loss be recognized before the cash payments are made to plan participants?

Answer: It depends. If the cash payments have yet to be made, the agreement itself may be revocable. Moreover, if the pension plan assets have not been used to effect the settlement, the employer may still be subject to risks related to these assets. Either of these conditions would preclude the employer from recognizing a settlement gain or loss.

Question C4: If an employer withdraws excess plan assets (cash) from a pension plan but is not required to settle a pension benefit obligation as part of the asset reversion transaction, should any of the net gain or loss included in accumulated other comprehensive income be immediately recognized in earnings?

Answer: No. A settlement has not occurred. Therefore, any net gain or loss should not be recognized in earnings.

Question C5: What is the accounting for the transaction described in paragraph C4?

Answer: The employer's withdrawal of cash is considered a negative plan contribution. The employer should debit cash and should credit the net pension asset or liability, as appropriate.

Question C6: If individual nonparticipating annuity contracts are to be used to settle a pension benefit obligation, may a settlement gain or loss be recognized if the individual annuity contracts have not been issued?

Answer: It depends. The issuance of individual annuity contracts is not the critical event in determining whether a settlement gain or loss can be recognized. However, the failure to issue individual contracts, along with other evidence, may indicate that the pension benefit obligation has not been effectively settled. In order for a settlement gain or loss to be recognized, an irrevocable transaction that relieves the employer (or the pension plan) from primary responsibility for the pension benefit obligation and that eliminates significant risks associated with the pension obligation and pension assets must have occurred. A commitment to purchase annuity contracts is not sufficient for a settlement gain or loss to be recognized.

Question C7: If individual nonparticipating annuity contracts are to be used to settle a pension benefit obligation, may a settlement gain or loss be recognized if the premium for the purchase of the individual annuity contracts has not been paid?

Answer: It depends. As discussed previously, for a settlement gain or loss to be recognized, an irrevocable transaction that relieves the employer (or the pension plan) of primary responsibility for the pension benefit obligation and that eliminates significant risks associated with the pension obligation and pension assets must have occurred. The failure to pay the insurance premium may indicate that the transaction is revocable. In addition, if pension plan assets have not been transferred to effect the settlement, they may still be at risk. In order for a settlement gain or loss to be recognized, the insurance company must have unconditionally assumed the legal obligation to provide the promised pension benefits.

Question C8: If a contract is entered into that requires an insurance company to pay only a portion of specific participants' pension benefits—for example, payments due retirees for the next five years—has a settlement occurred?

Answer: No. A contract to provide pension benefits for a specified period of time is a limited-term annuity. As such, it does not eliminate the risks associated with the pension benefit obligation. For example, the risk related to employee life expectancy (i.e., the duration of the pension benefits) remains. For an annuity contract with a life insurance company to qualify for settlement accounting, the contract needs to be a life annuity and not a limited-term annuity.

Question C9: Does the following constitute a settlement?

- An employer (or the pension plan) irrevocably purchases an insurance contract that guarantees payment of those pension benefits vested as of the date of the purchase.
- The purchase price of the insurance contract significantly exceeds the purchase price of a nonparticipating annuity contract covering the same pension benefits.

- As compensation for the risk of guaranteeing those pension benefits, the insurance company receives an annual fee based on a percentage of the actuarial present value of the covered pension benefits.
- If a specified ratio of assets to the covered pension benefit obligation is maintained, the employer (or the pension plan) continues to manage the assets used to effect the purchase; however, the insurance contract requires that a certain percentage of the assets be invested in high-quality bonds or a dedicated bond portfolio, depending on the ratio of assets to the covered pension benefit obligation.
- Upon final satisfaction of all of the pension benefit obligation covered by the insurance contract and payment of all of the contract's administrative fees due to the insurance company, the insurance company will remit to the employer (or the pension plan) any amounts remaining in the insurance contract's account balance. The employer (or the pension plan) is also permitted to make interim withdrawals from the account with prior notification of the insurance company, unless a withdrawal causes the ratio of assets to the covered pension benefit obligation to drop below a specified percentage.

Answer: No. The employer has not effectively transferred the risks and rewards associated with the pension plan assets and obligations. The type of annuity contract described in this question is a participating annuity contract. Because the employer is still subject to the pension plan's risks and rewards, the criteria for settlement accounting in ASC 715-30-15-6 and ASC 715-30-35-86 through 35-87 (paragraphs 3 and 5 of FAS-88) have not been met.

Question C10: What is the rationale for requiring settlement accounting for only certain participating annuity contracts?

Answer: The FASB had two basic reasons for requiring settlement accounting for only certain participating annuity contracts. First, some contracts that are essentially nonparticipating annuity contracts could be structured as participating contracts by requiring the payment of a small additional premium for a *de minimis* participation feature. Employers might have attempted to structure the purchase of an annuity contract in this manner to avoid having to recognize a pension plan settlement. Therefore, settlement plan accounting is applied to a participating annuity contract if the contract is essentially equivalent to a nonparticipating contract. Second, in some cases it might make economic sense for the employer to purchase a participating contract. Assuming that the requisite risks and rewards are transferred under the terms of the participating contract, settlement accounting is required. However, if the employer's exposure to pension plan gains and losses is substantially the same both before and after the employer enters into the participating annuity contract, settlement accounting would not be permitted.

Question C11: Are there quantitative criteria that can be used to determine whether the purchase of a participating annuity contract qualifies for settlement accounting?

Answer: No. Whether the purchase of a participating annuity contract qualifies for settlement accounting depends on the facts and circumstances of the particular case.

Question C12: If a parent company's wholly owned subsidiaries, Subsidiaries A and B, have separate pension plans, and Subsidiary B purchases nonparticipating annuity contracts from Subsidiary A (which is an insurance company) to provide the vested benefits under Subsidiary B's pension plan, does that purchase constitute a settlement in the parent company's consolidated financial statements? Does the transaction constitute a settlement in the separately issued financial statements of Subsidiary B?

Answer: The above transaction does not constitute a settlement in the parent company's consolidated financial statements. This Statement specifically precludes settlement accounting if an annuity contract is purchased from an insurance company controlled by the employer. In this case, the parent company is still subject to the risks associated with the pension benefit obligation and plan assets (all that has happened is that they have been transferred within the consolidated group, from Subsidiary B to Subsidiary A). The settlement would be recognized in Subsidiary B's separate financial statements, assuming the other criteria for settlement accounting have been met. The related-party nature of the pension settlement must be disclosed in the notes to the financial statements.

Question 13: Is the relative cost of the participation right (10%) used in Illustration 2, Example 2C, of this Statement (pp. 29-31) intended to be an indication of a criterion that could be used to determine whether the purchase of a participating annuity contract qualifies for settlement accounting?

Answer: No. The facts assumed in that example were chosen solely to illustrate the application of ASC 715-30-35-79 (paragraphs 9 and 10 of FAS-88).

Question C14: If an employer terminates its pension plan, settles a pension benefit obligation, withdraws excess plan assets, and establishes a successor pension plan that has the same pension benefit formula, have both a settlement and a curtailment occurred?

Answer: No. A settlement has occurred but not a curtailment. Although employees will no longer earn benefits for future service under the old plan, they will earn credit under the new plan. For accounting purposes, the old and new pension plans are viewed as essentially one plan. The settlement of the pension benefit obligation and the withdrawal of excess plan assets are recognized (i.e., the settlement). If the new pension plan provides increased (reduced) pension benefits for future service, a pension plan amendment (negative amendment) has occurred.

Question C15: If as part of the sale of a segment or a portion of a line of business (see the question in paragraph C37) there is a transfer of a pension benefit obligation to the purchaser (i.e., the purchaser assumes the pension benefit obligation for specific employees), have both a settlement and a curtailment occurred?

Answer: It depends. A settlement has occurred if the criteria in ASC 715-30-15-6 (paragraph 3 of FAS-88) are met. However, if there is a reasonable chance that the purchaser may not provide the promised pension benefits and if the employer remains contingently liable for such benefits, a settlement has not occurred. A curtailment has occurred if the sale significantly reduces the expected future years of employee service of present employees covered by the employer's pension plan.

Question C16: Are *annuity contracts* defined differently in ASC 715 (FAS-87) and ASC 715 (FAS-88)? If so, how are the definitions different, and why?

Answer: Yes. Under this Statement's guidance, annuity contracts purchased from an entity that is controlled by the employer are *not* eligible for settlement accounting. The FASB's rationale for this requirement is that pension plan risks are merely being shifted from one part of the entity to another part of the same entity. Under the guidance in ASC 715 (FAS-87), pension benefits covered by annuity contracts are excluded from the measurement of the projected benefit obligation and from plan assets. However, if the annuity contract is purchased from a captive insurer (a more limited definition than an insurer controlled by the employer), the projected benefit obligation is not reduced and the annuity contract purchased from the captive insurer is included among plan assets. This treatment is largely justified on the basis of practical expediency.

Question C17: If nonparticipating annuity contracts are purchased from a less-than-majority-owned investee that is not controlled by the employer and the criteria for a settlement are satisfied, is the resulting settlement gain or loss subject to partial recognition (i.e., should it be reduced to reflect the employer's ownership)?

Answer: No. The entire settlement gain or loss should be recognized in earnings. This treatment represents a departure from the normal practice of eliminating the applicable portion (based on ownership) of gains or losses from intercompany transactions. However, this treatment does not establish a new precedent for the treatment of nonpension intercompany transactions.

Question C18: Is there a specific threshold for determining if an event results in (*a*) a *significant* reduction of expected years of future service of present employees covered by a pension plan or (*b*) an elimination of the accrual of pension benefits for some or all of the future services of a *significant* number of employees covered by a pension plan?

Answer: No. Judgment should be exercised based on the facts and circumstances that are unique to each case.

Question C19: If an employer has a pension plan covering employees in several divisions and the employer terminates employees in one of those divisions, does a curtailment occur if the expected years of future service of present employees in that division are reduced significantly but the reduction is not significant in relation to the expected years of future service of all employees covered by the pension plan?

Answer: No. This Statement should be applied on an overall basis for each individual pension plan. In the above example, the reduction in the expected years of future service is not significant for the pension plan as a whole. The above example would give rise to a pension plan gain or loss (see ASC 715-30-35-18, 35-19, and 35-21 (FAS-87, paragraphs 29) ASC 715-30-35-24 (paragraph 32 of FAS-87), and ASC 715-30-35-25 (paragraph 33 of FAS-87), for additional details).

Question C20: Can a curtailment occur if an employer either (*a*) temporarily lays off a significant number of present employees covered by a pension plan or (*b*) temporarily suspends a pension plan so that employees covered by the pension plan do not earn additional pension benefits for some or all of their future services?

Answer: Yes. A curtailment occurs if there is a significant reduction in pension benefits for some or all of the future services of employees covered by the pension plan. This result holds regardless of whether the cause is a temporary employee layoff or a temporary suspension of the pension plan.

Question C21: If unrelated, individually insignificant reductions of expected years of future service of employees covered by a pension plan accumulate to a significant reduction over a single year or more than one year, does that constitute a curtailment?

Answer: No. Each of these reductions leads to a pension plan gain or loss (see ASC 715-30-35-18, 35-19, and 35-21 (FAS-87, paragraphs 29), ASC 715-30-35-24 (paragraph 32 of FAS-87) andASC 715-30-35-25 (paragraph 33 of FAS-87), for additional details).

Question C22: If individually insignificant reductions of expected years of future service of employees covered by a pension plan are (*a*) caused by one event, such as a strike, or (*b*) related to a single plan of reorganization and those reductions accumulate to a significant reduction during more than one fiscal year, does a curtailment occur?

Answer: Yes. The fact that the significant reduction occurs over a period of time does not change the fact that an event giving rise to curtailment accounting has occurred.

Question C23: Does a curtailment occur if an employer terminates a pension plan and establishes a successor pension plan that provides additional but reduced pension benefits for all years of employees' future service?

Answer: No. In this case the pension plan continues to provide benefits for future employee service, albeit at a reduced level. In accordance with the guidance in this Statement, a curtailment involves the elimination, for a significant number of employees, of pension credit for some or all of their expected future service. This situation represents a reduction of future benefits, not an elimination of such benefits. ASC 715 (FAS-87) requires that a reduction in future pension benefits be treated as a negative plan amendment.

Question C24: Can a curtailment occur if a pension plan is terminated and replaced by a successor pension plan?

Answer: Yes. A curtailment involves the elimination, for a significant number of employees, of the accrual of defined pension benefits for some or all of their expected future service. The substitution of a new pension plan for an existing pension plan would represent a curtailment if (*a*) a significant number of employees covered under the old pension plan are not covered under the new pension plan or (*b*) a significant number of years of future employee service do not result in the accrual of defined pension benefits.

Illustration of Substituting New Plan for Existing Plan

Rorer Industries offers a pension plan that provides employees a flat pension benefit of $1,000 for each year of service. At December 31, 20X4, Rorer terminates this plan and replaces it with a new pension plan. Under the new plan, employees will be provided with a pension benefit of $500 for each year of service. At December 31, 20X4, Employee A had worked for Rorer for five years. The typical Rorer employee has five years of service.

Given the above facts, Rorer needs to account for the substitution of a new pension plan for its existing plan as a curtailment. At December 31, 20X4, the accumulated pension benefit obligation for Employee A was $5,000. Given the terms of the new pension plan, Employee A will not earn additional defined pension benefits under the new plan until the year 20Y0 (the accumulated pension benefit obligation for Employee A under the new plan will not reach $5,000 until December 31, 20X9). Therefore, Employee A will provide five years of future service without accruing any additional defined pension benefits. Since Employee A is a typical Rorer employee, these facts are consistent with a significant reduction in the accrual of additional pension benefits for future years of employee service.

30.12 *Pension Plans—Settlements and Curtailments*

Question C25: If an employer disposes of a segment or a portion of a line of business (see the question in paragraph C37) that results in a termination of some employees' services earlier than expected but does not significantly reduce the expected years of future service of present employees covered by the pension plan, should the effects of the reduction in the workforce on the pension plan be measured in the same manner as a curtailment (pars. 12–13) to determine the gain or loss on the disposal pursuant to ASC 205-20-45-3 (paragraph 43 of FAS-144, Accounting for the Impairment or Disposal of Long-Lived Assets)?

Answer: Yes. The above facts do not represent a curtailment, since the expected years of future service of present employees covered by the pension plan have not been significantly reduced. However, the effects of the reduction in the workforce should be treated in the same manner as a curtailment for the purpose of calculating the gain or loss on disposal.

Question C26: What is considered a successor pension plan for purposes of applying this Statement?

Answer: This question is relevant because if a pension obligation is settled and the pension plan is terminated without being replaced by a successor plan, a pension plan termination and curtailment have both occurred.

An employer that terminates a pension plan may establish a new plan, or it may amend one or more existing pension plans. The new plan or the amended plan may provide for the accrual of defined pension benefits for the future services of present employees who were covered by the previous (terminated) pension plan. In these cases, a successor plan would exist unless (*a*) the defined pension benefits provided by the new plan are significantly fewer than the pension benefits provided by the old plan or (*b*) the present employees covered by the new plan are significantly fewer than the employees covered by the old plan.

This Statement does not apply to an employer's withdrawal from a multiemployer pension plan. If an employer withdraws from a multiemployer plan and establishes a new pension plan for its employees, the new plan is not considered a successor plan. In some cases the employer may be responsible for a portion of the plan's unfunded pension obligation. If the requirements of ASC 450-FAS-5 (Accounting for Contingencies) are met, the employer should accrue a liability for its share of the unfunded obligation.

Question C27: If settlement of the pension benefit obligation as part of a pension plan termination occurs (and there is no successor pension plan) in a financial reporting period that differs from the period in which the effects of the curtailment resulting from the pension plan termination ordinarily would be recognized, should the effects of both the settlement and the curtailment be recognized in the same financial reporting period?

Answer: Generally not. The effects of a settlement should be recognized in accordance with paragraph 9 of this Statement (ASC

715-30-35-79); the effects of a curtailment should be recognized in accordance with paragraph 14 of this Statement (ASC 715-30-35-94). This may result in the effects of the settlement and the curtailment being recognized in different financial reporting periods.

> **PRACTICE POINTER:** The effects of a pension plan curtailment are recognized on the date of the pension plan amendment. The effects of a settlement are recognized when the employer is relieved of its obligation for providing the pension plan benefits.

Question C28: This question has been deleted.

Question C29: If, in terminating its pension plan (old assets), an employer settles the pension benefit obligation and withdraws excess plan assets and then contributes and allocates those assets to participants' accounts in a new defined contribution pension plan, may the employer combine any net gain or loss from the settlement and curtailment of the old plan with the net periodic pension cost from the contribution to the defined contribution pension plan and thereby report both on a net basis for purposes of classification in the income statement or disclosure in accompanying footnotes?

Answer: No. In the facts at hand, both a pension plan termination and a contribution to a defined contribution plan have taken place. These are two separate events and they need to be recognized in earnings as such. As a result of the pension plan termination, all net pension amounts included in accumulated other comprehensive income are recognized in earnings. Net periodic pension cost is recognized for the amount contributed to the defined contribution pension plan. Therefore, it is inappropriate to net the results of the separate events.

Question 30: If a market-related value of plan assets other than fair value is used for purposes of determining the expected return on plan assets, is that basis also to be used in determining the maximum gain or loss subject to pro rata recognition in earnings when a pension benefit obligation is settled?

Answer: No. The fair value of the plan assets on the date of settlement is to be used.

Question C31: As of what date should plan assets and the projected benefit obligation be measured in determining the accounting for a settlement?

Answer: Plan assets and the projected benefit obligation should be measured as of the date of the settlement, which is the date on which the FAS-88 criteria for settlement accounting have been met. The appropriate date for measuring plan assets and the projected benefit obligation is important because these amounts determine (*a*) the maximum gain or loss subject to pro rata recognition in earnings (e.g., if 100% of the projected benefit obligation is settled, then 100% of the maximum gain or loss is recognized in earnings) and (*b*) the percentage reduction in the projected benefit obligation.

Question C32: If the interest rates implicit in the purchase price of nonparticipating annuity contracts used to effect a settlement are different from the assumed discount rates used to determine net periodic pension cost, should the employer measure the portion of the projected benefit obligation being settled (and the remaining portion, if appropriate) using the implicit annuity interest rates and include any resulting gain or loss in the maximum gain or loss subject to pro rata recognition in earnings?

Answer: Yes. As discussed in the answer to the question in paragraph C31, plan assets and the projected benefit obligation are measured as of the settlement date. In measuring the portion of the projected benefit obligation being settled, the employer should use the purchase price of the nonparticipating annuity contracts. Any gain or loss resulting from remeasuring the plan assets and the projected benefit obligation as of the settlement date are included in computing the maximum gain or loss subject to pro rata recognition in earnings.

Question C33: If a settlement occurs in the circumstances described in the question in paragraph C32 and the interest rates implicit in the purchase price of nonparticipating annuity contracts used to effect the settlement are different from the assumed discount rates used to determine net periodic pension cost, is it appropriate to measure the unsettled portion of the projected benefit obligation using the implicit annuity interest rates?

Answer: Maybe. The employer should consider measuring the projected benefit obligation for the unsettled portion of the pension obligation using the interest rate implicit in the annuity contract under the following circumstances:

- If the demographics of the participants for whom the PBO was settled are similar to the demographics of participants for whom the PBO was *not* settled (in particular, the length of time until pension payments will be made should be similar for each group)
- If the interest rates implicit in the annuity contracts represent the best estimate of the interest rates at which the unsettled portion of the PBO could be effectively settled

Question C34: If an employer settles a pension benefit obligation and withdraws excess plan assets as part of terminating its pension plan, should the settlement gain or loss determined pursuant to paragraph 9 (ASC 715-30-35-79) be adjusted to eliminate any gains or losses relating to securities issued by the employer if those securities are included in the plan assets withdrawn?

Answer: No. It is the settlement of the pension plan, not the withdrawal of plan assets, that precipitates the recognition in earnings of any net gain or loss included in accumulated other comprehensive income. The withdrawal of plan assets does not affect the recognition of the settlement gain or loss. In addition, the nature of the plan assets that are withdrawn does not affect the recognition of the settlement gain or loss.

Question C35: If the transition asset or obligation is reduced when a settlement gain is recognized, how is any balance of the transition asset or obligation remaining in accumulated other comprehensive income amortized in future periods?

Answer: The balance of the transition asset or obligation asset is amortized on a straight-line basis over the remainder of the amortization period established at transition.

Question C36: If a negative pension plan amendment adopted shortly before the date of initial application of the guidance in ASC 715 (FAS-87) is the reason that a transition asset exists in accumulated other comprehensive income, should any portion of the transition asset remaining in accumulated other comprehensive income as of the date of a settlement be included in the maximum gain or loss subject to pro rata recognition in earnings?

Answer: Yes. Any transition asset or obligation remaining in accumulated comprehensive income at the time of a settlement is included in determining the maximum gain or loss subject to pro rata recognition in earnings.

Question C37: If an employer sells a segment of a component of an entity as defined in paragraph 41 of FAS-144 (ASC, *Glossary*) and the employer settles a pension benefit obligation related to the employees affected by the sale, should the settlement gain or loss recognized in accordance with ASC 715-30-35-79, 35-82 through 35-83 (paragraphs 9 through 11 of FAS-88) be classified separately in discontinued operations?

Answer: According to ASC 360 (FAS-144), a settlement is directly related to a disposal transaction if a cause-and-effect relationship is established and the settlement occurs one year or less after a disposal transaction, unless the settlement is delayed by events not under the entity's control. A direct cause-and-effect relationship would exist if a condition of the sale of a component of an entity were to require settlement of the pension benefit obligation for employees affected by a sale. The timing of a settlement that occurs because of a disposal of a component of an entity may be at the employer's discretion. An employer's decision to settle a pension benefit obligation when a sale occurs may cause a coincidence of events that would not by itself signify that there is a cause-and-effect relationship between the transactions. In this case, paragraphs 9 through 11 of FAS-88 (ASC 715-30-35-79, 35-82, 35-83) would apply.

Question C38: This question has been deleted.

Question C39: How should an employer determine and report a gain or loss from a settlement or curtailment that occurs as a direct result of a disposal of a component of an entity?

Answer: Under the guidance in ASC 715-30-35-94 (paragraph 14 of FAS-88), a curtailment loss should be recognized in earnings if it is probable that a curtailment will occur and the related amount is estimable. Consequently, if it is probable that a disposal of a component of an entity will occur and the disposal loss is estimable, a curtailment loss should be recognized even if the reporting entity has not yet met all of the criteria required in ASC 360 (FAS-144) to classify the disposal group's operations as discontinued operations. Gain recognition on a curtailment gain also is required under paragraph 14 of FAS-88 (ASC 715-30-35-94) if the related employees are terminated or a suspension or amendment of a plan is adopted. A curtailment gain or loss should be classified in income from continuing operations until the reporting entity meets the criteria required in FAS-144 to report discounting operations. A gain or loss from the settlement of a pension benefits obligation should be recognized when a settlement occurs.

Question C40: If an employer incorporates a division of its operations and subsequently spins it off to owners of the enterprise and also transfers to the new entity's pension plan either (*a*) a pension benefit obligation related to the employees transferred as part of the spinoff or (*b*) plan assets, how should the employer and the new entity account for the transaction?

Answer: ASC 845 (APB-29, Accounting for Nonmonetary Transactions) precludes the recognition of a gain or loss on the distribution of nonmonetary assets to owners of the enterprise spinoff. In a similar fashion, the recognition of a gain or loss resulting from the transfer of pension assets or of the pension plan obligation in a spinoff also is prohibited. Any (*a*) transition asset or obligation remaining in accumulated other comprehensive income, and (*b*) net gain or loss included in accumulated other comprehensive income should be allocated between the employer's existing pension plan and the pension plan of the spun-off new entity in proportion to the projected benefit obligation of each pension plan. Prior service costs included in accumulated other comprehensive income should be allocated between the two pension plans based on an analysis of the prior service of the individuals that will be covered under each of the pension plans. The accounting for a transfer of plan assets and the pension benefit obligation to a new entity established as a result of a spinoff is illustrated below.

Illustration of Incorporation and Subsequent Spinoff of a Pension Plan

XYZ, Inc., incorporated one of its divisions, ABC, Inc. ABC is later spun off to XYZ's shareholders. ABC assumes XYZ's pension obligation that relates to ABC's employees. The accumulated benefit obligation assumed by ABC (all of which is vested) is $60,000. ABC's projected benefit obligation is $12,000 higher than this amount based on the expected future salary levels of these employees. In addition, XYZ transfers to ABC $56,000 in plan assets. The appropriate accounting treatment for XYZ, Inc., and ABC, Inc., is illustrated below.

	Old Plan Before Spinoff	Old Plan	After Spinoff New Plan
Assets and obligations:			
Accumulated benefit obligation	$(144,000)	$(84,000)	$(60,000)
Effects of future compensation levels	(36,000)	(24,000)	(12,000)
Projected benefit obligation	(180,000)	(108,000)	(72,000)
Plan assets at fair value	320,000	264,000	56,000
Funded status and recognized asset/liability	$(140,000)	$156,000	$(16,000)
Amounts remaining in accumulated other comprehensive income:			
Transition asset	(80,000)	(48,000)	(32,000)
Prior service cost	50,000	35,000	15,000
Net gain	(110,000)	(66,000)	(44,000)
	$(140,000)	$79,000	$(61,000)

Spreadsheet Notes

1. The allocation of the $180,000 projected benefit obligation between the two plans was based on an analysis of the individual employees covered by each plan.
2. The allocation of the $320,000 of plan assets between the two plans was chosen by XYZ's management (we assume that no regulatory requirements apply).
3. The allocation of the transition asset or obligation remaining in accumulated other comprehensive income and the net gain or loss included in accumulated other comprehensive income between the two plans was based on the percentage of the total projected benefit obligation assumed by each plan (60% for the old plan, 40% for the new plan).
4. The allocation of prior service cost included in accumulated other comprehensive income between the two plans was based on an analysis of the individual employees covered by each plan (for illustrative purposes we have assumed that this allocation differs from the PBO assumed by each plan).

Journal Entries

XYZ, Inc.

Pension asset	16,000	
Accumulated other comprehensive income—transition asset	32,000	
Accumulated other comprehensive income—net gain	44,000	
Stockholders' equity		77,000
Accumulated other comprehensive income—prior service cost		15,000

To record the transfer of plan assets, a pension benefit obligation, and net deferred amounts from XYZ, Inc. to ABC, Inc. Note that the credit to stockholders' equity represents the net of all assets and liabilities transferred from XYZ, Inc. to ABC, Inc.

ABC, Inc.

Stockholders' equity	77,000	
Accumulated other comprehensive income—prior service cost	15,000	
Pension asset		16,000
Accumulated other comprehensive income—transition asset		32,000
Accumulated other comprehensive income—net gain		44,000

To record the receipt of plan assets, a pension benefit obligation, and net deferred amounts from XYZ, Inc. Note that the debit to stockholders' equity represents the net of all assets and liabilities received from XYZ, Inc.

Question C41: What is the proper sequence of events to follow in measuring the effects of a settlement and a curtailment that are to be recognized at the same time?

Answer: Although the method selected may affect the determination of the aggregate gain or loss recognized, management decides whether the effects of the settlement are recognized first or the effects of the curtailment. Once management has selected a method, however, that method must be followed in future years when a settlement and a curtailment occur simultaneously.

Question C42: Because the amount of the vested benefit obligation settled and the amount of plan assets used to purchase non-participating annuity contracts are equal in Illustrations 1 and 2 of this Statement, is it appropriate to conclude that no gains and losses occurred when the projected benefit obligation and the plan assets were measured as of the date of the settlement?

Answer: No. The "Before" columns in these illustrations reflect the measurement of the plan assets and the projected benefit obligation as of the settlement date. Any gains and losses arising from measuring these two accounts at the settlement date have already been recognized. (See Question 31 for additional discussion.)

Question C43: Is the method in Illustration 2, Examples 2B and 2C, of this Statement that allocates an amount equal to the settlement gain on a pro rata basis to the transition asset or obligation remaining in accumulated other comprehensive income and the net gain included in accumulated other comprehensive income the only method of allocation permitted under those circumstances by ASC 715 (FAS-88)?

Answer: No. An amount equal to the settlement gain could first be applied to the transition asset or obligation remaining in accumulated other comprehensive income. If any settlement gain remains, it would be applied against the net gain included in accumulated comprehensive income. If this method is selected, it must be applied consistently across years. Although this alternative method is acceptable, allocating the settlement gain based on the projected benefit obligation is preferable because (a) it is a more unbiased method, and (b) the allocation method can affect the determination of net periodic pension cost in subsequent periods.

Question C44: Is the method in Illustration 2, Example 2C, of this Statement that determines the maximum gain subject to pro rata recognition in earnings by first reducing the net gain included in accumulated other comprehensive income by the cost of the participation right the only method of allocation permitted under those circumstances by this Statement?

Answer: No. In the determination of the maximum gain subject to pro rata recognition in earnings, the cost of the participation right could be allocated as follows:

1. To the transition asset or obligation remaining in accumulated other comprehensive income
2. To the net gain included in accumulated other comprehensive income
3. On a pro rata basis between those two amounts based on their relative amounts.

Any one of the three methods is acceptable. The method illustrated in Example 2C of Illustration 2 allocates the cost of the participation right to the net gain included in accumulated other comprehensive income. However, the preferred method is to allocate the cost of the participation right on a pro rata basis between

30.20 *Pension Plans—Settlements and Curtailments*

those two amounts for the same reasons discussed in the answer in paragraph C43. Whichever method is selected must be applied on a consistent basis from year to year.

Question C45: May an employer adopt an accounting policy that requires recognition in earnings of gains and losses from all settlements during the year for a pension plan if the cost of those settlements exceeds the service cost component of net periodic pension cost for that pension plan for the year?

Answer: Yes. Recognition in earnings of gains and losses from pension plan settlements is required if the cost of those settlements exceeds the sum of the service cost and interest cost components of net periodic pension cost for the year in question. However, recognition of settlement gains and losses is permitted, but *not* required, if the aggregate settlement cost is below the sum of service cost and interest cost. The accounting policy adopted for recognition in earnings gains and losses from settlements must be applied on a consistent basis from year to year.

Question C46: If an employer's accounting policy is not to recognize in earnings a gain or loss from a settlement if the cost of all settlements during the year does not exceed the sum of the service cost and interest cost components of net periodic pension cost for the pension plan for the year, how should the employer account for the following situation: (*a*) it is estimated at the beginning of the year that the cost of all settlements during the year will not exceed the threshold amount described above; (*b*) a pension benefit obligation is settled during the first quarter and a settlement gain or loss is not recognized; and (*c*) in the second quarter and subsequent to the issuance of the first quarter's interim report, it is determined that the cost of all settlements during the year will exceed the threshold amount?

Answer: In this case, the change in handling settlement gains and losses should be treated as a change in accounting estimate. The settlement gain or loss would be recognized in the second quarter.

Question C47: How should an employer determine the amount of prior service cost included in accumulated other comprehensive income that should be recognized in earnings in the event of a curtailment if the employer amortizes prior service cost on a straight-line basis over the average remaining service period of employees expected to receive the related pension benefits?

Answer: Paragraph 12 of this Statement (ASC 715-30-35-92) requires that the prior service cost included in accumulated other comprehensive income associated with future years of employee service that is no longer expected to be rendered should be recognized in earnings as part of a curtailment. This basic approach applies even if the employer amortizes prior service cost included in accumulated other comprehensive income on a straight-line basis over the employees' average remaining service period. However, if the employer amortizes prior service cost included in accumulated other comprehensive income using this alternate approach, the determination of the prior service cost included in accumulated other comprehensive income associated with the curtailment may be less precise. As a practical matter, the prior service cost included in accumulated other comprehensive income associated with the curtailment may have to be determined by referring to the reduction in the (remaining) expected future years of service. For example, assume that as of January 1, 20X8, the remaining expected future years of service that pertain to prior service costs included in accumulated other comprehensive income is ten years. As the result of a curtailment during 20X8, the remaining expected years of future service is five years. In this case, 50% of the prior service cost included in accumulated other comprehensive income is associated with the curtailment. Consequently, the employer would recognize in earnings 50% of the prior service cost included in accumulated other comprehensive income.

Question C48: If a curtailment occurs because an employer terminates or suspends a pension plan (so that employees do not earn additional pension benefits for future service) but the employees continue to work for the employer, should any prior service cost included in accumulated other comprehensive income that is associated with the employees who are affected by the pension plan termination or suspension be included in determining the net gain or loss to be recognized for the curtailment?

Answer: Yes. One reason why recognition of prior service cost in net periodic pension cost as a result of a retroactive pension plan amendment is deferred is the likelihood that the employer will receive future benefits as a result of the plan amendment. These future benefits are associated with future employee service for those employees active at the date of the plan amendment who are expected to receive benefits under the plan. Any future economic benefits the employer was expecting to receive as a result of the retroactive plan amendment are in all likelihood dissipated by the suspension or termination of the pension plan. As such, some, or all, of the prior service cost included in accumulated other comprehensive income should no longer be deferred and recognized in earnings. Further, if the pension plan is terminated, all prior service cost included in accumulated other comprehensive income must be recognized in earnings.

Question C49: If a curtailment results from a pension plan suspension that may be only temporary (e.g., the pension plan suspension will end as soon as the employer's financial condition sufficiently improves), how is the net gain or loss from the curtailment determined?

Answer: The curtailment gain or loss should be determined based on the probable duration of the pension plan suspension. [The term *probable* is defined in accordance with ASC 450 (FAS-5, Accounting for Contingencies).] In some cases, it may be possible to determine only a range for the likely duration of the pension plan suspension. If no length of time estimated within that range is more likely than any other length of time, the expected duration of the pension plan suspension is to be calculated to produce minimum curtailment gain or loss.

Question C50: If the transition asset or obligation remaining in accumulated comprehensive income is reduced as part of the accounting for a curtailment, how is any remaining balance amortized in future periods?

Answer: The balance of the transition asset or obligation remaining in accumulated other comprehensive income should be amortized on a straight-line basis over the remainder of the amortization period determined at the time ASC 715 (FAS-87) was adopted. (See the question in paragraph C35 for additional discussion.)

Question C51: If a curtailment occurs that causes almost all of the pension plan's participants to become permanently inactive, should the employer continue to amortize any balance of the transition asset remaining in accumulated other comprehensive income using the amortization period determined at transition?

Answer: Yes. The transition asset remaining in accumulated other comprehensive income should continue to be amortized over the remainder of the amortization period determined at transition. (See the question in paragraph C35 for additional discussion.)

Question C52: If both a transition asset remaining in accumulated other comprehensive income and a larger (smaller) net loss included in accumulated other comprehensive income exist at the date of a curtailment that decreases (increases) the projected benefit obligation, how should the effects of the curtailment be applied to those pension amounts?

Answer: The appropriate accounting treatment is as follows:

- Any reduction in the projected benefit obligation that is not recognized as a curtailment gain should be offset against the net loss included in accumulated other comprehensive income.
- Any increase in the projected benefit obligation that is not recognized as a curtailment loss should be offset against the transition asset remaining in accumulated other comprehensive income.

No further offsetting of amounts is permitted.

The first illustration below presents the appropriate accounting treatment when the transition asset remaining in accumulated other comprehensive income is less than the net loss. The second illustration presents the appropriate accounting treatment when the transition asset remaining in accumulated other comprehensive income exceeds the net loss included in accumulated other comprehensive income.

Illustration of Pension Plan Curtailment: Transition Asset Remaining in Accumulated Other Comprehensive Income Is Less Than Net Loss Included in Accumulated Other Comprehensive Income

Herring's Haberdashery sponsors a defined benefit pension plan. Herring's terminates a significant number of employees in an attempt to lower manufacturing costs. Herring's management makes the termination decision on September 30, 20X8, and the effects of the terminations are reasonably estimable at that time. The termination date is November 30, 20X8. Herring's has a transition asset remaining in accumulated other comprehensive income. As a result of the plan curtailment, Herring's escapes a pension liability for employees whose benefits are not yet vested, and its pension obligation is reduced to the extent that future compensation levels are no longer relevant for the terminated employees. Herring's projected benefit obligation is reduced by $220,000 ($180,000 from the elimination of future compensation levels on pension benefits to be received and $40,000 from the elimination of nonvested accumulated benefits). The appropriate accounting for this curtailment is as follows:

Since the projected benefit obligation is reduced, Herring's will recognize a net gain on the curtailment. In accordance with the guidance in this Statement, if the effect of a curtailment is the recognition of a net gain, the gain is recognized in earnings on the date the employees terminate (November 30, 20X8). In the following schedule, plan assets and the projected benefit obligation are also measured as of that date.

	11/30/X8		
	Before Curtailment	Effects of Curtailment	After Curtailment
Assets and obligations:			
Vested benefit obligation	$(3,100,000)		$(3,100,000)
Nonvested benefits	(500,000)	$ 40,000	(460,000)
Accumulated benefit obligation	(3,600,000)	40,000	(3,560,000)
Effects of future compensation levels	(800,000)	180,000	(620,000)
Projected benefit obligation	(4,400,000)	220,000	(4,180,000)
Plan assets at fair value	4,200,000		4,200,000
Funded status and recognized asset (liability)	$(200,000)	220,000	$20,000

30.24 Pension Plans—Settlements and Curtailments

Amounts recognized in accumulated
other comprehensive income:

Transition asset	(400,000)		(400,000)
Net loss	600,000	(200,000)	400,000
	$ 200,000	$(200,000)	-0-

Spreadsheet Notes

1. Under the guidance in this Statement, the potential curtailment gain—the $220,000 decrease in the projected benefit obligation—first should be offset against any net loss included in accumulated other comprehensive income. In this case, there is a net loss of $200,000 (a $600,000 net loss, net of the $400,000 transition asset remaining in accumulated other comprehensive income). Therefore, the curtailment gain recorded by Herring's Haberdashery is $20,000.

Journal Entry

Pension asset	$20,000	
Pension liability	$200,000	
Gain from Curtailment		$20,000
Other comprehensive income—net loss		$200,000

Illustration of Pension Plan Curtailment: Transition Asset Remaining in Accumulation Other Comprehensive Income Exceeds Net/Loss Included in Other Comprehensive Income

The facts are the same as in the previous illustration except for the following:

1. Herring's supplements the retirement benefits of the employees who are terminated. This increases the projected benefit obligation by $440,000.
2. The net loss included in other comprehensive income is $200,000.

Since the projected benefit obligation is increased, Herring's will recognize a net loss on the curtailment. In accordance with the guidance in this Statement, if the effect of a curtailment is the recognition of a net loss, which is recognized in earnings when it is probable that the curtailment will occur and the effects are estimable (September 30, 20X8). In the following schedule, plan assets and the projected benefit obligation are also measured as of that date.

Pension Plans—Settlements and Curtailments

	9/30/X8		
	Before Curtailment	Effects of Curtailment	After Curtailment
Assets and obligations:			
Vested benefit obligation	$(3,100,000)	$(440,000)	$(3,540,000)
Nonvested benefits	(500,000)	40,000	(460,000)
Accumulated benefit obligation	(3,600,000)	(400,000)	(4,000,000)
Effects of future compensation levels	(800,000)	180,000	(620,000)
Projected benefit obligation	(4,400,000)	(220,000)	(4,620,000)
Plan assets at fair value	4,200,000		4,200,000
Funded status and recognized liability	$(200,000)	$(220,000)	$(420,000)
Amounts recognized in other comprehensive income:			
Transition asset	(400,000)	200,000	(200,000)
Net loss	200,000		200,000
	$ (200,000)	$ 200,000	$ -0-

Spreadsheet Notes

1. Under the guidance in this statement the potential curtailment loss—the $220,000 increase in the projected benefit obligation—first should be offset against any net gain included in accumulated other comprehensive income. In this case, there is a net gain of $200,000 ($400,000 transition asset in accumulated comprehensive income, net of the $200,000 of net loss included in accumulated other comprehensive income). After $220,000 increase in the projected benefit obligation is offset against the $200,000 gain included in other comprehensive income the curtailment loss recorded by Herring's Haberdashery is $20,000.

Journal Entry

Loss from curtailment	$20,000	
Other comprehensive income—transition asset	$200,000	
Pension liability		$220,000

Question C53: If both a transition asset remaining in accumulated other comprehensive income and a net gain included in accumulated other comprehensive income exist at the date of a curtailment that increases the projected benefit obligation, should the effects of the curtailment be offset (*a*) initially against a transition asset remaining in accumulated other comprehensive income, (*b*) initially against a net gain included in accumulated other comprehensive income, or (c) against both on a pro rata basis?

Answer: Any one of those approaches is acceptable, as long as the approach selected is applied on a consistent basis. However, the preferable approach is to apply the curtailment loss against both on a pro rata basis. (See the question in paragraph C43 for additional discussion.)

Question C54: How should (a) the liability and the loss from employees' acceptance of an offer of special termination benefits and (b) the change in the projected benefit obligation due to the related curtailment be determined?

Answer: The liability and the loss from employees' acceptance of an offer of special termination benefits are computed as the difference between:

- The actuarial present value of the accumulated benefit obligation for those employees receiving special termination benefits before consideration of the effects on the accumulated benefit obligation of those benefits *and*
- The actuarial present value of the accumulated benefit obligation for those employees receiving special termination benefits after consideration of the effects on the accumulated benefit obligation of those benefits.

Those amounts are determined as of the date the employees accept the offer of special termination benefits.

The change in the projected benefit obligation due to the related curtailment is determined as the difference between:

- The projected benefit obligation for the affected employees before their acceptance of the special termination benefits *and*
- The projected benefit obligation for the affected employees determined by applying the normal pension plan formula and assuming no future service due to the termination.

The following illustration presents the applicable accounting treatment for this circumstance.

Illustration of Curtailment: Termination Benefits Offered to Employees

On July 1, 20X8, AHB, Inc., offers its employees special pension benefits in connection with their voluntary termination of employment. Employees who accept this offer will receive an additional ten years of credited service, and employees can retire at age 50 instead of at age 55. Employees must elect to receive these special benefits, in exchange for their voluntary termination of employment, by November 1, 20X8.

On November 1, 20X8, employees representing 20% of AHB's workforce accept the special termination benefits. The actuarial present value of the accumulated benefit obligation for these employees, before consideration of the special termination benefits, as of November 1, 20X8, is $1,050,000. After consideration of the special termination benefits, the actuarial present value of the accumulated benefit obligation is $1,250,000.

Future compensation levels are no longer relevant for the 20% of AHB's workforce who accept the special termination benefits and who voluntarily leave AHB. This has the effect of reducing AHB's projected benefit obligation by $160,000.

At the time the special termination benefits are accepted, the transition obligation remaining in other comprehensive income unrecognized net obligation at transition was $1,600,000. Of that amount, $300,000 was assigned to the future years of service of the 20% of employees who accepted AHB's special termination offer. The appropriate accounting is as follows:

On November 1, 20X8, AHB will recognize a loss of $340,000 in earnings (this includes the loss from issuing the special termination benefits and the loss on the curtailment). Note that the loss is recognized on November 1, 20X8, because it is not until this date that the number of employees accepting the special termination benefits is known. The following schedule analyzes the effects of the special termination benefits on the applicable pension-related accounts.

	11/1/X8		
	Before Employee Terminations	Effects of Terminations	After Employee Terminations
Assets and obligations:			
Vested benefit obligation			
Employees accepting offer	$(1,050,000)	$(200,000)	$(1,250,000)
Other employees	(1,550,000)		(1,550,000)
Nonvested benefits	(400,000)		(400,000)
Accumulated benefit obligation	(3,000,000)	(200,000)	(3,200,000)
Effects of future compensation levels	(1,000,000)	160,000	(840,000)
Projected benefit obligation	(4,000,000)	(40,000)	(4,040,000)
Plan assets at fair value	2,800,000		2,800,000
Funded status and recognized liability	$(1,200,000)	$(40,000)	$(1,240,000)
Amounts recognized in accumulated other comprehensive income:			
Transition obligation	1,600,000	(300,000)	1,300,000
Net Gain	(600,000)		(600,000)
	$1,000,000	$(300,000)	$700,000

30.28 Pension Plans—Settlements and Curtailments

Spreadsheet Notes

1. The loss from the issuance of the special termination benefits is $200,000 ($1,250,000 − $1,050,000).
2. The $160,000 decrease in future compensation levels is a potential gain. Under the guidance in this Statement, this amount should first be offset against any net loss included in accumulated other comprehensive income. Because AHB has a net gain in accumulated other comprehensive income, the entire potential gain of $160,000 is recognized in earnings (this amount represents a curtailment gain).
3. Under the guidance in this Statement, the transition obligation remaining in accumulated other comprehensive income must be treated as prior service cost included in accumulated other comprehensive income for the purpose of applying the guidance in FAS-88. The reduction in prior service cost associated with the years of future service the terminated employees had been expected to work is $300,000. This amount represents a curtailment loss.
4. The total loss recognized in earnings is $340,000 (the $200,000 loss from issuing the special termination benefits, the $160,000 gain from the reduction in future compensation, and a $300,000 loss from the immediate recognition of a portion of the transition obligation remaining in accumulated other comprehensive income.

Journal Entry

Loss on Employee Terminations	$340,000	
Other comprehensive income—transition obligation		$300,000
Pension liability		$40,000

Question C55: If (a) an employer adopts a plan to terminate employees that will significantly reduce the expected years of future service of present employees covered by a pension plan and (b) the sum of the effects of the resulting curtailment identified in paragraphs 12 and 13 (ASC 715-30-35-92, 35-93) of this Statement is expected to be a net gain, should that gain be recognized in earnings when the related employees terminate or when the plan is adopted?

Answer: The curtailment gain should be measured and recognized when the employees terminate.

Question C56: If (a) an employer amends its pension plan to provide for the plan's termination (or suspension) and thereby eliminates for a significant number of employees the accrual of all (or some) of the pension benefits for their future services after a subsequent date (i.e., the effective date of the pension plan termination or suspension is subsequent to the amendment date) and (b) the sum of the effects of the resulting curtailment identified in paragraphs 12 and 13 of FAS-88

(ASC 715-30-35-92, 93) is a net gain, should that gain be recognized in earnings when the employer amends its pension plan or when the pension plan termination (or suspension) is effective?

Answer: The curtailment gain should be measured and recognized when the pension plan is amended.

Question C57: If an employer's offer of special termination benefits results in a curtailment, is it possible that the offer of termination benefits could be recognized in a reporting period different from the period in which the curtailment is recognized?

Answer: Yes. These two events may be recorded in different reporting periods. A loss from a curtailment is recognized when the curtailment is probable and its effects are reasonably estimable. The costs of termination benefits are recorded when the employees elect to receive the special termination benefits and the cost of these benefits is reasonably estimable.

Question C58: This question has been deleted.

Question C59: If an employer sponsors a pension plan that provides supplemental early retirement benefits, should those pension benefits be accounted for as contractual termination benefits?

Answer: No. The provision of supplemental early retirement benefits should be included in the computation of net periodic pension cost. Contractual termination benefits arise from the occurrence of a specific event that results in involuntary employee termination.

Question C60: Should termination indemnities that are associated with preretirement termination of employment be accounted for as contractual termination benefits?

Answer: *Termination indemnities,* which are more common outside the United States, are amounts payable to employees, often as a lump sum, upon termination of employment. The payment of termination indemnities should be accounted for as contractual termination benefits if they are paid only as the result of a specific event that results in involuntary termination. In these cases, a liability and a loss should be accrued when it is probable that employees will receive this benefit and the amount can be reasonably estimated. If virtually all employees who terminate their employment receive these benefits, the payments are in substance a pension plan and they should be accounted for under the provisions of ASC 715 (FAS-87).

Question C61: If an employer offers for a short period of time special termination benefits to employees, may the employer recognize a loss at the date the offer is made based on the estimated acceptance rate?

Answer: No. Before the employer can recognize a liability and a loss, employees must accept the offer and the amount of the special termination benefits must be reasonably estimable. However, if the offer of special termination benefits is directly related to the disposal of a segment or a portion of a line of business, these benefits should be accounted for in accordance with ASC 225-20-45 (APB-30) (including Interpretation 1 of APB-30).

Question C62: This question has been deleted.

Question C63: Would a gain or loss from a settlement or curtailment or the cost of termination benefits normally be classified as an extraordinary item?

Answer: Not unless the requirements of ASC 225-20-45 (APB-30) for classification as an extraordinary item—i.e., unusual in nature and infrequent in occurrence—are met. In most cases, a pension plan settlement, curtailment, or offer of special termination benefits would not meet the requirements for classification as an extraordinary item.

Question C64: Do any of the following meet the "unusual nature and infrequency of occurrence criteria" of ASC 225-20-45 (APB-30), thereby causing any resulting gain or loss to be classified as extraordinary?

1. An employer terminates its only pension plan and does not establish a successor pension plan.
2. An employer terminates its only pension plan, withdraws excess plan assets, and establishes a successor pension plan, but because of current regulatory guidelines is not permitted to effect the same series of transactions again for 15 years.
3. An employer terminates one of its foreign pension plans, withdraws excess plan assets, and establishes a successor pension plan. The employer has never effected this series of transactions in the past and has no intention of repeating these actions in the future.
4. An employer terminates its underfunded pension plan, and a regulatory agency takes over the pension plan and initiates a lien against 30% of the employer's net worth.

Answer: No. The basic problem with 1. through 4. above is that although they may be infrequent in occurrence, they are not unusual in nature. Terminating a pension plan is a normal occurrence in the current business environment.

Question C65: This question has been deleted.

Question C66: If an employer withdraws excess plan assets from its pension plan and is subject to an excise tax, is the excise tax an expense in the period of the withdrawal or should it be accounted for under the guidance in ASC 740 (FAS-109) as an income tax and deferred if related gains (such as a settlement gain) will be recognized for financial reporting purposes in subsequent periods?

Answer: An excise tax due to an employer's withdrawal of excess plan assets does not constitute an income tax. This excise tax follows a particular transaction, and the presence of taxable income is not a prerequisite for its imposition. Therefore, the excise tax should be recognized in the period the excess assets are withdrawn, and it should not be displayed as part of income tax expense on the income statement.

Questions 67–70: These questions have been deleted.

EITF Issue 91-7 (Accounting for Pension Benefits Paid by Employers after Insurance Companies Fail to Provide Annuity Benefits) (ASC 715-30-35-89 through 35-91)

OVERVIEW

Based on the guidance in ASC715 (FAS-88), a company purchases annuity contracts from an insurance company to settle its obligation under a defined benefit pension plan; the company may or may not terminate the plan. The insurance company subsequently becomes insolvent and is unable to meet its obligation under the annuity contracts. The company decides to make up some or all of the shortfall in payments to the plan's retirees.

ACCOUNTING ISSUE

How should a company account for the cost of making up the shortfall of payments to retirees caused by an insurance company's failure to fulfill its obligation under annuity contracts?

EITF CONSENSUS

The EITF reached a consensus that an employer's assumption of the cost of making up a shortfall in payments to retirees as a result of an insurance company's failure to meet its obligations under annuity contracts should be recognized as a loss to the extent of a gain, if any, and recognized on the original settlement. The loss recognized would be the lesser of (a) a gain recognized on the original settlement and (b) the amount of the benefit obligation assumed by the employer. The excess of the obligation assumed by the employer over the loss recognized should be accounted for as a plan amendment or a plan initiation in accordance with the provisions of ASC 715-30-35-10 through 35-11, 35-13 through 35-14, 35-17 (paragraphs 24 through 28 of FAS-87, Employers' Accounting for Pensions). The accounting thereafter should be in accordance with the provisions of ASC 715 (FAS-87 and FAS-88).

DISCUSSION

Although employers previously settled pension obligations by purchasing annuity contracts, the failure of a number of insurance companies during 1991 caused this Issue to be brought before the EITF. No accounting pronouncement specifically addresses how to account for the obligation discussed in this Issue. Because the employer may or may not be required to assume responsibility for the shortfall, it is not always clear that it is, in fact, a legal obligation.

Under current accounting literature, a pension obligation settled by the purchase of annuity contracts is not included in the accumulated benefit obligation and the projected benefit obligation. Similarly, the value of the annuity contracts is not included in plan assets.

The EITF's consensus adopted one of several approaches discussed by the Task Force, which is based on the view that the transaction consists of two components: a change in estimate and a plan amendment. Proponents of this approach believed that the gain recognized on the settlement was based on an estimate that did not materialize. According to paragraph 10 of APB-20 (Accounting Changes), "accounting estimates change as new events occur, as more experience is acquired, or as additional information is obtained." (Although APB-20 was superseded by FAS-154 (Accounting Changes and Error Corrections) the quote still applies.) They argued that although recognition of a gain was appropriate at the time the obligation was settled, subsequent events resulted in a change in estimate and loss recognition in the period in which additional information became available.

Proponents of this approach believed that the shortfall exceeding the loss recognized as a change in estimate should be accounted for as a plan amendment. The amortization period of prior service cost related to a plan amendment depends on whether employees are active, inactive, or, as stated in ASC 715-30-35-13 (paragraph 26 of FAS-87), costs may be amortized over a shorter period "during which the employer expects to realize economic benefits from an amendment." Employers would have to base their decision on the specific facts and circumstances. Those who supported this approach believed that employers should be able to choose the amortization period that represents the substance of the transaction.

EITF Issue 05-5 (Accounting for Early Retirement or Postemployment Programs with Specific Features (Such as Terms Specified in Altersteilzeit Early Retirement Arrangements)) (ASC 715-30-55-81 through 55-86)

OVERVIEW

The German government has established an early retirement program, referred to as the Altersteilzeit (ATZ) arrangement, under which employees that meet certain age and other requirements transition from full or part-time employment to retirement before their legal retirement age. The German government reimburses employers that participate in the program for bonuses paid to participating employees and for additional contributions paid into the German government's pension program under an ATZ arrangement for a maximum of six years. The program, which was developed in 1996, will expire in 2009.

Typical features of ATZ arrangements include the following:

- Type I: Participants work 50% of a normal full-time schedule during each year of the ATZ period and receive 50% of their salaries each year.
- Type II: Participants work full time for half of the ATZ period (the active period) and do not work for the other half of the ATZ period (the inactive period). They receive 50% of their salary each year of the ATZ period.
- For both Type I and Type II arrangements: The participants receive an annual bonus. Although the amount of the bonus may vary by employer, it generally equals 10–15% of the employee's most recent regular pay before the ATZ period. Therefore, during the ATZ period, employees generally receive 60–65% of their regular pay before the ATZ period. Employers also make additional contributions for the participants into the German government's pension program.

ACCOUNTING ISSUES

1. How should a termination/retirement benefit under a Type II ATZ arrangement be accounted for?
2. How should a government subsidy under Type I and Type II ATZ arrangements be accounted for?

EITF CONSENSUS

The EITF reached the following consensus positions:

1. For Type II ATZ arrangements, employers should account for the bonus feature and additional contributions into the German government's pension program as postemployment benefits under the guidance in ASC 712 (FAS-112, Employers' Accounting for Postemployment Benefits). Additional compensation should be recognized from the time an employee signs an ATZ contract until the end of the employee's active service period.
2. Under Type I and Type II arrangements, employers should recognize the government's subsidy when they meet the necessary criteria and are entitled to receive it.

The FASB staff noted that employers should recognize the salary components of Type I and Type II ATZ arrangements, other than the bonus and additional contributions to the German government's pension arrangement, from the beginning of the ATZ period to the end of the active service period. Under Type II arrangements, the deferred portion of an employee's salary should be discounted if it is expected that the payment will be deferred for longer than a year. The EITF agreed with the FASB staff's view.

FASB RATIFICATION

The FASB ratified the EITF's consensus positions at its June 29, 2005, meeting.

RELATED CHAPTERS IN 2011
GAAP GUIDE, VOLUME II

Chapter 29, "Pension Plans—Employers"
Chapter 32, "Postemployment and Postretirement Benefits Other Than Pensions"

RELATED CHAPTERS IN 2011
GAAP GUIDE, VOLUME I

Chapter 33, "Pension Plans"
Chapter 34, "Postemployment and Postretirement Benefits Other Than Pensions"

RELATED CHAPTERS IN 2011
INTERNATIONAL ACCOUNTING/FINANCIAL REPORTING STANDARDS GUIDE

Chapter 7, "Business Combinations"
Chapter 13, "Employee Benefits"
Chapter 16, "Financial Instruments"
Chapter 22, "Interim Financial Reporting"

CHAPTER 31
PERSONAL FINANCIAL STATEMENTS

CONTENTS

Overview	31.01
Authoritative Guidance	
ASC 274 Personal Financial Statements	31.02
SOP 82-1 Accounting and Financial Reporting for Personal Financial Statements	31.02

OVERVIEW

Standards for the preparation of financial statements that have been issued by the FASB and other standard-setting bodies are generally intended for business enterprises. As a general rule, those standards are not intended for use in preparing financial statements for individuals.

SOP 82-1 (Accounting and Financial Reporting for Personal Financial Statements) is the source of GAAP for the preparation of personal financial statements.

AUTHORITATIVE GUIDANCE

ASC 274 Personal Financial Statements

SOP 82-1 (Accounting and Financial Reporting for Personal Financial Statements) (ASC 274-10-05-1 through 05-3; 15-1, 15-2; 25-1; 35-1 through 35-15; 45-1 through 45-13; 50-1, 50-2; 55-1 through 55-7, 55-9 through 55-14)

BACKGROUND

The guidance in ASC 274 (SOP 82-1) addresses the preparation and presentation of personal financial statements for individuals or groups of related individuals (e.g., a husband and wife, a family).

The primary focus of personal financial statements is a person's assets and liabilities. Users of those financial statements normally consider estimated current value information to be more relevant to their decision-making than historical cost information. The guidance in ASC 274 (SOP 82-1) explains how the estimated current amounts of assets and liabilities should be determined and applied in the presentation of personal financial statements.

STANDARDS

Form of the Statements

Personal financial statements consist of the following:

- *Statement of financial condition* Presents the estimated current values of assets, estimated current amounts of liabilities, estimated income taxes on the differences between the estimated current values of assets and the estimated current amounts of liabilities and their tax bases, and net worth as of a specified date.

    The term *net worth* is used to designate the difference between total assets and total liabilities, after deduction of estimated income taxes on the differences between the current amounts of these items and their tax bases.

- *Statement of changes in net worth* Presents the major sources of increases and decreases in net worth (e.g., income (loss), changes in the estimated current values of assets, changes in the estimated amounts of liabilities, changes in the estimated income tax on the differences between the estimated current value of assets and the estimated current amount of liabilities and their related tax bases).

- *Comparative financial statements* Presents information about the current period and one or more prior periods (optional).

Methods of Presentation

Assets and liabilities should be recognized on the accrual basis rather than on the cash basis. The most useful presentation of assets and liabilities is in their order of liquidity and maturity, respectively, without classification as current and noncurrent.

In personal financial statements for one of a group of joint owners of assets, the statements should include only the person's interest as a beneficial owner. Business interests that constitute a large part of a person's total assets should be shown separately from other investments. The estimated current value of an investment in a separate entity should be shown in one amount as an investment if the entity is marketable as a going concern. Assets and liabilities of the separate entity should not be combined with similar personal items.

The estimated current values of assets and the estimated current amounts of liabilities of limited business activities not conducted in a separate business entity (e.g., investment in real estate and a related mortgage) should be presented in separate amounts, particularly if a large portion of the liabilities may be satisfied with funds from sources unrelated to the investment.

Guidelines for Determining Current Values and Amounts

The estimated current value of an asset in personal financial statements is the amount at which the item could be exchanged between a buyer and a seller, each of whom is well informed and willing, and neither of whom is compelled to buy or sell. Costs of disposal should be considered in estimating current values. Recent transactions involving similar assets and liabilities in similar circumstances ordinarily provide a reasonable basis for determining the current value of an asset and the estimated current amount of a liability. In the absence of recent similar transactions, adjustments of historical cost for changes in a specific price index, appraisals, and discounted amounts of projected cash receipts and payments may be appropriate.

Receivables

Receivables should be presented at amounts of cash the person estimates will be collected, using appropriate interest rates at the date of the financial statements.

Marketable Securities

Marketable securities should be based on quoted market prices, if available, based on the closing price on the date of the financial statements if the securities were traded on that date. Bid-and-ask quotations may be used to estimate the current value. An adjustment to market price may be required if the investor owns sufficient amounts of securities that his or her sale of the securities would influence the market price.

Options

If published prices of options are unavailable, the current value of options should be determined on the basis of the values of the assets subject to option, taking into consideration such factors as the exercise prices and length of the option period.

Investments in Life Insurance

The estimated current value of life insurance is the cash value of the policy less the amount of any loans against it. The face value of the policy should be disclosed.

Investments in Closely Held Businesses

There is no one generally accepted procedure for determining the estimated current value of an investment in a closely held business. Alternative valuation procedures include the following:

- Multiple of earnings
- Liquidation value
- Reproduction value
- Appraisal
- Discounted amounts of projected cash receipts and payments
- Adjustments of book value or cost of the person's share of equity

The objective should be to approximate the amount at which the investment could be exchanged between a buyer and a seller, each of whom is well informed and willing, and neither of whom is compelled to buy or sell.

Real Estate

Investments in real estate, including leaseholds, should be presented at current value, with consideration given to information such as the following:

- Sales of similar property in similar circumstances
- The discounted amount of projected receipts and payments relating to the property or the net realizable value of the property, based on planned courses of action
- Appraisals based on estimates of selling prices and costs
- Appraisals used to obtain financing
- Assessed value for property taxes

Intangible Assets

Investments in intangible assets should be based on discounted amounts of projected cash receipts and payments arising from the planned use or sale of the assets. The cost of a purchased intangible asset may be used if no other information is available.

Future Interests and Similar Assets

Nonforfeitable rights to receive future sums should be presented as assets at their discounted amounts if those rights have all of the following characteristics:

- The rights are for fixed or determinable amounts.
- The rights are not contingent on the holder's life expectancy or the occurrence of a particular event, such as disability or death.
- The rights do not require future performance of service by the holder.

Examples of rights that may have these characteristics are guaranteed minimum portions of pensions, deferred compensation contracts, and beneficial interests in trusts.

Payables and Other Liabilities

Payables and other liabilities should be presented at their discounted amounts of cash to be paid. The discount rate should be the rate implicit in the transaction in which the debt was incurred—unless the debtor is able to discharge the debt currently at a lower amount, in which case the debt should be presented at the lower amount.

Noncancelable Commitments

Noncancelable commitments to pay future sums should be presented as liabilities at their discounted amounts if those commitments have all of the following characteristics:

- The commitments are for fixed or determinable amounts.
- The commitments are not contingent on others' life expectancies or on the occurrence of a particular event, such as disability or death.
- The commitments do not require future performance of services by others.

Income Taxes Payable

The liability for income taxes should include unpaid income taxes for completed tax years and an estimate of the amount of income taxes accrued for the elapsed portion of the current year of the financial statements.

Estimated Income Taxes on the Difference between the Estimated Current Values of Assets and the Current Amounts of Liabilities and Their Tax Bases

A provision should be made for estimated income taxes on the difference between the estimated current values of assets and the estimated current amounts of liabilities and their tax bases. This estimate should include consideration of negative tax bases of tax shelters, if any. This amount should be presented between liabilities and net worth in the statement of financial condition. Methods and assumptions used to estimate the income taxes should be disclosed.

Financial Statement Disclosure

Personal financial statements should include information to make the statements adequately informative. The items in the following list, which is not all-inclusive, indicate the nature and type of information that should be disclosed:

- The name(s) of individual(s) covered by the financial statements
- A statement that assets are presented at their estimated current values and liabilities at their estimated current amounts
- The method used to estimate current values of assets and current amounts of liabilities
- If assets are held jointly by the person and others, the nature of the joint ownership
- If the person's investment portfolio is material in relation to other assets and is concentrated in one or a few companies, the names of the companies or industries and the current values of their securities
- If the person has a material investment in a closely held business:
  — The name of the company and the person's percentage ownership
  — The nature of the business
  — Summarized financial information about the assets, liabilities and results of operations of the business
- Descriptions of intangible assets and their estimated useful lives
- Amount of life insurance
- Nonforfeitable rights (that do not have the characteristics described above)
- Tax information as follows:
  — The methods and assumptions used to compute the estimated income taxes on the difference between the estimated current values of assets and the estimated current amounts of liabilities and their tax bases

- Unused operating losses and capital loss carryforwards
- Other unused deductions and credits and their expiration dates
- The difference between the estimated current values of major assets and the estimated current amounts of liabilities or categories of assets and liabilities and their tax bases
* Maturities, interest rates, collateral, and other details related to receivablesand debt
* Noncancelable commitments (that do not have the characteristics described above)

☞ **PRACTICE POINTER:** Generally accepted accounting principles other than those described in ASC 274 (SOP 82-1) may be applicable to personal financial statements. For example, ASC 450 (FAS-5, Accounting for Contingencies), and ASC 850 (FAS-57 (Related Party Disclosures), may provide useful guidance in preparing personal financial statements.

CHAPTER 32
POSTEMPLOYMENT AND POSTRETIREMENT BENEFITS OTHER THAN PENSIONS

CONTENTS

Overview		32.02
Authoritative Guidance		
ASC 715 Compensation—Retirement Benefits		32.04
FSP FAS-106-2	Accounting and Disclosure Requirements Related to the Medicare Prescription Drug Improvement and Modernization Act of 2003	32.04
FIG FAS-106	Guide to Implementation of Statement 106 on Employers' Accounting for Postretirement Benefits Other Than Pensions	32.09
EITF Issue 92-12	Accounting for OPEB Costs by Rate-Regulated Enterprises	32.27
EITF Issue 93-3	Plan Assets under FASB Statement No. 106	32.33
EITF Issue 06-4	Accounting for Deferred Compensation and Postretirement Benefit Aspects of Endorsement Split-Dollar Life Insurance Arrangements	32.34
EITF Issue 06-10	Accounting for Deferred Compensation and Postretirement Benefit Aspects of Collateral Assignment Split-Dollar Life Insurance Arrangements	32.37
Related Chapters in 2011 GAAP Guide, Volume II		32.40
Related Chapters in 2011 GAAP Guide, Volume I		32.40
Related Chapters in 2011 International Accounting/Financial Reporting Standards Guide		32.40

32.02 *Postemployment and Postretirement Benefits Other Than Pensions*

OVERVIEW

ASC 715 (FAS-106, Employers' Accounting for Postretirement Benefits Other Than Pensions) requires the accrual of postretirement benefits in a manner similar to the recognition of net periodic pension cost under FAS-87 (Employers' Accounting for Pensions). The provisions of ASC 715 (FAS-106) are similar in most respects to those of FAS-715 (FAS-87). They would differ only if there are compelling reasons for different treatments.

Similar to ASC 715 (FAS-87), the following features are incorporated in ASC 715 (FAS-106) to address the required accounting for postretirement benefits:

- *Delayed recognition* Certain changes in the obligation for postretirement benefits and in the value of plan assets are not required to be recognized as they occur. Instead, they can be recognized systematically over future periods.

- *Net cost* The recognized consequences of events and transactions affecting a postretirement benefit plan are reported as a single amount in the employers' financial statements. That amount includes at least three types of events or transactions that might otherwise be reported separately—exchanging a promise of deferred compensation for current employee services, the interest cost arising from the passage of time until those benefits are paid, and the returns from the investment in plan assets if the plan is funded.

- *Offsetting* Plan assets (assets that have been segregated and restricted for the payment of postretirement benefits) offset the accumulated postretirement benefit obligation in determining amounts in the employer's statement of financial position. Also, the return on plan assets reduces postretirement benefit cost in the employer's statement of income. That reduction is reflected, even though the obligation has not been settled and the investment in the assets may be largely controlled by the employer, and substantial risks and rewards associated with both the obligation and the assets are borne by the employer.

The FASB has also established accounting standards for employers that provide benefits for former or inactive employees after employment, but before retirement (*postemployment benefits*). ASC 712 (FAS-112, Employers' Accounting for Postemployment Benefits) requires employers to recognize the obligation to provide postemployment benefits in accordance with the guidance in ASC 710 and ASC 420 (FAS-43, Accounting for Compensated Absences) if the criteria for accrual established in that pronouncement are met. If the criteria in ASC 710 and ASC 420 (FAS-43) are not met, an employer should account for postemployment benefits when it is probable that a liability has been incurred and the amount of that liability can be reasonably estimated, in accordance with ASC 450 (FAS-5, Accounting for Contingencies).

The following pronouncements, which are the sources of GAAP for postemployment and postretirement benefits other than pensions, are discussed in the 2011 *GAAP Guide, Volume I,* Chapter 34, "Postemployment and Postretirement Benefits Other Than Pensions."

ASC 360; 710	Omnibus Opinion—1967 (APB-12)
ASC 715	Employers' Accounting for Postretirement Benefits Other Than Pensions (FAS-106)
ASC 712	Employers' Accounting for Postemployment Benefits (FAS-112)
ASC 715	Employers' Disclosures about Pensions and Other Postretirement Benefits—An Amendment of FASB Statements No. 87, 88, and 106 (FAS-132(R))
ASC 715; ASC 958	Employers' Accounting for Defined Benefit Pension and Other Postretirement Plans—An Amendment of FASB Statements No. 87, 88, 106, and 132(R) (FAS-158)

32.04 *Postemployment and Postretirement Benefits Other Than Pensions*

AUTHORITATIVE GUIDANCE

ASC 715 Compensation—Retirement Benefits

FSP FAS-106-2 Accounting and Disclosure Requirements Related to the Medicare Prescription Drug Improvement and Modernization Act of 2003 (ASC 715-60-05-8 through 05-11; 15-11 through 15-13; 35-133 through 35-148; 50-2B, 50-4, 50-6; 55-103; 715-740-10-55 through 10-57, 10-166 through 10-167)

OVERVIEW

The Medicare Prescription Drug Improvement and Modernization Act (the Act) will provide Medicare participants with a prescription drug benefit under Medicare Part D. In addition, sponsors of retiree health care benefit plans providing prescription drug benefits that are at least "actuarially equivalent" to those provided under Medicare Part D will be entitled to receive a federal subsidy.

Under the guidance in ASC 715-60-35-91 (paragraph 35 of FAS-106, Employer's Accounting for Postretirement Benefits Other Than Pensions), plan sponsors are required to consider Medicare in measuring a plan's accumulated postretirement benefit obligation (APBO) and net periodic postretirement benefit cost.

New Features of Medicare under the Act

Two new features have been added to Medicare as a result of the Act: (1) plan sponsors will receive subsidies based on 28% of the annual prescription drug costs between $250 and $5,000 incurred by individual beneficiaries (subject to indexing and the Act's provisions regarding *allowable retiree costs*) and (2) retirees will have the option to decide whether to enroll in a prescription drug benefit under Medicare Part D.

The amount of a plan sponsor's subsidy will depend on how many of the plan's beneficiaries that are eligible for Medicare decide *not* to enroll in Medicare Part D, which is voluntary. The Secretary of Health and Human Services has not yet issued detailed regulations on how to implement the Act, including how to determine whether a plan's prescription drug benefit is "actuarially equivalent" to the benefit under Medicare Part D, the evidence needed to demonstrate actuarial equivalency, documentation requirements for the subsidy, and the manner in which the subsidy will be paid by the appropriate agency.

The per capita claims cost of a plan that has been providing a prescription drug benefit to retirees will depend on (*a*) the extent that current and future retirees will voluntarily enroll in Medicare

Part D and pay a monthly premium, which initially will be $35, and (b) how the Act will affect the trend in health care costs and consumers' behavior.

Other Effects of the Act

Under the Act, plan sponsors will be able to exclude the federal subsidy from their taxable income for federal income tax purposes, which means that the temporary difference related to the APBO that results in a deferred tax asset under ASC 740 (FAS-109, Accounting for Income Taxes) will be affected, depending on how the subsidy is accounted for.

In addition, the Act provides for a two-year transition period during which plan sponsors may amend existing plans or establish new ones in response to the legislation in order to maximize the financial benefit to the entity or improve employee relations. Changes in the benefit formula as a result of plan amendments will affect the APBO.

FASB STAFF POSITION

Question 1: How should the effect of the subsidy on the following matters be accounted for?

1. Benefits attributable to past service
2. Current measures of net periodic postretirement benefit cost
3. Changes in estimates
4. Plan amendments
5. Income tax accounting

Answer: The subsidy's effect should be accounted for as follows:

1. On initial application of the guidance in this FSP, the effect of the subsidy on the APBO should be accounted for as an actuarial experience gain in accordance with the guidance in ASC 715-60-35-23, 35-25, 35-29 through 35-30 (paragraphs 56 and 59 of FAS-106).
2. The subsidy should be included in measuring the cost of benefits attributable to current service because it affects the sponsor's share of the plan's costs. By including the subsidy in the calculation of net periodic postretirement benefit cost, the sponsor's service cost—which is defined in ASC 715-60-35-10 (paragraph 47 of FAS-106)—is reduced.
3. A change in estimate is an actuarial experience gain in accordance with the guidance in ASC 715-60-35-23 through 35-25 (paragraph 56 of FAS-106), if the amount of the estimated expected subsidy changes because of changes in regulations or legislation, changes in the underlying estimates of postretirement prescription drug costs, or other changes that are *not* plan amendments.

4. Sponsors that amend a plan to make it actuarially equivalent to Medicare Part D should combine the direct effect on the APBO and the effect on the APBO from the subsidy that the sponsor expects to receive. If actuarial equivalency under the Act of a plan's prescription drug benefits is disqualified as the result of a subsequent plan amendment that *reduces* the coverage, there is *no* effect on an actuarial experience gain, if any, that was previously recognized. Nevertheless, the combined net effect on the APBO of the plan's loss of (i) actuarial equivalency under the Act as a result of the plan amendment reducing coverage and (ii) the subsidy's elimination should be accounted for as a prior service cost or credit as of the date on which the amendment is adopted.

5. Because the subsidy is exempt from federal taxation, it has *no* effect on temporary differences, if any, under the guidance in ASC 740 (FAS-109) that are related to the plan.

Question 2: What disclosures are required?

Answer: Sponsors that have not yet determined whether the prescription drug benefits are actuarially equivalent to Medicare Part D under the Act should disclose the following information in their interim or annual financial statements:

- The Act's existence
- The fact that a subsidy has not been considered in amounts presented for the APBO or net periodic postretirement benefit cost because it has not been determined whether the benefits under the plan are actuarially equivalent to Medicare Part D under the Act

The following disclosures should be made in the financial statements of the first interim or annual period in which the effects of the subsidy are included in measuring the APBO and in the first period in which the effects of the subsidy are included in measuring net periodic postretirement benefit cost:

- The amount by which the APBO is reduced for the subsidy related to benefits attributed to past service
- The subsidy's effect on the measurement of net periodic postretirement benefit cost in the current period, including the(i) amortization of the actual experience gain, if any, as a component of the net amortization under the guidance in ASC 715-60-35-29 through 35-30 (paragraph 59 of FAS-106); (ii) reduction in current period service cost as a result of the subsidy; and (iii) consequent reduction in interest cost on the APBO due to the subsidy
- Other disclosures under the guidance in ASC 715-20-50-1 (paragraph 5r of FAS-132(R)), which requires an explanation of significant changes, if any, in a plan's benefit obligation or assets that would *not* be obvious in the Statement's other required disclosures

Question 3: What are the effective dates and transition requirements of the FSP?

Answer: This FSP is effective for the first interim or annual period that begins after June 15, 2004. However, the FSP is effective for fiscal years beginning after December 15, 2004, for *nonpublic* entities—under the definition in FAS-87 (Employers' Accounting for Pensions)—that sponsor one or more defined benefit postretirement health care plans that provide prescription drug coverage if no plan has more than 100 participants. Earlier adoption is encouraged in financial statements for periods including or following the Act's enactment if the financial statements have not yet been issued as of the issuance date of this FSP.

After this FSP's effective date, if a sponsor concludes that the effects of the Act (including a subsidy, if any, changes in participation rates, and changes in estimated care cost) do *not* constitute a significant event under the guidance in ASC 715-60-35-126 (paragraph 73 of FAS-106), those effects should be included in the next measurement of the plan's assets and obligations, as required under the guidance in ASC 715 (FAS-106). However, if a sponsor concludes that the effects of the Act constitute a significant event, the sponsor should measure the effects of the Act, if any, other than the subsidy, at the next measurement date for plan assets and obligations in accordance with the guidance in this FSP, even if the plan's benefits are *not* actuarially equivalent to those under Medicare Part D or the sponsor is unable to determine whether any of the plan's benefits are actuarially equivalent.

The effective date and transition of this FSP also apply to sponsors that elected deferral under FSP FAS-106-1, which has been superseded by this FSP, but whose deferral expired as a result of a subsequent event, such as a plan amendment, before the issuance of this FSP.

Question 4: What is the transition for a sponsor that elected deferral if (*a*) the plan provides actuarially equivalent benefits as of the Act's enactment date based on information available at the date this FSP is adopted and (*b*) enactment of the Act was a significant event for the plan?

Answer: The FSP provides the following transition methods:

- *Retroactive application to the date of enactment* Under this transition method, the plan's assets and APBO—including the effects of the subsidy, if applicable, and other effects of the Act—should be remeasured (i) when this FSP is first adopted as of the usual measurement date that would have followed the Act's enactment or (ii) at the end of the sponsor's interim annual period that includes the date of the Act's enactment, whichever is earlier. However, sponsors also are permitted to remeasure as of the date of enactment. The APBO should be measured based on the plan's existing provisions on the measurement date. Plan amendments that occur after the measurement date on (i) or (ii), above, should *not* be anticipated and should *not* be included in that measurement. If, however, a plan was amended before this FSP's effective date so that the plan would *not* be actuarially equivalent, the effects of the subsidy should *not* be included in the transition measurement under this FSP. The effects of an amendment of a prescription drug plan and the resulting effects of the subsidy should be accounted for in accordance with the guidance in paragraph (e) of the answer to Question 1.

The accrued or prepaid postretirement benefit cost reported in a sponsor's balance sheet generally will *not* be affected by the measurement of plan assets and obligations in accordance with the guidance in the previous paragraph. However, the amount of net periodic postretirement benefit cost for periods *after* the remeasurement date will be affected by those remeasurements and should be accounted for in accordance with the guidance in ASC 250-10-45-5 (paragraph 7 of FAS-154). The guidance in ASC 250-10-45-14 through 45-17 (paragraphs 15 through 16 and paragraph 19 of FAS-154, and paragraph 28 of APB-28) should be followed if previously issued financial reports for periods *before* the effective date of this FSP would have been affected by the remeasurement guidance in the previous paragraph. The guidance in paragraph (e) of the answer to Question 1 of this FSP applies to the calculation of the effects on prior periods of plan amendments adopted after the measurement date discussed in the paragraph above but before the effective date of this FSP. The effects of such an amendment should be determined as of the date of the plan amendment's adoption.

- *Prospective application as of the application date*   The plan's assets and APBO—including the effects of the subsidy, if applicable, and other effects of the Act—should be remeasured in accordance with the guidance in ASC 715-60-35-125 (paragraph 73 of FAS-106) as of the beginning of the period in which this FSP is first adopted. The APBO should be measured based on the plan's existing provisions at the measurement date and should include the best available information about actuarial assumptions and discount rates. Net periodic postretirement benefit cost in interim periods *after* the adoption date and until the measurement date otherwise required in ASC 715 (FAS-106) should be determined based on those measurement results.

Question 5: How should a *nonpublic* entity with only small plans account for the effects of the Act?

Answer: A *nonpublic* entity that meets the criteria in the first paragraph of the answer to Question 3 and for whose plan the Act is a significant event should follow the guidance in paragraph (a) of the answer to Question 4, including the related transition guidance. Alternatively, the entity may include the effects of the Act prospectively in measurements of net periodic postretirement benefit cost and plan assets and obligations for fiscal years beginning after December 15, 2004.

Question 6: How should sponsors that did *not* elect deferral account for the effect of the Act?

Answer: Sponsors that did *not* elect deferral under FSP FAS-106-1 and whose previous accounting for the effects of the Act differs from the provisions of this FSP should account for the adoption of this FSP as a change in accounting principle under the guidance in FAS-154 (*ASC 250, Accounting Changes and Error Corrections*). Such entities should present in their financial statements the cumulative effect of retroactive application of this FSP to the date on which the Act was enacted in accordance with the guidance in ASC 250-10-45-5 and ASC 250-10-45-14 through 45-16, as applicable.

Question 7: After adoption of this FSP, how should an employer determine a plan's actuarial equivalence without a plan amendment?

Answer: A sponsor that was unable to determine whether its plan is actuarially equivalent to Medicare Part D on adoption of this FSP may receive new information about the Act, such as regulations clarifying actuarial equivalency or interpretive information. If after reconsideration of actuarial equivalency of the plan's benefits the sponsor concludes that there is actuarial equivalence, that conclusion may be a significant event under the guidance in ASC 715-60-35-126 (paragraph 73 of FAS-106). If the effects of the subsidy on the plan are significant, the plan's assets and obligations should be measured as of the date that actuarial equivalency was determined. The subsidy's effect on the APBO should be presented as an actuarial gain in accordance with the guidance in paragraph (a) of the answer to Question 1 of this FSP. The amount of net periodic postretirement benefit cost in later periods should include the effects of those measurements. However, prior financial statements should *not* be retroactively adjusted. A cumulative effect for prior periods also should *not* be recognized in income.

FIG FAS-106 Guide to Implementation of Statement 106 on Employers' Accounting for Postretirement Benefits Other Than Pensions (ASC 715-20-55-1, 55-2; 715-60-15-5,15-6; 25-4; 35-21, 35-33, 35-64 through 35-65, 35-96, 35-111 35-113, 35-168; 55-1 through 55-25, 55-27 through 55-30, 55-32 55-34, 55-106 through 55-111, 55-140, 55-142 through 55-175; 715-70-55-2, 55-3; 80-55-3 through 55-5; 710-10-55-2, 55-5 through 55-6; 60-3)

OVERVIEW

The following Implementation Guide is based on the guidance in FSP FAS-158-1, which superseded the guidance in the Implementation Guide for ASC 715 (FAS-106, A Guide to Implementation of Statement 106 on Employers' Accounting for Pensions), which consisted of questions and answers developed by the FASB staff in response to inquiries from constituents. The guidance below, which was included in the Implementation Guide, was carried over into ASC 715 (FAS-106) as Appendix F and is included in the Accounting Standards Codification as noted above.

ASC 715-FAS-106—APPENDIX F

Scope

Question F1: Does this Statement apply to long-term disability benefits paid to former employees on disability retirement under an employer's postretirement benefit plan?

Answer: Yes, as long as the benefits provided are postretirement benefits. Disability benefits paid to former or inactive employees who are not on disability retirement should be accounted for in accordance with ASC 712 (FAS-112, Employers' Accounting for Postemployment Benefits). Similarly, if disability income benefits are paid pursuant to a pension plan, the applicable accounting guidance is found in ASC 715 (FAS-87, Employers' Accounting for Pensions).

Question F2: If some employees, upon their retirement, voluntarily elect under the provisions of the Consolidated Omnibus Budget Reconciliation Act of 1985 (COBRA), as amended, to continue their health care coverage provided through the active employee health care plan and the cost to the employer of their continuing coverage exceeds the retirees' contributions, should the employer account for that cost under the guidance in ASC 715 (FAS-106)?

Answer: No. The right to continue health care coverage under COBRA is not based on employee retirement. This right generally is available to any terminated employee. Therefore, employers should follow the guidance in ASC 712 (FAS-112) when the cost of continuing health care coverage under COBRA exceeds the former employees' contributions.

Question F3: A collectively bargained defined benefit postretirement health care plan of a single employer may stipulate that benefits will be provided for the duration of the collective-bargaining agreement, or the plan may imply or explicitly state that benefits are subject to renegotiation upon the expiration of the current collective-bargaining agreement. Past negotiations have resulted in the continuation of the plan, although the plan has been amended at various times. Should the accumulated postretirement benefit obligation (APBO) be measured based only on benefits expected to be paid during the period in which the current agreement will be in force?

Answer: No. The APBO should be measured assuming that the defined benefit postretirement health care plan will continue after the expiration of the existing collective-bargaining agreement. Unless there is evidence to the contrary, a postretirement benefit plan that currently exists is expected to continue in the future.

Contracts Involving Deferred Compensation

Question F4: How should an employer account for a deferred compensation contract that does not provide a vested benefit for the employee's prior service at the date the contract is entered into? For example, an employee must render 30 years of service to receive benefits under a deferred compensation contract and has rendered 16 years of service at the date of entering into the contract. Credit is granted for that prior service in determining eligibility for the benefit to be provided. Should the total obligation be accrued over the remaining 14 years of service, or should the employer immediately recognize the portion related to the 16 years of service already rendered?

Answer: The total obligation under the deferred compensation contract should be accrued over the remaining 14 years of service. An obligation related to the prior service would be accrued only if the employee was entitled to part of the benefit without regard to future service (i.e., if the credit for prior service results in a vested benefit).

Question F5: An employee becomes fully eligible for benefits under a deferred compensation contract five years after entering into the contract. The contract states, however, that if the employee dies or becomes disabled, benefits will be payable immediately. The contract is not one of a group of contracts that possess the characteristics of a pension plan. What is the attribution period?

Answer: If the employee is expected to provide service over the five-year period, the obligation should be accrued over this time period. If the employee dies or becomes disabled before the five-year period expires, any remaining unrecognized cost would be recognized in the period in which the death or disability occurred. No accrual is required if the employee is not expected to work for the employer for the next five years.

Substantive Plan

Question F6: Can future amendments to a written postretirement health care plan that change the amount of a defined dollar cap be anticipated as part of the substantive plan?

Answer: Yes, if the employer's past practices indicate that plan amendments are a common occurrence. For example, the employer may have a history of regularly increasing (or decreasing) the defined dollar cap under a postretirement health care plan.

Question F7: Is a postretirement health care plan with a defined dollar cap considered to be a plan that provides benefits defined in terms of monetary amounts as discussed in paragraph 26 (ASC 715-60-35-56)?

Answer: No. In this scenario, the benefit is reimbursement of specified eligible medical claims. The fact that the employer's reimbursement of these claims is limited to a specific dollar amount (i.e., the dollar cap) does not indicate that the benefits are defined in monetary amounts.

Measurement

Question F8: Should the assumed discount rates used to measure an employer's postretirement benefit obligation be the same rates used to measure its pension obligation under the guidance in ASC 715 (FAS-87)?

Answer: Not necessarily. As in FAS-87, the discount rate chosen to measure the liability for postretirement benefit obligations should reflect the interest rate on high-quality debt instruments of a duration comparable to that of the benefit obligation. However, a different discount rate may be appropriate, because the timing of expected payments under the postretirement benefit plan may differ from the expected timing of pension payments.

Question F9: An employer sponsors a health care plan that provides benefits to both active employees and retirees under age 65. The plan requires active employees and retirees to contribute to the plan. Can the contributions of active employees ever be used to reduce the employer's cost of providing benefits to retirees?

Answer: Yes, but only if contributions by active employees exceed the cost of providing health care benefits for this group over its working life and the employer has no obligation to refund the excess contributions. The cost of providing health care coverage for active employees should be measured on the assumption they are the only group covered by the plan (i.e., retirees would be excluded in this computation).

Question F10: An employer has a contributory health care plan covering active employees and retirees under which retirees pay 100% of the average cost of benefits determined based on the combined experience of active employees and retirees. The employer pays all of the remaining cost. The active employees do not contribute to the plan. Under this arrangement, does the employer have an obligation under this Statement?

Answer: Yes, if the actual cost of providing health care benefits to retirees exceeds their contributions. If this is the case, the employer is subsidizing the retirees' health care benefits. The employer has an obligation for the difference between the expected cost of the retirees' benefits and the expected contribution amounts.

Question F11: Are there any circumstances under which an employer may measure its postretirement health care benefit obligation by projecting the cost of premiums for purchased health care insurance?

Answer: Yes, if the postretirement benefit plan provides that the benefit to be received by retirees is a payment of their future health care insurance premiums.

Question F12: If an employer has measured its postretirement health care benefit obligation by projecting the cost of premiums for purchased health care insurance, does that reduce or eliminate the applicability of any provisions of this Statement, for example, the calculation and disclosure of service and interest cost?

Answer: No. All of the provisions in this Statement, including the disclosure of service and interest cost, still apply.

Question F13: Should employers assume a trend of decreasing (or increasing) Medicare reimbursement rates if Medicare has consistently reduced (or increased) the portion of benefits it will cover? For example, certain health care costs may have increased by 15% last year but Medicare may have covered only a smaller increase, which increased the employer's or retirees' share of the cost of benefits. When determining its postretirement benefit obligation, should an employer assume that such a reduction in Medicare coverage would continue?

Answer: Generally not. Changes in Medicare coverage should be projected only if they result from currently enacted legislation or regulations. Future changes in Medicare legislation or regulations should not be anticipated even if past experience indicates that such changes are likely.

Attribution

Question F14: An employer modifies the eligibility requirements under its postretirement benefit plan by changing the plan's credited service period from "25 years of service after age 40" to "15 years of service after both (*a*) reaching age 50 and (*b*) rendering 10 years of service." What is the beginning of the attribution period?

Answer: The credited service period for this pension plan is undefined. Therefore, the attribution period begins on the date of hire. The net effect of the above change is to lengthen the attribution period for employees under age 40.

Question F15: An employer provides retiree health care and life insurance benefits under one plan. Employees are eligible for health care and death benefits upon attaining age 55 and having rendered 20 years of service; however, the life insurance benefits are based on final pay. Does basing the life insurance benefits on final pay extend the full eligibility date to a plan participant's expected retirement date? For example, if an employee is expected to fulfill the 20-year service requirement before age 55 and is expected to retire at age 62 with salary increases in all years of service, is the employee's full eligibility date the date he or she reaches age 62?

Answer: Yes, assuming the additional life insurance benefits earned between age 55 and the employee's expected retirement date are not trivial in relation to the total benefit to be received. This postretirement benefit plan has an indefinite credited service period. Therefore, the attribution period begins on the date of hire and ends on the full eligibility date. The full eligibility date is the date on which an employee has earned all of the benefits that he or she will receive under the postretirement benefit plan. In this case, the full amount of life insurance benefits to be received will not be known until the employee retires.

Question F16: Would the answer to the question in paragraph F15 be different if the benefits were provided and accounted for under two separate plans, one providing life insurance benefits and the other providing health care benefits?

Answer: Yes. If health care and life insurance benefits are provided under separate plans, the full eligibility date would be determined separately for each plan.

Question F17: If the terms of the plan in the question in paragraph F15 specified which 20-year service period constituted the credited service period—for example, the first 20 years after date of hire, or the first 20 years of service after age 35—would basing life insurance benefits on final pay still extend the full eligibility date to the expected date of retirement?

Answer: Yes, assuming the additional life insurance benefits earned between age 55 and the employee's expected retirement date are not trivial in relation to the total benefit to be received.

Question F18: Under what conditions would a plan be considered a frontloaded plan?

Answer: A plan is considered frontloaded if all, or a disproportionate portion of, expected benefits to be received under the plan are attributed to employees' early years of service. If a plan is frontloaded, the expected postretirement benefit obligation (EPBO) should not be attributed ratably to each year of credited service in the credited service period but should be attributed in accordance with the plan benefit formula. The employee group as a whole is evaluated in determining whether the plan is frontloaded.

Illustration of a Frontloaded Plan

TWR, Inc., offers a postretirement benefit plan that provides both health care and life insurance benefits. Employees are eligible for health care and death benefits upon attaining age 55 and after having completed 20 years of service. Life insurance benefits are based on final pay, and employees are expected to receive annual pay raises between age 55 and their expected retirement age, 62. An employee named Jane Doe is hired at age 20 at a starting salary of $30,000. TWR assumes annual pay increases of 4%, a life expectancy of 75 years, and a discount rate of 7%.

Assume that the EPBO for Jane Doe at age 40 is $43,091 ($28,500 for health care benefits and $14,591 for life insurance benefits). A ratable allocation of the EPBO over her expected working life, 42 years, would result in an accumulated postretirement benefit obligation (APBO) of $20,519 at the end of year 20 ($13,571 for health care benefits and $6,948 for life insurance benefits; both of these amounts are 20/42 of the applicable EPBO). Based on the respective benefit formulas, assume that the APBO at the end of 20 years is $28,500 for health care benefits and $6,157 for life insurance benefits. Because the APBO based on the benefit formulas of $34,657 is a significantly greater amount than a ratable allocation of the EPBO of $20,519, the postretirement plan is considered to be frontloaded. For frontloaded benefit plans, benefits should be attributed using the respective benefit formulas. Therefore, TWR would report an APBO of $34,657 for Jane Doe at the end of year 20.

Question F19: An employer has a retiree health care plan that bases benefits on length of service; to be eligible for any benefits under it, employees must render a minimum of ten years of service after they reach age 45. However, upon attaining age 45, employees receive credit for 3% of the maximum benefit for each year of service before age 45. For example, at age 45 an employee hired at age 25 receives credit for 60% (3% × 20 years) of the plan's postretirement health care benefits. When does the credited service period begin?

Answer: The credited service period begins at the date of hire. The total benefits to be received are a function of the total years of service, including service before age 45.

Question F20: An employer requires that, in order to be eligible to participate in its retiree health care plan, an employee must participate in its contributory active health care plan. An employee can join the active plan at any time before retirement but must have worked 10 years and attained age 55 while in service to be eligible for benefits under the retiree plan. When does the attribution period begin?

Answer: At the date of hire if the employee is expected to participate in the active health care plan. This is because the plan does not specify which ten years of service must be worked in order to qualify for benefits under the plan. If an employee is not expected to participate in the active health care plan, the employee would not be considered a plan participant for purposes of the postretirement benefit plan.

Question F21: Should an employer's annual accrual for the service cost component of net periodic postretirement benefit cost relate to only those employees who are in their credited service periods?

Answer: In most cases, yes. However, in some cases a plan will establish a nominal service period in relation to the employee's expected total years of service. For example, an employee is hired at age 25 and is expected to work until age 62. The plan may specify that the credited service period begins at age 55 and runs until retirement. In this case, the credited service period according to the plan would be nominal in relation to the total expected years of service. In such instances, the attribution period, and the recognition of service cost, would begin at the date of hire.

Question F22: In determining the attribution period, what is considered a nominal credited service period?

Answer: Judgment is required in determining what qualifies as a nominal credited service period. Generally the service period would be considered nominal if it is very short in relation to the total expected years of employee service before full eligibility for benefits.

Curtailments and Negative Plan Amendments

Question F23: An employer's previous accounting for postretirement benefits has considered the written plan to be the substantive plan. On July 1, 20X4, its Board of Directors approves a negative plan amendment (i.e., an amendment that reduces benefits attributable to prior service) that will be effective on January 1, 20X6. The employer intends to announce the negative plan amendment to plan participants on July 1, 20X5. When should the effects of the negative plan amendment be considered for accounting purposes?

Answer: July 1, 20X5, the date on which the negative plan amendment is communicated to employees. It would have been appropriate to account for the effects of the negative plan amendment on July 1, 20X4, the date the amendment was approved by the Board, if the amendment had been communicated to employees at that time or within a reasonable period of time thereafter. A reasonable period of time would be the time it would normally take to prepare information about the amendment and to distribute it to employees and retirees. A one-year period is excessive for this purpose.

Question F24: Is it important to distinguish between a reduction in the accumulated postretirement benefit obligation (APBO) caused by a negative plan amendment and a reduction caused by a curtailment?

Answer: Yes. A reduction in the APBO caused by a curtailment is potentially recognizable as a current component of income. Conversely, a reduction in the APBO caused by a negative plan amendment that exceeds any prior service cost or transition obligation included in accumulated other comprehensive income is *not* immediately recognized as a reduction of current postretirement benefit costs.

Question F25: What is the difference between a negative plan amendment and a curtailment that reduces the APBO?

Answer: A negative plan amendment is a change in the terms of the plan that reduces or eliminates benefits for employee services already rendered. A curtailment reduces the APBO by reducing the number of employees covered under the plan and/or by eliminating the benefits attributable to future service for some or all plan participants.

Illustration of a Negative Plan Amendment and a Curtailment That Reduces the APBO

Company A sponsors a postretirement health care plan that previously was noncontributory. A plan amendment requiring current and future retirees to contribute $200 per month toward the cost of benefits provided would be a negative plan amendment because this change reduces the APBO for employee service already rendered.

Company B sponsors a postretirement life insurance plan. Life insurance benefits previously were defined based on final pay. Company B changes this plan on December 31, 20X4, to fix the life insurance benefits payable based on salaries in effect on that date. This change qualifies as a curtailment because the accrual of additional death benefits based on future employee service has been eliminated.

Question F26: Company B sponsors a postretirement life insurance plan. Life insurance benefits previously were defined based on final pay. Company B changes this plan on December 31, 20X4, to fix the life insurance benefits payable based on salaries in effect on that date. Before this change, the APBO at December 31, 20X4, included an amount—$400,000—based on projected future employee pay levels. Thus, the APBO at December 31, 20X4, decreases by $400,000 as a result of the plan amendment because increases in employees' future pay levels will no longer increase their death benefits under the plan. Why is the $400,000 a "potentially" currently recognizable curtailment gain?

Answer: Whether any or all of the $400,000 curtailment gain should be recognized currently as a component of net periodic postretirement benefit cost depends on the existence and amount of a net loss included in accumulated other comprehensive income for prior service cost, or a transition obligation included in accumulated other comprehensive income that must be offset before a curtailment gain can be recognized.

Question 27: Should the accounting for a curtailment always consider any prior service cost included in accumulated other comprehensive income or a transition obligation included in accumulated other comprehensive income?

Answer: Yes. The theoretical reason for not immediately recognizing prior service cost as a current component of postretirement benefit cost is that amendments of the postretirement benefit plan will result in a positive future economic benefit (e.g., a more motivated and committed workforce). A curtailment raises doubt about the existence of these future economic benefits. Therefore, this Statement requires recognition in net periodic postretirement benefit cost of any prior service cost included in accumulated other comprehensive income. In the case of a curtailment, any transition obligation remaining in accumulated other comprehensive income is considered to be a prior service cost.

Question F28: Does a curtailment result only from events that occur outside a postretirement benefit plan?

Answer: No. Although many curtailments result from events that occur outside the postretirement benefit plan—for example, (*a*) closing a plant, (*b*) selling a division or subsidiary, or (*c*) laying off a number of employees—a curtailment can also result from events that occur inside—for example, from a negative plan amendment that has the effect of eliminating the accrual of some or all of the future benefits for a significant number of plan participants.

Question F29: Does a gain result if, at the time of a curtailment, there exists negative prior service cost included in accumulated other comprehensive income due to a previous plan amendment that reduced benefits under the plan?

Answer: Yes. In accounting for a curtailment, a (negative) prior service cost included in accumulated other comprehensive income that results from a reduction in benefits (a negative plan amendment) is treated the same as a prior service cost that results from an increase in benefits. Therefore, any *negative* prior service cost included in accumulated other comprehensive income associated with future years of service that are affected by the curtailment is a gain. To the extent that this gain is not offset by any other curtailment losses, it is recognized currently as a component of income.

Question F30: What are examples of the accounting for a negative plan amendment that results in a curtailment?

Answer: The first illustration that follows is an example of a negative plan amendment that results in a curtailment gain. The second illustration is an example of a negative plan amendment that results in a curtailment loss.

Illustration of Negative Plan Amendment—Curtailment Gain

X, Inc., sponsors a defined benefit postretirement benefit plan. The only benefit provided under the plan is a life insurance benefit. The amount of life insurance provided under the plan is based on final pay levels. On December 31, 20X8, X, Inc., eliminates this benefit for employees who are not age 45 or older. This group constitutes a significant portion of the workforce of X, Inc. This change in the postretirement benefit plan results in two separate reductions in the APBO. First, benefits earned by employees under age 45, based on prior pay levels, are eliminated (resulting in a $300,000 reduction in the APBO). Second, the APBO had been calculated based on assumptions about the future of those employees' pay levels. Because employees under age 45 will no longer be plan participants, the future pay levels of those employees, which were considered in calculating the APBO, are no longer relevant (resulting in a $500,000 reduction in the APBO). This change in the postretirement benefit plan results in the elimination of future benefit accruals for that group of employees. As such, the $500,000 reduction in the APBO is potentially recognizable as a current curtailment gain. This curtailment would be accounted for in the following manner:

	December 31, 20X8					
	Before Negative Plan Amendment	Negative Plan Amendment	After Negative Plan Amendment	Curtailment	After Curtailment
(APBO)	$(1,500,000)	$ 300,000	$(1,200,000)	$ 500,000	$(700,000)
Recognized liability					
Prior service cost	100,000	(100,000)	-0-		
Transition obligation	140,000	(140,000)	-0-		

Net loss	200,000		200,000	(200,000)	
Negative prior service cost		(60,000)	(60,000)		(60,000)
	$ 440,000	$ (300,000)	$ 140,000	$ (200,000)	$ (60,000)

The journal entry to record the negative plan amendment is as follows:

Postretirement benefit liability	$300,000	
Other comprehensive income		$300,000

The journal entry to record a curtailment gain is as follows:

Postretirement benefit liability	$500,000	
Other comprehensive income		$200,000
Curtailment gain		$300,000

The following facts should be noted about the above accounting:

1. Any decrease in the APBO as a result of a negative plan amendment is used first to reduce any existing prior service cost included in accumulated other comprehensive income and then to reduce any transition obligation included in accumulated other comprehensive income. Any amount that remains from the negative plan amendment is treated as "negative prior service cost." The negative prior service cost, $60,000, is recognized by amortization over future periods beginning January 1, 20X8. The negative prior service cost is amortized and recognized in net periodic postretirement benefit cost by assigning an equal amount to each remaining year of service up to the full eligibility date for each plan participant who was active at the date of the amendment but was not yet fully eligible for benefits at that date. Only participants who are over age 45 and who do not yet qualify for plan benefits qualify under this definition.

2. The decrease in the APBO as a result of the curtailment is used first to reduce any net loss included in accumulated other comprehensive income on the curtailment date. Any remaining curtailment amount is recognized currently in income. The curtailment gain currently recognized is *not* a component of net periodic postretirement benefit cost and should be disclosed separately.

Illustration of Negative Plan Amendment—Curtailment Loss

Crown Color, Inc., sponsors an unfunded postretirement health care plan covering employees at three locations. On December 1, 20X8, Crown Color amends its benefit plan. Any employee of its Butte, Montana, plant who does not retire by December 31, 20X8, is not entitled to receive benefits under the plan. Employees of the Butte plant who retire by December 31, 20X8, will receive benefits under the terms of the postretirement health care plan. Crown Color's employees at its other two locations are not affected by this change in the postretirement benefit plan.

32.20 *Postemployment and Postretirement Benefits Other Than Pensions*

As a result of the above, Crown Color's accumulated postretirement benefit obligation is reduced by $200,000. This reflects an elimination of benefits attributed to years of service already rendered by employees who are not yet eligible to retire and to service rendered by eligible employees who choose not to retire (this reduction represents the results of the negative plan amendment). As a result of the early retirement of other (eligible) employees at the Butte plant, Crown Color's APBO increases by $100,000 (this represents a curtailment).

Before these changes, Crown Color's transition obligation included in accumulated other comprehensive income was $400,000. At the date of transition to this Statement, the remaining expected years of service of employees at the Butte location represented 35% of the total remaining expected years of service of all of Crown Color's employees. This will be accounted for in the following manner:

	December 31, 20X8				
	Before Negative Plan Amendment	Negative Plan Amendment	After Negative Plan Amendment	Curtailment	After Curtailment
(APBO) Recognized liability	$(475,000)	$ 200,000	$ (275,000)	$(100,000)	$(375,000)
Amounts recognized in accumulated other comprehensive income:					
Prior service cost	50,000	(50,000)	- 0 -		
Transition obligation	400,000	(150,000)	250,000	(87,500)	162,500
Net gain	(75,000)				
	$375,000	$(200,000)	$175,000	$(12,500)	$162,500

The journal entry to record the negative plan amendment is:

Postretirement benefit liability	$200,000	
Other comprehensive income		$200,000

The journal entry to record the curtailment loss is:

Curtailment loss	$100,000	
Other comprehensive income	$12,500	
Postretirement benefit liability		$112,500

The following facts should be noted about the above accounting:

1. The increase in the APBO as a result of the curtailment is used first to reduce any net gain recognized in accumulated other comprehensive income at the date of the curtailment.

2. As a result of the plan amendment, 35% of the total expected remaining years of service, for all of Crown Color's locations, have been eliminated. Therefore, Crown Color should accelerate the recognition of 35% of the transition obligation remaining in accumulated other comprehensive income *after* the negative plan amendment is recorded (i.e., 35% of $250,000, the transition obligation remaining in accumulated other comprehensive income after the negative plan amendment becomes effective, is immediately recognized).

3. The curtailment loss is not a component of net periodic postretirement benefit cost and therefore should be disclosed separately.

Question F31: An employer adopts an amendment to its postretirement health care plan that has the dual effect of expanding the plan's coverage and increasing the deductible. Should the increase in the deductible be measured and recognized separately from the benefit improvement?

Answer: No. It is not unusual for numerous plan changes to be made at the same time. Some of the changes may increase benefits; other changes may decrease benefits. All of the changes should be considered together to determine whether there has been a net increase in benefits (a positive plan amendment) or a net decrease in benefits (a negative plan amendment).

Gains and Losses

Question F32: In applying the provisions of paragraphs 59 and 60 (ASC 715-60-35-29, 35-32) for the recognition of gains and losses as a component of net periodic postretirement benefit cost is it appropriate for an employer to elect annually a new method of amortization of gains and losses included in accumulated other comprehensive income?

Answer: No. The employer should choose a method of amortizing gains and losses and follow the chosen method consistently from period to period. Any change in the method of recognizing gains and losses would fall within the scope of ASC 250 (FAS-154, Accounting Changes and Error Corrections) and would need to meet the preferability requirement of ASC 250 (FAS-154) for an accounting change. Although the employer has some discretion in choosing how to recognize gains and losses, the amortization of these items must equal or exceed the minimum amortization as set forth in paragraph 59 of this Statement (ASC 715-60-35-29, 35-30).

Question F33: An employer sponsors a contributory postretirement health care plan that has an annual limitation on the dollar amount of the employer's share of the cost of benefits (a defined dollar-capped plan). The cap on the employer's share of annual costs and the retirees' contribution rates are increased 5% annually. Any amount by which incurred claims costs exceed the combined employer and retiree contributions is initially borne by the employer but is passed back to retirees in the subsequent year through supplemental retiree contributions for that year. In 20X8, incurred claims costs exceed the combined employer and retiree contributions, requiring a supplemental retiree contribution in 20X9. If the employer decides in 20X9 to absorb the excess that arose in 20X8 rather than pass it on to the retirees, when should the employer recognize as a component of net periodic postretirement benefit cost the loss due to that temporary deviation from the substantive plan?

Answer: The loss should be recognized as a component of net periodic postretirement benefit cost at the time the employer makes the decision to deviate from the substantive plan. In this case, the loss would be recognized in 20X9.

Question F34: If an employer previously projected that health care costs under a defined dollar capped plan would exceed the cap in 20X8, but actual claims in that year do not exceed the cap, should a gain be recognized immediately as a component of net periodic postretirement benefit cost in 20X8 in accordance with paragraph 61 (ASC 715-60-35-34, 35-35)?

Answer: No. The above situation represents a situation where the experience of the benefit plan is better than expected. This situation gives rise to an unrealized gain. Under the provisions of FAS-106, paragraph 56 (ASC 715-60-35-23 35-25), this type of gain should be recognized in accumulated other comprehensive income (see question in paragraph F59). A gain is recognized immediately as a component of net periodic postretirement benefit cost only when the employer deviates, on a temporary basis, from the provisions of the substantive plan and, as a result, there is a reduction in the APBO.

Question F35: What situation would result in a gain that would be recognized immediately as a component of net periodic postretirement benefit cost in accordance with paragraph 61 (ASC 715-60-35-34, 35-35)?

Answer: A gain would be recognized immediately as a component of net periodic postretirement benefit cost if plan participants agreed to make a one-time voluntary contribution to the plan that exceeds the amount called for under the terms of the substantive plan, and future contributions by plan participants are expected to revert to the level specified by the substantive plan.

Plan Assets

Question F36: May an employer include in plan assets the assets of a "rabbi trust" (so named because the first grantor trust to receive a favorable ruling from the Internal Revenue Service was one formed for a rabbi)?

Answer: No. Plan assets held in a rabbi trust are *explicitly* available to the employer's creditors in the event of bankruptcy. Under the guidance in this Statement, assets must be segregated and restricted (typically in a trust) to qualify as plan assets. EITF Issue 93-3 (Plan Assets under FASB Statement No. 106) (see page 33) states that a trust does not have to be "bankruptcy-proof" for the trust assets to qualify as plan assets under the guidance in ASC 715 (FAS-106). However, the EITF states that trust assets would *not* qualify as plan assets if such assets were *explicitly* available to the employer's general creditors in the event of bankruptcy.

Question F37: An insurance contract with a captive insurance company does not qualify as a plan asset. However, can an investment contract with a captive insurance company qualify as a plan asset if it meets the criteria in paragraph 63 (ASC, *Glossary*)?

Answer: Yes, assuming the investment contract with the captive insurance company is segregated and restricted for the payment of plan benefits (see paragraphs 7 and 8 of FAS-97 (Accounting and Reporting by Insurance Enterprises for Certain Long-Duration). Contracts and for Realized Gains and Losses from the Sale of Investments) (ASC 944-20-25-16, 25-19)) for a definition of *investment contract)*. An investment contract with a captive insurance company represents an obligation of the employer to pay cash to the benefit plan to be used for the purpose of providing postretirement benefits. Since an accrued liability of the employer to pay cash is not considered a plan asset, the investment contract should be considered a debt security of the employer. This debt security must be currently transferable to be included in plan assets.

Question F38: If an employer issues its own debt or equity securities directly to its postretirement benefit trust, may those securities be included in plan assets under the guidance in this Statement?

Answer: Yes, provided there are no restrictions on the transfer of these assets. The plan trustee must have the unilateral right to unconditionally sell, transfer, or otherwise dispose of the securities. Assets that are not currently transferable but that can be converted into transferable assets should not be considered plan assets. For example, nontransferable convertible preferred stock does not qualify as a plan asset even if it can be converted into transferable common stock.

Disclosures

Question F39: This question has been deleted.

Question F40: Should an employer's disclosure of the weighted average of the assumed discount rates for its postretirement benefit obligation be the same as its disclosure for its pension benefit obligation?

Answer: Not necessarily (see the answer to the question in paragraph F8 for additional discussion). Even if the assumed discount rates are the same, the weighted average of those rates may differ between the timing and pattern of benefits to be provided and may be different for a postretirement benefit plan than for a pension plan. A pension plan typically provides a fixed yearly benefit, which is not expected to change over time. However, a postretirement health care plan is likely to pay more of its benefits as retirees age (since health typically deteriorates with age). If the timing or pattern of postretirement benefits differs from the timing or pattern of pension benefits because of the expected cost of health care, the difference should be considered in the weighting of the assumed discount rates.

Multiple Plans—Employers

Question F41: An employer has two legally separate postretirement benefit plans. Both plans are unfunded (defined benefit) plans covering the same employees. One plan provides postretirement medical care and the other provides postretirement dental care. May the employer account for the two plans as one plan?

Answer: Yes. Paragraph 76 of this Statement (ASC 715-60-35-130), allows the employer to combine unfunded (defined benefit) postretirement health care plans if either (*a*) different benefits are provided to the same group of employees or (*b*) the same benefits are provided to different groups of employees. However, if either of these plans were funded (i.e., if they held plan assets), they could not be combined but must be measured separately.

Question F42: When is it appropriate for the employer in the question in paragraph F4 to change from one-plan accounting to two-plan accounting—that is, to accounting for each plan separately?

Answer: The employer must move to two-plan accounting if the provisions of paragraph 76 (ASC 715-60-35-130) of this Statement are no longer met. For example, two-plan accounting would become mandatory if either (*a*) different benefits were provided to different groups of employees or (*b*) one or both of the plans became funded (i.e., held plan assets). If the conditions of paragraph 76 (ASC 715-60-35-130) continue to be met, the employer would have to meet the preferability requirement of FAS-154 (ASC 250) in order to support a voluntary change from one-plan accounting to two-plan accounting.

Multiemployer Plans

Question F43: An employer that has a single-employer postretirement benefit plan decides to provide health care benefits to its retirees by participating with several unrelated employers in a group postretirement health care benefit arrangement that does not result from collective bargaining. The arrangement is administered by an independent board of trustees and provides a uniform level of benefits to all retirees by utilizing group medical insurance contracts. Each participating employer is assessed an annual contribution for its share of insurance premiums, plus administrative costs. Employers may require their respective retirees to pay a portion of the annual assessment. Retirees whose former employer stops paying the annual assessment have the right to continue participation if they assume the cost of the annual premiums needed to maintain their existing benefits. Should the employer account for this arrangement as a multiemployer plan?

Answer: No. The key factor is that in a multiemployer plan the obligation to retirees does not depend on the former employer's continued participation. This feature is lacking from the above example.

Question F44: May a multiemployer plan be considered a substantially equivalent replacement plan (a successor plan) for an employer that terminates its single-employer defined benefit postretirement plan in such a way that acceleration of the recognition of prior service cost included in accumulated other comprehensive income as a component of net periodic postretirement benefit cost is not required?

Answer: No. Multiemployer plans and single-employer plans are sufficiently different from each other that either one is precluded from being a successor plan for the other. In a multiemployer plan, the employer promises to make a defined contribution. A single employer plan that gives rise to prior service cost is a defined benefit plan. The nature of the employer's promise—to make a defined contribution or to provide defined benefits—is fundamentally different between these two types of plans.

Question F45: This question has been deleted.

Plan Settlements

Question F46: An employer that immediately recognized its transition obligation in income upon adopting the guidance in this Statement subsequently amends its plan to eliminate its obligation for postretirement benefits and partially compensates affected participants by increasing their pension benefits. How should those events be accounted for?

Answer: In this case, the employer has terminated its postretirement benefit plan and has effectively settled its postretirement benefit obligation by increasing the pension benefits that it will provide. The cost to the employer in providing enhanced pension benefits is the cost of settling the postretirement benefit plan. This increase in pension benefits results in an increase in pension liability (or a decrease in pension assets). The obligation for the postretirement benefit plan should be eliminated. The difference between the reduction in the postretirement benefit liability and the increase in the pension liability benefits equals the gain on the plan termination that should be recognized in accordance with the guidance in FAS-88.

Illustration of Immediate Termination of Plan

GPP, Inc., sponsors a postretirement benefit plan and a pension plan. On December 31, 20X8, GPP terminates its postretirement benefit plan. As partial compensation to the employees who are affected, GPP amends its pension plan so that current and future retirees will receive a pension benefit equal to 2% of final salary for each year of employment (GPP's previous pension benefit formula was 2% of an employee's salary over the employee's last five years of service). GPP's postretirement benefit liability at December 30, 20X8, is $4,400,000; the expected benefit obligation on that date is $7,800,000. As a result of the change in the pension plan formula, GPP's pension liability increases by $750,000. GPP wants to determine the gain on the plan termination.

The gain on the plan termination is the difference between the reduction in the accumulated postretirement benefit obligation and the increase in the expected benefit obligation. Therefore, GPP would recognize a gain of $3,650,000 ($4,400,000 − $750,000).

Special Termination Benefits

Question F47: What is the intent of paragraph 102 of this Statement (ASC 715-60-25-6) on special termination benefits?

Answer: This paragraph provides guidance for the employer in accounting for the special termination benefits offered to employees in exchange for early retirement.

Question F48: How should an employer measure the postretirement benefit incentive that employees are to receive in exchange for their early termination of employment?

Answer: The termination incentive typically is measured as the difference between (1) the actuarial present value of the accumulated benefits for the terminating employees considering the enhanced benefits (it is assumed that the employees retire immediately) *and* (2) the actuarial present value, based on benefits attributable to prior service, of the accumulated benefits for the terminating employees without the enhanced benefits. (It is assumed that the employees retire at the earliest date on which they would be eligible for postretirement benefits.)

Defined Contribution Plans

Question F49: An employer has two legally separate postretirement benefit plans: (1) a defined benefit plan and (2) a defined contribution plan. The terms of the defined benefit plan specify that the employer's obligation under that plan is reduced to the extent that a participant's account balance in the defined contribution plan will be used to pay incurred health care costs covered by the defined benefit plan. For purposes of applying the guidance in this Statement, should those plans be considered a single plan or two plans?

Answer: Two plans. The nature of the promises under each plan, the manner in which those promises are satisfied, the availability of plan assets to pay benefits, and the respective accounting for each type of plan are all so dissimilar as to preclude accounting for a defined benefit and a defined contribution plan as a single plan for the purposes of applying the guidance in this Statement.

Question F50: If any assets of the defined contribution plan described in the question in paragraph F49 have not yet been allocated to participants' individual accounts, do they reduce the accumulated postretirement benefit obligation of the defined benefit plan?

Answer: No. The employer's intent to allocate these assets to the accounts of individual employees in the future is not sufficient to reduce the employer's present obligation under the defined benefit plan. Under such an arrangement, the assets of individual employees in the defined contribution plan would be used to pay health care costs incurred in the future (the employer's obligation under the defined benefit plan is limited to covering health care costs in excess of amounts held in individual defined contribution accounts). When unallocated assets are assigned to the accounts of individual employees, the employer's obligation under the defined benefit plan is reduced. This reduction is recognized immediately as a component of net periodic postretirement benefit cost.

EITF Issue 92-12 (Accounting for OPEB Costs by Rate-Regulated Enterprises) (ASC 715-60-60-6; 980-715-25-4 through 25-7; 50-1)

OVERVIEW

Like other entities, rate-regulated entities were required to apply the provisions of FAS-106 (Employers' Accounting for Postretirement

Benefits Other Than Pensions) for fiscal years beginning after December 15, 1992. Under the guidance in ASC 715 (FAS-106), postretirement benefits are considered to be deferred compensation arrangements, which involve an exchange of a promise of future benefits for current services performed by employees. The Statement requires recognition of an obligation over the employees' related service period associated with providing future postretirement benefits to retired employees.

Before the guidance in ASC 715 (FAS-106) became effective, most companies, including regulated entities, were accounting for costs of other postretirement benefits (OPEB costs) on a pay-as-you-go or cash basis. OPEB costs were paid and recognized in the period in which they were incurred. Rate regulators generally permitted including such costs in rates when they were paid. On adoption of under the guidance in ASC 715 (FAS-106), regulated entities not only had to accrue postretirement benefit obligations in their financial statements in the current period, but also had to either recognize a transition obligation relating to prior service costs immediately or amortize that obligation over the employees' average remaining service period, or 20 years, whichever is longer. Therefore, costs recognized under the guidance in ASC 715 (FAS-106) would be significantly higher than those recognized on a cash basis.

As rate-regulated entities were getting ready to adopt the guidance in ASC 715 (FAS-106) for financial reporting, the question arose as to how costs recognized under the requirements of the guidance in ASC 715 (FAS-106) would affect OPEB costs included in rates. If regulators were to permit entities to include in rates all of the costs under the guidance in ASC 715 (FAS-106), (including amortization of the transition obligation), the costs reported in the entity's financial statements and the costs included in rates would not differ. In this case, no deferral of costs or recognition of a regulatory asset would be necessary. However, if regulated entities were not allowed by the applicable regulator to include in rates, the entire amount of the costs charged to customers under the guidance in ASC 715 (FAS-106), some questioned whether regulated entities would have sufficient evidence to meet the criteria in paragraph 9 of FAS-71,Accounting for the Effects of Certain Types of Regulation) for deferral of the difference between the amount charged in rates and the total cost recognized in the financial statements under the guidance in ASC 715 (FAS-106). Under that paragraph, all or part of an incurred cost that would otherwise be charged to expense may be capitalized as a regulatory asset if two conditions are met: (*a*) it is probable that by including the cost in rates charged to customers the capitalized cost will be recovered from future revenues and (*b*) future revenue will result in recovery of a previously incurred cost instead of providing for similar levels of future costs.

ACCOUNTING ISSUES

1. What additional criteria or evidence does a rate-regulated entity need in order to meet the requirements in paragraph 9 of FAS-71 (ASC 980-340-25-1) for recognition of a regulatory

asset related to costs under the guidance in ASC 715 (FAS-106) for which rate recovery has been deferred?
2. Should the conclusions reached in this Issue apply to discontinued plans under the guidance in ASC 715 (FAS-106)?
3. If a rate-regulated entity initially fails to meet the regulatory asset recognition criteria in this Issue, should a regulatory asset be recognized in a subsequent period when the criteria are met?

EITF CONSENSUS

The EITF reached the following consensus positions, which are limited to accounting for regulatory assets related to costs accounted for under the guidance in ASC 715 (FAS-106) by regulated entities that apply the guidance in ASC 980 (FAS-71).

1. Recognition of a regulatory asset should be based on the following guidelines:
   a. *No* regulatory asset should be recognized for costs under the guidance in ASC 715 (FAS-106) if the regulator continues to include OPEB costs of a continuing plan in rates on a pay-as-you-go basis.
   [Several Task Force members noted that ASC 715 (FAS-106) costs should be included in current rates, because they represent current costs of providing the regulated service or product that must be recovered through rates under the provisions of ASC 980 (FAS-71).]
   b. A regulatory asset related to a continuing plan should be recognized for the difference between costs under the guidance in ASC 715 FAS-106) and OPEB costs included in rates if:
      (1) It is probable that at least the amount of the regulatory asset will be recovered from future revenues that include the cost in rates, *and*
      (2) All of the following criteria are met:
         (a) Deferral of costs under the guidance in ASC 715 (FAS-106) and subsequent inclusion of those deferred costs in the entity's rates is allowed by the entity's regulator under a rate order, which includes a policy statement or generic order that applies to entities in the regulator's jurisdiction.
         (b) Annual costs under the guidance in ASC 715 (FAS-106), including amortization of the transition obligation, will be included in rates within approximately five years of adopting the guidance in ASC 715 (FAS-106). Conversion to full accrual accounting may occur in steps, but additional amounts should not be deferred longer than approximately five years.
         (c) The regulator's authorized period for combined deferral and recovery of the regulatory asset should not

be longer than approximately 20 years from adoption of the guidance in ASC 715 (FAS-106). If a regulator requires a deferral period that exceeds 20 years, only the proportionate amount of costs that will be recovered within 20 years should be recognized as a regulatory asset.

(d) For each year, the percentage by which rates increase under the regulatory recovery plan should not exceed the percentage by which rates increased in the immediately preceding year. This criterion is similar to that for phase-in plans discussed in paragraph 5d of FAS-92 (Regulated Enterprises—Accounting for Phase-in Plans) (ASC 980-340-25-3). The Task Force noted that this criterion would be met by recovering the regulatory asset in rates on a straight-line basis.

c. *Transition requirement* The consensus positions discussed above apply to rate-regulated entities that elect to immediately recognize the transition obligation in accordance with the guidance in ASC 715 (FAS-106) and to entities that elect to delay recognition of the transition obligation and amortize it in accordance with the guidance in ASC 715 (FAS-106).

d. *Disclosure* Rate-regulated entities should disclose the following information about costs urecognized under the guidance in ASC 715 (FAS-106) in their financial statements:

(1) A description of the regulatory treatment of OPEB costs

(2) The status of any pending regulatory action

(3) The amount of any costs recognized under the guidance in ASC 715 that have been deferred as a regulatory asset at the balance sheet date

(4) The expected period of recovery of deferred amounts through rates

2. A regulatory asset of a discontinued plan related to costs recognized under the guidance in ASC 715 (FAS-106) should be recognized if it is probable that an amount at least equal to the deferred asset will be included in rates and recovered in future revenues within approximately 20 years after adopting the guidance in ASC 715 (FAS-106). During that period, rate recovery may continue on a pay-as-you-go basis. For the purpose of this consensus, a discontinued plan is one in which employees do not earn additional benefits for future service (it has no current service costs).

3. The EITF reached a tentative conclusion that a rate-regulated entity that initially does not meet the criteria for recognizing a regulatory asset but that meets the criteria in a subsequent period should recognize a regulatory asset for the cumulative difference between costs under the guidance in ASC 715 (FAS-106) and OPEB costs included in rates since the date the guidance in ASC 715 (FAS-106) was adopted.

SUBSEQUENT DEVELOPMENT

The above consensus was affirmed during the Task Force's discussion of Issue 93-4 in March 1993. At that meeting, the Task Force also reached a consensus on the broader issue, which applies to *all* regulatory assets, not only those for costs accounted fot under the guidance in ASC 715 (FAS-106):

> A regulatory asset should be recognized when a cost meets the asset recognition criteria in paragraph 9 of FAS-71 (ASC 980-340-25-1), even though the cost did not meet those criteria when it was incurred.

During the discussion of Issue 93-4, the Task Force reached a consensus on accounting for impairment of regulatory assets. That consensus was nullified by FAS-121 (Accounting for the Impairment of Long-Lived Assets and for Long-Lived Assets to Be Disposed Of), which amended FAS-71 to provide that a regulated asset should be charged to earnings if it no longer meets the criteria in paragraph 9 of FAS-71 (ASC 980-340-25-1). That requirement continues to apply even though FAS-121 has been superseded by ASC 360 (FAS-144) (Accounting for the Impairment or Disposal of Long-Lived Assets).

DISCUSSION

1. This Issue was brought to the EITF because of concerns about the recoverability of a regulatory asset for costs recognized under the guidance in ASC 715 (FAS-106) through rates in future periods. The underlying premise of ASC 980-340 (FAS-71) is that rates charged to current customers include current costs of providing the regulated service. However, paragraph 9 of FAS-71 (ASC 980-340-25-1) provides for situations in which some costs may be deferred because they are not recovered in rates in the same period in which they are recognized in the financial statements. Some believed that the judgmental criteria in paragraph 9 (ASC 980-340-25-1) are adequate and analogized to accounting for pensions, compensated absences, and taxes by rate-regulated entities.

    However, others were concerned about the changing regulatory environment and questioned the probability that capitalized costs would be recovered. They were concerned whether regulators would permit including costs recognized under the guidance in ASC 715 (FAS-106) in rates because such costs are noncash expenses that represent estimates of costs that will be incurred in the future. Generally, rates charged by regulated entities include costs incurred to provide services in the current period. A further concern was related to the extended time period for recovery of the liability recognized under the guidance in ASC 715 (FAS-106) including the transition obligation, which is related to prior service and could be amortized over more than 20 years.

    The EITF resolved the concerns about recoverability by adding criteria that would tighten the requirements in paragraph 9 of FAS-71 (ASC 980-340-25-1) and by requiring that costs recognized under the guidance in ASC 715 (FAS-106) costs be fully included in rates within approximately 20 years from adoption of the guidance in ASC 715 (FAS-106). Those who supported a 20-year recovery period for the regulatory asset argued that the period should not be shorter for rate-regulated entities than for other entities and that at the end of that period, regulated entities would present costs recognized under the guidance in ASC 715 (FAS-106) in their financial statements in the same manner as other entities.

Another concern was that regulated entities may *backload* the recovery of the regulatory asset for FAS-106 costs. For example, if a portion of costs recognized under the guidance in ASC 715 (FAS-106) is deferred during the first five years, but the asset will not be recovered through rates until years 16 to 20, there was a concern about the probability of recovery.

The Task Force dealt with this concern by adopting the requirement for phase-in plans in under the guidance in ASC 980-340 (FAS-92) which requires a decreasing or steady percentage increase in rates over the recovery period. The Task Force decided not to differentiate between entities that elect immediate recognition of the transition obligation and those electing to amortize it in accordance with the requirements under the guidance in ASC 715 (FAS-106), because the transition method elected would not affect the entity's revenues, net income, or equity during the recovery period if the entity meets the criteria for recognizing a regulatory asset. Although the regulatory asset of an entity that elects immediate recognition of the transition obligation would be larger than that of an entity that elects to recognize it over approximately 20 years, both entities would be recovering the cost through rates based on the guidance in this Issue.

2. The Task Force considered whether a regulated entity with a discontinued OPEB plan—a plan having a transition obligation related to employees' prior service but no current service costs—should be prohibited from recording a regulatory asset like an entity with a continuing plan, if OPEB costs are included in rates on a pay-as-you-go basis. The issue was raised because of concerns that significant amounts of current period operating costs would continue to be deferred over long periods if OPEB costs were to be recovered through rates on a pay-as-you-go basis. Those who supported permitting recognition of a regulatory asset in this situation argued that unlike a continuing plan, which may have increasing deferrals over 30 to 40 years, no current costs would be deferred. Therefore, they did not object to pay-as-you-go recovery if deferred costs will be recovered through rates within approximately 20 years after adoption of the guidance in ASC 715 (FAS-106).

3. Those who supported recognizing a regulatory asset for an incurred cost when it meets the criteria in paragraph 9 of

FAS-71 (ASC 980-340-25-1)—even though the criteria were not met when the cost was incurred—believed that the asset is created by the regulator's rate action rather than by incurring the cost. They referred to paragraph 180 in SFAC-6 (Elements of Financial Statements) (not in ASC), which states that "[t]he ultimate evidence of the existence of assets is the future economic benefit, not the cost incurred." They argued that the regulatory asset should be recognized when it becomes probable that it will be recovered in future rates, even if recovery occurs in a period other than the one in which the cost was incurred. Another argument was that recognition of the regulatory asset when its recovery becomes probable is consistent with a balance sheet approach to financial reporting.

EITF Issue 93-3 (Plan Assets under FASB Statement No. 106) (ASC 715-60-55-26; 710-10-60-2)

OVERVIEW

According to Title I of the Employee Retirement Income Security Act (ERISA), the assets of a pension, profit-sharing, or stock bonus plan must be held in a trust created or organized in the United States. ERISA specifically provides that plan assets held in a trust are protected from the claims of general creditors and are considered bankruptcy-proof. This protection does not appear to extend to assets held to fund other postretirement employee benefits (OPEBs), which are addressed in under the guidance in ASC 715 (FAS-106).

The guidance in ASC 715 (FAS-106) sets standards for accounting for other postretirement benefit costs, specifically health care benefit costs. It requires entities to report their obligations to provide postretirement benefits at the time employees render services necessary to earn benefits. For example, Company X has a policy that all employees with 20 years of service are guaranteed lifetime health insurance coverage. In accordance with the guidance in ASC 715 (FAS-106), the company must currently accrue the expected cost of providing health insurance to match the cost to each employee's actual service period.

Accounting for OPEB plans is similar to accounting for pension plans. Like pension and profit-sharing plans, OPEB plans must maintain sufficient plan assets to fund the expected costs of a postretirement plan. According to paragraph 63 of FAS-106 (ASC, *Glossary*), a plan's assets include stocks, bonds, and other investments that are segregated in a trust and restricted for the purpose of providing postretirement benefits. In accordance with the guidance in ASC 715 (FAS-106), many employers have established trusts to fund OPEB plans. However, some of those trusts are not protected from general creditors in the event of a bankruptcy. Therefore, some have questioned whether a trust established to fund postretirement plans must be bankruptcy-proof.

ACCOUNTING ISSUE

Does a trust established to pay postretirement benefits in accordance with the provisions of ASC 715 (FAS-106) have to be protected from the claims of general creditors in bankruptcy for the trust's assets to qualify as plan assets?

EITF CONSENSUS

- It is not necessary to determine that a trust is bankruptcy-proof for the trust's assets to qualify as plan assets under the guidance in ASC 715 (FAS-106).
- Assets held by a trust that explicitly provides that its trust assets are available to the employer's general creditors if the employer declares bankruptcy would *not* qualify as plan assets under FAS-106.

The Task Force discussed the FASB's conclusion in ASC 715-60-25-111 (paragraph 308 of FAS-106) that "if assets set aside in a separate trust or similar funding vehicle can be used for other purposes at the employer's discretion, then the trust assets should not be considered plan assets." Certain Task Force members stated that if a trust arrangement explicitly makes segregated assets available to satisfy claims of creditors in bankruptcy, that provision would effectively permit using those assets for other purposes at the employer's discretion.

DISCUSSION

Even though the guidance in ASC 715 (FAS-106) is clear that plan assets must be restricted solely to the provision of postretirement benefits and to the payment of retirees' benefits, and that the requirement is consistent with pension accounting, the Task Force's consensus confirms the view that plan assets do not have to be maintained in a bankruptcy-proof trust to qualify as plan assets. Furthermore, proponents of this view argued that accounting is generally based on the "going concern" notion—the possibility of an employer's bankruptcy is remote and protection in bankruptcy is not relevant. Also, in the event of a bankruptcy, the employer would no longer control plan assets, so the issue of proper asset segregation and usage would no longer apply.

Nevertheless, even though the Task Force does not require an explicit protection of plan assets in bankruptcy, its second consensus prohibits an explicit statement that plan assets are available to creditors.

EITF Issue No. 06-4 (Accounting for Deferred Compensation and Postretirement Benefit Aspects of Endorsement Split-Dollar Life Insurance Arrangements) (ASC 715-60-05-14 through 05-15; 15-20 through 15-21; 35-177 through 35-179; 55-176 through 55-177, 55-179)

OVERVIEW

A company may purchase life insurance to protect against a loss of "key" employees, to fund deferred compensation and postretirement benefit obligations, and to provide investment return. Split-dollar life insurance, the structure of which may be complex and varied, is one type of life insurance that may be purchased by a company. The most common types of such arrangements are *endorsement split-dollar* life insurance (owned and controlled by the company) and *collateral assignment split-dollar* life insurance (owned and controlled by the employee).

There is diversity in practice in accounting for the deferred compensation and postretirement features of *endorsement* split-life insurance policies, the terms of which may be as follows:

- The employer pays a single premium at the inception of a policy to insure an employee's life.

- The insurer may charge or credit the policyholder based on negative or positive experience for a specific risk (e.g., mortality risk). The insurer usually realizes an additional premium by adjusting the policy's cash surrender value.

- The employer and an employee enter into a separate agreement whereby the policy's benefits are split between the employer and the employee with the employer endorsing a portion of the death benefits to the employee.

- The employer owns and controls the policy and may terminate the arrangement at will.

- Upon the death of an employee, the employee's beneficiary receives the portion of the death benefits designated to the employee and the employer keeps the remainder.

- An employee's beneficiary may receive the benefit directly from the insurance company or from the employer.

An employee's portion of the death benefits is commonly based on (*a*) the amount by which the employee's portion of the death benefits exceeds the gross premiums, (*b*) the amount by which the employee's portion of the death benefits exceeds the gross premiums plus an additional fixed or variable investment return on those premiums, (*c*) the face amount of the death benefit under the policy less the employee's portion of the policy's cash surrender value, or (*d*) an amount equal to a multiple of the employee's base salary at retirement or death (e.g., twice the employee's base salary).

SCOPE

This Issue applies only to the recognition of a liability and the related compensation costs for endorsement split-life insurance arrangements that are owned and controlled by an employer. It does *not* apply to split-dollar life insurance arrangements that provide a specific benefit to an employee only during the period that the employee is the employer's active employee. The question is how employers should account for the aspects of those policies that are related to deferred compensation, postretirement, or postemployment benefits.

ACCOUNTING ISSUE

When an employer and an employee enter into a split-dollar life insurance arrangement, should the postretirement benefit associated with the arrangement be accounted for in accordance with the guidance in ASC 715 (FAS-106, Employers' Accounting for Postretirement Benefits Other Than Pensions) or that in ASC 715 (APB-12, Omnibus Opinion—1967)?

EITF CONSENSUS

The EITF reached a consensus that an employer should recognize a liability for future benefits associated with an *endorsement* split-dollar life insurance arrangement that is based on a substantive agreement with an employee in accordance with the guidance in ASC 715 (FAS-106, Employers' Accounting for Settlements and Curtailments of Defined Benefit Pension Plans and for Termination Benefits) if a substantive postretirement benefit plan exists. If an arrangement is in substance an individual deferred compensation contract with an employee, the guidance in APB-12 (Omnibus—1967) should be followed based on the substantive arrangement with an employee. The EITF believes that the purchase of a standard endorsement split-dollar life insurance policy does *not* settle an employer's liability for a benefit obligation under the provisions of ASC 715 (FAS-106) or ASC 710-10-25-9 through 25-11 (paragraph 6A through 7 of APB-12). For example, an employer that agrees to maintain a life insurance policy during an employee's retirement should accrue the cost of the insurance policy under the guidance in ASC 715 (FAS-106, or ASC 710-10-25-9 through 25-11 (paragraph 6A through 7 of APB-12). Likewise, an employer that has agreed to provide an employee with a death benefit should accrue a liability in accordance with the guidance in ASC 715 (FAS-106) or ASC 710-10-25-9 through 25-11 (paragraph 6A through 7 of APB-12) over the employee's service period for the actuarial present value of the future death benefit as of the employee's expected retirement date.

The EITF noted that the substance of an arrangement should be determined based on the available evidence, such as an arrangement's explicit written terms, communications from the employer to an employee, and the conclusion as to who is the primary obligor for the postretirement benefit, the employer or the insurance company. For example, an employer's promise to pay a postretirement death benefit even if the insurance company defaults on a payment indicates that the employer has promised to provide a postretirement benefit and is the primary obligor. In addition, if the amount of a death benefit is *not* explicitly related to the insurance policy, the amount of the postretirement benefit should be the amount of the death benefit promised to the employee. In contrast, if under the terms of an arrangement, an employer has *no* obligation to pay a death benefit if the insurance company defaults on a payment, it is an indication that the employer has promised to maintain a life insurance policy during the employee's retirement. Employers should follow the guidance in ASC 715 (FAS-106) and ASC 710-10-25-9 through 25-11 (paragraph 6A through 7 of APB-12), as applicable, to determine how to measure and attribute their cost or obligation under an arrangement.

FASB RATIFICATION

The FASB ratified the EITF's consensus on this Issue at its September 20, 2006, meeting.

EITF Issue 06-10 (Accounting for Deferred Compensation and Postretirement Benefit Aspects of Collateral Assignment Split-Dollar Life Insurance Arrangements) (ASC 715-60-05-15; 35-180 through 35-185; 55-178, 55-180 through 55-181)

OVERVIEW

A company may purchase life insurance to protect against a loss of "key" employees, to fund deferred compensation and postretirement benefit obligations, or to provide an investment return. Two types of split-dollar life insurance arrangements exist: *endorsement* split-dollar life insurance, which is owned and controlled by the company, and *collateral assignment* split-dollar life insurance, which is owned and controlled by the employee.

At its September 7, 2006, meeting, the EITF reached a consensus that an employer should recognize a liability for future benefits associated with an *endorsement* split-dollar life insurance arrangement that is based on a substantive agreement with the employee in accordance with the guidance in ASC 715 (FAS-106, Employers' Accounting for Settlements and Curtailments of Defined Benefit Pension Plans and for Termination Benefits) if a substantive postretirement benefit plan exists. If an arrangement is, in substance, an individual deferred compensation contract with an employee, the guidance in APB-12 (Omnibus—1967) should be followed based on a substantive arrangement with an employee.

In this Issue, the EITF addresses how an employer should account for *collateral assignment* split-dollar life insurance arrangements. Under this type of arrangement, although an employee owns and controls the policy, the employer usually pays all of the premiums and in turn, the employee irrevocably assigns all or a portion of the death benefits to the employer as collateral for the employer's payment of the premiums, which are considered to be a loan. Usually, the employer is entitled to receive a portion of the death benefits equal to the amount of premiums paid by the employer or that amount plus an additional fixed return on the premiums. An employee that retires may have the option or be required to transfer the policy to the employer to satisfy the outstanding loan. Under the Sarbanes Oxley Act of 2002, all public and private entities are required to account for such arrangements as employer loans in accordance with the provisions of ASC 835-30 (APB-21).

Interest on Receivables and Payables. The employer must recognize a receivable from the employee at a discounted amount for the premiums paid.

ACCOUNTING ISSUES

1. Based on a substantive agreement with an employee, should an employer recognize a liability for a postretirement benefit related to a *collateral assignment* split-dollar life insurance arrangement in accordance with the guidance in ASC 715 (FAS-106), if, in substance, a postretirement benefit exists, or in accordance with the guidance in APB-12, if an arrangement is, in substance, an individual deferred compensation contract?

2. How should an employer recognize and measure the asset in a *collateral assignment* split-dollar life insurance arrangement?

EITF CONSENSUS

The EITF reached the following consensus positions:

1. If a substantive postretirement benefit plan exists, an employer should recognize a liability for a postretirement benefit associated with a *collateral assignment* split-dollar life insurance arrangement in accordance with the guidance in ASC 715 (FAS-106). The guidance in ASC 710-10-25-9 through 25-11 (paragraph 6A through 7 of APB-12) should be followed for an arrangement that is, in substance, an individual deferred compensation contract with an employee and if, based on that contract, the employer has agreed to maintain a life insurance policy during the employee's retirement or to provide the employee with a death benefit. If in the past an employer has had a stated or implied commitment to provide an employee with a loan to pay premiums on an insurance policy during an employee's retirement or is currently promising to provide loans in the future, it may be presumed that the employer has in effect agreed to maintain the life insurance policy, unless

there is opposing evidence. An employer that has committed to maintain a life insurance policy or to provide a death benefit after an employee's retirement should account for those obligations as follows:

- Accrue the estimated cost of maintaining the life insurance policy after an employee's retirement in accordance with the guidance in ASC 715 (FAS-106), or
- Accrue a liability for the actuarial present value of a future death benefit as of an employee's expected retirement date in accordance with the guidance in ASC 710-10-25-9 through 25-11 (paragraph 6A through 7 of APB-12).

During its discussions, the EITF noted that to determine whether an arrangement is substantive, all relevant information should be considered, such as the explicit written terms of an arrangement, an employer's communications to the employee, an employer's past administrative procedures for the same or similar arrangements, and whether an employer has the primary obligation for an employee's postretirement benefit. For example, if under the terms of an arrangement, an employer has *no* stated or implied obligation to provide loans to an employee to pay for premiums on a life insurance policy, the employer may have *no* postretirement obligation. In contrast, if under a collateral assignment arrangement with an employee, an employer has a stated or implied obligation to provide an employee with loans to cover the insurance company's gains or losses, the employer may have a postretirement obligation. The guidance in ASC 715 (FAS-106) or ASC 710-10-25-9 through 25-11 (paragraph 6A through 7 of APB-12), as applicable, should be consulted to determine how to measure and assign the cost of the obligation under an arrangement

The EITF noted further that collateral assignment split-dollar insurance arrangements should be reevaluated in periods after their inception based on the guidance in ASC 715 (FAS-106) to determine whether the substance of an arrangement has changed as a result of a change in facts and circumstances, such as an amendment to an arrangement or a change from an employer's past practice, and may require that a liability be recognized or that a previously recognized liability for a postretirement obligation be adjusted.

2. An employer should recognize and measure an asset based on the nature and substance of a collateral assignment split-dollar life insurance arrangement. The EITF noted that to determine the nature and substance of an arrangement, an employer should evaluate (*a*) future cash flows to which the employer is entitled, if any, and (*b*) an employee's obligation and ability to repay the employer. For example, at the balance sheet date, an employer's asset would be limited to the cash surrender value of an insurance policy, if the amount the employer could recover from an

employee or retiree is limited to the amount of the insurance policy's cash surrender value, even if the employer's loan to the employee or retiree exceeds that amount. In contrast, an employer should recognize the value of a loan, including accrued interest, if applicable, based on the guidance in ASC 835-30 (APB-21), if under the arrangement, an employee or retiree is required to repay the employer regardless of the collateral assigned and the employer (*a*) has determined that the employee's or retiree's loan is collectible and (*b*) intends to try to recover the amount by which the loan exceeds the insurance policy's cash surrender value. To determine the nature and substance of a collateral assignment split-dollar life insurance arrangement, an employer should consider all the available information.

FASB RATIFICATION

The FASB ratified the EITF's consensus positions at its March 28, 2007, meeting.

RELATED CHAPTERS IN 2011 GAAP GUIDE, VOLUME II

Chapter 29, "Pension Plans—Employers"
Chapter 30, "Pension Plans—Settlements and Curtailments"

RELATED CHAPTERS IN 2011 GAAP GUIDE, VOLUME I

Chapter 33, "Pension Plans"
Chapter 34, "Postemployment and Postretirement Benefits Other Than Pensions"

RELATED CHAPTERS IN 2011 INTERNATIONAL ACCOUNTING/FINANCIAL REPORTING STANDARDS GUIDE

Chapter 7, "Business Combinations"
Chapter 13, "Employee Benefits"
Chapter 16, "Financial Instruments"

CHAPTER 33
REAL ESTATE TRANSACTIONS

CONTENTS

Overview		33.02
Authoritative Guidance		
ASC 310 Receivables		
EITF Issue 86-21	Application of the AICPA Notice to Practitioners Regarding Acquisition, Development, and Construction Arrangements to Acquisition of an Operating Property	33.04
EITF Issue 89-14	Valuation of Repossessed Real Estate	33.05
ASC 323 Investments—Equity Method and Joint Ventures		
EITF Issue 94-1	Accounting for Tax Benefits Resulting from Investments in Affordable Housing Projects	33.08
ASC 360 Property, Plant and Equipment		
FTB 86-2	Accounting for an Interest in the Residual Value of a Leased Asset	33.11
EITF Issue 84-17	Profit Recognition on Sales of Real Estate with Graduated Payment Mortgages or Insured Mortgages	33.13
EITF Issue 86-6	Antispeculation Clauses in Real Estate Sales Contracts	33.14
EITF Issue 87-9	Profit Recognition on Sales of Real Estate with Insured Mortgages or Surety Bonds	33.15
EITF Issue 88-12	Transfer of Ownership Interest as Part of Down Payment under FASB Statement No. 66	33.17
EITF Issue 88-24	Effect of Various Forms of Financing under FASB Statement No. 66	33.18

33.02 *Real Estate Transactions*

EITF Issue 98-8	Accounting for Transfers of Investments That Are in Substance Real Estate	**33.23**
EITF Issue 00-13	Determining Whether Equipment Is "Integral Equipment" Subject to FASB Statements No. 66 and No. 98	**33.24**
EITF Issue 06-8	Applicability of the Assessment of a Buyer's Continuing Investment under FASB Statement No. 66, *Accounting for Sales of Real Estate*, for Sales of Condominiums	**33.25**
EITF Issue 07-6	Accounting for the Sale of Real Estate Subject to the Requirements of FASB Statement No. 66, *Accounting for Sales of Real Estate*, When the Agreement Includes a Buy-Sell Clause	**33.27**

ASC 970 Real Estate—General

EITF Issue 85-27	Recognition of Receipts from Made-Up Rental Shortfalls	**33.29**
EITF Issue 86-7	Recognition by Homebuilders of Profit from Sales of Land and Related Construction Contracts	**33.31**
EITF Issue 97-11	Accounting for Internal Costs Relating to Real Estate Property Acquisitions	**33.32**

ASC 974 Real Estate Investment Trusts

EITF Issue 95-6	Accounting by a Real Estate Investment Trust for an Investment in a Service Corporation	**33.34**

ASC 978 Real Estate—Time Sharing Activities

SOP 04-2	Accounting for Real Estate Time-Sharing Transactions	**33.37**
Related Chapters in 2011 GAAP Guide, Volume II		**33.47**
Related Chapters in 2011 GAAP Guide, Volume I		**33.47**

OVERVIEW

The timing of revenue recognition is a significant financial reporting issue encountered in accounting for real estate transactions. That issue is addressed in GAAP by classifying real estate transactions into the following three categories:

1. Real estate sales, except retail land sales
2. Sale-leasebacks involving real estate
3. Retail land sales

Standards for the acquisition, development, construction, and sale and rental costs related to real estate projects are also addressed in GAAP. In addition, guidance is provided for the accounting for initial rental operations, as well as rules for ascertaining when a real estate project is substantially completed and available for occupancy.

The following pronouncements, which provide guidance on financial reporting for those types of real estate transactions, are discussed in the 2010 *GAAP Guide Volume I,* Chapter 37, "Real Estate Transactions":

ASC 360	Accounting for Sales of Real Estate (FAS-66)
ASC 970	Accounting for Costs and Initial Rental Operations of Real Estate Projects (FAS-67)
ASC 840	Accounting for Leases:

- Sale-Leaseback Transactions Involving Real Estate
- Sales-Type Leases of Real Estate
- Definition of the Lease Term
- Initial Direct Costs of Direct Financing (FAS-98)

ASC 360   Real Estate Sales (FIN-43)

AUTHORITATIVE GUIDANCE

ASC 310 Receivables

Issue 86-21 (Application of the AICPA Notice to Practitioners Regarding Acquisition, Development, and Construction Arrangements to Acquisition of an Operating Property) (ASC 310-10-05-9; 815-15-55-9, 55-10)

OVERVIEW

Company A, not necessarily a financial institution, makes a 10- to 15-year loan to Company B to acquire an operating property. In addition to paying a market interest rate and fees, Company B agrees that upon sale or refinancing of the loan, it will share with Company A a certain percentage of the property's appreciation, which is calculated as the difference between the original loan balance and the net proceeds from the sale of the property or the property's appraised value. Company B may discontinue paying a portion of accrued interest during the term of the loan but will pay that interest at maturity.

ACCOUNTING ISSUES

1. Does ASC 310-10-5-9;15-5; 25-15 through 25-30; 45-15; 40-3 40-5; 310-35-55-61 (the AICPA's Notice to Practitioners, *ADC Arrangements* (known as the third Notice)) apply to financing of acquisitions of operating properties?
2. If yes, how should its guidance be applied?

EITF CONSENSUS

1. The guidance in the third Notice should be considered by preparers and auditors in accounting for shared appreciation mortgages, loans on operating real estate properties, and real estate acquisition, development, and construction (ADC) arrangements entered into by entities that are not financial institutions, even though the third Notice discussed only ADC arrangements of financial institutions.
2. The nature of expected residual profit should be determined based on the guidance in ASC 310-10-25-15 through 25-17 (paragraphs 3 to 5 of the third Notice, which discuss various profit-sharing arrangements, such as a specific percentage of the borrower's profit on a sale).
3. The Task Force believed that the third Notice is the best guidance available to preparers and auditors on this subject.

OBSERVATION: ASC 810 (FIN-46(R), Consolidation of Variable Interest Entities) requires the consolidation of variable interest entities by an entity that absorbs a majority of a variable entity's expected losses or has the right to receive a greater part of the variable entity's expected residual returns or both.

EFFECT OF ASC 815 (FAS-133)

The embedded equity kicker discussed in this Issue should be analyzed to determine whether it is a separate derivative under the definition in ASC (FAS-133). If not, the above consensus positions continue to apply.

SEC OBSERVER COMMENT

The SEC Observer stated that *all* SEC registrants are expected to follow the guidance in the third Notice for existing and future real estate ADC arrangements.

SUBSEQUENT DEVELOPMENTS

The following events occurred after the EITF's discussion of this Issue:

- The SEC staff issued SAB-71, which incorporates the guidance in the third Notice in its discussion of mortgage loans having the economics of a real estate investment or joint venture instead of a loan. The SAB also refers to the consensus in this Issue and was supplemented by SAB-71A.
- The AICPA's Accounting Standards Executive Committee issued Practice Bulletin 1, which incorporates the third Notice as Appendix I.
- The Federal Home Loan Bank Board (FHLBB) issued a notice that requires all financial institutions insured by the Federal Savings and Loan Insurance Corporation (FSLIC) or its affiliates to follow the principles in the third Notice in classifying and accounting for ADC arrangements in reports or financial statements filed with the FSLIC and the FHLBB.

EITF Issue 89-14 (Valuation of Repossessed Real Estate) (ASC 310-40-40-6A, 40-7; 55-12)

OVERVIEW

A seller finances a sale of real estate. Although the buyer's initial investment is insufficient for full accrual profit recognition under the guidance in ASC 360 (FAS-66), the transaction qualifies for sales recognition, with profit deferred and recognized on the installment or cost recovery methods. Some time after the sale, the buyer defaults on the seller's mortgage, and the seller forecloses the property. The property's fair value at foreclosure is less than the seller's gross receivable, which includes the cost of the property and deferred profit, but is greater than the net receivable, which consists of principal and interest receivable reduced by deferred profit and related allowances.

ACCOUNTING ISSUE

At what amount should the seller recognize the foreclosed property?

EITF CONSENSUS

The EITF reached a consensus that the seller should recognize the foreclosed property at the lower of the net receivable or the property's fair value.

The Task Force emphasized that the consensus assumes it is appropriate under the circumstances to include any accrued interest income on the financing in the net receivable, as it is defined under the consensus. However, some questioned whether such amounts should be included on sales accounted for on the installment or cost recovery methods.

It was noted that ASC 470 FAS-15, Accounting by Debtors and Creditors for Troubled Debt Restructurings) does not apply in this situation, because deferred profit is not considered a valuation allowance account, as contemplated in ASC 470 (FAS-15). The Statement would apply, however, if profit had been recognized on the full accrual method, with recognition of the property at fair value, if appropriate.

> **OBSERVATION:** ASC 360 FAS-144, Accounting for the Impairment or Disposal of Long-Lived Assets) provides guidance on accounting for long-lived assets held for sale as well as specific criteria on how to determine when a long-lived asset should be classified as held for sale. Under the Statement's provisions, a newly acquired foreclosed asset classified as held for sale should be recognized at the lower of its carrying amount or fair value less selling costs.

Illustration of Valuation of Foreclosed Real Estate

	Installment Method	Cost Recovery Method
Sales transaction:		
Seller's financing	$475,000	$475,000
Buyer's initial investment	25,000	25,000
Sales value	$500,000	$500,000
Sales value	$500,000	$500,000

Cost	350,000	
Gain	150,000	150,000
Amount recognized	(7,500)	0
Deferred profit	$142,500	$150,000
Foreclosure at end of first year:		
Original principal balance	$475,000	$475,000
Accrued interest in first year at 8%	38,000	38,000
Gross receivable at foreclosure	513,000	513,000
Less: Deferred profit	(142,500)	(150,000)
Net receivable	$370,500	$363,000
Property's fair value at foreclosure	$430,000	$430,000

Under the consensus, the foreclosed property would be recognized at $370,500 under the installment method or at $363,000 under the cost recovery method.

DISCUSSION

As stated above, the Task Force noted that ASC 470 (FAS-15 does not apply in this transaction, because deferred profit is not considered a valuation allowance under the guidance in ASC 470 (FAS-15). That comment is based on the guidance in paragraph 7 of FAS-15 (ASC 470-60-15-12), which states that a foreclosure is not considered a troubled debt restructuring if the fair value of the receivable is at least equal to the "recorded investment in the receivable." The primary focus of of the guidance in ASC 470 (FAS-15) is on transactions that would result in a loss. In the case of a sale on which profit has been deferred—as in the transaction in this Issue—the net receivable, not the gross receivable, should be considered the seller's recorded investment in the receivable and compared to fair value, because it does not include deferred profit on the sale. If profit had been recognized on the full accrual method, the gross receivable would have been compared to fair value.

Recognition of foreclosed real estate at the net receivable amount results in no gain or loss on foreclosure. The original cost of the property is increased or decreased by gains and interest income recognized in prior periods and cash collected on the sale and financing. More cash may be received than recognized as gains and interest income under the installment method if the gain is a small percentage of the sales price. The same may occur under the cost recovery method, because no gain is recognized until the cost has been recovered. In those situations, the property would be recognized at less than its original cost because of the excess cash. In the above Illustration, a $3 gain was recognized on the sale, $15 of interest income was accrued, and $10 cash was received on the down payment. When the property is recognized at foreclosure, the original cost of $140 would be increased by $8 (3 + 15 − 10) to $148, which also equals the $205 receivable less deferred profit of $57.

The journal entry to recognize the foreclosed property would be as follows:

Property	$370,500	
Deferred profit	142,500	
Receivable		$513,000

SUBSEQUENT DEVELOPMENT

The AICPA issued SOP 92-3 (Accounting for Foreclosed Assets) in April 1992 (see Chapter 5, "Bankruptcy and Reorganization," for further details). It provides guidance on the balance sheet treatment of foreclosed assets after foreclosure.

ASC 323 Investments—Equity Method and Joint Ventures

EITF Issue 94-1 (Accounting for Tax Benefits Resulting from Investments in Affordable Housing Projects) (ASC 323-740-05-3, S25-1, 25-1 through 25-5; 35-2; 45-2; 55-2 through 55-10, S99-2; 325-20-35-5, 35-6)

OVERVIEW

The affordable housing credit, which had expired after June 30, 1992, is a tax benefit that was retroactively extended and made permanent under the Revenue Reconciliation Act of 1993. Investors commonly receive such tax benefits by purchasing interests in limited partnerships that operate qualified affordable housing projects; the tax benefits are passed through to the limited partners. Credits are available if a sufficient number of units are rented to qualifying tenants at a rental that does not exceed statutory amounts. For example, a housing project with 20% or more residential units that are rent-restricted and occupied by individuals whose income is 50% or less of the community's median gross income qualifies for the credit. The affordable housing credit may be taken on the tax return each year for ten years and is subject to recapture over 15 years, beginning with the first year tax credits are earned.

ACCOUNTING ISSUE

How should investors in qualified affordable housing project limited partnerships account for their investments?

EITF CONSENSUS

1. A receivable for tax benefits to be received over the term of the investment should *not* be recognized at the time an investment in a qualified affordable housing project is purchased.
2. Income from affordable housing credits should *not* be recognized for financial reporting purposes before they are reported for tax purposes.
3. Limited partnership investments in qualified affordable housing projects should be reviewed periodically for impairment.
4. A liability should be recognized for (*a*) unconditional and legally binding delayed equity contributions and for (*b*) equity contributions contingent on a future event when it becomes probable.

The Task Force observed that additional guidance on accounting for delayed equity contributions may be found in ASC 450 (FAS-5), EITF Issue 85-16, and SFAC-6 (not in the ASC).

5. Limited partnership investments in affordable housing projects should be accounted for as follows.

Effective yield method

   a. The effective yield method should be elected if a limited partnership investment in an affordable housing project meets *all* of the following conditions:

     (1) A creditworthy entity guarantees the availability of tax credits to the investor by a letter of credit, a tax indemnity agreement, or a similar arrangement.

     (2) A positive yield is expected on the investment, based only on cash flows from guaranteed tax credits.

     (3) The investor's partnership interest is limited for legal and tax purposes with liability limited to the capital investment.

   b. The effective yield method should be applied as follows:

     (1) Tax credits are recognized as they are allocated.

     (2) The initial cost of an investment is amortized so that it results in a constant effective yield over the period tax credits are received. (The effective yield is the investor's internal rate of return on the investment, determined by the cost of the investment and guaranteed tax credits.)

     (3) Any expected residual value is excluded from the effective yield calculation.

     (4) Income for cash received from the limited partnership's operations or sale of the property is recognized when it is realized or realizable.

     (5) The investor's share of the tax credit, net of amortization of the investment in the limited partnership, is

presented in the income statement as a component of income taxes related to continuing operations.

(6) Other tax benefits received are accounted for in accordance with ASC 740 (FAS-109).

The Task Force observed that the effective yield method should not be applied whenever an individual investment meets the required conditions, but rather because it is the entity's accounting policy to do so. In addition, the SEC Observer stated that the SEC staff believes that the effective yield method should not be used in analogous situations.

Equity method

For investments not accounted for on the effective yield method or the cost method, the guidance in ASC 970-323 and ASC 323 (SOP 78-9) and consensus positions not related to the effective yield method should be followed.

The Task Force observed that ASC 970-323 and ASC 323 (SOP 78-9) generally requires using the equity method to account for limited partnership investments in real estate ventures unless the limited partner has only a minor interest with practically no influence over the partnership's operating and financial policies.

OBSERVATION: Because limited partnerships are excluded from the guidance in ASC 323 (APB-18), the equity method may be used to account for such investments even if an ownership interest does not meet the 20% presumption of significant influence. See Topic D-46 in Chapter 15 for a discussion of the SEC staff's position on the use of the equity method to account for limited partnership investments.

Cost method

- The cost method should be used only if an investment is so minor that there is virtually no influence over operating and financial policies.
- The difference between the carrying amount of the investment and its estimated residual value should be amortized during the periods in which the investor receives allocated tax credits.

    —The estimated residual value is the value of the investment at the end of the last period in which tax credits are allocated to the investor without considering anticipated inflation.

    —Annual amortization is calculated based on the ratio of tax credits received in the current year to total estimated tax credits that will be allocated to the investor.

OBSERVATION: ASC 810 (FIN-46(R), Consolidation of Variable Interest Entities) requires the consolidation of variable interest entities by an entity that absorbs a majority of a variable entity's expected losses or has the right to receive a greater part of the variable entity's expected residual returns or both.

DISCUSSION

The EITF's discussions of the accounting for investments in limited partnership interests in affordable housing projects indicated that such investments may be made for two different reasons:

1. Some invest in these limited partnerships solely for the purpose of receiving tax benefits, not as real estate equity investments. Those investors attribute no residual interest to the investment and believe that other aspects of the investment are insignificant. They believe that no risks or rewards, other than the tax benefits, are transferred to the investor. Proponents of this view argue that the cost of an investment should be amortized over the life of the project, based on an effective yield. Others argue that the cost method should be used with tax benefits recognized when they are realized. An investment would not be amortized but evaluated for impairment periodically and written off at the end of the tax-benefit period.

2. Another view was that an investment in a limited partnership is a real estate investment. Proponents of this view argue that the limited partners share in the risks and rewards of ownership and that receipt of tax benefits is uncertain. In addition, limited partners may share in the partnership's taxable income or loss over the life of the project.

The Task Force's consensus limiting the effective yield method to situations in which specific conditions are met reflects the Task Force's effort to differentiate between investments in limited partnerships that are purchased for tax purposes and as real estate investments. Use of the effective yield method is limited to investments entered into for the purpose of realizing tax benefits if there is assurance that the tax benefits will be realized, mitigating the real estate business risks. In addition, lack of control over operations and limited liability provide assurance that an investor's cash flows will not be negative in future periods and is another indicator that the intent of the investment was to realize tax benefits.

ASC 360 Property, Plant, and Equipment

FTB 86-2 (Accounting for an Interest in the Residual Value of a Leased Asset) (ASC 360-10-25-2 through 25-4; 30-3, 30-4; 30-13, 30-14; 840-30-35-21, 35-53)

BACKGROUND

FTB 86-2 responds to five questions related to accounting for the residual value of a leased asset.

STANDARDS

Question 1: How should an enterprise account for the acquisition from a lessor of the unconditional right to own and possess, at the end of the lease term, an asset subject to the lease? How should an enterprise account for the acquisition of the right to receive all or a portion of the proceeds from the sale of a leased asset at the end of the lease?

Answer: At the date the rights are acquired, both transactions involve a right to receive, at the end of the lease term, all or a portion of the future benefit included in the leased asset. This right should be accounted for as the acquisition of an asset.

Question 2: How should an enterprise acquiring an interest in the residual value of a leased asset determine the cost at acquisition?

Answer: The cost is the amount of cash disbursed, the fair value of other consideration given (which could include noncash assets or services rendered), and the present value of liabilities assumed. The fair value of the interest in the residual value at the date of the agreement should be used to measure the cost of the interest if that fair value is more clearly evident than the fair value of the assets surrendered, services rendered, or liabilities assumed.

Question 3: How does an enterprise that acquires an interest in the residual value of a leased asset account for that asset during the lease term?

Answer: An enterprise that acquires an interest in the residual value of a leased asset should not recognize increases in the asset's estimated value over the remaining term of the lease. The asset should be reported at no more than its acquisition cost until sale or disposition. If the value of the asset declines below its carrying amount and that decline is considered other than temporary, the asset should be written down to fair value and the amount of the write-down should be recognized as a loss. Subsequent increases in fair value before sale or disposition should not be recorded.

Question 4: Do the provisions indicated in the answer to Question 3 apply to lease brokers?

Answer: Yes.

Question 5: If a lessor sells substantially all of the minimum rental payments associated with a sales-type, direct financing, or leveraged lease and retains an interest in the residual value of the leased asset, how should the lessor account for that asset over the remaining lease term?

Answer: The lessor should not recognize increases in the leased asset's residual value over the remaining lease term. If the fair value of the residual declines, however, that decline should be recognized as a loss if the decline is considered other than temporary. Subsequent recoveries in fair value should not be recorded.

EITF Issue 84-17 (Profit Recognition on Sales of Real Estate with Graduated Payment Mortgages or Insured Mortgages) (ASC 360-20-40-35)

OVERVIEW

A sale of real estate is financed by a graduated payment mortgage. Such mortgages may have negative amortization of principal in the early years and may be partially or fully insured.

ACCOUNTING ISSUES

- Do graduated payment mortgages meet the requirements for the buyer's initial and continuing investment under the full accrual method?
- Can government or private mortgage insurance be considered part of the buyer's initial and continuing investment?

EITF CONSENSUS

- The EITF reached a consensus that a graduated payment mortgage with negative amortization of principal does not meet the continuing investment test in FAS-66 (Accounting for Sales of Real Estate). Therefore, profit should not be recognized based on the full accrual method.
- No consensus. (See Issue 87-9 for the Task Force's consensus on this issue.) (ASC 360-20-40-11,40-12; 55-3)

DISCUSSION

FAS-66 is based on AICPA accounting guides that were issued in the 1970s to curb profit recognition abuses in the real estate industry. The purpose of the buyer's initial and continuing investment requirements is to demonstrate that the buyer has an economic commitment to the property. Under paragraphs 9 and 12 (ASC 360-20-40-10, 40-19, 40-20), which provide guidance on those requirements, the buyer must be contractually obligated to make sufficient annual payments to *reduce* the indebtedness on the property. In contrast, a negative amortization mortgage *increases* the buyer's indebtedness, because the balance of the loan increases.

SUBSEQUENT DEVELOPMENT

At a subsequent meeting, the EITF reached a consensus that profit recognition using the full accrual method is permitted if a loan is insured under a current FHA or VA program. This consensus does not apply to private mortgage insurance.

EITF Issue 86-6 (Antispeculation Clauses in Real Estate Sales Contracts) (ASC 360-20-40-39)

OVERVIEW

An antispeculation clause is included in some land sales contracts to assure that the buyer develops the land according to a master plan. Under such contracts, the buyer is required to develop the land within a specified period of time and may be prohibited from developing it for certain uses. If the buyer does not comply with the contract, the seller has the right, but not the obligation, to repurchase the property, which represents a potential penalty to the buyer for not complying with the sales contract. The buyer does not, however, have the right to put the property back to the seller.

According to paragraph 26 of FAS-66 (ASC 360-20-40-38), the seller should not recognize profit on a sale on the full accrual method, if a sales contract includes a repurchase option. Such a transaction should be accounted for as a financing, leasing, or profit-sharing arrangement instead of as a sale.

ACCOUNTING ISSUE

Is a seller precluded from recognizing a sale if a real estate sales contract includes an antispeculation clause?

EITF CONSENSUS

The EITF reached a consensus that a seller is not precluded from recognizing a sale if there is only a *remote probability* that the buyer will not comply with a sales contract's antispeculation clause.

The Task Force stated that using a probability test is not appropriate if the seller has an option to repurchase the property that is not contingent on the buyer's compliance with a specific requirement.

DISCUSSION

The Task Force discussed the following factors that would indicate that there is only a remote probability that the buyer will not comply with the contract's antispeculation clause:

- The buyer has the ability and intent to follow the provisions of the sales contract. If the buyer is a substantive party and the seller does not expect to have a right to repurchase the property, no option exists on sale.

- The risks and rewards of ownership have been transferred to the buyer. The buyer will benefit from the appreciation of the property if it is developed according to the contract, while the seller has no obligation and would have no incentive to repurchase the property if its value depreciates. The seller does not share in the appreciation or depreciation of the property.

- There are business reasons for the option. The seller includes the antispeculation clause in the contract only to enforce the buyer's promise to develop the property as agreed in the contract. The clause is more like a restriction in a deed than a repurchase option. In practice, deed restrictions in retail land sales that limit the type of home that can be built on a property do not preclude full accrual profit recognition.

EITF Issue 87-9 (Profit Recognition on Sales of Real Estate with Insured Mortgages or Surety Bonds) (ASC 360-20-40-11, 40-12; 55-3)

OVERVIEW

Sellers financing residential or other properties may require mortgage insurance on a portion of the loan. They often accept surety bonds instead of letters of credit to support the buyer's notes. Under paragraph 9 of FAS-66 (ASC 360-20-40-10), one of the conditions for the buyer's initial investment under the full accrual method is that the buyer's notes be accompanied by a letter of credit from an independent lending institution.

ACCOUNTING ISSUES

1. Can a financial instrument, such as a surety bond, that meets the following conditions be considered equivalent to an irrevocable letter of credit in determining whether the buyer's notes should be included in the buyer's initial investment, so profit can be recognized on the full accrual method?
    a. The seller has the same rights of collection as under an irrevocable letter of credit.
    b. The surety has the same obligation to the seller as under an irrevocable letter of credit.
    c. The surety has the same recourse to the buyer in the case of default as under an irrevocable letter of credit.
2. Can government or private insurance covering part of the balance of a mortgage be considered equivalent to an irrevocable letter of credit and included in the buyer's initial and continuing investment, in determining whether to recognize profit on a sale using the full accrual method?
3. Do the minimum down payment percentages stated in paragraphs 53 and 54 of FAS-66 (ASC 360-20-55-1, 55-2) apply, or should the loan limits in governmental programs be used if a buyer of a single-family residential property qualifies for a loan from the Federal Housing Administration (FHA) or Veterans

Administration (VA), which insure or guarantee a part or the full amount of the mortgage, but require no down payments or down payments of less than 5%?

EITF CONSENSUS

1. A seller may consider an irrevocable financial instrument, such as a surety bond from an independent insurer that meets the conditions stated in Issue 1 above, to be equivalent to an irrevocable letter of credit that can be used to support the buyer's notes, which are included in the buyer's initial investment in determining whether profit can be recognized under the full accrual method. The buyer's commitment to pay is an important criterion in FAS-66 that must be met for full profit recognition.

2. Mortgage insurance is not considered equivalent to an irrevocable letter of credit in determining whether the full accrual method is appropriate, because purchasing mortgage insurance does not demonstrate the buyer's commitment to meet the obligation to pay for the property.

3. The normal down payment requirements or loan limits under FHA or VA government-insured programs may be used by a seller for sales of owner-occupied single-family homes financed under those programs instead of the minimum initial investment percentages stated in paragraphs 53 and 54 of FAS-66 (ASC 360-20-55-1, 55-2) to determine whether a seller may recognize profit on the full accrual method if the mortgage receivable is insured under the FHA or VA program. (The Task Force's initial consensus required that the mortgage receivable be *fully* insured by a governmental agency. The Task Force subsequently reached a consensus that all loans insured by the VA or FHA qualify for full accrual profit recognition. This consensus does not apply to private mortgage insurance.) The Task Force justified its departure from the requirements of FAS-66 in this situation, because government insurance transfers the risk on the mortgage receivable to the governmental agency.

Representatives of the VA and FHA mortgage insurance programs indicated that FHA mortgage insurance usually covers 100% of the outstanding principal, and VA insurance usually provides first-dollar loss coverage of 40% or 50% of the qualified amount of the loan, but no more than $36,000; coverage is reduced pro rata as the loan principal is paid off. Neither program splits its coverage with private insurers, and both provide for recourse against the borrower in case of default. (See Issue 88-12 below regarding what may be included in a buyer's initial investment under FAS-66.)

DISCUSSION

1. A surety bond differs from mortgage insurance, because the bond exposes the buyer to the same risk of loss as under an irrevocable letter of credit. If a buyer defaults on the notes, the surety has recourse to the buyer's general assets for the amount of the bond. Those who believed that a surety bond is equivalent to an irrevocable letter of credit and should therefore qualify under the requirements of ASC 360 (FAS-66) argued that it (a) demonstrates the buyer's commitment to pay for the property and (b) increases the likelihood that the seller will collect the receivable supported by the bond. The FASB staff agreed with that view and recommended that the Task Force accept surety bonds as equivalent to irrevocable letters of credit if they meet the conditions stated in Issue 1 above.

2. Mortgage insurance should not be considered equivalent to an irrevocable letter of credit, because it does not demonstrate the buyer's commitment to pay for the property—a requirement of ASC 360 (FAS-66)—even though it increases the likelihood that the sales price will be collected.

EITF Issue 88-12 (Transfer of Ownership Interest as Part of Down Payment under FASB Statement No. 66) (ASC 360-20-55-66, 55-67)

OVERVIEW

An income-producing property is owned in a partnership by two parties. One of the parties, which holds a 75% interest in the property, sells its interest to the party holding a 25% interest in the property. The buyer receives a 10% down payment and a note for the balance secured by 100% of the property, which has no outstanding debt. Paragraph 54 of FAS-66 (ASC 360-20-55-2) specifies a minimum initial investment of 15% of the sales value of the property as an initial investment for this type of transaction.

ACCOUNTING ISSUES

- Does the buyer's pledge of 100% of the purchased property as security for a note meet the requirements for the buyer's initial investment in determining whether profit may be recognized on the full accrual method?

- If yes, can a note collateralized by assets other than the purchased property, such as other real estate or marketable securities, be included as part of the buyer's initial investment in determining whether profit can be recognized on the full accrual method?

EITF CONSENSUS

The EITF reached a consensus that under the provisions of ASC 360 (FAS-66), full accrual profit recognition is not permitted for this transaction, because the buyer's initial investment should not include the purchased property or other assets pledged as security for a note.

DISCUSSION

Under the criteria stated in paragraph 9 of FAS-66 (ASC 360-20-40-10), only the buyer's cash down payment in this transaction qualifies to be included in the buyer's initial investment. A note would have to be supported by an irrevocable letter of credit from an independent lending institution. In Issue 87-9, the Task Force reached a consensus that a surety bond meeting certain conditions could be substituted for an irrevocable letter of credit, but mortgage insurance was not acceptable because it did not demonstrate the buyer's commitment to pay for the property. Under a strict interpretation of paragraph 9 (ASC 360-20-40-10), a note collateralized by the property or other assets would not qualify.

In addition, this transaction would not qualify for full accrual profit recognition, because the 10% down payment does not meet the minimum down payment required in paragraph 54 for an income-producing property, which is 15% of sales value.

EITF Issue 88-24 (Effect of Various Forms of Financing under FASB Statement No. 66) (ASC 360-20-40-14 through 40-17, 40-32; 55-55, 55-56)

OVERVIEW

Real estate sales are financed in various ways. The financing may be provided by independent third parties, by the seller, or both. Also, the financing may be nonrecourse to the buyer; that is, the lender's only recourse in the event the buyer defaults is to foreclose on the property. The financing also may involve the buyer's assumption of the seller's preexisting recourse or nonrecourse mortgage obligations.

The guidance in ASC 360 (FAS-66) establishes accounting standards for recognizing profit or loss on sales of real estate. The Statement is unclear, however, as to how various forms of financing affect the seller's profit recognition.

Paragraph 3 of FAS-66 (ASC 360-20-40-3) states that a seller recognizes profit on the full accrual method if *both* of the following conditions are met:

1. The profit can be determined; there is reasonable assurance that the sales price is collectible; and it is possible to estimate the amount that will not be collectible.
2. The earnings process is essentially complete; the seller has no obligation to perform significant activities after the sale.

In applying condition 1, collectibility is demonstrated by the buyer's initial and continuing investments, which must be adequate to demonstrate a commitment to pay for the real estate. A sufficient investment puts the buyer at risk of loss through default and motivates the buyer to pay on the debt. Unless both conditions are met, the seller must defer all or a part of the profit. Deferred profit would be recognized in the future on the installment, cost-recovery, or the reduced-profit method.

ACCOUNTING ISSUE

How should profit be recognized on sales of real estate that involve various forms of financing?

EITF CONSENSUS

- The initial and continuing investment requirements of ASC 360 (FAS-66) apply. However, a seller can recognize profit on the full accrual method if consideration received by the seller for the *full* sales value of the property consists of the following:
  - Cash, as long as the seller has no contingent liability on debt the buyer might incur or assume
  - The seller's existing nonrecourse debt on the property assumed by the buyer
  - Recourse debt on the property assumed by the buyer with the seller's *complete release* from those obligations
  - Any combination of the above
- In determining the adequacy of the buyer's initial investment for purposes of recognizing profit by the full accrual method, *neither* of the following forms of financing should be included as part of the buyer's initial investment:
  - Debt secured by the property, whether borrowed directly from the seller or others or indirectly by the buyer's assumption of the seller's existing debt
  - Payments to the seller from the proceeds of debt secured by the property
- Neither of the following should be considered the buyer's cash payments in the seller's computation of the amount of profit that can be recognized initially under the installment, cost recovery, or reduced-profit method:

A seller may, however, recognize as income deferred profit in excess of the total amount of (*a*) the seller's financing and (*b*) the buyer's outstanding debt secured by the property for which the seller is contingently liable.

—A buyer's debt secured by the property, either incurred directly from the seller or others or indirectly by assuming the seller's existing debt

—Cash paid to the seller from the proceeds of a buyer's debt secured by the property

The buyer's commitment to pay for the property is demonstrated only by the payment of a sufficient amount of cash or other qualifying form of investment, not by a borrowing secured by the property. Items included or excluded from the initial investment are discussed in paragraphs 9 and 10 of FAS-66 (ASC 360-20-40-10, 40-13).

DISCUSSION

- The first consensus is intended to clarify the guidance in FAS-66—that the initial and continuing investment requirements do not apply if the seller has no receivable and is not contingently liable on the buyer's debt. Sales that include the following components qualify for full accrual profit recognition:

    —The buyer makes an adequate cash down payment, and the remainder is financed by a first mortgage from an independent lender.

    —The total sales price is financed by a first mortgage from an independent lender.

    —The buyer makes an adequate cash down payment and assumes the seller's nonrecourse mortgage for the remainder of the sales price.

    —The buyer assumes the seller's nonrecourse mortgage for the total sales price.

- Under this consensus, profit may be recognized on the full accrual method if the buyer makes an adequate initial investment based on the criteria in paragraphs 53 and 54 of FAS-66 (ASC 360-20-55-1, 55-2), and if the buyer's payments on the mortgage obligation meet the requirements for the continuing investment. Any financing secured by the property is excluded. Sales that include the following components qualify for full accrual profit recognition:

    —Adequate cash initial investment and first mortgage seller financing

    —Adequate cash initial investment and assumption of seller's recourse mortgage, on which the seller remains contingently liable

Real Estate Transactions 33.21

—Adequate cash initial investment, first mortgage from an independent lender, and seller financing
—Adequate cash initial investment, assumption of seller's nonrecourse mortgage, and seller financing
—Adequate cash initial investment, seller financing, and assumption of seller's recourse mortgage

- Under the cost recovery method, no profit is recognized until the seller has recovered the cost of the property. Paragraph 62 of FAS-66 (ASC 360-20-55-13) states that "no profit is recognized until cash payments by the buyer, including principal and interest on debt due to the seller *and on existing debt assumed* by the buyer, exceed the seller's cost of the property sold." (Emphasis added.) However, paragraph 14 of SOP 78-4 (Application of the Deposit, Installment, and Cost Recovery Methods in Accounting for Sales of Real Estate) which has been incorporated in FAS-66, states that "no profit is recognized until cash collections, including both principal and interest, *and existing debt assumed* by the buyer exceed the cost of the property sold." (Emphasis added.)

There was some controversy as to whether a seller's debt assumed by a buyer should be considered a payment by the buyer at closing, as it had been interpreted under SOP 78-4. It seems that some believed that the FASB changed that provision of the SOP in the process of drafting FAS-66 and thus changed the accounting under the cost recovery method. The problem was that in some instances a literal interpretation of paragraph 62 (ASC 360-20-55-13) would result in no profit recognition, even if the buyer's cash payments exceeded the amount due to the seller or the debt assumed by the buyer. Based on the Task Force's consensus, profit can be recognized if cash payments at closing, a first mortgage from an independent lender, the borrower's assumption of the seller's nonrecourse mortgage, or a combination of these exceeds seller financing and debt secured by the property, for which the seller is contingently liable.

Illustration of Profit Recognition When Buyer's Initial Investment Is Inadequate

Assumptions

Sales price	$250,000
Seller's basis in property sold	$187,500
Seller's profit	$ 62,500
Initial investment requirement	20%
Continuing investment test is met.	
a. Buyer's initial cash investment	0
Seller's recourse mortgage assumed*	$250,000

33.22 Real Estate Transactions

  No profit recognized
*The seller remains contingently liable on the mortgage.
 b. Buyer's initial cash investment   0
   Seller financing $250,000
   No profit recognized
 c. Buyer's initial cash investment   0
   Seller financing $ 50,000
   Seller's recourse mortgage assumed* $200,000
   No profit recognized
 d. Buyer's initial cash investment   0
   First mortgage from independent lender $200,000
   Seller financing $ 50,000
   Profit recognized on cost recovery or installment method on excess over seller financing $ 12,500
 e. Buyer's initial cash investment $ 25,000
   Seller financing $225,000
   Profit recognized on the installment method ($25,000 × .25) $ 6,250
 f. Buyer's initial cash investment $ 25,000
   Seller's recourse mortgage assumed* $225,000
   Profit recognized on the installment method ($25,000 × .25) $ 6,250
 g. Buyer's initial cash investment $ 25,000
   First mortgage from independent lender $200,000
   Seller financing $ 25,000
   Profit recognized on cost recovery or installment method on excess of seller financing ($62,500 − $25,000) $ 37,500
 h. Buyer's initial cash investment $ 25,000
   Seller's nonrecourse mortgage assumed $200,000
   Seller financing $ 25,000
   Profit recognized on cost recovery or installment method on excess of seller financing $ 37,500
 i. Buyer's initial cash investment $ 25,000
   Seller's recourse mortgage assumed* $200,000
   Seller financing $25,000
   Profit recognized on the installment method ($25,000 × .25) $ 6,250

*The seller remains contingently liable on the mortgage.

EITF Issue 98-8 (Accounting for Transfers of Investments That Are in Substance Real Estate) (ASC 360-20-15-3)

OVERVIEW

The guidance in ASC 860 FAS-140, Accounting for Transfers and Servicing of Financial Assets and Extinguishments of Liabilities) on accounting for transfers of financial assets differs substantially from the guidance in ASC 360 (FAS-66) on accounting for sales of real estate. This Issue was raised because some believe that sales or exchanges of financial assets, such as corporate stock of enterprises with substantial real estate assets, partnership interests, and timesharing interests, that are in substance real estate should be accounted for under the guidance in ASC 360 (FAS-66), not under the guidance in ASC 860 (FAS-140).

Under the guidance in ASC 860 (FAS-140, a transfer of financial assets is accounted for as a sale if it meets the criteria in paragraph 9 (ASC 860-10-40-4, 40-5). The requirements for profit recognition on sales of real estate assets are discussed in paragraph 5 of FAS-66 (ASC 360-20-40-5). Although both pronouncements require that the transferor relinquish control over the asset by prohibiting the transferor from maintaining a continuing involvement with the asset, the Statements have very different requirements for sales recognition and for subsequent accounting for transactions that do not meet their respective criteria.

ACCOUNTING ISSUE

Should sales or transfers of financial assets that are in substance real estate be accounted for under the provisions of ASC 360 (FAS-66) or the provisions of ASC 860 (FAS-140)?

EITF CONSENSUS

The EITF reached a consensus that sales or transfers of investments in the form of financial assets that are in substance real estate should be accounted for under the provisions of ASC 360 (FAS-66).

The Task Force noted that the consensus would apply to transfers of acquisition, development, and construction loans (ADC loans), which are considered to be investments that are in substance real estate according to EITF Issue 84-4. However, the consensus would not apply to marketable investments in real estate investment trusts (REITs) accounted for under the provisions of ASC 320 (FAS-115, Accounting for Certain Investments in Debt and Equity Securities), because they are not considered to be investments that are in substance real estate. Sales or exchanges of such investments should be accounted for under the guidance in ASC 860 (FAS140).

> **OBSERVATION:** FAS-125 was superseded by ASC 860 (FAS-140, *Accounting for Transfers and Servicing of Financial Assets and Extinguishments and Liabilities*). The guidance in ASC 860-

10-15-4 (paragraph 4 of FAS-140) provides that transfers of ownership interests that are in substance real estate are not under its scope. Such transactions should be accounted for under the guidance in ASC 360 (FAS-66). That provision affirms the guidance in this Issue. ASC 860-10-35-4, 35-6; 860-10-05-8; 860-20–25-5; 460-10-60-35; 860-20-55-46 through 55-48; 860-50-05-2 through 05-4; 30-1, 30-2; 35-1A, 35-3, 35-9 through 35-11; 25-2, 25-3, 25-6; 50-5 (FAS-166), which amends the guidance in ASC 860 (FAS-140), did not reconsider that provision.

DISCUSSION

Proponents of the view that the guidance in ASC 360 (FAS-66) should apply to transfers of assets that are in substance real estate believe that the substance of an investment is more important than its form. They argued that it would be unacceptable to change the revenue recognition model for real estate by changing the form of the investment. In addition, they noted that paragraph 101 of FAS-66 (ASC 976-10-15-4) cites corporate stock of enterprises with substantial real estate, sales of interests in a partnership that was formed for the purpose of acquiring real estate directly from third parties, and sales of time-sharing interests in real estate properties as examples of financial assets that are in substance real estate. They suggested that paragraph 101 (ASC 976-10-15-4) should be consulted to determine which financial assets should be accounted for under the guidance in ASC 360 (FAS-66).

EITF Issue 00-13 (Determining Whether Equipment Is "Integral Equipment" Subject to FASB Statements No. 66 and No. 98) (ASC 360-20-15-4 through 15-8; 55-58, 55-59)

OVERVIEW

ASC 360 (FIN-43, Real Estate Sales), which concludes that sales of "integral equipment" should be accounted for under the guidance in ASC 360 (FAS-66), defines that term, as it is used in the Interpretation, as "... any physical structure or equipment attached to the real estate that cannot be removed and used separately without incurring significant cost." An office building, a manufacturing facility, a power plant, and a refinery are cited as examples. Some are concerned that in applying the provisions of ASC 840 and ASC 360 (FASB Statements 13, 66, and 98), there will be diversity in determining which assets are considered "integral equipment," because the accounting literature on real estate sales and leasing transactions does not provide guidance on how to interpret the phrase "... cannot be removed and used separately without incurring significant cost."

ACCOUNTING ISSUE

How should entities determine whether equipment is "integral equipment"?

EITF CONSENSUS

- The Task Force agreed that the phrase "cannot be removed and used separately without incurring significant cost" raises the following two questions: (*a*) whether the equipment can be removed without incurring significant cost and (*b*) whether the equipment can be moved to another location to be used by another entity without significantly diminishing its value or usefulness.

- The Task Force reached a consensus that to determine whether an asset should be considered to be integral equipment, it is necessary to know (*a*) the significance of the cost of removing the equipment from its existing location, including the cost of repairing damage caused by its removal, and (*b*) the diminution in the equipment's value due to its removal. The Task Force agreed that the cost of shipping and reinstalling equipment at a new location should be considered the minimum amount of diminution in the value of equipment due to its removal. To determine whether there is additional diminution in value, it is necessary to consider the nature of the equipment and its likely use by other potential users.

- Equipment should be considered to be "integral equipment" if the combined cost of removal and the equipment's decrease in value exceeds 10% of the fair value of the installed equipment. For leasing transactions, estimates of the costs of removal, the decrease in the equipment's value, as well as its fair value should be based on information as of the inception of the lease.

EITF Issue 06-8 (Applicability of the Assessment of a Buyer's Continuing Investment under FASB Statement No. 66, *Accounting for Sales of Real Estate*, for Sales of Condominiums) (ASC 360-20-40-50-55)

OVERVIEW

Developers of condominium units usually sell individual units during a project's construction phase. Paragraph 5 of FAS-66 (Accounting for Sales of Real Estate) (ASC 360-20-40-5) provides guidance on accounting for real estate sales. Under the guidance in paragraph 5d of FAS-66 (ASC 360-20-40-5), one of the requirements for the seller to recognize profit under the full accrual method is that the buyer must demonstrate a commitment to pay by having an adequate continuing investment in the property. However, that requirement may not be met during a condominium's construction phase, because of the length of time it takes to complete such a project. In addition, because the risks and rewards of ownership have *not* been transferred to the buyer during the construction phase, the developer's continuing involvement is discussed further in paragraph 37 (ASC 360-20-40-50).

Under the guidance in paragraph 37 (ASC 360-20-40-50), a developer may recognize profit on individual condominium units using the percentage-of-completion method during a project's construction phase, if certain criteria are met. One of those criteria is the collectibility of the sales price. Paragraph 4 of FAS-66 (ASC 360-20-40-4) states that a buyer that makes a substantial initial and continuing investment in a property demonstrates a commitment to pay the remainder of the sales price, because the buyer will not want to lose that investment through a default. Additional factors to consider in an evaluation of collectibility are the buyer's credit standing, the property's age and location, and the adequacy of cash flow from the property. Some have questioned whether a developer needs to apply the continuing investment test discussed in paragraph 12 of FAS-66 (ASC 360-2-40-19, 20) in order to conclude that the sales price is collectible and profit may be recognized on the percentage-of-completion method.

ACCOUNTING ISSUES

1. Does an entity that recognizes profit on the percentage-of-completion method need to evaluate the adequacy of a buyer's continuing investment under the guidance in paragraph 12 of FAS-66 (ASC 360-20-40-19, 40-20)?

2. When the criteria in paragraph 37 of FAS-66 (ASC 360-20-40-50) are applied to reassess whether profit may be recognized on the percentage-of-completion method, should the initial and continuing investment tests be applied on a cumulative basis (*a*) from the date the seller and the buyer entered into a contract or (*b*) prospectively from the date on which a reassessment is made to determine whether profit may be recognized on the percentage-of-completion method on a transaction that previously did *not* meet the criteria in paragraph 37 (ASC 360-20-40-50) for profit recognition on that method?

EITF CONSENSUS

The EITF reached the following consensus positions:

1. When evaluating the collectibility of the sales price of an individual condominium unit under the guidance in paragraph 37d of FAS-66 (ASC 360-20-40-50), a seller's conclusion should be based on whether the buyer's initial and continuing investment is adequate. The EITF noted that just as for other types of real estate sales, a buyer's initial and continuing investment should be made in the form required in paragraph 9 of FAS-66 (ASC 360-20-40-10) and that only the nonrefundable portion of such investments should be counted toward the buyer's initial and

continuing investment. The continuing investment criterion in paragraph 12 of FAS-66 (ASC 360-20-40-19, 40-20) has been met if a buyer is required to either (1) pay additional amounts during the construction term that are at least equal to the level annual payments required to fund principal and interest on an amortizing customary mortgage for the property's remaining purchase price, which is the difference between the purchase price and the buyer's initial investment; or (2) increase the minimum initial investment by an equivalent total amount. The remaining purchase price is calculated based on the property's sales price. This test should be performed by using a hypothetical loan between a seller and a buyer for the amount of the purchase price *less* the buyer's initial investment. The EITF agreed that using the remaining purchase price is consistent with the guidance in paragraph 12 of FAS-66 (ASC 360-20-40-19, 40-20), because it refers to a buyer's "debt for the purchase price of the property."

2. The deposit method discussed in paragraphs 65 through 67 of FAS-66 (ASC 360-20-55-17, 55-19, 55-20) should be used until a buyer's payments meet the criteria in paragraph 37 of FAS-66 (ASC 360-20-40-50), including an assessment of collectibility using the initial and continuing investment tests discussed in paragraphs 8 through 12 of FAS-66 (ASC 360-20-40-9, 40-10, 40-13, 40-18 40-20). When an entity reevaluates whether profit should be recognized under the percentage-of-completion method, all of the criteria in paragraph 37 of FAS-66 (ASC 360-20-40-50) should be reevaluated.

3. The initial and continuing investment tests should be applied *prospectively* from the date on which the collectibility of the sales price is reevaluated, as if the deposit was received on that date.

FASB RATIFICATION

The FASB ratified the consensus at its November 29, 2006, meeting.

EITF Issue 07-6 (Accounting for the Sale of Real Estate Subject to the Requirements of FASB Statement No. 66, *Accounting for Sales of Real Estate*, When the Agreement Includes a Buy-Sell Clause) (ASC 360-20-55-21A; 65-1)

OVERVIEW

Issue 07-6 addresses a situation in which two entities have created a jointly owned entity and one of the entities has sold real estate to the newly formed entity. Under those circumstances, the agreement between the investors may include a buy-sell clause, which gives both investors the opportunity to offer to purchase the other investor's interest. If one investor makes an offer under a buy-sell clause, the other investor may decide to sell its interest for the offered amount or to buy the offering investor's interest at the offered amount. The buy-sell clause may stipulate that an offer be made at fair value, at a contractually specified amount, or at the amount set by the offeror. Commonly, the amount of the offer is set by the offeror.

Under the guidance in ASC 360 (FAS-66, Accounting for Sales of Real Estate), one of the criteria for profit recognition on the full accrual method is that a seller has transferred to a buyer all of its risks and rewards of ownership in a sale of real estate and has *no* substantial continuing involvement with the property. In Issue 07-6, the seller is the investor that sold the real estate property to the jointly owned entity and the buyer is the other investor in that entity. Under the guidance in FAS-66, a seller that has met all of the requirements for full accrual revenue recognition but has retained an equity interest in the real estate or has an equity interest in the *buyer* (the jointly owned entity) must account for the sale as a partial sale.

Furthermore, under the guidance in paragraph 26 of FAS-66 (ASC 360-20-40-38), if a seller is obligated to repurchase the real estate or if under the transaction's terms, the buyer is permitted to or can require the seller or give an option to the seller to repurchase the real estate, the seller has a prohibited form of continuing involvement, which rules out any profit recognition. Questions have been raised as to whether a buy-sell clause is such a form of prohibited continuing involvement so that a partial sale and profit recognition would *not* be permitted.

EITF CONSENSUS

At its November 29, 2007 meeting, the EITF reached consensus positions on Issue 07-6.

SCOPE

The guidance in Issue 07-6 applies to real estate sale transactions accounted for under the guidance in FAS-66 that include a buy-sell clause. That is, the guidance in Issue 07-6 applies if an individual who owns an entity jointly with another investor sells real estate to the entity and the arrangement between the seller and the other investor in the entity includes a buy-sell clause. The seller of the real estate would meet the criteria for partial sale recognition under the guidance in ASC 360 (FAS-66), except for the potential effect of the buy-sell clause. The guidance in Issue 07-6 applies only to transactions accounted for under the guidance in ASC 360 (FAS-66).

RECOGNITION

Judgment should be used to determine whether a seller has transferred the usual risks and rewards of ownership under the terms of a buy-sell clause and has *no* continuing involvement with the real estate in accordance with the guidance in paragraph 26 of FAS-66 (ASC 360-20-40-38). All of the relevant facts and circumstances of the transaction at the time of the real estate sale should be considered to make that determination.

A buy-sell clause alone would *not* be considered a prohibited form of continuing involvement that would rule out a partial sale or profit recognition under the guidance in ASC 360 (FAS-66). However, all of the relevant facts and circumstances should be considered in the effort to determine whether a buy-sell clause in-substance provides the buyer with a *put option* to acquire the seller's interest in the jointly owned entity or gives the seller an in-substance option to acquire the buyer's interest in the jointly owned entity, and thus the ability to reacquire the real estate.

FASB RATIFICATION

The FASB ratified the EITF's consensus positions in issue 07-6 at its December 12, 2007 meeting.

ASC 970 Real Estate—General

EITF Issue 85-27 (Recognition of Receipts from Made-Up Rental Shortfalls) (ASC 970-360-25-1, 55-1 through 55-3)

OVERVIEW

A public real estate syndication (buyer) purchases a newly constructed office building from a developer (seller). At the date of the sale, the buyer's general partner negotiates a master leaseback agreement with the seller for the building, which is only partially occupied. The agreement provides that the seller will lease vacant space for two years at a market rate and the buyer will pay the seller a reasonable fee, which is described as a fee in exchange for signing a master lease or as an escrowed portion of the purchase price. If a sublease meets certain conditions, the seller will not be required to make future lease payments on space the seller leases to others. The seller's rental payments would exceed the buyer's fee, if the seller is unable to lease the vacant space during the two-year lease period.

ACCOUNTING ISSUE

How should a buyer account for (*a*) a fee paid to the seller and (*b*) rental payments received from the seller?

EITF CONSENSUS

The EITF reached a consensus that the buyer should account for the fee paid to the seller and rental payments received from the seller as adjustments to the basis of the acquired property that will affect future depreciation.

The buyer's fee paid to the seller was considered by some Task Force members, including the SEC Observer, to be an escrowed portion of the purchase price that is conditional on the seller's ability to rent the space.

EFFECT OF ASC 815 (FAS-133)

The guidance in ASC 815 (FAS-133) applies if the agreement in this Issue meets the definition of a derivative in ASC 815 (FAS-133).

DISCUSSION

In a related discussion in Issue 84-37, the Task Force did not reach a consensus, but agreed that the following factors may be helpful in identifying a rental shortfall agreement that a buyer should account for as an adjustment of the purchase price, not as a sale-leaseback transaction:

- The seller is paid a fee as an incentive to enter the lease agreement. However, some noted that no fee does not necessarily indicate that it is a sale-leaseback.
- The seller makes a short-term lease commitment and has no renewal option.
- The buyer relieves the tenant of the lease obligation as the seller rents the space to tenants.
- Subleases are for longer periods than the sale-leaseback.
- The seller's lease commitment equals the difference between lease rents at the time of sale and market rents over some period, if the building is fully leased at the time of sale.

Some Task Force members noted that the transaction may be more like a sale-leaseback if the seller-lessee has a firm commitment, is not relieved of the primary obligation on the subleased space, and the lease agreement is for a long term.

The Task Force generally agreed during its discussion of Issue 85-27 that the consensus on that Issue applies if a seller agrees to make up a decrease in rentals that result from rent terminations during a specified period after the sale of a building that was fully rented at the time of sale. Such receipts should not be recognized as income, but as adjustments to the buyer's basis in the property.

EITF Issue 86-7 (Recognition by Homebuilders of Profit from Sales of Land and Related Construction Contracts) (ASC 970-360-55-4, 55-5)

OVERVIEW

A homebuilder enters into a contract with a buyer to construct a single-family house on a lot owned by the homebuilder. The sales price stated in the contract does not distinguish between the sale of the lot and construction of the house. Title on the lot is not transferred to the buyer until completion of construction and closing.

If, instead, the house was built on a lot owned by the buyer, the homebuilder would be able to recognize profit on the construction of the house based on the percentage-of-completion method discussed in SOP 81-1 (Accounting for Performance of Construction-Type and Certain Production-Type Contracts).

ACCOUNTING ISSUE

Should a builder recognize profit on the construction of a house on the builder's lot (*a*) separately for the construction of the house using the percentage-of-completion method regardless of the transfer of title on the lot or (*b*) for the construction of the house and sale of the lot when title passes at closing, based on the guidance in FAS-66?

EITF CONSENSUS

The EITF reached a consensus that profit recognition on the transaction should be recognized when the conditions for full accrual profit recognition in paragraph 5 of FAS-66 (ASC 360-20-40-5) have been met. Until then, proceeds received for the land and construction of the house should be accounted for based on the deposit method discussed in paragraphs 65 and 66 of FAS-66 (ASC 360-20-55-17, 55-19). This consensus was based on the views of the AICPA's Real Estate Committee.

DISCUSSION

The consensus is based on a strict application of paragraph 5 of FAS-66 (ASC 360-20-40-5). Under that paragraph, profit should not be recognized under the full accrual method until: the sale has closed; the buyer's initial and continuing investments meet the conditions in paragraphs 8-16 (ASC 360-20-40) of the Statement; the seller's receivable cannot be subordinated to the buyer's other obligations, except for a first mortgage on the property or a loan, the proceeds of which will be used to pay the seller; and the seller has transferred the risks and rewards of ownership to the buyer and will have no continuing involvement with the property.

EITF Issue 97-11 (Accounting for Internal Costs Relating to Real Estate Property Acquisitions) (ASC 970-340-25-1, 25-2, 5 through 25-7; 35-3, 35-4; 720-25-1, 25-2)

OVERVIEW

FAS-67 (Accounting for Costs and Initial Rental Operations of Real Estate Projects) provides guidance for the treatment of costs related to the acquisition, development, construction, sale, and rental of real estate projects. The costs addressed in FAS-67 include preacquisition costs and project costs. Under the Statement, preacquisition costs (e.g., for surveying, zoning studies, or obtaining an option on the property, which are incurred before its acquisition) (*a*) should be capitalized if they are related directly to the property, (*b*) would be incurred if the property were owned, and (*c*) should be capitalized only if it is probable that the property will be acquired or the purchaser will obtain an option to acquire the property.

Paragraph 7 of FAS-67 (ASC 970-360-25-2, 25-3) states that project costs are those that are "clearly associated with the acquisition, development and construction of a real estate project" and should be capitalized. Indirect project costs associated with more than one project also should be capitalized and allocated to the related projects.

This Issue has been raised because many real estate companies have full-time property acquisition departments that are involved in finding and acquiring properties and that perform services, such as appraisals and feasibility studies, which otherwise may be provided by outsiders. Because FAS-67 does not distinguish between the accounting for internal and external costs, the treatment of the costs of internal acquisition departments has been diverse—some companies capitalize those costs while others expense them. Opinions also differ as to whether FAS-67 applies to all real estate acquisitions or only to properties requiring further development and construction.

ACCOUNTING ISSUE

Should any costs incurred by an internal acquisitions department of a real estate entity to identify and acquire real estate properties be capitalized as part of the acquired property?

EITF CONSENSUS

- Costs related to preacquisition activities that are incurred by a real estate entity's internal department to identify and acquire a property that will be classified as *nonoperating* when it is acquired should be *capitalized* as part of the cost of acquiring the property if the costs can be directly identified with the acquired property and were incurred *after* the acquisition was considered probable. If the entity later decides to classify the property as operating when it is acquired, capitalized costs should be expensed and additional costs should be expensed as incurred.

- Preacquisition costs incurred *internally* in connection with the acquisition of a property that will be classified as *operating* on acquisition should be *expensed* as incurred. However, if the entity later decides that the property should be classified as nonoperating when it is acquired, amounts that had already been expensed should *not* be capitalized as part of the cost of acquiring the property. An operating property is (*a*) a property on which major construction activities, not routine maintenance or cleanup activities have been substantially *completed* by the acquisition date; (*b*) a property that will be available for occupancy when tenant improvements are completed; or (*c*) a property that is already income producing. The EITF also stated that preacquisition costs related to properties that are partially operating and partially nonoperating should be accounted for based on the guidance in paragraph 23 of FAS-67 (ASC 970-360-25-17), which requires that the two components be accounted for as separate projects and that preacquisition costs incurred be allocated between the respective portions.

- The FASB staff noted that guidance on distinguishing between external and internal costs can be found in questions 9 and 10 of the implementation guide on FAS-91. In addition, related guidance on accounting for a service corporation established by a REIT can be found in EITF Issue 95-6.

DISCUSSION

- The Task Force's original charge was to determine whether the accounting for preacquisition costs incurred by a real estate entity's internal property acquisitions department should differ from that for costs incurred for the same services provided by a third party. The Task Force's final consensus on this Issue is based on the guidance in paragraph 4 of FAS-67 (ASC 970-360-25-3), which requires that (*a*) only costs that can be directly identified with a specific property be capitalized, that is, not all costs incurred to identify acquisitions are capitalizable, (*b*) the costs would be capitalizable if the property had already been acquired, and (*c*) it is probable that the property will be acquired. In addition, members who supported this consensus argued that there is no conceptual reason that the accounting for preacquisition costs incurred by an internal department should differ from costs incurred if the same services are provided by an unrelated third party.

  The Task Force decided that capitalization of preacquisition costs is appropriate only for properties that will be *acquired*, because those costs will be recovered over the life of the property through its revenue stream. The benefit of costs related to properties not acquired expires in the period in which the costs were incurred, because they will not be recovered from revenues earned in future periods.

- In its discussion of the Issue, the Task Force distinguished between internal costs related to the identification and acquisition of real estate properties that need further development (*nonoperating* properties) and those incurred to identify and acquire *operating* real estate properties. Some Task Force members argued that the acquisition of an operating property is similar to a business combination and should be accounted for based on the principles in ASC 815 (FAS-141(R), Business Combinations). Interpretation 33 of APB-16 (Costs of Maintaining an "Acquisitions" Department) states that "[a]ll internal costs associated with a business combination are deducted *as incurred*" and further that costs that are capitalized under purchase accounting, such as finder's fees and fees paid to outside consultants, are direct costs not "recurring internal costs which may be directly related to an acquisition." In addition, some argued that the guidance in FAS-67 (see ASC references above) was intended to apply only to nonoperating properties.

The FASB staff, who supported the EITF's consensus, analogized to (*a*) the guidance on the capitalization of interest costs in paragraph 9b and 10a of FAS-34 (ASC 835-20-25-5, 25-6) under which capitalization ceases when the status of a property changes from nonoperating to operating and (*b*) the guidance in ASC 310 (FAS-91) and ASC 840 (FAS-13), both of which distinguish between the treatment of costs related to *originating* loans and leases and those related to *acquiring* existing loans or leases.

ASC 974 Real Estate Investment Trusts

EITF Issue 95-6 (Accounting by a Real Estate Investment Trust for an Investment in a Service Corporation) (ASC 974-323-25-1; 840-25-1)

> **OBSERVATION:** FIN-46(R) requires the consolidation of variable interest entities by an entity that absorbs a majority of a variable entity's expected losses or has the right to receive a greater part of the variable entity's expected residual returns or both. FIN-46 and ASC 810 (FIN-46(R)) nullify the consensus in this Issue for service corporations that are considered to be variable interest entities under the provisions of ASC 810 (FIN-46(R)), which must be accounted for under the Interpretation's provisions. The consensus continues to apply, however, to service corporations that are *not* variable interest entities.

OVERVIEW

To retain their favorable tax status (that is, be able to deduct dividends in arriving at taxable income), real estate investment trusts (REITs) may be established in the form of trusts, associations, or corporations, and may distribute a substantial amount of their taxable income to their shareholders annually. Because the Internal Revenue Code restricts the types of operating activities performed by a REIT to retain its qualification, some REITs have established service corporations (SCs) to perform certain services for the REIT or for third parties, such as property management, leasing services, and services involving the acquisition, development, construction, financing, or sale of real estate projects.

REITs are not permitted to own more than 10% of an SC's voting stock for federal income tax purposes. Consequently, a REIT may own a minimal interest in an SC's voting stock while holding a substantial interest in the SC's nonvoting preferred stock or nonvoting common stock, so that the REIT enjoys substantially all of the SC's economic benefits. A majority of an SC's voting stock is owned by the REIT's sponsors, officers, or affiliates. Generally, transfers of voting stock are not restricted. Owners of the majority of an SC's voting common stock generally contribute minimal amounts of equity to the SC.

ACCOUNTING ISSUES

1. Should an SC be considered an independent third party, as the term is used in ASC 310 (FAS-91, Accounting for Nonrefundable Fees and Costs Associated with Originating or Acquiring Loans and Initial Direct Costs of Leases), when determining the amount of costs a REIT should capitalize for leasing services?
2. Should a REIT account for its investment in an SC on the cost method, the equity method, or the consolidation method, if the REIT receives substantially all of the economic benefits generated by the SC?

EITF CONSENSUS

The EITF reached the following consensus positions:

1. A REIT should not consider an SC to be an independent third party, regardless of how it accounts for its investment in the SC. A REIT should not capitalize costs for leasing services provided by the SC in excess of the amount of such costs that would have been capitalized under the provisions of ASC 840 (FAS-13, Accounting for Leases), as amended by ASC 310 (FAS-91) if the REIT had incurred such costs directly.

    This consensus should be applied prospectively as of July 21, 1995.

2. A REIT should not account for its investment on the cost method if some or all of the following factors—which indicate the REIT's ability to exercise at least significant influence over an SC—exist:
   a. The SC's activities are performed primarily for the REIT.
   b. The REIT receives substantially all of the SC's economic benefits.
   c. The REIT can designate a seat on the SC's board of directors.
   d. Individuals serving on the REIT's board of directors also serve on the SC's board of directors.
   e. The REIT and SC share officers and/or employees.
   f. Owners of a majority of an SC's voting common stock contributed a minimal amount to the SC's equity.
   g. The SC's operations are influenced by the views of the REIT's management.
   h. The REIT can obtain the necessary financial information to account for its investment in the SC on the equity basis.

The Task Force agreed that the decision whether to consolidate the SC or account for it on the equity basis depends on facts and circumstances.

> **OBSERVATION:** The guidance in ASC 840 (FAS-154, Accounting for Changes and Error Corrections) supersedes APB-20 (Accounting Changes), but carries forward many of the Opinion's provisions without change, including those related to reporting a change in accounting estimate, a change in the reporting entity, and the correction of an error. Under the guidance in ASC 250 (FAS-154), a voluntary change in accounting principle must be applied *retrospectively* to the financial statements in all prior periods.

The Task Force also observed that if application of the consensus on Issue 2 results in a change in the method of accounting for a REIT's investment in an SC, the change should be accounted for based on the guidance in ASC 250 (FAS-154, which superseded APB-20) for reporting a change in accounting entity. The EITF reached a consensus that a restatement should be reported in the next annual financial statements issued by the REIT after September 21, 1995.

DISCUSSION

1. This Issue initially was considered a secondary issue because the consensus might depend on the primary issue—the REIT's accounting for the SC. That is, if an SC provides leasing services to the REIT, a consensus on the accounting for the REIT's investment in the SC would affect the amount of initial direct leasing costs capitalized by the REIT. Under the guidance in ASC 840

(FAS-13), as amended by FAS-91, initial direct leasing costs are limited to (*a*) those that would be incurred in transactions with independent third parties to originate a lease and to (*b*) certain costs incurred by a REIT for specific activities related to obtaining a lease. If an SC is consolidated, the amount of leasing costs permitted under the guidance in ASC 310 (FAS-91) would be limited to certain internal costs.

During the Task Force's discussion of a REIT's accounting for an investment in an SC, the SEC Observer expressed his discomfort with a conclusion that a REIT can capitalize fees paid to an SC that would not be capitalizable if the REIT had incurred those costs directly. The Task Force's consensus was influenced by that view. It was also influenced by the fact that the decision on the method used by the REIT may be subject to judgment.

2. A REIT's voting interest in an SC is usually less than 10%. Under a strict interpretation of APB-18, a 20% or greater voting interest in an investee connotes significant influence. The Task Force believed that a REIT often has significant influence over an SC's operations, even if it has less than a 20% voting interest in the SC. The Task Force therefore developed a list of factors that would indicate that a REIT has significant influence and could overcome the 20% ownership presumption in APB-18.

ASC 978 Real Estate—Time Shares

SOP 04-2 (Accounting for Real Estate Time-Sharing Transactions) (ASC 978-10-05-3 through 05-6, 15-3 through 15-6; ASC 978-230-45-1; ASC 978-250-35-1; ASC 978-310-05-2 through 05-3; 30-1 through 30-2; 35-1 through 35-6, 40-1 through 40-2; 978-340-25-1 through 25-5; 40-1 through 40-2; 60-1; 978-605-10-1; 15-1; 25-1 through 25-17, 25-19; 30-1 through 30-10; 55-1 through 55-25, 55-27 through 55-62; 55-64 through 55-95; 978-720-05-2 through 05-4; 25-1 through 25-3; 978-810-25-1; 978-840-25-1 through 25-2)

BACKGROUND

The volume of sales of interests in real estate time-sharing intervals has grown enormously during the past 20 years. In addition, the variety of ways in which interests in time-sharing intervals are structured has increased. For example, interests in time-sharing intervals may be purchased for a fixed time, such as a specific week; for a floating time, such as a specific season; or in the form of points, vacation clubs, or fractional interests. Also, buyers may have the right to exchange their time-sharing intervals for other time periods and venues, as well as for other products, such as cruises, through a third-party exchange company. Some sellers of time-sharing intervals establish time-sharing special-purpose entities to which they transfer title in the real estate.

STANDARDS

Scope

SOP 04-2 applies to the accounting for *real estate* time-sharing transactions in which a seller:

- Passes title and ownership of the real estate to a buyer or SPE in a fee simple transaction without recourse
- Retains title and ownership of all or a portion of the real estate
- Passes to a buyer title and ownership of all or a portion of the real estate, which subsequently revert to the seller or are transferred to a third party

The SOP also applies to transactions involving a time-share reseller.

Profit Recognition under ASC 360 (FASB Statement No. 66)

Sellers should recognize revenue on sales of real estate time-sharing intervals in accordance with the guidance in FAS-66 for sales of real estate other than retail land sales. The guidance in paragraphs 25 through 43 of the Statement (FASB Accounting Standards Codification (ASC) 360-20-40-37, 40-38, 40-40 through 40-50, 40-56, 40-57 through 40-64; 460-10-60-3; 840-10-25-60) regarding continuing involvement should be followed. Revenue may be recognized in accordance with the percentage-of-completion method if the criteria in paragraph 37 (ASC 360-20-40-50) have been met, but related selling and marketing costs should not be included in computing costs. Contract-for-deed arrangements qualify for profit recognition. Transactions in which title can revert to a seller, however, should be accounted for as operating leases.

Seller Identification of Projects and Phases

Time-share interval projects may be constructed in a single phase or in multiple phases. This SOP requires sellers of time-sharing intervals to (*a*) define a project at its inception in terms of the number of phases to be developed and (*b*) to account separately for each phase of a project.

If the definition of a project or its phases changes because of significant changes in facts and circumstances related to the development of a project, that is, a change in the nature of a project, the change should be accounted for as a change in an accounting estimate by making an adjustment in the current period. Significant changes may include changes in sales prices or discount programs, changes in construction contract prices or inflation, temporary construction delays, design changes, or a seller's decision to significantly increase the proportion of a project's luxury units as compared to the number of standard units in the project. If a change in the definition of a project is *not* the result of a significant change in facts or circumstances in the project's development, such as a change in the number of phases into which a project is divided, which is a change in the way the project is accounted for but is *not* a change in the facts and circumstances of the project, the change should be accounted for as a cumulative effect of a change in the application of an accounting principle in accordance with FAS-154 (Accounting Changes and Error Corrections) (ASC 250-120-45-5 through 45-10).

Determination of Sales Value

Under the guidance in ASC 360 (FAS-66) the *sales value* of a sale of real estate must be calculated in order to determine whether a buyer's initial and continuing investment is adequate for full accrual revenue recognition. To determine the sales value of a real estate sale, the stated sales price should be adjusted as follows:

- Reduce the stated sales price of a time-sharing interval by the difference between the amount paid by a buyer to a seller and the fair value of products or services a seller provides or is legally or otherwise committed to provide to a buyer as part of consummating a sale. Such products or services often are used as sales incentives and should be accounted for in accordance with the guidance in EITF Issue 01-9 (Accounting for Consideration Given by a Vendor to a Customer (Including a Reseller of the Vendor's Products), which differentiates between cash and noncash incentives. Noncash incentives should be accounted for as separate deliverables that have an associated cost of sales. Cash incentives should be accounted for as discounts of the stated sales prices.

    A seller may give a buyer a *cash* incentive in cash or by waiving a payment that the buyer would otherwise have to make, for example, payment for closing costs or for the first year of owners association maintenance fees. A *noncash* incentive is one that a buyer could purchase, such as a first-year membership in a time-share exchange program or a voucher for airline tickets. If a *noncash* incentive such as a voucher for airline tickets is provided free as an incentive to consummate a sale, the stated sales price of the time-sharing interval should be *reduced* by the fair value of the voucher, which should be recognized as a separate item in revenue.

    If a time-sharing interval is sold together with a membership in a time-share exchange program, however, and the first year of membership in the program is provided for free, the fair value of the fee for the exchange program should be accounted for as a *cash* incentive, because the buyer would otherwise have to pay the fee. In that case, the fair value of the fee for the exchange program should be deducted from the sales price and accounted for as a reduction of the seller's cost for fees instead of as a separate revenue item. Incentives do *not* include products or services that are included in future maintenance charges or other fees that a buyer pays for at market rates.

Inducements provided by a seller to prospective buyers regardless of whether they make a purchase are considered to be selling costs, which should be accounted for in accordance with the SOP discussion in the section on costs to sell time-sharing intervals.

- Increase the stated sales price for the purpose of determining sales value by fees charged to a buyer that are unrelated to financing, such as fees for document preparation. Fees that a seller collects for third parties, such as municipalities or taxing authorities, however, should *not* be added to the stated sales price and should *not* be included in a buyer's initial and continuing investment. Fees that are related to financing of time-share purchases, such as loan origination fees, should be accounted for as adjustments to the stated interest rate on financings, in accordance with the guidance in ASC 310 (FAS-91, Accounting for Nonrefundable Fees and Costs Associated with Originating or Acquiring Loans and Initial Direct Costs of Leases). Sellers that offer buyers at the time of sale programs under which buyers can reduce their payments by prepaying their notes, or sellers that consistently make such offers during the term of buyers' notes should include estimated payment reductions in their calculations of sales value.

- Sellers that partially or fully finance buyers' time-sharing transactions at stated interest rates that are less than prevailing market rates for buyers with similar credit ratings in similar transactions should reduce the sales value and the amount of the note in accordance with the guidance in ASC 835 (APB-21, Interest on Receivables and Payables).

Application of Test of Buyer's Commitment

When testing for the adequacy of a buyer's commitment under paragraph 5(b) of FAS-66 (ASC 360-20-40-5), sellers should reduce the amount of buyers' initial and continuing investments by the amount that the fair value of products or services offered to buyers as incentives exceeds the amount paid by a buyer for such goods or services. That requirement does not apply if a buyer does *not* receive the incentive until the buyer has met certain contractual obligations related to the purchase of a time-sharing interval. For example, a seller requires a buyer to make timely payments on a note for six months in order for the seller to pay the buyer's owners association fees in the second year. In that situation, a seller has to determine whether future performance meets the initial and continuing investment criterion for a buyer's commitment. To meet that criterion, a buyer's future payments required for eligibility to receive an incentive should at least equal the incentive's fair value. The required payments should equal the value of an incentive and interest on the amount *not* paid for the incentive.

When applying the criterion in paragraph 5(b) of FAS-66 (ASC 360-20-40-5), a seller should reduce the measurement of a buyer's commitment by the amount that the fair value of an incentive exceeds the amount the buyer paid for the incentive if future performance is deemed *not* to be sufficient. If a portion of a buyer's down payment is considered to apply as a payment for an incentive because the buyer's future payment does *not* at least equal the fair value of the incentive, that amount should *not* be included in the buyer's initial and continuing investment.

Upgrade and Reload Transactions

In a *reload* transaction, an existing owner of a time-sharing interval purchases a new interval, which is accounted for as a separate transaction. The buyer must meet the commitment criterion in paragraph 5(b) of FAS-66 (ASC 360-20-40-5) by making an additional cash payment or providing other consideration that qualifies. The buyer's initial and continuing investments from the initial transaction should *not* be included in measuring the buyer's commitment for the additional purchase.

In an *upgrade* transaction, a buyer modifies an existing time-share interval. In that case, the buyer's initial and continuing investments in the original transaction are included in determining whether the buyer meets the commitment criterion. The guidance in FAS-66 for profit recognition is applied to the sales value of the new interval.

Accounting for Uncollectibility

Receivables of interest and principal on sales of time-sharing intervals become uncollectible when a seller determines that less than the total amount of the note will be collected. Uncollectibility should be based on a seller's actual collection experience, regardless of who services the receivables, not based on amounts a seller receives as proceeds. In accounting for uncollectible receivables, sellers should:

- Recognize estimates of uncollectible receivables as a reduction of sales revenue when recognizing profit on sales of time-sharing intervals under the full accrual or the percentage of completion methods. To recognize the reduction in revenue on estimated uncollectible amounts accounted for under the relative sales value method, a corresponding adjustment is made to cost of sales and inventory by applying the cost-of-sales percentage.

- Charge uncollectible accrued interest income receivable to interest income when it is determined that a receivable is uncollectible.
- Consider modifications, deferments, or downgrades of receivables, which involve only modifications of the terms of notes receivable, as troubled debt restructurings, and account for them under the guidance in ASC 310 (FAS-114, Accounting by Creditors for Impairment of a Loan). The allowance for uncollectible accounts should be charged when a recorded investment in a note receivable is reduced under the provisions of ASC 310 (FAS-114). That treatment is necessary, because estimated losses were charged against revenue when a sale was recognized or was subsequently charged against revenue as a change in estimate. Direct costs associated with uncollectible receivables, such as collection costs, should be expensed as incurred.
- Account for assumptions of notes receivable as two separate activities with two different parties as follows:
  —Charge the allowance for uncollectible receivables with the remaining investment in the original note receivable, which becomes uncollectible when an arrangement with the original buyer is terminated.
  —Account for a time-sharing transaction with a new buyer in accordance with the profit recognition guidance in ASC 360 (FAS-66).
- Account for the allowance for uncollectibles the same as for any receivables after the initial recognition of a sale when revenue is reduced for estimated uncollectibles, except that *no* bad debt expense is recognized.
- Evaluate receivables in each reporting period, and, at least quarterly, estimate the amount of ultimate collections and evaluate the adequacy of the allowance under the guidance in ASC 450 (FAS-5, Accounting for Contingencies). Adjust the allowance and current-period revenue through the account for uncollectibles, which is a contra-revenue account. Adjust cost of sales and inventory for a corresponding amount.
- Determine the amount of the allowance for uncollectibles by considering uncollectibles by year of sale and the aging of notes receivable and other factors such as the location of time-share units, contract terms, collection experience, economic conditions, and other qualitative factors.
- Adjust interest income if a gain or loss on a sale of a portfolio of receivables without recourse is attributable to a change in market interest rates between the date receivables were generated and the date they were sold. Adjust revenue for a gain or loss on the transaction attributable to other factors, such as a change in the perceived credit quality of the portfolio between the date receivables were generated and the date they were sold.

Accounting for Cost of Sales and Inventory

The following guidance applies only to transactions accounted for under the full accrual, percentage-of-completion, cost recovery, installment, or reduced profit revenue recognition methods discussed in FAS-66. It does *not* apply to transactions accounted for under the deposit method, which is also discussed in ASC 360 (FAS-66).

Sellers should account for the cost of sales and time-sharing inventory by the *relative sales value method*, which is similar to a gross profit method. It is used to allocate inventory cost and to determine the cost of sales in conjunction with a sale. Under this method, cost of sales is calculated as a percentage of net sales using a cost-of-sales percentage, which is a ratio of total costs to the total remaining estimated time-sharing revenue. Different phases should be accounted for separately under this method. Common costs, including costs of amenities, should be allocated to inventory by the phase they will benefit.

Estimated total revenue, which is the actual amount to date, and expected future revenue, should include factors such as incurred or estimated uncollectibles, changes in sales prices or sales mix, repossession of intervals the seller may or may not be able to sell, effects of upgrade programs, and past or expected sales incentives to sell slow-moving inventory. Those estimates should be recalculated at least quarterly. The cost-of-sales percentage should be recalculated whenever estimated revenue or cost is adjusted based on newly estimated total revenue and total cost, including costs to complete, if any. The *effects* of changes should be accounted for prospectively in the period in which a change occurred so that the revised estimates will be reported in the balance sheet and in subsequent periods as if those estimates had been made at inception. The effects of changes should be disclosed in accordance with the guidance in FAS-154 (Accounting Changes and Error Corrections) (ASC 250-10-50-4). The inventory balance in the balance sheet, estimated costs to complete the inventory, if any, is the pool of costs that will be charged against future revenue.

If the relative sales value method is used, inventory is *not* affected if a time-sharing interval is repossessed or reacquired, unless there is a change in expected uncollectibles. Sellers should test inventory for impairment based on the guidance in ASC 360 (FAS-144, Accounting for the Impairment or Disposal of Long-Lived Assets).

Costs to Sell Time-Sharing Intervals

Costs incurred to sell time-sharing intervals should be expensed as incurred unless the costs qualify for capitalization under ASC 978 SOP 04-2). Deferral of recognition until a sale transaction occurs, however, is permitted for costs that (*a*) are reasonably expected to be recovered from the sale of time-sharing intervals or from incidental operations and (*b*) are incurred for (1) tangible assets used directly during the selling period for the purpose of making sales (for example, model units and furnishings, sales property and equipment, and semi-permanent signs), and (2) services required to obtain regulatory approval of sales, for example, legal fees and costs of preparing, printing, and filing prospectuses. Such costs should be allocated proportionately to sale transactions based on the number of intervals available for sale in a project or phase to which those selling costs apply.

Other costs may be deferred until a sale occurs if they are (*a*) reasonably expected to be recovered from a sale of time-sharing intervals; (*b*) directly associated with sales transactions accounted for under the percentage of completion, installment, reduced profit, or deposit methods of accounting, such as commissions; and (*c*) incremental costs that a seller would *not* have incurred if a sales transaction had not occurred. Deferred selling costs should be expensed in the period in which the related revenue is recognized. Deferred selling costs related to sales contracts that are canceled before profit has been recognized on the transaction should be expensed in the period in which the cancellation occurred.

Costs of call centers and direct and incremental costs related to bringing potential buyers to tour a property should be expensed as incurred. Other costs that should be expensed as incurred are costs incurred for unsuccessful sales transactions and sales overhead, such as rent for on-site and off-site sales offices, utilities, maintenance, and telephone expenses. The cost of nonrefundable airline tickets purchased for potential buyers who will be touring a property should be expensed on the date of the visit.

Operations During Holding Periods

The holding period for time-sharing operations begins when intervals are available for sale, that is, when they are legally registered for sale as time-sharing intervals, which should be accounted for as inventory during holding periods and should *not* be depreciated. Operating costs during holding periods include (*a*) seller subsidies to an owners association and (*b*) maintenance and other costs related to time-sharing intervals held for sale.

Units rented in periods other than the holding period should be depreciated with rental activities accounted for under the guidance in ASC 840 (FAS-13, Accounting for Leases) and related authoritative literature. In each reporting period, sellers should evaluate whether to continue classifying time-sharing intervals as held and available for sale.

During a holding period, revenue and costs of rental and other operations should be accounted for as incidental operations. If incremental revenue from incidental operations exceeds related incremental costs, the pool of inventory costs under the relative sales value method should be reduced by that excess amount. Estimates of future excess amounts should *not* be considered in calculations under the relative value method. Incremental costs that exceed incremental revenue should be expensed as incurred.

Costs related to rentals and other operations (for example, sampler programs and mini-vacations) during a holding period should be deferred if they are (*a*) directly related to rental activities during a holding period and are reasonably expected to be recovered from those activities and (*b*) incremental costs that a seller would not have incurred if a particular rental transaction had not occurred. Such deferred costs should be expensed or netted against inventory costs in the period in which a rental occurs.

Sampler Programs and Mini-Vacations

If a seller applies a portion of a buyer's payment for a sampler program or mini-vacation that has *not* been used in its entirety against the sales price of a time-sharing interval, the payment should be considered a part of the buyer's initial and continuing investment when evaluating the buyer's commitment. A seller should *not* include such a payment in a buyer's initial and continuing investments, however, if the buyer has fully used the sampler program or mini-vacation, even if legal documents state that the payment would be applied to the sales price.

Special Entities, Point Systems, Vacation Clubs, and Similar Structures

Interests in time-sharing intervals structured as special entities established to facilitate sales, point systems, vacation clubs, and variations of those structures, should be accounted for based on the guidance for profit recognition in ASC 360 (FAS-66). The transactions should be evaluated primarily based on whether a seller has transferred title to an interest in a time-sharing interval without recourse and whether the seller has a continuing involvement with the buyer, and other requirements necessary to meet the profit recognition criteria in ASC 360 (FAS-66). Profit should only be recognized if a time-sharing interval has been sold to an end user. No profit should be recognized on a transfer of time-sharing intervals to a special purpose entity (SPE), which should be considered to have no economic substance for balance sheet reporting purposes if it (*a*) was structured for legal purposes and (*b*) has no debt, and its only assets are the time-sharing intervals. Interests in an SPE not yet sold to end users should be presented in the balance sheet as time-sharing inventory. SPEs that do not meet the conditions in (*a*) and (*b*) above should be accounted for in the same manner as investments in other SPE's structures.

A seller, its affiliate, or a related party that operates a points program, vacation, or exchange program should be considered to have a continuing involvement with the buyer. A seller's accounting should be determined based on whether compensation for those services is set at prevailing market rates. If there is no compensation for the services, or if the fee is at below prevailing market rates, compensation should be imputed when a sale is recognized and charged against the sales value of the interval. Profit should be recognized under the guidance on continuing involvement in FAS-66. Revenue on those services should be recognized as it is earned.

Owners Associations

Until all time-sharing intervals have been sold, a seller is the owner of all unsold units and is required to pay the owners association dues or maintenance fees for those units. Also, sellers will frequently subsidize the operations of an owners association for a limited time rather than pay dues or maintenance fees on unsold units. Sellers' payments for maintenance fees should be expensed as incurred. Subsidies to an owners association also should be expensed. A seller that is contractually entitled to recover all or a portion of its subsidy to an owners association should recognize a receivable only if recovery is probable and the measurement of the receivable is reasonably reliable. A seller that is hired to manage an owners association for a fee should recognize that fee as revenue only if it is earned and realized or realizable. A seller that subsidizes an owners association's operations while acting as its manager should offset its revenue from fees on seller-owned intervals against its subsidy expense.

> **OBSERVATION:** The guidance in the previous paragraph applies if a timeshare development's Owners Association (OA) is not consolidated in the seller's financial statements, but this SOP does not provide guidance regarding issues related to consolidation of an OA. Such guidance is provided in ARB-51 (Consolidated Financial Statements), as amended by FAS-94 (Consolidation of All Majority-Owned Subsidiaries), FAS-144 (Accounting for the Impairment or Disposal of Long-Lived Assets), and FAS-160 (Noncontrolling Interests in Consolidated Financial Statements); FIN-46R (Consolidation of Variable Interest Entities); and related EITF Issues. AcSEC noted that the amendment of ARB-51 by FAS-144 removed the previous exception that allowed an entity not to consolidate a controlled entity if control is likely to be temporary.

Presentation and Disclosures

In its balance sheet, a seller should present gross notes receivable from time-sharing sales, a deduction from notes receivable for the allowance for uncollectibles, and a deduction from notes receivable for deferred profit under FAS-66, if any.

Sellers of time-sharing intervals should make the following disclosures in their financial statements:

- The effects of changes in estimate in the relative sales value method, in accordance with the guidance in ASC 250-10-50-4 (FAS-154).
- Maturities of notes receivable for each of the five years following the date of the financial statements and the total for all following years. The total of notes receivable balances displayed with various maturity dates should be reconciled to the amount of notes receivable on the balance sheet.
- The weighted average and range of stated interest rates of notes receivable
- Estimated cost to complete improvements and promised amenities
- Activity in the allowance for uncollectibles, including the balance at the beginning and end of the period, additions related to sales in the current period, direct write-offs charged against the allowance, and changes in estimates related to sales in prior periods. The same disclosures should be made for receivables with recourse, if applicable.
- Policies related to meeting the criteria for a buyer's commitment and collectibility of sales prices in ASC 360 (FAS-66)

Changes in time-sharing notes receivable, including sales of those notes, should be reported as cash flows from operations in the statement of cash flows.

RELATED CHAPTERS IN 2011 *GAAP GUIDE, VOLUME II*

Chapter 11, "Consolidated Financial Statements"
Chapter 23, "Interim Financial Reporting"

RELATED CHAPTERS IN 2011 *GAAP GUIDE, VOLUME I*

Chapter 7, "Consolidated Financial Statements"
Chapter 26, "Interim Financial Reporting"
Chapter 37, "Real Estate Transactions"

CHAPTER 34
RESEARCH AND DEVELOPMENT

CONTENTS

Overview	34.01
Authoritative Guidance	
ASC 730 Research and Development	34.02
EITF Issue 07-3 Accounting for Nonrefundable Advance Payments for Goods or Services to Be Used in Future Research and Development Activities	34.02
ASC 810 Consolidation	34.03
EITF Issue 99-16 Accounting for Transactions with Elements of Research and Development Arrangements	34.03
Related Chapter in 2011 GAAP Guide, Volume I	34.05

OVERVIEW

The accounting for research and development (R&D) costs is carefully defined in the authoritative accounting literature. Once R&D costs are appropriately identified, GAAP require that they be expensed in the period incurred. Some costs related to R&D activities, however, may be capitalized and carried forward as assets if the R&D has alternative future uses. Assets related to R&D may include property, plant, and equipment and intangible assets used in an entity's ongoing R&D effort.

The following pronouncements, which are the sources of GAAP for the costs of research and development, are discussed in the 2011 *GAAP Guide, Volume I*, Chapter 39, "Research and Development":

    ASC 730   Accounting for Research and Development Costs (FAS-2)

    ASC 730   Research and Development Arrangements (FAS-68)

34.02 *Research and Development*

AUTHORITATIVE GUIDANCE

ASC 730 Research and Development

EITF Issue No. 07-3 (Accounting for Nonrefundable Advance Payments for Goods or Services to Be Used in Future Research and Development Activities) (ASC 730-10-55-3; 730-20-25-13 through 25-14; 35-1; 65-1)

OVERVIEW

This Issue addresses the accounting for *nonrefundable* portions of advance payments made by entities involved in research and development activities (R&D entities) on purchases of goods and services that will be used in their activities in the future, such as payments to contract research organizations (CRO), which perform clinical trial management services. Prepayments to CROs are generally for activities, such as per-patient clinical trial treatment costs and for travel costs of a CRO's personnel. In addition, CROs often enter into contracts with third parties to deliver the goods or services to the R&D entity and must pay those third parties even if the R&D activities are terminated. Advance payments are usually made three to six months before the R&D activity begins.

R&D entities usually purchase goods and services for a specific project and can not use them for another future project. A portion of the advance may sometimes be refundable, but usually some portion of the advance payment is nonrefundable.

There is diversity in the way that R&D entities account for the nonrefundable portion of advance payments. Some defer the costs of advance payments until the R&D activities have been performed while others expense them as the payments are made.

SCOPE

The guidance in this Issue applies only to *nonrefundable* advance payments for goods and services to be used or rendered in future R&D activities under executory contractual arrangements. The accounting guidance in ASC 730 (FASB Statement No. 2, *Accounting for Research and Development Costs* (FAS-2)), applies to nonrefundable advance payments for materials, equipment, facilities, and purchased intangible assets having an alternative future use to be used in future R&D activities. The consensus position reached on this Issue should not be applied by analogy to other types of advance payments.

ACCOUNTING ISSUE

Should *nonrefundable* advance payments for goods or services that will be used or rendered for research and development activities be expensed when the advance payment is made or when the research and development equity has been performed?

EITF CONSENSUS

The EITF reached a consensus that R&D entities should defer and capitalize as assets *nonrefundable* advance payments for goods and services that will be used or rendered in future R&D activities. Amounts related to goods delivered and services performed should be recognized as expenses. Entities should continue to evaluate whether they expect that purchased goods will be delivered and purchased services will rendered. If they will *not* be used in future R&D activities, capitalized advanced payments for those goods and services should be expensed.

FASB RATIFICATION

The FASB ratified the EITF's consensus on this Issue at its June 27, 2007, meeting.

ASC 810 Consolidation

EITF Issue 99-16 (Accounting for Transactions with Elements of Research and Development Arrangements) (ASC 810-30-15-2, 15-3; 25-1, 25-3; 30-1; 35-1; 45-1, 45-2; 55-1 through 55-4)

OVERVIEW

This Issue applies only to certain new transactions, such as in the following example. A Sponsor capitalizes a *wholly owned* subsidiary (Newco) with $110 million in cash and the right to technology developed by the sponsor, which has no book value, in exchange for shares in Class A and Class B common stock in Newco, which have a nominal fair value. Simultaneously, the Sponsor and Newco enter into agreements that include a *development contract* and a *purchase option*. Thereafter, the Sponsor distributes the Class A common shares in Newco, which have a fair value of $80 million, to its shareholders. The Sponsor continues to hold all of the Class B common shares that give the Sponsor no financial interest and no voting interest except for certain blocking rights. Newco, which has no employees—except for a CEO—and has only nominal office facilities, is required to spend all of the cash contributed by the Sponsor on R&D, which will be performed by the Sponsor under a cost plus 10% development contract with Newco. The Sponsor will be paid $55 million for each of two years, at the end of which all of the cash will have been expended.

The Sponsor has the right to exercise the option to purchase all of Newco's Class A common shares at any time during the term of the development contract at a price that approximates the fair value of the shares. During that two-year period, Newco is not permitted to change the Sponsor's rights under the purchase option without the Sponsor's previous approval. Newco also is prohibited from merging, liquidating, selling a substantial portion of its assets, or amending its certificate of incorporation to change the purchase option, Newco's authorized capitalization, or the certificate of incorporation's provisions regarding Newco's board of directors without the Sponsor's previous approval.

Arrangements in which funds are provided by third parties are not included under the scope of this Issue, because they generally would be accounted for under the provisions of ASC 730 (FAS-68, Research and Development Arrangements).

Under the provisions of ASC 730 (FAS-68), an enterprise accounts for an R&D arrangement that gives the enterprise the right to the results of R&D funded partially or entirely by others based on the nature of the obligation incurred under the arrangement. An enterprise that must repay funds provided by others, regardless of the results of the R&D, is required to estimate and recognize that liability. However, the enterprise would account for its obligation under the arrangement as a contract to perform R&D for others if the repayment obligation occurs only if the R&D has a future economic benefit.

ACCOUNTING ISSUE

How should a Sponsor account for a research and development arrangement under the scope of this Issue?

EITF CONSENSUS

- The Sponsor should account as follows for an R&D arrangement under the scope of this Issue:
    - —On distribution of Newco's Class A common stock, reclassify cash contributed to Newco as restricted cash and recognize R&D expense as those activities are performed.
    - —Account for the distribution of the Class A common stock as a dividend to the Sponsor's common stockholders.
    - —Calculate the amount of the dividend based on the fair value of Newco's Class A common stock and recognize the transaction when the stock is distributed.
    - —Present Newco's Class A common stock outside permanent equity, similar to a minority interest.
- In determining the amount of net income or earnings available to the Sponsor's common stockholders for the EPS calculation, the Sponsor should *not* allocate any portion of R&D expense to Newco's Class A common stock. The Task Force noted that the accounting result under this consensus is in essence the same as

it would be in consolidation with the incurred R&D costs allocated to Newco's Class B common stock held by the Sponsor, because the value of the Class A common stock is related to the value of the purchase option, *not* to the Sponsor's original funding of the arrangement

- The Sponsor should account for the purchase option as follows:

    —*Purchase option is exercised* Account for the exercise of the option to acquire the Class A common stock like an acquisition of a minority interest by allocating the excess of the option's exercise price over its carrying amount to the assets acquired (in-process or completed R&D) and liabilities assumed, if any.

    —*Purchase option is not exercised* When an option expires, reclassify Newco's Class A common stock to additional paid-in capital as an adjustment to the initial dividend.

- *Effective date and transition* The consensus positions apply to R&D arrangements consummated after May 18, 2000, and to existing arrangements in which any form of commitment (e.g., Sponsor's guarantee of Newco's debt) exists. An arrangement has been consummated if the Sponsor has distributed Newco's shares to its shareholders and the related agreements, including the following, have been executed:

    —Creation and commitment to a specified amount of Newco's capitalization

    —Development and purchase option agreements

    —Other related agreements, such as a sponsor's financing guarantees

    Commitments made after May 18, 2000, that involve additional financing for existing arrangements should be accounted for based on the consensus positions in this Issue by reporting the revised accounting for the arrangement as a cumulative effect of a change in accounting principle under ASC 250 (APB-20).

    > **OBSERVATION:** ASC 810 (FIN-46(R)) (Consolidation of Variable Interest Entities) requires the consolidation of variable interest entities by an entity that absorbs a majority of a variable entity's expected losses or has the right to receive a greater part of a variable entity's expected residual returns or both. The Interpretation applies to many special-purpose entities involved in research and development activities.

RELATED CHAPTER IN 2011 GAAP GUIDE, VOLUME 1

Chapter 39, "Research and Development"

CHAPTER 35
RESULTS OF OPERATIONS

CONTENTS

Overview		**35.02**
Authoritative Guidance		
ASC 205 Presentation of Financial Statements		**35.04**
EITF Issue 87-24	Allocation of Interest to Discontinued Operations	**35.04**
EITF Issue 03-13	Applying the Conditions in Paragraph 42 of FASB Statement No. 144, *Accounting for the Impairment or Disposal of Long-Lived Assets*, in Determining Whether to Report Discontinued Operations	**35.07**
ASC 210 Balance Sheet		**35.12**
Topic D-43	Assurance That a Right of Setoff Is Enforceable in a Bankruptcy under FASB Interpretation No. 39	**35.12**
ASC 225 Income Statement		**35.13**
EITF Issue 01-13	Income Statement Display of Business Interruption Insurance Recoveries	**35.13**
AIN APB-9	Reporting the Results of Operations: Unofficial Accounting Interpretations of APB Opinion No. 9	**35.14**
AIN APB-30	Reporting the Results of Operations: Accounting Interpretations of APB Opinion No. 30	**35.14**
ASC 325 Investments—Other		**35.15**
FTB-85-4-1	Accounting for Life Settlement Contracts by Third-Party Providers	**35.15**
ASC 330 Inventory		**35.20**
EITF Issue 96-9	Classification of Inventory Markdowns and Other Costs Associated with a Restructuring	**35.20**

ASC 410 Asset Retirement and Environmental Obligations	35.21
EITF Issue 89-13 Accounting for the Cost of Asbestos Removal	35.21
ASC 605 Revenue Recognition	35.22
EITF Issue 01-14 Income Statement Characterization of Reimbursements Received for "Out-of-Pocket" Expenses Incurred	35.22
Issue 06-3 How Taxes Collected from Customers and Remitted to Governmental Authorities Should Be Presented in the Income Statement (That Is, Gross versus Net Presentation)	35.23
ASC 710 Compensation—General	35.25
EITF Issue 06-2 Accounting for Sabbatical Leave and Other Similar Benefits Pursuant to FASB Statement No. 43, *Accounting for Compensated Absences*	35.25
ASC 720 Other Expenses	35.26
SOP 98-5 Reporting on the Costs of Start-Up Activities	35.26
ASC 808 Collaborative Arrangements	35.28
EITF Issue 07-1 Accounting for Collaborative Arrangements	35.28
ASC 855 Subsequent Events	35.32
Topic D-86 Issuance of Financial Statements	35.32
ASC 954-450 Health Care Entities—Contingencies	35.33
EITF Issue 09-L Health Care Entities: Presentation of Insurance Claims and Related Insurance Recoveries	35.33
Related Chapters in 2011 GAAP Guide, Volume II	35.35
Related Chapters in 2011 GAAP Guide, Volume I	35.35
Related Chapter in 2011 International Accounting/Financial Reporting Standards Guide	35.36

OVERVIEW

Reporting the results of operations, primarily determining and presenting net income and comprehensive income, is one of the most important aspects of financial reporting. GAAP provide specific guidance concerning how certain items should be presented in the income statement.

The following pronouncements, which are the sources of GAAP for reporting the results of operations are discussed in the 2011 *GAAP Guide, Volume I,* Chapter 40, "Results of Operations."

ASC 225; ASC 250	Reporting the Results of Operations (APB-9)
ASC 225	Reporting the Results of Operations—Reporting the Effects of Disposal of a Segment of a Business, and Extraordinary, Unusual, and Infrequently Occurring Events and Transactions (APB-30)
ASC 250; ASC 270	Prior Period Adjustments (FAS-16)
ASC 220	Reporting Comprehensive Income (FAS-130)
ASC 420	Accounting for Costs Associated with Exit or Disposal Activities (FAS-146)
ASC 250	Accounting Changes and Error Corrections (FIN-154)
ASC, *Glossary*	Accounting for a Loss on a Sublease (FIN-27)

AUTHORITATIVE GUIDANCE

ASC 205 Presentation of Financial Statements

EITF Issue 87-24 Allocation of Interest to Discontinued Operations (ASC 205-20-45-6 through 45-69; S50-1; S99-3)

OVERVIEW

A company selling a business segment (or line of business) reports the sale separately as a discontinued operation. The company has debt on its balance sheet.

ACCOUNTING ISSUES

1. Can interest expense be allocated to discontinued operations based on the debt's principal amount that will or could be paid with proceeds from the sale of operations?
2. If so, how should such interest be allocated?
3. Can general overhead expenses be allocated to discontinued operations?

EITF CONSENSUS

1. Allocation of interest to discontinued operations is permitted but not required. (See the subsequent development section below.)
2. The following method should be used if allocation of interest to discontinued operations is elected:
   a. Allocate other consolidated interest not attributable to the entity's other operations based on a ratio of net assets to be sold or discontinued less debt required to be paid due to the disposal transaction to the sum of the consolidated entity's total net assets plus consolidated debt *other than:*
      (1) Debt of the discontinued operation that will be assumed by the buyer,
      (2) Debt required to be paid due to the disposal transaction, and
      (3) Debt that can be directly attributed to the entity's other operations.
   b. A uniform consolidated debt-to-equity ratio for all operations is assumed. If that is not the case because the assets being sold are atypical, as in a finance company, a normal debt-to-equity ratio for that type of business can be used.

c. Allocate interest to discontinued operations based on debt that can be identified as specifically related to those operations, if allocation based on net assets would not provide meaningful results.

The consensus applies to the income statement presentation of both continuing and discontinued operations and including presentation of the gain or loss on disposal of a component of an enterprise. The decision whether to allocate interest should be applied consistently to all discontinued operations.

3. General and corporate overhead should not be allocated to discontinued operations.

SUBSEQUENT DEVELOPMENT

Under the guidance in this Issue, which was based on the framework of APB-30, an entity has been permitted to, but not required to, allocate interest expense related to discontinued operations based on the principal amount of debt that will or could be paid with proceeds received on the sale of discontinued operations. The EITF's consensus has also limited the maximum amount of interest that could be allocated and has provided guidance on the appropriate allocation method. Although ASC 360; ASC 205 (FAS-144, Accounting for the Impairment or Disposal of Long-Lived Assets) supersedes the guidance in APB-30 regarding discontinued operations, the requirement that discontinued operations be reported separately in the income statement from continuing operations has been retained.

At its June 2002 meeting, the EITF reached a consensus requiring that interest on debt that will be assumed by a buyer and debt that must be repaid when the disposal of discontinued operations occurs be allocated to discontinued operations. This consensus modifies the original consensus in Issue 1, but it does *not* affect the allocation of other consolidated interest to discontinued operations, which has been permitted but not required.

SEC STAFF COMMENT

The SEC Observer stated that registrants that elect to allocate interest in accordance with the consensus will be expected to clearly disclose their accounting policy, including the method of allocation, and the amount allocated to and included in discontinued operations for all periods presented.

35.06 Results of Operations

Illustration of Allocation of Interest to Discontinued Operations

Assets	
Assets of discontinued operations	$ 400,000
Other assets	800,000
Total assets	$1,200,000
Liabilities and Equity	
Trade payables and other noninterest-bearing debt	$ 250,000
Debt related to discontinued operations to be assumed by the buyer	100,000
Debt required to be paid due to disposal	150,000
Debt related to other operations	150,000
Debt unrelated to other operations	250,000
Deferred taxes	50,000
Total liabilities	$ 950,000
Stockholders' equity	250,000
Total liabilities and equity	$1,200,000

Total interest expense (10% average interest rate × $650,000 interest-bearing debt) = $65,000

Allocation of interest on consolidated interest not attributable to other operations is computed as follows:

$$\frac{\text{Net assets to be discontinued less debt required to be paid due to disposal}}{\text{Sum of consolidated net assets* plus debt unrelated to other operations}} = \frac{\$400,000 - \$100,000 - \$150,000}{\$250,000 + \$250,000} = .3$$

*($1,200,000 − $950,000 = $250,000)

Interest on debt unrelated to other operations = $250,000 × .10
= $25,000 × .3
= $7,500

Interest on debt assumed by buyer = $100,000 × .10
= $10,000

Interest allocated to discontinued operations = $7,500 + $10,000
= $17,500

DISCUSSION

This Issue was raised by the FASB staff, who noted that practice is varied. The allocation approach chosen by the Task Force is based on the rationale that interest is a cost that should be associated with the assets financed with the debt. The Task Force favored an allocation approach based on the amount of debt that will be repaid with the proceeds of the sale of discontinued operations. However, they decided to limit that amount to debt that will be assumed by the buyer and other debt unrelated to operations, such as general corporate debt.

EITF Issue 03-13 (Applying the Conditions in Paragraph 42 of FASB Statement No. 144, *Accounting for the Impairment or Disposal of Long-Lived Assets*, in Determining Whether to Report Discontinued Operations) (ASC 205-20-50-4,50-6; 55-4 through 55-26, 55-35, 55-37 through 55-40, 55-49 through 55-58, 55-60 through 55-65, 55-67 through 55-79)

OVERVIEW

Paragraph 42 of FAS-144 (Accounting for the Impairment or Disposal of Long-Lived Assets) (ASC 205-20-45-1), which provides guidance on whether the results of operations of a component of an entity that has been disposed of or that is classified as held for sale should be reported in discontinued operations, requires that both of the following two criteria be met: (1) the component's operations and cash flows have been or will be eliminated from the ongoing entity's operations as a result of the disposal transaction and (2) the ongoing entity should have no significant continuing involvement in the disposed of component's operations after a disposal transaction has occurred. This Issue was raised because the FASB had received questions as to whether a disposed of component can have any continuing cash flows that have gone through the ongoing entity's operations.

ACCOUNTING ISSUES

1. How should an ongoing entity evaluate whether operations and cash flows of a component that it has disposed of have been or will be eliminated from the ongoing entity's operations?

2. What types of continuing involvement represent a significant continuing involvement in the operations of a component that has been disposed of?

EITF CONSENSUS

The EITF reached the following consensus positions on an approach for determining whether an ongoing entity that has *eliminated* from its ongoing operations the operations and cash flows of a component it has disposed of has met the criteria in paragraph 42 of FAS-144 (ASC 205-20-45-1) for presentation in discontinued operations of the results of operations of a component that has been disposed of or one being held for sale:

1. The process of evaluating whether the operations and cash flows of a disposed of component have been or will be eliminated from an entity's ongoing operations requires a determination of whether the ongoing entity expects to continue generating *direct* or *indirect* cash flows from activities related to that component. Direct and indirect cash flows are distinguished based on their *nature* and *significance* in accordance with management's expectations and the best available information. Generating *direct* cash flows from a disposed of component is an indicator that an entity has *not* eliminated the component from its operations and, therefore, should *not* present the component in discontinued operations; however, the requirement in paragraph 42(a) (ASC 205-20-45-1), the purpose of which is to determine whether an entity continues a disposed of component's revenue-producing or cost-generating activities after a disposal has occurred, would be met and the component would qualify for presentation in discontinued operations if continuing cash flows are *indirect*.

2. A component's continuing revenue-producing and cost-generating activities are considered to be *direct* cash inflows or outflows if the ongoing entity expects to:
   a. Recognize significant cash inflows and outflows as a result of *migration*, which is the sale of similar commodities or services to specific customers of the disposed of component, *or*
   b. Recognize significant cash inflows and outflows as a result of the continuation of revenue-producing or cost-generating activities with the disposed of component.

Activities That Generate Continuing Cash Flows

An ongoing entity's cash flows after disposal of a component would be considered to be *direct* cash flows if:

- It is likely that revenues and costs being generated by the entity would have been generated by the disposed of component had the disposal not occurred (*migration*), or

- The ongoing entity's revenues and costs are generated as a result of an active involvement with the disposed of component (*continuation of activities*).

If an ongoing entity is generating cash flows as a result of a migration or continuation of activities, the entity should determine whether the cash flows are significant. Although the significance of continuing cash flows generated as a result of other factors need not be determined, an ongoing entity should evaluate the criteria in paragraph 42(b) (ASC 205-20-45-1) to determine whether its continuing involvement in the disposed of component's operations is significant. Interest earned on financing provided by a seller, contingent consideration in a business combination, dividends on an investment, and passive royalty interests in the operations of a component that has been disposed of are examples of continuing cash flows that would *not* be direct.

Significance of Continuing Cash Flows

Judgment is required to determine the significance of continuing cash flows as a result of migration or continuation of activities between an ongoing entity and the disposed of component. The continuing cash flows that an ongoing entity expects to generate after a disposal of a component should be compared to the cash flows that an entity would have expected if the disposal had not occurred. The latter cash flows should include cash flows from transactions with third parties and from intercompany transactions, which should be determined as if they had occurred between the component and a third party. Continuing cash inflows and outflows should be considered separately, regardless of how they are presented in the income statement (gross or net). If it is determined that cash inflows are *direct* cash flows, it is not necessary to evaluate cash outflows.

Significant Continuing Involvement

An ongoing entity that eliminates the operations and cash flows of a disposed of component from its ongoing operations due to a disposal transaction should evaluate whether it will have a significant continuing involvement in the component's operations *after* the transaction has occurred.

The EITF reached a consensus that a continuing involvement in a disposed of component's operations enables the ongoing entity to influence that component's operating and financial policies. An evaluation of whether an ongoing entity has that ability should consider whether the entity retains any risks or is able to obtain benefits from the disposed of component's ongoing operations. Risk retention or the ability to obtain benefits, however, is not by itself an indicator of an ongoing entity's ability to influence a disposed of component's operating and financial policies. Rather, to determine whether an ongoing entity has a continuing involvement with a disposed of component, it is necessary to evaluate the existence of an interest in the disposed of component or a contractual or other type of arrangement with that component, if any.

Qualitative and quantitative factors from the perspective of the disposed of component should be considered in determining whether a continuing involvement is significant. All types of continuing involvement should be considered individually and in total. The following are some factors that should be considered when determining whether an ongoing entity has a *significant* continuing involvement in a disposed of component:

- The entity has retained a sufficiently large interest in a disposed of component that enables it to significantly influence the disposed of component's operating and financial policies. Interests other than common stock or in-substance common stock may provide such influence, but a cost method investment in common stock or in-substance common stock would *not* be considered a significant continuing involvement.

- The ongoing entity and the buyer or the disposed of component have entered into a contractual agreement that provides the previous owner with significant influence over the disposed of component's operating and financial policies. Determining whether a contract or other arrangement provides the ongoing entity with significant continuing involvement requires judgment and consideration of all available information. The following factors, which are *not* individually presumptive or determinative, should be considered:

    —The contract's significance to the disposed of component's overall operations

    —The extent of an ongoing entity's involvement in a disposed of component's operations

    —Each party's rights under the contract

    —The contract or arrangement's pricing terms

Period of Assessment

The EITF reached a consensus that the *assessment period* should include the point when the component initially meets the criteria to be classified as held for sale or is disposed of and should last for one year after the component is actually disposed of. The assessment should be based on all the facts and circumstances including the intent and ability of the ongoing entity's management:

- To eliminate the disposed of component from its operations, and

- To avoid a continuing involvement with the disposed of component's operations.

If during the year following the disposal, significant events or circumstances occur that may change the ongoing entity's current assessment, the entity should reassess whether it expects to meet the criteria in paragraph 42 of FAS-144 (ASC 205-20-45-1). The component's operations should *not* be presented in discontinued operations if such an event occurs and causes the ongoing entity to expect that the criteria in paragraph 42 (ASC 205-20-45-1) will *not* be met by the end of the assessment period. If it is expected that the criteria in paragraph 42 will be met by the end of the assessment period, however, presentation in discontinued operations is permitted. The occurrence of such events may result in the reclassification of a disposed of component into and out of discontinued operations for all periods during the assessment period.

If as a result of circumstances beyond an ongoing entity's control, eliminating a disposed-of component's cash flows from its operations or eliminating its significant involvement in a disposed of component's operations requires more than one year from the actual date of disposal, the assessment period may be extended if the ongoing entity takes the necessary actions to resolve the situation and expects that the disposed of component's direct cash flows and its continuing involvement will be eliminated.

If a component is either disposed of or classified as held for sale at the balance sheet date, significant events or circumstances that occur *after* the balance sheet date but *before* the financial statements are issued should be included in determining whether the criteria in paragraph 42 (ASC 205-20-45-1) are expected to be met so that discontinued operations will be presented in accordance with that paragraph.

Disclosure

An ongoing entity should disclose in the notes to its financial statements the following information about each discontinued operation that generates continuing cash flows:

- The nature of activities generating continuing cash flows
- The period of time over which continuing cash flows are expected to be generated
- The primary factors causing the entity to conclude that expected continuing cash flows are *not* direct cash flows of the disposed-of component
- Intercompany revenues and expenses for all periods presented before the disposal of components (*a*) with which the ongoing entity is involved in *continuation of activities* after their disposal and (*b*) for which the ongoing entity presents in continuing operations after their disposal revenues and expenses that

had been accounted for as intercompany transactions before the disposal of those components

- In the period in which operations are initially classified as discontinued, the types of continuing involvement, if any, that the ongoing entity will have after a disposal transaction

TRANSITION

The consensus positions should be applied to a component of an entity that is either disposed of or classified as held for sale in fiscal periods beginning after December 15, 2004. Operating results related to a component disposed of or classified as held for sale within an entity's fiscal year that includes the date on which the consensus is ratified may be reclassified based on the consensus.

The FASB ratified the consensus positions in this Issue at its November 30, 2004, meeting.

ASC 210 Balance Sheet

Topic D-43 (Assurance That a Right of Setoff Is Enforceable in a Bankruptcy under FASB Interpretation No. 39) (ASC 210-20-45-9)

At the November 1994 meeting of the EITF, the FASB staff clarified the meaning of the phrase "the right of setoff is enforceable at law," which is one of the conditions for offsetting in paragraph 5d of FIN-39 (Offsetting of Amounts Related to Certain Contracts) (ASC 210-20-45-1).

Some have questioned whether the right of setoff is effective if a debtor is in bankruptcy. Two opposing views were suggested about the relationship between paragraph 6 of the Interpretation (ASC 210-20-45-8), which states that "legal constraints should be considered to determine whether the right of setoff is enforceable," and paragraph 48 (not in ASC), which states that "this Interpretation does not include a separate requirement for protection in bankruptcy." Some believed that the effectiveness of the right of setoff in bankruptcy needs to be proved, while others believed that it is unnecessary to consider bankruptcy in financial statements that are prepared under the going-concern concept.

The FASB staff's views about the amount of certainty needed to determine whether the right of setoff should be upheld in bankruptcy straddles those two views. They believe that because the phrase "enforceable at law" includes the concept that the right of setoff should be recognized in bankruptcy, FIN-39 does not include a requirement for protection in bankruptcy. To assert in financial statements that the right of setoff is enforceable at law requires support that depends on cost-benefit constraints, and facts and circumstances. Amounts should be offset only if—based on all available positive and negative information about the ability to legally enforce the setoff—"there is reasonable assurance that the right of setoff would be upheld in bankruptcy."

ASC 225 Income Statement

EITF Issue 01-13 (Income Statement Display of Business Interruption Insurance Recoveries) (ASC 225-30-05-2, 45-1, 50-1; 450-30-60-2, 3)

OVERVIEW

Business interruption (BI) insurance is discussed in the authoritative accounting literature in ASC 605 (FIN-30, Accounting for Involuntary Conversions of Nonmonetary Assets to Monetary Assets) and in SOP 96-1 (Environmental Remediation Liabilities) (see Chapter 11). ASC 605 (FIN-30) provides broad guidance on the recognition, measurement, and classification of insurance recoveries related to property and equipment. Under the Interpretation, gains or losses on involuntary conversions of property and equipment into insurance proceeds should be measured as the difference between the carrying amount of the property or equipment and the insurance proceeds received. Such recoveries are reported in the financial statements on the same line as a reduction of the related loss.

SOP 96-1 (see Chapter 11), which applies to insurance recoveries for environmental remediation costs, requires that expenses related to environmental remediation be reported in *operating* income in financial statements that classify items as operating or nonoperating. Credits from recoveries of such expenses should be reported on the same income statement line as a reduction of the expense.

BI insurance differs from the types of insurance discussed above, because it protects an insured entity's future earnings or profits if its operations are suspended because of a loss of use of equipment and property as a result of a covered event. Such insurance usually reimburses the insured entity for certain costs and losses incurred during a reasonable period in which the entity rebuilds, repairs, or replaces the damaged property. Covered losses include costs related to gross margin not earned because normal operations have been halted, a portion of fixed charges and expenses related to a loss of gross margin, and other expenses such as the rental of temporary facilities and equipment.

ACCOUNTING ISSUE

How should recoveries of business interruption insurance be displayed in the income statement?

EITF CONSENSUS

The Task Force reached a consensus that permits entities to decide how to present recoveries from business interruption insurance in their financial statements as long as the presentation is acceptable under current GAAP. In addition, the following disclosures should be made in the period in which such recoveries are reported:

- The nature of the event that caused losses due to business interruption.
- The total amount of recoveries from business interruption insurance reported during the period and the income statement line items in which recoveries are reported (including amounts reported as extraordinary items under ASC 225 (APB-30)).

AIN APB-9 (Reporting the Results of Operations: Unofficial Accounting Interpretations of APB Opinion No. 9) (ASC 225-20-55-4)

BACKGROUND

ASC 225-20-55-4 (AIN-APB 9) addresses whether a regulatory-agency requirement to recognize a particular write-off as an extraordinary loss is applicable in reports to shareholders.

STANDARDS

Question: The Interstate Commerce Commission has ruled that railroads must write off certain receivables from other railroads as extraordinary losses. Is this accounting treatment appropriate for annual reports to shareholders and for annual reports of entities other than railroads?

Answer: No. Regulatory authorities often rule on the accounting treatment of companies under their jurisdiction. Despite the appropriateness of this practice for regulatory reporting purposes, ASC 225-20-55-4 (APB-9), as amended by ASC 225 (APB-30), specifies that, regardless of size, losses from receivables do not constitute extraordinary losses. Treatment of uncollectible receivables as an extraordinary item in the financial statements should result in a qualified audit opinion.

AIN APB-30 (Reporting the Results of Operations: Accounting Interpretations of APB Opinion No. 30) (ASC 225-20-55-3 through 55-4)

BACKGROUND

ASC 225-20-55-3 through 55-4 (AIN-APB 30) presents three issues that pertain to the application of ASC 225 (APB-30).

STANDARDS

Question 1: What factors should be considered in determining whether a particular event or transaction (*a*) is an extraordinary item or (*b*) should otherwise be set forth in the income statement? How are these factors applied in practice?

Answer: The unusual nature and the infrequency of occurrence of events and transactions should be considered when determining whether a transaction qualifies for treatment as an extraordinary item. Paragraphs 19–22 (ASC 225-20-15, 45, 55) discuss the relationship of those two criteria to the environment in which an entity conducts its business. Gains and losses that meet those criteria and therefore are reported in the financial statements as extraordinary items should result directly from a major casualty, an expropriation, or a prohibition under a newly enacted law or regulation. ASC 225-20-55-3 through 55-4 (AIN-APB 30) presents four examples each of transactions that do and do not meet the APB-30 criteria. For example, if a large portion of a tobacco manufacturer's crops are destroyed by a hail storm in a locality where hail storms are rare, the criterion for extraordinary classification would be met. On the other hand, if a citrus grower's Florida crop is damaged by frost and experience indicates that frost damage occurs every three or four years, the criterion of infrequent occurrence is not met and the loss would not be presented as extraordinary.

Question 2 is not covered since it deals with the initial application of APB-30. APB-30 was effective over 25 years ago.

Question 3: The guidance on this question has been superseded by the guidance in ASC 360; ASC 225 (FAS-144, Accounting for the Disposal and Impairment of Long-Lived Assets).

ASC 325 Investments—Other

FSP FTB-85-4-1 (Accounting for Life Settlement Contracts by Third-Party Providers) (ASC 325-30-15-6; 25-2; 30-1C through 30-2; 35-8 through 35-12; 40-1A; 45-1 through 45-5; 50-2 through 50-10)

OVERVIEW

In this FASB Staff Position (FSP), the FASB Staff provides guidance for the initial and subsequent measurement, financial presentation, and disclosure of third-party investors' investments in life settlement contracts, which for the purpose of this FSP are contracts between owners of life insurance policies and third-party investors with the following features:

- The investor does not have the insurable interest (i.e., an interest in the insured's survival) necessary to issue an insurance policy.
- Consideration given by an investor to the policy's owner exceeds the policy's current cash surrender value.
- Under the contract, the investor will be paid the face value of the insurance policy when the insured dies.

Investments in such contracts had been accounted under the guidance in ASC 325-30-15-2 through 15-3; 35-1 through 35-2; 25-1;05-3 through 05-5 (FTB 85-4, Accounting for Purchases of Life Insurance), under which investors reported the amount that could be realized on such insurance contracts as assets. As a result, investors recognized the excess of the purchase price of a life settlement contract over the cash surrender value of the underlying insurance policy as an expense.

Owners of life insurance policies enter into life settlement contracts for various reasons, such as for estate planning, compensation arrangements, and for the purpose of investing. Some have questioned whether the guidance in ASC 325-30-15-2 through 15-3; 35-1 through 35-2; 25-1;05-3 through 05-5 (FTB 85-4) should apply to life settlement contracts entered for investing purposes, because they believe that a policy's cash surrender value does *not* present the economic substance of the investing activity.

This FSP applies to transactions in which a broker assists in the settlement transaction between a policy owner and an investor and to those that occur without a broker's assistance.

Certain provisions of ASC 325-30-15-2 through 15-3; 35-1 through 35-2; 25-1;05-3 through 05-5 (FTB 85-4) and of ASC 815 (FAS-133, Accounting for Derivative Instruments and Hedging Activities) are amended by the guidance in this FSP.

FASB STAFF POSITION

Under the guidance in this FSP, investors may elect to account for investments in life settlement contracts by the investment method or the fair value method. That election, which is irrevocable, should be made based on the facts of the specific contract and should be supported by contemporaneous documentation or a documented policy permitting an automatic election.

Investment Method

Under the investment method, an investor should account for an investment in a life settlement contract as follows:

- The initial investment is recognized at the price of the transaction plus all initial direct external costs.
- Continuing costs, such as policy premiums and direct external costs, if any, to keep the policy in force should be capitalized.

- No gain should be recognized until the insured dies.
- When the insured dies, an investor should recognize in earnings, or other performance indicators if an entity does not report earnings, the difference between a life settlement contract's carrying amount and the proceeds received from the underlying life insurance policy.
- An investment in a life settlement contract should be tested for impairment whenever an investor becomes aware of new or updated information indicating that, when the insured dies, the carrying amount of the investment plus expected undiscounted future premiums and capitalizable direct external costs, if any, will exceed the expected proceeds from the insurance policy. That information includes, but is not limited to, a change in expected mortality and in the creditworthiness of the underlying insurance policy's issuer. Testing a life settlement contract for impairment is *not* necessary if only a change in interest rates occurs.
- An impairment loss should be recognized if expected undiscounted cash inflows (generally, the insurance proceeds) are less than an investment's carrying amount plus expected undiscounted future premiums and capitalizable direct external costs, if any. If there are expected discounted future premiums and capitalizable direct external costs, the investment should be written down to fair value.
- Current interest rates should be considered in the fair value measurement.

Fair Value Method

Under the fair value measurement method, an investor should account for an investment in a life settlement contract as follows:

- An initial investment in a life settlement contract should be accounted for at its transaction price.
- In subsequent periods, the entire investment should be remeasured at fair value at each reporting period and changes in the investment's fair value should be recognized in earnings in the period in which they occur or by other performance indicators if an entity does not report earnings.
- Premiums paid and life insurance proceeds received should be reported on the same financial reporting line in which changes in fair value are reported.

Financial Statement Presentation

1. *Balance sheet presentation* Investments that are remeasured at fair value should be reported on the face of the balance sheet separately from investments reported under the investment

method. Investors may elect to use one of the following presentation alternatives:
  a. Display the carrying amounts of investments accounted for under the fair value method on a separate line from those accounted for under the investment method.
  b. Display the total carrying amount of investments accounted for under the fair value method and those accounted for under the investment method and parenthetically disclose separate information about the carrying amounts of the investments accounted for under each method.
2. *Income statement presentation* Investment income from investments in life settlement contracts that are remeasured at fair value should be presented separately on the face of the income statement from investment income on such investments accounted for under the investment method. Investors may elect one of the following presentation alternatives:
  a. Display income from investments in life settlement contracts accounted for under the fair value method and income from such investments accounted for under the investment method as separate line items.
  b. Display the total amount of investment income from investments in life settlement contracts accounted for under the fair value method with the investment income from such contracts accounted for under the investment method and parenthetically disclose separate information about the investment income from investments accounted for under each method.
3. *Statement of cash flows presentation* Cash receipts and cash payments related to life settlement contracts under the guidance in ASC 230 (FAS-95, Statement of Cash Flows), as amended, should be classified based on the nature and purpose for which the life settlement contracts were acquired.
4. *Disclosures* Investors should disclose the following information:
  a. The accounting policy for life settlement contracts, including the classification of cash receipts and disbursements in the statement of cash flows.
  b. The disclosures required in other U.S. pronouncements of generally accepted accounting principles, including other disclosure requirements regarding the use of fair value.
  c. Life settlement contracts accounted for under the investment method:
    (1) Based on the remaining life expectancy for each of the first five succeeding years from the balance-sheet date and thereafter, as well as the total, the number of life settlement contracts, the carrying values, and the death benefits of the underlying insurance policies.

(2) The nature of new or updated information that causes a change in an investor's expectations on the timing of realization of proceeds from investments in life settlement contracts, including the information in item (1) above. However, investors are *not* required to seek out such information to update the assumptions used to determine the remaining life expectancy of their life settlement contracts.

d. Life settlement contracts accounted for under the fair value method:

(1) The methods and significant assumptions used to estimate the fair value of investments in life settlement contracts, including mortality assumptions, if any.

(2) Based on the remaining life expectancy for each of the first five succeeding years from the balance-sheet date and thereafter, the total number of life settlement contracts, the carrying values, and the death benefits of the underlying insurance policies.

(3) Reasons for changes in the expectation of the timing of realization of investments in life settlement contracts, including significant changes to amounts disclosed in item (2) above.

e. For each period reported in the income statement:

(1) Gains and losses recognized during the period on investments sold during the period.

(2) Unrecognized gains or losses recognized during the period on investments still held at the balance sheet date.

Amendment to ASC 325-30-15-2 through 15-3; 35-1 through 35-2; 25-1; 05-3 through 05-5 (FTB 85-4)

Footnote 1 to FASB Technical Bulletin No. 85-4 has been amended as follows:

—Add at the end of the first sentence, "other than life settlement contracts referred to in the last sentence of this paragraph."

—Add after the last sentence, "A purchase of a life settlement contract that meets the scope requirement of FASB Staff Position FTB 85-4-1 (Accounting for Life Settlement Contracts by Third-Party Investors) should be accounted for under FSP 85-4-1 and is not addressed by this Technical Bulletin."

Amendment to ASC 815 (FAS-133)

ASC 815-10-15-67 (paragraph 10(g) of FAS-133, FASB Accounting Standards Codification (ASC) 815-10-15-67) has been amended as follows:

— In the first sentence after the title of FTB 85-4, insert "or FASB Staff Position FTB 85-4-1" (Accounting for Life Settlement Contracts by Third-Party Investors).

— At the beginning of the second sentence, delete "The exception in this subparagraph affects only the accounting by the policyholder; it" and insert "This" before "does."

ASC 330 Inventory

EITF Issue 96-9 (Classification of Inventory Markdowns and Other Costs Associated with a Restructuring) (ASC 330-10-S35-2; 420-10-S45-2; S99-3)

OVERVIEW

EITF Issue 94-3 (which was superseded by ASC 420 (FAS-146), provided guidance on the timing of liability recognition related to exit or restructuring costs. That Issue also provided guidance on the types of costs that could be accrued when an exit or restructuring plan is adopted. It specifically did not address asset impairments that result from an exit plan, nor did the Issue provide guidance as to whether the liability for such costs should be presented in the income statement with restructuring charges.

ACCOUNTING ISSUE

Should inventory markdowns associated with an exit plan or a restructuring activity be classified in the income statement as a cost of goods sold or as an exit or restructuring cost?

EITF CONSENSUS

Although the Task Force agreed not to address the Issue, they observed that disclosure of the amount of inventory markdowns related to an exit plan or restructuring activity may be appropriate, regardless of how the inventory markdowns are classified.

SEC OBSERVER COMMENT

At the May 1996 meeting, the SEC Observer stated that the SEC staff prefers classification of such inventory markdowns as a cost of goods sold in the income statement. At the July 1996 meeting, the SEC Observer reiterated that the staff's preference is based on the view that (1) it is difficult to distinguish inventory markdowns due to the decision to restructure a business or to exit an activity from markdowns caused by external market conditions that are independent of that decision and that (2) decisions about the timing, method, and pricing of inventory dispositions are normal recurring activities related to the management of an ongoing business.

ASC 410 Asset Retirement and Environmental Obligations

EITF Issue 89-13 (Accounting for the Cost of Asbestos Removal) (ASC 410-20-15-3, 30-45-6)

OVERVIEW

Many jurisdictions require "dangerous asbestos" found in buildings to be treated by removal or containment. In addition, many companies have voluntarily treated asbestos in buildings they own.

ACCOUNTING ISSUES

The following issues were discussed:

- Should costs incurred to treat an asbestos problem that was known when a property was acquired be capitalized or recognized as an expense? (Discussed in Chapter 7, "Capitalization and Expense Recognition Concepts.")
- Should costs incurred to treat an asbestos problem in an existing property that was identified after acquiring the property be capitalized or recognized as an expense? (Discussed in Chapter 7, "Capitalization and Expense Recognition Concepts.")
- If those costs are charged to expense, should they be reported as an extraordinary item?

EITF CONSENSUS

The EITF reached a consensus that costs of asbestos treatment charged to expense do not qualify for reporting as extraordinary items.

DISCUSSION

Classification as an extraordinary item requires an event or transaction to be unusual and infrequent. Some argued that although asbestos treatment may not meet both criteria for an extraordinary item, such events occur infrequently. Consequently, related costs might qualify under the guidance in ASC 225-20-45-16 (paragraph 26 of APB-30) to be classified as a separate component of income from continuing operations. Although the Task Force agreed that expenses related to asbestos treatment are not extraordinary, the consensus does not address whether such costs may be accounted for as infrequent items.

SUBSEQUENT DEVELOPMENT

The guidance in ASC 410 (FAS-143, Accounting for Asset Retirement Obligations) does not apply to an asbestos removal obligation that does not result from the normal operation of an asset. The consensus positions reached in this Issue or the provisions of SOP 96-1 (see Chapter 11) may apply in those circumstances. The guidance in the Statement, which requires recognition of the fair value of a liability for an asset retirement obligation in the period in which it is incurred, would apply to an acquisition of a tangible long-lived asset with an existing asset retirement obligation. The liability would be recognized when the asset is acquired as if it were incurred on that date. The consensus positions in this Issue no longer apply to obligations for asbestos removal under the scope of ASC 410 (FAS-143).

ASC 605 Revenue Recognition

EITF Issue 01-14 (Income Statement Characterization of Reimbursements Received for "Out-of-Pocket" Expenses Incurred) (ASC 605-45-15-2, 15-4; 45-22, 45-23)

OVERVIEW

The EITF addressed the accounting for reimbursements received from customers for a service provider's "out-of-pocket" expenses incurred, such as expenses related to mileage, airfare, hotel stays, out-of-town meals, photocopies, and telecommunication and facsimile charges. Reimbursements may be based on actual amounts incurred or are included in a negotiated flat fee for professional services provided and out-of-pocket expenses incurred.

This Issue does not apply to the following transactions for which other guidance already exists in the authoritative accounting literature:

- Sales of financial assets, including debt and equity securities, loans, and receivables
- Lending transactions
- Insurance and reinsurance premiums
- Broker-dealer transactions under the scope of ASC 940 (the AICPA's Audit and Accounting Guide, *Brokers and Dealers in Securities*), and reimbursements received for expenses incurred

by entities that follow the guidance in other specialized industry AICPA Audit and Accounting Guides, which include accounting guidance for reimbursements

EITF CONSENSUS

The EITF reached a consensus that service providers should include reimbursements for out-of-pocket expenses incurred in revenue in the income statement by analogy to the guidance in EITF Issues 99-19 (Reporting Revenue Gross as a Principal versus Net as an Agent) (see chapter 36) and 00-10 (Accounting for Shipping and Handling Fees and Costs) (see chapter 36). In addition, the EITF believes that this guidance is consistent with the guidance in ASC 605-35 (AICPA Statement of Position 81-1, Accounting for Performance of Construction-Type and Certain Production-Type Contracts) (See chapter 27).

EITF Issue 06-3 (How Taxes Collected from Customers and Remitted to Governmental Authorities Should Be Presented in the Income Statement (That Is, Gross versus Net Presentation)) (ASC 605-45-15-2; 50-3, 50-4)

OVERVIEW

Entities are assessed for taxes on all kinds of transactions—from sales taxes on a broad range of goods and services to excise taxes on specific kinds of transactions—by various governmental authorities. Because such taxes are calculated, remitted to the governmental authority, and administered differently, there is no one model to follow in accounting and reporting for them. In addition, some taxes (such as sales taxes) are collected from customers and transmitted by vendors to the appropriate governmental agencies, and other taxes (such as income taxes) are paid by the entity.

The SEC staff has received questions regarding the income tax presentation of various taxes. For example, the SEC's Chief Accountant stated in March 2002 in the minutes of the SEC Regulation Committee that franchise fees in the Cable industry should be presented in the income statement on a gross basis rather than net of revenue. A member of the SEC staff stated at the 2005 AICPA National Conference on Current SEC and PCAOB Developments that in response to questions regarding how changes in the party responsible for paying state and local sales taxes would affect a vendor's presentation on the income statement, the SEC staff has recommended that pass-through taxes be accounted for in accordance with the guidance in EITF Issue 99-19 (Reporting Revenue Gross as a Principal versus Net as an Agent) (see chapter 36) and Issue 01-14 (Income Statement Characterization of Reimbursements Received for "Out-of-Pocket" Expenses Incurred) (discussed in this chapter). The SEC staff continues to hold that view.

ACCOUNTING ISSUES

1. Should the scope of this Issue include all nondiscretionary amounts assessed by governmental authorities, all nondiscretionary amounts assessed by governmental authorities in connection with a transaction with a customer, or only sales, use, and value-added taxes?
2. Should taxes assessed by a governmental authority under the scope of Issue 1 be presented in the income statement on a gross or net basis?

EITF CONSENSUS

1. The scope of this Issue includes any tax assessed by a governmental authority that is both imposed on and that occurs at the same time as a specific revenue-producing transaction between a seller and a customer and may include, but is not limited to, sales, use, value added, and some excise taxes. Tax schemes based on gross receipts and taxes imposed while acquiring inventory are *excluded* from the scope of this Issue.
2. An entity's decision to present taxes discussed under the scope of this Issue in revenues and costs (gross basis) or to exclude them from revenues and costs (net basis) should be disclosed as an accounting policy under the guidance in ASC 235-10-05-3 through 05-4; 50-1 through 50-6 (APB-22, Disclosure of Accounting Policies). However, existing policies related to taxes assessed by a governmental authority as a result of this consensus need *not* be reevaluated. If an entity reports its taxes on a gross basis, the amounts of those taxes should be disclosed in interim and annual financial statements for each period for which an income statement is presented, if the amounts are significant. The total amount of those taxes may be disclosed.

The consensus positions in this Issue do *not* affect the consensus positions reached in Issue 99-19 (Reporting Revenue Gross as a Principal versus Net as an Agent) (chapter 36), Issue 00-10 (Accounting for Shipping and Handling Fees and Costs), and Issue 01-14 (Income Statement Characterization of Reimbursements Received for "Out-of-Pocket" Expenses Incurred) (this chapter).

FASB RATIFICATION

The FASB ratified the EITF's consensus positions at its June 28, 2006, meeting.

ACS 710 Compensation—General

EITF Issue 06-2 (Accounting for Sabbatical Leave and Other Similar Benefits Pursuant to FASB Statement No. 43, *Accounting for Compensated Absences*) (ASC 710-10-15-3; 25-5)

> **OBSERVATION:** This Issue does *not* apply to *public* colleges and universities, even those that have adopted GASB-20 (Accounting and Financial Reporting for Proprietary Funds and Other Governmental Entities That Use Proprietary Fund Accounting), because the guidance in ASC 710 (FAS-43) conflicts with the guidance in GASB-16 (Accounting for Compensated Absences).

OVERVIEW

Some entities, such as colleges and universities, provide a benefit to their employees, known as a sabbatical leave. Under sabbatical leave, employees are entitled to a compensated absence for a specified period of time, such as three months, after having worked for the employer for a specified period of time (i.e., seven years). The employee is compensated during the sabbatical but is not required to perform any duties for the employer. Employees are not entitled to compensation for unused sabbatical leave if their employment terminates before having worked for the full eligibility period. Further, employees that have worked for the specified period but did not avail themselves of the benefit are not entitled to the benefit if their employment is terminated.

The guidance in ASC 710-10-25-1 (paragraph 6 of FAS-43 (Accounting for Compensated Absences) provides that employers should accrue a liability for employees' compensation for future absences if certain conditions are met. Condition 6b states that "the obligation relates to rights that vest or accumulate." In addition, ASC 710-10-25-1(b) (footnote 2 of paragraph 6 of FAS-43) defines *accumulate* to mean "that earned but unused rights to compensated absences may be carried forward to one or more periods subsequent to that in which they are earned even though there may be a limit to the amount that can be carried forward." Based on that guidance, some question whether a sabbatical benefit should be accrued even though the benefit does not vest.

ACCOUNTING ISSUE

Does an employee's right to a compensated absence under a sabbatical or similar benefit accumulate in accordance with the guidance in paragraph 6b of FAS-43 (ASC 710-10-25-1) if the employee must complete a minimum service period and if the benefit does not increase with additional years of service?

SCOPE

The guidance in this Issue is limited to sabbatical or similar arrangements under which an employee is *not* required to perform direct or indirect services for or on behalf the employer during the absence. It does not apply to public colleges or universities, even those that have adopted GASB-20, because ASC 710 (FAS-43) conflicts with GASB-16.

EITF CONSENSUS

The EITF reached a consensus that compensation costs associated with an employee's right to a sabbatical or other similar arrangement should be accrued over the required service period if, under that arrangement, (a) the employee is required to complete a minimum period of service and (b) the benefit does *not* increase with additional years of service accumulated in accordance with the guidance in ASC 710-10-25-1(b) (paragraph 6b of FAS-43, Accounting for Compensated Absences) for arrangements under which an employee is *not* required to perform duties for the employer during a compensated absence. All of the other conditions in ASC 710-10-25-1 (paragraph 6 of FAS-43) also must be met.

FASB RATIFICATION

The FASB ratified the consensus positions in this Issue at its June 28, 2006, meeting.

ASC 720 Other Expenses

SOP 98-5 (Reporting on the Costs of Start-Up Activities) (ASC 720-15-15-1 through 15-5; 25-1; 55-1, 55-3, 55-5, 55-7, 55-9, 55-10)

BACKGROUND

SOP 98-5 is the second in a series of projects by AcSEC to consider reporting the costs of activities that are undertaken to create future economic benefits. The first project led to SOP 93-7 (Reporting on Advertising Costs) (see chapter 3).

Start-up activities are defined broadly as those onetime activities related to all of the following:

- Opening a new facility
- Introducing a new product or service
- Conducting business in a new territory
- Conducting business with a new class of customer or beneficiary
- Initiating a new process in an existing facility

- Commencing some new operation
- Organizing a new entity (i.e., organization costs)

In practice, start-up costs are referred to in different ways, including preoperating costs and organization costs. In SOP 98-5, they are referred to as start-up costs.

Certain costs are not considered start-up costs and should be accounted for in accordance with existing authoritative accounting pronouncements. They include the following:

- Costs of acquiring or constructing long-lived assets and getting them ready for their intended use
- Costs of acquiring or producing inventory
- Costs of acquiring intangible assets
- Costs related to internally developed assets
- Costs that are covered by ASC 730 (FAS-2, Accounting for Research and Development Costs)
- Costs of fund-raising incurred by not-for-profit organizations
- Costs of raising capital
- Costs of advertising
- Costs incurred in connection with existing contracts in accordance with ASC 605-35 (SOP 81-1, Accounting for Performance of Construction-Type and Certain Production-Type Contracts)

STANDARDS

According to SOP 98-5, costs of start-up activities, including organization costs, are to be expensed as incurred.

> ☛ **PRACTICE POINTER:** SOP 98-5 continues a general trend (begun with FAS-2) of expensing those expenditures where the amount, timing, or uncertainty of future cash flows is uncertain. The costs associated with start-up activities, although clearly incurred with the expectation of generating future benefits, may not meet the definition of an asset or may not be measurable with sufficient accuracy because of the following:
>
> - The expenditure fails to generate future benefits (i.e., no asset).
> - The timing of any future benefits that might be generated is uncertain (i.e., measurement difficulties in valuing the resulting asset).
> - The amount of such future benefits may not exceed the costs of generating those benefits (i.e., no asset).

The following pronouncements are amended by SOP 98-5 to incorporate the conclusion that costs of start-up activities should be expensed as incurred:

- ASC 605-35 (SOP 81-1, Accounting for Performance of Construction-Type and Certain Production-Type Contracts)
- ASC 908 (SOP 88-1, Accounting for Developmental and Preoperating Costs, Purchases and Exchanges of Take-off and Landing Slots, and Airframe Modifications)
- ASC 946 (SOP 93-4, Foreign Currency Accounting and Financial Statement Presentation for Investment Companies)
- ASC 924 (Audit and Accounting Guide, *Audits of Casinos*)
- ASC 910 (Audit and Accounting Guide, *Construction Contractors*)
- ASC 912 (Audit and Accounting Guide, *Audits of Federal Government Contractors*)
- ASC 946 (Audit and Accounting Guide, *Audits of Investment Companies*)
- ASC 908 (Industry Audit Guide, *Audits of Airlines*)

ASC 808 Accounting for Collaborative Arrangements

EITF Issue 07-1 (Accounting for Collaborative Arrangements) (ASC 808-10-10-1, 15-2 through 15-13; 45-1 through 45-5; 50-1; 55-1 through 55-19; 65-1)

OVERVIEW

In Issue 07-1, the EITF addresses the accounting for arrangements entered into by entities in a number of industries, such as the pharmaceutical, biotechnology, motion picture, software, and computer hardware industries, under which intellectual property is jointly developed and commercialized with other entities; usually, without creating a separate legal entity for that activity. All of the activities are conducted by the parties to the arrangement using their own employees and facilities. For example, one of the participants may be responsible for performing the research and development of a product while the other participant may be responsible for the product's commercialization. Because the accounting for such arrangements is diverse (i.e., arrangements may be accounted for on a gross basis or a net basis), the EITF was asked to develop accounting and disclosure guidance to improve the comparability of financial statements.

The guidance in Issue 07-1 applies to collaborative arrangements conducted by parties that participate in such arrangements without creating a separate legal entity for that purpose. The guidance in Issue 07-1 is *not* limited to specific industries or to intellectual property. However, arrangements for which specific guidance exists under other current authoritative literature are excluded from the scope of Issue 07-1 and should be accounted for according to the existing guidance. In addition, Issue 07-1 does *not* apply to arrangements that involve a financial investor.

EITF CONSENSUS

At its November 29, 2007, meeting, the EITF reached a consensus on the following positions.

Scope

A contractual arrangement under which the parties are involved in a joint operating activity and are exposed to significant risks and rewards that depend on the activity's ultimate success is referred to as a "collaborative arrangement." Although for the most part the activities of a collaborative arrangement under the scope of Issue 07-1 are *not* conducted through a separate legal entity created for that purpose, the existence of a specific legal entity for specific activities related to *part* of the arrangement or for a specific geographic location for part of the arrangement's activities does *not* exclude an arrangement from the definition of a collaborative arrangement in this Issue. However, the guidance in ASC 810 (ARB-51, Consolidated Financial Statements), ASC 840-10-45-4; ASC 810-10-60-4 (FAS-94, Consolidation of All Majority-Owned Subsidiaries), ASC 323-10 (APB-18, The Equity Method of Accounting for Investments in Common Stock), ASC 810 (FIN-46R, Consolidation of Variable Interest Entities), or other related literature should be applied to account for any part of a collaborative arrangement performed in a separate legal entity. The disclosure requirements in Issue 07-1 apply to the total arrangement, regardless of the parts that are conducted in a separate legal entity.

Participants should determine at the inception of an arrangement whether it is a collaborative arrangement based on the facts and circumstances at that time. However, a collaborative arrangement may begin at any time during an activity on which the participants have been collaborating. If the facts or circumstances of the participants' roles or their exposure to risks and rewards change, the arrangement should be reevaluated. Exercising an option is an example of a situation that might change a participant's role in an arrangement.

Joint Operating Activity

Participants in a collaborative arrangement may jointly develop and bring to market intellectual property, pharmaceutical products, software, computer hardware, or a motion picture. One participant may be primarily responsible for a specific activity or two or more participants may be jointly responsible for certain activities. Joint operating activities may include research and development, marketing, general and administrative activities, manufacturing, and distribution. A joint operation of a hospital is an example of a collaborative arrangement.

Active Participation

Active participation in a collaborative arrangement may consist of, but may not be limited to:

- Significant involvement in directing and carrying out joint activities;
- Participation on a steering committee or other means of oversight or governance; or
- Holding a contractual or other legal right to underlying intellectual property.

However, if an entity's only responsibility is to provide financial resources to a venture, that entity generally is *not* an active participant in a collaborative arrangement under the scope of Issue 07-1.

Significant Risks and Rewards

To determine whether participants in a collaborative arrangement are exposed to significant risks and rewards that depend on the joint operating activity's commercial success, an arrangement's specific facts and circumstances, including, but not limited to, the arrangement's terms and conditions, should be considered. Based on an arrangement's terms and conditions, participants in an arrangement may *not* be exposed to *significant risks and rewards* if:

- Services are performed for fees at fair market value rates.
- A participant can leave an arrangement without cause and recover a significant portion or all of its cumulative economic participation to date.
- Only one participant receives an initial allocation of profits.
- The amount of a reward that a participant can receive is limited.

The following factors should be considered in evaluation of risks and rewards:

- The stage of the endeavor's life cycle in which collaboration begins.
- The expected time period or financial commitment that participants will devote to the arrangement as it relates to an endeavor's total life span or expected value.

Consideration exchanged for a license related to intellectual property may *not* be an indicator that the participants are *not* exposed to risks or rewards on the ultimate success of their effort. Judgment is necessary to determine whether the participants are exposed to risks and rewards.

Income Statement Classification

Participants in a collaborative arrangement may report costs incurred and revenues generated from transactions with third parties in an appropriate line item in the participant's respective financial statements in accordance with the guidance in EITF Issue 99-19 (Reporting Revenue Gross as a Principal versus Net as an Agent). Collaborative arrangements should *not* be accounted for using the equity method of accounting in APB-18. A participant in a collaborative arrangement who under the guidance in Issue 99-19 is considered to be the principal participant in a specific revenue or cost transaction with a third party, should report that transaction on a gross basis in its financial statements.

The income statement description of payments between participants under a collaborative arrangement should be evaluated based on the arrangement's nature and contractual terms and the nature of each entity's business operations. If such payments fall under the scope of other authoritative literature, they should be accounted for under that guidance. Otherwise, the payments should be reported in the income statement based on an analogy to authoritative accounting literature, or if no appropriate analogy exists, the accounting policy selected should be applied in a reasonable, rational, and consistent manner.

Disclosure

Participants in a collaborative arrangement should disclose the following information in the initial reporting period and annually thereafter:

- The nature and purpose of collaborative arrangements.
- The entity's rights and obligations under a collaborative arrangement.
- The entity's accounting policy for collaborative arrangements in accordance with the guidance in APB-22 (Disclosure of Accounting Policies).
- Income statement classification and amounts related to transactions as a result of the collaborative arrangement between participants for each period in which an income statement is presented.

Separate disclosure should be made about information related to collaborative arrangements that are significant individually.

TRANSITION

The EITF reached a consensus that the guidance in Issue 07-1 should be effective for annual periods that begin after December 15, 2008, and interim periods within those fiscal years. The effect of applying the guidance in Issue 07-1 should be accounted for as a change in accounting principle by *retrospective* application to all prior periods presented for all collaborative arrangements that exist as of the effective date. If retrospective application of the effects of a change in accounting principle in accordance with paragraph 11 of FAS-154 (Accounting Changes and Error Corrections) (ASC 250-10-45-9, 45-10), is impractical, the reasons why amounts were not reclassified and how reclassification would affect the current period in accordance with the guidance in paragraph 9 of FAS-154 (ASC 250-20-45-7) should be disclosed. Entities should decide on an arrangement-by-arrangement basis whether retrospective application is impractical.

When the guidance in Issue 07-1 is first applied, disclosure of the following information is required:

- A description of prior-period information *retrospectively* adjusted, if any; and

- The effect of a change on revenue and operating expenses (or other appropriate captions of changes in the applicable net assets or performance indicator) and other affected line items in the financial statements, if any.

FASB RATIFICATION

The FASB ratified the EITF's consensus positions in Issue 07-1 at its December 12, 2007, meeting.

ASC 885 Subsequent Events

Topic D-86 (Issuance of Financial Statements) (ASC 855-10-S25-1, S99-2)

In response to inquiries as to when financial statements are considered to have been issued, the SEC staff announced that financial statements are issued as of the date they are distributed for "general use and reliance" in a form and format that complies with GAAP. Annual financial statements should include an audit report stating that the auditors complied with generally accepted auditing standards (GAAS) in completing the audit. Financial statements would be considered to have been issued when the annual or quarterly financial statements are widely distributed to the registrant's shareholders and other users of financial statements or filed with the Commission, whichever is earlier. The SEC staff's position is based on the view that in accordance with the 1934 Securities Exchange Act, registrants and their auditors have a responsibility to issue financial statements that are not misleading as of the date they are filed with the Commission.

In addition, the SEC staff notes that the issuance of an earnings release should not be considered the issuance of financial statements, because its form and format do not comply with GAAP and GAAS.

ASC 954-450 Health Care Entities—Contingencies

EITF Issue No. 09-K   Health Care Entities: Presentation of Insurance Claims and Related Insurance Recoveries (ASC 954-450-25-2; 65-1; 954-720-25-1)

OVERVIEW

Issues related to an insured entity's claims incurred under claims-made insurance and retroactive insurance contracts were addressed in EITF Issue No. 03-8, "Accounting for Claims-Made Insurance and Retroactive Insurance Contracts by the Insured Entity," which is codified in FASB Accounting Standards Codification™ (ASC) 720, *Other Expenses* (ASC 720-20). According to that guidance, it is inappropriate to offset prepaid insurance and receivables for expected recoveries from insurers against a recognized incurred but *not* reported liability or a liability incurred due to a past insurable event, unless the transaction meets the conditions in ASC 210, *Balance Sheet* (ASC 210-20-45) (FASB Interpretation No. 39, *Offsetting of Amounts Related to Certain Contracts*). As a result of that guidance, liability claims and related anticipated insurance recoveries are usually recognized on a gross-basis.

Some constituents have asked whether the guidance in ASC 720-20 applies to health care entities because the language in the AICPA Audit and Accounting Guide, *Health Care Organizations*, has been interpreted by some to permit or require that insurance recoveries be netted against an organization's estimated accrual for medical malpractice claims.

ACCOUNTING ISSUE

How should health care entities record liabilities for medical malpractice and other similar claims and related insurance recoveries?

SCOPE

The guidance in Issue 09-K clarifies that the requirements in ASC 210-20 apply to health care entities accounted for under the scope of ASC 954, *Health Care Entities*, which report medical malpractice claims and similar contingent liabilities, as well as related anticipated insurance recoveries on their balance sheets. In accordance with the guidance in ASC 210-20, entities are not permitted to offset anticipated insurance recoveries from third parties against conditional or unconditional liabilities.

EITF CONSENSUS

At its July 29, 2010 meeting, the EITF affirmed as a consensus its consensus-for-exposure reached at the March 2010 meeting that health care entities, similar to entities in other industries, should determine whether to present claims and insurance recoveries in the balance sheet on a gross or net basis based on the guidance in ASC 210-20-45. The EITF believes that a gross presentation shows that the entity is obligated on the claim even though an insurance company may be paying to defend the claim and may eventually pay for a portion of the claim or the total claim. In addition, the gross presentation of an insurance receivable required in ASC 210-20 is a better presentation of the retained credit risk if an insurer is unable to pay a claim.

The EITF discussed the recognition of a receivable if a health care entity will be indemnified by its insurer. Some members noted that such a receivable should be recognized at the same time as the liability and should be measured on the same basis as the liability, conditional on a need for a valuation allowance for uncollectible amounts. They asked the FASB staff to amend the existing guidance in ASC 954-450-25-2, accordingly.

Some commentators on the proposed ASU questioned the industry-specific guidance in ASC 954 requiring that legal costs related to litigation or settlement of claims be accrued upon the occurrence of incidents that will result in claims. The EITF discussed whether the guidance on the treatment of such legal costs should be conformed with the guidance for other industries. As a result of that discussion and the agreement of the FASB Chairman, who was present at the meeting, Issue 10-F was added to the EITF's agenda and discussed at the July 29, 2010 meeting.

EFFECTIVE DATE, TRANSITION METHOD, AND TRANSITION DISCLOSURES

The EITF affirmed as a consensus its previous consensus-for-exposure related to the application of the guidance in Issue 09-K, which is as follows:

- Adopt the guidance for fiscal years, and interim periods within those years, that begin after December 15, 2010. Early adoption is permitted.
- Record a cumulative-effect-adjustment to opening retained earnings (or unrestricted assets) as of the beginning of the period in which the guidance is adopted, if necessary.
- Calculate the cumulative-effect-adjustment as the difference between the following amounts: (1) the liability recognized in the balance sheet after the initial application of the guidance in Issue 09-K that was not previously recognized; and (2) the receivable recognized in the balance sheet for expected insurance

recoveries after the initial application of the guidance in Issue 09-K that was not previously recognized.
- Provide the disclosures in ASC 250, *Accounting Changes and Error Corrections* (ASC 250-10-50-1 through 50-3), in the period in which the guidance in Issue 09-K is adopted.

In addition, the EITF reached a consensus permitting, but not requiring, retrospective application of the guidance in Issue 09-K to all prior periods. That treatment may be necessary in rare situations if the amount of the liability on a claim and the receivable from insurance are not completely offset.

FASB RATIFICATION

The FASB ratified the EITF's consensus positions in Issue 09-K at its August 18, 2010 meeting.

ACCOUNTING STANDARDS UPDATE

The FASB issued ASU 2010-24, which incorporates the EITF's guidance in Issue 09-K.

AICPA Accounting Interpretations

RELATED CHAPTERS IN 2011
GAAP GUIDE, VOLUME II

Chapter 23, "Interim Financial Reporting"
Chapter 24, "Inventory"
Chapter 32, "Postemployment and Postretirement Benefits Other Than Pensions"
Chapter 37, "Segment Reporting"

RELATED CHAPTERS IN 2011
GAAP GUIDE, VOLUME I

Chapter 26, "Interim Financial Reporting"
Chapter 27, "Inventory"
Chapter 34, "Postemployment and Postretirement Benefits Other Than Pensions"
Chapter 40, "Results of Operations"
Chapter 42, "Segment Reporting"

RELATED CHAPTER IN 2011 INTERNATIONAL ACCOUNTING/FINANCIAL REPORTING STANDARDS GUIDE

Chapter 26, "Non-Current Assets Held for Sale and Discontinued Operations"

CHAPTER 36
REVENUE RECOGNITION

CONTENTS

Overview		36.03
Authoritative Guidance		
ASC 325 Investments—Other		36.05
EITF Issue 88-5	Recognition of Insurance Death Benefits	36.05
ASC 460 Guarantees		36.06
EITF Issue 03-12	Impact of FASB Interpretation No. 45, *Guarantor's Accounting and Disclosure Requirements for Guarantees, Including Indirect Guarantees of Indebtedness of Others,* on EITF Issue No. 95-1, *Revenue Recognition on Sales with a Guaranteed Minimum Resale Value*	36.06
ASC 470 Debt		36.07
EITF Issue 88-18	Sales of Future Revenues	36.07
ASC 605 Revenue Recognition		36.09
FTB 90-1	Accounting for Separately Priced Extended Warranty and Product Maintenance Contracts	36.09
EITF Issue 91-9	Revenue and Expense Recognition for Freight Services in Process	36.10
EITF Issue 95-1	Revenue Recognition on Sales with a Guaranteed Minimum Resale Value	36.13
EITF Issue 95-4	Revenue Recognition on Equipment Sold and Subsequently Repurchased Subject to an Operating Lease	36.17
EITF Issue 99-19	Reporting Revenue Gross as a Principal versus Net as an Agent	36.18

36.02 *Revenue Recognition*

EITF Issue 00-10	Accounting for Shipping and Handling Fees and Costs	36.22
EITF Issue 01-9	Accounting for Consideration Given by a Vendor to a Customer (Including a Reseller of the Vendor's Products)	36.23
EITF Issue 02-16	Accounting by a Reseller for Cash Consideration Received from a Vendor	36.32
EITF Issue 03-10	Application of EITF Issue No. 02-16, "Accounting by a Customer (Including a Reseller) for Certain Consideration Received from a Vendor," by Resellers to Sales Incentives Offered to Consumers by Manufacturers	36.34
EITF Issue 06-1	Accounting for Consideration Given by a Service Provider to Manufacturers or Resellers of Equipment Necessary for an End-Customer to Receive Service from the Service Provider	36.36
EITF Issue 08-1	Revenue Arrangements with Multiple Deliverables	36.38
EITF Issue 08-9 (ASU 2010-17)	Milestone Method of Revenue Recognition	36.44
Topic D-96	Accounting for Management Fees Based on a Formula	36.47
ASC 924 Entertainment—Casinos		36.49
EITF Issue 09-F (ASU 2010-16)	Accruals for Casino Jackpot Liabilities	36.49
ASC 932 Extractive Activities—Oil and Gas		36.51
EITF Issue 90-22	Accounting for Gas-Balancing Arrangements	36.51
ASC 944-605 Financial Services—Insurance		36.54
FSP FAS-97-1	Situations in Which Paragraphs 17(b) and 20 of FASB Statement No. 97, *Accounting and Reporting by Insurance Enterprises for Certain Long-Duration Contracts and for Realized Gains and Losses from the Sale of Investments,* Permit or Require Accrual of an Unearned Revenue Liability	36.54

ASC 946-605 Financial Services—Investment Companied   **36.56**

    FSP EITF 85-24-1   Application of EITF Issue No. 85-24, "Distribution Fees by Distributors of Mutual Funds That Do Not Have a Front-End Sales Charge," When Cash for the Right to Future Distribution Fees for Shares Previously Sold Is Received from Third Parties   **36.56**

    EITF Issue 85-24   Distribution Fees by Distributors of Mutual Funds That Do Not Have a Front-End Sales Charge   **36.59**

ASC 954-605 Health Care Entities—Revenue Recognition   **36.60**

    EITF Issue 09-L (ASU 2010-23)   Health Care Entities: Measuring Charity Care for Disclosure   **36.60**

ASC 980 Regulated Operations   **36.62**

    EITF Issue 91-6   Revenue Recognition of Long-Term Power Sales Contracts   **36.62**

    EITF Issue 92-7   Accounting by Rate-Regulated Utilities for the Effects of Certain Alternative Revenue Programs   **36.66**

    EITF Issue 96-17   Revenue Recognition under Long-Term Power Sales Contracts That Contain Both Fixed and Variable Pricing Terms   **36.69**

Related Chapter in 2011 GAAP Guide, Volume I   **36.73**

Related Chapter in 2011 International Accounting/Financial Reporting Standards Guide   **36.73**

OVERVIEW

GAAP, as well as recognized industry practices, generally require revenue recognition at the point of sale. One aspect of a sale that complicates this generally simple rule is a buyer's right of return. Revenue from sales in which a right of return exists is recognized at the time of sale only if certain specified conditions are met. If those conditions are met, sales revenue and cost of sales are reduced to reflect estimated returns and costs of those returns. If they are not met, revenue recognition is postponed.

The following pronouncements, which are the source of GAAP for revenue recognition, are discussed in the 2009 *GAAP Guide, Volume I*, Chapter 41, "Revenue Recognition."

ASC 952 Accounting for Franchise Fee Revenue (FAS-45)
ASC 605 Revenue Recognition When Right of Return Exists (FAS-48)

AUTHORITATIVE GUIDANCE

ASC 325 Investments—Other

EITF Issue 88-5 (Recognition of Insurance Death Benefits) (ASC 325-30-35-1)

OVERVIEW

Some companies purchase life insurance policies to cover the lives of certain employees, with the company as the beneficiary. Such policies, referred to as corporate-owned life insurance (COLI) policies, are used for various purposes: (*a*) to protect the company if a key employee dies; (*b*) to accumulate funds to finance a shareholder/partner buy/sell agreement in case a shareholder/partner dies or leaves the company; or (*c*) to fund the employer's obligations to certain employee benefit plans, such as pension plans, by borrowing against the policy.

In the past, companies have recognized income on COLI policies when proceeds were received upon the death of an employee. Because companies were taking out policies on certain groups of employees, it was suggested that income from death benefits on COLI policies could be recognized over the estimated period of the employees' lives on an actuarially projected basis.

ACCOUNTING ISSUES

1. Should an entity recognize income on death benefits from COLI policies on an actuarially projected basis or upon the death of the insured?

2. If a company intends to retain COLI policies in force until the death of the insured and to borrow against them, should the company recognize the policy as an asset at the policy's net loan value, which is the maximum amount that the entity can contractually borrow against the policy, or at its cash surrender value?

EITF CONSENSUS

1. The purchaser of life insurance should not recognize income from death benefits based on actuarial projections. The Task Force noted that under the guidance in ASC 325-30-15-2 through 15-3; 35-1 through 2; 25-1; 05-3 through 05-5 (FTB 85-4, Accounting for Purchases of Life Insurance) a purchaser is required to recognize an asset for the amount at which the policy could be realized on the date of the financial statements. Because a death benefit may not be realized before the insured's actual death, recognition of death benefits on an actuarially projected basis is an inappropriate means of measuring the asset.

36.06 *Revenue Recognition*

2. The Task Force did not reach a consensus on this Issue. It was noted that FTB 85-4 specifies that the asset be measured at its cash surrender value and that changes in that value be used to adjust policy premiums. The Task Force discussed whether it is appropriate to recognize the difference between the cash surrender value and premiums paid as a temporary difference. That issue was resolved by paragraph 14 of FAS-109 (Accounting for Income Taxes) (ASC 740-10-25-30), which states that "[t]hat excess is a temporary difference if the cash surrender value is expected to be recovered by surrendering the policy, but it is not a temporary difference if the asset is expected to be recovered without tax consequences upon the death of the insured (there will be no taxable amount if the insurance policy is held until the death of the insured)."

DISCUSSION

The following arguments were made against income recognition on an actuarially projected basis:

- Income should be recognized only when it is realized and earned upon the death of the insured.
- The death benefit is earned as a result of an event—the death of the insured—not as a function of the passage of time.
- Paragraph 17 of FAS-5 (Accounting for Contingencies) precludes income recognition of gain contingencies (ASC 450-30-25-1).
- Income should not be accrued based on assumed experience.

ASC 460 Guarantees

EITF Issue 03-12 (Impact of FASB Interpretation No. 45, *Guarantor's Accounting and Disclosure Requirements for Guarantees, Including Indirect Guarantees of Indebtedness of Others*, on EITF Issue No. 95-1, *Revenue Recognition on Sales with a Guaranteed Minimum Resale Value*) (ASC 460-10-55-17)

OVERVIEW

Issue 95-1 addresses whether a manufacturer should recognize a sale on equipment sold with a resale value guarantee. The EITF reached a consensus in that Issue that a manufacturer should *not* recognize a sale on a transfer of equipment if the buyer receives a resale value guarantee. The EITF also reached a consensus that the transaction should be accounted for as a lease, based on the guidance in FAS-13 (Accounting for Leases), because the buyer has the right to use the equipment from the sales date to the date on which the manufacturer guarantees a minimum resale value for the equipment. Classification as a sales-type lease or an operating lease should be based on the calculation of the minimum lease payments, as defined in paragraph 5 of FAS-13 (ASC 840-10-25-4), which would be the difference between the proceeds on the initial transfer of the equipment to the buyer (the selling price) and the manufacturer's residual value guarantee at the first date on which the buyer can exercise the guarantee.

When ASC 460 (FIN-45, Guarantor's Accounting and Disclosure Requirements for Guarantees, Including Indirect Guarantees of Indebtedness of Others) was issued, the FASB staff determined that the consensus in Issue 95-1 for sales-type leases is nullified by the Interpretation because the guarantee would be related to an asset removed from the manufacturer's books under that type of lease. Some constituents questioned that decision, because under a sales-type lease, a manufacturer would be required to recognize two guarantees for the same asset, that is, once when a sales-type lease transaction is recorded with the amount of the residual value of the equipment remaining on the manufacturer's books and again in accordance with the requirements of ASC 460 (FIN-45), at the fair value of the guarantee at inception.

ACCOUNTING ISSUE

How does ASC 460 (FIN-45) affect the consensus in Issue 95-1?

EITF CONSENSUS

The consensus in Issue 95-1 concerns a sales-type lease, under which a manufacturer guarantees the residual value of equipment transferred under the lease and continues to recognize an asset for the residual value of the guaranteed equipment. The EITF reached a consensus that the provisions of ASC 460 (FIN-45) do *not* affect the guidance in Issue 95-1 related to sales-type leases, because the Interpretation does *not* apply to a guarantee for an asset related to an underlying lease recorded on the guarantor's books.

ASC 470 Debt

EITF Issue 88-18 (Sales of Future Revenues) (ASC 470-10-25-1, 25-2; 35-3)

OVERVIEW

Company G enters into an agreement with Company H (an investor) to receive a sum of cash in exchange for a specified percentage or amount of Company G's future revenues or another measure of income, such as gross margin or operating income, for a particular product line, business segment, trademark, patent, or contractual right, for a specified period. The future revenue or income may be from a foreign contract, transaction, or operation denominated in a foreign currency.

ACCOUNTING ISSUES

1. Assuming the proceeds received from the sale of future revenues are appropriately accounted for as a liability, should the liability be characterized as debt or deferred income? (Discussed in Chapter 4, "Balance Sheet Classification and Related Display Issues.")
2. How should debt or deferred income be amortized?
3. How should the foreign currency effects of classifying the proceeds as deferred income or debt be recognized? (Discussed in Chapter 18, "Foreign Operations and Exchange.")

EITF CONSENSUS

The Task Force reached the following consensus on the second Issue:

- If the proceeds are classified as debt, they should be amortized under the interest method.
- If the proceeds are recognized as revenue, they should be amortized under the units-of-revenue method.
- Amortization for a period under the units-of-revenue method is calculated based on the ratio of the proceeds received from the investor to the total payments expected to be made to the investor over the term of the agreement. That ratio is applied to the cash payment for the period.

DISCUSSION

Deferred income resulting from the sale of future revenues differs from traditional deferred income, which is generally satisfied by delivering goods or services (for example, a service agreement), and which is amortized on a straight-line basis. The units-of-revenue method is more appropriate in these circumstances, because future cash flows will not be level from year to year.

ASC 605 Revenue Recognition

FTB 90-1 (Accounting for Separately Priced Extended Warranty and Product Maintenance Contracts) (ASC 460-10-15-9; 60-41; 605-20-25-1 through 25-6)

BACKGROUND

An *extended warranty* is an agreement to provide warranty protection in addition to that covered in the manufacturer's original warranty, if any, or to extend the period of coverage beyond that provided by the manufacturer's warranty. A *product maintenance contract* is an agreement to perform certain agreed-upon services to maintain a product for a specified period. Some contracts cover both an extended warranty and product maintenance. A *separately priced contract* is one in which the customer has the option to purchase the services provided under the contract for a stated amount that is separate from the price of the product.

STANDARDS

Question: How should revenue and costs from a separately priced extended warranty or a product maintenance contract be recognized?

Answer: Revenue should be deferred and recognized over the contract period on a straight-line basis, except when sufficient historical evidence indicates that the costs of performing under the contract are incurred in a pattern other than straight-line. In those circumstances, revenue should be recognized over the contract period in proportion to the costs expected to be incurred in performing the services required under the contract.

Costs that are directly related to the acquisition of the contract and that would not have been incurred if the contract had not existed should be deferred and charged to expense in proportion to the revenue recognized. All other costs should be charged to expense as incurred.

Illustration of Recognition of Revenue and Costs on a Separately Priced Extended Warranty Contract—Warranty Costs Not Incurred on a Straight-Line Basis

Dorf Motors sells a separately priced extended warranty contract for $1,200 on 1/1/20X4 in conjunction with the sale of its Spitfire model. The extended warranty contract extends the manufacturer's warranty (three years, 36,000 miles) by an additional three years and 36,000 miles. Dorf has sufficient warranty experience to predict claim costs under the extended warranty as follows: year 1: $0 (manufacturer's warranty in effect), year 2: $0, year 3: $0, year 4: $100, year 5: $200, and year 6: $300. Dorf incurred $200 of costs directly related to the sale of the extended warranty contract and that would not have been incurred if the contract had not been sold.

36.10 *Revenue Recognition*

On 1/1/X4, Dorf would record a liability for deferred revenue of $1,200. None of this deferred revenue would be recognized in X4, X5, and X6, since any warranty work performed by Dorf falls under the manufacturer's warranty, not under the extended warranty. Revenue, and amortization of direct costs, would be recognized as follows during X7–X9:

	Revenue Recognized	Amortization of Direct Costs
20X7	$200	$33
	[($100 / $600) × $1,200]	[($200 / $1,200)] × $200
20X8	$400	$67
	[($200 / $600) × $1,200]	[($400 / $1,200)] × $200
20X9	$600	$100
	[($300 / $600) × $1,200]	[($600 / $1,200)] × $200

A loss exists if the total of the expected costs of providing services under the contract and unamortized acquisition costs exceeds the related unearned revenue. A loss is recognized by first charging any unamortized acquisition costs to expense and then by recognizing a liability for the excess.

EITF Issue 91-9 (Revenue and Expense Recognition for Freight Services in Process) (ASC 605-20-25-13; S25-1 S99-2)

OVERVIEW

Motor carriers provide a variety of services to their customers. The services can be (*a*) limited, involving only pickup and delivery (usually of a full trailer loaded by the customer—known as "truckload carriers"), or (*b*) extensive, including pickup of small loads, consolidation of loads from different customers, transportation to the motor carrier's terminal, transfer at hub terminals, and final delivery.

Revenues are recognized when customers are billed, usually at the time freight is received from the customer (shipper). Direct expenses are incurred throughout the freight service process from pickup to delivery and completion.

This Issue addresses revenue and expense recognition at the balance sheet date for freight that has been received but has not been delivered.

The following five alternative methods of revenue recognition are currently used in practice:

1. Revenue is recognized when freight is received from the shipper (or when freight leaves the carrier's terminal), and expenses are recognized when incurred.
2. Revenue is recognized when freight is received from the shipper (or when freight leaves the carrier's terminal), and

estimated costs to complete are accrued at the end of each reporting period.
3. Revenue and direct costs are recognized when the shipment is completed, and expense is recognized as incurred.
4. Revenue is recognized when the shipment is completed, and expense is recognized as incurred.
5. Revenue is allocated between reporting periods based on relative transit time in each reporting period, and expense is recognized as incurred.

ACCOUNTING ISSUE

How should motor carriers recognize revenue and expense for freight services in process at the balance sheet date?

EITF CONSENSUS

The EITF reached a consensus that Alternative 1 is not an acceptable method of revenue recognition for freight carriers. The Task Force noted that this consensus is not limited to motor carriers.

The Chairman of the AICPA's Accounting Standards Executive Committee stated that in its 1980 discussions of a proposed Issues Paper, *Accounting for Recognition of Revenue for the Motor Carrier Industry*, which was prepared by the AICPA Motor Carriers Special Committee, AcSEC had tentatively concluded that Alternatives 3 or 5 were acceptable. The proposed Issues Paper was to be included in an Audit and Accounting Guide for the motor carrier industry; this Guide was not issued because AcSEC believed that reported net income based on any of the other alternatives would not differ materially.

SEC OBSERVER COMMENT

The SEC Observer indicated that a change from Alternative 1 to Alternative 2 would not be acceptable, because under Alternative 2, revenue is recognized before performance and liabilities are recognized before they are incurred.

DISCUSSION

The following illustration shows the potential income statement effect of revenue and expense recognition under the five alternatives. However, because only one shipment in one reporting period is considered, the results are not as extreme as for companies that have a large number of shipments and report revenue and expense over a number of periods.

36.12 Revenue Recognition

Illustration of Revenue and Expense Recognition by Motor Carriers

Assumptions

Amount billable for shipment A	$2,000
Total expected direct costs associated with shipment A	$1,400
Date freight is received from shipper	June 29, 20X1
Date of final delivery	July 2, 20X1
Reporting date	June 30, 20X1
Direct costs (expenses) incurred through June 30, 20X1	$ 800
Amount billable and billed at June 30, 20X1	$2,000

Revenue and expense recognition at June 30, 20X1

	Alternative				
	1	2	3	4	5
Revenue	$2,000	$ 2,000	$ 0	$ 0	$ 1,000
Expense	800	1,400	0	800	800
Gross profit (loss)	$1,200	$ 600	$ 0	$(800)	$ 200

When this Issue was discussed, predominant industry practice was to recognize revenue based on Alternative 1. The appeal of that method was its simplicity; other methods could involve extensive record keeping. Proponents believed that because of the short-term nature of the service (normally no more than five days), using Alternative 1 would not lead to abuse or distortion. Opponents argued that the earnings process is not complete when the shipment is picked up, because the carrier still must perform significant services, including final delivery.

Paragraph 83 of CON-5 (not included in ASC) refers to two factors for revenue recognition: (*a*) revenues must be realized and realizable and (*b*) revenues must be earned. Alternative 1 does not conform to that guidance.

Although Alternative 2 attempts to match expenses to revenues recognized, it is unacceptable because revenue is recognized before delivery of the shipment. Thus, it does not meet the revenue recognition criteria in CON-5 (not included in ASC). In addition, direct operating expenses are accrued before they have been incurred and the benefits consumed.

Proponents of Alternative 3 believed that the act of delivering the freight is significant because it indicates performance of the service. They believed that revenue is not earned until performance.

Alternative 4 is the most conservative method. Under this alternative, revenue is recognized the same as in Alternative 3, but there is no deferral (or matching) of expenses. There are also no onerous record-keeping requirements. Those who supported this alternative agreed with the revenue recognition criteria in Alternative 3, but believed that direct costs should not be deferred but treated as period costs. In addition, they argued that the cost of estimating and allocating direct costs to different periods is not warranted. Those who supported Alternative 3 argued that revenues and expenses would not be matched properly under Alternative 4.

Proponents of Alternative 5 argued that it provides the best measure of revenue earned during the period and is most faithful to the revenue recognition criteria in CON-5 (not included in ASC), because revenue recognized under that alternative is based on proportional performance, i.e., relative transit time in each reporting period. In addition, an attraction of this alternative was that direct costs are charged to expense as incurred and not allocated between reporting periods. Proponents believed that allocation of such costs would be too subjective. Opponents of the proportional performance alternative argued that there is no reliable way to estimate the degree of performance.

Issue 95-1 (Revenue Recognition on Sales with a Guaranteed Minimum Resale Value) (ASC 460-10-55-17; 60-22; 605-50-60-1; 840-10-55-12 through 55-25)

OVERVIEW

Some manufacturers selling equipment to end users offer an incentive program, under which the manufacturer contractually guarantees the purchaser a minimum resale value on disposition of the equipment, which has an expected useful life of several years. If the equipment meets certain conditions, such as no excess wear and tear, manufacturers may guarantee its resale price in one of two ways: the equipment will be reacquired at a guaranteed price at specified times periods, or the purchaser will be paid for any difference between the proceeds received on the sale of the equipment at the guaranteed minimum resale value. The purchaser is not required, however, to resell the asset to the manufacturer under the incentive program.

Although equipment dealers may be involved in those transactions, the manufacturer is the party responsible for the resale value guarantee. Manufacturers using such programs have been recognizing revenue on the sale of the equipment to independent dealers and have considered the resale protection as a sales incentive. They have recorded the estimated cost of the incentive as a sales discount in the period in which the equipment is sold to the dealer based on historical data, such as amounts realized on resale at auction.

ACCOUNTING ISSUE

Should manufacturers recognize a sale on equipment sold to purchasers with a resale value guarantee?

EITF CONSENSUS

- A manufacturer should not recognize a sale on a transfer of equipment if purchasers receive a resale value guarantee.
- The transaction should be accounted for as a lease, based on the guidance in ASC 840 (FAS-13, Accounting for Leases).
- The difference between the proceeds on the initial transfer of the equipment to the purchaser (the selling price) and the manufacturer's residual value guarantee at the purchaser's first exercise date of the guarantee should be used as the amount of minimum lease payments in determining whether to classify the lease as an operating or as a sales-type lease.

A manufacturer should account for a transfer of equipment under an operating lease as follows:

- Record a liability for the net proceeds received when the equipment is transferred.
- Reduce the liability on a pro rata basis to the guaranteed amount on the first date on which the buyer can exercise the guarantee, and credit revenue for corresponding amounts.
- Continue reducing the liability in a similar manner if the buyer decides to use the equipment beyond the first exercise date.
- Report the equipment in the balance sheet and depreciate it based on the entity's customary depreciation policy.
- Account for potential impairment of the equipment based on the guidance in ASC 205; ASC 360 (FAS-144, Accounting for the Impairment or Disposal of Long-Lived Assets).
- Account for the buyer's exercise of the resale value guarantee as follows:
  —If a buyer exercises the resale value guarantee by selling the equipment to another party, (a) reduce the liability by any amount paid to the purchaser, (b) remove the undepreciated carrying amount of the equipment and any remaining liability from the balance sheet, and (c) include the amounts in (a) and (b) in determining income for the period in which the buyer sells the equipment.
  —If a buyer exercises the resale value guarantee by selling the equipment back to the manufacturer at the guaranteed amount, (a) reduce the liability by the amount paid to the purchaser and (b) include any remaining liability in determining income for the period in which the guarantee is exercised.

OBSERVATION: ASC 460 (FIN-45, Guarantor's Accounting and Disclosure Requirements for Guarantees, Including Indirect Guarantees of Indebtedness of Others), which requires a guarantor to recognize the fair value of a liability at the inception of a guarantee, does *not* affect the consensus in this Issue. Because the manufacturer continues to carry the residual value of the equipment (which is guaranteed) as an asset, the guarantee does *not* meet the characteristics in paragraph 3 of FIN-45 (ASC 460-10-15-4). (See Issue 03-12.)

DISCUSSION

The Task Force initially had reached a tentative conclusion that sales recognition should not be precluded when a manufacturer guarantees the resale value of equipment, but that conclusion was opposed by the FASB's and SEC's staffs and was subsequently withdrawn by the Task Force. The FASB staff and the SEC staff both believed that such transactions should be accounted for under the guidance in ASc 840 (FAS-13), because the manufacturer has retained the risk of reselling the equipment. In effect, the purchaser has the right to use the equipment for a predetermined period of time without the risk of resale at the end of that period.

Illustration of Revenue Recognition on Sales with a Guaranteed Minimum Resale Value

On June 1, 20X4, ABC Motor Co. enters into an agreement with Affordable Auto Rental Co. under which ABC sells ten automobiles to Affordable for $15,000 cash per automobile. ABC conditionally guarantees Affordable either (*a*) a maximum resale value (residual value guarantee) of $7,500 per automobile sold back to ABC starting on December 1, 20X5, the first exercise date (subject to wear and tear), or (*b*) the difference between the residual value guarantee and the amount Affordable receives in a sale to an unrelated party. ABC's inventory cost of each automobile is $12,000. ABC, which accounts for the transaction as an operating lease under the consensus in EITF Issue 95-1, depreciates the automobiles over an estimated economic life of five years on a straight-line basis. The company has a November 30th year-end.

Under the two scenarios below, ABC should account for the transaction initially, during the term of the lease, and when Affordable exercises the residual value guarantee as follows:

Scenario 1 On December 1, 20X5, Affordable sells nine automobiles (one was destroyed in a fire) to another party for $60,000 and exercises ABC's residual value guarantee for the nine automobiles.

Scenario 2 On December 1, 20X5, Affordable exercises the residual value guarantee by selling nine automobiles back to ABC.

At June 1, 20X4—Date of Transfer with Residual Value Guarantee.

Under both scenarios, ABC recognizes the leased automobiles as an asset at its inventory cost and recognizes a liability (deferred revenue) for the net proceeds it received from Affordable on the transfer. (Net proceeds are assumed to be the cash payment received.)

36.16 Revenue Recognition

Cash	$150,000		
Leased automobiles	120,000		
Deferred revenue		$150,000	
Inventory—automobiles		120,000	

At November 30, 20X4

Under both scenarios, ABC reduces the residual value guarantee by a proportionate amount and recognizes a corresponding amount of revenue [$75,000 × (6/18)]. Six months of depreciation is recognized for the automobiles [$120,000 × (6/60)].

Deferred revenue	$25,000		
Depreciation expense	12,000		
Revenue		$25,000	
Accumulated depreciation		12,000	

At November 30, 20X5

Under both scenarios, ABC reduces the residual value guarantee by a proportionate amount and recognizes a corresponding amount of revenue [$75,000 × (12/18)]. Six months of depreciation is recognized for the automobiles [$120,000 × (12/60)].

Deferred revenue	$50,000		
Depreciation expense	24,000		
Revenue		$50,000	
Accumulated depreciation		24,000	

Scenario 1: Exercise of the Residual Value Guarantee

On December 1, 20X5, Affordable sells nine automobiles to an unrelated party for $60,000 and exercises the residual value guarantee. ABC pays Affordable $7,500 (the difference between the guaranteed amount of $67,500 for nine automobiles and $60,000). ABC removes the remaining residual value guarantee and the undepreciated carrying amount of the asset from its balance sheet and uses those amounts to determine income for the quarter ending February 29, 20X6.

Deferred revenue	$75,000		
Accumulated depreciation	36,000		
Cost of sales—automobiles	84,000		
Sale—automobiles		$ 67,500	
Leased automobiles		120,000	
Cash		7,500	

Scenario 2: Exercise of the Residual Value Guarantee

On December 1, 20X5, Affordable exercises the residual value guarantee by selling nine automobiles back to ABC. ABC pays Affordable $67,500 and credits revenue for the amount of the remaining residual value guarantee after the payment.

Deferred revenue	$75,000	
Cash		$67,500
Revenue		$7,500

Issue 95-4 (Revenue Recognition on Equipment Sold and Subsequently Repurchased Subject to an Operating Lease) (ASC 605-15-05-6; 15-2; 25-5; 840-10-60-3)

OVERVIEW

Finished products are sold by a manufacturer to an independent dealer that sells those products to customers, who may be individuals or other independent entities. Customers may purchase such products by (a) paying cash, (b) using their own financing sources, or (c) using traditional consumer financing or lease financing arranged by the dealer and provided by unrelated commercial banks, other finance companies, or by the manufacturer's wholly owned subsidiary.

ACCOUNTING ISSUE

Should a manufacturer recognize a sale on a product sold to an independent dealer if the dealer's customer subsequently enters into an operating lease with the manufacturer or its finance subsidiary, which acquires title to the product subject to the lease?

EITF CONSENSUS

The EITF reached a consensus that a manufacturer can recognize a sale when the product is transferred to the dealer if *all* of the following conditions exist:

- The dealer is a substantive and independent entity whose business with the manufacturer and retail customers is conducted separately.
- The manufacturer has delivered the product and passed the risks and rewards of ownership to the dealer, including responsibility for the ultimate sale of the product and for insurability, theft, or damage. The dealer cannot return the product to the manufacturer if the customer does not enter into a lease with the manufacturer or its finance subsidiary.
- At the time the product is delivered to the dealer, the manufacturer or its finance affiliate has no legal obligation to provide a lease to the dealer's potential customer.
- Other financing alternatives are available to the customer from sources that are not affiliated with the manufacturer, and the customer makes the selection from the financing alternatives.

DISCUSSION

The Task Force's consensus was based on the following views:

- The manufacturer's sale of the product to the dealer is a legal sale. Because the manufacturer has no further obligation related to the product, other than warranty obligations, the dealer's transaction with the retail customer is a separate transaction.
- The sale to the dealer meets the criteria for revenue recognition in paragraph 83 of CON-5 (not included in the ASC), because revenue was earned when the manufacturer sold the product to the dealer. The manufacturer has no obligation related to future sales to retail customers.
- The manufacturer's involvement in financing alternatives is not a primary issue in the dealer's sales process as long as the customer can choose between financing from the manufacturer's subsidiary and alternative financing sources from unaffiliated parties.
- The manufacturer does not guarantee the dealer's recovery of its investment in the product.
- The economic substance of the operating lease is independent of the manufacturer's sale to the dealer, because title, risks, and rewards of ownership have been transferred to the dealer, including the product's ultimate sale and disposition in case of theft or damage.

EITF Issue 99-19 (Reporting Revenue Gross as a Principal versus Net as an Agent) (ASC 605-45-05-1, 05-2; 15-3 through 15-5; 45-1, 45-2, 45-4 through 45-14, 45-6 through 45-18; 50-1; 55-2, 55-3, 55-5, 55-6, 55-8, 55-9, 55-11 through 55-14, 55-16, 55-18, 55-20, 55-22, 55-24, 55-25, 55-27 through 55-31, 55-33, 55-34, 55-36 through 55-38, 55-40 through 55-45)

OVERVIEW

As a result of the proliferation of sales of goods and services over the Internet, the SEC staff has noted diversity in registrants' revenue recognition practices. Frequently, a vendor does not stock the merchandise sold on its Internet site, but rather arranges for a supplier to ship the merchandise directly to the buyer. Similarly, services sold on an Internet site are frequently performed by a third party, not by the Internet vendor. In some cases, the vendor's profit on the transaction consists of a commission or fee for selling a third party's products or services. The importance of a company's revenue recognition method has increased in the current economic environment because some investors value Internet companies—especially start-ups that may show losses or very little net income in the early years—based on multiples of revenues instead of multiples of gross profit or earnings.

SAB-101 addresses the question whether Company A, which sells Company T's products on the Internet, should recognize (*a*) both the gross amount of the sale and the related costs or (*b*) the net revenue earned on the sale. In determining how a company should recognize revenue, the SEC staff considers whether the company

1. Is acting as a principal in the transaction
2. Takes title to the merchandise
3. Has the risks and rewards of ownership, such as risks of loss for collection, delivery, or returns
4. Is acting as an agent or broker (including performing services as an agent or broker) and is compensated by a commission or fee

The SEC also requires a company that performs as an agent or broker to report sales on a net basis if no risks and rewards of ownership of the goods are assumed.

Because the SEC staff believes that additional factors may exist, the staff asked the EITF to develop an accounting model that is consistent with the requirements of SAB-101. The EITF's guidance is not limited to Internet transactions, but also may apply to transactions with travel agents, magazine subscription brokers, and sales of products through catalogs, consignment sales, or special-order retail sales.

This Issue does not address the timing of revenue recognition and whether revenue should be deferred if the earnings process is not complete. Further, it does not apply to transactions under guidance that had been included in categories (a) or (b) of the GAAP hierarchy (guidance issued by the FASB and AICPA) before July 1, 2009 when the FASB Accounting Standards Codification™ became effective, nor those addressed in Issues 00-10 (in this chapter) and 00-14 (codified in Issue 01-9).

ACCOUNTING ISSUE

Under what circumstances should a company report revenue based on (*a*) the *gross* amount billed to a customer for the sale of a product or service on which the company earns revenue or (*b*) the *net* amount retained (the amount billed less the amount paid the supplier), because the supplier or service provider paid the company a commission or fee?

EITF CONSENSUS

The decision whether to report revenue at (*a*) the *gross* amount billed to a customer, because the company earned the revenue from a sale of goods or services, or (*b*) the *net* difference between the amount billed to a customer less the amount paid to the supplier, because the company earned a commission or fee, depends on judgment based on the facts and circumstances. The following factors, which should not be considered to be presumptive or determinative, should be considered in that decision based on their strength:

- Indicators of Gross Revenue Reporting
    - *Acting as the primary obligor*   The fact that a company is responsible for fulfilling a customer's order, including whether the product or service is acceptable to the customer, is a strong indicator that the company has the risks and rewards of a principal and should report revenue at the *gross* amount billed to the customer. A company's marketing representations and the terms of a sales contract indicate whether the company or the supplier is fulfilling the order.
    - *General inventory risk before the order is placed or on product return*   If a company (*a*) takes title to the product before it is ordered by a customer who has the right of return and (*b*) takes title to the product if it is returned, the company has general inventory risk, which indicates that it has the risk and rewards of a principal in the transaction and is a strong indicator that it should report revenue at the gross amount. The company and the supplier should have no arrangement to reduce or mitigate inventory risk, for example, the right to return unsold products to the supplier.
    - *Latitude in establishing the price*   A company's ability, within economic constraints, to establish the price of a product or service charged to the customer may indicate that the company is acting as a principal in the transaction.
    - *Addition of meaningful value to a product or service*   The fact that a company adds meaningful value (the selling price is greater because of the addition) to a product or provides a significant portion of a service ordered by a customer may indicate that the company has primary responsibility for fulfillment, including customer satisfaction with the component of the product or portion of total services provided by the supplier.
    - *Discretion in selecting the supplier*   The fact that a company can select a supplier among several to provide a product or service ordered by a customer may indicate that the company has primary responsibility for fulfillment.
    - *Involvement in determining product or service specifications*   The requirement for a company to determine the nature, type, characteristics, or specifications of a product or service ordered by a customer may indicate that the company has primary responsibility for fulfillment.
    - *Retention of the risk of physical loss of inventory after a customer's order or during shipping*   The risk of physical loss of inventory exists (*a*) from the time the company takes title to the product at the point of shipment (e.g., the supplier's facilities) until the product is transferred to the customer on delivery or (*b*) from the time the company takes title to the product after the cus-

tomer's order has been received until the product is delivered to a carrier for shipment to the customer. This indicator provides less persuasive evidence than general inventory risk that the gross amount of revenue should be reported.

—*Assumption of credit risk*   The company assumes credit risk if it is responsible for collecting the sales price from the customer and has to pay the supplier regardless of whether it collects the full sales price. The company's assumption of credit risk for the amount billed to the customer may provide weak evidence that the company has the risks and rewards of a principal in the transaction and should report revenue gross. No credit risk is assumed if the company collects the full sales price before delivering the product or service to the customer.

- Indicators of Net Revenue Reporting
  - *The supplier is the primary obligor*   The fact that the supplier is responsible for fulfillment, including whether the product or services ordered or purchased by the customer are acceptable, may indicate that the company does not have the risks and rewards as a principal in the transaction and should report revenue based on the amount retained after paying the supplier. The company's representations while marketing the product and the sales contract generally provide evidence of whether the company or the supplier is required to fulfill the order or service.
  - *The company earns a fixed amount*   The fact that the company earns a fixed amount on the transaction regardless of the amount billed for the product or service indicates that the company is acting as an agent for the supplier.
  - *The supplier assumes the credit risk*   The fact that the supplier assumes the credit risk, because the full sales price has not been collected before the product or service is delivered to the customer, indicates that the company is acting as an agent for the supplier.

Some members noted that voluntary disclosures of an entity's gross volume of transactions that are reported may be useful to users. The information could be disclosed parenthetically in the income statement or in the notes to the financial statements. Gross amounts disclosed on the face of the income statement should not be described as revenues and should not be reported in a column that is included in the sum of net income or loss. Such amounts may be described as gross billings.

SEC OBSERVER COMMENT

The SEC Observer reminded registrants that under Regulation S-X, Rule 5-03(b)(1), they are required separately to present in the income statement revenues from the sale of products and revenues from the provision of services. Because commissions and fees earned from activities reported net are service revenues, separate presentations are usually made for revenues reported gross and revenues reported net.

The SEC Observer also noted that the SEC staff stated in Topic D-85 (not in the codification) that registrants should retroactively apply the guidance in SAB-101 to income statement classification of all periods presented in their next interim or annual financial statements filed with the Commission after January 20, 2000, if the information is available. He reiterated that the same guidance applies to any income statement reclassification required by this Issue. In addition, the staff expects companies registering shares in an initial public offering to comply with SAB-101 in their filing of an initial registration statement with the SEC.

EITF Issue 00-10 (Accounting for Shipping and Handling Fees and Costs) (ASC 605-45-05-2, 05-3; 15-2, 15-4; S45-1; 45-19 through 45-21; 50-2; S99-1)

OVERVIEW

The income statement classification of amounts charged to customers for shipping and handling and related costs differs among companies. Some report charges to customers in revenue and report costs incurred as expenses, but others report only the net amount of costs and revenues. In addition, the costs included in the shipping and handling category also differ by company. Some include only amounts paid to third-party shippers, but others may also include internal costs, such as salaries and overhead related to the preparation of the goods for shipment. Some charge customers for shipping costs incurred and direct incremental handling costs. Many charge amounts for shipping and handling that are not a direct reimbursement of costs incurred.

This Issue applies only to shipping and handling fees and costs reported by companies that report revenue at the gross amount billed, as discussed in Issue 99-19 above.

ACCOUNTING ISSUES

1. How should a seller of goods classify in the income statement amounts billed to a customer for shipping and handling?

2. How should a seller of goods classify in the income statement costs incurred for shipping and handling?

EITF CONSENSUS

1. The classification of shipping and handling costs is an accounting policy decision that should be disclosed in accordance with the guidance in ASC 235 (APB-22, Disclosure of Accounting

Policies). A company's policy may be to include shipping and handling costs in costs of sales. A company should disclose the amounts of such costs and the line items in which they are included on the income statement, if such costs are significant and are not included in cost of sales, but rather are accounted for together or separately as other income statement line items.

2. The Task Force noted that it decided not to reach a consensus on Issue 2, even though it may result in a diversity of types of costs being classified as shipping and handling.
3. Netting shipping and handling costs against shipping and handling revenues is inconsistent with the consensus on Issue 1.
4. Application of the consensus in 1 above is subject to the SEC Observer's comments, which are discussed below.

SEC OBSERVER COMMENT

The SEC Observer noted that the SEC staff stated in Topic D-85 (not in the ASC) that registrants should retroactively apply the guidance in SAB-101 to income statement classification of all periods presented in their next interim or annual financial statements filed with the Commission after January 20, 2000, if the information is available. He reiterated that the same guidance applies to the reclassification of shipping and handling revenues required in this Issue.

Registrants are expected to evaluate the significance of shipping and handling costs so that the consensus positions reached in this Issue are applied based on the significance of such costs to (*a*) each line item on the income statement in which they are included and (*b*) the total gross margin.

EITF Issue 01-9 (Accounting for Consideration Given by a Vendor to a Customer (Including a Reseller of the Vendor's Products)) (ASC 330-10-35-13; 605-50-05-1; 15-2, 15-3; 25-1 through 25-9; S45-1; 45-1 through 45-11; 55-1, 55-3, 55-5, 55-8 through 55-12, 55-14, 55-15, 55-17 through 55-22, 55-24, 55-25, 55-27, 55-28, 55-30, 55-31, 55-33 through 55-37; 55-40 through 55-44, 55-46, 55-47, 55-49, 55-50, 55-52, 55-53, 55-55 through 55-69, 55-71, 55-72, 55-74 through 55-77, 55-79 through 55-95, 55-97 through 55-107; S99-1; 908-360-55-1)

OVERVIEW

This Issue is a codification of the guidance provided and consensus positions reached in Issues 00-14 (Accounting for Certain Sales Incentives), Issue 3 from Issue 00-22 (Accounting for "Points" and Certain Other Time-Based or Volume-Based Sales Incentive Offers, and Offers for Free Products or Services to be Delivered in the Future), and Issue 00-25 (Vendor Characterization of Consideration to a Reseller of a Vendor's Products). It applies to vendors that earn revenue by providing products or services, or both.

This Issue also discusses how a vendor, which is a manufacturer or distributor, should report in its income statement consideration given to a retailer. Although there are three parties to the transactions—the vendor, the retailer, and the end consumer—only the accounting for consideration from a vendor to a retailer is addressed.

Consideration from a vendor to a retailer may be in the form of cash, but it can also be in the form of credits that the retailer can apply against trade amounts owed to the vendor, or in the form of the vendor's equity instruments. EITF Issue 96-18 provides guidance on accounting for such equity instruments.

The Issue applies to the following kinds of arrangements:

1. Slotting fees, which are fees that a vendor pays to a retailer for shelf space for the vendor's products. The scope of the Issue also applies to other product placement arrangements, such as brand development or new product introduction arrangements, for which a vendor pays fees to a retailer to display the vendor's products in favorable locations in the store, for end-cap placement, and for additional shelf space. A vendor may incur slotting fees (*a*) before selling any of the products to the retailer, (*b*) on a regular schedule to maintain a shelf space allocation or to continue being a regular vendor, or (*c*) periodically as negotiated. The vendor may or may not receive stated rights for those fees.

2. Cooperative advertising arrangements, in which a vendor reimburses a retailer for a portion of the costs incurred to advertise the vendor's products. The vendor is generally required to participate in advertising costs based on the actual cost. The retailer may be reimbursed for an amount limited to a specified percentage of its purchases from the vendor. In other arrangements, the amount of reimbursement is based on a percentage of the retailer's purchases from the vendor during a specific time period, regardless of actual costs incurred by the retailer to advertise the vendor's products.

3. Buydowns, which are arrangements under which a vendor agrees to reimburse a retailer up to a specified amount for shortfalls in the sales price received by the retailer for the vendor's products over a specified time period. Under such arrangements, the vendor reimburses, compensates, or issues credit memos to the retailer for a decrease in revenue per product unit during a specified promotion period for a product. Under those arrangements, the retailer is not required to make any expenditures for advertising or promotions. Other related arrangements in which a vendor reduces the net price paid by the retailer for the vendor's products include factory

incentives, dealer holdbacks, price protection, and factory-to-dealer incentives.

4. Arrangements under which a vendor agrees to pay all or a portion of a customer's financing costs for a designated time period.

Issues 1 and 2 provide guidance on the income statement presentation of such consideration given by a vendor to a customer.

Because the accounting literature does not provide guidance on the accounting for sales incentives, such as discounts, coupons, rebates and free products, or services offered voluntarily by vendors to their customers at no charge, the EITF was asked to address this Issue. It applies to sales incentives offered by manufacturers to customers of retailers or other distributors and the following types of offers:

- To purchase a product or receive a service at a reduced price at the point of sale
- To receive a reduction in the price of a product or service after paying the full price at the point of sale by submitting a claim for a refund or rebate of a specified amount of the purchase price
- To receive a free product or service at the point of sale when purchasing another specified item

Issue 3, on which the EITF did not reach a consensus, addresses whether a vendor should recognize as an asset consideration given to a customer in the form of up-front, nonrefundable consideration or whether the vendor should recognize the cost immediately. Issues 4, 5, and 6 address the cost of sales incentives and how they should be measured. The guidance in Issues 4 and 5 apply only to arrangements that link an incentive to a single sale for which the vendor receives no identifiable benefit from the customer in exchange. If a customer, however, does provide an identifiable benefit to the vendor in exchange for an offer, and the fair value of that benefit is less than the amount of the offer, the amount by which the offer exceeds the benefit received should be accounted for under the guidance in Issues 4 and 5. The guidance in Issue 5 on loss recognition does *not* apply to arrangements in which a vendor must deliver a minimum amount of goods or services to a customer during a contractually specified period.

Issue 6 applies to rebates or refunds of a determinable amount of cash to customers having a cumulative level of revenue transactions with a vendor or that remain a customer for a specified period of time and the vendor receives no identifiable benefit from the customer. However, if a customer does provide an identifiable benefit to a vendor in exchange for an offer, and the fair value of that benefit is less than the amount of the offer, the amount by which the offer exceeds the benefit received should be accounted for under the guidance in Issue 6.

The scope of this Issue does *not* include the following:

36.26 *Revenue Recognition*

- Coupons, rebates, and other forms of rights for free or significantly discounted products or services that a customer received in an earlier exchange transaction and that the vendor accounted for as a separate element of that transaction.
- Offers for free or significantly discounted products or services that a customer can exercise in the future without an additional exchange with the vendor as a result of a current revenue transaction.

ACCOUNTING ISSUES

Income Statement Presentation

1. When an incentive or other consideration is given by a vendor to a customer (reseller or retailer) (*a*) should an adjustment of the vendor's selling price for products sold be deducted from revenue in the vendor's income statement or (*b*) should cost the vendor incurs for assets or services that a customer provides to the vendor be accounted for as a cost or expense in the vendor's income statement?
2. Should a vendor that has "negative revenue" as a result of a revenue deduction for consideration given to customers based on the guidance in Issue 1 recharacterize that amount as an expense in the income statement?

Recognition and Measurement

3. When should a vendor recognize as an asset upfront nonrefundable consideration that the vendor gives to a customer instead of immediately recognizing a cost in the income statement?
4. When should a vendor recognize and how should the vendor measure the cost of sales incentives offered voluntarily to customers at no charge that customers can exercise in a single transaction if *no* loss is incurred on the sale of the product or service?
5. When should a vendor recognize and how should the vendor measure the cost of sales incentives discussed in Issue 4 if a loss is incurred on the sale of the product or service?
6. How should a vendor account for an offer to a customer to rebate or refund a specified amount of cash that may be redeemed only if the customer completes a specified cumulative level of revenue transactions or remains a customer for a specified period of time?

EITF CONSENSUS

The Task Force reached the following consensus positions:

Income Statement Presentation

1. It is presumed that a vendor's consideration to a customer related to the vendor's products is a reduction of the vendor's prices that results in a reduction of revenue in the income statement. However, that presumption may be overcome, and the vendor should account for the consideration as a cost if the vendor has received or will receive a benefit that meets the following two conditions:

    a. In return for the consideration, the vendor has received or will receive an identifiable benefit from the customer in the form of goods or services. The benefit should be one for which the vendor would have entered into an exchange transaction with a third party that is separate from its sales of goods or services.

    b. The fair value of the benefit can be reasonably estimated. Otherwise, an excess of consideration over the fair value of the benefit, if any, should be deducted from revenue presented in the income statement.

    The Task Force noted that the effect of the requirement for separability in (a) above would generally result in the recognition of slotting fees or similar fees related to product development or placement as a reduction of revenue. For example, a vendor's agreement to reimburse a customer for a reduction in a product's sales price would always be recognized as a revenue reduction. Buydowns, which would never meet criterion (a), should always be accounted for as reductions of revenue.

    In addition, this Issue also applies to consideration from a vendor to a customer that resells the product in another format or uses the product as a component of another product, for example, a payment for cooperative advertising from a fabric manufacturer to a clothing manufacturer.

    A vendor should report as an *expense* in its income statement the cost of consideration consisting of a free product or service, such as a gift from a vendor or a free airline ticket to be honored by an unrelated entity, and other noncash consideration in the form of equity or credits to be applied against further purchases from the vendor or equity, because the free item is an element in the exchange transaction and *not* a refund or rebate of a portion of the sales price. The EITF did not state how that expense should be classified, but the SEC staff believes that expenses related to free products or services delivered when a customer purchases another product or service should be reported in cost of sales.

2. Although it is presumed that no portion of amounts required under this Issue, or other authoritative accounting literature, to be classified as a reduction of revenue should be reclassified as an expense, a vendor may be permitted to reclassify as an

expense a cumulative shortfall of revenue from doing business with a particular customer if the vendor can demonstrate that the reduction of cumulative revenue earned by the vendor since the inception of the customer relationship will result in a shortfall, referred to as *negative revenue*. In doing that customer analysis, a vendor that sells a product directly to resellers that subsequently sell it to retailers receiving the vendor's consideration must be able to identify the reseller from which a retailer purchased the vendor's product. The Task Force noted that reclassification of negative revenue as an expense would be permitted if a vendor gives a fixed amount of consideration to a new customer before the customer has purchased any products or placed or committed to place any orders. Reclassification as an expense would *not* be permitted if a vendor has an existing arrangement with a customer under which the vendor is an exclusive supplier of a specific product for a certain period of time and it is probable that the customer will place an order or if the customer is required to order a minimum amount of the vendor's products in the future.

Revenue earned by a vendor from a particular customer also may include revenue earned from other entities in a consolidated group that includes the customer. The term *customer* is used in this Issue as it is defined in paragraph 39 of FAS-131 (ASC 280-10-50-42), which states that each of the following is considered to be a single customer: a group of entities under common control, the federal government, a state government, a local government, or a foreign government. Also, the *inception of an overall relationship* with a customer may occur when a new relationship is established or when a relationship is reestablished with a customer with whom the vendor previously had a business relationship that had been terminated.

Each financial reporting period should stand on its own when applying the guidance in Issue 2 on the recharacterization of "negative revenue" if that amount fluctuates during multiple reporting periods. Amounts presented as an expense in one period should not be reclassified in a later period even if a credit to expense results. A credit up to the expense previously recognized should be presented in the income statement as a reduction of expense if a reduction in the measured fair value of consideration occurs due to changes in estimates or other factors. A remaining credit, if any, should be presented in revenue.

The guidance in this Issue regarding the recharacterization as an expense of "negative revenue" that results when a vendor recognizes a reduction in revenue for cash consideration given to a customer (*a*) applies to consideration with a variable measurement (e.g., an equity instrument accounted for under Issue 96-18 for which the measurement date has yet to occur), (*b*) prohibits a vendor from recharacterizing as an expense a portion of consideration received from a customer that was not immediately reported in the income statement and the vendor has cumulative revenue from the customer when that portion of the consideration is finally reported in the income statement, and (c) does not prohibit a vendor from recognizing as an expense a portion of the consideration that a vendor pays or is obligated to pay to a customer at the beginning of an overall relationship if that amount exceeds the amount of probable future revenue the vendor expects to receive from the customer. The conclusion that future revenue is probable does not require the existence of a purchase commitment or exclusivity arrangement.

SEC OBSERVER COMMENT

Registrants are reminded to consider whether under the requirements in Item 303 of Regulation S-K information about the incentives discussed in this Issue should be disclosed in *Management's Discussion and Analysis of Financial Condition and Results of Operations*.

The SEC Observer stated that the staff believes that arrangements under which a vendor agrees to pay all or a portion of a customer's financing costs for a designated time might affect a vendor's timing of revenue recognition on products sold to a customer or reseller, depending on the arrangement's specific facts and circumstances.

In addition, the SEC Observer stated that registrants that would have been required to apply the guidance in Issues 1 and 2 in a previous period under the earlier transition guidance requiring adoption in annual financial statements for the fiscal year beginning after December 15, 1999, should disclose the following information in SEC filings for intervening periods. That is, registrants should disclose the amount of consideration for the current period and, if practicable, for all other periods presented, as well as the line item in which they are classified if the registrant did not classify consideration from a vendor to a customer discussed in Issue 1 in accordance with the consensus on that Issue.

Recognition and Measurement

3. The EITF agreed to discontinue its consideration of Issue 3 regarding whether a vendor should recognize an asset instead of an immediate expense for up-front nonrefundable consideration given to a customer. This Issue applied specifically to fees paid by vendors to obtain shelf space for their products (slotting fees). Vendors that recognized an asset for such consideration should recharacterize such amounts in subsequent income statements in accordance with the guidance for Issues 1 and 2.
4. Vendors should recognize the cost of sales incentives offered voluntarily and without charge to customers if such incentives

do *not* result in a loss on a sale or service on either of the following dates, whichever occurs later:

a. The date on which the vendor recognizes the related revenue.

b. The date on which the sales incentive is offered. (This would occur if the vendor offers the sales incentive after having recognized revenue on the sale, for example, if a manufacturer offers discount coupons to retailers subsequent to the sale of the product.)

A liability or deferred revenue should be recognized at the later of the above dates based on an estimated amount of refunds or rebates that will be claimed if customers must submit a form to receive refunds or rebates of specific amounts. A maximum potential liability or deferred revenue should be recognized for refunds or rebates if it is not possible to make a reasonable and reliable estimate of the amount of *future* refunds or rebates. Although that estimate depends on many factors, the Task Force reached a consensus that a vendor's ability to make a reasonable and reliable estimate may be impaired as a result of the following:

(1) The period during which refunds or rebates can be claimed is relatively long.

(2) The vendor has no historical experience with similar types of sales incentives or is unable to apply that experience because circumstances have changed.

(3) The volume of relatively homogeneous transactions is insufficient.

5. A vendor should *not* recognize a liability for sales incentives voluntarily offered to customers at no cost that will result in a loss on the sale of products or services before recognizing revenue on the transactions. The Task Force noted that a sales incentive that will result in a loss on the sale of a product may indicate that existing inventory is impaired under the guidance in ASC 330 (ARB-43).

SEC OBSERVER'S COMMENTS

The SEC Observer stated that registrants that would have been required to apply the guidance in Issues 4 and 5 in a previous period under an the earlier transition guidance requiring adoption in annual financial statements for the fiscal year beginning after December 15, 1999, should disclose the following information in SEC filings for intervening periods:

- All disclosures required in SAB Topic 11M, including anticipated effects of reclassifications, if any, of prior period financial statements presented. If previously reported revenue would be reduced as a result of application of the consensus positions in Issues 4 and 5, that fact should be explicitly disclosed.

- If a registrant's accounting has historically been different from the consensus positions reached in Issues 4 and 5, the entity should disclose the recognition policy followed as well as the following information for all fiscal periods of fiscal years beginning after December 15, 1999:

    —The liability or deferred revenue reported as of the beginning of the period,

    —The amount of additional revenue deferred or liability accrued during the period,

    —Amounts refunded to customers during the period,

    —Adjustments made during the period for changes in estimates and other adjustment, if any, and

    —The balance of the liability or deferred revenue at the end of the period.

The SEC Observer also reminded registrants to consider whether to disclose in *Management's Discussion and Analysis of Financial Condition and Results of Operations* information about the incentives discussed in this Issue, in accordance with the requirements in Item 303 of Regulation S-K.

EITF CONSENSUS

1. A vendor should *reduce* revenue by the amount recognized as an obligation for a rebate or refund to a customer. The cost of honoring claims for rebates or refunds should be allocated on a rational and systematic basis to each underlying revenue transaction with a customer that will enable the customer to reach a cumulative level at which a rebate or refund will be earned. The total rebate or refund obligation should be based on an estimated number of customers that will earn and claim refunds under the offer. "Breakage" should be included if the amount of future rebates can be reasonably estimated. Otherwise, the vendor should recognize a liability for the maximum rebate or refund, without a reduction for breakage. Although the ability to make that estimate may vary on a case-by-case basis, a vendor's ability to make a reasonable estimate may be affected by the following factors:

    a. The period during which a rebate or refund can be claimed is relatively long.

    b. The vendor has no historical experience with similar types of sales incentives for similar products or is unable to use that experience because the circumstances differ.

c. The volume of homogenous transactions is not large enough to make a reasonable estimate.

Under some programs, the amount of a cash rebate or refund may increase, based on the customer's volume of purchases. If a vendor can reasonably estimate the volume of a customer's future purchases, a liability should be recognized for the *estimated* amount of the cash rebate or refund. Otherwise, the vendor should recognize a liability for the maximum potential refund or rebate under the program.

2. Changes in the estimated amounts of cash rebates or refunds from a previous offer, such as a retroactive increase or decrease in the amount of the rebate, should be recognized immediately as a cumulative catch-up adjustment to adjust the balance of the rebate obligation. Revenue on future sales should be reduced based on the *revised* rate of the refund obligation.

SUBSEQUENT DEVELOPMENT

At its June 15–16, 2005, meeting, the EITF agreed with the recommendation of the FASB staff that a footnote be added to clarify the scope of Issue 4. The footnote will state that the accounting guidance in Issue 4 does not apply if a vendor offers a customer in connection with a current transaction free or discounted products or services that the customer can redeem at a future date without making a further exchange transaction with the vendor.

EITF Issue 02-16 (Accounting by a Reseller for Cash Consideration Received from a Vendor)
(ASC 605-50-05-1; 15-2; 25-10 through 25-12; 45-12 through 45-15; 55-116, 55-117, 55-119, 55-120, 55-122, 55-123)

OVERVIEW

In Issue 01-9 (Accounting for Consideration Given by a Vendor to a Customer [Including a Reseller of the Vendor's Products]), the EITF provides guidance on (*a*) how *vendors* should account for consideration given to customers that are resellers of their products and entities that purchase their products from a reseller, and (*b*) how to measure and when to recognize such consideration in the income statement. This Issue addresses how *resellers* of a vendor's products should account for cash consideration received from vendors.

ACCOUNTING ISSUES

1. Under what circumstances should a reseller account for cash consideration received from a vendor as (*a*) an adjustment of the vendor's prices for its products or services and presented as a reduction of cost of sales in the reseller's income statement,

(b) an adjustment of a cost incurred by the reseller and presented as a reduction of that cost in the reseller's income statement, or (c) a payment received for assets or services delivered to a vendor and presented as revenue in the reseller's income statement?

2. How should a reseller measure the amount of and when should a reseller recognize a vendor's offer of a rebate or refund of a specific amount of cash consideration payable only if the reseller makes a specified amount of purchases or remains a reseller for a specified time period?

EITF CONSENSUS

Issue 1

- It is presumed that cash consideration received by a reseller from a vendor is a *reduction* of the vendor's prices for its products or services and should be reported as a reduction of cost of sales in the reseller's income statement.
- That presumption may be overcome, however, if a vendor's cash consideration to a reseller is (a) a payment for assets or services delivered to the vendor that should be presented as revenue or other income in the reseller's income statement, depending on the circumstances, or (b) a reimbursement of the reseller's costs to sell the vendor's products or services that should be reported as a reduction of the reseller's selling costs in the income statement.
- If a vendor receives or will receive in exchange for its cash consideration an identifiable benefit (e.g., goods or services) that is sufficiently separable from the reseller's purchases of the vendor's products, the reseller should report the payment as revenue in its income statement. Indicators supporting that treatment include (a) the fact that the reseller could have entered into an exchange transaction with another party to provide the benefit and (b) the fair value of the benefit provided can be reasonably estimated. A reseller should reduce its cost of sales reported in the income statement if the vendor's cash consideration for the benefit exceeds the benefit's estimated fair value.

Issue 2

- If cash consideration paid by a vendor to a reseller is a reimbursement of the reseller's specific, incremental, identifiable costs incurred to sell the vendor's products or services, that amount should be reported in the reseller's income statement as a reduction of that cost. Cash consideration in excess of a reseller's cost, if any, should be reported in the reseller's income statement as a reduction of cost of sales.

- If a vendor's rebate or refund for a specified amount of cash consideration payable under a binding arrangement will occur only if a reseller achieves a cumulative level of purchases or remains a customer for a specified time period, the reseller should reduce its cost of sales based on a systematic and rational allocation of the cash consideration related to each of the underlying transactions resulting in the reseller's progress toward earning the rebate or refund only if receipt of the rebate or refund is *probable* and reasonably estimable. Otherwise, the consideration should be recognized as milestones are achieved.

- Although the EITF noted that a reasonable estimate of the amount of future cash rebates or refunds depends on many factors and circumstance that may vary on a case-by-case basis, the EITF reached a consensus that the following factors may impair a customer's ability to determine the probability and to reasonably estimate the amount of a rebate or refund:

  —The purchases will occur over a relatively long period.

  —No historical experience with similar products exists or such experience cannot be applied because of changing circumstances.

  —In the past, expected cash rebates or refunds needed significant adjustments.

  —The product is affected by significant external factors, such as technological obsolescence or changes in demand.

- Changes in estimates of cash rebates or refunds and a vendor's retroactive changes of a previous offer, such as a retroactive increase or decrease in a rebate's amount, are changes in estimates that should be accounted for with a cumulative catch-up adjustment. The EITF noted that entities should consider whether any portion of such an adjustment would affect inventory, thus requiring that only a portion of the adjustment be reported in the income statement.

EITF Issue 03-10 **(Application of EITF Issue No. 02-16, "Accounting by a Customer (Including a Reseller) for Certain Consideration Received from a Vendor," by Resellers to Sales Incentives Offered to Consumers by Manufacturers) (ASC 605-50-45-16 through 45-20; 55-125 through 55-127)**

OVERVIEW

Issue 02-16 (Accounting by a Customer (Including a Reseller) for Certain Consideration Received from a Vendor) provides that a customer receiving cash from a vendor should reduce its cost of sales in the income statement based on the presumption that the vendor's price is reduced by the cash received. That presumption may be overcome, however, if the cash received is (*a*) a payment for assets or services received from the customer that should be accounted for as revenue or other income in the customer's income statement, or (*b*) a payment to reimburse the customer for costs incurred to sell the vendor's products that should be accounted for as a reduction of those costs in the customer's income statement.

This Issue addresses a reseller's accounting for sales incentives, such as coupons, offered by manufacturers (vendors) directly to consumers for products that will be purchased from resellers. Depending on the form of the incentive, some are tendered by a consumer directly to a reseller for a reduction in the sales price of a product, while others are sent by the consumer to the manufacturer for a rebate after the product has been purchased from a reseller. In either case, the reseller's gross margin for the product is unaffected. A reseller that agrees to accept an incentive as partial payment of a product's sales price will be reimbursed by the vendor for the amount of the incentive.

This Issue applies only to incentives that meet the following criteria: (*a*) consumers can use the incentives at *any* reseller in partial payment of the reseller's price for a particular product, (*b*) the vendor reimburses resellers at the face amount of the incentive, (*c*) the incentive is *not* part of a broader incentive program between a specific vendor and reseller or a cooperative promotional program, and (*d*) the incentive creates an expressed or implied *agency* relationship between the vendor and the reseller for the particular sales incentive transaction.

ACCOUNTING ISSUE

Should consideration received by a reseller from a vendor as a reimbursement for honoring the vendor's sales incentives offered directly to consumers be recognized as a reduction of the cost of the reseller's purchases from the vendor and, therefore, be accounted for as a reduction of cost of sales under the guidance in Issue 02-16?

EITF CONSENSUS

The EITF reached a consensus that the consensus positions in Issue 02-16 do *not* apply to vendors' sales incentives offered directly to consumers if (*a*) customers can use the incentives at any reseller that accepts the manufacturer's incentive as partial or full payment of the reseller's price for the vendor's product, (*b*) the vendor reimburses resellers directly for the face amount of the incentive, (*c*) the terms governing a reseller's reimbursement for the vendor's sales incentive offered to consumers can be determined only on the basis of the terms of that incentive and must not be influenced by or negotiated in connection with any other incentive arrangement between the vendor and the reseller, and (*d*) the reseller is subject to an expressed or implied agency relationship with the vendor regarding the sales incentive transaction between the vendor and the consumer.

For example, a reseller would recognize $4 in revenue and $3 as a cost of sales for a $4 box of cereal with a $3 cost if a customer pays $3.50 in cash and presents a 50-cent coupon for which the vendor reimburses the reseller. Sales incentives with characteristics that do not meet the criteria in this Issue should be accounted for under Issue 01-9 or Issue 02-16, whichever applies.

EITF Issue 06-1 (Accounting for Consideration Given by a Service Provider to Manufacturers or Resellers of Equipment Necessary for an End-Customer to Receive Service from the Service Provider) (ASC 605-50-15-2; 25-13 through 25-18; 50-1; 55-108, 55-110 through 55-114)

OVERVIEW

Frequently, the customers of a service provider must purchase equipment produced by a manufacturer and sold by a third-party reseller that distributes the equipment without having a direct involvement with the service provider. A service provider, to increase demand for its service, may induce third-party manufacturers or resellers to reduce the price of equipment. Such consideration was not included under the scope of Issue 01-9 (Accounting for Consideration Given by a Vendor to a Customer (Including a Reseller of the Vendor's Products)) because third-party manufacturers and resellers were *not* considered part of a service provider's distribution chain.

ACCOUNTING ISSUES

1. Should consideration given by a service provider to a third-party manufacturer or reseller of equipment (that is *not* the service provider's customer) that provides a benefit to a service provider's customer be described as "cash consideration" or as "other than cash" consideration when the guidance in Issue 01-9 is applied?

2. If a customer needs certain equipment in order to receive a service from a service provider, is consideration given by the service provider to a third-party manufacturer or a reseller of equipment benefiting a customer of both the service provider and the equipment manufacturer or reseller, in substance, the same as if the service provider had given the consideration directly to the end-customer?

3. Should consideration given by a service provider to a manufacturer or a reseller of equipment (that is *not* the service provider's customer) be accounted for under the model in Issue 01-9 if the customer needs the equipment in order to receive a service from a service provider and the consideration can be linked to the benefit received by the service provider's customer?

EITF CONSENSUS

The EITF reached the following consensus positions:

- If consideration given by a service provider to a third-party manufacturer or reseller that is *not* the service provider's customer can be linked contractually to the benefit that the service provider's customer receives, the service provider should account for that consideration under the guidance in Issue 01-9 as cash or as other than cash.

    This consensus is based on the view that consideration given by a service provider to a third-party manufacturer or a reseller that can be linked contractually to the service provider's customer is in substance the same as if the service provider had given the consideration directly to its customer.

- There is a presumption in Issue 01-9 that cash consideration should be accounted for as a *reduction* of revenue unless *both* of the following two conditions are met: (*a*) the vendor receives or will receive an identifiable benefit in exchange for the consideration, and (*b*) the vendor can make a reasonable estimate of the fair value of the benefit in condition (*a*). Under the guidance in Issue 01-9, other than cash consideration should be accounted for as an expense.

- A service provider that gives consideration to a third-party manufacturer or a reseller that provides a benefit to the service provider's customer should describe that consideration based on the form in which the service provider has instructed the third-party manufacturer or reseller that it be given. That is, if a service provider requires that consideration given to its customer by a third-party manufacturer or reseller be in a form other than "cash consideration," as defined in Issue 01-9, the service provider should describe that consideration as "other than cash" in its application of the guidance in Issue 01-9. A service provider also should describe such consideration as "other than cash" if the service provider does *not* control the form in which the consideration is given to its customer. It was noted that if a reseller or third-party manufacturer uses the consideration to reduce a customer's price on equipment purchased, the service provider should describe the consideration given to the third-party manufacturer or reseller as "other than cash."

Disclosure

The following information should be disclosed about such incentive programs:

- The program's features, and
- Amounts recognized in the income statement for such incentive programs and how they were classified in each period presented, if significant.

FASB RATIFICATION

The FASB ratified the EITF's consensus positions on this Issue at its September 20, 2006, meeting.

EITF Issue No. 08-1 (ASU 2009-13) (Revenue Arrangements with Multiple Deliverables) (ASC 605-25-15-3A; 25-2; 30-2, 30-5, 30-6A through 30-6B, 30-7; 50-1 through 50-2; 55-1, 55-3, 55-7, 55-12, 55-25, 55-29, 55-32, 55-34, 55-36 through 55-47, 55-52, 55-54, 55-6A through 55-57, 55-61, 55-69, 55-75 through 55-6B, 55-93; 65-1)

OVERVIEW

In Issue 08-1, the EITF is addressing practice issues related to: (1) the determination of the unit of accounting for arrangements under which a vendor performs multiple activities that generate revenue (e.g., the delivery of multiple products or the performance of multiple services under arrangements that consist of products that cannot function separately and for which evidence of the separate fair values of the deliverables is unavailable); and (2) issues related to allocation methods used in revenue recognition. (ASC 605, Revenue Recognition, ASC 605-25-05-1 and 05-02). Although paragraph 83 of Financial Accounting Standards Board (FASB) Concepts Statement No. 5, Recognition and Measurement in Financial Statements of Business Enterprises (CON-5) (not included in the ASC), provides guidance on the fundamental factors to consider regarding the timing of revenue recognition, many issues encountered by entities in practice are not addressed in the current accounting literature.

SCOPE

The guidance in Issue 08-1, which amends the guidance in ASC 605-25, Multiple-Element Arrangements, applies to all deliverables under contractually binding arrangements, regardless of their form (i.e., written, oral, or implied), in all industries, if a vendor will perform multiple revenue-generating activities unless it is stated otherwise in ASC 605-25-15-3A and 15-4, which is the scope section of ASC 605-25.

The guidance in another ASC Topic or the guidance in ASC 605-25 should be applied as follows in determining how to: (1) separate units of accounting; and (2) allocate consideration to each unit of accounting in an arrangement:

- If guidance on determining separation and allocation is provided under another ASC Topic, the arrangement should be accounted for under the guidance in that Topic. (ASC 605-25-15-3A(a))
- If guidance on determining separation but not allocation is provided in another ASC Topic, the allocation of consideration to separate units, some of which may be accounted for under the guidance in that other ASC Topic and others under the guidance in ASC 605-25, should be based on the relative selling price of the deliverables under the scope of the other ASC Topic and the selling prices of the deliverables not under the scope of that ASC Topic. To allocate consideration for deliverables accounted for under the guidance of another ASC Topic and those accounted for not under the guidance of that ASC Topic, the selling prices of the deliverables should be determined based on the guidance in ASC 605-25-30-6A and 30-6B (discussed below). Thereafter, the guidance in ASC 605-25 would apply to the identification of separate units of accounting and the allocation of consideration under an arrangement should be allocated to deliverables not subject to the guidance in the other ASC Topic. (ASC 605-25-15-3A(b))
- If no guidance for determining separation or allocation exists under another ASC Topic, the guidance in ASC 605-25 should be followed to determine the separation of units of accounting and the allocation of consideration. However, if a deliverable subject to the guidance of another ASC Topic does not meet the criteria in ASC 605-25-25-5, as amended (criterion b., which required "objective and reliable evidence of the fair value of the undelivered item(s)" is superseded by the guidance in ASC 605-25) for a deliverable to be considered a separate unit of accounting, consideration allocated to that deliverable should be combined with the amount allocated to other undelivered items under the arrangement. Revenue for those combined deliverables should be recognized as one unit of accounting. (ASC 605-25-15-3A(c))

ACCOUNTING ISSUES

The following issues have been raised regarding the model of revenue recognition when there are multiple payment streams:

- How should an entity determine whether an arrangement with multiple deliverables consists of more than one unit of accounting?

- How should consideration be allocated among separate units of accounting in an arrangement that consists of more than one unit of accounting?

EITF CONSENSUS

At its meeting on September 9 and 10, 2009, the EITF reached consensus positions affirming that the following principles and application guidance should be used to determine: (1) how to measure consideration on an arrangement; (2) whether to divide an arrangement into separate units of accounting; and (3) how consideration on an arrangement should be allocated to separate units of accounting.

The agreed upon principles are:

- Divide revenue arrangements with multiple deliverables into separate units of accounting if a deliverable meets the criteria to be considered a separate unit of accounting;
- Allocate consideration on an arrangement among separate units of accounting based on their relative selling prices, except as specified in ASC 605-25-30-4 and 30-5; and
- Consider recognition criteria separately for each unit of accounting. (ASC 605-25-25-2)

Units of Accounting

At the inception of an arrangement and as each item is delivered, a vendor should evaluate all of the deliverables in an arrangement to determine whether they are separate units of accounting. For an arrangement with multiple deliverables, a delivered item should be considered to be a separate unit of accounting if it meets both of the following criteria, which should be applied consistently to arrangements with similar characteristics and in similar circumstances:

1. A delivered item has value to the customer on its own (i.e., the item can be sold separately by a vendor or the customer can resell it on its own). An observable market for a deliverable is not required in the case of a customer's resale of a deliverable.
2. If an arrangement includes a general right of return for a delivered item, the delivery or performance of an undelivered item is considered probable and substantially under the vendor's control. (ASC 605-25-25-5)

A delivered item under an arrangement that does not meet those two criteria should be combined with other applicable undelivered items under the arrangement. Revenue on such an arrangement should be allocated and recognized for the combined deliverables as a single unit of accounting. (ASC 605-25-25-6)

Measurement and Allocation of Consideration Received on an Arrangement

The total amount of consideration on an arrangement should be fixed and determinable, except for the effect of: (1) a customer's right to a refund, if any, or other concessions; or (2) performance bonuses to which a vendor may be entitled. (ASC 605-25-30-1)

At the inception of an arrangement, consideration should be allocated to all of the deliverables under an arrangement based on their relative selling prices, except as discussed in ASC 605-25-30-4 and 30-5. To apply the relative selling price method, it is necessary to determine the selling price for a deliverable by using vendor-specific objective evidence (VSOE) of the selling price, if available. Otherwise, evidence of a third party's selling price should be used, as discussed in ASC 605-25-30-6B. If information about neither of those selling prices exists, a vendor should use its best estimate of a deliverable's selling price when applying the relative selling price method. When a vendor decides whether to use VSOE or third-party evidence of a deliverable's selling price, the vendor should not overlook information that is reasonably available without excessive cost or effort. (ASC 605-25-30-2)

If a separate unit of accounting in an arrangement must be recognized at fair value under the guidance in another ASC Topic and marked to market in each subsequent period, the amount allocated to that deliverable should be its fair value. In that case, all other consideration on an arrangement should be allocated to other units of accounting based on their relative selling prices. (ASC 605-25-30-4)

The amount that may be allocated to a delivered unit(s) of accounting should not exceed the amount that is not contingent on: (1) the delivery of additional items; or (2) meeting other specified performance conditions. Although the guidance in FASB Statement No. 48, Revenue Recognition When Right of Return Exists (FAS-48) (ASC 605-15), may affect the amount of revenue recognized, the allocated amount is not adjusted for the effect of a general right of return under FAS-48. (ASC 605-25-30-5)

Revenue recognized in a period should not exceed an amount that has been measured based on the assumption that the arrangement will not be canceled. An asset recognized for amounts in excess of revenue that has been recognized under an arrangement for cash payments or other consideration that a vendor has received from a customer since the arrangement's inception should not exceed all of the consideration to which the vendor is legally entitled, including cancellation fees if a customer cancels the order. However, a vendor's intent to enforce its contractual right if a customer cancels an order should be considered in determining the amount of asset recognition. (ASC 605-25-30-6)

VSOE of a selling price should not exceed the price charged for: (1) a deliverable sold separately; or (2) a deliverable not yet sold separately if it is probable that the established price will not change before the product is introduced. (ASC 605-25-30-6A)

Third-party evidence of a selling price consists of the price the vendor or a competitor would charge for interchangeable products or services sold separately to customers under similar circumstances. (ASC 605-25-30-6B)

A vendor's best estimate of a selling price should be consistent with the objective of determining VSOE of a deliverable's selling price. Market conditions and factors specifically related to an entity should be considered in estimating a selling price. (ASC 605-25-30-6C)

It should not be presumed that prices for individual products or services in an arrangement with multiple deliverables stated in a contract represent VSOE or third-party evidence of a selling price or a vendor's best estimate of a selling price. (ASC 605-25-30-7)

Disclosure

The objective of the guidance in this Issue related to disclosures is to provide financial statement users with qualitative and quantitative information about: (1) a vendor's revenue arrangements; (2) significant judgments made in applying the guidance in Issue 08-1; and (3) how changes in those judgments or in the application of the guidance in Issue 08-1 may significantly affect the timing or amount of revenue recognized. Consequently, to comply with this requirement, a vendor should disclose other qualitative and quantitative information, as necessary, in addition to the required disclosures. (ASC 605-25-50-1)

The following information should be disclosed for similar types of arrangements:

- The nature of a vendor's arrangements for multiple-deliverables;
- All significant deliverables under the arrangements;
- The general timing of delivery or performance of a service for deliverables under the arrangements;
- Provisions related to performance, cancellation, and refunds;
- A discussion of the significant factors, inputs, assumptions, and methods used to determine a selling price, based on VSOE, third-party evidence, or an estimated selling price, for significant deliverables;
- Whether significant deliverables under an arrangement qualify as separate units of accounting, and, if applicable, the reasons why they do not qualify;
- The general timing of revenue recognition for significant units of accounting; and
- Separate information about the effect of changes in either the selling price or the method or assumptions used to determine the selling price of a specific unit of accounting if either one of those changes significantly affects the allocation of consideration for an arrangement. (ASC 605-25-50-2)

EFFECTIVE DATE AND TRANSITION

The following is the transition and effective date guidance related to Issue 08-1 in ASC 605-25-65-1:

- The guidance in Issue 08-1 should be applied prospectively for revenue arrangements entered into or materially modified in fiscal years that begin on or after June 15, 2010. However, a vendor may elect to early adopt the guidance retroactively in accordance with the guidance in ASC 605-25-65-1(e).
- Early application is permitted:
- A vendor that elects to early adopt the guidance in a reporting period other than the first period of the entity's fiscal year should apply the guidance in Issue 08-01 retrospectively from the beginning of the entity's fiscal year.
- The following information should be disclosed at a minimum for all interim periods reported in the fiscal year in which the guidance in Issue 08-1 has been adopted: (1) revenue; (2) income before income taxes; (3) net income; (4) earnings per share; and (5) the effect of the change for the relevant captions presented.
- In the year in which the guidance in Issue 08-1 is adopted, an entity should disclose information that helps financial statement users to understand the effect of a change in accounting principle if the guidance in Issue 08-1 is adopted prospectively. The following is the minimum qualitative information that should be disclosed about similar types of arrangements:
- A description of the change in units of accounting, if any.
- A description of the change in how the vendor allocates consideration on an arrangement to various units of accounting.
- A description of changes in the pattern and timing of revenue recognition.
- Whether adoption of the guidance in Issue 08-1 is expected to materially affect the entity's financial statements after initial adoption.
- If adoption of the guidance in Issue 08-1 will materially affect the information in the financial statements, quantitative information should be provided in addition to the qualitative information disclosed in the period in which the guidance in Issue 08-1 is adopted to help users understand the effect of a change in accounting principle. That objective may be met by using the following methods, among others, depending on a vendor's facts and circumstances:
- The amount of revenue a vendor would have recognized if an arrangement or a modification of an arrangement had been accounted for based on the guidance in ASC 605-25 before it was amended by the guidance in Issue 08-1.

- The amount of revenue a vendor would have recognized in the year before the year the guidance in Issue 08-1 had been adopted if an arrangement that had been accounted for under the guidance in ASC 605-25 before it was amended by the guidance in Issue 08-1 had been subject to the guidance in Issue 08-1.
- The amount of revenue a vendor recognized in a reporting period and the amount of deferred revenue as of the end of the period for: (1) arrangements that were entered into before the guidance in Issue 08-1 was adopted and were accounted for under the guidance in ASC 605-25 before it was amended by the guidance in Issue 08-1; and (2) arrangements that were entered into or materially modified after the effective date of the guidance in Issue 08-1 and were accounted for based on that guidance.
- A vendor may elect, but is not required, to adopt the guidance in Issue 08-1 retrospectively based on the guidance in ASC 250, Accounting Changes and Error Corrections, ASC 250-10-45-5 through 45-10. A vendor that elects to do so should disclose the information required in ASC 250-10-50-1 through 50-3.

EFFECT OF ISSUE 08-1 ON EXISTING GUIDANCE

The guidance in Issue 00-21 is superseded by the guidance in Issue 08-1. Existing guidance is affected as follows:

1. *New paragraphs:* ASC 605-25-30-6A through 6C; 50-2; 55-56A through 55-6B; 55-75 through 55-93; 65-1.
2. *Amended paragraphs:* ASC 605-25-05-1 through 05-2; 15-3A, 15-4; 25-2, 25-5 through 25-6; 30-2, 30-4 through 30-5, 30-7; 50-1; 55-1 through 55-3, 55-7 through 55-9, 55-11 through 55-12, 55-15, 55-17, 55-19, 55-23 through 55-30, 55-32, 55-34 through 55-47, 55-51 through 55-56, 55-58 through 55-61, 55-68 through 55-69, 55-73.
3. *Superseded paragraphs.* ASC 605-25-30-3, 30-8 through 30-9,; 55-48 through 55-50.

FASB RATIFICATION

At its September 23, 2009 meeting, the FASB ratified the EITF's consensus positions.

EITF Issue 08-9: Milestone Method of Revenue Recognition (ASC 605-1-05-1, 25-2A, ASC 605-25-15-2A, ASC 605-28-15-1; 25-1 through 25-3, 65-1, 50-1 through 50-2, 15-2 through 15-4, 05-1 (ASU 2010-17)

OVERVIEW

In EITF Issue No. 08-1, "Revenue Arrangements with Multiple Deliverables" (Financial Accounting Standards Board (FASB)

Accounting Standards Codification™ (ASC) 605, *Revenue Recognition*), the EITF provides guidance regarding the accounting for arrangements under which a vendor performs multiple activities that generate revenue. One of the practice issues raised during the discussion of Issue 08-1 was whether the EITF should develop guidance for the application of the milestone method as a means of allocating contingent consideration when revenue on such an arrangement becomes fixed or determinable. At its September 10, 2008 meeting, the EITF agreed with a recommendation made by the staff of the FASB that the milestone method should be discussed as a separate Issue.

SCOPE

The EITF reached a consensus that the guidance related to the milestone method of revenue recognition should be applied only to research or development arrangements under which a vendor satisfies its performance obligation to provide deliverables or units of accounting over a period of time and a portion or all of the consideration to the vendor is contingent on the achievement of uncertain future events and circumstances (i.e., a milestone), such as the successful completion of phases in a drug study or a specific result from research or development endeavors.

EITF CONSENSUS

The EITF affirmed as consensus positions the following consensus-for-exposure positions reached at previous meetings:

- The guidance in Issue 08-9 may be applied to arrangements under which: (1) a vendor's obligations to a customer are satisfied over a period of time; and (2) all or a portion of the consideration under the arrangement is contingent on the achievement of one or more milestones, unless this guidance conflicts with other guidance in ASC 605.
- A milestone is an event: (1) for which there is substantive uncertainty at the date an arrangement is entered into that the event will be achieved; (2) that can only be achieved based in whole or in part on the vendor's performance or a specific outcome resulting from the vendor's performance; and (3) if achieved, would result in additional payments being due to the vendor. Further, a milestone does *not* include an event that is contingent only on the passage of time or on the vendor's performance.
- For the purpose of Issue 08-9, a milestone is an event: (1) for which there is *substantive* uncertainty about its occurrence at the date a customer enters into an arrangement with a vendor; (2) that will be achieved in whole or in part as a result of the vendor's performance or a specific outcome that occurs as a result of

that performance; and (3) that triggers additional payments to the vendor as a result of its achievement.
- A vendor applying the guidance in Issue 08-9 may not elect to follow another accounting method under which the vendor recognizes consideration on a milestone in its entirety in the period in which the milestone has been achieved. However, a vendor that meets the criteria in Issue 08-9 is not prohibited from electing to apply a different accounting policy under which revenue related to a portion of the consideration for achieving a milestone would be deferred.
- Although determining at the inception of an arrangement whether a milestone is *substantive* is based on judgment, that determination should be based on the following principles related to the consideration earned when a substantive milestone has been achieved : The consideration is (1) proportionate either to the vendor's performance that results in a specific outcome or to an increase in the value of the delivered item(s); (2) related only to *past* performance; and (3) reasonable comparative to all of the deliverables and payment terms under the arrangement, including other consideration on potential milestones.
- A milestone is *not* considered to be substantive if any portion of the consideration for its achievement does *not* apply exclusively to *past* performance but is related to remaining deliverables in the unit of accounting under the arrangement. If so, not all of the consideration paid for reaching the milestone would be recognized as revenue. Further, since recognition of all consideration paid when a milestone is achieved must be related to a *substantive* milestone, a milestone cannot be separated into substantive and nonsubstantive portions. Consideration on the achievement of a milestone that is subject to a refund or an adjustment based on the vendor's future performance also is *not* considered to be related to past performance and, therefore, the milestone would not be considered to be substantive. However, a vendor would *not* be precluded from applying the milestone method to substantive milestones under an arrangement if one of the milestones under that arrangement is *not* substantive because the consideration paid for that milestone is *not* related exclusively to past performance.
- The revenue attribution model for consideration on an arrangement contingent on the achievement of a milestone in Issue 08-9 is *not* the only acceptable, revenue recognition method regardless of whether the milestone is considered to be substantive. However, a vendor's revenue recognition policy for arrangements under which the consideration is contingent on the vendor's achievement of a milestone should be applied *consistently* to similar deliverables or units of accounting.

DISCLOSURE

The EITF also reached a consensus that entities that elect to apply the guidance in Issue 08-9 should disclose the following information in the notes to their financial statements for each arrangement that includes a material milestone payment:

- A description of the overall arrangement;
- A description of the individual milestones and related contingent consideration;
- Whether the milestones are considered to be substantive;
- The factors considered in determining whether a milestone is substantive; and
- The amount of consideration recognized on milestones during the period.

EFFECTIVE DATE AND TRANSITION

The EITF reached a consensus that the guidance in Issue 08-9 should be applied *prospectively* to milestones achieved in fiscal years and interim periods in those years that begin after June 15, 2010, but earlier application is permitted.

A vendor that elects to early adopt the guidance in a period other than the first period in its fiscal year is required to apply that guidance *retrospectively* from the beginning of the entity's fiscal year. In that case, the effect of the change on (a) revenue, (b) income before income taxes, (c) net income, and (d) earnings per share should be disclosed for all previously reported interim periods in the fiscal year of adoption.

To enable financial statement users to understand the effect of a change in financial principle, if the guidance in Issue 08-9 is adopted *prospectively*, a vendor should disclose the information in ASC 250, *Accounting Changes and Error Corrections* (ASC 250-10-50-1 through 50-3), in the year of adoption.

The EITF reached a consensus that a vendor may elect, but is not required to adopt the guidance in Issue 08-9 *retrospectively* by applying the guidance in ASC 250-10-45-5 through 45-10. If so, the disclosures in ASC 250-10-50-1 through 50-3 also should be made.

FASB RATIFICATION

The FASB ratified the EITF's consensus positions on this Issue at its March 31, 2010, meeting.

Topic D-96 (Accounting for Management Fees Based on a Formula) (ASC 605-20-S25-2; S99-1)

Certain fee-based arrangements, which are common in the investment advisory and real estate management businesses, include an incentive fee related to performance in addition to a base fee—for example, based on cost savings generated by a real estate management company. Under such arrangements, the amount of the fee generally is not confirmed until the end of a contractual time period. This announcement states the views of the SEC staff on the accounting for revenue from incentive fees at interim dates before the final amount has been confirmed. It does not apply to revenue arrangements discussed in SOP 81-1 (Accounting for Performance of Construction-Type and Certain Production-Type Contracts). The SEC staff has been asked to address this Issue because sometimes performance that exceeds the required target in the early part of the measurement period may be reversed if the performance target is not achieved in a later measurement period. The SEC staff provided the following example:

> An investment advisor managing a mutual fund is paid a monthly base fee. However, the advisor is also paid an incentive fee equal to 20% of the Fund's returns that exceed the S&P 500's return for the year. The contract can be terminated by each party with reasonable notice at the end of each quarter. At termination, the Advisor's incentive fee will be calculated based on the Fund's returns to date compared to those of the S&P 500 during that period. If the Fund's return exceeds the S&P 500's returns by $200,000 in the first quarter, $100,000 in the second quarter, and $50,000 in the fourth quarter, but is $75,000 less than the S&P 500's returns in the third quarter, the Fund's total return for the year would exceed the S&P 500's return by $275,000. The Advisor's total incentive fee for the year would be $55,000 in the fourth quarter.

A survey conducted by the SEC staff indicated that a majority of investment advisors and property managers recognize no income until the end of the contract period. However, others recognize the amount of revenue that would be receivable at a point in time as if the contract were terminated at that date. Under this second method, the advisor would recognize $40,000 as an incentive fee at the end of the first quarter ($200,000 × .2) and $20,000 at the end of the second quarter ($100,000 × .2). At the end of the third quarter, the advisor would reduce previously recognized revenue by $15,000 ($75,000 × .2) and would recognize $10,000 ($50,000 × .2) at the end of the fourth quarter.

Although the SEC Staff prefers the first method, because it believes it is more consistent with the guidance in Question 8 of SAB-101 (Revenue Recognition in Financial Statements), the staff would not object if companies use the second method, which provides better information about a manager's actual performance during the quarter.

The SEC Staff objects, however, to the use of another method under which revenue recognized under the second method discussed above would be reduced by an amount that management believes will be lost as a result of future performance. The Staff believes that this method is inconsistent with the guidance in Question 8 of SAB-101 and the requirement that the fee be fixed or determinable.

SEC OBSERVER COMMENTS

The following are the views of the SEC Staff on some variations of the methods discussed above:

- Unless an arrangement has been terminated, revenue should not be recognized based on amounts that would be receivable at termination as a result of provisions for penalties or liquidated damages in addition to the amount payable under the incentive fee formula.

- Revenue recorded at an interim date should not exceed the amount a customer would be required to pay on termination if a customer can terminate an arrangement at will and thus avoid paying all or some of the fee due to the manager.

- Revenue should be recognized in interim periods under the second method for a *fixed* incentive fee (e.g., a fixed amount for exceeding the S&P 500) only if the target has been exceeded and should be limited to a proportionate amount of the fixed payment due.

- The SEC Staff's views apply even if a manager or adviser has no termination rights during the contract term.

The SEC Staff encourages registrants to submit to the Staff for preclearance any questions regarding revenue accounting for such arrangements.

DISCLOSURE

The accounting policy for such arrangements should be disclosed in accordance with ASC 235 (APB-22, Disclosure of Accounting Policies) and SAB 101. Disclosure is required about previously recognized revenue that may be lost due to future performance contingencies, as well as disclosure of the nature of the contracts causing the contingencies, and the amount of revenue that would be affected, if material.

ASC 924 Entertainment—Casinos

EITF Issue 09-F Accruals for Casino Jackpot Liabilities (ASC 924-605-25-2, 55-1 through 55-2, 65-1) (ASU 2010-16)

OVERVIEW

Entities that earn their revenue from gaming activities classify slot machine jackpots as follows:

- "Nonprogressive" jackpots are *fixed* payouts that have been programmed into a slot machine based on certain combinations that are identified on the machine's payout table. Because in most jurisdictions a gaming entity is permitted to remove a machine paying such jackpots from the floor at any time, even if no fixed jackpots have been paid on that machine, a gaming entity is not required to make any payouts on such machines as long as a machine's payouts are within a preapproved percentage, which has been programmed into the machine.

- "Progressive" jackpots are payouts based on a percentage that is programmed into a slot machine and conforms to a machine's payout table, which increases as more customers play the machine. The amount that would be paid out the first time a slot machine is played or immediately after a jackpot has been paid out is referred to as the "base" amount of a progressive jackpot. Any amount paid above the base amount and until a customer wins a jackpot is referred to as the "incremental" amount of a progressive jackpot. The base amount of a jackpot is funded by the gaming entity while the incremental amount is funded by customers who play the machine. Therefore, in most jurisdictions, a gaming entity that removes a machine paying progressive jackpots from the floor is usually required to: (1) transfer the incremental amount to a different machine on the floor; or (2) award that amount in some sort of prize drawing. In some jurisdictions, a gaming entity that removes a progressive slot machine from the floor also has to retain and award the base amount of a progressive jackpot. In those circumstances, the gaming entity usually accrues a liability for the base amount before the jackpot has been won. However, some gaming entities also are accruing the incremental amount as a liability based a specific amount (e.g., five cents) per coin played by customers.

This Issue, which is related to how gaming entities should account for base jackpot liabilities if payment of a jackpot can be avoided, was brought before the EITF because some gaming entities are accruing a liability for progressive and nonprogressive base jackpots before a jackpot has been won. Those who support this approach base their view on the guidance in ASC 924-605-25-2, which states that "[b]ase jackpots shall be charged to revenue ratably over the period of play expected to precede payout." However, those who believe that a liability should not be accrued for a base jackpot's amount if the gaming entity is not required to make an award, as in a nonprogressive jackpot, cite the guidance in ASC 924-605-25-1, which states that "[r]evenue recognized and reported by a casino is generally defined as the win from gaming activities, that is, the difference between gaming wins and losses, not the total amount wagered."

SCOPE

The consensus positions in this Issue apply to base jackpots and incremental amounts in progressive jackpots paid by entities that earn revenue from gaming activities.

EITF CONSENSUS

At its March 18, 2010 meeting, the EITF reconfirmed its consensus-for-exposure reached at the November 19, 2009 meeting that a liability should *not* be accrued until an entity incurs an obligation to pay a base jackpot. The EITF reached a consensus that an obligation to pay incremental amounts in progressive jackpots should be accounted for in the same manner as the obligation to pay a base jackpot because the same principle applies.

EFFECTIVE DATE AND TRANSITION

The EITF reached a consensus that the guidance in Issue 09-F is effective for fiscal years, and interim periods within those fiscal years, that begin on or after December 15, 2010. The guidance should be applied through a cumulative-effect adjustment to retained earnings as of the beginning of the fiscal year in which it was adopted. Earlier application is permitted. However, an entity that chooses early adoption in a period other than the first reporting period in its fiscal year must apply the guidance in Issue 09-F *retrospectively* to the beginning of its fiscal year.

FASB RATIFICATION

The FASB ratified the EITF's consensus positions at its March 31, 2010 meeting.

ASC 932 Extractive Activities—Oil and Gas EITF

EITF Issue 90-22 (Accounting for Gas-Balancing Arrangements) (ASC 932-10-S25-1; S50-2; S99-5; 55-1, 55-2)

OVERVIEW

Partners in a gas well may arrange to share in the gas well's production. One partner, Company A, may decide not to sell its share of the gas production because it does not have a customer or market conditions are unfavorable. In that situation, the other partner,

Company B, may agree to take Company A's gas production and sell it. At a future date, Company A will have the right to take more than its share of the gas production to make up for the extra amount taken ("the overtake") by Company B. Alternatively, Company B pays for the overtake, either in cash or with gas from another well. Such transactions are known as *gas-balancing arrangements*.

The two predominant methods used to account for those arrangements are the *entitlements method* and the *sales method*. The entitlements method assumes that each unit of gas is jointly owned by the well's partners. In the above scenario, Company B would recognize revenue from sales only to the extent of its proportionate share of the gas sold, recording a payable to Company A. Conversely, Company A would recognize a receivable and a sale for the overtake. Under the sales method, Company B would recognize sales revenue for the entire amount, recognizing no payable to Company A, which would record no receivable or revenue currently. Under the sales method, the partners track the imbalance by making memorandum entries. The partners may not use the same accounting method, because each partner makes that choice independently.

To illustrate the difference between the two methods, consider a situation in which Company A has a 40% interest and Company B has a 60% interest in a gas well. Production of the entire well during November is 6,000 MCF (thousand cubic feet) and the price is $1.50 per MCF. The allocation of gas production and revenue according to the terms of the partnership agreement would be as follows:

	Percentage Interest	Gas Production	Revenue at $1.50/MCF
Company A	40%	2,400MCF	$3,600
Company B	60%	3,600MCF	5,400
Total	100%	6,000MCF	$9,000

Company A gives up its share of the November production to Company B. The accounting under the entitlements method and the sales method would be as follows:

	Entitlements Method			Sales Method		
	Co. A	Co. B	Total	Co. A	Co. B	Total
Cash received	$0	$9,000	$9,000	$0	$9,000	$9,000
Receivable	3,600	0	$3,600	0	0	0
Payable	0	($3,600)	($3,600)	0	0	0
Revenue	$3,600	$5,400	$9,000	$0	$9,000	$9,000

ACCOUNTING ISSUE

How should participants in a gas-balancing arrangement account for the transactions?

EITF CONSENSUS

Although the EITF noted that practice for accounting for gas-balancing arrangements is not uniform, it decided to refer the Issue to the AICPA's Committee on Regulated Industries because the Issue is industry-specific and established practice exists.

EFFECT OF FAS-133

The terms of the arrangements discussed in this Issue should be analyzed to determine whether an arrangement meets the definition of a derivative under the guidance in ASC 815 (FAS-133). Even though the derivative may always have a zero value, the disclosures in paragraphs 44-45 (ASC 815-30-50-1), as amended by FAS-161, of the Statement would be required. Further, the option feature may not qualify for the exception for normal purchases and normal sales in paragraph 10(b) of FAS-133 (ASC 815-10-15-13).

SEC OBSERVER COMMENT

The SEC Observer made the following comments:

- The SEC staff has not taken a position on which of the two methods is preferable.
- Under the entitlements method, the recorded receivable or liability should be valued at the lower of (*a*) the price at the time of production, (*b*) current market value, or (*c*) the contract price if there is a contract.
- Receivables should be recognized net of selling expenses.
- Registrants are required to disclose their accounting method and the amount of an imbalance in units and value, if significant.
- Management's Discussion and Analysis should include information about the effect of gas imbalances on operations, liquidity, and capital resources.

In addition, the SEC Observer noted that the same method should be used to account for gas imbalances consistently. An overtaker (Company B in this Issue) using the sales method that has insufficient reserves to offset the imbalance should recognize a liability for the shortfall at the current market prices; if a different price is specified in the contract, it should be used instead.

ASC 944-605 Financial Services—Insurance

FSP FAS-97-1 (Situations in Which Paragraphs 17(b) and 20 of FASB Statement No. 97, *Accounting and Reporting by Insurance Enterprises for Certain Long-Duration Contracts and for Realized Gains and Losses from the Sale of Investments,* Permit or Require Accrual of an Unearned Revenue Liability) (ASC 944-605-25-9 through 25-11)

OVERVIEW

Guidance on the timing of recognition of unearned revenue can be found in a number of paragraphs of FAS-97 (Accounting and Reporting by Insurance Enterprises for Certain Long-Duration Contracts and for Realized Gains and Losses from the Sale of Investments). Under the guidance in paragraph 19 of FAS-97 (FASB Accounting Standards Codification (ASC) 944-605-25-5), insurers are required to recognize revenue from universal life contracts in the period in which the contracts are assessed unless there is evidence that the amount assessed is for services that will be performed over more than one period. Paragraph 20 (ASC 944-605-25-6, 25-7) states further that amounts assessed for services that will be performed in the future should be recognized as unearned revenue and recognized in income in the periods in which those services will be performed.

In paragraph 54 of the Statement's Basis of Conclusions section, the FASB argued against commentators' suggestions that revenue be recognized ratably over the life of a contract to show a "level pattern of service." The FASB's view is that revenue should be recognized according to a contract's terms and conditions, unless the substance of the agreement differs from the contract's terms. In paragraph 54, the FASB again stated that amounts related to services that will be provided in the future should be deferred and recognized over the period during which the insurer will provide the service.

An example of an assessed amount that is unearned is discussed in paragraph 61 of FAS-97. Such an amount would be assessed only in certain contract periods or in such a manner that the insurer would have current profits and incur future losses from a specific function of the contract. The FASB concludes that under those circumstances, specific assessments might result in the recognition of unearned revenue, but that it is necessary to consider the facts and circumstances of the particular situation to reach that conclusion. The issue of when insurers should recognize unearned revenue has been raised again because of diversity in the interpretation of paragraph 26 of SOP 03-1 (Accounting and Reporting by Insurance Enterprises for Certain Nontraditional Long-Duration Contracts and for Separate Accounts) (ASC 944-605-25-8), which states:

For a contract determined to meet the definition of an insurance contract ... if the amounts assessed against the contract holder each period for the insurance benefit feature are assessed in a manner that is expected to result in profits in earlier years and losses in subsequent years from the insurance benefit function, a liability should be established in addition to the account balance to recognize the portion of such assessments that compensates the insurance enterprise for benefits to be provided in future periods.

Paragraph 26 (ASC 944-605-25-8) also can be interpreted as limiting the circumstances in which insurers are required to recognize unearned revenue to those in which current profits will be followed by future losses.

FASB STAFF POSITION

The FASB staff believes that under the guidance of FAS-97, insurers should accrue an unearned revenue liability for amounts assessed to contract holders that represent compensation for services to be provided in future periods. The staff further states that the situation discussed in paragraph 26 (ASC 944-25-8) does *not* amend FAS-97 and does *not* restrict the recognition of unearned revenue for insurance benefit features of universal life contracts to situations in which profits are expected to be followed by losses. The staff reiterates the requirement in paragraphs 17(b) and 20 of FAS-97 (ASC 944-605-30-16; 944-605-35-2; 944-605-25-6, 25-7) that an unearned revenue liability be accrued for "any amounts that have been assessed to compensate the insurer for services to be performed over future periods."

The FASB staff's comments in paragraphs 54, 60, and 61 of FAS-97 express the staff's views regarding the impropriety of recognizing unearned revenue to show a level gross profit over the life of a contract or to produce a level gross profit from a death benefit over the life of a contract. The FASB staff also stresses the need to consider the facts and circumstances of each situation. Further, the staff notes that if the amount of an insurance benefit liability is determined according to paragraph 26 of SOP 03-1 (ASC 944-605-25-8), unearned revenue liabilities accrued in accordance with paragraphs 17(b) and 20 of FAS-97 (ASC 944-605-30-16; 944-605-35-2; 944-605-25-6, 25-7) should be considered. For that purpose, an increase in the unearned revenue liability during a period should be excluded from amounts assessed against a contract holder's account balance for the period, and a decrease in the unearned revenue liability during a period should be included in that period's assessment.

EFFECTIVE DATE AND TRANSITION

The guidance in this FSP is effective for financial statements beginning after June 18, 2004, the date this FSP was posted on the FASB's web site. If previously reported information changes as a result of applying this FSP, a cumulative effect of the accounting change should be reported as of the beginning of the first fiscal period following June 18, 2004.

ASC 946–605 Financial Services—Investment Companies

FSP Issue 85-24-1 (Application of EITF Issue 85-24, "Distribution Fees by Distributors of Mutual Funds That Do Not Have a Front-End Sales Charge," When Cash for the Right to Future Distribution Fees for Shares Previously Sold Is Received from Third Parties) (ASC 946-605-05-5 through 05-11; 25-4 through 7; 50-1)

OVERVIEW

Mutual fund shares referred to as "B shares" are usually sold by a fund's distributor without a sales commission (front-end load) on purchase. Rather, the distributor usually receives an asset-based fee on such shares, known as a 12b-1 fee, which is charged to investors over a period of six to eight years (12b-1 period). In addition, investors that redeem B-shares before the expiration of the 12b-1 plan period usually are charged an asset-based fee, known as a contingent deferred sales charge (CDSC), which also may be referred to as a back-end load or a sales charge. The amount of that fee declines over time until the 12b-1 plan period has expired. Fees related to shares previously sold by a distributor are referred to as "Rights" in this FSP.

The 12b-1 fees are calculated periodically as a percentage of net asset value. The CDSC is calculated as a percentage of the current net assets or the original cost of shares being redeemed, whichever is less. Both fees are intended to compensate a fund's distributor for costs incurred in the form of sales commissions to broker-dealers, and for other costs related to the distribution of mutual fund shares, such as advertising, marketing, and financing costs. A distributor is usually a subsidiary of a fund's sponsor, but is a separate entity so that the distribution function is separate from the fund's investment advisory function and its record keeping and transaction services functions. However, if a fund replaces its distributor, the original distributor continues to receive 12b-1 fees and CDSC for shares it has sold.

Distributors sometimes sell their Rights to third parties and receive lump sum cash payments. The agreements may include provisions to protect buyers on default as well as indemnities in case a fund's independent board decides to terminate its 12b-1 plan. Under Issue 85-24 (Distribution Fees by Distributors of Mutual

Funds That Do Not Have a Front-End Sales Charge), distributors are *not* permitted to recognize revenues on fees until cash is received. However, Issue 85-24 does *not* provide guidance regarding the accounting for the receipt of cash from parties *other* than investors or the mutual fund. Consequently, some distributors have accounted for sales of Rights to third parties as sales of unrecognized financial assets. Others have recognized revenue on the receipt of cash from a third party for sales of Rights. Still others have accounted for such transactions as loans.

FASB STAFF POSITION

Question: How should a distributor account for cash received from a third party for a sale of Rights?

Answer: The FASB staff believes that a distributor should recognize revenue on a sale of Rights when cash is received from a third party if the distributor has *no* recourse to those Rights or any continuing involvement with them. That is, neither the distributor nor any member of the consolidated group to which the distributor belongs: (1) retains an excessive interest in the risks and rewards related to the Rights sold; (2) guarantees or provides assurances related to a purchaser's rate of return on the Rights sold; or (3) can restrict the ability of a consolidated group or a mutual fund's independent board to remove, replace, or subcontract any of the entities or individuals that provide services to the fund. Deferred costs, if any, related to shares sold by a distributor to which the Rights pertain should be written off to earnings in the period in which revenue on the sale of those Rights is recognized.

This FSP is *not* intended to provide guidance to mutual funds, investors in mutual funds, or third party investors that obtain the Rights regarding how to account for those Rights. Mutual Funds should follow the accounting guidance provided in SOP 95-3 (Accounting for Certain Distribution Costs of Investment Companies). No analogies should be made to this FSP when accounting for other transactions.

> **OBSERVATION:** The FASB issued ASC 250 (FAS-154, Accounting Changes and Error Corrections), which supersedes FAS-3 and APB-20. The Statement is effective for accounting changes and corrections of errors made in accounting periods beginning after December 15, 2005.

Basis for Conclusions

The FASB staff's conclusions are based on the following concepts:

- *Revenue recognition* If a distributor has *no* recourse or continuing involvement with Rights that have been sold, revenue recognition is appropriate when the distributor receives cash for the sale of those Rights because there is no uncertainty about the amount the distributor will receive on the sale. A sale of Rights is *not* analogous to sales of software as some have suggested because a distributor's right to receive 12b-1 fees or CDSC does *not* require the distributor to perform additional services to receive those Rights, which result from past services.

- *Continuing involvement* Services to investors performed by other members of a mutual fund's consolidated group are distinct and separable from a distributor's services and are *not* affected by the distributor's sale of Rights. However, a distributor maintains a continuing involvement if an arrangement includes the following provisions: (*a*) the distributor or any member of its consolidated group is required to perform future services in connection with the sale of the Rights, including actual or expected performance of a separate service with separate pricing that is a direct result of the transaction between the distributor and the buyer of the Rights, and (*b*) the distributor or any member of its consolidated group is permitted to participate in future risks or rewards in the Rights that are not proportionate to the portion of the Rights sold, for example, retention of risks or rewards of 60% when only 50% of the Rights have been sold.
- *Recourse* A distributor or its consolidated group would have recourse to a buyer that would preclude revenue recognition if an arrangement includes the following provisions:
  —The consolidated group must make a payment to the buyer if its independent board decides to change the nature of the Rights, for example, provisions related to the computation of fees and the timing of payments
  —The consolidated group must make a payment to the buyer if its independent board decides to change service providers such as the distributor, advisor, or transfer agent
  —The arrangement includes provisions that protect the buyer from risks related to fluctuations in a mutual fund's net asset value or to legal or regulatory risks that might result in termination of the 12b-1 plan
  —The arrangement restricts changes in a fund's investment objectives in accordance with the fund's prospectus or similar restrictions

Separate-Company Financial Statements

Revenue recognition in a distributor's separate-company financial statements is not affected if any member of the consolidated group that includes the distributor has a continuing involvement with a buyer as a result of the retention of a proportionate or pro rata interest. The provisions of this FSP apply to the determination of revenue recognition in a distributor's separate-company financial statements. For example, a distributor should recognize revenue in its separate-company financial statements when receiving cash from an arrangement in which a distributor transfers all or a pro rata interest in Rights to a member of its consolidated group that is *not* the distributor's subsidiary.

EITF Issue 85-24 (Distribution Fees by Distributors of Mutual Funds That Do Not Have a Front-End Sales Charge) (ASC 946-605-25-8)

OVERVIEW

Under Rule 12b-1 of the Investment Company Act of 1940, an investment company that sponsors a mutual fund can adopt a plan, known as a 12b-1 plan, which permits it to finance the cost of distributing its mutual fund's shares with the fund's assets, rather than charging a fee (front-end load) to investors when they purchase shares. Funds that have adopted such plans are known as no-load funds.

The fund usually enters into an agreement with a distributor, under which the distributor is paid a fee based on either an annual percentage of the fund's average net assets or an annual percentage of the fund's average net assets limited to actual costs incurred. Although distribution agreements usually continue from year to year, under the rules of a 12b-1 plan the agreement must be approved annually by the investment company's directors and may be terminated at any time with no penalty to the fund.

Because investors do not pay a front-end load, they are required to pay a contingent-deferred sales load (back-end load), which is a sales charge based on a percentage of the redemption proceeds or original cost, whichever is less, if the shares are held for less than a specified period. The percentage decreases (usually by 1% a year) until it is eliminated. The fee is deducted from the shareholder's proceeds on redemption and is paid to the distributor, even if the distribution agreement has been terminated.

When this Issue was discussed in 1985, distributors of mutual fund shares were recognizing distribution fees in income when they were received. Incremental direct costs related to distribution activities, such as sales commissions, were deferred and amortized over six years (the period shareholders would have to hold shares without incurring a fee on redemption). All other distribution costs were expensed as incurred. Because this method resulted in the deferral of a large amount of costs to future accounting periods (so they could be matched with future revenues), some in the industry suggested recognizing the discounted amount of the distribution fee in the period in which shares are sold.

ACCOUNTING ISSUE

Should fees that are expected to be received over a specified future period be recognized at a discounted amount when shares are sold, together with all related distribution costs, or on receipt with deferral of incremental direct costs?

EITF CONSENSUS

The EITF reached a consensus that distributors should continue to recognize fees on receipt, defer incremental direct costs, and expense indirect costs when they are incurred.

DISCUSSION

The Task Force supported the more conservative approach of recognizing revenue when the fee is realized and earned, which is consistent with the guidance in CON-5 (Recognition and Measurement in Financial Statements of Business Enterprises) (not included in the ASC).

ASC 954-605 Health Care Entities—Revenue Recognition

EITF Issue 09-L Health Care Entities: Measuring Charity Care for Disclosure (ASC 954-605-50-3; 65-1) (ASU 2010-23)

OVERVIEW

Health care entities provide charity care, which is any service provided without the expectation of payment to patients that meet certain guidelines established by the health care entity. Under the guidance in ASC 954-605-25-10 and 25-11, no revenue should be recognized for charity care in the financial statements and judgment should be used to distinguish between bad debts and charity care, which should be based on established criteria. Under the guidance in ASC 954-605-50-3, an entity is required to disclose in the notes to the financial statements management's policy for charity care and the level of such care, which is determined based on a provider's rates, costs, units of service, or other statistical measurements. Some have asked whether the measurement of charity care disclosed in the financial statements should be standardized for improved comparability among health care entities.

ACCOUNTING ISSUE

How should a health care entities measure charity care?

SCOPE

The guidance in Issue 09-L applies to entities that provide health care services.

EITF CONSENSUS

After reviewing comment letters related to the proposed guidance in Issue 09-L at its July 29, 2010 meeting, the EITF affirmed as a consensus its consensus-for-exposure that information about charity care disclosed in the financial statements of health care entities should be based on the entity's measurement of the direct and indirect costs of providing such services, which should be determined in a manner that is consistent with that used to report charity care to the IRS for regulatory purposes. The EITF asked the FASB staff to clarify in the final ASU that such information may be determined by various means, such as by using: (1) information from a cost accounting system; (2) reasonable techniques to estimate the cost of providing charity care; or (3) other reasonable methods. In addition, the EITF noted that subsidies related to charity care, such as those from an uncompensated care fund or from gifts and grants, should *not* be offset against the costs of charity care. Rather, the cost and subsidies for charity care should be provided gross to increase transparency.

In addition to disclosing the costs of providing charity care, health care entities also should separately disclose the following information: (1) amounts received from various sources to compensate the entity for providing charity care; and (2) the method used to determine the costs of providing charity care.

EFFECTIVE DATE AND TRANSITION

The EITF reached a consensus that the guidance in Issue 09-L should be effective for fiscal years that begin after December 15, 2010, with early adoption permitted. The guidance should be applied *retrospectively*. In addition, the disclosures in ASC 250-10-50-1 through 50-3 should be made in the period in which the guidance in Issue 09-L is adopted.

FASB RATIFICATION

The FASB ratified the EITF's consensus-for-exposure positions at its August 18, 2010 meeting.

ASC 980 Regulated Operations

EITF Issue 91-6 (Revenue Recognition of Long-Term Power Sales Contracts) (ASC 440-10-60-20; 980-605-25-5 through 25-8, 25-11 through 25-15)

OVERVIEW

Nonutility generators (NUGs) are facilities that supply power to other entities (often rate-regulated utilities), usually under long-term sales contracts (20-30 years), or to builder/users for their own needs.

A long-term contract includes pricing and other specifics that create practical issues in accounting, particularly in recognizing revenue. Pricing arrangements may include the following:

- Specified prices per unit (e.g., per kilowatt hour or kwh) that increase, decrease, or remain fixed over the term of the contract
- Formula-based prices per kwh (e.g., a price determined annually based on the current cost of power from other sources or on published rates)

A combination of those pricing arrangements is used in the following billing methods:

- Billings based on specified prices but adjusted at the end of the contract according to a formula approach (e.g., adjusted to the cost of power from other sources), which results in either an increase or a decrease in the sales price
- Billings based on specified prices and adjusted at the end of the contract according to a formula approach, but the adjustment is made only if it results in a decrease in the sales price

Because NUGs are not regulated entities, the provisions of ASC 980 (FAS-71) do not apply.

The EITF's discussion was based on the following three examples of long-term contracts:

Type 1 Contract

The customer (utility) is obligated to take or pay for all power made available by the NUG for the term of the contract (20 years). The price per kwh is specified and increases in years 11 to 20.

Type 2 Contract

The customer is obligated to take or pay for all power made available by the NUG for the term of the contract. Billings are based on specified prices per kwh that increase during the term. However, total payments over the term of the contract will be based on a formula used by the customer annually to compute its *avoided cost*, which is the cost that would have been incurred if power had been purchased from another source or had been self-generated (the source is specified in the contract). Over the term of the contract, the customer uses what is referred to as a "tracker account" to record its avoided cost and to offset actual billings against that amount. At the end of the contract, the tracker account is adjusted, if necessary, and may result in an additional payment to the NUG, if avoided cost is greater than actual billings, or in a refund to the customer, if billings exceed avoided cost.

Type 3 Contract

The contract is the same as a Type 2 contract, except the formula is used to limit the NUG's total revenue to the lesser of total avoided cost or total actual billings (i.e., an adjustment is made only if the customer's cost decreases).

ACCOUNTING ISSUES

1. Should revenue on a power sales contract that provides for scheduled price changes (Type 1 contract) be recognized based on the price schedule or ratably over the term of the contract?
2. Should the accounting required for contracts described in Issue 1 change if the power sales contract provides that total revenues for the term of the contract be determined based on a separate, formula-based pricing arrangement (Type 2 contract)?
3. Should the accounting required for contracts described in Issue 1 change if the power sales contract provides that total revenues for the term of the contract be limited by a separate formula-based pricing arrangement (Type 3 contract)?

EITF CONSENSUS

1. NUGs should account for Type 1 contracts as follows:
   a. Recognize revenue at the lesser of
      i. the amount billable under the contract
      ii. an amount determined by the kwhs available to the customer during the period multiplied by the estimated average revenue per kwh over the term of the contract.
   b. Determine the lesser amount annually based on the cumulative amount that would have been recognized under either method had it been applied consistently from the beginning of the contract.
2. Recognize revenue for Type 2 and 3 contracts in each period based on a contract's separate formula-based pricing arrange-

ment if *total* revenues billed under the contract are determined or limited by that arrangement, but not if the separate formula-based pricing arrangement is used only to establish liquidating damages.
3. Recognize a receivable only if (*a*) the contract requires the customer to pay the NUG for the difference between the amount billed and the amount calculated according to the formula-based pricing arrangement at the end of the contract, and (*b*) it is probable that the receivable will be recovered.

The EITF also agreed on the following:

- Contracts that are considered leases are outside the scope of this Issue and should be accounted for in accordance with the provisions of ASC 840 (FAS-13, Accounting for Leases).
- NUGs are required to recognize revenue on contracts entered into after May 21, 1992, based on the consensus positions reached in this Issue.

EFFECT OF ASC 815 (FAS-133)

Long-term power sales contracts that meet the definition of a derivative in ASC 815 (FAS-133) should be marked to fair value through earnings, unless a contract has been designated as a hedged instrument. Contracts that do not meet the definition of a derivative should be analyzed to determine whether they contain embedded derivatives that should be accounted for separately under the Statement. Otherwise, the consensus position on this Issue continues to apply.

DISCUSSION

1. The consensus on Issue 1 was based on two views. Under one view, revenue on a long-term power sales contract should be recognized as an amount that is billable under the contract. Under the second view, periodic revenue should be recognized based on estimated average revenue per kwh over the life of the contract.

    Proponents of the first view believed that these contracts are executory contracts under which customers have no obligation to pay unless the NUG makes power available to them.

    Under the second view, long-term power sales contracts are similar to operating leases and kwhs made available to customers annually are similar to property used by a lessee.

    The EITF's consensus on Issue 1 represents a compromise between those two views; it results in recognition of the most conservative amount of revenue, regardless of the method used. It attempts to associate revenue with the periods in which it was earned while allocating revenue more evenly over the term of the contract. That approach also addresses concerns about possible abuses or manipulation under the first approach; for example, structuring a contract to front-end revenue by charging higher rates in the early years, thereby recognizing revenue before it has been earned and distorting revenue recognized over the term of the contract.

2. Those who supported recognizing revenue on Type 2 and Type 3 contracts based on the avoided-cost formula believed that the tracker account used to monitor the cumulative difference between amounts billed and amounts calculated with the avoided-cost formula shifts the customer's substantial risk of changes in the utility's avoided cost to the NUG over the term of the contract. They further believed that the contract is in substance an arrangement under which the customer provides financing to the NUG in the early years and the NUG sells power to the customer at the avoided cost over the term of the contract. Although proponents of this view agreed that a power sales contract is not a lease, they argued that if a lease with escalating rents had an alternative calculation based on rents adjusted to, for example, the consumer price index, under FAS-13 the lessor would be permitted to recognize revenue based on the CPI only in the early years of the lease.

An EITF working group met with industry representatives to discuss the characteristics of contracts similar to those referred to above as Type 2 and Type 3 contracts, except that they also may have some of the characteristics of Type 1 contracts. All those contracts use a tracking account. They were described as Category A and Category B contracts in the working group's discussions. Some contracts under Category A use a tracking account only to measure liquidated damages if the NUG does not perform under the contract. Revenue is not limited to avoided cost, and the NUG can retain all amounts billed if it performs under the contract. Another type of contract in this category has specified rates in the early years of the contract and fluctuating rates based on avoided cost in the later years. A balance of billings over avoided cost in the tracker account in the early years of the contract is forgiven over the years when rates are based on avoided cost. If the NUG performs over the contract term, the tracker account is amortized to zero. Industry representatives believed that the economic substance of Category A contracts is the same as for Type 1 contracts in Issue 1. That is, the NUG keeps all amounts billed, but here the customer has the additional security that the NUG will perform. They argued that because the NUG's total revenue is not determined by or limited to revenues based on the avoided-cost formula and the tracker account is used only to determine liquidation damages, if necessary, revenue on this category should not be based on the avoided-cost formula. Rather, revenue on those contracts should be recognized the same as for contracts in Issue 1.

In Category B contracts, which measure total revenue on a contract based on the avoided-cost formula, the tracker account is used to accumulate the difference between billings and actual annual avoided cost. The balance of the tracker account must be settled at the end of such contracts with the customer paying no more than total actual avoided cost. The economic substance of such contracts is that the NUG takes on the risk that there will be unexpected changes in avoided-cost projections over the term of the contract or that the projections of avoided cost on which the contract's rates were based were inaccurate. Although they have adequate cash flows, NUGs that recognize revenue based on avoided cost in this category of contracts incur losses in the early years of a contract, because avoided cost is too low to cover the NUG's financing and construction costs. In contrast, actual amounts billed on the contract are based on avoided costs over the long term and always exceed annual avoided cost in the early years and reverse in later years.

The Task Force's consensus requires revenue on Type 2 and 3 contracts to be recognized based on avoided cost, because that amount represents revenue earned in each period. Because the NUG's *total* revenue on Type 3 contracts is determined by or limited to total revenue based on the avoided-cost formula over the *term* of the contract, the EITF believed that revenue recognition based on the avoided-cost formula also best represents revenue earned over the term of the contract.

EITF Issue 92-7 (Accounting by Rate-Regulated Utilities for the Effects of Certain Alternative Revenue Programs) (ASC 980-605-25-1 through 25-4)

OVERVIEW

Utility customers generally are billed for their usage based on predetermined rates, which are regulated and approved by the utility's regulatory commission. The rates are set based on costs of service and are designed to recover the utility's allowable costs, which include a return on shareholders' investments.

Certain utility regulators have authorized the use of alternative revenue programs that reduce the volatility in the utility's earnings and have the following objectives:

- To protect the utilities, their investors, and their customers from unexpected fluctuations in sales and earnings caused by changes in weather patterns or by reduced demand because of conservation efforts
- To reward utilities for meeting certain goals

The two major alternative revenue programs addressed in this Issue allow utilities to adjust future billings to consider certain past events:

Type A

Type A programs are intended to reduce the effects on a utility's revenue of differences between actual sales volume and estimated sales used to set base rates. Such differences may be caused by abnormal weather patterns, conservation efforts, and other external factors. For example, 50% more kilowatt hours of electricity may be used during a very hot summer, or user conservation efforts may result in decreased usage. Variations between forecasted revenue and actual usage may be adjusted by billing surcharges that are added to or deducted from base rates in future billings. For example, in a period following a hot summer, customers' billings would be increased by a surcharge. Surcharges are most commonly used to recover fuel costs that differ from estimated costs included in base rates. Under Type A programs, the utility recognizes revenue in the future when customers are provided with service at the base rate plus or minus a surcharge.

Type B

Type B programs involve incentive awards that are related to a utility's performance. Such programs commonly set goals that may be achieved by measurable improvement in a utility's effectiveness or efficiency of operations. Examples of such goals are controlling growth in demand, reducing costs, and reducing the number of customer complaints. Achievement of those goals may be measured subjectively and objectively and usually involves an audit by the regulatory authority. If the goals are achieved, Type B programs provide utilities with additional revenue. If they are not achieved, there may be penalties for the utility and refunds for its customers.

ACCOUNTING ISSUES

- What is the appropriate accounting for alternative revenue programs (Type A and Type B) of regulated utilities?
- Should the accounting for Type A and Type B programs be the same?

EITF CONSENSUS

The EITF reached a consensus that if the specific events that would allow a utility to bill additional revenues under Type A or Type B programs have occurred, a utility should recognize those additional revenues if all of the following conditions are met:

- The utility's regulatory commission has approved the additional revenue program, which allows the utility to adjust future rates automatically. Such adjustments are considered automatic even before the regulator has verified the adjustment to future rates.
- The utility can determine the amount of additional revenue for the period objectively, and recovery is probable.
- Additional revenues will be collected no later than 24 months from the end of the annual period in which they were recognized.

A regulated utility operating under an approved alternative revenue program that does not conform to the above conditions at the date of the consensus (July 23, 1992) may continue to recognize such revenue if:

- The utility has filed a rate application to amend the plan to meet the above conditions or intends to do so as soon as possible.
- It is probable that the regulator will change the terms of the alternative revenue program to meet the conditions in the consensus.

DISCUSSION

When the EITF was discussing this Issue, industry practice was to recognize revenue and the related asset when the condition resulting in future billings occurred, the amount was known, and it was probable that it would be recovered.

The EITF was asked to consider when the economic benefit of alternative rate programs should be recognized in a utility's financial statements. The following alternatives were considered:

- Recognize when the amount of additional revenue is known and realization is probable
- Capitalize incurred costs in accordance with FAS-71, and recognize revenue when a future service is provided
- Recognize an asset for the additional revenue when the future service is provided at the higher rate

Proponents of the first alternative, which was supported by the Task Force, noted that paragraph 7 of FAS-71 (Accounting for the Effects of Certain Types of Regulation) (ASC 980-10-15-5) states that regulated enterprises should follow GAAP, except if GAAP conflict with the Statement's provisions. They argued that because the Statement does not specifically address this issue, GAAP for all entities should be followed in recognizing amounts to be received under those programs. CON-5 states that revenue may be recognized when it is realized and has been earned. Assets are defined in CON-6 (Elements of Financial Statements) as "probable future economic benefits obtained or controlled by a particular entity as a result of past transactions." Thus, this view supports recording the revenue and related asset in the year the earnings process and performance were completed, even though the surcharge billing occurs in the future.

EITF Issue 96-17 (Revenue Recognition under Long-Term Power Sales Contracts That Contain Both Fixed and Variable Pricing Terms) (ASC 980-350-35-3 through 35-5; 605-35-17 through 35-18)

OVERVIEW

This Issue addresses contracts that consist of fixed and variable pricing arrangements that were not considered in Issue 91-6. (See the consensus.) For example, billings under such contracts are based on a stated price schedule for a certain period of time, such as the first ten years of a 30-year contract, with billings at a variable rate for the remainder of the contract. Unlike the contracts discussed in Issue 91-6, total revenues billed under the contracts addressed in this Issue are not limited by a tracker account that the NUG maintains to record the difference between a utility's avoided costs and amounts that can be billed under the contract, with the difference, if any, repaid at the end of the contract. *Avoided energy cost* is the cost that a utility would have incurred had it purchased the power from another source or had the power been self-generated.

Power sales contracts negotiated on a competitive basis by NUGs prior to developing and constructing a power generation facility usually are long-term contracts (20 to 30 years) that are intended to minimize the NUG's financial risk. Although the contracts usually provide for payments based on both an energy and a capacity component, this Issue only discusses revenue recognition for the energy component. The energy component is arrived at through a complex formula that represents the utility's avoided energy cost.

NUGs generally price long-term powers sales contracts to recover expected fixed and variable costs and to earn a reasonable rate of return. Rates must be sufficiently firm to assure financing for construction of the facility. Utilities are motivated by cost so they usually seek rates that agree with their estimated long-range avoided costs. Most of the contracts addressed in this Issue were negotiated in California in the early to mid-1980s. The initial terms of the contracts were at fixed or scheduled prices based on avoided cost to guarantee a revenue stream. It was expected at that time that avoided costs would increase significantly over the term of the contracts (30 years). In reality, avoided costs have decreased.

ACCOUNTING ISSUE

How should NUGs recognize revenue on long-term power sales contracts that consist of separate, specified terms for (a) a fixed or scheduled price per kwh for one period of the contract and (b) a variable price per kwh (which is based on market prices, actual avoided costs, or formula-based pricing arrangements), for a different portion of the contract, if total revenues billable under the contract over its entire term are not determined or limited by a tracker account or other form of adjustment?

EITF CONSENSUS

The EITF reached a consensus that the contracts addressed in this Issue should be bifurcated and accounted for as follows:

- Revenue earned during the contract period in which prices are fixed or scheduled should be recognized in accordance with the consensus on Issue 1 of Issue 91-6; that is, at the lesser of (a) the amount billable under the contract or (b) an amount based on the kwh made available during the period multiplied by the estimated average revenue per kwh over the term of the contract. The lesser amount should be determined annually based on the cumulative amounts that would have been recognized had each method been applied consistently from the beginning of the term of the contract.
- During the contract period in which variable prices are used, revenue should be recognized as billed, in accordance with the contract's provisions for that period.

The Task Force noted that revenue for the entire contract should be recognized based on the consensus on Issue 1 of Issue 91-6 if the contractual terms during the separate fixed and variable portions of the contract do not approximate the expected market rates at the inception of the contract.

The Task Force also observed that such contracts should be reviewed periodically to determine whether they are profitable or whether immediate loss recognition is required. Premiums related to a contractual rate in excess of current market rates should be amortized over the remaining portions of the respective periods of long-term power sales contracts acquired in purchase business combinations. For example, a premium resulting from an above-market rate related to the fixed or scheduled portion of a contract would be amortized over the remaining portion of that period of the acquired contract.

EFFECT OF ASC 815 (FAS-133)

Long-term power sales contracts that meet the definition of a derivative in ASC 815 (FAS-133) and are not designated as hedging instruments should be marked to fair value through earnings. However, some contracts that meet the definition of a derivative may meet the scope exception in paragraph 10(b) of the Statement (ASC 815-10-15-13) for normal purchases and normal sales. Contracts that do not meet the definition of a derivative should be analyzed to determine whether they contain embedded derivatives that should be accounted for separately under the the guidance in ASC 815 (FAS-133). The consensus continues to apply to all contracts that do not meet the above conditions.

DISCUSSION

The approach adopted by the Task Force accounts for each phase of the contract separately. Proponents believed that revenues earned during each contract period are not affected by revenues in another contract period. They argued further that total revenues under the contracts discussed in this Issue are not the sum of revenues earned in each period of the contract. They noted that the consensus in Issue 1 of Issue 91-6 specifically states that it applies only to contracts with scheduled price changes that are determined by the contract and do not require estimating a utility's future avoided cost. They argued that if the EITF had wanted NUGs to recognize level revenues over the contract term, such estimates would have been required for formula-based contracts discussed in Issue 91-6, which usually are based on avoided cost.

Market rates are used in the variable-rate period of the contracts discussed in this Issue. Proponents analogized to the revenue recognition practices of oil or natural gas producers who enter into long-term contracts and recognize revenue as billed at current market prices on delivery. Similar accounting is followed by the mineral extractive industries and for agricultural commodities.

Illustration of Revenue Recognition on Long-Term Power Sales Contracts with Fixed and Variable Pricing Terms

Highpower Resources Co. has entered into a ten-year contract to provide energy. There is no tracker account. During the first five years of the contract, the rates are fixed at amounts stated in the contract; for the following five years, rates are at the utility's actual avoided energy cost. It is expected that actual avoided costs in the second half of the contract will be higher than those at the time the contract is entered into. Actual avoided costs decrease over the contract term. Annual demand is 1 million kwh per year.

The following energy rates are used in years 1-5 (the fixed portion of the contract):

Year 1	$.06
Year 2	.07

36.72 Revenue Recognition

Year 3	.08
Year 4	.09
Year 5	.10

Actual avoided energy costs in years 6-10 are as follows:

Year 6	$.041
Year 7	.038
Year 8	.035
Year 9	.031
Year 10	.027

Revenue recognition during the fixed portion of the contract

1. Calculate the estimated average rate per kwh:

$$\frac{\text{Total revenue per kwh based on contract}}{\text{Number of years}} = \frac{\$.4}{5} = \$.08$$

2. Calculate the cumulative amounts using estimated revenue that is based on the average rate and that is the billable amount. Recognize the amount that results in a lower cumulative amount had each method been applied consistently from the beginning of the contract term. (For example, in year 4, recognizing $90,000 at the billable rate results in the lower cumulative amount of $300,000; had $90,000 been recognized at the average rate, the resulting cumulative amount would be $320,000.)

		Cumulative Amounts		
	Estimated Avg. Rate	Avg. Rate	Billable Rate	Revenue Recognition
Year 1	$.08	$ 80,000	$ 60,000	$ 60,000
Year 2	.08	160,000	130,000	70,000
Year 3	.08	240,000	210,000	80,000
Year 4	.08	320,000	300,000	90,000
Year 5	.08	400,000	400,000	100,000

Revenue recognition during the variable portion of the contract

Recognize revenue based on actual avoided energy costs.

	Actual Avoided Energy Cost	Revenue Recognition
Year 6	$.041	$41,000
Year 7	.038	38,000
Year 8	.035	35,000
Year 9	.031	31,000
Year 10	.027	27,000

RELATED CHAPTER IN 2011
GAAP GUIDE, VOLUME I

Chapter 41, "Revenue Recognition"

RELATED CHAPTER IN 2011
INTERNATIONAL ACCOUNTING/FINANCIAL REPORTING STANDARDS GUIDE

Chapter 30, "Revenue"

CHAPTER 37
SEGMENT REPORTING

CONTENTS

Overview		37.01
Authoritative Guidance		
ASC 205 Presentation of Financial Statements		37.03
FIG-FAS 131	Guidance on Applying Statement 131	37.03
ASC 280 Segment Reporting		37.12
FTB 79-4	Segment Reporting of Puerto Rican Operations	37.12
EITF Issue 04-10	Determining Whether to Aggregate Operating Segments That Do Not Meet the Quantitative Thresholds	37.12
Topic D-70	Questions Related to the Implementation of FASB Statement No. 131	37.14
ASC 350 Intangibles—Goodwill and Other		37.16
Topic D-101	Clarification of Reporting Unit Guidance in Paragraph 30 of FASB Statement No. 142	37.16
ASC 954-280 Health Care Entities—Segment Reporting		37.16
FTB 79-5	Meaning of the Term "Customer" as It Applies to Health Care Facilities under FASB Statement No. 131	37.16
Related Chapter in 2011 GAAP Guide, Volume I		37.17
Related Chapter in 2011 International Accounting/Financial Reporting Standards Guide		37.17

OVERVIEW

The term *segment reporting* refers to the presentation of information about certain parts of an enterprise, in contrast to information about the entire enterprise. The need for segment information became increasingly apparent in the 1960s and 1970s as enterprises diversified their activities into different industries and product lines, as well as into different geographic areas. Financial analysts and other groups of financial statement users insisted on the importance of disaggregated information—in order for them to assess risk and perform other types of analyses. The following pronouncement, which is the source of GAAP for segment reporting, is discussed in the 2011 *GAAP Guide, Volume I*, Chapter 42, "Segment Reporting."

ASC 280   Disclosures about Segments of an Enterprise and Related Information (FAS-131)

AUTHORITATIVE GUIDANCE

ASC 205 Presentation of Financial Statements

FIG FAS 131 (Guidance on Applying Statement 131) (ASC 205-20-60-3; 280-10-50-26, 50-33, 50-36, 50-39; 50-55-2 through 55-11; 55-15 through 55-24, 55-27, 55-29 through 55-31, 55-33 through 55-36, 55-39 through 55-45)

BACKGROUND

The FASB has received a number of questions regarding the implementation of ASC 280 (FAS-131, Disclosures about Segments of an Enterprise and Related Information). To provide additional guidance to the financial reporting community in applying ASC (FAS-131), the FASB has published 23 of these questions and its responses to the questions in the FASB's newsletter, *Viewpoints*.

ASC 280 (FAS-131)—like its predecessor, FAS-14 (Financial Reporting for Segments of a Business Enterprise)—requires disclosures relating to operating segments, major products and services, major customers, and geographic areas of operation. However, unlike FAS-14, ASC 280 (FAS-131) adopts a "management approach" for determining the segment information to be disclosed. That is, each company adopts its own approach for dividing its operations into segments. Management typically makes operating decisions and assesses performance on a segment basis. Segments disclosed under the provisions of ASC (280) (FAS-131) should correspond with the segments used by company management in assessing the performance of the overall entity. Another difference between FAS-14 and FAS-131 is that segment disclosures are now required on an annual *and* an interim basis.

STANDARDS

Scope

Question 1: If, in accordance with SEC Regulation S-X, Rule 3-09, "Separate Financial Statements of Subsidiaries Not Consolidated and 50% or Less Owned Persons," the separate financial statements of a joint venture or an investee accounted for by the equity method are provided in the annual report of the investor, is segment information required to be provided for the significant equity method investee or joint venture?

Answer: No. Segment financial information is not required in the separate financial statements of an investee or joint venture if these entities are not public companies. However, segment information

37.04 *Segment Reporting*

must be disclosed in these separate financial statements if the investee (or joint venture) is a public company. This same requirement applies to financial statements filed under SEC Regulation S-X, Rule 3-10, "Financial Statements of Guarantors and Affiliates Whose Securities Collateralize an Issue Registered or Being Registered."

Definition of Operating Segments

Question 2: Can an investee account for by the equity method, by itself, qualify as an operating segment?

Answer: Yes. Management of the investor can be expected to review the operating performance of the investee for purposes of determining whether to maintain the investor-investee relationship. This result holds even though the management of the investor may not control the investee and may not have operating authority over how the investee allocates resources internally.

Question 3: Can a corporate division that earns revenues (e.g., a treasury operation that earns interest income) and incurs expenses qualify as an operating segment?

Answer: Yes. A corporate division can be considered an operating segment if it (1) earns revenues, (2) prepares discrete financial information, and (3) has its performance reviewed regularly by the entity's chief operating officer. This result holds even if the revenues earned by the corporate division are incidental to the entity's overall revenues.

Question 4: Can a component of an entity that earns revenues and incurs expenses but has no assets allocated to it for internal reporting purposes be considered an operating segment? For example, assume Division A of an entity conducts business with a separate class of customers using assets shared with Division B. Division B allocates expenses associated with those shared assets to Division A, but the assets are presented in the internal financial reports of Division B.

Answer: Yes. However, the fact that no assets are disclosed for a reportable segment should be disclosed as well as the reasons for this fact. In addition, ASC 280 (FAS-131) requires disclosure of (1) the basis of accounting for transactions between reportable segments, (2) how assets used jointly by more than one segment are allocated, and (3) situations in which expenses might be allocated to a segment (e.g., depreciation) without allocating the related assets.

Question 5: Can a discontinued operation be considered an operating segment?

Answer: FAS-131 is silent on this issue, but the FASB believes that a discontinued operation cannot be an operating segment. The required disclosures for a discontinued operation are fully specified in APB-30 (Reporting the Results of Operations—Reporting the Effects of Disposal of a Segment of a Business, and Extraordinary, Unusual, and Infrequently Occurring Events and Transactions). However, entities should recognize that the disposal of a segment categorized as reportable under FAS-131 may not meet the APB-30 definition of a *segment*. APB-30 defines a *segment* differently than does FAS-131.

A reportable segment (per FAS-131) that is being disposed of may meet the APB-30 criteria for treatment as a discontinued operation. The information disclosed for such a segment in comparative financial reports before the measurement date (for determining the gain or loss on disposition) does not have to be restated. If, however, the balance sheet and income statement information for the segment being disposed of have been restated in comparative financial statements, the required disclosures in ASC 280 (FAS-131) about the segment being disposed of do not have to be provided in the comparative financial statements.

Question 6: A public company has multiple subsidiaries. One of these subsidiary companies is a public company because it has public debt outstanding. This public subsidiary reports three reportable segments (Dept. Y, Dept. Z, and Division 7) in its separate filings. In preparing the segment information for the public company, should Dept. Y, Dept. Z, and Division 7 automatically be considered reportable segments because they are reportable segments of the parent company's public subsidiary?

Answer: No. Reportable segments of a public subsidiary company are not automatically reportable segments to the parent company itself.

Determining Reportable Segments

The following information pertains to Questions 7 through 10. Assume that a company has identified eight operating segments before applying the FAS-131 aggregation criteria. Segments C and E are reportable segments since they meet the 10% threshold criteria (based on revenues) contained in FAS-131. Revenues from sales to external customers (no intersegment sales exist) are as follows:

	Revenue
Segment A	$ 5
Segment B	4
Segment C	35
Segment D	7
Segment E	32
Segment F	4
Segment G	9
Segment H	4
Total Revenues	$100

Under the guidance in ASC 280 (FAS-131) an entity is permitted to aggregate operating segments if it has similar economic characteristics and if they are similar on the following five dimensions: (1) nature of products and services, (2) nature of production process, (3) types of customers, (4) distribution methods, and (5) nature of its regulatory environment (if applicable).

Question 7: May Segment G (below the 10% thresholds) be aggregated with Segment E (above the 10% thresholds) if only a majority of the aggregation criteria are met?

Answer: No. The sequence for aggregating segments is as follows:

1. Identify operating segments.
2. Aggregate segments (at management's discretion) if *all* five of the aggregation criteria are met.
3. Determine which segments are reportable (based on quantitative thresholds for revenues, profit or loss, assets) after the aggregation in step 2 has taken place.
4. After determining reportable segments, any segment that does not meet the thresholds that mandate separate disclosure may be combined with any other segment that does not require separate disclosure if a *majority* of the aggregation criteria are met.

In the present example, assuming a majority of the aggregation criteria are met, Segment G could be combined with segments A, B, D, F, and H. Segment G cannot be combined with Segment C or Segment E unless all of the aggregation criteria are met.

Question 8: For purposes of this question only, assume that Segments B and C meet all of the five criteria for aggregation and have similar economic characteristics; however, this year certain economic performance measures differ. For example, gross margins differ slightly and sales of the segments, which typically move in tandem, trended slightly differently this year. Those differences were due to inventory problems caused by the company's suppliers, and it is expected that the margins and sales trends of Segments B and C will again be similar next year. May Segment B be aggregated with Segment C for the current-year segment disclosures?

Answer: Yes. FAS-131 states that future prospects are more important in evaluating the similarity of operating segments than are current-period results. In a related fashion, two segments that normally do not exhibit similar economic characteristics and performance measures should not necessarily be combined just because economic performance measures may be similar in the current year.

Applying Quantitative Thresholds

Question 9: How is the quantitative threshold for segment profit or loss applied when the measure of segment profit or loss used by the chief operating decision maker is a different measure for each segment (e.g., the chief operating decision maker uses net income for purposes of evaluating the performance of Segments A, B, and H, but uses operating income for purposes of evaluating the performance of Segments C, D, E, F, and G)?

Answer: The chief operating decision maker uses different measures of income for assessing segment performance. In such cases, a single income measure—calculated for all segments on a consistent basis for internal purposes—should be selected for applying the 10% of profit or loss criterion in FAS-131 to determine whether a segment is reportable. This is the case regardless of whether the income measure selected is used in assessing the operating performance of each segment. Therefore, in this case, either operating income or net income would be chosen as the single income measure for applying the 10% profit or loss criterion in FAS-131.

Once reportable segments are determined using the above approach, the income number disclosed in the financial statement notes would continue to be the income figure used by the entity's chief operating decision maker for assessing the performance of each segment. Therefore, net income would be disclosed for Segments A, B, and H; operating income would be disclosed for Segments C, D, E, F, and G. See Topic D-70 (Questions Related to the Implementation of FASB Statement No. 131) in Chapter 35 for an additional discussion of this issue.

Question 10: Because total external revenues of the segments identified as reportable constitute only 67% of consolidated external revenues (35% + 32%), an additional segment must be identified for reporting. In meeting the 75% revenue test, must Segment G (the next largest segment by percentage of external revenues) be identified as a reportable segment?

Answer: No. The next largest segment by percentage of external revenues does not necessarily have to be identified as a reportable segment. Any one or more additional segments can be identified as reportable segments by management as long as the segments presented account for at least 75% of consolidated external revenue.

Question 11: Assume that operating income (loss) of six segments is as follows:

	Operating Income (Loss)
Segment A	$ 2
Segment B	(10)
Segment C	4
Segment D	18
Segment E	18
Segment F	(2)
Consolidated income	$30

Assume, based on the above information (and after considering revenues and assets for each segment), that Segments A and C do not meet the quantitative threshold criteria as reportable segments. Management decides to apply the aggregation criteria in FAS-131, and Segments B and E meet *all* of the aggregation criteria. As a result, these two segments are combined into one segment. After the combination of Segments B and E into one segment, Segment C now meets the 10% of profit or loss threshold (10% of the aggregate profit for those segments reporting a profit or 10% of the absolute value of the aggregate loss for those segments reporting a loss, whichever is greater).

Would Segment C, which previously did not meet the quantitative thresholds but subsequent to the first level of aggregation (in accordance with all five FAS-131 criteria being met) meets one of the quantitative thresholds, be considered a reportable segment?

Answer: Yes. The sequence of determining reportable segments is outlined in the answer to Question 7.

Question 12: If segments have been aggregated in accordance with either paragraph 17 or paragraph 19 of FAS-131 (ASC 280-10-50-11, 50-13), is an entity required to disclose the fact that segments have been aggregated?

Answer: Yes, the factors that an entity uses in identifying reportable segments should be disclosed. This includes disclosing whether individual segments have been aggregated.

Measuring Segment Profit and Loss and Assets

Question 13: If, in measuring the performance of its equity investees, an entity internally uses the proportionate consolidation method, can that method be used in reporting the results of segments externally?

Answer: Yes, proportionate consolidation should be used in reporting the results of segments externally if that is the method used in reporting results to the entity's chief operating decision maker. If proportionate consolidation is used for segment reporting, the following additional items must be disclosed: (1) the accounting policy used for segment reporting, (2) the amount of the investee's revenues and assets eliminated in reconciling to consolidated totals, and (3) the investor's equity and investment in the investee. However, just because proportionate consolidation is appropriate in some situations in reporting segment data, proportionate consolidation still cannot be used in preparing general-purpose financial statements.

Question 14: If an entity uses multiple performance measures in evaluating segment performance and allocating resources, including both pre-tax and after-tax measures, how should it determine the most appropriate measure to use externally?

Answer: An entity's chief operating decision maker may use multiple measures in assessing a segment's profit or loss or asset level. In such cases, the performance measure used for external reporting purposes should be that measure which is most consistent with how the corresponding amounts were determined in the entity's consolidated financial statements.

Question 15: Assume that the chief operating decision maker evaluates the performance of the entity's segments based on earnings before interest, taxes, depreciation, and amortization (EBITDA). Included in the management reports reviewed by the chief operating decision maker are summaries of depreciation and amortization expense related to each of the segments. Must depreciation and amortization expense be disclosed for each of the reportable segments?

Answer: Yes. FAS-131 requires disclosure of certain amounts if such amounts are included in the measure of operating profit or loss used by the chief operating decision maker. Although depreciation and amortization are not subtracted in computed EBITDA, such amounts typically would be reviewed along with EBITDA by the chief operating decision maker. Therefore, it is reasonable to assume that the amounts of depreciation and amortization are considered in evaluating the performance of a segment. As such, they are to be disclosed. Refer to Topic D-70 (Questions Related to the Implementation of FAS-131) in Chapter 35 for an additional discussion of this topic.

Question 16: For internal reporting purposes, assume that included in the measure of performance of Segment A is interest expense charged from Segment B on advances from Segment B to Segment A. Should the amounts of intercompany interest be included in the interest expense and interest income amounts disclosed for Segment A and Segment B, respectively?

Answer: Yes. Since intercompany interest is included in determining the measure of operating profit or loss reviewed by the chief operating decision maker, such intercompany interest amounts are to be included in reporting interest income and interest expense. Given that a management approach is used in ASC 280 (FAS-131), amounts reported for a segment should be same the amounts that are used by management. No adjustments may be made to those amounts. However, an entity is required to disclose how it accounts for transactions between segments.

Segment Information in Interim Financial Statements

Question 17: FAS-131, paragraph 33 (ASC 280-10-50-32), requires disclosures of certain segment information in interim financial reports. That paragraph does not discuss identification of reportable segments in interim periods. Are entities required to apply the quantitative tests to their operating segments for each interim period when determining their reportable segments for the interim period?

Answer: No. Segment information in interim statements is generally viewed as an extension of the segment information presented in the annual financial statements. This answer assumes that no change has occurred during the interim period that would suggest that the entity's reportable segments have changed. If a change has occurred that suggests that application of the quantitative thresholds would reveal a reportable segment that had previously not been reportable and that segment is expected to continue to be reportable in the future, the quantitative threshold tests are to be applied at the interim reporting date.

Question 18: Are enterprise-wide disclosures required for interim reporting?

Answer: No. Enterprise-wide disclosures are only required in annual financial statements. Segment disclosures at an interim date are limited to the following items:

- Revenues from external customers
- Intersegment revenues
- A measure of segment profit or loss
- Total assets if there has been a material change from the amount disclosed in the most recent annual report
- Any change from the last annual report in determining segments or segment profit or loss
- A reconciliation of the profit figure reported for reportable segments to the entity's consolidated income before income taxes, extraordinary items, discontinued operations, and the cumulative effect of changes in accounting principles

Question 19: Are the interim disclosures required only for the current quarter or are they required for the year-to-date amounts as well?

Answer: Interim disclosures are required both for the current quarter and for the year-to-date period.

Enterprise-Wide Disclosures: Geographic Information

Question 20: Should the required supplemental geographic disclosures be based on the "management approach" (i.e., using the amounts and measurement principles that management uses to evaluate the performance of an entity's operations in foreign countries)?

Answer: No. The amounts and measurement principles used in preparing the general-purpose financial statements should be the basis for the supplemental geographic disclosures. The entity must disclose if it is not practicable for it to present geographic information.

Question 21: Paragraph 38 (ASC 280-10-50-41) requires disclosure of revenues from external customers attributed to all foreign countries in total from which the enterprise derives revenues and separate disclosure of revenues from external customers attributed to an individual foreign country, if material. How should those revenues be determined?

Answer: Any method of allocating revenues from external customers to geographic segments is acceptable as long as the method is reasonable, consistently applied, and disclosed. For example, revenues may be allocated based on the location of the unit selling goods, the location of the customer, or the destination to which the goods are shipped.

Illustration of Disclosure of Revenues Attributed to Foreign Countries

Global Enterprises, a U.S.-based firm, has operations throughout Western Europe, as follows:

Foreign Country	Revenues Derived from Operating Units Located In	Revenues Derived from Sales to Customers Located In	Revenues from Shipments Made To
United Kingdom	$200,000	$300,000	$100,000
Germany	$150,000	$400,000	$250,000
France	$150,000	$250,000	$200,000
Spain	$300,000	$ 40,000	$200,000
Portugal	$200,000	$ 10,000	$250,000

Global has worldwide revenues of $2 million, and it considers revenues of 10% or more of total revenues in a particular country as material. If foreign revenues are determined based on the unit selling the goods, Spain, Portugal, and the United Kingdom would be the geographic segments separately disclosed. If foreign revenues are determined based on the location of the customer buying the goods, Germany, the United Kingdom, and France would be the geographic segments separately disclosed. If foreign revenues are determined based on the location to which the goods are shipped, all countries would be separately disclosed except the United Kingdom.

Question 22: Paragraph 38 (ASC 280-10-50-41) requires disclosure of long-lived assets in geographic areas. What is meant by the term *long-lived assets*? Would intangible assets be included in that disclosure?

Answer: The guidance in ASC 280 (FAS-131) does not specifically define what is meant by *long-lived assets*. The FASB interprets *long-lived assets* to be assets that cannot be readily moved (i.e., fixed assets). As such, intangible assets would not be included in the disclosure of long-lived assets by geographic area.

Question 23: Subsequent to the introduction of the European Monetary Union (EMU), which is intended to result in a single economic community, will geographic information by individual country still be required for the European countries that participate in the EMU?

Answer: Yes. The required geographic information in ASC 280 (FAS-131) is required to be disclosed separately by individual country, if material.

ASC 280 Segment Reporting

FTB 79-4 (Segment Reporting of Puerto Rican Operations) (ASC 280-10-55-25)

BACKGROUND

Under the guidance in ASC 280 (FAS-131, Disclosures about Segments of an Enterprise and Related Information), an entity is required to disclose certain information about its foreign operations and export sales. Further, according to the guidance, foreign operations include an entity's revenue-producing operations that are located outside its home country (e.g., the United States for U.S. enterprises).

STANDARDS

Question: Are Puerto Rican operations and operations in other areas under U.S. sovereignty or jurisdiction (e.g., Virgin Islands, American Samoa) considered foreign for purposes of applying the guidance in ASC 280 (FAS-131)?

Answer: Puerto Rican operations, as well as those in other non-self-governing U.S. territories, should be considered domestic operations. Factors such as proximity, economic affinity, and similarities of business environments indicate this classification for these operations.

EITF Issue 04-10 (Determining Whether to Aggregate Operating Segments That Do Not Meet the Quantitative Thresholds) (ASC 280-10-50-13)

OVERVIEW

Under the guidance in ASC 280-10-50-10 (paragraph 16 of FAS-131, Disclosures about Segments of an Enterprise and Related Information), entities are required to report separate information about each operating segment that has been identified in accordance with the guidance in ASC 280-10-50-1-9 (paragraphs 10–15 of FAS-131) or that has been created by combining two or more segments in accordance with the guidance in ASC 280-10-50-11 (paragraph 17 of FAS-131) and exceeds the quantitative thresholds in ASC 280-10-50-12 (paragraph 18 of FAS-131). Under the guidance in ASC 280-10-50-11 (paragraph 17 of FAS-131), the combination of two or more operating segments into a single operating segment is permitted if the combination is consistent with the objective and basic principles of ASC 280 (FAS-131), the segments have similar economic characteristics, and they are similar in each of the following areas:

- The nature of the products and services
- The nature of the production processes
- The type or class of customer for their products or services
- The methods used to distribute their products or provide their services
- The nature of the regulatory environment, for example, banking, insurance, or public utilities, if applicable.

Segments about which information must be reported separately are referred to as reportable segments.

ACCOUNTING ISSUE

How should an entity evaluate the criteria in ASC 280-10-50-11 (paragraph 17 of FAS-131) that are used to combine two or more operating segments into a single segment when determining whether operating segments that do not meet the quantitative thresholds may be aggregated in accordance with ASC 280-10-50-13 (paragraph 19 of FAS-131)?

EITF CONSENSUS

The EITF reached a consensus that operating segments that do *not* meet the quantitative thresholds can be combined only if: (*a*) the combination is consistent with the objective and basic principles of ASC 280 (FAS-131), (*b*) the segments have similar economic characteristics, and (*c*) the segments share a majority of the criteria for combination listed in ASC 280-10-50-11 (paragraph 17(a) through (e) of FAS-131).

The FASB ratified the consensus positions in this Issue at its October 13, 2004, meeting.

SUBSEQUENT DEVELOPMENTS

At the EITF's November 2004 meeting, the FASB staff reported that a proposed FASB Statement of Position (FSP) that would provide guidance for determining whether two or more operating segments have similar economic characteristics is being developed. The proposed FSP is expected to be posted on the FASB's web site for comments and is likely to be effective for fiscal periods ending after March 15, 2005. Because the guidance in the proposed FSP and the consensus in this Issue, which would have been effective for fiscal years ending after October 13, 2004, are interrelated, the EITF reached a consensus that the Issue's effective date should be delayed to coincide with the proposed FSP's effective date; however, early application of the consensus in this Issue is permitted. The FASB ratified this consensus at its November 30, 2004, meeting.

At the EITF's June 2005 meeting, the FASB staff recommended that Issue 04-10 become effective for fiscal years ending after September 15, 2005, because the FASB decided not to issue proposed FSP FAS-131-a (Determining Whether Operating Segments Have Similar Economic Characteristics under Paragraph 17 of FAS-131 (ASC 280-10-50-11)). The EITF agreed with the recommendation of the FASB staff and reached a consensus to implement that recommendation.

Topic D-70 (Questions Related to the Implementation of FASB Statement No. 131) (ASC 280-10-55-12 through 55-14)

The FASB staff reported on the following technical questions about ASC 280 (FAS-131) received from constituents and the staff's responses:

Question 1: Is an entity required to disclose the amount of depreciation and amortization for each reportable segment if the entity's chief operating decision maker uses the amount of earnings before interest, taxes, depreciation, and amortization (EBITDA) to evaluate the performance of the entity's segments but management reports reviewed by the operating decision maker also include summaries of depreciation and amortization expense related to each reportable segment?

Answer: Yes. Based on the guidance in ASC 280-10-50-22 and 50-25 (paragraphs 27 and 28 of FAS-131), depreciation and amortization expense should be disclosed for each reportable segment under the above circumstances. ASC 280-10-50-22 (paragraph 27 of FAS-131) requires enterprises to report a measure of profit or loss for each reportable segment, and ASC 280-10-50-22 and 50-25 (paragraphs 27 and 28 of FAS-131) require that other amounts be disclosed about each reportable segment if they are *included* in the measure of profit or loss reviewed by the chief operating decision maker. The staff's view that amortization and depreciation expense should be reported for each reportable segment in the circumstances stated above, even though those amounts are *not* included in the measure of segment profit and loss used by the chief operating decision maker to evaluate each business segment's performance, is based on the guidance in ASC 280-10-50-22 and 50-25 (paragraph 29 of FAS-131), which states that "the amount of each segment item reported shall be the measure reported to the chief operating decision maker for purposes of making decisions about allocating resources to the segment and assessing its performance." The staff noted that this guidance can be applied to other amounts reported to the chief operating decision maker that are not included in the amount of segment profit or loss used to evaluate a segment's performance.

Question 2: ASC 280-10-50-12 (paragraph 18 of FAS-131) provides a choice of three quantitative thresholds to determine whether an entity should report separate information about an operating segment. Specifically, ASC 280-10-50-12 (paragraph 18b) states that separate information should be reported about an operating segment if "the absolute amount of its reported profit or loss is 10% or more of the greater, in absolute amount, of (1) the combined reported profit of all operating segments that did not report a loss or (2) the combined reported loss of all operating segments that did report a loss." If a chief operating decision maker uses different measures of profit or loss to evaluate the performance of separate segments (e.g., the performance of three of seven segments is evaluated based on operating income and the performance of the remaining four segments is evaluated based on net income), how should the quantitative threshold for segment profit or loss be applied?

Answer: The purpose of the guidance in ASC 280-10-50-12 (paragraph 18 of FAS-131) is to identify the segments for which to report separate information. Therefore, the size of each segment's profit or loss must be compared on a consistent basis to the entity's total profit and loss, which should be similar to the amount used in the consolidated financial statements (without reconciling items), because the total amount would include segments and business activities that do not meet the criterion for a reportable segment and consequently are reported in the "all other" classification. The requirement that a reportable segment should be one that makes up 10% or more of an the entity's *total* reported profit or loss (or revenue or assets) is similar to the requirement in FAS-14 (Financial Reporting for Segments of a Business Enterprise), which also requires as in ASC 280-10-50-14 (paragraph 20 of FAS-131), that reportable segments should account for at least 75% of an entity's total consolidated revenue from *external* sources.

If an entity's chief operating decision maker does not evaluate the performance of all segments based on the same measures of profit and loss, the criterion in ASC 280-10-50-12 (paragraph 18b of FAS-131) should, nevertheless, be applied to a consistent measure of segment profit and loss to determine the entity's reportable segments. That procedure does not affect the requirement in ASC 280-10-50-22 (paragraph 27 of FAS 131) that the actual measure of profit or loss used by the chief operating decision maker to evaluate each reportable segment's performance be disclosed.

The staff noted that the above guidance for ASC 280-10-50-12 (paragraph 18b of FAS-131) also applies if the criteria in ASC 280-10-50-12 (paragraphs 18a or 18c of FAS-131) are used, that is, the 10% threshold of revenue or assets should be applied to total revenues or assets, which should be similar to the amount of consolidated revenues or assets (without reconciling items).

ASC 350 Intangibles—Goodwill and Other

Topic D-101 (Clarification of Reporting Unit Guidance in Paragraph 30 of FASB Statement No. 142) (ASC 350-20-55-1 through 55-9)

To clarify the guidance in ASC 350-20-35-33, 35-36 (paragraph 30 of FAS-142, Goodwill and Other Intangible Assets), the FASB staff provided the following guidance on how to determine whether a component of an operating segment is a reporting unit:

- Judgment should be used based on the specific facts and circumstances related to the entity.
- No single characteristic or factor among those listed in ASC 350-20-35-33, 35-36 (paragraph 30) is determinative.

The way an entity's operations are managed and the way it has integrated an acquired entity with its own operations are significant. ASC 350-20-35-33, 35-36 (paragraph 30 of FAS-142) states that "[a] component of an operating segment is a reporting unit if the component constitutes a business for which discrete financial information is available and segment management regularly review the operating results of the component." Judgment based on the specific facts and circumstances is necessary to determine whether a component is a business. The guidance in ASC 805 (FAS-141(R), Business Combinations) should be used to determine whether a group of assets represents a business.

This pronouncement has been amended by the guidance in ASC 958-805 (FAS-164), which states that any references to a "business or businesses" likewise refer to a "nonprofit activity" and "nonprofit activities," respectively.

ASC 954-280 Health Care Entities—Segment Reporting

FTB 79-5 (Meaning of the Term "Customer" as It Applies to Health Care Facilities under FASB Statement No. 131) (ASC 954-280-45-1)

BACKGROUND

Under the guidance in ASC 280 (FAS-131) disclosure is required if 10% or more of an entity's revenue is derived from sales to a single customer. The disclosures should state that fact and should give the amount of revenue derived from each customer. A group of customers under common control is considered a single customer.

STANDARDS

Question: Is an insuring entity (e.g., Blue Cross) considered a "customer" of a health care facility?

Answer: An insuring entity should not be considered a customer of a health care facility as the term *customer* is used in ASC 280 (FAS-131). The fact that the insuring entity is a paying agent for the patient does not make the insuring entity the customer of the health care facility. The paying entity does not decide which services to purchase and from whom those services will be purchased.

RELATED CHAPTER IN 2011 *GAAP GUIDE, VOLUME I*

Chapter 42, "Segment Reporting"

RELATED CHAPTER IN 2011 *INTERNATIONAL ACCOUNTING/FINANCIAL REPORTING STANDARDS GUIDE*

Chapter 31, "Segment Reporting"

CHAPTER 38
STOCK-BASED PAYMENTS

CONTENTS

Overview		**38.03**
Authoritative Guidance		
ASC 470 Debt		**38.04**
EITF Issue 01-1	Accounting for a Convertible Instrument Granted or Issued to a Nonemployee for Goods or Services and Cash	**38.04**
ASC 480 Distinguishing Liabilities from Equity		**38.06**
FSP FAS-150-4	Issuer's Accounting for Employee Stock Ownership Plans under FASB Statement No. 150, *Accounting for Certain Financial Instruments with Characteristics of both Liabilities and Equity*	**38.06**
ASC 505 Equity		**38.07**
EITF Issue 96-18	Accounting for Equity Instruments That Are Issued to Other Than Employees for Acquiring, or in Conjunction with Selling, Goods or Services	**38.07**
EITF Issue 00-8	Accounting by a Grantee for an Equity Instrument to Be Received in Conjunction with Providing Goods or Services	**38.15**
EITF Issue 00-18	Accounting Recognition for Certain Transactions Involving Equity Instruments Granted to Other Than Employees	**38.17**
Topic D-90	Grantor Balance Sheet Presentation of Unvested, Forfeitable Equity Instruments Granted to a Nonemployee	**38.20**

ASC 715   Compensation—Retirement Benefits

| EITF Issue 86-27 | Measurement of Excess Contributions to a Defined Contribution Plan or Employee Stock Ownership Plan | **38.21** |

ASC 718   Compensation—Stock Compensation

FSP FAS-123 (R)-1	Classification and Measurement of Freestanding Financial Instruments Originally Issued in Exchange for Employee Services under FASB Statement No. 123(R)	**38.25**
FSP FAS-123 (R)-2	Practical Accommodation to the Application of Grant Date as Defined in FASB Statement No. 123(R)	**38.27**
FSP FAS-123 (R)-4	Classification of Options and Similar Instruments Issued as Employee Compensation That Allow for Cash Settlement upon the Occurrence of a Contingent Event	**38.28**
SOP 93-6	Employers' Accounting for Employee Stock Ownership Plans	**38.30**

FTB 97-1 Accounting under Statement 123 for Certain Employee Stock Purchase Plans with a Look-Back Option   **38.52**

EITF Issue 00-16	Recognition and Measurement of Employer Payroll Taxes on Employee Stock-Based Compensation	**38.57**
EITF Issue 09-J	EITF Issue: Effect of Denominating the Exercise Price of a Share-Based Payment Award in the Currency of the Market in Which the Underlying Equity Security Trades	**38.57**
Topic D-83	Accounting for Payroll Taxes Associated with Stock Option Exercises	**38.59**
Topic D-110	Escrowed Share Arrangements and the Presumption of Compensation	**38.59**

ASC 815   Derivatives and Hedging

| EITF Issue 02-8 | Accounting for Options Granted to Employees in Unrestricted, Publicly Traded Shares of an Unrelated Entity | **38.60** |

Grandfathered Pronouncements

SOP 76-3	Accounting Practices for Certain Employee Stock Ownership Plans	38.61
EITF Issue 89-8	Expense Recognition for Employee Stock Ownership Plans	38.63
EITF Issue 89-12	Earnings-per-Share Issues Related to Convertible Preferred Stock Held by an Employee Stock Ownership Plan	38.66
EITF Issue 92-3	Earnings-per-Share Treatment of Tax Benefits for Dividends on Unallocated Stock Held by an Employee Stock Ownership Plan (Consideration of the Implications of FASB Statement No. 109 on Issue 2 of EITF Issue No. 90-4)	38.71

Authoritative Guidance Not Included Separately in the Codification but Incorporated with Other Guidance on the Same Subject — 38.72

FAS-123(R)-5	Amendment of FASB Staff Position FAS 123(R)-1	38.72
FAS-123(R)-6	Technical Corrections of FASB Statement No. 123(R)	38.74

Related Chapters in 2011 GAAP Guide, Volume II — 38.78

Related Chapter in 2011 GAAP Guide, Volume I — 38.78

Related Chapter in 2011 International Accounting/Financial Reporting Standards Guide — 38.78

OVERVIEW

Stock issued to employees may include compensation (compensatory plan) or may not include compensation (noncompensatory plan). A *compensatory plan* is one in which services rendered by employees are partially compensated for by the issuance of stock. The measurement of compensation expense included in compensatory plans is the primary problem encountered in accounting for stock issued to employees.

The following pronouncement, which is discussed in the 2011 *GAAP Guide, Volume I,* Chapter 43, "Stock-Based Payments":

ASC 718   Share-Based Payment (FAS-123(R))

AUTHORITATIVE GUIDANCE

ASC 470 Debt

EITF Issue 01-1 (Accounting for a Convertible Instrument Granted or Issued to a Nonemployee for Goods or Services and Cash) (ASC 470-20-05-12; 25-17 through 25-19; 30-22-26)

OVERVIEW

In addition to the guidance in ASC 470 (APB-14, Accounting for Convertible Debt and Debt Issued with Stock Purchase Warrants), the EITF has issued guidance on accounting for convertible securities with beneficial conversion features in Issue 98-5 (Accounting for Convertible Securities with Beneficial Conversion Features or Contingently Adjustable Conversion Ratios) and in Issue 00-27 (Application of EITF Issue 98-5 to Certain Convertible Instruments (both Issues are discussed in chapter 12)). In addition, ASC 718 (FAS-123 (R), Share-Based Payment) and Issue 96-18 (Accounting for Equity Instruments That Are Issued to Other Than Employees for Acquiring, or in Conjunction with Selling, Goods or Services) provide guidance on accounting for equity securities (including convertible securities) that are issued in exchange for goods or services. However, neither the FASB nor the EITF has provided recognition and measurement guidance for transactions in which convertible instruments are issued to nonemployees in exchange for goods or services or combined with cash. The convertible instruments addressed in this Issue contain a nondetachable conversion option that allows the holder to convert the instrument into the issuer's stock.

ACCOUNTING ISSUES

1. Should the intrinsic value of the conversion option of a convertible instrument issued in exchange for goods or services or combined with cash be measured under the model in Issue 98-5, as interpreted by Issue 00-27, at (a) the instrument's commitment date as defined in Issue 00-27, (b) the measurement date under Issue 96-18, or (c) the later of the two dates?

2. How should the fair value of the convertible instrument be measured?

3. Should distributions paid or payable on such convertible instruments be recognized as a financing cost (interest expense or dividend) or as a cost of the goods or services received from the counterparty?

4. Should a purchaser of a convertible instrument with a beneficial conversion option for cash account for goods or services

provided (received) as an adjustment to the consideration for the convertible instrument if the purchaser also provides (receives) goods or services to (from) the issuer under a different contract?

EITF CONSENSUS

The Task Force noted that existing guidance should be applied as follows:

1. To determine the fair value of a convertible equity or debt instrument issued in exchange for goods or services (or combined with cash) that can be converted into the issuer's equity securities, apply FAS-123(R), as interpreted by Issue 96-18.
2. To determine whether a convertible instrument includes a beneficial conversion option, apply the requirements of Issue 98-5 and Issue 00-27 so that the fair value determined in (a) above is considered the proceeds from issuing the instrument.
3. To measure the intrinsic value, if any, of the conversion option under Issue 98-5, as interpreted by Issue 00-27, compare the proceeds received for the instrument (fair value calculated under (a) above) to the fair value of the common stock the counterparty would receive when the option is exercised.

The following are the Task Force's consensus positions on the Issues:

1. The fair value of a convertible instrument issued in exchange for goods or services and the intrinsic value, if any, of a conversion option under Issue 98-5 should be determined using the *measurement date* in Issue 96-18, not the commitment date in Issue 00-27.
2. The following guidelines should be used to determine the fair value of a convertible instrument:
    a. The fair value of the goods or services received should be used if that amount can be determined with reliability and the issuer has not recently issued similar convertible instruments.
    b. The best evidence of a convertible instrument's fair value may be found in recent issuances of similar convertible instruments for cash to parties having only an investor relationship with the issuer.
    c. The fair value of a convertible instrument should not be less than the fair value of equity shares to which it would be converted if reliable information about (a) or (b) above does not exist.
3. Distributions paid or payable under a convertible instrument should be accounted for as a cost of goods or services received

until the instrument is considered to have been issued under FAS-123(R) and Topic D-90 (Grantor Balance Sheet Presentation of Unvested, Forfeitable Equity Instruments Granted to a Nonemployee), which provides that forfeitable equity instruments are considered unissued until future services have been provided. Thereafter, distributions under such instruments should be accounted for as financing costs. A discount on a convertible instrument as a result of a beneficial conversion feature should not be accreted until the instruments are considered to have been issued for accounting purposes.

4. To determine whether the fair value of goods and services and that of a convertible instrument equal the separately stated pricing of an agreement for goods or services and of a convertible instrument, it is necessary to evaluate the terms of both. If the fair value and separately stated pricing are not equal, the terms of those transactions should be adjusted by recognizing the fair value of the convertible instrument and adjusting the fair value of the purchase or sales price of the goods or services. To determine the fair value of a convertible instrument issued to a provider of goods or service that is part of a larger issuance, evidence of the fair value of that convertible instrument may be found in the amount paid by unrelated investors making a substantive investment in the issuance.

ASC 480 Distinguishing Liabilities from Equity

FSP FAS-150-4 (Issuers' Accounting for Employee Stock Ownership Plans under FASB Statement No. 150, Accounting for Certain Financial Instruments with Characteristics of both Liabilities and Equity) (ASC 480-10-15-8)

OVERVIEW

Employee Stock Ownership Plans (ESOPs) are employee benefit plans under the Employee Retirement Income Security Act of 1974 (ERISA) and the Internal Revenue Code (IRC) of 1986. Employers that sponsor ESOPs are required by law to provide employees with a put option or another means of redeeming shares that cannot be readily traded. ESOPs often require that shares be sold back to the employer at fair value when an employee dies, retires, or reaches a certain age. Shares that must be redeemed meet the definition of mandatorily redeemable shares in ASC 480 (FAS-150, (Accounting for Certain Financial Instruments with Characteristics of both Liabilities and Equity), which does *not* apply to obligations under stock-based compensation arrangements accounted for under APB-25 (Accounting for Stock Issued to Employees), FAS-123(R)

(Accounting for Stock-Based Compensation), SOP 93-6 (Employers' Accounting for Employee Stock Ownership Plans), or related guidance. However, according to paragraph 17 of FAS-150 (ASC 480-10-15-8), the Statement does apply to freestanding financial instruments issued under stock-based compensation arrangements that are no longer required to be accounted for under the guidance in, ASC 718 (FAS-123(R)), SOP 93-6, or related guidance.

FASB STAFF POSITION

Question: Does the guidance in ASC 480 (FAS-150) apply to mandatorily redeemable ESOP shares or freestanding agreements to repurchase ESOP shares?

Answer: No. The guidance in ASC 480 (FAS-150) does *not* apply to mandatorily redeemable ESOP shares or freestanding agreements to repurchase those shares, because until they are redeemed, such shares are accounted for under the provisions of SOP 93-6 or its related guidance, such as that in EITF Issue 89-11. The SEC's requirement that registrants classify amounts related to mandatorily redeemable stock outside of permanent equity in accordance with the guidance in the SEC's ASR-268 (Presentation in Financial Statements of "Redeemable Preferred Stocks") is discussed in Issue 89-11.

ASC 505 Equity

EITF Issue 96-18 (Accounting for Equity Instruments That Are Issued to Other Than Employees for Acquiring, or in Conjunction with Selling, Goods or Services) (ASC 505-50-05-3,05-8; 15-2 through 15-3; 25-2, 25-4, 25-9; 30-2 through 30-4 through 30-7, 30-11 through 30-14, 30-21 through 30-23, 30-25 through 30-28, 30-30 through 30-31; 35-3, 35-5 through 35-10; 55-2 through 55-11, 55-13 through 55-17, 55-20 through 55-24, 55-28, 55-31 through 55-40; 440-10-60-4)

OVERVIEW

FAS-123 (before its revision in 2004) provided guidance on the measurement principles for stock options issued to nonemployees in exchange for goods and services. The guidance in ASC 505-50-30-2 states (paragraph 8 of FAS-123 that stock option transactions with nonemployees that involve the receipt of goods and services "shall be measured at the fair value of the consideration received or the fair value of the equity instruments issued, whichever is more reliably measurable." However, FAS-123 did not provide guidance on the *measurement date* for *nonemployee* stock options; nor does it state whether the measurement date guidance established for employee stock options should be used as a model. It also does not provide guidance for the issuance of nonemployee stock options involving the *sale* of goods and services, such as stock options used as sales incentives.

The guidance in FAS-123 generally required that compensation cost for equity instruments issued to employees be measured based on the fair value of the award at the grant date, but paragraph 22 provided an exception for certain situations, in which it is impossible to "reasonably estimate" the fair value of a stock option or other equity instrument on that date, for example, if the option exercise price changes by a specified amount based on a change in the price of the underlying security. Paragraph 22 provided that under such circumstances, the award's fair value should be measured based on the stock price and other relevant information on the "first date at which it is reasonably possible to estimate that value." However, it required using the intrinsic value of the award at the grant date to estimate compensation cost in those situations. FAS-123(R), which was issued in 2004, also did not provide guidance on the accounting for share-based payment transactions with nonemployees but referred readers to EITF Issue 96-18 for such guidance.

In Issue 96-3, the Task Force reached a consensus on the date on which the fair value of nonemployee stock options should be determined as well as a consensus on the number of equity instruments that should be recognized when that number is contingent on future events. The transactions discussed in Issue 96-18 differ from those in Issue 96-3, because (*a*) they may extend over more than one reporting period and (*b*) the quantity and terms of the equity instruments to be issued to the counterparty under the exchange arrangement are known at the date of the arrangement or only within a range on that date. For example, the option price may vary based on the passage of time or the occurrence of certain events, such as the counterparty's performance or a change in the price of the underlying security.

This Issue provides guidance on the measurement date and the recognition of *all* stock-option transactions with nonemployees, therefore superseding Issue 96-3. It does not apply, however, to equity instruments issued in a business combination or to those issued to lenders or investors providing financing to the issuer.

ACCOUNTING ISSUES

1. What date should an issuer use to measure the fair value of equity instruments in all transactions under the scope of this Issue?

2. In what period(s) and in what manner (capitalize or expense) should an issuer recognize the fair value of equity instruments in all transactions under the scope of this Issue?

3. How should the cost of equity instruments be recognized *before the measurement date* if the quantity and terms are all known in advance, because they do not depend on the counterparty's performance or market conditions?
4. If the quantity or terms of the equity instruments are not all known in advance, because they are based on the counterparty's performance or market conditions:
    a. How should the equity instruments be measured *at the measurement date?*
    b. How should the cost of the equity instruments be recognized *before the measurement date?*
    c. How should the equity instruments be accounted for *after the measurement date* if the quantity or terms of the equity instruments change as a result of the counterparty's performance or market conditions?

EITF CONSENSUS

1. The fair value of equity instruments in all nonemployee awards should be measured based on the stock price and other measurement assumptions on one of the following dates (the measurement date), whichever occurs first:
    a. The date on which the issuer and the counterparty reach a commitment for the counterparty's performance to earn the equity instruments. The counterparty's performance is considered probable (there is a performance commitment) because of a strong enough disincentive for nonperformance (in addition to forfeiture of the equity instruments) resulting from the relationship between the issuer and the counterparty. However, performance is not assured merely because the issuer can sue the counterparty for nonperformance. The Task Force did not consider that to be a large enough disincentive, because the option to sue for nonperformance always exists. In addition, there may not be sufficient assurance that damages will be collected.
    b. The date on which the counterparty's performance is concluded, because the counterparty has delivered or purchased, as appropriate, the goods or services, even though on that date the quantity and all the terms of the equity instruments may still depend on other events, such as a target stock price. (This date is used if the counterparty made no performance commitment.) In some cases, a counterparty may be required to perform over a period of time, such as over several years; the equity award is fully vested, cannot be forfeited, and can be exercised on the date the parties enter into the contract. The Task Force members noted that this fact pattern would be rare, because usually there is a required vesting period. However, they agreed

that in that situation, the fair value of the award could be measured on the date the parties enter into a contract even if the services are yet to be performed.
2. The EITF did not discuss the period(s) in which the entity should recognize the fair value of the instruments that will be issued or whether the amounts should be expensed or capitalized. However, the Task Force reached the following consensus positions on the period and manner of recognition for all transactions:
   a. An asset, expense, or sales discount should be recognized (or previous recognition reversed) in the same period(s) and in the same manner as if the issuer had paid for the goods or services in cash or used cash rebates as a sales discount instead of paying with equity instruments.
   b. An asset, expense, or sales discount that had been recognized should not be reversed, if a counterparty does not exercise a stock option and the option expires unexercised.
3. Equity instruments should be measured at their current fair values at each interim financial reporting date, if the quantity and terms of the transaction are known and it is appropriate under GAAP for an issuer to recognize costs related to the transaction during financial periods preceding the measurement date. The methods illustrated in ASC 505-50-55-28 should be used to ascribe the changes in fair values to interim reporting dates.
4. If the quantity or any of the transaction's terms are unknown initially, the equity instruments should be accounted for as follows:
   a. The fair value of the equity instruments should be recognized as follows at the measurement date:
      (1) The issuer should recognize the equity instruments at their fair value on the measurement date, if the quantity or any of the transaction's terms depend on the achievement of market conditions, which are related to achieving a specified market target, such as a specified stock price or intrinsic value of a stock option. The fair value of the equity instruments should be computed without considering the market condition plus the fair value of the issuer's commitment to change the quantity or terms of the equity instruments, based on whether the market condition is met.
      (2) The issuer should recognize, on the measurement date, the lowest total amount (i.e., the variable terms multiplied by the applicable number of equity instruments) within a range of total fair values for the equity instruments based on different possible outcomes, if the quantity or any terms of the equity instruments on that date depend on the achievement of performance conditions by the counterparty, such as increasing mar-

ket share for a specified product by a specified amount. The amount recognized may be zero.

(3) The consensus in 4(a)(2) above applies, if the transaction requires the counterparty to meet performance conditions and market conditions.

b. If the quantity or the terms of a transaction are unknown and it is appropriate for the issuer to recognize the cost of the transaction in reporting periods *before* the measurement date, the equity instruments should be accounted for as follows:

(1) The equity instruments should be recognized at their fair value on the date of recognition, as in the consensus on Issue 3 above, if the outcome of the transaction depends only on market conditions. (See ASC 505-50-30-28 for application guidance).

(2) The equity instruments should be recognized at the lowest total fair value at each interim date, if the outcome depends only on the counterparty's performance. The method illustrated in ASC 505-50-55-28; 55-33 through 40 should be used to ascribe the changes in fair values between interim reporting dates (ASC 505-50-30-25).

(3) The guidance in 4(a)(2) above also applies, if the outcome of the transaction depends both on the counterparty's performance and on market conditions (ASC 505-50-30-26).

c. If the quantity or any of the terms of the transaction are unknown initially, the accounting after the measurement date should be as follows:

(1) For transactions that depend only on market conditions, the Task Force noted that after measuring the current fair value of the issuer's commitment related to the market condition, in accordance with 4(a)(1) above, the issuer should, if necessary, recognize and classify future changes in the fair value of the commitment in accordance with accounting guidance on financial instruments, such as that in EITF Issue 96-13, which has been codified in Issue 00-19 with Issues 99-3 and 00-7 (ASC 505-50-35-5 through 35-6).

(2) For transactions that depend only on the counterparty's performance, the lowest total fair value measured, based on the consensus in 4(a)(2) above, should be adjusted to recognize the additional cost of the transaction using the method for modification accounting in ASC 718-20-35-3 through 35-4 as each quantity and term of the transaction becomes known and until all such information becomes known as a result of the counterparty's performance.

38.12 *Stock-Based Payments*

Under that method, the adjustment is measured at the date the quantity or terms of the equity instruments are known as the difference between (*a*) the current fair value of the *revised* instruments, using the current known quantity or term, and (*b*) the fair value of the equity instruments before knowing the revised quantity or term. The current fair value is calculated using the assumptions that result in the lowest total fair value, if the quantity or any term remains unknown (ASC 505-50-35-7).

(3) For transactions that depend on the counterparty's performance and on market conditions, the issuer should apply the method discussed in ASC 718-20-35-3 through 35-4 until the last condition related to the counterparty's performance has been met. The issuer should measure the current fair value of the commitment to issue additional equity instruments or change the terms of the equity instruments, based on whether the market condition is met, if the counterparty has met the last performance condition but one or more market conditions remain unresolved. This amount is an additional cost of the transaction. The EITF noted that the issuer should, if necessary, recognize and classify future changes in the fair value of the commitment in accordance with accounting guidance on financial instruments, such as EITF Issue 00-19, after measuring the current fair value of the issuer's commitment related to market conditions (ASC 505-50-35-8 through 35-10).

SUBSEQUENT DEVELOPMENT

The EITF agreed that a grantee's ability to immediately exercise an award is *not* required to attain a measurement date at the date two parties enter into a contract under which Company X grants to Company Y a fully vested and nonforfeitable equity award, even though Company Y's performance will occur over a period of time (e.g., over several years). To clarify that point, the EITF decided to delete the word *exercisability* from the two instances in which it is used in footnote 5 in the abstract for Issue 96-18 in the FASB's *EITF Abstracts*.

EFFECT OF ASC 815 (FAS-133)

The terms of the stock options in this Issue should be analyzed to determine whether they meet the definition of a derivative in ASC 815 (FAS-133). Although paragraph ASC 815-10-15-74 (11(b) of FAS-133) exempts *issuers* of contracts related to stock-based compensation arrangements under the provisions in ASC 718 from accounting for those contracts as derivatives the guidance in ASC 815-10-55-49 through 55-51, 55-53 through 55-55; 15-75 (Issue C3, Exception Related to Stock-Based Compensation Arrangements, of the

FAS- 133 Implementation Guide) provides that the exception in ASC 815-10-15-74 (paragraph 11(b) of FAS-133) does not apply to nonemployee *holders* of derivatives who receive the options as compensation for goods or services. Those parties are required to account for the options as derivatives under the guidance in ASC 815 (FAS-133). However, all or a portion of the contract may be exempt if the underlying is a specified volume of sales or service revenue of one of the counterparties in the arrangement. The guidance in ASC 815-10-15-122, 15-125 through 15-127 (Issue A10) and ASC 815-10-15-133 through 13-138 (Issue A14) of the FAS-133 Implementation may also be relevant.

DISCUSSION

The SEC Observer stated that recognition of compensation cost at the grant date is acceptable in the case of stock options granted to employees, because the employee model looks at employment as an ongoing situation. In contrast, because a nonemployee does not have the same kind of commitment to perform, it would be inappropriate to recognize a liability for the fair value of the equity instruments to be issued until completion of performance. The Task Force decided that the fair value of the equity instruments to be issued should be measured when the issuer and the counterparty reach a commitment for the counterparty's performance if the counterparty has a strong enough disincentive for nonperformance. In other words, the counterparty's performance is assured because both parties have incurred a contingent liability for a future transfer of consideration. Otherwise the cost of the transaction should not be measured until performance has been completed.

This approach is analogous to the guidance in the following pronouncements: (*a*) the guidance in ASC 470-20-25-2 (paragraph 16 and footnote 2 of APB-14), which require the portion of the proceeds of debt securities issued with stock warrants that is allocable to the warrants to be allocated based on the relative fair value of the securities when the securities are issued, which is when an agreement about the terms of the debt has been reached and announced; and (*b*) the guidance in ASC 730-20-25-12 (paragraph 13 of FAS-68, Research and Development Arrangements), which requires that warrants or similar instruments issued in connection with a research and development arrangement be measured at their fair value on the date of the arrangement.

Illustration of Accounting for Nonemployee Stock Options with Variable Terms

1. In the following arrangement, the counterparty's commitment to perform is made before performance is completed. However, the quantity of the equity instruments to be issued is unknown. On 8/1/X7, Gary and Harry

38.14 *Stock-Based Payments*

Real Estate Corp. (the Company) enters into an agreement with APEX Painters, Inc., under which APEX would paint five of the Company's office buildings beginning on 9/1/X7. The agreement provides that, in exchange for its services, the Company will pay APEX $50,000 and will issue to APEX 5,000 stock options that are exercisable over five years at an exercise price of $10, if APEX completes the project by 12/31/X7. No stock options will be issued if the project is completed after that date, and the contract price will be reduced by $10,000 for each week completion is delayed. The project is completed on time. Assuming the total fair value of the award on 8/1/X7—the date the agreement is reached—is $50,000, the Company should measure the fair value of the award on the commitment date—8/1/X7—in accordance with the consensus in 1(a), because it is probable that APEX will perform. In accordance with the consensus in paragraph 4(a)(ii), the Company should recognize a fair value of zero at the commitment date, because that is the lowest total fair value if the project is not completed by the deadline. The fair value of the award should be measured at the award's current fair value on 12/31/X7, when the project is completed.

2. In the following example, there is no commitment to perform until the counterparty has completed performance:

A manufacturer of a new type of oven offers its customers 5,000 shares of its stock as an incentive to purchase a minimum of 500 ovens over the following two years. For every additional 100 ovens purchased, the manufacturer offers its customers an additional 1,000 shares. Customers have no performance commitment, because they are not required to purchase the ovens. The manufacturer will recognize the fair value of the 5,000 shares on the date the customer has purchased the minimum number of ovens as discussed in paragraph 4 (a)(ii). The cost of the incentive should be adjusted for each additional 100 ovens purchased by a customer in accordance with paragraph 4(c)(ii) using modification accounting.

3. In the following example, the guidance on the measurement date is applied to a transaction that has a market condition:

On 7/1/98, the XYZ Insurance Co. hires ABC Software Company to modify the company's software to comply with the requirements for the year 2000. XYZ will pay ABC $50,000 in cash and will issue 500 stock options if the modifications are completed by 6/30/99. There is a performance commitment, because ABC will incur a substantial penalty, which is considered to be a "sufficiently large disincentive for non-performance," if the software modifications are not completed by that date. XYZ and ABC agreed on the quantity and terms of the stock options when the contract was signed on 7/1/98. The fair value of the stock options is $50,000 on the commitment date. However, if ABC completes the project by 6/30/99 and the fair value of XYZ's shares is less than $50,000 on 12/31/01, XYZ will issue an additional five stock options for each dollar that the stock price is below $100 per share, up to 125 stock options. Initially, XYZ will measure the 500 stock options (one option per share) at their fair value on 7/1/98, the day ABC made a commitment to perform. The fair value of the shares on that date is $40,000. In addition, XYZ would also recognize an additional $10,000 for the fair value of the additional stock options that could potentially be issued, regardless of whether the commitment is in-the-money. The total cost to be recognized for the options would be $50,000. After the initial recognition on the commitment date, XYZ would account for the 125 stock options that may be issued in accordance with existing authoritative guidance on financial instruments, including EITF Issue 96-13.

EITF Issue 00-8 (Accounting by a Grantee for an Equity Instrument to Be Received in Conjunction with Providing Goods or Services) (ASC 505-50-05-1, 4, 5; 25-5; 30-18, 30-19, 30-29; 35-13 through 35-15; 50-2; 55-25 through 55-27; 845-10-50-2)

OVERVIEW

Issue 96-18 provide guidance to grantors on the accounting for equity instruments issued to other than employees in exchange for products or services. Those documents address the amount at which such equity instruments should be recognized and the date on which recognition should occur. However, the *grantee's* accounting for such transactions, which may span over more than one reporting period and may contain terms contingent on the grantee's performance, is currently not addressed in the authoritative literature.

ACCOUNTING ISSUES

1. On what date should a *grantee* measure the fair value of revenue received in the form of equity instruments in exchange for goods or services provided to a grantor?

2. If the terms of equity instruments received by a *grantee* for goods or services provided to a grantor can be adjusted after the measurement date based on the resolution of a contingency, such as performance above a level to which the grantee has committed, performance after the instrument was earned, or market conditions, how should the grantee account for an increase in the fair value of revenue received in the form of equity instruments after the contingency has been resolved?

EITF CONSENSUS

1. A grantee should measure the fair value of equity instruments received in exchange for providing goods or services to a grantor based on the stock price and other measurement assumptions on either of the following dates, whichever is earlier (the measurement date):

    a. When the parties agree on the terms of the compensation arrangement in the form of equity instruments and on the grantee's performance commitment to earn the equity instruments

b. When the grantee's performance required to earn the equity instruments is completed (i.e., the vesting date)

2. The accounting is as follows if on the measurement date, the quantity or any of the terms of the equity instruments depend on:

   a. **Achieving a market condition** Revenue is measured based on the fair value of the equity instruments, including the adjustment provisions. The fair value of the equity instruments is used without considering the market condition plus the fair value of the commitment to change the quantity or terms of the equity instruments if the market condition is met.

   b. **Additional grantee performance** Changes in fair value as a result of an adjustment to the instrument for a condition requiring additional grantee performance should be measured as additional revenue based on the guidance in ASC 718-20-35-3 through 35-4 for modification accounting. At the date on which the quantity or terms of the equity instrument are revised, the adjustment is measured as the difference between (*a*) the current fair value on that date of the revised equity instrument using the known quantity and terms and (*b*) the current fair value on that date of the old equity instrument before the adjustment. If the fair value of the equity instruments changes after the measurement date for reasons that are unrelated to the achievement of performance conditions, those fair value changes should be accounted for in accordance with the relevant literature on accounting and reporting for investments in equity instruments. For example, on July 1, 2000, the date the parties agreed on the grantee's performance commitment, the fair value of an equity instrument granting options to the contractor is $500,000. On July 1, 2001, the original instrument is adjusted because the grantee has met a condition for additional performance. The equity instrument's fair value is $1 million on that date. If the fair value of the *original* instrument is $650,000 on July 1, 2001, the increase in its fair value due to the performance condition is $350,000 ($1 million less $650,000). The $150,000 increase in the fair value of the original instrument from $500,000 to $650,000 is unrelated to the grantee's performance and should be accounted for based on other relevant literature.

The Task Force noted that although the Issue does not address the timing of revenue recognition, a grantee would recognize deferred revenue or revenue in the same periods and in the same manner as cash, rather than equity instruments, received for goods or services.

DISCLOSURE REQUIREMENTS

The Task Force noted that in accordance with paragraph 28 of APB-29 (ASC 845-10-50-1), the amount of gross operating revenue recognized as a result of the nonmonetary transactions discussed in this Issue should be disclosed in the financial statements of each reporting period. In addition, the SEC Observer reminded registrants of Item 303(a)(3)(ii) of Regulation S-K, which requires disclosure of known trends or uncertainties that have had or that are reasonably expected to have a materially favorable or unfavorable effect on revenues.

EITF Issue 00-18 (Accounting Recognition for Certain Transactions Involving Equity Instruments Granted to Other Than Employees) (ASC 505-50-05-6, 05-7; 25-7 through 25-8; 30-15 through 30-16; 35-11 through 35-12; 45-1)

OVERVIEW

Issue 96-18 (Accounting for Equity Instruments That Are Issued to Other Than Employees for Acquiring, or in Conjunction with Selling, Goods or Services) provides guidance to grantors on the measurement of the fair value of equity instruments granted to other than employees. Issue 00-8 (Accounting by a Grantee for an Equity Instrument to Be Received in Conjunction with Providing Goods and Services) provides guidance to grantees on the measurement of the fair value of such equity instruments for revenue recognition purposes. Those Issues do not provide guidance on the period or manner in which to recognize the fair value of the transaction; they state only that recognition should be in the same period and the same manner as if cash had been exchanged.

Both Issues provide that the measurement date occurs when a performance commitment is reached or if there is no performance commitment, on the vesting date when performance is complete, whichever occurs earlier. Since the Task Force reached its consensus positions on the measurement date, some grantors have been structuring equity instruments so that they are nonforfeitable and the grantee is fully vested at the date the parties enter into the contract, thereby establishing the measurement date. Those arrangements do not require a grantee to achieve a specific future performance to earn or retain the equity instruments. That is, the grantee can exercise the instruments immediately or at a specified future date whether or not future performance is met. Because instruments with such provisions are considered to be issued for accounting purposes under the guidance in ASC 718, the grantor recognizes the issuance of the instrument as a credit in equity at the fair value of the instrument measured in accordance with the guidance in Issue 96-18.

Although the equity instruments cannot be forfeited, under many arrangements, they cannot be exercised until a future date. Instruments with such provisions provide, however, that they can be exercised if the grantee meets certain performance requirements. Some question whether the grantee's rights under those instruments are truly vested before the grantee's performance, which accelerates exercisability. In addition, some equity instruments are being structured with sufficiently large disincentives to nonperformance. Some question whether it is appropriate for grantees to recognize equity instruments with those provisions as assets at the measurement date.

ACCOUNTING ISSUES

1. In what period and manner should a *grantor* recognize the measured cost of a transaction if a grantor issues a fully vested, exercisable, nonforfeitable equity instrument at the date the grantor and grantee enter an agreement for goods or services and no specific performance is required of the grantee?

1a. When, if ever, should a grantor present an asset in the balance sheet as contra-equity, if the grantor believes that an asset (other than a note or a receivable) has been received in return for fully vested, nonforfeitable equity instruments issued at the date the grantor and grantee enter into an agreement for goods or services under which the grantee retains the equity instruments without a specific performance requirement?

2. How should a *grantor* that issues a fully vested, exercisable, nonforfeitable equity instrument that can be exercised only after a specific period of time, measure and recognize the equity instrument at the date of the arrangement, and thereafter, if the grantee achieves a performance condition that accelerates exercisability under the terms of the instrument?

3. How should a *grantee* account for a contingent right to receive a grantor's equity instrument as consideration for future performance under an instrument that includes the grantee's performance commitment?

EITF CONSENSUS

1. The Task Force decided not to reach a consensus on Issue 1 on the period and manner in which a grantor should recognize the measured cost of fully vested, nonforfeitable equity instruments issued at the date a grantor and grantee enter into an agreement for goods or services. The Task Force noted, however, that a grantor should recognize the measured cost of the goods or services as if it had paid for them in cash or used cash rebates as sales discounts rather than granting equity instruments.

1a. The EITF reached a consensus that a grantor that issues fully vested, nonforfeitable equity instruments in exchange for an asset (other than a note or a receivable) should *not* report the acquired asset as a contra-equity in the balance sheet. This consensus applies only when a grantor issues equity instruments to *nonemployees* in exchange for goods or services. Some members noted that this consensus may be inconsistent with the consensus reached in Issue 85-1 regarding a note or a receivable. The FASB staff was asked to consider whether to codify the consensus on this Issue with Issue 85-1 and to consider how to make the two consensus positions more consistent. In addition, the staff was asked to consider whether the type of asset received in the circumstances discussed in this Issue affects whether that asset is presented as contra-equity.

2. The Task Force reached the following consensus on the accounting for fully vested, nonforfeitable equity instruments that can be exercised only after a specified time period, but that a grantee may exercise earlier if specified performance conditions are achieved:

    a. Measure the fair value of the equity instruments at the *grant* date and recognize the measured cost in the same period and manner as if paid for in cash.

    b. If exercisability is accelerated because a grantee has met specified performance requirements, account for an increase in the equity instruments' fair value as a modification in accordance with paragraph 35 of FAS-123 and measure the adjustment at the date the terms of the agreement are revised as the difference between (i) the current fair value of the *revised* equity instruments at the date they are exercisable and (ii) the current fair value of the *old* equity instruments immediately before their exercisability is accelerated. The EITF noted, however, if acceleration of a grantee's ability to exercise the option is the only change in terms, a significant additional charge will only occur if the expected dividend on the underlying instrument is greater than the sum of (i) the effect of discounting the exercise price and (ii) a loss in the time value of money because the equity instrument has been exercised early.

3. At its March 15, 2007, meeting, the EITF agreed to delete issue 3 from its agenda, because the question will be addressed by the FASB in two of its related projects.

SEC OBSERVER'S COMMENTS

Regarding Issue 1, the SEC Observer stated that registrants should consider the facts and circumstances of the transaction in determining the period and manner of cost recognition. In addition, if the cost of equity instruments is capitalized, the SEC staff would object to any approach other than those required in EITF Issue 85-1, SAB 40, and Regulation S-X, Rule 5-02.30.

For Issue 2, the SEC Observer stated that grantees and grantors should use the same commitment date and similar values for such transactions, or the staff would challenge their accounting. In addition, registrants are reminded to disclose (*a*) the amount of revenues from equity transactions in accordance with EITF Issue 00-8 and (*b*) known trends and uncertainties that a registrant *reasonably expects* would have a material favorable or unfavorable effect on revenues, as required in Item 303(a)(3)(ii) of Regulation S-K.

During the EITF's discussion of Issue 3, the SEC Observer stated his concern about the number and complexity of the issues that have been raised as a result of the consensus positions reached in Issues 96-18 and 00-8.

Topic D-90 (Grantor Balance Sheet Presentation of Unvested, Forfeitable Equity Instruments Granted to a Nonemployee) (ASC 505-50-S25-1; S99-1)

The SEC Observer discussed the following guidance, which addresses the balance sheet classification of unvested forfeitable equity instruments granted to nonemployees for future services instead of cash. Under such arrangements, a grantor has the right to recover the consideration paid as well as to impose a large penalty as damages for nonperformance. Issue 96-18 (Accounting for Equity Instruments That Are Issued to Other Than Employees for Acquiring, or in Conjunction with Selling, Goods or Services (see ASC references in Issue 96-18 above)) provides that the commitment and measurement date for such instruments is the date that equity instruments were issued to the grantee if the grantee has a large enough disincentive for nonperformance.

Because practice is diverse as to the recognition of such transactions on the measurement date, the SEC staff will require registrants that receive a right to receive future services in exchange for unvested, forfeitable equity instruments to consider such instruments as *unissued* for accounting purposes until the instruments vest, which occurs when the future services have been received. Therefore, there is no recognition at the measurement date and the transaction is not recorded.

This announcement does not apply to arrangements under which fully vested, nonforfeitable, equity instruments are exchanged for future services that will be addressed in Issue 00-18 (Accounting Recognition for Certain Transaction Involving Equity Instruments Granted to Other Than Employees) (See ASC references in Issue 00-18 discussed above.).

ASC 715 Compensation—Retirement Benefits

EITF Issue 86-27 (Measurement of Excess Contributions to a Defined Contribution Plan or Employee Stock Ownership Plan) (ASC 715-70-55-4 through 55-9)

Note: The EITF's consensus positions below in Issues 1d, 1e, and 2a to 2e relating to employers' accounting for unallocated shares contributed to an ESOP as a result of a pension reversion have been nullified by the guidance in ASC 718-40 (SOP 93-6). However, under the SOP's transition provisions, employers may elect not to apply the provisions of the SOP to shares purchased in a pension reversion that occurred before December 31, 1992. The consensus positions in this Issue may continue to apply to such shares, if the employer so elects. In addition, the consensus positions related to employers' accounting for unallocated shares contributed to defined contribution plans are not affected by the guidance in ASC 718-40 (SOP 93-6, which is discussed in this chapter. and continue to apply.

OVERVIEW

An employer terminates a defined benefit pension plan and contributes the withdrawn assets to a defined contribution plan or to an employee stock ownership plan (ESOP). If the amount contributed exceeds the employer's required (or maximum) annual contribution to the plan, the excess assets are held in a suspense account until they are allocated to plan participants. The employer retains the risks and rewards of ownership related to those assets while they are held in the suspense account. Excess contributions made to an ESOP must either be converted to the employer's stock within 90 days of the asset reversion or be used to retire debt incurred to acquire the employer's stock.

ACCOUNTING ISSUES

1. Contributions to a defined contribution plan
    a. How should an employer initially account for the excess contribution not allocated to individual participants?
    b. If an employer recognizes the unallocated amount as an asset, how should it be measured and classified in subsequent periods, until it is allocated to individual participants?
    c. How should an employer measure compensation expense?
    d. How should an employer account for its own common stock?

e. How should an employer account for its own debt securities and third-party debt securities?
2. Contributions to an ESOP
    a. How should an employer initially account for the excess contribution not allocated to individual participants?
    b. How should an employer measure compensation expense?
    c. How should an employer account for its own common stock and debt securities and third-party debt securities?
    d. How should an employer account for dividends on unallocated shares?
    e. How should an employer treat its own unallocated common stock in determining EPS?

EITF CONSENSUS

The following consensus positions apply to *defined contribution plans* only:

1a. Recognize an excess contribution as an asset regardless of whether the excess unallocated contribution results from a plan reversion or from another source.

1b. Account for unallocated contributions in subsequent periods as follows:

   a. Recognize an unallocated amount as an asset and treat it as if it were part of the employer's investment portfolio. For example, an unallocated amount that consists of marketable equity securities should be accounted for in accordance with ASC 320 (FAS-115). Employers such as investment companies and broker-dealers subject to specialized industry accounting rules are exempt from the provisions of ASC 320 (FAS-115). They should recognize income from such securities, including dividends, interest, and realized gains and losses, the same as for similar items.

   OBSERVATION: The consensus referred to FAS-12, which was superseded by FAS-115.

1c. Recognize compensation expense at the time of plan allocation based on the assets' fair market value at that time.

The following consensus positions apply to both *defined contribution plans* and *ESOPs*:

1d. In the employer's financial statements, recognize as treasury stock the portion of the plan's unallocated assets consisting of the employer's common stock.

1e. Account for unallocated assets consisting of employer debt securities as follows:

   a. Recognize the portion of the plan's unallocated assets consisting of the employer's debt securities as an asset, not as an extinguishment of debt.

   b. Measure employer debt securities or debt securities issued by a third party that are included in the plan's unallocated assets at fair value, and recognize unrealized gains or losses in a separate component of equity in accordance with ASC 320 (FAS-115).

   OBSERVATION: The original consensus required measuring such debt securities at the lower of cost or market, with losses reflected in income.

   This consensus applies only to employer debt securities included in the unallocated assets of a defined contribution plan or an ESOP and does *not* apply in other circumstances in which an entity reacquires its own debt securities.

The following consensus positions apply to *ESOPs* only:

2a. Reduce shareholders' equity for unallocated shares in the employer's own stock, as if they were treasury stock.

2b. Recognize compensation expense at the date of allocation based on the then-current market price of the stock, and recognize the difference between the purchase price and the current market price as an increase or decrease to shareholders' equity.

2c. Same as Issues 1d and 1e above.

2d. Account for dividends on an employer's own common stock as follows:

   a. Increase treasury stock for dividends on employer common stock that are invested in additional employer common stock. Such dividends are not considered income and should not reduce retained earnings. In conformity with the 1986 Tax Reform Act, an ESOP's sponsor receives a tax deduction for cash dividends paid to participants within 90 days or that are used to repay the ESOP's loan in a leveraged ESOP.

   b. Charge compensation expense for dividends paid to participants on unallocated shares.

   c. Charge dividends on allocated shares to retained earnings.

   d. Charge prepayments on ESOP debt as compensation expense, and account for dividends on unallocated shares as treasury stock.

   e. Follow the guidance in SOP 76-3 for other dividends.

> **OBSERVATION:** The guidance in SOP 76-3 is not included in the FASB Accounting Standards Codification™, but has been grandfathred for existing ESOPs and, therefore, is included in this chapter.

2e. Unallocated shares of employer common stock should not be considered outstanding in the earnings-per-share computation.
    It was noted that this accounting differs from that required in paragraph 11 of SOP 76-3. The Task Force reached this conclusion because they believed that unallocated employer common stock resulting from a pension reversion differs sufficiently from unallocated employer shares contemplated in the discussion of leveraged ESOPs in SOP 76-3.

DISCUSSION

The consensus positions reached in this Issue apply to two vehicles used for a similar purpose: to compensate employees. The generic term *defined contribution plan* is used to describe plans under which employers make regular periodic awards to participants' accounts, which are subject to vesting provisions. A defined contribution plan—as contemplated in this Issue—is a type of pension plan, which is accounted for under the guidance in ASC 715 (FAS-87). While an ESOP meets the definition of a defined contribution plan, it may be established for a variety of reasons, such as to raise new capital, create a market for the employer's stock, or to replace benefits lost on the termination of a defined benefit plan. ESOPs differ from other defined contribution plans because they invest only in shares of the employer's stock, whereas defined contribution plans invest primarily in debt and equity securities of other entities. Special accounting applies to ESOPs because of their specialized nature; they were accounted for under SOP 76-3 until the issuance of SOP 93-6. The EITF's consensus positions consider the differences between those plans.

1a. Two alternative methods of accounting for the excess contribution to defined contribution plans were suggested to the Task Force. One was to recognize that amount as prepaid pension cost, consistent with the requirement in paragraph 35 of FAS-87 (ASC 715-30-25-1) for a defined benefit pension plan. Another was to recognize the entire contribution as net periodic pension cost. The Task Force's consensus that the employer should recognize the unallocated contribution as an asset was based on the view that the employer retains the risks and benefits of the excess contribution until it is actually allocated to participants. Because the employer will use the excess contributions to make future contributions to the plan, a gain or loss on those funds will determine whether the employer has to contribute additional assets in future years.

1b. This consensus is consistent with the Task Force's consensus on Issue 1a. If the excess contribution is recognized as the employer's asset, it should be accounted for the same as other such assets held by the employer.

1c. This consensus is a further extension of the view that the employer retains the risks and rewards of the excess contribution, which ultimately should be reflected in compensation expense. That is, the difference between the carrying amount of the unallocated shares and their market value is recognized as a realized gain or loss.

1d. The Task Force's consensus on this Issue is the same as that reached in Issue 2a for ESOPs, which hold shares only in the employer's own stock. The rationale for treating an ESOP's unallocated shares in the employer's own stock as treasury stock in the employer's financial statements was that the shares were under the employer's control and that such shares do not differ from treasury stock held for the purpose of meeting the requirements of other employee stock plans. Those who supported this view argued that although the plans may differ, the substance of the transaction is the same.

1e. The Task Force supported the recognition of unallocated assets consisting of employer debt securities as assets rather than as extinguishment of debt, because they believed that the conditions for extinguishment of debt in FAS-76 (not in ASC) have not been met. That is, a debtor/creditor relationship continues to exist because control over the debt instrument has not been returned to the debtor (employer); the ESOP's trustee continues to control the debt instrument. In addition, some argued that FAS-76 was not intended to apply to such transactions.

ASC 718 Compensation—Stock Compensation

FSP FAS-123(R)-1 (Classification and Measurement of Freestanding Financial Instruments Originally Issued in Exchange for Employee Services under FASB Statement No. 123(R)) (ASC 718-10-35-9, 35-10, 35-11, 65-1)

OVERVIEW

This FSP has been issued for the following reasons:

- To defer the requirement in ASC 718 (FAS-123(R), Share-Based Payment) (revised 2004) that freestanding financial instruments accounted for under the guidance in ASc 718 (FAS-123(R)) that were conveyed to a holder by an employer and linked to the holder's employment should be accounted for in accordance with the recognition and measurement guidance in other applic-able generally accepted accounting principles (GAAP) if the instrument's rights no longer are linked to the holder's employment.

- To supersede the guidance in FSP EITF 00-19-1 (Application of EITF Issue No. 00-19 to Freestanding Financial Instruments Originally Issued as Employee Compensation).
- To amend paragraph 11(b) of FAS-133 (Accounting for Derivative Instruments and Hedging Activities) (FASB Accounting Standards Codification (ASC) 815-10-15-74) and Statement Statement 133 Implementation Issue No. C3 (Scope Exceptions: Exception Related to Share-Based Payment Arrangements) by adding a footnote to both documents stating that FSP FAS 123 (R)-1 defers the guidance in paragraph A231 of FAS-123(R) (ASC 718-10-35-13) under certain circumstances for employee awards and provides additional guidance for awards that no longer are within the scope of FAS-123(R). Such awards should be analyzed to determine whether they should be accounted for under the guidance in FAS-133..

Entities that offer stock-based compensation to employees are required to account for such arrangements under the guidance in (FAS-123(R) Share-Based Payment); however, (FAS-123(R) provides that the rights conveyed by freestanding instruments issued under those arrangements are *excluded* from the scope of (FAS-123(R)) if the holder's rights under the instruments no longer are linked to the holder's employment by the issuer. According to paragraph A231 of FAS-123(R) (ASC 718-10-35-13) those instruments should be accounted for under the measurement and recognition guidance in other applicable GAAP. Paragraphs A231 and A232 of FAS-123(R) (ASC 718-10-35-13, 14) and the related footnotes 123 and 124 provide guidance as to when an award no longer is linked to employment.

To determine whether a financial instrument should be classified as a liability or equity, examples of differences between the accounting in ASC 718 (FAS-123(R)) and that in other GAAP are discussed in paragraphs B119-B135 of FAS-123(R) (not included in the ASC). As a result of those differences, freestanding financial instruments initially accounted for as equity under the guidance in ASC 718 (FAS-123(R)) or as liabilities may be classified differently under other GAAP. Those differences may be related to practical exceptions in ASC 718 (FAS-123(R)), some of which have been carried over from the existing literature on stock compensation as interim guidance while the FASB continues its work on a project related to the distinction between liabilities and equity and the unique nature of the employee-employer relationship.

The requirement in ASC 718 (FAS-123(R)) that instruments no longer linked to employment be evaluated under other GAAP was based on the view that the recognition and measurement principles used to account for freestanding financial instruments should be the same regardless of how they were acquired by a holder.

Because the FASB's project considering the distinction between liabilities and equity could change other applicable GAAP significantly, the FASB decided to defer the requirement in ASC 718 (FAS-123(R)) that freestanding financial instruments no longer linked to a holder's employment be accounted for under the measurement and recognition principles of other applicable GAAP.

FASB STAFF POSITION

The recognition and measurement guidance in ASC 718 (FAS-123(R)) for freestanding financial instruments issued to employees in exchange for their past or future services that currently is being applied or that was applied to such instruments when ASC 718 (FAS-123(R)) was initially adopted should continue to apply for the life of those instruments, unless the instrument's terms are modified or a holder is no longer employed by the entity. Modifications should be accounted for in accordance with the guidance in paragraph A232 of FAS-123(R) (ASC 718-10-35-14). After an instrument has been modified, it should be accounted for in accordance with the recognition and measurement guidance of other applicable GAAP.

When the guidance in FSP FAS 123(R)-1 is applied, financial instruments issued, in whole or in part, as consideration for the delivery of goods or services, *not* employee services, should *not* be considered to have been issued in exchange for employee services regardless of whether the award's recipient was an employee on the grant date.

FSP FAS-123(R)-2 (Practical Accommodation to the Application of Grant Date as Defined in FASB Statement No. 123(R)) (ASC 718-10-25-5)

OVERVIEW

The *grant date* of a share-based payment award is defined in Appendix E of ASC 718 (FAS-123(R), Share-Based Payment) (revised 2004)) based on certain criteria, one of which is the concept that an employer and employee have a "mutual understanding" of a share-based payment award's most important terms. That concept was initially included in the definition of the grant date in FAS-123 (Accounting for Stock-Based Compensation).

In practice, an award's grant date is the date on which an award is approved in accordance with an entity's corporate governance provisions if the approved grant is communicated to the entity's employees within a short period of time after the award's approval. Communicating the key terms and conditions of an award to employees receiving share-based payments immediately after the board of directors' approval or the approval of management with the relevant authority may be difficult for many companies with large numbers of employees that are located in different geographic locations, because the companies prefer to communicate with their employees personally.

To address those concerns, the FASB believes that there should be a *practical* solution to the manner in which the concept of "mutual understanding" is applied. Because this solution is unique to the circumstances described, the concepts in this FSP should *not* be applied by analogy to other concepts in ASC 718 (FAS-123(R)) or other generally accepted accounting principles.

FASB STAFF POSITION

It is presumed that there is a mutual understanding of the key terms and conditions of an award made to an individual employee at the date an award is approved by the board of directors or management with the relevant authority if all the other criteria in the definition of the grant date *and* the following two conditions have been met:

1. The award was made unilaterally so that a recipient is *unable* to negotiate its key terms and conditions with the employer.

2. It is expected that the employer will communicate the award's key terms and conditions to the individual recipients within a short period of time from the date on which the award was approved (i.e., within a reasonable period of time in which an entity could communicate information about the awards to the recipients in accordance with the entity's customary human resource practices).

FSP FAS-123(R)-4 (Classification of Options and Similar Instruments Issued as Employee Compensation That Allow for Cash Settlement upon the Occurrence of a Event) (ASC 718-10-35-15)

OVERVIEW

The subject of this FSP is the classification of options and similar instruments issued to employees as compensation that can be settled in cash when a contingent event occurs. ASC 718-10-25-11 (paragraphs 32 and A229 of FAS-123(R), Share-Based Payment) (revised 2004) are amended by this FSP.

This issue was addressed because under some share-based payment plans, cash settlement of an option or similar instrument is required if a contingent event occurs. Settlement of an option in cash is required or permitted, at a holder's option, if the issuer has a change in control or another event affecting its liquidity occurs or if the holder dies or becomes disabled. Under APB-25 (Accounting for Stock Issued to Employees), as interpreted, an option or similar instrument would have been classified as a liability or as equity based on an assessment of the *probability* that an event requiring cash settlement, such as a change of control, would occur. Therefore, an option or similar instrument would have been classified as equity if it had been determined that occurrence of a contingent event was *not* probable *and not* under the employee's control. In contrast, under the guidance in ASC 718-10-25-11 (paragraphs 32 and A229 of FAS-123(R), options or similar instruments must be classified as liabilities if settlement in cash or other assets is required "under any circumstances." Because cash settlement of an entity's options or similar instruments issued as employee compensation *may* be required on the occurrence of a change in control, those instruments would have to be classified as liabilities under the guidance in ASC 718-10-25-11 (paragraphs 32 and A229 of FAS-123(R).

FASB STAFF POSITION

This FSP amends the guidance in ASC 718-10-25-11 (paragraphs 32 and A229 of FAS-123(R), to incorporate the notion that the conditions in those paragraphs would *not* be met until the occurrence of a contingent event requiring cash settlement that is *not* under an employee's control, such as an initial public offering, becomes *probable*.

An option or similar instrument should be accounted for as a modification from equity to a liability award if that instrument is reclassified from equity to a liability, because it becomes *probable* that an event requiring cash settlement will occur. On the date it becomes probable that a contingent event will occur, the issuer should:

- Recognize a share-based liability equal to the portion of the award attributed to past service (considering a provision, if any, for accelerated vesting) multiplied by the award's fair value on that date.
- Charge an offsetting debit to equity if the liability is equal to or less than the amount previously recognized in equity.
- Recognize compensation cost for an amount, if any, by which the liability exceeds the amount previously recognized in equity.

Total compensation cost recognized for an award that has a contingent cash settlement feature must be at least equal to the award's fair value at the grant date.

The accounting guidance in this FSP, which applies only to options or similar instruments issued in connection with employee compensation arrangements, should *not* be applied by analogy to instruments that are *not* related to employee share-based arrangements.

AMENDMENT OF ASC 718-10-25-11 (PARAGRAPHS 32 AND A229 OF FAS-123(R))

The following footnotes are being added to ASC 718-10-25-11 (paragraphs 32 and A229 of FAS-123(R)).

- "A cash settlement feature that can be exercised only upon the occurrence of a contingent event that is outside the employee's control (such as an initial public offering) would not meet condition (b) until it becomes probable that event will occur."
- "SEC registrants are required to consider the guidance in ASR 268. Under that guidance, options and similar instruments subject to mandatory redemption requirements or whose redemption is outside the control of the issuer are classified outside permanent equity."

SOP 93-6 (Employers' Accounting for Employee Stock Ownership Plans) (ASC 718-40-05-2 through 05-4; 15-2 through 15-4; 25-2 through 25-6, 25-9 through 25-17, 25-19, through 25-20 through 25-21; 30-1 through 30-5; 35-1; 40-2 through 40-7; 45-2 through 45-9; 50-1; 55-1 through 55-33)

BACKGROUND

An employee stock ownership plan (ESOP) is an employee benefit plan described by the Employee Retirement Income Security Act (ERISA) of 1974 and the Internal Revenue Code of 1986. An ESOP can be either a qualified stock bonus plan or a combination of a qualified stock bonus plan and a money purchase pension plan. In both cases, the ESOP is expected to invest primarily in stock of the sponsoring employer.

SOP 76-3, which was issued in December 1976, primarily provided accounting and reporting guidance for leveraged ESOPs. ASC 718-40 (SOP 93-6), which supersedes it, must be applied for ESOP shares acquired after December 30, 1992; at the company's discretion, it can be applied to ESOP shares acquired before December 31, 1992. Alternatively, SOP 76-3 can continue to be applied to ESOP shares acquired before December 31, 1992. A number of changes affecting ESOPs occurred between the release of SOP 76-3 and the issuance of SOP 93-6. For instance, Congress passed a number of laws affecting ESOPs, and numerous regulatory changes in this area have emanated from the Internal Revenue Service and from the U.S. Department of Labor. A number of these changes sparked a substantial growth in the number of ESOPs. Not only has the number of ESOPs grown, but also their complexity has increased. ESOPs are now formed for a number of different purposes:

- To fund a matching program for one or more employee benefit plans of the sponsor (e.g., 401(k) savings plan, formula-based profit-sharing plan)
- To raise new capital or to create a market for the existing stock
- To replace benefits lost from the termination of other employee benefit plans (e.g., retirement plans, other postretirement benefit plans)
- To help finance a leveraged buy-out
- To be used by owners to terminate their ownership interests in the entity on a tax-advantaged basis
- To be used as a deterrent against hostile takeovers

The financing of ESOPs also has changed significantly since SOP 76-3 was issued. When SOP 76-3 was issued, ESOP borrowing was typically from an outside lender. In today's environment, it is not unusual for an ESOP to be internally leveraged (the ESOP borrows from the employer sponsoring the ESOP, with or without an outside loan to the employer). In addition, some ESOPs use dividends on shares held by the ESOP largely to fund required debt payments. When SOP 76-3 was issued, most debt repayments were funded through employer contributions.

Finally, AcSEC issued SOP 93-6 to resolve some continuing controversies regarding the measurement of compensation cost and how dividends on shares held by the ESOP should be treated. These two issues had been problematic since the issuance of SOP 76-3.

STANDARDS

The conclusions in SOP 93-6 apply to all ESOPs, both leveraged and nonleveraged. SOP 93-6 provides guidance to the employer that sponsors the ESOP. Accounting guidance for the ESOP itself can be found in the AICPA Audit and Accounting Guide titled *Audits of Employee Benefit Plans* (see CCH's *GAAS Guide* for coverage of this AICPA Accounting and Auditing Guide).

The accounting for leveraged and nonleveraged ESOPs is discussed separately on the following pages. In addition, pension reversion ESOP and the disclosures required by SOP 93-6 are covered.

Accounting for Leveraged ESOPs

A leveraged ESOP borrows money to acquire shares of the employer sponsoring the ESOP. An ESOP may borrow either from the employer sponsor or directly from an outside lender. The shares acquired from the debt proceeds initially are held in a suspense account (i.e., they are not immediately allocated to the accounts of employees participating in the ESOP). The ESOP's debt is liquidated through (*a*) contributions of the employer to the ESOP and (*b*) dividends on the employer's stock held by the ESOP. As the ESOP's debt is repaid, shares are released from the suspense account. Released shares must be allocated to participants' accounts by the end of the ESOP's fiscal year.

Purchase of Shares

The ESOP may purchase either newly issued shares or treasury shares from the employer. The employer should record the issuance or sale of shares to the ESOP at the time it occurs, based on the fair value of its shares at that time. The offsetting debit is to unearned ESOP shares, a contra-equity account, which is to be shown as a separate line item on the employer's balance sheet.

In some cases, the ESOP may acquire shares of the employer through secondary market purchases. Even in this case, the employer should debit unearned ESOP shares for the cost of the shares purchased by the ESOP. If the ESOP is internally leveraged (i.e., the ESOP has borrowed from the employer), the offsetting credit recorded by the employer is to cash. If the ESOP is externally leveraged (i.e., the ESOP has borrowed directly from an outside lender), the offsetting credit recorded by the employer is to an appropriately titled debt account.

Illustration of Issuance of ESOP Shares as a Form of Employee Compensation

Pfeiffer, Bryant & Co. sponsors an ESOP for its employees. During the first quarter of 20X4, the employees of Pfeiffer, Bryant & Co. earn the right to receive 10,000 shares. The ESOP holds 25,000 shares of Pfeiffer Bryant's stock, acquired at an average cost of $20 per share. Pfeiffer Bryant's stock price was $22 at 1/1/X4, $29 at 3/31/X4, and was $25 on average during the first quarter of 20X4. Pfeiffer Bryant would record this transaction as follows:

Compensation cost (10,000 × $25)	$250,000	
Unearned ESOP shares (10,000 × $20)		$200,000
Additional paid-in capital		50,000

Release of ESOP Shares—General

ESOP shares are released for one or more of three purposes: (1) to compensate employees directly, (2) to settle a liability for other employee benefits, and (3) to replace dividends on allocated shares when these dividends are used to pay debt service.

The allocation of shares to employees typically is based on employee service. The number of shares to be released for each period (quarter or year) of employee service is usually specified in ESOP documents. As employees provide services, the release of ESOP shares is earned (hence they are committed to be released whether or not they have yet to be legally released). ESOP shares are legally released for distribution to participant accounts when debt payments are made.

When shares are committed to be released (which may occur before the shares are legally released), unearned ESOP shares should be credited for the cost of the shares to be released. The offsetting debit, which is based on the fair value of the shares, depends on the purpose for which the ESOP shares are being released. If the committed-to-be-released shares relate to employee compensation, the debit is to compensation cost. If the committed-to-be-released shares relate to the settlement of a liability for other employee benefits, the debit is to employee benefits payable. If the committed-to-be-released shares are to replace dividends on allocated shares, the debit is to dividends payable. Therefore, in most cases, the debit for committed-to-be-released shares, which is based on fair value, will differ from the credit for these same shares, which is based on cost. This difference is accounted for as a debit or credit to shareholders' equity, typically through the use of the additional paid-in capital account.

Release of ESOP Shares—Direct Compensation of Employees

As employees provide services over the accounting period (quarter or year), they ratably earn the right to receive ESOP shares. In essence, the commitment to release shares occurs ratably throughout the period. Therefore, compensation cost should be measured based on the average fair value of the stock over the relevant time period. Compensation cost recognized in previous interim periods should not be changed to reflect changes in the stock's fair value in later interim periods in the same fiscal year.

Release of ESOP Shares—Satisfaction of Other Employee Benefits

In some cases, an employer will settle its liability to provide other employee benefits by allocating shares of stock held by the ESOP to participant accounts. For example, some employers may allocate ESOP shares to satisfy a commitment to fund a 401(k) plan or a profit-sharing plan. The employer should recognize the expense and the liability for employee benefits (e.g., 401(k) contributions, profit-sharing contributions) in the same manner as if the ESOP was not used to fund the benefit. The employer should debit the liability account (for employee benefits) when ESOP shares are committed to be released to settle the liability. The number of shares to be released depends on the amount of the liability and the fair value of the ESOP shares at the time the liability is settled.

Release of ESOP Shares—Replacement of Dividends on Allocated Shares When Such Dividends Are Used to Service Debt

Dividends on shares of stock already allocated to participants' accounts can be used to service debt. However, if dividends on allocated shares are used in this manner, unallocated shares with a fair value equal to the dividends diverted must be allocated to participants' accounts.

When shares are committed to be released to replace the dividends on allocated shares used for debt service, the employer should debit dividends payable. In addition, only those dividends that pertain to shares already allocated are charged to retained earnings.

Determination of Fair Value

A number of the provisions of SOP 93-6 require the use of the fair value of the employer's stock. The fair value of such stock is the amount that would be received in a sale, in the normal course of business, between a willing buyer and a willing seller. If the stock is publicly traded, the market price of the stock is the best estimate of fair value. If the employer's stock is not publicly traded, the employer's best estimate of fair value should be used.

Dividends on Unallocated ESOP Shares

Dividends declared on unallocated ESOP shares are not charged against retained earnings by the employer. If dividends on unallocated shares are used for debt service, the employer debits debt and/or interest payable (the credit is to cash). In some cases, dividends on unallocated shares may be paid to participants or added to participants' accounts. In these cases, the offsetting debit is to compensation cost.

Dividends on Allocated ESOP Shares

Dividends declared on allocated ESOP shares are charged against retained earnings by the employer. The employer can satisfy its liability for the distribution of dividends in one of three ways: (1) by contributing cash to participant accounts; (2) by contributing additional shares, with a fair value equal to the amount of the dividends, to participant accounts; or (3) by releasing ESOP shares held in suspense, with a fair value equal to the amount of the dividends, to participant accounts.

Redemption of ESOP Shares

Employers are required to offer a put option to holders of ESOP shares that are not readily tradable (required for both leveraged and nonleveraged ESOPs). The employer is required to purchase the employee's stock at its fair value at the time the put option is exercised. The employer would record its purchase of the employee's stock in a manner identical to the purchase of treasury shares.

Reporting of Debt and Interest—General

The employer's accounting for ESOP-related debt and interest depends on the type of ESOP debt. The three types of ESOP-related debt can be described as follows:

1. *Direct loan*   The loan is from an outside lender to the ESOP.
2. *Indirect loan*   The loan is from the employer to the ESOP, and the employer borrows a comparable sum from an outside lender.
3. *Employer loan*   The loan is from the employer to the ESOP. There is no related outside borrowing by the employer.

Reporting of Debt and Interest—Direct Loan

The ESOP's liability to the lender should be recorded by the employer (in essence, the ESOP's debt is treated as the debt of the employer). In addition, accrued interest payable on the loan is recorded by the employer. Cash payments that the employer makes to the ESOP, which are to be used to service debt payments, are recorded as a reduction in the related debt and the accrued interest payable amounts. The employer should record the reduction in these two liability accounts when the ESOP remits a loan or interest payment to the lending institution. The source of the cash contribution from the employer to the ESOP does not affect this accounting treatment (i.e., the accounting treatment is as specified above, regardless of whether the source of cash is an employer contribution or dividends on ESOP stock).

Recording of Debt and Interest—Indirect Loan

Because the employer borrows from an outside lender, the employer obviously records this borrowing as a liability. In addition, in the case of an indirect loan, the ESOP has borrowed from the employer (typically an amount equal to what the employer has borrowed from an outside lender). Although the employer has a loan receivable from the ESOP, the employer does not recognize this asset in its financial statements. Because the employer does not record the loan receivable, the employer also does not recognize interest income. The employer may make a cash contribution to the ESOP for the purpose of funding the ESOP's debt repayments—concurrent payments from the ESOP back to the employer. Neither the cash contribution from the employer to the ESOP nor the concurrent debt repayment from the ESOP to the employer is recognized in the employer's financial statements.

Recording of Debt and Interest—Employer Loan

The employer has made a loan to the ESOP, and the employer has not borrowed a comparable amount from an unrelated lender. Although the employer has a note receivable, it is not recognized in the employer's financial statements. Therefore, interest income also is not recognized. (The ESOP's note payable and related interest cost also are not recognized in the employer's financial statements.)

Earnings per Share

Shares that are committed to be released are treated as outstanding in computing both basic and diluted EPS. Shares not committed to be released are not treated as outstanding in either computation.

ESOPs holding convertible preferred stock may encounter the following unique EPS issues (however, some complexity in this area has been reduced by the issuance of ASC 260-10 (FAS-128, Earnings per Share)):

- How to compute the number of shares outstanding for the application of the if-converted method
- How earnings applicable to common stock in if-converted computations should be adjusted for the effects of dividends on allocated shares used for debt service
- Whether prior periods' EPS should be restated for a change in the conversion ratio

Convertible preferred stock—Number of common shares outstanding The number of common shares that would be issued on conversion of preferred stock, where the convertible preferred stock is committed to be released, should be considered outstanding for the purpose of applying the if-converted method. This treatment applies to the computation of both basic and diluted EPS (assuming the effects are dilutive).

A participant's account balance may contain convertible preferred stock when it is withdrawn. The participant may be entitled to receive either (*a*) common stock or (*b*) cash with a value equal to (1) the fair value of convertible preferred stock or (2) a stated minimum value per share. The common stock that would have been issuable (upon conversion) may have a fair value that is less than the fair value of the convertible preferred stock or less than the stated minimum value per share. If this is the case, the participant will receive common stock or cash with a value greater than the fair value of the common stock that would have been issuable given the stated conversion rate. The presumption is that any shortfall will be made up by the issue of additional shares of common stock. However, this assumption can be overcome if past experience or a stated policy indicates that any shortfall will be paid in cash.

When the employee applies the if-converted method, the number of common shares issuable on assumed conversion is the greater of:

- The shares issuable at the stated conversion rate *or*
- The shares issuable if participants were to withdraw the convertible preferred shares from their accounts.

The shares issuable, if participants were to withdraw the convertible preferred shares from their accounts, are to be computed as the ratio of:

- The average fair value of the convertible stock or, if greater, its stated minimum value *to*
- The average fair value of the common stock.

Convertible preferred stock—Adjustment to earnings If employers use dividends on allocated shares to pay debt service, earnings applicable to common shares should be adjusted for the purpose of applying the if-converted method. Earnings applicable to common stock would be adjusted for the difference (net of tax) between:

- The amount of compensation cost reported *and*
- The amount of compensation cost that would have been reported if the allocated shares had been converted to common stock at the beginning of the period.

Convertible preferred stock—Changes in conversion rates Earnings per share for prior periods should not be restated for changes in conversion rates.

Accounting for income taxes Differences between book ESOP-related expense and the ESOP-related expense allowed for tax purposes may result from the following:

- The fair value of committed-to-be-released shares is different from the cost of these shares *and/or*
- The timing of expense recognition is different for book purposes than for tax purposes.

In either case, the guidance in ASC 740 (FAS-109, Accounting for Income Taxes) is to be followed. The tax effects of differences between book and tax reporting are to be recognized as a component of stockholders' equity (i.e., these differences do not give rise to deferred tax assets and liabilities).

If the cost of shares committed to be released exceeds their fair value, the expense deductible for tax purposes will exceed the book expense. The tax effect of this difference should be credited to stockholders' equity. If the cost of shares committed to be released is less than their fair value, the expense deductible for book purposes will exceed the expense deductible for tax purposes. The tax effect of this difference should be charged to stockholders' equity to the extent that prior credits to stockholder's equity that are related to cost exceeding the fair value of shares that were committed to be released in previous years.

Dividends paid on ESOP shares frequently result in a tax deduction. The tax-advantaged nature of ESOPs is a contributing factor behind their growth. The tax benefit of tax-deductible dividends on allocated ESOP shares is to be recorded as a reduction in income tax expense from continuing operations.

Accounting for terminations If an ESOP is terminated, either in whole or in part, all outstanding debt related to the shares terminated must be repaid or refinanced. The ESOP may repay the debt through one or more of the following sources:

- Employer contributions
- Dividends on ESOP shares
- Proceeds from selling suspense shares, either to the employer or to another party

The number of suspense shares the employer may purchase is limited. The employer can purchase only those shares that have a fair value equal to the applicable unpaid debt. Any shares that remain must be allocated to participants' accounts.

For example, if the ESOP sells suspense shares and uses the proceeds to repay the debt, the employer would account for this transaction as follows:

- Debit the book value of the debt and the accrued interest payable that relate to the shares being terminated.
- Credit unearned ESOP shares for the cost of the shares being terminated.
- Debit or credit any resulting difference to paid-in capital.

If the employer reacquires the suspense shares, the employer should account for the purchase in a manner similar to the purchase of treasury stock. The employer debits treasury stock based on the fair value of the suspense shares acquired (on the date the employer reacquires them). The employer credits unearned ESOP shares based on their cost. Any difference between the cost and the fair value of the suspense shares reacquired is assigned to paid-in capital.

If the fair value of the suspense shares on the termination date of the ESOP is greater than the ESOP's unpaid debt, the remaining suspense shares are released to participants. The release of these remaining suspense shares to participants is charged to compensation cost. The charge is equal to the fair value of the shares released to participants, determined as of the date the ESOP-related debt is extinguished.

Accounting for Nonleveraged ESOPs

A nonleveraged ESOP is less complex than a leveraged ESOP, and the accounting guidance on it is less complex and less voluminous. An employer contributes shares of its stock or cash to the ESOP for the benefit of employees. If the employer's contribution is cash, the ESOP uses the cash contribution to purchase employer securities. The employer shares that are donated or acquired by the ESOP may be outstanding shares, treasury shares, or newly issued shares. The shares held by the ESOP are allocated to participants' accounts; they are held by the ESOP and are distributed to employees at a future date (e.g., termination, and retirement). Shares obtained by the ESOP must be allocated to individual accounts by the ESOP's fiscal year-end.

Purchase of Shares

The employer records compensation cost based on the contribution that the terms of the plan require the employer make to the ESOP in the reporting period. Compensation cost includes the fair value of shares contributed, the fair value of shares committed to be contributed, cash contributed, and cash committed to be contributed.

Dividends

The employer should record a charge to retained earnings for dividends declared on shares held by a nonleveraged ESOP, with one exception to this requirement: Dividends on suspense account shares held by a pension reversion ESOP are to be accounted for in a manner similar to dividends on suspense account shares held by a leveraged ESOP.

Redemptions

As was the case with leveraged ESOPs, the employer is required to provide ESOP participants with put options if the employer shares held by the ESOP are not readily tradable. If a participant exercises his or her put option, the employer is to record the reacquisition of its stock from the participant in a manner similar to the purchase of treasury stock.

Earnings per Share

In general, all shares held by a nonleveraged ESOP are to be treated as outstanding by the employer in computing its EPS, with one exception: Suspense account shares of a pension reversion ESOP should not be treated as outstanding until they are committed to be released to participants' accounts.

Income Taxes

Compensation cost for financial reporting purposes may be accrued earlier than it is deductible for tax purposes, which creates a FAS-109 temporary difference.

Accounting for Pension Reversion ESOPs

An employer may terminate a defined benefit pension plan and recapture excess pension plan assets, although such a reversion of pension plan assets exposes the employer to an excise tax on the reversion of the pension assets. The employer may avoid some of the excise tax by transferring the pension assets to an ESOP (either new or existing, either leveraged or nonleveraged). The ESOP uses the (reverted) pension plan assets to acquire shares of the employer or to retire ESOP-related debt.

The ESOP may use the pension assets it receives to acquire shares of the employer. If the shares are acquired from the employer (either new shares or treasury shares), the employer would debit unearned ESOP shares (the offsetting credit is to common stock or treasury stock). If the shares are acquired on the secondary market, the employer would still debit unearned ESOP shares (the offsetting credit is to cash).

The ESOP may use the pension plan assets received on the reversion to repay debt. If this is the case, ESOP shares will be committed to be released from the suspense account. The guidance for leveraged ESOPs should be followed in determining the appropriate accounting. For instance, the employer will record the reduction in debt as it is repaid. The employer also will reduce the account "unearned ESOP shares" as these shares are committed to be released. How these committed-to-be-released shares are used determines the offsetting debit (see the earlier discussion on this issue for leveraged ESOPs).

Disclosures

An employer that sponsors an ESOP (both for leveraged and nonleveraged plans) is required to make the following disclosures:

1. A description of the ESOP, employee groups covered, the method of determining contributions, and the nature and effects of any significant changes that would affect comparability across periods
2. The accounting policies followed by the ESOP, which include the method of determining compensation, the classification of dividends on ESOP shares, and the treatment of ESOP shares for EPS computations
3. The amount of compensation cost for the period
4. As of the balance sheet date, the number of (*a*) allocated shares, (*b*) committed-to-be-released shares, and (*c*) suspense shares
5. As of the balance sheet date, the fair value of unearned ESOP shares
6. The existence and nature of any repurchase obligation (if such an obligation exists, the fair value of shares already allocated that are subject to the repurchase obligation)

Shares of an ESOP acquired before December 31, 1992, can continue to be accounted for under the provisions of SOP 76-3. For employers that elect to continue to account for these "old shares" under SOP 76-3, the disclosures required by items 2 and 4 above need to be made separately for shares accounted for under SOP 93-6 and SOP 76-3. Also, the fair value of unearned ESOP shares as of the balance sheet date (item 5) does not have to be disclosed for "old shares."

For leveraged and pension reversion ESOPs only, the following additional disclosures are required:

- The basis for releasing shares
- How dividends on allocated and unallocated shares are used

Examples

Appendix A of SOP 93-6 provides a number of detailed examples on the application of this Statement. Accounting is illustrated for the following types of ESOPs: (1) a common-stock leveraged ESOP with a direct loan, (2) a common-stock leveraged ESOP used to fund the employer's match of a 401(k) savings plan with an indirect loan, (3) a common-stock nonleveraged ESOP, (4) a convertible-preferred-stock leveraged ESOP with a direct loan, and (5) a convertible, preferred stock, leveraged ESOP used to fund a 401(k) savings plan with an employer loan. Appendix A of SOP 93-6 also presents an example of an ESOP termination and of the required ESOP note disclosures. The first illustration that follows is a simplified example of the accounting for a common-stock leveraged ESOP with a direct loan; the second illustration is for a common-stock nonleveraged ESOP.

Illustration of a Common-Stock Leveraged ESOP with a Direct Loan

Neal and Neel (N&N) established a common-stock leveraged ESOP with a direct loan on January 1, 20X4. Relevant information regarding the ESOP is as follows:

1. The ESOP borrows $2,500,000 from an outside lender at 8% for four years. The proceeds are used to purchase 50,000 shares of newly issued N&N stock that has a market value of $50 per share.
2. The ESOP will fund the debt service with cash contributions from N&N and with dividends on the employer stock it holds.
3. Dividends on all shares of stock held by the ESOP, allocated and unallocated, are used for debt service.
4. N&N makes cash contributions to the ESOP at the end of each year.
5. The average market price of N&N's common stock during each year is as follows: 20X4, $54; 20X5, $47; 20X6, $56; 20X7, $60.
6. At the end of each quarter, N&N pays dividends of $.50 per share on its common stock. Therefore, dividends on ESOP shares are $100,000 per year (50,000 shares × $.50 dividend per share per quarter × 4 quarters per year). Because dividends on allocated shares are used for debt service, N&N must provide the ESOP with additional shares of common stock. The number of additional shares of common stock required is determined by dividing the dividends on allocated shares by the average market price of N&N's stock.
7. Both principal and interest payments on the ESOP's debt are due in equal annual installments at the end of each year. Yearly debt service is as follows:

Table 1—Debt Service

Year	Principal	Interest	Total Debt Service
20X4	$ 554,802	$ 200,000	$ 754,802
20X5	599,186	155,616	754,802
20X6	647,121	107,681	754,802
20X7	698,891	55,911	754,802
Total	$2,500,000	$ 519,208	$3,019,208

8. The number of shares of N&N stock released to participants' accounts each year is as follows:

Table 2—Shares Released for Compensation and Dividends

Year	Dividends	Compensation	Total
20X4	0	12,500	12,500
20X5	532	11,968	12,500
20X6	893	11,607	12,500
20X7	1250	11,250	12,500

The number of shares released for dividends is determined by dividing the amount of dividends on allocated shares (which are being used for debt service) by the average market price of the common stock during the year in question. For example, in the year 20X5, 12,500 shares of common stock were allocated (see Table 3 below). Dividends on these 12,500 shares are $25,000 (12,500 shares × $2 per year). Dividing $25,000 by $47 (the average market price of N&N's common stock during 20X5) results in the issuance of 532 shares during 20X5 to replace the dividends on allocated shares used for debt service. In this example, the remaining shares are released as compensation to ESOP participants.

9. Shares released and allocated are based on total debt service payments made during the year (both principal and interest). Because 25% of debt service payments are made in each year, 25% of the shares (12,500) are released each year. Shares released in a particular year are allocated to participants' accounts during the next year. See Table 3.

Table 3—Shares Released and Allocated

Year	Cumulative Number of Shares Released	Cumulative Number of Shares Allocated	Average Shares Released	Year-End Suspense Shares
20X4	12,500	0	6,250	37,500
20X5	25,000	12,500	18,750	25,000
20X6	37,500	25,000	31,250	12,500
20X7	50,000	37,500	43,750	0

10. N&N's income before giving effect to the ESOP is as follows: 20X4, $2,600,000; 20X5, $2,800,000; 20X6, $3,100,000; 20X7, $3,200,000.
11. All interest cost and compensation cost are charged to expense each year.
12. Excluding ESOP shares, the weighted average equivalent number of shares outstanding is 2,000,000 each year.
13. N&N's combined statutory tax rate is 36% each year.
14. The only book/tax difference is that associated with the ESOP.
15. No valuation allowance is necessary for any deferred tax asset.

The following tables and journal entries illustrate the results of applying SOP 93-6.

Table 4—Summary of the Effects of Applying SOP 93-6

Year	Principal	Unearned ESOP Shares	Paid-In Capital	Dividends	Interest Expense	Compensation Expense	Cash
Notes:	(1)	(2)	(3)	(4)	(1)	(5)	(6)
20X4	$ 554,802	$ (625,000)	$ (50,000)	$ 0	$200,000	$ 675,000	$ (754,802)
20X5	599,186	(625,000)	37,500	25,000	155,616	562,496	(754,802)
20X6	647,121	(625,000)	(75,000)	50,000	107,681	649,992	(754,802)
20X7	698,891	(625,000)	(125,000)	75,000	55,911	675,000	(754,802)
Total	$2,500,000	$(2,500,000)	$(212,500)	$150,000	$519,208	$2,562,488	$(3,019,208)

Notes:

(1) Principal paid and interest expense from Table 1.

(2) The credit to unearned ESOP shares is calculated by multiplying the number of ESOP shares released each year (12,500) by the cost of these shares to the ESOP ($50 per share).

(3) The debit or credit to paid-in capital is computed by multiplying the number of ESOP shares released each year (12,500) by the difference between the average market price per share (for the particular year) and the cost per share ($50). For example, in 20X4 this calculation resulted in a $50,000 credit [($54 − $50) × 12,500].

(4) The dividend amount is calculated by multiplying the cumulative number of shares allocated (see Table 3) by the dividend per share, $2 per year.

(5) Compensation expense is computed by multiplying the number of shares released for compensation (see Table 2) by the average market price per share (for the particular year).

(6) The cash disbursed each year comprises a yearly contribution of $654,802 and $100,000 of dividends. Also note that this amount equals the yearly debt service.

Table 5—Tax Computations

	20X4	20X5	20X6	20X7
Current provision:				
Income before ESOP	$2,600,000	$2,800,000	$3,100,000	$3,200,000
ESOP contribution	(654,802)	(654,802)	(654,802)	(654,802)
ESOP dividends	(100,000)	(100,000)	(100,000)	(100,000)
Taxable income	$1,845,198	$2,045,198	$2,345,198	$2,445,198
Multiplied by 36%	664,271	736,271	844,271	880,271
Deferred provision:				
Reduction in unearned ESOP shares for financial reporting	$625,000	$625,000	$625,000	$625,000
Related tax deduction (1)	554,802	599,186	647,121	698,891
Difference	$(70,198)	$(25,814)	$22,121	$73,891
Tax rate	36%	36%	36%	36%
Deferred tax expense (benefit)	$(25,271)	$(9,293)	$7,964	$26,601

Notes:

(1) The tax deduction in computing the deferred income tax provision is equal to the amount of the principal repayment.

Table 6—Reconciliation of Effective Tax Rate to Provision for Income Taxes

	20X4	20X5	20X6	20X7
Pretax income (1)	$1,725,000	$2,081,888	$2,342,327	$2,469,089
Tax at 36% (statutory rate)	621,000	749,480	843,238	888,872
Benefit of ESOP dividends (2)	0	(9,000)	(18,000)	(27,000)
Effect of difference between average fair value and cost of released shares (3)	18,000	—	13,500 (4)	45,000
Provision as reported	$ 639,000	$ 740,480	$ 838,738	$ 906,872

Notes:

(1) See Table 7 for the computation of the pretax income.

(2) Computed by multiplying the yearly ESOP dividend amount (see Table 4) by the statutory tax rate, 36%.

(3) Computed by multiplying the number of shares released during the year (12,500 each year) by the difference between the average market value during the year and the cost of the ESOP shares and then multiplying this amount by the statutory tax rate. This computation is as follows for 20X4: [12,500 × ($54 − $50) × 36%]. This

amount cannot be negative; therefore, this amount is zero during any year in which the cost of the ESOP shares exceeds the average market value during the year (e.g., year 20X5).

(4) Computed as explained in item 3 minus the excess cost of the ESOP shares released in year 20X5 over their fair value multiplied by the tax rate. The entire computation is [(($56 − $50) × 12,500) × 36%] − [(($50 − $47) × 12,500) × 36%].

Table 7—Tax and EPS Computations

	20X4	20X5	20X6	20X7
Income before ESOP	$2,600,000	$2,800,000	$3,100,000	$3,200,000
Interest expense	(200,000)	(155,616)	(107,681)	(55,911)
Compensation expense	(675,000)	(562,496)	(649,992)	(675,000)
Pretax income	$1,725,000	$2,081,888	$2,342,327	$2,469,089
Provision for income tax:				
Currently payable	$ 664,271	$ 736,273	$ 844,271	$ 880,271
Deferred	(25,271)	(9,293)	7,964	26,601
Shareholders' equity (1)	0	13,500	(13,500)	0
Total	$ 639,000	$ 740,480	$ 838,735	$ 906,872
Net income	$1,086,000	$1,341,408	$1,503,592	$1,562,217
Average shares outstanding (2)	2,006,250	2,018,750	2,031,250	2,043,750
Earnings per share	$ 0.54	$ 0.66	$ 0.74	$ 0.76

Notes:

(1) Calculated by multiplying the shares released during the year (12,500) by the excess of ESOP cost over the average market value of the stock ($50 − $47) and then multiplying this amount by the statutory tax rate (36%). This amount reverses in full in 20X6 since the fair value of the N&N stock in that year, $56, is more than $3 above the cost of N&N's stock to the ESOP, $50.

(2) Calculated by adding the cumulative average number of shares released in each year (see Table 3) to the weighted average number of common shares otherwise outstanding.

Journal Entries

January 1, 20X4 (Date N&N Establishes the ESOP)

Cash	$2,500,000	
Debt		$2,500,000

[To record the ESOP loan]

Unearned ESOP shares (contra-equity)	$2,500,000	
Common stock and paid-in capital		$2,500,000

[To record the issuance of 50,000 shares to the ESOP at $50 per share—the fair value of the stock at the time it is issued]

December 31, 20X4

Interest expense	$200,000	
Accrued interest payable		$200,000

[To record interest expense]

Accrued interest payable	$200,000	
Debt	554,802	
Cash		$754,802

[To record the debt payment. The cash disbursement consists of $100,000 of dividends (none of which is charged to retained earnings in 20X4, because none of the shares has yet to be allocated) and $654,802 of additional employer contributions to the ESOP.]

Compensation expense	$675,000	
Paid-in capital		$ 50,000
Unearned ESOP shares		625,000

[To record release of 12,500 shares at average fair value of $54. The ESOP's cost is $50.]

Deferred tax asset	$ 25,271	
Provision for income taxes	639,000	
Income taxes payable		$664,271

[To record income taxes for 20X4; see Tables 5-7 for the computations of these amounts]

December 31, 20X5

Interest expense	$155,616	
Accrued interest payable		$155,616

[To record interest expense]

Accrued interest payable	$155,616	
Debt	599,186	
Cash		$754,802

[To record the debt payment. The cash disbursement consists of $100,000 of dividends ($25,000 of which is charged to retained earnings in 20X5 (see Table 4)) and $654,802 of additional employer contributions to the ESOP.]

Retained earnings	$25,000	
Dividends payable		$25,000

[To record declaration of a $2.00-per-share dividend on 12,500 allocated shares]

Compensation expense	$562,500*	
Dividends payable	25,000	
Paid-in capital	$ 37,500	
Unearned ESOP shares		$625,000

38.48 *Stock-Based Payments*

[To record the release of 12,500 shares (11,968 for compensation and 532 for dividends) at an average fair value of $47 per share. The per-share cost is $50.]

*$4 rounding difference

Deferred tax asset	$ 9,293	
Provision for income taxes	740,480	
Paid-in capital		$ 13,500
Income taxes payable		736,273

[To record income taxes for the year 20X5; see Tables 5-7 for the computations of these amounts.]

December 31, 20X6

Interest expense	$107,681	
Accrued interest payable		$107,681

[To record interest expense]

Accrued interest payable	$107,681	
Debt	647,121	
Cash		$754,802

[To record the debt payment. The cash disbursement consists of $100,000 of dividends ($50,000 of which is charged to retained earnings in 20X6 (see Table 4)) and $654,802 of additional employer contributions to the ESOP.]

Retained earnings	$50,000	
Dividends payable		$50,000

[To record declaration of a $2.00-per-share dividend on 25,000 allocated shares]

Compensation expense	$650,000*	
Dividends payable	50,000	
Paid-in capital		$75,000
Unearned ESOP shares		625,000

[To record the release of 12,500 shares (11,607 for compensation and 893 for dividends) at an average fair value of $56 per share. The per-share cost is $50.]

*$8 rounding difference

Provision for income taxes	$838,735	
Paid-in capital	13,500	
Deferred income taxes		$ 7,964
Income taxes payable		844,271

[To record income taxes for 20X6; see Tables 5-7 for the computations of these amounts.]

December 31, 20X7

Interest expense	$55,911	
Accrued interest payable		$55,911

[To record interest expense]

Accrued interest payable	$ 55,911	
Debt	698,891	
Cash		$754,802

[To record the debt payment. The cash disbursement consists of $100,000 of dividends ($75,000 of which is charged to retained earnings in 20X7 (see Table 4)) and $654,802 of additional employer contributions to the ESOP.]

Retained earnings	$75,000	
Dividends payable		$75,000

[To record declaration of a $2.00-per-share dividend on 37,500 allocated shares]

Compensation expense	$675,000	
Dividends payable	75,000	
Paid-in capital		$125,000
Unearned ESOP shares		625,000

[To record the release of 12,500 shares (11,250 for compensation and 1,250 for dividends) at an average fair value of $60 per share. The per-share cost is $50.]

Provision for income taxes	$906,872	
Deferred income taxes		$ 26,601
Income taxes payable		880,271

[To record income taxes for 2002; see Tables 5-7 for the computations of these amounts]

Illustration of a Common-Stock Nonleveraged ESOP

Melton, Inc. established a common-stock nonleveraged ESOP on January 1, 20X4. Melton is to contribute 15% of its pretax profit before ESOP-related charges as of the end of each of the next four years. The ESOP will use this contribution to purchase newly issued shares at the current market price (the year-end price, since contributions to the ESOP are made at year-end). Melton's stock price at December 31 of each year is as follows: 20X4, $52; 20X5, $49; 20X6, $54; 20X7, $63. With the exception of these new facts, all of the relevant facts are identical to the assumptions used in the previous illustration. The following table and journal entries illustrate the results of applying SOP 93-6.

38.50 Stock-Based Payments

Table 1—Summary of the Effects of Applying SOP 93-6

Year	Compensation Expense	Dividends	Number of ESOP Shares Purchased	Cumulative ESOP Shares
Notes:	(1)	(2)	(3)	(4)
20X4	$390,000	$ —	7,500	7,500
20X5	420,000	15,000	8,571	16,071
20X6	465,000	32,142	8,611	24,682
20X7	480,000	49,364	7,619	32,301

Notes:

(1) Compensation expense is equal to pretax profit before ESOP-related charges multiplied by 15%.

(2) Dividends are equal to cumulative ESOP shares, as of the beginning of the year, multiplied by the annual dividend per share, $2.

(3) The number of ESOP shares purchased is computed by dividing the yearly employer contribution (i.e., compensation expense) by the year-end market price of Melton's common stock. For example, in 20X4, 7,500 shares are purchased ($390,000/$52 per share).

(4) Cumulative ESOP shares are shares held at the beginning of the year plus shares purchased during the year.

Journal Entries

December 31, 20X4

Compensation expense	$390,000	
Common stock and paid-in capital		$390,000

[To record Melton's contribution, the sale of shares to the ESOP, and compensation expense]

Provision for income taxes	$795,600	
Income taxes payable		$795,600

[To record income taxes at 36% on taxable income of $2,210,000 ($2,600,000 of pre-ESOP income less $390,000 of compensation expense)]

December 31, 20X5

Compensation expense	$420,000	
Retained earnings	15,000	
Common stock and paid-in capital		$420,000
Dividends payable		15,000

[To record Melton's contribution, the sale of shares to the ESOP, declaration of dividends, and compensation expense]

Dividends payable	$15,000	
Cash		$15,000

[To record the payment of dividends]

Provision for income taxes	$856,800	
Income taxes payable		$856,800

[To record income taxes at 36% on taxable income of $2,380,000 ($2,800,000 of pre-ESOP income less $420,000 of compensation expense)]

December 31, 20X6

Compensation expense	$465,000	
Retained earnings	32,142	
Common stock and paid-in capital		$465,000
Dividends payable		32,142

[To record Melton's contribution, the sale of shares to the ESOP, declaration of dividends, and compensation expense]

Dividends payable	$32,142	
Cash		$32,142

[To record the payment of dividends]

Provision for income taxes	$948,600	
Income taxes payable		$948,600

[To record income taxes at 36% on taxable income of $2,635,000 ($3,100,000 of pre-ESOP income less $465,000 of compensation expense)]

December 31, 20X7

Compensation expense	$480,000	
Retained earnings	49,364	
Common stock and paid-in capital		$480,000
Dividends payable		49,364

[To record Melton's contribution, the sale of shares to the ESOP, declaration of dividends, and compensation expense]

Dividends payable	$49,364	
Cash		$49,364

[To record the payment of dividends]

Provision for income taxes	$979,200	
Income taxes payable		$979,200

[To record income taxes at 36% on taxable income of $2,720,000 ($3,200,000 of pre-ESOP income less $480,000 of compensation expense)]

FTB 97-1 (Accounting under Statement 123 for Certain Employee Stock Purchase Plans with a Look-Back Option) (ASC 718-50-30-1 through 30-3; 35-1 through 35-2; 55-2 through 55-9, 55-22 through 55-33)

> **NOTE:** ASC 718 (FAS-123(R), Share-Based Payment) (revised 2004) amends the guidance in FAS-123 (Accounting for Stock-Based Compensation) and supersedes the guidance in APB-25 (Accounting for Stock Issued to Employers).

BACKGROUND

ASC 718 (FAS-123(R), Stock Based Payment) states that the objective of the fair value method of accounting for stock-based compensation is to estimate the fair value of the equity instrument—based on the stock price and other measurement assumptions at the grant date—that is issued in exchange for employee services. This objective also applies to the fair value measurement of grants under a compensatory employee stock purchase plan (ESPP), and is the basis for Illustration 19 of FAS-123(R)).

A *look-back option* is a feature that provides the employee a choice of purchasing stock at two or more times (e.g., an option to purchase stock at 85% of the stock price at the grant date or at a later exercise date). Section 423 of the Internal Revenue Code provides that the employee will not be immediately taxed on the difference between the fair value of the stock and a discounted purchase price if the following requirements are met:

- The option price is not less than 85% of the market price when the option is granted or when the option is exercised.
- The choice does not have a term in excess of 27 months.

The criteria for evaluating whether an ESPP qualifies for noncompensatory treatment are established in ASC 718-50-25-1 (paragraph 12 of FAS-123(R)); if it does, the employer is not required to recognize compensation expense. If an ESPP satisfies *all* of the following criteria, the discount from market price to the employee is not stock-based compensation and simply reduces the proceeds from issuing the shares of stock:

- The plan incorporates no option features.
- The discount from the market prices does not exceed the greater of (*a*) a per-share discount that would be reasonable in an offer of stock to stockholders or others or (*b*) the per-share amount of stock issuance costs avoided by not having to raise a significant amount of capital by a public offering of the stock.
- Substantially all full-time employees meeting limited employment qualifications may participate on an equitable basis.

A look-back option is one feature that causes an ESPP to be considered compensatory. In reaching this conclusion, the FASB observed that a look-back option can have substantial value, because it enables the employee to purchase the stock for an amount that *could be* significantly less than the fair value at the date of purchase. A look-back option is not an essential element of a plan aimed at promoting broad employee stock ownership; a purchase discount also provides incentive for participation. Based on these observations, the FASB concluded that broad-based plans that contain look-back options cannot be treated as noncompensatory.

> **OBSERVATION:** A look-back option in an employee stock purchase plan (ESPP) is treated differently under the guidance FAS-123(R) than under APB-25. An ESPP with a look-back option is treated as compensatory under the guidance in FAS-123.

STANDARDS

FTB 97-1 responds to three questions concerning how Illustration 19 of ASC 718 (FAS-123(R)) applies to the different types of ESPP plans with look-back options described above. Following are a recap of Illustration 19 of FAS-123(R)) and an analysis of the three questions and the FASB's response.

Illustration of Look-Back Option without Dividends

On January 1, 2004, Company S offered employees the opportunity to purchase its stock at either 85% of the current price ($50) or 85% of the price at the end of the year when the options expire. For purposes of valuing the option, expected volatility is assumed to be .30, and the risk-free interest rate for the next 12 months is 6.8%.

The value of this look-back option can be estimated at the grant date by combining its two components, as follows:

1. 15% of a share of nonvested stock
2. 85% of a 1-year call option held with an exercise price of $50

The option holder will receive value of at least 15% of a share of stock upon exercise, regardless of the stock price after the grant date. In this example, the stock price is $50 when the grant is made. If the price falls to $40 and the option is exercised at that price, the holder pays $34 ($40 × .85) and receives value of $6, which is 15% of the market price at the date of exercise. On the other hand, if the market price increases to $60, the holder can purchase stock at only $42.50 ($50 × .85) and receive value of $17.50 ($60 − $42.50).

Using an option-pricing model to value the look-back option under the stated assumptions (e.g., .30 expected volatility and 6.8% risk-free interest rate) results in the following:

15% of a share of nonvested stock ($50 × .15)	$ 7.50
Call on 85% of a share of stock with an exercise price of $50 ($7.56 × .85)	6.43
Total grant date value	$13.93

This calculation is based on the idea that the value of the look-back option consists of two components: (1) the 15% reduction from a $50 market value ($7.50) and (2) 85% of a call option with an exercise price of $50. The $7.56 figure in the second component is the value of the call option as computed by an option-pricing model.

Illustration of Look-Back Option with Dividends

This example assumes the same facts as in the previous case, except that Company S pays a 2.5% annual dividend quarterly (i.e., .625% per quarter). Calculation of the value of the look-back option is similar to the calculation in the previous illustration, except that the components are *reduced to reflect the dividends that the holder of the option does not receive* during the term of the option. The value of the two components of the option is calculated as follows:

15% of a share of nonvested stock ($50 × .15 × .9754)	$ 7.32
Call on 85% of a share of stock, $50 exercise price, 2.5% dividend yield ($6.78 × .85)	5.76
Total grant date value	$13.08

The first component is the minimum benefit to the holder, regardless of the price of the stock at the exercise date. The second component is the additional benefit to the holder if the stock price exceeds $50 at the exercise date. The $6.78 in the second component is the value of the call option as computed by an option-pricing model.

FTB 97-1 Questions and Answers

Question 1: Illustration 19 of ASC 718 FAS-123(R)) provides the only specific guidance on measuring the compensation cost associated with an award under a compensatory ESPP with a look-back option. Is the fair value measurement technique described in that illustration applicable to all types of ESPPs with a look-back option?

Answer: No. The measurement approach in ASC 718 (FAS-123(R)), Illustration 19, was intended to illustrate how the fair value of an award under a basic type of ESPP with a look-back option could be determined at the grant date by focusing on the substance of the arrangement and valuing each feature of the award separately. The fundamental components of a look-back option may differ from plan to plan, affecting the individual calculations. For example, the illustration in ASC 718 (FAS-123(R)) assumes that the number of shares that may be purchased is fixed at the grant date based on the grant date stock price and the amount the employee elects to have withheld (Type A plan). Some plans (e.g., Type B plans) do not fix the number of shares that the employee is permitted to purchase, requiring modification to the determination of fair value.

Question 2: How should the Illustration 19 measurement approach be modified to determine the fair value of an ESPP award plan with a Type B look-back option (i.e., the plan does *not* fix the number of shares that an employee is permitted to purchase)?

Answer: In a Type A plan, the number of shares an employee is permitted to purchase is limited to the number based on the price of the stock at the origin of the agreement. For example, if an employee had $4,250 withheld from salary, and the plan permitted him or her to purchase shares at 85% of the $50 current stock price, he or she could purchase 100 shares, as follows:

$$\$4{,}250/(85\% \times \$50) = 100 \text{ shares}$$

In a Type B plan, the employee is permitted to purchase as many shares as the $4,250 withheld will permit. If, for example, the market price falls to $30, the employee is not limited to purchasing 100 shares and may actually purchase 167 shares, determined as follows:

$$\$4{,}250/(85\% \times \$30) = 167 \text{ shares}$$

Following the ASC 718 (FAS-123(R)), Illustration 19, approach of combining the components of the plan, and using the same underlying assumptions as in that illustration, the value of the Type B option is calculated at the grant date as follows:

15% of a share of nonvested stock ($50 × 15%)	$ 7.50
One-year call on 85% of a share of stock, exercise price of $50 ($7.56 × 85%)	6.43
One-year put on 15% of a share of stock, exercise price of $50 ($4.27 × 15%)	.64
	$14.57

This Illustration is the same as that presented earlier (the "no dividend" case) with the addition of a third component: a one-year put option on the employer's stock, valued with a standard option-pricing model. The same assumptions are applied. This has the effect of adding $.64 to the value of the option, raising the total to $14.57 ($7.50 + $6.43 + $.64).

Total compensation is measured at the grant date based on the number of shares that can be purchased using the total withholdings and the grant date market price, rather than on the potentially greater number of shares that may be purchased if the market price falls. For example, in the above Illustration, an employee who had $1,275 withheld could purchase 30 shares based on the grant date price [$1,275/($50 × .85)], and total compensation expense recognized for that employee would be $437 (30 × $14.57).

Question 3: The characteristics of Type A and Type B plans are incorporated into other types of ESPP plans with a look-back option. The measurement approach in ASC 718 (Illustration 19 of FAS-123(R)) for a Type A plan, as modified by Question 2 of FTB 97-1 for a Type B plan, forms the basis for determining the fair value of the award under the other types of ESPP with a look-back option. What additional modifications are necessary to determine the fair value of awards under other types of ESPPs?

Answer: The fair value of an award under an ESPP plan with a look-back option with multiple purchase periods (Type C plan) should be determined in the same manner as an award under a graded vesting stock option plan. Such awards under a two-year plan with purchase periods at the end of each year would be valued as having two separate options, both starting with the initial grant date and having different lives (12 and 24 months, respectively).

This same approach should be used to value ESPP awards with multiple purchase periods that incorporate reset or rollover mechanisms (Type D and Type E plans). At the date the reset or rollover mechanism becomes effective, the terms of the award have been modified. This is, in substance, an exchange of the original award for a new award with different terms. Similarly, an election by an employee to increase withholdings (Types F, G, and H plans) is a modification of the terms of the award, which is similar to an exchange of the original award for a new award with different terms.

The guidance in ASC 718 (FAS-123(R)) indicates that a modification of the terms of an award that makes it more valuable should be treated as an exchange of the original award for a new award. In substance, the employer repurchases the original instrument by issuing a new instrument of greater value and incurs additional compensation cost for that incremental value.

A Type I plan permits an employee to increase withholdings retroactively. An employee may elect not to participate, or to participate at a minimal level, until just before the exercise date. This makes it difficult to determine when there is a mutual understanding of the terms of the award and, thus, when the grant date actually occurs. In this situation, the later date when the employee remits an amount to the company should be considered the grant date for purposes of valuing the option.

Changes in compensation resulting from salary increases, commissions, or bonus payments are not plan modifications and do not represent changes in the terms of the plan. The only incremental compensation cost is that which results from the additional shares that may be purchased with the additional amounts withheld.

EITF Issue 00-16 (Recognition and Measurement of Employer Payroll Taxes on Employee Stock-Based Compensation) (ASC 718-10-25-22)

OVERVIEW

As a result of the increased use of employee stock options as a means of compensating employees and the rapid growth of the market value of stock in certain sectors of the economy, the significance of payroll taxes incurred by employers on employee stock-based compensation is increasing. Under the guidance in ASC 718-10-25-23 (Topic D-83, Accounting for Payroll Taxes Associated with Stock Option Exercises), employers are required to recognize an expense for payroll taxes incurred in connection with stock-based compensation. There is no guidance, however, on when the employer should recognize that expense. Currently, employers recognize a cost when an event, such an employee's exercise of a stock option, results in a payment to the taxing authority. Some question whether the timing of cost recognition for an employer's payroll taxes on stock-based compensation under the guidance in ASC 718 (FAS-123(R)) is appropriate.

ACCOUNTING ISSUE

When should an employer recognize a liability and the corresponding cost for employer payroll taxes on employee stock-based compensation?

EITF CONSENSUS

Employers should recognize a liability for payroll taxes on an employee's stock-based compensation on the date that the measurement and payment of the tax to the taxing authority is triggered. For example, in the case of a nonqualified option in the United States, a liability would generally be recognized on the exercise date.

EITF Issue 09-J: Effect of Denominating the Exercise Price of a Share-Based Payment Award in the Currency of the Market in Which the Underlying Equity Security Trades (ASC 718-10-25-14A; 65-02) (ASU 2010-13)

OVERVIEW

Guidance on the classification of share-based payment awards as equity or a liability is provided in ASC 718, *Compensation—Stock Compensation*. The exercise price of employee stock options granted by a public company to its employees is usually denominated in the currency in which the underlying equity securities trade. Such awards are usually classified in equity. However, ASC 718-10-25-13 provides that if an award is indexed to a factor that is "not a market, performance, or service condition, the award should be classified as a liability...."

Share-based awards of public companies that regularly raise capital in a country other than their home country and whose securities trade on an exchange in that foreign country frequently are denominated in the foreign country's functional currency, which may differ from the issuer's functional currency, the functional currency of the subsidiary that has issued the share-based payment awards, or the currency in which the employees receiving the awards are paid. Under the guidance in ASC 718-10-25-13, if an award is indexed "to a factor in addition to the entity's share price" and that "additional factor is not a market, performance, or service condition, the award shall be classified as a liability." Because there is no guidance in ASC 718 regarding which currency is considered the "ordinary" currency of a share-based payment award that qualifies for classification in equity, some believe that it is the issuer's functional currency, while others believe that it is the functional currency of the country in which the shares are traded. Therefore, the question has been raised whether awards denominated in the currency of the market in which the underlying equity security trades should be classified as equity or as liability awards.

SCOPE

The guidance in this Issue applies to share-based payment awards accounted for under the scope of ASC 718.

EITF CONSENSUS

The EITF reaffirmed as a consensus the following consensus-for-exposure positions reached at its November 19, 2009 meeting:

- Equity treatment of an employee share-based payment award is appropriate if an award is denominated in the currency of a market in which a substantial portion of the entity's equity securities are traded and all of the other criteria for classification in equity have been met
- An employee share-based payment award denominated in a currency other than the functional currency of the foreign operation or in the currency in which the employee is paid should *not* be classified in equity because it contains a condition that is *not* a market, performance, or service condition. Such an award should be accounted for as a liability.

EFFECTIVE DATE AND TRANSITION

The EITF reached a consensus that the guidance in this Issue should be effective for fiscal years, and interim periods within those years, beginning on or after December 15, 2010. The guidance in Issue 09-J should be applied through a cumulative effect adjustment to the opening balance of retained earnings for all awards that are outstanding as of the beginning of the fiscal year in which the guidance is initially applied.

Early adoption of the guidance is permitted. An entity that elects early adoption in a fiscal period other than the first reporting period of the entity's fiscal year is required to apply the guidance *retrospectively* from the beginning of its fiscal year. Presentation of the transition disclosures in ASC 250, *Accounting Changes and Error Corrections* (250-10-50-1 through 50-3) is required.

FASB RATIFICATION

The FASB ratified the EITF's consensus positions at its March 31, 2010 meeting.

Topic D-83 (Accounting for Payroll Taxes Associated with Stock Option Exercises) (ASC 718-10-25-3)

The FASB staff has been asked to clarify the accounting for payroll taxes paid by an employer under the Federal Insurance Contributions Act (FICA) and Medicare taxes that the employer pays when an employee exercises stock options.

The FASB staff believes that because the difference between the exercise price paid by an employee and the fair value of the acquired stock on the exercise date is treated as if it were compensation paid to the employee, payroll taxes on those amounts should be recognized as operating expenses and included in the income statement. This announcement should be applied prospectively for stock options exercised after September 23, 1999.

Topic D-110 (Escrowed Share Arrangements and the Presumption of Compensation) (ASC 718-10-S25-1; S99-2; 505-50-S25-3)

As a result of requests for clarification of the SEC staff's position regarding the presumption that escrowed share arrangements represent compensation for certain shareholders, the SEC Staff Observer made the following announcement regarding such arrangements at the EITF's June 18, 2009, meeting.

Sometimes when an entity has an initial public offering or enters into another transaction to raise capital, some of the entity's shareholders may agree to put a portion of their shares in escrow. An escrowed share arrangement can occur between a company and its shareholders or between the shareholders and new investors. Under the terms of some escrowed share arrangements, the shares are released back to the shareholders only if specified criteria related to performance are met.

In the past, the SEC staff has held the view that there is a presumption that an escrowed share arrangement that involves the release of shares to certain shareholders when those shareholders have met certain criteria related to performance is compensatory and that it is like a reverse stock split under which shareholders subsequently receive a restricted stock award under a plan based on performance.

To determine whether the presumption of compensation has been overcome, a registrant should consider the substance of an arrangement and whether a shareholder has entered into the arrangement for a purpose that is not related to, or contingent on, continued employment. For example, as a condition of a financing transaction, an investor may request that specific shareholders who own a significant portion of an entity's shares and who also may be the entity's officers or directors participate in an escrowed share arrangement. Under those circumstances, if the shares are released or cancelled, regardless of whether a shareholder's employment will continue, the facts and circumstances may indicate that the arrangement was entered into by the shareholders to make the financing transaction possible and *not* for the purpose of compensation. The SEC staff believes that if the presumption that an escrow arrangement is compensatory has been overcome based on the facts and circumstances, the arrangement should be recognized and measured based on its nature and accounted for as a reduction of proceeds allocated to newly issued securities.

The SEC staff also believes that consistent with the principle stated in ASC 805-10-55-25 (paragraph A87 of FAS-141(R), if shares in an escrowed share arrangement are automatically forfeited on the termination of employment of a participant in the arrangement, such an arrangement is considered to be compensatory.

ASC 815 Derivatives and Hedging

EITF Issue 02-8 (Accounting for Options Granted to Employees in Unrestricted, Publicly Traded Shares of an Unrelated Entity) (ASC 815-10-45-10; 55-46 through 55-48)

OVERVIEW

This Issue addresses how an employer that grants to its employees stock option awards in the publicly traded shares of an unrelated entity should account for those awards.

ACCOUNTING ISSUE

How should an employer account for stock option awards issued to employees in unrestricted, publicly traded shares of an unrelated entity?

EITF CONSENSUS

The EITF reached the following consensus positions:

- Option awards granted to employees in the stock of an unrelated entity that require employees to remain employed for a specified time period and specify the exercise price meet the definition of a derivative in ASC 815 (FAS-133) that should be accounted for at its fair value at inception. Subsequent changes in the derivative's fair value should be included in determining net income. The options should continue to be accounted for as a derivative after the award has vested.
- Before an award has vested, an employer should present changes in an option award's fair value as *compensation* expense in the income statement.
- After an award has vested, an employer may present changes in an option award's fair value elsewhere in the income statement.

Grandfathered Pronouncements

SOP 76-3 (Accounting Practices for Certain Employee Stock Ownership Plans)

BACKGROUND

An employee stock ownership plan (ESOP) is an employee benefit plan sponsored under the provisions of the Employee Retirement Income Security Act (ERISA) of 1974. An ESOP can be either a qualified stock bonus plan or a combination of a qualified stock bonus plan and a money purchase pension plan. In both cases, the ESOP is expected to invest primarily in "qualifying employer securities."

At the time SOP 76-3 was issued, there were two essential differences between an ESOP and other qualified stock bonus plans. First, the ESOP generally is permitted to borrow money for the purpose of purchasing the employer's stock. Second, the allowable investment tax credit percentage that the employer can claim may increase by as much as 1.5% if that amount is contributed to the ESOP.

In borrowing money for the purpose of purchasing the employer's stock, the ESOP typically borrows from a bank or another commercial lender. The employer shares purchased can be outstanding shares, treasury shares, or newly issued shares. The ESOP holds these shares until they are distributed to employees. The shares may be allocated to individual employees even though the actual shares may not be distributed until a later date. In some cases, the ESOP issues notes to existing shareholders in exchange for their stock.

The employer typically collateralizes the ESOP debt by pledging the stock (purchased from the debt proceeds), and by either guaranteeing or committing to make ESOP contributions sufficient to service the related debt. The employer's annual contribution to the ESOP is tax-deductible (subject to certain limitations). The employer's annual contribution is used to fund (1) amortization of the debt principal, (2) interest payments on the debt, (3) working capital needs, and (4) other expenses. If the employer's annual ESOP contribution exceeds items 1 through 4, the excess can be used to purchase additional employer securities.

SOP 76-3 was issued because several accounting questions arose relating to ESOPs that borrowed money from a bank or other lender to acquire shares, or that issued notes directly to existing shareholders in exchange for their shares.

STANDARDS

The provisions of SOP 76-3 were largely superseded by SOP 93-6 (Employers' Accounting for Employee Stock Ownership Plans). However, shares acquired by an ESOP before December 31, 1992, or shares acquired after that date that were committed to be released before the beginning of the year in which SOP 93-6 was adopted, can continue to be accounted for under the guidance in SOP 76-3.

If the employer has either guaranteed or committed to funding the ESOP in a manner sufficient to cover debt service payments, the related debt (i.e., obligation of the ESOP) is to be recorded as a liability on the employer's balance sheet. AcSEC concluded that the employer's guarantee or commitment was in substance the assumption of the ESOP's debt; as such, the related debt amount should be shown as a liability in the employer's financial statements.

The offsetting debit that the employer records upon recognizing a liability for the ESOP's debt is to shareholders' equity. The employer does not recognize the assets of the ESOP; employees of the ESOP—not the employer—own these assets.

As the ESOP makes payments on its debt, the employer is to reduce its liability. As the employer reduces its liability, the offsetting credit is to shareholders' equity. Symmetry should exist between the liability for ESOP-related debt and the corresponding entry to shareholders' equity.

The annual ESOP contribution (or contribution commitment) that the employer makes is recognized as an expense. This requirement applies to all ESOPs—whether the ESOP has borrowed money from a bank or another lender or has issued a note directly to existing shareholders for their shares. The employer's contribution or contribution commitment is recognized in the year it was made, regardless of whether such contribution is concurrently used to reduce the ESOP's debt.

The expense is to be divided between interest expense and compensation expense, and the employer should disclose the interest rate and terms of the ESOP's debt in its financial statements (since SOP 76-3 essentially views such debt as that of the employer).

The employer should treat all shares held by the ESOP as outstanding for the purpose of calculating the employer's EPS (whether or not the shares have been allocated to individual employees). The employer should charge all dividends pertaining to shares held by the ESOP to retained earnings.

If the employer receives any additional investment tax credit (ITC) as a result of an ESOP contribution, such incremental ITC is to be recorded as a reduction in income tax expense in the year that the applicable ESOP contribution is made. This accounting treatment applies, regardless of the method generally utilized by the employer in accounting for the ITC (flow-through or deferral) for property acquisitions.

EITF Issue 89-8 (Expense Recognition for Employee Stock Ownership Plans)

> **Note:** SOP 93-6 supersedes SOP 76-3 and nullifies the consensus positions in this Issue. However, under the SOP's transition provisions, employers that elect not to apply SOP 93-6 to shares purchased before December 31, 1992, can continue to apply the provisions of SOP 76-3 and applicable EITF consensus positions to those shares.

OVERVIEW

An employer may establish a leveraged employee stock ownership plan (ESOP) to benefit its employees by granting them shares of its stock. The employer also realizes tax benefits on its contributions to the ESOP.

A leveraged ESOP is established by forming a trust that borrows money to acquire shares of the employer's stock, which are restricted to common stock and convertible preferred stock. Usually, the ESOP borrows from a financial institution and pledges the stock as security. Alternatively, the employer may borrow from a financial institution, and, in turn, lend the money to the trust to purchase the employer's stock. When the employer recognizes the ESOP debt as a liability, an equivalent amount is recognized as a debit in shareholders' equity, similar to unearned compensation, as discussed in paragraph 14 of APB-25. In both cases, the debt is serviced with proceeds from employer contributions to the ESOP and dividends on unallocated shares of the employer's stock. As payments are made on the debt, shares are released and allocated to employees' individual accounts, and the debit in shareholders' equity is reduced. The amount of shares to be released and allocated to employees is based on a percentage of the total number of shares the ESOP purchased. The percentage may be determined in one of two ways:

1. The ratio of principal and interest paid in the current period to the total principal and interest to be paid.
2. The ratio of principal paid in the current period to the total debt principal.

SOP 76-3 was the primary source of guidance when this Issue was discussed. It viewed a leveraged ESOP as a deferred compensation plan and provided that annual expense be based on the amount contributed or committed to be contributed for the year. Because the structure of ESOPs had changed since the issuance of the SOP in 1976, the guidance on expense recognition needed to be updated. Specifically, because loan repayment terms had changed, loan repayments on ESOPs were not always level over the term of the loan, with some repayment schedules tied to an employer's expected cash flow or compensation costs. Other repayment schedules required only interest payments in early years, with principal payments delayed for a number of years, or otherwise had nonlevel repayment terms. Some debt agreements permitted voluntary prepayments or required prepayments if the employer's cash flow exceeded certain amounts. Some questioned whether such changes in repayment terms should affect an employer's expense recognition for contributions to a plan.

ACCOUNTING ISSUE

How should an employer recognize expense for contributions to an ESOP?

EITF CONSENSUS

1. Expense recognition for contributions to an ESOP should be as follows for shares acquired after December 14, 1989:
    a. Recognize contributions to an ESOP as expense in accordance with the shares-allocated method, discussed below, for shares with level and nonlevel repayment terms. Under the shares allocated method, interest expense is recognized each period as incurred. Expense related to the principal

portion (the compensation element) is recognized based on the cost of shares allocated for the period. It is computed as follows:

$$\frac{\text{Shares allocated for the period}}{\text{Total shares purchased}} \times \text{Original principal}$$

$$+ \text{ Interest incurred for the period} = \frac{\text{Expense related}}{\text{to the principal}}$$

    b. Reduce compensation expense recognized each period by dividends used to service the ESOP debt.

2. Expense recognition for contributions to an existing ESOP for shares acquired before December 15, 1989, should be as follows:

    a. The current method may continue to be used if cumulative expense, before dividends are deducted, is at least equal to 80% of cumulative expense under the shares-allocated method before dividends are deducted.

    b. Recognize an additional amount in the current period if cumulative expense under the current method is less than 80% of cumulative expense under the shares-allocated method (total cumulative expense should equal 80% of expense under the shares-allocated method).

    c. Expense recognition should not be reduced if the cumulative amount under the current method exceeds 80% of the amount under the shares-allocated method.

3. Report the effect of initial application of this consensus as a cumulative effect of a change in accounting principle, in accordance with APB-20.

4. Adjust the debit in shareholders' equity related to the ESOP loan for the difference between the periodic expense and cash contributions, if any, in each period.

SEC OBSERVER COMMENT

The SEC Observer stated that SEC registrants should fully disclose their method of accounting for ESOPs in accordance with the pension plan disclosure requirements in paragraph 65 of FAS-87. Accordingly, the following information should be disclosed:

- A description of the plan, including employee groups covered
- The basis for determining contributions
- The nature and effect of significant matters affecting comparability of information for all periods presented
- The cost of contributions to the ESOP recognized during the period

In addition, the SEC staff expects the following information to be disclosed for each period presented:

- Actual interest incurred on ESOP debt
- Amount contributed to the ESOP
- Amount of dividends paid by the ESOP on shares held by the ESOP for ESOP debt service

The SEC Observer suggested that registrants consider the need to discuss the potential effect of leveraged ESOPs in the results of operations and liquidity sections of "Management's Discussion and Analysis of Financial Condition and Results of Operations," as required by Item 303 of Regulation S-K. An example is a large scheduled increase in contributions to an ESOP.

At a meeting subsequent to the issuance of SOP 93-6, the SEC Observer stated that the above disclosure requirements should continue to be made by registrants for shares grandfathered from the accounting provisions of that SOP.

DISCUSSION

The Task Force believed that the shares-allocated method is consistent with the guidance in paragraph 9 of SOP 76-3, which required the employer's expense to be the amount contributed or committed to be contributed to the ESOP for the year. (The employer is committed to the extent that interest is accrued and shares are allocated.) Task Force members noted that if shares are allocated based on principal, expense recognition is the same whether the cash payments or shares-allocated methods are used.

The Task Force noted that sometimes the debt payments, the allocation of related shares to participants, and the period over which participants earned those shares may not occur in the same reporting period. If this is the case, the employer may have to accrue or defer compensation expense recognition. The cost of shares should be recognized in the period in which they were earned, regardless of whether debt payments were made in that period. However, expense recognition for prepaid debt should not be deferred for more than one period. Accruals and deferrals should be consistent. Interest should be charged as incurred.

EITF Issue 89-12 (Earnings-per-Share Issues Related to Convertible Preferred Stock Held by an Employee Stock Ownership Plan)

Note: SOP 93-6 supersedes SOP 76-3 and nullifies the consensus positions in this Issue. However, under the SOP's transition provisions, employers that elect not to apply SOP 93-6 to shares purchased *before* December 31, 1992, can continue to apply the provisions of SOP 76-3 and applicable EITF consensus positions to those shares.

OVERVIEW

An employer sponsoring an ESOP issues high-yield convertible preferred stock to the ESOP, which finances that purchase with debt. The ESOP repays the debt by using the dividends from the convertible preferred stock and the employer's contributions. In accordance with the guidance in SOP 76-3, the employer charges such dividends to retained earnings.

The employer may redeem the convertible preferred stock in common stock, cash, or a combination of both at a redemption price that equal's the stock's initial value. Each share may be converted into a fixed number of shares of common stock. The employer also may guarantee ESOP participants that on retirement or termination they will receive at least the redemption price in common stock, cash, or a combination of both.

ACCOUNTING ISSUES

The EITF discussed the following issues related to the calculation of EPS under the if-converted method:

1. Should convertible preferred shares issued to an ESOP be considered common stock equivalents?
2. Should net income be reduced by the additional ESOP contribution that would be necessary to meet the debt service requirement if the preferred stock is assumed to be converted, thus eliminating the availability of dividends on the convertible preferred stock?
3. If the employer guarantees that participants will receive at least the redemption price of the preferred stock on retirement or termination, should the number of shares assumed to be outstanding be increased, and if so, to what extent, if the market price of the underlying common stock is less than the redemption price of the preferred stock?
4. What would be the effect on the answer in Issue 3 if the redemption price guarantee can be paid in cash?

EITF CONSENSUS

The EITF reached the following consensus positions, which apply regardless of how the convertible stock is classified in the employer's balance sheet. (Publicly held companies must classify convertible shares as temporary equity. In addition, the if-converted method should not be applied if it is antidilutive.)

1. FAS-128 nullified the consensus in Issue 1.

2. If the preferred stock is assumed to be converted, dividends on those shares would no longer be paid and the ESOP would receive only dividends on the common stock into which the shares were converted. As a result, the employer would have to make an additional contribution to the ESOP for debt service. The employer should therefore adjust net income for the difference between the current dividends on the convertible preferred stock and the dividends on the common stock considered outstanding under the if-converted method.

   EITF members noted that under the provisions of some employee benefit plans, an employer may be required to make other nondiscretionary adjustments related to the conversion of preferred stock and the additional ESOP contribution.

3. The calculation of EPS in paragraph 63 of APB-15 and FAS-128, which requires using the market price at the end of the reporting period to determine the number of shares to be issued, applies if the market price of the underlying common stock is less than the guaranteed value of the convertible stock. The number of common shares to be used in calculating EPS under the if-converted method is the sum of the following: for unallocated shares—the number of common shares based on the stated conversion, *plus* for allocated shares—the number of common shares equivalent to the redemption value, but not less than the number of shares at the stated conversion rate for convertible preferred stock allocated as of the reporting date. As required in paragraph 63 APB 15, EPS for prior periods should be restated if the number of shares issued or contingently issuable changes as a result of changes in the market price.

4. An employer that is required or has the ability and intent to satisfy a guarantee in cash should use the stated conversion rate for all shares in calculating EPS; the employer need not assume the issuance of additional shares for the guarantee feature.

   OBSERVATION: The disclosure requirements in FIN-45 (Guarantor's Accounting and Disclosure Requirements for Guarantees, Including Indirect Guarantees of Indebtedness to Others) apply to guarantees of the value of the preferred stock by employers that continue to apply the guidance in SOP 76-3 to shares acquired before January 1, 1993. The other provisions of FIN-45 do *not* affect the consensuses in this Issue.

SEC OBSERVER COMMENT

The SEC Observer noted that registrants should not analogize these consensus positions to other situations involving the calculation of EPS. In addition, registrants should apply the consensus positions retroactively to EPS calculations for all periods presented in SEC filings subsequent to the consensus. Although the SEC staff would accept the calculations required in the consensus, the SEC staff will deal with unusual situations based on the specific case.

FASB STAFF COMMENT

The FASB staff stated that consensus positions 2, 3, and 4 apply to basic (referred to as "primary" when this Issue was discussed) and diluted EPS calculations if the convertible preferred stock is a common stock equivalent.

DISCUSSION

Issue 2 In computing diluted EPS under the provisions of APB-15 (and FAS-128) a convertible security is assumed to have been converted at the beginning of the period, thus requiring appropriate adjustments to net income. In the case of convertible preferred stock held by an ESOP, if it is assumed that the stock has been converted to common stock, the ESOP will receive dividends on the common stock, but dividends from preferred shares would no longer be available to the ESOP for debt service. Consequently, the employer's contribution for debt service would increase to compensate for a potential deficiency resulting from the difference between dividends on the preferred stock and on the common stock. To illustrate, assume that an ESOP has an annual debt service requirement of $2,000,000, and dividends on the employer's preferred stock held by the ESOP are $1,000,000. The employer would thus contribute $1,000,000 for debt service. However, if it is assumed that (a) the ESOP converts the preferred stock, (b) dividends from the common stock are only $600,000, and (c) there is no change in the debt service requirement, the employer would have to increase the debt service contribution by $400,000 to make up the deficiency.

The EITF's consensus was based on the view that regardless of the source of the proceeds (i.e., whether from dividends on the preferred stock or from an additional employer contribution), the ESOP made debt service payments during the year. Because dividends on the preferred stock would not have been available during the year—as a result of the assumed conversion of the preferred stock at the beginning of the year—it is assumed that the deficiency between the higher dividends on the preferred stock and the dividends on the common stock into which it is converted is made up by an additional employer contribution, which is considered a nondiscretionary adjustment to net income in accordance with paragraph 51 of APB-15.

Issue 3 Sometimes an ESOP that invests in the employer's convertible securities guarantees that the value the employee would receive at the time of conversion would not be less than a specified amount per share of preferred stock. To illustrate, assume the following: A preferred stock that is convertible into common stock on a one-for-one basis has a guarantee that the employee would receive at least

38.70 Stock-Based Payments

$12 for each share of preferred stock at the date of conversion. If an employee converts 100 shares of preferred stock when the fair value of the common stock is more than $12 per share, the employee would receive 100 shares of common stock. If, however, the common stock's fair value is less than the $12 per share guaranteed minimum value, the employee would receive additional shares or cash so that the total value received is equal to the guaranteed amount. For example, at $10 per share, the employee would receive 120 shares of common stock, 100 shares of common stock plus $200, or a combination of common stock and cash worth $1,200.

The following illustrates the EITF's consensus on Issue 3. An ESOP holds 100,000 shares of convertible preferred stock, of which 60,000 shares are allocated to participants and 40,000 shares are unallocated. One share of preferred stock is convertible into two shares of common stock, and participants are guaranteed a market value of common stock equivalent to $10 per preferred share. On December 31, 1989, the market price per share of common stock is $4. The number of shares to be included in diluted EPS is calculated as follows:

Unallocated shares:		
40,000 shares × 2		80,000
Allocated shares:		
Guaranteed value (60,000 shares × $10)	$600,000	
Market price per share	$ 4	
Shares required to satisfy guarantee ($600,000/$4)	150,000	
Shares based on conversion rate (60,000 shares × 2)	120,000	
Shares used:		150,000
		230,000

Issue 4 The consensus reached by the Task Force analogized to the guidance in paragraph 6 of FIN-31, which dealt with whether stock appreciation rights that are payable in stock or in cash should be considered common stock equivalents. Under the Interpretation, the decision was made based on "the terms most likely to be elected based on the facts available each period." FAS-128 carried forward that guidance but provides that it should be presumed that settlement will be in common stock. The potential common shares would, therefore, be included in diluted EPS. The presumption that the rights will be paid in stock may be overcome based on past experience and on the company's stated policy that the rights will be paid partially or wholly in cash. Similarly, this consensus depends on the requirement or the employer's ability and expressed intent to satisfy the guarantee in cash.

EITF Issue 92-3 (Earnings-per-Share Treatment of Tax Benefits for Dividends on Unallocated Stock Held by an Employee Stock Ownership Plan (Consideration of the Implications of FASB Statement No. 109 on Issue 2 of EITF Issue No. 90-4))

Note: SOP 93-6 supersedes SOP 76-3 and nullifies the consensus positions in this Issue. However, under the SOP's transition provisions, employers that elect not to apply SOP 93-6 to shares purchased *before* December 31, 1992, can continue to apply the provisions of SOP 76-3 and applicable EITF consensus positions to those shares.

OVERVIEW

Under current federal income tax laws, an employer that sponsors an employee stock ownership plan (ESOP) is entitled to deduct dividends on stock held by the ESOP in computing the employer's corporate taxable income. When this Issue was discussed in March 1992, FAS-109 had just been issued but its application was not required until 1993. Consequently, companies were accounting for income taxes based on the guidance in APB-11, FAS-96, or had early adopted FAS-109. Under paragraph 37 of FAS-109 (ASC 740-20-45-3), tax benefits related to dividends on unallocated ESOP shares must be credited directly to retained earnings. That requirement is similar to the requirement in APB-11, except that APB-11 does not distinguish between allocated and unallocated shares. FAS-96 required recognizing the benefit as a reduction of income tax expense.

ACCOUNTING ISSUES

- In computing EPS, should entities applying the provisions of FAS-109 adjust net income for tax benefits related to dividends on unallocated common stock held by an ESOP?
- Should the same treatment apply to convertible preferred stock ESOPs when computing EPS under the if-converted method?

EITF CONSENSUS

- In computing EPS, companies applying FAS-109 should not adjust net income for tax benefits related to dividends on unallocated common stock held by an ESOP, because under FAS-109, tax benefits on such shares must be charged to retained earnings.
- The same treatment applies to convertible preferred stock ESOPs in computing EPS under the if-converted method.

DISCUSSION

The Task Force's consensus positions on this Issue were based on the view that the amount used in EPS computations should be consistent with the calculation of net income based on the provisions of FAS-109.

This consensus was nullified by SOP 93-6 for shares acquired by an ESOP *after* December 31, 1992.

Authoritative Guidance Not Included Separately in the Codification but Incorporated with Other Guidance on the Same Subject

FAS-123(R)-5 (Amendment of FASB Staff Position 123(R)-1)

OVERVIEW

Entities that offer stock-based compensation to employees are required to account for such arrangements under the guidance in FAS-123(R) (Share-Based Payment). When it was initially issued, FAS-123(R) provided that rights conveyed by freestanding instruments issued under those arrangements should be *excluded* from the scope of FAS-123(R) if a holder's rights under the instruments no longer are linked to the holder's employment by the issuer. Paragraph A231 of FAS-123(R) (ASC 718-10-35-13) provided that those instruments should be accounted for under the measurement and recognition guidance in *other* applicable GAAP. Paragraphs A231 and A232 of FAS-123(R) (ASC 718-10-35-13, 14) and the related footnotes 123 and 124 provided guidance as to when an award no longer is linked to employment.

To determine whether a financial instrument should be classified as a liability or as equity, examples of differences between the accounting in FAS-123(R) and that in other GAAP are discussed in paragraphs B119–B135 of FAS-123(R). As a result of those differences, freestanding financial instruments initially accounted for under the guidance in FAS-123(R) as equity or as liabilities may be classified differently under other GAAP. Those differences may be related to practical exceptions in FAS-123(R), some of which were carried over from the existing literature on stock compensation as interim guidance while the FASB continued its work on a project related to the distinction between liabilities and equity, and the unique nature of the employee-employer relationship.

The requirement in FAS-123(R) that instruments no longer linked to employment be evaluated under *other* GAAP was based on the view that the recognition and measurement principles used to account for freestanding financial instruments should be the same regardless of how they were acquired by a holder. Because the FASB's project, considering the distinction between liabilities and equity might change other applicable GAAP significantly, the FASB decided to defer indefinitely the application of the guidance in paragraph A231 of FAS-123(R) (ASC 718-10-35-13), which requires that freestanding financial instruments no longer linked to a holder's employment be accounted for under the measurement and recognition principles of other applicable GAAP.

Consequently, FAS-123(R) was amended by FSP FAS-123(R)-1 to provide that the Statement's recognition and measurement guidance for freestanding financial instruments issued to employees in exchange for their past or future services be applied to such instruments when FAS-123(R) was initially adopted should continue to apply for the *life* of those instruments, unless an instrument's terms are *modified* when a holder no longer is employed by the entity. Such modifications must be accounted for in accordance with the guidance in paragraph A232 of FAS-123(R) (ASC 718-10-35-14). After an instrument has been modified, it should be accounted for in accordance with the recognition and measurement guidance of *other* applicable GAAP.

Paragraph 53 of FAS-123(R) (ASC 718-20-35-6) provides that "Exchanges of share options or other equity instruments or changes to their terms in conjunction with an equity restructuring or a business combination are modifications for purposes of this Statement." However, since the issuance of FSP FAS-123(R)-1, the FASB staff has been asked whether guidance in *other* applicable GAAP, such as EITF Issue 00-19 (Accounting for Derivative Financial Instruments Indexed to, and Potentially Settled in, a Company's Own Stock) would apply to an instrument whose holder no longer is employed by an entity if that entity (*a*) has executed an equity restructuring, or (*b*) has modified or exchanged share-based payment awards in a business combination.

FASB STAFF POSITION

Entities should *continue* to apply the recognition and measurement guidance in FAS-123(R) to instruments originally issued as employee compensation awards to holders who are no longer employed by the issuer at the time of an award's modification if the award's terms have been modified only for the purpose of indicating that an equity restructuring has occurred and the following two conditions are met:

1. The fair value of the awards to the holders has *not* increased or the ratio of the awards' intrinsic value to the exercise price has been maintained so that the holder is made whole, or an antidilution provision added to an award's terms was *not* added in contemplation of an equity restructuring; and

38.74 *Stock-Based Payments*

2. All holders of the same class of equity instruments, such as stock options, are treated the same.

Paragraph 5 of FSP FAS-123(R)-1 (ASC 718-10-35-10) is amended by that guidance noting that only for the purpose of this FSP, a modification is *not* considered to be a change in an award's terms. Other modifications to an award that occur after a holder has left an issuer's employment should be accounted for under the guidance in paragraph A232 of FAS-123(R) (ASC 718-10-35-14).

FAS-123(R)-6 (Technical Corrections of FASB Statement No. 123(R))

INTRODUCTION

The purpose of this FSP is to make the following technical corrections to the guidance in FAS-123(R) (Share-Based Payment):

- Paragraph A240(d)(1) (ASC 718-10-50-2) is amended to exempt nonpublic entities from the requirement to disclose the total intrinsic value of outstanding fully vested share options, share units, and share options expected to vest;
- Paragraph A102 (ASC 718-20-55-32) of Illustration 4(b) is amended to revise the calculation of the minimum compensation cost that should be recognized to comply with the guidance in paragraph 42 of the Statement (ASC 718-10-35-8);
- Paragraph A170 (ASC 718-10-55-121) of Illustration 13(e) is amended to specify that previously recognized compensation cost, if any, should have been reversed at the date that it was no longer probable that the awards in the illustration would vest; and
- Paragraph E1 (ASC, *Glossary*) is amended to exclude an offer to settle an award from the definition of *short-term inducement*.

BACKGROUND

Disclosure Requirements for Nonpublic Entities

Although under the guidance in paragraph A240(d)(2) of FAS-123(R) (ASC 718-10-50-2) nonpublic entities are specifically exempted from the requirement to disclose the total intrinsic value of share options or share units that can be currently exercised or converted, under the guidance in paragraph A240(d)(1) (ASC 718-10-50-2), those entities are *not* exempted from the requirement to disclose the total intrinsic value of outstanding fully vested share options or units and share options *expected* to vest. As a result, a nonpublic entity would have to determine the *fair value* of its equity at each reporting period.

Amendment of Illustration 4(b)

Under the existing guidance in paragraph 42 of FAS-123(R) (ASC 718-10-35-8), compensation cost for awards with *graded* vesting based only on service may be recognized using one of the following alternative methods:

- On a straight-line basis over the required service period for individual portions of an award, each of which would have a separate vesting period (i.e., as if there were multiple awards [graded vesting]); or
- On a straight-line basis over the required service period for the total award.

Nevertheless, the amount of compensation cost recognized at any date is conditional on a minimum amount that equals the portion of an award's value at the grant date that is vested at that date.

Illustration 4(b) is an example of the accounting for an award with *graded* vesting, including the minimum amount of compensation cost that must be recognized if an entity uses the straight-line method and has determined a specific value for each separate portion of an award that vests. That is, the value per share option changes for each year of vesting.

The example in paragraph A102 (ASC 718-20-55-32) is intended to illustrate how to calculate the minimum amount of compensation cost at the vesting date, as required in paragraph 42 (ASC 718-10-35-8), when calculating compensation cost on a straight-line basis over the required service period for the total award. Because one of the assumptions used in Illustration 4(b) is changed in the example in paragraph A102 (ASC 718-20-55-32), the calculation in that paragraph is inconsistent with the guidance in paragraph 42 (ASC 718-10-35-8) because (1) it does *not* consider that the *total* value of an award changes if the vesting schedule is front loaded; and (2) it is implied that an average value is used per award based on the award's total value, even though the total compensation cost in the example in Illustration 4(b) was calculated based on a different value for each separate portion of the award that vested on different dates.

According to the guidance in footnote 86 to paragraph 102A, an award may be valued using a single weighted-average expected life resulting in a single value for the total award being attributed on a straight-line basis over the required service period for (1) each portion of an award that vests separately as if there were multiple awards or (2) the total award.

Amendment of Illustration 13(e)

Illustration 13(e) in Appendix A of FAS-123(R) is an example of a Type III modification in which the probability that the original vesting conditions will be satisfied changes from probable to improbable. It is assumed in the example that until an entity decides to close a plant in which all of the award holders are employed, it is probable that an award will vest. Because on the date on which an entity decides to close a plant it is no longer probable that the awards will vest, previously recognized compensation cost should be reversed. However, it is implied in the illustration that the reversal should occur on the date on which an award is modified to accelerate its vesting terms. According to the guidance in paragraph A170 (ASC 718-20-55-121), the original award's service condition is *not* expected to be satisfied at the modification date (June 30, 2008) because the employees cannot meet the service requirement. As a result, compensation cost, if any, recognized as of the modification date for the original award would be reversed at that date.

Amendment of the Definition of Short-Term Inducement

The phrase *or settlement of an award*, which is included in the definition of "short-term inducement" in Appendix E of FAS-123(R), raises a question regarding the interaction of the accounting guidance for short-term inducement in paragraph 52 of the Statement (ASC 718-20-35-5) and that for a settlement of an award under the guidance in paragraph 55 of the Statement (ASC 718-20-35-7). If an entity offers for a limited time period to repurchase a vested equity award for cash, at fair value or at an amount that exceeds fair value, under the guidance in paragraph 55 (ASC 718-20-35-7), the fair value of the equity instrument at the date on which an employee accepts the offer (acceptance date) would be charged to equity. If the repurchase price exceeds the equity instrument's fair value on the acceptance date, the excess would be recognized as additional compensation cost. On the other hand, an offer to repurchase an award for cash that is considered to be a short-term inducement based on the definition in Appendix E would be accounted for as a modification for those that accept the offer.

It was not the FASB's intent that a short-term inducement considered to be a settlement should affect the award's classification for the period it remains outstanding, for example, that an award should be changed from an equity instrument to a liability instrument. Consequently, the definition of a short-term inducement should not include an offer to repurchase an award for a limited time period and should not be accounted for as a modification under the guidance in paragraph 52 of FAS-123(R) (ASC 718-20-35-5). Nevertheless, an entity that has a history of settling its awards in cash, should consider at the inception of an award whether it has a substantive liability in accordance with the guidance in paragraph 34 of FAS-123(R) (ASC 718-10-25-15).

FASB STAFF POSITION

Disclosure Requirements for Nonpublic Entities

The guidance in paragraph A240(d)(1) (ASC 718-10-50-2) is amended as follows (added text is underlined):

> The number, weighted-average exercise price (or conversion ratio), aggregate intrinsic value (except for nonpublic entities), and weighted-average remaining contractual term of options (or share units) outstanding.

Amendment of Illustration 4(b)

The guidance in paragraph A102 (ASC 718-20-55-32) is amended as follows (added text is underlined and deleted text struck out):

> Entity T could use the same computation of estimated cost, as in Table 3 above, but could elect to recognize compensation cost on a straight-line basis for all graded vesting awards. In that case, total compensation cost to be attributed on a straight-line basis over each year in the three-year vesting period is approximately $3,988,868 ($11,966,606/3). However, this Statement requires that compensation cost recognized at any date must be at least equal to the amount attributable to options that are vested at that date. For example, if 50% of this same option award vested in the first year of the three-year vesting period, ~~$5,983,303 ($11,966,606/2)~~ 436,500 options [2,910 × 150 (300 × 50%)] would be vested at the end of 20X5. Compensation cost amounting to $5,855,560 (436,500 × $13.44) attributable to the vested awards would be recognized in the first year [footnote omitted].

Amendment of Illustration 13(e)

Paragraph A170 (ASC 718-20-55-121) is amended as follows (new text is underlined and deleted text is struck out):

> On January 1, 20X7, Entity Z issues 1,000 at-the-money options with a four-year explicit service condition to each of 50 employees that work in Plant J. On December 12, 20X7, Entity Z decides to close Plant J and notifies the 50 Plant J employees that their employment relationship will be terminated effective June 30, 20X8. On June 30, 20X8, Entity Z accelerates vesting of all options. The grant date fair value of each option is $20 on January 1, 20X7, and $10 on June 30, 20X8, the modification date. At the date Entity Z decides to close Plant J and terminate the employees, ~~of modification~~ the service condition of the original award is not expected to be satisfied because the employees cannot render the requisite service; therefore, any compensation cost recognized as of ~~of the modification date for the original award would be reversed at the modification date. However, the modified award is fully vested as a result of the vesting acceleration. Therefore, a~~

December 12, 2007, for the original award would be reversed. At the date of the modification, the fair value of the original award, which is $0 ($10 × 0 options expected to vest under the original terms of the award), is subtracted from the fair value of the modified award $500,000 ($10 × 50,000 options expected to vest under the modified award). The total recognized compensation cost of $500,000 will be less than the fair value of the award at the grant date ($1 million) because at the date of the modification, the original vesting conditions were *not* expected to be satisfied.

Amendment of the Definition of Short-Term Inducement

The guidance in paragraph E1 of FAS-123(R) (ASC, *Glossary*) is amended as follows (Deleted text is struck out):

Short-term inducement

An offer by the entity that would result in modification ~~settlement~~ of an award to which an award holder may subscribe for a limited period of time.

RELATED CHAPTERS IN 2011
GAAP GUIDE, VOLUME II

Chapter 14, "Earnings per Share"
Chapter 39, "Stockholders' Equity"

RELATED CHAPTERS IN 2011
GAAP GUIDE, VOLUME I

Chapter 13, "Earnings per Share"
Chapter 43, "Stock-Based Payments"
Chapter 44, "Stockholders' Equity"

RELATED CHAPTER IN 2011
INTERNATIONAL ACCOUNTING/FINANCIAL
REPORTING STANDARDS GUIDE

Chapter 32, "Share-Based Payments"

CHAPTER 39
STOCKHOLDERS' EQUITY

CONTENTS

Overview		39.02
Authoritative Guidance		
ASC 272 Limited Liability Entities		39.03
PB-14	Accounting and Reporting by Limited Liability Companies and Limited Liability Partnerships	39.03
ASC 325 Investments—Other		39.05
EITF Issue 99-4	Accounting for Stock Received from the Demutualization of a Mutual Insurance Company	39.05
ASC 505 Equity		39.06
FSP FAS-129-1	Disclosure Requirements under FASB Statement No. 129, *Disclosure of Information about Capital Structure*, Relating to Contingently Convertible Securities	39.06
FTB 85-6	Accounting for a Purchase of Treasury Shares at a Price Significantly in Excess of the Current Market Price of the Shares and the Income Statement Classification of Costs Incurred in Defending against a Takeover Attempt	39.08
EITF Issue 86-32	Early Extinguishment of a Subsidiary's Mandatorily Redeemable Preferred Stock	39.09
EITF Issue 99-7	Accounting for an Accelerated Share Repurchase Program	39.11
EITF Issue 02-11	Accounting for Reverse Spinoffs	39.12
EITF Issue 09-E Accounting for Distributions to Shareholders with Components of Stock and Cash		39.13
Related Chapter in 2011 GAAP Guide, Volume I		39.15

39.02 *Stockholders' Equity*

OVERVIEW

The various elements constituting stockholders' equity in the statement of financial position are classified according to source. Stockholders' equity may be broadly classified into four categories: (1) legal capital, (2) additional paid-in capital, (3) noncontrolling interests, and (4) retained earnings. Detailed information is presented in the body of the statement, in related notes, or in some combination thereof.

The following pronouncements, which are the sources of GAAP for stockholders' equity, are discussed in the 2011 *GAAP Guide, Volume I*, Chapter 44, "Stockholders' Equity."

	Chapter 1, Prior Opinions (ARB-43)
ASC 605	A. Rules Adopted by Membership
	B. Opinions Issued by Predecessor Committee
	Chapter 7, Capital Accounts (ARB 43)
ASC 852	A. Quasi-Reorganizations
ASC 505	Omnibus Opinion—1967, Paragraphs 9 and 10, Capital Changes, Chapter 10 (APB-12)
ASC 470	Paragraph 16, Debt with Stock Purchase Warrants (APB-14)
ASC 505	Disclosure of Information about Capital Structure (FAS-129)

AUTHORITATIVE GUIDANCE

ASC 272 Limited Liability Companies

PB-14 (Accounting and Reporting by Limited Liability Companies and Limited Liability Partnerships) (ASC 272-10-05-1, 05-2, 05-5, 05-6; 45-1 through 45-7; 50-1 through 50-5; 850-10-60-9)

BACKGROUND

Limited liability companies and limited liability partnerships (referred to hereafter as LLCs) are formed under the laws of individual states and therefore have characteristics that are not uniform. Generally, however, they have the following characteristics:

- They are unincorporated associations of two or more persons.
- Their members have limited personal liability for the obligations of the LLC.
- They are treated as partnerships for federal income tax purposes.
- At least two of the following corporate characteristics are lacking:
  — Limited liability
  — Free transferability of interests
  — Centralized management
  — Continuity of life

PB-14 provides guidance for U.S. LLCs that prepare financial statements in accordance with generally accepted accounting principles.

STANDARDS

An LLC that is subject to U.S. federal, foreign, state, or local taxes (including franchise taxes) must account for those taxes in accordance with ASC 740 (FAS-109, Accounting for Income Taxes), including accounting for a change in tax status.

Financial Statement Display

- A complete set of financial statements must include the following:
  — Statement of financial position
  — Statement of operations

- —Statement of cash flows
- —Notes to financial statements
- Disclosure is required of changes in members' equity for the period, either in a separate statement or in notes to the financial statements.
- The equity section of the statement of financial position is referred to as "members' equity." Information about the different classes of members' equity is required, including the amount of each class, stated separately, either in the financial statements (preferable) or in notes to the financial statements (acceptable).
- If the members' equity is less than zero, the deficit should be reported, even though the members' liability may be limited.
- If the LLC maintains separate accounts for components of members' equity (e.g., undistributed earnings, earnings available for withdrawal, unallocated capital), disclosure of these accounts is required in the financial statements or notes.
- If the LLC records amounts due from members for capital contributions, such amounts receivable should generally be presented as deductions from members' equity, with the very limited exception of instances where there is substantial evidence of ability and intent to pay within a reasonably short period.
- Comparative financial statements are encouraged, but not required. Any exceptions to comparability must be disclosed in the notes to the financial statements.
- If the formation of an LLC results in a new reporting entity, the guidance in ASC 250-10-45-21 (FAS-154, Accounting Changes and Error Corrections) should be followed with regard to a change in reporting entity. In accordance with an amendment in Accounting Standards Update (ASU) 2010-8, a change should be applied retrospectively to prior periods presented to show financial information for the new reporting entity for those periods.

Disclosures

- The following information is required to be disclosed:
  - —Description of any limitation of members' liability
  - —The different classes of members' interests and the respective rights, preferences, and privileges of each class
  - —The amount of each class of members' equity included in the statement of financial position
  - —If the LLC has a limited life, the date on which the LLC will cease to exist

ASC 325 Investments—Other

EITF Issue 99-4 (Accounting for Stock Received from the Demutualization of a Mutual Insurance Company) (ASC 325-30-05-59A; 25-1A; 30-1B; 40-1)

OVERVIEW

A mutual insurance company is not owned by stockholders, but by its policyholders who are members with rights by virtue of their insurance contract, the corporation's bylaws and charter, or its articles of incorporation and various laws. Such rights may include sharing in the mutual's excess capital, participating in corporate governance, receiving the corporation's remaining value on liquidation, and the expectation that the corporation will be operated to benefit the members.

Although policyholders' membership interests in a mutual differ significantly for a number of reasons from stockholders' ownership interests in a corporation, their rights are important when a mutual insurance company is demutualized and there are changes to a corporation owned by its stockholders. In that situation, the mutual entity values each policyholder's membership rights and distributes those amounts to the policyholders in stock, cash, policy enhancements, or in combination. The members' rights are extinguished in a demutualization—the members become customers and perhaps stockholders as well.

GAAP does not permit policyholders in a mutual insurance company to recognize their membership interests as an asset, because the members receive no information as to the value of those interests. Further, those interests are forfeited if the policy lapses.

ACCOUNTING ISSUE

How should a policyholder account for stock received in a demutualization of a mutual insurance company?

EITF CONSENSUS

The EITF reached a consensus that a member receiving stock in a demutualization of an insurance company should determine the fair value of the stock and recognize it in income as a gain from continuing operations.

DISCUSSION

- Those who support the view that policyholders should recognize stock received in a demutualization of an insurance company at fair value believe that the policyholders have received something of value to which they were previously not entitled. They point to the guidance in FTB 85-1, which used the same reasoning to reach the conclusion that member institutions should recognize the preferred stock received at fair value. The FTB referred to ASC 845-10-30-1 (paragraph 18 of APB-29), which states that "a nonmonetary asset received in a nonreciprocal transfer should be recorded at the fair value of the asset received."

- Although proponents agree that policyholders already had some rights related to the mutual insurance company, stock received in a demutualization provides policyholders with additional rights, for example, one vote per share of stock rather than one vote for all policies owned. Because policyholders have received additional value, they should recognize a gain equivalent to the fair value of the stock.
- Others view the stock received as a distribution, which is a return on capital, when the mutual insurance company is liquidated in its current format and becomes a stock corporation. That is, assets have been distributed to the policyholders and should be recognized in income as a cash dividend would be.
- Proponents of recognition of the gain in income from continuing operations believe that demutualizations are not unusual and infrequent events and consequently a gain realized from such an event would not qualify as an extraordinary item. In addition, treatment as an extraordinary item would be inappropriate if the distribution of stock is analogized to a dividend.

ASC 505 Equity

FAS-129-1 (Disclosure Requirements under FASB Statement No. 129, *Disclosure of Information about Capital Structure,* **Relating to Contingently Convertible Securities) (ASC 505-10-15-2; 50-6, 50-8A, 50-9, 50-10; 470-10-60-2)**

Question: How do the disclosure requirements in ASC 505-10-50-3 (paragraph 4 of FAS-129, Disclosure of Information about Capital Structure), which requires entities to explain the significant rights and privileges of their outstanding securities, including (*a*) conversion or exercise prices and rates and relevant dates, (*b*) sinking-fund requirements, (*c*) unusual voting rights, and (*d*) significant terms of contracts to issue additional shares, apply to contingently convertible securities, such as instruments with contingent conversion requirements that have not been met and that are not otherwise required to be included in computing diluted earnings per share (EPS)?

Answer: The FASB staff believes that the provisions of ASC 505 (FAS-129) apply to all contingently convertible securities, including those with contingent conversion requirements that have not been met and that otherwise would not be included in the computation of EPS under the provisions of FAS-128 (Earnings per Share). To help users of financial statements understand the conditions of a contingency, entities should disclose the significant terms of the conversion features of contingently convertible securities and the possible effect of conversion in accordance with the guidance in ASC 505-10-50-3 (paragraph 4 of FAS-129). Disclosing the following quantitative and qualitative terms of contingently convertible securities would be useful to users:

- A description of (i) events or changes in circumstances under which a contingency causing conversion would be met and (ii) significant features of a security necessary to understand the conversion rights and their timing, for example, the periods in which a contingency might be met and in which securities might be converted
- The conversion price and the number of shares into which the security might be converted
- A description of events or changes in circumstances, if any, that might result in an adjustment or change in a contingency, the conversion price, or the number of shares, including the significant terms of those changes
- The manner in which a transaction will be settled when conversion occurs or alternative settlement methods, such as settlement in cash, shares, or a combination of the two

The following disclosures also may be useful to users:

- Whether a diluted EPS calculation includes shares that would be issued if contingently convertible securities were to be converted if the contingency is met, and if it does not, why.
- As required under the guidance in ASC 815 (FAS-133, Accounting for Derivative Instruments and Hedging Activities), ASC 480 (FAS-150, Accounting for Certain Financial Instruments with Characteristics of both Liabilities and Equity), and ASC 815 (EITF Issue 00-19, Accounting for Derivative Financial Instruments Indexed to, and Potentially Settled in, a Company's Own Stock), information about derivative transactions entered into as a result of the issuance of contingently convertible securities, such as the terms of derivative

transactions, including the settlement terms, how the transactions are related to contingently convertible securities, the number of shares underlying the derivatives, and the possible effect of the issuance of contingently convertible securities. A purchase of a call option with terms that presumably would substantially offset changes in the value of a written call option embedded in a convertible security is an example of such a transaction.

FTB 85-6 (Accounting for a Purchase of Treasury Shares at a Price Significantly in Excess of the Current Market Price of the Shares and the Income Statement Classification of Costs Incurred in Defending against a Takeover Attempt) (ASC 225-20-55-4; 505-30-25-3, 25-4; 30-2, 30-4; 50-3, 50-4; 60-1)

BACKGROUND

Most treasury stock transactions engaged in by an enterprise are solely capital transactions and do not involve recognition of revenue and expense. In some cases, however, treasury stock transactions may involve the receipt or payment of consideration in exchange for rights or privileges, which may require recognition of revenue or expense. FTB 85-6 was issued to clarify this and other issues that may arise in a takeover attempt.

STANDARDS

Purchase Price in Excess of Market Price

Question 1: How should a company account for a purchase of treasury shares at a price that is significantly in excess of the current market price of the shares?

Answer: This situation creates an assumption that the purchase price includes amounts attributable to items other than the shares purchased. The price paid in excess of the current market price of the shares should be attributed to the other elements in the transaction. If the fair value of those other elements is more clearly evident than the market value of the stock, the former amount should be assigned to those elements and the difference should be recorded as the cost of the treasury shares. If no stated or unstated consideration in addition to the capital stock can be identified, the entire purchase price should be assigned to the treasury stock.

Illustration of the Accounting for "Greenmail" Payments

Saul Rainwood buys 1 million shares of Old Steel Inc. over a period of time at prices ranging from $10 to $19 per share. On May 29, 20X5, shares of Old Steel Inc. close at $15 per share. On May 30, 20X5, Old Steel reacquires all of Rainwood's shares at $30 per share, and Rainwood enters into an agreement to not reacquire more than 5% of Old Steel's common stock for a period of three years. As a result of this transaction, Old Steel would recognize treasury stock of $15 million and record a $15 million expense for the excess purchase price over the stock's closing market price on May 29th. The $15 million charged to expense is the consideration Rainwood received, over and above the stock's market price, for disposing of his shares and agreeing not to reacquire a substantial ownership stake for a period of time (i.e., a greenmail payment).

Agreements with a Shareholder or Former Shareholder Not to Purchase Additional Shares

Question 2: Should amounts an enterprise pays to a shareholder (or former shareholder) that are attributed to an agreement precluding that shareholder (or former shareholder) from purchasing additional shares be capitalized as assets and amortized over the period of the agreement?

Answer: No, such payments should be expensed as incurred.

Costs of Defense and "Standstill" Agreement in a Takeover Attempt

Question 3: Should the costs a company incurs to defend itself in a takeover attempt or the costs of a "standstill" agreement be classified as extraordinary?

Answer: No. Neither meets the criteria for an *extraordinary* item as defined in APB-30 (Reporting the Results of Operations—Reporting the Effects of Disposal of a Segment of a Business, and Extraordinary, Unusual, and Infrequently Occurring Events and Transactions).

EITF Issue 86-32 (Early Extinguishment of a Subsidiary's Mandatorily Redeemable Preferred Stock) (ASC 505-10-60-4; 810-10-40-1, 40-2, 40-2A)

> **OBSERVATION:** FAS-150 (Accounting for Certain Financial Instruments with Characteristics of both Liabilities and Equity) requires that a financial instrument that is mandatorily redeemable at a specified or determinable date, or on the occurrence of a certain event, be accounted for as a liability, except if the redemption is required to occur when a reporting entity is being liquidated or terminated. Consequently, FAS-150 nullifies

the consensus in Issue 86-32 as it relates to mandatorily redeemable preferred stock. In addition, FAS-150 requires that amounts paid to holders of those contracts in excess of the initial amount at which they were measured should be accounted for as an interest cost rather than as a charge to a noncontrolling interest in the entity. The consensus in this Issue continues to apply to a financial instrument with a redemption feature that is *not* considered a mandatorily redeemable financial instrument under the provisions of FAS-150.

OVERVIEW

Company X acquires Company Z in a purchase business combination. Subsequent to the business combination, Company Z issues mandatorily redeemable preferred stock with a fixed dividend and no voting rights. The carrying amount of that stock is $75 million. Eighteen months after the redeemable stock is issued, its market value declines. Company X purchases the subsidiary's redeemable preferred stock for $60 million on the open market and holds it until it is due to be redeemed.

ACCOUNTING ISSUE

How should Company X account for the purchase of its wholly owned subsidiary's mandatorily redeemable preferred stock?

EITF CONSENSUS

The EITF reached a consensus that the company should treat the acquisition of the subsidiary's mandatorily redeemable preferred stock as a capital transaction. Thus, the company should recognize no gain or loss from the acquisition in its consolidated financial statements.

The EITF noted that dividends on a subsidiary's preferred stock, regardless of whether it is redeemable, should be included in minority interest as a charge against income.

DISCUSSION

The authoritative accounting literature does not provide guidance on accounting for this transaction. The decision to treat the purchase of the subsidiary's mandatorily redeemable preferred stock as a capital transaction was based on the view that the subsidiary's redeemable preferred stock is an equity security. Proponents of this view noted that the same as for other equity securities, dividends on such securities are charged to retained earnings. The stock is reported in the balance sheet as treasury stock with the discount credited to paid-in capital.

EITF Issue 99-7 (Accounting for an Accelerated Share Repurchase Program) (ASC 260-10-55-89; 505-30-25-5, 6; 55-1, 55-3, 55-5, 55-6; 60-2)

OVERVIEW

In an accelerated share repurchase program, an entity purchases a specified number of shares immediately, but the purchase price for those shares is based on the average market price of the shares over a specified period of time. Such programs combine the benefits of an immediate share retirement of a tender offer with the price benefits of repurchases on the open market. They may be structured as a treasury stock purchase or a forward contract:

- *Treasury stock purchase* An investment banker who is an unrelated third party borrows 1 million shares of Company A's common stock from investors, becomes the shares' owner of record, and sells the shares short to Company A on 7/1/X9 for $50 a share and is paid $50 million in cash on that date. Company A has legal title to the shares, which are held as treasury stock, and no other party can vote those shares.
- *Forward contract* Company A enters into a forward contract with an investment banker on 1 million shares of Company A's common stock. If the volume-weighted average daily market price during the contract period from July 1, 20X9, to October 1, 20X9, exceeds the $50 initial purchase price (net of the investment banker's commission), the Company has the option to deliver to the investment banker on October 1, 20X9, cash or shares of common stock equal to the price difference times 1 million. If the volume-weighted average daily market price during the contract period is less than the $50 purchase price, the investment banker delivers to Company A on October 1, 20X9, cash or shares of common stock equal to the price difference times 1 million.

ACCOUNTING ISSUE

How should accelerated share repurchase programs be accounted for?

EITF CONSENSUS

The Task Force reached a consensus position that accelerated repurchase programs should be accounted for as two separate transactions as follows:

1. As a treasury stock transaction in which shares of the company's stock are acquired and recognized on the acquisition date (e.g., July 1, 20X9)
2. As a forward contract that is indexed to its own stock

According to the guidance in Issue 99-3 (codified in Issue 00-19), the forward contract in the example discussed above would be classified as an equity instrument, because the entity would receive cash when there is a gain on the contract, but has the option to pay in cash or stock when there is a loss on the contract. Therefore, no fair value changes of the contract would be recognized and the contract's settlement would be recognized in equity.

In calculating basic and diluted earnings per share (EPS), the number of shares used to calculate the weighted-average common shares outstanding would be reduced by the shares repurchased as treasury stock. The guidance in FAS-128, as interpreted in Topic D-72, should be used to measure the effect of the forward contract on EPS.

EITF Issue 02-11 (Accounting for Reverse Spinoffs) (ASC 505-60-05-2 through 05-4; 15-2; 25-2, 25-4 through 25-5, 25-7 through 25-8; 45-1; 55-2, 55-5, 55-7, 55-8 through 55-12)

OVERVIEW

A *spinoff* is a transaction in which a company (a *spinnor*) transfers assets (usually a subsidiary) into a new legal entity (the *spinnee*) and distributes the shares in that entity to its shareholders, who do *not* give up any shares held in the spinnor. Spinoff transactions benefit companies in several ways. For example, neither the spinnor nor its shareholders recognize a gain on the distribution of shares if the spinoff qualifies as a nontaxable reorganization. A spinoff also avoids the double taxation that would result from a sale of a subsidiary and distribution of the proceeds to the company's shareholders.

ASC 845-10-30-10 (paragraph 23 of APB-29, Accounting for Nonmonetary Transactions) as amended by ASC 360 (FAS-144, Accounting for the Impairment or Disposal of Long-Lived Assets), provides guidance on accounting for spinoff transactions, which are nonreciprocal transfers to owners. It requires that a spinoff be accounted for based on the carrying value of the assets distributed to its shareholders. The transaction should *not* be accounted for as a sale of a spinnee followed by a distribution of the proceeds.

Some companies have been accounting for spinoffs based on the form of the transaction rather than on its substance—that is, the spinnee becomes the continuing entity. It is important to determine which entity will be treated as the spinnee for accounting purposes, because under the provisions of FAS-144, a spinnor must report a spinnee as a discontinued operation if the spinnee is a component of an entity and meets the conditions in ASC 205-20-45-1 (paragraph 42 of the FAS-144) for such reporting.

ACCOUNTING ISSUE

Should a spinoff that treats a spinnee as the continuing entity be accounted for as a *reverse* spinoff, in which the spinnee is treated as the spinnor for accounting purposes based on the substance rather than the form of the transaction?

EITF CONSENSUS

1. A transaction should be accounted for as a *reverse* spinoff if the substance of the transaction is most accurately depicted for shareholders and other users of financial statements by treating a legal spinee as the accounting spinnor. Judgment based on an evaluation of the relevant facts and circumstances should be used to determine whether a transaction should be accounted for as a reverse spinoff.

2. Although it should be presumed that the *legal* spinnor is also the spinnor for *accounting* purposes, that presumption may be tested by considering the following indicators, neither of which should be considered presumptive or determinative:

   a. The accounting spinnor (legal spinnee) is larger than the accounting spinnee (legal spinnor) based on assets, revenues, and earnings.

   b. The fair value of the accounting spinnor (legal spinnee) exceeds that of the accounting spinnee (legal spinnor).

   c. The former combined entity's senior management remains with the accounting spinnor (legal spinnee).

   d. The accounting spinnor (legal spinnee) has been held longer than the accounting spinnee (legal spinnor).

(EITF Issue 09-E Accounting for Distributions to Shareholders with Components of Stock and Cash) (ASC 505-20-15-3A)

OVERVIEW

Real estate investment trusts (REITs) are required by the Internal Revenue Service (IRS) to distribute at least 90 percent of their taxable income. REITS occasionally issue a "special" dividend distribution above the REIT's recurring quarterly dividend in periods in which a REIT has had large nonrecurring earnings. Frequently, those special dividends have been issued in cash and stock subject to IRS approval in a private letter ruling. In 2008, the IRS issued a ruling that permits REITS to make their annual required distributions in cash and stock if shareholders are permitted to elect to receive their total distribution in cash or in stock equal to the amount of the cash distribution. If too many shareholders elect to receive their distribution in cash, those electing to receive cash must receive a pro rata amount of cash that corresponds to their proportionate interest in the distribution. However, shareholders making that election cannot receive less than 10 percent of their total distribution in cash. This guidance in that ruling has also been extended to closed-end investment funds, which also must distribute at least 90 percent of their taxable income. Entities that want to declare regular or special dividends in cash and stock must obtain a private letter ruling from the IRS.

As a result of this IRS ruling, the following diversity in practice has developed:

- Some entities account for the portion of the dividend issued in stock as a new stock issuance, which is included in earnings per share (EPS) *prospectively*. Others who consider it to be a stock dividend follow the guidance in ASC 260, *Earnings Per Share* (ASC 260-10-55-12), and *retrospectively* restate shares outstanding and EPS.

- Some believe that a stock dividend should be included in EPS on the date the dividend is declared, while others believe that a stock dividend should be included in EPS when the shares' trading price has been adjusted to include the effects of the stock dividend or when a dividend is settled.

EITF CONSENSUS

Rather than confirming its consensus-for-exposure positions reached at the September 2009 meeting, the EITF reached a consensus at its November 19, 2009 meeting that the stock portion of a distribution to shareholders that contains components of cash and stock and allows the shareholders to select their preferred form of distribution should be considered to be an issuance of stock in applying the EPS provisions of ASC 260. The EITF reached this consensus, which is based on the alternative view presented in the proposed ASU exposed for comment because some EITF members expressed the view that under this type of distribution a shareholder's' ownership position changes unlike in the case of a stock dividend in which the shareholder is left in the same ownership position as before the transaction had occurred. EITF members noted that such a distribution should be classified as a liability when an entity becomes obligated to make the distribution in accordance with the guidance in ASC 480, *Distinguishing Liabilities from Equity* (ASC 480-10-25-14). Further, a distribution classified as a liability would be included in diluted EPS in accordance with the guidance in ASC 260-10-45-45 through 45-47 for contracts that may be settled in stock or in cash.

Disclosure. The EITF reached a consensus that in accordance with the guidance in ASC 260-10-50-2, an entity should disclose any transaction that occurs *after* the end of the most recent period but *before* the financial statements are issued or are available to be issued that would cause a material change in the number of common shares or potential common shares outstanding at the end of the period had that transaction occurred *before* the end of the period.

EFFECTIVE DATE AND TRANSITION

The EITF affirmed its consensus that this guidance is effective for interim and annual periods that end on or after December 15, 2009, and should be applied *retrospectively*.

FASB RATIFICATION

The FASB ratified the EITF's consensus positions in Issue 09-E at its December 2, 2009 meeting.

RELATED CHAPTER IN 2011 *GAAP GUIDE, VOLUME I*

Chapter 44, "Stockholders' Equity"

CHAPTER 40
TRANSFER OF FINANCIAL ASSETS

CONTENTS

Overview		**40.02**
Authoritative Guidance		
ASC 310 Receivables		**40.04**
SOP 03-3	Accounting for Certain Loans or Debt Securities in a Transfer	**40.09**
ASC 325 Investments—Other		**40.09**
FSP FAS EITF 99-20-1	Amendments to the Impairment Guidance of EITF Issue No. 99-20	**40.09**
EITF Issue 99-20	Recognition of Interest Income and Impairment on Purchased Beneficial Interests and Transferor's Beneficial Interests in Securitized Financial Assets Obtained in a Transfer Accounted for as a Sale	**40.17**
ASC 860 Transfers and Servicing		**40.22**
FSP FAS-140-1	Accounting for Accrued Interest Receivable under FAS-140 Securitizations	**40.22**
FSP FAS-140-3	Accounting for Transfers of Financial Assets and Repurchase Financing Transactions	**40.23**
EITF Issue 85-13	Sale of Mortgage Service Rights on Mortgages Owned by Others	**40.26**
EITF Issue 87-30	Sale of a Short-Term Loan Made under a Long-Term Credit Commitment	**40.27**
EITF Issue 88-22	Securitization of Credit Card and Other Receivable Portfolios	**40.30**
EITF Issue 90-21	Balance Sheet Treatment of a Sale of Mortgage Servicing Rights with a Subservicing Agreement	**40.33**

EITF Issue 95-5	Determination of What Risks and Rewards, If Any, Can Be Retained and Whether Any Unresolved Contingencies May Exist in a Sale of Mortgage Loan Servicing Rights	40.36
EITF Issue 97-3	Accounting for Fees and Costs Associated with Loan Syndications and Loan Participations after the Issuance of FASB Statement No. 125	40.38
EITF Issue 99-8	Accounting for Transfers of Assets That Are Derivative Instruments but That Are Not Financial Assets	40.40
EITF Issue 02-9	Accounting for Changes That Result in a Transferor Regaining Control of Financial Assets Sold	40.41
FIG FAS-140	A Guide to Implementation of Statement 140 on Accounting for Transfers and Servicing of Financial Assets and Extinguishments of Liabilities	40.43

Related Chapters in 2011 GAAP Guide, Volume II	40.66
Related Chapters in 2011 GAAP Guide, Volume I	40.66
Related Chapter in 2011 International Accounting/Financial Reporting Standards Guide	40.66

OVERVIEW

Transfers of financial assets take many forms. Depending on the nature of the transaction, the transferor may have a continuing interest in the transferred asset. Accounting for transferred assets in which the transferor has no continuing involvement with the transferred asset, or with the transferee, has been relatively straightforward and not controversial. Transfers of financial assets in which the transferor has some continuing interest, however, have raised issues about the circumstances in which a transfer should be considered a sale of all or part of the assets or a secured borrowing, and how transferors and transferees should account for sales of financial assets and secured borrowings.

GAAP for transactions involving the transfer of financial assets, which are established in the following authoritative pronouncements, are discussed in the 2010 *GAAP Guide, Volume I,* Chapter 45, "Transfer and Servicing of Financial Assets."

ASC 860	Accounting for Transfers and Servicing of Financial Assets and Extinguishments of Liabilities (FAS-140)
ASC 815	Accounting for Certain Hybrid Financial Instruments—An Amendment of FASB Statements No. 133 and 140 (FAS-155)
ASC 860	Accounting for Servicing of Financial Assets—An Amendment of FASB Statement No. 140 (FAS-156)

ASC 860 (FAS-140, Accounting for Transfers and Servicing of Financial Assets and Extinguishments of Liabilities) establishes accounting and reporting standards for transfers and servicing of financial assets and extinguishments of liabilities based on a consistent application of the financial-components approach. That approach requires the recognition of financial assets and servicing assets that are controlled by a reporting entity, the derecognition of financial assets when control is surrendered, and the derecognition of liabilities when they are extinguished. Specific criteria are established for determining when control has been surrendered in a transfer of financial assets. FAS-140 supersedes the guidance in FAS-125 and carries forward most of the provisions of FAS-125 without reconsideration.

AUTHORITATIVE GUIDANCE

ASC 310 Receivables

SOP 03-3 (Accounting for Certain Loans or Debt Securities in a Transfer) (ASC 310-10-50-18; 30-05-2 through 05-3; 15-1 through 15-4, 15-6 through 15-10; 25-1; 30-1; 35-2 through 35-3, 35-5 through 35-6, 35-8 through 35-15; 40-1; 45-1; 50-1 through 50-3; 55-2, 55-5 through 55-29; 60-3)

OVERVIEW

Since the AICPA issued PB-6 (Amortization of Discounts on Certain Acquired Loans) in August 1989, the FASB has issued ASC 310-10-35 (FAS-114, Accounting by Creditors for Impairment of a Loan) ASC 320 (FAS-115, Accounting for Certain Investments in Debt and Equity Securities) and ASC 310-10-35-40; 50-16 through 50-17, 50-20; ASC 310-40-35-6; 50-6 (FAS-118, Accounting by Creditors for Impairment of a Loan-Income Recognition and Disclosures), and has amended the guidance in ASC 450 (FAS-5, Accounting for Contingencies).

SOP 03-3 amends the guidance in paragraph 15 of PB-6 for decreases in estimated cash flows expected to be collected. In addition, SOP 03-3 limits application of the guidance in PB-6, as amended, to loans purchased in fiscal years beginning on or before December 15, 2004. Amendments of PB-6 should be applied prospectively for fiscal years beginning after December 15, 2004. All of the guidance in PB-6 applies, as amended, for fiscal years beginning after December 15, 2004, to loans under the scope of the PB.

Scope

The SOP applies to all nongovernmental entities that acquire loans, including not-for-profit organizations. Loans under the scope of this SOP (1) have had a deterioration in credit quality since origination; (2) have been acquired in a transfer (*a*) that meets the conditions in ASC 860-10-40-4 through 40-5 (paragraph 9 of FAS-140 (Accounting for Transfers and Servicing of Financial Assets and Extinguishments of Liabilities, as amended by FAS-166) to be accounted for as a sale or purchase, (*b*) that is a purchase business combination, (*c*) to a newly created subsidiary if the investor wrote down the loan to its fair value with the intent of transferring the subsidiary's stock as a dividend to the parent company's shareholders, or (*d*) that is a contribution receivable or a transfer in satisfaction of a prior promise to give; and (3) it is probable at acquisition, as defined in ASC 860-10-35-3 (paragraph 10 of FAS-114), that all contractually required payments receivable will not be collected, with the following exceptions:

- Loans measured at fair value with all changes in fair value included in earnings or, for not-for-profit organizations, loans measured at fair value with all changes in fair value included in the statement of activities and included in the performance indicator, if one is presented
- Mortgage loans classified as held for sale under paragraph 4 of FAS-65 (Accounting for Certain Mortgage Banking Activities) (ASC 948-310-35-1)
- Leases defined in ASC 840 (FAS-13, Accounting for Leases)
- Loans acquired in a business combination accounted for at historical cost
- Loans held by liquidating banks
- Revolving credit agreements (e.g., credit cards and home equity loans), if the borrower has revolving privileges at the acquisition date
- Loans that are retained interests

Loans that are derivative instruments accounted for under the provisions of ASC 815 (FAS-133, Accounting for Derivative Instruments and Hedging Activities) also are excluded from the SOP's scope. However, if a loan that would normally come under the scope of this SOP has an embedded derivative accounted for under the provisions of ASC 815 (FAS-133), the host instrument would be accounted for under the scope of this SOP if it meets the scope requirements of the SOP.

Recognition, Measurement, and Display

A loan loss allowance should *not* be established at acquisition for loans acquired in a transfer. Loans acquired in a business combination should be initially recognized at the present value of amounts expected to be received. A valuation allowance should be established only for incurred losses at the present value of cash flows that were expected at acquisition but not received.

Income recognition should be based on a reasonable expectation about the timing and amount of cash flows to be collected. If after acquisition, an investor is unable to calculate a yield on a loan because of a lack of information necessary to reasonably estimate the cash flows expected to be collected, the investor is permitted to place the loan on a nonaccrual status and recognize income by the cost recovery method or on a cash basis. If, however, the timing and amount of cash flows expected to be collected, for example, from a sale of a loan into the secondary market or a sale of loan collateral, is reasonably estimable, the cash flows should be used to apply the interest method under this SOP. Interest income should *not* be recognized if it would cause the net investment in the loan to exceed the payoff amount. Income should *not* be accrued on loans acquired primarily for the rewards of owning the underlying collateral, such as for the use of the collateral in the entity's operations or to improve it for resale.

Changes in Cash Flows Expected to Be Collected

Investors should account for changes in cash flows expected to be collected as follows:

1. For loans accounted for as debt securities, cash flows expected to be collected over the life of a loan should continue to be estimated, unless a subsequent evaluation reveals that:
   a. The debt security's fair value is *less* than its amortized cost basis. In that case, it should be determined whether the decline is other than temporary and the guidance on impairment of securities in ASC 320-20-45-9 paragraph 16 of FAS-115) should be applied. The timing and amount of cash flows expected to be collected should be considered in determining the probability of collecting all cash flows that were expected to be collected at acquisition as well as additional cash flows as a result of changes in estimates made after acquisition.
   b. It is probable, based on current information and events, that cash flows previously expected to be collected have significantly increased or actual cash flows significantly exceed previously expected cash flows. The amount of the accretable yield for the loan should be recalculated as the excess of the revised cash flows expected to be collected over the sum of (i) the initial investment *less* (ii) cash collected *less* (iii) other-than-temporary impairments *plus* (iv) the yield accreted to date. The amount of accretable yield should be adjusted by reclassifying amounts from the nonaccretable difference. This adjustment should be accounted for as a change in estimate in accordance with the guidance in ASC 250 (FAS-154, Accounting Changes and Error Corrections). The amount of periodic accretion should be adjusted over the remaining life of the loan.
2. For loans *not* accounted for as debt securities, cash flows expected to be collected over the life of a loan should continue to be estimated, unless a subsequent evaluation reveals that:
   a. It is probable, based on current information and events, that all cash flows originally expected to be collected and additional cash flows expected to be collected as a result of changes in estimates after acquisition will *not* be collected, in which case, the condition in ASC 450-20-25-2 (paragraph 8(a) of FAS-5) is met. Therefore, the loan should be considered impaired when applying the measurement and other provisions of ASC 450 (FAS-5) or the provisions of ASC 310 (FAS-114), if applicable.

b. It is probable based on current information and events that cash flows originally expected to be collected have increased significantly or actual cash flows significantly exceed cash flows previously expected to be collected. In that case:

   (1) The remaining valuation allowance or allowance for loan losses established after the loan's acquisition should be reduced by the increase in the present value of cash flows expected to be collected; *and*

   (2) The amount of the loan's accretable yield should be recalculated as the excess of revised cash flows expected to be collected over the sum of (1) the initial investment *less* (2) cash collected *less* (3) write-downs *plus* (4) the yield accreted to date. The amount of accretable yield should be adjusted by reclassifying the nonaccretable difference. This adjustment should be accounted for as a change in estimate in accordance with the guidance in ASC 250 (FAS-154). The amount of periodic accretion should be adjusted over the remaining life of the loan.

Prepayments

The treatment of expected prepayments should be consistent in accounting for cash flows expected to be collected and for projections of contractual cash flows so that the nonaccretable difference will *not* be affected. The nonaccretable difference also should *not* be affected if actual prepayments differ from expected prepayments.

Restructured or Refinanced Loan

A loan that is refinanced or restructured subsequent to acquisition, other than by a troubled debt restructuring, should *not* be accounted for as a new loan. The provisions of SOP 03-3, including those related to changes in cash flows expected to be collected continue to apply.

Variable Rate Loans

Contractually required payments receivable on a loan with a contractual interest rate that varies based on subsequent changes in an independent factor, for example, the prime rate, should be based on the factor as it changes over the life of the loan. The loan's effective interest rate or cash flows expected to be collected should *not* be based on projections of future changes in that factor. At acquisition, the amount of cash flows expected to be collected should be calculated based on the rate in effect at the acquisition date. Increases in cash flows expected to be collected should be

40.08 *Transfer of Financial Assets*

accounted for according to the guidance in 1(b) and 2(b), above, in the discussion of changes in cash flows expected to be collected. The amount of cash flows originally expected to be collected and the accretable yield should be reduced if cash flows expected to be collected decrease as a direct result of a change in the contractual interest rate. This change should be accounted for according to the guidance in 1(a) and 2(a), above, in the discussion of changes in cash flows originally expected to be collected and recognized prospectively as a change in accounting estimate according to the guidance in ASC 250 (FAS-154). In this case, *no* loss will be recognized, but the future yield will be reduced.

Multiple Loans Accounted for as a Single Asset

SOP 03-3 permits investors to recognize, measure, and disclose information about loans *not* accounted for as debt securities as a similar single asset if the loans were acquired in the same fiscal year and have similar credit risks or risk ratings, and have one or more common major characteristic, such as financial asset type, collateral type, size, interest rate, date of origination, term, or geographic location, so that a composite interest rate and expectation of cash flows to be collected for the pool can be used. However, each individual loan should meet the scope criteria of this SOP. The total cost of the acquired assets should be allocated to the individual assets based on their relative fair values at the acquisition date. The amount by which contractually required payments receivable exceed an investor's initial investment for a specific loan or a pool of loans with common risk characteristics should not be used to offset changes in cash flows expected to be collected from another loan or another pool of loans with different risk characteristics.

Once aggregated, the carrying amounts of individual loans should *not* be removed from the pool unless the investor sells, forecloses, writes off, or pays off the loan in another manner. The percentage yield calculation used to recognize accretable yield on a pool of loans should *not* be affected by the difference between a loan's carrying amount and the fair value of the collateral or other assets received.

Disclosures

The notes to the financial statements should include the following information about loans that meet the scope criteria in this SOP:

- How prepayments are considered in determining contractual cash flows and cash flows expected to be collected
- Disclosures required in ASC 310-10-50-12 through 50-13 and 35-34 (paragraphs 20(a) and 20(b) of FAS-114), if the condition in ASC 320-20-45-9 (paragraph 16 of FAS-115) or ASC 450-20-25-

2 (paragraph 8(a) of FAS-5) related to the discussion in this SOP of changes in cash flows expected to be collected is met
- Separate information about loans accounted for as debt securities and those that are *not*, including:
  —The outstanding balance, which consists of the undiscounted sum of all amounts, including amounts considered to be principal, interest, fees, penalties, and other amounts under the loan owed to the investor at the reporting date, except for amounts irrevocably forgiven in a debt restructuring; amounts legally discharged and interest, fees, penalties, and other amounts that would be accrued after the reporting date for loans with a net carrying amount; and the related carrying amount at the beginning and end of the period.
  —The accretable yield at the beginning and at the end of the period, reconciled for additions, accretion, disposals of loans, and reclassifications to or from the nonaccretable difference during the period.
  —Contractually required payments receivable, cash flows expected to be collected, and the fair value at the acquisition date of loans acquired during the period.
  —The carrying amount at the acquisition date of loans under the scope of this SOP not accounted for in accordance with the income recognition model in the SOP that are acquired during the period and the carrying amount of all such loans at the end of the period.
- The following disclosures are required only for loans *not* accounted for as debt securities:
  —For each period for which an income statement is presented, the amount of (a) expenses, if any, recognized in accordance with the guidance in 2(a) of the section on changes in cash flows expected to be collected and (b) reductions of the allowance recognized in accordance with the guidance in 2(b)(1) of the section on changes in cash flows expected to be collected.

The amount of the allowance for uncollectible accounts at the beginning and end of the period.

ASC 325 Investments—Other

FSP EITF 99-20-1 (Amendments to the Impairment Guidance of EITF Issue No. 99-20) (ASC 325-40-65-1)

OVERVIEW

The objective of FSP EITF 99-20-1 is to amend the guidance in EITF Issue 99-20 (Recognition of Interest Income and Impairment on

Purchased Beneficial Interests and Beneficial Interests That Continue to Be Held by a Transferor in Securitized Financial Assets) to assist users in determining whether an other-than-temporary impairment has occurred. The guidance in ASC 320 (FAS-115) is retained and underscored in the guidance provided in this FSP.

This project was undertaken by the FASB staff for several reasons. One reason is that the current authoritative accounting guidance in ASC 320 (FAS-115, Accounting for Certain Investments in Debt and Equity Securities) and EITF Issue 99-20 (discussed below) provides two different models for an assessment of whether an impairment is other-than-temporary.

Under GAAP in the U.S., entities are required to determine whether an impairment of a debt security's fair value is other-than-temporary. If that is the case, the amount of that impairment must be recognized in earnings. The two current models are as follows:

1. Under the guidance in Issue 99-20, which applies to debt securities that are beneficial interests in securitized financial assets under the Issue's scope, a reporting entity would determine that an impairment of a debt security's fair value is other than temporary if there has been an unfavorable change in the estimated cash flows from the beneficial interest based on the entity's best estimate of cash flows that market participants would use to determine the beneficial interests' fair value. Management's judgment about the probability that it will collect all the cash in its previous projections cannot mitigate that determination.

2. Under the guidance in ASC 320 (FAS-115), which applies to debt securities *not* under the scope of Issue 99-20, a reporting entity is permitted to use management's reasonable judgment about the probability that previously projected cash flows will be collected and is not required to rely solely on the assumptions of market participants about future cash flows.

Another reason for undertaking this project is that the FASB staff received comments from some constituents that under the current adverse market conditions, reporting entities required to apply the guidance in Issue 99-20 would have to automatically recognize an other-than-temporary impairment if a debt security's fair value is less than its cost basis without having determined whether it is probable that all projected cash flows will not be collected even though based on current information, it is expected that the underlying assets will fully perform.

In addition, although the guidance in Issue 99-20 and that in ASC 320 (FAS-115) applies to different types of debt instruments, for example, beneficial interests versus corporate bonds, both types of instruments have similar economic risks. Further, similar beneficial interests with the same current credit quality might be evaluated differently for other-than-temporary impairment under the two different models because their credit quality differed when the beneficial interests were first recognized.

PRINCIPLES FOR THE EVALUATION OF OTHER-THAN-TEMPORARY IMPAIRMENT

The following is guidance for the evaluation of whether an other-than-temporary impairment has occurred:

- The objective of an evaluation is to determine whether it is probable that the holder will realize some part of an unrealized loss on an impaired security. Under GAAP, a holder may realize an unrealized loss on an impaired security if (a) it is probable that the holder will *not* collect all of the contractual or estimated cash flows, considering the timing and the amount, or (b) the holder does not have the intent or the ability to hold the security to recovery.
- The fact that all of the scheduled payments to date have been received should *not* lead to an automatic conclusion that a security is *not* other-than-temporarily impaired. Similarly, the fact that that a security's fair value has declined should not lead to an automatic conclusion that an other-than-temporary impairment has occurred. Judgment and an analysis of the situation are required to determine whether a decline in a security's fair value is a sign that it is probable that a holder will not collect all of the contractual or estimated cash flows from a security. In accordance with the guidance in SEC Staff Accounting Bulletin (SAB) 5M, it may be possible to determine whether an impairment is other than temporary based "on the length of time and the extent to which [fair] value has been less than cost." If the amount of a decline in fair value is steep and has been occurring over a lengthy period of time, the requirement for persuasive evidence increases to overcome the probability that a holder will not collect all of a security's contractual or estimated cash flows.
- A holder of a security evaluating whether an impairment is other than temporary should consider all relevant information regarding whether cash flows from a security are collectible, including information about past events, current conditions, as well as reasonable and supportable forecasts in estimating future cash flows. The information should include the security's remaining payment terms, prepayment speeds, the issuer's financial condition, expected defaults, and the value of underlying collateral, if any. The following should be considered: industry analyst's reports and forecasts, sector credit ratings, and other market data relevant to the security's collectibility. Also to be considered are how other credit enhancements, such as guarantees, affect the security's performance, including the guarantor's current financial condition and/or whether subordinated

interests, if any, could absorb estimated losses on the loans underlying the security. Because a security's remaining payment terms could significantly differ from those in prior periods, a holder should consider whether a security backed by loans that are currently performing will continue to perform if required payments increase in the future, for example, balloon payments. How the value of collateral, if any, affects a security's expected performance also should be considered. If the value of collateral has been declining, the effect of that decline on the holder's ability to collect a balloon payment also should be considered.
- As stated in SAB Topic 5M, a holder may have to realize an unrealized loss because of an inability or intent to hold a security for sufficient time to recover its market value. Further guidance on this matter may be found in ASC 320-10-35-33 paragraph 14 of FSP FAS–115/ FAS-124-1 The Meaning of Other-Than-Temporary Impairment and Its Application to Certain Investments).

The following are sources of GAAP and other sources, which are mentioned in footnote 4 of FAS-115 that support this FSP's objective and principles discussed above:

- ASC 320-10-S55-1 (SAB Topic 5.M) discusses the fact that the market price of a security may be influenced by general conditions in the market that represent expectations for the total economy, for a specific industry, or a specific company. Management should investigate such declines in value assuming that a write-down may be necessary and consequently should consider all available evidence to determine an investment's realizable value. Many factors should be considered in that evaluation. The relevance of those factors will vary from case to case.
- ASC 320-10-S55-1 (SAB Topic 5.M) also states that an issuer's financial condition and near-term prospects should be considered as well as specific events that may affect an issuer's operations, such as changes in technology or the discontinuance of a segment of a business that may weaken an investment's earnings potential. If the evidence does not support a realizable value that equals or exceeds an investment's carrying value, it should be written down to fair value and a realizable loss should be recognized.
- ASC 325-20-35-2 (Paragraph 6(a) of APB-18, The Equity Method of Accounting for Investments in Common Stock) states that if an investee has a series of operating losses or other factors indicating that an investment's decrease in value is other than temporary, a loss should be recognized.
- Paragraph 47 of SAS-92 (Auditing Derivative Instruments, Hedging Activities, and Investments in Securities) states that to determine whether a loss is other than temporary, it is often necessary to estimate the outcome of future events, which requires judgment based on subjective and objective factors that include knowledge and experience about past and

current events and assumptions about future events, for example:
—Fair value is significantly below cost,
—A decline is due to adverse conditions specifically related to a security or to an industry's or geographic area's specific conditions,
—Management does not have the intent and the ability to hold a security until an anticipated recovery in its fair value.
- A security has been downgraded by a rating agency.
- An issuer's financial condition has deteriorated.
- An entity has reduced or eliminated a security's dividend payments, or scheduled interest payments have not been made.
- The entity recognized losses from a security after the end of the reporting period.

Disclosures. The objective of the disclosures required in ASC 320-10-50-6 through 50-8B, 50-1 (paragraphs 17 and 18 of FSP FAS 115-1/FAS-124-1) is to provide information about all investments with an unrealized loss, including those under the scope of Issue 99-20, for which an entity has *not* recognized an other-than-temporary impairment. That information also should include the evidence a holder considered in reaching a conclusion that an other-than-temporary impairment has *not* occurred.

International convergence. One of the differences between U.S. GAAP and International Financial Reporting Standards is eliminated by reducing the number of impairment models for debt securities in U.S. GAAP. The remaining impairment models will be reconsidered in a joint project of the FASB and the International Accounting Standards Board (IASB) that addresses complexity in existing accounting standards.

FASB STAFF POSITION

The guidance in this FSP applies to beneficial interests under the scope of Issue 99-20. The guidance in paragraphs 12, 13, and 15 of Issue 99-20 is amended by the guidance in this FSP to conform the guidance on impairment Issue 99-20 with that in ASC 320-10-35-18; 45-9 (paragraph 16 of FAS-115) and related implementation guidance.

Footnote 21c of FAS-157 (Fair Value Measurements), as added by FSP FAS 157-3 (Determining the Fair Value of a Financial Asset When the Market for That Asset Is Not Active), is amended by the guidance in this FSP as follows: [Added text is underlined and deleted text is struck-out.]

> The discount rate adjustment technique described in paragraph B7-B11 of Statement 157 would not be appropriate when determining whether there has been an other-than-temporary the change in fair value results in an impairment and/or necessitates a change in yield

under EITF Issue No. 99-20, "Recognition of Interest Income and Impairment on Purchased Beneficial Interests That Continue to Be Held by a Transferor in Securitized Financial Assets," because that technique uses contractual cash flows rather than <u>estimated</u> cash flows ~~expected by market participants.~~

EFFECTIVE DATE AND TRANSITION

This FSP is effective for interim and annual reporting periods ending after December 15, 2008, and should not be applied retrospectively to previous interim or annual reporting periods.

As required in paragraph 15 of FSP FAS 15-1/FAS 124-1, an other-than-temporary impairment, if any, that results from the application of the guidance in ASC 320 (FAS-115) or Issue 99-20, the amount that must be recognized in earnings should equal the difference between an investment's cost and its fair value at the balance sheet date of the reporting period for which an assessment has been made.

AMENDMENTS TO ISSUE 99-20

The following are the amendments to paragraphs 5e, 12, 13, 15, of Issue 99-20 to insert the guidance in FSP EITF 99-20-1. Paragraphs 28, 29, and 30 are also added. [Added text is <u>underlined</u> and deleted text is ~~struck out.~~]

- Paragraph 5e., last sentence—"Instead, interest income on such beneficial interests should be recognized in accordance with the provisions of Statement 91, and determining whether an other-than-temporary impairment of such beneficial interests exists should be based on FSP EITF 99-20-1, FSP FAS 115-1/124-1, Statement 115, SAB 59, SAS-92 and Statement 115 Special Report."
- Paragraph 12—first sentence—The Task Force reached a consensus that "The original Task Force Consensus was superseded by FSP EITF 99-20-1.] The holder of a beneficial interest should continue to update the estimate of cash flows over the life of the beneficial interest. If upon evaluation:"
- Paragraph 12(a)—First sentence—"Based on current information and events that the holder of the beneficial interest estimates a market participant would use in determining the current fair value of the beneficial interest, it is probable that there is a favorable...."
- Paragraph 12(a)—Second sentence—"The adjustment should be accounted for prospectively as a change in estimate in conformity with Opinion 20 Statement 154 [Note: See paragraph 25 of the Status Section.] with the amount of periodic accretion adjusted over the remaining life of the beneficial interest."

- Paragraph 12(b). —Second and third sentences—"An entity should apply the impairment of securities guidance in paragraph 16 of FAS-115 and the related implementation guidance (see paragraphs 13, 13A, 13B, and 15 of this Issue). If based on current information and events it is probable that there a holder's best estimate of cash flows that a market participant would use in determining the current fair value of the beneficial interest, there has been an adverse change in estimated cash flows (in accordance with paragraph 12(a) above), then the condition in paragraph 8(a) of Statement 5 is met and (1) an other-than-temporary impairment...."

- Paragraph 13—Second and third sentences—"Subsequent to the transaction date, estimated cash flows are defined as the holder's estimate of the amount and timing of estimated principal and interest cash flows based on the holder's best estimate of current information and events that a market participant would use in determining the current fair value of the beneficial interest. In this Issue, "a favorable or (or an adverse) change in estimated cash flows" (as used in paragraph 12(a)) is considered in the context of both timing and amount of the estimated cash flows."

- New paragraph 13A—

  It is inappropriate to automatically conclude that a security is not other-than-temporarily impaired because all of the scheduled payments to date have been received. However, it also is inappropriate to automatically conclude that every decline in fair value represents an other-than-temporary impairment. Further analysis and judgment are required to assess whether a decline in fair value indicates that it is probable that the holder will not collect all of the contractual or estimated cash flows from the security. In addition, SAB Topic 5M states that "the length of time and extent to which the [fair] value has been less than cost" can indicate a decline is other-than-temporary. The longer and/or the more severe the decline in fair value, the more persuasive the evidence that is needed to overcome the premise that it is probable that the holder will not collect all of the contractual estimated cash flows from the issuer of the security.

- New paragraph 13B—

  In making its other-than-temporary impairment assessment, the holder should consider all available information relevant to the collectibility of the security, including information about past events, current conditions, and reasonable and supportable forecasts, when developing the estimate of future cash flows. Such information generally should include the remaining payment terms of the security, prepayment speeds, financial condition of the issuer(s), expected defaults, and value of any underlying financial collateral. To achieve that objective, the holder should consider, for example, industry analyst reports and forecasts, sector credit ratings, and other market data that are relevant to the collectibility of the security. The holder also should consider how other credit enhancements affect the expected performance of the security, including consideration of the current financial condition of the guarantor of a security (if the guarantee is not a separate contract[1a]) and/or whether any subordinated interests are capable of absorbing estimated losses on the loans underlying the security. The remaining payment terms of the security could be significantly different from the payment terms in prior periods (such as for securities backed by "nontraditional loans"[1b]). Thus, the holder should consider whether a security backed by currently performing loans will continue to perform when required payments increase in the future (including "balloon" payments). The holder also should consider how the value of any collateral would affect the expected performance of the security. If the fair value of the collateral has declined, the holder needs to assess the effect of that decline on the ability of the holder to collect the balloon payment.

- Paragraph 15—Insert between the first and second sentence. "[Note: See paragraph 28 of the STATUS section.]"

- Paragraph 15—Add as the last sentence. For example, an other-than-temporary impairment exists if as SAB Topic 5M states, "[The holder does not have] the intent and ability... to retain an investment in the issuer for a period of time sufficient to allow for any anticipated recovery in market value."

- New paragraph 28—FSP FAS 115-1/FAS 124-1 supersedes Topic D-44 (Recognition of Other-Than-Temporary Impairment upon the Planned Sale of a Security Whose Cost Exceeds Fair Value). However, paragraph 14 of FSP FAS 115-1/FAS 124-1 indicates, "... questions sometimes arise about whether an investor shall recognize an other-than-temporary impairment only when it intends to sell a specifically identified available-

---

[1a] As discussed in paragraph 8 of FSP FAS 115-1/124-1.
[1b] As indicated in FSP SOP 94-6-1, nontraditional loans may have features such as (a) terms that permit principal payment deferral or payments smaller than interest accruals (negative amortization), (b) a high loan-to-value ratio, (c) multiple loans on the same collateral that when combined result in a high loan-to-value ratio, (d) option adjustable-rate mortgages (option ARMs) or similar products that may expose the borrower to future increases in repayments in excess of increases that result solely from increases in the market interest rate (e.g., once negative amortization results in the loan reaching a maximum principal accrual limit), (e) an initial interest rate that is below the market interest rate for the initial period of the loan term and that may increase significantly when the period ends, and (f) interest-only loans that should be considered in developing estimates of future cash flows.

for-sale debt or equity security at a loss shortly after the balance sheet date. When an investor has decided to sell an impaired available-for-sale security and the investor does not expect the fair value of the security to fully recover prior to the expected time of sale, the security shall be deemed other-than-temporarily impaired in the period in which the decision to sell is made. However, an investor shall recognize an impairment loss when the impairment is deemed other than temporary even if a decision to sell has not been made."

- New Paragraph 29—FSP EITF 99-20-1 issued in January 2009, amends paragraphs 12, 13, and 15 of Issue 99-20 to align the impairment guidance in Issue 99-20 with that in paragraph 16 of Statement 115 and related implementation guidance. The FSP also amends Issue 99-20 for required status updates for the issuance of Statements 140, 154, and other literature.
- New paragraph 30—No further EITF discussion is planned.

EITF Issue 99-20 (Recognition of Interest Income and Impairment on Purchased Beneficial Interests and Transferor's Beneficial Interests in Securitized Financial Assets Obtained in a Transfer Accounted for as a Sale) (ASC 310-20-60-1, 2; 30-15-5; 320-10-35-38; 55-2; 325-40-05-1, 05-2; 15-2 through 9; 25-1 through 25-3; 30-1 through 30-3; 35-1 through 35-13, 35-15, 35-16; 45-1; 55-1 through 55-25; 60-7)

OVERVIEW

> **OBSERVATION:** FAS-140, which superseded FAS-125, did not affect the guidance in this Issue. FAS-125 established guidance on the accounting for interests retained in securitization transactions accounted for as sales. However, when the EITF reached its consensus positions in Issue 99-20, no guidance existed on the recognition and measurement of interest income from retained beneficial interests that continue to be held by a transferor. In June 2009, the FASB issued ASC 860-10-35-4; 35-6; 860-10-05-8; 860-20-25-5; 460-10-60-35; 860-20-55-46 through 55-48; 860-50-05-2 through 05-4; 30-1, 30-2; 35-1A, 35-3, 35-9 through 35-11; 25-2, 25-3, 25-6; 50-5 (FAS-166, *Transfers of Financial Assets — An Amendment of FASB Statement No. 140*), which has amended the guidance in Issue 99-20.

> **OBSERVATION:** See FSP EITF Issue 99-20-1 for amendments to Issue 99-20.

Scope

This Issue applies to a transferor's beneficial interests that a transferor *acquires as proceeds* in securitization transactions

40.18 *Transfer of Financial Assets*

accounted for as sales under the guidance in ASC 860 (FAS-140), as amended by ASC 860-10-35-4; 35-6; 860-10-05-8; 860-20–25-5; 460-10-60-35; 860-20-55-46 through 55-48; 860-50-05-2 through 05-4; 30-1, 30-2; 35-1A, 35-3, 35-9 through 35-11; 25-2, 25-3, 25-6; 50-5 (FAS-166), and to *purchased* beneficial interests in securitized financial assets. The guidance in this issue also applies to beneficial interests that are:

1. Debt securities accounted for under the guidance in ASC 310 (FAS-115), or required to be accounted for like such debt securities in accordance with ASC 860-20-35-2; ASC 320-35-45 (paragraph 14 of FAS-140), as amended by ASC 860-10-35-4; 35-6; 860-10-05-8; 860-20–25-5; 460-10-60-35; 860-20-55-46 through 55-48; 860-50-05-2 through 05-4; 30-1, 30-2; 35-1A, 35-3, 35-9 through 35-11; 25-2, 25-3, 25-6; 50-5 (FAS -166).

2. Securitized financial assets that have contractual cash flows, such as loans, receivables, and guaranteed lease residuals (The guidance in Issue 96-12 applies to securitized financial assets that do not involve contractual cash flows, such as common stock equity securities.)

3. Financial instruments that do not cause an entity holding the beneficial interests to consolidate the entity that issued the beneficial interests (e.g., a special purpose entity).

4. Not included under the scope of AICPA Practice Bulletin 6 (not in ASC), as amended by ASC 310-10-35-12 through 35-14, 35-16 through 35-26, 35-28 through 35-29, 35-32, 35-34, 35-37, 35-39; 45-5 through 45-6; 50-13, 50-15, 50-19; 310-30-30-2; 310-40-35-8 through 45-9, 45-12; 310-40-50-2 through 50-3, 50-12 (FAS-114) and 320-10-05-2; 15-2 through 15-5, 15-7; 25-1, 25-3 through 25-6, 25-9, 25-12, 25-14 through 25-16, 25-18; 30-1; 35-1 through 35-2, 35-4 through 35-5, 35-10 through 35-13, 35-18; 45-1 through 45-2, 45-8 through 45-11, 45-13; 50-1A through 50-3, 50-5, 50-9 through 50-11; 55-3; 942-320-50-1 through 50-3 (FAS-115) and 310-30-05-2 through 05-3 15-1 through 15-4, 15-6 through 15-10; 25-1; 30-1; 35-2 through 35-3, 35-6, 35-8 through 35-15; 40-1; 45-1; 50-1 through 50-3, 50-18; 55-5, 55-29; ; 835-10-60-3 (SOP 03-3) or the scope of SOP 03-3.

5. (a) Not beneficial interests in securitized financial assets with high credit quality (e.g., guaranteed by the U.S. government) so that the possibility of credit loss is remote and (b) do not permit the debtor to prepay or settle the obligation so that the holder would not recover substantially all of its recorded investment. Interest income on such beneficial interests should be recognized in accordance with the guidance in ASC 310-20 (FAS-91). The guidance in FSP EITF 99-20-1, FSP 115-1/FAS-124-1, ASC 320 (FAS-115), SEC Staff Bulletin 59, Statement of Auditing Standards 92, the FASB Special Report on FAS-115 should be followed to determine whether an other-than-temporary impairment of such beneficial assets exists.

6. Issued in equity form but meet the definition of a debt security in paragraph 137 of FAS-115 (ASC, Glossary), such as (a) a right to receive a future stream of cash flows under specified terms and conditions or (b) that must be redeemed by the issuer or must be redeemable at the investor's option.
7. Classified as trading securities under FAS-115, because under GAAP, entities in certain industries, such as banks and investment companies, are required to report investment income as a separate item in the income statement even though those entities report their investments at fair value and report changes in value in earnings. The Task Force believed that whether beneficial interests are classified as held-to-maturity, available-for-sale, or trading should not affect the recognition and measurement of interest income on those instruments.
8. The portions of hybrid beneficial interests referred to as host contracts, if they meet this Issue's scope requirements. A host contract must be separated from the hybrid instrument's embedded derivative, which must be accounted for separately according to the guidance in ASC 815-15-05-1; 35-2A; 25-1, 25-14, 25-26 through 25-29; 815-10-15-72 through 15-73 (paragraphs 12 through 14 of FAS-133). Hybrid beneficial interests measured at fair value in accordance with ASC 815-15-30-1 (paragraph 16 of FAS-133) are not included under the scope of this Issue if a transferor does not report interest income from those instruments as a separate item in the income statement.

This Issue applies to beneficial interests that would be covered under the AICPA's proposed SOP on accounting for certain purchased loans until that SOP is issued and becomes effective.

ACCOUNTING ISSUE

How should a transferor that retains an interest in securitized financial assets or an entity that purchases a beneficial interest in securitized financial assets account for income and impairment?

EITF CONSENSUS

1. The holder of a beneficial interest should estimate at the date the beneficial interest is acquired (the transaction date) the amount by which all cash flows that will be received from the beneficial interest will exceed the initial investment (the accretable yield). The holder should use the effective yield method to recognize that amount as interest income over the life of the beneficial interest. The initial investment is the fair value the beneficial interest as of the transfer date if the holder is also the transferor as required in ASC 860 (FAS-140), as amended by ASC 860-10-35-4, 35-6; 860-10-05-8; 860-20-25-5;

460-10-60-35; 860-20-55-46 through 55-48; 860-50-05-2 through 05-4; 30-1, 30-2; 35-1A, 35-3, 35-9 through 35-11; 25-2, 25-3, 25-6; 50-5 (FAS-166). The accretable yield should not be presented in the balance sheet.

2. The estimated cash flows should be adjusted over the life of the beneficial interest if:

   a. Based on the estimated fair value of the beneficial interest, using current information and events, it is probable that estimated cash flows will be more or less than the previous projection. An investor should recalculate the amount of the accretable yield for the beneficial interest on that date as the excess of estimated cash flows over the sum of (*a*) the initial investment *less* (*b*) cash received to date *less* (*c*) other-than-temporary impairment recognized to date *plus* (*d*) the yield accreted to date. The adjustment should be recognized prospectively as a change in estimate in accordance with APB-20 and the periodic accretion should be adjusted over the life of the beneficial interest. Based on cash flows, interest income may be recognized on a beneficial interest, even if accretion of the net investment in the beneficial interest results in an amount that exceeds the amount at which the beneficial interest could be settled if the entire amount were prepaid immediately.

   b. The beneficial interest's fair value is less than its reference amount. The guidance on impairment of securities in ASC 320-10-45-9 (paragraph 16 of FAS-115) should be applied to determine whether a decline is other-than-temporary. If based on the holder's best estimate of cash flows, all of the cash flows estimated in accordance with paragraph 2a above will not be collected, an other-than-temporary impairment has occurred and the beneficial interest should be written down to fair value. The change in value should be included in income. However, an other-than-temporary impairment need not be recognized if a change in the interest rate of a *plain vanilla* variable rate beneficial interest occurs without other indicators of impairment. To determine whether a favorable or adverse change in estimated cash flows from the amount previously projected (based on the timing and amount of estimated cash flows) has occurred, the present value of the remaining cash flows estimated at the initial transaction date, or the last date on which the amount was previously revised, should be compared to the present value of estimated cash flows at the current financial reporting date. Cash flows should be discounted at a rate that equals the current yield used to accrete the beneficial interest. A change is considered to be favorable—that is, an other-than-temporary impairment has *not* occurred—if the present value of the current estimated cash flows exceeds the present value of the estimated cash flows at the initial transaction date or the last date at which the amount was previously revised. A change is considered to be adverse—that is, an other-than-temporary impairment has occurred—if the present value of the current estimated cash flows is less than the present value of estimated cash flows at the initial transaction date or the last date at which the amount was previously revised.

3. At the transaction date, estimated cash flows are defined as the estimate of the amount and timing of future cash flows of principal and interest used to determine the purchase price or the holder's fair value for gain or loss recognition under ASC 860 (FAS-140, as amended by FAS-166). Thereafter, estimated cash flows are defined as the holder's estimate of the amount and timing of estimated cash flows from principal and interest payments, based on the holder's best assessment of current information and events a market participant would use to determine the current fair value of a beneficial interest. A favorable or adverse change in estimated cash flows is considered in terms of the timing and amount of estimated cash flows.

4. The Task Force noted that in accordance with the guidance in Topic D-44 (not included in the ASC), an entity that intends to sell a retained interest classified as available-for-sale should recognize a loss on an other-than-temporary impairment at the time the decision to sell is made, if the retained interest will be sold at a loss shortly after the balance sheet date, its fair value is less than its carrying amount, and it is not expected to recover before the date of an expected sale. The guidance in SAB-59, SAS-81, and ASC 860 (FAS-115) should also be considered in determining whether an other-than-temporary impairment exists.

5. The cost recovery method should be used if a beneficial interest is placed on nonaccrual status or if the holder cannot reliably estimate the security's cash flows.

> **OBSERVATION:** ASC 810 (FIN-46(R), Consolidation of Variable Interest Entities) requires the consolidation of a variable interest entity by an entity that absorbs a majority of a variable entity's expected losses or has the right to receive a greater part of a variable entity's expected residual returns or both.

> **OBSERVATION:** The guidance in ASC 815 (FAS-133, Accounting for Derivative Instruments and Hedging Activities) is amended by the guidance in ASC 815-15-25-4 through 25-5 (FAS-155, Accounting for Certain Hybrid Financial Instruments), which provides an election for the fair value measurement of certain hybrid financial instruments with embedded derivatives that otherwise would have to be bifurcated. If an entity elects to account for an entire hybrid financial instrument at fair value, that financial instrument should not be used as a hedging instrument in a hedging relationship under the guidance in ASC 815 (FAS-133).

OBSERVATION: Although the guidance in ASC 860-50-35-3, 35-6 through 35-7; 50-5 (FAS-156, Accounting for Servicing of Financial Assets—An Amendment of FASB Statement No. 140) amends the accounting guidance in ASC 860 (FAS-140, as amended by FAS-166) for separately recognized servicing assets and servicing liabilities, it does not affect the guidance in this Issue. Issue 99-20 represents the FASB's decision in ASC 860-50-35-3, 35-6 through 35-7; 50-5 (FAS-156) to replace the term "retained interests" with "interests that continue to be held by a transferor".

OBSERVATION: The guidance in ASC 860 (FAS-166), which was issued in June 2009, should be applied as of the beginning of an entity's first annual reporting period that begins after November 15, 2009, for interim periods in that first annual reporting period and for interim and annual reporting periods thereafter. Its guidance must be applied to transfers that occur on or after the effective date. FAS-166 amends the guidance in ASC 860 (FAS-140) by eliminating the concept of a special-purpose entity and the scope exception that exempted special-purpose entities from following the guidance in ASC 810 (FIN 46(R)). Under the guidance in ASC 810 (FAS-140, as amended by FAS-166), derecognition provisions should be applied to a transfer of an entire financial asset, a group of entire financial assets, or a participating interest in an entire financial asset. In addition, interests acquired by a transferor on completion of a transfer of an entire financial asset or an entire group of financial assets that meet the conditions to be accounted for as a sale should be recognized and measured initially at fair value. The term "interests that continue to be held by a transferor" as it is used In ASC 860 (FAS-140, as amended by FAS-166), applies only if a transferor retains participating interests on completion of a transfer of participating rights in a transaction that meets the conditions to be accounted for as a sale. Under the guidance in FAS-166, that term should be used only for such retained participation rights.

ASC 860 Transfers and Servicing

FSP FAS-140-1 (Accounting for Accrued Interest Receivable under FAS-140 Securitizations) (ASC 860-20-35-6; 55-17 through 55-19)

Question: How should the accrued interest receivable related to securitized and sold receivables be accounted for and reported under the guidance in ASC 860 (FAS-140, Accounting for Transfers and Servicing of Financial Assets and Extinguishments of Debt)?

Answer: When credit card receivables are securitized, a pool of receivables is transferred to a trust and the trust receives the right to future collections of principal, finance charges, and fees. Assuming that the transfer of receivables meets the ASC 860 (FAS-140) criteria for treatment as a sale, the transferor will carry on its balance sheet only its retained interests in the transferred receivables.

Some companies that securitize credit card receivables continue to recognize accrued interest receivable as an asset on their balance sheet, even thought the right to receive this accrued interest receivable has been transferred to the trust. The accrued interest receivable represents the investors' portion of the accrued fees and finance charges on the transferred credit card receivables. According to the final FSP that was recently issued, this accounting treatment is generally no longer acceptable.

Assuming that the securitization meets the requirements to be treated as a sale and the accrued interest receivable is subordinated, the accrued interest receivable should be considered one of the components of the sales transaction. The accrued interest receivable should be treated as retained beneficial interest. It is not acceptable to refer to the accrued interest receivable as "loans receivable," or as any other title that fails to communicate that the accrued interest receivable has been subordinated to the senior interests in the securitization.

The accrued interest receivable cannot be prepaid or settled in a manner in which the owner would suffer a significant loss of its investment. Therefore, the accrued interest receivable is not subsequently measured like an investment in debt securities that is treated as available-for-sale or trading under the guidance in ASC 320 (FAS-115, Accounting for Certain Investments in Debt Equity Securities). The subsequent measurement of retained interests that cannot be prepaid or settled in a manner in which the owner would suffer a significant loss on its investment, including accrued interest receivable, is accounted for in accordance with ASC 450 (FAS-5, Accounting for Contingencies). ASC 450 (FAS-5) provides guidance in providing for the uncollectibility of receivables including, as in this case, accrued interest receivable.

FSP FAS-140-3 (Accounting for Transfers of Financial Assets and Repurchase Financing Transactions) (ASC 860-10-05-21A, 212B; 40-42 through 46; 55-17A through 55-17C, 55-54; 65-1)

OVERVIEW

In this FSP, the FASB staff addresses the accounting for a transaction that has the following fact pattern: Party A (transferor) transfers a financial asset to Party B (transferee) who pays cash for the asset to Party A. Subsequently or at the same time, Party B enters into a repurchase agreement, as defined in ASC 860-10-05-20 through 05-21 (paragraph 97 of FAS-140, Accounting for Transfers and Servicing of Financial Assets and Extinguishments of Liabilities) with Party A.

Under that agreement, Party A lends cash to Party B, which transfers the financial asset or substantially the same asset, as defined SOP 90-3 (Definition of the Term "Substantially the Same" for Holders of Debt Instruments, as Used in Certain Audit Guides and a Statement of Position) to Party A as collateral for the loan. Under the terms of the arrangement, Party B must repurchase the financial asset, or substantially the same financial asset, from Party A at a fixed or determinable price within a prescribed time period. Party A returns the financial asset, or substantially the same financial asset, to Party B when Party B has made the required payment to Party A under the agreement. The repurchase agreement may occur at the same time as the original transfer of the financial asset by Party A to Party B or at a later date.

Under the guidance in ASC 860 (FAS-140), any involvement a transferor has with a transferred asset (even one that occurs some time after the initial transfer) must be considered in an analysis of whether the transferor has relinquished control over the transferred financial asset. ASC 860 (FAS-140) does not, however, provide guidance for the repurchase transaction discussed in this FSP. Further, there is a presumption in ASC 860 (FAS-140) that the counterparties to a transfer of a financial asset will account for the transaction symmetrically.

The question addressed in this FSP is whether there are circumstances in which the transfer of a previously transferred financial asset and a repurchase financing agreement related to the same asset between the same counterparties may be accounted for as two separate transactions. Although this question was first asked by entities in the mortgage real estate investment trust industry, the guidance in this FSP also will affect entities in other industries.

FASB STAFF POSITION

The presumption in this FSP is that an initial transfer and a repurchase agreement between the same counterparties should be linked and accounted for as one transaction under the guidance in ASC 860 (FAS-140), unless certain criteria are met. In that case, the two agreements should be evaluated separately under the guidance in ASC 860 (FAS-140).

The following three transactions occur in a transfer of a financial asset and a repurchase agreement between the same counterparties:

1. The initial transfer when a transferor transfers a financial asset to a transferee.

2. The execution of a repurchase agreement under which an initial transferee (borrower) transfers a previously transferred financial asset back to the initial transferor (lender) as collateral for a loan.

3. The settlement of the repurchase agreement under which a borrower repays a lender who then returns the collateral to the borrower.

Derecognition and recognition. The counterparties to a transfer of a financial asset and a related repurchase agreement are permitted to account for those transactions separately if: (1) there is a compelling and separate business or economic purpose for entering into the separate transactions; and (2) the repurchase agreement is *not* a means for the initial transferor to regain control over the transferred asset. A transaction that lacks a specific business or economic purpose and is entered into only to achieve a specific accounting result by circumventing an accounting standard does *not* qualify for separate accounting.

This FSP provides that an initial transfer and a related repurchase agreement entered into between the same counterparties simultaneously or at a later date should be considered to be *linked* and accounted for as one transaction, unless *all* of the following criteria are met:

- The initial transfer and the repurchase agreement do *not* contractually depend on each other and the counterparties have entered into *no* implied commitments, such as the pricing or performance of the initial transfer or the repurchase agreement, which depend on or affect the terms of the transactions and the execution of the other agreement.
- The initial transferor has full recourse to the transferee on default. That is, the initial transferor must be exposed to the initial transferee's, or its affiliates' credit risk, not only to the market risk of the transferred financial asset. In addition the transferee's repurchase agreement for the previously transferred financial asset, or substantially the same asset, must be for a fixed price, not fair value.
- There is a quoted price in an active market for the previously transferred financial asset and the repurchase agreement (i.e., Level 1 inputs as defined in ASC 820 (FAS-157, Fair Value Measurements)); in addition, the financial asset's initial transfer and the repurchase agreement are executed at market rates. This provision should *not* be circumvented by embedding off-market terms in a separate transaction at the time of the initial transfer or the repurchase financing.
- The repurchase agreement must be settled *before* the financial asset's maturity.

If *all* of the above criteria are met, the initial transfer and the repurchase agreement should be accounted for separately. In that case, (1) the initial transfer should be analyzed to determine whether the transaction meets the requirements for sale accounting in ASC 860 (FAS-140) without considering the repurchase agreement, and (2) the initial transferor and the initial transferee should analyze the repurchase financing as a repurchase agreement in accordance with [ASC 860-10-55-68 through 68A; 40-4 through 40-5; 35-3; ASC 860-20-40-1 through 40-2; 25-1 through 25-3; 30-1 through 30-2; 55-25 (paragraphs 9 through 12) ASC 860 -10-55-58; 40-24; 55-35; ASC 860–30-

25-7; ASC 860-20-40-1A (paragraphs 4 through 49) and ASC 860-10-05-19 through 21; 55-55 through 57, 55-1 through 55-3; 55-51 through 53 (paragraphs 96 through 101) of FAS-140]. The guidance in ASC 860 (FAS-140 as amended by FAS-166) requires that both parties to a repurchase agreement use the same criteria to determine how to account for the repurchase agreement.

The initial transfer and repurchase agreement in a transaction that does *not* meet all of the criteria for separate accounting should be accounted for as a *linked* transaction and evaluated to determine whether the requirements for sale accounting in ASC 860 (FAS-140 as amended by FAS-166) have been met. If the requirements for sale accounting have *not* been met, the linked transaction should be accounted for based on the economics of the combined transactions, generally, as a forward contract. In addition, it is necessary to determine whether a linked transaction should be accounted for as a derivative in accordance with the guidance in ASC 815 (FAS-133, Accounting for Derivative Instruments and Hedging Activities) and to consider whether other accounting literature applies to the linked transaction, such as how other aspects of a securitization transaction are affected if an initial transferor retains a financial asset that is subject to a repurchase agreement.

EFFECTIVE DATE AND TRANSITION

FSP FAS-140-3 is effective for financial statements issued for fiscal years that begin after November 15, 2008, and interim periods in those fiscal years. Earlier application is *prohibited*.

The guidance in the FSP should be applied prospectively to initial transfers and repurchase financings for which an initial transfer is executed on or after the beginning of the fiscal year in which the FSP is initially applied.

EITF Issue 85-13 (Sale of Mortgage Service Rights on Mortgages Owned by Others) (ASC 860-50-40-10, 50-11)

OVERVIEW

A company sells its portfolio of first-mortgage loans and retains the right to service the loans. Because there is a lag between the time the mortgage payments are collected and the time such payments are passed to the mortgage owners, the company invests that "float." As a result, the company can sell the mortgage servicing rights for cash or for participation in the future interest stream produced by the loans.

ACCOUNTING ISSUES

- Should a gain be recognized on the sale of mortgage servicing rights for a participation in the income stream of future interest?

- If so, how should the gain be measured?

EITF CONSENSUS

- A gain should be recognized at the date of the sale.
- The Task Force agreed that it is difficult to measure the gain if the sales price is based on the seller's participation in future payments; it also agreed that the accounting literature does not provide guidance on the upper limit of a computed sales price. All available information should be considered, including the gain that would be recognized if the servicing rights were sold for a fixed cash price.

> **OBSERVATION:** Although ASC 860-50-35-3, 50-5, 35-6 through 35-7 (FAS-156, Accounting for Servicing of Financial Assets—An Amendment of FASB Statement No. 140) does not affect the guidance in this Issue, changes in the fair value of separately recognized servicing assets or servicing liabilities that are measured at fair value subsequent to adoption of the Statement should be included in earnings in the period in which the fair value changes occur. An additional change in the fair value of servicing assets or servicing liabilities, if any, from the last measurement date to a date of sale should be included in earnings at the date of sale.

DISCUSSION

The Task Force discussed whether the gain should be calculated in the same way as on the sale of the related mortgage loan portfolio. They noted that the difficulty in determining the upper limit of the sales price is the result of uncertainty about prepayments and the duration of the underlying mortgage loans. They also discussed whether the gain on this transaction, plus the gain on the sale of the mortgage loan portfolio, should be limited to the gain if the servicing rights were sold for a fixed cash price.

EITF Issue 87-30 (Sale of a Short-Term Loan Made under a Long-Term Credit Commitment) (ASC 860-10-55-71, 55-72)

OVERVIEW

A financial institution has made a 90-day short-term loan to a borrower under a five-year long-term credit commitment and subsequently transfers the short-term loan without recourse to a third party. Under the transfer agreement, the risk of loss on the short-term loan is legally transferred to the purchaser, while the transferor retains no obligation to repurchase the short-term loan. The financial institution may relend to the borrower under the long-term credit commitment when the short-term obligation matures, but may refuse to do so based on an evaluation of the borrower's credit or because the borrower does not satisfy a covenant under the long-term credit commitment.

ACCOUNTING ISSUE

Should a transfer of a short-term loan under a long-term credit commitment be accounted for as a sale or as a financing transaction?

EITF CONSENSUS

1. A transfer of a short-term loan under the long-term credit commitment described above should be accounted for as a sale.
2. Loan covenants affect the accounting for a transfer as follows:
   a. A transfer of a short-term loan under a long-term credit commitment that includes a substantive *subjective* covenant should be accounted for as a sale.
   b. A transfer of a short-term loan under a long-term credit commitment that includes only *objective* covenants should be accounted for as a sale only if such objective covenants are substantive—that is, they specifically apply to the borrower and are expected to be meaningful and relevant in determining whether the long-term credit commitment obligates the financial institution to relend to the borrower.
3. Commitment fees received for long-term commitments should be recognized based on the guidance in FAS-91.

EFFECT OF ASC 815 (FAS-133)

The guidance in ASC 815 (FAS-133) applies if an analysis of the terms of the contract indicate that the put option qualifies as a derivative under the Statement.

EFFECT OF ASC 860 (FAS-140), AS AMENDED BY ASC 860 (FAS-166)

- The guidance in ASC 860 (FAS-140, as amended by FAS-166) affirms the Task Force's consensus that a short-term loan under a long-term credit commitment to a third-party purchaser without recourse should be accounted for as a sale under the circumstances described in this Issue. Such a transaction could meet the conditions for the surrender of control under the guidance in ASC 860-10-40-4 and 40-5 (paragraph 9 of FAS-140), as amended by the guidance in ASC 860 (FAS-166). Specific transactions should be evaluated based on the guidance in ASC 860-10-40-4 and 40-5 (paragraph 9 of FAS-140, as amended by ASC 860 (FAS-166)).
- If a transaction discussed in this Issue is accounted for as a transfer of a receivable with a put option, recognition of a sale

is required if the transaction meets the conditions in ASC 860-10-40-4 through 40-5 (paragraph 9 of FAS-140), as amended by the guidance in ASC 860 (FAS-166)), would apply.
- The guidance in ASC 860-10-40-4 through 40-5 (paragraph 9 of FAS-140, as amended by the guidance in ASC 860 (FAS-166)) is amended to require that a transferor that effectively retains control over transferred financial assets be precluded from recognizing a sale on the transaction. Examples of when a transferor effectively retains control over transferred financial assets are included in ASC 860-10-40-4 and 40-5 (paragraph 9 of FAS-140, as amended by ASC 860 (FAS-166)).
- The SEC Observer's concerns (see comment below) are partially resolved by the requirement in ASC 860-20-25-1 (paragraph 11 of FAS-140, as amended by FAS-166), that a liability be recognized for a put obligation incurred or proceeds in such transactions if the put obligation does not prohibit sales accounting.
- The guidance in ASC 860 (FAS-140) does not address a lender's refusal to relend to a borrower based on subjective or objective covenants. (See SEC Observer's Comment.) However, the put option's terms should be analyzed to determine whether the put meets the definition of a derivative in ASC 815 (FAS-133). If a loan cannot be readily converted to cash and there is no market mechanism to enable the holder to settle the option in net cash, the put option may not meet condition 6(c) of FAS-133, which is further discussed in ASC 860-10-40-4 through 40-5 (paragraph 9 of FAS-140, as amended by FAS-166).
- The recognition of commitment fees is not addressed in ASC 860 (FAS-140).

SEC OBSERVER COMMENT

The SEC Observer stated that he is uncomfortable with sales accounting and concerned about uncertainties related to the transaction, such as the accounting for commitment fees for long-term commitments under ASC 311 (FAS-91), the classification of the loan by the borrower as short-term or long-term, and the probability of whether the financial institution will relend to the borrower.

DISCUSSION

Although the risk of loss has been transferred in this transaction, and the transferor has no contractual obligation to repurchase the short-term loan receivable, the Issue is complicated by the fact that it deals with a short-term loan under a revolving long-term credit commitment. That is, if the transaction is viewed as a single loan that reprices periodically, the substance of the transaction is that the lender (transferor) either repays the transferee when the loan rolls over or the transferee agrees to purchase the additional portion of the loan.

Some Task Force members questioned the consistency of the transaction described with actual transactions and with a proposed AICPA Practice Bulletin, *Sales of Short-Term Loans under Long-Term Credit Commitments*. The Practice Bulletin (which was never issued as a final document) would have required sales recognition if the transaction meets certain conditions.

To address concerns about the probability that the financial institution will relend to the borrower, the EITF discussed the effect of loan covenants on the relending decision. The Task Force's consensus was based on a discussion of the following two types of financial-related covenants:

1. *Subjective covenants* Compliance is determined subjectively. For example, a provision that refers to a "material adverse change" may be evaluated differently by the parties to the agreement.

2. *Objective covenants* Compliance is determined objectively based on data such as financial ratios.

The Task Force reached the consensus on the accounting for commitment fees to address a concern expressed by the SEC Observer.

EITF Issue 88-22 (Securitization of Credit Card and Other Receivable Portfolios) (ASC 860-10-05-11; 20-35-10; 55-16)

OVERVIEW

Banks or other financial institutions form pools of receivables consisting of balances owed by credit card customers and transfer an interest in the receivables to a trust. A bank then sells undivided participation interests in the trust to investors. The trust is commonly referred to as a credit card securitization. It has a limited life that can be divided into two phases:

1. A reinvestment phase, during which all receivables generated by customers in the pool are kept by the trust while investors receive interest payments only

2. A liquidation phase, during which investors receive principal payments as well as interest

During the reinvestment phase, usually 18 to 36 months, the trust purchases additional credit card receivables as balances in the selected accounts increase. Although the percentage of the bank's and investors' participation in the trust's assets may fluctuate up or down during this phase, as a result of charge and payment activities in the selected accounts, the investors' dollar investment in the trust remains constant, because proceeds from repayments (principal payments) allocated to the investors are reinvested in additional credit card receivables.

For example, the following illustrates such activity for a month.

	Credit Card Balances	Investors' Interest	Percentage
Total receivables in trust, 1/1	$1,000,000	$750,000	75.0
Repayments	(100,000)	(75,000)	75.0
Charges	80,000	75,000	93.8
Total receivables in trust, 1/31	$ 980,000	$750,000	76.5

In this example, a larger percentage of charges (93.8% instead of 75%) was allocated to the investors in order to maintain their $750,000 investment in the trust.

During the liquidation period, principal payments on receivables in the trust are allocated to investors, based on the terms of the agreement. The following methods are used:

- The *participation method,* which consists of:

    —*Fixed participation* Based on investors' interests in the receivables at the end of the reinvestment period.

    —*Preset participation* Based on a preset percentage that is higher than investors' participation interests at the end of the reinvestment period. (Results in a faster payout than the fixed participation method.)

    —*Floating participation* Based on investors' actual participation interests in the trust each month. (Interests will decline each month because of repayments.)

- The *controlled amortization method,* which is based on a predetermined monthly payment schedule; investors' interests are liquidated over a specified period. One of the three participation methods is used to allocate principal payments to investors. If principal payments are greater than the predetermined monthly payment, they are allocated to the bank and used to increase the investors' ownership interests. If allocated principal payments are less than the predetermined monthly payment, payments to investors are reduced by the deficiency. The deficiency is recovered in subsequent months if the amount allocated to investors exceeds the predetermined payments.

Credit losses on receivables in the trust generally are allocated to investors based on their actual floating participation interest (participation interests may fluctuate monthly because of an imbalance between charges and payments on accounts), regardless of the liquidation method. However, some form of credit enhancement, such as a third-party letter of credit that exceeds expected credit losses, may be used to mitigate losses allocated to investors.

ACCOUNTING ISSUES

1. This issue has been nullified.
2. This issue has been nullified.
3. How should a gain or loss on transfer that is recognized as a sale be calculated?

EITF CONSENSUS

The EITF reached the following consensus positions:

1. This consensus has been nullified by the guidance in FAS-140, which as been amended by the guidance in ASC 860-10-35-4, 35-6; 860-10-05-8; 860-20-25-5; 460-10-60-35; 860-20-55-46 through 55-48; 860-50-05-2 through 05-4; 30-1, 30-2; 35-1A, 35-3, 35-9 through 35-11; 25-2, 25-3, 25-6; 50-5 (FAS-166):1.
2. The consensus on the effect of the liquidation method was nullified by the guidance in ASC 860 (FAS-140).
3. A gain, if any, on the sale of receivables should not exceed amounts related to existing receivables at the date of the sale. Amounts related to future receivables expected to be sold during the reinvestment period should *not* be included in the gain. (This consensus has been affirmed in ASC 860-50-25-9 (paragraph 78 of FAS-140)). Based on information about certain transactions, some Task Force members noted that a gain on such transactions generally would not be significant, because the receivables sold have a relatively short life, the high cost of servicing credit card loans, and the yields required by the current interest rate environment. In addition, they noted that a transaction's terms should be reviewed to determine whether a loss should be recognized for costs expected to be incurred for all future servicing obligations, including costs for receivables not yet sold. (This comment was affirmed in ASC 860 (FAS-140), which superseded FAS-125 and has been amended by ASC FAS-166). Under the guidance in ASC 860 (FAS-140), a servicer is required to recognize a servicing liability if the servicer expects that the costs of performing the service will exceed the benefits and the work is expected to be performed at a loss. Some members also observed that transaction costs related to sales of receivables may be recognized over the initial and reinvestment periods in a rational and systematic manner, unless a transaction results in a loss. (The Task Force members' comments were affirmed in ASC 860 (FAS-140) and were not reconsidered in ASC 860-10-35-4, 35-6; 860-10-05-8; 860-20-25-5; 460-10-60-35; 860-20-55-46 through 55-48; 860-50-05-2 through 05-4; 30-1, 30-2; 35-1A, 35-3, 35-9 through 35-11; 25-2, 25-3, 25-6; 50-5 (FAS-166), which amended the guidance in FAS-140.)

In addition, in accordance with the guidance in ASC 860 (FAS-140), transaction costs for a past sale are not an asset and consequently should be included in a gain or loss. However, some of the transaction costs incurred at the beginning of a credit card securitization can qualify for asset recognition because they are related to future sales that will occur during the revolving period. (The EITF's comments are consistent with this guidance.)

SUBSEQUENT DEVELOPMENT

The SEC Observer stated at the EITF's July 1995 meeting that the staff believes that the Task Force's consensus positions in Issue 88-22 also apply to securitizations of other types of receivables with similar arrangements. The Task Force agreed with that view.

> **OBSERVATION:** ASC 810 (FIN-46(R), Consolidation of Variable Interest Entities) requires the consolidation of variable interest entities by an entity that absorbs a majority of a variable interest entity's expected losses or has the right to receive a greater part of a variable interest entity's expected residual returns or both.

> **OBSERVATION:** Although the guidance in ASC 860-50-35-3, 35-6 through 35-7; 50-5 (FAS-156, *Accounting for Servicing of Financial Assets—An Amendment of FASB Statement No. 140*), which amends the accounting guidance in FAS-140 for separately recognized servicing assets and servicing liabilities, its guidance does not affect the guidance in this Issue. The FASB's decision in ASC 860-50-35-3, 35-6 through 35-7, 50-50-5 (FAS-156) to replace the term *retained interests* with the term *interests that continue to be held by a transferor* is reflected in this Issue.

EITF Issue 90-21 (Balance Sheet Treatment of a Sale of Mortgage Servicing Rights with a Subservicing Agreement) (ASC 460-10-60-37; 860-10-S40-1; S99-1; 50-40-7 through 40-9)

OVERVIEW

Mortgage servicers perform administrative services for mortgage investors for which they receive a fee. Among the services they perform are collection of mortgage payments, remittance of escrow taxes and insurance payments to the proper entities, and remittance of the net collections to the investor. The right to receive those fees is recognized in the mortgage servicer's financial statements as an asset referred to as "mortgage servicing rights." A mortgage servicer may sell the right to receive those fees, but may retain the obligation to service the mortgage through a subservicing agreement.

This issue was first discussed by the EITF in Issue 87-34. In that Issue, the Task Force reached a consensus that income should not be recognized immediately on the transaction, and that the accounting for the transaction as a financing or a sale depends on the specific circumstances. The Task Force agreed, however, that a loss should be recognized if the transferor has determined that future servicing would be performed at a loss because of prepayments on the loans. That consensus does not apply to temporary subservicing agreements in which subservicing is performed by the transferor only for a short time.

ACCOUNTING ISSUE

Should a transfer of mortgage servicing rights with a subservicing agreement be accounted for (a) always as a sale with a gain deferred, (b) always as a financing, or (c) based on the particular facts and circumstances of the transaction?

EITF CONSENSUS

1. A sale of mortgage servicing rights with a subservicing agreement should be accounted for as a sale with gain deferred, if substantially all of the risks and rewards inherent in owning the rights have been effectively transferred to the buyer.

2. The transaction should be treated as a financing if substantially all risks and rewards have *not* been transferred. Risks and rewards associated with a seller performing purely administrative functions under a subservicing agreement would not necessarily preclude sales treatment.

3. Certain factors, if present, provide *conclusive evidence* that substantially all risks and rewards have *not* been transferred and thus preclude sales treatment. Certain other factors, if present, are *presumed to indicate* that substantially all risks and rewards have *not* been transferred. The presumption can be overcome only if there is sufficient evidence to the contrary. Those factors are in the following table:

Conclusive Evidence—No Sales Recognition	*Must Be Overcome for Sales Recognition*
• The seller/subservicer directly or indirectly guarantees a yield to the buyer.	• The seller/subservicer directly or indirectly provides financing or guarantees the buyer's financing. Nonrecourse financing would indicate that risks have not been transferred.
• The seller/subservicer is obligated to make payments of all or a portion of the subservicing fees to the buyer on a nonre-	• The terms of the subservicing agreement unduly limit the purchaser's ability to exercise the rights associated with ownership. An example

course basis prior to receipt from the mortgagor.

- The seller/subservicer indemnifies the buyer for damages due to causes other than failure to perform its contractual duties.
- The seller/subservicer agrees to absorb losses on mortgage loan-foreclosures not covered by government agencies or other guarantors, including absorption of foreclosure costs of managing foreclosed property.
- Title to the servicing rights is retained by the seller/subservicer.

is a subservicing agreement that is not cancelable by either party (although a reasonable noncancellation period is allowed).

- The buyer is a special-purpose entity without sufficient capital at risk.

Some EITF members observed that there may be other factors that also indicate that the seller has not transferred substantially all risks and rewards associated with ownership to the buyer.

> **OBSERVATION:** Under the provisions of ASC 460 (FIN-45, Guarantor's Accounting and Disclosure Requirements for Guarantees, Including Indirect Guarantees of Indebtedness to Others), a guarantor is required to recognize a liability for the obligation assumed at the inception of a guarantee. The Interpretation also provides guidance on the appropriate disclosures.

> **OBSERVATION:** Although the guidance in ASC 860-50-35-3, 35-6 through 35-7, 50-5 (FAS-156, Accounting for Servicing of Financial Assets—An Amendment of FASB Statement No. 140) does not affect the guidance in this Issue, changes in the fair value of separately recognized servicing assets or servicing liabilities that are measured at fair value subsequent to adoption of the Statement should be included in earnings in the period in which the fair value changes occur. An additional change in the fair value of servicing assets or servicing liabilities, if any, from the last measurement date to a date of sale should be included in earnings at the date of sale.

SEC OBSERVER COMMENT

The SEC Observer noted that the SEC staff believes that if, in substance, a transaction transfers only a portion of the servicing revenue, substantially all the risks and rewards of ownership have not been transferred. Such a transaction should be accounted for under the guidance in EITF Issue 88-18.

DISCUSSION

The Task Force's primary concerns related to the transferor's continuing involvement with the loans and whether the risks and rewards have been transferred.

Those who believed that the determination of whether to account for the transaction as a sale or financing should be based on specific circumstances analogized to sale-leasebacks and to the specific criteria used to determine whether a transaction in Issue 88-18 is a sale or financing. They also looked to SEC SAB-30 (Accounting for Divestiture of a Subsidiary or Other Business Operation) and SAB-82 (Certain Transfers of Nonperforming Assets) for guidance on factors that would help determine whether the transaction is a sale or a financing.

Each of the factors that provide conclusive evidence that the transaction is *not* a sale is related to aspects of the transferor's retention of risks and rewards of ownership that cannot be overcome. Although the list of presumptive evidence includes factors that also indicate retention of the risks and rewards of ownership, those factors, such as the buyer's ability to cancel the subservicing agreement, may be overcome.

EITF Issue 95-5 (Determination of What Risks and Rewards, If Any, Can Be Retained and Whether Any Unresolved Contingencies May Exist in a Sale of Mortgage Loan Servicing Rights) (ASC 860-50-40-3 through 40-5)

OVERVIEW

A seller/transferor may provide a buyer/transferee with protection provisions in an agreement to sell or transfer servicing rights. Such provisions may include adjustment of the sales price for loan prepayments, defaults, or foreclosures occurring within a specific time period. In addition, most agreements include representations and warranty provisions that apply to eligibility defects discovered within a specific time period.

In EITF Issue 89-5 (Sale of Mortgage Loan Servicing Rights), the EITF had reached a consensus that a seller/transferor should *not* recognize a sale before the closing date, which is when title and all risks and rewards pass irrevocably to the buyer and no significant unresolved contingencies remain.

The issue was addressed again in Issue 94-5, in which the EITF was asked (*a*) whether Issue 89-5 precludes sales recognition, because *all* risks have not passed, if a sales agreement includes some or all of the protection, representation, or warranty provisions, or (*b*) whether Issue 89-5 does not preclude sales recognition of such an agreement, because the provisions are *insignificant unresolved contin-*

gencies for which the seller accrues a liability at the date of sale. The EITF reached a consensus that sales recognition would be precluded on the transfer of mortgage servicing rights until resolution of uncertainties related to the seller's retention of prepayment, credit, or similar risks, such as foreclosures and defaults. The Task Force retroactively rescinded the consensus on Issue 94-5 in January 1995 and agreed to reconsider it.

ACCOUNTING ISSUE

Is sales recognition precluded at the date title passes if the agreement includes any provision under which the seller retains specific risks, or could a sale be recognized at that date if:

- A seller can reasonably estimate and recognizes a liability for the costs related to protection provisions, or if
- A sales agreement provides for substantially all risks and rewards to irrevocably pass to the buyer, and the seller can reasonably estimate the minor protection provisions and recognizes a liability for that amount?

EITF CONSENSUS

- A transfer of a right to service mortgage loans should be recognized as a sale if the following conditions have been met:
  —Title has passed.
  —Substantially all risks and rewards of ownership have irrevocably passed to the buyer.
  —The seller has retained only minor protection provisions that are reasonably estimable.
- A liability should be accrued for the estimated obligation associated with the minor protection provisions.
- A seller retains only minor protection provisions if
  —The obligation related to those provisions does not exceed 10% of the sales price and
  —Prepayment risk is retained for a maximum of 120 days.

This consensus supersedes Issue 89-5. However, this consensus carries forward the consensus in Issue 89-5, under which recognition of a sale at the closing date would not necessarily be precluded if the seller enters into a temporary agreement to perform subservicing for a short period of time.

DISCUSSION

Proponents of the view adopted by Task Force noted that authoritative pronouncements such as ASC 605 (FAS-48). ASC 360 (FAS-66 and FAS-98) permit sales recognition when some risk has been retained by the seller. It also was argued that sufficient historical and projected information exists about the types of risks retained to enable a seller to estimate the effects of such uncertainties. In addition, provisions related to prepayment protection, early payment defaults, and investor approval are resolved within a short period of time, such as three months or less. The buyer's remedies usually are limited to a reduction of the sales proceeds for the disqualified portion, but the buyer cannot void the sale unless there is fraud. As a result, the seller can estimate the effect of the provisions.

The Task Force decided to define the term *minor* as 10% of the sales price to attain consistent application of the consensus. Ten percent was chosen as the maximum limit, because it is a common definition of minor found in the accounting literature, such as in lease accounting and pooling of interests. Ten percent also is considered a reasonable percentage of risk to be retained by the seller while recognizing a sale.

EITF Issue 97-3 (Accounting for Fees and Costs Associated with Loan Syndications and Loan Participations after the Issuance of FASB Statement No. 125) (ASC 310-20-25-20; 860-10-55-3)

OVERVIEW

Note: The guidance in ASC 860 (FAS-140 as amended by FAS-166), which superseded FAS-125, does not affect the guidance in this Issue. In Issue 88-17, the EITF discussed the characteristics of loan syndications and loan participations and the divergent accounting for nonrefundable fees and costs associated with those transactions under the provisions of ASC 310 (FAS-91). The EITF reached a consensus on Issue 88-17 that because there are no substantive differences between loan syndications and some loan participations, nonrefundable fees and costs on those transactions should be treated the same. The Task Force established criteria for transactions that are structured legally as participations but that should be accounted for as "in-substance loan syndications" and reached a consensus that all transactions legally structured as syndications must also meet those criteria, thus creating in-substance participations.

Loan participations, which are transfers of financial assets, were covered under the scope of FAS-125, as superseded by FAS-140, but loan syndications, which do not transfer financial assets, are not. In Topic D-52 the FASB staff had determined that FAS-125 nullifies the EITF's consensus in Issue 88-17 that loan participations meeting certain criteria should be considered "in-substance syndications" and thus accounted for the same as syndications. However, the FASB staff stated that the accounting for transactions structured legally as syndications is unaffected by the provisions of FAS-125. Such transactions would continue to be accounted for under the provisions of ASC 310 (FAS-91).

This Issue was brought to the EITF because some questioned the staff's interpretation that FAS-125 nullifies the EITF's consensus that certain participations should be accounted for as "in-substance syndications."

ACCOUNTING ISSUES

1. Does FAS-125 apply to loan participations even if they are considered to be in-substance syndications under the consensus in Issue 88-17?

2. If the conclusion to Issue 1 is that certain loan participations should no longer be accounted for as loan syndications, is the consensus in Issue 88-17 (that certain legal syndications may be in-substance participations) also no longer applicable?

EITF CONSENSUS

1. The EITF's consensus positions in Issue 88-17 should be superseded.

2. All loan participations should be accounted for under the provisions of FAS-125, which applies to all loan participations, even those having the characteristics of loan syndications discussed in Issue 88-17.

3. All transactions structured legally as loan syndications, including those described as in-substance loan participations in Issue 88-17, should be accounted under the provisions of FAS-91.

DISCUSSION

The FASB staff explained that lenders sometimes structure transactions as loan participations rather than syndications because of the administrative difficulties of structuring a syndication. In a participation, the lender originates and funds the total loan but very shortly thereafter sells interests in the loan to other lenders, whereas in a syndication, several lenders initially fund the loan. The fees are the same in both transactions, but the lender in a participation has the credit and interest rate risk until other participants are found. Those who supported accounting for loan participations and loan syndications based on their legal form argued that FAS-125 applies to all transfers of financial assets and that it would be counterproductive to make exceptions to that requirement.

EITF Issue 99-8 (Accounting for Transfers of Assets That Are Derivative Instruments but That Are Not Financial Assets) (ASC 815-10-40-2, 40-3; 860-10-15-5; 40-40)

OVERVIEW

> **OBSERVATION:** The guidance in ASC 860 (FAS-140 as amended by FAS-166), which superseded FAS-125, does not affect the guidance in this Issue. This Issue also was not reconsidered in ASC 860-10-35-4, 35-6; 860-10-05-8; 860-20–25-5; 460-10-60-35; 860-20-55-46 through 55-48; 860-50-05-2 through 05-4; 30-1, 30-2; 35-1A, 35-3, 35-9 through 35-11; 25-2, 25-3, 25-6; 50-5 (FAS-166), which amended ASC 860 (FAS-140).
>
> This Issue was raised because it was unclear how to account for transfers of nonfinancial assets that are accounted for as derivatives under the guidance in ASC 815 (FAS-133). Transfers of such derivatives are excluded from the scope of FAS-125, which applies only to transfers of financial assets and financial liabilities, as defined in paragraph 3 of FAS-107 (ASC, Glossary).

ACCOUNTING ISSUE

How should transfers of nonfinancial assets that are accounted for as derivatives under ASC 815 (FAS-133) be accounted for?

EITF CONSENSUS

1. Transfers of nonfinancial assets (e.g., a forward contract to purchase gold requiring physical settlement) that are considered to be derivatives under the definition in ASC 815 (FAS-133) should be accounted for by analogy to FAS-140. However, this consensus does not apply to contracts that may meet the definition of a derivative in ASC 815 FAS-133, for example, contracts issued by an entity in connection with stock-based compensation arrangements addressed in ASC 718 (FAS-123 (R)) that are excluded from the scope of ASC 815-10-15-74 (FAS-133, paragraphs 10 and 11).
2. If a derivative instrument could potentially be both a nonfinancial asset and a nonfinancial liability—for example, a commodity forward contract that is a nonfinancial derivative instrument—the instrument must meet the criteria in ASC 860 (FAS-140 as amended by FAS-166) to qualify for derecognition.

The Task Force also noted that a special purpose entity that receives nonfinancial assets in a transfer should not be accounted for as a securitization entity under the guidance in ASC 860 (FAS-140 as amended by FAS-166).

EITF Issue 02-9 (Accounting for Changes That Result in a Transferor Regaining Control of Financial Assets Sold) (ASC 860-20-25-11 through 25-13; 30-4; 35-9; 55-41 through 55-42, 55-62 through 55-92; 40-25-2; 50-25-10)

OVERVIEW

According to ASC 860-20-25-8 (paragraph 55 and 55A of FAS-140, Accounting for Transfers and Servicing of Financial Assets and Extinguishments of Liabilities) as amended by ASC 860 (FAS-166, Accounting for Transfers of Financial Assets), a transferor may regain control of financial assets previously accounted for as sold if the transferee no longer meets one of the conditions in ASC 860-10-40-4 through 40-5 (paragraph 9 of FAS-140) that are required for sale accounting. Failure to meet the conditions in ASC 860-10-40-4 through 40-5 (paragraph 9) is usually a result of a change in law, or other circumstances. If such circumstances occur, a portion of the transferred financial assets may no longer meet the conditions of a participating interest or the transferor may regain control of a transferred financial asset that had been accounted for as a sale because one or more of the conditions in ASC 860-10-40-4 through 40-5 (paragraph 9 of FAS-140) are no longer met. Under those circumstances, the transferor must account for the transferred financial assets as if they have been repurchased from the transferee in exchange for the liabilities assumed by the transferor. The transferor recognizes the transferred financial assets and liabilities at their fair value on the date the change occurs and thereafter reports the assets and the liabilities in its financial statements to the former transferee or other beneficial interest holders in those assets. The transferee derecognizes the transferred financial assets on that date and accounts for them as if they were sold in exchange for a receivable from the transferor. It is assumed in this Issue that the transferor does not consolidate the transferee. However, a transferor that subsequently consolidates an entity that had been involved in a transfer that was accounted for as a sale should apply current guidance.

ACCOUNTING ISSUES

1. How should a transferor account for retained beneficial interests if portions of the underlying assets that had been sold are rerecognized in accordance with the guidance in ASC 860-20-25-8 (paragraph 55 of FAS-140) because the transferor's contingent call option on the transferred assets, such as a removal of accounts provision (ROAP), becomes exercisable? How much of a gain or loss should be recognized under those circumstances?

2. Are there any circumstances under which an allowance should be recorded for assets that are rerecognized at fair value in accordance with ASC 860-20-25-8 (paragraph 55)?

3. How does the rerecognition of assets (or a portion thereof) sold in accordance with ASC 860-20-25-8 (paragraph 55) affect the accounting for a related servicing asset?
4. How should a transferor subsequently account for its interests, except for servicing assets, after the occurrence of an event that triggers the application of ASC 860-20-25-8 (paragraph 55)?

EITF CONSENSUS

1. When applying the guidance in ASC 860-20-25-8 (paragraph 55 of FAS-140), a transferor should recognize no gain or loss in earnings related to its beneficial interests. Such beneficial interests should be evaluated for impairment when applying the guidance in FAS-55 and periodically thereafter. However, a transferor may recognize a gain or loss when exercising a removal of accounts provision (ROAP) or a similar contingent right related to a repurchased transferred financial asset that is not a derivative accounted for under the guidance in FAS-133 and is not at-the-money. That is, the fair value of repurchased assets should not exceed or be less than the transferor's related obligation to the transferee.

> **OBSERVATION:** Although the guidance in ASC 860 (FAS-156, Accounting for Servicing of Financial Assets—An Amendment of FASB Statement No. 140) amends the accounting guidance in FAS-140 for separately recognized servicing assets and servicing liabilities, it does not affect the guidance in this Issue. Under the guidance in ASC 860 (FAS-156), separately recognized assets that had been transferred and accounted for as sold should be measured at fair value if and when they are reacquired.

> **OBSERVATION:** This Issue has been revised to include amendments of this Issue in FAS-166, which has amended the guidance in FAS-140. The guidance in both Statements is included in ASC 860 of the FASB Accounting Standards Codification™.

2. A transferor should never recognize a loan loss allowance on a loan that does not meet the definition of a security when that loan is initially rerecognized under the guidance in ASC 860-20-25-8 (paragraph 55 of FAS-140).
3. The accounting for a servicing asset related to a previously sold financial asset does not change if an event causing the application of ASC 860-20-25-8 (paragraph 55) occurs. The contractually required cash flows from the rerecognized assets continue to be paid to the securitization entity, which will use the proceeds to satisfy its contractual obligations, including those to beneficial interest holders. A transferor, as servicer, continues to be contractually required to collect the asset's cash flows for

the benefit of the securitization entity and to service the asset in other ways. Therefore, a transferor should continue to recognize the servicing asset and evaluate it for impairment as required in ASC 860 (FAS-140).

4. A transferor should not combine an interest in the underlying assets, other than the servicing asset, with rerecognized financial assets after an event occurs that requires the application of the guidance in ASC 860-20-25-8 (paragraph 55 of FAS-140). A transferor's interest should be combined, however, with the underlying assets, if as a result of a subsequent event, the transferor recovers the financial assets from a transferee—for example, by exercising a removal of accounts provision or by consolidating a securitization entity under GAAP, including FIN-46(R).

FASB RATIFICATION

The FASB ratified the EITF's consensus positions at its meeting on April 2, 2003.

FASB Implementation Guides

FIG FAS-140 (A Guide to Implementation of Statement 140 on Accounting for Transfers and Servicing of Financial Assets and Extinguishments of Liabilities) (ASC 320-10-25-5, 25-18; 405-20-55-5 through 55-9; 860-10-05, 10-9, 10-12, 10-13, 10-22; 15-4; 35-5, 35-8, 35-10 through 35-12; 40-7, 40-9, 40-11, 40-12, 40-14, 40-24, 40-26, 40-27, 40-29, 40-31, 40-33, 40-40; 55-3, 55-4, 55-7 through 55-18, 55-24A, 55-25A, 55-27 through 55-33, 55-38 through 55-42; 55-46, 55-51, 55-54, 55-58, 55-59, 55-69 55-62 through 55-64, 55-66 through 55-70, 55-75 through 55-79; 860-20-25-6; 35-2, 35-3, 35-5, 35-7, 35-8; 55-3 through 55-9, 55-11 through 55-16, 55-24, 55-25, 55-28, 55-31, 55-34 through 55-39, 55-60, 55-61, 55-101 through 55-107; 860-30-15-2, 15-3; 25-9; 35-2, 35-3; 45-2, 45-3; 860-40-05-6; 15-11, 15-15, 15-19 through 15-28; 40-11; 45-2, 45-4; 55-3, 55-11, 55-12, 55-14 through 55-16, 55-18 through 55-20, 55-23 through 55-25, 55-27 through 55-29; 860-50-25-7 through 25-9; 30-2 through 30-9; 35-11 through 35-14, 35-15; 50-5; 55-4 through 55-11, 55-13 through 55-18)

BACKGROUND

FIG FAS-140, reported on in this section, includes responses to 123 specific questions regarding the application of FAS-140.

STANDARDS

Scope

Question 1: If a right to receive the minimum lease payments to be obtained under an operating lease is transferred, could that right be considered a financial asset within the scope of FAS-140?

Answer: No. FAS-140 does not apply to an unrecognized financial asset.

Question 2: Is a transfer of servicing rights that are contractually separated from the underlying serviced assets within the scope of FAS-140? For example, does FAS-140 apply to an entity's conveyance of mortgage servicing rights that have been separated from an underlying mortgage loan portfolio that the entity intends to retain?

Answer: No. Paragraph 4 states that FAS-140 "does not address transfers of nonfinancial assets, for example, servicing assets." See the discussion of SOP 01-6. Accounting for Certain Entities (Including Entities with Trade Receivables) That Lend to or Finance the Activities of Others (SOP 01-6) (for ASC references, see SOP 01-6 in Chapter 11, "Contingencies, Risks, and Uncertainties") and EITF Issue 95-5 (Determination of What Risks and Rewards, If Any, Can Be Retained and Whether Any Unresolved Contingencies May Exist in a Sale of Mortgage Loan Servicing Rights) (for ASC references, see Issue 95-5 in this chapter for the treatment of servicing rights that have been separated from the underlying serviced assets).

Question 3: Is a debtor's conveyance of cash or noncash financial assets in full or partial settlement of an obligation to a creditor considered a transfer under FAS-140?

Answer: No. A transfer involves the conveyance of a noncash financial asset by and to someone other than the originator of the financial asset.

Question 4: Does FAS-140 address a reacquisition by an entity of its own securities by exchanging noncash financial assets (e.g., U.S. Treasury bonds or shares of an unconsolidated investee) for its common shares?

Answer: No. FAS-140 does not address either investments by, or distributions to, owners.

Question 5: Do the provisions of FAS-140 apply to "desecuritizations" of securities into loans or other financial assets?

Answer: No. See the discussion of EITF Topic D-51 (The Applicability of FAS-115 to Desecuritizations of Financial Assets) in Chapter 25, "Investments in Debt and Equity Securities," for additional information.

Question 6: Are securitized stranded costs of a utility company a financial asset, and would the transfer of the asset be within the scope of FAS-140?

Answer: No. Securitized stranded costs do not meet the definition of a financial asset. The cash flows that arise from securitized stranded costs are the result of government regulation; they do not flow from a contract between two or more parties.

Question 7: Would a transfer of beneficial interests in a securitization trust that holds nonfinancial assets, such as securitized stranded costs or other similar rights by third-party investors, be within the scope of FAS-140?

Answer: Yes. In general, the beneficial interests in such a trust would be considered financial assets by third-party investors.

Question 8: Is a judgment from litigation a financial asset?

Answer: Generally not. However, a financial asset exists when a court judgment is reduced to contractually specified payment terms.

Question 9: Is a judgment from litigation a financial asset if it is transferred to an unrelated third party (i.e., would the transfer be within the scope of FAS-140)?

Answer: Yes, if the judgment is enforceable and has been reduced to a contractually specified payment schedule.

Question 10: Does FAS-140 apply to a transfer of an ownership interest in a consolidated subsidiary by its parent if that consolidated subsidiary holds nonfinancial assets?

Answer: No. An ownership interest in a consolidated subsidiary denotes an interest in individual assets and liabilities. Some of these assets are nonfinancial in nature.

Question 11: This question was deleted because the concept of temporary control was eliminated by the guidance in FAS-144 (Accounting for the Impairment or Disposal of Long-Lived Assets).

Question 12: Would FAS-140 apply to a transfer of an investment in a controlled entity that has not been consolidated because that entity accounts for its investment at fair value (e.g., a broker-dealer or an investment company)?

Answer: Generally, yes. An entity that carries an investment in a subsidiary at fair value will realize its investment by transferring that investment, which is a financial asset, rather than by the realization of the underlying assets and liabilities, which might include nonfinancial assets.

Question 13: Is a transfer of an equity method investment within the scope of FAS-140?

Answer: Yes, unless the transfer is in substance a sale of real estate, as defined in FIN-43 (Real Estate Sales). The guidance in FAS-66 (Accounting for Sales of Real Estate) (ASC 360, *Property, Plant and Equipment*; 976, *Real Estate—Retail Land*), APB-29 (Accounting for Nonmonetary Transactions) (ASC 845, *Nonmonetary Transactions*), and EITF Issue 01-2 (Interpretation of APB Opinion No. 29) (ASC 845, *Nonmonetary Transactions*) for guidance.

Question 14: Is a forward contract on a financial instrument that must be (or may be) physically settled by the delivery of that financial instrument in exchange for cash a financial asset or liability, the transfer (or extinguishment in the case of a liability) of which would be within the scope of FAS-140?

Answer: Yes.

Question 15: Is a transfer of a recognized financial instrument that may be a financial asset or a financial liability at any point in time, such as during a forward or swap contract, subject to the provisions of both paragraph 9 and paragraph 16 (ASC 860-10-40-4; 40-5; 405-20-40-1)?

Answer: Yes. Certain financial instruments (e.g., forwards or swaps) may ultimately prove to be either financial assets or liabilities. Therefore, transfers of these types of financial instruments must meet the requirements of both paragraph 9 (regarding assets) (ASC 860-20-40-4; 40-5) and paragraph 16 (regarding liabilities) (ASC 405-20-40-1) to be derecognized.

Question 16: Does FAS-140 apply to a transfer of a recognized derivative instrument that is not a financial instrument?

Answer: Yes. FAS-140 does apply if the derivative involves a nonfinancial liability (e.g., a written commodity option) at the date of transfer, because FAS-140 applies to the extinguishments of all liabilities. Some derivatives have characteristics of both nonfinancial assets and nonfinancial liabilities (e.g., a commodity forward contract). In such cases, FAS-140 does apply. FAS-140 does *not* apply if the derivative involves a nonfinancial asset (e.g., an option to purchase a commodity) at the date of transfer. However, the transfer of nonfinancial derivative instruments, subject to the FAS-133 requirements, should be accounted for using the FAS-140 guidance (see EITF: Issue 99-8 (Accounting for Transfers of Assets That Are Derivative Instruments but That Are Not Financial Assets) for additional discussion of this issue).

Control Criteria—Isolation

Question 17: What type of evidence is sufficient to provide reasonable assurance that transferred financial assets are isolated beyond the reach of the transferor and its consolidated affiliates under FAS-140?

Answer: There must be reasonable assurance that the transferred financial assets could not be reached by creditors in bankruptcy or other receiver for the transferor or its consolidated affiliates, if any, included in the financial statements being presented and its creditors. The Audit Issues Task Force has issued guidance on evaluating legal interpretations in support of management's assertion that the isolation criterion has been met.

> ☞ **PRACTICE POINTER:** Evaluating whether transferred assets are isolated beyond the reach of the transferor (and the transferor's creditors, even in bankruptcy) is primarily a legal judgment. Therefore, the auditor will typically not be able to evaluate management's assertion that transferred assets are appropriately isolated in the absence of a legal letter. The legal letter must not (1) restrict the auditor's reliance on the letter, (2) disclaim an opinion, (3) restrict its scope to facts and circumstances not applicable to the particular transfer, and (4) express its conclusions using conditional language, such as that contained in the Audit Issues Task Force's interpretation (e.g., "In our opinion, the transfer should be considered a sale...").

> ☞ **PRACTICE POINTER:** In evaluating whether transferred assets are isolated beyond the reach of the transferor (and the transferor's creditors, even in bankruptcy), a legal specialist should consider the following factors: (1) the structure of the transfer, (2) the nature of the transferor's continuing involvement, if any, with the transferred assets, (3) the type of insolvency or other receivership proceedings applicable to the transferor if it fails, and (4) other applicable legal factors.

Question 18: Is the requirement of paragraph 9a (ASC 860-10-40-5) (i.e., the isolation requirement) satisfied if the likelihood of bankruptcy is remote?

Answer: No. The focus is not on whether bankruptcy is remote, but whether the transferred financial assets would be isolated from the transferor in the event of bankruptcy.

Question 19: Are transferred financial assets isolated from the transferor in those cases in which the Federal Deposit Insurance Corporation (FDIC) would act as a receiver if the transferor failed?

Answer: Generally, yes. The FDIC cannot recover, reclaim, or recharacterize financial assets transferred by an insured depository institution if the transfer met all the FAS-140 requirements for sale accounting treatment, except the requirement that the transferred assets be legally isolated for the transferor's creditors. Also see EITF Topic D-67 (Isolation of Assets Transferred by Financial Institutions under FAS-140) in this chapter for a discussion of this issue. Finally, the AICPA's Audit Issues Task Force has issued an Auditing Interpretation (the Use of Legal Interpretations As Evidential Matter to support Management's Assertion that a Transfer of Financial Assets Has Met the Isolation Criterion in Paragraph 9(a) of Statement of

Financial Accounting Standards No. 140) to help auditors assess when transferred assets would be beyond the reach of the FDIC.

Question 19A: Can financial assets transferred by an entity subject to possible receivership by the FDIC be considered isolated from the transferor (i.e., can the transfer meet the condition in paragraph 9(a)) of FAS-140 (ASC 860-10-40-4 and 40-5) if circumstances arise under which *the FDIC or another creditor* can require their return?

Answer: Yes. If an entity subject to possible receivership by the FDIC transfers financial assets, they are isolated from the transferor if the FDIC or another creditor cannot require that the financial assets be returned or can only require a return in receivership, after a default, and in exchange for payment of, at a minimum, principal and interest earned at the contractual yield to the date that investors paid. See Question 19C for guidance if a transferor can require that the transferred financial assets be returned.

Question 19B: Does the answer to Question 19A also apply to financial assets that an entity transferred subject to *the U.S. Bankruptcy Code*?

Answer: No. According to the guidance in paragraphs 81-83 of FAS-140 (ASC 860-10-55-19 through 55-23) transfers of financial assets by entities subject to the U.S. Bankruptcy Court meet the condition in paragraph 9A of FAS-140 (ASC 860-10-40-4 and 40-5) if the transferred financial asset have been "put presumptively beyond the reach of the transferor and its creditors, even in bankruptcy..." That treatment differs from the treatment for receivership under the FDIC.

Question 19C: Can financial assets transferred by any entity be considered isolated from *the transferor* (i.e., can the transfer meet the condition in paragraph 9(a) of FAS-140 (ASC 860-10-40-4 and 40-5)) if circumstances can arise under which *the transferor* can require their return, only in exchange for payment of principal and interest earned (at the contractual yield) to the date investors are paid?

Answer: No, unless the transferor has the ability to require the return of the transferred financial assets solely from a contract with the transferee.

Question 19D: Which of the answers in questions 19A–19C applies to entities subject to possible receivership under jurisdictions other than the FDIC or the U.S. Bankruptcy Code?

Answer: It depends on the circumstances that apply to those entities. Under the guidance in paragraph 84 of FAS-140 (ASC 860-10-55-24 and 55-25A), judgments about the isolation of transferred financial assets of entities that are subject to other possible bankruptcy, conservatorship, or other receivership procedures should be made in comparison to the powers of bankruptcy courts or trustees, conservators, or receivers in those jurisdictions. The same types of judgments may need to be made about the powers of a transferor and its creditors.

Question 20: Could a transfer from one subsidiary (the transferor) to another subsidiary (the transferee) of a common parent be accounted for as a sale for each subsidiary's separate-company financial statements?

Answer: Yes, if two conditions are met. First, the requirements of paragraph 9 of FAS-140 (ASC 860-10-40-4 and 40-5), including the isolation requirement, must be met. Second, the financial statements of the transferee cannot be consolidated with the separate-company financial statements of the transferor.

Question 21: This question has been deleted because FAS-166 (Accounting for Transfers of Financial Assets) has amended the definition of proceeds in FAS-140, as amended, to include beneficial interests.

Control Criteria—Conditions That Constrain a Transferee

Question 22: Assuming that all of the other requirements of paragraph 9 (ASC 860-10-40-4, 5) are met, has a transferor surrendered control over transferred financial assets if the transferee, which is not an entity whose sole purpose is to engage in securitization or asset-backed financing activities is precluded from exchanging the transferred assets but obtains the unconstrained right to pledge them?

Answer: It depends. If the transferee is able to obtain most of the cash flows associated with the transferred financial assets either by transferring or pledging those assets, the transferee would have control over the transferred assets.

Question 22A: Entity A transfers a financial asset to Entity B which has a significantly limited ability to pledge or exchange the transferred assets and is not an entity whose sole purpose is to engage in securitization or asset-backed financing activities. The transferor receives cash for the transferred financial assets and has *no* continuing involvement with those assets. Does this transfer qualify under the requirements in paragraph 9(b) of FAS-140 (ASC 860-10-40-5)?

Answer: Yes. The requirements in paragraph 9(b) (ASC 860-10-40-5) would *not* be met if Entity B were *not* permitted to pledge or exchange the transferred financial asset and the transferor received a benefit from that limitation that is more than insignificant. Paragraph 166 of FAS-140 states "transferred assets from which the transferor can obtain no further benefits are no longer its assets and should be removed from its statement of financial position." However, if a transferor has any continuing involvement after a transfer to an entity that is not a securitization entity, the transferor should evaluate whether the requirements in paragraph 9(b) (ASC 860-10-40-5) have been met, in accordance with the guidance in paragraphs 29 through 34 of FAS-140 (ASC 860-10-40-15-6, 15-7, 15-18).

Question 23: In certain loan participation agreements that involve transfers of participating interests, the transferor is required to approve any subsequent transfers or pledges of the interests in the loans held by the transferee. Would that requirement be a constraint that would prevent the transferee from taking advantage of its right to pledge or to exchange the transferred financial asset and, therefore, preclude accounting for the transfer as a sale?

Answer: It depends, and judgment clearly is necessary. A requirement that constrains the transferee from selling or pledging the transferred assets and that provides more than a trivial benefit to the transferor would result in sale accounting being precluded. In that case, the transferor has not given up control and should account for such transfers as secured borrowings. However, FAS-140 also indicates that a requirement to obtain the transferor's permission before selling or pledging the transferred assets—if such permission is not unreasonably withheld—typically does not constrain the transferee from selling or pledging the related assets.

Question 24: If a securitization entity issues beneficial interests in the form of Rule 144A securities and the holder of those beneficial interests may not transfer them unless an exemption from the 1933 U.S. Securities Act registration is available, do the limits on the transferability of the beneficial interests result in a constraint on the transferee's right to pledge or exchange those beneficial interests and, therefore, preclude sale accounting by the transferor?

Answer: It depends. The primary limitation on the sale of Rule 144A securities is that the buyer must be a sophisticated investor. If a large number of such investors exist, there would be no effective constraint on the transferee's right to pledge or exchange the asset.

Questions 24a through 30: These questions have been deleted because the concept of a qualifying special-purpose entity has been removed from FAS-140, as amended by FAS-166.

Question 31: Credit card securitizations often include a "removal-of-accounts provision" (ROAP) that permits the seller, under certain conditions and with trustee approval, to withdraw receivables from the pool of securitized receivables. Does a transferor's right to remove receivables from a credit card securitization preclude accounting for a transfer as a sale?

Answer: It depends on the rights that the transferor has under the ROAP. A ROAP that does not allow the transferor to unilaterally reclaim specific financial assets from the transferee does not preclude sale accounting.

Question 32: If a transferor is permitted to dissolve a securitization entity (e.g., through the beneficial interests that it holds) and reassume control of the transferred financial assets, is the transferor precluded from accounting for the transfer as a sale?

Answer: Yes. In this case, the transferor effectively maintains control over the assets through its ability to dissolve the securitization entity and reclaim the assets.

Questions 33 through 41: These questions have been deleted because the concept of a securitization entity has been removed from FAS-140, as amended by FAS-166.

Control Criteria—Effective Control

Question 42: Dollar-roll repurchase agreements (also called dollar rolls) are agreements to sell and repurchase similar but not identical securities. Dollar rolls differ from regular repurchase agreements in that the securities sold and repurchased, which are usually of the same issuer, are represented by different certificates, are collateralized by different but similar mortgage pools (e.g., conforming single-family residential mortgages), and generally have different principal amounts. Is a transfer of financial assets that are under a dollar-roll repurchase agreement within the scope of FAS-140?

Answer: Yes, if the dollar-roll repurchase agreement pertains to the transfer of securities that already exist.

Question 43: Does paragraph 9c (ASC 860-10-40-5) preclude sale accounting for a dollar-roll transaction that is subject to the provisions of FAS-140?

Answer: It depends. In order for sale accounting to be precluded, the transferred financial assets to be repurchased must be the same or substantially the same as the assets transferred. All of six characteristics discussed in paragraph 48 (ASC 860-40-24; 860-10-55-35) must exist in order to meet the substantially-the-same requirement (see paragraph 47a of FAS-140 (ASC 860-10-40-24) for further details).

Question 44: In a transfer of existing securities under a dollar-roll repurchase agreement, if the transferee is committed to return substantially the same securities to the transferor but that transferee's securities were to be announced at the time of transfer, would the transferor be precluded from accounting for the transfer as a secured borrowing?

Answer: No. The transferor is only required to obtain a commitment from the transferee to return substantially the same securities. The transferor is not required to determine that the transferee holds the securities that it is committed to return.

Question 45: Paragraph 49 (ASC 860-10-40-24) states that to be able to repurchase or redeem financial assets on substantially the agreed terms, even in the event of default by the transferee, a transferor must at all times during the contract term have obtained cash or other collateral sufficient to fund substantially all of the cost of purchasing replacement financial assets from others. Would a transferor maintain effective control if, under the arrangement, the transferor is substantially overcollateralized at the date of transfer even though the arrangement does not provide for frequent adjustments to the amount of collateral maintained by the transferor?

Answer: No. If a mechanism does not exist to ensure that adequate collateral is maintained—even for a transaction that is substantially overcollateralized—sale accounting would not be precluded.

Question 46: Paragraph 49 (ASC 860-10-40-24) requires that "... a transferor must at all times during the contract term have obtained cash or other collateral sufficient to fund substantially all of the cost of purchasing replacement financial assets from others." *Substantially all* is not specifically defined in FAS-140. Should entities interpret *substantially all* to mean 90% or more?

Answer: No. The FASB consciously decided not to provide a percentage test for the term *substantially all*. Judgment is required in interpreting this term, as well as interpreting the other criterion regarding whether the terms of a repurchase agreement fail to maintain effective control over the transferred asset.

Question 47: Does FAS-140 contain special provisions for differences in collateral maintenance requirements that exist in markets outside the United States?

Answer: No. The general provisions of FAS-140 apply. Therefore, the fact that some foreign markets typically do not require collateral for repurchase transactions would not preclude sale accounting.

Question 48: The example of effective control in paragraph 9(c)(1) of FAS-140 (ASC 860-10-40-5) states that the transferor maintains effective control over the financial transferred assets through "an agreement that both entitles and obligates the transferor to repurchase or redeem them before their maturity." What does the term *before maturity* mean in the context of the transferor that maintains effective control under the provisions of FAS-140?

Answer: FAS-140 does not define the term *before maturity*. However, in order for the agreement to be viewed as requiring repurchase or redemption before maturity, the remaining term in the life of the financial asset must be sufficient enough so that the asset could be sold again. That is, the remaining term must not be so short that a net cash payment would be made.

Question 49: How do different types of rights of a transferor to reacquire (call) transferred financial assets affect sale accounting under FAS-140?

Answer: Sale accounting is precluded if a transferor's right to reacquire (call) a transferred financial asset constrains the ability of a transferee to (or, if the transferee is an entity whose sole purpose is to engage in securitization or asset-backed financing activities and that entity is constrained from pledging or exchanging the assets it receives, each third-party holder of its beneficial interests) pledge or exchange the transferred financial assets (or beneficial interests) it received and provides more than a trivial benefit to the transferor.

In addition, paragraph 9(c) precludes sale accounting if a transferor, its consolidated affiliates included in the financial statements being presented, or its agents, maintain effective control over transferred financial assets. For example, sale accounting is precluded if a right to reacquire a transferred financial asset results in either of the following:

1. The transferor, its consolidated affiliates included in the financial statements presented, or its agents, maintain effective control through an agreement that both entitles and obligates the transferor to repurchase or redeem the transferred financial asset before its maturity; or
2. The transferor, its consolidated affiliates included in the financial statements, or its agents, maintains effective control through an agreement that provides the transferor with both the unilateral ability to have the holder return the specific transferred financial assets and a more-than-trivial benefit attributable to that ability, other than through a cleanup call.

A unilateral right to reclaim specific transferred financial assets permits a transferor to maintain effective control and precludes sale accounting if the transferor has the unilateral right to reacquire the transferred financial assets and if that right provides the transferor with more than a trivial benefit. Paragraph 50 of FAS-140 (ASC 860-10-40-9, 40-10, 40-33 and 40-34 states that "a call or other right conveys more than trivial benefit if the price to be paid is fixed, determinable or other otherwise potentially advantageous, unless because that price is so far out of the money or for other reasons it is probable when the option is written that the transferor will not exercise it. (See the table in FIG-140 for extensive details regarding provisions for different types of rights of a transferor to reacquire (call) transferred assets.)

Question 50: In certain transactions, the transferor is entitled to repurchase a transferred, amortizing, individual financial asset that is not readily obtainable elsewhere when its remaining principal balance reaches some specified amount, for example, 30% of the original balance. Does FAS-140 permit such a transfer to be accounted for partially as a sale and partially as a secured borrowing?

Answer: If yes, a call enables a transferor to unilaterally force the holder of a transferred financial asset to return the remaining portion of the entire financial asset to the transferor and gives the transferor more than a trivial benefit, the transferor should not account for a transfer of the total financial asset for as a sale. Under the guidance in FAS-140, the provisions related to derecognition should be applied to a transfer of a total financial asset, a group of total financial assets, or a participating interest in a total financial asset. Further, accounting for a transfer of a total financial asset or a participating interest in a total financial asset partially as a sale and partially as a secured borrowing is prohibited. (See Question 49.)

Question 51: Would a transferor's contractual right to repurchase a loan participation that is not a readily obtainable financial asset preclude sale accounting?

Answer: Yes, based on the guidance in paragraph 9(b) (ASC 860-10-40-5), each transferee should have the right to pledge or exchange the assets it received and that a transferor cannot (a) restrict a transferee from using its right to pledge or exchange its assets and (b) receive more than a trivial benefit. A transferor's contractual right to repurchase a loan is a call option written by a transferee to the transferor. According to paragraph 32 (ASC 860-10-40-18), a freestanding call option may benefit the transferor and may restrict a transferee if the transferred financial assets are not readily in the marketplace. If a transferor's right to repurchase a financial asset is not freestanding but is attached to the loan and may be transferred with it, paragraph 9(c)(2) (ASC 860-10-40-5) states that a transferor maintains effective control over the transferred financial asset.

Question 52: Deleted.

Question 53: Under FAS-140, does a transfer of a debt security classified as held-to-maturity that occurs for a reason other than those specified in paragraphs 8 and 11 of FAS-115 (Accounting for Certain Investments in Debt and Equity Securities) taint the entity's held-to-maturity portfolio?

Answer: It depends on how the transfer is handled. If the transfer of the debt security is treated as a sale, the entity's held-to-maturity portfolio would be tainted unless the transfer occurred for one of the reasons specified in paragraph 8 or 11 of FAS-115 (ASC 320-10-25-6, 25-9). If the transfer is accounted for as a secured borrowing, the held-to-maturity portfolio would not be tainted.

Question 54: Deleted the concept of a securitization entity is removed from FAS-140, as amended by FAS-166.

Question 55: Assuming that all of the other criteria of paragraph 9 (ASC 860-10-40-4,40-5) are met, is sale accounting appropriate if a cleanup call on a pool of assets in a qualifying SPE is held by a party other than the servicer? For example, sometimes the fair value of beneficial interests retained by a transferor of financial assets who is not the servicer or an affiliate is adversely affected by the amount of transferred financial assets declining to a "low level." If such a transferor has a call exercisable when assets decline to a specified low level, could that be a cleanup call?

Answer: No. Because the transferor is not the servicer or an affiliate of the servicer, the transferor's call on the assets in the qualifying SPE is not a cleanup call for accounting purposes. However, because the call option can only be exercised when the assets reach a certain pre-specified level, the transfer would be recorded as a partial sale (assuming the other provisions of paragraph 9 (ASC 860-10-40-4, 40-5) are met).

Question 56: In a securitization transaction involving not-readily-obtainable assets, may a transferor that is also the servicer hold a cleanup call if it "contracts out the servicing" to a third party (that is, enters into a subservicing arrangement with a third party) without precluding sale accounting?

Answer: Yes. This is due to the fact that from the SPE's perspective, the transferor remains the servicer. If the subservicer fails to perform under the contract, the transferor remains liable for servicing the assets. However, if the transferor sells the servicing rights to a third party, the transferor could not hold a cleanup call.

Measurement of Assets and Liabilities upon Completion of a Transfer

Question 57: Could a transferor's exchange of one form of beneficial interests in financial assets that have been transferred into a trust for an equivalent, but different, form of beneficial interests in the same transferred financial assets be accounted for as a sale under FAS-140?

Answer: No. This type of arrangement definitely does not qualify for sale accounting, and it may not even meet the FAS-140 definition of a transfer. If the exchange is with a trust that originally issued the beneficial interests, a transfer has not occurred.

Question 58: Deleted because FAS-140, as amended by FAS-166, requires that derecognition provisions be applied to a transfer of the whole financial asset, a group of whole financial assets, or a participating interest in a whole financial asset. See the guidance in paragraphs 10 and 11 of FAS-140, as amended (ASC 860-20-40-1; 860-20-25-1 through 25-3; 860-20-30-1, 30-2).

Question 59: Deleted because a beneficial interest obtained in a transfer of a whole financial asset or a group of whole financial assets accounted for as a sale are considered to be proceeds of the sale and are recognized initially and measured at fair value under the guidance in FAS-140, as amended by FAS-166.

Question 60: Deleted because a beneficial interest obtained in a transfer of a whole financial asset or a group of whole financial assets accounted for as a sale are considered to be proceeds of the sale and are recognized initially and measured at fair value under the guidance in FAS-140, as amended by FAS-166.

Question 61: An entity transfers debt securities to a qualifying SPE that has a predetermined life, in exchange for cash and the right to receive proceeds from the eventual sale of the securities. For example, a third party holds a beneficial interest that is initially worth 25% of the fair value of the assets of the qualifying SPE at the date of transfer. The qualifying SPE must sell the transferred securities at a predetermined date and liquidate the qualifying SPE at that time. In addition, the beneficial interests are issued in the form of debt securities, and prior to the transfer those securities are accounted for as available-for-sale in accordance with FAS-115. Does the transferor have the option to classify the debt securities as trading at the time of the transfer?

Answer: Generally, no. FAS-115 securities held by the transferor after the transfer convey rights to the same cash flows as the FAS-115 securities held before the transfer; FAS-115 explains that transfers into and from the trading category should be rare. If, however, the transferred securities were not FAS-115 securities prior to the transfer, then the transferor would have the opportunity to decide the appropriate classification of the transferred assets at the date of the transfer.

Question 62: In certain transfers, the transferor retains an interest that should be subsequently accounted for under EITF Issue 99-20. If the transferred asset was accounted for as available-for-sale under FAS-115 prior to the transfer, how should the transferor account for amounts in other comprehensive income at the date of transfer?

Answer: The application of EITF Issue 99-20 should not result in recognition of earnings of an unrealized gain or loss that had been recognized in accumulated other comprehensive income before it is realized.

Question 63: Deleted because FAS-140, as amended by FAS-166, deletes the concept of a securitization entity. Guidance is provided in Question 62 above.

Question 64: Assume an entity transfers a bond to a qualifying SPE for cash and beneficial interests. When the transferor purchased the bond, it paid a premium (or discount) for it and that premium (or discount) was not fully amortized (or accreted) at the date of the transfer. Would that existing premium or discount continue to be amortized (or accreted)?

Answer: Yes, but only to the extent a sale has not occurred because the transferor retained beneficial interests in the bond.

Question 65: Deleted because FAS-140, as amended by FAS-166, requires that derecognition provisions be applied to a transfer of the whole financial asset, a group of whole financial assets, or a participating interest in a whole financial asset. See the guidance in paragraphs 10 and 11 of FAS-140, as amended (ASC 860-20-40-1; 860-20-25-1 through 25-3; 860-20-30-1, 30-2).

Question 66: Deleted because FAS-157 (Fair Value Measurements) (ASC 820, *Fair Value Measurement*) defines fair value and establishes a framework for measuring fair value.

Question 67: Can the method used by the transferor for providing "recourse" affect the accounting for the transfer?

Answer: Yes. However, before evaluating the accounting treatment for the recourse provision, the transferor must first determine whether a sale has occurred. In some jurisdictions, the recourse provision may suggest that the transferred assets have not been appropriately isolated (i.e., the transferor and its creditors still have access to the assets). If a sale has occurred, the accounting depends on the manner in which the recourse provision is effected. The transferor may agree to reimburse the transferee for amounts not paid by debtors. The transferor would separately recognize a liability for this obligation. Alternatively, the transferor may retain a beneficial interest in the assets that is only receivable after other investors are paid. In such a manner, the transferor in essence retains credit risk. However, in this situation, no recourse liability is needed.

Question 68: What should the transferor consider when determining whether retained credit risk is a separate liability or a part of a retained beneficial interest in the asset?

Answer: If the transferor's liability is limited to a claim on its retained interest in the transferred assets, no separate liability is recognized. The transferor would recognize an asset valuation account for this recourse obligation on the date of transfer. However, if the transferor's obligation under the recourse provision could exceed its retained interest in the transferred assets, a separate liability is recognized.

Question 69: Deleted because the fair value practicability exception has been removed from FAS-140, as amended by FAS-166 (ASC 860).

Question 70: Deleted because FAS-157 (Fair Value Measurements) (ASC 820) defines fair value and establishes a framework for measuring fair value.

Question 71: Deleted because the fair value practicability exception has been removed from FAS-140, as amended by FAS-166 (ASC 860).

Question 72: Must a transferor recognize in earnings the gain or loss that results from a transfer of financial assets that is accounted for as a sale, or may the transferor elect to defer recognizing the resulting gain or loss in certain circumstances?

Answer: Sale accounting and the corresponding recognition of gain or loss is not optional if a transfer of financial assets meets the FAS-140 requirements for sale accounting.

40.58 *Transfer of Financial Assets*

Question 73: Does FAS-140 require disclosures about the assumptions used to estimate fair values of the transferor's retained interests in securitized financial assets or of other assets obtained and liabilities incurred as proceeds in a transfer?

Answer: Yes, see paragraph 17(f) of FAS-140, as amended by FAS-166 (ASC 860-20-50-1 through 50-4).

Question 74: Deleted because a beneficial interest obtained in a transfer of a whole financial asset or a group of whole financial assets accounted for as a sale are considered to be proceeds of the sale and are recognized initially and measured at fair value under the guidance in FAS-140, as amended by FAS-166.

Question 75: How should a transferor initially and subsequently measure credit enhancements provided in a transfer if the balance that is not needed to make up for credit losses is ultimately to be paid by the transferor?

Answer: Credit enhancements are measured at the date of transfer by allocating previous carrying amounts between assets sold and retained interests, based on relative fair values. Credit enhancements provided by other parties are initially measured at the fair value of the enhancement that is expected to benefit the transferor. FAS-140 does not provide guidance on the subsequent measurement of credit enhancements—other existing authoritative literature should be consulted (e.g., FAS-114 [Accounting by Creditors for Impairment of a Loan]).

Questions 76 and 77: Deleted because FAS-157 (Fair Value Measurements) (ASC 820) defines fair value and establishes a framework for measuring fair value.

Servicing Assets and Servicing Liabilities

Question 78: Paragraph 62 (ASC 860-50-30-2) states that "typically, the benefits of servicing are expected to be more than *adequate compensation* to the servicer for performing the servicing..." (Emphasis added). What is meant by the term *adequate compensation*?

Answer: *Adequate compensation* means the amount of compensation necessary to attract an alternate servicing entity, if one becomes necessary. This amount is determined by the marketplace and includes a provision for normal profit.

Questions 79 through 86: Deleted because the fair value practicability exception has been removed from FAS-140, as amended by FAS-166 (ASC 860).

Question 87: For sales of mortgage loans, is adequate compensation the same as normal servicing fees previously used in applying FAS-65?

Answer: No. FAS-140 defines *adequate compensation* as the amount of compensation necessary to attract an alternate servicing entity, should one become necessary. This amount is determined by the marketplace, and includes a provision for normal profit. FAS-65 defines *normal servicing* fees as the amount that was typically charged for servicing a particular type of loan. Often, a normal servicing rate as formerly determined under FAS-65 would exceed FAS-140's definition of *adequate compensation*.

Question 88: Do the types of assets being serviced affect the amount required to adequately compensate the servicer?

Answer: Yes, since different asset classes require different levels of effort to service. The nature of the assets being serviced should be considered a factor in determining the fair value of a servicing asset or servicing liability.

Question 89: Does a contractual provision that specifies the amount of servicing fees that would be paid to a replacement servicer affect the determination of adequate compensation?

Answer: No. A contractually specified amount that would be paid to a replacement servicer could be more or less than adequate compensation.

Question 90: If market rates for servicing a specific type of financial asset change subsequent to the initial recognition of a servicing asset or servicing liability, does FAS-140 include any requirement to adjust the recorded asset or liability?

Answer: Yes. In terms of a servicing asset, a change in market rates may indicate that the asset is impaired. In terms of a servicing liability, a change in market values may increase the liability. Such an increase in the liability would be recorded as a loss in the income statement.

Question 91: Do additional transfers under revolving-period securitizations (e.g., home equity loans or credit card receivables) result in the recognition of additional servicing assets or servicing liabilities?

Answer: Yes. Servicing assets and liabilities arise from the sale of new receivables.

Question 92: The question and answer have been nullified by FAS-156 (ASC 860, *Transfers and Servicing*), which provides specific guidance in its amendment to paragraph 13 of FAS-140 (ASC 860-50-45-1, 45-2; 860-50-25-1, 25-4; 860-50-30-1, 30-8; 860-35-1 through 35-5, 35-15)

Question 93: How should an entity account for rights to future income from serviced assets that exceed contractually specified servicing fees?

Answer: If the benefits to servicing are expected to exceed adequate compensation, the servicer should record a servicing asset, an interest-only strip, or both. For example, the servicer may be entitled to receive interest income from serviced assets that exceeds contractually specified servicing fees. This would represent a financial asset, not a servicing asset, and would effectively be an interest-only strip.

Question 94: Should a loss be recognized if a servicing fee that is equal to or greater than adequate compensation is to be received but the servicer's anticipated cost of servicing would exceed the fee?

Answer: No. Recognition of a servicing asset or a servicing liability depends on the marketplace, not on a servicer's cost of servicing.

Servicing—Other

Question 95: Should an entity recognize a servicing liability if it transfers all or some of a financial asset that meets the definition of a participating interest that is accounted for as a sale and retains an obligation to service the asset but is not entitled to receive a contractually specified servicing fee? Is the answer to this question affected by circumstances in which it is not customary for the transferor/servicer to receive a contractually specified servicing fee?

Answer: Yes. A servicer/transferor would be required to recognize a servicing at fair value if the benefits of servicing are less than adequate compensation.

Question 96: A selling entity (*a*) transfers a portion of a loan under a participation agreement that meets the definition of a participating interest and qualifies for sale accounting under FAS-140, (*b*) obtains the right to receive benefits of servicing that more than adequately compensate it for servicing the loan, and (*c*) and continues to service the loan, regardless of the transfer because it (the selling entity) retains part of the participated loan. In these circumstances, is the selling entity required to record a servicing asset?

Answer: Yes, the selling entity is required to record a servicing asset for the portion of the loans it sold. If the benefits of servicing are significantly greater than an amount that would be fair compensation for a substitute service provider, if one were to be required, the transferred portion does not meet the definition of a participating interest. Consequently, the transfer would not qualify for sale accounting.

Question 97: A transferor that sells mortgage loans in their entirety that it originated in a transfer that is accounted for as a sale takes on the obligation to service them. Immediately thereafter the transferor enters into an arrangement to subcontract the obligation to service with another servicer. How should the transferor account for the obligation to service in this situation?

Answer: The transferor should account separately for the two transactions. The sale of the mortgage loans and the obligation to service those loans should be accounted for in accordance with FAS-140, as amended by FAS-166. The obligation to service should be initially recognized and measured at fair value in accordance with paragraph 11 of FAS-140 (see reference in Question as proceeds obtained from the sale of the mortgage loans. The transferor's accounting for the subcontract with another servicer is not under the scope of FAS-140, but should be accounted for under existing guidance).

Question 98: When servicing assets are assumed without cash payment, what is the appropriate offsetting entry to be made by the transferee?

Answer: If an exchange has occurred, the transaction should be recorded based on the facts and circumstances. On the other hand, if the investor is in substance making a capital contribution to the investee, the investee should recognize an increase in equity from a contribution by owner.

Question 99: FAS-140 requires that an entity separately evaluate and measure impairment of designated strata of servicing assets. If more than one characteristic exists for stratifying servicing assets, must more than one predominant risk characteristic be used?

Answer: No. FAS-140, paragraph 63g(1) (ASC 860-50-35-9), requires servicers to stratify servicing assets based on one or more predominant risk characteristics of the underlying financial assets.

Question 100: FAS-140, paragraph 63g(1) (ASC 860-50-35-9), requires a servicer to stratify servicing assets based on one or more of the predominant risk characteristics of financial assets. Should the strata selected by the servicer be used consistently from period to period?

Answer: Yes, generally the strata selected should be used consistently from period to period. If a significant change is made, it should be accounted for prospectively as a change in accounting estimate in accordance with APB-20 (Accounting Changes).

Question 101: FAS-140 requires impairment of servicing assets to be recognized via a valuation allowance for an individual stratum. The valuation allowance should reflect changes in the measurement of impairment subsequent to initial measurement of impairment. Fair value in excess of the carrying amount of servicing assets for that stratum should not be recorded. How should an entity recognize subsequent increases in a previously recognized servicing liability?

Answer: The revised estimate of the liability should be recorded and a loss should be recognized in earnings. Similar to accounting for changes in the valuation allowance of an impaired asset, increases in the servicing obligation may be recovered, but the obligation should not be reduced below the amortized measurement of the initially recognized servicing liability.

Question 102: Deleted because the fair value practicability exception has been removed from FAS-140, as amended by FAS-166.

Question 103: Deleted because FAS-157 (Fair Value Measurements) (ASC 820) defines fair value and establishes a framework for measuring fair value.

Financial Assets Subject to Repayment

Question 104: If an entity recognizes both a servicing asset and the right to receive future interest income from serviced assets in excess of contractually specified servicing fees (an interest-only strip) in a transfer of a whole financial asset to an unconsolidated entity that meets the requirements for sale accounting, should the value of the right to receive future cash flows from ancillary sources (e.g., late fees) be included in measuring the servicing asset or in measuring the interest-only strip?

Answer: Yes, generally in the servicing asset. The value of the right to receive future cash flows from ancillary sources is included in the measurement of the servicing asset if the right to such future cash flow depends, as is customary, on servicing being performed satisfactorily. The value of the right to future cash flows from ancillary sources is generally not included in measuring the interest-only strip.

Question 105: FAS-140, paragraph 14 (ASC 860-20-35-2), requires that financial assets, except for instruments under the scope of FAS-133 (ASC 815) that contractually can be prepaid or otherwise settled in such a way that the holder will not recover substantially all of its recorded investment subsequently be measured like available-for-sale or trading debt securities in accordance with FAS-115. Does this mean that those financial assets are included in the scope of FAS-115?

Answer: This depends on the form of the assets, but in either case the measurement principles of FAS-115, including provisions for recognizing and measuring impairment should be applied.

Question 106: Can a financial asset that can be contractually prepaid or otherwise settled in such a way that the holder would not recover substantially all of its recorded investment be classified as held-to-maturity if the investor concludes that prepayment or other forms of settlement are remote?

Answer: No. This is not a relevant factor in determining whether the provisions of paragraph 14 (ASC 860-20-35-2) apply to those financial assets.

Question 107: A transferor transfers mortgage loans in their entirety to a third party in a transfer that is accounted for as a sale but retains servicing. Afterward, the transferor enters into a subservicing arrangement with a third party. If the transferor's benefit of servicing exceeds its obligation under the subservicing agreement, should the difference be accounted for as an interest-only strip?

Answer: No. The transferor should account for the two transactions separately. The transfer of mortgage loans and the obligation to service the loans should be accounted for by the transferor in accordance with FAS-140 and the contract with the subscriber should be separately accounted for (not within the scope of FAS-140).

Question 108: Can a debt security that is purchased late enough in its life that, even if prepaid, the holder would recover substantially all of its recorded investment, be initially classified as held-to-maturity?

Answer: Yes. The debt security can be classified as held-to-maturity if the conditions of paragraph 7 of FAS-115 (ASC 320-10-25-1, 25-5; 320-10-35-1) are met.

Question 109: May a loan (that is not a debt security), which when initially obtained could be contractually prepaid or otherwise settled in such a way that the holder would not recover substantially all of its recorded investment, be classified as held for investment later in its life?

Answer: Yes, if the following conditions are met: (1) it would no longer be possible for the holder not to recover substantially all of its recorded investment upon contractual prepayment or settlement and (2) the conditions for amortized cost accounting are met.

Question 110: FAS-140, paragraph 14 (ASC 860-20-35-2), requires that certain financial assets that are not in the form of debt securities be measured at fair value like investments classified as available-for-sale or classified as trading under FAS-115. How should instruments subject to provisions of paragraph 14 (ASC 860-20-35-2) be evaluated for impairment?

Answer: All of the measurement principles of FAS-115 apply. This includes recognition and measurement of impairment.

Question 111: Is a financial asset that is not a debt security under FAS-115 subject to the requirements of paragraph 14 (ASC 860-20-35-2) because it is denominated in a foreign currency?

Answer: No. An entity is not required to measure such an investment like a debt security unless it has provisions that allow it to be contractually prepaid or otherwise settled in a way that the holder would not recover substantially all of its recorded investment, as denominated in the foreign currency.

Question 112: Is a note for which the repayment amount is indexed to the creditworthiness of a party other than the issuer subject to the provisions of FAS-140, paragraph 14 (ASC 860-20-35-2)?

Answer: Yes, because the event that might cause the holder to receive less than substantially all of its recorded investment is based on a contractual provision, not on a default by the borrower.

Question 113: Can a residual tranche debt security in a securitization of financial assets using a securitization entity be classified as held-to-maturity?

Answer: The answer depends on the specific facts and circumstances. If the contractual provisions of the residual tranche debt security provide that the residual tranche can contractually be prepaid or otherwise settled so that the holder would not recover substantially all of its recorded investment, the residual tranche debt security should not be accounted for as held-to-maturity. On the other hand, if the only way the holder of the residual tranche would not substantially recover all of its recorded investment is via default of the borrower, then a held-to-maturity classification is acceptable if the conditions specified for that classification in FAS-115 are met.

Secured Borrowings and Collateral

Question 114: Are the collateral recognition requirements of paragraph 15 (ASC 860-30-25-5) limited to transfers by or to broker-dealer entities, or do they apply to other types of borrowings?

Answer: The collateral recognition provisions of paragraph 15 (ASC 860-30-25-5) apply to the accounting for all transfers of financial assets pledged as collateral that are accounted for as secured borrowings.

Question 115: What is the proper classification by the transferor of securities loaned or transferred under a repurchase agreement that is accounted for as a secured borrowing if the transferee is permitted to sell or repledge those securities, and rights of substitution or termination are not granted to the transferor?

Answer: Pledged assets should be reported in the statement of financial position separately from other assets not so encumbered, but otherwise FAS-140 does not specify the classification or terminology to be used. Paragraph 65 (ASC 860-50-55-22) illustrates possible classifications and terminology.

Question 116: What is the appropriate classification of liabilities incurred in connection with securities borrowing and resale agreement transactions?

Answer: FAS-140 does not specify classification or terminology to be used to describe liabilities by either the secured party or debtor in securities borrowing or resale transactions. Such liabilities should be separately classified.

Question 117: How should a transferor measure transferred collateral that must be reclassified?

Answer: FAS-140, paragraph 15a (ASC 860-30-25-5), requires transferred collateral that can be sold or repledged by the secured party to be reclassified and reported separately by the transferor. However, it does not change the transferor's measurement of that collateral.

Question 118: Does FAS-140 provide guidance on subsequent measurement of a secured party's obligation to return transferred collateral that the secured party recognized in accordance with paragraph 15 (ASC 860-30-25-5)?

Answer: No. FAS-140 generally does not address subsequent measurement of transferred financial assets or the obligation to return transferred collateral. The liability to return the collateral should be measured in accordance with other relevant authoritative literature.

Extinguishment of Liabilities

Question 119: Are liabilities extinguished by legal defeasances?

Answer: Yes, if the condition of FAS-140, paragraph 16b (ASC 405-20-40-1), is satisfied, which requires that the debtor has been legally released.

Question 120: How should a debtor account for the exchange of an outstanding debt instrument with a lender for a new debt instrument with the same lender but with substantially different terms? How should the debtor account for a substantial modification of a debt instrument?

Answer: FAS-140, paragraph 16 (ASC 405-20-40-1), permits derecognition of a liability only if it is extinguished by the debtor paying the creditor or the debtor being legally released as the primary obligor, either judicially or by the creditor.

Question 121: If an entity is released from being the primary obligor and it becomes a secondary obligor, should the entity recognize the resulting guarantee from being the secondary obligor in the same manner as a third-party guarantor?

Answer: Yes. The entity should recognize the guarantee in the same way it would have as a guarantor that had never been primarily liable.

Question 122: Does FAS-140 address impairment of financial assets?

Answer: FAS-140 does not address subsequent measurement of assets and liabilities, except for servicing assets and servicing liabilities and interest strips, other beneficial interests, loans, other receivables, or other financial assets that contractually may be prepaid or settled otherwise so that the holder would not recover all of its recognized investment. Generally impairment should be measured by reference to other applicable authoritative guidance.

Question 123: Many securitization structures provide for a disproportionate distribution of cash flows to various classes of investors during the amortization period (referred to as a turbo provision). What effect do such provisions have on the accounting for transfers of financial assets under FAS-140?

Answer: Distribution provisions that diverge from the stated ownership percentages of different parties do *not* affect whether (1) sale accounting is appropriate or (2) the transferred assets should be derecognized. Differential distribution provisions should be taken into consideration in determining the relative fair values of the portion of transferred assets sold and portions retained by the transferee.

RELATED CHAPTERS IN 2011
GAAP GUIDE, VOLUME II

Chapter 17, "Financial Instruments"
Chapter 25, "Investments in Debt and Equity Securities"

RELATED CHAPTERS IN 2011
GAAP GUIDE, VOLUME I

Chapter 17, "Financial Instruments"
Chapter 28, "Investments in Debt and Equity Securities"
Chapter 45, "Transfer and Servicing of Financial Assets"

RELATED CHAPTER IN 2011
INTERNATIONAL ACCOUNTING/FINANCIAL REPORTING STANDARDS GUIDE

Chapter 16, "Financial Instruments"

CHAPTER 41
TROUBLED DEBT RESTRUCTURING

CONTENTS

Overview		**41.02**
Authoritative Guidance		
ASC 310 Receivables		**41.03**
FTB 80-2	Classification of Debt Restructurings by Debtors and Creditors	**41.03**
EITF Issue 87-18	Use of Zero Coupon Bonds in a Troubled Debt Restructuring	**41.03**
EITF Issue 87-19	Substituted Debtors in a Troubled Debt Restructuring	**41.05**
EITF Issue 94-8	Accounting for Conversion of a Loan into a Debt Security in a Debt Restructuring	**41.06**
EITF Issue 96-22	(Applicability of the Disclosures Required by FASB Statement No. 114 When a Loan Is Restructured in a Troubled Debt Restructuring into Two (or More) Loans)	**41.10**
EITF Issue 09-I	Effect of a Loan Modification When the Loan Is Part of a Pool That Is Accounted for as a Single Asset	**41.12**
Topic D-80	Application of FASB Statements No. 5 and No. 114 to a Loan Portfolio	**41.14**
ASC 320 Investments—Debt and Equity Securities		**41.15**
FTB 94-1	Application of Statement 115 to Debt Securities Restructured in a Troubled Debt Restructuring	**41.15**
ASC 470 Debt		**41.16**
FTB 81-6	Applicability of Statement 15 to Debtors in Bankruptcy Situations	**41.16**

41.02 *Troubled Debt Restructuring*

ASC 942-310 Financial Services—Depository and Lending   **41.16**

    PB-5   Income Recognition on Loans to
                            Financially Troubled Countries   **41.16**

Related Chapter in 2011 GAAP Guide, Volume II   **41.17**

Related Chapter in 2011 GAAP Guide, Volume I   **41.17**

OVERVIEW

Debt may be restructured for a variety of reasons. A restructuring of debt is considered a troubled debt restructuring (TDR) if the creditor, for economic or legal reasons related to the debtor's financial difficulties, grants a concession to the debtor that it would not otherwise consider. The concession may occur as a result of an agreement between the creditor and the debtor, or it may be imposed by law or a court.

A loan is impaired if, based on current information and events, it is probable that the creditor will be unable to collect all amounts due according to the contractual terms of the loan agreement.

The following pronouncements, which are the sources of GAAP for a troubled debt restructuring, are discussed in the 2011 GAAP Guide, *Volume I*, Chapter 46, "Troubled Debt Restructuring."

    ASC 310;   Accounting by Debtors and Creditors for Troubled
    ASC 470   Debt Restructurings (FAS-15)

    ASC 310   Accounting by Creditors for Impairment of a Loan (FAS-114)

    ASC 310   Accounting by Creditors for Impairment of a Loan—Income Recognition and Disclosures (FAS-118)

AUTHORITATIVE GUIDANCE

ASC 310 Receivables

FTB 80-2 (Classification of Debt Restructurings by Debtors and Creditors) (ASC 310-40-15-3; 55-4; 470-60-15-3; 55-15)

BACKGROUND

ASC 310-40-15-3 through 15-12; 35-2, 35-5 through 35-7; 40-2, 40-5 through 40-6, 40-8; 25-1 through 25-2; 50-1; 55-2; 10-1 through 10-2; ASC 470-60-15-3 through 15-12; 55-3; 35 through 35-12; 45-1 through 45-2; 50-1 through 50-2; 10-1 through 10-2; ASC 450-20-60-12 (FAS-15, Accounting by Debtors and Creditors for Troubled Debt Restructurings) defines *troubled debt restructuring* as a restructuring in which the creditor, for economic or legal reasons related to the debtor's financial difficulties, grants a concession to the debtor that the creditor would not otherwise consider.

STANDARDS

Question: In applying FAS-15, can a debt restructuring be a troubled debt restructuring (TDR) for a debtor but not for a creditor?

Answer: Yes, a debtor may have a TDR even though the creditor does not have a TDR. The debtor and creditor individually apply FAS-15 in light of the specific facts and circumstances to determine whether a particular restructuring constitutes a TDR. Paragraph 7 of FAS-15 (FASB Accounting Standards Codification™ (ASC) 310-40-15-8, 12) is particularly helpful for creditors in determining whether a particular restructuring is a TDR for debtors and creditors. FAS-15 establishes tests for applicability that are not necessarily symmetrical between the debtor and the creditor, particularly when the debtor's carrying amount and the creditor's recorded investment are different amounts.

EITF Issue 87-18 (Use of Zero Coupon Bonds in a Troubled Debt Restructuring) (ASC 310-40-55-6 through 55-10)

OVERVIEW

A creditor agrees to a troubled debt restructuring on a collateralized loan. Under the terms of the agreement, the debtor liquidates some of the collateral and repays a portion of the loan. The remainder of the loan is restructured. The debtor then liquidates the remainder of the collateral, with the creditor's approval, and invests the proceeds in a series of zero coupon bonds that will mature each year at a value equal

41.04 Troubled Debt Restructuring

to the yearly debt service requirement under the restructured loan. The creditor holds the zero coupon bonds as the only collateral for the restructured loan.

ACCOUNTING ISSUE

Is the sale of the collateral and the creditor's receipt of the zero coupon bonds, which have a fair value lower than the net investment in the loan, a settlement of the debt that requires the creditor to recognize a loss?

EITF CONSENSUS

The EITF reached a consensus that the loan is settled with the zero coupon bonds and, therefore, the creditor should recognize (*a*) a loss on the difference between the fair value of the zero coupon bonds and the net investment in the loan and (*b*) an asset for the fair value of the zero coupon bonds.

> **OBSERVATION:** FAS-121 amended ASC 310-40-40-3 (paragraph 28 of FAS-15) and requires creditors to account at fair value less cost to sell for long-lived assets received from a debtor in full satisfaction of a receivable. A loss should be recognized if the recorded investment in the receivable exceeds the fair value of the assets less cost to sell. Such losses are included in the income for the period, unless all or a part of the loss is offset against the allowance for uncollectible accounts or other valuation accounts. This guidance is carried forward in FAS-144, which supersedes FAS-121.

EFFECT OF ASC 860 (FAS-140 and FAS-166)

The Task Force's consensus on loss recognition is *unaffected* by FAS-125 (Accounting for Transfers and Servicing of Financial Assets and Extinguishments of Liabilities) and FAS-140, which supersedes FAS-125. However, the guidance in paragraph 15 of FAS-140 (ASC 860-30-05-2, 05-3) provides guidance to debtors and creditors on the accounting for collateral based on whether the secured party has the right to sell or pledge the collateral. Under the circumstances in this Issue, the debtor would reclassify the zero coupon bond held by the creditor as an encumbered asset and report it in the balance sheet separately from other assets that are not encumbered in that manner.. That guidance was not reconsidered in ASC 860 (FAS-166). Under the guidance paragraph 17 of FAS-140 (ASC 860-50-50-4) as amended by ASC 860 (FAS-166), a creditor would report the fair value of the collateral and any portion that has been sold or repledged, if the creditor has the right to sell or pledge the collateral. If a creditor does not have that right, the *debtor* should report information about that collateral.

DISCUSSION

Most Task Force members believed that the transaction is an insubstance foreclosure or settlement of the loan, based on paragraph 34 of FAS-15 (ASC 310-40-40-6). Others noted that the creditor should not be able to avoid loss recognition by avoiding legal foreclosure. FAS-114 amends the concept of "in-substance foreclosure" in paragraph 34 of FAS-15 (ASC 310-40-40-6) by providing that the creditor must have physical possession of the collateral, regardless of whether it has been legally foreclosed, to account for the loan as in-substance foreclosed and recognize the fair value of the asset. That is, the creditor should continue to account for a loan for which foreclosure is probable as a loan until the creditor has possession of the collateral.

Although the creditor did not legally foreclose on the loan, the debtor's obligation on the restructured loan was settled with the zero coupon bonds because the creditor had possession of the bonds and was collecting annual payments. The creditor should therefore recognize a loss on that transaction. Under the amendment in FAS-114, this transaction qualifies for an in-substance foreclosure and the same accounting as that required under the consensus.

EITF Issue 87-19 (Substituted Debtors in a Troubled Debt Restructuring) (ASC 310-40-40-1)

OVERVIEW

A creditor and a debtor agree to a troubled debt restructuring on a mortgage loan receivable under which the debtor will make payments to the creditor for the next 30 years. With the creditor's permission, the debtor sells the house, collateralizing the loan on a contract for deed to a third party for less than the creditor's net investment in the loan. The debtor retains title to the house and the creditor retains a lien on the property. The debtor finances the sale of the house to the third party so that monthly principal and interest payments equal the debtor's required payments on the restructured loan. The third party makes the monthly payments directly to the creditor.

ACCOUNTING ISSUE

Should the sale of the collateral and subsequent payments by the third party to the creditor be considered a settlement of the restructured loan, thus requiring the creditor to recognize a loss for the difference between the carrying amount of the net investment in the restructured loan and the fair value of the payments to be received from the third party purchaser?

EITF CONSENSUS

The EITF reached a consensus that the creditor should recognize an asset for the fair value of the payments to be received from the third-party purchaser and a loss on the settlement of the restructured loan that is measured based on the difference between the net investment in the loan and the fair value of the asset received to satisfy the loan in accordance with the guidance in paragraph 28 of FAS-15 (ASC 310-40-40-3).

Some members of the Task Force believed that the transaction is an in-substance foreclosure or settlement of the loan, based on paragraph 34 of FAS-15 (ASC 310-40-40-6). Others believed it is an addition or substitution of a debtor, based on paragraph 42 of FAS-15 (ASC 310-40-25-2). Some members noted that a creditor should not be able to avoid loss recognition by avoiding a legal foreclosure even though the creditor essentially has repossessed the collateral by approving the sale and requiring that the third party make payments directly to the creditor instead of to the debtor.

DISCUSSION

This Issue is similar to Issue 87-18. Here, as in that Issue, the debtor has settled the restructured debt by turning over the economic benefits of the collateral without a legal foreclosure. Under FAS-15, as amended by FAS-114, the transaction qualifies for in-substance foreclosure and loss recognition. (See the discussion in Issue 87-18 of the amendment of FAS-15 on in-substance foreclosure.)

EITF Issue 94-8 (Accounting for Conversion of a Loan into a Debt Security in a Debt Restructuring) (ASC 310-40-40-8A, 40-9)

OVERVIEW

A creditor receives a debt security issued by the debtor in a debt restructuring. The fair value of the debt security differs from the creditor's basis in the loan on the date the debt is restructured because (*a*) there has been a direct write-off against the loan, in which case the fair value of the security exceeds the basis of the loan, or (*b*) there has been no direct write-off against the loan, in which case the basis of the loan exceeds the fair value of the security.

ASC 310-35-13 through 35-14, 35-16 through 35-26, 35-28, 35-29, 35-34, 35-37, 35-39; 45-5 through 45-6; 50-15, 50-19; ASC 310-30-30-2; ASC 310-40–35-8, 35-12; 50-2 through 50-3, 50-12 through 50-13 (FAS-114) provides guidance to creditors on accounting for impaired loans. ASC 320-10-05-2; 50-1A through 50-3, 50-5, 50-9 through 50-11; 55-3; 15-5; 30-1; 35-1 through 35-2, 35-4 through 35-5, 35-10 through 35-13, 35-18; 15-2 through 15-4, 15-7; 25-3 through 25-6, 25-9, 25-11 through 25-12, 25-14 through 25-16; 45-1 through 45-2, 45-8 through 45-11, 45-13 (FAS-115) discusses the accounting for investments in marketable securities and investments in all debt securities. ASC 320-10-15-6. 55-2 (FTB 94-1) states that the provisions of FAS-115 apply to securities received in a debt restructuring.

ACCOUNTING ISSUES

- At what amount should a creditor recognize a debt security issued by the debtor and received in a debt restructuring?
- How should a creditor account for a difference, if any, between the creditor's basis in the loan and the fair value of the debt security at the date of the restructuring?

EITF CONSENSUS

- The creditor should recognize a debt security issued by the debtor and received in a debt restructuring at the fair value of the security at the date of the restructuring.
- The creditor should account for the difference between the creditor's basis in the loan and the fair value of the debt security as follows:
  —Recognize the difference as a recovery of the loan if the fair value of the debt security exceeds the net carrying amount of the loan.
  —Recognize the difference as a charge to the allowance for credit losses if the net carrying amount of the loan exceeds the fair value of the debt security.
  —After the restructuring, account for the debt security in accordance with the guidance in ASC 320-10-05-2; 50-1A through 50-3, 50-5, 50-9 through 50-11; 55-3; 15-5; 30-1; 35-1 through 35-2, 35-4 through 35-5, 35-10 through 35-13, 35-18; 15-2 through 15-4, 15-7; 25-3 through 25-6, 25-9, 25-11 through 25-12, 25-14 through 25-16; 45-1 through 45-2, 45-8 through 45-11, 45-13 (FAS-115).
- If a security is received in a restructuring to settle a claim for past-due interest on a loan, the security should be measured at its fair value at the date of the restructuring and accounted for consistent with the entity's policy for recognizing cash received for past-due interest. After the restructuring, the security should be accounted for based on the guidance in FAS-115.

Illustration of the Conversion of a Loan into a Debt Security

Example 1—Conversion of a Loan with a Prior Write-down into a Security

Original recorded investment in the loan	$50,000
Write-down	(5,000)
Recorded investment in the loan as adjusted	$45,000
Fair value of security at restructuring:	
Scenario 1	$47,000
Scenario 2	$45,000
Scenario 3	$40,000

Accounting for a Debt Security Classified as Available-for-Sale

Scenario 1

Investment in debt security	$47,000	
Loan		$45,000
Allowance for credit losses—recovery		2,000

Scenario 2

Investment in debt security	$45,000	
Loan		$45,000

Scenario 3

Investment in debt security	$40,000	
Allowance for credit losses	5,000	
Loan		$45,000

Example 2—Conversion of a Loan with a Valuation Allowance into a Security

Recorded investment in the loan	$50,000
Valuation allowance	5,000
Net carrying amount of the loan	$45,000
Fair value of security at restructuring:	
Scenario 1	$47,000
Scenario 2	$45,000
Scenario 3	$40,000

Accounting for a Debt Security Classified as Available-for-Sale

Scenario 1

Investment in debt security	$47,000	
Valuation allowance	5,000	

Loan		$50,000
Allowance for credit losses—recovery		2,000
Scenario 2		
Investment in debt security	$45,000	
Valuation allowance	5,000	
Loan		$50,000
Scenario 3		
Investment in debt security	$40,000	
Valuation allowance	5,000	
Allowance for credit losses	5,000	
Loan		$50,000

DISCUSSION

- Debt securities are within the scope of ASC 320-10-05-2; 50-1A through 50-3, 50-5, 50-9 through 50-11; 55-3; 15-5; 30-1; 35-1 through 35-2, 35-4 through 35-5, 35-10 through 35-13, 35-18; 15-2 through 15-4, 15-7; 25-3 through 25-6, 25-9, 25-11 through 25-12, 25-14 through 25-16; 45-1 through 45-2, 45-8 through 45-11, 45-13 (FAS-115) and must be recognized at fair value, if they are classified as trading or available-for-sale.

- Two alternative approaches were discussed. Under one approach, the difference, if any, between the creditor's basis in the loan and the fair value of the debt security at the date of the restructuring would be accounted for as a FAS-115 fair value adjustment.

   The other approach—the one adopted by the Task Force—is that of settlement accounting. Proponents of this approach argued that assets carried at fair value are excluded by the modification-of-terms provisions in ASC 310-40-15-3 through 15-12; 35-2, 35-5 through 35-7; 40-2, 40-5 through 40-6, 40-8; 25-1 through 25-2; 50-1; 55-2; 10-1 through 10-2; ASC 470-60-15-3 through 15-12; 55-3; 35 through 35-12; 45-1 through 45-2; 50-1 through 50-2; 10-1 through 10-2; ASC 450-20-60-12 (FAS-15) as well as from the scope of ASC 310-35-13 through 35-14, 35-16 through 35-26, 35-28, 35-29, 35-34, 35-37, 35-39; 45-5 through 45-6; 50-15, 50-19; ASC 310-30-30-2; ASC 310-40–35-8, 35-12; 50-2 through 50-3, 50-12 through 50-13 (FAS-114), because modification-of-terms accounting and allowance for loan losses are unnecessary when an asset is accounted for at fair value. FAS-115 does not address the treatment of a recovery in value at the date of a restructuring or the treatment of an additional write-down. Proponents of this view believed that accounting for the debt security at fair value provides an embedded gain or loss that should be accounted for as a recovery, if there is a gain, or as a write-off, if there is a loss. They noted that recovery accounting is an established practice that measures historical loan-loss experience. The gain is a function of the market's evaluation of collectibility based on credit considerations instead of market interest rates. Proponents of this view also argued that a gain should not be considered a holding gain as contemplated in FAS-115, because the gain in that case occurred before the restructuring, whereas here the asset was a loan and it would be misleading to recognize it as a gain on the security. An adjustment of bad debt expense for the loan would therefore best present the economics of the transaction.

Some analogized the restructuring of the loan into a debt security by comparing it to the securitization of mortgage loans held for sale, which is accounted for under FAS-65 (Accounting for Certain Mortgage Banking Activities) as a sale of the mortgage loan and a purchase of a mortgage-backed security. They argued that if the loan was sold rather than exchanged for the debt security, a gain would be recognized as a recovery. Recognition of a previous write-off represents the economics of the transaction.

- The Task Force's consensus was based on the notion that a gain on securities received in payment for past-due interest that was never recognized on the balance sheet should be recognized as income, as if those claims were sold for cash.

EITF Issue 96-22 (Applicability of the Disclosures Required by FASB Statement No. 114 When a Loan Is Restructured in a Troubled Debt Restructuring into Two (or More) Loans) (ASC 310-40-50-5; S50-1; S99-1)

OVERVIEW

Under the provisions of ASC 310-35-13 through 35-14, 35-16 through 35-26, 35-28, 35-29, 35-34, 35-37, 35-39; 45-5 through 45-6; 50-15, 50-19; ASC 310-30-30-2; ASC 310-40-35-8, 35-12; 50-2 through 50-3, 50-12 through 50-13 (FAS-114), as amended by ASC 310-10-35-40; 50-16 through 50-17, 50-20; ASC 310-40-35-10; 50-6 (FAS-118, Accounting by Creditors for Impairment of a Loan-Income Recognition and Disclosures), creditors must disclose information about their investments in impaired loans and related allowances for credit losses. Creditors need not make those disclosures in years subsequent to the year in which a loan is restructured in a troubled debt restructuring that involves a modification of terms if the following two criteria are met: (*a*) the interest rate provided for in the restructuring agreement at least equals the rate the creditor was willing to accept for a new loan with comparable risk at the time the loan was restructured and (b) the loan is not impaired under the terms of the restructuring agreement.

Because it was expected that the above criteria would be applied to a single loan resulting from a loan restructuring, some have questioned whether loans resulting from a loan restructuring that involves a loan-splitting or other multiple-loan structure—in which the original loan is restructured into two or more loans—should be considered separately or together for the purpose of impairment disclosures. For example, a lender may restructure a loan by splitting it into two loans: Loan A, which meets the criteria for exemption from the disclosures after the year of the restructuring, and Loan B, which includes the remaining cash flows under the original loan that are not expected to be collected and have been charged off. Here, Loan B does not meet the criteria for exemption from disclosure. Loan B may be forgiven when Loan A is paid off, or the debtor may be required to make payments on Loan B only if its results of operations exceed certain sales levels.

ACCOUNTING ISSUE

Should two or more restructured loans that result from a troubled debt restructuring be considered independently or collectively when assessing whether the disclosures required in ASC 310-10-50-12 through 13, 35-34 (paragraphs 20a and 20c of FAS-114), as amended, apply?

EITF CONSENSUS

The EITF reached a consensus that two or more loan agreements resulting from a troubled debt restructuring, as defined in ASC 310-40-15-3 through 15-12; 35-2, 35-5 through 35-7; 40-2, 40-5 through 40-6, 40-8; 25-1 through 25-2; 50-1; 55-2; 10-1 through 10-2; ASC 470-60-15-3 through 15-12; 55-3; 35 through 35-12; 45-1 through 45-2; 50-1 through 50-2; 10-1 through 10-2; ASC 450-20-60-12 (FAS-15), should be considered separately when assessing whether the disclosures in ASC 310-10-50-12 through 13, 35-34 (paragraphs 20a and 20c of FAS-114), as amended, should be made in years subsequent to the year of the restructuring, because the loans are legally distinct from the original loan. Nevertheless, the creditor should continue measuring a loan's impairment based on the contractual terms of the *original* loan agreement, in accordance with ASC 310-10-35-20 through 35-22, 35-24 through 35-27, 35-32, 35-37; ASC 310-40-35-12; ASC 310-30-30-2 (paragraphs 11 through 16 of FAS-114), as amended.

SEC OBSERVER COMMENT

The SEC Observer stated the staff's concern that disclosures about impaired loans after the loans have been restructured into multiple loans in a troubled debt restructuring may imply under some circumstances that the quality of the loan portfolio has improved merely as result of a troubled debt restructuring. Consequently, the staff believes that registrants should inform users clearly about how multiple loan structures affect the disclosures about impaired loans.

Illustration of Required Disclosure Requirements When a Loan Is Restructured in a Troubled Debt Restructuring into Two (or More) Loans

MHR Corp. restructures a loan into two loans in a troubled debt restructuring. Loan A represents the portion of the contractual cash flows expected to be collected and meets the criteria for exemption from disclosure in the years following the restructuring. Loan B represents the portion of the contractual cash flows *not* expected to be collected and that will be written off.

MHR should disclose information about Loan B in years subsequent to the restructuring in conformity with the requirements of ASC 310-35-13 through 35-14, 35-16 through 35-26, 35-28, 35-29, 35-34, 35-37, 35-39; 45-5 through 45-6; 50-15, 50-19; ASC 310-30-30-2; ASC 310-40–35-8, 35-12; 50-2 through 50-3, 50-12 through 50-13 (FAS-114), as amended, because the recorded investment in that loan and the related allowance for credit losses would be zero.

DISCUSSION

As stated in the consensus, the Task Force believed that loans resulting from a troubled debt restructuring are legally separate loans that should, therefore, be considered separately when assessing whether they should be exempted from disclosure. They argued that although the combined loans meet the definition of an impaired loan and must be measured for impairment purposes based on the terms of the original loan agreement, the loans should be considered new loans for disclosure purposes, because the criteria for exemption from disclosure are based on the terms specified in the restructuring agreement—not on those stated in the original loan agreement.

EITF Issue 09-I Effect of a Loan Modification When the Loan Is Part of a Pool That Is Accounted for as a Single Asset

OVERVIEW

Under the guidance in ASC 310, *Receivables* (ASC 310-30-15-6), an entity is permitted to account for acquired assets with "common risk characteristics" in a pool of assets, which becomes a unit of accounting when it is established. Because the purchase discount for loans accounted for in a pool is not allocated to the individual loans, all the loans in a pool are accreted at a rate based on the cash flow projection for the pool. Also, impairment is tested on the total pool and not on the individual loans.

Guidance for evaluating whether a loan modification should be classified as a troubled debt restructuring (TDR) is provided in ASC 310-40-15-4, which states that a restructuring of debt represents a TDR if a creditor grants a concession to the debtor as a result of the debtor's financial difficulties. Questions have been raised about whether TDR accounting applies if acquired loans with credit deterioration are accounted for in a pool. If so, some believe that the troubled loan should be removed from the pool or that the whole pool should be accounted for as a TDR. A loan that is removed from a pool would no longer be accounted for under the guidance in ASC 310-30. However, others believe that such loans should not be removed from the pool.

SCOPE

The guidance in this Issue applies to modifications of loans accounted for as a pool that is established under the provisions of ASC 310-30-15-6. The guidance in this Issue does *not* apply to loans accounted for individually under the guidance in ASC 310-30 or those not under the scope of that guidance.

EITF CONSENSUS

The EITF affirmed its consensus-for-exposure reached at the November 19, 2009 meeting that TDR accounting should not be applied to loans accounted for as a pool under the guidance in ASC 310-30 that had deteriorating credit when they were acquired. The EITF decided *not* to require additional disclosures, because it is expected that as part of its project on loan loss disclosures, the FASB will consider whether additional disclosures should be required about loan modifications, including for loans accounted for within a pool under the guidance in ASC 310-30.

EFFECTIVE DATE AND TRANSITION

The EITF reached a consensus that this Issue should be effective for the modification of loans accounted for as a pool under the guidance in ASC 310-30 in interim or annual periods that end on or after July 15, 2010. Application of the amendments should be prospective only. Early application is permitted. For existing pools, an entity is permitted to make a one-time election on a pool-by-pool basis to change the unit of accounting from a pool to an individual basis when the guidance in this Issue is adopted. This election does not prohibit an entity from applying pool accounting to loans acquired after the effective date of this guidance.

FASB RATIFICATION

The FASB ratified the EITF's consensus positions in Issue 09-I at its March 31, 2010 meeting.

Topic D-80 (Application of FASB Statements No. 5 and No. 114 to a Loan Portfolio) (ASC 310-10-35-2, 35-4, 35-6, 35-8, 35-15, 35-19, 35-25, 35-27, 35-34 through 35-36, 35-38; 55-1 through 55-6; 40-50-4; 450-20-60-3)

The SEC staff issued this announcement in response to inquiries regarding the transition required for companies that change their application of generally accepted accounting principles as a result of the guidance in the FASB staff's Viewpoints article, "Application of FASB Statements 5 and 114 to a Loan Portfolio," which was published in the FASB's April 12, 1999, *Status Report*. The SEC staff noted that the guidance in that article is part of generally accepted accounting principles and should be followed by *all* creditors.

According to the SEC staff, if an SEC registrant's application of the guidance in the Viewpoints article results in a material adjustment, the change should be reported and disclosed in the first quarter ending after May 20, 1999, like a cumulative effect of a change in accounting principles in accordance with (ASC 250-10-45-5). Registrants should *not* restate financial statements for periods before May 20, 1999.

The SEC staff reported that a March 10, 1999, letter to financial institutions—which was issued jointly by the SEC, Federal Deposit Insurance Corporation, Federal Reserve Board, Office of the Controller of the Currency, and Office of Thrift Supervision (the Agencies)—encourages the FASB and its staff to issue additional guidance on accounting for loan losses. In addition, the letter states that the Agencies support the work of the AICPA's Allowance for Loan Losses Task Force in its effort to develop specific guidance on the measurement of credit losses and how to distinguish probable losses inherent in a portfolio at the balance sheet date from possible or future losses that are not inherent in the balance sheet at that date. The Agencies require that allowances be reported for probable losses. The letter also states that the senior staff of the Agencies are working jointly on guidance for (*a*) documentation to support the allowance in addition to that provided in the SEC Financial Reporting Release No. 28 (Accounting for Loan Losses by Registrants Engaged in Lending Activities) under the heading *Procedural Discipline in Determining the Allowance and Provision for Loan Losses to be Reported* and (*b*) improved disclosures about allowances for credit losses.

The EITF asked that the Viewpoints article and a May 21, 1999, letter from the Board of Governors of the Federal Reserve System, which provides guidance to supervisors and bankers regarding the

Viewpoints article, be attached to the announcement. The SEC staff supports that guidance.

ASC 320 Investments—Debt and Equity Securities

FTB 94-1 (Application of Statement 115 to Debt Securities Restructured in a Troubled Debt Restructuring) (ASC 320-10-15-6; 55-2)

BACKGROUND

FTB 94-1 was issued to clarify a perceived inconsistency between ASC 310-35-13 through 35-14, 35-16 through 35-26, 35-28, 35-29, 35-34, 35-37, 35-39; 45-5 through 45-6; 50-15, 50-19; ASC 310-30-30-2; ASC 310-40–35-8, 35-12; 50-2 through 50-3, 50-12 through 50-13 (FAS-114) and ASC 320-10-05-2; 50-1A through 50-3, 50-5, 50-9 through 50-11; 55-3; 15-5; 30-1; 35-1 through 35-2, 35-4 through 35-5, 35-10 through 35-13, 35-18; 15-2 through 15-4, 15-7; 25-3 through 25-6, 25-9, 25-11 through 25-12, 25-14 through 25-16; 45-1 through 45-2, 45-8 through 45-11, 45-13 (FAS-115, Accounting for Certain Investments in Debt and Equity Securities). This problem came to light during the FASB's discussion of the applicability of FAS-115 to Brady bonds that were received in a TDR. The term *Brady bonds* refers to bonds issued to financial institutions by foreign governments under a program designed by Treasury Secretary Nicholas Brady in the late 1980s to help developing countries refinance their debt to those institutions.

If FAS-115 did not apply to a debt security that was restructured in a TDR involving a modification of terms before the effective date of FAS-114, then the impairment provisions of FAS-114 and FAS-115 would not apply, leaving the accounting to be handled in accordance with ASC 310-40-15-3 through 15-12; 35-2, 35-5 through 35-7; 40-2, 40-5 through 40-6, 40-8; 25-1 through 25-2; 50-1; 55-2; 10-1 through 10-2; ASC 470-60-15-3 through 15-12; 55-3; 35 through 35-12; 45-1 through 45-2; 50-1 through 50-2; 10-1 through 10-2; ASC 450-20-60-12 (FAS-15), which would not require the recognition of the time value of money or the security's fair value.

STANDARDS

Question: For a loan that was restructured in a TDR involving a modification of terms, does FAS-115 apply to the accounting by the creditor if the restructured loan meets the definition of a *security* in FAS-115?

Answer: ASC 320-10-05-2; 50-1A through 50-3, 50-5, 50-9 through 50-11; 55-3; 15-5; 30-1; 35-1 through 35-2, 35-4 through 35-5, 35-10 through 35-13, 35-18; 15-2 through 15-4, 15-7; 25-3 through 25-6, 25-9, 25-11 through 25-12, 25-14 through 25-16; 45-1 through 45-2, 45-8 through 45-11, 45-13 (FAS-115) applies to all loans that meet the definition of the term *security* in that Statement. Therefore, any loan that was restructured in a TDR involving a modification of terms, including loans restructured before the effective date of FAS-114, are subject to the requirements of FAS-115.

ASC 470 Debt

FTB 81-6 (Applicability of Statement 15 to Debtors in Bankruptcy Situations) (ASC 470-60-15-10; 55-1, 55-2)

BACKGROUND

Some confusion arose over the applicability of ASC 310-40-15-3 through 15-12; 35-2, 35-5 through 35-7; 40-2, 40-5 through 40-6, 40-8; 25-1 through 25-2; 50-1; 55-2; 10-1 through 10-2; ASC 470-60-15-3 through 15-12; 55-3; 35 through 35-12; 45-1 through 45-2; 50-1 through 50-2; 10-1 through 10-2; ASC 450-20-60-12 (FAS-15) to bankruptcy situations, prompting the issuance of FTB 81-6. On the one hand, FAS-15 indicates that it applies to TDRs consummated under reorganization, arrangement, or other provisions of the Federal Bankruptcy Act or other federal statutes. On the other hand, FAS-15 indicates that it does not apply to situations in which liabilities are generally restated under federal statutes, a quasi-reorganization, or corporate adjustment.

STANDARDS

Question: Does FAS-15 apply to TDRs of debtors involved in bankruptcy proceedings?

Answer: FAS-15 does not apply to debtors who, in connection with bankruptcy proceedings, enter into TDRs that result in a general restatement of the debtor's liabilities.

ASC 942-310 Financial Services—Depository and Lending

PB-5 (Income Recognition on Loans to Financially Troubled Countries) (ASC 942-310-05-2; 35-1 through 35-4)

BACKGROUND

Many bank loans to financially troubled countries meet the criteria for accrual of losses in accordance with ASC 450 (FAS-5).

In those situations, banks should establish loan loss allowances by charges to income.

If a financially troubled country suspends interest payments, banks with outstanding loans from such a country should suspend the accrual recognition of interest income. Such financially troubled countries may later resume interest payments. Guidance on accounting by a creditor for the receipt of interest payments from a debtor that had previously suspended interest payments is included in the industry audit guide titled *Audits of Banks*.

STANDARDS

When a country becomes current as to principal and interest payments and has normalized relations with the international financial markets, assuming the allowance for loan losses is adequate, the creditor may recognize interest on an accrual basis. Even if these conditions are met, the bank should not automatically return the loan to accrual accounting status. Some period of payment performance generally is necessary to make an assessment of collectibility before returning the loan to accrual status.

RELATED CHAPTER IN 2011 GAAP GUIDE, VOLUME II

Chapter 5, "Bankruptcy and Reorganization"

RELATED CHAPTER IN 2011 GAAP GUIDE, VOLUME I

Chapter 46, "Troubled Debt Restructuring"

APPENDIX: LISTING OF SPECIALIZED INDUSTRY GUIDANCE

The 2011 *GAAP Guide, Volume II* contains a great number of authoritative accounting pronouncements that are included in Levels B, C, and D of the SAS-69 GAAP hierarchy. In compiling this volume, priority has been given to the authoritative literature that has general applicability to enterprises in many industries.

The FASB, AICPA, EITF, and other organizations have also issued pronouncements that apply to enterprises in certain specialized industries. The following listing has been prepared to provide assistance in locating authoritative accounting pronouncements that may be relevant in addressing complex accounting issues in a particular industry. Existing pronouncements are grouped by type for each industry.

AGRICULTURE

Statements of Position

SOP 85-3   Accounting by Agricultural Producers and Agricultural Cooperatives

Audit and Accounting Guides

AAG-APC   Audits of Agricultural Producers and Agricultural Cooperatives

COMPUTER SOFTWARE

FASB Statements

FAS-86   Accounting for the Costs of Computer Software to Be Sold, Leased, or Otherwise Marketed (ASC 985)

FIN-6   Applicability of FASB Statement No. 2 to Computer Software (ASC 730)

Statements of Position

*SOP 98-1 Accounting for Costs of Computer Software Developed or Obtained for Internal Use

*SOP 98-9 Modification of SOP 97-2, Software Revenue Recognition, with Respect to Certain Transactions

Audit and Accounting Guides

AAG-REV Auditing Revenue in Certain Industries

EITF Issues

*Issue 96-6 Accounting for the Film and Software Costs Associated with Developing Entertainment and Educational Software Products

*Issue 00-3 Application of AICPA Statement of Position 97-2 to Arrangements That Include the Right to Use Software Stored on Another Entity's Hardware

*Issue 03-5 Applicability of AICPA Statement of Position 97-2, *Software Revenue Recognition*, to Non-Software Deliverables in an Arrangement Containing More-Than-Incidental Software

*Issue 07-1 Accounting for Collaborative Arrangements Related to the Development and Commercialization of Intellectual Property

*Issue 09-3 (ASU 2009-14) Applicability of SOP 97-2 to Certain Arrangements That Include Software Elements

AICPA Staff Guidance

*AICPA Staff Guidance on Implementing SOP 97-2, Software Revenue Recognition

Employers' Accounting for Pensions (ASC 715)

*SOP 81-1 Accounting for Performance of Construction-Type and Certain Production-Type Contracts

Audit and Accounting Guides

AAG-CON Construction Contractors

---

*This pronouncement is essentially an industry standard but is covered in the 2011 *GAAP Guide, Volume II* under an appropriate subject matter heading. See cross-reference listings for specific location.

EMPLOYEE BENEFIT PLANS

APB Opinion

APB-12   Omnibus Opinion—1967 (ASC 360; 710)
Omnibus Opinion—1967 (ASC 360, ASC 710)

FASB Statements

FAS-87   Employers' Accounting for Defined Benefit Plans

FAS-88   Employers' Accounting for Settlements and Curtailments of Defined Benefit Pension Plans and for Termination Benefits (ASC 715)

FAS-106   Employers' Accounting for Postretirement Benefits Other Than Pensions (ASC 715)

FAS-112   Employers' Accounting for Postemployment Benefits (ASC 712)

FAS-132(R)   Employers' Disclosures about Pensions and Other Postretirement Benefits—An Amendment of FASB Statements No. 87, 88, and 106 (ASC 715)

FAS-158   Employers' Accounting for Defined Benefit Pension and Other Postretirement Plans—An Amendment of FASB Statements No. 87, 88, 106, and 132(R) (ASC 715; 958)

FASB Staff Positions

FAS-146-1   Determining Whether a One-Time Termination Benefit Offered in Connection with an Exit or Disposal Activity Is in Substance an Enhancement to an Ongoing Benefit Arrangement

AAG-INV-1/ SOP-94-4-1   Reporting of Fully Benefit-Responsive Investment Contracts Held by Certain Investment Companies Subject to the AICPA Investment Company Guide and Defined-Contribution Health and Welfare and Pension Plans

FAS 132(R)-1   Employers' Disclosures about Postretirement Benefit Plan Assets

*FAS-158-1   Conforming Amendments to the Illustrations in FASB Statements No. 87, No. 88, and No. 106 to the Related Staff Implementation Guides

---

*This pronouncement is essentially an industry standard but is covered in the 2011 *GAAP Guide, Volume II* under an appropriate subject matter heading. See cross-reference listings for specific location.

Statements of Position

SOP 92-6   Accounting and Reporting by Health and Welfare Benefit Plans

SOP 94-4   Reporting of Investment Contracts Held by Health and Welfare Benefit Plans and Defined-Contribution Pension Plans

SOP 99-2   Accounting for and Reporting of Postretirement Medical Benefit (401(h)) Features of Defined Benefit Pension Plans

SOP 99-3   Accounting for and Reporting of Certain Defined Contribution Plan Investments and Other Disclosure Matters

Audit and Accounting Guides

AAG-EBP   Audits of Employee Benefit Plans

EITF Issues

*Issue 88-1   Determination of Vested Benefit Obligation for a Defined Benefit Pension Plan

*Issue 90-3   Accounting for Empoloyers' Obligations for Future Contributions to a Multiemployer Pension Plan

*Issue 91-7   Accounting for Early Retirement Paid by Employers After Insurance Companies Fail to Provide Annuity Benefits

*Issue 92-12   Accounting for OPEB Costs by Rate-Regulated Enterprises

*Issue 93-3   Plan Assets Under FASB Statement No. 106

*Issue 03-2   Accounting for the Transfer to the Japanese Government of the Substitutional Portion of Employee Pension Fund Liabilities

*Issue 03-4   Accounting for "Cash Balance" Pension Plans

*Issue 05-5   Accounting for the Altersteilzeit Early Retirement Programs and Similar Type Arrangements

*Issue 06-4   Accounting for Deferred Compensation and Postretirement Benefit Aspects of Endorsement Split-Dollar Life Insurance Arrangements

---

*This pronouncement is essentially an industry standard but is covered in the 2011 *GAAP Guide, Volume II* under an appropriate subject matter heading. See cross-reference listings for specific location.

*Issue 06-10 Accounting for Deferred Compensation and Post-retirement Benefit Aspects of Collateral Assignment Split-Dollar Life Insurance Arrangements

FASB/SEC Staff Announcements

Topic D-27 Accounting for the Transfer of Excess Pension Assets to a Retiree Health Care Benefits Account

Topic D-36 Selection of Discount Rates Used for Measuring Defined Benefit Pension Obligations of Postretirement Plans Other Than Pensions

ENTERTAINMENT

FASB Statements

FAS-50 Financial Reporting in the Record and Music Industry (ASC 928)

FAS-51 Financial Reporting by Cable Television Companies (ASC 922)

FAS-63 Financial Reporting by Broadcasters (ASC 920)

Statement of Position

SOP 00-2 Accounting by Producers or Distributors of Films

Audit and Accounting Guides

AAG-CAS Audits of Casinos

EITF Issues

Issue 09-F (ASU 2010-16) Accruals for Casino Jackpot Liabilities

FINANCIAL INSTITUTIONS

FASB Statements

FAS-65 Accounting for Certain Mortgage Banking Activities (ASC 948)

FAS-91 Accounting for Nonrefundable Fees and Costs Associated with Originating or Acquiring Loans and Initial Direct Costs of Leases (ASC 310)

---

*This pronouncement is essentially an industry standard but is covered in the 2011 *GAAP Guide, Volume II* under an appropriate subject matter heading. See cross-reference listings for specific location.

FAS-140   Accounting for Transfers and Servicing of Financial Assets and Extinguishments of Liabilities—A Replacement of FASB Statement 125 (ASC 860)

FAS-156   Accounting for Servicing of Financial Assets—An Amendment of FASB Statement No. 140 (ASC 860)

Statements of Position

SOP 97-1   Accounting by Participating Mortgage Loan Borrowers

SOP 01-6   Accounting by Certain Entities (Including Entities With Trade Receivables) That Lend to or Finance the Activities of Others

Audit and Accounting Guides

AAG-DEP   Depository and Lending Institutions

EITF Issues

*Issue 84-19   Mortgage Loan Payment Modifications

*Issue 85-13   Sale of Mortgage Service Rights on Mortgages Owned by Others

*Issue 85-20   Recognition of Fees for Guaranteeing a Loan

*Issue 86-8   Sale of Bad-Debt Recovery Rights

*Issue 87-30   Sale of a Short-Term Loan Made under a Long-Term Credit Commitment

*Issue 88-20   Difference between Initial Investment and Principal Amount of Loans in a Purchased Credit Card Portfolio

*Issue 88-22   Securitization of Credit Card and Other Receivable Portfolios

Issue 89-3   Balance Sheet Presentation of Savings Accounts in Financial Statements of Credit Unions

*Issue 90-21   Balance Sheet Treatment of a Sale of Mortgage Servicing Rights with a Subservicing Agreement

*Issue 92-5   Amortization Period for Net Deferred Credit Card Origination Costs

---

*This pronouncement is essentially an industry standard but is covered in the 2011 *GAAP Guide, Volume II* under an appropriate subject matter heading. See cross-reference listings for specific location.

Appendix: Listing of Specialized Industry Guidance APP.07

    *Issue 93-1   Accounting for Individual Credit Card Acquisitions

    *Issue 95-5   Determination of What Risks and Rewards, If Any, Can Be Retained and Whether Any Unresolved Contingencies May Exist in a Sale of Mortgage Loan Servicing Rights

    *Issue 97-3   Accounting for Fees and Costs Associated with Loan Syndications and Loan Participations after the Issuance of FASB Statement No. 125

    *Issue 09-I (ASU 2010-18)   Effect of a Loan Modification When the Loan Is Part of a Pool That is Accounted for as a Single Asset

Practice Bulletins

    PB-6   Amortization of Discounts on Certain Acquired Loans

HEALTH CARE

FASB Interpretations

    FIN-46(R)   Consolidation of Variable Interest Entities

Statements of Position

    SOP 99-2   Accounting for and Reporting of Postretirement Medical Benefits (401(h)) Features of Defined Benefit Pension Plans

    SOP 02-2   Accounting for Derivative Instruments and Hedging Activities by Not-for-Profit Health Care Organizations, and Clarification of the Performance Indicator

Audit and Accounting Guides

    AAG-HCO   Health Care Organizations

EITF Issues

    *Issue 97-2   Application of FASB Statement No. 94 and APB Opinion No. 16 to Physician Practice Management Entities and Certain Other Entities with Contractual Management Arrangements

---

*This pronouncement is essentially an industry standard but is covered in the 2011 *GAAP Guide, Volume II* under an appropriate subject matter heading. See cross-reference listings for specific location.

*Issue 09-K   Health Care Entities: Presentation of Insurance
(ASU 2010-24)   Claims and Related Insurance Recoveries

*Issue 09-L   Health Care Entities: Measuring Charity Care
(ASU 2010-24)   For Disclosure

FASB/SEC Staff Announcements

Topic D-89   Accounting for Costs of Future Medicare Compliance Audits

INSURANCE

FASB Statements

FAS-60   Accounting and Reporting by Insurance Enterprises (ASC 944)

FAS-61   Accounting for Title Plant (ASC 950)

FAS-91   Accounting for Nonrefundable Fees and Costs Associated with Originating or Acquiring Loans and Initial Direct Costs of Leases (ASC 310)

FAS-97   Accounting and Reporting by Insurance Enterprises for Certain Long-Duration Contracts and for Realized Gains and Losses from the Sale of Investments (ASC 944)

FAS-113   Accounting and Reporting for Reinsurance of Short-Duration and Long-Duration Contracts (ASC 944)

FAS-120   Accounting and Reporting by Mutual Life Insurance Enterprises and by Insurance Enterprises for Certain Long-Duration Participating Contracts (ASC 944)

FAS-163   Accounting for Financial Guarantee Insurance Contracts—An Interpretation of FASB Statement No. 60 (ASC 944)

FASB Staff Positions

*FAS-97-1   Situations in Which Paragraphs 17(b) and 20 of FASB Statement No. 97, *Accounting and Reporting by Insurance Enterprises for Certain Long-Duration Contracts and for Realized Gains and Losses from the Sale of Investments*, Permit or Require Accrual of an Unearned Revenue Liability

---

*This pronouncement is essentially an industry standard but is covered in the 2011 *GAAP Guide, Volume II* under an appropriate subject matter heading. See cross-reference listings for specific location.

Statements of Position

SOP 92-5	Accounting for Foreign Property and Liability Reinsurance
SOP 94-5	Disclosures of Certain Matters in the Financial Statements of Insurance Enterprises
SOP 95-1	Accounting for Certain Insurance Activities of Mutual Life Insurance Enterprises
SOP 97-3	Accounting by Insurance and Other Enterprises for Insurance-Related Assessments
SOP 98-7	Deposit Accounting: Accounting for Insurance and Reinsurance Contracts That Do Not Transfer Insurance Risk
SOP 00-3	Accounting by Insurance Enterprises for Demutualizations and Formations of Mutual Insurance Holding Companies and for Certain Long-Duration Participating Contracts
SOP 03-1	Accounting and Reporting by Insurance Enterprises for Certain Nontraditional Long-Duration Contracts and for Separate Accounts
SOP 05-1	Accounting by Insurance Enterprises for Deferred Acquisition Costs in Connection with Modifications or Exchanges of Insurance Contracts

Audit and Accounting Guides

AAG-LHI	Life and Health Insurance Entities
AAG-PLI	Audits of Property and Liability Insurance Companies

EITF Issues

*Issue 88-5	Recognition of Insurance Death Benefits
*Issue 99-4	Accounting for Stock Received from the Demutualization of a Mutual Insurance Company
*Issue 03-8	Accounting for Claims-Made Insurance and Retroactive Insurance Contracts by the Insured Entity
Issue 06-4	Accounting for Deferred Compensation and Postretirement Benefit Aspects of Endorsement Split-Dollar Life Insurance Arrangements

---

*This pronouncement is essentially an industry standard but is covered in the 2011 *GAAP Guide, Volume II* under an appropriate subject matter heading. See cross-reference listings for specific location.

Issue 06-5 — Accounting for Purchase Life Insurance—Determining the Amount That Could Be Realized in Accordance with FASB Technical Bulletin 86-4

09-B (ASU 2010-15) — Consideration of an Insurer's Accounting For Majority-Owned Investments When the Ownership Is through a Separate Account

Practice Bulletins

8 — Application of FASB Statement No. 97, *Accounting and Reporting by Insurance Enterprises for Certain Long-Duration Contracts and for Realized Gains and Losses from the Sale of Investments*, to Insurance Enterprises

15 — Accounting by the Issuer of Surplus Notes

FASB/SEC Staff Announcements

*Topic D-54 — Accounting by the Purchaser for a Seller's Guarantee of the Adequacy of Liabilities for Losses and Loss Adjustment Expenses of an Insurance Enterprise Acquired in a Purchase Business Combination

INVESTMENT COMPANIES

FASB Staff Positions

*EITF 85-24-1 — Application of EITF Issue No. 85-24, "Distribution Fees by Distributors of Mutual Funds That Do Not Have a Front-End Sales Charge," When Cash for the Right to Future Distribution Fees for Shares Previously Sold is Received from Third Parties

AAG-INV-1 and SOP-94-4-1 — Reporting of Fully Benefit-Responsive Investment Contracts Held by Certain Investment Companies Subject to the AICPA Investment Company Guide and Defined-Contribution Health and Welfare and Pension Plans

Statements of Position

SOP 93-1 — Financial Accounting and Reporting for High-Yield Debt Securities by Investment Companies

---

*This pronouncement is essentially an industry standard but is covered in the 2011 *GAAP Guide, Volume II* under an appropriate subject matter heading. See cross-reference listings for specific location.

*SOP 93-4   Foreign Currency Accounting and Financial Statement Presentation for Investment Companies

SOP 95-2   Financial Reporting by Nonpublic Investment Partnerships

SOP 95-3   Accounting for Certain Distribution Costs of Investment Companies

SOP 07-1   Clarification of the Scope of the Audit and Accounting Guide "Investment Companies" and Accounting by Parent Companies and Equity Method Investors for Investments in Investment Companies

Audit and Accounting Guides

AAG-BRD   Brokers and Dealers in Securities

AAG-INV   Audits of Investment Companies

EITF Issues

*Issue 85-12   Retention of Specialized Accounting for Investments in Consolidation

*Issue 85-24   Distribution Fees by Distributors of Mutual Funds That Do Not Have a Front-End Sales Charge

FASB/SEC Staff Announcements

*Topic D-76   Accounting by Advisors for Offering Costs Paid on Behalf of Funds, When the Advisor Does Not Receive both 12b-1 Fees and Contingent Deferred Sales Charges

NOT-FOR-PROFIT ORGANIZATIONS

FASB Statements

FAS-93   Recognition of Depreciation by Not-for-Profit Organizations (ASC 958)

FAS-116   Accounting for Contributions Received and Contributions Made (ASC 958)

FAS-117   Financial Statements of Not-for-Profit Organizations (ASC 958)

---

*This pronouncement is essentially an industry standard but is covered in the 2011 *GAAP Guide, Volume II* under an appropriate subject matter heading. See cross-reference listings for specific location.

FAS-124	Accounting for Certain Investments Held by Not-for-Profit Organizations (ASC 958)
FAS-136	Transfer of Assets to a Not-for-Profit Organization or Charitable Trust That Raises or Holds Contributions for Others (ASC 958)
FAS-164 (ASU 2010-07)	Not-for-Profit Entities: Mergers and Acquistions (ASC 958)

FASB Interpretations

FIN-46(R)	Consolidation of Variable Interest Entities

FASB Staff Positions

*FAS-117-1	Endowments of Not-for-Profit Organizations
SOP 94-3-1 and AAG HCO-1	Omnibus Changes to Consolidation and Equity Method Guidance for Not-for-Profit Organizations

Statements of Position

SOP 94-3	Reporting of Related Entities by Not-for-Profit Organizations
SOP 98-2	Accounting for Costs of Activities of Not-for-Profit Organizations and State and Local Governmental Entities That Include Fund Raising
SOP 02-2	Accounting for Derivative Instruments and Hedging Activities by Not-for-Profit Health Care Organizations, and Clarification of the Performance Indicator

Audit and Accounting Guides

AAG-NPO	Not-for-Profit Organizations
AAG-SLG/NFP	Government Auditing Standards and Circular A-133 Audits

OIL AND GAS

FASB Statements

FAS-19	Financial Accounting and Reporting by Oil and Gas Producing Companies (ASC 932)

---

*This pronouncement is essentially an industry standard but is covered in the 2011 *GAAP Guide, Volume II* under an appropriate subject matter heading. See cross-reference listings for specific location.

FAS-69   Disclosures about Oil and Gas Producing Activities (ASC 932)

FASB Interpretations

FIN-33   Applying FASB Statement No. 34 to Oil and Gas Producing Operations Accounted for by the Full Cost Method

FIN-36   Accounting for Exploratory Wells in Progress at the End of a Period

FASB Staff Positions

*FAS-19-1   Accounting for Suspended Well Costs

*FAS 142-2   Application of FASB No. 142, *Goodwill and Other Intangible Assets*, to Oil and Gas Producing Entities

Audit and Accounting Guides

AAG-OGP   Audits of Entities with Oil and Gas Producing Activities

EITF Issues

*04-2   Whether Mineral Rights Are Tangible or Intangible Assets and Related Issues

*04-3   Mining Assets: Impairment and Business Combinations

*04-6   Accounting for Stripping Costs Incurred during Production in the Mining Industry

Accounting Standards Updates (ASU)

ASU 2010-03   Oil and Gas Reserve Estimation and Disclosures (ASC 932)

REAL ESTATE

FASB Statements

FAS-66   Accounting for Sales of Real Estate (ASC 976)

FAS-67   Accounting for Costs and Initial Rental Operations of Real Estate Projects (ASC 970)

FAS-98   Accounting for Leases: (ASC 840)

---

*This pronouncement is essentially an industry standard but is covered in the 2011 *GAAP Guide, Volume II* under an appropriate subject matter heading. See cross-reference listings for specific location.

- Sale-Leaseback Transactions Involving Real Estate
- Sales-Type Leases of Real Estate
- Definition of the Lease Term
- Initial Direct Costs of Direct Financing

FASB Interpretations

FIN-43   Real Estate Sales

FASB Staff Positions

*FAS-13-1   Accounting for Rental Costs Incurred During a Construction Period

Statements of Position

SOP 75-2   Accounting Practices of Real Estate Investment Trusts

SOP 78-9   Accounting for Investments in Real Estate Ventures

SOP 92-1   Accounting for Real Estate Syndication Income

*SOP 04-2   Accounting for Real Estate Time-Sharing Transactions

Audit and Accounting Guides

AAG-RLE   Guide for the Use of Real Estate Appraisal Information

AAG-CIR   Common Interest Realty Associations

EITF Issues

*Issue 84-17   Profit Recognition on Sales of Real Estate with Graduated Payment Mortgages or Insured Mortgages

*Issue 85-16   Leveraged Leases: Real Estate Leases and Sale-Leaseback Transactions, Delayed Equity Contributions by Lessors

*Issue 85-27   Recognition of Receipts from Made-Up Rental Shortfalls

*Issue 86-6   Antispeculation Clauses in Real Estate Sales Contracts

---

*This pronouncement is essentially an industry standard but is covered in the 2011 *GAAP Guide, Volume II* under an appropriate subject matter heading. See cross-reference listings for specific location.

*Issue 86-7   Recognition by Homebuilders of Profit from Sales of Land and Related Construction Contracts

*Issue 86-21   Application of the AICPA Notice to Practitioners regarding Acquisition, Development, and Construction Arrangements to Acquisition of an Operating Property

*Issue 87-9   Profit Recognition on Sales of Real Estate with Insured Mortgages or Surety Bonds

*Issue 88-12   Transfer of Ownership Interest as Part of Down Payment under FASB Statement No. 66

*Issue 88-24   Effect of Various Forms of Financing under FASB Statement No. 66

*Issue 89-14   Valuation of Repossessed Real Estate

*Issue 90-20   Impact of an Uncollateralized Irrevocable Letter of Credit on a Real Estate Sale-Leaseback Transaction

*Issue 94-1   Accounting for Tax Benefits Resulting from Investments in Affordable Housing Projects

*Issue 95-6   Accounting by a Real Estate Investment Trust for an Investment in a Service Corporation

*Issue 97-11   Accounting for Internal Costs Relating to Real Estate Property Acquisitions

*Issue 98-8   Accounting for Transfers of Investments That Are in Substance Real Estate

*Issue 00-13   Determining Whether Equipment Is "Integral Equipment" Subject to FASB Statements No. 66 and No. 98

*Issue 03-16   Accounting for Investments in Limited Liability Companies

*Issue 05-6   Determining the Amortization Period for Leasehold Improvements

*Issue 06-8   Applicability of the Assessment of a Buyer's Continuing Investment under FASB Statement No. 66, *Accounting for Sales of Real Estate,* for Sales of Condominiums

---

*This pronouncement is essentially an industry standard but is covered in the 2011 *GAAP Guide, Volume II* under an appropriate subject matter heading. See cross-reference listings for specific location.

*Issue 07-06   Accounting for the Sale of Real Estate Subject to the Requirements of FASB Statement No. 66 When the Agreement Includes a Buy-Sell Clause

FASB/EITF Staff Announcements

*Topic D-46   Accounting for Limited Partnership Investments

REGULATED INDUSTRIES

FASB Statements

FAS-71	Accounting for the Effects of Certain Types of Regulation (ASC 980)
FAS-90	Regulated Enterprises—Accounting for Abandonments and Disallowances of Plant Costs (ASC 980)
FAS-92	Regulated Enterprises—Accounting for Phase-in Plans (ASC 980)
FAS-101	Regulated Enterprises—Accounting for the Discontinuation of Application of FASB Statement No. 71 (ASC 980)
FAS-106	Employers' Accounting for Postretirement Benefits Other Than Pensions (ASC 715)
FAS-109	Accounting for Income Taxes (ASC 740)
FAS-144	Accounting for the Impairment or Disposal of Long-Lived Assets (ASC 205; 360)

EITF Issues

*Issue 90-22	Accounting for Gas-Balancing Arrangements
*Issue 91-6	Revenue Recognition of Long-Term Power Sales Contracts
*Issue 92-7	Accounting by Rate-Regulated Utilities for the Effects of Certain Alternative Revenue Programs
*Issue 92-12	Accounting for OPEB Costs by Rate-Regulated Enterprises
*Issue 96-17	Revenue Recognition under Long-Term Power Sales Contracts That Contain both Fixed and Variable Pricing Terms

---

*This pronouncement is essentially an industry standard but is covered in the 2011 *GAAP Guide, Volume II* under an appropriate subject matter heading. See cross-reference listings for specific location.

*Issue 97-4   Deregulation of the Pricing of Electricity—Issues Related to the Application of FASB Statements Nos. 71 and 101

*Issue 04-6   Accounting for Stripping Costs Incurred During Production in the Mining Industry

TRANSPORTATION

FASB Staff Positions

AUG-AIR-1   Accounting for Planned Major Maintenance Activities

Statements of Position

SOP 88-1   Accounting for Developmental and Preoperating Costs, Purchases and Exchanges of Take-off and Landing Slots, and Airframe Modifications

Audit and Accounting Guides

AUG-AIR   Audits of Airlines

EITF Issues

*Issue 91-9   Revenue and Expense Recognition for Freight Services in Process

---

*This pronouncement is essentially an industry standard but is covered in the 2011 *GAAP Guide, Volume II* under an appropriate subject matter heading. See cross-reference listings for specific location.

Accounting Resources on the Web

The following World Wide Web addresses are just a few of the resources on the Internet that are available to practitioners. Because of the evolving nature of the Internet, some addresses may change. In such a case, refer to one of the many Internet search engines, such as Google (http://www.google.com) or Yahoo (http://www.yahoo.com).

Accounting Research Manager
http://www.accountingresearchmanager.com

AICPA http://www.aicpa.org

American Accounting Association
http://www.accounting.rutgers.com

CCH Integrated Solutions http://cchgroup.com/books/default

FASAB http://www.fasab.gov

FASB http://www.fasb.org

Federal Tax Law http://www.taxsites.com/federal.html

Fedworld http://www.fedworld.gov

GASB http://www.gasb.org

Government Accountability Office http://www.gao.gov

House of Representatives http://www.house.gov

International Accounting Standards Board
http://www.iasb.org.uk

IRS Digital Daily http://www.irs.ustreas.gov/prod.cover.html

Learning Center http://cch.learningcenter.com

Library of Congress http://www.loc.gov

National Association of State Boards of Accountancy
http://www.nasba.org

Office of Management and Budget http://www.gpo.gov

ProSystem fx Engagement http://www.epacesoftware.com

Public Company Accounting Oversight Board
http://www.pcaobus.org

Securities and Exchange Commission http://www.sec.gov

Thomas Legislative Research http://thomaslocal.gov

Cross-Reference

ORIGINAL PRONOUNCEMENTS TO 2011 *GAAP GUIDE*, Volume I CHAPTERS

This locator provides instant cross-reference between an original pronouncement and the chapter(s) in this publication in which a pronouncement is covered. Original pronouncements are listed chronologically on the left and the chapter(s) in which they appear in the 2011 *GAAP Guide volume I* in the center column. When an original pronouncement has been superseded, cross-reference is made to the succeeding pronouncement. Cross-references to the FASB's Accounting Standards Codification are listed on the right.

Pronouncements for which no sections in the FASB codification are indicated result from the fact that the pronouncement has been superseded or has not yet been codified.

Many pronouncements appear in the more than one place. In this cross-reference, the primary coverage is found in the section(s) indicated, but for an identification of all sections in the codification affected by a pronouncement, consult the "Cross-Reference" search function on the FASB web site.

ACCOUNTING RESEARCH BULLETINS (ARBs)

(Accounting Research Bulletins 1–42 were revised, restated, or withdrawn at the time ARB No. 43 was issued.)

ORIGINAL PRONOUNCEMENT	2011 *GAAP GUIDE*, VOLUME I REFERENCE	FASB ACCOUNTING STANDARDS CODIFICATION (ASC) TOPIC
ARB No. 43 Restatement and Revision of Accounting Research Bulletins		
Chapter 1—Prior Opinions		
1-A: Rules Adopted by Membership	Balance Sheet Classification and Related Display Issues, ch. 3	310, Receivables
		505, Equity
		605, Revenue Recognition
	Consolidated Financial Statements, ch. 7	850, Related Party Disclosures
	Installment Sales, ch. 22	
	Stockholders' Equity, ch. 44	
1-B: Opinion Issued by Predecessor Committee	Stockholders' Equity, ch. 44	505, Equity
Chapter 2—Form of Statements		
2-A: Comparative Financial Statements	Consolidated Financial Statements, ch. 7	205, Presentation of Financial Statements
2-B: Combined Statement of Income and Earned Surplus	Superseded	—

CR.01

CR.02 *Cross-Reference*

Chapter 3—Working Capital

3-A: Current Assets and Current Liabilities	Balance Sheet Classification and Related Display Issues, ch. 3	210, Balance Sheet 310, Receivables 340, Deferred Costs and Other Assets 470, Debt
3-B: Application of United States Government Securities Against Liabilities for Federal Taxes on Income	Superseded	—

Chapter 4

Inventory Pricing	Inventory, ch. 27	330, Inventory

Chapter 5

Intangible Assets	Superseded	—

Chapter 6

Contingency Reserves	Superseded	—

Chapter 7—Capital Accounts

7-A: Quasi-Reorganization or Corporate Readjustment	Stockholders' Equity, ch. 44	852, Reorganizations
7-B: Stock Dividends and Stock Split-Ups	Stockholders' Equity, ch. 44	505, Equity
7-C: Business Combinations	Superseded.	—

Chapter 8

Income and Earned Surplus	Superseded	—

Chapter 9—Depreciation

9-A: Depreciation and High Costs	Depreciable Assets and Depreciation, ch. 11	360, Property, Plant, and Equipment
9-B: Depreciation on Appreciation	Superseded	—
9-C: Emergency Facilities—Depreciation, Amortization, and Income Taxes	Depreciable Assets and Depreciation, ch. 11	—

Chapter 10—Taxes

10-A: Real and Personal Property Taxes	Property Taxes, ch. 36	720, Other Expenses
10-B: Income Taxes	Superseded	—

Chapter 11—Government Contracts

11-A: Cost-Plus-Fixed-Fee Contracts	Government Contracts, ch. 19	912, Contractors—Federal Government
11-B: Renegotiation	Government Contracts, ch. 19	912, Contractors—Federal Government
11-C: Terminated War and Defense Contracts	Government Contracts, ch. 19	912, Contractors—Federal Government

Chapter 12

Foreign Operations and Foreign Exchange	Superseded	—

Chapter 13—Compensation

13-A: Pension Plans—Annuity Costs Based on Past Service	Superseded	—

Cross-Reference **CR.03**

13-B: Compensation Involved in Stock Option and Stock Purchase Plans	Superseded	—
Chapter 14		
Disclosures of Long-Term Leases in Financial Statements of Lessees	Superseded	—
Chapter 15		
Unamortized Discount, Issue Cost, and Redemption Premium on Bonds Refunded	Superseded	—
ARB No. 44		
Declining-Balance Depreciation	Superseded	—
ARB No. 44 (Revised)		
Declining-Balance Depreciation	Superseded	—
ARB No. 45		
Long-Term Construction-Type Contracts	Long-Term Construction Contracts, ch. 30	605, Revenue Recognition
ARB No. 46		
Discontinuance of Dating Earned Surplus	Stockholders' Equity, ch. 44	—
ARB No. 47		
Accounting for Costs of Pension Plans	Superseded	—
ARB No. 48		
Business Combinations	Superseded	—
ARB No. 49		
Earnings per Share	Superseded	—
ARB No. 50		
Contingencies	Superseded	—
ARB No. 51		
Consolidated Financial Statements	Consolidated Financial Statements, ch. 7	810, Consolidation

ACCOUNTING PRINCIPLES BOARD OPINIONS (APBs)

ORIGINAL PRONOUNCEMENT	2011 *GAAP GUIDE, VOLUME I* REFERENCE	FASB ACCOUNTING STANDARDS CODIFICATION (ASC) TOPIC
APB Opinion No. 1		
New Depreciation Guidelines and Rules	Superseded	—
APB Opinion No. 2		
Accounting for the "Investment Credit"	Income Taxes, ch. 21	740, Income Taxes
APB Opinion No. 2—Addendum		
Accounting Principles for Regulated Industries	Superseded	740, Income Taxes

CR.04 *Cross-Reference*

APB Opinion No. 3

| The Statement of Source and Application of Funds | Superseded | — |

APB Opinion No. 4

| Accounting for the "Investment Credit" | Income Taxes, ch. 21 | 740, Income Taxes |

APB Opinion No. 5

| Reporting of Leases in Financial Statements of Lessee | Superseded | — |

APB Opinion No. 6

| Status of Accounting Research Bulletins | Depreciable Assets and Depreciation, ch. 11 | — |
| | Stockholders' Equity, ch. 44 | |

APB Opinion No. 7

| Accounting for Leases in Financial Statements of Lessors | Superseded | — |

APB Opinion No. 8

| Accounting for the Cost of Pension Plans | Superseded | — |

APB Opinion No. 9

| Reporting the Results of Operations | Results of Operations, ch. 40 | 225, Income Statement
250, Accounting Changes and Error Corrections |

APB Opinion No. 10

Omnibus Opinion—1966	Balance Sheet Classification and Related Display Issues, ch. 3	210, Balance Sheet 605, Revenue Recognition 740, Income Taxes
	Income Taxes, ch. 21	
	Installment Sales, ch. 22	

APB Opinion No. 11

| Accounting for Income Taxes | Superseded | — |

APB Opinion No. 12

Omnibus Opinion—1967	Deferred Compensation Contracts, ch. 10	310, Receivables 360, Property, Plant, and Equipment 710, Compensation—General
	Depreciable Assets and Depreciation, ch.11	
	Postemployment and Postretirement Benefits Other Than Pensions, ch. 34	
	Stockholders' Equity, ch. 44	

APB Opinion No. 13

| Amending Paragraph 6 of APB Opinion No. 9, Application to Commercial Banks | Results of Operations, ch. 40 | 225, Income Statement
250, Accounting Changes Error Corrections |

APB Opinion No. 14

| Accounting for Convertible Debt and Debt Issued with Stock Purchase Warrants | Convertible Debt and Debt with Warrants, ch. 9. | 470, Debt |

Cross-Reference CR.05

APB Opinion No. 15		
Earnings per Share	Superseded	—
APB Opinion No. 16		
Business Combinations	Superseded	—
APB Opinion No. 17		
Intangible Assets	Superseded	—
APB Opinion No. 18		
The Equity Method of Accounting for Investments in Common Stock	Equity Method, ch. 14	323, Investments—Equity Method and Joint Ventures
APB Opinion No. 19		
Reporting Changes in Financial Position	Superseded	—
APB Opinion No. 20		
Accounting Changes	Superseded	—
APB Opinion No. 21		
Interest on Receivables and Payables	Interest on Receivables and Payables, ch. 25	835, Interest
APB Opinion No. 22		
Disclosure of Accounting Policies	Accounting Policies and Standards, ch. 2	235, Notes to Financial Statements
APB Opinion No. 23		
Accounting for Income Taxes—Special Areas	Income Taxes, ch. 21	740, Income Taxes
APB Opinion No. 24		
Accounting for Income Taxes—Investments in Common Stock Accounted for by the Equity Method (Other Than Subsidiaries and Corporate Joint Ventures)	Superseded	—
APB Opinion No. 25		
Accounting for Stock Issued to Employees	Stock-Based Payments, ch. 43	—
APB Opinion No. 26		
Early Extinguishment of Debt	Extinguishment of Debt, ch. 15	470, Debt
APB Opinion No. 27		
Accounting for Lease Transactions by Manufacturer or Dealer Lessors	Superseded.	—
APB Opinion No. 28		
Interim Financial Reporting	Interim Financial Reporting, ch. 26	270, Interim Reporting
	Inventory, ch. 27	
APB Opinion No. 29		
Accounting for Nonmonetary Transactions	Nonmonetary Transactions, ch. 32	845, Nonmonetary Transactions

CR.06 *Cross-Reference*

APB Opinion No. 30

Reporting the Results of Operations—Reporting the Effects of Disposal of a Segment of a Business, and Extraordinary, Unusual, and Infrequently Occurring Events and Transactions	Results of Operations, ch. 40	225, Income Statement

APB Opinion No. 31

Disclosure of Lease Commitments by Lessees	Superseded	—

FINANCIAL ACCOUNTING STANDARDS BOARD STATEMENTS (FASs)

ORIGINAL PRONOUNCEMENT	2011 *GAAP GUIDE*, VOLUME I REFERENCE	FASB ACCOUNTING STANDARDS CODIFICATION (ASC) TOPIC
FASB Statement No. 1		
Disclosure of Foreign Currency Translation Information	Superseded	—
FASB Statement No. 2		
Accounting for Research and Development Costs	Inventory, ch. 27	730, Research and Development
	Research and Development, ch. 39	
FASB Statement No. 3		
Reporting Accounting Changes in Interim Financial Statements	Superseded	—
FASB Statement No. 4		
Reporting Gains and Losses from Extinguishment of Debt	Superseded	—
FASB Statement No. 5		
Accounting for Contingencies	Contingencies, Risks, and Uncertainties, ch. 8	450, Contingencies
FASB Statement No. 6		
Classification of Short-Term Obligations Expected to Be Refinanced	Balance Sheet Classification and Related Display Issues, ch. 3	210, Balance Sheet 470, Debt
FASB Statement No. 7		
Accounting and Reporting by Development Stage Enterprises	Development Stage Enterprises, ch. 12	915, Development Stage Entities
FASB Statement No. 8		
Accounting for the Translation of Foreign Currency Transactions and Foreign Currency Financial Statements	Superseded	—

Cross-Reference **CR.07**

FASB Statement No. 9		
Accounting for Income Taxes—Oil and Gas Producing Companies	Superseded	—
FASB Statement No. 10		
Extension of "Grandfather" Provisions for Business Combinations	Superseded	—
	Business Combinations, ch. 4	
FASB Statement No. 11		
Accounting for Contingencies—Transition Method	No longer relevant.	—
FASB Statement No. 12		
Accounting for Certain Marketable Securities	Superseded	—
FASB Statement No. 13		
Accounting for Leases	Leases, ch. 29	840, Leases
FASB Statement No. 14		
Financial Reporting for Segments of a Business Enterprise	Superseded.	—
FASB Statement No. 15		
Accounting by Debtors and Creditors for Troubled Debt Restructurings	Troubled Debt Restructuring, ch. 46	310, Receivables 470, Debt
FASB Statement No. 16		
Prior Period Adjustments	Results of Operations, ch. 40	250, Accounting Changes and Error Corrections 270, Interim Reporting
FASB Statement No. 17		
Accounting for Leases—Initial Direct Costs	Superseded	—
FASB Statement No. 18		
Financial Reporting for Segments of a Business Enterprise—Interim Financial Statements	Superseded	—
FASB Statement No. 19		
Financial Accounting and Reporting by Oil and Gas Producing Companies	Specific industry guidance not covered in 2011 GAAP Guide Vol. I	—
FASB Statement No. 20		
Accounting for Forward Exchange Contracts	Superseded	—
FASB Statement No. 21		
Suspension of the Reporting of Earnings per Share and Segment Information by Nonpublic Enterprises	Superseded	—

CR.08 *Cross-Reference*

FASB Statement No. 22

Changes in the Provisions of Lease Agreements Resulting from Refundings of Tax-Exempt Debt	Extinguishment of Debt, ch. 16	840, Leases
	Leases, ch. 29	

FASB Statement No. 23

Inception of the Lease	Leases, ch. 29	840, Leases

FASB Statement No. 24

Reporting Segment Information in Financial Statements That Are Presented in Another Enterprise's Financial Report	Superseded	—

FASB Statement No. 25

Suspension of Certain Accounting Requirements for Oil and Gas Producing Companies	Specific industry guidance not covered in 2011 GAAP Guide Vol. I	—

FASB Statement No. 26

Profit Recognition on Sales-Type Leases of Real Estate	Superseded	—

FASB Statement No. 27

Classification of Renewals or Extensions of Existing Sales-Type or Direct Financing Leases	Leases, ch. 29	840, Leases

FASB Statement No. 28

Accounting for Sales with Leasebacks	Leases, ch. 29	840, Leases

FASB Statement No. 29

Determining Contingent Rentals	Leases, ch. 29	840, Leases

FASB Statement No. 30

Disclosure of Information About Major Customers	Superseded	—

FASB Statement No. 31

Accounting for Tax Benefits Related to U.K. Tax Legislation Concerning Stock Relief	Superseded	—

FASB Statement No. 32

Specialized Accounting and Reporting Principles and Practices in AICPA Statements of Position and Guides on Accounting and Auditing Matters	Superseded	—

FASB Statement No. 33

Financial Reporting and Changing Prices	Superseded	—

FASB Statement No. 34

Capitalization of Interest Cost	Interest Costs Capitalized, ch. 24	835, Interest

Cross-Reference **CR.09**

FASB Statement No. 35

Accounting and Reporting by Defined Benefit Pension Plans	Specific industry guidance not covered in 2011 GAAP Guide Vol. I.	—

FASB Statement No. 36

Disclosure of Pension Information	Superseded	—

FASB Statement No. 37

Balance Sheet Classification of Deferred Income Taxes	Income Taxes, ch. 21	740, Income Taxes

FASB Statement No. 38

Accounting for Preacquisition Contingencies of Purchased Enterprises	Superseded	—

FASB Statement No. 39

Financial Reporting and Changing Prices: Specialized Assets—Mining and Oil and Gas	Superseded	—

FASB Statement No. 40

Financial Reporting and Changing Prices: Specialized Assets—Timberlands and Growing Timber	Superseded	—

FASB Statement No. 41

Financial Reporting and Changing Prices: Specialized Assets—Income-Producing Real Estate	Superseded	—

FASB Statement No. 42

Determining Materiality for Capitalization of Interest Cost	Interest Costs Capitalized, ch. 24	835, Interest

FASB Statement No. 43

Accounting for Compensated Absences	Balance Sheet Classification and Related Display Issues, ch.3	420, Exit or Disposal Cost Obligations 710, Compensation—General

FASB Statement No. 44

Accounting for Intangible Assets of Motor Carriers	Superseded	—

FASB Statement No. 45

Accounting for Franchise Fee Revenue	Revenue Recognition, ch. 41	952, Franchisors

FASB Statement No. 46

Financial Reporting and Changing Prices: Motion Picture Films	Superseded	—

FASB Statement No. 47

Disclosure of Long-Term Obligations	Long-Term Obligations, ch. 31	440, Commitments

FASB Statement No. 48

Revenue Recognition When Right of Return Exists	Revenue Recognition, ch. 41	605, Revenue Recognition

CR.10 *Cross-Reference*

FASB Statement No. 49

| Accounting for Product Financing Arrangements | Product Financing Arrangements, ch. 35 | 470, Debt |

FASB Statement No. 50

| Financial Reporting in the Record and Music Industry | Specific industry guidance is not covered in the 2011 GAAP Guide Vol. I | — |

FASB Statement No. 51

| Financial Reporting by Cable Television Companies | Specific industry guidance not covered in 2011 GAAP Guide Vol. I. | — |

FASB Statement No. 52

| Foreign Currency Translation | Foreign Operations and Exchange, ch. 18 | 830, Foreign Currency Matters |

FASB Statement No. 53

| Financial Reporting by Producers and Distributors of Motion Picture Films | Superseded | — |

FASB Statement No. 54

| Financial Reporting and Changing Prices: Investment Companies | Superseded | — |

FASB Statement No. 55

| Determining Whether a Convertible Security Is a Common Stock Equivalent | Superseded | — |

FASB Statement No. 56

| Designation of AICPA Guide and Statement of Position (SOP) 81-1 on Contractor Accounting and SOP 81-2 Concerning Hospital-Related Organizations as Preferable for Purposes of Applying APB Opinion 20 | Superseded | — |

FASB Statement No. 57

| Related Party Disclosures | Related Party Disclosures, ch. 38 | 850, Related Party Disclosures |

FASB Statement No. 58

| Capitalization of Interest Cost in Financial Statements That Include Investments Accounted For by the Equity Method | Interest Costs Capitalized, ch. 24 | 835, Interest |

FASB Statement No. 59

| Deferral of the Effective Date of Certain Accounting Requirements for Pension Plans of State and Local Governmental Units | Superseded | — |

FASB Statement No. 60

| Accounting and Reporting by Insurance Enterprises | Specific industry guidance not covered in 2011 GAAP Guide Vol. I. | — |

Cross-Reference **CR.11**

FASB Statement No. 61

| Accounting for Title Plant | Specific industry guidance not covered in 2011 GAAP Guide Vol. I. | — |

FASB Statement No. 62

| Capitalization of Interest Cost in Situations Involving Certain Tax-Exempt Borrowings and Certain Gifts and Grants | Interest Costs Capitalized, ch. 24 | 835, Interest |

FASB Statement No. 63

| Financial Reporting by Broadcasters | Specific industry guidance not covered in 2011 GAAP Guide Vol. I. | — |

FASB Statement No. 64

| Extinguishments of Debt Made to Satisfy Sinking-Fund Requirements | Superseded by FAS-145. | — |

FASB Statement No. 65

| Accounting for Certain Mortgage Banking Activities | Specific industry guidance not covered in 2011 GAAP Guide Vol. I. | — |

FASB Statement No. 66

| Accounting for Sales of Real Estate | Real Estate Transactions, ch. 37 | 360, Property, Plant, and Equipment
976, Real Estate—Retail Land |

FASB Statement No. 67

| Accounting for Costs and Initial Rental Operations of Real Estate Projects | Real Estate Transactions, ch. 37 | 970, Real Estate—General |

FASB Statement No. 68

| Research and Development Arrangements | Research and Development, ch. 39 | 730, Research and Development |

FASB Statement No. 69

| Disclosures about Oil and Gas Producing Activities | Specific industry guidance not covered in 2011 GAAP Guide Vol. I. | — |

FASB Statement No. 70

| Financial Reporting and Changing Prices: Foreign Currency Translation | Superseded | — |

FASB Statement No. 71

| Accounting for the Effects of Certain Types of Regulation | Specific industry guidance not covered in 2011 GAAP Guide Vol. I. | — |

FASB Statement No. 72

| Accounting for Certain Acquisitions of Banking or Thrift Institutions | Specific industry guidance not covered in 2011 GAAP Guide Vol. I. | — |

CR.12 *Cross-Reference*

FASB Statement No. 73

Reporting a Change in Accounting for Railroad Track Structures	Superseded	—

FASB Statement No. 74

Accounting for Special Termination Benefits Paid to Employees	Superseded	—

FASB Statement No. 75

Deferral of the Effective Date of Certain Accounting Requirements for Pension Plans of State and Local Governmental Units	Superseded	—

FASB Statement No. 76

Extinguishment of Debt	Superseded	—

FASB Statement No. 77

Reporting by Transferors for Transfers of Receivables with Recourse	Superseded	—

FASB Statement No. 78

Classification of Obligations That Are Callable by the Creditor	Balance Sheet Classification and Related Display Issues, ch. 3	470, Debt

FASB Statement No. 79

Elimination of Certain Disclosures for Business Combinations by Nonpublic Enterprises	Superseded	—

FASB Statement No. 80

Accounting for Futures Contracts	Superseded	—

FASB Statement No. 81

Disclosure of Postretirement Health Care and Life Insurance Benefits	Superseded	—

FASB Statement No. 82

Financial Reporting and Changing Prices: Elimination of Certain Disclosures	Superseded	—

FASB Statement No. 83

Designation of AICPA Guides and Statement of Position on Accounting by Brokers and Dealers in Securities, by Employee Benefit Plans, and by Banks as Preferable for Purposes of Applying APB Opinion 20	Superseded.	—

FASB Statement No. 84

Induced Conversions of Convertible Debt	Convertible Debt and Debt with Warrants, ch. 9	470, Debt

Cross-Reference **CR.13**

FASB Statement No. 85

Yield Test for Determining whether a Convertible Security Is a Common Stock Equivalent	Superseded	—

FASB Statement No. 86

Accounting for the Costs of Computer Software to Be Sold, Leased, or Otherwise Marketed	Specific industry guidance not covered in 2011 GAAP Guide Vol. I.	985, Software

FASB Statement No. 87

Employers' Accounting for Pensions	Specific industry guidance not covered in 2011 GAAP Guide Vol. I.	—

FASB Statement No. 88

Employers' Accounting for Settlements and Curtailments of Defined Benefit Pension Plans and for Termination Benefits	Not-for-Profit Organizations, Appendix.	715, Compensation— Retirement Benefits

FASB Statement No. 89

Financial Reporting and Changing Prices	Specific industry guidance not covered in 2011 GAAP Guide Vol. I.	—

FASB Statement No. 90

Regulated Enterprises— Accounting for Abandonments and Disallowances of Plant Costs	Specific industry guidance not covered in 2011 GAAP Guide Vol. I.	—

FASB Statement No. 91

Accounting for Nonrefundable Fees and Costs Associated with Originating or Acquiring Loans and Initial Direct Costs of Leases	Leases, ch. 29	310, Receivables

FASB Statement No. 92

Regulated Enterprises— Accounting for Phase-in Plans	Specific industry guidance not covered in 2011 GAAP Guide Vol. I.	—

FASB Statement No. 93

Recognition of Depreciation by Not-for-Profit Organizations	Not-for-Profit Organizations, Appendix	958, Not-for-Profit Entities

FASB Statement No. 94

Consolidation of All Majority-Owned Subsidiaries	Consolidated Financial Statements, ch. 7	810, Consolidation
	Equity Method, ch. 14	

FASB Statement No. 95

Statement of Cash Flows	Cash Flow Statement, ch.5	230, Statement of Cash Flows

FASB Statement No. 96

Accounting for Income Taxes	Superseded	—

FASB Statement No. 97

Accounting and Reporting by Insurance Enterprises for Certain Long-Duration Contracts and for Realized Gains and Losses from the Sale of Investments | Specific industry guidance not covered in 2011 GAAP Guide Vol. I.

FASB Statement No. 98

Accounting for Leases:
- Sale-Leaseback Transactions Involving Real Estate
- Sales-Type Leases of Real Estate
- Definition of the Lease Term
- Initial Direct Costs of Direct Financing Leases

Leases, ch. 29
Real Estate Transactions, ch. 37

840, Leases

FASB Statement No. 99

Deferral of the Effective Date of Recognition of Depreciation by Not-for-Profit Organizations | Not-for-Profit Organizations, Appendix | 958, Not-for-Profit Entities

FASB Statement No. 100

Accounting for Income Taxes—Deferral of the Effective Date of FASB Statement No. 96 | Superseded | —

FASB Statement No. 101

Regulated Enterprises—Accounting for the Discontinuation of Application of FASB Statement No. 71 | Specific industry guidance not covered in 2011 GAAP Guide Vol. I. | —

FASB Statement No. 102

Statement of Cash Flows—Exemption of Certain Enterprises and Classification of Cash Flows from Certain Securities Acquired for Resale | Cash Flow Statement, Ch. 5. | 230, Statement of Cash Flows
960, Plan Accounting—Defined Benefit Pension Plans

FASB Statement No. 103

Accounting for Income Taxes—Deferral of the Effective Date of FASB Statement No. 96 | Superseded | —

FASB Statement No. 104

Statement of Cash Flows—Net Reporting of Certain Cash Receipts and Cash Payments and Classification of Cash Flows from Hedging Transactions | Cash Flow Statement, ch. 5 | 230, Statement of Cash Flows

FASB Statement No. 105

Disclosure of Information About Financial Instruments with Off-Balance-Sheet Risk and Financial Instruments with Concentrations of Credit Risk | Superseded | —

Cross-Reference CR.15

FASB Statement No. 106

Employers' Accounting for Postretirement Benefits Other Than Pensions	Deferred Compensation Contracts, ch. 10	715, Compensation—Retirement Benefits
	Postemployment and Postretirement Benefits Other Than Pensions, ch. 34	

FASB Statement No. 107

Disclosures about Fair Value of Financial Instruments	Financial Instruments, ch. 17	825, Financial Instruments

FASB Statement No. 108

Accounting for Income Taxes—Deferral of the Effective Date of FASB Statement No. 96	Superseded	—

FASB Statement No. 109

Accounting for Income Taxes	Depreciable Assets and Depreciation, ch. 11	740, Income Taxes
	Income Taxes, ch. 21	

FASB Statement No. 110

Reporting by Defined Benefit Pension Plans of Investment Contracts	Specific industry guidance not covered in 2011 GAAP Guide Vol. I.	

FASB Statement No. 111

Rescission of FASB Statement No. 32 and Technical Corrections	Accounting Changes, ch. 1	—

FASB Statement No. 112

Employers' Accounting for Postemployment Benefits	Postemployment and Postretirement Benefits Other Than Pensions, ch. 34	712, Compensation—Nonretirement Postemployment Benefits

FASB Statement No. 113

Accounting and Reporting for Reinsurance of Short-Duration and Long-Duration Contracts	Specific industry guidance not covered in 2011 GAAP Guide Vol. I.	310, Receivables

FASB Statement No. 114

Accounting by Creditors for Impairment of a Loan	Impairment of Long-Lived Assets, ch. 20	310, Receivables
	Troubled Debt Restructuring, ch. 46	

FASB Statement No. 115

Accounting for Certain Investments in Debt and Equity Securities	Investments in Debt and Equity Securities, ch. 28	320, Investments—Debt and Equity Securities

FASB Statement No. 116

Accounting for Contributions Received and Contributions Made	Not-for-Profit Organizations, Appendix	720, Other Expenses 958, Not-for-Profit Entities

FASB Statement No. 117

Financial Statements of Not-for-Profit Organizations	Not-for-Profit Organizations, Appendix	958, Not-for-Profit Entities

FASB Statement No. 118

Accounting by Creditors for Impairment of a Loan—Income Recognition and Disclosures	Impairment of Long-Lived Assets, ch. 20	310, Receivables

FASB Statement No. 119

Disclosure about Derivative Financial Instruments and Fair Value of Financial Instruments	Superseded	—

FASB Statement No. 120

Accounting and Reporting by Mutual Life Insurance Enterprises and by Insurance Enterprises for Certain Long-Duration Participating Contracts	Specific industry guidance not covered in 2011 GAAP Guide Vol. I.	—

FASB Statement No. 121

Accounting for the Impairment of Long-Lived Assets and for Long-Lived Assets to Be Disposed Of	Superseded	—

FASB Statement No. 122

Accounting for Mortgage Servicing Rights	Superseded	—

FASB Statement No. 123

Accounting for Stock-Based Compensation	Superseded	—

FASB Statement No. 123 (revised 2004)

Share-Based Payment	Stock-Based Payments, ch. 43	505, Equity 718, Compensation—Stock Compensation

FASB Statement No. 124

Accounting for Certain Investments Held by Not-for-Profit Organizations	Not-for-Profit Organizations, Appendix	958, Not-for-Profit Entities

FASB Statement No. 125

Accounting for Transfers and Servicing of Financial Assets and Extinguishments of Liabilities	Superseded	—

FASB Statement No. 126

Exemption from Certain Required Disclosures about Financial Instruments for Certain Nonpublic Entities	Financial Instruments, ch. 17	825, Financial Instruments

FASB Statement No. 127

Deferral of the Effective Date of Certain Provisions of FASB Statement No. 125	Transfer and Servicing of Financial Assets, ch. 45	860, Transfers and Servicing

Cross-Reference CR.17

FASB Statement No. 128		
Earnings per Share	Earnings per Share, ch. 13	260, Earnings per Share
FASB Statement No. 129		
Disclosure of Information about Capital Structure	Stockholders' Equity, ch. 44	505, Equity
FASB Statement No. 130		
Reporting Comprehensive Income	Results of Operations, ch. 40	220, Comprehensive Income
FASB Statement No. 131		
Disclosures about Segments of an Enterprise and Related Information	Segment Reporting, ch. 42	280, Segment Reporting
FASB Statement No. 132		
Employers' Disclosures about Pensions and Other Postretirement Benefits	Superseded	—
FASB Statement No. 132 (revised 2003)		
Employers' Disclosures about Pensions and Other Postretirement Benefits	Pension Plans ch. 33 Postemployment and Postretirement Benefits Other Than Pensions, ch. 34	715, Compensation—Retirement Benefits
FASB Statement No. 133		
Accounting for Derivative Instruments and Hedging Activities	Financial Instruments, ch. 17	815, Derivatives and Hedging
FASB Statement No. 134		
Accounting for Mortgage-Backed Securities Retained after the Securitization of Mortgage Loans Held for Sale by a Mortgage Banking Enterprise	Specific industry guidance not covered in 2011 GAAP Guide Vol. I.	—
FASB Statement No. 135		
Rescission of Statement No. 75 and Technical Corrections	Specific industry guidance not covered in 2011 GAAP Guide Vol. I.	—
FASB Statement No. 136		
Transfer of Assets to a Not-for-Profit Organizationor Charitable Trust That Raises or Holds Contributions for Others	Not-for-Profit Organizations, Appendix	958, Not-for-Profit Entities
FASB Statement No. 137		
Deferral of the Effective Date of Statement No. 133	Financial Instruments, ch. 17	815, Derivatives and Hedging
FASB Statement No. 138		
Accounting for Certain Derivative Instruments and Certain Hedging Actvities	Financial Instruments, ch. 17	815, Derivatives and Hedging

FASB Statement No. 139

Rescission of FASB Statement No. 53 and amendments to FASB Statements No. 63, 89, and 121	Specific industry guidance not covered in 2011 GAAP Guide Vol. I.	—

FASB Statement No. 140

Accounting for Transfers and Servicing of Financial Assets and Extinguishments of Debt	Transfer and Servicing of Financial Assets, ch. 45	860, Transfers and Servicing

FASB Statement No. 141

Business Combinations	Superseded.	—

FASB Statement No. 141(R)

Business Combinations	Business Combinations, ch. 4	805, Business Combinations

FASB Statement No. 142

Goodwill and Other Intangible Assets	Intangible Assets, ch. 23	350, Intangibles—Goodwill and Other

FASB Statement No. 143

Accounting for Asset Retirement Obligations	Depreciable Assets and Deprecations, ch. 11	410, Asset Retirement and Environmental Obligations

FASB Statement No. 144

Accounting for the Impairment or Disposal of Long-Lived Assets	Impairment of Long-Lived Assets, ch. 20	205, Presentation of Financial Statements 360, Property, Plant, and Equipment

FASB Statement No. 145

Rescission of FASB Statements No. 4, 44, and 64, Amendment of FASB Statement No. 13, and Technical Corrections	Extinguishment of Debt, ch. 15	470, Debt
	Leases, ch. 29	

FASB Statement No. 146

Accounting for Costs Associated with Exit or Disposal Activities	Results of Operations, ch. 40	420, Exit or Disposal Cost Obligations

FASB Statement No. 147

Acquisitions of Certain Financial Institutions	Superseded	—

FASB Statement No. 148

Accounting for Stock-Based Compensation—Transition and Disclosure	Stock-Based Payments, ch. 43	505, Equity 718, Compensation—Stock Compensation

FASB Statement No. 149

Amendment of Statement 133 on Derivative Instruments and Hedging Activities	Financial Instruments, ch. 17	815, Derivatives and Hedging

FASB Statement No. 150

Accounting for Certain Financial Instruments with Characteristics of both Liabilities and Equity	Balance Sheet Classification and Related Display Issues, ch. 3, 157, and 162.	480, Distinguishing Liabilities from Equity

Cross-Reference CR.19

FASB Statement No. 151

| Inventory Costs | Inventory, ch. 27 | — |

FASB Statement No. 152

| Accounting for Real Estate Time-Sharing Transactions | Real Estate Transactions, ch. 37 | — |

FASB Statement No. 153

| Exchanges of Nonmonetary Assets | Nonmonetary Transactions, ch. 32 | — |

FASB Statement No. 154

| Accounting Changes and Error Corrections | Accounting Changes, ch. 1 | 250, Accounting Changes and Error Corrections |

FASB Statement No. 155

| Accounting for Certain Hybrid Financial Instruments | Financial Instruments, ch. 17 | — |

FASB Statement No. 156

| Accounting for Servicing of Financial Assets | Transfer and Servicing of Financial Assets, ch. 45 | 860, Transfers and Servicing |

FASB Statement No. 157

| Fair Value Measurements | Fair Value, ch. 16 | 820, Fair Value |

FASB Statement No. 158

| Employers' Accounting for Defined Benefit Pension and Other Postretirement Plans | Pension Plans, ch. 33
Postemployment and Postretirement Benefits Other Than Pensions, ch. 34 | 715, Compensation—Retirement Benefits
958, Not-for-Profit Entities |

FASB Statement No. 159

| The Fair Value Option for Financial Assets and Financial Liabilities | Investments in Debt
Fair Value, ch. 16 Securities, and Equity, ch. 28 | 825, Financial Instruments |

FASB Statement No. 160

| Noncontrolling Interests in Consolidated Financial Statements | Consolidated Financial Statements, ch. 7 | — |

FASB Statement No. 161

| Disclosures about Derivative Instruments and Hedging Activities | Financial Instruments, ch. 17 | 815, Derivatives and Hedging |

FASB Statement No. 162

| The Hierarchy of Generally Accepted Accounting Principles | Superseded. | — |

FASB Statement No. 163

| Accounting for Financial Guarantee Insurance Contracts | Specific industry guidance not covered in 2011 GAAP Guide Vol. I. | — |

FASB Statement No. 164

| Not-for-Profit Entities: Mergers and Acquisitions—Including an Amendment of FASB Statement No. 142 | Not-for-Profit Organizations, Appendix | — |

CR.20 *Cross-Reference*

FASB Statement No. 165

Subsequent Events	Accounting Policies and Standards, ch. **2**	855, Subsequent Events

FASB Statement No. 166

Accounting for Transfers of Financial Assets—an Amendment of FASB Statement No. 140	Transfer and Servicing of Financial Assets, ch. **45**	860, Transfers and Servicing

FASB Statement No. 167

Amendments to FASB Interpretation No. 46(R)	Consolidated Financial Statements, ch. **7**	810, Consolidation

FASB Statement No 168

The FASB Accounting Standards Codification and the Hierarchy of Generally Accepted Accounting Principles—a Replacement of FASB Statement No. 162	Accounting Policies and Standards, ch. **2**	105, Generally Accepted Accounting Principles

FINANCIAL ACCOUNTING STANDARDS BOARD INTERPRETATIONS (FINs)

ORIGINAL PRONOUNCEMENT	2011 *GAAP GUIDE, VOLUME I* REFERENCE	FASB ACCOUNTING STANDARDS CODIFICATION (ASC) TOPIC
FASB Interpretation No. 1		
Accounting Changes Related to the Cost of Inventory	Accounting Changes, ch.1	250, Accounting Changes and Error Corrections
	Inventory, ch. 27	330, Inventory
FASB Interpretation No. 2		
Imputing Interest on Debt Arrangements Made under the Federal Bankruptcy Act	Superseded.	—
FASB Interpretation No. 3		
Accounting for the Cost of Pension Plans Subject to the Employee Retirement Income Security Act of 1974	Superseded.	—
FASB Interpretation No. 4		
Applicability of FASB Statement No. 2 to Business Combinations Accounted for by the Purchase Method	Superseded.	—
FASB Interpretation No. 5		
Applicability of FASB Statement No. 2 to Development Stage Enterprises	Superseded.	—
FASB Interpretation No. 6		
Applicability of FASB Statement No. 2 to Computer Software	Research and Development, ch. 40	730, Research and Development

Cross-Reference **CR.21**

FASB Interpretation No. 7

| Applying FASB Statement No. 7 in Financial Statements of Established Operating Enterprises | Portions amended by FAS-154.

Development Stage Enterprises, ch. 13 | 915, Development Stage Entities |

FASB Interpretation No. 8

| | Portions amended by FAS-165. | |
| Classification of a Short-Term Obligation Repaid prior to Being Replaced by a Long-Term Security | Balance Sheet Classification and Related Display Issues, ch. 3 | 470, Debt |

FASB Interpretation No. 9

| Applying APB Opinions No. 16 and 17 When a Savings and Loan Association or a Similar Institution Is Acquired in a Business Combination Accounted for by the Purchase Method | Superseded. | — |

FASB Interpretation No. 10

| Application of FASB Statement No. 12 to Personal Financial Statements | Superseded. | — |

FASB Interpretation No. 11

| Changes in Market Value after the Balance Sheet Date | Superseded. | — |

FASB Interpretation No. 12

| Accounting for Previously Established Allowance Accounts | Superseded. | — |

FASB Interpretation No. 13

| Consolidation of a Parent and Its Subsidiaries Having Different Balance Sheet Dates | Superseded. | — |

FASB Interpretation No. 14

| Reasonable Estimation of the Amount of a Loss | Contingencies, Risks, and Uncertainties, ch. 9 | 450, Contingencies |

FASB Interpretation No. 15

| Translation of Unamortized Policy Acquisition Costs by a Stock Life Insurance Company | Superseded. | — |

FASB Interpretation No. 16

| Clarification of Definitions and Accounting for Marketable Equity Securities That Become Nonmarketable | Superseded. | — |

FASB Interpretation No. 17

| Applying the Lower of Cost or Market Rule in Translated Financial Statements | Superseded. | — |

FASB Interpretation No. 18

| Accounting for Income Taxes in Interim Periods | Income Taxes, ch. 21 | 740, Debt |

CR.22 Cross-Reference

FASB Interpretation No. 19

Lessee Guarantee of the Residual Value of Leased Property	Leases, ch. 29	840, Leases

FASB Interpretation No. 20

Reporting Accounting Changes under AICPA Statements of Position	Superseded.	—

FASB Interpretation No. 21

Accounting for Leases in a Business Combination	Superseded.	840, Leases

FASB Interpretation No. 22

Applicability of Indefinite Reversal Criteria To Timing Differences	Superseded.	—

FASB Interpretation No. 23

Leases of Certain Property Owned by a Governmental Unit or Authority	Leases, ch. 29	840, Leases

FASB Interpretation No. 24

Leases Involving Only Part of a Building	Leases, ch. 29	840, Leases

FASB Interpretation No. 25

Accounting for an Unused Investment Tax Credit	Superseded	—

FASB Interpretation No. 26

Accounting for Purchase of a Leased Asset by the Lessee during the Term of the Lease	Leases, ch. 29 Leases, ch. 29	840, Leases

FASB Interpretation No. 27

Accounting for a Loss on a Sublease	Leases, ch. 29 Results of Operations, ch.41	—

FASB Interpretation No. 28

Accounting for Stock Appreciation Rights and Other Variable Stock Option or Award Plans	Stock-Based Payments, ch. 44	505, Equity 718, Compensation, Stock Compensation

FASB Interpretation No. 29

Reporting Tax Benefits Realized on Disposition of Investments in Certain Subsidiaries and Other Investees	Superseded	—

FASB Interpretation No. 30

Accounting for Involuntary Conversions of Nonmonetary Assets to Monetary Assets	Nonmonetary Transactions, ch. 32	605, Revenue Recognition

FASB Interpretation No. 31

Treatment of Stock Compensation Plans in EPS Computations	Superseded.	—

Cross-Reference CR.23

FASB Interpretation No. 32		
Application of Percentage Limitations in Recognizing Investment Tax Credit	Superseded	—
FASB Interpretation No. 33		
Applying FASB Statement No. 34 to Oil and Gas Producing Operations Accounted for by the Full Cost Method	Specific industry guidance not covered in 2011 GAAP Guide Vol. I.	932, Extractive Industries—Oil and Gas
FASB Interpretation No. 34		
Disclosure of Indirect Guarantees of Indebtedness of Others	Superseded.	—
FASB Interpretation No. 35		
Criteria for Applying the Equity Method of Accounting for Investments in Common Stock	Equity Method, ch. 15	323, Investments—Equity Method and Joint Ventures
FASB Interpretation No. 36		
Accounting for Exploratory Wells in Progress at the End of a Period	Specific industry guidance not covered in 2011 GAAP Guide Vol. I.	—
FASB Interpretation No. 37		
Accounting for Translation Adjustments upon Sale of Part of an Investment in a Foreign Entity	Foreign Operations and Exchange, ch. 18	830, Foreign Currency Matters
FASB Interpretation No. 38		
Determining the Measurement Date for Stock Option, Purchase, and Award Plans Involving Junior Stock	Stock-Based Payments, ch. 44	505, Equity 718, Compensation, Stock Compensation
FASB Interpretation No. 39		
Offsetting of Amounts Related to Certain Contracts	Balance Sheet Classification and Related Display Issues, ch.3 Financial Instruments, ch. 17	210, Balance Sheet 815, Derivatives and Hedging
FASB Interpretation No. 40		
Applicability of Generally Accepted Accounting Principles to Mutual Life Insurance and Other Enterprises	Specific industry guidance not covered in 2011 GAAP Guide Vol. I.	325, Investments—Other
FASB Interpretation No. 41		
Offsetting of Amounts Related to Certain Repurchase and Reverse Repurchase Agreements	Balance Sheet Classification and Related Display Issues, ch. 3	210, Balance Sheet
FASB Interpretation No. 42		
Accounting for Transfers of Assets in Which a Not-for-Profit Organization Is Granted Variance Power	Superseded	—
FASB Interpretation No. 43		
Real Estate Sales	Real Estate Transactions, ch. 38	360, Property, Plant, and Equipment

FASB Interpretation No. 44

Accounting for Certain Transactions Involving Stock Compensation	Stock-Based Payments, ch. 44	505, Equity 718, Compensation, Stock Compensation

FASB Interpretation No. 45

Guarantor's Accounting and Disclosure Requirements for Guarantees, Including Indirect Guarantees of Indebtedness of Others	Contingencies, Risks, and Uncertainties, ch. 9	460, Guarantees

FASB Interpretation No. 46

Consolidation of Variable Interest Entities	Superseded	—

FASB Interpretation No. 46 (revised December 2003)

Consolidation of Variable Interest Entities	Consolidated Financial Statements, ch. 7	810, Consolidations

FASB Interpretation No. 47

Accounting for Conditional Asset Retirement Obligations	Depreciable Assets and Depreciation, ch. 12	410, Asset Retirement and Environmental Obligations

FASB Interpretation No. 48

Accounting for Uncertainty in Income Taxes	Income Taxes, ch. 21	740, Income Taxes

FASB ACCOUNTING STANDARDS UPDATES (ASUs)

[The following ASUs are omitted from this list because they are covered in the 2011 GAAP Guide Vol II: 2009-08, -10, -13, -14, -15; 2010-01, -05, -13, -15, -16, -17, -18. A complete list of pronouncements covered in the 2011 GAAP Guide Vol. II follows this listing of pronouncements covered in Vol. I.]

ORIGINAL PRONOUNCEMENT	2011 *GAAP GUIDE* VOLUME II REFERENCE	FASB ACCOUNTING STANDARDS CODIFICATION (ASC) TOPIC
Accounting Standards Update 2009-01		
Topic 105—Generally Accepted Accounting Principles	Accounting Policies and Standards, Ch. 2	—
Amendments based on Statement of Financial Accounting Standards No. 168—The FASB Accounting Standards Codification And the Hierarch of Generally Accepted Accounting Principles		
Accounting Standards Update 2009-02		
Omnibus Update	Consolidated Financial Statements, Ch. 7	—
Amendments to Various Topics for Technical Corrections		

Cross-Reference **CR.25**

Accounting Standards Update 2009-03

SEC Update	SEC guidance for public companies is not covered in the 2011 GAAP Guide, Vol. I	—
Amendments to Various Topics Containing SEC Staff Accounting Bulletins		

Accounting Standards Update 2009-04

Accounting for Redeemable Equity Instruments	SEC guidance for public companies is not covered in the 2011 GAAP Guide, Vol. I	—
Amendment to Section 480-10-S99		

Accounting Standards Update 2009-05

Fair Value Measurements and Disclosure	Consolidated Financial Statements, Ch. 7	820, Fair Value Measurement and Disclosure
Measuring Liabilities at Fair Value	Fair Value, Ch. 16	

Accounting Standards Update 2009-06

Income Taxes (Topic 740)	Income Taxes, Ch. 21	740, Income Taxes
Implementation Guidance On Accounting for Uncertainty in Income Taxes and Disclosure Amendments for Nonpublic Entities		

Accounting Standards Update 2009-07

Accounting for Various Topics	SEC guidance for public companies is not covered in the 2011 GAAP Guide Vol. I	—
Technical Corrections to SEC Paragraphs		

Accounting Standards Update 2009-09

Accounting for Investments— Equity	SEC guidance for public companies is not covered in the 2011 GAAP Guide Vol. I	—
Method and Joint Ventures and Accounting for Equity-Based Payments to Non-Employees		
Amendments to Sections 323-10-S99 and 505-50-S99		

Accounting Standards Update 2009-11

Extractive Activities—Oil and Gas	Specific industry guidance is not covered in the 2011 GAAP Guide Vol. I	—
Amendment to Section 932-10-S99		

CR.26   Cross-Reference

Accounting Standards Update 2009-12		
Fair Value Measurements and Disclosures	Specific industry guidance is not covered in the 2011 GAAP Guide Vol. I	—
Investments in Certain Entities That Calculate Net Asset Value per Share (or Its Equivalent)		
Accounting Standards Update 2009-16		
Transfers and Servicing (Topic 860)	Transfers and Servicing of Financial Assets, Ch. 45	—
Accounting for Transfers of Financial Assets		
Accounting Standards Update 2009-17		
Consolidations (Topic 810)	Consolidated Financial Statements, Ch. 7	810, Consolidation
Improvements to Financial Reporting by Enterprises Involved with Variable Interest Entities		
Accounting Standards Update 2010-02		
Consolidation (Topic 810)	Consolidated Financial Statements, Ch. 2 Equity Method, Ch. 14 Nonmonetary Transactions, Ch. 32	323, Investments 810, Consolidation 845, Nonmonetary Transactions
Accounting and Reporting for Decreases in Ownership of a Subsidiary—a Scope Clarification		
Accounting Standards Update 2010-03		
Extractive Activities—Oil and Gas Reserve Estimation and Disclosure	Specific industry guidance is not covered in the 2011 GAAP Guide Vol. I	—
Accounting Standards Update 2010-04		
Accounting for Various Topics	SEC guidance for public companies is not covered in the 2011 GAAP Guide Vol. I	—
Technical Corrections to SEC Paragraphs		
Accounting Standards Update 2010-06		
Fair Value Measurements and Disclosures (Topic 820)	Fair Value, Ch. 6	820, Fair Value Measurement and Disclosure
Improving Disclosures about Fair Value Measurements		

Accounting Standards Update 2010-07		
Not-for-Profit Entities (Topic 958)	Not-for-Profit Organizations, Appendix	958, Not-for-Profit Entities
Not-for-Profit Entities: Mergers and Acquisitions		
Accounting Standards Update 2010-08		
Technical Corrections to Various Topics	Multiple chapters	805, Business Combinations
Accounting Standards Update 2010-09		
Subsequent Events (Topic 855)	Accounting Policies and Standards, Ch. 2	855, Subsequent Events
Amendments to Certain Recognition and Disclosure Requirements		
Accounting Standards Update 2010-10		
Consolidation (Topic 810)	Specific industry guidance is not covered in the 2011 GAAP Guide Vol. I	—
Amendments for Certain Investment Funds		
Accounting Standards Update 2010-11		
Derivatives and Hedging (Topic 815)	Financial Instruments, Ch. 17	815, Consolidation
Scope Exception Related to Embedded Credit Derivatives		
Accounting Standards Update 2010-12		
Income Taxes (Topic 740)	Income Taxes, Ch. 21	740, Income Taxes
Accounting for Certain Tax Effects of the 2010 Health Care Reform Acts		
Accounting Standards Update 2010-14		
Accounting for Extractive Activities—Oil & Gas	Specific industry guidance is not covered in the 2011 GAAP Guide Vol. I	—
Amendments to Paragraphs 932-10-S99-1		
Accounting Standards Update 2010-19		
Foreign Currency (Topic 830)	SEC guidance for public companies is not covered in the 2011 GAAP Guide Vol. I	—
Foreign Currency Issues: Multiple Foreign Currency Exchange Rates		

Accounting Standards Update 2010-20

Disclosures about the Credit quality of Financing Receivables and the Allowance for Credit Losses	Contingencies, Risks, and Uncertainties, Ch 8	310, Receivables

ORIGINAL PRONOUNCEMENTS TO 2011 *GAAP GUIDE*, VOLUME II CHAPTERS

This locator provides instant cross-reference between an original pronouncement and the chapter(s) in this publication in which a pronouncement is discussed. Original pronouncements are listed chronologically on the left and the chapter(s) in which they appear in the 2011 *GAAP Guide*, Volume II are listed on the right. If an original pronouncement has been nullified or its guidance incorporated in another pronouncement, a cross-reference is made to the succeeding pronouncement.

Because of the number of citations for each pronouncement discussed in Volume II, cross references to the Codification for those pronouncements are included with the related text.

FASB TECHNICAL BULLETINS

ORIGINAL PRONOUNCEMENT	2011 *GAAP GUIDE* VOLUME II REFERENCE	
FTB 79-1 (R)		
Purpose and Scope of FASB Technical Bulletins and Procedures for Issuance	Accounting Policies and Standards, ch. 2	
FTB 79-3		
Subjective Acceleration Clauses in Long-Term Debt Agreements	Balance Sheet Classification and Related Display Issues, ch. 4	
FTB 79-4		
Segment Reporting of Puerto Rican Operations	Segment Reporting, ch. 37	
FTB 79-5		
Meaning of the Term "Customer" as It Applies to Health Care Facilities under FASB Statement No. 14	Segment Reporting, ch. 37	
FTB 79-8		
Applicability of FASB Statements 21 and 33 to Certain Brokers and Dealers in Securities	Superseded by FAS-131, paragraph 128(f).	—
FTB 79-9		
Accounting for Interim Periods for Changes in Income Tax Rates	Interim Financial Reporting, ch. 23	
FTB 79-10		
Fiscal Funding Clauses in Lease Agreements	Leases, ch. 26	
FTB 79-12		
Interest Rate Used in Calculating the Present Value of Minimum Lease Payments	Leases, ch. 26	—

FTB 79-13
Applicability of FASB Statement No. 13 to Current Value Financial Statements — Changing Prices, ch. 9

FTB 79-14
Upward Adjustment of Guaranteed Residual Values — Leases, ch. 26

FTB 79-15
Accounting for Loss on a Sublease Not Involving the Disposal of a Segment — Leases, ch. 26

FTB 79-16 (R)
Effect of a Change in Income Tax Rate on the Accounting for Leveraged Leases — Leases, ch. 26

FTB 79-17
Reporting Cumulative Effect Adjustment from Retroactive Application of FASB Statement No. 13 — Not in Codification — —

FTB 79-18
Transition Requirement of Certain FASB Amendments and Interpretations of FASB Statement No. 13 — Not in Codification — —

FTB 79-19
Investor's Accounting for Unrealized Losses on Marketable Securities Owned by an Equity Method Investee — Not in Codification — —

FTB 80-1
Early Extinguishment of Debt through Exchange for Common or Preferred Stock — Portions amended by FAS-111 and FAS-145.

Extinguishment of Debt, ch. 16

FTB 80-2
Classification of Debt Restructurings by Debtors and Creditors — Troubled Debt Restructuring, ch. 41

FTB 81-6
Applicability of Statement 15 to Debtors in Bankruptcy Situations — Troubled Debt Restructuring, ch. 41

FTB 82-1
Disclosure of the Sale or Purchase of Tax Benefits through Tax Leases — Not in Codification — —

FTB 84-1
Accounting for Stock Issued to Acquire the Results of a Research and Development Arrangement — Not in Codification — —

FTB 85-1

Accounting for the Receipt of Federal Home Loan Mortgage Corporation Participating Preferred Stock	Not in Codification	—

FTB 85-3

Accounting for Operating Leases with Scheduled Rent Increases	Leases, ch. 26

FTB 85-4

Accounting for Purchases of Life Insurance	Balance Sheet Classification and Related Display Issues, ch. 4

FTB 85-5

Issues Relating to Accounting for Business Combinations	Not in Codification	—

FTB 85-6

Accounting for a Purchase of Treasury Shares at a Price Significantly in Excess of the Current Market Price of the Shares and the Income Statement Classification of Costs Incurred in Defending against a Takeover Attempt	Stockholders' Equity, ch. 39

FTB 86-2

Accounting for an Interest in the Residual Value of a Leased Asset	Portions amended by FAS-140.
	Real Estate Transactions, ch. 30

FTB 88-1

Issues Related to Accounting for Leases	Leases, ch. 26

FTB 90-1

Accounting for Separately Priced Extended Warranty and Product Maintenance Contracts	Revenue Recognition, ch. 36

FTB 94-1

Application of Statement 115 to Debt Securities Restructured in a Troubled Debt Restructuring	Troubled Debt Restructuring, ch. 41

FTB 97-1

Accounting under Statement 123 for Certain Employee Stock Purchase Plans with a Look-Back Option	Stock-Based Payments, ch. 38

FTB 01-1

Effective Date for Certain Financial Institutions of Certain Provisions of Statement 140 Related to the Isolation of Transferred Assets	No longer relevant	—

AICPA STATEMENTS OF POSITION

ORIGINAL PRONOUNCEMENT	2011 *GAAP GUIDE* VOLUME II REFERENCE	
SOP 76-3 Accounting Practices for Certain Employee Stock Ownership Plans	Stock-Based Payments, ch. 38	—
SOP 81-1 Accounting for Performance of Construction-Type and Certain Production-Type Contracts	Long-Term Construction Contracts, ch. 27	
SOP 82-1 Accounting and Financial Reporting for Personal Financial Statements	Personal Financial Statements, ch. 31	—
SOP 90-3 Definition of the term *Substantially the Same for Holders of Debt Instruments*, as Used in Certain Audit Guides and a Statement of Position	Investments in Debt and Equity Securities, ch. 25	
SOP 90-7 Financial Reporting by Entities in Reorganization under the Bankruptcy Code	Bankruptcy and Reorganization, ch. 5	
SOP 93-3 Rescission of Accounting Principles Board Statements	Accounting Policies and Standards, ch. 2	
SOP 93-4 Foreign Currency Accounting and Financial Statement Presentation for Investment Companies	Foreign Operations and Exchange, ch. 18	
SOP 93-6 Employers' Accounting for Employee Stock Ownership Plans	Stock-Based Payments, ch. 38	
SOP 93-7 Reporting on Advertising Costs	Advertising, ch. 3	
SOP 94-6 Disclosure of Certain Significant Risks and Uncertainties	Contingencies, Risks, and Uncertainties, ch. 12	
SOP 96-1 Environmental Remediation Liabilities	Contingencies, Risks, and Uncertainties, ch. 12	
SOP 97-2 Software Revenue Recognition	Computer Software, ch. 10	
SOP 98-1 Accounting for Costs of Computer Software Developed or Obtained for Internal Use	Computer Software, ch. 10	

CR.32 *Cross-Reference*

SOP 98-5

Reporting on the Costs of Start-Up Activities	Results of Operations, ch. 35

SOP 98-9

Modification of SOP 97-2, Software Revenue Recognition, With Respect to Certain Transactions	Not in Codification

SOP 01-6

Accounting for Certain Entities (Including Entities with Trade Receivables) That Lend To or Finance the Activities of Others	Contingencies, Risks, and Uncertainties, ch. 11

SOP 03-3

Accounting for Certain Loans or Debt Securities Acquired in a Transfer	Transfer of Financial Assets, ch. 40

SOP 04-2

Accounting for Real Estate Time-Sharing Transactions	Real Estate Transactions, ch. 34

SOP 07-1

Clarification of the Scope of the Audit and Accounting Guide "Investment Companies" and Accounting by Parent Companies and Equity Method Investors for Investments in Investment Companies	Financial Investments, ch. 17

FASB STAFF POSITIONS

ORIGINAL PRONOUNCEMENT	2011 *GAAP GUIDE* VOLUME II REFERENCE	

FAS 13-1

Accounting for Rental Costs Incurred during a Construction Period	Real Estate Transactions, ch. 34

FAS 13-2

Accounting for a Change in the Timing of Cash Flows Relating to Income Taxes Generated by a Leveraged Transaction	Leases, ch. 26

FAS 19-1

Accounting for Suspended Well Costs	Capitalization and Expense Gas Recognition Concepts, ch. 7

FAS 97-1

Situations in Which Paragraphs 17(b) and 20 of FASB Statement No. 97, "Accounting and Reporting by Insurance Enterprises for Certain Long-Duration Contracts and for	Revenue Recognition, ch. 36

Realized Gains and Losses from the Sale of Investments," Permit or Require Accrual of an Unearned Revenue Liability

FAS 106-1

| Accounting and Disclosure Requirements Related to the Medicare Prescription Drug Improvement and Modernization Act of 2003 | Superseded by FSP FAS 106-2. | — |

FAS 106-2

Accounting and Disclosure Requirements Related to the Medicare Prescription Drug, Improvement and Modernization Act of 2003

Postemployment and Retirement Benefits Other Than Pensions, ch. 32

FAS 107-1 and APB 28-1

Interim Disclosures about Fair Value of Financial Instruments

Interim Financial Reporting, ch. 23

FAS 109-1

Application of FASB Statement No. 109, "Accounting for Income Taxes," to the Tax Deduction on Qualified Production Activities Provided by the American Jobs Creation Act of 2004

Income Taxes, ch. 20

FAS 109-2

Accounting and Disclosure Guidance for the Foreign Earnings Repatriation Provision within the American Jobs Creation Act of 2004

Not in Codification

FAS 115-1 and FAS 124-1

The Meaning of Other-Than-Temporary Impairment and Its Application to Certain Investments

Investments in Debt and Equity Securities, ch. 25

FAS 115-2 and FAS 124-2

Recognition and Presentation of Other-Than-Temporary Impairments

Investments in Debt and Equity Securities, ch. 25

FAS 117-1

Endowments of Not-for-Profit Organizations - Net Asset Classification of Funds Subject to an Enacted Version of the Uniform Prudent Management of Institutional Funds Act, and Enhanced Disclosures for All Endowment Funds

Balance Sheet Classification, ch. 4

FAS 123(R)-1

Classification and Measurement of Freestanding Financial Instruments Originally Issued in Exchange for Employee Services under FASB Statement No. 123(R)

Stock-Based Payments, ch. 38

FAS 123(R)-2

Practical Accommodation to the Application of Grant Date as Defined in FASB Statement No. 123(R) — Stock-Based Payments, ch. 38

FAS 123(R)-3

Transition Election Related to Accounting for the Tax Effects of Share-Based Payment Awards — Stock-Based Payments, ch. 38

FAS 123(R)-4

Classification of Options and Similar Instruments Issued as Employee Compensation That Allow for Cash Settlement upon the Occurrence of a Contingent Event — Stock-Based Payments, ch. 38

FAS 123(R)-5

Amendment of FASB Staff Position 123(R)-1 — Stock-Based Payments, ch. 38

FAS 123(R)-6

Technical Corrections of FASB Statement No. 123(R) — Stock-Based Payments, ch. 38

FAS 126-1

Applicability of Certain Disclosure and Interim Reporting Requirements for Obligors for Conduit Debt Securities — Financial Instruments, ch. 17

FAS 129-1

Disclosure Requirements under FASB Statement No. 129, "Disclosure of Information about Capital Structure, Relating to Contingently Convertible Securities" — Stockholders' Equity, ch. 39

FAS 132(R)-1

Employers' Disclosures about Postretirement Benefit Plan Assets — Postemployment and Postretirement Benefits Other Than Pensions, ch. 32

FAS 133-1 and FIN 45-4:

Disclosures about Credit Derivatives and Certain Guarantees - An Amendment of FASB Statement No. 133 and FASB Interpretation No. 45; and Clarification of the Effective Date of FASB Statement No. 161 — Financial Instruments, ch. 17

FAS 140-1

Accounting for Accrued Interest Receivable Related to Securitized and Sold Receivables under Statement No. 140 — Transfer and Servicing of Financial Assets, ch. 40

FAS 140-2

Clarification of the Application of Paragraphs 40(b) and 40(c) of FASB Statement No. 140 — Superseded by ASU 2009-16 (FAS-166)

FAS 140-3

Accounting for Transfers of Financial Assets and Repurchase Financing Transactions — Transfers of Financial Assets, ch. 40

FAS 141-1 and FAS 142-1

Interaction of FASB Statements No. 141, "Business Combinations," and No. 142, "Goodwill and Other Intangible Assets," and EITF Issue No. 04-2, "Whether Mineral Rights Are Tangible or Intangible Assets" — Nullified by FAS-141(R)

FAS 141(R)-1

Accounting for Assets Acquired and Liabilities Assumed in a Business Combination That Arise from Contingencies — Business Combinations, ch. 6

FAS 142-2

Application of FASB Statement No. 142, "Goodwill and Other Intangible Assets," to Oil- and Gas-Producing Entities — Intangible Assets, ch. 21

FAS 142-3

Determination of the Useful Life of Intangible Assets — Intangible Assets, ch. 21

FAS 143-1

Accounting for Electronic Equipment Waste Obligations — Capitalization and Expense Recognition Concepts, ch. 7

FAS 144-1

Determination of Cost Basis for Foreclosed Assets under FASB Statement No. 15, "Accounting by Debtors and Creditors for Troubled Debt Restructurings," and the Measurement of Cumulative Losses Previously Recognized under Paragraph 37 of FASB Statement No. 144, "Accounting for the Impairment or Disposal of Long-Lived Assets" — Impairment of Long-Lived Assets, ch. 19

FAS 146-1

Determining Whether a One-Time Termination Benefit Offered in Connection with an Exit or Disposal Activity Is, in Substance, an Enhancement to an Ongoing Benefit Arrangement — Pension Plans—Settlements and Curtailments, ch. 30

FAS 150-1

Issuer's Accounting for Freestanding Financial Instruments Composed of More Than One Option or Forward Contract Embodying Obligations under FASB Statement No. 150, "Accounting for Certain Financial Instruments with Characteristics of both Liabilities and Equity" — Financial Instruments, ch. 17

CR.36 *Cross-Reference*

FAS 150-2

Accounting for Mandatorily Redeemable Shares Requiring Redemption by Payment of an Amount That Differs from the Book Value of Those Shares, under FASB Statement No. 150, "Accounting for Certain Financial Instruments with Characteristics of both Liabilities and Equity"

Financial Instruments, ch. 17

FAS 150-3

Effective Date and Transition for Mandatorily Redeemable Financial Instruments of Certain Nonpublic Entities of FASB Statement No. 150, "Accounting for Certain Financial Instruments with Characteristics of both Liabilities and Equity"

Financial Instruments, ch. 17

FAS 150-4

Issuers' Accounting for Employee Stock Ownership Plans under FASB Statement No. 150, "Accounting for Certain Financial Instruments with Characteristics of both Liabilities and Equity"

Financial Instruments, ch. 17

FAS 150-5

Issuer's Accounting under FASB Statement No.150 for Freestanding Warrants and Other Similar Instruments on Shares That Are Redeemable

Financial Instruments, ch. 17

FAS 157-1

Application of FASB Statement No. 157 to FASB Statement No. 13 and Other Accounting Pronouncements That Address Fair Value Measurements for Purposes of Lease Classification or Measurement under Statement 13

Not in Codification

FAS 157-2

Effective Date of FASB Statement No. 157

Superseded by FSP FAS 157-4

FAS 157-4

Determining Fair Value When the Volume and Level of Activity for the Asset or Liability Have Significantly Decreased and Identifying Transactions That Are Not Orderly

Fair Value, ch. 16

FAS 158-1

Conforming Amendments to the Illustrations in FASB Statements No. 87, No. 88, and No. 106 and to Related Staff Implementation Guides

Pension Plans-Employers, ch. 29

Pension Plans-Settlements and Curtailments, ch. 30
Postemployment and Postretiremnt Benefits Other Than Pensions, ch. 32

FIN 39-1

| Amendment of FASB Interpretation No. 39 | Financial Instruments, ch. 17 |

FIN 45-1

| Accounting for Intellectual Property Infringement Indemnification under FIN-45 | Contingencies, Risks, and Uncertainties, ch. 11 |

FIN 45-2

| Whether FASB Interpretation No. 45, "Guarantor's Accounting and Disclosure Requirements for Guarantees, Including Indirect Guarantees of Indebtedness of Others," Provides Support for Subsequently Accounting for a Guarantor's Liability at Fair Value | Contingencies, Risks, and Uncertainties, ch. 11 |

FIN 45-3

| Application of FASB Interpretation No. 45 to Minimum Revenue Guarantees Granted to a Business or Its Owners | Contingencies, Risks, and Uncertainties, ch. 11 |

FIN 46(R)-1

| Reporting Variable Interests in Specified Assets of Variable Interest Entities under Paragraph 13 of FASB Interpretation No. 46 (Revised December 2003), "Consolidation of Variable Interest Entities" | Consolidated Financial Statements, ch. 10 |

FIN 46(R)-2

| Calculation of Expected Losses under FASB Interpretation No. 46 (Revised December 2003), "Consolidation of Variable Interest Entities" | Consolidated Financial Statements, ch. 10 |

FIN 46(R)-3

| Evaluating Whether As a Group the Holders of the Equity Investments at Risk Lack the Direct or Indirect Ability to Make Decisions about an Entity's Activities through Voting Rights or Similar Rights under FASB Interpretation No. 46 (Revised December 2003), "Consolidation of Variable Interest Entities" | Superseded by FAS-167 |

FIN 46(R)-4

| Technical Correction of FASB Interpretation No. 46 (revised December 2003), Consolidation of Variable Interest Entities, Relating to Its Effects on Question No. 12 of EITF Issue No. 96-21, "Implementation Issues in Accounting for Leasing Transactions Involving Special-Purpose Entities" | Leases, ch. 26 |

CR.38 *Cross-Reference*

FIN 46(R)-5

Implicit Variable Interests under FASB Interpretation No. 46 (revised December 2003), "Consolidation of Variable Interest"	Consolidated Financial Statements, ch. 10

FIN 46(R)-6

Determining the Variability to Be Considered in Applying FASB Interpretation No. 46(R)	Consolidated Financial Statements, ch. 10

FIN 46(R)-7

Application of FASB Interpretation No. 46(R) to Investment Companies	Consolidated Financial Statements, ch. 10

FIN 48-1

Definition of *Settlement* in FASB Interpretation No. 48	Income Taxes, ch. 20

FIN 48-2

Effective Date of FASB Interpretation No. 48 for Nonpublic Enterprises	No longer relevant

FIN 48-3

Effective Date of FASB Interpretation No. 48 for Certain Nonpublic Enterprises	No longer relevant

APB 14-1

Accounting for Convertible Debt Instruments That May Be Settled in Cash upon Conversion (Including Partial Cash Settlement)	Convertible Debt and Debt with Warrants, ch. 12

APB 18-1

Accounting by an Investor for Its Proportionate Share of Accumulated Other Comprehensive Income of an Investee Accounted for under the Equity Method in Accordance with APB Opinion No. 18 upon Loss of Significant Influence	Equity Method, ch. 15

FTB 85-4-1

Accounting for Life Settlement Contracts by Third-Party Providers	Results of Operations, ch. 35

SOP 78-9-1

Interaction of AICPA Statement of Position 78-9 and EITF Issue No. 04-5	Consolidated Financial Statements, ch. 10

SOP 90-7-1

An Amendment of AICPA Statement of Position 90-7	Bankruptcy and Reorganization, ch. 5

Cross-Reference   CR.39

SOP 94-3-1 and AAG HCO-1

Omnibus Changes to Consolidation and Equity Method Guidance for Not-for-Profit Organizations	Consolidated Financial Statements , ch. 10

SOP-94-6-1

Terms of Loan Products That May Give Rise to a Concentration of Credit Risk	Contingencies, Risks, and Uncertainties, ch. 11

SOP 07-1-1

Effective Date of AICPA Statement of Position 07-1	Consolidated Financial Statements, ch. 10

AAG INV-1 and SOP 94-4-1

Reporting of Fully Benefit-Responsive Investment Contracts Held by Certain Investment Companies Subject to the AICPA Investment Company Guide and Defined-Contribution Health and Welfare and Pension Plans	Not discussed in this Guide.

FSP AUG AIR-1

Accounting for Planned Major Maintenance Activities	Capitalization and Expense Recognition Concepts, ch. 7

EITF 85-24-1

Application of EITF Issue No. 85-24, "Distribution Fees by Distributors of Mutual Funds That Do Not Have a Front-End Sales Charge," When Cash for the Right to Future Distribution Fees for Shares Previously Sold Is Received from Third Parties	Revenue Recognition, ch. 36

EITF 99-20-1

Amendments to the Impairment Guidance of EITF Issue No. 99-20	Transfer and Service of Financial Assets, ch. 40

EITF 00-19-1

Application of EITF Issue No. 00-19 to Freestanding Financial Instruments Originally Issued as Employee Compensation	Superseded by FSP FAS 123(R)-1.

EITF 00-19-2

Accounting for Registration Payment Arrangements	Financial Instruments, ch. 17

EITF 03-1-1

Effective Date of Paragraphs 10–20 of EITFIssue No. 03-1, "The Meaning of Other-Than-Temporary Impairment and Its Application to Certain Investments"	Superseded by FSP FAS 115-1 and FSP FAS 124-1.

EITF 03-6-1 (As Amended)

Determining Whether Instruments Granted in Share-Based Payment Transactions Are Participating Securities	Earnings per Share, ch. 13

EITF CONSENSUS POSITIONS

ORIGINAL PRONOUNCEMENT	2011 *GAAP GUIDE* VOLUME II REFERENCE
84-1 Tax Reform Act of 1984: Deferred Income Taxes of Stock Life Insurance Companies	Resolved by FTB 84-3, which was superseded by FAS-96 and FAS-109.
84-2 Tax Reform Act of 1984: Deferred Income Taxes Relating to Domestic International Sales Corporations	No consensus. Resolved by FTB 84-2, which was superseded by FAS-96 and FAS-109.
84-3 Convertible Debt "Sweeteners"	Resolved by FAS-84.
84-4 Acquisition, Development, and Construction Loans	Resolved by PB-1, Exhibit I.
84-5 Sale of Marketable Securities with a Put Option	Not discussed in GAAP Vol. II.
84-6 Termination of Defined Benefit Pension Plans	Superseded by FAS-88.
84-7 Termination of Interest Rate Swaps	Nullified by FAS-133.
84-8 Variable Stock Purchase Warrants Given by Suppliers to Customers	Resolved by FAS-123(R).
84-9 Deposit Float of Banks	Not in Codification
84-10 LIFO Conformity of Companies Relying on Insilco Tax Court Decision	No consensus.
84-11 Offsetting Installment Note Receivables and Bank Debt ("Note Monetization")	Resolved by SAB-70, FTB 86-2, and FIN-39.

Cross-Reference **CR.41**

84-12

Operating Leases with Scheduled Rent Increases | Consensus nullified by FTB 85-3. FTB 88-1 provides additional guidance.

84-13

Purchase of Stock Options and Stock Appreciation Rights in a Leveraged Buyout | Nullified by FAS-123(R).

84-14

Deferred Interest Rate Setting | Nullified by FAS-133.

84-15

Grantor Trusts Consolidation | No consensus. Addressed in FTB 85-2, which was superseded by FAS-125.

84-16

Earnings-per-Share Cash-Yield Test for Zero Coupon Bonds | Resolved by FAS-85.

84-17

Profit Recognition on Sales of Real Estate with Graduated Payment Mortgages or Insured Mortgages | Real Estate Transactions, ch.33

84-18

Stock Option Pyramiding | Nullified by FAS-123(R).

84-19

Mortgage Loan Payment Modifications | Financial Instruments, ch. 17

84-20

GMNA Dollar Rolls | Partially resolved by guidance in paragraphs 9, 27-30-,68, and 70 of FAS-125.

84-21

Sale of a Loan with a Partial Participation Retained | Resolved by FAS-125, paragraphs 10 and 39.

84-22

Prior Years' Earnings per Share Following a Savings and Loan Association Conversion and Pooling | No consensus. Resolved by FAS-141.

84-23

Leveraged Buyout Holding Company Debt | No consensus. Guidance provided by SAB-73 and FAS-105.

84-24

LIFO Accounting Issues | No consensus. SAB-58 provides guidance.

84-25

Offsetting Nonrecourse Debt with Sales-Type or Direct Financing Lease Receivables | Resolved by FTB 86-2 and SEC Staff Accounting Bulletin No. 70.

84-26

Defeasance of Special-Purpose Borrowings — Resolved by FAS-125.

84-27

Deferred Taxes on Subsidiary Stock Sales — No consensus. Resolved by FAS-96, which was superseded by FAS-109.

84-28

Impairment of Long-Lived Assets — No consensus. Resolved by FAS-121.

84-29

Gain and Los Recognition on Exchanges of Productive Assets and the Effect of Boot — No consensus. Resolved by EITF Issues 86-29 and 87-29.

84-30

Sales of Loans to Special-Purpose Entities — Resolved by FIN-46 and FIN-46(R) for entities under the scope of those pronouncements.

84-31

Equity Certificates of Deposit — Resolved by FAS-133.

84-32

Not used.

84-33

Acquisition of a Tax Loss Carryforward— Temporary Parent-Subsidiary Relationship — Resolved by FAS-144.

84-34

Permanent Discount Restricted Stock Purchase Plans — Nullified by FAS-123(R), except for nonpublic entities under the scope of paragraph 83 of FAS-123(R).

84-35

Business Combinations: Sale of Duplicate Facilities and Accrual of Liabilities — Nullified by FAS-141(R).

84-36

Interest Rate Swap Transactions — Nullified by FAS-133.

84-37

Sale-Leaseback Transaction with Repurchase Option — No consensus. See FAS-98.

84-38

Identical Common Shares for a Pooling Of Interests — Nullified by FTB 85-5.

84-39

Transfers of Monetary and Nonmonetary Assets among Individuals and Entities Under Common Control — No consensus.

Cross-Reference **CR.43**

84-40

Long-Term Debt Repayable by a Capital Stock Transaction	Issue 1 nullified by FIN-46 and FIN-46 (R) and Issue 2 resolved by FAS-150.

84-41

Consolidation of Subsidiary Instantaneous Defeasance	Resolved by FAS-94.

84-42

Push-Down of Parent Company Debt to a Subsidiary	No consensus. See SAB 43.

84-43

Income Tax Effects of Asset Evaluation in Certain Foreign Countries	Nullified by FAS-109.

84-44

Partial Termination of a Defined Benefit Pension Plan	Resolved by FAS-88.

85-1

Classifying Notes Received for Capital Stock	Balance Sheet Classification and Related Display Issues, ch.4

85-2

Classification of Costs Incurred in a Takeover Defense	Nullified by FTB 85-6.

85-3

Tax Benefits Relating to Asset Dispositions Following an Acquisition of a Financial Institution	Consensus nullified by FAS-96, which was superseded by FAS-109.

85-4

Downstream Mergers and Other Stock Transactions between Companies under Common Control	No consensus. Resolved by FTB 85-5.

85-5

Restoration of Deferred Taxes Previously Eliminated by Net Operating Loss Recognition	No consensus. Resolved by FAS-96, which was superseded by FAS-109.

85-6

Futures Implementation Questions	Resolved by Q and A to FAS-80.

85-7

Federal Home Loan Mortgage Corporation Stock	No consensus. Resolved by FTB 85-1.

85-8

Amortization of Thrift Intangibles	Nullified by FAS-141(R).

85-9

Revenue Recognition on Options to Purchase Stock of Another Entity	Convertible Debt and Debt with Warrants, ch.12

85-10
Employee Stock Ownership Plan Contribution Funded by a Pension Plan Termination — Nullified by FAS-88.

85-11
Use of an Employee Stock Ownership Plan in a Leveraged Buyout — No consensus. See SOP 93-6.

85-12
Retention of Specialized Accounting for Investments in Consolidation — Not discussed.

85-13
Sale of Mortgage Service Rights on Mortgages Owned by Others — Transfer and Servicing of Financial Assets, ch. 40

85-14
Securities That Can Be Acquired for Cash in a Pooling of Interests — Nullified by FAS-141.

85-15
Recognizing Benefits of Purchased Net Operating Loss Carryforwards — Consensus nullified by FAS-96, which was superseded by FAS-109.

85-16
Leveraged Leases: Real Estate Leases and Sale-Leaseback Transactions, Delayed Equity Contributions by Lessors — Leases, ch. 26

85-17
Accrued Interest upon Conversion of Convertible Debt — Convertible Debt and Debt with Warrants, ch. 13

85-18
Earnings-per-Share Effect of Equity Commitment Notes — Superseded by FAS-128.

85-19
Not used.

85-20
Recognition of Fees for Guaranteeing a Loan — Contingencies, Risks, and Uncertainties, ch. 11

85-21
Changes of Ownership Resulting in a New Basis of Accounting — Business Combinations, ch. 6

85-22
Retroactive Application of FASB Technical Bulletins — No longer relevant.

85-23
Effect of a Redemption Agreement on Carrying Value of a Security — Not in Codification

85-24
Distribution Fees by Distributors of Mutual Funds That Do Not Have a Front-End Sales Charge — Revenue Recognition, ch. 36

Cross-Reference **CR.45**

85-25

| Sale of Preferred Stocks with a Put Option | Included in discussion of Issue 85-40. |

85-26

| Measurement of Servicing Fee under FASB Statement No. 65 When a Loan Is Sold with Servicing Retained | No consensus. Resolved by FTB 87-3 and FAS-125. |

85-27

| Recognition of Receipts from Made-Up Rental Shortfalls | Real Estate Transactions, ch. 33 |

85-28

| Consolidation Issues Relating to Collateralized Mortgage Obligations | Resolved by FAS-94. |

85-29

| Convertible Bonds with a "Premium Put" | Convertible Debt and Debt with Warrants, ch. 12 |

85-30

| Sale of Marketable Securities at a Gain with a Put Option | No consensus. Resolved by FAS-125. |

85-31

| Comptroller of the Currency's Rule on Deferred Tax Debits | Not discussed in this Guide. |

85-32

| Purchased Lease Residuals | Nullified by FTB 86-2. |

85-33

| Disallowance of Income Tax Deduction | Nullified by FAS-109. |

85-34

| Banker's Acceptances and Risk Participations | Resolved by FAS-125. |

85-35

| Transition and Implementation Issues for FASB Statement No. 86 | No longer useful. |

85-36

| Discontinued Operations with Expected Gain and Interim Operating Losses | Nullified by FAS-144. |

85-37

| Recognition of Note Received for Real Estate Syndication Activities | Resolved by SOP 92-1. |

85-38

| Negative Amortizing Loans | No longer useful. |

85-39

| Implications of SEC Staff Accounting Bulletin No. 59 on Noncurrent Marketable Equity Securities | Not in Codification |

85-40

Comprehensive Review of Sales of Marketable Securities with Put Arrangements — Not in the Codification

85-41

Accounting for Savings and Loan Associations and FSLIC Management Consignment Program — Not discussed in this Guide.

85-42

Amortization of Goodwill Resulting from Recording Time Savings Deposits at Fair Value — Nullified by FAS-141(R).

85-43

Sale of Subsidiary for Equity Interest in Buyer — Resolved by Issue 86-29.

85-44

Differences between Loan Loss Allowances — Not discussed in this Guide.

85-45

Business Combinations: Settlement of Stock Options and Awards — Nullified by FAS-123(R), except for an entity under the scope of paragraph 83 of FAS-123(R).

85-46

Partnership's Purchase of Withdrawing Partner's Equity — No consensus.

86-1

Recognizing Net Operating Loss Carryforwards — Nullified by FAS-109.

86-2

Retroactive Wage Adjustments Affecting Medicare Payments — No longer relevant.

86-3

Retroactive Regulations Regarding IRC Section 338 Purchase Price Allocations — The consensus on Issue 1 is no longer relevant. The consensus on Issue 2 was superseded by FAS-109.

86-4

Income Statement Treatment of Income Tax Benefit for Employee Stock Ownership Plan Dividends — Consensus nullified by FAS-96, which was superseded by FAS-109.

86-5

Classifying Demand Notes with Repayment Terms — Balance Sheet Classification and Related Display Issues, ch. 4

86-6

Antispeculation Clauses in Real Estate Sales Contracts — Real Estate Transactions, ch. 33

Cross-Reference CR.47

86-7

| Recognition by Homebuilders of Profit from Sales of Land and Related Construction Contracts | Real Estate Transactions, ch. 33 |

86-8

| Sale of Bad-Debt Recovery Rights | Financial Instruments, ch. 17 |

86-9

| IRC Section 338 and Push-Down Accounting | Income Taxes, ch. 20 |

Also see Issue 94-10.

86-10

| Pooling with 10 Percent Cash Payout Determined by Lottery | Nullified by FAS-141. |

86-11

| Recognition of Possible 1986 Tax Law Changes | Resolved by FTB 86-1, which was superseded by FAS-96 and FAS-109. |

86-12

| Accounting by Insureds for Claims-Made Insurance Policies | Codified in Issue 03-8. |

Contingencies, Risks, and Uncertainties, ch. 12

86-13

| Recognition of Inventory Market Declines at Interim Reporting Dates | Interim Financial Reporting, ch. 23 |

86-14

| Purchased Research and Development Projects in a Business Combination | Nullified by FAS-141(R). |

86-15

| Increasing-Rate Debt | Balance Sheet Classification and Related Display Issues, ch. 4 |

Interest on Receivables and Payables, ch. 22

86-16

| Carryover of Predecessor Cost in Leveraged Buyout Transactions | Superseded by Issue 88-16. |

86-17

| Deferred Profit on Sale-Leaseback Transaction with Lessee Guarantee of Residual Value | Leases, ch. 26 |

86-18

| Debtor's Accounting for a Modification of Debt Terms | Superseded by Issue 96-19 and resolved by FIN-39. |

86-19

| Change in Accounting for Other Postemployment Benefits | Resolved by FAS-106. |

86-20

Accounting for Other Postemployment Benefits Of an Acquired Company — Nullified by FAS-106.

86-21

Application of the AICPA Notice to Practitioners regarding Acquisition, Development, and Construction Arrangements to Acquisition of an Operating Property — Real Estate Transactions, ch. 33

86-22

Display of Business Restructuring Provisions in the Income Statement — No consensus. See SAB 67 and FAS-144.

86-23

Not used.

86-24

Third-Party Establishment of Collateralized Mortgage Obligations — No longer relevant because of the issuance of FAS-125 and FAS-140.

86-25

Offsetting Foreign Currency Swaps — Foreign Operations and Exchange, ch. 18

86-26

Using Forward Commitments as a Surrogate for Deferred Rate Setting — Resolved by FAS-133.

86-27

Measurement of Excess Contributions to a Defined Contribution Plan or Employee Stock Ownership Plan — Stock-Based Payments, ch. 38

86-28

Accounting Implications of Indexed Debt Instruments — Effectively nullified by FAS-133

86-29

Nonmonetary Transactions: Magnitude of Boot and the Exceptions to the Use of Fair Value — Codified in Issue 01-2.

86-30

Classification of Obligations When a Violation Is Waived by the Creditor — Balance Sheet Classification and Related Display Issues, ch. 4

86-31

Reporting the Tax Implications of a Pooling of a Bank and a Savings and Loan Association — Nullified by FAS-141.

86-32

Early Extinguishment of a Subsidiary's Mandatorily Redeemable Preferred Stock — Stockholders' Equity, ch. 39

Cross-Reference **CR.49**

86-33

Tax Indemnifications in Lease Agreements	Leases, ch. 26

86-34

Futures Contracts Used as Hedges of Anticipated Reverse Repurchase Transactions	Nullified by FAS-133.

86-35

Debentures with Detachable Stock Purchase Warrants	Superseded by Issue 96-13, which has been codified in Issue 00-19.
	Financial Instruments, ch.17

86-36

Invasion of a Defeasance Trust	Not in Codification

86-37

Recognition of Tax Benefit of Discounting Loss Reserves of Insurance Companies	Consensus nullified by FAS-96, which was superseded by FAS-109.

86-38

Implications of Mortgage Prepayments on Amortization of Servicing Rights	Consensus in Section A nullified by FAS-122.
	Consensus in Section B nullified by FAS-125.
	Consensus in Section C superseded by Issue 89-4.

86-39

Gains from the Sale of Mortgage Loans with Servicing Rights Retained	Nullified by FAS-125, which supersedes FAS-122. See paragraphs 10 and 39 of FAS-125 for guidance.

86-40

Investments in Open-End Mutual Funds That Invest in U.S. Government Securities	Consensus no longer applies. Resolved by FAS-115.

86-41

Carryforward of the Corporate Alternative Minimum Tax Credit	Consensus nullified by FAS-96, which was superseded by FAS-109.

86-42

Effect of a Change in Tax Rates on Assets and Liabilities Recorded Not-of-Tax in a Purchase Business Combination	Consensus nullified by FAS-96, which was superseded by FAS-109.

86-43

Effect of a Change in Tax Law or Rates on Leveraged Leases	Leases, ch. 26

86-44

Effect of a Change in Tax Law on Investments in Safe Harbor Leases	Leases, ch. 26

CR.50 *Cross-Reference*

86-45

Imputation of Dividends on Preferred Stock Redeemable at the Issuer's Option with Initial Below-Market Dividend Rate

No consensus.

86-46

Uniform Capitalization Rules for Inventory under the Tax Reform Act of 1986

Inventory, ch. 24

87-1

Deferral Accounting for Cash Securities That Are Used to Hedge Rate or Price Risk

Resolved by FAS-133.

87-2

Net Present Value Method of Valuing Speculative Foreign Exchange Contracts

Resolved by FAS-133.

87-3

Not used.

87-4

Restructuring of Operations: Implications of SEC Staff Accounting Bulletin No. 67

Not in Codification

87-5

Troubled Debt Restructurings: Interrelationship Between FASB Statement No. 15 and the AICPA Savings and Loan Guide

Nullified by FAS-114.

87-6

Adjustments Relating to Stock Compensation Plans

Nullified by FIN-44.

87-7

Sale of an Asset Subject to a Lease and Nonrecourse Financing: "Wrap Lease Transactions"

Not in Codification

87-8

Tax Reform Act of 1986: Issues Related to the Alternative Minimum Tax

Income Taxes, ch. 20

Leases, ch. 26

Consensuses on Issues 2–9 and 11 were nullified by FAS-109.

87-9

Profit Recognition on Sales of Real Estate with Insured Mortgages or Surety Bonds

Real Estate Transactions, ch. 33

87-10

Revenue Recognition by Television "Barter" Syndicators

Not in Codification

87-11		
	Allocation of Purchase Price to Assets to Be Sold	Nullified by FAS-144.
87-12		
	Foreign Debt-for-Equity Swaps	Foreign Operations and Exchange, ch. 18
87-13		
	Amortization of Prior Service Cost for a Defined Benefit Plan When There Is a History of Plan Amendments	No consensus. Resolved by Question and Answer No. 20 of FASB Special Report on FAS-87.
87-14		Not used.
87-15		
	Effect of a Standstill Agreement on Pooling-of-Interests Accounting	Nullified by FAS-141.
87-16		
	Whether the 90 Percent Test for a Pooling of Interests Is Applied Separately to Each Company or on a Combined Basis	Nullified by FAS-141.
87-17		
	Spinoffs or Other Distributions of Loans Receivable to Shareholders	Codified in Issue 01-2.
87-18		
	Use of Zero Coupon Bonds in a Troubled Debt Restructuring	Troubled Debt Restructuring, ch. 41
87-19		
	Substituted Debtors in a Troubled Debt Restructuring	Troubled Debt Restructuring, ch. 41
87-20		
	Offsetting Certificates of Deposit against High-Coupon Debt	Issue 1 resolved by FAS-125. Issue 2 superseded by Issue 96-19.
87-21		
	Change of Accounting Basis in Master Limited Partnership Transactions	Business Combinations, ch. 6
87-22		
	Prepayments to the Secondary Reserve of the FSLIC	No longer relevant. See Topics D-47 and D-57.
87-23		
	Book Value Stock Purchase Plans	Nullified by FAS-123(R), except for nonpublic entities under the scope of paragraph 83 of FAS-123(R); Issue 3 nullified by SOP 93-6.
87-24		
	Allocation of Interest to Discontinued Operations	Results of Operations, ch. 35

CR.52 *Cross-Reference*

87-25

Sale of Convertible, Adjustable-Rate Mortgages with Contingent Repayment Agreement	No consensus. Resolved by FAS-125 and FAS-140.

87-26

Hedging of a Foreign Currency Exposure with a Tandem Currency	Nullified by FAS-133.

87-27

Poolings of Companies That Do Not Have a Controlling Class of Common Stock	Nullified by FAS-141.

87-28

Provision for Deferred Taxes on Increases in Cash Surrender Value of Key-Person Life Insurance	Resolved by FAS-109.

87-29

Exchange of Real Estate Involving Boot	Codified in Issue 01-2.

87-30

Sale of a Short-Term Loan Made under a Long-Term Credit Commitment	Transfer and Servicing of Financial Assets, ch. 40

87-31

Sale of Put Options on Issuer's Stock	Codified in Issue 00-19.

87-32

	Not used.

87-33

Stock Compensation Issues Related to Market Decline	Nullified by FIN-44.

87-34

Sale of Mortgage Servicing Rights with a Subservicing Agreement	Not discussed.

88-1

Determination of Vested Benefit Obligation for a Defined Benefit Pension Plan	Pension Plans—Employers, ch.29

88-2

	Not used.

88-3

Rental Concessions Provided by Landlord	Resolved by FTB 88-1 and Issues 88-10 and 94-3.

88-4

Classification of Payment Made to IRS to Retain Fiscal Year	Capitalization and Expense Recognition Concepts, ch. 7

88-5

Recognition of Insurance Death Benefits	Revenue Recognition, ch. 36
	No consensus on Issue 2, but FAS-109 provides guidance.

Cross-Reference **CR.53**

88-6

Book Value Stock Plans in an Initial Public Offering	Nullified by FAS-123(R), except for nonpublic entities under the scope of paragraph 83 of FAS-123(R).
88-7	Not used.
88-8	Partially nullified and partially resolved by FAS-133.

88-9

Put Warrants	Nullified by FAS-128, FAS-133, and FAS-150 and superseded by Issue 96-13.

88-10

Costs Associated with Lease Modification or Termination	FAS-146 resolves Issue 1 and nullifies Issues 2 and 3.

88-11

Allocation of Recorded Investment When a Loan or Part of a Loan Is Sold	Nullified by FAS-156.

88-12

Transfer of Ownership Interest as Part of Down Payment under FASB Statement No. 66	Real Estate Transactions, ch. 33
88-13	Not used.

88-14

Settlement of Fees with Extra Units to a General Partner in a Master Limited Partnership	No consensus. Resolved by SOP 92-1.

88-15

Classification of Subsidiary's Loan Payable in Consolidated Balance Sheet When Subsidiary's and Parent's Fiscal Years Differ	Balance Sheet Classification and Related Display Issues, ch. 4

88-16

Basis in Leveraged Buyout Transactions	Nullified by FAS-141(R).

88-17

Accounting for Fees and Costs Associated with Loan Syndications and Loan Participations	Partially nullified by FAS-125 and superseded by Issue 97-3.

88-18

Sales of Future Revenues	Balance Sheet Classification and Related Display Issues, ch. 4
	Foreign Operations and Exchange, ch. 18
	Revenue Recognition, ch. 36

88-19

FSLIC-Assisted Acquisitions of Thrifts	Nullified by FAS-141(R).

88-20

Difference between Initial Investment and Principal Amount of Loans in a Purchased Credit Card Portfolio

Intangible Assets, ch. 21

88-21

Accounting for the Sale of Property Subject to the Seller's Preexisting Lease

Leases, ch. 26

88-22

Securitization of Credit Card and Other Receivable Portfolios

Transfer and Servicing of Financial Assets, ch. 40

88-23

Lump-Sum Payments under Union Contracts

Capitalization and Expense Recognition Concepts, ch. 7

88-24

Effect of Various Forms of Financing under FASB Statement No. 66

Real Estate Transactions, ch. 33

88-25

Ongoing Accounting and Reporting for a Newly Created Liquidating Bank

Not discussed in this Guide.

88-26

Controlling Preferred Stock in a Pooling of Interests

Nullified by FAS-141.

88-27

Effect of Unlocated Shares in an Employee Stock Ownership Plan on Accounting for Business Combinations

Nullified by FAS-141.

89-1

Accounting by a Pension Plan for Bank Investment Contracts and Guaranteed Investment Contracts

Resolved by FAS-110 and SOP 94-4.

89-2

Maximum Maturity Guarantees on Transfers of Receivables with Recourse

Not in Codification.

89-3

Balance Sheet Presentation of Savings Accounts in Financial Statements of Credit Unions

Not discussed.

89-4

Accounting for a Purchased Investment in a Collateralized Mortgage Obligation Instrument or in a Mortgage-Backed Interest-Only Certificate

Superseded by Issue 99-20.

89-5

Sale of Mortgage Loan Servicing Rights

Superseded by Issue 95-5.

Cross-Reference **CR.55**

89-6

Not used.

89-7

Exchange of Assets or Interest in a Subsidiary for a Noncontrolling Equity Interest in a New Entity

Codified in Issue 01-2.

89-8

Expense Recognition for Employee Stock Ownership Plans

Stock-Based Payments, ch. 38

89-9

Accounting for In-Substance Foreclosures

Nullified by FAS-114.

89-10

Sponsor's Recognition of Employee Stock Ownership Plan Debt

Nullified by SOP 93-6.

89-11

Sponsor's Balance Sheet Classification of Capital Stock with a Put Option Held by an Employee Stock Ownership Plan

Balance Sheet Classification and Related Display Issues, ch. 4

89-12

Earnings-per-Share Issues Related to Convertible Preferred Stock Held by an Employee Stock Ownership Plan

Stock-Based Payments, ch. 38

89-13

Accounting for the Cost of Asbestos Removal

Capitalization and Expense Recognition Concepts, ch. 7

Results of Operations, ch. 35

89-14

Valuation of Repossessed Real Estate

Real Estate Transactions, ch.33

89-15

Accounting for a Modification of Debt Terms When the Debtor Is Experiencing Financial Difficulties

Superseded by Issue 02-4.

89-16

Consideration of Executory Costs in Sale-Leaseback Transactions

Leases, ch. 26

89-17

Accounting for the Retail Sale of an Extended Warranty Contract in Connection with the Sale of a Product

Nullified by FTB 90-1.

89-18

Divestitures of Certain Investment Securities to an Unregulated Commonly Controlled Entity under FIRREA

Consensus no longer applies. Resolved by FAS-115.

CR.56 *Cross-Reference*

89-19

Accounting for a Change in Goodwill Amortization for Business Combinations Initiated Prior to the Effective Date of FASB Statement No. 72

Nullified by FAS-141(R).

89-20

Accounting for Cross Border Tax Benefit Leases

Leases, ch. 26

90-1

Not used.

90-2

Exchange of Interest-Only and Principal- Only Securities for a Mortgage-Backed Security

Nullified by FAS-125.

90-3

Accounting for Employers' Obligations for Future Contributions to a Multiemployer Pension Plan

Pension Plans—Employers, ch. 29

90-4

Earnings-per-Share Treatment of Tax Benefits for Dividends on Stock Held by an Employee Stock Ownership Plan

Issue 1 nullified by FAS-128. (See Appendix F of FAS-128 for discussion on deduction of dividends.) Issue 2 addressed in Issue 92-3.

90-5

Exchanges of Ownership Interests between Entities under Common Control

Not in Codification

90-6

Accounting for Certain Events Not Addressed in Issue No. 87-11 Relating to an Acquired Operating Unit to Be Sold

Nullified by FAS-144.

90-7

Accounting for a Reload Stock Option

Nullified by FAS-123(R), except for nonpublic entities under the scope of paragraph 83 of FAS-123(R).

90-8

Capitalization of Costs to Treat Environmental Contamination

Capitalization and Expense Recognition Concepts, ch.7

90-9

Changes to Fixed Employee Stock Option Plans as a Result of Equity Restructuring

Nullified by FIN-44.

90-10

Accounting for a Business Combination Involving a Majority-Owned Investee of a Venture Capital Company

Resolved by FAS-141.

90-11	Accounting for Exit and Entrance Fees Incurred in a Conversion from the Savings Association Insurance Fund to the Bank Insurance Fund	No longer useful.
90-12	Allocating Basis to Individual Assets and Liabilities for Transactions within the Scope of Issue No. 88-16	Nullified by FAS-141(R).
90-13	Accounting for Simultaneous Common Control Mergers	Not in Codification
90-14	Unsecured Guarantee by Parent of Subsidiary's Lease Payments in a Sale-Leaseback Transaction	Leases, ch. 26
90-15	Impact of Nonsubstantive Lessors, Residual Value Guarantees, and Other Provisions in Leasing Transactions	Nullified by FIN-46 and FIN-46(R) for entities under their scope.
90-16	Accounting for Discontinued Operations Subsequently Retained	Nullified by FAS-144.
90-17	Hedging Foreign Currency Risk with Purchased Options	Affirmed by FAS-133.
90-18	Effect of a "Removal of Accounts" Provision on the Accounting for a Credit Card Securitization	Not in Codification
90-19	Convertible Bonds with Issuer Option to Settle for Cash upon Conversion	Nullified by FSP APB-14-1.
90-20	Impact of an Uncollateralized Irrevocable Letter of Credit on a Real Estate Sale-Leaseback Transaction	Leases, ch. 26
90-21	Balance Sheet Treatment of a Sale of Mortgage Servicing Rights with a Subservicing Agreement	Transfer and Servicing of Financial Assets, ch. 40
90-22	Accounting for Gas-Balancing Arrangements	Revenue Recognition, ch. 36
91-1	Hedging Intercompany Foreign Currency Risks	Nullified by FAS-133.

91-2

Debtor's Accounting for Forfeiture of Real Estate Subject to a Nonrecourse Mortgage	No consensus. SEC and FASB staffs agree that FAS-15 applies.

91-3

Accounting for Income Tax Benefits from Bad Debts of a Savings and Loan Association	No consensus. Resolved by FAS-109 with additional guidance in SEC SAB-91.

91-4

Hedging Foreign Currency Risks with Complex Options and Similar Transactions	Resolved by FAS-133.

91-5

Nonmonetary Exchange of Cost-Method Investments	Business Combinations, ch. 6

91-6

Revenue Recognition of Long-Term Power Sales Contracts	Revenue Recognition, ch. 36

91-7

Accounting for Pension Benefits Paid by Employers after Insurance Companies Fail to Provide Annuity Benefits	Pension Plans—Settlements and Curtailments, ch. 30

91-8

Application of FASB Statement No. 96 to a State Tax Based on the Greater of a Franchise Tax or an Income Tax	Income Taxes, ch. 20

91-9

Revenue and Expense Recognition for Freight Services in Process	Revenue Recognition, ch. 36

91-10

Accounting for Special Assessments and Tax Increment Financing Entities	Contingencies, Risks, and Uncertainties, ch. 11

92-1

Allocation of Residual Value or First-Loss Guarantee to Minimum Lease Payments in Leases Involving Land and Building(s)	Leases, ch. 26

92-2

Measuring Loss Accruals by Transferors for Transfers of Receivables with Recourse	Not in Codification

92-3

Earnings-per-Share Treatment of Tax Benefits for Dividends on Unlocated Stock Held by an Employee Stock Ownership Plan (Consideration of the Implications of FASB Statement No. 109 on Issue 2 of EITF Issue No. 90-4)	Stock-Based Payments, ch. 38

92-4

Accounting for a Change in Functional Currency When an Economy Ceases to Be Considered Highly Inflationary — Foreign Operations and Exchange, ch. 18

92-5

Amortization Period for Net Deferred Credit Card Origination Costs — Financial Instruments, ch. 17

92-6

Not used.

92-7

Accounting by Rate-Regulated Utilities for the Effects of Certain Alternative Revenue Programs — Revenue Recognition, ch. 36

92-8

Accounting for the Income Tax Effects under FASB Statement No. 109 of a Change in Functional Currency When an Economy Ceases to Be Considered Highly Inflationary — Foreign Operations and Exchange, ch. 18

92-9

Accounting for the Present Value of Future Profits Resulting from the Acquisition of a Life Insurance Company — Nullified by FAS-141(R).

92-10

Loan Acquisitions Involving Table Funding Arrangements — Nullified by FAS-125.

92-11

Not used.

92-12

Accounting for OPEB Costs by Rate-Regulated Enterprises — Postemployment and Postretirement Benefits Other Than Pensions, ch. 32

92-13

Accounting for Estimated Payments in Connection with the Coal Industry Retiree Health Benefit Act of 1992 — Contingencies, Risks, and Uncertainties, ch. 12

93-1

Accounting for Individual Credit Card Acquisitions — Financial Instruments, ch. 17

93-2

Effect of Acquisition of Employer Shares for/by an Employee Benefit Trust on Accounting for Business Combinations — Resolved by FAS-141.

93-3

Plan Assets under FASB Statement No. 106 — Postemployment and Postretirement Benefits Other Than Pensions, ch. 32

93-4

Accounting for Regulatory Assets	See Subsequent Development in Issue 92-12. Postemployment and Postretirement Benefits Other Than Pensions, ch. 32.

93-5

Accounting for Environmental Liabilities	Incorporated in and nullified by SOP 96-1.

93-6

Accounting for Multiple-Year Retrospectively Rated Contracts by Ceding and Assuming Enterprises	Not discussed in this Guide.

93-7

Uncertainties Related to Income Taxes in a Purchase Business Combination	Nullified by FAS-141(R).

93-8

Accounting for the Sale and Leaseback of an Asset That Is Leased to Another Party	Leases, ch. 26

93-9

Application of FASB Statement No. 109 in Foreign Financial Statements Restated for General Price-Level Changes	Income Taxes, ch. 20

93-10

Accounting for Dual Currency Bonds	Resolved by FAS-133.

93-11

Accounting for Barter Transactions Involving Barter Credits	Nonmonetary Transactions, ch. 28

93-12

Recognition and Measurement of the Tax Benefit of Excess Tax-Deductible Goodwill Resulting from a Retroactive Change in Tax Law	Not in Codification

93-13

Effect of a Retroactive Change in Enacted Tax Rates That Is Included in Income from Continuing Operations	Income Taxes, ch. 20

93-14

Accounting for Multiple-Year Retrospectively Rated Insurance Contracts by Insurance Enterprises and Other Enterprises	Not discussed in this Guide.

93-15

Not used.

93-16

| Application of FASB Statement No. 109 to Basis Differences within Foreign Subsidiaries That Meet the Indefinite Reversal Criterion of APB Opinion No. 23 | Income Taxes, ch. 20 |

93-17

| Recognition of Deferred Tax Assets for a Parent Company's Excess Tax Basis in the Stock of a Subsidiary That Is Accounted for as a Discontinued Operation | Income Taxes, ch. 20 |

93-18

| Recognition of Impairment for an Investment in a Collateralized Mortgage Obligation Instrument or in a Mortgage-Backed Interest-Only Certificate | Superseded by Issue 99-20. |

94-1

| Accounting for Tax Benefits Resulting from Investments in Affordable Housing Projects | Real Estate Transactions, ch. 33 |

94-2

| Treatment of Minority Interests in Certain Real Estate Investment Trusts | Nullified by FAS-160. |

94-3

| Liability Recognition for Certain Employee Termination Benefits and Other Costs to Exit an Activity (including Certain Costs Incurred in a Restructuring) | Nullified by FAS-146. |

94-4

| Classification of an Investment in a Mortgage-Backed Interest-Only Certificate as Held-to-Maturity | Resolved by FAS-125. |

94-5

| Determination of What Constitutes All Risks and Rewards and No Significant Unresolved Contingencies in a Sale of Mortgage Loan Servicing Rights under Issue No. 89-5 | Superseded by Issue 95-5. |

94-6

| Accounting for the Buyout of Compensatory Stock Options | Nullified by FIN-44. |

94-7

| Accounting for Financial Instruments Indexed to, and Potentially Settled in, a Company's Own Stock | Codified in Issue 93-13, which has been codified in Issue 00-19. |

94-8

| Accounting for Conversion of a Loan into a Debt Security in a Debt Restructuring | Troubled Debt Restructuring, ch. 41 |

94-9

Determining a Normal Servicing Fee Rate for the Sale of an SBA Loan — Nullified by FAS-125.

94-10

Accounting by a Company for the Income Tax Effects of Transactions among or with Its Shareholders under FASB Statement No. 109 — Income Taxes, ch. 20

95-1

Revenue Recognition on Sales with a Guaranteed Minimum Resale Value — Revenue Recognition, ch. 36

95-2

Determination of What Constitutes a Firm Commitment for Foreign Currency Transactions Not Involving a Third Party — Nullified by FAS-133.

95-3

Recognition of Liabilities in Connection with a Purchase Business Combination — Nullified by FAS-141(R).

95-4

Revenue Recognition on Equipment Sold and Subsequently Repurchased Subject to an Operating Lease — Revenue Recognition, ch. 36

95-5

Determination of What Risks and Rewards, If Any, Can Be Retained and Whether Any Unresolved Contingencies May Exist in a Sale of Mortgage Loan Servicing Rights — Transfer and Servicing of Financial Assets, ch. 40

95-6

Accounting by a Real Estate Investment Trust for an Investment in a Service Corporation — Real Estate Transactions, ch. 33

95-7

Implementation Issues Related to the Treatment of Minority Interests in Certain Real Estate Investment Trusts — Nullified by FAS-160.

95-8

Accounting for Contingent Consideration Paid to the Shareholders of an Acquired Enterprise in a Purchase Business Combination — Nullified by FAS-141(R).

95-9

Accounting for Tax Effects of Dividends in France in Accordance with FASB Statement No. 109 — Income Taxes, ch. 20

95-10

Accounting for Tax Credits Related to Dividend Payments in Accordance with FASB Statement No. 109

Income Taxes, ch. 20

95-11

Accounting for Derivative Instruments Containing both a Written Option-Based Component and a Forward-Based Component

Resolved by FAS-133.

95-12

Pooling of Interests with a Common Investment in a Joint Venture

Nullified by FAS-141.

95-13

Classification of Debt Issue Costs in the Statement of Cash Flows

Cash Flow Statement, ch. 8

95-14

Recognition of Liabilities in Anticipation of a Business Combination

Nullified by FAS-146.

95-15

Recognition of Gain or Loss When a Binding Contract Requires a Debt Extinguishment to Occur at a Future Date for a Specified Amount

Superseded by Issue 96-19.

95-16

Accounting for Stock Compensation Arrangements with Employer Loan Features under APB Opinion No. 25

Nullified by FAS-123(R), except for nonpublic entities under the scope of paragraph 83 of FAS-123(R).

95-17

Accounting for Modifications to an Operating Lease That Do Not Change the Lease Classification

Leases, ch. 26

95-18

Accounting and Reporting for a Discontinued Business Segment When the Measurement Date Occurs after the Balance Sheet Date but before the Issuance of Financial Statements

Nullified by FAS-144.

95-19

Determination of the Measurement Date for the Market Price of Securities Issued in Purchase Business Combination

Codified in Issue 99-12.

95-20

Measurement in the Consolidated Financial Statements of a Parent of the Tax Effects Related to the Operations of a Foreign Subsidiary That Receives Tax Credits Related to Dividend Payments

Income Taxes, ch. 20

95-21

Accounting for Assets to Be Disposed of Acquired in a Purchase Business Combination	Resolved by FAS-144.

95-22

Balance Sheet Classification of Borrowings Outstanding under Revolving Credit Agreements That Include both a Subjective Acceleration Clause and a Lock-Box Arrangement	Balance Sheet Classification and Related Display Issues, ch. 4

95-23

The Treatment of Certain Site Restoration/Environmental Exit Costs When Testing a Long-Lived Asset for Impairment	Impairment of Long-Lived Assets, ch. 19

96-1

Sale of Put Options on Issuer's Stock That Require Or Permit Cash Settlement	Codified in Issue 00-19.

96-2

Impairment Recognition When a Nonmonetary Asset Is Exchanged or Is Distributed to Owners and Is Accounted for at the Asset's Recorded Amount	Codified in Issue 01-2.

96-3

Accounting for Equity Instruments That Are Issued for Consideration Other Than Employee Services under FASB Statement No.123	Superseded by Issue 96-18.

96-4

Accounting for Reorganizations Involving a Non–Pro Rata Split-off of Certain Nonmonetary Assets to Owners	Codified in Issue 01-2.

96-5

Recognition of Liabilities for Contractual Termination Benefits or Changing Benefit Plan Assumptions in Anticipation of a Business Combination	Business Combinations, ch. 6

96-6

Accounting for the Film and Software Costs Associated with Developing Entertainment and Educational Software Products	Computer Software, ch. 9

96-7

Accounting for Deferred Taxes on In-Process Research and Development Activities Acquired in a Purchase Business Combination	Nullified by FAS-141(R).

Cross-Reference **CR.65**

96-8

Accounting for a Business Combination When the Issuing Company Has Targeted Stock

Nullified by FAS-141.

96-9

Classification of Inventory Markdowns and Other Costs Associated with a Restructuring

Results of Operations, ch. 35

96-10

Impact of Certain Transactions on the Held-to-Maturity Classification under FASB Statement No. 115

Investments in Debt and Equity Securities, ch. 25

96-11

Accounting for Forward Contracts and Purchased Options to Acquire Securities Covered by FASB Statement No. 115

Investments in Debt and Equity Securities, ch. 25

96-12

Recognition of Interest Income and Balance Sheet Classification of Structured Notes

Financial Instruments, ch. 17

96-13

Accounting for Derivative Financial Instruments Indexed to, and Potentially Settled in, a Company's Own Stock

Codified in Issue 00-19.

96-14

Accounting for the Costs Associated with Modifying Computer Software for the Year 2000

No longer useful.

96-15

Accounting for the Effects of Changes in Foreign Currency Exchange Rates on Foreign-Currency-Denominated Available-for-Sale Debt Securities

Foreign Operations and Exchange, ch. 18

96-16

Investor's Accounting for an Investee When the Investor Has a Majority of the Voting Interest but the Minority Shareholder or Shareholders Have Certain Approval or Veto Rights

Consolidated Financial Statements, ch. 10

96-17

Revenue Recognition under Long-Term Power Sales Contracts That Contain both Fixed and Variable Pricing Terms

Revenue Recognition, ch. 36

96-18

Accounting for Equity Instruments That Are Issued to Other Than Employees for Acquiring, or in Conjunction with Selling, Goods or Services

Stock-Based Payments, ch. 38

96-19
Debtor's Accounting for a Modification or Exchange of Debt Instruments — Extinguishment of Debt, ch. 15

96-20
Impact of FASB Statement No. 25 on Consolidation of Special Purpose Entities — Nullified by FAS-140.

96-21
Implementation Issues in Accounting for Leasing Transactions Involving Special-Purpose Entities — Leases, ch. 26

96-22
Applicability of the Disclosures Required by FASB Statement No. 114 When a Loan Is Restructured in a Troubled Debt Restructuring into Two (or More) Loans — Troubled Debt Restructuring, ch. 41

96-23
The Effects of Financial Instruments Indexed to, and Settled in, a Company's Own Stock on Pooling-of-Interests Accounting for a Subsequent Business Combination — Resolved by FAS-141.

97-1
Implementation Issues in Accounting for Lease Transactions, Including Those Involving Special-Purpose Entities — Leases, ch. 26

97-2
Application of FASB Statement No. 94 and APB Opinion No. 16 to Physician Practice Management Entities and Certain Other Entities with Contractual Management Arrangements — Consolidated Financial Statements, ch. 10

97-3
Accounting for Fees and Costs Associated with Loan Syndications and Loan Participations after the Issuance of FASB Statement No. 125 — Transfer and Servicing of Financial Assets, ch. 40

97-4
Deregulation of the Pricing of Electricity— Issues Related to the Application of FASB Statements No. 71 and 101 — Not discussed.

97-5
Accounting for the Delayed Receipt of Option Shares upon Exercise under APB Opinion No.25 — Nullified by FAS-123(R), except for entities under the scope of paragraph 83 of FAS-123(R).

Cross-Reference CR.67

97-6

Application of Issue No. 96-20 to Qualifying Special-Purpose Entities Receiving Transferred Financial Assets Prior to the Effective Date of FASB Statement No. 125 — Nullified by FAS-140.

97-7

Accounting for Hedges of the Foreign Currency Risk Inherent in an Available for-Sale Marketable Equity Security — Not in Codification

97-8

Accounting for Contingent Consideration Issued in a Purchase Business Combination — Nullified by FAS-141(R).

97-9

Effect on Pooling-of-Interests Accounting of Certain Contingently Exercisable Options or Other Equity Instruments — Nullified by FAS-141.

97-10

The Effect of Lessee Involvement in Asset Construction — Leases, ch. 26

97-11

Accounting for Internal Costs Relating to Real Estate Property Acquisitions — Capitalization and Expense Recognition Concepts, ch. 7

97-12

Accounting for Increased Share Authorizations in an IRS Section 423 Employee Stock Purchase Plan under APB Opinion No. 25 — Nullified by FAS-123(R), except for nonpublic entities under the scope of paragraph 83 of FAS-123(R).

97-13

Accounting for Costs Incurred in Connection with a Consulting Contract or an Internal Project That Combines Business Process Reengineering and Information Technology Transformation — Capitalization and Expense Recognition Concepts, ch. 7

97-14

Accounting for Deferred Compensation Arrangements Where Amounts Earned Are Held in a Rabbi Trust and Invested — Consolidated Financial Statements, ch. 10

97-15

Accounting for Contingency Arrangements Based on Security Prices in a Purchase Business Combination — Nullified by FAS-141(R).

98-1

Valuation of Debt Assumed in a Purchase Business Combination — Nullified by FAS-141(R).

98-2

Accounting by a Subsidiary or Joint Venture for an Investment in the Stock of Its Parent Company or Joint Venture Partner	Not in Codification

98-3

Determining Whether a Nonmonetary Transaction Involves Receipt of Productive Assets or of a Business	Nullified by FAS-141(R).

98-4

Accounting by a Joint Venture for Business Received at Its Formation	Removed from EITF agenda; to be addressed in FASB's New Basis project.

98-5

Accounting for Convertible Securities with Beneficial Conversion Features or Contingently Adjustable Conversion Ratios	Convertible Debt and Debt with Warrants, ch. 12

98-6

Investor's Accounting for an Investment in a Limited Partnership When the Investor Is the Sole General Partner and the Limited Partners Have Certain Approval or Veto Rights	No consensus.

98-7

Accounting for Exchanges of Similar Equity Method Investments	Codified in Issue 01-2.

98-8

Accounting for Transfers of Investments That Are in Substance Real Estate	Real Estate Transactions, ch. 33

98-9

Accounting for Contingent Rent	Leases, ch. 26

98-10

Accounting for Contracts Involved in Energy Trading and Risk Management Activities	Superseded by Issue 02-3.

98-11

Accounting for Acquired Temporary Differences in Certain Purchase Transactions That Are Not Accounted for as Business Combinations	Income Taxes, ch. 20

98-12

Application of Issue No. 96-13 to Forward Equity Sales Transactions	Nullified by FAS-150.

98-13
Accounting by an Equity Method Investor for Investee Losses When the Investor Has Loans to and Investments in Other Securities of the Investee

Equity Method, ch. 14

98-14
Debtor's Accounting for Changes in Line-of-Credit or Revolving-Debt Arrangements

Extinguishment of Debt, ch. 15

98-15
Structured Notes Acquired for a Specified Investment Strategy

Financial Instruments, ch. 17

99-1
Accounting for Debt Convertible into the Stock of a Consolidated Subsidiary

Convertible Debt and Debt with Warrants, ch. 12

99-2
Accounting for Weather Derivatives

Financial Instruments, ch. 17

99-3
Application of Issue No. 96-13 to Derivative Instruments with Multiple Settlement Alternatives

Codified in Issue 00-19.

99-4
Accounting for Stock Received from the Demutualization of a Mutual Insurance Company

Nonmonetary Transactions, ch. 28

99-5
Accounting for Pre-Production Costs Related to Long-Term Supply Arrangements

Capitalization and Expense Recognition Concepts, ch. 7

99-6
Impact of Acceleration Provisions in Grants Made between Initiation and Consummation of a Pooling-of-Interests Business Combination

Nullified by FAS-141.

99-7
Accounting for an Accelerated Share Repurchase Program

Stockholders' Equity, ch. 39

99-8
Accounting for Transfers of Assets That Are Derivative Instruments but That Are Not Financial Assets

Transfer and Servicing of Financial Assets, ch. 40

99-9
Effect of Derivative Gains and Losses on the Capitalization of Interest

Financial Instruments, ch. 17

99-10
Percentage Used to Determine the Amount of Equity Method Losses

Equity Method, ch. 14

99-11

Subsequent Events Caused by Year 2000 — No longer relevant.

99-12

Determination of the Measurement Date for the Market Price of Acquirer Securities Issued in a Purchase Business Combination — Nullified by FAS-141(R).

99-13

Application of Issue No. 97-10 and FASB Interpretation No. 23 to Entities That Enter into Leases with Governmental Entities — Leases, ch. 26

99-14

Recognition of Losses on Firmly Committed Executory Contracts — Removed from EITF agenda.

99-15

Accounting for Decreases in Deferred Tax Asset Valuation Allowances Established in a Purchase Business Combination As a Result of a Change in Tax Regulations — Nullified by FAS-141(R).

99-16

Accounting for Transactions with Elements of Research and Development Arrangements — Research and Development, ch. 34

99-17

Accounting for Advertising Barter Transactions — Nonmonetary Transactions, ch. 28

99-18

Effect on Pooling-of-Interests Accounting of Contracts Indexed to a Company's Own Stock — Resolved by FAS-141.

99-19

Reporting Revenue Gross as a Principal versus Net as an Agent — Revenue Recognition, ch. 36

99-20

Recognition of Interest Income and Impairment on Certain Investments — Transfer and Servicing of Financial Assets, ch. 40

00-1

Balance Sheet and Income Statement Display under the Equity Method for Investments in Certain Partnerships and Other Unincorporated Noncontrolled Ventures — Equity Method, ch. 14

00-2

Accounting for Web Site Development Costs Capitalization or Expense Recognition — Capitalization and Expense Recognition Concepts, ch. 7

00-3

Application of AICPA Statement of Position 97-2 to Arrangements That Include the Right to Use Software Stored on Another Entity's Hardware	Computer Software, ch. 9

00-4

Majority Owner's Accounting for the Minority Interest in a Subsidiary and a Derivative	Financial Instruments, ch. 17

00-5

Determining Whether a Nonmonetary Transaction Is an Exchange of Similar Productive Assets	Codified in Issue 01-2.

00-6

Accounting for Freestanding Derivative Financial Instruments Indexed to, and Potentially Settled in, the Stock of a Consolidated Subsidiary	Financial Instruments, ch. 17

00-7

Application of Issue No. 96-13 to Equity Derivative Transactions That Contain Certain Provisions That Require Net Cash Settlement If Certain Events outside the Control of the Issuer Occur	Codified in Issue 00-19.

00-8

Accounting by a Grantee for an Equity Instrument to Be Received in Conjunction with Providing Goods or Services	Stock-Based Payments, ch. 38

00-9

Classification of a Gain or Loss from a Hedge of Debt That Is Extinguished	Not in Codification

00-10

Accounting for Shipping and Handling Fees and Costs	Revenue Recognition, ch. 36

00-11

Meeting the Ownership Transfer Requirements of FASB Statement No. 13 for Leases of Real Estate	Leases, ch. 26

00-12

Accounting for Stock-Based Compensation Granted by an Investor to Employees of an Equity Method Investee	Equity Method, ch. 14

00-13

Determining Whether Equipment Is "Integral Equipment" Subject to FASB Statements No.66 and No. 98	Real Estate Transactions, ch. 33

00-14

Accounting for Certain Sales Incentives — Codified in Issue 01-9.

00-15

Classification in the Statement of Cash Flows of the Income Tax Benefit Received by a Company upon Exercise of a Nonqualified Employee Stock Options — Nullified by FAS-123(R), except for nonpublic entities under the scope of paragraph 83 of FAS-123(R).

00-16

Recognition and Measurement of Employer Payroll Taxes on Employee Stock-Based Compensation — Stock-Based Payments, ch. 38

00-17

Measuring the Fair Value of Energy-Related Contracts in Applying EITF Issue No. 98-10, "Accounting for Contracts Involved in EnergyTrading and Risk Management Activities" — Superseded by Issue 02-3.

00-18

Accounting Recognition for Certain Transactions Involving Equity Instruments Granted to Other Than Employees — Stock-Based Payments, ch. 38

00-19

Determination of Whether Share Settlement is within the Control of the Issuer for Purposes of Applying Issue 96-13 — Earnings per Share, ch. 13

Financial Instruments, ch. 17

00-20

Accounting for Costs incurred to Acquire or Originate Information for Database Content and Other Collections Information — No longer relevant.

00-21

Accounting for Revenue Arrangements with Multiple Elements — Revenue Recognition, ch. 36.

00-22

Accounting for "Points" and Certain Other Time-Based Sales Incentive Offers, and Offers for Free Products or Services to Be Delivered in the Future — Removed from EITF agenda.

00-23

Issues Related to the Accounting for Stock Compensation under APB Opinion No. 25, *Accounting for Stock Issued to Employees*, and FASB Interpretation No. 44, *Accounting for Certain Transactions Involving Stock Compensation* — Nullified by FAS-123(R), except for nonpublic entities under the scope of paragraph 83 of FAS-123(R).

00-24

Revenue Recognition: Sales Arrangements That Include Specified-Price Trade-in Rights — Removed from EITF agenda.

00-25

Vendor Income Statement Consideration from a Vendor to a Retailer — Codified in Issue 01-9.

00-26

Recognition by a Seller of Losses on Firmly Committed Executory Contracts — Removed from EITF agenda.

00-27

Application of Issue No. 98-5 to Certain Convertible Instruments — Convertible Debt and Debt with Warrants, ch. 12

01-1

Accounting for Convertible Instrument Granted or Issued to a Nonemployee for Goods or Services and Cash — Stock-Based Payments, ch. 38

01-2

Interpretations of APB Opinion No. 29, Accounting for Nonmonetary Transactions — Nonmonetary Transactions, ch. 28

01-3

Accounting in a Purchase Business Combination for Deferred Revenue of an Acquiree — Nullified by FAS-141(R).

01-4

Accounting for Sales of Fractional Interests in Equipment — Removed from EITF agenda.

01-5

Application of FASB Statement No. 52, *Foreign Currency Translation*, to an Investment Being Evaluated for Impairment That Will Be Disposed Of — Foreign Operations and Exchange, ch. 18

01-6

The Meaning of "Indexed to a Company's Own Stock" — Financial Instruments, ch. 17

01-7

Creditor's Accounting for a Modification or Exchange of Debt Instruments — Extinguishment of Debt, ch. 15

01-8

Determining Whether an Arrangement Is a Lease — Leases, ch. 26

01-9

Accounting for Consideration Given by a Vendor to a Customer or a Reseller of the Vendor's Products — Revenue Recognition, ch. 36

CR.74 *Cross-Reference*

01-10

Accounting for the Impact of the Terrorist Attacks of September 11, 2001	Not in Codification

01-11

Application of EITF Issue No. 00-19, "Accounting for Derivative Financial Instruments Indexed to, and Potentially Settled in, a Company's Own Stock," to a Contemporaneous Forward Purchase Contract and Written Put Option	Resolved by FAS-150.

01-12

The Impact of the Requirements of FASB Statement No. 133, *Accounting for Derivative Instruments and Hedging Activities*, on Residual Value Guarantees in Connection with a Lease	Leases, ch. 26

01-13

Income Statement Display of Business Interruption Insurance Recoveries	Results of Operations, ch. 35

01-14

Income Statement Characterization of Reimbursements Received for "Out-of-Pocket" Expenses Incurred	Results of Operations, ch. 35

02-2

When Certain Contracts That Meet the Definition of Financial Instruments Should Be Combined for Accounting Purposes	Removed from EITF agenda. Partially resolved by FAS-150.

02-3

Issues Involved in Accounting for Derivative Contracts Held for Trading Purposes and Contracts Involved in Energy Trading and Risk Management	Financial Instruments, ch. 17

02-4

Debtor's Accounting for a Modification or an Exchange of Debt Instruments in accordance with FASB Statement No. 15, *Accounting by Debtors and Creditors for Troubled Debt Restructurings*	No consensus.

02-5

Definition of "Common Control" in Relation to FASB Statement No. 141, *Business Combinations*	Not in Codification

02-6

Classification of Cash Flows of Payments Made to Settle an Asset Retirement Obligation within the Scope of FASB Statement No. 143, *Accounting for Asset Retirement Obligations*	Cash Flow Statement, ch. 8

02-7

Unit of Accounting for Testing Impairment of Indefinite-Lived Intangible Assets	Impairment of Long-Lived Assets, ch. 19

02-8

Accounting for Options Granted to Employees in Unrestricted, Publicly Traded Shares of an Unrelated Entity	Stock-Based Payments, ch. 38

02-9

Accounting for Changes That Result in a Transferor Regaining Control of Financial Assets Sold	Transfer and Servicing of Financial Assets, ch. 40

02-10

Determining Whether a Debtor Is Legally Released as Primary Obligor When the Debtor Becomes Secondarily Liable Under the Original Obligation	Removed from EITF agenda.

02-11

Accounting for Reverse Spinoffs	Stockholders' Equity, ch. 39

02-12

Permitted Activities of a Qualifying Special-Purpose Entity in Issuing Beneficial Interests under FASB Statement No. 140, *Accounting for Transfers and Servicing of Financial Assets and Extinguishments Of Liabilities*	Nullified by FAS-166.

02-13

Deferred Income Tax Considerations in Applying the Goodwill Impairment Test in FASB Statement No. 142, *Goodwill and Other Intangible Assets*	Income Taxes, ch. 20

02-14

Whether the Equity Method of Accounting Applies When an Investor Does Not Have an Investment in Voting Stock of an Investee but Exercises Significant Influence Through Other Means	Equity Method, ch. 15

02-15

Determining Whether Certain Conversions of Convertible Debt to Equity Securities Are within the Scope of FASB Statement No. 84, *Induced Conversions of Convertible Debt*	Convertible Debt and Debt with Warrants, ch. 13

CR.76 *Cross-Reference*

02-16

Accounting by a Reseller for Cash Consideration Received from a Vendor	Revenue Recognition, ch. 36

02-17

Recognition of Customer Relationship Intangible Assets Acquired in a Business Combination	Nullified by FAS-141(R).

02-18

Accounting for Subsequent Investments in an Investee after Suspension of Equity Method Loss Recognition	Equity Method, ch. 14

03-1

The Meaning of Other-Than-Temporary Impairment and Its Application to Certain Investments	Nullified by FSP FAS 115-1 and FSP FAS 124-1

03-2

Accounting for the Transfer to the Japanese Government of the Substitutional Portion of Employee Pension Fund Liabilities	Pension Plans-Employers, ch. 29

03-3

Accounting for Claims-Made Insurance Policies by the Insured Entity	Codified in Issue 03-8.

03-4

Accounting for "Cash Balance" Pension Plans	Pension Plans—Employers, ch. 29

03-5

Applicability of AICPA Statement of Position 97-2, *Software Revenue Recognition*, to Non-Software Deliverables in an Arrangement Containing More-Than-Incidental Software	Computer Software, ch. 9

03-6

Participating Securities and the Two-Class Method under FASB Statement No. 128, *Earnings per Share*	Earnings per Share, ch. 13

03-7

Accounting for the Settlement of the Equity-Settled Portion of a Convertible Debt Instrument That Permits or Requires the Conversion Spread to Be Settled in Stock (Instrument C of Issue 90-19)	Nullified by FSP APB-14-1.

03-8

Accounting for Claims-Made Insurance and Retroactive Insurance Contracts by the Insured Entity	Contingencies, Risks, and Uncertainties, ch. 11

Cross-Reference CR.77

03-9

| Determination of the Useful Life of Renewable Intangible Assets under FASB Statement No. 142 | Removed from EITF agenda. |

03-10

| Application EITF Issue No. 02-16, "Accounting By a Customer (Including a Reseller) for Certain Consideration Received from a Vender," by Resellers to Sales Incentives Offered to Consumers by Manufacturers | Revenue Recognition, ch. 36 |

03-11

| Reporting Realized Gains and Losses on Derivative Instruments That Are Subject to FASB Statement No. 133, *Accounting for Derivative Instruments and Hedging Activities*, and Not "Held for Trading Purposes" as Defined in EITF Issue No. 02-3, "Issues Involved in Accounting for Derivative Contracts Held for Trading Purposes and Contracts Involved in Energy Trading and Risk Management Activities" | Financial Instruments, ch. 17 |

03-12

| Impact of FASB Interpretation No. 45 on Issue No. 95-1 | Revenue Recognition, ch. 36 |

03-13

| Applying the conditions in Paragraph 42 of FASB Statement No. 144 in Determining Whether to Report Discontinued Operations | Results of Operations, ch. 35 |

03-14

| Participants' Accounting for Emissions Allowances under a "Cap and Trade" Program | Removed from EITF agenda. |

03-15 Not used.

03-16

| Accounting for Investments in Limited Liability Companies | Equity Method, ch. 14 |

03-17

| Subsequent Accounting for Executory Contracts That Have Been Recognized on an Entity's Balance Sheet | Removed from EITF agenda. |

04-1

| Accounting for Pre-existing Contractual Relationships between the Parties to a Purchase Business Combination | Nullified by FAS-141(R). |

04-2

| Whether Mineral Rights Are Tangible or Intangible Assets and Related Issues | Nullified by FAS-141(R). |

04-3

Mining Assets: Impairment and Business Combinations	Business Combinations, ch. 6

04-4

Allocation of Goodwill to Reporting Units for a Mining Enterprise	Removed from EITF agenda.

04-5

Investor's Accounting for an Investment in a Limited Partnership When the Investor Is the Sole General Partner and the Limited Partners Have Certain Rights	Consolidated Financial Statements, ch. 10

04-6

Accounting for Stripping Costs Incurred during Production in the Mining Industry	Inventory, ch. 24

04-7

Determining Whether an Interest Is a Variable Interest In a Potential Variable Interest Entity	Removed from EITF agenda.
	See FSP FIN-46(R)-6.

04-8

The Effect of Contingently Convertible Debt on Diluted Earnings per Share	Earnings per Share, ch. 13

04-9

Accounting for Suspended Well Costs	Resolved by FSP FAS 19-1.

04-10

Determining Whether to Aggregate Operating Segments That Do Not Meet the Quantitative Thresholds	Segment Reporting, ch. 37

04-11

Accounting in a Business Combination for Deferred Postcontract Customer Support Revenue of a Software Vendor	Removed from EITF agenda.

04-12

Determining Whether Equity-Based Compensation Awards Are Participating Securities	Removed from EITF agenda.

04-13

Accounting for Purchases and Sales of Inventory with the Same Counterparty	Nonmonetary Transactions, ch. 28

05-1

Accounting for the Conversion of an Instrument That Becomes Convertible upon the Issuer's Exercise of a Call Option

Convertible Debt and Debt with Warrants, ch. 12

05-2

The Meaning of "Conventional Convertible Debt Instrument" in EITF Issue 00-19, "Accounting for Derivative Financial Instruments Indexed to and Potentially Settled in, a Company's Own Stock"

Financial Instruments, ch. 17

05-3

Accounting for Rental Costs Incurred During the Construction Period

Removed from EITF agenda. See FSP FAS 13-1.

05-4

The Effect of a Liquidated Damages Clause on a Freestanding Financial Instrument Subject to EITF Issue No. 00-19, "Accounting for Derivative Financial Instruments Indexed to, and Potentially Settled in, a Company's Own Stock"

Removed from EITF's agenda.

05-5

Accounting for Early Retirement or Postemployment Programs with Specific Features (such as Term Specified in Altersteilzeit [ATZ] Early Retirement Arrangements)

Pension Plans—Employers ch. 29

05-6

Determining the Amortization Period for Leasehold Improvements

Leases, ch. 26

05-7

Accounting for Modifications to Conversion Options Embedded in Debt Instruments and Related Issues

Superseded by Issue 06-6.

05-8

Income Tax Consequences of Issuing Convertible Debt with a Beneficial Conversion Feature

Income Taxes, ch. 20

06-1

Accounting for Consideration Given by a Service Provider to Manufacturers or Resellers of Equipment Necessary for an End-Customer to Receive Service from the Service Provider

Revenue Recognition, ch. 36

06-2

Accounting for Sabbatical Leave and Other Similar Benefits Pursuant to FASB Statement No. 43,"Accounting for Compensated Absences"

Results of Operations, ch. 35

CR.80 Cross-Reference

06-3

How Taxes Collected from Customers and Remitted to Governmental Authorities Should be Presented in the Income Statement (That Is, Gross versus Net Presentation)

Results of Operations, ch. 35

06-4

Accounting for Deferred Compensation and Postretirement Benefit Aspects of Endorsement Split-Dollar Life Insurance Arrangements

Postemployment and Postretirement Benefits Other Than Pensions, ch. 32

06-5

Accounting for Purchases of Life Insurance—Determining the Amount That Could Be Realized in Accordance with FASB Technical Bulletin No. 85-4

Balance Sheet Classification, ch. 4

06-6

Debtor's Accounting for a Modification (or Exchange) of Convertible Debt

Extinguishment of Debt, ch. 15

06-7

Issuer's Accounting for a Previously Bifurcated Conversion Option in a Convertible Debt Instrument When the Conversion Option No Longer Meets the Bifurcation Criteria in FASB Statement No. 133, *Accounting for Derivative Instruments and Hedging Activities*

Convertible Debt and Debt with Warrants, ch. 12

06-8

Applicability of the Assessment of a Buyer's Continuing Investment under FASB Statement No. 66, *Accounting for Sales of Real Estate*, for Sales of Condominiums

Real Estate Transactions, ch. 33

06-9

Reporting a Change in (or the Elimination of) a Previously Existing Difference between the Fiscal Year-End of a Parent Company and That of a Consolidated Entity or between the Reporting Period of an Investor and That of an Equity Method Investee

Accounting Changes, ch. 1

06-10

Accounting for Deferred Compensation and Postretirement Benefit Aspects of Collateral Assignment Split-Dollar Life Insurance Arrangements

Postemployment and Postretirement Benefits Other Than Pensions ch. 32

06-11

| Accounting for Income Tax Benefits of Dividends on Share-Based Payment Awards | Income Taxes, ch. 20 |

06-12

| Accounting for Physical Commodity Inventories for Entities within the Scope of the AICPA Audit and Accounting Guide, *Brokers and Dealers in Securities* | Not in Codification. |

07-1

| Accounting for Collaborative Arrangements Related to the Development and Commercialization of Intellectual Property | Results of Operations, ch. 35 |

07-2

| Accounting for Convertible Debt Instruments That Require or Permit Partial Cash Settlement upon Conversion | Removed from EITF's agenda. |

07-3

| Accounting for Advance Payments for Goods or Services to Be Used in Future Research and Development Activities | Research and Development, ch. 34 |

07-4

| Application of the Two-Class Method under FASB Statement No. 128, *Earnings per Share*, to Master Limited Partnerships | Earnings per Share, ch. 13 |

07-5

| Determining Whether an Instrument (or Embedded Features) Is Indexed to an Entity's Own Stock | Financial Instruments, ch. 17 |

07-6

| Accounting for the Sale of Real Estate Subject to the Requirements of FASB Statement No. 66, *Accounting for Sales of Real Estate*, When the Agreement Includes a Buy-Sell Clause | Real Estate Transactions, ch. 33 |

08-1 (ASU 2009-13)

| Revenue Arrangements with Multiple Deliverables | Revenue Recognition, ch. 36 |

08-2

| Lessor Revenue Recognition for Maintenance Services | Removed from the EITF's agenda. |

08-3

| Accounting by Lessees for Maintenance Deposits under Lease Arrangements | Leases, ch. 26 |

08-4

| Transition Guidance for Conforming Changes to Issue No. 98-5 | Convertible Debt and Debt with Warrants, ch. 12 |

08-5

| Issuer's Accounting for Liabilities Measured at Fair Value with a Third-Party Guarantee | Fair Value, ch. 16 |

08-6

| Equity Method Investment Accounting Considerations | Equiity Method, ch. 14 |

08-7

| Accounting for Defensive Intangible Assets | Intangible Assets, ch. 23 |

08-8

| Accounting for an Instrument (or an Embedded Feature) with a Settlement Amount That Is Based on the Stock of an Entity's Consolidated Subsidiary | Consolidated Financial Statements, ch. 10 |

08-9 (ASU 2010- 17)

| Milestone Method of Revenue Recognition | Revenue Recognition, ch. 36 |

08-10

| Selected Statement 160 Implementation Questions | Not in Codification |

09-1

| Accounting for Own-Share Lending Arrangements in Contemplation of Convertible Debt Issuance | Convertible Debt and Debt with Warrants, ch. 12 |

09-2

| Research and Development Assets Acquired in an Asset Acquisition | Removed from the EITF's agenda. |

09-3 (ASU 2009- 14)

| Applicability of SOP 97-2 to Certain Arrangements That Include Software Elements | Computer Software, ch. 9 |

09-4

| Seller Accounting for Contingent Consideration | Under Discussion |

09-B (ASU 2010-15)

| Consideration of an Insurer's Accounting For Majority-Owned Investments When the Ownership Is through a Separate Account | Consolidation, ch. 10 |

09-D

| Application of the AICPA Audit and Accounting Guide, *Investment Companies*, by Real Estate Investment Companies | Under discussion |

09-E (ASU 2010-1)

Accounting for Distributions to Shareholders With Components of Stock and Cash	Stockholders' Equity, ch. 39

09-F (ASU 2010-16)

Accruals for Casino Jackpot Liabilities	Revenue Recognition, ch. 36

09-G

Accruals for Casino Jackpot Liabilities	Revenue Recognition, ch. 36

09-G

Accounting for Costs Associated With Acquiring or Renewing Insurance Contracts	Under discussion

09-H

Health Care Enitites: Revenue Recognition	Under discussion

09-I (ASU 2010-18)

Effect of a Loan Modification When the Loan Is Part of a Pool That is Accounted for as a Single Asset	Troubled Debt Restructuring, ch. 41

09-J (ASU 2010-13)

Effect of Denominating the Exercise Price of a Share-Based Payment Award in the Currency of The Market in Which the Underlying Equity Security Trades	Share-Based Payments, ch. 38

09-K (ASU 2010-24)

Health Care Entities: Presentation of Insurance Claims and Related Insurance Recoveries	Results of Operations, ch. 35

09-L (ASU 2010-23)

Health Care Entities: Measuring Charity Care For Disclosure	Results of Operations, ch. 35

10-A

How the Carrying Amount of a Reporting Unit Should Be Calculated When Performing Step 1 of the Goodwill Impairment Test	Under discussion

Issue 10-B

Accounting for Multiple Foreign Exchange Rates	Under discussion

Issue 10-C

Reporting Loans to Participants by Defined Contribution Pension Plans	Under discussion

10-D

Accounting for Certain Fees Associated with Recently Enacted Health Care Legislation	Under discussion

CR.84   *Cross-Reference*

10-E

Debtor's Accounting for Real Estate Subject to a Nonrecourse Mortgage in Default Prior to Forfeiture	Under discussion

SEC/FASB STAFF ANNOUNCEMENTS

ORIGINAL PRONOUNCEMENT	2011 *GAAP GUIDE* VOLUME II REFERENCE
D-1	
Implications and Implementation of an EITF Consensus	Accounting Changes, ch. 1
D-2	
Applicability of FASB Statement No. 65 to Savings and Loan Associations	Not discussed in this Guide.
D-3	
International Loan Swaps	No longer relevant.
D-4	
Argentine Government Guarantee of U.S. Dollar-Denominated Loans to the Argentine Private Sector	Not discussed.
D-5	
Extraordinary Treatment Related to Abandoned Nuclear Power Plants	Resolved by FAS-90.
D-6	
Income Capital Certificates and Permanent Income Capital Certificates	No longer relevant.
D-7	
Adjustment of Deferred Taxes to Reflect Change in Income Tax Rate	Resolved by FAS-109.
D-8	
Accruing Bad-Debt Expense at Inception of a Lease	Not in Codification
D-9	
Lessor Accounting under FASB Statement No. 91	Resolved by FAS-98.
D-10	
Required Use of Interest Method in Recognizing Interest Income	Financial Instruments, ch. 17
D-11	
Impact of Stock Market Decline	Investments in Debt and Equity Securities, ch. 25
D-12	
Foreign Currency Translation—Selection of Exchange Rate When Trading Is Temporarily Suspended	Foreign Operations and Exchange, ch. 18

Cross-Reference CR.85

D-13

Transfers of Receivables in Which Risk of Foreign Currency Fluctuation is Retained — Superseded by FAS-125.

D-14

Transactions Involving Special-Purpose Entities — Nullified by FIN-46 and FIN-46(R).

D-15

Earnings-per-Share Presentation for Securities Not Specifically Covered by APB Opinion No.15 — Rescinded by SEC staff because FAS-128 issued.

D-16

Hedging Foreign Currency Risks of Future Net Income, Revenues, or Costs — Nullified by FAS-133.

D-17

Continued Applicability of the FASB Special Report on Implementation of Statement 96 — Nullified by FAS-109.

D-18

Accounting for Compensation Expense If Stock Appreciation Rights Are Cancelled — Nullified by FAS-123(R).

D-19

Impact on Pooling-of-Interests Accounting of Treasury Shares Acquired to Satisfy Conversions in a Leveraged Preferred Stock ESOP — Nullified by FAS-141.

D-20

Disclosure of Components of Deferred Tax Expense — No longer relevant.

D-21

Phase-in Plans When Two Plants Are Completed at Different Times but Share Common Facilities — Not discussed in this Guide.

D-22

Questions Related to the Implementation of FASB Statement No. 105 — Nullified by FAS-133.

D-23

Subjective Acceleration Clauses and Debt Classification — Balance Sheet Classification and Related Display Issues, ch. 4

D-24

Sale-Leaseback Transactions with Continuing Involvement — Leases, ch. 26

D-25

Application of APB Opinion No. 10, Paragraph 7, to Market Values Recognized for Off-Balance-Sheet Financial Instruments — Superseded by FIN 39.

CR.86 Cross-Reference

D-26

SEC Disclosure Requirements Prior to Adoption of Standard on Accounting for Postretirement Benefits Other Than Pensions

No longer relevant.

D-27

Accounting for the Transfer of Excess Pension Assets to a Retiree Health Care Benefits Account

Pension Plans—Employers, ch. 29

D-28

SEC Disclosure Requirements prior to Adoption of Standard on Accounting for Income Taxes

No longer relevant.

D-29

Implementation of FASB Statement No. 107.

No longer relevant.

D-30

Adjustment Due to Effect of a Change in Tax Laws or Rates

Income Taxes, ch. 20

D-31

Temporary Differences Related to LIFO Inventory and Tax-to-Tax Differences

Income Taxes, ch. 20

D-32

Intraperiod Tax Allocation of the TaxEffect of Pretax Income from Continuing Operations

Income Taxes, ch. 20

D-33

Timing of Recognition of Tax Benefits for Pre-reorganization Temporary Differences and Carryforwards

Income Taxes, ch. 20

D-34

Accounting for Reinsurance: Questions and Answers about FASB Statement No. 113

Not discussed in this Guide.

D-35

FASB Staff Views on Issue No. 93-6, "Accounting for Multiple-Year Retrospectively Rated Contracts by Ceding and Assuming Enterprises"

Not discussed in this Guide.

D-36

Selection of Discount Rates Used for Measuring Defined Benefit Pension Obligations and Obligations of Postretirement Benefit Plans Other Than Pensions

Pension Plans—Employers, ch. 29

D-37

Classification of In-Substance Foreclosed Assets

Nullified by FAS-114.

Cross-Reference **CR.87**

D-38

Reclassification of Securities in Anticipation of Adoption of FASB Statement No. 115 — No longer relevant.

D-39

Questions Related to the Implementation of FASB Statement No. 115 — **Investments in Debt and Equity Securities, ch. 25**

D-40

Planned Sale of Securities following a Business Combination Expected to Be Accounted for as a Pooling of Interests — Superseded by FAS-141.

D-41

Adjustments in Assets and Liabilities for Holding Gains and Losses as Related to the Implementation of FASB Statement No. 115 — **Investments in Debt and Equity Securities, ch. 25**

D-42

The Effect on the Calculation of Earnings per Share for the Redemption or Induced Conversion of Preferred Stock — Earnings per Share, ch. 13

D-43

Assurance That a Right of Setoff Is Enforceable in a Bankruptcy under FASB Interpretation No. 39 — Results of Operations, ch. 35

D-44

Recognition of Other-Than-Temporary Impairment upon the Planned Sale of a Security Whose Cost Exceeds Fair Value — Nullified by FSP FAS 115-1 and FSP FAS 124-1.

D-45

Implementation of FASB Statement No. 121 for Assets to Be Disposed Of — Superseded by FAS-144.

D-46

Accounting for Limited Partnership Investments — Equity Method, ch. 14

D-47

Accounting for the Refund of Bank Insurance Fund and Savings Association Insurance Fund Premiums — Not discussed in this Guide.

D-48

The Applicability of FASB Statement No. 65 to Mortgage-Backed Securities That Are Held to Maturity — Superseded by FAS-125.

CR.88   *Cross-Reference*

D-49

Classifying Net Appreciation on Investments of a Donor-Related Endowment Fund	Not discussed in this Guide.

D-50

Classification of Gains and Losses from the Termination of an Interest Rate Swap Designated to Commercial Paper	Superseded by ASU 2010-4

D-51

The Applicability of FASB Statement No. 115 to Desecuritizations of Financial Assets	Investments in Debt and Equity Securities, ch. 25

D-52

Impact of FASB Statement No. 125 on EITF Issues	No longer necessary.

D-53

Computation of Earnings per Share for a Period That Includes a Redemption or an Induced Conversion of a Portion of a Class of Preferred Stock	Earnings per Share, ch. 13

D-54

Accounting by the Purchaser for a Seller's Guarantee of the Adequacy of Liabilities for Losses and Loss Adjustment Expenses of an Insurance Enterprise Acquired in a Purchase Business Combination	Nullified by FAS-141(R).

D-55

Determining a Highly Inflationary Economy under FASB Statement No. 52	Foreign Operations and Exchange, ch. 18

D-56

Accounting for a Change in Functional Currency and Deferred Taxes When an Economy Becomes Highly Inflationary	Foreign Operations and Exchange, ch. 18

D-57

Accounting Issues Relating to the Deposit Insurance Funds Act of 1996	Not discussed.

D-58

Effect on Pooling-of-Interest Accounting of Certain Contingently Exercisable Options to Buy Equity Securities	Superseded by Issue 97-9.

D-59

Payment of a Termination Fee in Connection with a Subsequent Business Combination That Is Accounted for Using the Pooling-of-Interests Method	Nullified by FAS-141.

Cross-Reference **CR.89**

D-60

| Accounting for the Issuance of Convertible Preferred Stock and Debt Securities with a Nondetachable Conversion Feature | Superseded by Issue 98-5 for instruments issued *after* 5/20/99. |

D-61

| Classification by the Issuer of Redeemable Instruments That Are Subject to Remarketing Agreements | Balance Sheet Classification and Related Display Issues, ch. 4 |

D-62

| Computing Year-to-Date Diluted Earnings per Share under FASB Statement No. 128 | Earnings per Share, ch. 13 |

D-63

| Call Options "Embedded" in Beneficial Interests Issued by a Qualifying Special-Purpose Entity | Nullified by FAS 140. |

D-64

| Accounting for Derivatives Used to Hedge Interest Rate Risk | Nullified by FAS-133. |

D-65

| Maintaining Collateral in Repurchase Agreements and Similar Transactions under FASB Statement No. 125 | Not in Codification |

D-66

| Effect of a Special-Purpose Entity's Powers to Sell, Exchange, Repledge, or Distribute Transferred Financial Assets under FASB Statement No. 125 | Nullified by ASU 2009-16 (FAS- 166) |

D-67

| Isolation of Assets Transferred by Financial Institutions under FASB Statement No. 125 | No longer applies. |

D-68

| Accounting by an Equity Method Investor for Investee Losses When the Investor Has Loans to and Investments in Other Securities of an Investee | Equity Method, ch. 14 |

D-69

| Gain Recognition on Transfers of Financial Assets under FASB Statement No. 125 | Not in Codification |

D-70

| Questions Related to the Implementation of FASB Statement No. 131 | Segment Reporting, ch. 37 |

D-71
Accounting Issues Relating to the Introduction of the European Economic and Monetary Union (EMU) — Not in Codification

D-72
Effect of Contracts That May Be Settled in Stock or Cash on the Computation of Diluted Earnings per Share — Earnings per Share, ch. 13

D-73
Reclassification and Subsequent Sales of Securities in Connection with the Adoption of FASB Statement No. 133 — Resolved by FAS-133.

D-74
Issues Concerning the Scope of the AICPA Guide on Investment Companies — Not discussed in this Guide.

D-75
When to Recognize Gains and Losses on Assets Transferred to a Qualifying Special-Purpose Entity — Superseded by FAS-140.

D-76
Accounting by Advisors for Offering Costs Paid on Behalf of Funds, When the Advisor Does Not Receive both 12b-1 Fees and Contingent Deferred Sales Charges — Not discussed in this Guide.

D-77
Accounting for Legal Costs Expected to Be Incurred in Connection with a Loss Contingency — Capitalization and Expense Recognition Concepts, ch. 7

D-78
Accounting for Supervisory Goodwill Litigation Awards and Settlements — Not discussed in this Guide.

D-79
Accounting for Retroactive Insurance Contracts Purchased by Entities Other Than Insurance Enterprises — Codified in Issue 03-8.

D-80
Application of FASB Statements No. 5 and No.114 to a Loan Portfolio — Troubled Debt Restructuring, ch. 41

D-81
Accounting for the Aquisition of Consolidated Businesses — Rescinded by the SEC staff.

D-82

Effect of Preferred Stock Dividends Payable in Common Shares on Computation of Income Available to Common Stockholders — Earnings per Share, ch. 13

D-83

Accounting for Payroll Taxes Associated with Stock Option Exercises — Stock-Based Payments, ch. 38

D-84

Accounting for Subsequent Investments in an Investee After Suspension of Equity Method Loss Recognition When an Investor Increases Its Ownership Interest from Significant Influence to Control through a Market Purchase of Voting Securities — Superseded by ASU 2010-4

D-85

Application of Certain Transition Provisions in SEC Staff Accounting Bulletin No. 101 — Not in Codification

D-86

Issuance of Financial Statements — Results of Operations, ch. 35

D-87

Determination of the Measurement Date for Consideration Given by the Acquirer in a Business Combination When That Consideration Is Securities Other Than Those Issued by the Acquirer — Nullified by FAS-141(R).

D-88

Planned Major Maintenance Activities — Resolved by FSP AUG AIR-1.

D-89

Accounting for Costs of Future Medicare Compliance Audits — Capitalization and Expense Recognition Concepts, ch. 7

D-90

Grantor Balance Sheet Presentation of Unvested, Forfeitable Equity Instruments Granted to a Nonemployee — Stock-Based Payments, ch. 38

D-91

Application of APB Opinion No. 25, *Accounting for Stock Issued to Employees*, and FASB Interpretation No. 44, *Accounting for Certain Transaction Involving Stock Compensation*, to an Indirect Repricing of of a Stock Option — Nullified by FAS-123(R).

D-92

The Effect of FASB Statement No. 135, *Rescission of FASB Statement No. 75 and Technical Corrections*, on the Measurement and Recognition of Net Period Benefit Cost under FASB Statements No. 87, *Employers' Accounting for Pensions*, and No. 106, *Employers' Accounting for Postretirement Benefits Other Than Pensions*

Nullified by FAS-145.

D-93

Accounting for the Rescission of the Exercise of Employee Stock Options

Nullified by FAS-123(R).

D-94

Questions and Answers Related to the Implementation of FASB Statement No. 140

Incorporated in FIG-FAS-140

D-95

Effect of Participating Convertible Securities on the Computation of Basic Earnings per Share

Nullified by Issue 03-6.

D-96

Accounting for Management Fees Based on a Formula

Revenue Recognition, ch. 36

D-97

Push Down Accounting

Consolidated Financial Statements, ch. 10

D-98

Classification and Measurement of Redeemable Securities

Financial Instruments, ch. 17

D-99

Questions and Answers Related to Servicing Activities in a Qualifying Special-Purpose Entity under FASB Statement No. 140

Incorporated in *FASB Staff Implementation Guides*, Questions 22A, 24A, 25A-B, and 28A-D in Q&A 140.

D-100

Clarification of Paragraph 61(b) of FASB Statement No. 141 and Paragraph 49(b) of FASB Statement No. 142

Nullified by FAS-141(R).

D-101

Clarification of Reporting Unit Guidance in Paragraph 30 of FASB Statement No. 142

Segment Reporting, ch. 37

D-102

Documentation of the Methods Used to Measure Hedge Ineffectiveness under FASB Statement No. 133

Financial Instruments, ch. 17

Cross-Reference CR.93

D-103

Income Statement Characterization of Reimbursements Received for "Out-of-Pocket" Expenses Incurred — Renumbered as Issue 01-14

Results of Operations, ch. 35

D-104

Clarification of Transition Guidance in Paragraph 51 of FASB Statement No. 144 — Not in Codification

D-105

Accounting in Consolidation for Energy Trading Contracts between Affiliated Entities When the Activities of One but Not Both Affiliates Are within the Scope of EITF Issue No. 98-10, "Accounting for Contracts Involved in Energy Trading and Risk Management Activities" — Superseded by Issue 02-3.

D-106

Clarification of Q&A No. 37 of FASB Special Report, *A Guide to Implementation of Statement 87 on Employers' Accounting for Pensions* — Superseded by FAS-158.

D-107

Lessor Consideration of Third-Party Residual Value Guarantees — Leases, ch. 26

D-108

Use of the Residual Method to Value Acquired Assets Other Than Goodwill — Business Combinations, ch. 6

D-109

Determining the Nature of a Host Contract Related to a Hybrid Financial Instrument Issued In the Form of a Share under FASB Statement No. 133. — Financial Instruments, ch. 17

D-110

Escrowed Share Arrangements and the Presumption of Compensation — Share-Based Payments, ch. 38

AICPA PRACTICE BULLETINS

ORIGINAL PRONOUNCEMENT	2011 *GAAP GUIDE* VOLUME II REFERENCE

PB-1

Purpose and Scope of AcSEC Practice Bulletins and Procedures for Their Issuance — Accounting Policies and Standards, ch. 2

PB-2

Elimination of Profits Resulting from Intercompany Transfers of LIFO Inventories

Inventory, ch. 24

PB-4

Accounting for Foreign Debt/Equity Swaps

Financial Instruments, ch. 17

PB-5

Income Recognition on Loans to Financially Troubled Countries

Troubled Debt Restructuring, ch. 41

PB-11

Accounting for Preconfirmation Contingencies in Fresh-Start Reporting

Nullified by FSP SOP 90-7-1.

PB-13

Direct-Response Advertising and Probable Future Benefits

Advertising, ch. 3

PB-14

Accounting and Reporting by Limited Liability Companies and Limited Liability Partnerships

Stockholders' Equity, ch. 39

ACCOUNTING PRINCIPLES BOARD INTERPRETATIONS (AINs)

ORIGINAL PRONOUNCEMENT	2011 *GAAP GUIDE* VOLUME II REFERENCE

AIN-APB 4

Accounting for the Investment Tax Credit: Accounting Interpretations of APB Opinion No. 4

Not in Codification

AIN-APB-9

Reporting the Results of Operations: Unofficial Accounting Interpretations of APB Opinion No. 9

Results of Operations, ch. 35

AIN-APB 16

Business Combinations: Accounting Interpretations of APB Opinion No. 16

Superseded by FAS-141 for business combinations initiated after June 30, 2001.

AIN-APB 17

Intangible Assets: Unofficial Accounting Interpretations of APB Opinion No. 17

Superseded by FAS-142 for fiscal years beginning after December 15, 2001.

AIN-APB 18

The Equity Method of Accounting for Investments in Common Stock: Accounting Interpretations of APB Opinion No. 18

Equity Method, ch. 15

AIN-APB 21

Interest on Receivables and Payables: Accounting Interpretations of APB Opinion No. 21

Interest on Receivables and Payables, ch. 22

AIN-APB 25

Accounting for Stock Issued to Employees: Accounting Interpretations of APB Opinion No. 25

Not in Codification

AIN-APB 26

Early Extinguishment of Debt: Accounting Interpretations of APB Opinion No. 26

Extinguishment of Debt, ch. 16

AIN-APB-30

Reporting the Results of Operations: Accounting Interpretations of APB Opinion No. 30

Results of Operations, ch. 35

FASB STAFF IMPLEMENTATION GUIDANCE

ORIGINAL PRONOUNCEMENT	2011 *GAAP GUIDE* VOLUME II REFERENCE

FIG-FAS 109

A Guide to Implementation of Statement 109 on Accounting for Income Taxes

Income Taxes, ch. 20

FIG-FAS 5, 114

Application of FASB Statements 5 and 114 to a Loan Portfolio

Troubled Debt Restructuring, ch. 41

FIG-FAS 115

A Guide to Implementation of Statement 115 on Accounting for Certain Investments in Debt and Equity Securities

Investments in Debt and Equity Securities, ch. 25

FIG-FAS 131

Guidance on Applying Statement 31

Segment Reporting, ch. 37

FIG-FAS 140

A Guide to Implementation of Statement 140 on Accounting for Transfers and Servicing of Financial Assets and Extinguishments of Liabilities

Transfer and Servicing of Financial Assets, ch. 40

AICPA STAFF GUIDANCE

ORIGINAL PRONOUNCEMENT	2011 *GAAP GUIDE* *VOLUME II* REFERENCE	FASB ACCOUNTING STANDARDS CODIFICATION (ASC) TOPIC
AICPA Staff Guidance on Implementing SOP 97-2 Software Revenue Recognition	Computer Software, ch. 9	—

INDEX

A

Accelerated Cost Recovery System (ACRS), 2.06
Accelerated share repurchase program, 39.11–39.12
Acceleration clauses, subjective, 4.08, 4.16–4.18
Accounting by Lease Brokers (AICPA), 26.75–26.76
Accounting changes, 1.01–1.06
   in accounting estimate, 1.01
   corrections of errors, 1.01–1.02
   EITF consensus implications and implementation (Topic D-1), 1.04–1.05
   fresh-start reporting, 5.10–5.19
   overview, 1.01–1.02
   in reporting entity, 1.01
   reporting parent company and consolidated entity differences, 1.03–1.04
   reporting period of investor and equity method investee, 1.03–1.04
   retrospective application of, 1.01, 4.07, 4.29
Accounting policies and standards, 2.01–2.12
Accounting Principles Board (APB)
   interpretations issued by, viii
   rescission of statements, 2.03–2.05
   statements and opinions. *See* Appendix; Cross-Reference
Accumulated benefit obligation (ABO), 29.28–29.30
Accumulated postretirement benefit obligation (APBO), 32.14, 32.16–32.21
Acquisition, development, and construction (ADC) funding arrangements, 2.07–2.10
Acquisition combination, 6.02
Acquisition costs, allocation, 6.15, 6.16

Acquisition method accounting
   business combinations, 6.02
   contractual termination benefits, 6.12–6.14
   Master Limited Partnerships 6.09–6.12
   mining assets, 6.16–6.18
   nonmonetary exchanges of cost-method investments, 6.03–6.05
   ownership changes, 6.08–6.09
ACRS. *See* Accelerated Cost Recovery System
AcSEC. *See* AICPA Accounting Standards Executive Committee
ADC arrangements. *See* Acquisition, development, and construction funding arrangements
Advance payment
   interest on receivables and payables, 22.05
   in research and development, 34.02–34.03
Advertising costs, 3.01–3.10
   amortizing, 3.06–3.07
   assessment of realizability, 3.07–3.08
   barter transactions, 28.02–28.06
   capitalizing, 3.05
   communication, 3.02–3.03
   consideration given by vendors, 36.33, 36.37
   direct-response advertising (PB-13), 3.03–3.06, 3.08–3.09
   disclosures, 3.08
   expenditures, 3.01, 3.02, 3.08
   measurement, 3.06
   production, 3.02–3.03
   reporting on (SOP 93-7), 3.02–3.08
   results of operations, 35.26
   tangible assets, 3.08
Affinity group, 17.08

IND.02 *Index*

Afforable housing investments, 33.08–33.11
Agriculture, pronouncements related to. *See Appendix*
AICPA
  Allowance for Loan Losses Task Force, 41.13
  superseded by ASC, HL.01
AICPA Accounting Standards Executive Committee (AcSEC), 2.03, 2.04, 2.05, 2.06, 2.08, 33.46
AICPA AcSEC Practice Bulletins (PBs), viii, 2.05–2.10. *See also Appendix; Cross-Reference*
AICPA Code of Professional Conduct, 2.04
  Rule 203, 2.04
AICPA Committee on Regulated Industries, 36.13, 36.62
AICPA Motor Carriers Special Committee, 36.14
AICPA Statements of Position (SOPs), vii–viii, 2.03–2.05. *See also Appendix; Cross-Reference*
Allocation process, 11.17–11.18
Alternative minimum tax (AMT), 20.14–20.16, 26.39–26.40
Alternative revenue programs, 36.76–36.78
Altersteilzeit Early Retirement Arrangement (ATZ), 30.32–30.34
American Jobs Creation Act of 2004, deduction for qualified production activities, 20.08
Amortization period, leasehold improvements, 26.65–26.67
Annuity contracts, 30.05–30.06, 30.07–30.08, 30.14
Antispeculation clauses, 33.14–33.15
APB. *See* Accounting Principles Board
APB Opinions and Statements. *See also Cross-Reference*
  APB-28, Interim Financial Reporting (ASC 270), 23.01
Application software providers (ASPs), 9.17–9.18
Arrangement as lease, 26.59–26.63
Asbestos removal costs, 7.13–7.16, 35.21–35.22

ASC
  organization of, HL.02
  primacy of (FAS-168), HL.01
Asset classification of NFPO endowment funds, 4.25–4.29
Asset combination, 6.02
Asset construction, 26.23–26.32
Assets. *See* Impairment of long-lived assets; Transfer of financial assets
Audits of Banks (AICPA), 41.16
Authorization keys, 9.10
Available-for-sale securities, 18.03–18.05, 25.02, 25.07, 25.24, 25.26–25.27
Avoided-cost formula, 36.71–36.75, 36.78–36.82

B

Bad debt accrual, at lease inception, 26.76
Bad-debt recovery rights, 17.87–17.88
Balance sheet
  bankruptcy reporting, 5.06–5.08
  equity accounting method, 14.14–14.16
Balance sheet classification, 4.01–4.30
  borrowing, revolving credit agreement, 4.16–4.18
  capital stock, 4.20–4.24
  creditor-waived violations, 4.11–4.13
  demand notes, 4.08–4.09
  endowment funds of NFPOs subject to UPMIFA, 4.25–4.29
  equity instruments granted to nonemployees, 38.20
  future revenues sales, 4.14–4.16
  increasing-rate debt, 4.09–4.11, 22.02–22.04
  life insurance purchases, 4.04–4.08
  lock-box arrangement, 4.16–4.18
  long-term debt, 4.08
  overview, 4.02–4.03
  remarketing agreements, 4.19–4.20
  structured notes, 17.10–17.17
  subjective acceleration clauses, 4.08, 4.16–4.18
  subsidiary, 4.13–4.14

Bank Audit Guide (AICPA), 25.31
Banking and thrift institutions
  ADC funding, 2.07–2.10
  credit card securitization, 40.30–40.33
  FDIC-insured, 25.34
  lending to the activities of others, risks, 11.06–11.10
  loans to financially troubled countries, 41.15–41.16
Bankruptcy and reorganization, 5.01–5.21. *See also* Troubled debt restructuring
  accounting and finances, 5.04–5.06
  balance sheet reporting, 5.06–5.08
  cash flows, statement of, 5.09
  Chapter 7, 5.03–5.04
  Chapter 11, 5.01–5.02, 5.03, 5.05–5.12, 5.20
  claims, 5.03–5.04
  cram-down provisions, 5.04
  creation of MLP, 6.09–6.12
  disclosure statement, 5.05–5.06
  emerging entity issues, 5.10–5.11
  financial reporting, 5.03–5.19
    SOP 90-7 on. *See Cross-Reference*
  fresh-start reporting, 5.10–5.19
  income statement reporting, 5.01–5.02, 5.08–5.09
  legal summary, 5.03–5.04
  nonmonetary transactions, 28.16–28.18
  overview, 5.01–5.02
  professional fees, 5.09
  push-down accounting, 20.47–20.48
  recovery analysis, 5.14–5.17
  reorganization plan, 5.03–5.04
  reorganization value, 5.04–5.06
  right of setoff, 35.12–35.13
  split-off of nonmonetary assets, 28.11–28.15
Bargain purchase, business combinations, 6.02
Barter contract, 28.02–28.04
Barter transactions, 28.02–28.06
Bifurcation, 12.50–12.52
Bituminous Coal Operators' Association (BCOA), 11.38

Bonds
  convertible, premium put, 12.52–12.54
  foreign currency, 18.20
  inflation bonds, 17.11
  range bonds, 17.11
  special assessment, 11.43–11.46
  traditional convertible, 17.13
Bond swaps, 25.05, 25.13
Borrowing capacity, 15.15–15.16
Brady bonds, 25.33, 41. 14
Bridge financing, 22.04
Build-to-suit lease, 26.23–26.32
Business combinations, 6.01–6.18
  acquisition method accounting, 6.02
  acquisition or stock combination, 6. 02
  asset combination, 6. 02
  bargain purchase, 6. 02
  contingencies of assets and liabilities, accounting for, 6.05–6.08
  goodwill, 6. 02
  intangible assets, 21.05, 21.07, 21.08
  leasehold improvements, 26.65–26.67
  liabilities for termination benefits, 6.12–6.14
  Master Limited Partnerships, 6.09–6.12
  mining assets, 6.16–6.18
  nonmonetary exchange of cost-method investments, 6.03–6.05
  overview, 6.02
  ownership changes, 6.08–6.09
  PPM and physician practice, 10.24–10.35
  residual method, other than goodwill, 6.14–6.16
  subsidiary stock exchange, 6.09, 6.12
Business interruption, 35.13–35.14
Business process reengineering, 7.20–7.23
Buy-sell clause, real estate, 33.27–33.29

C

C corporations, 20.24, 20.44, 20.46
Call option
  purchased, 17.50, 17.68
  written, 17.51, 17.61–17.63

Call provisions, 15.05
Capitalization, 7.01–7.29
  asbestos removal costs, 7.13–7.16
  business process reengineering, 7.20–7.23
  derivative gains and losses, 17.73–17.74
  electronic equipment waste obligations, 7.10–7.13
  environmental contamination, 7.16–7.18
  expensing concepts, 7.01–7.29
  future Medicare compliance audits, 7.28–7.29
  interest, 17.46–17.48
  interest costs, 9.06
  internal software costs, 9.05
  inventory, 24.03–24.04
  IRS payments to retain fiscal year, 7.23–7.24
  legal costs of loss contingency, 7.18
  lump sum payments under union contracts, 7.19–7.20
  overview, 7.02
  planned major maintenance activities, 7.07–7.10
  pre-production costs, 7.03–7.05
  suspended well costs, 7.24–7.28
  web site development costs, 7.05–7.07
Capital lease, 26.04, 26.13, 26.18, 26.38, 26.43–26.44, 26.52–26.53, 26.62–26.66
Capital stock, 4.20–4.24
Carryforwards, 20.03, 20.08, 20.15, 20.16, 20.30–20.31, 20.36, 20.40–20.41, 20.43–20.45
Cash advances, 4.15
Cash balance plans, pension plans, 29.35–29.37
Cash flows
  disposal of long-lived assets, 35.07–35.12
  timing, leases, 26.71–26.74
Cash flow statement, 8.01–8.04
  bankruptcy reporting, 5.09
  debt issue cost classification, 8.02–8.03
  direct method, 5.09
  overview, 8.01–8.02
  payments to settle asset retirement obligation, 8.03–8.04
Cash settlements
  conversion of convertible debt, 12.03–12.12
  diluted EPS, 13.17–13.19
Casino jackpot accruals, 36.59–36.61
Change orders, 27.06
Changing prices, 16.02–16.03
Chapter 11 protection. *See* Bankruptcy and reorganization
Closely held businesses, 31.04, 31.06
Coal Industry Retiree Health Benefit Act, 11.38–11.39
Co-branding, 17.08
COLI policies, 36.05
Collaborative arrangements, 35.28–35.32
Collateralized notes, 4.16, 4.24
Collateral recognition, 40.64
Collateral repurchase agreements, 40.23–40.26, 40.51–40.52
Colleges and universities, 2.06–2.07
Compensated absence accounting, 2.06–2.07, 35.25–35.26
Completed contract method, 27.01, 27.02, 27.04
Computer software, 9.01–9.45
  amortization, 9.07
  capitalizing or expensing, 9.05
  collectibility, 9.10–9.11
  contract accounting, 9.15
  delivery issues, 9.09–9.10
  developed for internal use, 7.20–7.23, 9.04–9.08
  development stages, 9.03–9.06
  EE products, 9.15–9.17
  impairment, 9.07
  indemnification, 11.32
  internal costs as R&D, 9.05
  marketing, 9.07–9.08
  off-the-shelf, 9.14–9.15
  overview, 9.02–9.03
  post-contract customer support, 9.02, 9.11, 9.13–9.14, 9.34
  price, 9.10–9.11

pronouncements related to. *See Appendix*
purchased for internal use, 9.02, 9.06–9.07
revenue recognition, 9.08–9.15, 9.19–9.23, 9.24–9.44
revenue recognition of EE software development, 9.15–9.17
services, 9.14–9.15
stored on another entity's hardware, 9.17–9.18
upgrades and enhancements, 9.05–9.06, 9.12–9.13

Concentrations
of credit risk, 11.40–11.43
vulnerability from, 11.05–11.06

Conduit debt securities, disclosure and reporting, 17.90–17.95

Conforming changes transition, convertible debt, 12.43–12.45

Consolidated financial statements, 10.01–10.77. *See also* Financial statements
Chapter 11 protection, 5.09
contractual management arrangements, 10.24–10.35
determining variability, 10.12
elimination of intercompany profits, 24.04
fiscal year-end difference, 1.03–1.04
investment companies, 10.13–10.15, 10.58–10.72, 10.76–10.77
investments accounting, 10.16–10.24
investments held through separate accounts, 10.56–10.58
limited partnerships, 10.42–10.51, 10.73–10.75
overview, 10.03
rabbi trust, 10.36–10.42
real estate investments, 10.73–10.75
subsidiaries, 4.13–4.14, 10.51–10.55
variable interest entities (VIEs), 10.04–10.13

Construction contract
construction-type, 27.01–27.08
accounting for performance of (SOP 81-1).
See Cross-Reference
leases, 26.24, 26.26, 26.30

long-term, 27.01–27.08
production-type, 27.01–27.08
accounting for performance of (SOP 81-1).
See Cross-Reference
profit recognition, homebuilder, 33.31–33.32
rental costs during construction, 26.06

Construction financing, 11.43–11.46
Construction-in-progress, 26.49–26.51
Consulting contracts, 7.20–7.23
Consumer price index (CPI), 36.74
Contaminated soil cleanup, 7.16–7.18
Contingencies, 11.01–11.47. *See also* Risks and uncertainties
contingently convertible securities, 39.06–39.08
disclosures, 11.02
gain, 11.02
loss, 11.02
mortgage servicing rights sale, 40.36–40.38

Contingent rent, 26.55–26.58
Continuing operations, 20.19–20.21, 20.40
Contractor, 27.04
Contracts
antispeculation clauses, 33.14–33.15
construction-type, 27.01–27.08
accounting for performance of (SOP 81-1).
See Cross-Reference
production-type, 27.01–27.08
accounting for performance of (SOP 81-1).
See Cross-Reference
reclassification, 17.59–17.60
weather derivative, 17.43–17.46

Contractual management arrangements, 10.24–10.35
Contractual termination benefits, 6.12–6.14
Contra-equity account, 4.21–4.23
Convertible bonds
contingently adjustable conversion ratios, 12.14–12.24, 12.27, 12.42, 12.44

IND.06 *Index*

conversion features, 12.14–12.24
discounted, 12.52–12.54
premium put,
12.52–12.54Convertible debt, 12.01–12.54
accrued interest, 12.13–12.14
beneficial conversion, 12.14–12.24
bifurcation, 12.50–12.52
call option, 12.40–12.43
cash settlement, 12.03–12.12
conforming changes transition, 12.43–12.45
contingent conversion, 12.14–12.24
conventional instruments, 12.27–12.39, 12.48–12.50
conversion into subsidiary stock, 12.24–12.27
conversion price, 12.17
embedded conversion feature, 12.04–12.10, 12.15–12.17, 12.20–12.21, 12.24–12.38, 12.40–12.41, 12.45–12.46, 12.49–12.54
induced conversions, 12.39–12.40
overview, 12.02
own-share lending arrangements, 12.45–12.48
premium put, 12.52–12.54
revenue recognition, stock options, 12.12–12.13
Convertible instruments
conventional, 12.27–12.39, 12.48–12.50
effect on diluted earnings per share, 13.08–13.09
modification of convertible debt instruments, 15.19–15.21
stock transactions with nonemployees, 38.04–38.06
Convertible preferred stock, 38.66–38.70
Copyrights, 21.01
Corporate division, 37.04
Corporate-owned life insurance (COLI) policies, 36.05
Corrections of errors, 1.01–1.02
Cost method accounting, 33.10
Cost method investments, 6.03–6.05

Cost of sales and inventory, time-sharing, 33.37–33.47
Cost overruns, 26.24, 26.26, 26.31
Cost-plus contract, 27.04
Cost recovery method, 33.06–33.07, 33.21
Cost-type contract, 27.04, 27.07
CPA Letter, 2.05
Cram-down provision, 5.04
Credit cards
acquisitions of individual accounts, 17.08–17.10
cardholder relationships, 21.03–21.04
net-deferred origination costs, 17.06–17.08
origination fees, 17.06–17.08
private label, 17.06–17.08
securitization, 40.30–40.33
Creditor-waived violations, 4.11–4.13
Cross border tax benefit lease, 26.40–26.42
Cumulative catch-up method, 27.08
Current and prospective accounting, 1.01–1.02
Current value accounting, 16.02–16.03, 16.12–16.13
Customer support, 9.02, 9.11, 9.13–9.14, 9.34

D

Debt. *See* Convertible debt; Extinguishment of debt; Troubled debt restructuring; *headings below starting with "Debt"*
Debt and equity securities
available-for-sale, 25.02, 25.07, 25.24, 25.26–25.27
carrying value, 25.24, 25.39
classification criteria, 25.32–25.33
convertible, 12.01–12.54
desecuritization, 25.13
disclosures, 25.28–25.29
fair value, reporting changes, 25.24–25.25
FAS-115 implementation guide, 25.33–25.34
forward contracts, 25.06–25.11

held-to-maturity, 25.02, 25.04–25.06, 25.07, 25.15–25.22, 25.26–25.27
loan accounting, 40.04–40.09
noncurrent marketable, 25.27
other-than-temporary impairment, 25.03–25.04, 25.34–25.43
swaps, 18.06–18.07, 25.05, 25.13
trading, 25.02, 25.08, 25.23–25.24Debt instrument classification, 25.32–25.33
Debt instrument modification, 15.05–15.14, 15.16–15.19
Debt issue costs, 8.02–8.03
Debt securities, restructured, 41.06–41.09
Debt with warrants, 12.02
Default covenants, 26.54–26.55
Defensive assets, 21.07–21.09
Deferral method, 20.04–20.05
Deferred compensation, 32.10–32.11, 32.34–32.39
Deferred tax asset, 20.03
   discontinued operation, 20.21–20.23
   temporary differences, 20.16–20.19, 20.32–20.37, 20.39–20.40, 20.41–20.45, 20.49
Deferred tax liability, 20.03,, 20.16–20.19, 20.22, 20.32, 20.36, 20.38–20.39, 20.43–20.44, 20.48–20.52, 25.29–25.30
Defined-contribution plans, 32.27
Delayed equity investments, 26.34–26.35
Delayed recognition, 29.02, 32.02
Demand notes, 4.08–4.09
Depreciation, ACRS recovery deductions and, 2.06
Derivatives
   capitalization of interest, 17.46–17.48
   company's own stock, indexed to, 17.48–17.70
   consolidated subsidiary stock, indexed to, 17.24–17.27, 17.36–17.40
   framework for accounting (the Model) and, 17.52–17.54
   freestanding, 17.36–17.40
   minority owner's interest, indexed to, 17.24–17.25
   reporting gains/losses, 17.73–17.74

   trading purposes in energy and risk management, 17.70–17.73
   transfer, 40.39–40.40
   weather, 17.43–17.46
Desecuritizations of financial assets, 25.13
Detachable warrants, 12.12, 12.13, 12.15, 12.17, 12.31, 15.22–15.23
Dilution
   defined, 13.02
   earnings per share, 13.08–13.09, 13.15–13.19
Direct financing lease, 26.11, 26.18, 26.63, 26. 64
Direct marketing specialist, 17.08
Direct-response advertising
   amortizing, 3.06–3.07
   capitalizing, 3.05
   generating sales and traceability, 3.03–3.04
   incremental direct costs, 3.06
   payroll costs, 3.06
   probable future benefits, 3.04–3.05, 3.08–3.09
Disclosures
   credit derivatives and certain guarantees, 17.40–17.43
   debt and equity securities, 25.28–25.29
   enhanced, of endowment funds by NFPOs, 4.25–4.29
   fair value, 16.12–16.13
   financial instruments, 17.60–17.61
   personal financial statements, 31.06–31.07
   of risks and uncertainties (SOP 94-6). *See Cross-Reference*
   segment reporting, 37.03–37.06, 37.09, 37.10–37.11, 37.12, 37.16
Discontinued operations, 20.21–20.23
Discount amortization, 17.10
Discount rates, pension plans, 29.37–29.38
Distributed tax rate, 20.31
Dividend taxation, 20.28–20.31
Dollar-value LIFO method, 24.04
Downstream transaction, 14.28
Drop-down, 6.10, 6.11, 6.12

Dual index notes, 17.11
Due on demand clause, 4.09

E

Early retirement benefits, 30.32–30.34
Earnings before interest, taxes, depreciation, and amortization (EBITDA), 37.09, 37.14
Earnings per share (EPS), 13.01–13.22
   convertible instruments, effect of, 13.08–13.09
   diluted, 12.03–12.04, 12.38, 12.40, 12.43, 12.47–12.48, 13.02, 13.08–13.09, 13.15–13.19
   employee stock ownership plans (ESOPs), 38.66–38.70
   financial instruments indexed to company's own stock, 13.20–13.22
   overview, 13.02
   participating securities, determining, 13.03–13.05
   preferred stock, 13.13–13.15
      payable in common shares, 13.19
   rabbi trust, 10.36–10.42
   redeemable securities, 17.27–17.36
   tax benefits of ESOP dividends, 38.71–38.72
   two-class method, 13.05–13.08
      master limited partnerships, 13.09–13.13
Earnings per share calculations
   company's own stock, 13.20–13.22
   convertible debt instruments, 12.36–12.37
   diluted earnings per share, 13.08–13.09
   preferred stock dividends, 13.13–13.15
   two-class method, 13.05–13.08
      master limited partnerships, 13.09–13.13
   year-to-date, 13.15–13.19
Effective yield method, 33.09–33.10
Efforts-expended approach, 27.05
EITF Abstracts, 4.27
EITF consensus positions

asset retirement obligation payment classification (Issue 02-6), 8.03–8.04
   debt issue cost classification (Issue 95-13), 8.02–8.03
   implications and implementation of (Topic D-1), 1.04–1.05
   importance of, viii–ix
   inventory market decline recognition (Issue 86-13), 23.02–23.03
   procedure for issuance of, ix
EITF Issues. *See Cross-Reference*
   relevance to specific industries. *See Appendix*
Electronic equipment waste obligations
   accounting for, 7.10–7.13
   historical waste
      held by commercial users, 7.13
      held by private users, 7.12
Embedded beneficial conversion, 12.04–12.10, 12.15–12.17, 12.20–12.21, 12.24–12.38, 12.40–12.41, 12.45–12.46, 12.49–12.54
Emerging entity, 5.10–5.11
Emerging Issues Task Force (EITF), viii
Employee benefit plans. *See Appendix;* Employee stock ownership plans (ESOPs); Pension plans; Postretirement benefits (OPEBs)
Employee Retirement Income Security Act (ERISA), 11.39
Employee stock ownership plans (ESOPs)
   accounting issues, 38.06–38.07, 38.30–38.51, 38.61–38.63
   balance sheet classification, 4.20–4.24
   earnings per share and convertible stock, 38.66–38.70
   excess contributions, 38.21–38.25
   expense recognition, 38.63–38.66
   leveraged. *See* Leveraged ESOPs
   nonleveraged, 38.39–38.40, 38.49–38.51
   payroll taxes, 38.57, 38.59
   stock compensation, 38.59–38.60
   unallocated stock and earnings-per-share tax treatment, 38.71–38.72

unrelated entity options, 38.60–38.61
Employee stock purchase plans (ESPPs), 38.51–38.56
  employers' accounting for (SOP 93-6). *See Cross-Reference*
Employee termination. *See also* Employee stock ownership plans (ESOPs); Pension plans; Postretirement benefits (OPEBs)
  benefits, 6.12–6.14
  lump-sum payment, 7.19–7.20
  retiree pension and health benefits, 11.38–11.39
Endowment funds, disclosure of, 4.25–4.29
Energy trading and risk management, 17.70–17.73
Entertainment and educational software (EE) products, 9.15–9.17
  pronouncements related to. *See Appendix*
Enterprise-wide disclosures, 37.10–37.11
Entitlements method, 36.12–36.13, 36.61–36.62
Environmental cleanup guidance, 11.10–11.23
Environmental contamination treatment, 7.16–7.18
Environmental exit costs, 19.08–19.11
Environmental Protection Agency (EPA), 11.16–11.18
Environmental remediation liabilities, 11.10–11.23
  accounting guidance on (SOP 96-1). *See Cross-Reference*
  allocation, 11.17–11.18
  background, 11.10–11.11
  costs currently recognized, 11.23–11.24
  disclosure guidelines, 11.19–11.23
  estimates, 11.12–11.14
  financial statement guidelines, 11.18–11.19
  lessee responsibility, 26.53–26.54
  measurement, 11.14–11.18
  potential recoveries, 11.18
  PRPs, 11.16–11.17
  recognition, 11.12–11.114
  unasserted claims, 11.22

Environmental risk, 26.27, 26.30, 26.32, 26.52, 26.53–26.54
Environmental studies, 7.16
Equity accounting method, 14.01–14.31
  accounting considerations, 14.23–14.25
  AOCI upon a loss of significant influence, 14.25–14.26
  balance sheet, 14.14–14.16
  common stock, 14.28–14.29
    investments other than, 14.17–14.20
  equity securities, 25.03–25.04, 25.15, 25.23
  income statement, 14.14–14.16
  investee losses, 14.06–14.12, 14.13–14.14, 14.26–14.27, 14.30
  limited liability companies, 14.04–14.06
  limited partnership investments, 14.26
  loss recognition, 14.20–14.23
  overview, 14.02–14.03
  partnerships and joint ventures, 14.06–14.29
  stock-based compensation, 14.16–14.17
  subsequent investments, 14.20–14.23
  unrealized losses, marketable securities, 14.30
Equity instruments
  goods and services, with, 38.07–38.17
  issued to nonemployees, 38.07–38.14, 38.17–38.20
Equity interest
  business combinations, 6.10
  reorganization plan, 5.04–5.05
Equity-linked bear notes, 17.11
Equity method investments
  common stock, 14.28–14.29
  fiscal year-end difference, 1.03–1.04
  limited partner, 33.10
Equity securities. *See* Debt and equity securities; Investments in debt and equity securities
Escrowed share arrangements, 38.59–38.60

Index **IND.09**

Estimates
  accounting changes, 1.01
  long-term construction costs, 27.03–27.04, 27.08
  risk and uncertainties, 11.12–11.14
European Economic and Monetary Union (EMU), 37.11
Exchange rate, trading temporarily suspended, 18.13–18.14
Exchanges
  debt instruments, 15.03–15.04, 15.05–15.14, 15.16–15.19
  equity interests, between combining companies, 6.10
  nonmonetary, 28.01–28.21
  stock, to extinguish debt, 15.04–15.05
Executory costs, 26.18–26.19
Exit activity, pension plans, 30.03–30.04
Exit costs, environmental, 19.08–19.11
Exit plan, inventory markdowns, 35.20–35.21
Expense recognition, 7.01–7.29
  asbestos removal, 7.13–7.16
  business process reengineering, 7.20–7.23
  computer software modification, 9.05
  electronic equipment waste obligations, 7.10–7.13
  employee stock ownership plans (ESOPs), 38.63–38.66
  future Medicare compliance audit costs, 7.28–7.29
  legal costs, 7.18
  pre-production costs, 7.03–7.05
  Web site development costs, 7.05–7.07
Extended warranties, 36.08–36.10
External marketing, 9.07–9.08
Extinguishment of debt, 15.01–15.23
  detachable warrants, 15.22–15.23
  early, 15.02, 15.04–15.05, 15.12, 15.22, 15.22
  embedded beneficial conversion feature, 12.19, 12.39
  exchange of debt instruments, 15.03–15.04, 15.05–15.14, 15.16–15.19

  exchange of stock, 15.04–15.05
  line of credit arrangements, 15.14–15.16
  modification of convertible debt instruments, 15.19–15.21
  modification of debt instruments, 15.05–15.14, 15.16–15.19
  modification of debt terms, 15.03–15.04
  overview, 15.02
  revolving-debt arrangements, 15.14–15.16
  transfer of financial assets, 40.65
Extraordinary items, 35.14–35.15, 35.21–35.22

F

Fair value, 16.01–16.15
  current value financial statements, 16.12–16.13
  determination, 16.05–16.10
  financial instruments, 16.10–16.12
  lease classification, measurement for, 16.13–16.15
  nonmonetary transactions, 28.01–28.20
  overview, 16.02–16.03
  third-party credit enhancement, 16.04–16.05
FASB Accounting Standards Codification™ (ASC)
  U.S. GAAP and, HL.01
FASB Implementation Guide (FIG-FAS), viii. *See also Cross-Reference*
FASB Staff Positions (FSPs), viii, 2.03
FASB standards. *See Cross-Reference*
FASB Statements (FAS) and Interpretations (FIN), viii. *See also Appendix; Cross-Reference*
FAS-39 amendment, 17.95–17.98
FAS-123(R)
  amendment of staff position, 38.72–38.74
  technical corrections, 38.74–38.78
FAS-133 amendment, 17.40–17.43
FAS-141(R) on business combination contingencies, 6.02–6.10, 6.14–6.15

FAS-143 on asset retirement
obligations, 8.03
FAS-168 on primacy of ASC, HL.01
FASB Technical Bulletins (FTBs), viii,
2.10–2.11. *See also Cross-Reference*
FTB 79-9, (Accounting in Interim
Periods for Changes in
Income Tax Rates), 23.03
Federal Bankruptcy Code
Chapter 7, 5.03–5.04
Chapter 11, 5.01–5.02, 5.03, 5.05–5.12,
5.20
entity reorganization, 5.03–5.19
Federal Financial Institutions
Examination Council (FFIEC),
25.19, 25.34
Federal Home Loan Bank Board
(FHLBB), 33.05
Federal Home Loan Mortgage
Corporation (FHLMC), 25.32
Federal Housing Administration (FHA),
33.13, 33.15–33.16
Federal Savings and Loan Insurance
Corporation (FSLIC), 33.05
Financial Accounting Standards Board
(FASB) standards. *See Cross-
Reference*
Financial institutions. *See* Banking and
thrift institutions
pronouncements related to. *See
Appendix*
Financial instruments, 17.01–17.99. *See
also* Derivatives
classification and measurement,
17.27–17.36
conduit debt securities, disclosure
and reporting, 17.90–17.95
credit card acquisitions, 17.08–17.10
credit card origination costs,
17.06–17.08
disclosures about credit derivatives
and certain guarantees,
17.40–17.43
embedded features indexed to
entity's own stock,
10.51–10.55, 17.74–17.80
energy trading and risk
management, 17.70–17.73
fair value, disclosure, 16.10–16.12
FAS-39 amendment, 17.95–17.98

FAS-133 amendment, 17.40–17.43
foreign debt/equity swaps,
17.88–17.90, 18.06–18.07
freestanding, 17.17–17.19, 17.23,
17.36–17.40
hedge ineffectiveness, 17.80–17.81
hedging gains and losses,
17.73–17.74
hybrid, 4.11, 17.81
indexed to company's own stock,
17.48–17.70
interest gains and losses, 17.46–17.48
interest method, 17.86
mandatorily redeemable of
nonpublic entities, 17.20–17.22
mandatorily redeemable with shares
differing from book value,
17.19–17.20
mortgage payment modifications,
17.05–17.06
overview, 17.03–17.04
redeemable securities, 17.27–17.36
registration payment arrangements,
17.82–17.86
sale of bad-debt recovery rights,
17.87–17.88
structured notes, 17.10–17.17
subsidiary, 17.24–17.27, 17.36–17.40
transfers with constraints,
40.49–40.50
warrants, freestanding, 17.23
weather derivatives, 17.43–17.46
Financially troubled countries,
41.15–41.16
Financial statements. *See also*
Consolidated financial
statements; Interim financial
reporting; Personal financial
statements
advertising cost disclosures, 3.08
current value, 16.02–16.03,
16.12–16.13
environmental remediation liability,
11.18–11.19
foreign investments, 18.15–18.24
general price-level accounting,
16.02–16.03, 16.12–16.13
life settlement contracts,
presentation, 35.06–35.08

price-level adjusted, 20.48–20.50
results of operations, 35.32–35.33
risk disclosures, 11.03–11.06
vulnerability from concentrations, 11.05–11.06
First-loss guarantee, 26.43–26.44
Fiscal funding clauses, 26.07
Fiscal year-end difference, 1.03–1.04, 4.13–4.14
Fixed assets, 7.23
Fixed dollar conversion, 12.21–12.23
Fixed percentage conversion, 12.21–12.23
Fixed-price contract, 27.03
Floor put, 4.20, 4.21
FNMA, 25.32
Foreclosed property valuation, 33.05–33.08
Foreign debt-for-equity swaps, 17.88–17.90, 18.06–18.07
Foreign operations and exchange, 18.01–18.24
  available-for-sale securities, 18.03–18.05
  cash, 18.22
  currency accounting, 18.15–18.24
  currency swaps, offsetting, 18.05
  currency translation, 18.13–18.14
  debt-for-equity swaps, 17.88–17.90, 18.06–18.07
  disposal of impairment, 18.12–18.13
  dividends, 18.21
  exchangeability temporarily suspended, 18.13–18.14
  exchange rate changes, 18.03–18.05, 18.08–18.10, 18.11–18.12, 18.14–18.15
  expenses, 18.21
  financial statement presentation, 18.15–18.24
  forward exchange contracts, 18.22–18.23
  future net income, revenue, costs, 4.14
  highly inflationary economy, 18.07–18.12, 18.14–18.15
  income, 18.19–18.20
  income tax effects, 18.11–18.12
  investments, 18.18–18.19
  overview, 18.02
  receivables and payables, 18.21–18.22
  risks, 18.23
  unrealized gains and losses, 18.18–18.19
  withholding tax, 18.21
Foreign subsidiaries
  basis difference tax applications, 20.48–20.52
  dividend-related tax credits, 20.30–20.31
  highly inflationary economies, 18.07–18.12
  indefinite reversal criterion, 20.50–20.52
  temporary differences, 20.30–20.31
Forward contracts
  accelerated share repurchase program, 39.11–39.12
  securities acquisition, 25.06–25.11
Forward exchange contracts, 18.22–18.23
Forward purchase (sale) contracts, 17.50, 17.64–17.68
Forward sale contracts, 17.50, 17.61–17.63
France, tax effects of dividends, 20.26–20.28
Freestanding derivatives, 17.36–17.40
Freestanding financial instruments, 17.17–17.19, 17.23, 38.25–38.28
Freight services, 36.13–36.16
Fresh-start reporting
  criteria, 5.10
  disclosures, 5.11
  implementation, 5.10
  reorganization under bankruptcy code, 5.10–5.19
  transition, 5.11
Front-end load, 36.10, 36.65, 36.68
Frontloaded plan, illustration, postretirement benefits (OPEBs), 32.14
FTB. *See* FASB Technical Bulletins
Full accrual method, 33.06, 33.07, 33.13–33.20, 33.25, 33.28, 33.31

Functional currency
   determination, 18.15–18.24
   foreign subsidiaries, differences, 18.11–18.12
Future revenue sales
   classification, 4.14–4.16
   foreign transaction, 4.14
   revenue recognition, 36.07–36.08
Futures contracts, hedges, 17.73–17.74

G

Gain contingencies, 11.02
Gas-balancing arrangements, 36.11–36.13, 36.61–36.63
Gas production, 36.11–36.13, 36.61–36.63
General price-level accounting, 16.02–16.03, 16.12–16.13
Geographic information disclosures, 37.10–37.11
Ginnie Maes, 25.33
Golden parachute agreements, 6.13
Goodwill
   business combination accounting, 6.02
   capitalization, 7.05, 7.06, 7.21
   income taxes deferred, 20.04–20.05, 20.34
   as intangible asset, 21.05, 21.08, 21.09
Government National Mortgage Association (GNMA), 25.32
Graduated payment mortgages, 33.13
Grandfather clause, 25.32
Greenmail payments, 39.09
Guarantees, 2.08–2.09, 11.32–11.33
   disclosures about credit derivatives and certain guarantees, 17.40–17.43
   minimum revenue, 11.33–11.35
   loan fee, recognition, 11.35–11.38

H

Health care facilities, "customer," 37.16–37.17
Health care industry, 10.24–10.35
   charity, 36.69–36.71
   insurance claims and recoveries, 35.33–35.35

Health management organizations (HMOs), 10.24–10.35
Hedge accounting
   gains and losses, financial instruments, 17.73–17.74
   ineffectiveness under FAS-133, 17.80–17.81
Hedging activities, leases, 26.64–26.65
Held-to-maturity securities, 25.02, 25.04–25.06, 25.07, 25.15–25.22, 25.26–25.27
Hierarchy of GAAP, 2.03
Highly inflationary economies, 18.07–18.12, 18.14–18.15, 20.48–20.50
High-risk mortgage securities, 25.19, 25.34
Historical costs
   cost-method investors, 6.04
   transfers and exchanges, 6.09, 6.17
Historic dollar value, 4.28
Hybrid securities, 12.02, 12.20, 12.53–12.54

I

Impairment
   internal-use computer software marketing costs, 9.07
   investment disposal, 18.12–18.13
   long-lived assets, 19.01–19.11
   nonmonetary transactions, 28.05–28.06, 28.10
   other-than-temporary, 25.03–25.04, 25.34–25.43
   permanent, 23.02
   transfer of financial assets, 40.17–40.22
      EITF 99-20 amendments, 40.09–40.17
Impairment of long-lived assets, 19.01–19.11
   cumulative losses, measurement, 19.03–19.04
   environmental exit costs, 19.08–19.11
   FAS-15 costs and FAS-144 loss, 19.03–19.04
   foreclosed assets, cost determination, 19.03–19.04

IND.14 *Index*

intangible assets with indefinite lives, 19.05–19.07
loan, 41.10–41.12, 41.14
overview, 19.01–19.02
testing, 19.08–19.11
Implicit variable interests, 10.07–10.10
Income-producing property, 33.17–33.18
Income statement
  bankruptcy reporting, 5.01–5.02, 5.08–5.09
  business interruption insurance recoveries, 35.13–35.14
  equity accounting method, 14.14–14.16
  reimbursement for out-of-pocket expenses, 35.22–35.23
  shareholder transactions, 20.23–20.25
  takeover attempt defense costs, 39.08–39.09
Income taxes, 20.01–20.53. *See also* Investment tax credit; Tax credits
  accounting for (FAS-109 on). *See Cross-Reference*
  allocation of tax expense, 20.45
  alternative minimum tax, 20.14–20.16
  American Jobs Creation Act of 2004, 20.08
  business combinations, 20.45
  continuing operations, retroactive change in rates, 20.19–20.21
  convertible debt, 20.37–20.39
  deferred in applying goodwill, 20.04–20.05
  disclosure, 20.13, 20.45
  dividend payment tax credits, 20.28–20.31
  effective date of FASB Interpretation 48, 20.12–20.14
  enacted tax rates, retroactive, 20.19–20.21
  FASB-109 Implementation Guide, 18.11–18.12, 20.08–20.09, 20.40–20.46
  foreign earnings, 20.30–20.31, 20.48–20.52
  foreign operations, 18.11–18.12
  foreign subsidiaries, 20.30–20.31, 20.48–20.52
  French shareholders, 20.26–20.28
  functional currency changes, 18.11–18.12
  general price-level changes, 20.48–20.50
  goodwill, 20.04–20.05, 20.34
  indefinite reversal criterion, 20.50–20.52
  leveraged lease, 26.08–26.09, 26.71–26.74
  overview, 20.03
  parent company excess tax basis, 20.21–20.23
  personal financial statement, 31.05–31.06
  pretax income from continuing operations, 20.40
  push-down accounting, 20.47–20.48
  qualified production activities, 20.08–20.09
  rate changes, 20.39, 23.03, 26.08–26.09
  recognition and measurement, 20.43–20.44
  scheduling, 20.41–20.43
  settlement defined (FAS-48), 20.09–20.12
  share-based payment awards, 20.06–20.07
  shareholder-company transactions, 20.23–20.25
  state tax based on greater of franchise or income tax, 20.16–20.19
  tax-planning strategies, 20.45–20.46
  tax status changes, 20.44
  temporary differences, 20.03, 20.15–20.22, 20.25, 20.29–20.31, 20.32–20.37, 20.39–20.40, 20.41–20.45, 20.48–20.52
  Texas corporate franchise tax, 20.16–20.18
Increasing-rate debt classification, 4.09–4.11, 22.02–22.04
Incremental borrowing rate, 26.69–26.70
Indefinite-lived tangible assets, testing, 19.05–19.07
Indefinite reversal criterion, 20.50–20.52

Index amortizing notes, 17.10–17.11
Indexed debt instruments. *See* Structured notes
Indexed to a company's own stock, derivative financial instruments, 17.48–17.70
Inflation bonds, 17.11
Inflation rate, 18.08, 18.14
Information technology transformation, 7.20–7.23
Infrastructure construction financing, 11.43–11.46
Inside basis differences, 20.50–20.52
In-substance foreclosure, 41.05, 41.06
In-substance syndications, 40.38–40.39
Insurance
  claims-made, 11.23–11.32
  death benefits, reverse recognition, 36.05–36.06
  pronouncements related to. *See* Appendix
  retroactive, 11.23–11.32
Insurance contracts, weather derivatives, 17.43–17.46
Insurance policies, 4.04–4.08
Insured mortgages, 33.15–33.17
Intangible assets, 21.01–21.10
  accounting for, 21.07–21.09
  amortization, 21.05
  business combinations, 21.05, 21.07, 21.08
  capitalization, 7.02, 7.05, 7.06, 7.21
  credit cardholder relationships, 21.03–21.04
  disclosures, 21.06–21.07
  goodwill, 21.05, 21.08, 21.09
  mineral rights, 21.09
  oil and gas-producing entities, 21.09
  overview, 21.01–21.02
  personal financial statement, 31.05, 31.06
  useful life determination, 21.04–21.07
Integral equipment determination, real estate, 33.24–33.25
Intellectual property infringement indemnification, 11.32
Interactive software technology, 9.15–9.17

Intercompany profit or loss elimination, 24.04
Interest
  capitalization, 17.46–17.48
  gains and losses, financial instruments, 17.46–17.48
  receivables and payables, 22.01–22.05, 40.56–40.57
  transfer of financial assets, 40.17–40.22
Interest method, 17.86
Interest-only payments, 26.51–26.52
Interest rates
  modification of debt terms, 15.03–15.04
  troubled debt restructuring, 41.09–41.10
Interim financial reporting, 23.01–23.04
  income tax rate changes, 23.03
  inventory market declines, recognition of, 23.02–23.03
  issuance intervals, 23.01
  overview, 23.01
  segment information, 37.09–37.10
Internal cost recognition application guidance, 33.32–33.34
Internal Revenue Service (IRS) payments to retain fiscal year, 7.23–7.24
Intrinsic value method, 17.44
Inventory, 24.01–24.07. *See also* LIFO inventory
  market declines, recognition of, 23.02–23.03
  mining production costs, 24.05–24.06
  nonmonetary transactions, 28.18–28.21
  overview, 24.01–24.02
  profits from intercompany transfers, 24.04
  uniform capitalization rules, 24.03–24.04
Inventory markdowns, 35.20–35.21
Inverse floating-rate notes, 17.11
Investment accounting, 10.16–10.24

IND.16   Index

Investment companies, 18.15–18.24
  consolidated financial statements, 10.13–10.15, 10.58–10.72, 10.76–10.77
  pronouncements related to. See Appendix
Investment Company Act of 1940, 36.10, 36.68
Investments
  foreign operations and exchange, 18.18–18.19
  held through separate accounts, 10.56–10.58
Investments in debt and equity securities, 25.01–25.43
  accounting for, 25.14–25.31
  assets and liabilities for holding gains and losses, 25.11–25.12
  available-for-sale, 25.02, 25.07, 25.24, 25.26–25.27
  deferred tax implications, 25.29–25.30
  desecuritizations, financial assets, 25.13
  determining fair value, 25.30–25.31
  disclosures, 25.28–25.29
  FASB 115 implementation, 25.33–25.34
  financial statements, 25.28–25.29
  forward contracts, 25.06–25.11
  held-to-maturity, 25.02, 25.04–25.06, 25.07, 25.15–25.22, 25.26–25.27
  impairment, 25.27–25.28
  limited partnerships, 25.15
  noncurrent marketable equity securities, 25.27
  other-than-temporary impairment, 25.03–25.04, 25.34–25.43
  overview, 25.02
  purchased options, 25.06–25.11
  reporting fair value changes, 25.24–25.25
  substantially the same for holders or debt instruments, 25.31–25.33
  trading, 25.02, 25.08, 25.23–25.24
  transfers between category types, 25.25–25.27
Investment tax credit (ITC), leases, 26.37–26.38

Involuntary employee termination, 6.13

J

Japanese government, pension plans, 29.32–29.35
Joint venture
  ADC arrangements, 2.07–2.10
  equity method accounting, 14.06–14.29
Journal of Accountancy, 2.05

L

Land sales contracts, 33.14–33.15
Lease classification, fair value, 16.13–16.15
Leases, 26.01–26.76. See also Leveraged leases; Operating leases; Sale-leaseback transactions
  accounting for, 26.10–26.12
  alternative minimum tax, 26.39–26.40
  asset construction, lessee involvement effect, 26.23–26.32
  bad debts, 26.76
  business combination, leasehold improvements, 26.65–26.67
  cash flow timing, 26.71–26.74
  contingent rent, 26.55–26.58
  cross border tax benefit, 26.40–26.42
  determining if it is a lease arrangement, 26.59–26.63
  FAS-13 ownership transfer, 26.58–26.59
  FAS-133 requirements, 26.64–26.65
  fiscal funding clauses, 26.07
  governmental entities, 26.32–26.34
  leasehold improvements, amortization period, 26.65–26.67
  leveraged, 26.34–26.35, 26.71–26.74
  loss on a sublease, 26.08
  maintenance deposit accounting, 26.67–26.69
  minimum lease payments, 26.43–26.44, 26.69–26.70

operating leases,
  no change in lease classification, 26.45–26.46
  with scheduled rent increases, 26.09, 26.10–26.11
overview, 26.04–26.05
ownership transfer requirements, 26.58–26.59
preexisting lease, sale of property, 26.15–26.18
real estate, 26.34–26.35
rental costs during construction, 26.06
residual value, FASB 133, 26.64–26.65
residual value, upward adjustments, 26.07–26.08
sale-leaseback transaction, 26.34–26.35
  asset that is leased to another party, 26.22–26.23
  continuing involvement, 26.69
  deferred profit, 26.12–26.15
  executor costs, 26.18–26.19
  uncollateralized irrevocable letter of credit on real estate, 26.21–26.22
  unsecured guarantee, subsidiary, 26.19–26.20
securitization and VIEs, 26.70–26.71
special-purpose entities, 26.47–26.55
tax indemnification, 26.37–26.39
tax rate change on leveraged leases, 26.08–26.09, 26.36–26.37
Tax Reform Act of 1986, 26.39–26.40
termination of modification costs, 26.45–26.46
wrap lease transactions, 26.10, 26.74–26.76
Legal costs, 7.18, 8.03
Letter of credit, 4.19, 4.20, 4.24, 26.21–26.22
Leveraged buyout (LBO) transactions
  Master Limited Partnerships, 6.09–6.12
  nonmonetary exchange of cost-method investments, 6.03–6.05
  ownership changes, 6.08–6.09

Leveraged ESOPs, accounting for, 4.21, 38.32–38.39, 38.42–38.49
Leveraged leases
  accounting, 26.08–26.09
  alternative minimum tax, 26.71–26.74
  cash flow timing, 26.71–26.74
  delay equity contributions, 26.34–26.35
  income tax law or rate change, 26.08–26.09, 26.36–26.37
  real estate leases, 26.34–26.35
Liabilities, extinguishment of. *See* Extinguishment of debt
Liabilities, related to legal contingencies, 6.05–6.08
Life insurance
  investments, 31.04, 31.06
  purchases, 4.04–4.08
Life insurance policies
  COLI policies, 36.05
  death benefits, 36.05–36.06
Life settlement contracts, 35.15–35.20
  fair value method, 35.17
  financial statement presentation, 35.17–35.19
  investment method, 35.16–35.17
LIFO inventory
  intercompany transfers, 24.04
  market declines, 23.02
  temporary differences, 20.39–20.40
Limited liability companies (LLCs), 14.04–14.06, 39.03–39.04
Limited liability partnerships
  accounting and reporting, 39.03–39.04
  characteristics, 39.03–39.04
  disclosures, 39.04
  investments, 25.15, 33.08–33.11
Limited partnerships, 10.42–10.51, 10.73–10.75
  investments and equity accounting method, 14.26
  presumption of control, 10.32, 10.44, 10.74
  real estate investments, 33.08–33.11

whether to consolidate in general partnership, 10.42–10.51, 10.73–10.75
Line-of-credit, 15.14–15.16
Liquidity put, 4.20
Loan accounting, 40.04–40.09
Loan guarantee fees, 11.35–11.38
Loan guarantor, 11.35–11.38
Loan participations, 40.38–40.39
Loan-splitting, 41.10–41.11
Loan syndications, 40.38–40.39
Loans
   ADC arrangements, 2.07–2.10, 33.04–33.05, 33.23
   credit card, 21.03–21.04
   debt security conversion, 41.06–41.09
   dollar-denominated, 18.06
   equity method investor, 14.06–14.12, 14.26–14.27
   foreign debt/equity swaps, 17.88–17.90, 18.06–18.07
   impairment, 41.10–41.12, 41.14
   initial versus principal investment, 21.03, 21.05
   interest rates, 41.09–41.10
   multiple, 41.10–41.11
   own-share lending arrangements, 12.45–12.48
   restructured, 41.10–41.11
Local currency method, 18.06–18.10
Lock-box arrangement, 4.16–4.18
Locked-up assets, 21.07
Lock-up options, 17.77
Long-lived assets
   disclosure, 35.11–35.12
   disposal of, 35.07–35.12
   geographic area disclosures, 37.10–37.11
   impairment, 19.01–19.11
   mining assets, 6.16–6.18
Long-term construction contracts, 27.01–27.08
   accounting for, 27.02–27.08
   anticipated losses, 27.08
   basic contract price, 27.06
   change order, 27.06
   claims, 27.06
   completed-contract method, 27.01, 27.02, 27.04
   cost estimates, 27.03–27.04, 27.08
   income determination, cost, 27.07
   income determination, revenue, 27.06
   options and additions, 27.06
   overview, 27.01
   percentage of completion method, 27.01, 27.02, 27.04–27.05, 27.08
   pricing methods, 27.03–27.04
   profit center, 27.05
   progress measurement, 27.05
Long-term debt, 4.08
Long-term debt agreement, 4.08, 4.16–4.18
Long-term power sales contracts, 36.71–36.75, 36.78–36.82
Long-term supply arrangements, 7.03–7.05
Look-back option, 38.51–38.56
Loss contingencies, 11.02
   costs currently recognized, 11.22–11.23
   disclosure requirements, 11.20–11.23
   legal costs, 7.18
   not reasonably estimable, 11.22
   reasonably possible, 11.21
   related to recorded accruals, 11.21
   unasserted claims, 11.22
Lump-sum contract, 27.03
Lump-sum payments, 7.19–7.20, 30.02, 30.05

M

Maintenance, planned major, 7.07–7.10
Maintenance deposits, 26.67–26.69
Management approach, 37.03, 37.09–37.10
Mandatorily redeemable financial instruments
   of nonpublic entities, 17.20–17.22
   with shares differing from book value, 17.19–17.20
Mandatorily redeemable preferred stock, 39.09–39.10
Manufacturers, 24.03

Market price
  declines, recognition of, 23.02–23.03
  foreign transactions, 18.03, 18.17–18.18, 18.24
Market rentals, 26.45
Master Limited Partnerships (MLPs), 6.09–6.12
  business combinations, 6.09–6.12
  earnings per share, 13.09–13.13
Maximum guarantee test, 26.25–26.32
Medical services delivery, 10.24–10.35
Medicare
  compliance audit costs, 7.28–7.29
  Prescription Drug Improvement and Modernization Act of 2003, 32.04–32.09
Mergers, push-down accounting, 20.47–20.48
Mezzanine stock, 4.21
Milestone method, 36.54–36.57
Mineral rights, 21.09
Minimum lease payment
  calculation, 26.69–26.70
  residual value guarantee, 26.43–26.44
Minimum revenue guarantees, 11.33–11.35
Mining assets, impairment and business combinations, 6.16–6.18
Minority interest. *See also* Noncontrolling interest
  derivative indexed to, 17.24–17.27
Money-over-money lease transaction, 26.10, 26.12
Mortgage-backed securities (MBS), 25.32–25.33
Mortgage derivative products, 25.19, 25.34
Mortgage insurance, 33.15–33.17
Mortgage loan
  payment modifications, 17.05–17.06
  securitization, 41.09
Mortgage servicing rights, 40.26–40.27
  contingencies, 40.36–40.38
  subservicing agreement, 40.33–40.36
Motion picture companies, 9.15–9.17
Motor carrier services, 36.13–36.16
Multiemployer pension plan, 32.25

Multiple deliverables, revenue recognition, 36.27–36.32, 36.48–36.54
Mutual fund distribution fees, 36.10–36.11, 36.65–36.69
Mutual funds, 25.03
Mutual insurance company, demutualization stock, 39.05–39.06
Mutually exclusive approach, 26.23

N

National Conference of Commissioners on Uniform State Laws (NCCUSL), 4.25
Negative amortization mortgage, 33.13
Negative plan amendments, 32.15–32.21
Net cost, in accrual accounting, 29.02, 32.02
Net operating loss (NOL), 20.23, 20.32, 20.36
NFPOs. *See* Not-for-profit organizations
90 percent of fair value recovery test, 26.48
90 percent recovery-of-investment test, 26.25
Noncompensatory plan, 38.03
Noncontrolling interest
  derivative indexed to, 17.24–17.27
  stockholders' equity, 39.02
Nonemployee transactions, 38.04–38.06, 38.07–38.14, 38.17–38.20
Nonmonetary transactions, 28.01–28.21
  accounting issues, 28.06–28.18
  barter transactions, 28.02–28.04
    credits, 28.04–28.06
  cost-method exchanges, 6.03–6.05
  fair value, 28.01–28.20
  held for sale product or property, 28.09
  impairment, 28.05–28.06, 28.10
  involving monetary consideration, 28.09, 28.11–28.15
  nonreciprocal transfers to owners, 28.10, 28.16
  overview, 28.01
  purchases and sales of inventory, 28.18–28.21
  real estate, 28.09, 28.13–28.15

reorganizations, 28.16–28.18
similar productive assets, 28.08–28.09, 28.10–28.11
Nonrecourse financing
money-over-money lease, 26.10, 26.12
wrap lease transaction, 26.10, 26.74–26.76
Nonutility generators (NUGs), 36.71–36.75, 36.78–36.82
Notes
classified as assets, 4.23–4.24
received for capital stock, 4.23–4.24
repayment terms, 4.08–4.09
Not-for-profit organizations (NFPOs)
endowment funds of, 4.25–4.29
pronouncements related to. *See Appendix*
Notice to Practitioners, 2.05, 2.06

O

Offsetting
extinguishment of debt, 15.08
foreign currency swaps, 18.05
pension plans, 29.02
postretirement benefits, 32.02
Off-the-shelf software, 9.14–9.15
Oil and gas-producing entities
intangible assets, 21.09
pronouncements related to. *See Appendix*
Omnibus Budget Reconciliation Act (OBRA) of 1987, 20.42
Omnibus Budget Reconciliation Act (OBRA) of 1993, 20.19
Operating leases
changing interest rate, 22.03–22.04
described, 26.04
equipment sold, repurchased, 36.20–36.22
incentive payments, 26.10–26.12
modifications, 26. 26.45–26.46
scheduled rent increases, 26.09, 26.10–26.11
tax indemnification, 26.52
Operating real estate properties, 33.04–33.05
Operating segments, 37.04–37.05

aggregating, determining to, 37.12–37.14
Option-based derivatives
gains/losses reporting, 17.46–17.48
indexed, 17.48–17.70
trading purposes in energy and risk management, 17.70–17.73
weather derivatives, 17.43–17.46
Original equipment manufacturers (OEMs), 7.03
Origination fees, credit card, 17.06–17.08
Other comprehensive income, accumulated, upon a loss of significant influence, 14.25–14.26
Other-than-temporary impairment, 25.03–25.04, 25.34–25.43
Out-of-pocket expenses, 35.22–35.23
Output method, 27.05
Outside basis differences, 20.50–20.52
Own-share lending arrangements, 12.45–12.48
Ownership transfer requirements, leases, 26.58–26.59

P

Participating PRPs, 11.16–11.17
Participating securities, determining, 13.03–13.05
Partnership, annual payment to retain fiscal year, 7.23–7.24
Patents, 21.01
Payroll and payroll-related costs, 3.06, 9.06
Payroll taxes, employee stock ownership plans (ESOPs), 38.57, 38.59
PBs. *See* AICPA AcSEC Practice Bulletins
Pension plans, 30.01–30.34. *See also* Pension plans—employers; Postretirement benefits (OPEBs)
Altersteilzeit early retirement arrangement, 30.32–30.34
annuity contracts, 30.05–30.06, 30.07–30.08, 30.14
curtailment, 30.02, 30.08–30.09, 30.10–30.11, 30.15–30.16, 30.18, 30.21–30.31
early retirement, 30.32–30.34

employer paid after insurance fails to provide annuity benefits, 30.31–30.32
exit activity, 30.03–30.04
FAS-88 Implementation Guide, 30.04–30.31
lump-sum cash payment, 30.02, 30.05
overview, 30.02
settlement, 30.02, 30.04–30.05, 30.06–30.07, 30.09, 30.12–30.15, 30.18–30.21
spinoff, 30.16–30.18
Pension plans—employers, 29.01–29.38. *See also* Pension plans; Postretirement benefits (OPEBs)
accounting for, 29.03–29.27
cash balance plans, 29.35–29.37
delayed recognition, 29.02
discount rates, 29.37–29.38
excess pension assets transfer to retiree health care benefits, 29.37
future contributions, multi-employer, 29.31–29.32
Japanese government, 29.32–29.35
net cost, 29.02
offsetting, 29.02
overview, 29.02
retiree health care benefits account, 29.37
vested benefit obligations, 29.28–29.30
Percentage-of-completion method, 9.15, 27.01, 27.02, 27.04–27.05, 27.08
Percentage-of-taxable income (PTI) bad-debt deductions, 20.43
Personal financial statements, 31.01–31.07
accounting and financial reporting for (SOP 82-1) 31.03–31.07. *See also Cross-Reference*
current value determination, 31.03–31.07
disclosures, 31.06–31.07
form of, 31.02–31.03
future interests, 31.05
income taxes, 31.05–31.06
intangible assets, 31.05, 31.06
investments
in closely held businesses, 31.04, 31.06
in life insurance, 31.04, 31.06
marketable securities, 31.03–31.04
noncancelable commitments, 31.05, 31.07
nonforfeitable rights, 31.06
options, 31.04
overview, 31.01
payables, 31.05
presentation methods, 31.03
real estate, 31.04
receivables, 31.03
similar assets, 31.05
Personal guarantee, 2.08
Physician cosigning provision, 10.32–10.33
Physician practice, 10.24–10.35
Physician practice management entity (PPM), 10.24–10.35
Plan assets, OPEB, 32.27–32.33
Pooling-of-interest accounting, elimination of, 6.02
Post-contract customer support (PCS), 9.02, 9.11, 9.13–9.14, 9.34
Postemployment benefits. *See* Pension plans; Postretirement benefits (OPEBs)
Postretirement benefits (OPEBs), 32.01–32.40. *See also* Pension plans; Pension plans—employers
attribution, 32.13–32.15
curtailments, 32.15–32.21
deferred compensation, 32.10–32.11, 32.34–32.39
defined contribution plans, 32.27
delayed recognition, 32.02
disclosures, 32.24
discount rate selection, 29.37–29.38
FAS-106 Implementation Guide, 32.09–32.27
frontloaded plan, illustration, 32.14
gains and losses, 32.21–32.22
measurement, 32.11–32.13
Medicare prescription drugs, 32.04–32.09
multiemployer plans, 32.25

multiple plans, 32.24–32.25
negative plan amendments, 32.15–32.21
net cost, 32.02
offsetting, 32.02
overview, 32.02–32.03
plan assets, 32.23, 32.33–32.34
plan settlements, 32.25–32.26
rate-regulated enterprises, 32.27–32.33
special termination benefits, 32.26–32.27
split-dollar life insurance arrangements, 32.34–32.39
substantive plan, 32.11
Potentially responsible parties (PRPs)
categories, 11.16–11.17
liability allocation, 11.21–11.22
participating, 11.16
recalcitrant, 11.16
unproven, 11.16–11.17
Potential recoveries, 11.18
Power sales contracts, 36.71–36.75, 36.78–36.82
Practice Bulletins. *See* AICPA AcSEC Practice Bulletins; *Cross-Reference*
Precompte mobilier, 20.26
Preferred provider organizations (PPOs), 10.24–10.35
Preferred stock
dividends payable in common shares, 13.19
EPS calculation, 13.13–13.15
fixed-maturity, 15.04
induced conversion, 13.13–13.15
mandatorily redeemable, 39.09–39.10
Premium put, 12.52–12.54
Pre-production costs, 7.03–7.05
Prescription drugs. *See* Medicare
Price changes, 16.02–16.03
Price-level-adjusted financial statements, 20.48–20.50
Principal vs. net revenue reporting, 36.22–36.25
Probable future economic benefits, 3.04–3.05, 3.08–3.09

Product or property held for sale, nonmonetary transactions, 28.09
Production-type contracts, 27.01–27.08
Productive assets, 28.08–28.09
Product maintenance contracts, 36.08–36.10
Product master, 9.09, 9.28, 9.30
Profit center, 27.05
Profit recognition
by homebuilders, 33.31–33.32
real estate sales, 33.13, 33.15–33.17
Projected benefit obligation (PBO), 29.28–29.30
Protective rights, 10.20–10.23, 10.49
Public Securities Association, 25.33
Puerto Rican operations, 37.12
Purchase accounting. *See* Acquisition method accounting
Purchased options, 17.50, 17.61–17.63, 17.68
to acquire securities, 25.06–25.11
Push-down accounting, 6.09, 6.12, 20.47–20.48
Pushed down costs, 6.09, 6.12
Put option
balance sheet classification, 4.20–4.23
EPS calculation, 13.21–13.22
purchased, 17.50, 17.61–17.63
written, 17.50–17.51, 17.64–17.68
Put warrants, 17.69

Q

Quantitative thresholds, 37.06–37.08, 37.12–37.14
Quasi reorganization, 41.15

R

Rabbi trust, 10.36–10.42
Range bonds, 17.11
Rate-regulated enterprises, 32.27–32.33, 36.71, 36.76–36.78
Rate-regulated utilities, 36.71, 36.76–36.78
Real estate
acquisition, development, and construction (ADC) funding arrangements, 2.07–2.10, 33.04–33.05, 33.23

antispeculation clauses, 33.14–33.15
integral equipment determination, 33.24–33.25
nonmonetary transactions, 28.09, 28.13–28.15
personal financial statement, 31.04
pronouncements related to. *See Appendix*
tax benefits, 33.08–33.11
Real Estate Investment Trust (REIT)
asset construction, 26.23–26.32
minority interests, 33.34–33.37
service corporation investment, 33.34–33.37
Real estate leases
leveraged, 26.34–26.35, 26.71–26.74
sale-leaseback transactions, and, 26.34–26.35
Real estate transactions, 33.01–33.47
accounting for sales, 33.27–33.29
acquisition of operating property, 33.04–33.05
antispeculation clauses, 33.14–33.15
buyer's continuing investment, 33.25–33.27
buy-sell clause, 33.27–33.29
financing, 33.18–33.22
foreclosed property valuation, 33.05–33.08
graduated payment or insured mortgages, 33.13
integral equipment determination, 33.24–33.25
internal costs, 33.32–33.34
investments in affordable housing, 33.08–33.11
limited partnership investments, 33.08–33.11
overview, 33.02–33.03
profit recognition, 33.13, 33.15–33.17, 33.31–33.32
rental shortfall, 33.29–33.30
repossession, valuation, 33.05–33.08
residual value of a leased asset, interest in, 33.11–33.12
service corporation investment, 33.34–33.37

surety bonds and mortgage insurance, 33.15–33.17
time-sharing, 33.37–33.47
transfer of financial assets, 33.23–33.24
transfer of ownership as down payment, 33.17–33.18
Realized gain or loss, 6.03
Recalcitrant PRPs, 11.16
Receivables and payables, interest on, 22.01–22.05
Recourse obligation, 40.57
Redeemable securities, 17.27–17.36
Refinancing, 4.18
Regulated industries, pronouncements related to. *See Appendix*
Remarketing
agreement, 4.19–4.20
fees, 26.75
rights, 26.74–26.75
Removal of accounts provision, 40.42–40.43
Rentals
as future revenue, 4.15
leveraged lease transactions, 26.34–26.35
scheduled increases, 26.09, 26.10–26.11
shortfalls, 33.29–33.30
Rental shortfall agreement, 33.29–33.30
Reorganization. *See* Bankruptcy and reorganization
Reporting currency method, 18.09
Reporting unit guidance, 37.16
Repurchase agreements, 40.23–40.26, 40.51–40.52
Resale value guarantee, 36.06–36.07, 36.16–36.20
Research and development (R&D)
activities, 34.01–34.05
accounting for transactions of, 34.03–34.05
nonrefundable advance payments, 34.02–34.03
overview, 34.01
R&D-related assets, 34.01
stock issued to acquire results, 34.04, 34.05

Residual method to value acquired assets, 6.14–6.16
Residual value, 26.43–26.44, 33.11–33.12
Residual value guarantee
   deferred profit on sale-leaseback, 26.12–26.15
   FAS-133, 26.64–26.65
   upward adjustment, 26.07–26.08
Resource Conservation and Recovery Act (RCRA), 11.10, 11.15
Restatement of accounting changes, 1.01
Restructuring. *See also* Troubled debt restructuring
   costs related to operations, 35.20–35.21
   debt securities, 41.06–41.09
Results of operations, 35.01–35.36
   accounting interpretations, 35.14–35.15
   asbestos removal, 35.21–35.22
   business interruption, 35.13–35.14
   colloborative arrangements, 35.28–35.32
   compensated absences, 35.25–35.26
   discontinued operations, 35.04–35.07
      FASB 144 application, 35.07–35.12
   extraordinary items, 35.14–35.15, 35.21–35.22
   financial statement issuance, 35.32–35.33
   health care entities, insurance claims and recoveries, 35.33–35.35
   income statement presentation of taxes, 35.23–35.25
   interest allocation, 35.04–35.07
   inventory markdowns, 35.20–35.21
   life settlement contracts, 35.15–35.20
   out-of-pocket expenses, 35.22–35.23
   overview, 35.02–35.03
   restructuring costs, 35.20–35.21
   sabbatical leave, 35.25–35.26
   setoff right in bankruptcy, 35.12–35.13
   start-up costs, 35.26–35.28
   unofficial accounting interpretations, 35.14
Retained earnings, 39.02

Retiree health care benefits account, 29.37
Retrospective application of accounting changes, 1.01, 4.07, 4.29
Revaluation surplus, 20.51
Revenue recognition, 36.01–36.82
   alternative revenue program, 36.76–36.78
   cash consideration from vendor, 36.42–36.44
   casino jackpot accruals, 36.59–36.61
   computer software, 9.08–9.15, 9.19–9.23, 9.24–9.44
   computer software development of EE products, 9.15–9.17
   convertible debt, 12.12–12.13
   distribution fees, 36.10–36.11, 36.65–36.69
   equipment sold, repurchased, 36.20–36.22
   extended warranties, 36.08–36.10
   freight services in process, 36.13–36.16
   gas-balancing arrangements, 36.11–36.13, 36.61–36.63
   gross revenue reporting, 36.22–36.25
   guaranteed minimum resale value sales, 36.06–36.07, 36.16–36.20
   health care entities, charity, 36.69–36.71
   insurance death benefits, 36.05–36.06
   long-term power sales contracts, 36.71–36.75, 36.78–36.82
   management fees, 36.57–36.59
   milestone method, 36.54–36.57
   multiple deliverables, 36.27–36.32, 36.48–36.54
   mutual fund distribution fees, 36.10–36.11, 36.65–36.69
   net revenue reporting, 36.22–36.25
   overview, 36.03–36.04
   principal vs. net, 36.22–36.25
   product maintenance contracts, 36.08–36.10
   sales of future revenues, 36.07–36.08
   service provider, consideration given by, 36.46–36.47
   shipping and handling, 36.25–36.27

stock purchase options, 12.12–12.13
unearned revenue accrual, 36.63–36.65
vendor to customer consideration, 36.32–36.42, 36.44–36.45
Reverse spinoff, accounting for, 39.12–39.13
Reverse treasury stock method, 13.20–13.21
Revolving credit agreements, 4.16–4.18
Revolving-debt arrangements, 15.14–15.16
Right of setoff, 35.12–35.13
Risks and uncertainties, 11.01–11.47
    coal industry retiree estimated payments, 11.38–11.39
    concentration of credit risk, 11.40–11.43
    disclosures, 11.03–11.06, 11.09–11.10, 11.20–11.23
        accounting guidance on (SOP 94-6). *See Cross-Reference*
    environmental remediation liabilities, 11.10–11.23
    financial institutions that lend to activities of others, 11.06–11.10
    guarantees, 11.32–11.33
        minimum revenue, 11.33–11.35
        loan fee, recognition, 11.35–11.38
    insurance, 11.23–11.32
    intellectual property infringement indemnification, 11.32
    loan guarantee fees, 11.35–11.38
    overview, 11.02
    sale of mortgage servicing rights, 40.36–40.38
    special assessments, 11.43–11.46
    tax increment financing entities, 11.43–11.46
    terms of loan products, 11.40–11.43
Roll-out, 6.10, 6.11, 6.12
Roll-up, 6.10, 6.11, 6.12

S

Sabbatical leave, 35.25–35.26
Sale-leaseback transactions, 26.34–26.35
    asset leased to another party, 26.22–26.23
    build-to-suit lease, 26.23–26.32
    continuing involvement, 26.69
    deferred profit, 26.12–26.15
    executory costs, 26.18–26.19
    governmental leases, 26.32–26.34
    leased asset as real estate, 26.34–26.35
    lessee involvement in asset construction, 26.23–26.32
    leveraged leases, 26.34–26.35
    residual value guarantee, 26.64–26.65
    seller's pre-existing lease, 26.15–26.18
    uncollateralized letter of credit, 26.21–26.22
    unsecured parent guarantee, 26.19–26.20
    wrap lease, 26.10, 26.74–26.76
Sale of rights, third-party, cash received from, 36.66–36.67
Sales method, 36.12–36.13, 36.61–36.63
Sarbanes-Oxley Act, xv–xxvii
Savings and loan associations (S&Ls). *See* Banking and thrift institutions
S corporation, 20.12, 20.24, 20.44, 20.46, 20.52
Secondary revenue, 3.09
Secured borrowing, 40.64
Securities
    available-for-sale, 18.03–18.05, 25.02, 25.07, 25.24, 25.26–25.27
    foreign-currency-denominated, 18.03–18.05
    hybrid, 12.02, 12.20, 12.53–12.54
    marketable, unrealized losses, 14.30
    redeemable, classification and measurement of, 17.27–17.36
Securities and Exchange Commission (SEC), on EITF consensus positions, 1.04–1.05
Segment reporting, 37.01–37.17
    aggregating operating segments, 37.12–37.14
    determining reportable segments, 37.05–37.06
    disclosures, 37.03–37.06, 37.09, 37.10–37.11, 37.12, 37.16

enterprise-wide disclosures,
    37.10–37.11
FAS-131 guidance, 37.03–37.11,
    37.14–37.15
geographic disclosures, 37.10–37.11
health care facility "customer,"
    37.16–37.17
interim financial statements,
    37.09–37.10
operating segments, 37.04–37.05
overview, 37.01–37.02
performance measurement,
    37.08–37.09
Puerto Rican operations, 37.12
quantitative threshold application,
    37.06–37.08
reporting unit guidance, 37.16
Separately priced contract, 36.08–36.10
Sequential approach, 26.23
Service arrangements, 9.14–9.15
Service corporations (SCs), 33.34–33.37
Settlement
    defined (FAS-48), 20.09–20.12
    methods, 17.53–17.54
    types of, 17.36–17.37
Settlement, pension plan, 30.02,
    30.04–30.05, 30.06–30.07, 30.09,
    30.12–30.15, 30.18–30.21
Shareholders. *See also* Shareholders'
    rights; Stockholders' equity
    nominee, 10.25, 10.27, 10.29,
        10.31–10.35
    transactions with company, tax
        effects, 20.23–20.25
Shareholders' rights
    approval or veto, 10.18–10.24
    participation, 10.19, 10.34
    protective, 10.20–10.24, 10.49
    substantive participation, 10.48
Shipping and handling costs,
    36.25–36.27
Short-term letter of credit, 4.19
Short-term loan sale, 40.27–40.30
Similar assets
    nonmonetary transactions,
        28.08–28.09, 28.10–28.11
    personal financial statements, 31.05
Single-country fund, 18.16

Single-family residential mortgage,
    25.33
Site restoration costs, 19.08–19.11
Software companies, 9.16–9.17
Software revenue recognition, 9.08–9.15,
    9.19–9.23, 9.24–9.44
    accounting guidance on (SOPs 97-2
        and 98-9). *See Cross-Reference*
    arrangement exists, 9.09
    collectibility, 9.10–9.11
    delivery occurrence, 9.09–9.10
    fixed or determinable price,
        9.10–9.11
    multiple elements, 9.11–9.15
Software stored on another entity's
    hardware, 9.17–9.18
SOP. *See* AICPA Statements of Position
Special assessments, 11.43–11.46
Special-purpose entities (SPEs),
    26.47–26.55. *See also* Derivatives
    asset construction, 26.24, 26.31
    construction-in-progress transferred,
        26.50–26.51
    costs incurred by lessees, 26.49–26.50
    default provisions, 26.54–26.55
    environmental risk responsibility,
        26.53–26.54
    fees paid to, 26.49
    interest-only payments, 26.51–26.52
    lease transactions, 26.52–26.53
    lessee payments, 26.48
Spinoff
    pension plans, 30.16–30.18
Split-dollar life insurance arrangements,
    32.34–32.39
Springing lock box, 4.16–4.18
Stand-alone cost pool, 3.06
Standstill agreement, 39.09
Start-up costs, 7.02, 35.26–35.28
    accounting for (SOP 98-5).
        See Cross-Reference
State franchise tax, 20.16–20.19
Statements of Position. *See* AICPA
    Statements of Position (SOP);
    Cross-Reference
Stock-based payments, 38.01–38.78. *See
    also* Employee stock ownership
    plans (ESOPs)

compensatory plan, 38.03
convertible instrument to nonemployee, 38.04–38.06
employee stock ownership plans, 38.06–38.07, 38.21–38.25, 38.30–38.51, 38.61–38.63
  convertible stock and earnings-per-share, 38.66–38.70
  dividends on unallocated stock and earnings-per-share tax treatment, 38.71–38.72
  expense recognition, 38.63–38.66
employee stock purchase plans, 38.51–38.56
equity accounting method, 14.16–14.17
equity instrument granted to nonemployees, 38.07–38.14, 38.17–38.20
equity instrument with goods and services, 38.07–38.17
excess contributions, 38.21–38.25
FAS-123(R)
  amendment of staff position, 38.72–38.74
  technical corrections, 38.74–38.78
freestanding financial instruments, 38.25–38.28
grant date, 38.28–38.29
look-back option, 38.51–38.56
noncompensatory plan, 38.03
options classification, 38.29–38.30
overview, 38.03
payroll taxes, 38.57, 38.59
share arrangements as compensation, 38.59–38.60
share-based payment, 38.57–38.59
shares of an unrelated entity, 38.60–38.61
Stock combination, 6.02
Stockholders' equity, 39.01–39.15
accelerated share repurchase, 39.11–39.12
additional paid-in-capital, 39.02
contingently convertible securities, 39.06–39.08
disclosures, 39.06–39.08
distributions with stock and cash, 39.13–39.15
legal capital, 39.02
limited liability companies, 39.03–39.04
mandatorily redeemable preferred stock, 39.09–39.10
mutual insurance company, demutualization stock, 39.05–39.06
noncontrolling interests, 39.02
overview, 39.01–39.02
retained earnings, 39.02
reverse spinoffs, 39.12–39.13
subsidiary investment, 39.09–39.10
takeover attempt defense costs, 39.08–39.09
Structured notes, 17.10–17.17
Subjective acceleration clauses
  debt classification, 4.16–4.18
  demand provision versus, 4.09
  due on demand, 4.09
  long-term debt agreements, 4.08
Sublease, 26.08, 33.29–33.30
Subsequent event, 6.14
Subservicing agreement, 40.33–40.36
Subsidiaries. *See also* Foreign subsidiaries
  balance sheet classification, 4.13–4.14
  consolidated financial statements, 10.51–10.55
  deconsolidation of, 17. 32–17.33
  discontinued operation, 20.21–20.23
  exchange of ownership interest, 6.09
  exchange of stock, 6.09, 6.12
  freestanding indexed to, 17.36–17.40
  investment in parent's stock, 39.09–39.10
  long-lived assets, 6.09
  mandatorily redeemable preferred stock, 39.09–39.10
  minority interest derivative, 17.24–17.27
  pushed down costs, 6.09
  sale-leaseback transaction, 26.19–26.20
  venture capital, 10.16–10.17
  wholly owned, 26.19–26.20, 39.10

Substantive participating rights, 10.20–10.24, 10.45–10.49, 10.73
Substantive plan, 32.11
Substituted debtors, 41.05–41.06
Superfund, 11.10, 11.15
Surety bonds, 33.15–33.17
Suspended well costs, 7.24–7.28
Swaps
  bond, 25.05, 25.13
  foreign debt-for-equity, 17.88–17.90, 18.05, 18.06–18.07

T

Take-out commitment, 2.08
Takeover attempt defense costs, 39.08–39.09
Tax credits
  dividend-related, 20.28–20.31
  precompte mobilier, 20.26
Tax Equity and Fiscal Responsibility Act of 1982, 20.47
Tax Incremental Financing Entity (TIFE), 11.44–11.46
Tax indemnification, 26.37–26.39
Tax-planning strategies, 20.45–20.46
Tax Reform Act of 1986
  alternative minimum tax, 20.14–20.16, 26.37, 26.39–26.40, 26.74
  corporate tax rates, 26.36
  indemnification clauses, 26.37
  uniform capitalization rules, 24.03–24.04
Tax-to-tax differences, 20.39–20.40
Technical Bulletins. *See* FASB Technical Bulletins (FTB)
Temporary differences, 20.03, 20.15–20.22, 20.25, 20.29–20.31, 20.32–20.37, 20.39–20.40, 20.41–20.45, 20.48–20.52
Tenant improvements, 26.31
Termination benefits, 6.12–6.14, 32.26–32.27
Termination penalty, 26.45–26.46
Texas corporate franchise tax, 20.16–20.18
Third-party credit enhancement, fair value, 16.04–16.05
Third-party creditor, 15.09
Third-party intermediary, 15.09, 15.11
Third-party providers, life settlement contracts, 35.15–35.20
Time-and-material contract, 27.04
Time-sharing, 33.37–33.47
Tooling costs, 7.03
Trademarks, 21.01
Transfer of financial assets, 40.01–40.66
  accounting for (FAS-140), viii, 40.23–40.26
  accrued interest receivable, 40.22–40.23
  assets and liabilities at completion, 40.55–40.58
  credit card securitization, 40.30–40.33
  derivative instruments, 40.39–40.40
  effective control, 40.51–40.55
  extinguishment of liabilities, 40.65
  FAS-125 impact, 40.38–40.39
  FAS-140 Implementation Guide, 40.43–40.65
  gain and loss recognition, 40.05–40.06
  impairment, 40.17–40.22
    EITF 99-20 amendments, 40.09–40.17
  interest income, 40.17–40.22
  isolation, 40.46–40.49
  loan accounting, 40.04–40.09
  loan participations, 40.38–40.39
  loan syndications, 40.38–40.39
  mortgage service rights, 40.26–40.27, 40.33–40.38
  overview, 40.02–40.03
  receivable portfolio, 40.30–40.33
  receivables with recourse, 40.56–40.57
  recorded investment, loan sale, 40.62–40.63
  removal of accounts provision, 40.42–40.43
  repurchase agreements, 40.23–40.26, 40.51–40.52
  sale of short-term loan, 40.27–40.30
  secured borrowing and collateral, 40.64

servicing assets and liabilities, 40.58–40.59, 40.60–40.61
subject to repayment, 40.61–40.64
transferee constraints, 40.49–40.50
transferor control, 40.40–40.43
transfers of financial assets, 40.23–40.26
unresolved contingencies, 40.36–40.38
Transfer of investment, 33.23–33.24
Transfer of ownership interest, 33.17–33.18
leases, 26.58–26.59
Transportation, pronouncements related to. *See Appendix*
Treasury stock
accelerated share repurchase, 39.11–39.12
takeover attempt defense costs, 39.08–39.09
Troubled debt restructuring (TDR), 41.01–41.16. *See also* Bankruptcy and reorganization
bankruptcy, 41.15
Brady bonds, 41.14
classification by debtors and creditors, 41.03
defined, 41.03
disclosures, 41.10–41.11
FAS-5 and FAS-114 guidance, 41.13–41.14
FAS-115 application, 41.14–41.15
impairment measurement, 41.10–41.12, 41.14
income recognition, financially troubled countries, 41.15–41.16
interest rates, 41.09–41.10
loan impairment, 41.02, 41.10–41.11
loan to debt security conversion, 41.06–41.09
loan modification, pool accounted as single asset, 41.12–41.13
modification of debt terms, 25.14, 25.34, 41.09–41.10, 41.14–41.15
overview, 41.02
substituted debtors, 41.05–41.06
into two or more loans, 41.10–41.11

zero coupon bonds, 41.03–41.05
12b-1 plan, 36.10, 36.65–36.68
Two-class method, 13.05–13.08
master limited partnerships, 13.09–13.13

U

UMIFA. *See* Uniform Management of Institutional Funds Act
Uncertainty. *See* Contingencies; Risks and uncertainties
Uncollateralized letter of credit, 26.21–26.22
Undistributed tax rate, 20.29–20.31
Unearned revenue accrual, 36.63–36.65
Uniform capitalization rules, 24.03–24.04
Uniform Management of Institutional Funds Act (UMIFA), 4.25, 4.27, 4.28
Uniform Prudent Management of Institutional Funds Act of 2006 (UPMIFA), 4.25–4.29
Union agreements, 6.13
Union contracts, 7.19–7.20
United Mine Workers of America (UMWA), 11.38
United Mine Workers of America Combined Benefit Fund (Combined Fund), 11.38–11.39
Unit-price contract, 27.04
Units-of-delivery method. *See* Percentage-of-completion method
Units-of-revenue method, 36.08
Unproven PRPs, 11.16–11.17
Unsecured guarantee, 26.19–26.20
Upstream transaction, 14.28
Useful life determination, 21.04–21.07
Utilities, 36.71–36.75, 36.78–36.82

V

Valuation allowance, 20.23–20.25
Variable Interest Entities (VIEs)
consolidation, 10.04–10.13
determining variabilitiy, 10.12
implicit variable interest, 10.07–10.10

securitization and VIEs, leasing transactions, 26.70–26.71
Vendor-specific objective evidence (VSOE), fair value determination, 9.11–9.14, 9.20, 9.24–9.25, 9.27–9.33, 9.40–9.44
Vendor to customer consideration, revenue recognition, 36.32–36.42, 36.44–36.45
Venture capital company, 10.16–10.17
Vested benefit obligation (VBO), 29.28–29.30
Veterans Administration (VA), 33.15–33.16

W

Warranties, revenue recognition, 36.08–36.10
Warrants. *See also* Debt with warrants
 debt, 12.02
 detachable, 12.12–12.13, 12.15, 12.17, 12.31, 15.22–15.23
 freestanding, 17.23
 as freestanding derivatives, 12.26, 12.49
 put, 17.69
 stock purchase, 12.03, 12.13, 12.51, 17.68–17.69
 underlying, 12.29–12.30
Wash sales, 25.05, 25.13
Waste materials, mining industry, 24.05–24.06
Weather derivatives, 17.43–17.46
Web site development costs, 7.05–7.07
Withholding tax, 18.21
Wrap-lease transaction, 26.10, 26.74–26.76
Write-downs, loan restructuring, 41.07–41.09
Write-offs
 loan restructuring, 41.06, 41.09
 preexisting deferred tax assets, 20.24
 unamortized advertising costs, 3.07–3.08
Written options, 17.50–17.51

Z

Zero coupon bonds, 41.03–41.05